A HISTORY OF THE MEDITERRANEAN AIR WAR 1940-1945

Volume Two: North African Desert February 1942 – March 1943

A HISTORY OF THE MEDITERRANEAN AIR WAR 1940-1945

Volume Two: North African Desert
February 1942 – March 1943

Christopher Shores and Giovanni Massimello
with Russell Guest, Frank Olynyk
and Winfried Bock

GRUB STREET • LONDON

Published by
Grub Street
4 Rainham Close
London SW11 6SS

British Library Cataloguing in Publication Data
A CIP record for this title is available from the British Library

ISBN-13: 9781909166127

Cover design by Sarah Driver
Design by Roy Platten, Eclipse, Hemel Hempstead
roy.eclipse@btopenworld.com

Printed and bound by Berforts Group, UK

Grub Street Publishing only uses FSC
(Forest Stewardship Council) paper for its books.

CONTENTS

INTRODUCTION

This second volume of the planned series covers a period of 14 months, dealing with a wide spectrum of activities. Reactions to Volume 1 have been largely very gratifying for the team, but have raised some issues which we are trying to deal with.

1) Sources
Some readers have indicated that they had expected a considerably more comprehensive listing of our sources than the Bibliography included in the first volume. While in many cases our sources are similar, each member of the team has had their own particular lines of enquiry, many of them stretching over long periods from the 1960s onwards. Appended here therefore are notes relevant to each of us, indicating the basis of our research.

2) Addenda and Corrections
In a work of this nature we fully accept that there will be occasions when we get things wrong, or leave out matters which should have been included. We are very pleased and grateful for any such issue to be brought to our attention. It is our intention to incorporate such material appropriately within later volumes. We anticipate in the first instance that such a section will be included in Volume 3, dealing with any such errors or omissions in the first two.

In drawing such matters to our attention, however, we ask readers to 'treat us gently'. It needs to be kept in mind, perhaps, that no member of the team is a full-time professional author. We are all lifetime enthusiasts who operate in our spare time or retirement, and none of us is any longer in the first flush of youth. In short we are getting old and we tend to hurt easily!

3) Coverage
The question has been asked as to whether we include all operations, or only selective ones. The latter is certainly nearer to our intention. We consider that in a planned seven volumes to include all sorties etc where nothing of particular significance occurred would produce an indigestible amount of potentially not very interesting information.

We seek therefore, to include all those operational actions where something of note occurred such as an aircraft shot down or a victory claimed, a bombing raid of significant effectiveness, the sinking of a ship, or other events of this kind. Where large numbers of sorties were flown of a similar nature to each other, or where significant results cannot be said to have been achieved, we present examples supported by a general synopsis of activities. Large numbers of ground-attack missions would be typical of matters dealt with in this way, particularly when specific evidence of the actual results obtained is not available.

With regard to aircraft losses, we have generally left out those caused by accidents, particularly during training activities. However, on occasion we have included particularly notable losses of this nature where, for instance, a pilot of some significance was killed or seriously injured.

We have generally tried to maintain regular details of most of the moves, re-equipment and command of the vast majority of units involved in regard to all the four main air forces, the activities of which we have chronicled.

4) Times, Place Names and Distances

One matter we must draw to the reader's attention is the question of recorded times. Throughout the desert war the Allies employed GMT (Greenwich Mean Time) while the Axis used CET (Central European Time). For about half of each year these two times coincided, but during the other half they differed by approximately one hour. We have not tried to adjust recorded times during the period of the latter differential. However, readers are likely to find frequent examples during this period when the times recorded by each side for what are clearly matched reports of the same actions, will differ by the amount mentioned above.

As with Volume 1 we would mention that it has been our intention that place names and distances mentioned should as far as possible be those as employed by the Commonwealth forces during the period covered. On occasions the interpretation of these names in German and Italian records differed somewhat, (El Daba/Daba; El Alamein/Alamein; kilometres not miles etc.) and the reader will find such variations in this volume. Moreover, every effort has been made to be as accurate to the contemporary records as possible, but occasions may arise where our interpretation may not accord with current day spellings, particularly in regard to small and obscure locations which are not to be found in readily available atlases.

SOURCES AND ACKNOWLEDGEMENTS

Christopher Shores

I have been involved in researching the air operations in the Mediterranean Theatre of the Second World War for some 40 years. My sources started with access to the operations record books of the RAF and Commonwealth squadrons involved. This was subsequently expanded to incorporate the records of the RAF commands, groups and wings involved, and in interviewing and corresponding with a large number of the pilots who served there. This has usually been supported by access to their flying logbooks whenever possible. This primary research has taken place against an assiduous reading of all possible books relating to many of the aspects of the subject and to all the air forces dealt with. This reading has also covered the associated operations by the land and naval services over which, and in support of which, the air forces operated, although obviously not to anything like the depth associated with aviation matters. My own personal acknowledgements are included at the end of this section, following those of my colleagues which now follow.

Giovanni Massimello

By far the greatest part of our information regarding the Regia Aeronautica comes from the Diari Storici (historical diaries) drawn up each year by each squadriglia, gruppo, stormo and higher level units. There are about 1,100 such books preserved in the historical branch office of the Italian Air Force in Rome, and my search through these has given the best (and, in my opinion, largely unbiased) picture of the operations of Italian units. Unfortunately, their collection is incomplete; for instance, almost all the diaries for the year 1943-45 are missing, and some are also lost for the preceding years. Therefore the location of other sources became essential; these included mainly the many hundreds of pilot flight logs scattered amongst the same archive, the Archivo Centrale di Stato (National Archive) and some private collections. A third important source was the large quantity of serviceability reports (Situazioni efficienza bellica velivoli) compiled fortnightly at squadriglia level. In addition, I was able to check some other documents such as mission reports, missing personnel daily lists and claims reports. Many books have been published post war regarding single units and on individual pilots. A large quantity have been consulted and the most relevant publications are included in the Bibliography.

Finally, a most valuable source has been the quantity of interviews which I undertook, starting in the late sixties, with about one hundred Italian pilots and airmen. To them goes my grateful and everlasting memory.

I would now like to add that the demanding project of writing the history of the Mediterranean air war as a team headed by Chris Shores, has progressed during the years with growing satisfaction. The authors' intense co-operation proved to be a rewarding manner in which to integrate our various specialisations to produce a comprehensive and hopefully, a very accurate work. As per the first volume,

I wish to express my sincere gratitude to some good friends who provided me with their most valuable help in the preparation of this book. Giorgio Apostolo and Enrico Leproni let me scrutinise their large collections of photographs and generously allowed me to select several interesting pictures in order to include them in this volume. Erminio Bagnasco, whose deep knowledge of the history of the Italian Navy is well recognised internationally, regularly answered, promptly and accurately, the many questions that I posed regarding the naval operations.

I also wish to mention at least some of the many historians and enthusiasts who gave me their support and highly valued advice during this period, notably Gregory Alegy, Gregorio Baschirotto, Gabriele Brancaccio, Gianandrea Bussi, Gianni Cattaneo, Fulvio Chianese, Roberto Chiarvetto, Angelo Emiliani, Franco Farina, Giancarlo Garello, Daniele Gatti, Pierluigi Moncalvo and Paolo Varriale. Finally, I cannot forget the continuous assistance given in Rome by Tenente Colonnello Massimiliano Barlattani and Maresciallo Pasquale Rubertone; without their professional help and that of the whole staff of the historical branch office of the Italian Air Force, the section of this book regarding the activities of the Regia Aeronautica would have been impossible to complete.

Russell Guest

I initially met Chris Shores in 1980 when I first made the long flight from Australia to London, and have been working away, on and off, adding new information to his original books ever since. I have made ten trips back to the archives at Kew since then, and several trips to Canberra to visit the Australian War Memorial.

I have been fortunate over the years to have met or corresponded with a large number of RAAF pilots who flew in the period we are covering in these books. In alphabetical order they were: Nicky Barr, Dave Borthwick, Clive Caldwell, Fred Eggleston, Alan Ferguson, Bill Fordyce, Bob Gibbes, Peter Jeffrey, Max Jenkins, Murray Nash, Gus Officer, George O'Neill, Blake Pelly, Alan Rawlinson, Alec Richardson, Alan Righetti, Tom Russell, Easton Thwaites, Tom Trimble, I.H.S.'Jock' Watson, and Ken Watts. Amongst the groundcrews, my special thanks go to Ron Guymer and Bill Matthew.

A lot of assistance has come over the years from fellow enthusiasts Russell Brown, Ian Lawson, Brian Cull, John Foreman, Doug Norrie, Geoff Pentland, Ian Primmer and John Rayner. Of great help also have been the institutions that enable our interests to be fulfilled, the National Archives of the UK and of Australia, and the Australian War Memorial and Imperial War Museum, London.

Frank Olynyk

My main sources of information have been the US National Archives and Records Administration at College Park, Maryland, and the United States Air Force Historical Research Agency, Maxwell Air Force Base, Montgomery, Alabama. Between them these archives were able to provide me with the relevant records of the US 9th Air Force and with all the fighter and bomber groups serving in Egypt and Libya during the period under review. I also consulted the US Navy Deck Logs for the aircraft carrier USS *Ranger*. Additionally I have read carefully all the relevant literature that I have been able to access, all of the titles of which are included in the Bibliography listed at the back of this volume.

On a personal note, I am the Historian of the American Fighter Aces Association. Over the years I have put together a large collection of copies of mission and combat reports for the various fighter squadrons and groups. Gathering the material for the bomber and other units in the Mediterranean has been a new experience. I would like to thank Robin Cookson, archivist at the National Archives and Records Administration facility (NARA II) for his help in locating material in Record Group 18. I would also like to thank Tammy Horton at the USAF Historical Research Agency who has quickly turned around my requests for CDs and DVDs of the digitized versions of the agency's microfilm collection.

Winfried Bock

Winfried is a member of the team led by Jochen Prien, who have been producing the monumental multi-volume *Die Jagdfliegerverbände der Deutschen Luftwaffe 1934 bis 1945*. As such he has enjoyed wide access to the casualty records of WAST and the losses listed by the Luftwaffe Quartermaster General. He has also inspected the logbooks and diaries of many Luftwaffe pilots and others, particularly with the *Gemeinschaft der Jagdflieger*.

We have also received considerable help, for which we are most grateful, from Roger Hayward, author of the Air-Britain Publication *The Beaufort File*, who has sought to keep us mainly on the 'straight and narrow' particularly when dealing with nautical matters. He has provided his own bibliography in this regard, which is appended to ours. Our old friend, Dr Alfred Price, sadly no longer involved in aviation history, provided useful aid in regard to the high altitude interception work undertaken by 103 Maintenance Unit. We have also been fortunate to be made privy to the wide researches undertaken by our friends Morten Jessen and Andrew Arthy in connection with the service of the Focke-Wulf FW 190 in the Mediterranean area. Considerable assistance has also been provided by Sqn Ldr Andy Thomas from his wide archive and photographic collection relating to RAF squadrons. We have drawn frequently on the published work and specific knowledge of Wg Cdr C.G.'Jeff' Jefford, who has produced our maps for us, for which we are extremely grateful. Thanks also to Air Cdr Graham Pitchfork, Ian Simpson, Michael Schoeman, and to all those listed in the acknowledgements to Volume 1 for both help and the use of photographs.

Special thanks from us all to John Davies, our patient and long-suffering publisher. John's involvement on this occasion was far greater than normal editorial duties. Throughout a prolonged period fraught with almost endless additions and corrections, John's involvement, forebearance and considerable help was above and beyond the call of duty. In this he was greatly assisted by Natalie Parker, whose computer skills were put to our very great advantage. Bless you, Grub Street Guys and Gals – we are truly grateful and hope that we can give you a less traumatic time with the future volumes.

CHAPTER 1

HALFWAY BACK

The conclusion of Volume 1 found the 8th Army battered and somewhat bewildered at the end of January 1942, defending the Gazala Line, which was a few miles to the west of Tobruk, but east, not only of Derna, but of Benghazi by the full width of the Cyrenaican 'bulge'. In but a few days, more than half of the territory that it had taken in two months of costly fighting to gain, had been lost.

The RAF had learned many hard lessons since 1940, but also much that was of value. The recent performance of the army had, it may be recalled, led to a growing sense of bitterness that their colleagues on the ground had not seemed to be putting heart and soul into the conflict in the manner in which the air forces were. Poor leadership was much of the problem, and here the Western Desert Air Force had a distinct advantage. The overall air commander in the Middle East, Air Marshal Sir Arthur Tedder, was proving to be masterful in his role and his relationship with his immediate subordinate, Air Vice-Marshal Arthur Coningham, as commander of WDAF itself, was growing in confidence, trust and understanding.

Winston Churchill, the British prime minister, had complained to his advisors that they seemed incapable of offering him an army commander who could actually win battles. It was a desperately worrying time. Apart from the rebuff of the Crusader offensive during January, the Russians seemed only just to be holding on the Eastern Front, while in the Far East the early disasters resulting from the Japanese assaults on the USA and on the British territories in Malaya and Burma were still happening, or were at the least very fresh in the memory. It was less than two months since the shock of the sinking of the *Prince of Wales* and *Repulse* which had occurred immediately after the loss of so much of the US fleet at Hawaii.

Although the presence of the Soviet Union and the USA as allies gave an almost certainty of eventual victory, the way ahead before that could be achieved, looked long and hard. In only days ahead the German capital ships *Scharnhorst* and *Gneisenau*, bottled-up in Brest harbour for many months, would make their successful breakout up the English Channel, under the very noses of the main British defences. Before February was over Singapore would capitulate with the loss of a huge number of prisoners, further shattering British pride and morale.

There was still little that the United Kingdom could do; to launch an invasion of north-west France with the forces available was quite out of the question. Even maintaining the supply of the mother country with food and war materials was threatened still by the depredations of the Kriegsmarine's U-Boats on shipping in the Atlantic. Further evidence was becoming available that at this stage of the war the night bombing offensive against Germany was achieving little, and would require much development and production of heavier four-engined bombers and navigational aids before it could make any worthwhile contribution to the overall war effort. This left aid to Russia and holding on to North Africa as the only viable alternatives available for the immediate future.

Even these two activities could be mutually counter-productive. North Africa required much reinforcement of tanks and aircraft – just the items that Josef Stalin was demanding most vociferously for Russia. Moreover, the new war in the Far East made vast new demands for aircraft and warships, the latter requirement placing still greater pressure on the need to provide escort for the convoys seeking to be sent throughout a greatly widened war zone. It was hardly surprising that this was the period of the greatest shipping losses.

Of further concern to the British was the possibility that Russia might be defeated, or even enter into some separate agreement or armistice with Germany to bring the war in the east to a close. Either possibility opened the potential for the Germans to advance southwards through the Caucasus mountains down into the Middle East, threatening the British army with an attack from the rear. This also posed the threat of the oil-rich areas of Iran and Iraq falling into Axis hands, and endangered the main routes to the British possessions in India and Burma.

It was into this hugely problematic scenario that, on 1 December 1941, General Sir Alan Brooke had taken over the post of Chief of the General Staff from Field Marshal Sir John Dill. Considered probably to be the best military brain produced by the United Kingdom during the war, Brooke would work closely with Churchill for the rest of the conflict. His arrival commenced with a fight with Lord Beaverbrook, Minister for Aircraft Production, who was about to despatch 72 Hurricanes to Russia, with further supplies to follow. Subsequently, Brooke learned that the Chief of the Air Staff was suggesting sending six squadrons from the Middle East at a time when "we were at our wits end as to how to hold up adequate air forces" in the United Kingdom and Far East. Fortunately he was able to persuade the Prime Minister to postpone this proposal until after 8th Army had launched a new offensive in Cyrenaica, potentially planned for mid May.

Brooke had rapidly become aware that Churchill was not happy with the performance of General Auchinleck and was considering replacing him. Brooke had been worried for some time about Auchinleck's ability, and particularly about some of his advisers with whom he had surrounded himself. In an effort to improve this latter situation, Maj Gen R.L.McCreery, who had the relevant experience, was sent out, but was never consulted and was practically ignored. Regarding Auchinleck, Brooke wrote in his diary: "I have not the highest opinion of him!" However, by defending him from Churchill, he was seeking to ensure continuity. He wrote, most tellingly: "All depressing but made worse by lack of good military commanders. Half our Corps and Division (commanders) are totally unfit for their appointments, and yet if I were to sack them I could find no better; they lack character, imagination, drive and powers of leadership. The reason for this state of affairs is to be found in the losses we sustained in the last war of all our best officers, who should now be our Senior Commanders. I wonder if we will muddle through this time as we have done in the past." It is easy, 70 years later, to forget how close together the two great wars of the 20th Century were. However, that this was the view of Britain's senior soldier at the time augured ill for the immediate future.

Turning to the RAF itself, it does need to be stressed how different was its supply and maintenance position to that of the two opposing Axis air forces. For the Italians particularly, any need for rest, re-equipment, overhaul, etc. required no more than the relatively short flight across the Mediterranean home to Italy. For the Germans it was a little further, although bases were rapidly established in both Italy and Greece for immediate matters, while the flight on to southern Germany and Austria was not a vast distance further. Coupled with this, the Luftwaffe also had the advantage of a large force of transport aircraft, capable of carrying both men and urgent supplies in considerable quantities.

For the British, the position was very different (including the very substantial number of South African and Australian units sent to serve with the parent nation's units). To maintain a sizeable air force in the Middle East, capable of supporting 8th Army, defending the Egyptian base areas, and to maintain a presence further east against possible bombing attack and in case of a future threat from the Caucasus, required a huge administrative 'tail'. Volume 1 detailed the number of maintenance units, armaments depots, personnel holding units, operational training units, etc, which had already been set up by the end of 1941. These would continue to grow as the size of the 'spearhead' of squadrons grew to meet the ever-increasing planned strengths.

This required not only the creation of new units, but the building of a network of sub-contractors scattered through the back streets of Cairo, Alexandria, and other towns and cities. These were particularly valuable in overhauling and maintaining engines of both aircraft and vehicles, the work of recovery being achieved by the R & S units being particularly valuable. Study of the daily details of combats taking place will rapidly bring home the fact that the number of aircraft forced to land or crash-land due to damage or technical faults, made up a very high proportion of the losses suffered. The number of such aircraft picked up and removed for repair, or even rebuilding, was very considerable and a study of aircraft serial numbers indicates that having apparently been lost in action, the same aircraft would sometimes appear again in an active role.

As lines became more static, it rapidly became obvious how well both sides were served by mobile radar stations. Increasingly, no sooner did a formation take off to carry out a bombing or strafing attack, or a patrol over the front, than within minutes the opposing air force would be scrambling fighters to intercept. Indeed, study of information derived from Ultra transcripts or Y Service radio intercepts which are now available to the historian, indicates how considerable was the knowledge of the other side's 'comings and goings', personnel, etc. While not enjoying the level of information-gathering achieved by Ultra, the Axis listening services were no less efficient than those of their Allied opposite numbers.

Up to and during the Crusader offensive, the Luftwaffe had enjoyed some advantage over the WDAF fighters insofar as the Messerschmitt Bf 109E could outperform the Hurricane. The Regia Aeronautica's Fiat G.50bis and Macchi C.200 did not enjoy this 'spike' in performance, and met their opponents on relatively equal terms. The late months of 1941 had changed that situation considerably. The arrival of the Bf 109F introduced to North Africa a truly superb aircraft. At the same time the Italians brought to the area the C.202, powered by the same Daimler Benz engine as its German 'running mate'. Though less effectively armed than the Messerschmitt, and much less well provided with radio services, it nevertheless offered a distinct advantage over the WDAF aircraft available, including the latest models of the Curtiss P-40 series which were arriving in growing numbers.

The Luftwaffe fighter pilots particularly, many of whom had now been in fairly constant action for at least 18 months, had built up very significant skills and confidence. Above all, they had learned to make best use of the Bf 109F's superior performance to operate at higher altitude, diving to attack and climbing away again to regain height with a remarkable degree of invulnerability. They were also well-trained in addition to frequently being experienced. With many of its peacetime-trained pilots worn out by the Battle of Britain, or now involved in training, the RAF (and consequently the WDAF) was at this stage greatly dependent on the output of the Commonwealth Air Training Scheme which was under pressure to push through large quantities of new pilots, many of whom consequently arrived in North Africa with the minimum number of hours of flying time to allow them to have qualified for their 'wings'. Frequently they had received little or no training in aerial gunnery. Efforts were being made to rectify this after their arrival at the new OTUs, but demand for pilots with the units at this point of the war rendered them all too often as little more than a sophisticated form of cannon fodder. Inadequately trained, inexperienced, and provided with aircraft of inferior performance, they posed little threat and were 'easy pickings' for their Axis opponents.

This situation would ameliorate quite rapidly as the Allied fortunes improved, and this will become increasingly obvious in future volumes in this series. At this stage though, the air war in North Africa during 1942 was going to be a classic struggle between the fighters for air superiority. Initially this progresses much to the Axis advantage, but not to the extent that might have been expected. Rapidly, WDAF would learn how to protect its bombers and get them relatively safely to their targets – although this continued to be costly in terms of fighter losses until well into 1943. At first, the Axis proved equally successful in getting their bombers (nearly always Luftwaffe Ju 87 Stuka dive-bombers) to their own targets. Gradually, however, losses suffered by these increased. Perhaps more tellingly the number of WDAF squadrons which were enabled to carry bombs beneath the fuselages and wings of their fighter aircraft grew rapidly. The Luftwaffe was considerably slower to increase the use of their fighters in this way, although the Italians, whilst not doing so with their C.202s, rapidly brought to the front considerable numbers of older fighters to undertake this role.

If there is a primary criticism to be directed at the Luftwaffe, it was the enthusiastic adoption of the Richthofen ethos, developed during the Great War, whereby the pursuit by its fighter pilots of personal aerial victories was predominant. The awards of decorations and promotions rested so considerably on this factor that all else seems to have been restricted to a lower strata of duty. The tactics described for the Bf 109Fs were designed ideally to gain victories and minimise risk, but often resulted in German pilots sitting high above the WDAF bomber formations, picking out individual escorting fighters, but failing to get through to the bombers which increasingly suffered losses only to Flak.

Many WDAF fighter pilots criticised their opponents for not coming down to challenge them directly. This was partly frustration, for only in such circumstances could the advantages of the British fighters which related mainly to manoeuvrability, be utilised. For the Germans to become engaged in such 'dogfighting' was to throw away their greatest advantages to indulge in their least effective. Why should they? Since it was this fighter versus fighter battle which was to be so overwhelmingly important a factor in the operations covered throughout this volume, it is perhaps appropriate to commence by considering how it appeared at the time to some of the main protagonists amongst those 'at the sharp end'.

Eduard Neumann served throughout the period, initially as Kommandeur of I.Gruppe,

Jagdgeschwader 27 (I./JG 27), and then as Kommandeur of the whole Geschwader of three Gruppen:

"During the course of 1942 the Geschwader (two more Gruppen having arrived in Africa in the meantime) was equipped with the Bf 109F, and later with single specimens of the Bf 109G. These types had a lot of advantages over the 'Emil' (Bf 109E), but the ascendancy of performance over enemy types shrunk more and more. The British received a lot of aircraft of American origin in 1942, and between June and October of that year their operations were very reserved for good and right reasons. During these months of the regeneration of the WDAF the German fighters were worn out escorting the obsolete Stukas at a time when the Ju 87 was too slow and therefore very difficult to cover, and these missions were very costly to JG 27. The initiative passed over to the British in mid 1942.

"The North African theatre was considered by German pilots as not so hard as the Channel front, but much more difficult than the Russian front. On one hand this was the consequence of the excellent fighting spirit of the British pilots and their good aircraft, and on the other hand to the specific conditions of the desert. The food was defective because the supply over the sea did not function due to the failure of the transports. The climate injured the health of all pilots with a desert time of more than six months – these were the majority. Life on the ground was rendered more difficult by the activity of the extremely effective English commando troops. We could expect on any night that submarines would land sabotage troops, and during periods of bright moonlight, bombs fell. Altogether these efforts had a considerable effect.

"We really began to feel the British bombing attacks during the second half of 1942. It was just at the time when the German fighters were already weakened by losses and sickness, and they were also not skilled at fighting bomber formations. In my opinion this explains why the results against the bombers were apparently so small.

"We saw the defensive circle used by British fighter units until the end of 1942; in level flight they liked to be covered by higher-flying and permanently weaving pairs. The defensive circle seemed to be a necessity because of the technical performance of the British aircraft as they turned better but were slower in level flight and dive than the Bf 109. It is not surprising that the Germans used the technical advantages of their aircraft and avoided dogfights. I do not know if the covering pairs of the British formations proved successful, but it is a fact that a formation of permanently weaving and turning planes was more visible from a greater distance than the looser straight-flying formations favoured by the Germans.

"I have spoken so far only of the German fighter pilots but not the Italians. We were on friendly and often cordial terms with our Italian comrades, so far as was allowed by the Italian higher staff. The Italians were always willing to co-operate closely with us and when we flew together during Stuka escort missions for example, the Italian pilots provided valuable support. That the Italian aircraft were never good enough, and that the official political authorities in Italy seemed not to approve of too good relations between the German and Italian troops at the front, is another thing.

"It may be a little difficult for most people to understand today that the British flyers always enjoyed our respect and sympathy. This is more conceivable if one knows that in all German pilots' messes in peacetime the old veterans of World War One always spoke of the British pilots, of air combat with them, and of the British fairness in the most positive way. Many German pilots could speak English better than any other foreign language and were thus quickly on good terms with captured pilots. We endeavoured always to be as hospitable as possible in order to make their passage into captivity a little less bitter. We were again and again impressed to see how the captured pilots tried to conceal their regret and feign indifference and frivolity. For example, one time a very young Australian Flying Officer was rescued by the chief of our Desert Rescue Staffel immediately after landing in mid desert. When he got out of the Fi 156 he said to us with a bright smile: 'What a good service!'

"We registered the arrival of the American air force in great strength with great solicitude, but did not note the activity of American pilots before the autumn of 1942. During our withdrawal at the end of 1942 I met the first captured American fighter pilot at Gambut. I breakfasted with him and was astonished that he wore no soldierlike dress, only a dark, knitted combination suit, although his rank was Major. From now on we knew we had to fight not only against the American industrial power but against American soldiers. More impressive than the arrival of the Americans however was the arrival of the first Spitfires in the skies over North Africa. In my opinion it was thanks to the merits of Marseille that we were able to reduce the unquestionable threat from this aircraft to a bearable degree."

Professor Doctor Ludwig Franzisket, Staffelkapitän of 1.Staffel, JG 27 (1./JG 27) until wounded in October 1942:

"Our activity as fighter pilots over North Africa had positive and negative aspects for us. Absolutely positive was the unique good comradeship amongst the pilots and groundcrews. The psychological reason for this was probably the circumstance of our being in the desert where the conditions were equally hard for all ranks. For me as an inexperienced young officer who had never had to exercise leadership (as I was on arrival in 1941) it was not difficult to win the respect and obedience of the corporals and men who were mostly older than myself. The pilots dwelt in tents like the groundcrews, ate the same food, but their fighting was more dangerous and could be seen by all. Nobody envied the officers and pilots, and there was no resentment about anything.

"Another positive factor was the knowledge that we were fighting a very fair enemy in the air. We knew this from news received of our missing comrades from captured British pilots. Therefore we treated all British pilots very nobly. We respected and esteemed each other, but the British pilots stayed only a short while with our Geschwader before we had to send them back to Fliegerkorps headquarters.

"In the air we were superior to the British fighter aircraft (Hurricanes) particularly in 1941. The Curtiss Tomahawks and Kittyhawks were much better aircraft, but the Bf 109F had the better performance at high altitude. Over and above, our tactics seemed to be better than the British, but on the other hand the ever-growing superiority in numbers of the RAF was the reason why JG 27 was from summer 1942 onwards more and more decimated and weakened. This exhaustion finally led to the relief of the unit from the African war theatre.

"Negative points were the enormous technical difficulties and the lack of supply. An important but not decisive psychological factor was the news of the immense super-victories of the German pilots in Russia. But we all had the feeling that these victories were gained much more easily than ours. I never envied the German Jagdgeschwadern on the Channel front; I have a very unpleasant memory of my own tour of several months over England, and therefore I had the highest respect for the results of the pilots on the Western front."

George Keefer was a flight commander in 274 Squadron during 1942:

"My main impression of the desert war is still the tremendous camaraderie among those who were there – the Scots, Englishmen, Irishmen, Australians, New Zealanders, South Africans, Canadians, Palestinians, Danes, etc. The second principal impression is of the heat, dirt, flies, sand, smells, khamseens, and lack of water. I remember the few and far-between leaves in Alex and Cairo, when you tried to pack as much as possible into two or three days. Shepherd's, Pastroudi's, Dolls', the Excelsior, the Heliopolis Sports Club, the Mediterranean Dugout, the Cecil Hotel and the many other fun spots.

"Regarding the aircraft we flew, I guess I felt as most Hurricane pilots felt, that they were more than a match for the Italian aircraft, i.e. CR.42s, Fiat G.50s, Macchi 200s and Macchi 202s. On the other hand, in many respects, they were not equal to the 109s used by the Germans. I cannot think of one occasion when we encountered 109s and were above them. They were invariably on top of us every time we met. They seemed to be faster, had a better climb and much better altitude performance. Notwithstanding all this, the old 'Hurri' provided comfort in its ruggedness and extreme manoeuvrability. I certainly had the feeling that with this ruggedness and manoeuvrability no one could get me as long as I could see him coming.

"In the latter part of 1942 we flew in two groups of six aircraft (when serviceability would permit getting that many in the air at one time) with each group consisting of three pairs of aircraft with the No.1s flying roughly abreast of each other and the No.2s flying line astern of their No.1s. This was a fairly loose formation and 'weaving' was very much in vogue with the idea that everyone could have a better lookout behind by virtue of weaving. We used this both in fighter operations and in dive-bombing. In truth, I really don't think it was nearly as effective as that which we later used in England and Europe, i.e. the three groups of finger fours with no weaving. [The formation employed by the Luftwaffe in North Africa - Auth]

"We had a high respect for the 109 as an aircraft but little respect for the Italian aircraft as aircraft, but I don't think we had a very amiable feeling towards the pilots of either. I don't recall ever having heard the names of any of our opponents in the desert or anything about them personally in fact, though I guess mine was a very impersonal one altogether.

"There was a very high turnover of pilots in our squadron at that time with the result that the level of experience at any one time was certainly not high; however, this seemed to be a normal state of affairs and it never occurred to me that there might have been any other way of doing it. We did, however, from time to time receive a sprinkling of 'experienced' pilots out from England, but we felt, and I think they found, that the fighting in the Middle East was a very different kettle of fish from what it had been in England. I think the main difference consisted of fighting with what really amounted to inferior equipment under the most adverse conditions.

"Regarding the arrival of Spitfires, I can very well remember the first time we operated with them and this was after we had been pushed back to El Alamein. On this occasion we had a top cover of two Spitfires from 145 Squadron and the feeling of comfort was tremendous. There is no question, whatsoever, in my mind that the earlier arrival of Spits in the desert would have made a vast difference in the air fighting.

"Another strong memory I have was the nightly ritual in the mess tent when all the pilots would gather at 11 o'clock every night to hear Lala Anderson sing 'Lili Marlene' to the Germans from Radio Belgrade. This certainly was the only time when there was absolute silence in the mess tent.

"In summary, the overall impression remaining is one of living very intensely under incredibly trying conditions with a collection of the Commonwealth's finest young men, bound together by a tremendous purpose which seemed, at times, almost impossible to attain."

Ernst Düllberg served initially as a Staffelkapitän in II.Gruppe of JG 27, and then Kommandeur of III.Gruppe:

"During the course of the air combats in Africa in most cases only the unit leaders had the chance to gain victories. The reason for this was the effect of surprise in attacks on aircraft of an approximately equal performance. If combats lasted longer (as was the case generally only when inferior aircraft were met) the wingmen had chances to score. I very seldom encountered British bombers. They appeared only shortly before offensives and in the course of large ground operations. I believe it was much easier to shoot down a Ju 87 than a British or American bomber with its rear gunners. Generally, the African war theatre was not too difficult for German pilots. I had no problems with the climatic conditions personally. Of course, the enemy had superiority in numbers, but this was the picture on all fronts, east and west, and I did not feel that German losses were high over the desert, particularly when compared with those in Western Europe during the invasion, and on home defence. I respected the British pilots as very tough and fair opponents, but our main troubles were due to the supply situation. Often we had to use completely undamaged aircraft for parts to make others serviceable.

"The Bf 109F and G were superior to the Hurricane and Curtiss P-40, and during the earlier months the inferiority of the Hurricanes compensated for our lack of numbers. The Curtiss P-46 [this is an incorrect designation which appears actually to have related to the P-40F and Mark II version of the Kittyhawk – Auth] and Spitfire were equal to the Bf 109 in speed and rate of climb. The armament of British types was designed for fighter versus fighter combats and was superior to ours in dogfights, but in our surprise attacks the bigger calibre gun proved more profitable. I believe the double defensive circle sometimes used by the British (if numerically possible) was very effective if used properly. If the circle attacked lost height, the attacker was forced to go down too, and the second circle took over the top cover. If Marseille was often able to shoot down one aircraft after another out of a defensive circle, this was an isolated success. So far as I know his outstanding successes could not be repeated by other German pilots. The defensive circle was, however, of necessity; such a defensive manoeuvre could not produce victories and was only profitable when outnumbered by aircraft of equal speed.

"I am not surprised there was some confusion over the identification of types. At times I became involved in dogfights with Macchis before I recognised them. I believe the reason for this was the peculiar clearness of the air and the strong sunlight. We had little contact with the Italian air force. I remember that at times when we were in trouble and did not have enough serviceable aircraft, the Italians did not seem keen to take off. I know from experience that they refused to fly over the sea although they possessed air-sea rescue organisations in Sicily. The flying ability of their pilots was excellent, however, and when in the course of the war I had to re-train an Italian fighter Gruppo on Bf 109s we did not have a single crash, the Italians mastering the Bf 109 very well with a minimum number of flights.

"My longest combat in Africa lasted 15 minutes and was over our own airfield with a Curtis P-46 [Kittyhawk II – Auth]. I managed to shoot it down when it broke away to return to base, and I was able to cut it off. The pilot was unhurt and I was informed that he was a New Zealand Captain, but when I arrived at El Daba to meet him, he had already been taken away.

"My most memorable sortie was one on which we escorted an Fi 156 to pick up two force-landed Stuka flyers from a small island off the coast. A small British vessel, crewed by about eight men, tried to stop us, and although we strafed them incessantly they stuck to their purpose, jumping into shallow water and trying to reach the Stuka crew. The Storch was faster and picked them up, but suffered a puncture during the landing."

Neville Duke undertook two tours of operations in North Africa, the first flying Tomahawks and then Kittyhawks with 112 Squadron, and then with 92 Squadron on Spitfires:

"Before arriving in the desert I flew the first Spitfire Vs to go into service, with 92 Squadron (early in 1941), at the time these being the very latest equipment. To have to start flying the Curtiss Tomahawk was something of a change, not for the better as far as performance and fire power were concerned. The aircraft was very robust and was more sophisticated than contemporary British fighters, but as a result, was heavier and consequently not so manoeuvrable or fast-climbing. The armament of the Tomahawk was not heavy but a large supply of ammunition was carried and the nose-mounted .50in machine guns were conveniently situated for stoppages to be cleared from within the cockpit. The old fashioned ring-and-bead sight which was fitted in addition to the reflector sight could sometimes be used to advantage also. The armament of six .50in guns carried in the wings of the Kittyhawk was an improvement, but I sometimes removed two of them and carried a reduced load of ammunition in the interests of weight saving and resulting improved performance. Neither of these aircraft could really cope with the Bf 109 in speed or climb, or in the initial stages of a dive, but in a sustained dive could catch or get away from the German fighter.

"We flew in 'fluid sixes' or fours, all weaving. As the Germans nearly always had the advantage of height, when attacked we sometimes went into a defensive circle tactic which was derived from experience during shipping patrols and the inferior performance of our aircraft. The standard German attacks were either to dive and climb, or to dive, fire, and continue down through the formation, but on rare occasions a 109 pilot would turn with you, and this was a fair sign that you were in for trouble as they generally turned out to be tough customers. Fortunately the Germans used tracer ammunition and this helped us as it was possible to see where your opponent's fire was going and tighten or slacken your turn accordingly. Frequently the first indication you received of being attacked was when the ropes of tracer went smoking past your wingtips. The German pilots did seem to work much better in pairs than the RAF, and this team work was most effective.

"We felt we had the measure of the Italian fighters, particularly the MC.200s and G.50s, and the occasional CR.42s. The Italian pilots were much more inclined to engage in dogfights than the Germans but the lower performance and greater manoeuvrability of their aircraft accounted for this. They were certainly very fine aerobatic pilots but seemed to enter combat more in the spirit of a medieval joust than of a life and death struggle. They appeared to have many problems with inter-aircraft communication in the air and were consequently easier to bounce.

"As to bombers, we never met large formations of Ju 88s such as had been seen during the Battle of Britain, those that we did encounter were generally only in threes and fours, but we did see quite a lot of Ju 87s. Most of the transport aircraft we shot down were of the three-engined Ju 52 and S.82 type.

"Life in the desert was hard but healthy, and we were all very fit. With nowhere to go, we were thrown together a great deal, and the squadron tended to be much more of a unit than in other areas as a result. The sandstorms were bad, but generally it was a matter of adapting to the conditions and getting the 'feel' of the desert; in the air we learned to navigate by the desert tracks and by this feel. Maintenance was difficult, of course, and gun stoppages were frequent due to the sand, but in combat the main troubles were caused by the lack of cloud cover – there was nearly always a clear, bright blue sky and brilliant sunshine, and by windscreens and hoods getting sanded-up. During a formation take-off all but the first two or three aircraft off suffered from this, and when I was shot down at Tobruk in a Tomahawk it was mainly due to the fact that I could scarcely see out of my cockpit as well as to the fact that my radio had failed. Unfortunately perspex tended to attract the sand, and during the advance from Alamein 92 Squadron tried removing the cockpit canopies from their Spitfires, but the wind buffeting was so great that this was a failure.

"Due to our system of operational tours for pilots, there were never many experienced pilots in a squadron at one time, unlike the German system where pilots stayed with their units for long periods so that the number of experienced pilots and the level of experience tended to rise all the time. We did not hear much about the German pilots, or rumours that some of them were building up very big scores, but we did hear of Marseille as their leading pilot, although we were not aware of meeting him in the air other than to vaguely wonder if a particularly tough opponent had been he. Of course, we wanted an aircraft that would put us on an equal footing with the Bf 109 and were agitating for Spitfires from an early date, but they were a very long time coming. My old squadron, 92, which I rejoined in late 1942, were in the Canal Zone for months waiting for their aircraft before they arrived. 145 Squadron were the first to use these fighters in the desert and everyone tried to get posted to this unit. Had they arrived earlier they could have made a great difference to the situation."

Friedrich Körner served as an Oblt with I./JG 27 until shot down on 4 July 1942, when he became a prisoner of war:

"The reasons for the discrepancy between the number of German fighter victories and the number of successful pilots could be that some of the JG 27 pilots were strong individualists. Because of their successes they were looked upon benevolently by their leaders and were able to develop into 'aces'; other 'newcomers' had a hard time until they were able to assert themselves successfully, mainly against the opposition of the 'old hares'. A Jagdstaffel is a very interesting object of psychological study; sometimes there were Staffelkapitäne who led their units with the motto: 'There is only one man who has the right to shoot down enemy aircraft – me!' Other Staffeln had a normal relationship between the successes of Staffelkapitän, Schwarmführer and the most junior pilots. In order to raise the morale of the latter an effort was made for him to gain his first victory after some ten missions. Those pilots arriving in Africa who had completed a full training programme in the Ergänzungs-Gruppe of our Geschwader of some 250 flights for air firing, combat tactics and bomb dropping, were extremely good.

"It is not possible to compare the qualities of British and German pilots, we can only compare the differences in tactics. The Germans mostly flew Freie Jagd with one Schwarm, and on rare occasions with two Schwarme and a covering Rotte – rare because of the low serviceable strength of our aircraft. Often we met groups of 20 to 30 British fighters, which seemed unwieldy and whirled about in a confused fashion (perhaps to a pattern, though if so, this was not clear to the German pilots). When they were attacked by surprise they formed one, two or three defensive circles, but generally lost an aircraft before they could form these. From then on the progress of the combat was a question of endurance and fuel. Often the circle broke up when single aircraft left it in panic, and this resulted in other losses, often in the vicinity of enemy airfields, and even in the landing approach.

"Our top aces were very self-willed characters who had been able to develop their own methods of attack which could not be copied by the average pilots. The average pilots in Africa were very well trained and full of fighting spirit (an old slogan was 'Der Geist machts!' – It is the spirit which counts!) I believe our tactics of breaking formations into pairs at the start of a combat was the key to our success. It should be mentioned that all top aces had outstanding eyesight.

"The medium bombers, Blenheims, Bostons, Marylands, were mostly used for interdiction missions, the Beaufighters flying intruder missions. Counter air against our airfields and close air support for the ground troops were more rarely seen. For interdiction missions the bombers used to approach unseen from the sea or out of the desert. Counter air and close support missions always had strong fighter escorts. When we met medium bombers without escort (which very seldom happened) we were able to shoot some down, but in most cases we had long combats with the escorting fighters during which we broke formation to pairs to react more flexibly. These tactics facilitated breaking away from combat and never appeared to be recognised by the enemy. I never experienced our aircraft being pursued after breaking away.

"The Germans used for interdiction missions (Tobruk harbour, convoy battles) and for close air support to the front line, the Ju 87s. These needed fighter escort, being very slow and having poor defensive armament. They were scattered over a wide area after the dive and were very hard to protect. Interdiction and counter air with Ju 88s from Crete were out of range of Bf 109s. Ju 88 attacks on El Adem and Tobruk with fighter escorts succeeded without loss. At the time the known strengths were: 90 Bf 109s (60-70 per cent serviceable). Our losses in Africa were low, and I am very proud that I never lost a wingman. Regarding the losses inflicted on the enemy, we had the impression that these had no influence on their strength. Their limited appearance in periods before the bigger British ground operations was not the result of losses but a clear decision to economize power.

"Of course, we had difficulties of supply during the withdrawal in winter 1941 during which fuel and aircraft ran short. My 2 Staffel reached Sirte with only one Bf 109! However, we were accustomed to improvising and our technicians developed a great facility for invention. The difficulties of climate and nourishment were more trying for the groundcrews than for the flying personnel, as the pilots could escape into the cooler regions for some parts of the day. During my time in combat the numerical superiority of the enemy was not an important problem. If we met equal numbers, well and good. If they operated in great strength – why not? Our tactics – superior altitude, attack with great speed out of the sun (if possible) and climb away at a favourable angle – were used against all sizes of formations. And 'Den Letzten beissen die Hunde!' – 'The last is bitten by the dogs!' Our mental attitude to the enemy was without emotion and of a certain sporting spirit, but we had the will to destroy them. An air combat is a very serious matter and often ended in death.

"The Bf 109F was an excellent aircraft, and I flew it with enthusiasm. It was superior in operational height to Hurricane, Curtiss and Spitfire. Our tactics were the results of its performance; dive from height out of the sun, climb, renewed attack – no dogfight if possible. The MG 151 cannon was very good, and mostly I did not need to use the machine guns in the fuselage.

"I have sometimes observed the confusion in recognizing Spitfires, Hurricanes and Curtiss's. In the course of a combat between El Adem and Gambut in which we joined with 3 Staffel, I saw Marseille chasing a Hurricane which he shot down as it was about to shoot down a Curtiss itself! Generally I think that Bf 109s were not mistaken for Macchis because of the different camouflage, but it sometimes happened that we were attacked by Macchis. One time I was attacked by six of them which came down from a great height. I frantically waggled my wingtips to show them I was friendly. But they did not see, and I had the feeling that their reason was affected! To 'see red' happens more seldom than is thought, and to 'see red' sixfold seems very strange! Particularly as our friends were very quick to wave their wingtips when we outmanoeuvred them and were ready for the kill!

"I did not find it difficult to recognise nationalities – in most cases it was possible to see details like blue-white-red or blue-white-orange cockades, Lorraine crosses or red-white Polish 'chess-boards'. The British tactics corresponded with the performance of their aircraft – low wing loading, tight turning radius, good stunt flying abilities. The Bf 109 was devised for speed and therefore it is impossible to call a type good or bad. If the pilot was able to fly an aircraft to the limit of its performance he could obtain maximum results.

"I cannot understand why the Spitfire was introduced so late in the desert. Perhaps there was a priority for the defence of the motherland, or maybe the Spitfire was not ready for desert conditions earlier? The first news of the appearance of the Spitfires caused a certain anxiety and tension, especially among some of the older pilots who had experienced the Spitfire over the Channel in

1940. Fortunately some Spitfires were shot down in the first days of their appearance and the spell was broken. The Spitfire was equal in speed, superior in turning, but inferior in the dive. I have often experienced Spitfires not pursuing in a dive, or breaking off. After a few days we lost our fear of the Spitfire.

"My Kommandeur Neumann (later Kommodore) was on good terms with the Italian fighter pilots. For us other pilots the relations with the Italian air force were more neutral. Some joint missions to Tobruk and an evening with beer in our bar at Martuba were not enough to produce more friendly terms. Over and above this, there was the language difficulty. I doubt if officially there existed a real interest in better terms. For us the Italian air force was a great disappointment after the 'fame' of the Italians before the war. Their equipment was very bad, their aircraft obsolete. Some outstanding Italian pilots with dash and fighting spirit (aerobatic flying in low-level flight) could not alter that impression.

"It was relatively easy to watch the victories until they crashed, and mostly the wingman did this while the victorious pilot looked for other enemy aircraft. Crashes could be seen very easily and from a great height in the desert. Of course, there were errors, mostly double claims. JG 27 had a single radio frequency, and it often happened that comrades in other Staffeln, flying by chance in the same area, offered witness reports over the R/T."

John Waddy served in 250, 260 and 4 SAAF Squadrons flying Tomahawks and Kittyhawks, and then 92 Squadron, flying Spitfires. He subsequently became a member of the parliament of New South Wales, Australia:

"My main impression of the desert warfare was the spirit of the air force in all its ranks – something which I did not experience in any other theatre of war. There, we operated as a unit, sharing the same hard living conditions and all with a dedicated purpose, and this applied to ground staff as well as aircrew. In the air, of course, particularly flying P-40s I shall always remember 'looking up' to find the 109s. One will never forget the sand and the flies, the lack of amenities and the fighting, but one will always remember the friends one made and lost. We were amazed at the failure of the Luftwaffe and the Italians with their vastly superior aircraft, at least until the later part of 1942, to win and hold air supremacy.

"Apart from the fact that we always operated at a lower altitude than the enemy, the Curtiss P-40 was slower, had a slower rate of climb than the 109 and the MC.202 but, generally, it was a more manoeuvrable aircraft with an equivalent speed in the dive and approximately equal ground speed with a 109F which, I think, was a little faster than the MC.202. The P-40 had a better all-round vision. It was an extremely rugged aircraft and I believe the fire power of 6 x .50 machine guns was more effective than the one cannon firing through the prop boss of the 109s. I refer mainly to the Bf 109 because we did not, on many occasions, meet up with the Macchis. However, the 109, with its cannon firing through the prop boss, I believe had an advantage as I consider this a more desirable arrangement for the armament on fighter aircraft.

"Concerning the combat formations, these varied from time to time but I believe the final formations flown by the P-40s up to the time of El Alamein of the three sections of four was a most effective one. This allowed great flexibility as the sections of four operated in sub-sections of two and, of course, flying as we did, the sections were able to provide immediate cover for each other in the event of attack. It surprised me to learn that 50 per cent of Allied claims were for bombers or transport aircraft. The squadrons in which I flew would have had mainly claims for enemy fighters. Certainly we ran into a number of Ju 87s but we did not see much of the other bombers and certainly, very few transports. All in all, my 18 months in the Western Desert terminating after the Battle of El Alamein could briefly be described as one where we lived hard, fought hard against an equally determined enemy and experienced things one would never forget."

James 'Stocky' Edwards also flew Kittyhawks in 260 Squadron, rising from sergeant to flight lieutenant:

"I was posted to 94 Squadron on 15 January 1942 and was transported by Bombay aircraft to join the squadron at Antelat, a Western Desert airfield some 180 miles south of Benghazi. As the Bombay landed near the Mess tent at Antelat, we were welcomed by two Ju 88s appearing out of the clouds and dropping bombs on the airfield, accompanied by very loud ack-ack.

"The state of 94 Squadron appeared somewhat demoralised; in particular, we were told that there were only six pilots left on the squadron and few aircraft. Seven pilots, including the commanding officer and one flight commander, had been shot down the day before by Messerschmitt Bf 109s. We met two or three bedraggled pilot types in the Mess and learned that the others were on cockpit stand-by down near the airstrip, but they wouldn't be scrambled because their Hurricanes were over their wheels in mud and couldn't even be taxied. This was my introduction to an operational squadron in the Western Desert...! At this time the army had reached the limits of its first westward advance and had run out of steam and resources. From all appearances the area was a shambles. Retreating army personnel said that the front had been broken and the Jerries were now advancing – Rommel was beginning one of his famous pushes. In the early hours of the morning following our arrival, the four remaining Hurricanes were towed to drier ground and flown away east to more friendly territory, then the squadron camp was struck and everyone departed east across the desert.

"94 Squadron was re-grouped south of Tobruk at LG.110 and converted to Kittyhawks on 1 February 1942. On 14 February the squadron brought their new Kittyhawks to Gambut to re-commence operations, led by a new CO, Sqn Ldr E.M. 'Imshi' Mason, DFC, a famous desert pilot with 17 victories credited. However, the very next day, 94 Squadron suffered another serious setback in the air this time over the enemy airfield at Martuba. With only a few hours of conversion training on Kittyhawks, Mason led eight aircraft on a sweep and strafing mission in an attempt to catch the Bf 109s on the ground at Martuba. One or two alert Messerschmitt pilots saw the raid approaching and were able to get airborne, climb up, and come down on 94 Squadron as they crossed the field. They shot down the CO and four others. This unfortunate operation proved conclusively that the Kittyhawk, although an improvement over the Hurricane, was no match for the Bf 109 in the hands of an experienced pilot.

"On 16 February the squadron withdrew to LG.115 for further training with Sqn Ldr MacDougall as commanding officer. Here the squadron began flying a new type of formation, the 'finger four', with four aircraft in line-abreast. On 20 March we moved up again, this time to Gasr el Arid, to resume operations. Nevertheless, the squadron continued to lose both experienced and inexperienced pilots to Bf 109s; consequently the unit was next repatriated to the Delta area on 10 May, and I was then posted to 260 Squadron. With five other pilots I walked across the airfield to join this squadron, which was also flying Kittyhawk Is. By this time I had approximately 60 hours on the Kittyhawk, and while I felt quite comfortable with the aeroplane, I still knew very little about flying in combat against the 109s. In my estimation the Kittyhawk Mk I was not an easy aircraft to fly properly and as a result we lost a good number of pilots whilst training, and some experienced Hurricane pilots just flatly refused to fly it, preferring to go back to Hurricane squadrons.

"Regarding the Kittyhawk I, I found that one had to have a very strong right arm to control this aircraft during most manoeuvres. For instance, while dive-bombing the aircraft would pick up speed very quickly in a dive but had a great tendency to roll to the right. One could trim this out reasonably well with the left hand, but even then when one pulled up the fighter wanted to roll to the left quite violently; so I learned to trim out about halfway in the dive and hold the control stick central by bracing my arm against my leg and the cockpit wall. This way I found that I had more control and didn't have to take off so much trim when pulling out and the speed was reduced. However, it was distracting to have one's left hand on the trim all the time when it should have been on the throttle. Perhaps from this example the instability of the aircraft in the lateral plane at changing speeds can be understood – thus in a dogfight with violent changes of speed it was all one could do simply to fly the Kittyhawk. To avoid being shot down needed a head on a swivel – to look down into the cockpit even for a split second with 109s about was sure death. Since the Kittyhawk could fishtail and skid violently if not flown smoothly, which left little chance of hitting anything, I had the mercury ball portion of a needle and bank instrument placed right below my gunsight so that I could see it all the time, even without staring at it – this took all the guesswork out of flying smoothly.

"The Kittyhawk Mk II (P-40F) with Packard-Merlin engine – the Americans called it the Warhawk, but in 260 Squadron we called it the 'Gosh-Hawk' – was a definite improvement in lateral stability over the Mk I. 260 Squadron flew Kittyhawk IIs from September 1942 to December 1942, when we received Kittyhawk IIIs with many modifications and improvements added by the end of the Tunisian campaign. Eventually with the Mk III, the Kittyhawk became a good stable fighting aircraft, though it never did have enough power or climbing ability compared with a 109 or Spitfire. All Kittyhawks had six .50in guns -–excellent for strafing and blowing up ground targets. However, one annoying feature was the gun stoppages in the desert. When ground-strafing one could count on firing all ammunition without problems, but in dogfighting excessive 'G' forces came into play – the guns nearly always packed up after a few bursts, leaving the fighter in a most perilous position. The 109s never appeared to have any problems with their nose cannons – that big gaping hole in the centre of a white spinner with black puffs of smoke emitting from it.

"The cruising speed of the Kittyhawk II was reasonably fast, and about equal to that of the Spitfire V, while that of the Mk III compared to the Spitfire IX. However, the Kittyhawk didn't jump forward in answer to the throttle being advanced to full power, nor did it climb worth a damn compared with the Spitfire. It would turn inside the 109, but not as easily as a Spitfire. When the squadron's 'tame' Bf 109F flew with the Kittyhawks we found it necessary to throttle back to about 72 per cent power to stay with the formation. The Bf 109s definitely flew at higher cruising speeds – about 290/300mph – when operating with two or four aircraft.

"The month of June 1942 was another difficult period for everyone when the Germans were preparing for their advance, and 260 Squadron was primarily assigned to bomber escort duties over enemy concentrations. The enemy lines were only 25-30 minutes flying time from the Gambut airfields, so we would fall in as escort as the bombers passed over the field. All Kittyhawks carried 500lb bombs which we would drop after seeing the bombers safely on their way home. On most occasions we would go down and strafe after dropping the bombs. During that June the whole battle area appeared to be engulfed in dust and haze up to 12,000 feet. The sun shone through the haze with full intensity making the canopy tops glare. Messerschmitts were always over the target areas and attacked out of the sun as we turned. By the end of June the squadrons were in retreat, leap-frogging back in order to provide cover for our ground forces. At that time we didn't know why, but the Luftwaffe made no attempt to really support their advancing army. All desert squadrons re-grouped along the Alexandria-Cairo line and stabilised for the time being. Personnel were able to get a much-needed rest and change in Alexandria for a few days. Many new pilots arrived on the squadron and intensive training took place, while bomber escorts and sweeps continued. The squadron seemed to take on new life and knit together as a fighting team. By then – mid-September 1942 – I was leading the squadron on occasion as a sergeant.

"Administrative paper work had a very low priority. There was no feeling that we would move further east, or give up Alex or Cairo; it was a matter of recouping, building up, and going forward again. It was a different story now that our supply lines were down to almost zero, and it was the enemy's that were stretched out for miles. Many great air battles were fought over or near the Alamein line during July-November 1942. Our squadrons seemed to take on new strength and now there were three Spitfire squadrons operating in the area, making the 109s look up for the first time. We still lost pilots to 109s and ground fire, but the Luftwaffe was being hurt as their ablest sharp-shooters began to fall to Allied fighters. After the advance began in November 1942, it wasn't long before the bomber bases were too far behind the lines, so 260 Squadron joined 239 Wing with a primary role of dive-bombing and strafing, and occasional escort duties when the bombers were able to move up. This role continued until the end of the Tunisian campaign.

"Apart from flying, life in the desert generally was good – everyone soon adapted and learned to get along with the bare essentials. There was always a high degree of camaraderie, of living and fighting together, of trying to get the most of what was necessary to fight the enemy. Everyone was too busy or engrossed to become bored or lonely. Personally, I never thought much of being anywhere else – in fact, I was having the time of my life. Little things didn't matter – only important things counted. Uniforms and parades were unheard of and unnecessary, only rank insignia were worn with any regularity. There were no such things as social functions, parties, ot gatherings that might promote anyone's rank or position. At times during trying periods there would be shortages of food, with only bully beef and hard tack to eat, and only enough water to make tea, brush one's teeth, and wash one's face, but nobody went hungry or suffered ill effects. Most times there were lots of extras supplied in tins – tinned bacon, potatoes and fruit from South Africa and Australia – so there never were really any complaints regarding anything missing. Besides, there was no one to complain to, or no one cared to listen to such trivia. There were times we were able to shoot gazelle for fresh meat, or even quail. Except for three or four landing grounds such as Martuba, El Adem, Gazala, all Kittyhawk squadrons operated from new LGs levelled out of the desert some 20/30 miles from the coast. As a result we were seldom bothered by flies or other crawly creatures that were most surely prevalent at the older bases along the coast. Most important, there were none of the diseases common to inhabited areas.

"It should be noted, incidentally, that there was *no* air traffic control as such at the desert landing grounds throughout the entire desert campaigns, or even into Tunisia. Remarkably, when one contemplates a situation where four squadrons, sometimes more, operated from the same LG without mishap or waiting for take-off or landing. Usually the squadrons operated together, but on some occasions they conducted separate sorties. Except for the original airfields which were built along the coast, all others were simply graded out of the desert sand, approximately half a mile square, with a squadron widely dispersed on each side of the square. Group HQ would lay on operational duties; for example, for a bomber escort mission; Group HQ would notify the squadrons in order – close, medium, or top cover, or whatever, in relation to the bombers. The bombers formed up over their own field and then flew over the escort's field at 2/3,000 feet. When the bombers were seen approaching, all engines of the escort squadrons started up. As the bombers made a wide circuit of the field, the top cover escort took off first – usually 12 aircraft almost line-abreast across the field from their dispersal area. On take-off there was no lagging because one could be completely blinded by the dust kicked up from the leading aircraft's prop-wash. This was all very well, provided the leader lines up directly across the field to allow room for the aircraft on the extremes. There were occasions when pilots not fully aware of such hazards found themselves charging through dispersal areas, in amongst tents and slit trenches, while attempting to get airborne. Secondly, the medium bomber cover took off across the field from their dispersal, and finally the close cover squadron would follow from their side. By the time the bomber formation had completed a wide circuit of the field, all escort squadrons were in position around and above them, and the lot set course. On return to base the squadrons landed in reverse order to take-off. There was little waiting to land – the 109s had come into the circuit occasionally and caught aircraft with their wheels down. All pilots, therefore, learned to approach the field and land in the shortest time possible. Squadrons arranged landing priorities in the air, over the R/T, when necessary, but there was *no* air traffic control from the ground.

"The remarkable ability of the RAF to leap-frog its units in retreat as well as in advance to ensure full support to the ground troops seemed at times incredible. Someone had to be there in advance to prepare fields for the aircraft arrivals, usually on completion of an operation from the previous base. As the advance proceeded into Tripolitania, entire airfields had to be levelled out of the desert because of a shortage of landing grounds in new battle areas. Advance troops, including all squadron personnel who could be spared, would often pitch in with shovels and prepare a runway. While the desert was really a healthy place to live and operate, with only minor ailments throughout the year, the groundcrews suffered several privations. With no let-up from dawn to dusk, day after day, for more than two years for many, they were literally slaves to flying operations. No word good enough can be expressed to praise the groundcrews' outstanding achievements in keeping our aircraft flying throughout the desert war.

"Flying over the desert was an experience in itself. Seen from above it initially offered no evidence of habitation or life. There were shades of sand and brown with dark lines or spots intermixed, and to the novice this is best described as 'Bundoo' – nothing of note for miles in the great vastness below. Some pilots had more trouble finding their way around than others because as novices they could be right over an airfield and not recognise anything at first glance. Then the sun glinting off a perspex canopy or other object on the ground would help bring a whole camp into focus, with a very obvious airstrip in the middle. Of course, there was the Mediterranean coastline running roughly east-west, which everybody could recognise, and set course from some point on the coast.

"Bomber escort missions were sometimes flown out to sea, crossing back in near the target area, especially when said target was on the coast. Airfields such as El Daba, Gazala, Martuba, and enemy troop concentrations along the coast roads were attacked from out to sea. Most times operations were conducted over the desert where the coastline might be visible in the distance, depending on altitude flown. Strafing missions were flown right down on the deck, where surprise and accuracy in locating targets depended solely on the leadership of an experienced desert pilot. Experience could only be gained by actual close contact with the environment in hours flown, time in the area, and combat.

"The main and only reliable navigational aid in the desert was the sun. The desert was the sun, they were as one – sometimes annoying, sometimes a hindrance, but always helpful when attacking or navigating. With experience one learned to read the desert floor by light, and shadow. Every object, regardless of shape or size, cast a shadow, and by discerning these contrasts and knowing the actual ground environment in any given area, it was possible to understand and appreciate alien objects and movement amidst the normal surroundings. It was common practice to go down on the deck 60 to 80 miles from base and, with the aid of compass or directional gyro, align with the position of the sun, set course, and arrive over our own field. The sun was an important factor in all navigational and operational flying in the desert.

"In 260 Squadron we were fortunate in having Sqn Ldr O.V. Hanbury as commanding officer, who was probably one of the best all-round fighter leaders in the desert. He was a veteran of the Battle of Britain and completed two tours of ops in the desert. He was the CO when I joined 260 in May 1942, went off ops about 17 August for a rest, but returned to the squadron on 4 November 1942 and continued as CO until the end of the fighting in Tunisia. In the air he was the 'steely-grey' type, intent on destroying the enemy, and he expected the same from all his pilots. There were no excuses, no short-cuts, no line-shooting allowed or displayed at any time. He commanded respect from everyone on the squadron."

Werner Schroer, in 1942 an Oberleutnant, served in both I. and III./JG27:

"In my opinion the great variation in the scores of the German pilots in Africa is explained by the small number of fighter aircraft and the differing qualities of the pilots. Generally, the original pilots were better shots than the later arrivals, although some of the younger pilots, like Stahlschmidt, von Lieres and Remmer, were excellent. It was only natural, considering the low number of aircraft available, that the 'old hares' flew more sorties, were more often on the 'trigger' and were anxious to use every chance to gain a victory. Compared with the situation on the Channel front in 1940, there were a great many 'chances' in Africa. In the first months our opponents flew in a very conservative manner, and in most cases did not fly above 2,500 metres (7,500 feet). It was therefore relatively easy to climb above them and make surprise attacks. In their early combats with the Italians, the English pilots had not had the chance to gain the same experience that we had against the British home-based fighters over their own country the year before. The English pilots were generally very good; on my first sortie in Africa I was attacked by a Hurricane out of the sun and had 48 bullet holes in my aircraft, but was able to land close to our airfield at Gazala.

"I think one of the great vices of the German fighters was the growth of 'free-lance' hunting. Free-lance sorties (Freie Jagd) against enemy fighters were the most popular missions. Later, in the years of home defence in 1943-45 we were forced to abandon these sorties, but in Africa there were several reasons for this type of operation. Our early warning service (Freya and Kiebitz posts) was good, but in the opening months the British bombers flew mainly attacks on our ground forces and veered away when the German fighters approached, so that we mostly met only the covering fighters. Later on, when the bombers started to attack our airfields, they were excellently protected by fighters and we could seldom break through the fighter barrier. However, to tell the truth, the bombers did not come very often. Perhaps we could have shot down more bombers, but it is possible that we were not too interested – they had tail gunners. I have sometimes wished I could get a Ju 52 or Ju 87 in front of my guns, but I never had such luck!

"The number of our losses should be judged in relation to other factors. They were too high in comparison with our small strength but too low in relation to the possibilities which the RAF could have had if they had used their numerical superiority to best advantage against us. Often we only had two to five fighters serviceable due to lack of supplies of aircraft, fuel and engines.

"I feel the African air war was very difficult because of the unique conditions: the heat, the flies, the salt water, too few aircraft, no protection in the open desert, the numerical superiority of the enemy. Of course, now and then we had a feeling of superiority in combat. Often we took off with two or four fighters, shot down three enemies, but 30 or 50 escaped untouched – who can speak of superiority there? I believe we made some mistakes; like the RAF we should have concentrated on attacks on vehicles, tanks, forces, airfields, etc., but we shirked this as often as possible. I remember well the devastating effect on morale of such attacks on our forces. During the few ground attacks which I flew, the English soldiers lay on their backs and shot at us with their rifles. To the contrary, what did our men do? Out of their trucks, running away for cover – maybe it was the result of the constant British air attacks.

"We held the British pilots in high esteem. However, if I think it over soberly I have not experienced anything which I could add to the stories of British fair play, or anything to detract from them. There were rumours that German and British pilots had waved 'goodbye' with their wingtips when they had used all their ammunition – but these were fairy tales. The British pilots were well treated as long as they were with the German forces after capture. What happened to the German pilots I know only from the stories of Stahlschmidt, but he had the ill fortune to be captured by the Poles. We regretted that we had to fight against the English, but it was war and we had to fight. I confess that I had a certain degree of fear of them.

"I was only aware at the time that our Bf 109E, F and G were better than the Hurricanes and Curtiss's in climbing ability (long climbs). Dogfights in the style of Richthofen or Marseille I did not fight to a conclusion. The superiority of the British types in dogfights was notorious, and the Spitfire added their higher speed to this. The Spitfire arrived very late, but then the apprehension of our pilots was very great in memory of their experiences over the Channel. This fear was in many cases unfounded – because the excellent Spitfire needed an excellent pilot. I believe that our armament (a combination of heavy machine guns and cannons) was better than the armament of the Hurricane. Our Bf 109s were often able to return with 40 or 50 hits. Over and above this, our ammunition was superb. Often the pilots would arrange the sequence of loading the belts: tracer, explosive, and armour-piercing bullets. But you must hit – and that was the problem. How often I have missed, because accurate deflection shooting was not taught at training schools or during practice flights. My unforgettable Staffelkapitän 'Vati' Redlich, who was a wonderful person and a great leader, taught me shooting at the expense of many hours of his flying allowance for months, because I missed again and again. Maybe in fear or in haste, I started to fire on fighters from 1,000 to 500 metres (3,000 to 1,500 feet). Then one day I was alone and sat behind a Curtiss (merely by chance) – and from then on it was all right. However, there is no doubt that my true schoolmaster was Marseille; I studied his tactics for attacking the British defensive circles for a long time, tried it myself often without success – and finally learned the lesson.

"Mistakes in recognition of aircraft? I remember my scruples when meeting Macchis, but this was during the time when the Spitfires had arrived. Before this no Hurricane or Curtiss was to be expected at altitudes over 2,500 metres (7,500 feet), but the Macchis preferred to fly their freelance sorties at greater heights, and were sometimes taken for Spitfires. All fighter types of that time were similar in appearance and, of course, mistakes could have happened. At first the British flew in formations like bunches of grapes and were easy targets for our surprise attacks. They used no covering pairs 200 or 400 metres (600 or 1,200 feet) higher, and therefore we could attack in small numbers almost without risk. We attacked from above, the speed of the dive allowing us to climb at once. During the fights over the convoys to Tobruk, the British introduced the defensive circle. It was very efficient, but then Marseille disenchanted it; he would dive down near the circle, pull out and zoom into it from below. He reached the level of the circle just before stalling, just in time to level off, shoot down a Tommy and start to spin to sea level, where he pulled out at the last second (it was impossible to follow him). [But how often must this have given RAF pilots the impression that he had been shot down – Auth] He then climbed back to his own formation and repeated the performance until the circle broke up. No other German pilot was able to copy Marseille's tricks, although all made attempts to do so, and sometimes succeeded in breaking up the circle. During the convoy battles to Tobruk the circle was undoubtedly very effective for the British. I believe that it was one of the reasons why they could defend Tobruk for so long, as we spent most of our time and fuel trying to break the circle – and then there was no time left to attack the ships.

"I had very, very cordial relations with the Italian fighter pilots. But at that time we were of the opinion that they could have done somewhat more after they were equipped with Macchi 202s. Our Ju 87 and Ju 88 units may confirm this.

"I remember very well my first combat with a Spitfire in Africa. The pilot surprised me at 4,000 metres (12,000 feet); I was very frightened and made a bunt, then fell into a so-called negative dive. I was able to pull out at the very last second only by using the trim, which was very dangerous – trimming at such high speeds usually meant sure death. I was bathed in sweat and believe the British pilot must have seen that I was in trouble, although he finally lost me. It was my most exciting event of the whole war. We were very pleased that the Spitfire came to the desert so late. We did not ask why. The Spitfire was a wonderful aircraft and I shall never forget the blue-painted wings over us. Since the Channel days the German pilots were very biased about the Spitfire, but for me it affected my senses like a red rag to a bull – I must have a try at it.

"I personally knew that Polish and South African fighter units fought in the desert, but I knew nothing of Australians or French. To equalize our numerical inferiority our best chance was the surprise 'hit and run' attacks which the English did not like very much. Why accept a dogfight if I have the higher position and can return to it after the attack? To accept a dogfight was to venture voluntarily into an unfavourable position. When it happened, my reaction was to gain a better starting position by a prolonged climb. However, I never found that the English and South African pilots were too eager to accept combat when they had attacked our airfields and were pursued by us. All 'went on a journey' at full speed homeward. I cannot remember being very impressed by the new Kittyhawks. For me the Kittyhawk was the aircraft I could shoot down most easily. Why? Perhaps this type ran in my blood!"

The final Luftwaffe pilot to comment was Rudolf Sinner, technical officer of II./JG 27 during 1942:

"The air war in Africa favoured the 'experts' to a high degree. The wingmen, 'Kaczmareks' and No 2s had only a small chance to gain any victories. The majority of the victories of the German fighters were the result of surprise attacks, during which in most cases, only the leader was able to fire. Such quick, sparrowhawk-like attacks were seldom followed by a dogfight because the manoeuvrability and threefold numerical superiority made the British fighters very hard to attack. When there was time to zoom up and return for a second attack on a formation which did not have top cover, and had broken up into a defensive circle, or swirling 'beehive', again only the leader had the chance for attack and success.

"The German Staffeln were not able to operate more than three Rotten in most cases, and generally could not put in the air more than a Schwarm, or even a single Rotte. If you consider that each day only an average of six or eight Staffeln were on operations (the others were resting), it meant that each day the six or eight most experienced pilots were ordered to lead all the day's missions of half Staffel or Schwarm strength, and had to fly most of the missions in single pairs, again because of their experience. At best a further dozen pilots had a chance to fly as Rotten leaders; they only had a similar chance to score to the Staffel and Schwarm leaders if they were lucky enough to be given an independent assignment as a Rotte, or if the formation was split up in the course of a combat. The law of natural selection brought the more talented pilots quickly to the position of Rotten or Schwarm leader, and from that moment they had the opportunity to build up their personal scores. Simply expressed, it was a matter of cause and effect. However, it cannot be said from this that the pilots who were not prominent were below average, poor flyers or lacking in fighting spirit. Such generalizations are not possible, and likewise one cannot compare the German and the British pilots so far as their claims are concerned. The difference between the aircraft and tactics employed were too great.

"We only met British bomber formations occasionally. If we were able to attack, they were nearly always covered by a strong British fighter formation, and the attack generally split up into individual attacks between fighters. The Curtiss P-40, although not as good an aircraft to hunt the Bf 109s in, was an excellent aircraft to fly close escort to bombers. It was very dangerous to attack a bomber formation escorted by the manoeuvrable Curtiss's, and without prospects. Another reason for the relatively light losses of the British bombers was the excellent tight and clean formation flying. They held formation even in heavy Flak with admirable courage, and this enabled them to defend themselves with the very concentrated fire of their rear gunners, as well as helping the fighters covering them.

"The Germans operated in the hunting grounds of the British fighters, mainly with bombers (Ju

87s in the majority of cases). We did not fly many offensive missions with fighters, and for the British fighters it was relatively easy to attack our bombers with good chances of success. To attack the Bf 109 was very difficult for them, particularly in the pre-Spitfire times. In nearly all cases the initiative for attack lay with the German fighters, unless we were tied down to escort duties or asleep. Consequently, the relatively small success of the British fighters against the Bf 109s is easily explained. I always had the feeling that our losses were very low compared to the size of the effort made by the British and the losses they suffered in North Africa. During bombing attacks the Ju 87s and Ju 88s were forced to break up their formation and form a line of about a kilometre in length. They were not able to defend themselves with their own armament against the large numbers of British fighters attacking, and the scattered formation made it impossible for the German fighters to protect the bombers.

"Very seldom did we meet British formations of numerical inferiority. The rule was for two, four or six Bf 109s to meet enemy fighters in strengths of from 12 to 20 aircraft. The British units always flew very low, and always in very senseless combat formations. This pleased us, but we were unable to understand it. The British flying facilitated the German fighter pilots to see the enemy first, approach unseen, and choose the position of attack at will, while the British lost mobility and visibility. From one mission to the next I was afraid the British *must* recognise the cause of their helplessness, and change their formation to a looser one. But, God be praised! my fears were groundless! I met my first fighter opponents flying correct tactical formations over Tunisia, and they were Americans. I believe the British tactics in Africa were wrong; they were based on numbers, 'flock' tactics, and, as a last resort, defensive circles.

"If I compare the war theatres, I think the fight on the Channel front was somewhat harder for fighter pilots than in the desert. With the exception of the Murmansk region, the fighting in Russia in 1941-42 was much easier because of the technical inferiority of the Russians, allowing us to claim large numbers of aircraft. But this was compensated for in other areas by the chances of survival after a force-landing in enemy territory, whereas in Russia the pilots were killed. I personally had no trouble with the African climate, and preferred it to the Russian winter.

"We had the greatest regard for the British soldiers and flyers, though we knew them mainly by hearsay, rather than from personal experience as we seldom saw captured pilots. Of the few we saw we had different impressions; in some cases the reality did not agree with the idealistic conception we had of the British people. We were pleased that the captured pilots showed without exception a manly, correct attitude; they were very modest, not submissive, not aggressive, and not cringing. I remember only one Australian Curtiss pilot who we entertained at Martuba who left us with an unpleasant feeling. He contradicted our idea of the 'comrade of the other Feldpostnummer' in the most unpleasant way. He was a giant, but his behaviour, speech and appearance was like an uncivilised savage. His table manners were horrible, and 'Fifi' Stahlschmidt said: 'This man is a catastrophe, he is a matter for the firing squad!' I think we had some prejudices against the Poles and Australians, but we had the greatest respect for the British, South Africans, New Zealanders and French.

"It was unintelligible to me that the British built Hurricanes and used them against the Germans in 1942. Likewise I was astonished that they used the Curtiss for other tasks than bomber escort. These points, together with insufficient armament (machine guns in the wings) and bad cannon ammunition, were a blessing to us. It was a mistake that the Spitfires arrived in Africa so late. In the course of my not too frequent encounters with Spitfire squadrons in Africa, I had the impression that the pilots were not using the very dangerous merits of this type to the best advantage. The Spitfire squadrons in Africa – contrary to those on the Channel front – operated in a heavy and clumsy way. Perhaps the pilots had trouble getting accustomed to the new type. I can only shake my head that it was possible to mistake Curtiss's and Hurricanes. I feel that the ambition to have shot down the more efficient type was the secret reason for these mistakes; P-40 instead of Hurricane, Spitfire instead of P-40, Bf 109 instead of MC.202! n the desert it was impossible to observe the crash of an aircraft except at low altitudes, and then only in exceptional circumstances. Over the sea I think the pilot could see an aircraft ditching in a few cases. On most occasions the crashed aircraft in the desert burnt. If two pilots each shot down an aircraft at the same time then each pilot considered the observed crash as their victory, quite naturally.

"To sum up, we took advantage of the British 'flock' formations very often and surprised them, shot them down, or held up their strong formation, only with a pair or Schwarm of aircraft. We gave them only a few chances to use the excellent manoeuvrability of their weary 'dragons'. If it was necessary, we accepted dogfights (especially when escorting Stukas), and the better shots in our ranks were very successful even in the hottest of these. However, it is self-evident that we preferred to gain our victories with the least danger. I understand very well the bitter feeling the British pilots often had about the 'bad' Messerschmitts – but why should we expose ourselves unnecessarily.

"Finally some words about our Italian allies. I think that only a few Germans were able to judge them correctly and without bias, good or bad. Either we judged them as cowards or, to the contrary as cavaliers or kindred daredevils. I looked at the problem more objectively, as the character of the Italian people is so different to ours. I always regretted the small numbers of Italian soldiers who tried to rescue the honour of arms for their colours despite the unpleasant political and social omens. We watched with compassionate admiration the gallant Macchi 200 pilots die in their flying crates beside the Stukas they had to protect, and with great respect we observed the senseless, ineffectual ground attacks of the CR.42s through the Flak fire over the Deir el Raghil ridge. It was grand to celebrate a festival with the Italians, but generally we had the impression that the British treated them more seriously than we did. The African campaign was a question of supply. The supply of the Italians was so poor that their combat effectiveness, despite the heroism of some elite units, was miserable.

"Nevertheless, the Italians were generally excellent comrades, and in this respect were superior to the German soldier. They were always helpful, even in retreat or when badly frightened. The other ranks were more unassuming, more modest and more biddable than the average German privates. The Italian officers were, however, the extreme opposite in most cases. The true leaders of the troops were the active corporals and sergeants. The Italian pilots on average were better aerobats then the Germans and British. In combat they had nothing to offer, even after equipment with excellent aircraft like the MC.202. Our contacts were trifling, and besides some personal friendships, unfriendly, and from the Italian side, bureaucratic. For instance it was impossible for me, as acting Staffelkapitän, to speak with some Italian MC.202 pilots who had taken part in the fight from which Obfw Krenz did not return (1 September 1942), even when I had visited the Italians at their base!"

Finally, B.H.A.Playford arrived in North Africa as a flight officer at around the same time as 'Stocky' Edwards – just at the point where Volume 1 ends and Volume 2 starts!

"I arrived in the Western Desert at Advanced Air HQ, then at Tmimi, on 24 December 1941. This was the worst Christmas Eve I have ever spent, notable only for the fact that I met Basil Embrey, surely one of the bravest men ever. Next day I was awoken in my little tent around dawn by a tremendous outbreak of machine-gun fire. I leapt out of bed, put on my tin hat, drew my revolver, and shot out into a slit trench. I then felt very stupid and aggrieved – it was only the ground gunners welcoming Christmas morning. A miserable Christmas – nothing but bully beef and biscuits.

"On 29 December I went to El Adem, picked up a Hurricane IIa, and met George Keefer, then a pilot officer, who led me to 274 Squadron at Msus. The CO was 'Sid' Linnard (until March 1942), and subsequently Sqn Ldr E. 'Dixie' Dean. We were lucky to have such experienced COs. The flight commanders at that time were Flt Lts Andy Smith, a Canadian, and Aldridge. Andy Smith was a fantastic character. He had done something like 70 daylight shipping strikes on Blenheim Is, thoroughly deserving but never getting a gong. We had a very bad day on 26 January 1942. We went out ground-strafing all day in sections of four on the advancing Germans between Antelat and Msus. Aldridge would not fly as he said the weather was too bad, and when it was our turn my aircraft was unserviceable but flyable. Andy Smith promised me that if I went down he would land and pick me up. I took over B Flight from Aldridge, but poor Andy was killed on 12 February.

"Morale in 274 Squadron was not particularly high at this time, but nor was it low. It was a sort of resignation. Everybody was disenchanted with the desert Hurricane. A marvellous aeroplane, built like a tank, very manoeuvrable, but hopelessly slow. The Messerschmitt Bf 109F, apart from having superb armament, was nearly 100 mph faster, and climbed around 2,000 feet per minute faster as well. It flew with its hood closed, whereas the hooped Hurricane hood obscured vision, so we always flew with it open. On 15 August 1942, when I had become maintenance test pilot at 243 Wing base after being wounded, I did a proper speed test in level flight in a Hurricane IIc, and at 18,000 feet I achieved a maximum speed of 200 mph indicated, computed to be 270 mph true! The next day I did the same on a Spitfire Vb, and at 20,000 feet obtained 240 mph indicated, 320 mph true. The Bf 109F was faster in all respects than the desert Spitfire V. When Wally Conrad left 274 Squadron and went onto Spits, he said they were better but still not good enough. We also had a hopeless radio, the old TR9 sets, which were antiques and completely useless for air-to-air. As we had no radar, we did stand-by, which meant sitting in the aircraft ready for take-off for two hours at a time. As it was quite hot, even in January, after about one hour there was a great tendency to fall asleep; whereupon any evil-minded character who witnessed this would suddenly slam his transmitter on and shout down his mike, causing the sleeper to break wind violently in sheer terror!

"The food was awful but healthy. It was completely built around bully beef, hard biscuits, and a totally uneatable sausage immortalised by the name of pork and soya links. Meals consisted of a variety of bully and biscuit pie, bully and biscuit crumble, bully stew. Biscuits and jam crumble, bully fritters with mixed tinned veg, in a succulent salt water gravy, washed down with a mug of 'Tobruk 42' – salt tea!

"Our two outstanding pilots were George Keefer and Wally Conrad, both Canadians. They both survived the war, and happily remained good friends for many years. Although our average age, I suppose, was about 22, we had two pilots, Plt Off Sammy Samuels and 'Chiefy' (Flight Sergeant) O'Neill, a Canadian, who both looked incredibly young, particularly Sammy. English ladies on the tram from the junior officers' club into Alexandria often became visibly upset because Sammy looked so young.

"Summing up, I suppose we were just about an average squadron. Particularly in the desert, I think the type of commanding officer made a tremendous difference. We were fortunate in our two, although I understand 274 had not always been so happily placed in the past. We definitely had a 'First' and 'Second XI', and – looking back with hindsight – I can see now that there were many things that I could have done as a flight commander, particularly in regard to training and organising my flight, which I failed to do."

A captured Ju 52/3m transport put into Allied supply service as the 'Libyan Clipper' is seen here at Maaten Bagush.

Code Letters carried by British and Commonwealth Squadrons in North Africa, February 1942-March 1943

6 Squadron	JV	229 Squadron	HB
14 Squadron	LY	230 Squadron	NM
22 Squadron	OA	237 Squadron	DV
30 Squadron	RS	238 Squadron	VK
33 Squadron	NW	250 Squadron	LD
37 Squadron	LF	252 Squadron	BT
38 Squadron	HD	260 Squadron	ME,HS
39 Squadron	Nil	272 Squadron	XK
40 Squadron	BL	274 Squadron	YK
46 Squadron	Nil	335 Squadron	FG
47 Squadron	Nil	336 Squadron	Nil
55 Squadron	Nil	417 Squadron	AN
70 Squadron	DU (?)	450 Squadron	DJ,OK
73 Squadron	TP	451 Squadron	BQ
80 Squadron	EY	458 Squadron	MD
86 Squadron	BX	459 Squadron	GK
89 Squadron	Nil	2 PRU/680 Squadron	Nil
92 Squadron	QJ	601 Squadron	UF
94 Squadron	FZ,GO	800 Squadron	Nil
112 Squadron	GA	803 Squadron	Nil
117 Squadron	LD	805 Squadron	Nil
123 Squadron	XE	3 RAAF Squadron	CA
127 Squadron	BZ	1 SAAF Squadron	AX
145 Squadron	ZX	2 SAAF Squadron	TA,DB
148 Squadron	FS	3 SAAF Squadron	CA
159 Squadron	Nil	4 SAAF Squadron	KJ,DX
160 Squadron	Nil	5 SAAF Squadron	TJ
162 Squadron	Nil	7 SAAF Squadron	OZ
202 Squadron	TQ,AX	12 SAAF Squadron	VL
203 Squadron	Nil	15 SAAF Squadron	ZP
208 Squadron	Nil	21 SAAF Squadron	Nil
213 Squadron	AK	24 SAAF Squadron	OZ
217 Squadron	MW	40 SAAF Squadron	WR
223 Squadron	Nil	13 (RHAF) Squadron	Nil
227 Squadron	Nil		

Sunday, 1 February 1942

For the WDAF the first week of February was mainly occupied with ground-strafing activities, flown against the advancing Axis troops. In the air there was little aerial combat due to four days of pouring rain. Indeed, the Luftwaffe reported that its aircraft could not take off as they were sunk to the axles in mud. Nonetheless their fighter units managed to get into the air sufficiently to fly forward to Benina and Berka West. At the former base they were joined by the headquarters and 6° Gruppo of 1° Stormo CT with 21 serviceable MC.202s. From here 6° Gruppo would move again to Benghazi (K3 airfield) on 5 February and finally to Martuba on 11 February. At this time Gen DA Raoul da Barberino was replaced as commander of Settore Ovest (West Sector) by Gen BA Ruggero Bonomi. The Allied units were also on the move during the day, withdrawing this time to El Adem. At LG.110, Tmimi, 94 Squadron arrived, re-equipped with nine Kittyhawks and two Tomahawks, and led by a new commanding officer – none other than E.M. 'Imshi' Mason, DFC, the great ace of the First Libyan Campaign. 73 Squadron, meanwhile, undertook the unit's first offensive patrol as a full squadron since summer 1941. 274 Squadron welcomed back Sgt Persse, who had been shot down and wounded during December.

Italian Casualties

600ª Sq , 145°Gr T	S.81 crash-landed near Benina airfield, pilot S.Ten Vittorio Turco, copilot Serg Massimo Lucidi and most of crew, including S.Ten Luigi Caneppele of 363ª Sq, 150° Gr CT, killed

Monday, 2 February 1942

On this date 229 Squadron was taken off operations, passing nine Hurricanes to 1 SAAF Sqn. For 229 a new role was in the offing; it moved to LG.102 at Sidi Haneish on 7th where Sqn Ldr W.A.Smith rejoined the unit. However, its days of desert flying were nearly at an end for in March it would be posted to Malta, as will be recounted. Meanwhile, 4 SAAF Squadron moved to LG.110 to join the newly-arrived 94 Squadron. 2 SAAF Squadron would follow on 5th.

Further moves were also underway for some of the Italian units, 209ª and 236ª Squadriglie and 3° Gruppo CT, going from Agedabia to Benghazi K2 while 8° and 150° Gruppi CT moved to Benghazi K3.

British Casualties

208 Sqn	Hurricane Z4711 left 1705, soon after take-off developed engine failure and spun in; Lt B.V.Shields KiFA
1 SAAF Sqn	Hurricane II V7772 damaged by Flak during patrol over Tmimi-Derna road; Lt G.R.Connell safe

Tuesday, 3 February 1942

Mechili was evacuated by British forces, causing 112, 238 and 3 RAAF Squadrons to be withdrawn to Gambut, with 73 Squadron now moving to El Adem. At the same time 250 Squadron at Gazala No.1 was called back to El Gamil to replace its remaining Tomahawks with Kittyhawks and to undertake training on these new aircraft in the Canal Zone. During the afternoon six of 112 Squadron's Kittyhawks strafed vehicles on the Derna road, pilots claiming some ten vehicles shot-up. During this operation one aircraft was lost to ground fire.

British Casualties

112 Sqn	Kittyhawk I AK602 FTR from ground attack near Derna; Flg Off P.C.L.Brunton MiA
208 Sqn	Hurricane Z4085 Flg Off K.C.G.Davies off to reconnoitre road; attacked by two Bf 109s in Gorai area and evaded them in dust from the ground. However, oil tank had been hit and crash-landed 20m SW Tengender (probably on 31st Jan)

Wednesday, 4 February 1942

British Casualties

33 Sqn	Hurricane I badly damaged by Flak; Flg Off Tofield WiA

Italian Casualties

365ª Sq, 150° Gr CT	S.Ten Lorenzo Clerici killed by Allied bombing at Ain Gazala

Thursday, 5 February 1942

In the early dawn three Hurricanes of 73 Squadron were scrambled after raiders. A Bf 110 was damaged at 0525 and a second claim for one of these aircraft shot down was made five minutes later by Sgt Sands, who reported chasing this aircraft to the Tmimi area. One Ju 88 was claimed damaged at 1530 by the pilot of a 208 Squadron Hurricane. The unit's opponent appears to have been an aircraft of 1./LG 1 which recorded one bomber damaged 10% in combat with a reported five Hurricanes north of El Adem. However, this aircraft returned safely to its base with the wounded observer aboard.

British Claims

73 Sqn	Sgt E.L.Joyce	Hurricane IIb	Bf 110 Damaged	El Adem	0525
73 Sqn	Sgt A.H.Sands	Hurricane IIb Z5591	Bf 110	El Adem	0530
208 Sqn	Flg Off R.L.Macgregor	Hurricane II Z4772	Ju 88 Damaged		1530

British Casualties

73 Sqn	Flg Off R.I.Laing WiA on ground by bombing at El Adem
73 Sqn	Sgt H.W.E. Packham WiA on ground by bombing at El Adem
112 Sqn	Kittyhawk I AK685 crash-landed at base at 1625 due to Flak damage; Sgt W.E.Carson safe
1 SAAF Sqn	Hurricane II slightly damaged by Allied AA; Lt J.T.Seccombe safe
1 SAAF Sqn	Hurricane II damaged by Flak; Lt F.J.P.Collingwood safe

German Casualties	
1./LG 1	Ju 88A-4 10% damaged by Hurricanes N El Adem; observer WiA

Friday, 6 February 1942
The only known British claims related to Ju 88s claimed damaged during afternoon patrols.

British Claims					
274 Sqn	Flt Lt A.J.Smith	Hurricane IIb BD821	Ju 88 Damaged	El Adem	1520-1610
274 Sqn	Flt Lt F.J.Aldridge	Hurricane IIb DG914	Ju 88 Damaged	El Adem	1600-1700

Saturday, 7 February 1942
At this date the main units of Regia Aeronautica in North Africa were as follows:

Regia Aeronautica Order of Battle

13° Stormo BT	Col Antonio Pirino	BR.20 (30)
11° Gruppo	Magg Giuseppe Aini	
1ª Squadriglia	Cap Enrico Angelini	
4ª Squadriglia	Cap Giovanni Lazzarini	
43° Gruppo	T.Col Roberto Pagliocchini	
3ª Squadriglia	Cap Mario Persico	
5ª Squadriglia	Cap Vittorio Piccinelli	
174ª Squadriglia RST	Cap Vittorio Pini	S.79 (8)
175ª Squadriglia RST	Cap Vittorio Cantarella	S.79 (9)
176ª Squadriglia RST	Cap Remo Maccagnani	Cant.Z.1007bis (5)
279ª Squadriglia AS	Cap Giulio Marini	S.79 (4)
284ª Squadriglia AS	Cap Oscar Pegna	S.79 (5)
209ª Squadriglia Aut BaT	Ten Ezio Quarantelli	Ju 87 (2)
236ª Squadriglia Aut BaT	Cap Alessandro Cerutti	CR.42 (7)
1° Stormo CT	T.Col Alfredo Reglieri	MC.202 (38)
6° Gruppo	Magg Marco Larcher	
79ª Squadriglia	Cap Domenico Camarda	
81ª Squadriglia	Cap Giuliano Giacomelli	
88ª Squadriglia	Cap Dante Ocarso	
17° Gruppo	Magg Domenico Sciaudone	
71ª Squadriglia	Cap Pericle Baruffi	
72ª Squadriglia	Cap Pio Tomaselli	
80ª Squadriglia	Cap Clizio Nioi	
3° Gruppo Autonomo CT	T.Col Innocenzo Monti	CR.42 (26)
153ª Squadriglia	Ten Massimino Mancini	
154ª Squadriglia	Cap Giuseppe Tovazzi	
155ª Squadriglia	Cap Bruno Alessandrini	
12° Gruppo Autonomo CT	T.Col Bruno Codugnello	G.50 (36)
159ª Squadriglia	Cap Roberto Pastorelli	
160ª Squadriglia	Cap Vincenzo Sant'Andrea	
165ª Squadriglia	Cap Corrado Ceccacci	
150° Gruppo Autonomo CT	Magg Antonio Vizzotto	MC.200 (25)
363ª Squadriglia	Cap Luigi Mariotti	
364ª Squadriglia	Ten Mario Bellagambi	
365ª Squadriglia	Cap Domenico Bevilacqua	

160° Gruppo Autonomo CT	Magg Michele Mandara	CR.42 (35)
393ª Squadriglia	Cap Paolo Arcangeletti	
394ª Squadriglia	Cap Giovanni Giannini	
375ª Squadriglia	Cap Massimiliano Langosco di Langosco	
8° Gruppo Autonomo CT	Magg Mario Bacich	MC.200 (20)
92ª Squadriglia	Cap Nino Zannier	
93ª Squadriglia	Cap Riccardo Marcovich	
94ª Squadriglia	Cap Orfeo Cecchet	
69° Gruppo OA	Magg Ettore Zambaldi	Ca. 311 (22)
118ª Squadriglia	Cap Giuseppe Gaggi	
123ª Squadriglia	Cap Vittorio Falugi	
145ª Squadriglia RM	Cap Nicolò Albanese	Cant.Z.501 (9)
196ª Squadriglia RM	Cap Oreste Genta	Cant.Z.501 (5)

Overall 306 serviceable aircraft.

German paratroopers occupied the oasis of Gialo on this date, while the Luftwaffe fighters were able to move forward to Martuba at the same time. During the day I./JG 27 was able to record its first claim during the month (see also Chapter Three).

German Claims

2./JG 27	Lt Friedrich Körner	Blenheim	NE Derna 1427

Sunday, 8 February 1942

The Luftwaffe struck hard against the Commonwealth squadrons during a day of sustained action. At 0730 six Hurricanes of 274 Squadron patrolled over Martuba. Lt Marseille of I./JG 27 had taken off over his unit's airfield when he received warning that seven fighters were behind him. Pushing down the nose of his Messerschmitt to gain momentum, he then zoomed up above this formation and attacked, claiming two shot down, both of which were reportedly witnessed from the ground; one Hurricane was lost by 274 Squadron, Flt Sgt Hargreaves crash-landing and becoming a prisoner. In return Plt Off Conrad claimed a Bf 109 as a probable.

At 0900 two pilots of 112 Squadron scrambled after a Ju 88 which they chased over El Adem; here it was attacked by 274 Squadron Hurricanes, being claimed probably shot down. This may have been a reconnaissance aircraft of 1.(F)/122, which crash-landed at Gerbini airfield in Sicily 30% damaged, the crew surviving unharmed.

Hurricane IIa DG631 NH-C of 274 Squadron was being flown by Flg Off Wally Conrad on 8 February when he claimed a probable victory over a Bf 109.

Eight Hurricanes of 1 SAAF Squadron now moved to Gazala 2 for operations, from where at 1030 Lts Finney and MacLean were scrambled, followed by Lts Biden and Powell. Obfw Otto Schulz and his Röttenflieger from II./JG 27 bounced the first pair, Schulz hitting Finney's aircraft with a well-aimed burst which caused the South African pilot to crash-land at Gazala 1. Schulz at once swept in and strafed the crashed Hurricane to destruction. He then climbed swiftly to 9,000 feet to attack the other pair, hitting Powell's aircraft in the tail, and Biden's in the engine. This stopped and Biden went into a spin from which he subsequently pulled out, allowing him to crash-land, although into a wall! Schulz repeated his strafing attack, destroying this aircraft as well. The remaining four Hurricanes then took off, but failed to intercept.

Soon after midday 73 and 112 Squadrons took off to escort 11 Blenheims to Derna, joined by ten Kittyhawks of 3 RAAF Squadron. When circling over El Adem waiting to rendezvous with 73 Squadron, four of the Australian pilots had to return to base due to problems with their engines. Three Bf 109s then dived on the remaining aircraft, Oblt Keller of I./JG 27 shooting away the tail of Sgt Curtiss' aircraft, then repeating the process on Flg Off Threlkeld's fighter. The latter pilot baled out and was picked up safely by the army. Curtiss managed to stagger back to Gambut where he crash-landed. Four other pilots lost contact at this stage, and returned to base, only Sqn Ldr Gibbes remaining to accompany 112 Squadron to the target.

73 Squadron was providing top cover, but over Derna this unit's Hurricanes were attacked by Bf 109s and became involved in a dogfight. Two pilots made claims for probables, but Sgt Sands' aircraft received damage to the coolant system and he crash-landed ten miles from base. 112 Squadron, now alone over the Blenheims, fought a rearguard action as the formation headed for base. Over Bomba Bay three Messerschmitts were claimed shot down, but three of the unit's Kittyhawks failed to return. Four claims were made by the Luftwaffe in respect of this afternoon engagement.

This day's ten claimed – all identified as P-40s – matched fairly exactly with the Commonwealth losses, although no German losses actually occurred to confirm any of the Allied claims. The four credited to Jochen Marseille brought his personal score to 40, overtaking that of Oblt Homuth's 39, making him the top scorer in Africa to date. Otto Schulz was catching them fast, his two on this date bringing his total to 37.

174ª Squadriglia RST of the Regia Aeronautica moved from El Nofilia to Benghazi K2.

British Claims

274 Sqn	Plt Off W.A.G.Conrad	Hurricane IIb BD820 'D'	Bf 109 Probable	Tmimi-Derna	0745-0855
73 Sqn	Flg Off J.Irwin	Hurricane IIb	Bf 109F Probable	10-15m S Tmimi	0830
73 Sqn	Plt Off R.McDougal	Hurricane IIb	Bf 109E Probable	S Tmimi	0830
73 Sqn	Wt Off H.D.Price	Hurricane IIb	Ju 88 Probable	El Adem	1140
112 Sqn	Sgt H.G.Burney	Kittyhawk I AK702 'P'	Bf 109F	Derna	1250-1505
112 Sqn	Sgt H.G.Burney	Kittyhawk I AK702 'P'	Bf 109F (shared)	Derna	1250-1505
112 Sqn	Flt Lt P.H.Humphreys	Kittyhawk I AK682 'U'			
112 Sqn	Sgt G.W.Elwell	Kittyhawk I AK593	Bf 109	Derna	1250-1505

British Casualties

274 Sqn	Hurricane II Z4800 shot down ? Flak; Flt Sgt Hargreaves PoW 0745-0855
1 SAAF Sqn	Hurricane II Z5069 'AX-H' 'The Glamour King' damaged, crash-landed 1m SE Gazala, and then strafed; Lt A.J.Biden wounded on the ground by the strafe 1030-
1 SAAF Sqn	Hurricane II damaged; Lt W.F.Powell safe 1030-
1 SAAF Sqn	Hurricane II Z5069 crash-landed and strafed; Lt A.J.Biden safe 1030-
73 Sqn	Hurricane II Z5312; crash-landed; Sgt A.H.Sands safe 1200
3 RAAF Sqn	Kittyhawk I AK660 shot down; Flg Off T.L.Threlkeld baled out returned safe 1200
3 RAAF Sqn	Kittyhawk I AK655 tail shot away, crash-landed at base; Sgt V.F. Curtiss safe 1200
112 Sqn	Kittyhawk I AK593 took off at 1250; shot down; Sgt G.W. Elwell MiA nr Derna 1330
112 Sqn	Kittyhawk I AK652 took off at 1250; shot down; Sgt A.T.Donkin KiA nr Derna 1330
112 Sqn	Kittyhawk I AK585 took off at 1250; shot down; Sgt B.P.Hoare RNZAF MiA nr Derna 1330

German Claims

3./JG 27	Lt Hans-Joachim Marseille	2 P-40s	ENE Martuba and 20km from Martuba	0822 & 0825
4./JG 27	Obfw Otto Schulz	2 P-40s	Ain el Gazala l.g. & E Ain el Gazala	1035 & 1040
2./JG 27	Oblt Fritz Keller	2 P-40s	E and 30km WNW El Adem	1330 & 1335

3./JG 27	Lt Hans-Joachim Marseille	P-40	NW Bomba Bay	1420
2./JG 27	Lt Friedrich Körner	P-40	Bomba Bay	1427
3./JG 27	Lt Hans-Joachim Marseille	P-40	NE Bomba Bay	1430
3./JG 27	Oblt Gerhard Homuth	P-40	E Bomba Bay	1432

Monday, 9 February 1942

During a dawn raid on El Adem, Sqn Ldr Ward of 73 Squadron took off and shot down an He 111 of KG 26 into the sea north of Tobruk. At 0830 Flg Off Davies of 208 Squadron commenced a TacR sortie to the Gebel area, east of El Faidia; while so engaged, he attacked Martuba airfield and shot-up a radio truck. Oblt Düllberg of II./JG 27 was just taking off for an early patrol when this occurred, and giving chase, he shot the intruder down. At around the same time five Hurricanes of 274 Squadron intercepted a Ju 88 of II./LG 1 which Plt Off Weeks shot down, the bomber crash-landing south of Gazala. Somewhat later four of 73 Squadron's aircraft on a high patrol near El Adem were joined by two more from 274 Squadron. These aircraft became engaged with I./JG 27 Bf 109s, one of which was claimed shot down and one damaged, but a Hurricane was lost, the pilot being killed. The German pilots claimed two of the British fighters, one of these being the 40th for Oblt Homuth, equalling the total currently being claimed by his subordinate, Marseille. One Bf 109F was shot down with the loss of the pilot, although the JG 27 personnel thought it had fallen to AA fire; he crashed south of Gazala.

British Claims

73 Sqn	Sqn Ldr D.H. Ward	Hurricane IIb BD751	He 111	10-15m NW Tobruk	0700
274 Sqn	Plt Off R.N.Weeks	Hurricane IIb Z5064	Ju 88	El Adem	0800-0920
73 Sqn	Flg Off I.D.H.Duncan	Hurricane IIb	Bf 109 Damaged	El Adem	1045
73 Sqn	Flt Lt G.R.A.McG.Johnston	Hurricane IIc BD945	Bf 109F	15m S base, El Adem	1045

British Casualties

208 Sqn	Hurricane V7896 left 0830, shot down near Martuba; Flg Off K.G.C.Davies MiA
274 Sqn	Hurricane II Z4991 shot down; Sgt T.H.Johnston KiA

German Claims

5./JG 27	Oblt Ernst Düllberg	P-40	SE Martuba	0958
3./JG 27	Oblt Gerhard Homuth	Hurricane	S El Adem	1051
2./JG 27	Lt Karl von Lieres und Wilkau	Hurricane	SW El Adem	1051

German Casualties

5./KG 26	He 111H-6 WNr 4133 1H+EN shot down by Hurricane over Gambut; Uffz Willi Stender and 2 MiA; Oblt Heinz Birschel KiA
6./LG 1	Ju 88A-4 WNr 5576 L1+AP shot down by Hurricanes, crash-landed nr Tobruk; Fw Siegfried Haiderer and 3 PoW
2./JG 27	Bf 109F-4 trop WNr 8504 Red 10 shot down by AA S Ain el Gazala; Fw Gerhard Fuchs MiA

Tuesday, 10 February 1942

Axis forces reached Tmimi on this date, commencing the construction of strongpoints. They had at this stage re-captured the greater part of the Cyrenaican 'bulge', but here a line began to be established over which the opposing forces were to face each other for several months as both raced to build up their strength in preparation for a new offensive. This line began on the coast at Gazala, running southwards until it petered out around the fortress created at Bir Hacheim. Defences on both sides were strong on the coast, but became steadily more extended the further south they reached.

By now the Germans had started to fit some of their Bf 109Fs as fighter-bombers, JG 27 commencing operations of this nature on this date, pilots from 5.Staffel claiming to have destroyed 13 British vehicles. Bf 110s of III./ZG 26 were also active during the day, but one of their aircraft was lost attacking a column near Bir Hacheim when the pilot selected the wrong detonator setting, his bombs exploding too early, catching the Bf 110 in the explosion; the pilot died in the resulting crash. Otherwise, the day was marked only by a single clash between the opposing fighters.

2 SAAF and 4 SAAF Squadrons now moved to LG.115 to refit and to train new pilots. Elsewhere, 112 Squadron was joined by eight Polish pilots who immediately took the opportunity to paint their national 'chequerboard' emblem on the tails of their Kittyhawks. 80 Squadron was pulled back to LG.102 at Helwan for defensive duties. Amongst the Regia Aeronautica units, 67° Gruppo OA and its 129ª and 132ª Squadriglie were now disbanded at Sorman. The personnel were then posted to a newly-established

158° Gruppo Assalto comprising 236ª, 387ª and 388ª Squadriglie.

British Claims				
274 Sqn	Sgt J.P.MacDonnell	Hurricane IIb DG616	Bf 109 Probable	1145-1245

British Casualties		
73 Sqn	Hurricane II BD957 shot down ferrying to base LG at Sidi Haneish; Flt Sgt E.S.Foster MiA	1315-1330

German Claims				
3./JG 27	Lt Karl Kugelbauer	Hurricane	W Gambut	1308

German Casualties	
III./JG 27	Bf 109F-4 trop WNr 8706 50% damaged on ground at Martuba by bombs
III./ZG 26	Bf 110E-3 WNr 2329 3U+FR hit by blast of own bomb during low level attack, crashed 10km E Bir Hacheim; Oblt Ludwig Schott/Lt Speer KiA

Wednesday, 11 February 1942

112 Squadron despatched six Kittyhawks to patrol over the El Adem-Gazala area at 1430. During the return from this sortie there was some confusion on the R/T. Sgt Leu, who had been leading, handed over to Sgt Burney since his radio was not functioning well. At that stage it seems that Burney and Sgt Holman appear to have got left behind; reportedly, they were attacked by six Bf 109s and two MC.202s which were using dive and climb tactics. Their first attack on Holman was avoided, but the second got him. Burney fired at a Macchi, but this got away. On this occasion no claim appears to have been made for Holman's Kittyhawk by either German or Italian pilots.

During the day 23 MC.202s of 6° Gruppo, together with the 1° Stormo HQ, moved from Benghazi K3 to Martuba. At this location a new command was established under T.Col Alfredo Reglieri, to coordinate 6° and 150° Gruppi, 154ª Squadriglia CT and 209ª Squadriglia BaT. There were no other engagements leading to potentially confirmed claims being made, but from 274 Squadron, which was active during the day, Sqn Ldr Sid Linnard was posted to become wing leader with commensurate promotion to wing commander.

British Claims					
30 Sqn	Flt Lt R.T.P.Davidson	Hurricane I	Ju 88 Damaged	10m N Taifa Rocks	0930-
274 Sqn	Flt Lt B.H.A. Playford	Hurricane IIb DG204	Bf 109 Damaged	sweep over forward area	1500-1630
73 Sqn	Sgt E.L.Joyce	Hurricane IIb	Bf 109F Damaged	10-12m from base	1720

British Casualties	
112 Sqn	Kittyhawk I AK673 shot down by Bf 109 or MC.202 near Gazala; Sgt N. Holman KiA 1720
German Casualties	
9./JG 27	Bf 109F-4 trop WNr 8560 belly-landed at Martuba, 80% damaged

Thursday, 12 February 1942

At 0750 Plt Off Montagu of 208 Squadron took off on a TacR sortie during which he was attacked over Tmimi by two fighters which he identified as a Bf 109F and a Bf 109E, his aircraft being hit and damaged. Having reportedly got "a good burst" at one Messerschmitt, he and his pursuers flew over an Allied AA battery, following which he landed with hits in the oil and coolant systems. His attackers having broken off, he then tried to organise his Hurricane being towed 32 miles back to base. It seems that his assailants were from 4./JG 27, Obfw Schulze from this unit failing to get a claim for a P-40 shot down in the Tmimi area confirmed.

At 1315 the newly-promoted Wg Cdr Linnard led 73 and 274 Squadrons on a patrol over Tobruk where Ju 87s with escorting fighters were intercepted. Lt Marseille of 3./JG 27 at once attacked 274 Squadron's aircraft, claiming four shot down in eight minutes. Four were indeed lost, although both Sgt Parbury, who baled out, and Sgt Henderson, who crash-landed, were under the impression that their aircraft had been hit by Flak. Two aircraft went into the sea, one of these flown by Flt Lt A.J.Smith, a Canadian who had previously been a Blenheim fighter pilot with 30 Squadron. He was reported to have been seen to shoot down an MC.200 just before his demise, although no Italian fighters were actually lost.

The rest of the squadron and the wing leader claimed four of the dive-bombers shot down plus three damaged. The attacking formation, briefed to bomb shipping in Tobruk harbour, was comprised mainly of aircraft from StG 3 but incorporated a pair of Italian-flown Ju 87s of 209ª Squadriglia. Two of the

German aircraft were shot down with the loss of the crews, while one from the Italian unit was damaged. The gunner in the other claimed what he identified as a P-40 damaged, seeing this trailing smoke. These crews reported that their formation had been attacked by about 40 Hurricanes and P-40s!

Meanwhile the 12 pilots of 73 Squadron returned unscathed, one pilot claiming a Bf 109 shot down – although none were listed as lost. Later in the afternoon a further claim was made by this unit for a probable. A further claim for a Hurricane was submitted by Oblt Düllberg of 5./JG 27 which may have been against the 274 Squadron aircraft, or possibly against a Fleet Air Arm Fulmar patrolling over the coast above shipping heading for Tobruk (see also Chapter Three). Another pilot from Düllberg's unit failed to get confirmation for a claim which may have been in the Tobruk engagement, or in the earlier pursuit of the 208 Squadron Hurricane.

Hptmn Eduard Neumann, Kommandeur of I./JG 27, climbs out of his Bf 109F-4 after a sortie.

The GruppenAdjutant's Bf 109F of I./JG 27.

British Claims

274 Sqn	Plt Off W.A.G.Conrad	Hurricane IIb BG631	Ju 87	NE Tobruk	1300-1400
274 Sqn	Plt Off W.A.G.Conrad	Hurricane IIb BG631	Ju 87 Damaged	NE Tobruk	1300-1400
274 Sqn	Sgt R.W. Henderson	Hurricane IIb Z5381	Bf 109F Damaged	NE Tobruk	1300-1400
274 Sqn	Wg Cdr S.Linnard	Hurricane IIb Z5064	2 Ju 87s	NE Tobruk	1300-1400
274 Sqn	Sgt J.P.MacDonnell	Hurricane IIb DG204	Ju 87	NE Tobruk	1300-1400
274 Sqn	Sgt J.P.MacDonnell	Hurricane IIb DG204	Ju 87 Damaged	NE Tobruk	1300-1400
274 Sqn	Flt Lt A.J.Smith	Hurricane IIb BD821	MC.200	NE Tobruk	1300-1400
73 Sqn	Wt Off H.D.Price	Hurricane IIb	Bf 109	Tobruk	1330
73 Sqn	Sgt E.L.Joyce	Hurricane IIb	Bf 109F Probable	Gazala	1700

British Casualties

208 Sqn	Hurricane P2646 left 0750, attacked by two Bf 109s over Tmimi, force-landed at 0915 engine seized; Plt Off C.S.B.Montagu safe
274 Sqn	Hurricane II DG616 dived inverted into sea 1315; Plt Off S.E. van der Kuhle KiA 1315
274 Sqn	Hurricane II BD821 dived into sea pursued by MC.200 1315; Flt Lt A.J.Smith KiA 1315
274 Sqn	Hurricane II Z5381 reportedly hit twice by Flak and crash-landed S Tobruk, 1315; Sgt R.W.Henderson safe
274 Sqn	Hurricane II shot down reportedly by Flak, 1315; Sgt C.R.Parbury safe 1315
73 Sqn	Hurricane II BG750 engine failed in combat with Bf 109s, FTL; Flg Off J.A.Kirkpatrick safe

German Claims

5./JG 27	Oblt Ernst Düllberg	Hurricane	10-15km N Tobruk	1325
3./JG 27	Lt Hans-Joachim Marseille	4 P-40s	10-35km NW Tobruk	1330-1336
4./JG 27	Obfw Alfred Schulze	P-40 n.b.	Tmimi	
5./JG 27	Obfw Franz Woidich	P-40 n.	15km SW Fort Acroma	

German Casualties

3./StG 3	Ju 87R-2 WNr 6239 S1+EL shot down by Hurricanes Tobruk; Oblt Heinrich von Stromberg/Uffz Bernhard Goets KiA
3./StG 3	Ju 87R-2 WNr 6149 S1+BB shot down by Hurricane 15km NW Ain el Gazala; Fw Kurt Flath/Uffz Alfred Braun MiA

Italian Claims

209ª Sq BaT	Av Sc Enrico Terzoli gunner on Ju 87	P-40 damaged	Tobruk	1225-

Italian Casualties

209ª Sq BaT	Ju 87 damaged over Tobruk by fighters, S.Ten Giovanni Comici safe

Friday, 13 February 1942

From 13th to 28th the Regia Aeronautica carried out intense ground-attack activity in the Sidi Muftah, Ain el Gazala, El Adem, Bir Hacheim, Sidi Breghish, El Abidi areas to prevent Allied counterattacks. On the 13th around 0900 five Hurricanes of 274 Squadron and two of 1 SAAF Squadron took off to intercept Ju 87s and escorting fighters over Tobruk. At 12,000 feet their formation was dispersed by 'friendly' AA fire at which point Lt le Roux spotted two Bf 109s below him and dived on these. He was at once attacked from above by Lt Marseille, who pressed his attack so close that his own aircraft was hit by debris and his engine was damaged. Lt le Roux, his Hurricane on fire, crash-landed nine miles south-east of Tobruk. He had been afraid to bale out as Messerschmitts were still around, and on hitting the ground his cockpit hood slammed shut and jammed. Although wounded by exploding ammunition, he managed to get out and was picked up safely.

Marseille started gliding his powerless aircraft towards Axis lines when he saw another Hurricane below him. Diving towards this, he fired one burst sending the fighter down, then finishing his glide to safety. Meanwhile Lt Rudi Sinner claimed another Hurricane shot down at this time. Two more Hurricanes were indeed shot down during this engagement, although 274 Squadron recorded that the aircraft which Plt Off Weeks had been flying had fallen to Flak.

73 Squadron scrambled a little later to intercept another raid, forcing the bombers to jettison their bombs, but Flg Off Eiby was hit by Obfw Schulz of II./JG 27 and force-landed. During this raid one He 111 was claimed shot down by Flg Off Scade of 73 Squadron and one probably so by Plt Off Moriarty of 274 Squadron. Sgt Dodds of 274 Squadron claimed a Bf 109 shot down in the Mechili-Msus region, with a second claimed as a probable by Sqn Ldr Ward of 73 Squadron over Tobruk, one more being claimed damaged here. 8./JG 27 recorded the loss of Uffz Schmidt in combat with Hurricanes south of Bir Hacheim – almost certainly Dodds' victim. With evening two Hurricanes of 238 Squadron intercepted Ju 88s over a convoy, each pilot claiming one damaged.

British Claims

274 Sqn	Sgt J.Dodds	Hurricane IIb	Bf 109	Mechili-Msus	0815-0900
274 Sqn	Plt Off Moriarty	Hurricane IIb	He 111 Probable	Tobruk	0815-0900
73 Sqn	Sgt H.W.Coussens	Hurricane IIb	Bf 109 Damaged	Tobruk	0920
73 Sqn	Flg Off T.P.K.Scade	Hurricane IIb	He 111	Tobruk	0920
73 Sqn	Sqn Ldr D.H.Ward	Hurricane IIb	Bf 109 Probable	Tobruk	0920
238 Sqn	Flt Lt M.T.Judd	Hurricane I 'D'	Ju 88 Damaged	convoy patrol	1700-1845
238 Sqn	Sgt J.W.T.Purdy	Hurricane I 'N'	Ju 88 Damaged	convoy patrol	1700-1845

British Casualties

1 SAAF Sqn	Hurricane II MiA; Lt W.L.Herbert MiA
1 SAAF Sqn	Hurricane II Z2317 shot down 0935 by Bf 109s, crash-landed; destroyed by fire; Lt F.F.J.E.le Roux WiA, returned
274 Sqn	Hurricane II Z4426 shot down, reportedly by Flak; Plt Off R.N. Weeks KiA
73 Sqn	Hurricane II Z5681 Flg Off W.T.Eiby WiA, force-landed Tobruk at 0925
238 Sqn	Hurricane 'V' caught fire in combat with Ju 88, Sgt Smallwood baled out over convoy; safe

German Claims

3./JG 27	Lt Hans-Joachim Marseille	2 Hurricanes	20km SE Tobruk	0920 & 0925
2./JG 27	Lt Rudolf Sinner	Hurricane	ESE Tobruk	0923
4./JG 27	Obfw Otto Schulz	2 P-40s	NE Tobruk & Tobruk	1022 & 1030

German Casualties

8./JG 27	Bf 109F-4 trop WNr 8545 Black 10 +- combat with Hurricane S Bir Hacheim; Uffz Alfred Schmidt MiA
12./LG 1	Ju 88A-5 WNr 3355 shot down by Hurricanes, crashed nr Tobruk; pilot and two safe, observer KiA
3./LG 1	Ju 88A-4 10% damaged in combat; pilot and two safe; radio operator died of wounds 18 February 1942

Saturday, 14 February 1942

Commonwealth fighter pilots thought they had enjoyed a 'field day' when eight Kittyhawks of 3 RAAF Squadron and ten of 112 Squadron encountered a reported 32 Axis aircraft, claiming 20 shot down for no loss; every pilot of the 112 Squadron formation and all but one of the Australians prepared combat reports. The Kittyhawks had scrambled from El Adem at 1145, 112 Squadron flying ahead, followed by 3 RAAF whose pilots were 1,000 feet lower.

The formation which they had encountered was comprised of seven MC.202s of 6° Gruppo led by Magg Marco Larcher, which had taken off at 1115 to escort seven CR.42s of 154ª Squadriglia and 12 MC.200s of 150° Gruppo led by Magg Antonio Vizzotto to strafe British vehicles in the Bir Hacheim area. The Kittyhawk pilots first spotted the MC.200s below them, these trying to climb up into cloud, while the Australians reported a number of bombers with a close escort of six Bf 109s acting as top cover. These would appear actually to have been MC.202s which dropped on the Australians, but the latter broke in time and drove them off.

The Italian pilots engaged their attackers in a long clash in a cloudy sky which frequently allowed a temporary hide-out to the opposing contenders. They reported the British formation as about 20 strong, identified as 'Curtiss P-40 apparently of a new type'. In a confused multi-unit engagement such as this, overclaiming was almost certain to occur, and on this occasion it certainly did. Between them the 18 Kittyhawk pilots claimed nine MC.202s and Bf 109s (actually apparently all Macchis) shot down, one probable and two damaged, plus 11 MC.200s and one Ba 65 – which undoubtedly was another Macchi, mis-identified – plus one more probable and four damaged. Damage was also claimed to two Ju 87s which do not appear even to have been present!

Neville Duke:

> "Great Day. Best engagement yet. Got 16 Italian and Hun aircraft without a loss to ourselves. We intercepted some Macchi 200s and Breda 65s ground-strafing south-west of Acroma. Sighted them just as we came out of cloud at about 9,000 feet on our left. I was leading the left section and attacked ten Macchis just below us. Got on the tail of one straggling a bit and gave a long burst. He was hit around the engine and spun away. This was seen to crash by Sgt Evans.
>
> "A general dogfight started and I enjoyed myself more than I have ever done before. The cloud was just right and we dived down, had a squirt and climbed up into cloud again. 109 tactics! I finished up at ground level chasing a Macchi 200 with a chappie of 3 RAAF Squadron. After two or three attacks the Macchi crashed and burst into flames in an army camp where they had been strafing."

The Italian losses were quite severe, but of a considerably lower level then claimed, amounting to two MC.202s shot down and a third damaged, plus three MC.200s brought down and two more damaged. In return the MC.202 pilots claimed four of the attackers shot down and a fifth probably so – although no Allied losses had actually been suffered. However, for the Commonwealth pilots, justified or not, the day was certainly a boost to morale.

During the day a TacR Hurricane of 208 Squadron was shot down by fire from Allied troops soon after take-off, the pilot being killed. This unit suffered a further loss when another of its aircraft crashed on landing. The squadron complained vociferously that this was the third time during recent weeks that one of their aircraft had been hit or shot down by 'friendly' AA fire from the army. This day also saw the arrival at Gambut of 94 Squadron, now fully re-equipped with Kittyhawks and ready to resume operations. With the unit came a new commanding officer, Sqn Ldr E.M. 'Imshi' Mason, DFC.

British Claims

112 Sqn	Plt Off J.P.Bartle	Kittyhawk I AK700 'B'	MC.202 Probable	SW Acroma	1124-1235
112 Sqn	Plt Off J.P.Bartle	Kittyhawk I AK700 'B'	Bf 109F Damaged	SW Acroma	1124-1235
112 Sqn	Sgt H.G.Burney	Kittyhawk I AK702 'P'	Ba.65	SW Acroma	1124-1235
112 Sqn	Sgt R.H.Christie	Kittyhawk I AK761	2 MC.200s	SW Acroma	1124-1235
112 Sqn	Sgt R.H.Christie	Kittyhawk I AK761	MC.200 Damaged	SW Acroma	1124-1235
112 Sqn	Sgt W.E.G.Cordwell	Kittyhawk I AK630	Bf 109F	SW Acroma	1124-1235
112 Sqn	Plt Off E.Dickinson	Kittyhawk I AK804	MC.200	SW Acroma	1124-1235
112 Sqn	Sgt R.A.Drew	Kittyhawk I AK653 'G'	2 MC.200s	SW Acroma	1124-1235
112 Sqn	Sgt R.B.Evans	Kittyhawk I AK637	MC.200 Probable	SW Acroma	1145-1235
112 Sqn	Sgt R.M.Leu	Kittyhawk I AK781	2 MC.200s	SW Acroma	1145-1235
112 Sqn	Sgt R.E.Simonsen	Kittyhawk I AK682 'U'	MC.200	SW Acroma	1145-1235
112 Sqn	Sgt R.E.Simonsen	Kittyhawk I AK682	MC.200 Damaged	SW Acroma	1145-1235
3 RAAF Sqn	Flg Off P.R.Giddy	Kittyhawk I AK665	2 MC.202s	20m SE El Gazala	1200
3 RAAF Sqn	Flg Off P.R.Giddy	Kittyhawk I AK665	MC.202 Damaged	20m SE El Gazala	1200
3 RAAF Sqn	Flg Off R.H.Gray	Kittyhawk I AK621	Bf 109	20m SE El Gazala	1200
3 RAAF Sqn	Sgt W.H.A.Mailey	Kittyhawk I AK644	2 Bf 109s	20m SE El Gazala	1200
3 RAAF Sqn	Sgt W.H.A.Mailey	Kittyhawk I AK644	MC.200 Damaged	20m SE El Gazala	1200
3 RAAF Sqn	Sgt F.B.Reid	Kittyhawk I AK689 'W'	MC.200	20m SE El Gazala	1200
3 RAAF Sqn	Sgt F.B.Reid	Kittyhawk I AK689 'W' }	MC.200	20m SE El Gazala	1200-1215
112 Sqn	Plt Off N.F.Duke	Kittyhawk I AK578 'V' }			
3 RAAF Sqn	Sgt F.B.Reid	Kittyhawk I AK689 'W'	MC.200 Damaged	20m SE El Gazala	1200
3 RAAF Sqn	Sgt B.M.Thompson	Kittyhawk I }	MC.200	20m SE El Gazala	1200
3 RAAF Sqn	Flg Off H.G.Pace	Kittyhawk I AK691 }			
3 RAAF Sqn	Flg Off L.T.Spence	Kittyhawk I AK612	Bf 109	20m SE El Gazala	1200
3 RAAF Sqn	Sgt G.H.White	Kittyhawk I AK605	Bf 109	20m SE El Gazala	1200
3 RAAF Sqn	Sgt G.H.White	Kittyhawk I AK605	2 Ju 87s Damaged	20m SE El Gazala	1200
112 Sqn	Plt Off N.F.Duke	Kittyhawk I AK578 'V'	MC.200	SW Acroma	1215

British Casualties

208 Sqn	Hurricane Z4772 left 1650, shot down by Allied AA at Derna. Third time recently that a squadron aircraft hit or shot down by own AA; Flg Off B.A.B.Attwood KiA

German Casualties

5./StG 3	Ju 87R-2 WNr 6065 A5+FK shot down by AA 15km SW Ain el Gazala; Lt Günther Gästel KiA/Uffz Rudolf Arbeiter PoW

Italian Claims

6° Gr, 1°St CT	Magg Marco Larcher	MC.202	P-40 probable	Bir Hacheim 1115-1240
88ª Sq,6° Gr, 1°St CT	Ten Gino Ramarini	MC.202	P-40	Bir Hacheim 1115-1240
88ª Sq,6° Gr, 1°St CT	M.llo Natalino Stabile	MC.202	2 P-40s	Bir Hacheim 1115-1240
150° Gr CT	unidentified pilots	MC.202	P-40 shared	Bir Hacheim 1115-1240

Italian Casualties

88ª Sq,6° Gr, 1°St CT	MC.202 MM 7875 failed to return, Ten Raffaele Giannuzzi-Savelli MiA
88ª Sq,6° Gr, 1°St CT	MC.202 MM 7890 ran out of fuel and crash-landed, Serg Magg Alfredo Bordin slightly wounded
88ª Sq,6° Gr, 1°St CT	MC.202 MM 7784 '88-10' damaged and belly-landed, M.llo Natalino Stabile safe
88ª Sq,6° Gr, 1°St CT	MC.202 MM 7786 hit an aircraft on landing at Martuba, damaged
365ª Sq, 150° Gr CT	MC.200 failed to return, Ten Armando Badessi baled, MiA
364ª Sq, 150° Gr CT	MC.200 damaged in combat, Serg Magg Mario Angeloni unhurt
363ª Sq, 150° Gr CT	MC.200 failed to return, S.Ten Maurizio Nicolis di Robilant MiA
363ª Sq, 150° Gr CT	MC.200 failed to return, Serg Bruno Dellai MiA
150° Gr CT	MC.200 damaged in combat, Magg Antonio Vizzotto unhurt

This is what made II./JG 27's Obfw Otto Schulz believe that he was attacking Polish-flown Kittyhawks on 15 February. 94 Squadron had just returned to action with their new aircraft which had the unit's (short-lived) red-white chequerboard markings on the rudder. One of the unit's aircraft is seen here undergoing service.

Sunday, 15 February 1942

The tables were firmly turned on WDAF next day by the Luftwaffe. Soon after midday Bf 109s of I./JG 27 escorted Ju 88s over the Gambut area. As they turned for home following the bombing, Lt Marseille spotted two 3 RAAF Squadron Kittyhawks taking off to intercept. Having seen the bombers safely back over the lines, he and his Röttenflieger returned over the target area in time to bounce the two Australian aircraft out of the sun as they struggled for altitude. His fire hit Sgt Reid's aircraft which was too low for the pilot to bale out; he crashed and was killed instantly. Marseille's next burst hit Flg Off Briggs, who baled out, wounded, at 300 feet.

At 1645 Sqn Ldr Mason led eight of 94 Squadron's newly-arrived Kittyhawks on a sweep with 12 of 112 Squadron, streaking in to strafe Martuba airfield. As they swept over, Obfw Otto Schulz of II.Gruppe rushed to a Bf 109 which had just been serviced and took off within 30 seconds. Almost at once he sighted fighters which appeared to have Polish markings on their tails. In fact 94 Squadron had painted a red and white chequerboard strip around the fins and rudders of their aircraft as a unit marking.

Schulz attacked at once, shooting down Mason and three of his pilots within five minutes. After a further five minutes he spotted another fighter which appears to have been that flown by Sgt McQueen of 112 Squadron, attacking this too and inflicting serious damage which also wounded the pilot; nevertheless, McQueen managed to limp his Kittyhawk back to base. Flying just above the ground, he had few manoeuvre possibilities. He took in the close-range shots tucking in behind his armour plate. The sound of bullets hitting it resembled "hitting the keys of a grand piano without strings".

Lt Hans-Joachim Marseille at Martuba with his Bf 109F 'Yellow 14', WNr 8693 which demonstrates on the rudder 48 victory bars; the most recent pair were claimed on 15 February.

He didn't manage to avoid all of the bullets and was shot in the arms and legs. It's a mystery how he got out of the situation with his plane still in the air. McQueen had no idea that his attacker, having already shot down four planes, had simply run out of ammunition. Smoking, with a coughing engine, its wings riddled with bullet holes, the Kittyhawk flew toward the darkening horizon. The wounded pilot brought it to base, where he managed to land just before losing consciousness. McQueen's wounds were tended, but the ruined AK583 GA-X never flew again. Before the end of February it was crossed out of 112 Squadron's armament.

At precisely the same time and area, an MC.202 pilot of 6° Gruppo also claimed a P-40, and may also have attacked McQueen's aircraft. However, Schulz was credited with five victories partly on the evidence of a watching Afrika Korps tank officer, Lt Schorm, whose report gives an excellent account of the fight:

Oblt Otto Schulz in the cockpit of a Bf 109F of the II Gruppe Stab.

> "Shortly after 1700 hours about 20 British fighters flew over us near Bir Temrad, flying in a westerly direction. Sometime later they returned flying singly at low level. I stood on the deck of my tank and observed with my field glasses two of the aircraft crash in flames to the west. I was looking at the clouds of smoke when a third aircraft went into a vertical spin, touched the ground with its left wing tip, when it must have been dashed to pieces, as it did not burn, although I observed a cloud of dust for some time. In the meantime a fourth British fighter appeared from the left; a Bf 109 appeared from the point of the first crash, reducing the distance between them very rapidly. His first burst hit, and I could see the tracers and hits very well in the evening dusk. After a second the British fighter crashed on fire.
>
> "In the meantime a fifth British aircraft passed by my right, also on an easterly course. The German fighter flew over us, weaving his wingtips and we answered by waving our caps. As we had hoped, he had seen the fifth Tommy, turned left, and pursued him. At close range he gave a long burst, and I could see the hits very clearly. Both aircraft then disappeared behind a sand dune. Shortly after, I observed a little cloud of dust. The German fighter had pulled up steeply after the first burst, turned and veered off."

Technical Officer of II./JG 27, Lt Ernst Börngen in his Bf 109F. Beyond is the Stab aircraft flown early in the year by Obfw Otto Schulz.

Twenty minutes after take-off Schulz was back over his base, waggling his wingtips five times. He thought the Kittyhawk pilots he had attacked must have been novices under an instructional flight for newcomers, as no evasive action was taken by the apparently Polish (but actually British) pilots. Schulz was a steady, older pilot, 31 years of age at this time, and was known as 'Ein-Zwei-Drei – Otto' due to his swift scrambling and shooting; this combat brought his confirmed claims to 44. His fellow pilots made a large tin-plate Ritterkreuz replica, which they ceremoniously presented to him next morning. A few days later Feldmarschall Kesselring arrived at the airfield to present him with the genuine article. The loss of Sqn Ldr Mason was a particularly grave one for the WDAF; this outstanding fighter pilot had claimed the destruction of more than 17 aircraft in the Mediterranean area since the start of the war. Of the flight of five which he had been leading, only Sgt Phillips returned.

Meanwhile, during the day 260 Squadron handed its Hurricanes to 238 Squadron, receiving Tomahawks for training prior to the arrival of Kittyhawks, and moved to LG.115 for this purpose. 450 Squadron moved forward to Gambut and 1 SAAF Squadron withdrew from the front, having only six Hurricanes left on strength.

The Regia Aeronautica had again been active against targets on the ground when five MC.200s of 150° Gruppo led by Ten Mario Bellagambi strafed vehicles in the Bir Hacheim area, claiming four trucks set on fire and one damaged.

British Casualties

94 Sqn	Kittyhawk I AK807 off 1645, FTR from attack on Martuba a/f; Sqn Ldr E.M.Mason KiA
94 Sqn	Kittyhawk I AK858 off 1645, FTR from attack on Martuba a/f; Plt Off John Robert Vernall Marshall KiA
94 Sqn	Kittyhawk I AK601 off 1645, FTR from attack on Martuba a/f; Sgt Charles Llwyd Belcher KiA
94 Sqn	Kittyhawk I AK733 off 1645, FTR from attack on Martuba a/f; Sgt Edward Weightman KiA
112 Sqn	Kittyhawk I AK583 'X' damaged during attack on Martuba a/f; Sgt D.N.McQueen WiA
3 RAAF Sqn	Kittyhawk I AK605 shot down by Bf 109s near LG.110; Sgt F.B.Reid KiA
3 RAAF Sqn	Kittyhawk I AK594 damaged by Bf 109s, Flg Off P.J.Briggs baled out from 200 ft near LG.110

German Claims

3./JG 27	Lt Hans-Joachim Marseille	2 P-40s	3-5km WSW Gambut	1300 &1303
4./JG 27	Obfw Otto Schulz	5 P-40s	SE Martuba	1745, 1746 & 1747
			W Ain el Gazala	1750
			& 35km SE Martuba	1755

Italian Claims

81ª Sq, 6°Gr, 1°St CT	S.Ten Alberto Paggi	MC.202	P-40	Ain el Gazala	1735-1815

Monday, 16 February 1942

150° Gruppo again sent out six MC.200s to strafe a column south of Ain el Gazala between 1640-1805, this time the Italian pilots being escorted by nine 6° Gruppo MC.202s. Fifteen vehicles were claimed to have been damaged and four left in flames, but one MC.200 was hit by fire from the ground and crash-landed. Also during the day two Ju 87s from 209ª Squadriglia flown by S.Ten Giovanni Comici and Serg Guido Savini undertook the last mission to be flown by Italian Stukas in North Africa. The unit would be repatriated to Italy during March.

Meanwhile, at 0810 a 208 Squadron Hurricane had undertaken a TacR sortie to Mechili where it was attacked by Bf 109s, but without result. During his return flight Flg Off Macgregor was attacked again and was shot down near Acroma by Lt Hoffmann of I./JG 27. He was unhurt and later reported back to his unit on foot. In the afternoon six fighters from I./JG 27 attacked five Kittyhawks of 3 RAAF Squadron which had just taken off to escort bombers near El Adem, Oblt Keller shooting down Flg Off Threlkeld, who was killed, crashing in flames 20 miles south of El Adem.

Next day 94 Squadron having suffered crippling losses of both Hurricanes and Kittyhawks during the preceding six weeks, was withdrawn to Gasr el Arid, initially for further training.

British Claims

3 RAAF Sqn	Sgt G.H.White	Kittyhawk I AK623	Bf 109 Damaged	SE El Adem	1640

British Casualties

3 RAAF Sqn	Kittyhawk I AK691 shot down by Bf 109s 20m S El Adem; Flg Off T.Threlkeld KiA
208 Sqn	Hurricane Z4779 left 0810, attacked on start of TacR and again on return; shot down nr Acroma 0915; Flg Off R.L.Macgregor safe

German Claims

3./JG 27	Lt Friedrich Hoffmann	P-40	10km SE Fort Acroma	1018
2./JG 27	Oblt Fritz Kekker	P-40	30km SE El Adem	1635

German Casualties

5./JG 27	Bf 109F-4 trop WNr 8739 crash-landed at Martuba, 80% damaged

Wednesday, 18 February 1942

72ª and 80ª Squadriglie of the Regia Aeronautica's 17° Gruppo moved from Tamet to Benghazi K3 with nine MC.202s. 71ª Squadriglia with four Macchis would rejoin the sister units there on 2 March.

Thursday, 19 February 1942

British Claims

73 Sqn	Flt Lt G.R.A.McG.Johnston	Hurricane IIb	Bf 109E Damaged	E Martuba	0730

German Casualties

12./LG 1	Ju 88A-4 WNr 3355 L1+JV shot down by fighters, crashed into sea off Sidi Barrani; Fw Walter Kugler and 3 KiA

Saturday, 21 February 1942

Bad weather considerably restricted activities, rain, low clouds and sandstorms reducing flights of all types for the next few days. At midday on 20th six Bf 109s of I./JG 27 set off to patrol over Acroma, the three Rötten being led by Hptm Homuth with Lts Stahlschmidt and Marseille as section leaders. Stahlschmidt was in an unhappy frame of mind as he had been photographed before take-off by some soldiers – considered to be most inauspicious. Over Acroma they spotted 11 Kittyhawks of 112 Squadron and at once began to climb to get above them. Stahlschmidt was flying the slowest aircraft of the six, and was so busy watching the British fighters that he failed to give his aircraft full throttle, consequently falling behind the others.

Suddenly one of the Kittyhawks (that flown by Sqn Ldr Caldwell) pulled up vertically, fired, and hit his Messerschmitt. Upside down and in a spin, fire licking at his aircraft, he heard Homuth's angry voice in his earphones demanding: "Which idiot let himself be shot down?" He managed to pull out of the spin and crash-landed in no mans' land where he was picked up by an Axis patrol, being back at Martuba by evening. The remaining five Bf 109s fell on the Kittyhawks, two Polish pilots, Sgt Derma and Flg Off Jander, being shot down, while Sgt Elliott's aircraft was badly damaged and crashed at El Adem, the pilot dying of his wounds on 9 March. Apart from Caldwell, a second Kittyhawk pilot claimed a Messerschmitt shot down. Homuth and Marseille considered it a fabulous shot from such a distance to have brought down Stahlschmidt.

British Claims

112 Sqn	Sqn Ldr C.R.Caldwell	Kittyhawk I AK658 'Y'	Bf 109	Gazala	1030-1235
112 Sqn	Sgt K.F.Carson	Kittyhawk I AK762	Bf 109	Tmimi-Gazala	1030-1235

British Casualties

112 Sqn	Kittyhawk I AK781 badly damaged in combat over El Adem; Sgt P.T.Elliott landed at base
112 Sqn	Kittyhawk I AK678 'X' shot down in combat over El Adem; Sgt J.Derma safe (reported on 22nd)
112 Sqn	Kittyhawk I AK814 shot down in combat over El Adem; Flg Off W.Jander WiA, to Tobruk with broken leg
SRU	Maryland AH370 lost (or 21 July ?)

German Claims

3./JG 27	Lt Hans-Joachim Marseille	2 P-40s	19km W & 20km NE Fort Acroma	1210 & 1218
3./JG 27	Hptm Gerhard Homuth	P-40	20km SE Ain el Gazala	1211

German Casualties

Stab I./JG 27	Bf 109F-4 trop WNr 8528 shot down SE Gazala, 100%; Lt Hans-Arnold Stahlschmidt safe

Sunday, 22 February 1942

German fighters with drop-tanks strafed lorries and locomotives near Sidi Barrani and Mersa Matruh, while at 0915 13 MC.202s of 6° Gruppo led by Cap Dante Ocarso, took off to attack Acroma landing ground. Five provided top cover while the others attacked the parked aircraft there, claiming 15 Blenheims and Kittyhawks destroyed. All Macchis returned safely to Martuba at 1025. According to 208 Squadron the target was a landing ground known as Bir el Regal, where a detached flight of the unit was based.

The attackers were identified as MC.200s, four Hurricanes being badly damaged and one slightly. It appears that of the order of five or more other Hurricanes were also seriously damaged.

At noon Sqn Ldr Ward of 73 Squadron took off to intercept a reconnaissance Ju 88 of 1.(F)/121, but was beaten to the target by four Kittyhawks of 450 Squadron, Sgt Shaw claiming this unit's first victory by sending the intruder down from 20,000 feet south-east of Gazala. An hour later eight Hurricanes of 238 Squadron on a convoy escort patrol encountered a number of Ju 88s of II./LG 1, claiming one shot down, one probable and one damaged.

During the day 8./ZG 26 returned to Africa from Germany, and immediately Oblt Peter Habicht claimed an aircraft shot down, identified as a Boeing (for more information see Chapter Three).

Twelve MC.200s of 78ª Sq and 82ª Sq, 13° Gruppo, 2° Stormo, arrived at Castel Benito from Italy.

British Claims

450 Sqn	Sgt R.Shaw	Kittyhawk I AK 726 'O'	Ju 88	SE Gazala	1215
238 Sqn	Sgt G.H.Borham	Hurricane I 'N'	Ju 88	convoy patrol	1330-1530
	Sgt G.H.Borham	Hurricane I 'N'	Ju 88 Probable	convoy patrol	1330-1530
238 Sqn	Sgt G.H.Borham	Hurricane I 'N'	Ju 88 Damaged	convoy patrol	1330-1530

British Casualties

208 Sqn	Hurricanes damaged Cat II on ground, at Bir el Regal (detached flight) strafed by 9 MC.202s at 1030: V7780, Z4085, Z4388, Z4486, plus one slightly reported lost or struck off charge without details: Hurricanes Z4963, Z4968, Z5254, BD 772, BD898, BD957

German Claims

8./ZG 26	Oblt Peter Habicht	Boeing

German Casualties

1.(F)/121	Ju 88A-5 WNr 0522 7A+NH shot down by P-40 SE Ain el Gazala; Fw Willi Neumann, Lt Erwin Lieseberg and two PoWs; one, Uffz Bruno Mewes died in hospital in Tobruk on 23rd
6./LG 1	Ju 88A-4 WNr 5612 L1+LP shot down by AA over convoy African coast; Fw Werner Voigt and three MiA
2./(H)/14	Bf 109E-7 WNr 6109, badly damaged by AA, crash-landed nr Mechili, destroyed

Monday, 23 February 1942

450 Squadron experienced its first full-scale combat when the unit, in company with 3 RAAF Squadron, escorted six Bostons to bomb transport between Tmimi and Martuba at 1300. Lt Sinner and Fw Albers of I./JG 27 spotted the bombers attacking German tanks near Umm er Rzem and intercepted 450's aircraft. Although only one of his machine guns was operating, Sinner shot down one Kittyhawk and hit a second which made off trailing smoke. Sinner reported that the pilot baled out over El Adem, but in fact Sgt McBride in the second aircraft, spun and crashed while attempting a force-landing. He was thrown clear while his aircraft burnt out, but had been severely injured and died a while later. Sgt Nursey claimed one Bf 109 shot down and a second damaged, with another being claimed damaged by Sgt Young.

While this fight was taking place Fw Gromotka of II./JG 27, engaged in an intruder patrol over Sidi Barrani, intercepted a 14 Squadron Blenheim which was flying from Bir el Baheira to LG.116. He attacked four times, the bomber crash-landing with both engines on fire.

Lt Rudi Sinner, technical officer of I./JG 27 in early 1942, with his Bf 109F; he claimed two 'P-40s' shot down on 23 February.

Flt Lt P.C. Cotton, DFC, of 208 Squadron on a flight to Air HQ, was attacked by four Bf 109s while landing at LG.121, Sidi Barrani, with his wheels and flaps down. Five attacks were made on his aircraft, but it was not hit and he was even able to get a burst in at one of his attackers. Three claims were made by pilots of 8./JG 27 during the day for which no other matching British losses can be found, and it would seem possible that these claimants, all relatively inexperienced pilots, had been involved in this engagement with Cotton. They may also have been engaged in a strafing attack on LG.121 by four Bf 109s during which a Hurricane of 335 (Greek) Squadron was burnt out.

Eleven MC.200s of 150° Gruppo were led by Magg Vizzotto under an escort provided by MC.202s of 6° Gruppo to strafe vehicles in the Murtach area about noon. Seven MC.200s were hit by ground fire and one pilot was wounded.

British Claims					
450 Sqn	Sgt I.A.Nursey	Kittyhawk I AK606 'B'	Bf 109F	S El Adem	1300
450 Sqn	Sgt I.A.Nursey	Kittyhawk I AK606 'B'	Bf 109F Damaged	S El Adem	1300
450 Sqn	Sgt I.Young	Kittyhawk I AK732 'A'	Bf 109F Damaged	Gazala-Tmimi	1300
208 Sqn	Lt D.V.Maree	Hurricane Z4162	MC.202 Damaged	Martuba-Bomba	1500

British Casualties	
14 Sqn	Blenheim IV Z9729 'A' off from Bir el Baheira on relocation to LG.116.Attacked 4 times by Bf 109s and crash-landed with both engines on fire, elevator and rudder controls shot away. Sgt J.Bosworth plus one of crew and one passenger safe; one KiA, one WiA. (This may have occurred next day when a Blenheim was claimed by a Bf 110 pilot)
450 Sqn	Kittyhawk I AK734 'S' damaged in combat with Bf 109s and crash-landed at base; Sgt K.McBride KiA
450 Sqn	Kittyhawk I AK613 'K' shot down by Bf 109 SE Umm er Rzem; Flg Off C.K.T.Thompson PoW
335 Sqn	Strafe of airfield; Hurricane V7490 burnt out

German Claims				
6./JG 27	Fw Fritz Gromotka	Blenheim	W Sidi Barrani	1315
2./JG 27	Lt Rudolf Sinner	2 P-40s	SE Umm er Rzem	1323 & 1325
7./JG 27	Lt Wolf-Dietrich Sirc	P-40	N Tmimi	
8./JG 27	Lt Horst Heike	P-40	SE Sidi Rezegh	
8./JG 27	Obfw Hans Lampater	P-40	W Ain el Gazala	

Italian Casualties	
150° Gr CT	7 MC.200s damaged by ground fire, Ten Mario Bellagambi of 364ª Sq slightly wounded

Tuesday, 24 February 1942

According to a Luftwaffe report, a raid by British commandos destroyed two Bf 109s of III./JG 27 on Martuba airfield. During the day a fourth South African fighter squadron arrived in North Africa. This was 5 SAAF Squadron, equipped with Tomahawks, commanded by Maj J.E.Frost, DFC. On arrival it relieved 335 Squadron at LG.121.

Flg Off Macgregor of 208 Squadron was hit by Flak while on a TacR sortie over the Tmimi area, the glycol coolant tank of his Hurricane being punctured. He force-landed west of Gazala and was brought back by a South African armoured car.

British Casualties	
208 Sqn	Hurricane Z3734 hit by light AA at Tmimi, force-landed W Gazala; Flg Off R.L.Macgregor safe
238 Sqn	Hurricane Z4862 crashed on take-off, Gambut
60 SAAF Sqn	2 Bf 109s shoot-up Sidi Barrani; 2 Marylands damaged, 2 more Marylands, a Lodestar and a Hurricane hit

German Claims		
7./ZG 26	Uffz Fritz Lauff	Blenheim
Flak	recce a/c	

German Casualties	
7./JG 27	2 Bf 109F-4 trop WNrs 8422 and 8710 damaged 40% at Martuba – sabotage

Wednesday, 25 February 1942

14 Squadron Blenheims took off at 1640 from LG.116 to make independent attacks on Martuba airfield. Before reaching the target one bomber was badly damaged by Flak, the pilot jettisoning the bombs and turning for home. Over Allied territory the aircraft began to burn, the pilot and observer baling out.

However, the gunner was unable to get free, and was killed when the aircraft crashed. A second Blenheim ran out of fuel during the return flight and crashed into the sea.

On this date two BR.20s of 11° Gruppo BT flew from Benghazi K2 to bomb Tobruk, taking off in the dark at 0405. Just after take-off one bomber crashed into the ground. This war-weary unit was gradually repatriated in March.

British Casualties	
14 Sqn	Blenheim IV V5657 'O' damaged by Flak near Martuba l/g; bombs jettisoned and aircraft abandoned when caught fire; Flt Sgt J.T.Willis and one baled safely; one killed in aircraft
14 Sqn	Blenheim IV Z6443 'C' ran out of fuel on return from raid on Martuba l/g; ditched in sea; Plt Off F.R Brown and two safe
Italian Casualties	
4ª Sq, 11° Gr, 13° St BT	BR.20 MM 21891 crashed after take-off; pilot Cap Michele Pesso, copilot Serg Magg Eliseo Ghezzi and one KiA, two injured

Thursday, 26 February 1942

At 0750 Hptm Gerlitz of II./JG 27 on an early patrol with three other pilots, encountered a Wellington of 148 Squadron returning from a sortie over Benghazi; he quickly shot this down in flames (see also Chapter Eleven). Five minutes later the four German pilots attacked six Hurricanes of 274 Squadron which had scrambled over Gambut to intercept the Messerschmitts. Sgt Dodds spotted three of the German fighters diving on him, managed to evade them, and hit one which he claimed as probably destroyed. However, Gerlitz put a burst into Sgt Worthington's Hurricane, the latter pilot baling out. Sgt Harrington was also hit, force-landing at Baheira, but no claim was made for his aircraft.

Shortly after 1100 12 Kittyhawks of 450 and 3 RAAF Squadrons were scrambled to intercept aircraft over Tobruk. Here they were bounced by the Bf 109s of I. and II./JG 27. In the dogfight which followed five Kittyhawks were shot down while II./JG 27 lost two Bf 109s, both pilots being taken prisoner. Two or three of the Australian pilots survived unhurt.

Eleven Kittyhawks of 112 Squadron at Gambut Main which had been at readiness, had just landed from a scramble when five Bf 109s of 5./JG 27 swept in for a strafing attack, claiming five Kittyhawks destroyed on the ground. In fact two were burnt out, two badly damaged and three more suffered slight damage. Flt Sgt E.M. Jackson took off to pursue the strafers, but in doing so, crashed and was killed. The Germans also claimed to have destroyed a Boston on the ground, but this 24 SAAF Squadron aircraft had actually taken off when attacked by two Bf 109s. Lt Botha managed to belly-land the burning aircraft despite severe wounds, thereby saving the lives of his crew. Sadly, they were unable to pull him from the blazing wreck and he died.

While engaging in a reconnaissance mission to Bir Hacheim with Lt Keppler, Lt Stahlschmidt was shot down again, this time by ground fire. He had been attacking a column of trucks near Bir el Gobi when his engine suddenly cut in the midst of a firing pass and he force-landed, ramming a truck. He was hauled from his cockpit by troops who turned out to be members of the Polish Brigade. The angry Poles beat him with rifle butts and kicked him, ripping off his decorations and making him run the gauntlet of the column. He was then examined and interrogated by a Polish and a South African officer before being sent to another camp. After midnight he managed to escape, walking about five miles to the spot where he had originally crashed. Here he found a German outpost which returned him to his unit without more ado, his arrival there causing much jubilation. A few days later he returned to Germany on leave with Lt Marseille.

Twelve lorries were claimed destroyed south of Gazala by the pilots of four MC.202s of 79ª Squadriglia, 6° Gruppo at 1100. Also during the day a lone Bf 109F strafed 450 Squadron's airfield at 0830 slightly damaging three Kittyhawks. During the day 77ª Squadriglia of 13° Gruppo joined its sister units at Castel Benito.

British Casualties	
450 Sqn	three Kittyhawks slightly damaged on ground during strafe by Bf 109
German Casualties	
Stab I./JG 27	Bf 109F-4 trop WNr 8497 shot down by AA, Ain el Gazala area; Lt Hans-Arnold Stahlschmidt MiA, returned six days later

Friday, 27 February 1942

The Italians were out in strength again on this date, 6° Gruppo's MC.202s undertaking three sorties in the morning, strafing vehicles. During the second mission one aircraft was hit by AA but the pilot managed to get back to base safely. On the third operation, led by T Col Alfredo Reglieri, good results were reported with more than 20 vehicles claimed badly damaged. On this occasion two MC.202s were hit by AA, but both pilots managed to get their damaged aircraft back to base.

At 1000 ten MC.200s of 150° Gruppo set out to escort Luftwaffe Ju 87s to dive-bomb Tobruk. One Macchi was hit by AA and force-landed, the pilot becoming a prisoner.

Obfw Otto Schulz's 'White 2' after he had brought his victory total to 44 by 27 February.

Obfw Otto Schulz, victor over five Kittyhawks of 94 Squadron on 15 February.

British Claims

274 Sqn	Sgt J.Dodds	Hurricane IIb Z5469	Bf 109 Probable		0735-0845
450 Sqn	Sgt R.D.Dyson	Kittyhawk I AK633 'M'	Bf 109 Probable		1150-1200
3 RAAF Sqn	Sgt B.M.Thompson	Kittyhawk I AK622	2 Bf 109s	El Adem	1200

British Casualties

24 SAAF Sqn	Boston III Z2175 took off from LG.140 to return to LG.21 at 0730; shot down on take-off by 2 Bf 109s. Lt T.J.P.Botha, mortally wounded, made perfect belly landing, saving lives of crew. 2/Lt D.P.Bester tried to rescue him, but driven back by flames. One gunner wounded in attack, but helped out by other gunner
274 Sqn	Hurricane II Z5381 shot down early a.m. nr Gambut; Sgt Worthington baled out safe
274 Sqn	Hurricane II BD820 damaged in combat; Sgt Harrington force-landed at Baheira
274 Sqn	Hurricane II BD821 damaged in combat; Sgt Barwick force-landed at Gambut
3 RAAF Sqn	Kittyhawk I AK689 'W' shot down; Plt Off R.C.Hart baled out nr El Adem and returned safe
3 RAAF Sqn	Kittyhawk I AK665 shot down near XIII Corps HQ; Sgt R.M.Jennings KiA
450 Sqn	Kittyhawk I AK609 'C' shot down NE Acroma; Sgt E.J.Gray KiA
450 Sqn	Kittyhawk I AK717 'L' crash-landed at Tobruk; Sgt T.E.N.Crouch safe
450 Sqn	Kittyhawk I AK719 damaged by Bf 109s and crash-landed near Tobruk
112 Sqn	Kittyhawk AK707 'Y' destroyed on the ground by strafing at Gambut (Plt Off N.F.Duke's aircraft)
112 Sqn	Kittykawk AK658 'X' 'The Grim Jester' destroyed on the ground by strafing at Gambut (Sqn Ldr C.R.Caldwell's aircraft)
112 Sqn	2 Kittyhawks AK802, AK910 badly damaged on the ground at Gambut
112 Sqn	3 Kittyhawks slightly damaged on the ground at Gambut
112 Sqn	Kittyhawk I AK959 scrambled but crashed, chasing strafers; Flt Sgt E.M.Jackson KiFA

German Claims

Stab II./JG 27	Hptm Erich Gerlitz	Wellington	E Gambut	0750

Stab II./JG 27	Hptm Erich Gerlitz	Hurricane	W Gambut	0755
7./JG 27	Oblt Hermann Tangerding	P-40	El Adem	1152
8./JG 27	Fw Kurt Forbger	P-40	E Tobruk	1155
3./JG 27	Lt Hans-Joachim Marseille	P-40	10km ENE Ain el Gazala	1200
3./JG 27	Hptm Gerhard Homuth	P-40	NE Fort Acroma	1210
3./JG 27	Lt Hans-Joachim Marseille	P-40	10km ENE Fort Acroma	1212

German Casualties

7./JG 27	Bf 109F-4 trop WNr 8673 White 3 shot down by P-40 S Tobruk; Lt Wolf-Dietrich Sirc PoW
8./JG 27	Bf 109F-4 trop WNr 8541 Black 1 shot down by P-40 S Tobruk; Uffz Josef Lenz PoW

Italian Casualties

365ª Sq , 150° Gr CT	MC.200 shot down by AA over Tobruk, S.Ten Mario Gambari MiA, PoW

Saturday, 28 February 1942

The 150° Gruppo MC.200s were out again early in the morning when 15 of these fighters were led by Magg Vizzotto to attack El Adem airfield; here two aircraft were claimed to have been destroyed and ten damaged on the ground. During a morning patrol by 12 Hurricanes of 274 Squadron, the formation was attacked by what appeared to be two or three Bf 109s, and one Hurricane was shot down, the pilot baling out. However, no relevant German or Italian claims were recorded on this date. A photo-reconnaissance Hurricane of 2 PRU was also lost during the day. Hurricanes of 40 SAAF Squadron now moved up to Maaten Bagush, ready to commence tactical reconnaissance flights from here. The unit would soon move on to Sidi Aziez and then to El Adem.

Possibly Ju 88 of KG 30 was shot down near Benghazi flying from Sicily.

British Casualties

274 Sqn	Hurricane V7858 shot down by fighters; Plt Off J.Buckley baled out, safe
2 PRU	Hurricane PR lost; Plt Off R.H.Jacobs MiA

The Question of Spitfires

Since the arrival of the Messerschmitt Bf 109 in the Mediterranean and North Africa there had been a persistent appeal for Spitfires to be sent out, both to Malta and to Egypt. This appeal had been greatly enhanced since late 1941 when the F version of this formidable fighter had appeared in these skies highlighting the inadequacies of the Hurricane particularly. Until the start of 1942, with the exception of a few unarmed photographic reconnaissance versions of the Spitfire, every one of these aircraft had been retained in the home country in case of a resumption of the Luftwaffe's air assault in a manner similar to that of 1940. As it became clear that the Soviet Union was not going to collapse to the extent which had seemed possible prior to the winter of 1941/2, coupled with a steady growth in the number of squadrons available to Fighter Command and of the Spitfires coming off the production lines to equip them, a softening of the grasp upon these aircraft at last began to be felt.

While some of the weight being borne by the Hurricane units in North Africa was being ameliorated by the arrival of growing numbers of Curtiss Kittyhawks direct from the USA, the priority need was perceived to be Malta where the presence of high-quality interceptor fighters was seen to be the greatest. Nevertheless, during February 1942 moves were afoot to begin sending some of these desirable aircraft to both areas. As described in *Malta: The Spitfire Year, 1942*, relatively small deliveries of Spitfires were made to Malta during March. These were not despatched in squadron form; on arrival they and their pilots were amalgamated into, and began re-equipping two of the Hurricane squadrons already on the island. In the UK, however, two experienced units were ordered to pack up and commence embarkation for transfer to Egypt during 11/12 February. These were 92 and 145 Squadrons, commanded by Sqn Ldr J.H.Wedgwood, DFC, and Sqn Ldr A.D.J.Lovell, DFC & Bar, respectively. It appears, however, that only sufficient crated Spitfire Vbs were sent initially to equip one of these units on arrival, and it was 145 Squadron which received these during April. In the interim, as will be recounted, the pilots of 92 Squadron were attached to 80 Squadron and flew some of that unit's Hurricanes as their introduction to the North African war.

A month after the arrival of the first Spitfires on Malta, the urgent need for considerable reinforcements caused the air parties of two established squadrons to be carried to the island on the aircraft carrier USS *Wasp*, borrowed for the task from the US Navy. The three previous deliveries had taken just 31 Spitfires to the island, few of which now remained intact. Then on 20 April 47 more were flown off as 601 and 603 Squadrons, commanded respectively by Sqn Ldr J.D.Bisdee, DFC, and Sqn Ldr Lord David Douglas-Hamilton.

Even as delivery was underway, the ground parties of both units had been despatched via the ocean route, not initially at any rate to join the air parties on Malta, but to join RAF Egypt. Posted with them at the same time were four more squadrons, all of which had been flying Spitfires in the United Kingdom. These units all sailed on HMT K6 (ex SS *Rangitata*) on 15 April, reaching Durban, South Africa, during mid May, and then arriving in Egypt in the latter part of June. Amongst them was 601 Squadron's commanding officer, Sqn Ldr R.G.A.Barclay, DFC, who on arrival did not go on to Malta to rejoin his unit, but was instead posted to command 238 Squadron. On the island command had meanwhile passed to Sqn Ldr John Bisdee while on the way out on *Wasp*. Once more, aircraft did not actually accompany the units now arrived in Egypt, all of which (with the exception of 601 Squadron) were to wait many months to receive aircraft – and then these turned out in the first instance to be Hurricanes. Having despatched the personnel of so many units to the Middle East, one is bound to query just how experienced they were, given the critical months that slipped by before they were able to play any useful part in the proceedings.

Like 92 and 145 Squadrons, 74 Squadron (commanding officer Sqn Ldr G.P.H.Matthews, DFC) had seen considerable action during 1940 and early 1941, over Dunkirk, south-east England and Occupied France. Since then, however, it had spent many months on defensive duties in the north of England and in Northern Ireland; it no longer retained any of the experienced pilots of the early months of the war. 123 Squadron (Sqn Ldr D.M.Jack) was a recently-formed unit which had been acting as an OTU. 134 Squadron (Sqn Ldr A.M.D.Howes) had been one of the units forming 151 Wing which had delivered and operated Hurricanes in north Russia, but had been at Catterick in Yorkshire since its return in December 1941, having only recently become re-established in the UK and equipped with Spitfires. Finally, 417 Squadron (Sqn Ldr P.B.Pitcher) was an RCAF unit which had only been formed in late November 1941 and had been declared operational on Spitfires only one week before being ordered to prepare for the move to the Middle East. It would become the first, and the only, Canadian fighter unit to operate in the Mediterranean and Middle East.

In all cases the units had relatively experienced commanding officers and the occasional – very occasional – flight commanders who had actually been in combat. The vast majority of the pilots, as with the squadrons in the Middle East generally, were the rapidly-trained products of the Commonwealth Air Training Plan, now beginning to flow from their human production lines in rapidly growing numbers. Like the pilots of 92 Squadron, those of 74, 123 and 134 Squadrons ultimately found themselves attached to various of the resident units as temporary, or at times, permanent, reinforcements. The exception was 417 Squadron, which was held together more firmly because the commanders of the Royal Canadian Air Force had become very anxious (if not fixated) on achieving a high degree of 'Canadianisation' among its units.

All these units received Hurricanes before fully reverting to the Spitfires which ostensibly they had been sent out to fly, although in all cases it would be 1943 before they were fully so equipped. Perhaps the hardest-done-by unit was 123 Squadron which finally found itself at Habbaniya in Iraq in October 1942, receiving Gladiator II biplanes for a few weeks before sufficient Hurricanes became available.

Thus it was that by the summer the situation on Malta had been considerably ameliorated. Supplies of Spitfires had become adequate for the island's defence for the time being in any event. Given the beating that WDAF's fighters would have been taking following the opening of Rommel's Gazala offensive on 26 May, at the end of June the air party of 601 Squadron was sent from Malta to reinforce WDAF, the two parts of the unit being reunited at Maryut at the end of June. Although at that time 92 Squadron had still not received its Spitfires – and would not do so for several more weeks –the presence of both 145 and 601 at this critical juncture, at last began to be of some significance. For 603 Squadron, the story would be very different. In early August the air echelon was renumbered, the ground party then continuing to remain 'in limbo' for many more months before it became a full unit again, as will be described considerably later in our narrative.

March 1942

With the arrival of March the WDAF fighter units were reorganised in a new 211 Group within which 258 and 262 Wings became respectively 243 and 239 Wings, while a new wing, 233, was formed. Squadrons initially allotted were as follows:

233 Wing – 94, 260, 2 SAAF and 4 SAAF Squadrons
239 Wing – 3 RAAF, 112, 250 and 450 Squadrons
243 Wing – 33, 73, 80 and 274 Squadrons

These units were now in the main based at Gambut. From 233 Wing, 94 Squadron was away undertaking further training, whereas in 239 Wing 3 RAAF Squadron was at this point detached for a rest. 238 Squadron, retained currently for defensive duties associated with the coastal convoys to Tobruk, received a new commanding officer when Sqn Ldr O'Neill was replaced by Sqn Ldr C.J. 'Micky' Mount, DFC, a Battle of France veteran.

There was also a major change within the command structure of the Italian forces at this time when Gen Curio Barbasetti di Prun replaced Gen Giuseppe Gambara as chief of staff of armed forces in North Africa.

The first 14 days of March brought further bad weather with heavy rain and storms which continued to reduce operational activity of all types.

The ever-valuable work of the recovery units was very important to maintaining the strength of WDAF. Here a Hurricane of 73 Squadron, carrying the unit's pre-war fuselage flash, is loaded onto a 'Queen Mary' trailer after its wings have been removed. BD930 later served with 335 and 127 Squadrons after repair.

A number of shot-down Hurricanes are brought in for repair. To the right one aircraft painted with the fuselage flash of 73 Squadron may be seen, while in the left foreground is HB-D of 229 Squadron; behind this is an EZ-coded aircraft of 127 Squadron, and in the distance is probably EY of 80 Squadron.

A Little-known Diversion

Before proceeding with the diary of events in the Western Desert and over Egypt, at this point a new series of events occurred which barely touched upon Allied considerations, but which were of immediate concern to the Italians. At the start of the month a new threat to their Libyan colony and to their forces had been detected by the Regia Aeronautica deep in the south of the country, in the Fezzan desert area. About 30 kilometres east of Sebha, Caproni Ghiblis of Aviazione Sahariana had sighted and strafed motor vehicles approaching Italian garrisons. The intruders were mixed formations of Chevrolet, Bedford and Ford lorries belonging to Chad-based Free French forces led by Gen Jacques-Philippe Leclerc. Initially, he had planned an attack to penetrate Libya from the south to join the British forces advancing along the coast. However, the Axis offensive in January had forced him to revise his rather ambitious plans, greatly reducing its goals. The new version provided a 'touch and go' offensive to harass Italian garrisons in order to distract forces from the northern front. The Leclerc column was formed by four independent patrols, the aerial support being provided by the Groupe Bretagne, composed of Nantes and Rennes Escadrilles. The former was led by Lt Jean Mahé and had four Martin Marylands (ex-French Martin 167s, known simply as 'Glenns') and a Potez 540. The latter, commanded by Lt Marcel Finance, had five Lysanders and three Potez 29s. Leclerc had moved from Chad on 17 February and ten days later surprised and overwhelmed the small garrison of Uigh el Kebir. Here he established his command post and on 28 February his forces managed to capture the Gatrun and Tegerri garrisons, but a patrol led by Cne Jacques Massu met strong resistance at Umm el Araneb and was forced to retreat.

Fezzan – 3 March 1942

The four Glenns of the Nantes Escadrille entered operations but were hampered by bad visibility. Cdt André Noel returned to his base at Vur without completing a reconnaissance he had set out to undertake, while the other three sought to find and bomb a fort at Murzuch. Only one crew found the target, Lt François Court's aircraft releasing a single bomb on it. Court then became lost and belly-landed in the desert. The other two aircraft bombed unidentified forts, but one then ran out of fuel on its way back;

only Sous Lt Raymond managed to reach Vur safely.

French Casualties	
Nantes Esc	2 Marylands force-landed in desert; Lt Jean Mahé and Lt François Court and crews safe

Fezzan – 4 March 1942

Sous Lt Pierre Grillet took off from Uigh el Kebir on a reconnaissance sortie in a Lysander, but flew into a sandstorm which caused him to crash-land at Gatrun. His aircraft was damaged beyond repair and he suffered severe injuries.

French Casualties	
Rennes Esc	Lysander P9184 crash-landed in storm, DBR; S/Lt Pierre Grillet badly injured

Fezzan – 5 March 1942

As a result of the French aerial activity in Fezzan, Magg Michele Mandara, 160° Gruppo CT commanding officer, deployed four CR.42s to Sebha, led by Ten Eduardo Sorvillo. A single S.79 of 175ª Squadriglia RST was also sent as a reinforcement, flown by Ten Giuseppe Pellizzotti.

During the day the first sortie by Lysander P9181 was flown by Sgt Chef René Weill. Over Umm el Araneb, where Massu's force had been driven back, he was fired on by AA. He managed to complete his reconnaissance and reported the results to Leclerc. Cdt Noel, who had aborted his sortie on 3rd, now completed his mission in Glenn BS765, sighting the newly-arrived Italian aircraft at Sebha.

Fezzan – 6 March 1942

The CR.42s of 160° Gruppo undertook their first sorties from Sebha, hunting French vehicles between there and Zuila, but without result.

Fezzan – 7 March 1942

The four CR.42s at Sebha now moved to Umm el Araneb. After a reconnaissance to Gatrun, they were bombed and strafed by the French Lysander P9197 of the Rennes Escadrille, flown by Lt Finance. The fighter of Ten Sorvillo was set on fire, the pilot suffering severe injuries, while S.Ten Piero Bertonasso's CR.42 was slightly damaged. The pair of Fiats still serviceable took off immediately, flown by Serg Magg Duilio Bernardi and Serg Antonio Malavasi to hunt for the hostile aircraft. Bernardi found the Lysander and fired at it repeatedly, forcing it to land in the desert, trailing smoke. Finance took the gunner, Sgt Chef Fernand Leroy, who had been wounded in the leg, out of the aircraft and sought the cover of the smoke. It proved only to be a smoke bomb hit by a bullet from Bernardi's guns.

Meanwhile, Bernardi flew for some time over the grounded aircraft without attacking it further. Convinced that he had inflicted irreparable damage, he then departed. This allowed Finance, having got the gunner back on board, to take off and fly back to Uigh el Kebir.

At Umm el Araneb meantime, the wounded Sorvillo was put in an S.79 called to the spot and flown to Castel Benito. The S.79 flown by Ten Pellizzotti subsequently crashed at Sebha for unknown reasons, all crew being killed.

French Claims			
Rennes Esc	Lt Marcel Finance	Lysander P9197	CR.42 destroyed on ground at Umm el Araneb
Rennes Esc	Lt Marcel Finance	Lysander P9197	CR.42 damaged on ground at Umm el Araneb
French Casualties			
Rennes Esc	Lysander P9197 slightly damaged by CR.42, force-landed; Lt Marcel Finance safe, later flew out with gunner WiA		
Italian Claims			
393ª Sq , 160°Gr CT	M.llo Duilio Bernardi	CR.42	Lysander damaged and forced to land, Gatrun
Italian Casualties			
394ª Sq, 160°Gr CT	CR.42 MM 7627 '394-8', destroyed at Umm el Araneb by strafing, Ten Eduardo Sorvillo WiA		
375ª Sq, 160°Gr CT	CR.42 damaged at Umm el Araneb by strafing, S.Ten Piero Bertonasso safe		
175ª Sq RST	S.79 MM 21465 crashed to ground at Sebha, pilot Ten Giuseppe Pellizzotti, copilot Serg Giuseppe Zarattini and four KiA, one WiA		

Fezzan – 8 March 1942

Two more 160° Gruppo CR.42s were flown down to Sebha by Ten Raoul Francinetti and Serg Magg Aurelio Munich to replace the two which had been destroyed. Meanwhile, however, all the French aircraft left the area, retiring to their base at Faya in Chad, leaving Leclerc's patrols without air cover.

Fezzan – 9 March 1942

The two newly-arrived 160° Gruppo pilots strafed Massu's patrol, leaving one vehicle in flames and others damaged. Francinetti's CR.42 was slightly damaged by small-arms fire. In the afternoon Francinetti, Malavasi and Munich again attacked Massu's troops, this time near Uigh el Kebir, ten small trucks were claimed destroyed and others damaged. In practice, on 30 March an Italian patrol of 3ª Compagnia Sahariana found the wrecks of eight French vehicles. At this point the first Fezzan Campaign was at an end, French forces returning to Chad and the Italian garrisons being re-established.

The Main Campaign
Luftwaffe Order of Battle
March 1942

Fliegerführer Afrika	
Stab JG 27	Bf 109F-4
I./JG 27	Bf 109F-4
II./JG 27	Bf 109F-4
III./JG 27	Bf 109F-4
Stab StG 3	Ju 87R-4
	He 111H-5
	Bf 110
I./StG 3	Ju 87R-2
	Ju 87R-4
II./StG 3	Ju 87R-2
	Ju 87R-4
4.(H)/12	Personnel only
2.(H)/14	Bf 110E-2
	Bf 110E-3
	Hs 126B-1
	Bf 109E-7
Wüstennotstaffel	Fi 156C-3
X. Fliegerkorps	
Stab LG 1	Ju 88A-5
I./LG 1	Ju 88A-4
	Ju 88A-5
	He 111H-5

II./LG 1	Ju 88A-4
	Ju 88A-5
12./LG 1	Ju 88A-4
	Ju 88A-5
II./KG 26	He 111H-6
1.(F)/121	Ju 88A-1
	Ju 88A-5
	Ju 88D-5
	Bf 110E-3
1.(F)/122	Ju 88D-1
	Ju 88D-5
	Bf 109F-4
2.(F)/123	Ju 88A-5
	Ju 88D-1
	Ju 88D-2
	Bf 110E-3
2./SAGr 125	Ar 196A-3
SAGr 126	He 60
	Fokker T.VIII
	Ar 196A-3
	He 114A-2

Monday, 2 March 1942

To return to the main front, on this date 11 Hurricanes of 274 Squadron were on patrol over Tobruk when two of the unit's aircraft were shot down, both pilots suffering slight wounds and ending up together in Tobruk hospital. A third Hurricane crash-landed some 20 miles west of Gambut. These aircraft had all been shot down by 3./JG 27, Hptm Homuth and Lt Kugelbauer identifying them as P-40s – yet again. Sgt Dodds, flying in the lower of the two flights, became separated and reported meeting three MC.202s, one of which he claimed to have shot down in flames.

A 94 Squadron Kittyhawk I taxies out (without the ill-fated unit rudder markings) in the hands of newly-arrived Flt Sgt J.F.Edwards. He would make his first claim flying this aircraft on 23 March.

Eight MC.200s of 150° Gruppo, led as usual by Magg Vizzotto, with six CR.42s of 154ª Squadriglia, all escorted by 12 MC.202s of 6° Gruppo, took off at 1130 to strafe vehicles in the Taieb el Esem area. About 30 trucks were reported damaged but one CR.42 was shot down by AA, a second being damaged. Despite the presence of Bf 109s and MC.202s in the area during the morning, no engagements or losses have been discovered to match the claims of any of the Commonwealth pilots engaged.

British Claims					
274 Sqn	Sgt J.Dodds	Hurricane IIb Z5148	MC.202	Gazala	1030-1136
British Casualties					
274 Sqn	Hurricane II DG683 shot down by Bf 109 W Tobruk, 1050; Sgt K.F.Wildy baled out safe				
274 Sqn	Hurricane II BD881 shot down by Bf 109 W Tobruk, 1050; Sgt J.P.MacDonnell				
274 Sqn	Hurricane II Z5469 shot down by Bf 109 20m W Gambut, 1050, crash-landed; Sgt W.G.Eagle				
15 SAAF Sqn	Blenheim IV Z5864 crash-landed Amiriya				
German Claims					
3./JG 27	Lt Karl Kugelbauer	P-40	W Tobruk	1050	
3./JG 27	Hptm Gerhard Homuth	2 P-40s	W Tobruk & SE Fort Acroma	1051 & 1052	
Italian Casualties					
154ª Sq, 3° Gr CT	CR.42 MM 7630 shot down by AA, Ten Sergio Roveri MiA				

Tuesday-Wednesday, 3/4 March 1942

33 Squadron, based at Sidi Haneish where two Kittyhawks and a Tomahawk had been taken on strength, was now ordered to collect instead 12 Hurricane IIbs for re-equipment. Next day 80 Squadron moved to Gambut. 5 SAAF Squadron deployed forward to Maaten Bagush.

During 3rd an MC.202 of 17° Gruppo scrambled to intercept a Maryland from a detachment of 223 Squadron on reconnaissance duties, claiming to have probably shot this down. The Maryland crew returned, but with their aircraft shot-up, the crew reporting that they had been hit by both the Macchi and by Flak.

At this point 69° Gruppo OA was ordered to move its Ca.311s of 118ª and 123ª Squadriglie from Barce to Misurata.

British Casualties				
223 Sqn	Maryland shot-up by MC.202 and Flak			
Italian Claims				
72ª Sq , 17°Gr, 1° St CT	Serg Bruno Pellizzari MC.202	Maryland Probable	Martuba 1005	

Wednesday, 4 March 1942

British Casualties

213 Sqn	Hurricane FTR, left Port Said for Edcu, last plotted Lake Burillas, washed ashore at Baltim on 19th March; Sgt M.S.Lee KiA
208 Sqn	Hurricane I Z4064 hit by Flak NE Mechili, damaged Cat I; Sqn Ldr J.K.Rogers WiA

Thursday, 5 March 1942

Blue Section of 5 SAAF Squadron scrambled at 1619, Capt Duncan and Lt Thornhill-Cook intercepting and shooting down a Ju 88 of 2./LG 2 for the unit's first victory. Three members of the German crew baled out and were captured by pilots of 1 SAAF Squadron who were returning to Cairo by truck. A few minutes after this success, a further bomber was attacked by two more of the unit's pilots and claimed damaged. In the same area, however, another Ju 88 of the same unit involved in bombing Fuka airfield, encountered and shot down a Fleet Air Arm Albacore of 826 Squadron which was en route to Dekheila with four passengers aboard, all of whom were killed together with the crew.

British Claims

5 SAAF Sqn	Capt A.Duncan	Tomahawk IIb AN247	Ju 88	Maaten Bagush-Fuka	1610
5 SAAF Sqn	Lt B.S.Thornhill-Cook	Tomahawk IIb AN420 'P' }	Ju88 Damaged	N Ras el Kanaysis	1615
5 SAAF Sqn	Lt R.Pare	Tomahawk II AN383 'N' }			
5 SAAF Sqn	Lt J.V.Lindbergh	Tomahawk AK455			

British Casualties

5 SAAF Sqn	Tomahawk IIb AN420 'P' one bullet in wing; Lt B.S.Thornhill-Cook safe
826 Sqn	Albacore T9238 shot down by Ju 88 over Fuka; Lt C.W.B.Smith, CO of 821 Sqn, Ldg Air W.Stuttle of that unit, and three groundcrew all KiA

German Claims

I./LG 1	Lt Gerhard Brenner & crew	Albacore shot down into sea

German Casualties

2./LG 1	Ju 88A-4 WNr 5548 L1+FK shot down by P-40 1612, crashed nr Fuka; Lt Werner Ziegler and crew safe

Saturday, 7 March 1942

Magg Vizzotto led 18 MC.200s of 150° Gruppo off at 0915 to attack a large concentration of armoured vehicles south of Ain el Gazala, cover to his formation being provided by 17 MC.202s of 17° Gruppo. Ten vehicles were claimed to have been left in flames with many more damaged. However, all but two of the MC.200s were hit by small-arms fire, and three of these force-landed at Tmimi while a fourth did likewise at Martuba. On return from this sortie an 81ª Squadriglia MC.202 collided with another such aircraft from 88ª Squadriglia; the 81ª Squadriglia aircraft burst into flames, but the pilot escaped with only slight injuries.

British Casualties

33 Sqn	Hurricane Z5311 dived into ground W LG.115

Italian Casualties

81ª Sq, 6°Gr, 1°St CT	MC.202 MM 7769 burnt after collision with MC.202 MM 7715 at Martuba, M.llo Giovanni Collovini WiA

Sunday, 8 March 1942

At 1400 Sgt Persse of 274 Squadron was attacked by a Bf 109 while landing at Gambut Main, and crashed, suffering leg wounds. Nine Bf 109s then shot-up the airfield, damaging nine Hurricanes on the ground there.

Ten 150° Gruppo MC.200s were off again at 1630, led by Cap Luigi Mariotti, on this occasion to escort Luftwaffe Ju 87s attacking Tobruk harbour. Indirect support was provided by Bf 109s, but these did not intervene when a reported 20 P-40s attacked. Six Kittyhawks each from 450 and 3 RAAF Squadrons had taken off at 1700 to intercept 15 Ju 87s with a very close escort identified as MC.200s and 202s. These were reported to be flying in a very tight formation made up of two echelons of five and four aircraft, and two Bf 109s above. It seems that the Italians initially mistook the Kittyhawks for friendly fighters and in consequence were hard-hit. The Australians claimed five MC.200s shot down, plus two MC.202s and two Ju 87s, adding three more MC.200s and one 202 as probables, and two damaged.

German and Italian reports were quite specific that no Ju 87s were lost, and this seems to be borne out by 112 Squadron which was patrolling over the forward area at the same time, meeting 15 Ju 87s escorted only by two MC.200s and two Bf 109s. The pilots of this unit claimed one Stuka and one Macchi shot down. 3./StG 3 reported that one aircraft was damaged in combat with Curtiss fighters some 30km north-east of Gazala, but that this aircraft landed safely at base. Similarly, after suffering the loss of five MC.200s, 150° Gruppo had one more force-land at Tmimi. Following this engagement the Regia Aeronautica demanded better co-operation from the German fighters.

40 SAAF Squadron pilots were at this time attached to 208 Squadron, both to undertake some operations and to gain relevant experience before the latter unit was withdrawn for a rest.

British Claims

112 Sqn	Sgt R.B.Evans	Kittyhawk I AK766	Ju 87	into sea 5m N Gazala	1730
112 Sqn	Flt Lt D.F.Westenra	Kittyhawk I AK762	MC.200	N Gazala	1730
450 Sqn	Sgt D.H.McBurnie	Kittyhawk I ..717 'V'	MC.200		1725
450 Sqn	Sgt R.Shaw	Kittyhawk I ..592 'P'	MC.202		1725
450 Sqn	Flg Off Thompson	Kittyhawk I ..895 'K'	MC.200 Damaged		1725
3 RAAF Sqn	Flt Lt A.W.Barr	Kittyhawk I AK903	MC.202	15m N Tobruk	1735
3 RAAF Sqn	Flt Lt A.W.Barr	Kittyhawk I AK903	MC.202 Probable	15m N Tobruk	1735
3 RAAF Sqn	Flt Lt A.W.Barr	Kittyhawk I AK903	2 MC.200s Probable	15m N Tobruk	1735
3 RAAF Sqn	Sgt W.A.Beard	Kittyhawk I AK623 }	MC.202 Damaged	15m N Tobruk	1735
3 RAAF Sqn	Sgt T.E.Packer	Kittyhawk I AK898 }			
3 RAAF Sqn	Plt Off V.F.Curtis	Kittyhawk I AK622	Ju 87	15m N Tobruk	1735
3 RAAF Sqn	Plt Off V.F.Curtis	Kittyhawk I AK622	MC.200	15m N Tobruk	1735
3 RAAF Sqn	Flg Off P.R.Giddy	Kittyhawk I AK876	Ju 87	15m N Tobruk	1735
3 RAAF Sqn	Flg Off P.R.Giddy	Kittyhawk I AK876	MC.200	15m N Tobruk	1735
3 RAAF Sqn	Flg Off H.G.Pace	Kittyhawk I AK712	MC.200	15m N Tobruk	1735
450 Sqn	Sgt F.W.Beste	Kittyhawk I ..493 'W'	MC.200		1735
450 Sqn	Sgt R.D.Dyson	Kittyhawk I ..732 'A'	MC.200 Probable		1735

British Casualties

274 Sqn	Hurricane II Z5327 shot down by Bf 109 on landing approach, crash-landed 12.45-14.10; Sgt W.P.Persse WiA
	Gambut Main airfield shot-up; 9 Hurricanes damaged

German Casualties

3./StG 3	Ju 87R-2 WNr 5995 S1+GL , 20% damaged, combat P-40 30km NE Ain el Gazala; pilot safe/Uffz Gustav Riegel WiA

Italian Casualties

363ª Sq, 150°Gr CT	MC.200, Tobruk area 1730, Ten Enea Atti MiA
363ª Sq, 150°Gr CT	MC.200 MM 6661, Tobruk area 1730, Serg Ugo Rodorigo KiA
363ª Sq, 150°Gr CT	MC.200 MM 6490, Tobruk area 1730, Serg Enrico Micheli PoW
365ª Sq, 150°Gr CT	MC.200 MM 5332, Tobruk area 1730, Serg Raffaele Badalessi KiA
365ª Sq, 150°Gr CT	MC.200 MM 5333, Tobruk area 1730, Serg Magg Leopoldo Ierai PoW
77ª Sq, 13°Gr, 2°St CT	MC.200 MM 5852, crashed in flames near Misurata, Serg Camillo Stevani baled out

Monday, 9 March 1942

Nine Kittyhawks of 112 Squadron were scrambled early from Gambut Main to which the unit had now moved, their task being to intercept four Bf 109s which strafed the airfield, damaging a Hurricane of 238 Squadron. On return to the field Sgt Elliott suddenly dived from 10,000 feet and crashed, being killed instantly. He was not seen to be shot down and no cause for his

In the foreground is the tail of a Cant.Z.1007bis, the main bomber type employed by the Regia Aeronautica during 1942. Behind is a Bf 110 of III./ZG26.

death could be ascertained. During the afternoon Messerschmitts of I./JG 27 on a Freie Jagd patrol intercepted and shot down a Wellington of 38 Squadron and an Albacore of 826 Squadron which were preparing for a night operation. Full details of these engagements may be found in Chapter Three.

British Casualties			
112 Sqn	Kittyhawk I AK700 'B' shot down near Gambut Main; Sgt P.T.Elliott KiA		
826 Sqn	Albacore T9149; Sub Lt R.S.Nathan		
38 Sqn	Wellington Ic Z9099 'C' shot down by 2 Bf 109s near Fort Maddalena on a positioning flight with 2 torpedoes fitted. Two of crew KiA in crash-landing; Wg Cdr J.H.Chaplin, DFC, slightly injured and with two walked back to Allied lines		
12 SAAF Sqn	Boston III AL671 'F' strafed during raid on Wellington airfield adjacent to LG.21		
German Claims			
2./JG 27	Gefr Herbert Romeikat	Wellington	SW Sidi Barrani 1635
2./JG 27	Lt Friedrich Körner	Albacore	SW Sidi Barrani 1650
German Casualties			
4./KG 26	He 111H-6 15% damaged by AA nr Qotaifiya, landed safely, one WiA		

Tuesday, 10 March 1942

In the very early hours Plt Off Fraser and Sgt Sands of 73 Squadron flew to El Adem to undertake a night strafing sortie from there. However, Fraser was unable to take off again, so Sands went alone. During this sortie he was hit by ground fire and caused to bale out. This he achieved safely, returning to the unit three days later.

During another Freie Jagd operation, two pilots of I./JG 27 intercepted and shot down a bomber when east of Sidi Barrani, identified as a Boston. However, this may in fact have been a Beaufort of 39 Squadron since no Boston losses were recorded. On the other hand a Ju 88 of 3./LG 1 flown by Oblt Iro Ilk, also engaged a British bomber, in this case identified as a Blenheim, the German crew claiming to have shot this down north of Derna. Again, more details of this engagement will be found in Chapter Three.

It was on this date that Sqn Ldr C.R.Caldwell of 112 Squadron heralded a new form of operation for the Kittyhawk units when he made the first test drop of a 250lb bomb from one of these fighters. Now re-equipped and fully converted to these aircraft, 260 Squadron moved to Gasr el Arid, bringing the number of Kittyhawk units at the front to four, supported by two more with Tomahawks.

Lt Friedrich Körner of 2./JG 27 claimed his 10th victory on 9 March.

The Regia Aeronautica's 5ª Squadra HQ received a visit on this date from Gen SA Rino Corso Fougier, Regia Aeronautica chief of staff. He would undertake a tour of the main Italian fighter bases during the next few days. The date of his visit coincided with the return to Italy of all S.81s of 103ª Squadriglia of the Aviazione Sahariana; they would be replaced by Ghiblis. That night two BR.20s of 43° Gruppo bombed Tobruk.

British Casualties			
73 Sqn	Hurricane Z5377 shot down by Flak W El Adem at 0350 ; Sgt.A.H.Sands baled out and walked back		
4 SAAF	Tomahawk IIb AN412 lost		
German Claims			
2./JG 27	Oblt Fritz Keller	Boston	E Sidi Barrani 0935

Wednesday, 11 March 1942

Next morning 4 SAAF Squadron joined 260 Squadron at Gasr el Arid, but the main activities of the day occurred during escort missions over a convoy making for Tobruk. Here three sections of Tomahawks from 5 SAAF Squadron patrolled north of Gambut, Capt Hewitson sending a Ju 88 of 12./LG 1 crashing into the sea at 1600, with a second bomber claimed as a probable a couple of hours later. It appears that one of the patrols was intercepted by MC.202s, six of these fighters from 79ª Squadriglia undertaking a reconnaissance mission off Tobruk at much the same time in the morning. During this mission S.Ten Alessandro Rosa reported seeing two fighters at lower level, bouncing these and claiming damage to both. Although the times and location coincide, no such engagement was recorded by the South African unit.

British Claims

5 SAAF Sqn	2/Lt T.Finlayson	Tomahawk IIb AN427 'D'	Ju 88 Damaged	75m N Gambut	1600
5 SAAF Sqn	Capt J.L.Hewitson	Tomahawk IIb AN448 'H'	Ju 88	75m N Gambut	1600
5 SAAF Sqn	Lt J.D.W.Human	Tomahawk IIb AM401 'F'	} Ju 88 Damaged	75m N Gambut	1630
5 SAAF Sqn	Lt K.C.Kemsley	Tomahawk IIb AN468 'J'			
5 SAAF Sqn	Lt K.C.Whyte	Tomahawk IIb AN271	} He 111 Probable	N Gambut	1800
5 SAAF Sqn	Maj J.E.Frost	Tomahawk IIb AK195 'W'			

British Casualties

5 SAAF Sqn	Tomahawk IIb AN271 crashed on landing in the dark, after combat; Lt K.C.Whyte safe

German Casualties

12./LG 1	Ju 88A-4 WNr 142014 L1+BW shot down by fighters 150km NE Derna; Lt Heinz Althaus and three MiA

Italian Claims

79ª Sq , 6°Gr, 1°St CT	S.Ten Alessandro Rosa	MC.202	2 P-40s Damaged off Tobruk	0655-0810

Thursday, 12 March 1942

British Claims

5 SAAF Sqn	Lt R.L.Morrison	Tomahawk II b AN426	} Ju 88 Damaged	20m NE LG.21	1100
5 SAAF Sqn	Lt B.S.Thornhill-Cook	Tomahawk II b AN420 'P'			

Friday, 13 March 1942

At midday five Hurricanes of 274 Squadron and 12 Kittyhawks of 112 Squadron took off to intercept an incoming raid in the Tobruk area. Flg Off Bartle and Sgt Rozanski of the latter unit were bounced by Bf 109s diving out of heavy cloud, and Obfw Schulz shot down Rozanski's aircraft, the Polish pilot belly-landing and climbing out of his aircraft just before it burst into flames. Sgt Burney claimed to have attacked and destroyed an MC.202; Sgt Dodds of 274 Squadron reported that he had spotted three Ju 87s escorted by two MC.200s, one of which he climbed after and attacked. He claimed that this crashed on its back 20 miles west of Tobruk.

British Claims

112 Sqn	Sgt H.G.Burney	Kittyhawk I AK772	MC.202	into sea 12-15m N Tobruk	1225
112 Sqn	Plt Off J.P.Bartle	Kittyhawk I AK632	Bf 109 Probable	Acroma	1225
274 Sqn	Sgt J.Dodds	Hurricane IIb BD173	MC.200	20m W Tobruk	1205-1320

British Casualties

112 Sqn	Kittyhawk I AK834 shot down by Bf 109s near Gambut Main, crash-landed; Sgt J.W. Rozanski safe
112 Sqn	Kittyhawk I AK632 shot down by Bf 109s near Gambut Main: Plt Off J.P.Bartle safe

German Claims

4./JG 27	Obfw Otto Schulz	P-40	SW Tobruk 1235

German Casualties

1./StG 3	Ju 87R-2 30% damaged by AA Tobruk but landed safely at base; Uffz Fritz Poth WiA

Saturday, 14 March 1942

Twelve Kittyhawks each from 450 and 3 RAAF Squadrons escorted 12 Bostons to bomb Martuba, while 12 more Kittyhawks of 112 Squadron flew a diversionary sweep in the area. As they approached, seven MC.202s of 6° Gruppo were scrambled from Martuba at 1310, led by Cap Dante Ocarso to intercept the formation which was appearing over their base. They pursued with some success, claiming eight P-40s shot down and others damaged, including one of the Bostons. Cap Ocarso himself claimed two P-40s and Serg Magg Borreo claimed three.

112 Squadron had arrived as the dogfight was taking place and dived straight in, claiming two fighters shot down but losing two of their own in doing so, Sgt Simonsen being shot down in flames as Sgt Evans baled out. Meanwhile, two of 450 Squadron's aircraft were damaged, although the pilots managed to get back to base. As often happened, the Macchis were identified as Messerschmitts by several pilots, but 3

RAAF Squadron could claim only one aircraft shot down, plus two probables, while 450 Squadron made no claims at all. During this raid the bombing damaged four German aircraft, including three Bf 109s. On this date 2.(H)/14 lost a Bf 109E shot down by Curtiss fighters and crashed near Tobruk. This may have been the subject of one of the claims for such an aircraft – possibly that of the 112 Squadron pilots.

At 1700 16 150° Gruppo MC.200s and 16 MC.202s of 6° Gruppo raided a large concentration of armoured cars south of Ain el Gazala, claiming ten destroyed and many damaged, but lost three MC.200s to AA. One fell in flames in the target area, Serg Magg Zandonai being killed, a second crash-landed at Martuba, the pilot of this also losing his life, and the third force-landed within Axis lines.

British Claims

112 Sqn	Sqn Ldr C.R.Caldwell	Kittyhawk I AK772 'Y'	MC.202	15-25m W Bir Hacheim	1345
112 Sqn	Sqn Ldr C.R.Caldwell	Kittyhawk I AK772 'Y'	} Bf 109	W Bir Hacheim	1340
112 Sqn	Sgt Z.Urbanczyk	Kittyhawk I AK957 'D'	}		
3 RAAF Sqn	Flg Off G.T.Chinchen	Kittyhawk I AK891	} Bf 109	Martuba l.g. area	1350
3 RAAF Sqn	Sgt T.E.Packer	Kittyhawk I AK896	}		
3 RAAF Sqn	Flt Lt R.C.Hart	Kittyhawk I AK849	MC.202 Probable	Martuba a/f	1350
3 RAAF Sqn	Sgt E.K.Kildey	Kittyhawk I AK677	MC.200 Probable	Martuba a/f	1350
1 SAAF Sqn	Lt A.D.Maclean	Hurricane II	He 111 Damaged	Ras el Kanaysis	1855

British Casualties

112 Sqn	Kittyhawk I AK900 'A' shot down by Bf 109s near Bir Hacheim; Sgt R.E.Simonsen MiA
112 Sqn	Kittyhawk I AK878 'C' shot down by MC.202, Bir Hacheim; Sgt R.B.Evans baled out WiA
450 Sqn	Kittyhawk I AK671 'R' badly damaged by 2 MC.202s, Martuba area; Sgt E.J.Quirk safe
450 Sqn	Kittyhawk I AK592 'P'slightly damaged by 2 MC.202s Martuba area; Sgt D.R.Law safe
208 Sqn	Hurricane Z4687 left 0615, force-landed in desert while seeking evidence of previous night's bombing. 2/Lt H.W.Marchant safe, picked up by armoured car and returned next day, reporting engine failure

German Casualties

2.(H)/14	Bf 109E-7 WNr 5278 shot down by P-40, crashed nr Tobruk; Obfw Henry Schönbarth MiA

Italian Claims

88ª Sq, 6°Gr, 1°St CT	Cap Dante Ocarso	MC.202	2 P-40s	S Ain el Gazala	1310-1400
88ª Sq, 6°Gr, 1°St CT	Serg Magg Anano Borreo	MC.202	3 P-40s	S Ain el Gazala	1310-1400
88ª Sq, 6°Gr, 1°St CT	S.Ten Alfredo Civetta	MC.202	P-40	S Ain el Gazala	1310-1400
79ª Sq, 6°Gr, 1°St CT	M.llo Dino Forlani	MC.202	P-40	S Ain el Gazala	1310-1400
79ª Sq, 6°Gr, 1°St CT	S.Ten Alessandro Rosa	MC.202	P-40	S Ain el Gazala	1310-1400

Italian Casualties

364ª Sq, 150° Gr CT	MC.200 MM 5858 shot down by AA; Serg Magg Renato Zandonai MiA
365ª Sq, 150° Gr CT	MC.200 MM 6677 damaged by AA; Serg Magg Bruno Zotti crash-landed within lines, KiA

Sunday, 15 March 1942

450 Squadron again despatched 12 Kittyhawks to escort Bostons to Martuba, this time accompanied by 260 Squadron, as 12 Tomahawks of 2 SAAF Squadron flew a diversionary sweep. Bf 109s of II./JG 27 and six MC.202s of 6° Gruppo, led by Magg Marco Larcher, took off to intercept, the Italian pilots claiming four P-40s shot down near Martuba, with Obfw Woidich and Schulz each claiming one in the Gazala-Acroma area. Cap Giuseppe Pesola of 79ª Squadriglia attacked four fighters but was unable to observe the results; he was then attacked by a Kittyhawk that badly damaged the radiator of his aircraft. Pesola managed to escape his adversary by flying over the sea at very low altitude, but after a few minutes he was forced to head for the coast to try and belly-land. Once landed, still within British lines, he quickly abandoned his Macchi, looking for a place to hide. He spent the night hidden among the beach dunes, but next morning was taken prisoner by a South African patrol, alerted by some Arabs. Taken to Camp 310 near Suez, he managed to escape three months later but, after more than one year spent in Egypt on the run, he was again captured and taken to Camp 304 at Helwan. He would return to Italy after the armistice.

Pilots of 3 RAAF Squadron claimed two fighters probably shot down, but 2 SAAF Squadron had two Tomahawks damaged, 260 Squadron one Kittyhawk and 450 Squadron one more. The South African unit recorded that its pilots appeared to have panicked slightly when attacked, and their formation broke up in confusion.

Cap Giuseppe Pesola prepares to climb into his MC.202 '79-5' MM 7885. This pilot was forced to land in Allied-held territory on 15 March and became a prisoner of war.

2 SAAF Squadron was up again in the afternoon on an interception scramble over Tobruk, during which one claim was made for a Bf 109 and one for a damaged. Lt Isaacs, who made the latter claim, then had his own aircraft slightly damaged. The claim for the Messerschmitt shot down – the only confirmed claim of the day – may relate to Pesola's MC.202 which belly-landed within British lines. However, it was reported that Sgt Taylor of 450 Squadron in Kittyhawk AR706 AK-X, noted: "knocked hell out of a 109F and tried to get it confirmed later – was." Evidence that this was the case has not been discovered. This was the last combat in which Obfw Otto Schulz would take part for several weeks as he was now sent home to Germany on leave, which was to be followed by an officer's course.

Sgt Joe Bernier sits on the tail of a 260 Squadron Kittyhawk which had been shot-up by a Bf 109 of III./JG 27 on 15 March, the pilot (Sgt T.'Polly' Parrott) being wounded. Note that at this stage the unit's aircraft carried the codes MF, soon to be changed to HS.

During the night a bombing raid on Martuba seriously impaired 150° Gruppo's aircraft serviceability as at least four MC.200s were destroyed and some others damaged. On this date as well, a communications Bf 108 of StG 3 was destroyed.

British Claims

3 RAAF Sqn	Plt Off V.F.Curtis	Kittyhawk I AK708	Bf 109 Probable	Martuba satellite l.g.	1120
3 RAAF Sqn	Flg Off L.T.Spence	Kittyhawk I AK808	Bf 109F Probable	Martuba satellite l.g.	1120
2 SAAF Sqn	Capt E.M.Baker	Tomahawk IIb AN334 'R'	Bf 109F	5m N Tobruk	1610
2 SAAF Sqn	Lt W.J.Isaacs	Tomahawk IIb AK451	Bf 109F Damaged	5m N Tobruk	1610

British Casualties

2 SAAF Sqn	Tomahawk IIb AN321 damaged by Bf 109s on Tmimi op, 0930-1050; Lt N.G.Ford safe
2 SAAF Sqn	Tomahawk IIb AN354 damaged by own AA nr Gazala; Lt G.D.Reynolds slt WiA
2 SAAF Sqn	Tomahawk IIb AN399 damaged by Bf 109 at 1025; Lt V.M.L.Lindsay slt WiA in leg

British Casualties

2 SAAF Sqn	Tomahawk IIb AK451 damaged by Bf 109,1545-1645; Lt W.J.Isaacs safe
260 Sqn	Kittyhawk I badly damaged by Bf 109 over Gazala; Sgt T.Parrott safe
450 Sqn	Kittyhawk I damaged

German Claims

5./JG 27	Obfw Franz Woidich	P-40	20km SE Ain el Gazala	1125
4./JG 27	Obfw Otto Schulz	P-40	10km S Fort Acroma	1132

German Casualties

I.StG 3	Bf 108B-1 WNr 1124 destroyed in air raid at Martuba

Italian Claims

79ª Sq, 6°Gr, 1°St CT	Cap Domenico Camarda	MC.202	P-40	near Martuba	1120-1225
79ª Sq, 6°Gr, 1°St CT	Ten Paolo Cattaneo	MC.202	P-40	near Martuba	1120-1225
79ª Sq, 6°Gr, 1°St CT	S.Ten Rinaldo Bottoni	MC.202	P-40	near Martuba	1120-1225
81ª Sq, 6°Gr, 1°St CT	S.Ten Alberto Paggi	MC.202	P-40	near Martuba	1120-1225

Italian Casualties

79ª Sq, 6°Gr, 1°St CT	MC.202 MM 7885 '79-5' crash-landed in enemy territory, Cap Giuseppe Pesola PoW
150° Gr CT	4 MC.200s (MM 5293, 5343, 7679, 5334) destroyed by fire at Martuba after a British raid, two casualties among ground personnel

Monday, 16 March 1942

17° Gruppo moved from Benghazi K3 to Martuba with 16 serviceable MC.202s, bringing the whole 1° Stormo together at this base. On this date, however, 209ª Squadriglia BaT was ordered to fly its Ju 87s home to Italy.

British Casualties

208 Sqn	Hurricane Z4798 left 0945, lost propeller and crash-landed in Mechili area; 2/Lt J.W.F.Somerville in desert two days and nights before being picked up safely
4 SAAF Sqn	Tomahawk IIb bombed on ground by two Bf 109s and damaged
14 Sqn	Blenheim IV V5446 'M' force-landed on road Agedabia-Agheila for unknown reason. Crew walked for nine days until picked up by British armoured unit. Sqn Ldr A.C.Mills and two safe

Tuesday, 17 March 1942

British Claims

274 Sqn	Sgt W.G.Eagle	Hurricane IIb Z5382	Bf 110 Probable	W Gazala	1010-1130

British Casualties

14 Sqn	Blenheim T2124 'B' off 1130 on shipping strike, collided with Z7991 on forming up and crashed; Sgt R.J.Good and two KiFA
14 Sqn	Blenheim Z7991 off 1130 on shipping strike, collided with T2124 on forming up and crashed; Sgt. R.S.Linley and two KiFA

Wednesday, 18 March 1942

This was a mystery day. Luftwaffe reports indicate that 14 bombers and eight fighters attacked Martuba, damaging some Bf 109s on the ground. The groundcrews of the alert Schwarme kept working on their aircraft during the attack, suffering sprained hands and feet from the blast of the bomb explosions. II./JG 27 reported attacking British fighters over Gazala and Tobruk, claiming four victories against P-40s, one of which was not confirmed. However, during this fight an aircraft of 8.Staffel was shot down in combat with bombers, the pilot becoming a PoW. One claim for a Bf 109 damaged was made at this time in the Martuba area by a pilot of 260 Squadron, but no other details of this day's action have been found in British records.

It had been a week of sustained action for the Boston crews of 3 SAAF Wing, which undertook daily attacks on the Axis airfields as a diversion while a convoy for Malta was to be fought through from Alexandria from the 20th. Starting on 14 March the Bostons had been much involved. The raid undertaken on the 15th had been classed as 'quite exceptional', although the next day's attack had been all but aborted due to bad weather. A full-scale attack by 12 SAAF Squadron had been made on Martuba on the 17th, but now came the operation of 18 March. Bursts of heavy Flak were experienced and Axis fighters were seen climbing upwards, while during the return flight the bombers were fired on by 'friendly' Bofors guns – but no losses or serious damage was noted, and of the escorting fighters there was no mention!

British Claims

260 Sqn	Sgt W.R.McKay	Kittyhawk I	Bf 109F Damaged	Martuba area	0725-0855

British Casualties

14 Sqn	Blenheim IV Z5886 landed with undercarriage partly retracted at LG.116

German Claims

Stab II./JG 27	Obfhr Willi Kientsch	P-40	15km SW Ain el Gazala	0820
6./JG 27	Uffz Johann Walchhofer	P-40 Probable	SE Tobruk	0825
6./JG 27	Fw Fritz Gromotka	P-40	SE Tobruk	0830
Stab II./JG 27	Obfhr Willi Kientsch	P-40	10km SE Tobruk	0840

German Casualties

8./JG 27	Bf 109F-4 trop WNr 8724 Black 1 shot down during interception, crashed nr Ain el Gazala; Lt Horst Heike PoW
2.(H)/14	Bf 110E-3 WNr 2408, 40% damaged by AA nr Tmimi, landed safely at base

Thursday, 19 March 1942

Martuba East was again the target for 3 SAAF Wing, but once more the Bostons were fired on by 8th Army Bofors as they returned. During the morning 80 and 2 SAAF Squadrons were scrambled on an interception patrol over the Gambut area around 1030. One Bf 109 was claimed shot down and one probable, but one Hurricane was shot down into the sea and others were damaged.

At 1245 11 MC.202s of 6° Gruppo were scrambled over the Martuba area, led by Magg Larcher to intercept the Bostons' raid, but only two pilots managed to get within range, claiming one fighter shot down and one damaged. Some considerable time later a further victory was claimed by Uffz Niederhöfer of II./JG 27. At 1500 two pilots of 80 Squadron took off for a weather reconnaissance to the Gulf of Bomba, but they were intercepted by four Bf 109s. Flt Lt Trollip went into a spin to evade them, subsequently recovering and returning to base at 1550. Sgt Smith's aircraft, however, was badly damaged and he landed at Tobruk. The times recorded indicate that his was probably the aircraft claimed by Niederhöfer. Once more all the four fighters claimed by the Axis fighters during the day were listed as P-40s but all the British losses were Hurricanes.

Above right: **Oberfahnrich Willi Kientsch, serving as a young cadet with Stab II./JG 27, would remain active in the Mediterranean area for many months with this Gruppe.**

Right: **Bf 109Fs of II./JG 27 at Martuba in early 1942.**

British Claims					
80 Sqn	Plt Off F.Mason	Hurricane IIc BE410	Bf 109	Tobruk area	1030-1105
80 Sqn	Plt Off R.W.Richardson	Hurricane IIc BE407	MC.202 Damaged	Tobruk area	1030-1105
2 SAAF Sqn	Capt E.M.Baker	Tomahawk IIb AN334 'R'	Bf 109F Probable	Gambut	1055
450 Sqn	Sgt R.Shaw	Kittyhawk I AK726 'O'	Bf 109F Damaged	Martuba area	1200-1330

British Casualties	
80 Sqn	Hurricane IIc BE493 shot down into sea N Gambut by Bf 109 1030-1105; Flt Sgt P.Rivalent WiA
80 Sqn	Hurricane IIc BE407 badly damaged by Bf 109 1030-1105; Flg Off R.W.Richardson safe
80 Sqn	Hurricane IIc BE410 badly damaged by Bf 109 W Tobruk, 1500-1550; Sgt Smith safe

German Claims				
2./JG 27	Lt Friedrich Körner	P-40	N Gambut	1035
2./JG 27	Lt Willi Kothmann	P-40	N Gambut	1035
5./JG 27	Fw Hans Niederhöfer	P-40	W Tobruk	1530

German Casualties	
2.(H)/14	Bf 109E-7 WNr 3583, destroyed in air raid at Martuba

Italian Claims					
79ª Sq, 6°Gr, 1°St CT	Ten Paolo Cattaneo	MC.202	P-40	Martuba area	1245-1345
79ª Sq, 6°Gr, 1°St CT	M.llo Italo Bertinelli	MC.202	P-40 Damaged	Martuba area	1245-1345

Friday, 20 March 1942

The 3 SAAF Wing raid went in early, 260 Squadron being amongst the fighter units providing escort. Bf 109s of I./JG 27 were scrambled, as were six MC.202s of 17° Gruppo. The German pilots claimed three Curtiss fighters shot down without loss, but amongst the Italians claims could only be made for one fighter and one bomber damaged. However, Serg Magg Remo Broilo failed to return, but survived and was back at Martuba two days later. He reported that he had become engaged with five P-40s and had managed to shoot down two of these before his Macchi was hit and set on fire, and he was slightly wounded. He then managed to bale out into no mans' land from where he was rescued by a German patrol.

260 Squadron's Kittyhawks had been heavily involved, two pilots being shot down near Gazala, one of whom crash-landed at Tobruk. Meanwhile Flt Sgt Hindle's aircraft was damaged as was Sgt Wareham's. Flt Sgt Willmott was attacked by a reported four Bf 109s, one of which he claimed to have shot down, seeing this crash-land (this may have been Broilo's Macchi), following which he and Hindle landed at El Adem.

3 SAAF Wing recorded that the bomber crews had noted the aircraft on the ground at Martuba to have been well dispersed, with ground fire heavier than ever. Nonetheless, their bombs had destroyed a TacR Bf 109E for the second day running. The wing noted with satisfaction that although some of the escorting RAF fighters had suffered some losses, they had beaten off all attacks on the Bostons.

British Claims					
260 Sqn	Flt Sgt T.Hindle	Kittyhawk I	Bf 109F Probable	Martuba area	0700-0845
260 Sqn	Flt Sgt T.W.Willmott	Kittyhawk I	Bf 109F	Martuba area	0700-0845
2 SAAF Sqn	Lt G.D.van der Veen	Tomahawk IIb AN545	Bf 109/MC 202 Damaged		0800-0930

British Casualties	
260 Sqn	Kittyhawk I shot down by Bf 109 Gazala; Sgt F.W.Tregear safe
260 Sqn	Kittyhawk I shot down by Bf 109 Tobruk area; Sgt J.H.Alexander safe
260 Sqn	Kittyhawk I badly damaged by Bf 109s Gazala area; Sgt Wareham safe
260 Sqn	Kittyhawk I badly damaged by Bf 109s Gazala area; Sgt T.Hindle safe

German Claims				
2./JG 27	Lt Willi Kothmann	P-40	SE Martuba	0800
2./JG 27	Lt Friedrich Körner	2 P-40s	S Martuba & S Gazala	0803 & 0808

German Casualties	
I./StG 3	Ju 87 R-2 WNr 8512 15% damaged and WNr 6141 10% in air raid at Martuba

Italian Claims					
80ª Sq, 17°Gr, 1°St CT	Serg Magg Remo Broilo	MC.202 MM 7753	2 P-40s	Martuba area	0730
71ª Sq, 17°Gr, 1°St CT	Serg Egidio Buogo	MC.202	bomber Damaged	Martuba area	0730
71ª Sq, 17°Gr, 1°St CT	Ten Ottorino Capellini	MC.202	P-40 Damaged	Martuba area	0730

Italian Casualties

71ª Sq, 17°Gr, 1°St CT	MC.202 MM 7753 shot down; Serg Magg Remo Broilo WiA, baled, rescued by German patrol, returned

Saturday, 21 March 1942

By morning on this date the convoy for Malta had reached the eastern end of 'Bomb Alley', the passage between Crete and Cyrenaica, the scene of heavy attacks during previous convoys. Eighth Army had taken part in providing diversions, 50th Division, 1st South African Division and the Free French Brigade having launched raids which drew off the air forces. Admiral Cunningham attributed the success of the convoy to have been largely achieved as a result of these diversions. The main ground column got close enough to Martuba and Tmimi to shell the airfields here and as a result was heavily attacked from the air, although 120 Axis troops were taken prisoner. While these attacks were underway, 3 SAAF Wing was ordered to raid further west at Barce. Lt Col J.A.Mossop, commander of 24 SAAF Squadron, led the first such attack by four Bostons, bombing through heavy cloud and destroying a BR.20 bomber of 4ª Squadriglia, 11° Gruppo, on the ground.

Because of the intensity of the action, 94 Squadron had been called back onto operations, now sending out sections of four Kittyhawks at 20-minute intervals to patrol over the Gazala-Tobruk area. The second such flight encountered six Bf 109s of I./JG 27 over the sea north of Gazala, one Kittyhawk being shot down and a second damaged. A Schwarm of Bf 109s from I./JG 27 had been sent back to Derna early in the morning in order to be able to intercept the first bombing raid of the day and two of these, flown by Lts Körner and von Lieres, intercepted the 24 SAAF Squadron formation led by Lt Col Mossop. Once clear of the coastal cloud, Mossop had led his bombers down to about 100 feet above the ground. Having made their attacks, the bombers were on their way back to base and were flying well to the south of Bir Hacheim when Flt Sgt van Eyssen gave the warning: "Three enemy fighters at 200 feet." Reportedly, their attackers comprised two Messerschmitts and one MC.200, the latter turning away as soon as the Bostons' guns opened up. The South Africans had thought that fighters would not attack them at such a low level, or even if they did, would only make a single pass. They were sadly disillusioned as the two Germans continued maintaining a running attack. Capt J.P.Verster, who had only been in Egypt for 11 days and who was on his first operational flight, had the starboard engine of his aircraft shot out and Air Sgt F.A.J.Bender, his rear gunner, killed. A second attack hit the remaining engine and Verster made a high speed crash-landing. As he and the rest of the crew climbed out of the burning aircraft, the Messerschmitt roared past, continuing to fire at the wreck.

Meanwhile, Mossop's aircraft was also under attack and was being hit. Part of the tail was shot away and the fuselage was filled with the cordite of the exploding cannon shells. Both Mossop and Flt Sgt van Eyssen suffered broken legs; the rear gunner, Air Sgt R.E.M.Hague, had been half knocked out by the explosion of a shell close to his head. As Mossop attempted to keep control, the Messerschmitt attacked again, hitting the fuselage and the starboard engine. He managed to throttle back and like Verster, made a belly-landing. Plt Off B.A.Colebourne, an RAAF observer attached to the squadron, and Hague between them got the wounded top gunner out of the aircraft. Mossop was thus alone in the aircraft when during a further pass, a cannon shell pierced the rear seat armour, "blowing a fearsome hole in his back" as a broken oil lead sprayed over the engine. The other members of the crew got him out just before the petrol tank blew up, at which point Körner and von Lieres departed.

After Mossop's wounds had been dressed, Colebourne set off on foot to seek help. He found no-one at the site of Verster's crash since the crew had already set off on a two-day walk to safety. At Mossop's aircraft, the pilot held on, gravely wounded, in the hope and belief that the observers in the other Bostons would have maintained a note of their route and position to allow rescue to be organised. In fact they had not done so, and this considerably delayed any rescue. However, Colebourne walked for two days and nights by which time his flying boots were worn through and his feet lacerated, but reached Allied-held territory. The positional information he provided made it at last possible to send out a Lysander under the protection of a fighter patrol, a doctor that this aircraft was carrying providing treatment until an air ambulance aircraft could arrive and evacuate Mossop and the other wounded crewman. Jack Mossop subsequently recovered to lead 3 SAAF Wing in Italy many months later. Colebourne, after a long spell in hospital, was awarded a MBE. Meanwhile, Lt Körner's claim was recorded as I./JG 27's 1,000th of the war, which was celebrated in the proper fashion.

Meanwhile, during the day the well-camouflaged British column had approached Martuba airfield and at midday commenced shelling. The airfield staff at once began a defensive action and an emergency call was sent for 88mm guns. Unwisely, the British troops had taken up positions on a slope *towards* the airfield instead of on the reverse side, thereby leaving themselves exposed to counter-attack. Stukas arrived and took part in strafing attacks, joined by every available fighter.

The vehicles accompanying the column had initially been spotted approaching the airfield by a pair of MC.202 pilots of 17° Gruppo who were undertaking a tactical reconnaissance sortie at 1300. Within half an hour six more Macchis from 6° Gruppo led by Cap Domenico Camarda, took off to strafe, claiming to have left three vehicles in flames. Fifteen more 1° Stormo MC.202s followed at 1350 (eight of 17° and seven of 6° Gruppi) and led by Cap Guido Beggiato, took up the attack, reporting 11 vehicles in flames and many others damaged. One Macchi was hit by AA and crashed in flames. No more losses were suffered as further attacks were undertaken. The MC.200s of 150° Gruppo also took part, ten of these aircraft strafing vehicles south of Martuba between 1440-1515.

After about 30 minutes 88mm guns arrived and a battle lasting some six hours ensued. In the evening tanks and motorized infantry reached Martuba, and sallying out, brought back a number of prisoners. Later in the day Cap Camarda led eight MC.202s to Barce to protect that airfield from further attack. At the end of the day Gen Hans-Ferdinand Geisler called Col Alfredo Reglieri, 1° Stormo's commander, to congratulate him on the effectiveness of the Italian attacks. Also, 1° Stormo now received 13 new MC.202s directly from Italy, increasing the unit's serviceability to about 40 fighters.

The Regia Aeronautica did suffer further loss during the day, however, when an SAS raid by night on Benghazi led by the redoubtable 'Paddy' Mayne, destroyed a Ca.133 and two CR.42s, severely damaging four more of the biplane fighter-bombers. This had the result of increasing the protection of Axis airfields against further such commando raids.

Elsewhere during the day 2 SAAF Squadron flew patrols over the Tobruk-Gazala area on one of which its Tomahawks were bounced by fighters while returning to base, one pilot having to force-land near the airfield with the side of the cockpit partly shot away. A Hurricane of 40 SAAF Squadron was also lost during a TacR sortie. In the evening Hurricanes of 274 Squadron flew close escort to Bostons raiding Martuba again, one of the fighters being shot down in flames by Flak. Meanwhile, 3 RAAF Squadron had spent the day away from the battle zone, flying patrols over the Malta convoy, their aircraft fitted with long-range tanks.

British Claims

94 Sqn	Sqn Ldr I.M.MacDougall	Kittyhawk I AK...	Bf 109	6m W Gazala	0800

British Casualties

24 SAAF Sqn	Boston III Z2225 off 0615 from LG.140 to attack Barce. Shot down on return flight 30m SW Bir Hacheim. Capt J.P.Verster and two walk for two days without water until picked up by Free French; one of crew KiA. Nav 2/Lt D.P.Bester on first operational flight had been in Boston Z2175 shot down on 27 February
24 SAAF Sqn	Boston III AL733 shot down as above; Lt Col A.J.M.Mossop and three all badly injured, Mossop during strafe of the downed aircraft. Plt Off B.A.Colebourne, RAAF, badly burned, walked to lines and brought help
94 Sqn	Kittyhawk I AK748 left 0710, presumed shot down by Bf 109 near Gazala; Plt Off R.H.McKillop KiA
94 Sqn	Kittyhawk I AK739 left 0710, damaged, FTR; Plt Off A.J.Crosbie safe
274 Sqn	Hurricane II Z5313 shot down by Flak nr Martuba 1700-1815; Sgt E.A.Mullis KiA
274 Sqn	Hurricane II DG631 shot down by Flak nr Martuba 1700-1815
274 Sqn	Hurricane P4207/Z4015 flown by 40 SAAF Sqn crashed 10m SE Benghazi at 0915; Lt R.D.Mellor PoW
2 SAAF Sqn	Tomahawk IIb AN454 damaged by Bf 109 and Lt G.T.van der Veen slt WiA; damaged again before force-landing NW Bir el Baheira at 0915

German Claims

1./JG 27	Oblt Ludwig Franzisket	P-40	N Ain el Gazala	0755
2./JG 27	Lt Friedrich Körner	Boston	SE Bir Hacheim	0855
2./JG 27	Lt Karl von Lieres und Wilkau	Boston	SE Bir Hacheim	0856

German Casualties

2./JG 27	Bf 109F-4 trop WNr 8709 35% damaged by AA, crash-landed Martuba; pilot safe
6./JG 27	Bf 109F-4 trop WNr 8715 shot-up in combat, belly-landed at Martuba, 35% damaged
I./StG 3	Ju 87R-2 WNr 6198 hit by AA, force-landed at Martuba, 60% damaged

Italian Casualties

81ª Sq, 6°Gr, 1°St CT	MC.202 MM 7773 '81-5'shot down, S.Ten Alberto Paggi KiA
4ª Sq, 11°Gr, 13° St BT	BR.20 MM 24111 destroyed by bombs at Barce

3° Gr CT	2 CR.42s, 1 Ca.133 destroyed and 4 CR.42s MM 7030, 7604, 7623, 8439 damaged at Benghazi K2 by SAS patrol led by Capt 'Paddy' Mayne

Sunday, 22 March 1942

Following an uneventful night around Martuba three MC.202s of 81ª Squadriglia led by Cap Giuliano Giacomelli, undertook an early reconnaissance but saw no movement of British vehicles. The sortie was repeated at 0730 by Ten Luigi Zamana, but again nothing was to be seen. German fighters later attacked the remaining forces, now in retreat, destroying most of their surviving vehicles. What became known to JG 27 as 'The Battle of Martuba' was at an end. Following these actions the Malta convoy – MW10 – at last came under sustained air attack, as recorded in Chapter Three.

Italian Casualties

3ª Sq, 43°Gr, 13°St BT	BR.20 MM 22709 crashed near Barce; pilot Ten Aldo Nebbiolo and three WiA, copilot Serg Virgilio Guicciardi died of injuries

Monday, 23 March 1942

Martuba West was again the target for 24 SAAF Squadron during the morning, 94 and 260 Squadrons providing the escort on this occasion, but the defences were ready for them. The 12 Bostons approached from over the sea, flying into a veritable hurricane of Flak, as Messerschmitts from III./JG 27 and ten Macchis of 1° Stormo were scrambled to intercept. The Boston flown by Maj Ritchie Tennant was seen to lurch out of control and go down in flames with the loss of the crew. Lt Steyn lost control of his bomber as it was buffeted by shell bursts, and he ordered his crew to bale out. However, the intercom system had been damaged and only one man, Lt J.H.O.Dellow, heard him and got out. He reported: "As I went floating down I saw him fight the aircraft into level flight and escape." Realising that the others were still on board and despite 70 splinter holes in his Boston, Steyn sat back into his cockpit, evaded an attack by a lone fighter, and crash-landed near Tobruk. Whilst he was doing so, his gunner, Sgt S.F.Oostheuizen, claimed to have shot down one Messerschmitt in flames.

A third Boston, flown by Lt P.O'Donovan, was hit and set on fire by Flak, but the pilot kept the aircraft steady until the bombs had been released. With the gunner wounded, he then crash-landed near Sidi Rezegh, the crew all escaping. Sgt G.Catchlove, the gunner and a member of the RAAF, was wounded while fighting off one of the attacking fighters. A fourth bomber, also hit by ground fire, was attacked repeatedly by fighters, Lt Elliot-Wilson crash-landing this aircraft at El Baheira. The remaining bombers held formation as their escorts engaged the Axis fighters, the gunners in two of them claiming to have shot down one attacker by the cross-fire between them.

Amongst the Kittyhawks, each squadron lost one aircraft, 94 Squadron claiming two Bf 109s shot down and a third damaged in return. Luftwaffe pilots claimed two P-40s and one Boston shot down with two more Bostons claimed by the Flak gunners. One Messerschmitt force-landed at Martuba 85% destroyed in the combat, but the pilot escaped unscathed. The Italian pilots claimed a further three P-40s shot down and three probables, plus a Boston damaged; they suffered no loss or damage. One more JG 27 Messerschmitt was badly damaged on the ground during the bombing.

As a result of this series of raids, 24 SAAF Squadron had now lost both the commanding officer and his deputy, Maj Tennant. Maj C.Gey van Pittius took over on an acting basis until Lt Col J.A.Rademan, DFC, could arrive from the Union to assume command.

British Claims

94 Sqn	Flt Sgt J.F.Edwards	Kittyhawk I AK858	Bf 109	Martuba West	1000
94 Sqn	Flt Sgt M.M.Maxwell	Kittyhawk I AK821	Bf 109	Martuba West	1000

British Claims

94 Sqn	Flt Sgt R.H.Phillips	Kittyhawk I AK759	Bf 109 Damaged	Martuba West	1000

British Casualties

24 SAAF Sqn	Boston III Z2206 hit by Flak, Lt J.J.B.Steyn briefly lost control. Ordered bale-out but only observer, Lt J.H.O.Dellow heard and did so as intercom damaged. Steyn recovered control, evaded attack by lone Bf 109, and crash-landed near Tobruk. He and two safe; Dellow PoW
24 SAAF Sqn	Boston III Z2287 attacked and set on fire, one gunner wounded. Crash-landed on Trigh Capuzzo, 4km W Sidi Rezegh; Lt G.P.O'Donovan and two safe

British Casualties

24 SAAF Sqn	Boston III AL800 shot down over Martuba East, reportedly by flak. Maj R.Tennant and three KiA
94 Sqn	Kittyhawk I AK964 MiA left 0915, presumed shot down by Bf 109 nr Martuba; Flt Lt Hawthord PoW
260 Sqn	Kittyhawk I shot down by Bf 109 at Martuba; Sgt A.D.Saunders MiA
260 Sqn	Kittyhawk I shot down by Bf 109 at Martuba

German Claims

8./JG 27	Uffz Artur Liebold	P-40	NE Ain el Gazala
8./JG 27	Lt Hans Nietzsche	P-40	SE Tobruk
9./JG 27	Fw Walter Hillgruber	Boston	10km W Ain el Gazala
Flak		2 Bostons	

German Casualties

9./JG 27	Bf 109F-4 trop WNr 8717 combat with P-40, force-landed at Martuba 85%; pilot safe
7./JG 27	Bf 109F-4 trop WNr 8740 60% damaged by bombs on ground at Martuba

Italian Claims

81ª Sq, 6°Gr, 1°St CT	Ten Antonio Palazzeschi	MC.202	P-40	SE Tobruk	1015-1120
81ª Sq, 6°Gr, 1°St CT	Ten Antonio Palazzeschi	MC.202	2 P-40s Probable	SE Tobruk	1015-1120
81ª Sq, 6°Gr, 1°St CT	Ten Giorgio Falchi	MC.202	P-40	SE Tobruk	1015-1120
81ª Sq, 6°Gr, 1°St CT	Ten Giorgio Falchi	MC.202	P-40 Probable	SE Tobruk	1015-1120
88ª Sq, 6°Gr, 1°St CT	Serg Roberto Sgorbati	MC.202	P-40	SE Tobruk	1015-1120
88ª Sq, 6°Gr, 1°St CT	Serg Roberto Sgorbati	MC.202	Boston Damaged	SE Tobruk	1015-1120

Tuesday, 24 March 1942

In very bad weather an MC.200 of 8° Gruppo crashed when patrolling over Benghazi harbour with the loss of the pilot. The reason for his demise was not discovered. The pilot was killed and his MC.200 destroyed.

Italian Casualties

92ª Sq, 8°Gr, 2°St CT	MC.200 MM 5902 crashed to ground for u/k cause at Benghazi, Serg Magg Vito Copersino KiFA

Thursday, 26 March 1942

Early in the afternoon Hurricanes of 80 Squadron were scrambled over Tobruk, encountering Bf 109s of III./JG 27. Flg Off Frank Mason claimed one of these probably shot down, but his own aircraft was badly damaged by Fw Waibel, who claimed to have shot it down. Reportedly, Mason's Hurricane was also hit by the 'friendly' AA from within Tobruk.

Later on that same afternoon nine Kittyhawks of 94 Squadron provided close cover to nine Bostons of 12 SAAF Squadron, which had now relieved the hard-hit 24 SAAF, while 12 more fighters of 260 Squadron formed the top cover. Five MC.202s of 17° Gruppo were scrambled, followed some minutes later by ten more from 6° Gruppo; Bf 109s of III./JG 27 also took off. Four of the latter attacked the escort all the way back to Tobruk, shooting down one 94 Squadron aircraft and badly damaging a second – the German pilots claiming both on this occasion. This time the Italian pilots were able only to claim a P-40 as a probable and a second damaged. Three of the Bostons were hit by Flak, but all returned safely.

An S.79 of 174ª Squadriglia RST took off from Benghazi at 1320 on a reconnaissance mission to the Bir Tengender area, but failed to return.

British Claims

80 Sqn	Flg Off F.Mason	Hurricane IIc BE556 'C'	Bf 109F Probable	W Tobruk	1330-1415
260 Sqn	Sgt W.R.McKay	Kittyhawk I	Bf 109F Damaged	Tobruk area	1605-1730

British Casualties

94 Sqn	Kittyhawk I AK739 'R' left 1545, shot down S Tobruk by Bf 109; Sgt V.A.Laurence KiA
260 Sqn	Kittyhawk I badly damaged Cat II by Bf 109 S Tobruk; Plt Off N.Glew safe
80 Sqn	Hurricane IIc BE556 badly damaged by Bf 109 SE Tobruk at 1415; Flg Off F.Mason safe

German Claims

7./JG 27	Fw Karl Waibel	Hurricane	SE Tobruk	1355
7./JG 27	Fw Karl Waibel	P-40	S Tobruk	1355
8./JG 27	Uffz Viktor Gruber	P-40	S Tobruk	1702

German Casualties

Stab JG27	Bf 108B-1 WNr 1667 engine failure, force-landed at Sirte, 70% damaged
I./StG 3	Ju 87R-2 WNr 5785 and WNr 5875 shot down by AA nr Gazala

Italian Claims

79ª Sq, 6°Gr, 1°St CT	S.Ten Rinaldo Bottoni	MC.202	P-40 Probable	Martuba area	1620-1740
88ª Sq, 6°Gr, 1°St CT	S.Ten Alfredo Civetta	MC.202	P-40 Damaged	Martuba area	1640-1745

Italian Casualties

174ª Sq RST	S.79 MM 21559 failed to return, pilot Ten Italo Bignotti, copilot M.llo Alceo Toni and entire crew MiA

Friday, 27 March 1942

274 and 450 Squadrons took off on a morning interception sortie over Tobruk and El Adem, but four of the 12 Hurricanes of the former unit were forced to return early due to engine troubles. Five MC.202s of 17° Gruppo had also scrambled to intercept bombers and fighters reported to be raiding Martuba again. They were joined 15 minutes later by four 6° Gruppo aircraft. Over Tobruk two pilots from the latter unit engaged fighters to the east which they identified as Spitfires, each claiming one of these shot down. They had obviously in fact engaged 274 Squadron's Hurricanes, the pilot of this unit reporting being attacked from above by MC.202s, one of which was claimed shot down by Plt Off Conrad and one probably so by Sgt Barwick. The latter pilot, however, crash-landed at Bir Saliema when his Hurricane was hit and badly damaged. After the initial clash, S.Ten Sparapani reported that they had a second engagement as they headed for home, this time with P-40s, when S.Ten Rosa disappeared – he had actually crash-landed his Macchi and become a PoW. There were no claims by Kittyhawk pilots at this time, and it is likely that the Italian pilots had again been involved with 274 Squadron and that Rosa's aircraft had fallen victim to Wally Conrad. Taken to Camp 310, Rosa met there Cap Pesola, captured on 16 March, and shared all his adventures, escaping and being re-captured after one year on the run in Egypt.

At 1645 Hurricanes of 80 Squadron and Tomahawks of 2 SAAF Squadron were scrambled over Tobruk to intercept 15 Ju 87s of I./StG 3 escorted by ten Bf 109s. Lt Lipawsky claimed one of the Stukas probably destroyed, and it appears that he had damaged the aircraft of the Staffelkapitän of 3./StG 3, Ritterkreuzträger Hptm Helmut Naumann, who was wounded in combat with Curtiss fighters but managed to get back to base with his aircraft 10% damaged. A second Stuka was damaged to the same extent by AA. Meanwhile Lipawsky was then shot down and crash-landed, suffering wounds; his aircraft was strafed on the ground and burnt out. A second Tomahawk, flown by Lt E.Smith, was also shot down and crash-landed, it too being strafed as it did so, but Smith escaped unhurt. A third of this unit's aircraft suffered minor damage.

Flt Sgt Comfort of 80 Squadron was also attacked by a Bf 109, his Hurricane being badly damaged. During this engagement, Oblt Franzisket of 1./JG 27 claimed one P-40 at 1655, while in the later stages of the fight three more were claimed by pilots of II./JG 27, two of them by Oblt Rödel.

On this date 250 Squadron became the sixth WDAF unit to convert to Kittyhawks, these aircraft replacing the unit's Tomahawks.

British Claims

274 Sqn	Plt Off W.A.G.Conrad	Hurricane IIb BD226	MC.202	5m S El Adem	1130-1235
274 Sqn	Sgt Barwick	Hurricane IIb	MC.202 Probable	El Adem	1135-1230
2 SAAF Sqn	Lt G.B.Lipawsky	Tomahawk IIb AN295	Ju 87 Probable	El Adem-Tobruk	1645-1800
2 SAAF Sqn	Lt D.Paddon	Tomahawk IIb AN334 'R'	Bf 109F Probable	El Adem-Tobruk	1645-1800

British Casualties

2 SAAF Sqn	Tomahawk IIb AN295 crash-landed S Gazala; strafed by e/a at 1800, burnt out; Lt G.B.Lipawsky slt WiA
2 SAAF Sqn	Tomahawk IIb AN439 'J' shot down by Bf 109 and crash-landed S Gazala 1755 a/c burnt out; Lt E.Smith safe
2 SAAF Sqn	Tomahawk IIb AN278 'E' tailplane minor damage from Bf 109; Lt P.D.Bryant safe

British Casualties

80 Sqn	Hurricane IIc BE482 badly damaged by Bf 109 over Tobruk at 1735; Flt Sgt A.C.Comfort safe
55 Sqn	Blenheim IV Z5905 lost
274 Sqn	Hurricane shot down by fighters, El Adem, 1135-1230, crash-landed; Sgt Barwick

German Claims

1./JG 27	Oblt Ludwig Franzisket	P-40	S Ain el Gazala	1655
4./JG 27	Oblt Gustav Rödel	2 P-40s	W Tobruk & SW Ain el Gazala	1710 & 1724

German Claims

5./JG 27	Fw Hans Niederhöfer	P-40	S Bomba Bay	1730

German Casualties

3./StG 3	Ju 87R-2 10% damaged in combat with P-40 E Tmimi; Hptm Helmut Naumann WiA
I./StG 3	Ju 87R-2 WNr 6136 10% damaged by AA nr Tobruk

Italian Claims

88ª Sq, 6°Gr, 1°St CT	S.Ten Roberto Sparapani	MC.202	Spitfire	30km E Tobruk 1155-
79ª Sq, 6°Gr, 1°St CT	S.Ten Alessandro Rosa	MC.202 MM 7899	Spitfire	30km E Tobruk 1155-

Italian Casualties

79ª Sq, 6°Gr, 1°St CT	MC.202 MM 7899 damaged in combat, force-landed in enemy territory, S.Ten Alessandro Rosa PoW

Saturday, 28 March 1942

Nine Kittyhawks of 94 Squadron provided middle cover to the Bostons on a raid at 1245, 12 more of 450 Squadron flying top cover with the Tomahawks of 2 SAAF Squadron as close escort. Three MC.200s of 150° Gruppo were being led by S.Ten Giovanni Dell'Innocenti and were on patrol over Martuba as the raid approached. They immediately engaged but one of these fighters was at once shot down and the pilot killed. Eleven MC.202s of 17° Gruppo and three of 6° Gruppo were then scrambled to pursue the raiders, claiming two P-40s shot down, plus three and one Boston damaged. One more fighter was claimed by Fw Steinhausen of 1./JG 27. However, one Bf 109 of this unit was hit in the engine by one of the Curtiss fighters and crash-landed at Tmimi, 95% destroyed, although the pilot was not hurt.

During this fight Plt Off Crosbie of 94 Squadron was shot down, and Sgt Halliday of 450 Squadron was also hit, force-landing just west of the front line, suffering wounds; he was picked up by an army unit. So too was Crosbie, whose unit was advised that he was in a field hospital, only slightly wounded. However, on 5 April came the news that he had died.

Despite the losses of one Messerschmitt and one MC.200, the only claims to be submitted on this occasion were made by 450 Squadron and were for three Bf 109s as probables and one damaged. The bombing on this date had resulted in considerable damage when an ammunition dump was hit and exploded, destroying three Bf 109s of JG 27 and damaging three more. Another Messerschmitt was lost when the 4.Staffel aircraft flown by Lt Endmann was shot down by AA 20km west of Gazala; Endmann was seen to bale out but failed to return.

British Claims

450 Sqn	Plt Off A.E.Kelsall	Kittyhawk I AK895 'K'	Bf 109F Damaged	Martuba-base	1245-1423
450 Sqn	Sgt I.A.Nursey	Kittyhawk I AK668 'H'	Bf 109F Probable	Martuba-base	1245-1423
450 Sqn	Sgt N.H.Shillabeer	Kittyhawk I AK799 'R'	Bf 109F Probable	Martuba-base	1245-1423
450 Sqn	Sqn Ldr G.H.Steege	Kittyhawk I AK692 'C'	Bf 109F Probable	Martuba-base	1245-1423

British Casualties

94 Sqn	Kittyhawk I AK858 crash-landed, shot down by Bf 109s during bomber escort; Plt Off J.A.Crosbie WiA; Died of wounds 4 April
450 Sqn	Kittyhawk I AK659 'G' shot down by MC.202 and force-landed in the desert; Sgt W.J.Halliday safe
450 Sqn	Kittyhawk I AK706 'S' damaged by MC.202 Cat II, landed safely; Sgt E.J.Quirk safe

German Claims

1./JG 27	Fw Günther Steinhausen	P-40	S Tmimi	1340

German Casualties

1./JG 27	Bf 109F-4 trop WNr 8716 shot down by P-40, engine hit, crash-landed Tmimi 90%, pilot safe
2./JG 27	Bf 109F-4 WNr 7382 50% damaged & WNr 7396 40% damaged by bombs at Martuba
2./JG 27	Bf 109F-4 trop WNr 8596 30% & WNr 8481 90% damaged by bombs at Martuba
Stab II./JG 27	Bf 109F-4 trop WNr 8712 destroyed on ground by bombs at Martuba
4./JG 27	Bf 109F-4 trop WNr 8705 destroyed on ground by bombs at Martuba
4./JG 27	Bf 109F-4 trop WNr 8508 White 10, shot down by AA 20km W Gazala Bay; Lt Gerhard Endmann baled, but MiA

Italian Claims

80ª Sq,17°Gr, 1°St CT	Cap Clizio Nioi	MC.202	P-40	W Tobruk	1335-1430
80ª Sq,17°Gr, 1°St CT	Cap Clizio Nioi	MC.202	Boston Damaged	W Tobruk	1335-1430
80ª Sq,17°Gr, 1°St CT	Serg Magg Mario Host	MC.202	P-40 Damaged	W Tobruk	1335-1430
81ª Sq, 6°Gr, 1°St CT	S.Ten Bruno Ganda	MC.202	P-40	W Tobruk	1335-1435
71ª Sq,17°Gr, 1°St CT	S.Ten Gastone Petrucci	MC.202	P-40 Damaged	W Tobruk	1340-1415

72ª Sq,17°Gr, 1°St CT	Ten Mario Carini	MC.202	P-40 Damaged	W Tobruk	1340-1415

Italian Casualties

364ª Sq, 150°Gr CT	MC.200 MM 5827 shot down, Serg Magg Mario Angeloni KiA

A CR.42 of 3° Gruppo carries the unit's 'red devil' insignia on the wheel spat. On the right is Cap Giuseppe Tovazzi, commanding officer of 154 Squadriglia, who failed to return from a strafing sortie on 28 May. (*Gatti*)

Sunday-Monday, 29/30 March 1942

During the night 19 CR.42s of 3° Gruppo led by Cap Giuseppe Tovazzi raided Tobruk harbour and vehicle concentrations along Via Balbia, reporting hits on the docks and many lorries left in flames.

Monday, 30 March 1942

The Hurricanes of 1 SAAF Squadron were again engaged in a convoy patrol, this time from LG.110, when they intercepted and shot down a bomber, identified this time as a Ju 88. It proved to have been a Blenheim of 14 Squadron which crashed into the sea near Ras el Rumb with the loss of the crew.

British Claims

1 SAAF Sqn	2 pilots	Hurricane IIs	Ju 88* coast near Ras el Rumb

British Casualties

14 Sqn	Blenheim IV Z7627* shot down in error by Hurricane of 1 SAAF Sqn. Crashed in sea nr Ras el Rumb; Flt Lt H.K.Keck & two KiA
TC A	Blenheim Mk IV Z9832, left Luqa 0310 for Egypt and MiA; Sgt H.Janney, Sgt J.M.Shiner, Sgt C.E.Johnson MiA

Tuesday, 31 March 1942

During the day 2 SAAF Squadron flight tested all its aircraft prior to undertaking a mission. As Lt Hopkins returned from one such sortie at 0800, his aircraft was suddenly bounced by a Bf 109 of III./JG 27 out on a Freie Jagd, and was shot down, the pilot being killed. The German fighters at Martuba received a visit on this date from General Rommel.

British Casualties

2 SAAF Sqn	Tomahawk IIb AN429 shot down in the circuit by Bf 109s, aircraft burnt out; Lt A.E.M.Hopkins KiA

German Claims

7./JG 27	Oblt Hermann Tangerding	P-40	Gasr el Arid	0800

Wednesday, 1 April 1942

On a TacR sortie a Hurricane of 40 SAAF Squadron was hit by Flak, force-landing. 33 Squadron moved to Gambut. 133° Gruppo AS was formed at Benghazi K2. It was created when the reconnaissance unit, 174ª Squadriglia RST, changed its role to that of torpedo-bombing and joined with 175ª Squadriglia, which was based at Tripoli. 5ª Squadra assumed command of the Aviazione Sahariana and all reconnaissance units formerly under army control.

British Casualties

40 SAAF	Hurricane hit by AA force-landed between lines, rescued by army who destroyed the aircraft; Lt W.J.A.Webb safe
80 Sqn	Hurricane IIc BE706 left 1610, spun in, no one saw what happened; Flt Sgt A.D.Nightingale MiA

Thursday, 2 April 1942

Eleven MC.202s of 17° Gruppo were off at 1105 to escort seven MC.200s of 150° Gruppo to Tengender on a strafing mission. One MC.200 was hit and damaged. In the early afternoon four Bf 109s of I./JG 27 on a Freie Jagd attacked four Hurricanes of 238 Squadron patrolling over nine ships, claiming two shot down. Only one was recorded as lost when Sgt Cartwright's aircraft crashed straight into the sea. Plt Off Milne claimed to have damaged one of the Messerschmitts, and it seems that this was the aircraft flown by Lt Willi Kothmann, one of those who were thought to have shot down the Hurricanes, for this 13-victory ace failed to return after his aircraft was hit in the cooling system and was subsequently seen to crash into the sea 30km north of Marsa Luch.

At 1725 eight Bf 109s of I./JG 27 with belly tanks fitted, eight of II.Gruppe and 15 of III.Gruppe escorted 12 Ju 87s of I./StG 3 to attack shipping near Tobruk. Ten Kittyhawks of 260 Squadron and a number of 80 and 238 Squadron Hurricanes were scrambled to intercept north-west of Tobruk. 80 Squadron was attacked by I.Gruppe which was forming the top cover, and two of the unit's Hurricanes were shot down.

238 and 260 Squadrons attacked the Stukas, between them claiming one shot down and two damaged, the Kittyhawk pilots also claiming damage to three fighters, two of which were thought to be MC.202s. On this occasion two Ju 87s were actually shot down, both coming down in the sea about 20km north-west of Tobruk. III./JG 27 claimed one P-40 shot down, while Uffz Monska of II.Gruppe claimed to have caused one fighter to crash-land, although this was not confirmed due to lack of witnesses and there appeared to be no corroboratory evidence. In fact 260 Squadron lost one aircraft and its pilot. During the fight one of the Messerschmitts of III.Gruppe was hit by AA and force-landed near El Adem.

The final engagement of the day was subsequently recorded by 2 SAAF Squadron on the wrong day (4 April) – and with some uncertainty regarding the classification of the claims or the identity of the opponents claimed. At 1835 Wg Cdr Beresford, the new wing leader of 233 Wing led eight Tomahawks on a scramble over the Tobruk-Gazala area, encountering 15-20 fighters variously identified as Bf 109s or MC.202s; there was some debate regarding this on the unit's return to base. Beresford claimed one shot down as it was attacking Lt de Villiers, though it may have been classified as a probable. De Villiers and Lt Higgo shared in damaging another – although it is possible that they shared with Beresford. Meanwhile, Lt Eric Saville hit one that was last seen losing height and speed, then attacking another that was seen going down very fast, and then damaged a third. The squadron operations record book seems to credit Beresford with one MC.202 and Saville with two and one damaged – but in either case the credits could have been as probables. However, the authors have stuck with the ORB since this accords with the total number of victories Saville had achieved according to the citation when he was awarded a DFC in September.

British Claims

238 Sqn	Plt Off Milne	Hurricane I 'F'	Bf 109 Damaged	convoy patrol	1415-1540
238 Sqn	Plt Off F.D.B.Collenette	Hurricane I 'T'	Ju 87 Damaged	convoy patrol	1800-1915
238 Sqn	Sgt M.L.Lawrence-Smith	Hurricane I	Ju 87 Damaged	convoy patrol	1800-1915
260 Sqn	Plt Off N.V.Glew	Kittyhawk I	Bf 109F Damaged	5m NW Tobruk	1825-1945
260 Sqn	Flt Sgt T.Hindle	Kittyhawk I	MC.202 Damaged	5m NW Tobruk	1825-1945
260 Sqn	Sgt W.R.McKay	Kittyhawk I	MC.202 Damaged	5m NW Tobruk	1825-1945
260 Sqn	Flt Sgt T.W.Willmott	Kittyhawk I	Ju 87	5m NW Tobruk	1825-1945
2 SAAF Sqn	Wg Cdr T.B.de la P. Beresford	Tomahawk IIb	MC.202	20m SW Gazala road	1900
2 SAAF Sqn	Lt E.C.Saville	Tomahawk IIb	2 MC.202s	off Gazala road	1915
2 SAAF Sqn	Lt E.C.Saville	Tomahawk IIb	MC.202 Damaged	N Gazala Point	1915
2 SAAF Sqn	Lt A.Higgo	Tomahawk IIb AK524 'G' }	Bf 109/MC.202 Damaged	20m SW Gazala	1900
2 SAAF Sqn	Lt T.V. de Villiers	Tomahawk IIb AK249 'A' }			

British Casualties

80 Sqn	Hurricane IIc BE427 shot down by fighters 5m out to sea NW Tobruk at 1845; Flg Off P.K Crowther MiA
80 Sqn	Hurricane IIc BE335 shot down by fighters 5m out to sea NW Tobruk at 1845; Plt Off J.F.Kelham MiA
80 Sqn	Hurricane IIc BE338 damaged by Bf 109 5m out to sea NW Tobruk at 1845 Cat I; Flt Lt E.C.W.Trollip safe
238 Sqn	Hurricane shot down by Bf 109 N Gambut 1415-1500; Sgt H.Cartwright KiA, (possibly Z4579 'E')
450 Sqn	Kittyhawk AK592 'P' crashed on landing due to hitting spikes; Sgt D.R.Law safe
260 Sqn	Kittyhawk I shot down by Bf 109 into sea off Tobruk, 1825-1945; Sgt Plt Off A.S.Morley MiA
33 Sqn	Hurricane IIb destroyed on the ground by bombing; Plt Off MacKenzie WiA

German Claims

2./JG 27	Lt Willi Kothmann	Hurricane	N Gambut	1425
2./JG 27	Lt Friedrich Körner	Hurricane	N Gambut	1428
3./JG 27	Lt Julius Wildau	P-40	15km NE Fort Acroma	1805
9./JG 27	Oblt Hans-Joachim Heinecke	P-40	W Tobruk	1805

3./JG 27	Hptm Gerhard Homuth	P-40	30km N Fort Acroma	1807
6./JG 27	Uffz Otto Monska	P-40 o.Zg.	15km SE Tobruk	1810

German Casualties

2./JG 27	Bf 109F-4 trop WNr 8733 Red 5, combat with Hurricane over sea 30km NE Marsa Luch; Lt Willi Kothmann KiA
9./JG 27	Bf 109F-4 trop WNr 8558 20% damaged by AA Tobruk, force-landed SE El Adem; Fw Walter Hillgruber safe
3./StG 3	Ju 87R-4 WNr 6331 S7+HL combat with P-40 20km NW Tobruk and ditched; Lt Otto Rietdorf/Fw Rudolf Klünder PoW
1./StG 3	Ju 87R-4 WNr 6333 S7+BH combat with P-40 and crashed 20km NW Tobruk

Friday, 3 April 1942

During the morning eight Kittyhawks of 260 Squadron and ten of 94 Squadron escorted Bostons to Derna. Here Plt Off Usher of 94 Squadron claimed a Bf 109 shot down east of the town. This appears to have been I./JG 27's Lt Julius Wildau who crashed near the Via Balbia following an engagement with P-40s, and was killed.

Flying a diversionary sweep at this time, 274 Squadron's eight Hurricanes also encountered Messerschmitts which shot down one Hurricane in flames, the pilot of which was killed. The other pilots claimed two Bf 109s and an MC.202 probably shot down. The Axis fighters then met 260 Squadron over Bomba Bay, this unit's pilots claiming two Bf 109s shot down and a Macchi probable. 94 Squadron was in action in the same area, losing two of its aircraft at this time. 450 Squadron was also engaged, claiming damage to three Macchis.

During this series of engagements, Luftwaffe claims amounted to three P-40s, with a fourth claimed by Uffz Schwekusch as having belly-landed; again, this was not confirmed due to lack of witnesses. Apart from the loss of Wildau, a second Messerschmitt was force-landed in Axis territory by Lt Rainer. Italian fighters had also been heavily involved, ten 6° Gruppo MC.202s having scrambled at 1015. These engaged P-40s over Ain el Gazala, and one was claimed as a probable. However, one Macchi was shot down and the pilot killed in the Bomba Bay area. Fifteen minutes behind them, 11 more Macchis of 17° Gruppo had followed, five of these engaging 12 Curtiss fighters, four of which were claimed shot down, plus one probable and one damaged. In summary therefore, two Kittyhawks and one Hurricane had been lost by WDAF against Axis claims for eight (five by Italian pilots and three by Germans); WDAF claims totalled three Bf 109s plus two and two MC.202s as probables, with actual Axis losses as one or two Bf 109s and one Macchi.

British Claims

260 Sqn	Sgt J.V.Carlisle	Kittyhawk I	Bf 109 (shared)	5m NW Bomba, over Menelao Bay	1030-1215
260 Sqn	Sqn Ldr O.V.Hanbury	Kittyhawk I AK867			
260 Sqn	Flt Sgt T.Hindle	Kittyhawk I	Bf 109F	5m NW Bomba, over Menelao Bay	1030-1215
260 Sqn	Flt Sgt T.Hindle	Kittyhawk I	MC.202 Probable	12m SSW Gazala	1030-1215
450 Sqn	Sgt D.H.McBurnie	Kittyhawk I AK895 'K'	MC.202 Damaged	El Adem-Tobruk	1040-1202
450 Sqn	Sgt I.A.Nursey	Kittyhawk I AK606 'B'	MC.202 Damaged	S Gazala	1040-1202
450 Sqn	Sqn Ldr G.H.Steege	Kittyhawk I AK717 'V'	MC.202 Damaged	El Adem-Tobruk	1040-1202
274 Sqn	Plt Off R.H.Hunter	Hurricane IIb	Bf 109 Probable	Gazala area	1050
274 Sqn	Plt Off H.Garwood	Hurricane IIb	Bf 109 Probable	Gazala area	1050
274 Sqn	Sgt W.E.Marsh	Hurricane IIb BD820 'D'	MC.202 Probable	Gazala area	1050
94 Sqn	Plt Off G.L.Usher	Kittyhawk I AK741	Bf 109E	E Derna	1150

British Casualties

94 Sqn	Kittyhawk I AK769 shot down by Bf 109s crashed at Gazala from bomber escort; Sgt Musker WiA
94 Sqn	Kittyhawk I AK942 FTR from escort to Bostons to Derna; Plt Off R.W.M.Moon MiA
5 SAAF Sqn	Tomahawk IIb AN239 crashed in flames at Amiriya, 1655, enemy activity noted in the area; Lt M.J.Bartels KiA
274 Sqn	Hurricane II shot down by fighters, Gazala area; Sgt A.E.Howell WiA

German Claims

6./JG 27	Uffz Johann Walchhofer	P-40	SW Ain el Gazala	1030
6./JG 27	Gefr Otto Schwekutsch	P-40 o.Zg.	SW El Alamein	1032

German Claims

2./JG 27	Lt Karl von Lieres und Wilkau	P-40	W El Adem	1040
6./JG 27	Uffz Johann Walchhofer	P-40	30km E Ain el Gazala	1040

German Casualties

3./JG 27	Bf 109F-4 trop WNr 8411 combat with P-40, crashed 2km W Casa Cantoniera on Via Balbia; Lt Julius Wildau KiA

Italian Claims

79ª Sq, 6°Gr, 1° St CT	S.Ten Paolo Cattaneo	MC.202	P-40	Ain el Gazala	1015-1115
79ª Sq, 6°Gr, 1° St CT	Serg Magg Amedeo Benati	MC.202	P-40 Damaged	Ain el Gazala	1015-1115
81ª Sq, 6°Gr, 1° St CT	M.llo Giovanni Collovini	MC.202	P-40 Probable	Ain el Gazala	1015-1115
80ª Sq, 17°Gr, 1°St CT	Cap Clizio Nioi	MC.202	P-40	Derna	1030-1120
80ª Sq, 17°Gr, 1°St CT	Cap Clizio Nioi	MC.202	P-40 Probable	Derna	1030-1120
80ª Sq, 17°Gr, 1°St CT	Serg Magg Mario Host	MC.202	P-40	Derna	1030-1120
80ª Sq, 17°Gr, 1°St CT	Serg Magg Alvise Andrich	MC.202	P-40	Derna	1030-1120
80ª Sq, 17°Gr, 1°St CT	M.llo Bruno Castellani	MC.202	P-40	Derna	1030-1120
80ª Sq, 17°Gr, 1°St CT	Ten Renato Talamini	MC.202	P-40 Damaged	Derna	1030-1120

Italian Casualties

79ª Sq, 6°Gr, 1° St CT	MC.202 MM 7860 shot down by P-40 near Gulf of Bomba, M.llo Italo Bertinelli KiA

Saturday, 4 April 1942

Two MC.202s undertook a reconnaissance over the Bir Amarin-Bir Tengender area during which one pilot force-landed due to a fuel leakage. He was rescued and the aircraft recovered. Late in the afternoon eleven 17° Gruppo Macchis provided cover for nine MC.200s of 150° Gruppo to strafe a column south of Bir Amarin. Seven vehicles were reported set on fire and 27 damaged. One MC.202 force-landed in the desert, the pilot returning on foot next day.

In the afternoon 450 Squadron lost two pilots in unusual circumstances. Six of the unit's Kittyhawks were patrolling over Gambut at 6,000 feet when Plt Off Evatt lost control and went into a spin, followed a few minutes later by Plt Off Macpherson, both being killed. Both were new and inexperienced pilots, but no reasons could be found for their loss.

80 Squadron's commanding officer, Sqn Ldr J.R.Urwin-Mann, was posted away, tour-expired, command of the unit passing to Flt Lt C.R.A.Forsyth from 94 Squadron.

153ª Squadriglia of 3° Gruppo CT moved from Benghazi K2 to Martuba.

German Casualties

6./JG 27	Bf 109F-4 trop, combat, cabin hit by AA with minimal damage, but Uffz Otto Monska WiA

Italian Casualties

150° Gr CT	MC.200 MM 5268 force-landed due to combat, Magg Antonio Vizzotto returned

Sunday, 5 April 1942

Early in the day six aircraft each from 94 and 4 SAAF Squadrons, plus four of 260 Squadron, undertook a wing sweep. Two Bf 109s of II./JG 27, returning from escorting a reconnaissance Bf 110, spotted the formation and attacked the 260 Squadron Kittyhawks. Flt Sgt Burrill's blew up following Lt Jenisch's attack, although the wounded pilot survived to bale out. A second Kittyhawk was also damaged. During the return flight a Ju 88 of 1.(F)/121 was seen over El Adem and this was shot down 30 miles south of Gasr el Arid by four pilots jointly. This was 4 SAAF Squadron's first sortie since returning to the forward area.

British Claims

4 SAAF Sqn	Capt A.C.Bosman	Tomahawk Ib	Ju 88 (shared)	30m S Gasr el Arid	1045
4 SAAF Sqn	Lt N.W.Hancock	Tomahawk IIb			
94 Sqn	Sqn Ldr I.N.MacDougall	Kittyhawk I AK96			
94 Sqn	Flt Lt D.F.O.Shelford	Kittyhawk AK765			

British Casualties

260 Sqn	Kittyhawk I shot down by Bf 109 10m S Gazala 0955-1115; Sgt R.J.Burrill WiA
260 Sqn	Kittyhawk I damaged by Bf 109 S Gazala, 0955-1115; Flt Sgt Kempsey safe
450 Sqn	Kittyhawk I AK895 'K' scrambled at 1519, spun and crashed during patrol; Plt Off J.Evatt KiFA
450 Sqn	Kittyhawk I AK732 'A' scrambled at 1519, spun and crashed during patrol; Plt Off G.D.McPherson KiFA
73 Sqn	Hurricane Z5444 shot down El Adem
4 SAAF Sqn	Tomahawk IIb damaged Cat I on ground during an 0845 bombing attack by two Bf 109s

German Claims

5./JG 27	Lt Kurt Jenisch	P-40	15km S Ain el Gazala	0925

German Casualties

1.(F)/121	Ju 88D-1 WNr 1560 7A+FH shot down by P-40 50km S Gasr el Arid; Fw Friedrich Weger, Lt August Kleine and two KiA

Monday, 6 April 1942

On this date Axis forces began to move forward again, to consolidate their positions around Sidi Breghish and Segnali. This led to heavy fighting again. Early in the morning 12 Bostons set out to bomb Derna, escorted by 94, 2 SAAF and 4 SAAF Squadrons. Fifteen Bf 109s of I. and II./JG 27 took off to intercept, joined by 17 MC.202s of 1° Stormo (nine of 6° Gruppo and eight of 17°). The German pilots claimed three Curtiss fighters shot down but a further claim by Fw Heidel was not confirmed and may have been a double-claim on one by Lt Kalista. The Italian pilots claimed a further three P-40s, plus three damaged.

On this occasion the Axis pilots seem to have over-claimed fairly heavily, for the only loss by 233 Wing was the Kittyhawk flown by Flt Lt Shefford of 94 Squadron. Wg Cdr Beresford and Capt Bosman chased at least four Bf 109s off the tails of 4 SAAF Squadron, while Flt Lt Laubscher of 2 SAAF Squadron became separated and was repeatedly attacked on the way home, claiming one of his attackers shot down and one damaged. A further claim for a Bf 109 was made by Lt E.Smith.

Charles Laubscher:

> "Squadron top cover to Bostons raiding Martuba. Three aircraft in my flight forced to return to base so I roved alone above squadron. Attacked on homeward run by a 109F, diving almost vertically, about five miles SE of Martuba. Turned tightly to port in standard evasive action. Saw him half-roll on to his back which enabled him to lay off a deflection. Pulled on my stick to tighten my turn and promptly my Tomahawk went into a spin. Straightened out at approx. 5,000 ft and found myself in a hornets' nest of 109Fs all flying in sections of three line-astern at different altitudes. Saw that one section would pass almost directly ahead of me at a range of approx. 250 yards and laid off a full beam deflection on their No.3. Fired a long burst. His port wing dropped and he slid into a gentle dive. Did not wait to see what happened to him but headed back to our lines at full throttle. Two 109Fs attacked but I out-turned them at about 300 feet.
>
> "Northwest of Gazala I saw that a section of three 109Fs, flying in echelon port were overhauling me and as I now guessed that two were almost certainly pilots in training, I did a steep turn to port back towards them and did a head-on attack on No.3. Fired a good burst into him as we closed without any return fire. Immediately did a steep turn to port and headed back to Gazala, ducking over the escarpment down to the level of the mud flats. Only two aircraft closed on me, now more appropriately in line-astern. Never saw what happened to their No.3. Waited until they were committed to a quarter stern attack from left then turned tightly towards them, at about fifty feet above the ground. They were obviously unable, or too nervous, to turn as tightly as I did at this almost zero altitude. As they overshot I again headed for our lines, which were now close, and they left me. I prayed that our army types would not be trigger happy but I was low enough for our chaps to see my roundels and no shots were fired. I thought that I could only claim a probable and a damaged but a telephone call was received from the Bomber Wing that a rear gunner had seen an aircraft go in south-east of Martuba. As no other aircraft had fired a shot, this was clearly my 109F."

Whilst the pursuit of the departing WDAF formation was still underway, Hptm Homuth of I.Gruppe spotted a TacR Hurricane of 40 SAAF Squadron north of Tmimi, which he shot down. It is possible that some of the 1° Stormo pilots were also involved, Cap Camarda claiming to have damaged a Hurricane. The reconnaissance pilot, Lt Egner, baled out and became a PoW. Meanwhile 274 Squadron was scrambled to 'de-louse' the returning formation, undertaking a sweep with 12 Hurricanes over Gazala. Here the pilots became involved in a general dogfight with Bf 109s and Macchis, claiming Italian fighters (identified as MC.200s) as a probable and a damaged, one claim being made for a Bf 109 by Sgt Eagle.

More Regia Aeronautica reinforcements now reached North Africa, 86° Gruppo BT, led by T.Col Goffredo Marrama, arriving at Barce from Italy with 14 Cant.Z.1007bis. The two Squadriglie were 190ª (Cap Leo Vecellio-Reane) and 191ª (Cap Aurelio Salvadori). 13° Gruppo CT headquarters moved to Benghazi K3 with 77ª Squadriglia; 78ª and 82ª Squadriglie would follow later.

British Claims

274 Sqn	Sgt J.Dodds	Hurricane IIb	MC.200 Probable	off Gazala	0855-
274 Sqn	Sgt J.Dodds	Hurricane IIb	MC.200 Damaged	off Gazala	0855-
274 Sqn	Sgt W.G.Eagle	Hurricane IIb 'H'	Bf 109	off Gazala	0855-
2 SAAF Sqn	Flt Lt C.J.Laubscher	Tomahawk IIb 'H'	Bf 109E	E Derna	0930
2 SAAF Sqn	Flt Lt C.J.Laubscher	Tomahawk IIb	Bf 109 Damaged	NW Gazala Bay	0930
2 SAAF Sqn	Lt E.Smith	Tomahawk IIb 'B'	Bf 109	NW Gazala Bay	0930
94 Sqn	Plt Off G.L.Usher	Kittyhawk I AK741	Bf 109E Damaged	Derna-Gazala	0920
94 Sqn	Sgt W.T.Wallace	Kittyhawk I	MC.202 Damaged	Derna-Gazala	1000

British Casualties

94 Sqn	Kittyhawk I AK861 shot down by Bf 109s on escort to Bostons to Derna; Flt Lt D.F.O.Shelford KiA
2 SAAF Sqn	Tomahawk IIb slt damaged in wing by Bf 109; Lt R.D.B.Morton safe
40 SAAF Sqn	Hurricane left 0845, shot down by fighters; Lt Egner baled out, PoW

German Claims

4./JG 27	Oblt Gustav Rödel	P-40	Tmimi/Martuba	0823
2./JG 27	Lt Karl von Lieres und Wilkau	P-40	Ain el Gazala	0830
5./JG 27	Lt Alexander Kalista	P-40	20km SW El Adem	0840
3./JG 27	Hptm Gerhard Homuth	Hurricane	NW Tmimi	0910
4./JG 27	Fw Alfred Heidel	P-40 o.Zg. n.b.		

Italian Claims

88ª Sq, 6°Gr, 1°St CT	Cap Dante Ocarso	MC.202	P-40	Ain el Gazala	0815-0915
79ª Sq, 6°Gr, 1°St CT	Cap Domenico Camarda	MC.202	Hurricane Damaged	Ain el Gazala	0815-0915
80ª Sq, 17°Gr, 1°St CT	Cap Clizio Nioi	MC.202	P-40	Ain el Gazala	0820-0940
80ª Sq, 17°Gr, 1°St CT	Cap Clizio Nioi	MC.202	P-40 Damaged	Ain el Gazala	0820-0940
80ª Sq, 17°Gr, 1°St CT	Ten Emilio Marchi	MC.202	P-40 Damaged	Ain el Gazala	0820-0940
80ª Sq, 17°Gr, 1°St CT	Serg Magg Alvise Andrich	MC.202	P-40	Ain el Gazala	0820-0940
80ª Sq, 17°Gr, 1°St CT	Ten Giovanni B. Ghiglia	MC.202	P-40 Damaged	Ain el Gazala	0820-0940

Italian Casualties

175ª Sq RST	S.79 MM 23880 crash-landed at Castel Benito, pilot Ten Carlo Dell'Antonio, copilot Serg Salvatore Liberto and crew wounded

Tuesday, 7 April 1942

In the morning nine Kittyhawks of 260 Squadron provided top cover to six Bostons attacking Axis vehicles. Over Gazala they were intercepted by four Bf 109s of I./JG 27 when one was shot down and one damaged. Later in the morning Hurricanes of 33 and 80 Squadrons carried out a de-lousing sweep over the Gazala area meeting Messerschmitts and Macchis, claiming one of the latter shot down and one damaged.

In the afternoon Kittyhawks again escorted Bostons on a raid, this time with eight of 94 Squadron as top cover. One pilot was reported to have baled out due to engine failure, but the formation was then attacked by nine Bf 109s of II.Gruppe which shot the tail off Flg Off Thompson's aircraft. He baled out, returning on foot next day. Pilots of the German unit claimed that from two of the aircraft they shot down the pilots baled out, while the third, claimed by Oblt Fluder, crashed. It therefore appears that Oblt Rödel and Obfw Kientsch double-claimed on Thompson's aircraft.

During the day III./JG 27 lost two aircraft when engaged in fighter-bomber (Jabo) sorties. One of these, flown by Oblt Tangerding, came down near Tmimi due to engine failure. The German fighters had been reinforced further by the arrival at Derna from Sicily the day before of 6./JG 3, led by Oblt Jürgen Waldhelm. This unit moved on to Martuba but on arrival here two aircraft crash-landed, both suffering 10% damage.

British Claims

80 Sqn	Flg Off F.Mason	Hurricane IIc BE358	MC.202	SW Gazala	0930
80 Sqn	Flg Off F.Mason	Hurricane IIc BE358	MC.202 Damaged	SW Gazala	0930

British Casualties

450 Sqn	Kittyhawk I AK774 'O' shot down by Bf 109 S Gazala from 7,000ft; Flg Off E.T.Thompson baled out safely
450 Sqn	Kittyhawk I AK 663 'I' engine failed 15 minutes after take-off, and crashed at 1606; Sgt W.J. Metherall safe

260 Sqn	Kittyhawk I AK956 shot down by Bf 109s SW Gazala; Sgt J.H.Alexander MiA
260 Sqn	Kittyhawk I badly damaged by Bf 109 SW Gazala; Flt Sgt T.Hindle safe
4 SAAF Sqn	Tomahawk IIb slt damaged by Bf 109 1550-1730; Lt J.S.Warden safe

German Claims

3./JG 27	Hptm Gerhard Homuth	P-40	SW Ain el Gazala	0837
4./JG 27	Oblt Gustav Rödel	P-40	N Mteifel Chebir	1543
6./JG 27	Oblt Emmerich Fluder	P-40	30km S Ain el Gazala	1544
6./JG 27	Obfhr Willy Kientsch	P-40	S Ain el Gazala	1545

Thursday, 9 April 1942

176ª Squadriglia RST was disbanded and its six Cant.Z.1107bis and their crews were assigned to the newly-arrived 86° Gruppo BT, three to each squadriglia.

In the afternoon Lt Gouws of 40 SAAF Squadron undertaking a TacR sortie in a Tomahawk, was intercepted over the Chichiba-Ezzeiat area by two Bf 109s of II./JG 27 which were also engaged in a reconnaissance sortie. The South African was shot down by Oblt Rödel, belly-landing on fire south of Mteifel Chebir. Lt Blaauw of the same unit force-landed later in the day with engine trouble.

British Claims

40 SAAF	Lt D.N.Stott	Hurricane	Bf 109 Damaged	El Adem to Rotunda Segnali	1530

British Casualties

40 SAAF Sqn	Hurricane left 1746, intercepted by 2 Bf 109s; Lt Gouws seen to crash-land
40 SAAF Sqn	Hurricane Z4162 attacked and force-landed when engine seized at 1315; Lt J..P.Blaauw
40 SAAF Sqn	Hurricane crash-landed to Bf 109 El Adem 1530; Lt D.N.Stott safe

German Claims

4./JG 27	Oblt Gustav Rödel	P-40	30km SW Mteifel Chebir	1425

German Casualties

3./JG 27	Bf 109F-4 trop WNr 8617 hit obstruction during take-off at Derna, engine cut, destroyed; Obfw Herbert Kowalski WiA

Friday, 10 April 1942

A further pilot of 40 SAAF Squadron failed to return from an afternoon TacR. The unit was equipped at this time with 19 Hurricanes and two Tomahawks, borrowed from 208 Squadron which was resting.

British Casualties

40 SAAF Sqn	Hurricane FTR from Eluet el Daba (believed to be Z4320); Lt J.W.van Niekerk MiA

Saturday, 11 April 1942

At 1000 I./JG 27 provided close cover and II.Gruppe direct cover to 18 Ju 87s of I./StG 3 to attack vehicles in the Sidi Mansur-Bir Habex area. They were joined by 13 MC.202s of 17° Gruppo, currently at almost full strength. Seven Tomahawks of 4 SAAF Squadron led by Maj Moodie dived in haphazardly after the Axis formation had been spotted. Only two returned, each pilot claiming to have damaged a Stuka. Two pilots were reported safe but slightly wounded, both having crash-landed, and Lt Duff-Richardson was reported to be in Tobruk hospital, badly wounded; he subsequently claimed to have shot down a Bf 109 and a Ju 87, and damaged two more of the dive-bombers. Of two more pilots there was no news. British Intelligence later reported that two Ju 87s and one Bf 109 had been seen to go down, but evidence does not support this. One Ju 87 was shot down, although reportedly by AA as well as fighters, crashing 25km north-east of Sidi Mansur, where it burst into flames on impact; four more were damaged. One Bf 109 of I./JG 27 ditched in the sea, 80-100km north of Derna, but this was due to engine failure. On this occasion Luftwaffe claims matched South African losses quite exactly, I.Gruppe claiming two and II.Gruppe four.

From LG.13 1 SAAF Squadron was withdrawn eastwards for patrol duties over Port Said (see more in Chapter Three).

British Claims

4 SAAF Sqn	Lt M.Duff-Richardson	Tomahawk IIb	Bf 109	Gasr el Arid	1135

British Claims

4 SAAF Sqn	Lt M.Duff-Richardson	Tomahawk IIb	Ju 87	Gasr el Arid	1135
4 SAAF Sqn	Lt M.Duff-Richardson	Tomahawk IIb	2 Ju 87s Damaged	Gasr el Arid	1135
4 SAAF Sqn	Lt R.E.Jackson	Tomahawk IIb	Ju 87 Damaged	Gasr el Arid	1135
4 SAAF Sqn	Lt R.E.Jackson	Tomahawk IIb	MC.202 Damaged	Gasr el Arid	1135
4 SAAF Sqn	Maj D.D.Moodie	Tomahawk IIb 'I'	Ju 87 Damaged	Gasr el Arid	1135

British Casualties

4 SAAF Sqn	Tomahawk IIb 'I' damaged by Bf 109; Maj D.D.Moodie safe
4 SAAF Sqn	Tomahawk IIb AN297 shot down by Bf 109s, crash-landed in flames nr Bir Hacheim 1130; Lt W.M.Langerman slt WiA
4 SAAF Sqn	Tomahawk IIb shot down by Bf 109s SW Gazala; Lt M.Duff-Richardson badly WiA; left foot amputated
4 SAAF Sqn	Tomahawk IIb AM442 shot down 80km SW Gazala; Lt G.M.K.Donaldson KiA
4 SAAF Sqn	Tomahawk IIb AN339 shot down by Bf 109s; Lt R.H.Denehy WiA in leg, died of wounds in field hospital
4 SAAF Sqn	Tomahawk IIb AK368 shot down by Bf 109s 80km SW Gazala; 2/Lt D.C.Frye PoW

German Claims

1./JG 27	Fw Günther Steinhausen	P-40	N Bir Habex	1050
5./JG 27	Fw Hans Niederhöfer	P-40	10km NW	1050
			Sidi Mansour	1052
5./JG 27	Lt Kurt Jenisch	P-40	10km SSE Gadd el Ahmar	1054
5./JG 27	Hptm Ernst Düllberg	P-40	ESE Sidi Mansur	1055
5./JG 27	Lt Alexander Kalista	P-40	10km SE Gadd el Ahmar	1055
1./JG 27	Oblt Ludwig Franzisket	P-40	20km NE Bir Habex	

German Casualties

1./StG 3	Ju 87R-2 WNr 6155 S7+HL combat with P-40 AA Sidi Mansour, burst into flames; Fw Claus Neumann/Uffz Rudolf Krause KiA

Monday, 13 April 1942

A small expedition was undertaken jointly by German and Italian forces to neutralize a British landing ground which had been spotted in the eastern Libyan desert. Two S.82s of 145° Gruppo T, escorted by six Bf 110s of 7./ZG 26, carried a group of 60 Italian airmen, carabineri and German sappers with five machine guns and an anti-tank gun, the whole force commanded by T.Col Dazio Gilardoni of 5ª Squadra Comando Est (Eastern Command). Taking off at 0735, the transport aircraft landed on the deserted landing ground, as did several of the Bf 110s, three of which remained airborne as cover. Dumps of fuel and lubricant were shot-up, and it was noted that the wrecks of four Blenheims were present. By 1000 the operation had been completed.

At about this time nine MC.202s of 17° Gruppo which had taken off on a free sweep, encountered a formation of P-40s, two of which were claimed shot down. The Macchi flown by one of the claiming pilots was hit in the radiator and force-landed within Axis lines. Three more claims for aircraft damaged were also made by pilots of 2 SAAF Squadron who claimed an MC.202 damaged, while suffering no losses.

260 and 4 SAAF Squadrons had just arrived at El Adem from where the latter unit put up four Tomahawks. Early in the afternoon six Bf 109s appeared, carrying bombs, and two, from 6./JG 3, providing escort. The first Jabo missed hitting anything, but the second released 12 small bombs which destroyed one of 260 Squadron's Kittyhawks and damaged several South African Tomahawks of 40 SAAF Squadron, Sgt McKay of the former unit being wounded.

The patrolling Tomahawks dived to the attack, Capt Harrison shooting down one of the escorting pair, then giving chase to a second Messerschmitt which also failed to return, crash-landing west of El Adem. The pilot turned up on foot a few days later. German records indicate that this aircraft was also shot down in combat with Curtiss fighters, although it does not seem to have been credited to Capt Harrison, but to AA.

British Claims

2 SAAF Sqn	Lt D.Paddon	Tomahawk IIb	MC.202 Damaged	El Adem area	1100
4 SAAF Sqn	Capt L.E.Harrison	Tomahawk IIb	Bf 109	El Adem	1525

British Casualties

260 Sqn	Kittyhawk I destroyed on ground; Sgt W.R.McKay injured
40 SAAF Sqn	one Tomahawk damaged on ground

German Casualties

6./JG 3	Bf 109F-4 trop WNr 10019 Yellow 12 combat with P-40, force-landed nr El Adem, destroyed; Uffz Josef Fritz PoW
7./JG 27	Bf 109F-4 trop WNr 8533 White 8 shot down by P-40 W El Adem on Jabo operation; Fw Karl Waibel MiA, returned on foot a few days later

Italian Claims

71ª Sq, 17°Gr, 1°St CT	Cap Pericle Baruffi	MC.202 MM7895	P-40	S Ain el Gazala	0920-1030
71ª Sq, 17°Gr, 1°St CT	M.llo Achille Martina	MC.202	P-40	S Ain el Gazala	0920-1030
80ª Sq, 17°Gr, 1°St CT	Cap Clizio Nioi	MC.202	2 P-40s Damaged	S Ain el Gazala	0920-1030
80ª Sq, 17°Gr, 1°St CT	Serg Magg Aldo Bersani	MC.202	P-40 Damaged	S Ain el Gazala	0920-1030
80ª Sq, 17°Gr, 1°St CT	Serg Magg Mario Host	MC.202	P-40 Damaged	S Ain el Gazala	0920-1030

Italian Casualties

71ª Sq, 17°Gr, 1°St CT	MC.202 MM 7895 hit in radiator, force-landed, Cap Pericle Baruffi unscathed, returned

Tuesday, 14 April 1942

I./JG 27 despatched two Bf 109s to attack vehicles and Bofors emplacements near Gadd el Ahmar during the morning but Uffz Grimm's aircraft was hit by AA and he baled out to become a PoW.

On 14 April AVM Arthur Coningham visited 112 Squadron at Sidi Haneish to present the unit with its badge, and to undertake an inspection. In front of two of the unit's Kittyhawks he addresses the parade; he is flanked by the commanding officer, Sqn Ldr C.R.Caldwell (right).

German Casualties

I./JG 27	Bf 109F-3 trop WNr 8737 White 5 shot down by AA SE Gadd el Ahmar; Uffz Josef Grimm baled, PoW

Italian Casualties

79ª Sq, 6°Gr, 1°St CT	MC.202 MM 7776 '79-7' damaged by bombs at Martuba

Wednesday, 15 April 1942

During the evening 11 Kittyhawks of 260 Squadron were ordered off on an interception patrol, but were attacked by Bf 109s. Sgt Parrott's aircraft was hit and damaged, causing him to force-land near El Gobi. I./JG 27 claimed one fighter damaged.

British Casualties

260 Sqn	Kittyhawk I shot down by Bf 109 nr Bir el Gobi; Sgt Parrott safe

Thursday, 16 April 1942

250 Squadron, now fully re-equipped with Kittyhawks, moved to LG.12 at Sidi Haneish and 112 Squadron returned to Gambut Satellite. 40 SAAF squadron lost another Hurricane during a TacR, Lt Rose failing to return from a sortie to Gazala.

British Casualties

40 SAAF Sqn	Hurricane V7431 shot down by Flak on recce Gazala; Lt N.M. Rose MiA

Saturday, 18 April 1942

It was the anniversary of I./JG 27's arrival in North Africa, and the Kommandeur, Maj Neumann, organised 'Neumann's Grosse Wüstenrummel' (Neumann's big desert revels). Some of the groundcrew presented Neumann with a spade made from the control column of a Hurricane he had shot down; the spade had a most significant part in desert life, known to the German pilots as the 'Spatengang' (literally, walk to relieve nature). During the day all members of the unit wore fancy dress which they had concocted, and many booths were set up, including ball and dice games, wheels of fortune, a merry-go-round and a miniature rifle range. One of the biggest attractions was 'Maack's Weltschau', a 'world show' presented by Hptm Maack which included such wonders as 'the wife behind the lattices of the harem', etc. Neumann himself performed creditably as a magician. During the evening a large tent arranged as a casino was packed with guests from all branches of the Afrika Korps, and a musical variety show was laid on, Werner Schroer acting as master of ceremonies, broadcasting to outlying units over 'Radio Martuba'. This was jammed by the British and another frequency was tried, but this too was jammed. However, the day was a great success and caused a big sensation, helping considerably for a while to conquer the lethargy and boredom of desert life.

Geschwader Kommodore of Stukageschwader 3, Oberstlt Walter Sigel, led the unit throughout 1942 from April onwards.

Monday, 20 April 1942

80 Squadron carried out an early sweep over the Bir Hacheim-Tmimi area, Plt Off Foskett and Flt Sgt Campbell catching and shooting down a lone Bf 109E of 4.(H)/12 on a TacR 15 miles south-west of Bir Hacheim. This unit had replaced 2.(H)/14 for reconnaissance duties at this time.

At 1055 14 Bf 109s of II./JG 27 set off on a Freie Jagd, eight of them encountering 33 Squadron which had been scrambled on patrol over Tobruk. Two of the Hurricanes were shot down, both pilots baling out, with two more force-landing. On this occasion the German pilots claimed only the first two aircraft

– identified yet again as P-40s! As this engagement was taking place, eight Kittyhawks of 260 Squadron provided top cover to Bostons on a raid. No Axis interceptors were met, but near El Adem whilst on the way to the target, Plt Off Black was obliged to bale out – reason unknown.

British Claims

80 Sqn	Flt Sgt D.A.Campbell	Hurricane IIc BE713 'E'	Bf 109E	15m SW Bir Hacheim	0800-0900
80 Sqn	Sgt R.G.Foskett	Hurricane IIc BM974 'B'			

British Casualties

33 Sqn	Hurricane IIb BG883 'D' damaged by Bf 109s and abandoned nr Tobruk; Sgt Stott WiA
33 Sqn	Hurricane IIb BG916 shot down by Bf 109s and abandoned S Gambut; Sgt Griffiths safe
33 Sqn	Hurricane IIb 2416 force-landed, shot down by Bf 109 Gambut area; Plt Off K.C.Rolls safe
33 Sqn	Hurricane IIb BG862 force-landed, shot down by Bf 109 Gambut area; Sgt F.G.Woollard safe
260 Sqn	Kittyhawk I; Plt Off G.J.Black baled out

German Claims

5./JG 27	Fw Horst Reuter	P-40	2km SSE Rezegh	1150
5./JG 27	Hptm Ernst Düllberg	P-40	8km S Gambut	1155

German Casualties

4.(H)/12	Bf 109E-7 WNr 3325 shot down 20km E Bir el Harmat by Hurricanes; Obfw Ewald Handt KiA

Tuesday, 21 April 1942

At dawn Flt Lt Scade of 73 Squadron intercepted a Ju 88 of I./LG 1, but defensive fire hit the glycol system of his Hurricane, causing him to force-land at El Gobi at once. 86° Gruppo BT detached a flight of four Cant.Z.1007bis to Derna's El Fteiah airfield, to undertake strategic reconnaissance missions, mainly to the oases of Kufra, Gialo and Giarabub.

British Claims

73 Sqn	Flt Lt T.P.K.Scade	Hurricane BN165	Ju 88 Damaged	El Gobi	0645

British Casualties

40 SAAF Sqn	Hurricane Z4776 crash-landed at El Adem; Lt B.H.Nichol
73 Sqn	Hurricane BN165 force-landed Tobruk after combat with Ju 88; Flt Lt T.P.K.Scade safe

Wednesday, 22 April 1942

24ª Squadriglia of 68° Gruppo OA, equipped with Ca.311s, arrived at Misurata from Italy.

77ª and 82ª Squadriglie of 13° Gruppo moved from Benghazi to Martuba. 78ª Squadriglia remained at Benghazi to provide harbour protection. During the day a Ghibli of 12ª Squadriglia APC sighted a Blenheim IV abandoned deep in the desert (30°15'-21°40') by its crew. The pilot landed nearby and set fire to the aircraft.

British Casualties

33 Sqn	Hurricane IIb BG350 shot down by Flak; Flt Lt D.C.Cloete safe

Thursday, 23 April 1942

During the day 250 Squadron moved up to Gambut to resume operations. A reconnaissance Bf 110 of 4.(H)/12 was shot down by AA at Bir el Chaualat with the loss of the crew. With evening four Cant.Z.1007bis of 191ª Sq took off at 1935 to bomb Tobruk. During taxying, one collided with a parked S.79, damaging a wing. Three reached the target and two released fragmentation and incendiary bombs. A fifth aircraft went up in flames during take-off and was completely destroyed, pilot Ten Vittorio Vinciguerra and his crew being badly burnt.

German Casualties

4.(H)/12	Bf 110E-3 WNr 2525 shot down by AA Bir el Chaualat; Lt Josef Lengitz, Obfw Karl Hirschberger, Obgefr Wilhelm Hopfeld KiA

Italian Casualties

191ª Sq, 86°Gr, 35°St BT	Cant.Z.1007bis MM 23418 destroyed by fire on taking off from Barce, pilot S.Ten Vittorio Vinciguerra, copilot Serg Lures Paltrinieri and observer S.Ten Antonio Desiderio wounded

Italian Casualties

191ª Sq, 86°Gr, 35°St BT	Cant.Z.1007bis MM 23415 damaged after collision in taxying, pilot T.Col Goffredo Marrama safe

Friday, 24 April 1942

Early in the morning three 260 Squadron aircraft strafed four lorries west of Bir Hacheim, all of which blew up. Sgt Tregear failed to return and was thought to have flown into the explosion of his target and crashed. Eleven Tomahawks of 2 SAAF Squadron then carried out a sweep over the Bir Hacheim area where they were attacked by three Bf 109s. These comprised a pair of III./JG 27 aircraft and a Bf 109E of 4.(H)/12 which they were escorting. Lt E.Smith shot down the reconnaissance aircraft in flames, the two escorts being claimed hit by other pilots.

During the day 2 SAAF Squadron received a new commanding officer, Maj Andrew Bosman, late of 4 SAAF Squadron. Exulted the record book: "....he is acknowledged not only by us, but by the RAF, as not only one of the best, but the best fighter pilot in the Western Desert!" He arrived just in time to lead the unit in the heaviest fighting of the month next day.

Five Cant.Z.1007bis of 190ª Squadriglia took off at 1920 to bomb Tobruk again.

British Claims

2 SAAF Sqn	Lt A.D.Allen	Tomahawk IIb	Bf 109F Damaged	N Gazala	0905
2 SAAF Sqn	Flt Lt C.J.Laubscher	Tomahawk IIb	Bf 109F Damaged	N Gazala	0905
2 SAAF Sqn	Lt E.Smith	Tomahawk IIb 'V'	Bf 109E	E Gazala	0905

British Casualties

260 Sqn	Kittyhawk I AK966; Sgt F.W.Tregear RAAF KiA strafing W Bir Hacheim
203 Sqn	Blenheim V6014; Flt Lt W.R.Hole and crew MiA. Likely to fighter

German Casualties

4.(H)/12	Bf 109E-7 WNr 5263 shot down by P-40s Ain el Gazala; Fw Franz Reinisch KiA

Saturday, 25 April 1942

At dawn Flt Lt Scade and Flg Off Chatfield of 73 Squadron each claimed to have damaged a Ju 88 over Tobruk. Early in the morning 12 Ju 87s of I./StG 3 took off to attack shipping in Tobruk harbour, escorted by eight Bf 109s of 6./JG 3 as close cover, 14 of I./JG 27 as top cover, 17 of II./JG 27 as indirect cover, 13 of III.Gruppe and 13 Italian fighters of 6° Gruppo in a waiting position to provide additional cover during the return flight.

Against this force, eight Kittyhawks of 260 Squadron, 12 Tomahawks of 4 SAAF Squadron, and several Tomahawks with two Kittyhawks (which had just been passed to 2 SAAF Squadron by 94 Squadron) were scrambled. Six of the 260 Squadron aircraft made the initial interception, catching 11 Ju 87s just as they finished bombing; Sqn Ldr Hanbury claimed one and also claimed an MC.202, but he was hit and force-landed near Gazala. No Italian claims or losses were recorded, and it remains possible therefore, that his second opponent may have been a Messerschmitt. A second Ju 87 was claimed by Plt Off Miller, but he too was shot down and another two of the unit's aircraft were damaged. Two more Axis fighters were claimed by the unit's pilots and two were indeed shot down in the Gazala area, both pilots surviving and returning safely later.

The South Africans had less success and suffered fairly severe casualties. Lt de Waal of 2 SAAF Squadron was shot down after repeated attacks by three Bf 109s, having himself claimed a probable and a damaged. He only just got out of his fighter before it burst into flames. One more of the unit's aircraft was hit and was badly damaged. 4 SAAF Squadron again "just jumped in", Maj Moodie having his controls shot away and crash-landing five miles south-east of Gazala. Lt Langaard baled out over the sea and got into his dinghy, but had suffered severe burns. He reached the coast, but was lost on 10 May when the hospital ship *Ramb IV*, on which he was a patient, was sunk by enemy action. Meanwhile, the squadron's haul was limited, amounting to one probable and three aircraft damaged, to which the wing leader, Wg Cdr Beresford, added two more.

The Luftwaffe claims were once again very accurate considering the involved nature of the fight, ten fighters being claimed for an actual WDAF loss of seven destroyed or crash-landed, and four damaged, two of them badly. Apart from the two JG 27 Bf 109s that had been shot down, six Stukas had been hit by fighters or AA, one of these being shot down by the former. One of the JG 3 Messerschmitts had also been hit by AA and crash-landed at Martuba on return, although suffering only 10% damage, while a

III./JG 27 aircraft crash-landed here, 25% damaged.

Charles Laubscher had a somewhat different recollection of this particular mission:

"As 2 Squadron was only on standby I borrowed a Kittyhawk for a brief test flight [Laubscher gives the impression that he has borrowed this from 4 SAAF Squadron but at that time the only unit in 233 Wing with Kittyhawks was 260 Squadron – Author]. I tried out the guns (6 x .5") and was impressed by their fire power and the tracer which were clearly visible – also by the machine's power and manoeuvrability, the excellent field of vision from the cockpit and, inter alia, the pilot's relief tube! Landed after 20 minutes and, as I was taxying in, all squadrons in the wing were scrambled. Took off without changing aircraft, with 11 Tomahawks from 2 Squadron, 12 Kittyhawks from 4 Squadron [No – Tomahawks at this time – Author] and 12 Kittyhawks from a RAF squadron in the wing [Yes – 260 Squadron – Author]. Climbed at full bore as Control's orders had been 'Buster', all aircraft virtually in a straight line hoping to catch a Stuka squadron which had bombed the troops etc at Tobruk. The squadron at the north end of the line [? No 4] tallyhoed as they saw the Stukas flying low over the Gulf of Gazala, and the other two squadrons swung north-west towards them in time to be met by a mixed gaggle of 109Fs and Macchi 202s, numbering about 35 to 40 aircraft. What I believed to be the biggest dogfight of the desert war developed. One moment two or three of us would be firing at a single enemy aircraft, the next you were dodging an attack from two or three 109s or Macchis. Classic remark over the R/T from Lt Syd Cohen of 4 Squadron who was being given a particularly torrid time by four 109Fs: 'Christ, do these bloody Germans think I'm the only Jew in the South African Air Force!'

"Whilst weaving around I saw a 109F creeping up the tail of a Kittyhawk about 300 feet below and the same distance ahead of me. I yelled out over the R/T: 'Kittyhawk below me – turn, for Christ's sake turn!!' He must have heard me loud and clear for he went into a steep turn to starboard immediately, followed by the 109F which could not lay off a deflection. I cut the corner diving towards them, allowed as much deflection as I dared (my reflector sight dot was on the Kittyhawk's fuselage) and fired a long burst. Saw good strikes on the 109F's wings and fuselage and he slid slowly downwards into a steep dive. Couldn't follow him as I had to dodge an aircraft attacking me from my port stern quarter. Attacked another 109F head on and saw a streak of fire along his cowling as I passed over him. Chased another 109F to Tmimi, firing at long range. Tracers appeared to strike him, but tracers can be deceptive and he did not go down. Nearly jumped twice by 109Fs but outmanoeuvred these aircraft. Chased another 109F out to sea but could not catch him so I returned to the combat area. Sky was now clear of aircraft so I headed back to base, guns almost limp from all their efforts. Armourers advised that I had fired 1,100 rounds (including the short test burst naturally). The wing lost six aircraft in the engagement and we heard later that enemy losses were similar." [Such was the power of wartime propaganda and wishful thinking! – Author]

British Claims					
73 Sqn	Flt Lt T.P.K.Scade	Hurricane IIb	Ju 88 Damaged	Tobruk	0600
73 Sqn	Flg Off R.M.Chatfield	Hurricane IIb	Ju 88 Damaged	Tobruk	0605
260 Sqn	Sgt J.V.Carlisle	Kittyhawk I	Bf 109	2-3m off Gazala	1026-1135
British Claims					
260 Sqn	Sqn Ldr O.V.Hanbury	Kittyhawk I AK801	Ju 87	2-3m off Gazala	1026-1135
260 Sqn	Sqn Ldr O.V.Hanbury	Kittyhawk I AK801	MC.202	2-3m off Gazala	1026-1135
260 Sqn	Plt Off T.Hindle	Kittyhawk I	Bf 109	on shore, nr Ras el Tin	1026-1135
260 Sqn	Plt Off Miller	Kittyhawk I	Ju 87	2-3m off Gazala	1026-1135
2 SAAF Sqn	Lt J.O.de Waal	Tomahawk IIb AM464	Bf 109F Probable	Tobruk-Gazala area	1200-1250
2 SAAF Sqn	Lt J.O.de Waal	Tomahawk IIb AM464	Bf 109F Damaged	Tobruk-Gazala area	1200-1250
2 SAAF Sqn	Lt E.K.Ismay	Tomahawk IIb	Bf 109F Damaged	Tobruk-Gazala area	1200-1250
2 SAAF Sqn	Flt Lt C.J.Laubscher	Tomahawk IIb	Bf 109F Damaged	Tobruk-Gazala area	1200-1250
2 SAAF Sqn	Flt Lt C.J.Laubscher	Kittyhawk I	Bf 109F Probable	Tobruk-Gazala area	1200-1250
233 Wg	Wg Cdr T.B.de la P.Beresford	Tomahawk IIb	2 Bf 109Fs Damaged	Tobruk-Gazala area	1200-1250
British Casualties					
2 SAAF Sqn	Tomahawk IIb AK354 shot down by Bf 109s at Derna, 1200-1250; Lt H.F.Howard KiA				

British Casualties

2 SAAF Sqn	Tomahawk IIb AK475 shot down by Bf 109 over sea off Gazala/Tobruk area, 1200-1250; Lt F.J.Ball KiA
2 SAAF Sqn	Tomahawk IIb AM464 shot down by Bf 109, 1200-1250; Lt J.O.de Waal returned
2 SAAF Sqn	Tomahawk IIb AN454 damaged Cat II, 1200-1250; 2/Lt R.G.Harrison slt WiA
2 SAAF Sqn	Tomahawk IIb AN278 damaged Cat II, 1200-1250; Lt H.S.McMaster returned
4 SAAF Sqn	Tomahawk IIb AK469 'M' damaged by MC.202 and crash-landed nr Bir Gabeli c1100 Cat II; Maj D.D.Moodie safe
4 SAAF Sqn	Tomahawk IIb AK555 shot down by Bf 109 and baled out badly burned into sea 16km NW Gazala; Lt C.K.Langaard reached coast in dinghy; died when hospital ship *Ramb IV* sunk by enemy action on 10 May 1942
260 Sqn	Kittyhawk I shot down by Bf 109 N Gazala; Sgt J.W.Wareham MiA
260 Sqn	Kittyhawk I AK801 shot down by Bf 109s nr Gazala; Sqn Ldr O.V.Hanbury safe
260 Sqn	Kittyhawk I badly damaged
260 Sqn	Kittyhawk I slt damaged
260 Sqn	Kittyhawk I shot down by Bf 109s nr Gazala; Plt Off Miller safe
208 Sqn	Hurricane W9300 DBR

German Claims

5./JG 27	Fw Horst Reuter	2 P-40s	5km N El Giahir & 8km SE Ain el Gazala	0950 & 0955
4./JG 27	Oblt Gustav Rödel	P-40	6km N Ain el Gazala	0955
7./JG 27	Lt Wilhelm Scheiter	P-40	7km NNE Gazala over sea	0955
7./JG 27	Fw Walter Fink	P-40	7km NNE Gazala over sea	0955
2./JG 27	Hptm Ernst Maack	P-40	8km NE El Giahir	1002
2./JG 27	Lt Karl von Leres und Wilkau	P-40	4km NE Ain el Gazala	1004
3./JG 27	Lt Hans-Joachim Marseille	2 P-46s	2km and 10km N Ain el Gazala	1006 & 1008
1./JG 27	Fw Günther Steinhausen	P-40	ESE Ain el Gazala	1010

German Casualties

3./JG 27	Bf 109F-4 trop WNr 8692 shot down by P-40, force-landing on the coast nr Ras el Tin, 100%; Lt Karl Kugelbauer safe
III./JG 27	Bf 109F-4 trop crash-landed Martuba, 25%; pilot safe
5./JG 27	Bf 109F-4 trop WNr 8516 shot down by P-40s, crashed NE Ain el Gazala, 100%; Lt Kurt Jenisch safe
1./StG 3	Ju 87R-2 shot down by P-40 20km NE Ain el Gazala; Lt Rudolf Braun WiA/ Uffz Josef Wörner KiA
6./JG 3	Bf 109F-4 hit by AA, belly-landed at Martuba on return, 10% damaged; Uffz Waldemar Eyrich safe

Italian Casualties

3 MC.200s badly damaged at Martuba by strafing, 2300-2400, 6 slightly damaged

Sunday, 26 April 1942

During an early Freie Jagd, Hptm Maack of I./JG 27 shot-up and claimed to have set alight two armoured cars. An hour later at 1015, four III.Gruppe aircraft undertook a similar mission; over Tengender when flying at low level, they intercepted two aircraft which were identified as both being Curtiss fighters. In fact these were a Tomahawk, flown by Lt Booth, and a Hurricane, flown by Capt Nel, both of 40 SAAF Squadron on a TacR sortie. Lt Gruber shot down Booth's aircraft, the pilot crash-landing and the aircraft nosing over, but Nel made good his escape and returned to base.

During the day 3 RAAF Squadron moved to Gambut to join 112, 250 and 450 Squadrons, 239 Wing now being established here under the leadership of Wg Cdr H.C.Mayers. From Martuba, 6./JG 3 now returned to Sicily, having gained no victories during its short stay in North Africa.

British Casualties

40 SAAF Sqn	Tomahawk AN456 covering Hurricane of Capt Nel, intercepted over Tengender by four Bf 109s crash-landed, 1145; Lt J.H.Booth died on way to hospital, Nel escaped and returned

German Claims

8./JG 27	Uffz Viktor Gruber	P-40	W Gadd el Ahmar	1945

Monday, 27 April 1942

German Casualties

Wüstennotstaffel	Fi 156C-1 WNr 0701 damaged beyond repair on the ground at Martuba by raid

Tuesday, 28 April 1942

In the afternoon six III./JG 27 Bf 109s again flew a Freie Jagd over Gazala, reporting an engagement with 18 Curtiss fighters, one of which was claimed to have been shot down in flames by Oblt Heinecke. The WDAF unit involved has not been discovered.

Four 190ª Squadriglia's Cant.Z.1007bis bombers took off at 1935 to bomb Tobruk. Over the target the fourth to arrive was hit by heavy AA, the pilot being wounded in one arm; the copilot and one gunner were also wounded by splinters. Despite his serious injury, the pilot, Ten Umberto Lorenzi, managed to reach Derna where he force-landed at 2215. All those with wounds were taken to Derna hospital, but Lorenzi died there next day. He was awarded a Medaglia d'Argento al valor militare 'in memoriam'.

German Claims

9./JG 27	Oblt Hans-Joachim Heinecke	P-40	20km SE Gazala

Italian Casualties

190ª Sq, 86°Gr , 35°St BT	Cant.Z.1007bis MM 24257 hit by AA at Tobruk, pilot Ten Umberto Lorenzi and copilot Serg Magg Angelo Nodari wounded

Wednesday, 29 April 1942

Two Bf 109Fs of II./JG 27 escorted two Bf 109Es on a reconnaissance mission during which the pilots reported being attacked by four fighters near El Adem. Obfw Krenz's Bf 109F was badly damaged, but he returned to base. Again, the identity of the WDAF unit involved has not been identified. 450 Squadron now left 239 Wing for the moment, being withdrawn for a short rest at this point.

German Casualties

6./JG 27	Bf 109F-4 trop 20% damaged by P-40 SW El Adem, landed safely at base; Obfw Herbert Krenz safe

Thursday, 30 April 1942

On this date a most memorable event occurred when 145 Squadron, which had just arrived at Helwan, unloaded its Spitfire Vbs, the first to reach North Africa.

The Middle East Training Squadrons

At this stage five Middle East training squadrons were set up, initially within AHQ, Egypt, to provide a variety of advanced training. The first of these actually to come into being on 23 March 1942 was 3 METS at Amman which took over the Ground Gunner School at Helwan, training personnel in administration, gunnery, fire fighting and aircraft recognition. It was followed on 5 April by 1 METS at El Ballah. This unit was formed from within 233 (Fighter) Wing, which had set up a Conversion and Refresher School in late February. It now comprised an air fighting squadron with ten Hurricane Is, four Mark IIs and eight Kittyhawks, a conversion and refresher squadron with ten Kittyhawks, six Tomahawks, four Harvards, two Blenheims and two Baltimores to provide appropriate courses for all OTU fighter pilots out from the UK, and air fighting and firing courses for fighter pilots generally. It was intended that an instructor's training school would subsequently be added.

The third unit, 2 METS, was formed within 235 Wing of 205 Group at Shallufa to provide refresher and conversion courses for medium and heavy bomber crews. It moved to 238 Wing at Kabrit on 27 May. Also formed within 205 Group was 4 METS, mainly to train general reconnaissance and transport crews, for which it was equipped with four Wellingtons. This unit was formed on 1 May and was also based at Kabrit. Finally came 5 METS, also within 238 Wing at Kabrit, and formed on 16 May. This was actually the ex-Torpedo Bombing School, which provided a six weeks course on torpedo bombing, employing a variety of aircraft, notably Beauforts, Wellington VIIIs, and ultimately Marauders, Beaufighters and Baltimores.

Friday, 1 May 1942

At 0040 Sqn Ldr Ward and two other pilots of 73 Squadron took off to carry out a night strafe of Barce. Arriving there at 0130, Ward spotted what he took to be a four-engined transport aircraft over the airfield and shot this down in flames. A Cant.Z.1007bis of 191ª Squadriglia had set off at 2100 to bomb Gambut and Menastir airfields, but on return from the sortie to Barce, the aircraft was attacked just before landing by a night fighter which was believed to be a Beaufighter, and the bomber was shot down at 0025 the next day. In practice this all seems to be the same combat, despite the very faulty aircraft recognition. During this attack, Flg Off Badger's Hurricane was hit in the wing by Flak and caught fire, but after ten minutes the flames subsided and he got back safely.

Soon after dawn 2 SAAF Squadron on a wing sweep near Bir Hacheim, fought briefly with three Bf 109s of I./JG 27, but neither unit suffered any loss. 208 Squadron, which had been off operations during April, returned to the front area, re-organised on a three-flight basis, one with eight Tomahawks, the other two with 12 Hurricane Is, three of which were unarmed photo-reconnaissance machines. The unit's duties were now specified as being tactical reconnaissance rather than army co-operation. Training continued and the unit was promised re-equipment with Kittyhawks, but in the event this never happened.

British Claims

73 Sqn	Sqn Ldr D.H.Ward	Hurricane IIc BN131 'P'	FW 200*	Barce	0130
2 SAAF Sqn	Lt T.V.de Villiers	Tomahawk IIb AK438 'O'	Bf 109F Damaged	Bir Hacheim-Gazala area	0910

*claimed thus, but almost certainly a Cant.Z.1007bis trimotor bomber

British Casualties

73 Sqn	Hurricane possibly BG867 badly damaged by Flak nr Barce; Flg Off J.J.Badger safe

Italian Casualties

191ª Sq, 86°Gr , 35°St BT	Cant.Z.1007bis MM 23386 shot down 0025 on 2 May by a night fighter, pilot S.Ten Paolo Bianchi, copilot Serg Giancarlo Rossi and engineer 1°av Giovanni Gambino KiA, two WiA

Saturday, 2 May 1942

Three Bf 109s escorted nine Bf 110s to strafe east of Segnali South. One Bf 110, apparently struck by ground fire, hit the ground and crashed, another at once landed alongside to pick up the crew.

Eleven MC.202s of 17° Gruppo took off at 1005 from Martuba to escort a lone Cant.Z.1007bis MM 24258 flown by Ten Enzo Antonozzi of 190ª Squadriglia on a photo-reconnaissance mission over the El Mtelin area.

British Casualties

112 Sqn	Kittyhawk I AK578 'V' damaged in combat Cat II; Plt Off F.F.J.Edwards safe
112 Sqn	Kittyhawk I AK957 'D' damaged in combat Cat II; Plt Off F.Knoll safe

German Casualties

III./ZG 26	Bf 110E-2 WNr 3733 crashed due to ground fire; crew picked up and rescued by another aircraft of the unit

Sunday, 3 May 1942

British Casualties

80 Sqn	Hurricane IIc BE360 collided with BE712 nr Gazala; Sgt R.H.Thomas KiA
80 Sqn	Hurricane IIc BE712 collided with BE360; Plt Off C.N.Maynard injured, then died or killed on a hospital ship 10 May 1942, DoI

Sunday-Wednesday, 3-6 May 1942

The weather was very bad, operations being severely curtailed.

Wednesday, 6 May 1942

238 and 274 Squadrons moved to Gambut, the former unit at last receiving Hurricane IIs. The British and Commonwealth forces were now building up ready for a new offensive which it was intended should be launched from the Gazala line during June. WDAF fighter strength particularly, was being augmented. On patrol during the afternoon, Capt Duncan of 5 SAAF Squadron intercepted and claimed to have probably destroyed a Ju 88 over a convoy north of Sidi Barrani. This may have been an aircraft of 1.(F)/122 which crash-landed at Trapani, Sicily.

British Claims

5 SAAF Sqn	Capt A.Duncan	Tomahwak IIb AN247 'K'	Ju 88 Probable	N Barrani over convoy	1445

Thursday, 7 May 1942

Two Tomahawks of 40 SAAF Squadron set off on a TacR sortie. Two MC.200s of 82ª Squadriglia, 13º Gruppo, also took off on an early morning reconnaissance of the Tengender-Segnali South area. While so involved, they were engaged by the two South African pilots and were both shot down, one pilot being killed and the other returning on foot.

Bf 109F WNr 8480 crash-landed near Tmimi by Lt Hans-Arnold 'Fifi' Stahlschmidt of 2./JG 27 on 7 May after being hit by ground fire.

In the evening six Kittyhawks of 3 RAAF Squadron and six of 112 Squadron were scrambled over Tobruk, then sweeping over the Axis lines. On return they were attacked by two Bf 109s of I./JG 27 which had taken off to intercept. Lt Stahlschmidt had got into a good position behind one of the Kittyhawks, when one of his guns blew up, damaging his engine. He fled, crash-landing near Tmimi where his Messerschmitt was burnt out. Sqn Ldr Gibbes, the Australian unit commander, and Plt Off Edwards of 112 Squadron each claimed a Messerschmitt shot down. Bobby Gibbes: "Two 109Es tried to attack us north of Bir Hacheim. A 112 pilot got one and the other was given to me. It seems that they both went down and were confirmed by the army. I didn't even claim it as damaged. Fired a couple of bursts at it and then forced it into a head-on. Last I saw it was going like hell in a dive towards its territory. Pilot must have died of fright!"

British Claims

40 SAAF Sqn	Lt E.I.H.Sturgeon *	Hurricane V7753	MC.200	Tengender	0700
40 SAAF Sqn	Lt W.J.Webb	Hurricane Z4643	MC.200	Tengender	0700
112 Sqn	Plt Off F.F.J.Edwards	Kittyahwk I AK787	Bf 109	W Tobruk	1800-2030
3 RAAF Sqn	Sqn Ldr R.H.Gibbes	Kittyhawk I AK874	Bf 109F	Gazala	1900

* Sturgeon 'weaver' to Webb on TacR

British Casualties

112 Sqn	Kittyhawk I AK762 GA-G struck by lightning on ground and burnt out

German Casualties

2./JG 27	Bf 109F-4 trop WNr 8480 combat with P-40s N Bir Hacheim, force-landed atTmimi where aircraft destroyed by fire; Lt Hans-Arnold Stahlschmidt safe

Italian Casualties

82ª Sq, 13°Gr, 2°St CT	MC.200 MM 4545, shot down by P-40 SW Segnali 0600, S.Ten Gilberto Cerofolini KiA
82ª Sq, 13°Gr, 2°St CT	MC.200 MM 5914, combat with P-40, force-landed SW Segnali 0600, Serg Giacomo Magnani returned

Friday, 8 May 1942

Two I./JG 27 Bf 109s flew a Freie Jagd in the Sidi Barrani area, meeting what they took to be a Beaufighter, and this was shot down by Lt von Lieres; this appears actually to have been a Maryland of 60 SAAF Squadron on a mapping sortie which was shot down by a Bf 109 soon after taking off. Two Tomahawk pilots of 5 SAAF Squadron were practising formation flying and shadow firing when they spotted a vertical column of smoke, obviously from the crashed Maryland, and were about to investigate when they were jumped by the two Messerschmitts, von Lieres shooting down one, which crash-landed; the second was also hit by cannon shells and the pilot was slightly wounded.

British Casualties

5 SAAF Sqn	Tomahawk IIb AN426 'R' damaged by Bf 109 when on training flight, crash-landed E LG.121 at 1215, Cat II; Lt R.L.Morrison
5 SAAF Sqn	Tomahawk IIb AN421 'Z' damaged by Bf 109 when on training flight; 15m SE Sidi Barrani and crash-landed; Capt L.C.Botha slt WiA
60 SAAF Sqn	Maryland AH366 shot down by Bf 109 soon after take-off

German Claims

2./JG 27	Lt Karl von Lieres und Wilkau	Beaufighter	Sidi Barrani	1104
2./JG 27	Lt Karl von Lieres und Wilkau	P-40	40km SSW Sidi Barrani	1114

German Casualties

2./LG 1	Ju 88A-4 WNr 149167 L1+PK shot down by AA and crashed in Qotaifiya area; Lt Hans-Joachim Migura and three MiA

Saturday, 9 May 1942

Between 0255-0530 three Cant.Z.1007bis of 86° Gruppo bombed the water reservoir and aqueduct south-west of Tobruk, claiming that the targets were hit.

In covering the withdrawal of Bostons which had been attacking shipping in Benghazi harbour, pilots of 12 Kittyhawks of 3 RAAF Squadron spotted a Bf 110 with a top cover of Bf 109Es almost certainly aircraft of 4.(H)/12. Sqn Ldr Gibbes attacked the Bf 110, claiming to have inflicted some damage before returning to base. Lt Jack Webb of 40 SAAF Squadron on a TacR had to crash-land in Axis-held territory.

British Claims

3 RAAF Sqn	Sqn Ldr R.H.Gibbes	Kittyhawk I AK874	Bf 110 Damaged	NW Bir Hacheim	1210

British Casualties

40 SAAF Sqn	Hurricane Z4703 shot down and crash-landed in flames deep in Axis territory, aircraft blew up; Lt W.J.Webb rescued

Sunday, 10 May 1942

40 SAAF Squadron was involved in action again when two of the unit's Hurricanes were intercepted near Martuba by a pair of I./JG 27 Bf 109s on a Freie Jagd. Oblt Marseille, newly-promoted, shot down both, one crashing and the other belly-landing; he then landed at his own base at 0930. This engagement was the first in North Africa for the Luftwaffe to be directed from a 'Freya' radar set. In the afternoon 250 Squadron suffered the first loss of one of its Kittyhawks when Sgt Tweedie, one of six pilots on a strafing mission, was shot down by Flak and killed.

During the day 94 Squadron received a great shock when ordered to pass all Kittyhawks to 2 SAAF Squadron and withdraw to the Delta area. Flt Lt J.E.A.Williams, Flt Sgt J.F.Edwards and five of the other more experienced pilots were posted to 260 Squadron. Having taken such a beating on both Hurricanes and Kittyhawks, 94 had, despite intensive retraining, still suffered losses which far outstripped claims. The unit was re-equipped with Hurricanes for patrol duties in the Eastern Mediterranean and later, over the Greek Aegean islands. However, it would be many months before it would return to front-line duties. In taking over this new equipment, 2 SAAF Squadron, which had carried the code letters TA on its Tomahawks, was now allocated DB. Similarly, when moving from Tomahawks to Kittyhawks in July, the 4 SAAF Squadron code would change from DX to KJ. On reverting to Hurricanes after passing

Martin Baltimore IIs of 55 Squadron; the aircraft in the foreground is AG781 'B'.

its Kittykawks to the South African unit meanwhile, 94 was changed from FZ to GO, and indeed at much the same time 260 Squadron changed from MF to HS.

Eighth Army and WDAF were now preparing for further intensive action, but so too were the Luftwaffe and the Regia Aeronautica. At this stage an additional 40 Ju 87s, 30 Bf 109s and 15 Bf 110s were despatched from Sicily to Africa, bringing Luftwaffe strength to some 260 aircraft. New Allied squadrons had also arrived, but these were mainly allocated to relieve more experienced units in the rear areas, freeing the latter for the front. 7 SAAF Squadron arrived from South Africa, being equipped with Hurricanes as the fifth pure fighter unit from the Union. The squadron was initially sent to Palestine where it was joined by 134 and 417 Squadrons from England – the latter the first unit of the Royal Canadian Air Force to reach the Middle East – but both squadrons at this stage were without aircraft.

As already described, 92 and 145 Squadrons had also been posted to North Africa, the latter with their Spitfires. 46 Squadron had been in the area for some months awaiting aircraft, its own Hurricanes having been delivered direct to Malta where they had remained and been renumbered as 126 Squadron (see *Malta: The Hurricane Years, 1940-41*). The ground party thus now formed the basis for the second Beaufighter night fighter squadron, moving to Edcu during May to begin operations.

6 Squadron, after months of relative inactivity, moved to Shandur to convert to Hurricane IId anti-tank aircraft which carried a 40mm gun firing armour-piercing ammunition, beneath each wing. The unit received a high-level visit at this time to advise the commanding officer that at least one flight was required to be fully trained and ready to move up to the front by the end of the month.

Two of the bomber units, 55 and 223 Squadrons, received new equipment in the form of the Martin Baltimore, a development of the already familiar Maryland. These aircraft, however, would be delayed in entering action fully due to considerable and on-going problems with their defensive armament. More details of these various units during the period when they were serving in the rear areas will be found in Chapter Three until such time as they moved forward into the battle area.

British Casualties

250 Sqn	Kittyhawk I AL111 left 1455, FTR from sweep near Barce – Flak; Sgt Tweedie KiA
40 SAAF Sqn	Hurricane; Capt D. Cobbledick shot down KiA
40 SAAF Sqn	Hurricane; Lt N.Flesker shot down PoW
	(aircraft were V7780 and Z4377)

German Claims

3./JG 27	Oblt Hans-Joachim Marseille	2 Hurricanes	25km SE Martuba	0913 & 0915

Monday, 11 May 1942

A lone Cant.Z.1007bis of 191[a] Squadriglia flown by Ten Aldo Ulmi, set off from Derna at 1410 on a photo-reconnaissance sortie over the Giarabub-Siwa area. Analysis of the photos taken showed a number of tents and about 80 vehicles around Giarabub which were interpreted as being units of the LRDG.

Tuesday, 12 May 1942

The day was marked by a WDAF offensive to intercept formations of Ju 52/3m transport aircraft carrying supplies and reinforcements from Crete to North Africa. Full details of this day's activities will be found in Chapter Three, as it involved operations considerably different to those being undertaken over the front, even though including certain of the same units. For that reason the claims and losses related to the units taking part are repeated here as well.

British Claims

250 Sqn	Sgt G.G.Buckland	Kittyhawk I AK825	Ju 52/3m	60m N Derna	0920
250 Sqn	Sgt G.G.Buckland	Kittyhawk I AK825	Ju 52/3m Damaged	60m N Derna	0920
250 Sqn	Sgt G.G.Buckland	Kittyhawk I AK825	Bf 110 Damaged	60m N Derna	0920
250 Sqn	Sqn Ldr M.T.Judd	Kittyhawk I AK911	2 Ju 52/3ms	65m N Derna	0920
252 Sqn	Flt Sgt R.Ivey	Beaufighter Ic T4831 'D'	2 Ju 52/3ms	55m from Derna	0920
252 Sqn	Flt Sgt R.Ivey	Beaufighter Ic T4831 'D'	Ju 52/3m Damaged	55m from Derna	0920
252 Sqn	Sqn Ldr A.G.Wincott	Beaufighter Ic T4881 'N'	2 Ju 52/3ms	55m from Derna	0920
252 Sqn	Sqn Ldr A.G.Wincott	Beaufighter Ic T4881 'N'	Ju 52/3m Damaged	55m from Derna	0920
239 Wg	Wg Cdr H.C.Mayers	Kittyhawk I AK890	Ju 52/3m	60m N Derna	0920
239 Wg	Wg Cdr H.C.Mayers	Kittyhawk I AK890	Ju 52/3m Damaged	60m N Derna	0920
250 Sqn	Flg Lt J.L.Waddy	Kittyhawk I AK846 'H'	2 Ju 52/3ms	70m N Derna	0930
250 Sqn	Flg Lt J.L.Waddy	Kittyhawk I AK846 'H'	2 Bf 110s	70m N Derna	0930
250 Sqn	Plt Off C.E.Casbolt	Kittyhawk I AK583	2 Ju 52/3ms	45m N Derna	0930
250 Sqn	Sgt L.J.Devlin	Kittyhawk I AK953 'M'	2 Ju 52/3ms	45m N Derna	0930

British Casualties

252 Sqn	Beaufighter IIc T5028 shot down while attacking Ju 52/3ms off Derna; Sgt R.A.Cripps /Sgt T.Bateman KiA
250 Sqn	Kittyhawk I AK918 badly damaged by return fire from Ju 52/3ms N Derna; Plt Off W.J.Whitside safe

German Claims

7./ZG 26	Uffz Julius Baumann	Hurricane	0840

German Casualties

7./ZG 26	Bf 110C-4 WNr 3277 shot down by P-40 70km N Derna; Uffz Julius Baumann and bordfunker WiA
8 Ju 52/3ms	see Chapter Three
Wüstenotstaffel	Fi 156C-3 WNr 5591 crashed to sea 80km N Derna for u/k reason, Hptm Heinz Kroseberg/Uffz Walter Büchner MiA

Wednesday, 13 May 1942

Twelve Kittyhawks of 3 RAAF Squadron were scrambled on an interception patrol over El Adem, but were then ordered to Bir Hacheim. A further vector to Gazala followed, where they were bounced by two Bf 109s of I./JG 27, Oblt Marseille shooting down two of them in flames, one pilot being killed and the other baling out, slightly wounded. The dead pilot, Flg Off Pace, was found to have been killed by a single bullet that had passed vertically through the top of his cockpit canopy. Marseille's own aircraft was hit in the oil tank and propeller by fire from Chinchen's Kittyhawk.

British Claims

3 RAAF Sqn	Flg Off G.T.Chinchen	Kittyhawk I AK854	Bf 109F Damaged	Gazala	1105

British Casualties

3 RAAF Sqn	Kittyhawk I AL172 shot down by Bf 109s nr Gazala 1100; Flg Off H.G.Pace KiA
3 RAAF Sqn	Kittyhawk I AK855 shot down in flames by Bf 109s nr Gazala 1100; Sgt C.S.McDiarmid baled out, slt WiA

German Claims

3./JG 27	Oblt Hans-Joachim Marseille	2 P-40s	16km SE Gazala & 14km ESE Gazala Bay	1010 & 1015

German Casualties

3./JG 27	BF 109F-4 slt damaged in combat with P-40s, Oblt Hans-Joachim Marseille safe

Thursday, 14 May 1942

238 Squadron, re-equipped with Hurricane IIbs, moved to LG.121 at Sidi Barrani as part of 234 Wing. A Cant.Z.1007bis of 191ª Squadriglia flown by Ten Generali, took off from Gialo where it had landed on the previous day. As Generali headed back for Derna, he ran out of fuel and had to force-land 40km east of Marada. The aircraft would be recovered two days later when Cap Vecellio-Reane sighted the lost aircraft and landed alongside, slightly damaging his own aircraft in doing so. He therefore refuelled Generali's aircraft from his own and flew it back to Barce.

British Casualties	
40 SAAF Sqn	Hurricane 2627, unspecified enemy action, force-landed out of fuel; Lt D.F.Acutt

Friday, 15 May 1942

274 Squadron despatched eight Hurricanes to escort two TacR aircraft over the front. Due to the recent heavy losses suffered by the TacR units, it had been decided that in future these aircraft should receive a fighter escort again whenever possible. This was the first such occasion for the new policy, but in this case it was intense Flak which was encountered near Bir Hacheim, damage causing Sgt Dodds to force-land and inflicting damage on a second Hurricane. Later in the day six Kittyhawks of 250 Squadron strafed the Derna-Barce road, but during this sortie Plt Off Copeland also force-landed due to Flak damage, returning on 17 May.

Regia Aeronautica units were on the move, 150° Gruppo withdrawing from Martuba to Benghazi K3, committed mainly to harbour defence. The unit's place nearer the front would be taken by 8° Gruppo, also equipped with MC.200s. At the same time 158° Gruppo Assalto, led by Cap Alessandro Cerutti (236ª, 387ª and 388ª Squadriglie), equipped with CR.42s, moved from Sorman to K3. Ghiblis of 12ª Squadriglia APC were active searching for the force-landed 191ª Squadriglia Cant.Z.1007bis in the desert. Next day this unit would move to Agedabia.

British Casualties	
250 Sqn	Kittyhawk I AL104 left 1520, shot down by Flak, Derna-Barce flew back two days later; Plt Off P. Copeland safe
274 Sqn	Hurricane II force-landed, Flak; Sgt J.Dodds
274 Sqn	Hurricane II damaged by fighter; Sgt T.B.Hamilton

Saturday, 16 May 1942

40 SAAF Squadron experienced its first full escort when six Tomahawks of 4 SAAF Squadron accompanied one of its own aircraft over the front. On this date 112 Squadron became the first Kittybomber unit when Flt Lt Bartle led six bomb-carrying aircraft to attack Tmimi. During the day also 5 SAAF Squadron arrived at LG.115, Gasr el Arid, to join 233 Wing, moving into 94 Squadron's old dispersal area. The other members of the wing were now 260 and 2 SAAF Squadrons with Kittyhawks, and 4 SAAF Squadron, which like 5 SAAF, still flew Tomahawks.

At 1810 12 Kittyhawks of 3 RAAF Squadron and nine of 450 Squadron were scrambled to patrol over the Gazala area where they were attacked by three Bf 109s. These aircraft were from I./JG 27 and had taken off a little earlier for a Freie Jagd four-strong; one had returned early. Seeing the 3 RAAF aircraft at 1905, flying at 16,000 feet, Oblt Marseille dived on them, but was attacked by six. He broke away and climbed up behind the other six, shooting down Sgt Teede in a sharp turn to port; Teede crash-landed on fire west of El Adem.

Marseille pulled up again as he was once more attacked by six Kittyhawks, circling this formation and making a series of short diving attacks without result. By this time the Kittyhawks were down to about 1,900 feet, and he then shot down the leading aircraft of a flight of four from 450 Squadron at 1915 while in a wide turn to port. The pilot baled out, his falling aircraft striking another which crashed. Marseille was already on his way back to base and failed to see this, claiming only two victories.

British Casualties	
260 Sqn	Kittyhawk I AK693 shot down by Flak; Wt Off J.S.E.M.Bernier safe
3 RAAF Sqn	Kittyhawk I AL120 shot down by Bf 109, crash-landed about 1815, 12m W El Adem; Sgt E.V.Teede safe
450 Sqn	Kittyhawk I AK604 crashed during combat when aircraft hit by another Kittyhawk which had been abandoned due to battle damage; Sgt W.K.Metherall KiA

450 Sqn	Kittyhawk I AK697 shot down by Bf 109 2m E Acroma; Plt Off F.E.Parker baled, WiA			
94 Sqn	Kittyhawk I AK777 lost			
208 Sqn	Tomahawk IIb AK446 lost			
208 Sqn	Hurricane Z4872 lost			
274 Sqn	Hurricane II Z5435 lost			
German Claims				
3./JG 27	Oblt Hans-Joachim Marseille	2 P-40s	20km E Ain el Gazala & 3km E Fort Acroma	1805 & 1815

Sunday, 17 May 1942

250 Squadron welcomed back one of its pilots, Sgt Baron, who had been shot down four and a half months previously. 208 Squadron moved from Ismailia to Sidi Aziez to resume operations with one flight of Tomahawks and two of Hurricanes.

Monday, 18 May 1942

Early in the day six Kittybombers of 112 Squadron, covered by four more in fighter mode, undertook a bombing and strafing attack during which Plt Off Fisher was shot down in flames by Flak, while Sgt Davey crashed near Bir Temrad. Sgt Drew hit the ground with his propeller and force-landed 12 miles south of Gambut; Flak crews claimed two P-40s shot down. Two hours later six Bf 109s of newly-formed 10.(Jabo)/JG 27 attacked a tented camp east of the El Adem-Tobruk road. Lt Weinfurtner failed to return, ditching in the sea and drowning.

Two RAF squadrons received new commanders during the day. Sqn Ldr G.V.W.Kettlewell, a Greek campaign veteran, was now replaced as leader of 213 Squadron by Sqn Ldr M.H.Young, DFC, recently a flight commander in 73 Squadron and in 1940 a Defiant pilot in the Battle of Britain. 33 Squadron was taken over by Sqn Ldr J.E.Proctor, DFC, another Battle of Britain pilot who already had some 12 victories to his credit.

British Casualties		
112 Sqn	Kittyhawk I AK763 shot down by Flak during ground attack; Plt Off J.R.Fisher KiA	
112 Sqn	Kittyhawk I AK766 damaged by Flak during ground attack; Plt Off W.A.J.Johnston safe	
112 Sqn	Kittyhawk I AK994 shot down over Temrad during ground attack; Sgt J.V.Davey MiA	
112 Sqn	Kittyhawk I AK906 force-landed near Gambut; Sgt R.A.Drew safe	
80 Sqn	Hurricane II BE973, crashed on take-off; Sgt G.D.Nicholls KiFA	
German Claims		
Flak		2 P-40s

Tuesday, 19 May 1942

At 0715 nine Kittyhawks of 450 Squadron carried out a patrol near Gazala. Two aircraft returned early, the others splitting up into two sections of three and four respectively. At 0820 Oblt Marseille and his wingman on a Freie Jagd, dived on the smaller section, hitting one Kittyhawk which fell out of the formation, damaged in wing and rudder, and force-landed at Gambut Main. The second aircraft in the formation tried to engage, but fell into a spin, recovered in cloud, but thereby left Sgt Young alone. The intrepid Young climbed after the attackers to 20,000 feet where both Messerschmitts turned on him, so he dived for the clouds. However, Marseille put a burst into his engine, which stopped. Young weaved and crash-landed, his aircraft being shot-up on the ground by the German pilots and burnt out. Young evacuated the aircraft safely and was picked up by the army, returning safely to Gambut.

British Casualties				
450 Sqn	Kittyhawk I AK842 shot down by Bf 109 3m S Acroma, crash-landed, strafed and destroyed; Sgt I.C. Young safe			
450 Sqn	Kittyhawk I AK993 damaged by Bf 109, force-landed near Gazala; Sgt E.P.Oakley safe			
German Claims				
3./JG 27	Oblt Hans-Joachim Marseille	2 P-46s	8km SW & 5km S Fort Acroma	0720 & 0730

Wednesday, 20 May 1942

This day saw the return of III./JG 53 to Martuba from Sicily and Crete, and Maj Gerlitz was posted from JG 27 to command this unit. With his departure, Hptm Rödel took over command of II./JG 27, Oblt Düllberg becoming the Geschwader Adjutant. At this stage the Staffelkapitäne of III./JG 53 were Oblt Franz Götz (33 victories) 9.Staffel, Hptm Helmut Belser (32 victories) 8.Staffel, and Oblt Wilfried Pufahl (ten victories) 7.Staffel.

Thursday, 21 May 1942

Nine Kittyhawks of 260 Squadron carried out a sweep from 0735 to cover returning SAAF bombers in the Tmimi-Gazala area. Here the unit attacked two Bf 109s of JG 27's Geschwaderstab to the east of Tmimi, Fw Gromotka crash-landing. 33 Squadron flew an escort to a pair of TacR aircraft, but over Bir Hacheim the unit's new commanding officer, Sqn Ldr Proctor, was hit by Flak and force-landed.

British Claims					
260 Sqn	Flt Lt T.Hindle	Kittyhawk I	Bf 109F	Tmimi-Gazala area	0735-0850
British Casualties					
33 Sqn	Hurricane IIb Z5065 force-landed due to Flak Bir Hacheim; Sqn Ldr J.E.Proctor safe				
112 Sqn	Kittyhawk I AK766 DBR by a shell during ground attack sortie (this appears to have been the aircraft damaged by Flak three days earlier)				
German Casualties					
6./JG 27	Bf 109F-4 WNr 7410 combat with P-40 E Tmimi, force-landed nr Gazala 100%; Fw Fritz Gromotka safe				

Friday, 22 May 1942

The Luftwaffe's fighters now began operating from Tmimi as well as Martuba, and activity on both sides increased as each opponent strove to be ready, each being well aware that the other was fast approaching readiness to launch a new offensive.

At 0730 on this date 12 Kittyhawks from 250 Squadron with others of 112 Squadron, escorted nine Bostons of 24 SAAF Squadron, now back on operations, to bomb the familiar targets at Martuba. At the same time 12 3 RAAF Squadron fighters with 260 Squadron as close cover and 450 Squadron higher up, carried out a freelance bomber escort as a diversion to the main thrust. Around much the same time four Bf 109s of II./JG 27 had commenced a Freie Jagd, and these encountered the diversionary formation, diving on the top cover and shooting down two Australian Kittyhawks 30 miles east of Tmimi, also damaging two more; three claims were made by the Germans, all for aircraft reported to have crashed into the sea. Two Bf 109s were claimed in return by pilots of 3 RAAF and one probable by 450 Squadron; no losses were recorded by the Luftwaffe on this occasion.

Sqn Ldr Gibbes:

> "Were attacked by four 109s over Gulf of Bomba. Got split up and didn't carry out original job. Two 109s attacked top cover and two attacked by section. Attacks nicely executed. Subsequently, attacks rather weak and showed pilots of 109s to be very inexperienced. Got shot at one 109 which attacked 'Yellow 2' (Sgt Thomas). Pulled round and got a good burst into it. Later Sgt Kildey confirmed it for me. I didn't even claim it as damaged as I did not know if I hit it. Out-dived two 109s and got a burst into each. Didn't observe results as was busy clearing own tail. Formation by this time split up, so climbed to 15,000 feet over Gazala and joined bombers on their way home."

Meanwhile from Martuba eight Messerschmitts of I.Gruppe and three of III.Gruppe plus six MC.202s of 17° Gruppo scrambled, attacking 112 and 250 Squadrons, the German pilots claiming six Curtiss fighters plus one unconfirmed; two were actually lost by 112 Squadron and one from 250 Squadron was damaged, crash-landing on return. During the return flight Flg Off Waddy claimed one Messerschmitt shot down. The Italian pilots were able only to claim damage to one of the Bostons on this occasion. One III.Gruppe Bf 109 was lost during the day, the pilot baling out south of Martuba following engine failure, while a Bf 110 of 4.(H)/12 crash-landed at Martuba, suffering 40% damage. A Ju 88 of 5./LG 1 was shot down by AA over the Mersa Matruh area.

Somewhat later in the morning a lone MC.202 of 79ª Squadriglia flown by Serg Magg Amedeo Benati scrambled at 1005 to intercept a reconnaissance aircraft sighted over Benghazi. Catching this, he identified it as a Blenheim which he claimed to have shot down 30km off the coast (see also Chapter Three).

Bf 109F 'White 11' of 4./JG 27 with the Staffel emblem beneath the cockpit and that of II Gruppe on the nose.

Barce received reinforcements for its resident Cant.Z.1007bis when 15 more of these aircraft arrived, led by the 35° Stormo BT commander, Col Bruno Borghetti. These were aircraft of 95° Gruppo (Magg Pietro Zigiotti) comprising 230ª and 231ª Squadriglie led by Cap Augusto Fusco and Cap Francesco Casadio respectively.

British Claims

3 RAAF Sqn	Flt Lt A.W.Barr	Kittyhawk I AL199	Bf 109F	Gulf of Bomba	0825
3 RAAF Sqn	Sqn Ldr R.H.Gibbes	Kittyhawk I AK874	Bf 109F	Gulf of Bomba	0825
250 Sqn	Sgt J.A.Seabrook	Kittyhawk I AK704 'S'	Bf 109 Damaged	SW Tmimi	0910
250 Sqn	Flg Off J.L.Waddy	Kittyhawk I AK846 'H'	Bf 109	SW Tmimi	0910

British Casualties

450 Sqn	Kittyhawk I AK634 shot down by Bf 109s 5m S Gazala; Sgt E.J.Quirk MiA
450 Sqn	Kittyhawk I AK717 shot down by Bf 109 3m S Ras el Tin; Sgt A.L.Williams KiA
450 Sqn	Kittyhawk I AK981 force-landed at Gambut; Sgt I.A.Nursey safe
450 Sqn	Kittyhawk I AK702 'P' crashed into 40 SAAF Hurricane on landing at El Adem; Plt Off J.T. Bell safe
450 Sqn	Kittyhawk I AK998 force-landed after combat at Gambut Main; Flt Lt I.F. Rose safe
112 Sqn	Kittyhawk I AK787 FTR, presumed shot down by Bf 109 near Bomba at 0840; Plt Off K.C.Gundry KiA
112 Sqn	Kittyhawk I AK908 damaged Cat II by Bf 109 near Martuba; Flg Off F.Knoll safe
250 Sqn	Kittyhawk I AL116 'V' damaged by Bf 109, force-landed at Gambut Main 0930; Plt Off M.Rogerson safe
335 Sqn	Hurricane Z41101 ditched off El Daba
40 SAAF	Hurricane damaged by collision with shot-up Kittyhawk

German Claims

4./JG 27	Obfw Karl-Heinz Bendert	P-40	30km E Tmimi	0733
4./JG 27	Uffz Heinrich Steis	P-40	30km E Tmimi	0736
1./JG 27	Hptm Ludwig Franzisket	P-40	20km E Derna	0741
4./JG 27	Obfw Karl-Heinz Bendert	P-40	3km N Ain el Gazala	0745
1./JG 27	Fw Günther Steinhausen	P-46	20km S Martuba	0750
2./JG 27	Lt Hans-Arnold Stahlschmidt	P-40	SW Tmimi	0750
2./JG 27	Lt Karl von Lieres und Wilkau	P-40	S Tmimi	0751
1,/JG 27	Hptm Ludwig Franzisket	P-40	S Tmimi	0751
9./JG 27	Obfw Heinrich Rosenberg	P-40	10km S Martuba l.g.	0755
2./JG 27	Lt Karl von Lieres und Wilkau	P-40 o.Zg.	20km W Fort Acroma	0756

German Casualties

8./JG 27	Bf 109F-4 WNr 8723 crashed S Martuba due to engine failure; Uffz Gerhard Sdun baled, safe
4.(H)/12	Bf 110E-2 WNr 4427 crash-landed Martuba, 40% damaged; crew safe
5./LG 1	Ju 88A-4 WNr 5603 L1+LN shot down by AA Mersa Matruh; Fw Bruno Scharnowski KiA, three crew PoW

Italian Claims

72ª Sq,17°Gr, 1°St CT	Cap Pio Tomaselli	MC.202	Boston Damaged	Martuba	0745-0900
79ª Sq, 6°Gr, 1°St CT	Serg Magg Amedeo Benati	MC.202	Blenheim	30km off Benghazi	1005-1035

Italian Casualties

77ª Sq, 13°Gr, 2° St CT	MC.200 MM 7678 destroyed by bombs at night at Martuba
82ª Sq, 13°Gr, 2° St CT	MC.200 MM 7683 destroyed by bombs at night at Martuba
78ª Sq, 13°Gr, 2° St CT	5 MC.200s MM 8204, 8300, 5305, 8303, 8294 damaged by bombs at Martuba
Unidentified unit	2 CR.42s destroyed by bombs at Martuba, one damaged

Saturday, 23 May 1942

During a busy day six separate engagements took place, these involving in the main the Bf 109s of II./JG 27. This unit submitted a considerable number of claims, some of which have defied attempts to verify.

At 0815 80 Squadron's Hurricanes took off to patrol over El Adem, as a number of Kittyhawks were refuelling there. They were jumped by four Bf 109s of II.Gruppe on a Freie Jagd, two of them being shot down in flames, both crashing near Tobruk with one more crash-landing. About an hour later four more of this Gruppe's Messerschmitts attacked Hurricanes of 33 Squadron as these were patrolling over a convoy, claiming three which were confirmed plus one probable. However, the latter was credited to the pilot of a 6º Gruppo MC.202, four of this unit's aircraft having scrambled from Martuba and become engaged in this combat. Oblt Rödel, who made two of the claims, reported that he had shot down the leader of the British formation which went into the sea, seeing the pilot swimming away. This would appear to have been Flt Lt Wade who had been leading the 33 Squadron patrol; his was one of two of this unit's Hurricanes which failed to return. This was D.P.Wade not to be confused with Lance Wade who also served with this unit. Six more Bf 109s had followed Rödel's Schwarme a few minutes later, and one of the pilots of these, Obfw Bendert, claimed a fighter in flames ten miles south of Gazala, reporting that another disappeared into cloud trailing black smoke. Almost needless to say, in every case II.Gruppe identified its opponents as P-40s. Only the Italian pilot correctly claimed his victim as a Hurricane.

An hour later eight Bf 109s of I.Gruppe were scrambled, intercepting the Baltimore bombers of 223 Squadron on their first operational flight. These were incorrectly identified as Douglas DB-7s (i.e. Bostons). As with every new light or medium bomber to arrive in the Middle East, the Baltimores were sent out initially without fighter escort – the authorities had apparently still not accepted the lesson that in daylight and where fighter opposition could be expected, bombers must be escorted. On this occasion four Baltimores had been despatched to bomb Baheira satellite airfield, and one of them had lagged behind. This was caught north of Acroma by Hptm Homuth and was badly shot-up. The pilot turned back and just managed to crash-land it at base where the crew reported that the .30in rear machine guns had failed to operate. The Messerschmitts had immediately attacked the other three bombers, the rear guns of which all failed at the crucial moment, allowing the fighters to press home their attacks from 50-75 yards. Oblt Marseille shot down two in three minutes, and two minutes later the survivor was shot down by Obfw Mentnich. Two of the Baltimores fell in flames, the third crash-landing at Bir el Gobi. The surviving crew members claimed that one Bf 109 had been shot down by 'scare' guns fixed in the rear of the engine nacelles, although in the circumstances this was rather unlikely. Following this disastrous mission, Baltimores, like Bostons, were always escorted on day raids and the American .30in Browning machine guns in the dorsal and ventral gunners' positions were replaced with British .303in weapons.

In the meantime a further four II.Gruppe Bf 109s had taken off, Uffz Gierster claiming a fighter shot down, and Fw Reuter on his second sortie of the morning, claiming two, all three being claimed to have fallen into the sea near Tobruk. Eleven Kittyhawks of 2 SAAF Squadron escorted Bostons to attack airfields at Derna, but were attacked by a number of Bf 109s during the return journey. Lt Bryant lost formation and was attacked and his aircraft badly damaged by four Messerschmitts. He thought he had shaken them off when he spotted a truckload of soldiers waving frantically; looking round, he found a 109 on his tail. He turned sharply, flew through the fire of some British AA guns, and reached his airfield safely. The time of this engagement indicates that he was probably attacked by the II./JG 27 quartette mentioned.

During the day 80 Squadron, joined by two Hurricanes of 274 Squadron, provided escort to two 40 SAAF Squadron TacR aircraft over the front. Here Sgt Cormack's aircraft was damaged by an enemy fighter and he crash-landed at El Adem. However, Col Biden, flying one of the reconnaissance aircraft, claimed to have probably shot down an MC.202. He was probably engaged with aircraft from 6º Gruppo, eight of which had scrambled at 1040, led by Cap Giuliano Giacomelli, one pilot claiming damage to a fighter – identified as a P-40, of course!

During the afternoon four more II.Gruppe Messerschmitts were scrambled, attacking seven Kittyhawks of 450 Squadron which were escorting two more TacR Hurricanes over II.Gruppe's own airfield at Tmimi. At first there was no result arising from the general dogfight which ensued until Uffz Gierster, on his second sortie, claimed one victory south-east of Gadd el Ahmar, before being shot down himself and baling out, pilots of 450 Squadron claiming two Bf 109s destroyed. The Australians suffered no losses during this engagement.

WDAF bombing raids had achieved some success during this rather costly day, a Ju 88 of IV./LG 1 being destroyed at Berka airfield with a 1./StG 3 Ju 87 suffering a similar fate at Derna.

British Claims

260 Sqn	Flt Sgt T. Hindle	Kittyhawk I	Bf 110 Damaged	Martuba	0935-1100
450 Sqn	Flt Sgt D.H.McBurnie	Kittyhawk I AK998	Bf 109	20m S Tmimi	1530-1945
450 Sqn	Flt Sgt I.A.Nursey	Kittyhawk I AK606	Bf 109E	20m S Tmimi	1530-1945
40 SAAF	Lt Col E.A.Biden	Hurricane	MC.202 Probable	Segnali	1700-1815

British Casualties

223 Sqn	Baltimore I AG703 badly damaged, crash-landed at LG.170 at 1225, Plt Off D.G.W.Leakem RAAF and one safe, two WiA
223 Sqn	Baltimore I AG708 shot down by Bf 109s; Flg Off L.W.Bangley and three KiA
223 Sqn	Baltimore I AG717 shot down by Bf 109s; Sgt H.C.Horsfield and three KiA
223 Sqn	Baltimore II AG762 attacked by Bf 109s and badly damaged. Returned to LG.167 but w/o on 25th
33 Sqn	Hurricane IIb BG923 'Z' dived into ground and blew up after attack by Bf 109; Flt Lt D.P.Wade KiA
33 Sqn	Hurricane IIb Z5654 'T' badly damaged by Bf 109 N Ras el Tin; Sgt H.M.Laflamme safe
80 Sqn	Hurricane IIc BE339 shot down by Bf 109s near El Adem, 0930; Sgt Cormack safe
80 Sqn	Hurricane IIc BE707 'B' FTR from escort to Tmimi 0930; Flt Sgt W.R.Scott KiA
80 Sqn	Hurricane IIc BM974 shot down, crash-landed 0930; Sgt J.J.V.Howard KiA
2 SAAF Sqn	Kittyhawk I AK963 'K' badly damaged by four Bf 109s, 1030, Cat II; Lt P.D.Bryant safe

German Claims

5./JG 27	Fw Horst Reuter	P-40	10km NW El Adem	0835
5./JG 27	Lt Kurt Jenisch	2 P-40s	10km NW & 5km NE El Adem	0836 & 0839
Stab II./JG 27	Oblt Gustav Rödel	2 P-40s	10km N & 40km NE Ras el Tin	0940, 0947
Stab II./JG 27	Obfhr Willy Kientsch	P-40	10km N Ras el Tin	0940
Stab II./JG 27	Obfhr Willy Kientsch	P-40 n.b.	3km NE Ain el Gazala	0955
5./JG 27	Uffz Helmut Gierster	P-40	5km SE Tobruk	1105
4./JG 27	Obfw Karl-Heinz Bendert	P-40	5km S Ain el Gazala	1005
3./JG 27	Oblt Hans-Joachim Marseille	2 Douglas DB-7s	3 & 4km SE Tobruk harbour	1105 &1106
3./JG 27	Obfw Karl Mentnich	Douglas DB-7	SE Tobruk harbour	1108
5./JG 27	Fw Horst Reuter	2 P-40s	2km NE & 19km E Tobruk harbour	1113 &1116
3./JG 27	Hptm Gerhard Homuth	Douglas DB-7	N Fort Acroma	1118
5./JG 27	Uffz Helmut Gierster	P-40	15km SE Gadd el Ahmar	1652

German Casualties

5./JG 27	Bf 109F-4 WNr 7390 Black 5 shot down by P-40 1655 SE Gadd el Ahmar; Uffz Helmut Gierster baled, WiA
6./LG 1	Ju 88A-4 WNr 5633 L1+BP shot down by fighters Alexandria; Oblt Otto Obernhuber and three MiA
12./LG 1	Ju 88A-4 WNr 5728 destroyed on ground by bombs at Berka
1./StG 3	Ju 87R-4 WNr 6240 destroyed on ground by bombs at Derna

Italian Claims

81ª Sq, 6°Gr, 1°St CT	Serg Magg Luigi Morosi	MC.202	Hurricane	Ain el Gazala	0925-1020
81ª Sq, 6°Gr, 1°St CT	Ten Antonio Palazzeschi	MC.202	P-40 Damaged	Ain el Gazala	1040-1145

Sunday, 24 May 1942

It was obvious that the Axis forces were going to beat 8th Army 'to the punch', and attack somewhere along the line. At this critical moment 145 Squadron was ordered to move its Spitfires forward to Gambut. Axis reinforcement was proceeding apace, for on the evening of this day the 54 MC.202s of 4° Stormo CT, which had been operating over Malta, arrived at Martuba, led by T Col Armando François. They joined 1° Stormo, forming a force of more than 100 MC.202s, the largest concentration of these fighters ever to be achieved in Libya. Meanwhile 50° Stormo Assalto moved to Derna's El Fteiah airfield, ready for operations. This latter Stormo was newly-established under T Col Ferruccio Vosilla with the arrival of 159° Gruppo (389ª, 390ª and 391ª Squadriglie) to join 158° Gruppo, both units equipped with CR.42s fitted as fighter-bombers. Vosilla had previously commanded 18° Gruppo CT which had taken part in the Italian expeditionary force in Belgium during autumn 1940 for operations over England.

A patrol of MC.202s of 96ª Squadriglia, 9° Gruppo, 4° Stormo CT in flight. In the foreground is '96-8' MM 7927.

Next day a Comando Caccia (Fighter Command) would be established at Martuba under the 1° Stormo commander, Col Alfredo Reglieri, to co-ordinate the activities of the four MC.202-equipped units:

6° Gruppo (1° Stormo)	Magg Mario Larcher
17° Gruppo (1° Stormo)	Magg Domenico Sciaudone
9° Gruppo (4° Stormo)	Magg Antonio Larsimont-Pergameni
10° Gruppo (4° Stormo)	Magg Paolo Maddalena

The three squadriglie of newly arrived 9° Gruppo were led by S.Ten Alvaro Querci (73ª), Cap Ezio Viglione-Borghese (96ª) and S.Ten Jacopo Frigerio (97ª), who would be replaced by Ten Fernando Malvezzi on 1 June. The commanders of the three squadriglie of 10° Gruppo were Cap Franco Lucchini (84ª), Cap Ranieri Piccolomini (90ª) and Ten Orlando Mandolini (91ª).

For the Luftwaffe, the whole of III./ZG 26 had now gathered in Libya where the unit would remain until 4 August. With StG 3 and 12./LG 1, the three units now formed a special task force known as Gefechtsverband Sigel.

British Casualties	
73 Sqn	Hurricane IIc BD774 shot down by Flak at night in Tmimi area; Plt Off J.Beaumont MiA
German Casualties	
1./LG 1	Ju 88A-4 WNr 5553 L1+GH shot down by fighters, crashed nr Bir el Abd; Lt Hetterich and 3 MiA
III./ZG 26	Bf 110F-2 WNr 4543 3U+BD crashed W Benghazi during recce off Great Sirte; Lt Helmut Scheid and 2 MiA

German Casualties

KGrzbV102	Ju 52/3m WNr 6809, destroyed by own forces in the desert

Italian Casualties

82ª Sq, 13°Gr, 2°St CT	MC.200 MM 5911 damaged by bombs at Martuba
78ª Sq, 13°Gr, 2°St CT	3 MC.200s slightly damaged by bombs at Martuba

Monday, 25 May 1942

Early in the morning Flt Sgt Comfort of 80 Squadron escorted Lt Nichol of 40 SAAF Squadron on a sortie over Tmimi where they were attacked by four Bf 109s of II./JG 27 and both shot down, one in flames by Lt Jenisch and one crash-landed by Fw Niederhöfer.

In the later afternoon 12 Hurricanes of 274 Squadron were scrambled over Tobruk and then flew to Gazala where they were engaged in a dogfight in which Flt Lt Playford was shot down, crash-landing with slight wounds. Their opponents appear to have been ten MC.202s of 6° Gruppo (four of 79ª Squadriglia and six of 88ª Squadriglia) which were on a free sweep over the Ain el Gazala-Bir Hacheim area. South-east of Gazala a formation identified as 20 P-40s were seen at lower level and were bounced. The Macchi pilots reported what appeared to be a very successful attack, claiming nine of the British fighters shot down and others damaged for no loss. This does seem to have been a case of quite massive overclaiming, for the only WDAF unit which appears to have been involved was 274 Squadron and that unit suffered only the one loss. The Hurricane pilots took this attack to have been by Bf 109s, claiming one probable and two damaged in return.

One of the first of the new Spitfire Vs to reach Egypt. The aircraft carries a single number at this stage, prior to receiving squadron code letters.

Allied bombing of the Axis airfields had achieved a fair amount of success during the day, two Bf 109s being damaged at Martuba, with one more destroyed at Tmimi where another also suffered damage. Three MC.202s were also destroyed at Martuba.

Sqn Ldr B.Drake, DFC, arrived to take over command of 112 Squadron as Sqn Ldr C.R.Caldwell was being posted to England to convert to Spitfires before going home to Australia to lead a wing of these aircraft in the war with Japan. Awarded DFC & Bar during his tour as well as achieving very rapid promotion and gaining the nickname 'Killer', he had claimed 20 German and Italian aircraft shot down and one more shared – the highest total for any Allied pilot while operating over the Western Desert. His successor, Billy Drake, had flown in France with 1 Squadron and in the later stages of the Battle of Britain. He had claimed seven and two shared aircraft shot down by this time and would rapidly prove to be a worthy replacement for Caldwell, becoming one of the most successful RAF fighter pilots in the Mediterranean theatre.

British Claims

73 Sqn	Flg Off J.F.Pain	Hurricane IIc BM157	MC.200 Damaged	8-10m NE Tmimi	2110
274 Sqn	Plt Off C.D.A.Browne	Hurricane IIc	Bf 109 Damaged	Gazala	1705-
274 Sqn	Flt Lt G.C.Keefer	Hurricane IIc BE229 'S'	Bf 109 Probable	Gazala	1705-
274 Sqn	Plt Off F.B.Samuel	Hurricane IIc	Bf 109 Damaged	Gazala	1705-

British Casualties

73 Sqn	Hurricane BD774 lost to Flak; left at 2250 on the 24th for Tmimi; Plt Off J.Beaumont MiA
40 SAAF Sqn	Hurricane Z4033 shot down over Tmimi by 4 Bf 109s; Lt B.H. Nichol KiA and also pilot of 80 Sqn escorting
80 Sqn	Hurricane IIc BN413 left 0745, shot down by Bf 109 12m E Tmimi; Flt Sgt A.C.Comfort MiA
274 Sqn	Hurricane II BE398 damaged by Flak 15m SE El Alamein, crash-landed; Flt Lt B.H.A.Playford WiA
450 Sqn	Kittyhawk I AL217 force-landed Bir el Baheira, DBR; Sgt J.D.Gleeson safe

German Claims

5./JG 27	Lt Kurt Jenisch	P-40	20km E Tmimi	0725
5./JG 27	Fw Hans Niederhöfer	P-40	20km E Tmimi	0725

German Casualties

Stab/JG 27	Bf 109F-4 trop WNr 10191 50% damaged by bombs at Martuba
4./JG 27	Bf 109F-4 trop WNr 10044 destroyed by bombs on ground at Tmimi
4./JG 27	Bf 109E-4 trop WNr 8432 25% damaged by bombs on ground at Tmimi
9./JG 27	Bf 109F-4 trop WNr 8557 40% damaged by bombs on ground at Martuba

Italian Claims

79ª Sq, 6°Gr, 1°St CT	Cap Domenico Camarda	MC.202	P-40	SE Ain el Gazala	1620-1740
79ª Sq, 6°Gr, 1°St CT	S.Ten Adelmo Ferrazza	MC.202	P-40	SE Ain el Gazala	1620-1740
79ª Sq, 6°Gr, 1°St CT	Serg Ercole Paroli	MC.202	P-40	SE Ain el Gazala	1620-1740
88ª Sq, 6°Gr, 1°St CT	M.llo Gianlino Baschirotto	MC.202	2 P-40s	SE Ain el Gazala	1620-1740
88ª Sq, 6°Gr, 1°St CT	S.Ten Alfredo Civetta	MC.202	P-40	SE Ain el Gazala	1620-1740
88ª Sq, 6°Gr, 1°St CT	S.Ten Roberto Sgorbati	MC.202	P-40	SE Ain el Gazala	1620-1740
88ª Sq, 6°Gr, 1°St CT	M.llo Natalino Stabile	MC.202	2 P-40s	SE Ain el Gazala	1620-1740

Italian Casualties

88ª Sq, 6°Gr, 1°St CT	MC.202 MM 7904 set on fire by bombs at Martuba
71ª Sq, 17°Gr, 1°St CT	MC.202 MM 7888 destroyed by bombs at Martuba
97ª Sq, 9°Gr, 4°St CT	MC 202 MM 7911 '97-11' destroyed by bombs at Martuba
79ª Sq, 6°Gr, 1°St CT	MC 202 MM 7772 '79-6' damaged by bombs at Martuba
80ª Sq, 17°Gr, 1°St CT	MC 202 MM 7789 damaged by bombs at Martuba

Monday-Tuesday, 25/26 May 1942

The night brought a heavy raid in the opposite direction as LG.143, at Gasr el Arid was bombed in an effort by the Luftwaffe and Regia Aeronautica to destroy as many WDAF fighters as possible before the new offensive began. The raiders approached before midnight on 25 May, resulting in some confusion in the records since the British claims were listed as occurring on the 25th whereas Axis losses were listed next day. The first claim was made by Flt Lt Scade of 73 Squadron at 2230, followed by a second by Flt Sgt Joyce at 2256. Their victims were both Ju 88s of LG 1. Around the same time nine CR.42s of 3° Gruppo CT made a low level attack on Gambut, releasing around 50 small bombs and strafing; one of these biplanes was shot down by Flg Off Selby. At 2345 a Ju 88C night fighter of NJG 2 was lost to AA west of Bardia; the crew were all wounded, but escaped capture and walked back.

Between 0515-0730 Gambut was again attacked by 27 MC.202s of 4° Stormo, covered by 22 more MC.202s of 1° Stormo. The Italian pilots reported strafing 24 aircraft on the ground, claiming all of them destroyed or damaged.

Despite all these attacks, WDAF losses seem to have been restricted to a single Tomahawk of 4 SAAF Squadron damaged Cat II and several more such aircraft of 4 SAAF and 5 SAAF Squadrons slightly damaged by splinters. The South Africans reported that at dawn six MC.202s strafed at 0630, but inflicted no further damage, whereas 250 Squadron reported two Kittyhawks damaged. This would have been a great disappointment to the Italian command had they been aware.

Around the same time another Ju 88, this one from 12./LG 1, was shot down by Bofors gunners and two Hurricane pilots of 33 Squadron jointly, the crew of this aircraft being captured. This aircraft may also have been attacked and claimed damaged by 3 RAAF Squadron. At 0655, shortly after the attack on Gambut by the Italian fighters, 12 Kittyhawks of 3 RAAF Squadron were scrambled over El Adem to intercept four Ju 88s and six Bf 109s at 11,000 feet. Sqn Ldr Gibbes claimed a probable Messerschmitt before attacking a Ju 88 – probably the one then shot down by 33 Squadron and the Bofors gunners. Return fire from the rear gunner set Gibbes' engine alight, causing him to bale out at 4,000 feet, striking the tailplane and getting an aerial wire entangled in his parachute. He landed heavily and broke his ankle, which caused his removal to hospital.

Claims and losses related to the Axis attacks on Allied airfields during the night of 25/26 May 1942

British Claims					
73 Sqn	Flt Lt T.P.K.Scade	Hurricane IIc BN165	Ju 88	Gambut area	2230
73 Sqn	Flt Sgt E.L.Joyce	Hurricane IIc BM156 'L'	Ju 88		2256
73 Sqn	Flt Lt J.B.Selby	Hurricane IIc BM975 'F'	CR42	Gambut Satellite	2155-2330
33 Sqn	Sgt M.J.H.M.Belleau	Hurricane IIb BG761 'V' }	Ju 88*	Gambut Main a/f	early a.m.
33 Sqn	Lt H.Inglesby	Hurricane IIb BE168 'N' }			
3 RAAF Sqn	Sgt G.E.S.Clabburn	Kittyhawk I AL145	Ju 88 Damaged	El Adem	0720
3 RAAF Sqn	Sqn Ldr R.H.Gibbes	Kittyhawk I AK874	Bf 109 Probable	El Adem	0720
* shared with Bofors guns					
British Casualties					
4 SAAF Sqn	night 25/26th heavy raid on Gambut 2200-0500 Tomahawk IIb AN485 damaged Cat II at 0400				
4 SAAF/ 5 SAAF Sqns	several Tomahawks slt damaged by splinters, during raid on Gambut				
260 Sqn	2 Kittyhawk Is damaged on ground				
3 RAAF Sqn	Kittyhawk I AK874 damaged by Ju 88 rear gunner and abandoned over El Adem; Sqn Ldr R.H. Gibbes WIA				
Italian Claims					
1° Stormo CT	24 fighters destroyed or damaged on ground at Gambut				
Italian Casualties					
153ª Sq, 3°Gr Aut CT	CR.42 failed to return from raid on Gambut 2330-0230, Serg Magg Luigi Modesti PoW				

CHAPTER 2

DISASTERS ON THE GAZALA LINE

RAF AND COMMONWEALTH AIR FORCES

Western Desert Air Force Order of Battle as at 26 May 1942

AHQ, Western Desert – Gambut (Advanced AHQ) – Maaten Bagush(Rear AHQ)

Under direct control of AHQ, WD		
1 Air Ambulance Unit	Gerawla	DH-86
2 PRU (Det from HQ, RAF, ME)	Gambut	Spitfire
15 SAAF Sqn	Amiriya	Blenheim
15 SAAF Sqn (Det)	Kufra	Blenheim
40 SAAF, 208 Sqn	El Adem	Hurricane, Tomahawk
60 SAAF Sqn	Sidi Barrani	Maryland
1437 Strat Recce Flt	Maktila	Maryland, Baltimore
Comm Flt	Maaten Bagush	Various
3 SAAF Wing	**Baheira**	
12 SAAF, 24 SAAF Sqns	Baheira	Boston
223 Sqn	Baheira	Baltimore
211 GROUP		
233 Wing	**El Adem**	
4 SAAF, 5 SAAF Sqns	Gambut	Tomahawk
2 SAAF, 260 Sqns		Gambut
Kittyhawk		
239 Wing	**Gambut**	
3 RAAF, 112, 250, 450 Sqns	Gambut	Kittyhawk
243 Wing	**Gambut**	
33, 80, 335 Sqns	Gambut	Hurricane
145 Sqn	Gambut	Spitfire
73 Sqn	El Adem	Hurricane

Available to reinforce WDAF but not under its control

205 GROUP	**Ismailia**	
231 Wing	**Qotafiya**	
37, 70, 108 Sqns	El Daba	Wellington

236 Wing	**El Daba**	
104 Sqn (less Det in Malta)	El Daba	Wellington
148 Sqn	El Daba	Wellington
238 Wing		
38 Sqn (less torpedo-bomber a/c)	Maaten Bagush	Wellington
40 Sqn	Shallufa	Wellington
201 GROUP	**Alexandria**	
252, 272 Sqns	Qasaba	Beaufighter
821, 826 Sqns (FAA)	Maaten Bagush	Albacore

Tuesday, 26 May 1942

The long months of stalemate were at last over, and the morning saw the start of Rommel's offensive against the Gazala-Bir Hacheim line, marking the start of some six weeks of confused, exhausting, violent and costly fighting, which was to include one of the most disastrous retreats for the British Commonwealth throughout the war. It was, however, ultimately to lead to the downfall of Rommel's forces in Africa.

The offensive began with an attack by four Italian divisions on the northern end of the line, which was launched as a diversion to draw British mobile forces towards this end of the front which was the most strongly held. At the same time the 15th and 21st Panzer Division and 20th Light Division by-passed Bir Hacheim in the far south, the two former units then making for Acroma and the latter for El Adem.

The first casualty over the front for WDAF on this day occurred when Plt Off Samuel of 274 Squadron was hit by Flak near Acroma and force-landed. Later in the day 3 RAAF Squadron undertook the unit's first mission in the fighter-bomber role. At midday eight MC.200s of 8° Gruppo led by the unit commander, Magg Mario Bacich, undertook a strafing attack during which it was claimed that several vehicles had been destroyed in the Mteifel Chebir area. Three aircraft returned damaged by AA fire, one of them force-landing 6km from Bir Temrad.

During the afternoon five Bf 109s escorted Ju 87s over Gazala, where three of the dive-bombers were shot down by AA, the crew of a I./StG 3 aircraft being killed. The other two missing aircraft, both of the latest Ju 87D version, were from III./StG 3 which had been sent to Africa from Sicily to bring the Geschwader to full strength. Four more Bf 109s of II./JG 27 were scrambled over Gazala, attacking a formation of Kittyhawks. Fw Reuter singled out one and claimed to have shot it down, reporting that the aircraft crashed on the edge of the airfield, somersaulting; Lt Jenisch shot-up a second without result. Reuter was pursued by about six Kittyhawks and while attempting to turn into these, was hit by several. He broke away through some cloud, and returned to base. Seventeen bullet strikes were counted on his aircraft. It is uncertain which squadron was involved in this action, but during the day Flg Off Waddy, now flying with 260 Squadron, claimed a Bf 109 probably destroyed.

Towards evening a concentration of vehicles was strafed by ten CR.42s of 158° Gruppo on their first mission along the Via Balbia, east of Gazala. A little later five Cant.Z.1007bis of 190ª Squadriglia took off to bomb facilities at Tobruk and one to attack the railway line south of Ridotta Capuzzo.

British Claims

260 Sqn	Flg Off J.L.Waddy	Kittyhawk I AK956	Bf 109F Probable	El Adem	1520-1630

British Casualties

274 Sqn	Hurricane II (possibly BN124) force-landed; Plt Off F.B.Samuel
260 Sqn	Kittyhawk I crash-landed at El Adem approx 1600; Sgt D.C.Copping
112 Sqn	Kittyhawk AK682 'U' damaged Cat II by Bf 109, crash-landed at Gambut; Plt Off K.H.Knapik injured

German Claims

5./JG 27	Fw Horst Reuter	P-40	2km NE Ain el Gazala	1335

German Casualties

1./StG 3	Ju 87R-4 WNr 6333 S7+BH AA 30km SE Tmimi; Lt Arno Jänicke/ Gefr Helmut Dittrich KiA
7./StG 3	Ju 87D-1 WNr 2059 30% damaged by AA W Ain el Gazala; gunner Lt Heinrich Bruckner WiA, pilot safe
7./StG 3	Ju 87D-1 WNr 2076 S7+JM shot down by AA W Ain el Gazala; Uffz Ludwig Kochner/Uffz Heinrich Blumbach MiA

12./LG 1	Ju 88 A-4 WNr8617 L1+EW; shot down by AA, crashed nr Bir el Henassia; Fw Hans Wittlad and three PoW
1./LG 1	Ju 88 A-4 WNr5615 L1+RL shot down by Hurricane, crashed by Bir el Acra; Oblt Hans Riha and three MiA
4./LG 1	Ju 88 A-4 WNr8631 L1+GM shot down by Hurricane, crashed SW Gambut; Uffz Friedrich-Wilhelm Redlich and three MiA
8./ZG 26	Bf 110E-2 WNr 4419 damaged by AA at Martuba, crash-landed nr Derna North, 100%, radio operator Uffz Hugo Konrad WiA

Italian Casualties

88ª Sq, 6°Gr, 1°St CT	MC.202 MM 7783 damaged by bombs at Martuba
72ª Sq, 17°Gr, 1°St CT	MC.202 MM 7726 '72-7' destroyed by bombs at Martuba
91ª Sq, 10°Gr, 4°St CT	MC.202 MM 7790 '91-1' collided on taxying with MC.202 of 1°St, badly damaged
93ª Sq, 8°Gr, 2°St CT	MC.200 MM 5271 hit by AA, force-landed within Axis lines, Serg Magg Orazio Antonicelli safe
93ª Sq, 8°Gr, 2°St CT	MC.200 MM 5187 damaged in take-off accident, Serg Magg Bartolo Palumbo safe

Ju 87B of StG 3 features the typical desert paint scheme applied to many of the unit's aircraft in North Africa.

Wednesday, 27 May 1942

Twelve Kittyhawks of 2 SAAF Squadron were scrambled at dawn to intercept four Bf 109s of II./JG 27 escorting two Bf 109E reconnaissance aircraft over Gazala. From 0600 14 MC.200s of 13° Gruppo took off to strafe vehicles along the Via Balbia between Gazala and Tobruk; they were escorted by 16 MC.202s of 6° Gruppo. Near Gazala a reported 25 P-40s were engaged by the Italian escorts, the pilots of which claimed six shot down and seven damaged without loss. However, one MC.200 was shot down by ground fire and two more were damaged. For the Germans Obfw Krenzke claimed one Kittyhawk shot down in flames. 2 SAAF Squadron lost two Kittyhawks and their pilots, their commanding officer, Maj Human, claiming one Messerschmitt.

At 0950 5 SAAF Squadron's Tomahawks intercepted ten bombers escorted by ten fighters near Gazala. In the records of this newly-arrived unit, these were initially identified as Ju 87s, then being altered to BR.20s and subsequently to Do 215s! Two of these were claimed shot down and three damaged, plus a Bf 110 damaged. The latter seems to have indicated the true opponents of the 'green' South Africans, for such aircraft of III./ZG 26 led by Oblt Wehmeyer had taken off at 0910 from Derna. Over Tobruk the crews reported meeting a squadron of Hurricanes (probably actually 5 SAAF's Tomahawks) and formed a defensive circle. Wehmeyer, Fw Wein and Uffz Neitzke each claimed one fighter shot down, but one Bf 110 was shot down, the crew becoming PoWs.

Ju 87s were encountered by 4 SAAF Squadron, but only at the South Africans' airfield while they were on the ground; two of the unit's aircraft were badly damaged in the dive-bombing attack. At 1050 the unit scrambled 12 Tomahawks over Bir Hacheim where four Bf 109s of III./JG 53 were met as they were escorting a TacR Bf 110. Obfw Stumpf shot down one Tomahawk in flames and Lt Woodliffe crash-landed this aircraft near El Adem, returning safely later. Four Bf 109s of II./JG 27 escorting two Bf 109Es in the early afternoon became involved in combat with eight Kittyhawks. On the return flight Fw Reuter, whose aircraft had been damaged, encountered 11 Kittyhawks of 450 Squadron which were escorting bombers to El Adem. He attacked and damaged Sgt Oakley's aircraft, but was bounced by Sgt Shillabeer of 450 Squadron and was shot down, becoming a PoW. Reuter had been flying a very old and

Magg Marco Larcher's MC.202 being refuelled. The Gruppo commander's pennant can be clearly seen below the cockpit – a fairly rarely seen insignia.

slow Bf 109F on this occasion due to his usual mount having been damaged on the previous day. He baled out within sight of the front line but landed in the middle of a British tank concentration. He was picked up and enjoyed the dubious privilege of being taken along as a passenger into a heavy tank battle which lasted for the rest of the day. He had been credited with 20 confirmed victories by this date. Meanwhile, between 1240-1430 15 CR.42s of 158° Gruppo, escorted by 27 Macchis of 4° Stormo, attacked vehicles in the Acroma area.

3 RAAF Squadron flew many fighter-bomber sorties during the day, one by four Kittyhawks at 1345 meeting four Bf 109s of I./JG 27, Lt Körner shooting down Sgt Thomas, who crash-landed on fire south of Gambut, but survived to return next day. At 1605 four more Australian Kittybombers took off, but were intercepted by three Bf 109s of II./JG 27, this time Sgt Clabburn being shot down south of El Adem by Lt Jenisch, crash-landing. He too returned safely next day. Four more went out at 1650 and were attacked by two Bf 109s, again from II./JG 27, Sgt Norman being shot down by Obfw Krenzke, and baling out to become a PoW. Between 1630-1740 24 MC.200s of 2° Stormo (8° and 13° Gruppi) once again attacked MT between el Mrassas and Tobruk; one was hit by ground fire and force-landed safely within Axis lines. Escorting 17° Gruppo MC.202s intercepted about 15 P-40s over el Mrassas, claiming two probables. However, one of these fighters was also hit by ground fire and force-landed at Tmimi.

5 SAAF Squadron was ordered to scramble at 1745, arriving over Gazala and Tobruk where 2/Lt Stevens was shot down and captured, with two more Tomahawks being shot-up and badly damaged. At 1815 Hurricanes of 274 Squadron intercepted Ju 87s and Bf 109s south of Tobruk, one Stuka being claimed shot down plus one and one Messerschmitt claimed damaged. During the day 112 Squadron was engaged in fighter-bombing sorties all day, during one of which Flt Lt Dickinson was shot down. Like several others on this date, he survived to return next day.

73 Squadron, following its successes by night, withdrew from El Adem to Gambut due to the approach of 90th Light Division, but this force was held by the defenders. The panzer divisions were also held at Knightsbridge, and a great tank battle commenced which was to last for several days. On this date also the Italian Trieste Division attempted to break through the minefields at Sidi Muftah. During the day, Flt Sgt Sands of 73 Squadron was detailed to fly Hurricane BN 282 from El Adem to Gambut West. He departed separately from the rest of the Squadron as the aircraft was temporarily unserviceable, taking off somewhat later, but failed to arrive. Although reported missing, his remains were later found in the Sollum-Tobruk area by troops of the 2nd Cameronians, identified by his pay book.

British Claims

73 Sqn	Flg Off J.B.Selby	Hurricane IIc BM975 'F'	Ju 88 Damaged	Gambut Main	0420
2 SAAF Sqn	Lt A.D.Allen	Kittyhawk I AK642 'T'	Bf 109F Damaged	Gazala	0745

2 SAAF Sqn	Maj J.D.W.Human	Kittyhawk I AL186 'G'	Bf 109	Gazala	0745
2 SAAF Sqn	Lt G.D.Reynolds	Kittyhawk I AK747 'L'	MC.202 Probable	Gazala	0745
5 SAAF Sqn	Maj J.E.Frost	Tomahawk IIb AK195 'W'	Do 215	15m SW El Adem	0950
5 SAAF Sqn	2/Lt C.A.Golding	Tomahawk IIb AN468 'J'	Do 215 Damaged	15m SW El Adem	0950
5 SAAF Sqn	Capt J.L.Hewitson	Tomahawk IIb AN448 'H'	Bf 109	15m SW El Adem	0950
5 SAAF Sqn	Lt K.C.Morgan	Tomahawk IIb AN354 'X'	Do 215 Damaged	15m SW El Adem	0950
5 SAAF Sqn	Lt R.L.Morrison	Tomahawk IIb AN421 'Z'	Do 215	15m SW El Adem	0950
5 SAAF Sqn	Lt V.S.Muir	Tomahawk IIb AN262 'C'	Bf 110 Damaged	15m SW El Adem	0950
5 SAAF Sqn	Lt L.B.van der Spuy	Tomahawk IIb AN533 'Y'	Do 215 Damaged	nr Gazala	0950
4 SAAF Sqn	Lt J.S.Warden	Tomahawk II b AN378 'X'	Bf 109F Damaged	Bir Hacheim	1200
450 Sqn	Sgt N.H.Shillabeer	Kittyhawk I AK787	Bf 109	10m SW Gambut	1615
274 Sqn	Sgt J.Dodds	Hurricane IIc	Bf 109 Damaged	S Tobruk	1815-
274 Sqn	Flt Sgt J.W.Neil	Hurricane IIc	Ju 87	S Tobruk	1815-
274 Sqn	Plt Off F.B.Samuel	Hurricane IIc	Ju 87 Damaged	S Tobruk	1815-
274 Sqn	Sgt R.H.N.Walsh	Hurricane IIc	Bf 109 Damaged	S Tobruk	1815-

British Casualties

2 SAAF Sqn	Kittyhawk I AK904 'A' shot down 10m SW Gazala 0745; Lt N.S.Ford KiA
2 SAAF Sqn	Kittyhawk I AL138 'R' shot down 10m SW Gazala 0745; Lt D.Paddon KiA
4 SAAF Sqn	Tomahawk IIb AN378 'X' damaged Cat II by cannon shell in wing; Lt J.S.Warden safe
4 SAAF Sqn	Tomahawk IIb AN414 'L' damaged by Bf 109s Cat II, forced to land El Adem 1230; 2/Lt D.Woodliffe safe
4 SAAF Sqn	Tomahawk IIb 'Y' force-landed; Maj D.D.Moodie safe
5 SAAF Sqn	Tomahawk IIb AK195 'W' damaged by e/a Cat II 0930-1025; Maj J.E.Frost safe
5 SAAF Sqn	Tomahawk IIb AN354 'X' damaged Cat II by Bf 109s, 0930-1025; Lt K.C.Morgan safe
5 SAAF Sqn	Tomahawk IIb AN533 'Y' damaged Cat II, 0930-1025; Lt L.B.van der Spuy safe
5 SAAF Sqn	Tomahawk IIb AK421 'Z' damaged Cat I, 0930-1025; Lt R.L.Morrison safe
5 SAAF Sqn	Tomahawk IIb AN427 'D' engine cut, crash-landed – possible combat damage, 1025; Lt T.Finlayson safe
5 SAAF Sqn	Tomahawk IIb AN263 'V' shot down at 1745 18m NW El Adem; 2/Lt F.L.Stevens PoW escaped back next day
3 RAAF Sqn	Kittyhawk I AK965 left 1345 to strafe, force-landed 10m S El Adem; Sgt W.W.Thomas safe
3 RAAF Sqn	Kittyhawk I AK854 left 1605 to strafe MT SW El Adem, force-landed due to Flak; Sgt G.E.S.Clabburn safe
3 RAAF Sqn	Kittyhawk I AL183 left 1650 to attack tanks 5m E Bir Hacheim; Sgt.H.A.Norman PoW
112 Sqn	Kittyhawk I AL122 MiA from attack on MT; Flt Lt E.Dickinson shot down, returned
73 Sqn	Hurricane IIc BN 282 missing on transfer flight; Flt Sgt A.H.Sands MiA
450 Sqn	Kittyhawk AL184 damaged Cat II by a Bf 109; Sgt E.P.Oakley safe
40 SAAF Sqn	Hurricane hit by Flak at Sidi Rezegh, crash-landed at Gambut; Lt J.G.Grimes safe (he did not know Sidi Rezegh had been captured)

German Claims

6./JG 27	Obfw Erich Krenzke	P-40	20km S Ain el Gazala	0655
7./ZG 26	Oblt Alfred Wehmeyer	P-40	El Adem	0852
7./ZG 26	Uffz Helmut Neitzke	P-40	El Adem	0854
7./ZG 26	Fw Hans Wein	P-40	El Adem	0856
9./JG 53	Obfw Werner Stumpf	P-40	SE El Adem	0910
9./JG 53	Fw Heinz Herkendorff	P-40 (u/c)	3km SE El Adem	0911
2./JG 27	Lt Friedrich Körner	P-40	S Gambut	1530
6./JG 27	Obfw Erich Krenzke	P-40	15km E Bir Hacheim	1640
5./JG 27	Lt Kurt Jenisch	P-40	S El Adem	1710

German Casualties

5./JG 27	Bf 109F-4 WNr 7369 Red 6 combat with P-40; motor hit and force-landed between Tobruk and El Adem, 100%; Fw Horst Reuter PoW
III./ZG 26	Bf 110C-5 WNr 2195 3U+MR shot down by P-40 nr El Adem 0855; Uffz Arno Frickmann/Uffz Josef Ammersbach PoW
9./ZG 26	Bf 110E-2 WNr 3797 3U+ET hit by AA over Tobruk; crashed SW Tobruk; Oblt Johannes Bergfleth/Fw Schüpfner KiA
III./ZG 26	Bf 110E-2 WNr 2384 hit by AA, crash-landed nr Martuba, 80% damaged, crew safe
2./LG 1	Ju 88A-4 WNr 140215 L1+QK shot down by night fighter; crashed nr Bir el Gobi; Lt Hans Liebsch and three MiA
6./KG 100	He 111H-6 WNr 7218 6N+CJ shot down by AA, crashed nr Fuka; Uff Leopold Schneider and one PoW, two MiA, one KiA

A pair of Bf 109Fs of 9./JG 53.

Italian Claims

6° Gr, 1°St CT	Magg Marco Larcher	MC.202	2 P-40s Damaged	S Ain el Gazala	0610-0720
88ª Sq, 6° Gr, 1° St CT	Cap Dante Ocarso	MC.202	P-40	S Ain el Gazala	0610-0720
88ª Sq, 6° Gr, 1° St CT	M.llo Natalino Stabile	MC.202	P-40	S Ain el Gazala	0610-0720
88ª Sq, 6° Gr, 1° St CT	M.llo Natalino Stabile	MC.202	2 P-40s Damaged	S Ain el Gazala	0610-0720
88ª Sq, 6° Gr, 1° St CT	Serg Magg Alfredo Bordin	MC.202	P-40	S Ain el Gazala	0610-0720
80ª Sq, 17°Gr, 1°St CT	Ten Renato Talamini	MC.202	P-40	Ain Gazala-Tobruk	0615-0715
80ª Sq, 17°Gr, 1°St CT	Ten Renato Talamini	MC.202	3 P-40s Damaged	Ain Gazala-Tobruk	0615-0715
80ª Sq, 17°Gr, 1°St CT	Serg Magg Mario Host	MC.202 MM7752	P-40	Ain Gazala-Tobruk	0615-0715
80ª Sq, 17°Gr, 1°St CT	Serg Magg Alvise Andrich	MC.202 MM7892	P-40	Ain Gazala-Tobruk	0615-0715
71ª Sq, 17°Gr, 1°St CT	Serg Carlo Ermo	MC.202	P-40 Probable	el Mrassas	1635-1735
80ª Sq, 17°Gr, 1°St CT	Ten Emilio Marchi	MC.202	P-40 Probable	el Mrassas	1635-1735

Italian Casualties

80ª Sq, 17°Gr, 1°St CT	MC.202 MM 7752 damaged, Serg Magg Mario Host safe
80ª Sq, 17°Gr, 1°St CT	MC.202 MM 7892 '80-2' damaged, Serg Magg Alvise Andrich safe
90ª Sq, 10°Gr, 4°St CT	MC.202 MM 7938 '90-12' damaged on landing at Castel Benito from Pantelleria, S.Ten Steno Soprana safe
81ª Sq, 6°Gr, 1°St CT	MC.202 MM 7873 destroyed by bombs at Martuba
81ª Sq, 6°Gr, 1°St CT	MC.202 MM 7893 damaged by splinters at Martuba
88ª Sq, 6°Gr, 1°St CT	MC.202 MM 7783 damaged by bombs at Martuba
71ª Sq, 17°Gr, 1°St CT	MC.202 MM 7863 '71-5' hit in combat, force-landed at Tmimi, M.llo Andrea Stella (72ª Sq) safe
78ª Sq, 13°Gr, 2°St CT	MC.200 MM 5253 hit by ground fire, force-landed near Tmimi, Serg Cassio Poggi slightly wounded
94ª Sq, 8°Gr, 2°St CT	MC.200 MM 8331 hit by ground fire, force-landed 8km from Tmimi, Cap Orfeo Cecchet safe

Thursday, 28 May 1942

By night ten CR.42s of 3° Gruppo attacked artillery positions in the Ain el Gazala-Acroma area, one aircraft failing to return. 73 Squadron was also active during the pre-dawn period, intercepting and claiming one Ju 88 of I./LG 1 shot down, with two more claimed as probables and three damaged. With daylight 8th Army requested AVM Coningham to ignore air superiority operations and concentrate all possible aircraft on ground-attack sorties against columns, so serious was the position considered to be. This, of course, put the WDAF aircraft and their pilots and crews at a disadvantage and more directly in the way of danger than when undertaking offensive operations, or indeed, on defensive interceptions. Nevertheless, Coningham concurred with the request and a period which can only be described as being 'on the rack' began, particularly for the fighter squadrons.

Cyrenaica – Gazala to El Alamein, spring-summer 1942

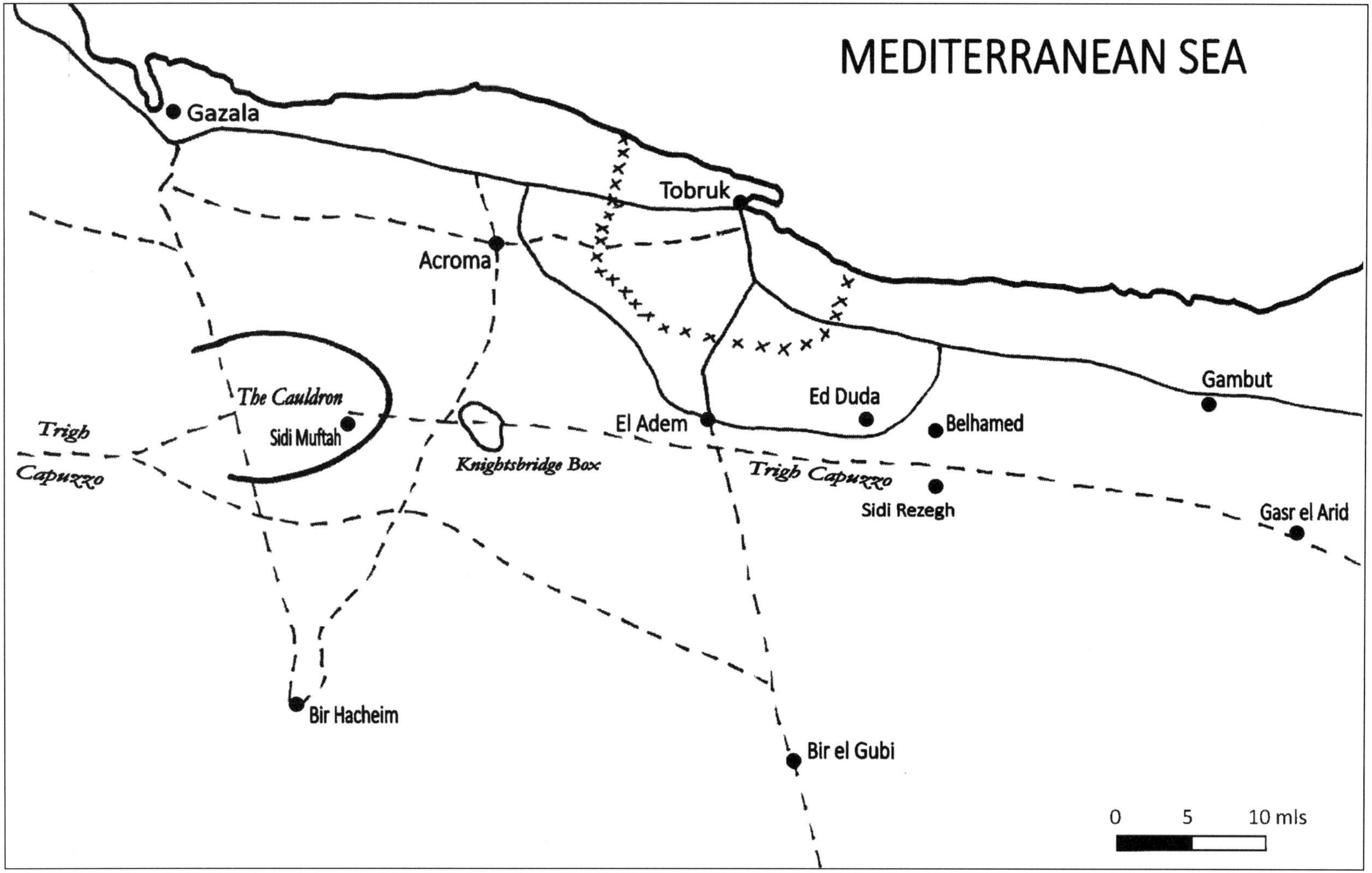

At 0935 four Hurricanes of 80 Squadron were carrying out a patrol when they were bounced by four Bf 109s of I./JG 27 near Gambut, which shot down two of the British fighters. Four more Bf 109s, these from II./JG 27, reported intercepting eight fighters engaged in a ground-attack mission, claiming two shot down in flames. One of these may have been an aircraft of 112 Squadron which lost Flt Lt Dickinson for the second time in two days, but this time permanently.

At 1025 six MC.202s of 6° Gruppo on a free sweep over the Bir Hacheim area, were contacted by radio from the ground (an unusual event for Italian fighters) and were directed to intercept a formation of five Bostons heading towards the coast road north of el Mrassas. Ten Piero Polizzy attacked the bombers, claiming one shot down; a 12 SAAF Squadron Boston was damaged, and this was probably the aircraft which he attacked. A little later at 1115 158° Gruppo despatched 15 CR.42s to attack a vehicle concentration north of Acroma. The biplanes were escorted by 12 MC.202s of 6° Gruppo, the pilots of which reported engaging a formation of 12 P-40s, claiming two shot down and a third shared with a German pilot.

Around half an hour later Maj Frost and two of his 5 SAAF Squadron pilots intercepted and shot down a lone Bf 109E of 4.(H)/12 on a TacR sortie near Gazala, the pilot being killed. Shortly after this, nine Kittyhawks of 250 Squadron were flying top cover to 450 Squadron escorting nine Bostons to bomb west of Acroma. Six Bf 109s were escorting two Ju 87s, but one of the latter was shot down by AA fire and the escort then lost the other. They then met the Allied bombers on their return trip and Oblt Otto Schulz, back from his leave, commissioned and promoted, shot down Sgt Overstone of 250 Squadron in flames.

In the early afternoon III./JG 27's fighters escorted Stukas near Acroma, together with a number of MC.200s. Fifteen of the latter aircraft of 8° Gruppo were out on a ground attack mission in the Bir Taieb el Esem area. 33 Squadron climbed to intercept these raiders, but were bounced by the Bf 109s, one Hurricane being shot down and two were damaged, the pilot of the first of these managing to bale out. Obgefr Vandeveert claimed one which crashed and Lt Doyé one which he thought had belly-landed, but as he had no witness, this was not confirmed. Plt Off Lance Wade claimed one Ju 87 and one MC.202 shot down. At about the same time Uffz Gruber of III./JG 27 claimed one victory in the Acroma area when on patrol with one other aircraft.

Amongst the Italian fighters at this time, one was shot down, reportedly by AA; he was picked up by a British patrol and made prisoner; five other aircraft were damaged. Meanwhile 15 MC.200s of 13° Gruppo strafed vehicles on the Via Balbia near Zaviet el Mrassas, three of these fighter-bombers being hit by small-arms fire.

The final combat of the day occurred when two Bf 109s of II.Gruppe escorted a Bf 110 on a reconnaissance sortie. After encountering several British fighters, Oblt Schulz attacked Lt Pare of 5 SAAF Squadron who was also on a reconnaissance in his Tomahawk of the El Adem-Bir el Gobi area, shooting him down. Pare baled out, walking back to the squadron. During the day Lt Webb of 40 SAAF Squadron out on a TacR sortie claimed a probable victory over an aircraft which intercepted him. On this same day 335 Squadron moved from LG.20 to LG.10 at Gerawla.

British Claims

73 Sqn	Plt Off C.S.Fraser	Hurricane IIc BE570 'S'	Ju 88 Damaged	20m W Gambut	0330-0445
73 Sqn	Sgt M.S.Jones	Hurricane IIc BN402	Ju 88 Damaged	19m E Gambut	0450
73 Sqn	Flt Lt T.P.K.Scade	Hurricane IIc BN165	Ju 88 Probable	E Gambut	0515
73 Sqn	Flt Lt T.P.K.Scade	Hurricane IIc BN165	Ju 88	15m E Tobruk	0525
73 Sqn	Flt Lt T.P.K.Scade	Hurricane IIc BN165	Ju 88 Probable	10m W Bardia, N road	0530
73 Sqn	Sgt D.R.Wiseman	Hurricane IIc	Ju 88 Damaged		
5 SAAF Sqn	Maj J.E.Frost	Tomahawk IIb AN434 'F'	}		
5 SAAF Sqn	2/Lt J.M.S.Martin	Tomahawk IIb AM401 'I'	} Bf 109E	nr Tmimi	1145
5 SAAF Sqn	Lt J.H.Slater	Tomahawk IIb AN433 'B'	}		
260 Sqn	Flt Lt T.Hindle	Kittyhawk I	Bf 109 Damaged	Acroma area	1150-1240
33 Sqn	Plt Off L.C.Wade	Hurricane IIb BG974 'D'	Ju 87	Acroma	1435
33 Sqn	Plt Off L.C.Wade	Hurricane IIb BG974 'D'	MC.202	Acroma	1435
40 SAAF Sqn	Lt W.J.A.Webb	Tomahawk AK312	Macchi Probable	SW Sidi Rezegh	1520-1610

British Casualties

80 Sqn	Hurricane IIc BE706 FTR, shot down by Bf 109, 12m SE Gambut 1030; Flt Sgt Pierre Wintersdorf safe

80 Sqn	Hurricane IIc BN567 FTR, damaged Cat II by Bf 109s nr Bir Hacheim; Sgt R.S.Sykes safe
112 Sqn	Kittyhawk I AK829 FTR from ground attack; Flt Lt E.Dickinson MiA
250 Sqn	Kittyhawk I AK877 shot down by Bf 109s 4m SW El Adem at about 1320-25; Sgt H.D.Ovenstone MiA
33 Sqn	Hurricane IIb Z5444 shot down 15m W El Adem 1745; Sgt G.H.Lyons KiA
33 Sqn	Hurricane IIb BG757 damaged El Adem 1745; Sqn Ldr J.E.Proctor safe
33 Sqn	Hurricane IIb BG949 'U' damaged El Adem 1745; Plt Off J.F.Allan safe
5 SAAF Sqn	Tomahawk IIb AK383 'N' shot down by Bf 109 N Sidi Rezegh at 1710; Lt R.Pare baled out safe
12 SAAF Sqn	Boston III AL773 damaged, NFD
73 Sqn	Hurricane II BD916 shot down, SOC, no details

German Claims

4./JG 27	Oblt Ferdinand Vögl	Hurricane	5km E Bir Hacheim	0845
4./JG 27	Obfw Alfred Schulze	Hurricane	5km E Bir Hacheim	0846
1./JG 27	Fw Günther Steinhausen	Hurricane	5km N Gasr el Arid	1000
Stab II./JG 27	Oblt Otto Schulz	P-40	15km NW El Adem	1220
8./JG 27	Uffz Viktor Gruber	P-40	8km N Fort Acroma	1405
6./JG 27	Obgefr Heinrich Vandeveert	P-40	39km SW El Adem	1445
Stab II./JG 27	Lt Hans Doyé	P-40 o.Zg. n.b.	11km SE El Adem	1455
Stab II./JG 27	Oblt Otto Schulz	P-40	15km E El Adem	1612

German Casualties

1./JG 27	Bf 109F-4 trop crash-landed for u/k reason at Tmimi at 1550, slightly damaged
4.(H)/12	Bf 109E-7 WNr 3489 shot down by P-40 nr Tmimi at 1145; Fw Willi Langer KiA

Italian Claims

79ª Sq, 6°Gr, 1°St CT	Ten Piero Polizzy	MC.202	Boston	N el Mrassas	1025-
81ª Sq, 6°Gr, 1°St CT	Ten Antonio Palazzeschi	MC.202	P-40	Acroma-El Adem	1135-1300
81ª Sq, 6°Gr, 1°St CT	M.llo Giovanni Collovini	MC.202	P-40	Acroma-El Adem	1135-1300
81ª Sq, 6°Gr, 1°St CT	M.llo Giovanni Collovini	MC.202	P-40 w German pilot	Acroma-El Adem	1135-1300

Italian Casualties

94ª Sq, 8°Gr, 2°St CT	MC.200 MM 6674 shot down by ground fire S Ain el Gazala 1500, Serg Magg Alberto Bottazzi PoW
154ª Sq, 3° Gr CT	CR.42 failed to return from Ain el Gazala-Acroma raid, Cap Giuseppe Tovazzi MiA
91ª Sq, 10°Gr, 4°St CT	MC.202 MM 7796 '91-3' destroyed by bombs at Martuba
91ª Sq, 10°Gr, 4°St CT	MC.202 MM 7902 '91-5' damaged by bombs at Martuba
91ª Sq, 10°Gr, 4°St CT	MC.202 MM 7799 '91-6' damaged by bombs at Martuba
91ª Sq, 10°Gr, 4°St CT	MC.202 MM 7907 '91-7' damaged by bombs at Martuba
91ª Sq, 10°Gr, 4°St CT	MC.202 MM 7910 '91-8' damaged by bombs at Martuba
91ª Sq, 10°Gr, 4°St CT	MC.202 MM 7808 '91-9' damaged by bombs at Martuba
91ª Sq, 10°Gr, 4°St CT	MC.202 MM 7934 '91-11' damaged by bombs at Martuba
90ª Sq, 10°Gr, 4°St CT	MC.202 MM 7810 '90-3' destroyed by bombs at Martuba
90ª Sq, 10°Gr, 4°St CT	MC.202 MM 7930 '90-2' damaged in landing at Martuba

Friday, 29 May 1942

73 Squadron Hurricanes were patrolling again during the early hours, Flg Off McDougal claiming a Ju 88 shot down at 0430 over the sea near Gambut; he was also to claim damage to two more during the next 45 minutes. At 0630 the Hurricanes of 80 Squadron took off for a sweep over the El Adem-Acroma-Bir Hacheim area at 6,000 feet. Six Bf 109s of II./JG 27 had taken off at the same time on a Freie Jagd of the Mteifel Chebir area, and seven more from III./JG 53 roamed over El Adem and Acroma. Fifteen minutes later seven Kittyhawks of 2 SAAF Squadron took off on a wing sweep. At 1710 the aircraft of II./JG 27 attacked 80 Squadron between El Adem and Bir Hacheim, Obfw Kenzke claiming a Hurricane in flames. 80 Squadron actually lost four aircraft during these engagements; one pilot returned next day while Sgt Swire was reported safe in hospital, wounded in chest and arm. Meanwhile, III./JG 53 continued its patrol, encountering 2 SAAF Squadron south of Gazala at 0740, Obfw Kronschnabel shooting down 2/Lt Brown who was on his first operational sortie.

Ten minutes later ten of 450 Squadron's Kittyhawks took off to patrol over Acroma as six Bf 109s of III./JG 27 commenced escorting Ju 87s of II./StG 3 on a raid. Over Acroma four of the Messerschmitt pilots attacked the Kittyhawks, but without result. The Australians were then ordered to intercept the Stuka, chasing them over Gazala, shooting two down, including that flown by the Staffelkapitän of

4./StG 3. Having shared in the destruction of these, Flt Sgt McBurnie then also shot down a Bf 109 flown by Lt von Fritsch, who force-landed on the coast near Bu Hama, becoming a PoW. In the meantime seven more Bf 109s from I./JG 27 had departed on a Freie Jagd, these spotting the combat between 450 Squadron and the Ju 87s, four of these German pilots at once joining the fray, immediately shooting down three of the Kittyhawks. II./JG 27 carried out another Stuka escort at 1150 during which Obfw Schulze had to undertake an emergency landing 15 miles south-east of Tmimi due to engine trouble. Oblt Schulz flew out to pick him up in a Fieseler Storch.

It was another busy day for the CR.42s of 158ª Gruppo which undertook two ground-attack missions in the Trigh Capuzzo-Mteifel Chebir-El Adem area. A third attack, designed to neutralize artillery batteries south-east of Gasr el Regem was undertaken, pilots claiming to have put one of these targets out of action and damaged two more, but one CR.42 was hit and damaged by AA, the pilot force-landing within Axis territory. From 1515 nine MC.202s of 4° Stormo made a free sweep of the Acroma-Bir Harmat-Bir Hacheim area, reporting meeting 15 P-40s over Acroma, three of which were claimed shot down for the Stormo's first victories since its recent arrival in North Africa. One of these was credited to Serg Teresio Martinoli, later to become Italy's top-scoring fighter pilot of WWII; one probable was also claimed, but one MC.202 failed to return.

Their opponents were 11 Hurricanes of 274 Squadron and nine Tomahawks of 5 SAAF Squadron which had been scrambled at 1540 on a wing sweep over Bir Hacheim. The pilots of these reported meeting a similarly mixed force of Bf 109s and MC.202s, Sgt Dodds of the former unit claiming damage to one Messerschmitt while Maj Frost of the latter unit claimed a Macchi shot down, three of his pilots each claiming a fighter damaged. Lt Slater was attacked by one fighter which was driven off by Capt Hewitson, who identified it as a Bf 109, but Slater had to crash-land five miles south of Tobruk.

At 2100 12 Bostons of 24 SAAF Squadron carried out a night raid, but were attacked by fighters nonetheless. A rear gunner claimed a Bf 109 in flames, but one bomber was hit and force-landed on the way back to base. During April and May III./ZG 26 had undertaken several night-fighting sorties and during this night Oblt Wehmeyer claimed a Boston shot down over Derna with the aid of searchlights; it seems likely that the aircraft lost during this night was therefore his victim. During much the same time period, 13 Cant.Z.1007bis bombers of 35° Stormo BT again bombed the harbour and strongpoints at Tobruk.

Douglas Boston III Z2223 OZ-F of 24 SAAF Squadron.

On the ground 80 Squadron had been rejoined by Flt Sgt Wintersdorf who had been shot down on the previous day. He reported that he had managed to bale out in the nick of time.

British Claims

73 Sqn	Flg Off R.McDougal	Hurricane IIc BN415 'D'	Ju 88	Gambut area, 10m to sea	0430
73 Sqn	Flg Off R.McDougal	Hurricane IIc BN415 'D'	Ju 88 Damaged	20m E Gambut	0445
73 Sqn	Flg Off R.McDougal	Hurricane IIc BN415 'D'	Ju 88 Damaged	10m E Gambut	0515
450 Sqn	Flt Sgt D.H.McBurnie	Kittyhawk I AK897	Bf 109F	20m E Gazala	0750-0911
450 Sqn	Flt Sgt D.H.McBurnie	Kittyhawk I AK897	Ju 87 (shared)	Gazala area	0750-0911
450 Sqn	Sgt M.A.Jenkins	Kittyhawk AK789			
450 Sqn	Flt Sgt I.A.Nursey	Kittyhawk I AK606	Ju 87	2m N coast, Gazala area	0750-0911

Hurricane IIcs of 213 Squadron. AK-U, BE653 was often flown by Plt Off Bert Houle. The aircraft displays the unit's special roundel on the fuselage where the central red spot was over-painted with a wasp.

274 Sqn	Sgt J.Dodds	Hurricane IIc	Bf 109F Damaged		1540
208 Sqn	Plt Off H.Rawlinson	Hurricane	Bf 109F Damaged	Gazala Bay	
5 SAAF Sqn	Maj J.E.Frost	Tomahawk IIb AN523 'R'	MC.202	10m E Gazala	1610
5 SAAF Sqn	Capt J.L.Hewitson	Tomahawk IIb AN448 'H'	Bf 109F Damaged	nr Gazala	1610
5 SAAF Sqn	Lt J.V.Lindbergh	Tomahawk IIb AN366 'O'	MC.202 Damaged	nr Gazala	1610
5 SAAF Sqn	Lt P.H.Saunders	Tomahawk IIb AM495 'T'	MC.202 Damaged	nr Gazala	1615
40 SAAF Sqn	Lt W.J.A.Webb	Tomahawk AK445	Ju 87 Damaged		1715

British Casualties

80 Sqn	Hurricane IIc BM991 shot down by Bf 109 El Adem-Bir Hacheim 0630-0730; Plt Off P.Pearson MiA
80 Sqn	Hurricane IIc BN354 shot down by Bf 109 El Adem-Bir Hacheim 0630-0730, force-landed; Flt Sgt D.A.Campbell safe
80 Sqn	Hurricane IIc BN396 shot down by Bf 109 El Adem-Bir Hacheim 0630-0730; Sgt C.Swire WiA
80 Sqn	Hurricane IIc BN547 shot down by Bf 109 El Adem-Bir Hacheim 0630-0730; Sgt R.S.Sykes safe
250 Sqn	Kittyhawk I AL213 shot down by Bf 109, 7m SE Acroma, 1555-1635; Sgt L.J.Devlin KiA
250 Sqn	Kittyhawk I AK846 'H' damaged by Flak, crash-landed at base 1310-1420; Sgt D.W.Cairns safe
250 Sqn	Kittyhawk I ET242 shot down by Flak nr Bir Hacheim
450 Sqn	Kittyhawk I AL163 shot down by Bf 109 10m W Tobruk; Sgt T.Packer KiA
450 Sqn	Kittyhawk I AK973 shot down by Bf 109 Acroma; Sgt J.N.Dean KiA
450 Sqn	Kittyhawk I AK998 'O' shot down by Bf 109 N Acroma; Sgt R.Shaw KiA
2 SAAF Sqn	Kittyhawk I AK870 shot down by Bf 109; 2/Lt I.Brown baled but parachute failed to open, KiA
5 SAAF Sqn	Tomahawk IIb AN433 'B' engine failure after combat and belly-landed 6m S Tobruk 1640; Lt J.H.Slater safe
3 RAAF Sqn	Kittyhawk I AL199, damaged by Flak, Cat II; Flg Off G.T.Chinchen safe
73 Sqn	Hurricane II BE169 SOC due to enemy action
24 SAAF Sqn	Boston III Z2176 off 2100 to attack shipping in Derna harbour; FTR, possibly Flak; Lt H.Murrow and three KiA
24 SAAF Sqn	Boston III AL673 'W' off 2100 to attack shipping in Derna harbour; port engine disabled by Flak; Lt I.H.Butler crash-landed at base; he and one injured, two safe

German Claims

6./JG 27	Obfw Erich Krenzke	Hurricane o.Zg. n.b.	20km NE Bir Hacheim	0610
9./JG 53	Lt Hermann Munzert	Hurricane	20km S El Adem	0613
9./JG 53	Obfw Josef Kronschnabel	P-40	S Ain el Gazala	0630
2./JG 27	Lt Hans-Arnold Stahlschmidt	P-40	N Fort Acroma	0749
2./JG 27	Hptm Hans Maack	P-40	W Tobruk	0750
2./JG 27	Lt Friedrich Körner	P-40	W Tobruk	0752

German Casualties

9./JG 27	Bf 109F-4 trop WNr 8575 Yellow 5 combat; crash-landed on coast nr Borde-Bou-Hasna; Lt Erik Freiherr von Frisch PoW
Stab II./StG 3	Ju 87D-1 WNr 2469 S7+QC shot down by P-40 Ain el Gazala; Oblt Erich Olfermann/Obfw Paul Kostrewa KiA
3./StG 3	Ju 87D-1 WNr 2450 S7+JM shot down by P-40 Ain el Gazala; Hptm Johann-Georg Drescher/Uffz Rudolf Tuffeck PoW

Italian Claims

90ª Sq, 10°Gr, 4°St CT	Serg Magg Massimo Salvatore	MC.202	P-40	Acroma	1415-
90ª Sq, 10°Gr, 4°St CT	Serg Magg Massimo Salvatore	MC.202	P-40 Probable	Acroma	1415-
73ª Sq, 9°Gr, 4°St CT	Serg Teresio Martinoli	MC.202	P-40	Acroma	1415-
73ª Sq, 9°Gr, 4°St CT	S.Ten Alvaro Querci	MC.202	P-40 Probable	Acroma	1415-
73ª Sq, 9°Gr, 4°St CT	Serg Mario Guerci	MC.202	P-40	Acroma	1415-

Italian Casualties

73ª Sq, 9°Gr, 4°St CT	MC.202 MM 7824 '73-5' failed to return, S.Ten Mario Massa MiA
91ª Sq, 10°Gr, 4°St CT	MC.202 MM 7794 '91-2' damaged by bombs at Martuba

Saturday, 30 May 1942

This proved to be a day of even heavier aerial activity, WDAF undertaking massive attacks by fighter-bombers and Bostons on the German armour in 'The Cauldron' area. Part of the panzer force withdrew west, smashing through a British minefield. The Commonwealth fighters had few chances to make claims against opposing aircraft during the day, but losses to the aggressive Messerschmitts and Macchis were very heavy. Ten Kittyhawks of 250 Squadron took off at 0650 as close cover to 450 Squadron on a recce-strafe in the Bir Hacheim area. Four Bf 109s of I./JG 27 were off at 0933, attacking the Kittyhawks out of the sun, splitting up the formation between Tobruk and El Adem, where Oblt Marseille shot down Sgt Buckland's aircraft, the pilot baling out. Sgt McWilliams's engine seized as he was about to dive on a Messerschmitt and he force-landed in a minefield.

Bf 109F-4/Z of 7./JG 53 in flight over the sea in the hands of Oblt Wilfried Pufahl, shot down in error by the crew of a Ju 88 on 30 May.

Fifteen MC.200s of 8° Gruppo were also out early, escorted by 11 MC.202s of 6° Gruppo. The former unit strafed vehicles in the Zaviet el Mrassas area, their pilots claiming one lorry and three armoured cars in flames and several others damaged. Eight Bf 109s of III./JG 53 escorted six Bf 110s on a reconnaissance at 0710, but during this one Bf 109 was shot down in error by the crew of a Ju 88 which they came upon and the pilot undertook an emergency landing south of Gazala. At 1020 nine Kittyhawks of 2 SAAF Squadron on a reconnaissance patrol were jumped by a number of MC.202s, eight of which from 17° Gruppo were engaged in a free sweep over the Bir el Harmat area. The Italian pilots claimed four shot down for the loss of one Macchi and its pilot. The South Africans lost one of their aircraft, claiming one MC.202 in return.

Four Bf 109s of I./JG 27 on a Freie Jagd of the Mteifel-Harmat area attacked nine bombers and 15 escorting fighters which were flying at a low altitude. Fw Keppler claimed one fighter to the south-east of Sidi Rezegh, reporting that the aircraft somersaulted as it reached the ground; he also claimed to have damaged a second. However, Uffz Timmermann's aircraft was hit and he force-landed north of Tmimi on the Via Balbia.

There was very heavy fighting during the early afternoon. Four Bf 109s of III./JG 53 took off on a Freie Jagd at 1405 followed 45 minutes later by four from I./JG 27, both formations attacking nine Bostons which were being escorted by 260 Squadron on a raid at 1445, at about the same time as six Kittyhawks of 250 Squadron with four of 3 RAAF Squadron were out on a strafing mission. Probably engaging both forces, the Luftwaffe fighter pilots claimed seven shot down. Nine MC.202s of 6° Gruppo were also out on a free sweep at this time, reporting a combat with nine P-40s over Bir el Harmat, where four were claimed shot down although one of the successful pilots was then shot down and killed.

Allied losses were heavy during this part of the day. Two of 260 Squadron's aircraft were shot down, as were two of 3 RAAF Squadron. 250 Squadron and 112 Squadron each lost one while in 2 SAAF Squadron 2/Lt Fulton, an American citizen attached to the unit, also failed to return, having baled out and become a PoW.

Four Kittyhawks of 112 Squadron took off at 1420 from Gambut Satellite No.1, to attack motor transport. Over the target heavy Breda AA was experienced as the formation swept down to strafe,Burney's aircraft being hit and crashing in flames, the pilot killed, his body never being found. Four Bf 109s of III./JG 53 took off at 1630 to escort six Bf 110s, but in doing so six Allied fighters were encountered, one of which was claimed shot down by Lt Harder. Ten minutes later four Bf 109s of II./JG 27 departed on a Freie Jagd, the pilots of these reporting combat with six fighters in the Acroma-Tobruk-Harmat area, this unit claiming three Kittyhawks and a Hurricane.

Once again the Italian units were active between 1350-1525 with four CR.42s of 158° Gruppo, escorted by four MC.202s of 6° Gruppo, strafing in the Harmat area. They were followed at 1535 by 15 MC.200s of 13° Gruppo which strafed in three waves in the Gasr el Regem area, tasked with attacking forces threatening the XXI Corpo d'Armata. These aircraft ran into intense AA fire and many were hit; one was shot down, the pilot being killed, while another force-landed at Tmimi.

At 1745 three aircraft of 450 Squadron joined others of 250 and 3 RAAF Squadrons to escort fighter-bombers of 112 Squadron. Two Tomahawks of 5 SAAF and ten of 4 SAAF Squadrons set off to escort bombers and fighter-bombers also. At 1720 four Bf 109s of II./JG 27 on a Freie Jagd were followed five minutes later by six of I.Gruppe to escort Ju 87s. Both units met the Allied fighters at 1810 when three claims were made. Two of 450 Squadron's aircraft and one of 5 SAAF Squadron were shot down, but the Stukas were forced to jettison their bombs on their own troops and were then pursued by the South Africans, Maj Human of 2 SAAF Squadron claiming a Bf 109 shot down at 1800.

In the course of the day an S.81 transport of 600ª Squadriglia which was carrying a number of high-ranking officers, was hit by small-arms fire and force-landed south of Ain el Gazala where the crew and passengers were all taken prisoner. The day had cost WDAF 16-18 Kittyhawks and Tomahawks, while the Axis fighter pilots had claimed 24 plus one Hurricane. Amongst the Allied pilots brought down, three were reported killed or missing, two had become prisoners, but eight-ten survived, only one of whom was wounded, the rest all returning within a day or two to resume operations.

British Claims

73 Sqn	Flt Lt R.McDougal	Hurricane IIc BN415 'D'	Ju 88 Damaged	20m N Gambut on coast	0525
2 SAAF Sqn	Lt L.J.P.Berrange	Kittyhawk I AK735 'E'	MC.202		1145
260 Sqn	Flt Sgt J.F.Edwards	Kittyhawk Ia 'O'	Bf 109F Damaged	N Rotunda Walib Gap	1530

British Claims

260 Sqn	Flt Sgt J.S.Bernier	Kittyhawk Ia	Bf 109F Probable	El Adem	1530
5 SAAF Sqn	Lt K.C.Whyte	Tomahawk IIb AN354 'X'	Bf 109F Probable	SW Acroma	1545
250 Sqn	Sgt H.R.Hannaford	Kittyhawk I AK884 'Y'	Bf 109E Damaged	El Adem area	1630
250 Sqn	Sgt F.MacK.Twemlow	Kittyhawk I AK921 'T'	Bf 109E Damaged	El Adem area	1630
3 RAAF Sqn	Flt Lt A.W.Barr	Kittyhawk I AK899	Bf 109 Probable *	Knightsbridge	1630-1700
2 SAAF Sqn	Maj J.D.W.Human	Kittyhawk I AL186 'G'	Bf 109F	just W Knightsbridge	1800

*One source credits Barr with a Bf 109 and a G.50 before he was shot down

British Casualties

112 Sqn	Kittyhawk I AK772 'Y' FTR from ground attack; Plt Off H.G.Burney MiA
250 Sqn	Kittyhawk I AK648 'E' badly damaged in Rezegh-Acroma area by Bf 109s; Sgt D.W.Cairns safe
250 Sqn	Kittyhawk I AK704 'S' MiA from sweep, NW El Adem 0715; Sgt G.G. Buckland KiA
250 Sqn	Kittyhawk I AK943 shot down by ground fire at Segnali
250 Sqn	Kittyhawk I AL162 'I' in a fight NW El Adem 0715 engine seized and Sgt C. F.McWilliam RAAF force-landed in a minefield
260 Sqn	Kittyhawk I AK836 shot down by MC.202s near El Adem at 1530; Plt Off H.Hale baled out
260 Sqn	Kittyhawk I AK696 shot down by MC.202 at 1530 nr El Adem; Flt Lt M.D.Wylie
260 Sqn	Kittykawk I damaged by Bf 109, crash-landed at base; Flt Sgt D.C.Copping safe
450 Sqn	Kittyhawk I AL200 shot down by Bf 109s nr El Adem, 1805; Flt Sgt I.A.Nursey
450 Sqn	Kittyhawk I AL206 shot down by Bf 109s 17m S Gambut, 1815; Sgt D.H.McBurnie,WiA
450 Sqn	Kittyhawk I 'W' forced to land at 1230 by Bf 109; Sgt M.A.Jenkins safe
450 Sqn	Kittyhawk I AK897 forced to land at 1230 by Bf 109; Sgt W.J.Halliday safe
3 RAAF Sqn	Kittyhawk I AL153 shot down by 4 Bf 109s, c1620-1700; Sgt C.S.MacDiarmid
3 RAAF Sqn	Kittyhawk I AK889 shot down by 4 Bf 109s, c1620-1700; Flt Lt A.W.Barr safe, returned two days later
2 SAAF Sqn	Kittyhawk I AK735 'E' MiA, shot down by MC.202s near Rotunda Walib 1530; 2/Lt W.E.S.Fulton PoW
2 SAAF Sqn	Kittyhawk I AK841 'K' damaged by MC.202, crash-landed Acroma 1145; Lt R.G.Harrison PoW
5 SAAF Sqn	Tomahawk IIb AM495 'T' shot down on bomber escort SW Acroma c1800; Lt P.H.Saunders KiA
208 Sqn	Hurricanes T9536 and Z4555 and Tomahawk AN287 damaged by night bombing at Sidi Aziez l.g. (30th/31st night)

German Claims

3./JG 27	Oblt Hans-Joachim Marseille	P-40	1km NW El Adem	0605
1./JG 27	Fw Gerhard Keppler	P-40	SW Sidi Rezegh	1130
Stab I./JG 27	Oblt Rudolf Sinner	P-40	Bir el Harmat	1405

Fw Emil Kaiser (left) with Oblt Marseille and Lt Hans-Arnold Stahlschmidt (far right).

Stab I./JG 27	Lt Werner Schroer	P-40	NE Bir Hacheim	1405
Stab I./JG 27	Fw Emil Kaiser	P-40	E Bir Hacheim	1407
Stab I./JG 27	Fw Emil Kaiser	P-40	SE Bir el Harmat	1409
9./JG 53	Obfw Werner Stumpf	P-40	SW El Adem	1425
8./JG 53	Hptm Helmut Belser	P-40	30km S Ain el Gazala	1435
8./JG 53	Lt Karl-Heinz Quaritsch	P-40	SW El Adem	1458
4./JG 27	Obfw Karl-Heinz Bendert	P-40	E Fort Acroma	1603
4./JG 27	Oblt Ferdinand Vögl	2 P-40s	SW Tobruk	1605 & 1610
7./JG 53	Lt Jürgen Harder	P-40	E Ain el Gazala	1617
4./JG 27	Oblt Ferdinand Vögl	Hurricane	NE Bir el Harmat	1618
2./JG 27	Lt Karl von Lieres und Wilkau	P-40	30km E El Adem	1702
5./JG 27	Oblt Ernst Börngen	P-40	SE Fort Acroma	1705
2./JG 27	Hptm Ernst Maack	P-40	E Sidi Rezegh	1708

German Casualties

1./JG 27	Bf 109F-4 trop WNr 8654 u/k reason force-landed by Via Balbia, 12km N Tmimi, 40% damaged; Uffz Walter Timmermann safe
7./JG 53	Bf 109F-4 trop WNr 10126 left 0710 shot down by Ju 88 by accident, force-landed S Gazala; Oblt Wilfried Pufahl safe

Italian Claims

71ª Sq,17°Gr, 1°St CT	Cap Pericle Baruffi	MC.202			
71ª Sq,17°Gr, 1°St CT	M.llo Marcello Lui	MC.202	P-40	Bir el Harmat	0950-1105
71ª Sq,17°Gr, 1°St CT	Ten Sergio Morandi	MC.202			
72ª Sq,17°Gr, 1°St CT	Ten Mario Carini	MC.202	P-40	Bir el Harmat	0950-1105
80ª Sq,17°Gr, 1°St CT	Ten Emilio Marchi	MC.202			
80ª Sq,17°Gr, 1°St CT	Ten Giovanni B.Ghiglia	MC.202	2 P-40s	Bir el Harmat	0950-1105
80ª Sq,17°Gr, 1°St CT	Serg Magg Alvise Andrich	MC.202			
81ª Sq, 6°Gr, 1°St CT	Cap Giuliano Giacomelli	MC.202	P-40	Bir el Harmat-Bir Hacheim	1440-1600
81ª Sq, 6°Gr, 1°St CT	Serg Magg Nello Meneghetti	MC.202 MM 7881			
81ª Sq, 6°Gr, 1°St CT	Ten Antonio Palazzeschi	MC.202	P-40	Bir el Harmat-Bir Hacheim	1440-1600
88ª Sq, 6°Gr, 1°St CT	Serg Luigi Bartesaghi	MC.202	P-40	Bir el Harmat-Bir Hacheim	1440-1600
88ª Sq, 6°Gr, 1°St CT	Serg Magg Anano Borreo	MC.202	P-40	Bir el Harmat-Bir Hacheim	1440-1600

Italian Casualties

72ª Sq, 17°Gr, 1°St CT	MC.202 MM 7735 '72-3', M.llo Giuseppe Magli MiA
81ª Sq, 6°Gr, 1°St CT	MC.202 MM 7881, M.llo Nello Meneghetti KiA
78ª Sq, 13°Gr, 2°St CT	MC.200 MM 8300 shot down by ground fire at Gars el Regem, Serg Giuseppe Allevot KiA
78ª Sq, 13°Gr, 2°St CT	MC.200 MM 5305 damaged by AA, Serg Gardo Ravasio safe
78ª Sq, 13°Gr, 2°St CT	MC.200 MM 8303 damaged by AA, S.Ten Plinio Pellegrini safe
600ª Sq, 145°Gr Tras	S.81 MM 20343 force-landed near Ain Gazala in enemy territory, pilot Ten Ettore Mineo, copilot Serg Francesco Tisi, crew and passengers PoW

Sunday, 31 May 1942

Heavy sandstorms did little to curtail operations which began at 0600 when five Hurricanes of 274 Squadron took part in an offensive sweep over El Adem-Bir Hacheim, meeting 15 Ju 87s escorted by seven Bf 109s of II./JG 27. They attacked at once, claiming one Stuka damaged, but lost at least one aircraft and its pilot. 5 SAAF Squadron, which had contributed 11 Tomahawks to the sweep, enjoyed rather more success, Capt Duncan claiming one Bf 109 shot down while others added claims for two probables and three damaged German aircraft. The II./JG 27 pilots claimed four Allied fighters shot down during this engagement, but lost three of their own in the Acroma area. Oblt Emmerich Fluder, who had been credited with eight victories, was killed and Obfw Erich Krenzke became a PoW, only Fw Fritz Gromotka managing to return safely; with only one claim for a Messerschmitt arising from this combat, it has to be considered whether possibly two of these aircraft collided, or whether AA fire was responsible for their demises.

I./JG 27 and III./JG53 each provided four Bf 109s at 0758 to escort 12 more Ju 87s to Harmat. 4 SAAF Squadron scrambled 12 Tomahawks over Gazala to intercept, two of the Stukas being claimed shot down with a third as a probable. However, I.Gruppe then attacked the South Africans, four pilots claiming eight shot down, three of them by Oblt Marseille and two by Fw Steinhausen. At much the

Maj Erich Gerlitz took over command of III./JG 53 in May. He is in his Bf 109F, having gained his 17th victory on the last day of that month.

same time pilots of III./JG 53 added three more claims. 4 SAAF Squadron's casualties on this occasion appear to have been four shot down and one damaged, with the pilot of the latter slightly wounded.

260 Squadron sent out 12 Kittyhawks on a bomber escort mission at 1315, attacking Italian troops withdrawing in the Segnali area. Pilots reported that Bf 109s maintained a continuous attack to and from the target, one Kittyhawk being shot down and two damaged. The squadron later attacked eight Ju 87s, Flg Off Waddy claiming one shot down, two probables and one damaged. During this operation at least one of the squadron's Kittyhawks was lost, its pilot being killed. Lionel Sheppard, then a Sgt :

> "Then came the great day – I was to fly number 2 to the CO, Sqn Ldr Hanbury, on a bomber escort. It was 31 May 1942 and 19 months after joining the RAF. May Day had arrived – or so I thought. I followed 'Pedro' Hanbury all over the sky as, after the bombers had dropped their load on target and we began the return journey, we ran into a gaggle of Stuka 87s and ME 109s. Occasionally I was where I should be – about 100 yards to Pedro's right. Most of the time I was behind him or above him, up to 40-50 yards away, but I was there – I must confess that I saw nothing although Pedro was chasing a 109. It was all I could do to be approximately in the right place. In the event Flt Sgt Vesey was shot down, but Plt Off Waddy claimed an 87. In summing up, Pedro gave everyone a severe dressing down except me, saying I had been the only one maintaining station throughout the whole show. Somewhere, however, I must have picked up a bit of shrapnel or maybe a bullet because, on landing, one oleo leg of my aircraft collapsed."

As on the preceding two days, the Regia Aeronautica's main task was to support the ground troops advancing along the coast. 50° Stormo's CR.42s undertook three ground-attack missions in the Acroma area, covered by MC.202s of 1° and 4° Stormi. During the morning Ten Renato Bagnoli claimed two P-40s damaged, while during the day's third operation, which began at 1620, nine MC.202s of 9° Gruppo sighted and engaged a formation described as including 25 mixed fighter types, identified as Hurricanes, Spitfires and P-40s, four of which were claimed by Italian pilots. Two MC.200s of 94ª Squadriglia of 8° Gruppo, flown by Cap Orfeo Cecchet and Ten Mario D'Agostini, carried out a TacR sortie over the area between Trigh Capuzzo and the sea, just in front of the forward positions of XXI Corpo d'Armata. D'Agostini was wounded in his right leg by a splinter.

Soon after 1900 four Tomahawks of 4 SAAF Squadron and eight of 5 SAAF Squadron provided cover for Kittyhawks trying to locate the headquarters of a German general. South-west of El Adem they were jumped by Bf 109s of II./JG 27, 12 of which were escorting Ju 87s south of Acroma. Oblt Schulz shot down Maj Andrew Duncan, DFC, 5 SAAF's commanding officer, and Capt Copeland of 4 SAAF Squadron. On his return flight to base, Schulz also attacked and claimed damage to a Curtiss fighter which was attacking a Bf 110. While the South Africans had been taking off, six Kittyhawks of 260 Squadron had also set off on an interception patrol, encountering four Bf 109s of III./JG 53, the pilots of which claimed three Kittyhawks shot down. Flt Lt Hindle, whose aircraft had been damaged during one of the earlier engagements, was shot down and this time did not return. It seems that Flt Sgt Carlisle was also shot down, although he survived unhurt.

112 Squadron carried out 24 fighter-bomber sorties during the day, dropping 19 250lb bombs. From one sortie at 1845, in conjunction with 450 Squadron, Plt Off Mitchell failed to return, being reported missing in the Bir Hacheim area, possibly a victim of III./JG 53. 450 Squadron lost Flt Lt Eric 'Mick' Thompson, who was killed and Sgt Gordon 'Blondie' Lindsay who claimed a Bf 109 but was shot down and baled out unhurt.There is an interesting side note to this day's operations. John Waddy, when returning to his native Australia in the *Queen Mary* some months later in company with the Australian 9th Division, met a captain of anti-aircraft artillery who described the battle to him. Checking from his diary, the soldier told him that he recorded the date, time, place and circumstances as apparently identical to Waddy's combat with the Stukas, thus appearing to confirm that all three Ju 87s he had fired at had in fact crashed. Waddy had by then left the area and took no further action to obtain confirmation of his probables. Luftwaffe losses of such aircraft actually tie up fairly precisely with Allied claims for the day, although many examples have been given of the inexactitudes and errors often connected with such ground witnesses. Nonetheless, this note is included here as a matter of interest.

British Claims

5 SAAF Sqn	Maj J.E.Frost	Tomahawk IIb AN385 'W'	Ju 87 Probable	nr Acroma	0655
5 SAAF Sqn	Lt K.C.Morgan	Tomahawk IIb AN354 'X'			
5 SAAF Sqn	2/Lt J.M.S.Martin	Tomahawk IIb AM401 'I'	Bf 109F Damaged	Gazala	0655
5 SAAF Sqn	Lt C. Sommerville	Tomahawk IIb AN431 'S'	Ju 87 Damaged	nr Acroma	0700
5 SAAF Sqn	Maj J.E.Frost	Tomahawk IIb AN385 'W'			
5 SAAF Sqn	Capt A.Duncan	Tomahawk IIb AN523 'R'	Bf 109	nr Acroma	0700
4 SAAF Sqn	Capt G.G.Bayly	Tomahawk IIb AN242 'P'	Ju 87 Probable	Bir el Harmat	0750-0900
4 SAAF Sqn	Maj D.D.Moodie	Tomahawk I 'N'	Ju 87	30m S Gazala	0820
4 SAAF Sqn	Lt T.P.L.Murray	Tomahawk I AH988 'Q'	MC.202 Damaged	30m S Gazala	0820
4 SAAF Sqn	Lt W.J.Wheeler	Tomahawk I 'E'	Ju 87	Gazala-El Adem	0820
274 Sqn	Sgt W.M.Bruckshaw	Hurricane IIc	Ju 87 Damaged	El Adem-Bir Hacheim	
33 Sqn	Sgt W.H.Swan	Hurricane IIb BG940	Bf 109 Damaged	Acroma	
260 Sqn	Flg Off J.L.Waddy	Kittyhawk I AK956	Ju 87	Segnali area	1315-1435
260 Sqn	Flg Off J.L.Waddy	Kittyhawk I AK956	2 Ju 87s Probable	Segnali area	1315-1435
260 Sqn	Flg Off J.L.Waddy	Kittyhawk I AK956	Ju 87 Damaged	Segnali area	1315-1435
450 Sqn	Sgt G.Lindsey	Kittyhawk I AL190	Bf 109	10m W El Adem	1845-2020
5 SAAF Sqn	Lt B.S.Thornhill-Cook	Tomahawk IIb AN420 'P'	Bf 109F Probable	SW El Adem	2000

British Casualties

73 Sqn	Hurricane II Flt Sgt D.G.Barrie FTR
274 Sqn	Hurricane IIc El Adem-Bir Hacheim; Plt Off W.H.Ismay KiA
274 Sqn	Hurricane IIc El Adem-Bir Hacheim, shot down; Plt Off Bell returned
112 Sqn	Kittyhawk I AK999 took off at 1845, direct hit by AA, exploded bomb; Plt Off S.S.Mitchell KiA, found and buried by army
250 Sqn	Kittyhawk I crashed Halfaya; Sgt D.M.Webster safe
260 Sqn	Kittyhawk I shot down by Bf 109 16m S Knightsbridge; Sgt C.P.Vesey KiA
260 Sqn	Kittyhawk I shot down by Bf 109 16m S Knightsbridge; Sgt L.J.Sheppard safe
260 Sqn	Kittyhawk I badly damaged by Bf 109s S Knightsbridge; Flt Lt T.Hindle safe
260 Sqn	Kittyhawk I shot down by Bf 109s, Flt Lt T.Hindle KiA (second sortie)
260 Sqn	Kittyhawk I shot down by Bf 109s; Flt Sgt J.V.Carlisle safe
450 Sqn	Kittyhawk I AL190 shot down by Bf 109s over El Adem; Sgt G.Lindsey baled out, safe
450 Sqn	Kittyhawk I AK789 shot down by Bf 109; Flt Lt E.T.Thompson, MiA
2 SAAF Sqn	Kittyhawk I AL176 shot-up by fighters, rudder controls damaged, belly-landed at Gambut Satellite at 1955; Lt J.O. de Waal safe
4 SAAF Sqn	Tomahawk IIb AN242 'P' damaged by Ju 87, shot down by Flak, crash-landed Bir Belefaa; Capt G.G.Bayly returned
4 SAAF Sqn	Tomahawk IIa AH914 'T' shot down by fighter, crash-landed SW El Adem; 2/Lt N.W.Hancock returned
4 SAAF Sqn	Tomahawk IIb AN360 shot down by Bf 109; 2/Lt R.F.Marillier KiA
4 SAAF Sqn	Tomahawk IIb AK509 shot down by Bf 109 50m W Tobruk; Lt R.E.Jackson KiA

British Casualties

4 SAAF Sqn	Tomahawk IIb probably shot down by Bf 109; Capt W.M.Copeland returned
4 SAAF Sqn	Tomahawk IIb AM406 'B' damaged; 2/Lt D.Woodliffe slt WiA
5 SAAF Sqn	Tomahawk IIb AN354 'X' crashed on return from bomber escort nr El Adem 1930; Lt K.C.Morgan safe
5 SAAF Sqn	Tomahawk IIb AK523 'R' FTR from escort near El Adem 2000; Maj A.Duncan KiA

German Claims

4./JG 27	Oblt Ferdinand Vögl	2 P-40s	SW Fort Acroma & 2km NE Mteifel Chebir	0615 & 0620
4./JG 27	Fw Franz Stigler	P-40	SW Fort Acroma	0623
4./JG 27	Fw Alfred Heidel	P-40	W Fort Acroma	0624
1./JG 27	Fw Günther Steinhausen	P-40	N Bir Hacheim	0725
8./JG 53	Lt Rudolf Müller	2 P-40s	W Bir el Harmat & SW Fort Acroma	0725 & 0735
3./JG 27	Oblt Hans-Joachim Marseille	2 P-40s	5km & 8km W Bir el Harmat	0726 & 0728
3./JG 27	Obfw Karl Mentnich	P-40	W Bir el Harmat	0730
2./JG 27	Lt Karl von Lieres und Wilkau	P-40	SW Fort Acroma	0732
3./JG 27	Oblt Hans-Joachim Marseille	P-40	10km SW Fort Acroma	0734
1./JG 27	Fw Günther Steinhausen	P-40	N Bir Hacheim	0735
8./JG 53	Hptm Helmut Belser	P-40	SW Fort Acroma	0742
7./JG 53	Oblt Wilfried Pufahl	P-40	W El Adem	1850
7./JG 53	Lt Jürgen Harder	P-40	W El Adem	1852
Stab II./JG 27	Oblt Otto Schulz	2 P-40s	29km SW & 15km SW El Adem	1857 & 1900
Stab III./JG 53	Maj Erich Gerlitz	P-40	W El Adem	1908

German Casualties

6./JG 27	Bf 109F-4 trop WNr 8660 Yellow 3 shot down by P-40 Bu Amud; Oblt Emmerich Fluder KiA
6./JG 27	Bf 109F-4 trop WNr 8774 Yellow 9 shot down by P-40 Bu Amud; Obfw Erich Krenzke PoW
6./JG 27	Bf 109F-4 trop WNr 8548 Yellow 4 shot down by P-40 Bu Amud; Fw Fritz Gromotka MiA, returned
1./StG 3	Ju 87R-4 WNr 6237 S7+JH shot down by P-40 20km NW El Adem, 10% damaged; Uffz Dieter Kretschmar PoW
1./StG 3	Ju 87R-4 WNr 6230 shot down by P-40 NW El Adem; Uffz Johann Danninger/Gefr Josef Mittendorfer returned
2./StG 3	Ju 87R-4 WNr 6272 S7+EK AA 25km NW El Adem, 10% damaged; gunner Fw Ludwig Kirner WiA
2./StG 3	Ju 87R-4 WNr 6233 S7+HK AA 30km SW Ain el Gazala, 10% damaged; gunner Gefr Josef Meyer WiA
3./StG 3	Ju 87R-2 WNr 5995 S7+GL shot down by P-40 25km SW Fort Acroma; Uffz Johann Krieger WiA/ Gefr Josef Jennen PoW

Italian Claims

80ª Sq,17°Gr, 1°St CT	S.Ten. Renato Bagnoli	MC.202	2 P-40s Damaged	Bir el Harmat	1050-1210
96ª Sq, 9°Gr, 4°St CT	Ten Emanuele Annoni	MC.202	Spitfire	SW Acroma	1620-
9° Gr, 4° St	u/i pilots	MC.202	2 Hurricanes	SW Acroma	1620-
90ª Sq, 10°Gr, 4°St CT	Serg Magg Massimo Salvatore	MC.202	P-40	SW Acroma	1620-

Italian Casualties

94ª Sq, 8°Gr, 2°St CT	MC.200 hit by AA, Ten Mario D'Agostini WiA
80ª Sq, 17°Gr, 1°St CT	MC.202 MM 7787 damaged on ground

LUFTWAFFE ORDER OF BATTLE JUNE 1942

Fliegerführer Afrika

Stab JG 27	Bf 109F-4	10.(Jabo)/JG 27	Bf 109F-4
I./JG 27	Bf 109F-4	III./JG 53	Bf 109F-4
II./JG27	Bf 109F-4	10.(Jabo)/JG 53	Bf 109F-4
III./JG 27 (less Kommando Kreta)	Bf 109F-4	I./NJG 2	Ju 88A-5 Ju 88A-4

I./NJG 2	Ju 88C-2 Ju 88C-4 Ju 88C-6
III./ZG 26	Bf 110C-5 Bf 110C-6 Bf 110C-7 Bf 110D-0 Bf 110D-1 Bf 110D-2 Bf 110D-3 Bf 110E-1 Bf 110E-2 Bf 110E-3 Bf 109E-7 Bf 110F-2 Bf 109F-4
10./ZG 26	Do17Z-2
Stab StG 3	He 111H-5 Bf 110E-3
I./StG 3	Ju 87R-2 Ju 87R-4
II./StG 3	Ju 87R-2 Ju 87R-4
III./StG 3	Ju 87D-1
4.(H)/12	Personnel only
2.(H)/14	Bf 110E-2 Bf 110E-3 Bf 109E-7 Bf 109F-4

X. Fliegerkorps

Kommando Kreta	Bf 109F-4 (part of III./JG 27)
Stab LG 1	Ju 88A-4
I./LG 1	Ju 88A-4
II./LG 1	Ju 88A-4
12./LG 1	Ju 88A-5 Ju 88A-4
II./KG 100	He 111H-6
1.(F)/121	Ju 88A-5 Ju 88D-1 Ju 88D-5 Bf 109F-4
1.(F)/122	Ju 88D-1 Ju 88D-5 Bf 109F-4
2.(F)/123	Ju 88A-5 Ju 88D-1 Ju 88D-2 Ju 88D-5 Ju 86R-1
2./SAGr 125	Ar 196A-3
SAGr 126	He 60A-1 Fokker T.VIII Ar 196A-3 Bv 138C-1

Transportverbande Ob.Süd

III./KGzbV 1	Ju 52/3m
KGrzbV 400	Ju 52/3m

Monday, 1 June 1942

Sandstorms continued throughout the day, preventing operations to any great extent until the afternoon. At 1620 4 SAAF and 5 SAAF Squadrons put up four and six Tomahawks respectively to escort Kittybombers to the Knightsbridge-Bir Hacheim area. Near Gazala the Tomahawks were jumped by four Bf 109s of III./JG 53 which were out on a Freie Jagd, Lt Murray of 4 SAAF Squadron being shot down by Obfw Stumpf and force-landed near El Adem. He was picked up by the army. 2/Lt Golding of 5 SAAF claimed one Messerschmitt.

At 1745 145 Squadron flew the first Spitfire sorties over the desert, two pilots claiming damage to a reconnaissance Ju 88. Five Kittyhawks of 112 Squadron and six from 3 RAAF Squadron were then scrambled at 1830 to intercept four Ju 88s of I./KG 54 and four Bf 110s, with an escort of Bf 109s. Four of these fighters of III./JG 53 attacked the Kittyhawks, Lt Quaritsch shooting down Plt Off Wilson of 112 Squadron in flames; the pilot baled out and became a PoW. Obfw Kronschnabel claimed one fighter shot-up and belly-landed, but this was not confirmed. It is possible that a claim for a Hurricane was also made by the pilot of one of the Bf 110s, although this may also have failed to obtain confirmation since

Spitfire Vb AB326 ZX-A of 145 Squadron in which Plt Off Sabourin made the first claim for the Spitfire in North Africa on 1 June when he claimed damage to a Ju 88.

it is not included in Luftwaffe records. However, one Kittyhawk of 3 RAAF Squadron was hit and the pilot slightly wounded, but Flt Lt Barr, who claimed a Bf 109, also claimed damage to a Bf 110; two more of the Australian pilots claimed Bf 109s, and two others claimed two such fighters damaged. Lt Quaritsch was shot down, crash-landing near El Adem. 112 Squadron pilots claimed damage to two Ju 88s, but one of the KG 54 bombers was shot down by the fighters, crashing between Acroma and Bir Hacheim.

The Luftwaffe's main protagonist on this date was from other causes. Whilst attacking vehicles, two Bf 110s of 9./ZG 26 were both shot down by AA, with a third from 7./ZG 26 hit by the blast of a tank which exploded as the pilot was strafing it, the big Messerschmitt crashing near Martuba and blowing up. Lost with this aircraft was the successful Oblt Alfred Wehmeyer and his gunner, while the crews of the other aircraft were also killed. A Ju 87 of 4./StG 3 was also the victim of AA south of Gazala in similar circumstances; in this case the pilot survived as a PoW.

II./JG 27 sent out six Bf 109s to escort two Bf 109E TacR aircraft over the Tobruk-Acroma area, Hptm Düllberg spotting a Wellington standing on an airfield north-west of Bir Hacheim which he strafed, causing it to burst into flames. At 1945 four Bf 109s of I./JG 27 undertook a ground-attack sortie near El Cheimar, claiming to have destroyed a scout car, a 20mm self-propelled gun, an armoured car, a car and a tank. Then at 2005 Fw Pöttgen claimed to have shot down a fighter north-west of Gadd el Ahmar, and ten minutes later Oblt Marseille claimed another south-west of Mteifel in flames. The first of these was Pöttgen's first claim in over 100 sorties as Marseille's Röttenflieger. The identity of their victims has not been discovered; however, due to the circumstances which devolved during the month, June 1942 proved to be the worst-recorded month of the war for the WDAF, presenting the researcher with probably the greatest number of unanswered questions of the whole North African campaign.

Throughout the day between 0510-1720 24 MC.200s of 2° Stormo strafed concentrations of Allied troops and vehicles between Mteifel Chebir and Bir Hacheim during five missions. The last of these saw a 78ª Squadriglia aircraft force-land within British lines, the pilot being captured. The day also saw the first sorties flown by the Free French GC 1 Alsace (or GC III.2 as it became known) from LG.16 at Fuka.

British Claims

1 SAAF Sqn	Lt I.R.Pride	Hurricane IIb 5348 'Z'	Ju 88 Damaged	scramble Edcu, NW Dekheila	0806
5 SAAF Sqn	2/Lt C.A.Golding	Tomahawk IIb AN468 'J'	Bf 109F	Knightsbridge-Bir Hacheim	1730
274 Sqn	Sgt W.G.Eagle	Hurricane IIc	Bf 109F Damaged	Bir Hacheim-El Adem	1730

Ju 87B S1 + HK of I./StG3 in flight between Maleme Crete and Derna.

145 Sqn	Sgt H.G.James	Spitfire Vb AB324 'L'	Ju 88 Damaged	Gambut	1735-1825
145 Sqn	Flt Lt J.J.P.Sabourin	Spitfire Vb AB326 'A'			
33 Sqn	Flt Lt S.V.P. Bird	Hurricane IIb BG940 'H'	Bf 109 Damaged		1815
33 Sqn	unstated		MC.202 Damaged		1815
3 RAAF Sqn	Flt Lt A.W.Barr	Kittyhawk I AL178 'W'	Bf 110 Damaged	30-35m SSE Gazala	1825-2020
3 RAAF Sqn	Flt Lt A.W.Barr	Kittyhawk I AL178 'W'	Bf 109F	30-35m SSE Gazala	1825-2020
3 RAAF Sqn	Sgt L.L.Boardman	Kittyhawk I AK816 'R'	Bf 109F Damaged	30-35m SSE Gazala	1825-2020
3 RAAF Sqn	Sgt W.D.Finlayson	Kittyhawk I AK745 'Z'	Bf 109F Damaged	30-35m SSE Gazala	1825-2020
3 RAAF Sqn	Sgt G.A.Neill	Kittyhawk I AL148 'F'	Bf 109F	30-35m SSE Gazala	1825-2020
3 RAAF Sqn	Plt Off G.C.Coward	Kittyhawk I AK992 'V'	Bf 109F	30-35m SSE Gazala	1825-2020
112 Sqn	Plt Off F.F.J.Edwards	Kittyhawk I AK907	Ju 88 Damaged	1830-2030	
112 Sqn	Flt Lt R.M.Leu	Kittyhawk I AK985	Ju 88 Damaged	1830-2030	

British Casualties

112 Sqn	Kittyhawk I AL196 FTR from sweep at 2000; Plt Off R.K.Wilson PoW
3 RAAF Sqn	Kittyhawk I AK729 damaged Cat II by fighters, near Bir Hacheim at 1900; Sgt E.H.T.Alderson slt WiA
4 SAAF Sqn	Tomahawk IIb AK988 shot down by Bf 109s and force-landed nr El Adem 1530-1630; Lt T.P.L.Murray safe
4 SAAF Sqn	Tomahawk IIb AN242 'P'shot down, crash-landed at Knightsbridge 0845; Capt G.G.Bayly safe

German Claims

9./JG 53	Obfw Werner Stumpf	P-40	15km SW Fort Acroma	1630
8./JG 53	Lt Karl-Heinz Quaritsch	Spitfire	Mteifel Chebir	1855
7./JG 53	Lt Heinrich Hesse	P-40	30km NW Bir Hacheim	1855
7./JG 53	Oblt Ernest Kläger	P-40	15km NW Bir Hacheim	1858
3./JG 27	Fw Rainer Pöttgen	P-40	NW Gadd el Ahmar	1905
3./JG 27	Oblt Hans-Joachim Marseille	P-40	20km ENE El Cheimar	1915

German Casualties

I./JG 27	Bf 109F-4 trop WNr 8508 50% damaged by air raid at Martuba
I./JG 27	Bf 109F-4 trop WNr 10146 10% damaged by air raid at Martuba
8./JG 53	Bf 109F-4 trop WNr 10134 lost in combat with P-40 nr El Adem; Lt Karl-Heinz Quaritsch
4./StG 3	Ju 87D-1 WNr 2365 S7+CM AA 15km S Ain el Gazala; Uffz Rudolf Holler PoW, Uffz Julius Roth KiA
7./ZG 26	Bf 110C-5 WNr 2233 3U+HR hit by blast of exploding tank, crashed SE of Martuba; aircraft exploded on impact; Oblt Alfred Wehmeyer/Uffz Karl-Heinz Biwer KiA
9./ZG 26	Bf 110F-2 WNr 4548 3U+US shot down by AA, crashed 4km NE of Segnali-North airfield; Oblt Karl-Heinz Bittner/Fw Ernst Hörning KiA
9./ZG 26	Bf 110F-2 WNr 4574 3U+BS shot down by AA , crashed N of Segnali-North airfield; Obfw Otto Polenz/Uffz Kurt Zitzmann KiA

Italian Casualties

78ª Sq, 13°Gr, 2°St CT	MC.200 MM 5312 hit by ground fire, force-landed in enemy territory, Serg Paolo Borgis PoW

Monday-Tuesday, 1/2 June 1942

Seven Cant.Z.1007bis of 35° Stormo bombed railway line and facilities N of Trigh Capuzzo.

German Casualties

6./KG 100	He 111H-6 WNr 7224 6N+D6, damaged by AA over Tobruk but landed safely at base, two WiA
3./KG 54	Ju 88A-4 WNr 3678 B3+AH, take-off 0100, shot down in combat with Hurricanes and crashed between Fort Acroma and Bir Hacheim;. Fw Theodor Kirner and crew MiA

Tuesday, 2 June 1942

Italian forces, supported by Stukas, began an attack on Free French forces dug in at the southern fortress of Bir Hacheim, hoping to quickly wipe out this outpost and roll-up the British southern flank. Air activity on the Allied side was limited due to continual sandstorms.

Two Hurribombers of 274 Squadron on a mission to the area known as 'The Cauldron' were attacked at 1722 by three Bf 109s of II./JG 27 on a Freie Jagd. Obfw Schulze surprised Flt Lt Pat Moriarty as he was strafing, shooting his aircraft down in flames, the Hurricane shattering on the ground. Flt Sgt Parbury set course for base, but ran into a sandstorm and crash-landed at Capuzzo. An 80 Squadron Hurricane was also lost, failing to return from a search for a missing Wellington – probably that destroyed during the previous day by Hptm Düllberg.

At 1916 two Bf 109s of II./JG 27 escorted a reconnaissance Bf 110 of 4.(H)/12 over Gazala, but this was shot down by AA when at 1,500 feet and crash-landed in flames south-west of Acroma, the crew being killed. The pilot, Hptm von Kühlwetter, had been the commanding officer, and was subsequently replaced by Hptm Scheffer. MC.200s of 2° Stormo and CR.42s of 50° Stormo continued to undertake strafing missions in the Trigh Capuzzo-Mteifel Chebir area.

British Claims

73 Sqn	Sqn Ldr D.H.Ward	Hurricane IIc BN131 'P'	Ju 88 Damaged	Gasr el Arid	0148

British Casualties

80 Sqn	Hurricane IIc BM977 took off at 1315, searching for Wellington SE Sollum; Sgt J.A.Glynn MiA
274 Sqn	Hurricane IIc p.m. fighter-bomber sortie over 'The Cauldron', shot down in flames; Flt Lt P.D.Moriarty KiA
274 Sqn	Hurricane IIc crash-landed at Capuzzo in sandstorm; Flt Sgt C.R.Parbury safe

German Claims

4./JG 27	Obfw Alfred Schulze	P-40	5km SW Ain el Gazala	1622

German Casualties

4.(H)/12	Bf 110E-2 WNr 4433 2S-HA shot down by AA Bu Alusk; Lt Hans Kahrt, Hptm Hubert von Kühlwetter, Obfw Heinz Preuss KiA

Bf 109Fs of 3./JG 27.

Wednesday, 3 June 1942

The WDAF fighter force was now switched to the priority task of defending the embattled French at Bir Hacheim, fighter-bombers claiming to have put some 60 Axis vehicles out of action here during the day. At 0620 eight MC.202s of 6° Gruppo on a free sweep in the Bir el Harmat-Bir Hacheim area, engaged a formation identified as 15 P-40s which were attacking German Ju 87s. These were attacked, three being claimed shot down plus one more probably. 33 Squadron reported meeting six MC 202s, claiming two damaged but having two of the unit's Hurricanes shot-up.

Around the same time two II./JG 27 Bf 109s were escorting a Bf 110 to Bir Hacheim, but were repeatedly attacked by three British fighters. Lt Jenisch force-landed ten miles from the target area and was strafed on the ground, but returned safely later to his own lines on foot.

The British unit responsible for this attack is uncertain, but may have been 145 Squadron which flew 12 sorties during the day, Sqn Ldr Overton claiming a Bf 109 damaged, though apparently at a later time. However, nine Tomahawks of 4 SAAF Squadron were scrambled at 0655, intercepting Ju 87s over Bir Hacheim, escorted by six Bf 109s each from I., II. and III./JG 27, and this certainly seems to have been the formation spotted by the 6° Gruppo Macchi pilots. Only one escorting Messerschmitt attacked the South Africans, Wg Cdr Beresford being slightly wounded. One Stuka was shot down by AA, the pilot, Hptm Spangeberg, the Staffelkapitän of 2./StG 3, becoming a PoW.

At 1215 11 Tomahawks of 5 SAAF Squadron were ordered off on a sweep, but Lts Hirst and Groble collided head-on taxying, both aircraft being damaged. Nine therefore took off, engaging Ju 87s of I./StG 3 near Bir Hacheim. The squadron noted that its Tomahawks were flying in line astern and turned "rather shakily" to the attack but hitting the Stukas squarely. Capt Botha claimed three shot down and shared a fourth with Wg Cdr Beresford, who also claimed another himself. Maj Frost and three other pilots claimed one apiece; one of these, 2/Lt Golding, shared a second with Capt Morrison. Four Ju 87s were actually lost during this combat, and a fifth damaged.

Six Bf 109s of I./JG 27 were flying escort and one of these, flown by Oblt Marseille, turned in behind the South African aircraft and attacked with apparent considerable effect. Reportedly, his cannon jammed after only ten rounds had been fired, leaving him only with his two machine guns. First to fall was Capt Pare who went down in flames at 1322, although reported to have first shot down a Bf 109. 2/Lt Martin then crashed, slightly wounded, at Bir Hacheim. Three more pilots also failed to return, however all were reported to be safe two days later, although all wounded and in Tobruk hospital. Capt Botha's aircraft also suffered damage, but he managed to get back to base where he force-landed.

Marseille landed at 1352, claiming to have shot down six Tomahawks between 1322-1333, this engagement being lauded throughout the Luftwaffe. There are, however, some anomalies here which, coupled with the failure so early in the engagement of his aircraft's main weapon, require careful consideration. It seems that Messerschmitts of III./JG 53 were also involved in the escort of the Stukas, two experienced pilots from this unit claiming between them three P-40s at precisely the same time as Marseille was making his attacks. Four II./JG 27 aircraft were on a Freie Jagd in the same area, again at the same time, one pilot from this unit claiming one of the fighters.

It is not suggested that Marseille deliberately exaggerated his claims, but it seems at the least very possible that three of the Messerschmitt pilots were firing at some of the Tomahawks at the same time as he was, or immediately afterwards. Perhaps, with only his machine guns working, he sprayed each in turn swiftly, confident that he had shot each down, leaving damaged aircraft in his wake to be finished off by the others. What can be said with certainty, however, is that claims for ten Tomahawks (or 'P-40s') were made between 1322-1333, during which period 5 SAAF Squadron suffered the loss of five aircraft plus a sixth damaged – perhaps a more typical claim-loss ratio. Following the report submitted on his return by Capt Botha, he was recommended for the immediate award of a DFC for his part.

During the day 3° Gruppo was disbanded and its personnel repatriated to Italy. The unit's CR.42s were left to 50° Stormo Assalto, with a few assigned to 1° and 4° Stormo for night-fighter duties.

British Claims

1 SAAF Sqn	Capt P.C.R.Metelerkamp	Hurricane IIb BG764 'W'	Ju 88 Damaged	25m NW Alexandria	0845
145 Sqn	Sqn Ldr C.N.Overton	Spitfire Vb AB339 'M'	Bf 109 Damaged	1100-1155	
233 Wg	Wg Cdr T.B.de la P.Beresford	Tomahawk IIb AM406	Ju 87	Bir Hacheim	1315
233 Wg	Wg Cdr T.B.de la P.Beresford	Tomahawk IIb AM406	Ju 87	Bir Hacheim	1315
5 SAAF Sqn	Capt L.C.Botha	Tomahawk IIb AN448 'H'			

British Claims

5 SAAF Sqn	Capt L.C.Botha	Tomahawk IIb AN448 'H'	3 Ju 87s	Bir Hacheim	1315
5 SAAF Sqn	Maj J.E.Frost	Tomahawk IIb AN385 'W'	Ju 87	Bir Hacheim	1315
5 SAAF Sqn	Lt H.G.Gaymans	Tomahawk IIb AN345 'M'	Ju 87	Bir Hacheim	1315
5 SAAF Sqn	2/Lt C.A.Golding	Tomahawk IIb AN468 'J'	Ju 87	Bir Hacheim	1315
5 SAAF Sqn	Capt R.L.Morrison	Tomahawk IIb AK 421 'Z' }	Ju 87	Bir Hacheim	1315
5 SAAF Sqn	unstated	Tomahawk IIb }			
5 SAAF Sqn	Lt V.S.Muir	Tomahawk IIb AN262 'C'	Ju 87	Bir Hacheim	1315
5 SAAF Sqn	Capt R.Pare	Tomahawk IIb AK384 'V'	Bf 109F	Bir Hacheim	1315
33 Sqn	unstated	Hurricane II	MC.202 Damaged		
33 Sqn	unstated	Hurricane II	MC.202 Damaged		

British Casualties

233 Wg	Tomahawk IIb AM406 slt damaged by Bf 109; Wg Cdr T.B.de la P.Beresford
112 Sqn	Kittyhawk I AL121 damaged Cat II in combat; Sgt N.A.Clark safe
5 SAAF Sqn	Tomahawk IIb AM401 'I' shot down, force-landed in desert 1315; 2/Lt J.M.S.Martin returned
5 SAAF Sqn	Tomahawk IIb AN262 'C' shot down by Bf 109, crash-landed NW Bir Hacheim; Lt V.S.Muir WiA
5 SAAF Sqn	Tomahawk IIb AK421 'Z' shot down by Bf 109 and crash-landed 1315; Capt R.L.Morrison WiA
5 SAAF Sqn	Tomahawk IIb AN468 'J' shot down and crash-landed 1315; 2/Lt C.A.Golding safe
5 SAAF Sqn	Tomahawk IIb AK384 'V' presumed shot down by Bf 109 1315; Capt R.Pare KiA
4 SAAF Sqn	Tomahawk IIb lost to 15 plus Bf 109s, Bir Hacheim 0745; Lt G.W.McGregor ?
33 Sqn	2 Hurricanes damaged by MC.202s

German Claims

7./JG 53	Oblt Ernst Kläger	P-40		1220
3./JG 27	Oblt Hans-Joachim Marseille	6 P-40s	W Bir Hacheim	1222, 1225, 1227, 1228, 1229, 1233
5./JG 27	Uffz Helmut Gierster	P-40	10km E Bir Hacheim	1223
8./JG 53	Hptm Helmut Belser	2 P-40s		1225 & 1228

German Casualties

5./JG 27	Bf 109F-4 trop WNr 8677 combat with P-40, force-landed 15km NW Bir Hacheim 0630, strafed 100%; Lt Kurt Jenisch safe
1./StG 3	Ju 87R-2 WNr 6015 S7+DH combat with P-40 25km SW Fort Acroma; Uffz Werner Nusswitz/Uffz Heinrich Dierking KiA
1./StG 3	Ju 87R-2 WNr 5969 S7+HH combat with P-40 25km SW Fort Acroma; Lt Karl Schneider KiA/Gefr Alfred Pobel PoW
1./StG 3	Ju 87R-4 WNr 6236 S7+LH combat with P-40 25km SW Fort Acroma, landed at base; Obfw Anton Braun (gunner) KiA
2./StG 3	Ju 87R-2 WNr 5967 S7+FK AA Ain el Gazala; Hptm Herbert Spangenberg/Fw Josef Motzet PoW
3./StG 3	Ju 87R-2 WNr 6066 S7+FL combat with P-40 15km NW Bir Hacheim; Lr Hans Deibel PoW/ Uffz Wilhelm Luberichs KiA
3./StG 3	Ju 87R-2 WNr 6043 S7+DK combat with P-40 15km NW Bir Hacheim ; Gefr August Brandt (gunner) PoW; pilot safe
III./ZG 26	Bf 110E-1 WNr 4562, badly shot-up in error by own Flak, and crash-landed near Gazala, 80% damaged

Italian Claims

81ª Sq, 6°Gr,1°St CT	Cap Edoardo Baldini	MC.202	P-40	Bir Hacheim-Bir el Harmat 0620-0730
81ª Sq, 6°Gr,1°St CT	M.llo Italo Baldelli	MC.202	P-40 Probable	Bir Hacheim-Bir el Harmat 0620-0730
81ª Sq, 6°Gr,1°St CT	S.Ten Bruno Ganda	MC.202	P-40	Bir Hacheim-Bir el Harmat 0620-0730
79ª Sq, 6°Gr,1°St CT	Serg Magg Amedeo Benati	MC.202	P-40	Bir Hacheim-Bir el Harmat 0620-0730

Thursday, 4 June 1942

WDAF squadrons were now operating flat-out, pilots frequently undertaking three or four sorties a day. The vast majority of these were directed over Bir Hacheim. At 0748 I./JG 27 escorted Ju 87s of II./StG 3 to attack the fortress where one of the bombers was shot down by AA fire. Seven Tomahawks each from 4 SAAF and 5 SAAF Squadrons with Kittyhawks of 2 SAAF Squadron, were ordered to patrol over Bir Hacheim where the South African pilots got in a good attack on the Stukas before the escorts

Serg Luciano Perdoni of 84ª Squadriglia (on the left) in front of his MC.202 '84-2' MM 7805.

were able to interfere, claiming eight shot down, three of them by Maj Frost. Five of the dive-bombers actually went down, including that flown by the Gruppenkommandeur, Hptm Heinrich Eppen, Ritterkreuzträger, he and his gunner failing to return.

The Tomahawks were then attacked by three Bf 109s of II./JG 27 which were out on a Freie Jagd, the German pilots claiming two, both of which they reported had crash-landed. Nine MC.202s of 10° Gruppo were also on a free sweep in the area at this time, reporting engaging P-40s, claiming four and two probables. During this fight 4 SAAF Squadron lost three aircraft, two of the pilots becoming PoWs. The third, Lt Lane, was picked up by a Hurricane of 274 Squadron flown by Plt Off George Keefer. Maj Meaker, who was flying with 5 SAAF Squadron, had to force-land when his aircraft was hit by the gunner in the Ju 87 he was attacking; he also was picked up, in his case by Lt Horne, and was flown back to base two-up in the Tomahawk. 260 Squadron claimed a Bf 109 destroyed and one damaged at 0910, the latter aircraft crash-landing.

2 SAAF Squadron, apparently flying top cover to the Tomahawks, became engaged with four Bf 109s, Lt de Waal claiming one shot down, with two claimed damaged. Having made one of the latter claims, Lt Burdon was shot down and crash-landed; he got clear before his aircraft exploded in flames, returning safely next day. Meanwhile, during the return flight, 5 SAAF Squadron flew through a heavy concentration of Flak, Lt Thornhill-Cook being shot down and killed. Lt Whyte's aircraft was shot-up, although he was able to nurse it back to base.

Hptm Heinrich Eppen was Kommandeur of I./StG 3 when he was shot down and killed by SAAF fighters on 4 June.

During the early afternoon ten CR.42s of 159° Gruppo strafed vehicles in the Bir Hacheim area, but four aircraft failed to return, one shot down by AA, one crash-landed, one landing due to fuel shortage and a fourth undamaged, but apparently for technical reasons. At much the same time Cap Franco Lucchini, a leading fighter pilot who at the time was credited with seven victories, led nine 10° Gruppo

MC.202s over Bir Hacheim again, where a large formation of British fighters was encountered, two P-40s being claimed by Lucchini and another pilot, while a number of unidentified 9° Gruppo pilots claimed four Hurricanes. Meanwhile, at 1520 ten Bf 109s of III./JG 27 had undertaken another Stuka escort over the area. Lt Nitzsche left the formation and force-landed, returning next morning – reason unknown.

At 1720 six Kittybombers of 260 Squadron, with 4 SAAF and 5 SAAF Squadron Tomahawks as cover, scrambled over Bir Hacheim where CR.42s escorted by MC.202s were met. These comprised five Fiats of 158° Gruppo and four of 390ª Squadriglia led by Cap Alessandro Cerutti, escorted by nine Macchis of 17° Gruppo. The attacking WDAF fighters were identified as P-40s and Spitfires – probably denoting the somewhat different appearance of the noses of the Kittyhawks and Tomahawks – and two of the CR.42s were shot down, one pilot being lost and the other becoming a PoW. The MC.202s were not able to protect their charges fully on this occasion and could only claim damage to one P-40. There was some confusion regarding the identity of the successful 233 Wing pilots, but one CR.42 was claimed by Flg Off Waddy of 260 Squadron, Capt Botha and Lt Patterson of 5 SAAF Squadron being awarded a half share each in the second biplane.

At the time that this engagement was occurring, eight Bf 109s of II./JG 27 escorted three Ju 87s over the area, one of the latter carrying Feldmarschall Kesselring as an observer, but this aircraft had to force-land 20 miles south of Tmimi. In the evening Bf 109s escorted a Fieseler Storch to pick up the stranded Feldmarschall. Plt Off Atkinson of 112 Squadron failed to return from one fighter-bomber attack which had departed at 1735, and a Hurricane of 213 Squadron was also lost, the pilot being killed.

The engagements by the South African units caused General Koenig, the French commander at Bir Hacheim to send his famous signal: "Bravo! Merci pour le RAF!" to which AVM Coningham responded: "Bravo a vous! Merci pour le sport!" Despite this, support for the fortress would be reduced next day in order that more sorties could be flown over the now-decisive Knightsbridge area.

A section of four S.82s of 145° Gruppo, led by T.Col Felice Mazzetti moved from Castel Benito to Derna to operate as a night bombing and transport unit; three more S.82s would follow later.

First SAAF unit to be re-equipped with Kittyhawk Is was 2 SAAF Squadron. This is DP-P of that unit, believed to be AL103 or AL223. In the background can be seen Tomahawks of 4 SAAF Squadron (coded KJ), both these units serving with 233 Wing at this time.

British Claims

5 SAAF Sqn	Lt B.S.Thornhill-Cook	Tomahawk IIb AK380 'R' }	Ju 87	NW Bir Hacheim	0855
5 SAAF Sqn	Lt K.C.Whyte	Tomahawk IIb AN313 'X' }			
5 SAAF Sqn	Maj J.E.Frost	Tomahawk IIb AM385 'W'	3 Ju 87s	Bir Hacheim	0900
4 SAAF Sqn	Capt G.G.Bayly	Tomahawk IIb AM418 'S'	Ju 87	Bir Hacheim	0910
4 SAAF Sqn	Capt G.G.Bayly	Tomahawk IIb AM418 'S'	Ju 87 Damaged	Bir Hacheim	0910
2 SAAF Sqn	Lt V.R.Burdon	Kittyhawk I AK392 'B'	Bf 109F Damaged	2m SE Bir Hacheim	0910
2 SAAF Sqn	Lt J.O.de Waal	Kittyhawk I AL126 'R'	Bf 109F	6m SE Bir Hacheim	0910
2 SAAF Sqn	Lt J.O.de Waal	Kittyhawk I AL126 'R'	Bf 109 Damaged	SE Bir Hacheim	0910
260 Sqn	unstated	Kittyhawk I	Bf 109F	Bir Hacheim	0910
260 Sqn	unstated	Kittyhawk I	Bf 109F Damaged*	Bir Hacheim	0910
4 SAAF Sqn	Lt S.Cohen	Tomahawk IIb 'N'	Ju 87 Damaged	Bir Hacheim	0915
4 SAAF Sqn	Maj J.L.Hewitson	Tomahawk IIb AN452 'M'	Ju 87	Bir Hacheim	0915
4 SAAF Sqn	Lt W.J.Wheeler	Tomahawk IIb AN428 'K'	Ju 87	SW Bir Hacheim	0915

4 SAAF Sqn	Capt J.Morphew	Tomahawk IIb AN393	Ju 87^	Bir Hacheim	0915
260 Sqn	Flg Off J.L.Waddy	Kittyhawk I AL198	CR.42	Bir Hacheim area	1720-1840
4 SAAF Sqn	Lt M.P. Ironside	Tomahawk IIb AN452 'M' sh	CR.42**		
4 SAAF Sqn	Lt A.C.Paterson	Tomahawk IIb AN462 'K' sh	CR.42**		
5 SAAF Sqn	Capt L.C.Botha	Tomahawk IIb AN448 'H' sh	CR.42**		c 1800

^Morphew, who became a PoW, did not claim this Ju 87

*claimed initially as damaged, but crash-landed

**Paterson claimed to have shared a CR.42 with RAF fighters – probably 260 Sqn but did not claim this; Botha claimed a share in this CR.42 at around 1800

British Casualties

260 Sqn	Kittyhawk I badly damaged by Bf 109, crash-landed Bir Hacheim 0910
112 Sqn	Kittyhawk I AL219 MiA from ground attack; Plt Off E.Atkinson KiA
213 Sqn	Hurricane II; Plt Off W.H.Thomlinson KiA
2 SAAF Sqn	Kittyhawk I AK611 'B' shot down and crash-landed at 0925 SW Bir Hacheim; Lt V.R.Burdon returned
4 SAAF Sqn	Tomahawk IIb AN393 shot down by four Bf 109s; Capt J.Morphew WiA, PoW; escaped 1943
4 SAAF Sqn	Tomahawk IIb AN460 shot down by Ju 87 rear gunner S Tobruk; Lt J. de la H.Lane picked up by Hurricane of 274 Sqn, flown by Plt Off G.C.Keefer
4 SAAF Sqn	Tomahawk IIb AN461 shot down by Bf 109; 2/Lt K.H.Lawler PoW
4 SAAF Sqn	Tomahawk IIb AK509 reportedly lost over Bir Hacheim, but no details
5 SAAF Sqn	Tomahawk IIb AK380 'R' shot down by Flak 15km S Bir Hacheim; Lt B.S.Thornhill-Cook KiA
5 SAAF Sqn	Tomahawk IIb AN388 'N' shot down by Ju 87 rear gunner; force-landed 16km SE Bir Hacheim 0925; Maj F.J.M.Meaker picked up by Lt C.J.C.Horne (AK415 'T')

German Claims

Stab II./JG 27	Oblt Gustav Rödel	P-40	3km SE Bir Hacheim	0815
Stab II./JG 27	Obfhr Willi Kientsch	P-40	10km SW Mteifel Chebir	0820

German Casualties

Stab II./JG 27	Bf 109F-4 trop WNr 10140 40% damaged by AA, force-landed at Tmimi
Stab I./StG 3	Ju 87R-2 WNr 6146 S7+AB combat P-40 15km WNW Bir Hacheim; Hptm Heinrich Eppen/Obfw Adalbert Betzler KiA
1./StG 3	Ju 87R-2 WNr 6163 S7+NH combat P-40 15km WNW Bir Hacheim; Uffz Michael safe; Heinz Schellenberg (gunner) WiA
2./StG 3	Ju 87R-4 WNr 6306 S7+GK combat P-40 15km NW Bir Hacheim; Lt Horst Heritsch/Gefr Gerhard Beck WiA
2./StG 3	Ju 87R-4 WNr 6205 S7+JK combat P-40 20km WNW Bir Hacheim; Ogfr Heinz Kaufold (gunner) KiA; pilot safe, 60% dam
5./StG 3	Ju 87D-1 WNr 2465 S7+KM AA Bir Hacheim; one baled, Lt Robert Hübel/ Uffz Fritz Müller KiA
3./LG 1	Ju 88A-4 WNr 140217 L1+WL, shot down by own Flak, crashed 100km W Tobruk; Lt Karl Blume KiA, 1 MiA, two PoW

Italian Claims

84ª Sq, 10°Gr, 4°St CT	M.llo Luigi Bignami	MC.202 MM 7928 '84-9'	P-40	S Bir Hacheim	0745-0850
84ª Sq, 10°Gr, 4°St CT	Serg Livio Barbera	MC.202 MM 7814 '84-5'	P-40 Probable	S Bir Hacheim	0745-0850
90ª Sq, 10°Gr, 4°St CT	M.llo Angelo Savini	MC.202	P-40	S Bir Hacheim	0745-0850
90ª Sq, 10°Gr, 4°St CT	Cap Ranieri Piccolomini	MC.202	P-40 Probable	S Bir Hacheim	0745-0850
91ª Sq, 10°Gr, 4°St CT	M.llo Leonardo Ferrulli	MC.202	2 P-40s	S Bir Hacheim	0745-0850
91ª Sq, 10°Gr, 4°St CT	Magg Paolo Maddalena	MC.202 MM 7805 '84-2'	P-40 (shared?)	S Bir Hacheim	0745-0850
84ª Sq, 10°Gr, 4°St CT	Cap Franco Lucchini	MC.202 MM 7797 '84-0'	P-40	Bir Hacheim	1300-1415
84ª Sq, 10°Gr, 4°St CT	Serg Luciano Perdoni	MC.202 MM 7805 '84-2'	P-40	Bir Hacheim	1300-1415
10° Gr, 4° St CT	unidentified pilots	MC.202s	4 Hurricanes	Bir Hacheim	1300-1415
80ª Sq, 17°Gr, 1°St CT	Cap Clizio Nioi	MC.202	P-40 damaged	Bir Hacheim	1600-1725
80ª Sq, 17°Gr, 1°St CT	M.llo Bruno Castellani	MC.202			

Italian Casualties

391ª Sq, 159°Gr, 50°St Ass	CR.42 MM 8528 shot down near Bir Hacheim 1205-1430, Ten Eugenio Antonelli MiA
391ª Sq, 159°Gr, 50°St Ass	CR.42 MM 8545 crash-landed near Beda Littoria 1430, Serg Renato Faresi wounded
390ª Sq, 159°Gr, 50°St Ass	CR.42 MM 8527 failed to return from Bir Hacheim, 1550-1750, Serg Magg Francesco Marcati MiA
388ª Sq, 158°Gr, 50°St Ass	CR.42 MM 5059 failed to return, 1550-1750, Serg Magg Pietro Bartolozzi PoW
389ª Sq, 159°Gr, 50°St Ass	CR.42 MM 8867 '389-11' destroyed by bombs at Derna

Friday, 5 June 1942

At 0500 eight MC.202s of 71ª Squadriglia, 17° Gruppo, undertook a free sweep over the overcrowded Bir Hacheim area where the pilots reported engaging about 20 P-40s, claiming six destroyed and three probables. This was considered to be somewhat of an exaggeration and was reduced by the command to three shot down and six forced to land. Their opponents appear actually to have been Hurricanes of 274 Squadron on an early sweep over the area which suffered no casualties, two of the British pilots claiming damage to fighters identified as Bf 109s. Later in the morning 14 MC.200s of 8° Gruppo strafed armoured vehicles in the Gabr el Abid area.

At 1215 four Bf 109s of II./JG 27 carried out a Freie Jagd in the same area, where Fw Niederhöfer attacked a lone fighter which he claimed as shot down in flames. This was probably the Hurricane flown by Lt van der Riet of 40 SAAF Squadron who was attacked and wounded by a Bf 109 while on a TacR sortie, and was chased back to his own airfield by his attacker, where he was shot down. Ten minutes later the Messerschmitt pilots attacked a fighter-bomber formation, Oblt Börngen and Fw Niederhöfer each claiming one of the escort, one on fire and one which crashed, but Lt Kalista was shot down and wounded. The Allied unit has not been identified, neither claims nor losses being recorded at this time.

At 1750 eight Bf 109s from III./JG 53, four from I.Gruppe, eight from II.Gruppe and eight from III./JG 27 escorted Ju 88s to the Bir Hacheim-Acroma area, the German pilots reporting engagements as the bombing was taking place, with ten Curtiss fighters and one Hurricane. Six Kittyhawks of 260 Squadron and eight Tomahawks of 5 SAAF Squadron had taken off at 1815 on an interception patrol over the Knightsbridge area, and these encountered the Luftwaffe formation and some accompanying MC.202s. Maj Frost was shot down and crash-landed in the lines of the 1st South African Division; Lt Derham was shot-up and crashed on landing, while Lt Whyte's aircraft was badly shot-up and he was wounded. 260 Squadron had two of its Kittyhawks damaged. In return the unit's pilots claimed damage to four Bf 109s and an MC.202; 5 SAAF Squadron claimed damage to two Ju 88s. The Luftwaffe pilots were definitely over-optimistic on this occasion, claiming nine Allied fighters shot down between 1740-1750, three of them by Obfw Alfred Schulze, for the loss of Oblt Tangerding's Messerschmitt which he force-landed near the Italian Trento Division command post.

During the night of 5th/6th, a British counter-attack was launched, but failed completely. Meanwhile Italian bombers continued to attack Tobruk in small numbers by night. On this particular night, however, an unusual attack was undertaken by three S.82 transport aircraft of 145° Gruppo T which released 80 medium and small-calibre bombs on the railway facilities at Capuzzo.

British Claims

274 Sqn	Sgt J.Dodds	Hurricane IIc	Bf 109F Damaged	Bir Hacheim area	0615-
274 Sqn	Flt Sgt J.W.Neil	Hurricane IIc	Bf 109F Damaged	Bir Hacheim area	0615-
5 SAAF Sqn	Lt L.B.van der Spuy	Tomahawk IIb AK533 'Y'	Ju 88 Damaged	SW Knightsbridge	1845
5 SAAF Sqn	Lt K.C.Whyte	Tomahawk IIb AN313 'X'	Ju 88 Damaged	SW Knightsbridge	1845
260 Sqn	unstated	Kittyhawk Is	4 Bf 109Fs Damaged		1845
260 Sqn	unstated	Kittyhawk I	MC.202 Damaged		1845

British Casualties

5 SAAF Sqn	Tomahawk IIb AM385 'W' shot down by ground fire 120km W Gambut 1900; Maj J.E.Frost safe
5 SAAF Sqn	Tomahawk IIb AN313 'X' damaged by fighters 128km W Gambut at 1850, Cat II; Lt K.C.Whyte WiA
5 SAAF Sqn	Tomahawk IIb AN247 'K' damaged by fighters and crashed on landing, Cat II; Lt R.C.Derham safe
260 Sqn	Kittyhawk I damaged 1845
260 Sqn	Kittyhawk I damaged 1845
40 SAAF Sqn	Hurricane Z4608 damaged by Bf 109 and followed back to base at 50ft and then shot down; Lt T.V.R.van der Riet WiA

German Claims

5./JG 27	Fw Hans Niederhöfer	P-40	5km W Fort Acroma	1100
5./JG 77	Fw Hans Niederhöfer	P-40	1km SW El Adem	1140
5./JG 27	Oblt Ernst Börngen	P-40	20km NE Mteifel Chebir	1151
2./JG 27	Lt Karl von Lieres und Wilkau	Hurricane	20km SW Fort Acroma	1740
7./JG 53	Oblt Ernst Kläger	P-40	SW Fort Acroma	1740
4./JG 27	Obfw Alfred Schulze	2 P-40s	S & E Gazala Bay	1742 & 1743
9./JG 27	Uffz Hans-Günther Junge	P-40	5km N Mteifel Chebir	1744
8./JG 53	Lt Karl-Heinz Quaritsch	Hurricane	SW Fort Acroma	1745

7./JG 53	Fw Rudolf Schmidt	P-40	25km SE Gazala Bay	1750
7./JG 53	Oblt Ernst Kläger	P-40	40km NW Bir Hacheim	1750
4./JG 27	Obfw Alfred Schulze	P-40	3km SE Ain el Gazala	1758

German Casualties

3./JG 27	Bf 109F-4 trop WNr 8580 Yellow 1 destroyed by bombing at Martuba
5./JG 27	Bf 109F-4 trop Red 11 LK SW Fort Acroma, 100%; Lt Alexander Kalista WiA
7./JG 27	Bf 109F-4 trop WNr 10032 LK, force-landed Mteifel Chebir ESE of Trento Division; Oblt Hermann Tangerding safe

Italian Claims

71ª Sq, 17°Gr, 1°St CT	Cap Ferdinando Vicentini	MC.202	P-40	Bir Hacheim	0500-0615
71ª Sq, 17°Gr, 1°St CT	Ten Glauco Vatta	MC.202	P-40	Bir Hacheim	0500-0615
71ª Sq, 17°Gr, 1°St CT	Ten Sergio Morandi	MC.202	P-40	Bir Hacheim	0500-0615
71ª Sq, 17°Gr, 1°St CT	M.llo Marcello Lui	MC.202	P-40	Bir Hacheim	0500-0615
71ª Sq, 17°Gr, 1°St CT	above pilots	MC.202			
71ª Sq, 17°Gr, 1°St CT	Ten Vittorio Bacchi-Andreoli	MC.202			
71ª Sq, 17°Gr, 1°St CT	Cap Pericle Baruffi	MC.202	2 P-40s	Bir Hacheim	0500-0615
71ª Sq, 17°Gr, 1°St CT	Ten Ottorino Capellini	MC.202			
71ª Sq, 17°Gr, 1°St CT	Serg Egidio Buogo	MC.202			
71ª Sq, 17°Gr, 1°St CT	Cap Pericle Baruffi	MC.202	P-40 Probable	Bir Hacheim	0500-0615
71ª Sq, 17°Gr, 1°St CT	Ten Ottorino Capellini	MC.202	P-40 Probable	Bir Hacheim	0500-0615
71ª Sq, 17°Gr, 1°St CT	Serg Egidio Buogo	MC.202	P-40 Probable	Bir Hacheim	0500-0615

Saturday, 6 June 1942

The Kittyhawks of 239 Wing concentrated mainly on fighter-bomber attacks on the panzer forces which were engaged in a heavy armoured battle at Knightsbridge, where Rommel had ordered his tanks forward again. Seventy vehicles were claimed during the day by the pilots of this wing. At 0600 11 Kittyhawks of 250 Squadron carried out a reconnaissance sweep over the Acroma-Knightsbridge area, encountering four Bf 109s of II./JG 27 and eight MC.202s of 9° and 10° Gruppi on a Freie Jagd/free sweep; two MC.202s and a Bf 109 were claimed damaged without loss, although the Italian pilots claimed two P-40s and a probable for the loss of 10° Gruppo's Cap Ezio Viglione-Borghese, who force-landed near Bir Hacheim and became a PoW; he had claimed seven victories by that date. Ten Emanuele Annoni took his place as commander of 96ª Squadriglia.

Sqn Ldr M.T.Judd of 250 Squadron claimed to have damaged two Axis fighters during operations on 6 June.

At 0830 five Bf 109s of II./JG 27 escorted two Bf 109Es of 4.(H)/12 over Tobruk on a reconnaissance mission, one of the latter crash-landing north-west of Bir Hacheim. This may have been the formation which ten Kittyhawks of 112 Squadron attacked in the area at 1015 when on a fighter-bomber mission. Sqn Ldr Drake claimed one Messerschmitt probable, other members of the squadron claiming three shot down. 4.(H)/12 lost three of its Bf 109Es on this date, probably at least two of them falling to 112 Squadron. Lt Hans Pickl was shot down and killed, Obfw Wilhelm Ritter crash-landed, and Lt Fritz Hülle's aircraft was reportedly shot down by AA. Hülle was captured, but was later released by Axis troops on 11 June. A fourth loss for this unit was an Fi 156, shot down by AA in the Rotonda-Mteifel Chebir area, the pilot being killed and the observer, Lt Rolf Mitlacher, captured. 2 SAAF Squadron on a bomber-escort mission at 1200 reported being attacked by two Bf 109s which inflicted severe damage on Lt Allen's aircraft.

The ever-suave Sqn Ldr Billy Drake (with cap) enjoys a cigarette with some of his 112 Squadron pilots. On his left is Flg Off Whitamore; the other two have not been identified.

Italian ground-attack aircraft were again active during the day. Ten CR.42s of 50° Stormo attacked targets in the Acroma area during the morning, three aircraft being shot down by AA and a fourth damaged. At around the same time four MC.200s of 94ª Squadriglia strafed three armoured cars and a truck near Gabr el Abidi, but three were hit by AA here also, although all reached their home base safely.

During the night of 6th/7th a raid badly damaged three MC.202s of 1° and 4° Stormi at Martuba, with eight suffering minor splinter damage.

British Claims

250 Sqn	Sqn Ldr M.T.Judd	Kittyhawk I AL157 'B'	Bf 109 Damaged	Acroma	0610-0705
250 Sqn	Sgt F.MacK.Twemlow	Kittyhawk I AK921 'T'	MC.202 Damaged	Acroma	0610-0705
250 Sqn	Sgt D.J.Cormack	Kittyhawk I AK799	MC.202 Damaged	Acroma	0610-0705
260 Sqn	unstated	Kittyhawk I	CR.42		0700-0800
260 Sqn	unstated	Kittyhawk I	CR.42 Damaged		0700-0800
112 Sqn	Sgt E.Adye	Kittyhawk I AK988	Bf 109	nr Bir Hacheim	1015-1140
112 Sqn	Sgt E.Adye	Kittyhawk I AK988	} Bf 109	nr Bir Hacheim	1015-1140
112 Sqn	Plt Off W.E.Carson	Kittyhawk I AL235			
112 Sqn	Plt Off A.C.Baker	Kittyhawk I AL107	Bf 109	nr Bir Hacheim	1015-1140
112 Sqn	Sqn Ldr B.Drake	Kittyhawk I AL161	Bf 109 Probable	nr Bir Hacheim	1015-1140

British Casualties

2 SAAF Sqn	Kittyhawk I badly damaged; Lt Allen
4 SAAF Sqn	Tomahawk IIb AN360 crash-landed 24km E Bir Hacheim; Lt N.W.Hancock
112 Sqn	Kittyhawk I AK985 damaged by fighters, Cat II, landed safely; Sgt R.A.Drew safe
112 Sqn	Kittyhawk I AL211 force-landed after AA damage, Cat II; Sgt D.J.B.White safe

German Casualties

4.(H)/12	Bf 109E-7 WNr 1299 White 11 shot down by AA 15km E Bir Hacheim; Lt Fritz Hülle PoW
4.(H)/12	Fi 156C-2 WNr 4449 shot down by AA, crashed Mteifel Chebir; Uffz Walter Kanoldt PoW, Lt Rolf Mitlacher KiA
4.(H)/12	Bf 109E-7 WNr 6314 White 14 shot down by P-40 Bir Hacheim, exploded on impact; Uffz Hans Pickl KiA
4.(H)/12	Bf 109E-7 WNr 0762 White 6 shot down, crash-landed; Obfw Wilhelm Ritter returned

Italian Claims

91ª Sq, 10°Gr, 4°St CT	Ten Orlando Mandolini	MC.202	P-40	Bir Hacheim	0510-
91ª Sq, 10°Gr, 4°St CT	M.llo Leonardo Ferrulli	MC.202	P-40	Bir Hacheim	0510-
73ª Sq, 9° Gt, 4° St CT	Ten Ferruccio Zarini	MC.202	P-40 Probable	Bir Hacheim	0510-

Italian Casualties

96ª Sq, 9°Gr, 4°St CT	MC.202 MM 7822 '96-1' force-landed near Bir Hacheim, Cap Ezio Viglione-Borghese PoW
72ª Sq, 17°Gr, 1°St CT	MC.202 MM 7882 '72-9'collided on landing with MC.202 MM 7766, M.llo Andrea Stella injured
81ª Sq, 6°Gr, 1°St CT	MC.202 MM 7766 collided with MC.202 MM 7882, burnt out
387ª Sq, 158°Gr, 50°St Ass	CR.42 MM 8467 failed to return, S.Ten Mario Ingino KiA
390ª Sq, 159°Gr, 50°St Ass	CR.42 MM 8845 failed to return, Serg Magg Giorgio Righetti PoW
390ª Sq, 159°Gr, 50°St Ass	CR.42 MM 8863 failed to return, Serg Magg Giacinto Fiascaris PoW
390ª Sq, 159°Gr, 50°St Ass	CR.42 hit by ground fire, Ten Giovanni Galfetti WiA
94ª Sq, 8° Gr, 2°St CT	MC.200 damaged by AA, Cap Orfeo Cecchet safe
94ª Sq, 8° Gr, 2°St CT	MC.200 damaged by AA, Serg Magg Danilo Billi safe
94ª Sq, 8° Gr, 2°St CT	MC.200 damaged by AA, Serg Alessandro Ruzzene safe
88ª Sq, 6°Gr, 1°St CT	MC.202 MM 7864 damaged by splinters at Martuba
4° Stormo CT	2 MC.202s damaged by bombs at Martuba

Sunday, 7 June 1942

The weight of operations was now so intense that 73 Squadron was ordered temporarily to return to day flying. At 0930 therefore, 12 of this unit's Hurricanes swept over the Gazala-Acroma area. When so engaged, these were attacked by four Bf 109s of III./JG 53, the pilots of that unit reporting 15-20 fighters, and claimed three shot down. For some reason these claims were not confirmed, but in fact three of the British unit's pilots had indeed been shot down, one of them being killed, another baling out, and the third, Sgt Wiseman, crash-landing after an unidentified attacker knocked the propeller off his aircraft. The lack of confirmation may have been because at just this time Macchi pilots of 10º Gruppo, led by Magg Maddalena, on a free sweep from 0835-1005, reported having encountered about 20 P-40s and claimed five shot down west of Acroma, two by Maddalena himself.

At 1030 ten Kittyhawks of 260 Squadron and eight Tomahawks of 5 SAAF Squadron escorted bombers to Knightsbridge. During this raid one Kittyhawk was damaged and Maj Frost claimed a Bf 109 probable. Later, at 1245, four Bf 109s of II./JG 27 escorted two TacR Bf 109Es over the Harmut-El Adem area, but at 1250 Italian fighters attacked the reconnaissance aircraft in error, being driven off by the escort. Twenty minutes later two British fighters attacked, Uffz Schwekutsch claiming to have shot down one of these, which he observed to belly-land. This was not confirmed as he had no witnesses. It may have been a TacR Tomahawk of 40 SAAF Squadron which was lost on this date.

Thirteen Bf 109s of I.Gruppe and eight of III./JG27, plus nine from III./JG 53, escorted Ju 87s over Acroma, encountering 2 SAAF Squadron Kittyhawks which were escorting Bostons. On spotting this large German formation the Bostons were ordered to return to base as the Kittyhawks attacked the Stukas. Capt Human claimed one of the escorting Messerschmitts shot down which was probably that flown by Lt Scheiter of III./JG 53 who failed to return; he turned up later on foot. Meanwhile, Oblt Marseille saw two Kittyhawks about to attack the aircraft of Hptm Homuth and Fw Pöttgen, who on this occasion was flying on the Gruppenkommandeur's wing. Marseille at once shot down one in flames from which it seems that Lt Frewen baled out. A second was then claimed by Hptm Belser of III./JG 53, and a third by Marseille, both of these also in flames. Lt Berrange was shot down and killed, and it is possible that the two German pilots double-claimed on this victory. Lt Quaritsch of JG53 claimed to have inflicted some damage on two more aircraft.

Having moved up to Gambut on 4 June, it was on this day that the new Hurricane IId 'tank-busters' of 6 Squadron took off for their first sorties, Flt F.E.G.Hayter and Flt Lt P.S.A.Miller leading five in search of a tank concentration, although in the event this sortie proved to be abortive. The 239 Wing diary recorded: "Now that 6 Squadron has started in action appreciation of the new weapon can be made." However, in the light of the first day's experience the returning pilots advised that the situation was not favourable to the tank-buster if the tanks they were seeking to attack were dispersed amongst other vehicles.

British Claims					
5 SAAF Sqn	Maj J.E.Frost	Tomahawk IIb AN422 'B'	Bf 109F Probable	Knightsbridge	1100
2 SAAF Sqn	Lt V.M.L.Lindsay	Kittyhawk I AL173 'Q'	Bf 109F Damaged		1100
2 SAAF Sqn	Maj J.D.W.Human	Kittyhawk I AL186 'G'	Bf 109F	SW El Adem	1800

British Casualties	
2 SAAF Sqn	Kittyhawk I AL193 'S' shot down SW El Adem 1820; Lt P.R.Frewen baled out, returned next day
2 SAAF Sqn	Kittyhawk I AK628 'P' shot down by Bf 109s SW El Adem; Lt L.J.P.Berrange KiA
40 SAAF Sqn	Tomahawk IIa AK456
73 Sqn	Hurricane II BN330 shot down Gazala-Acroma; Flt Lt C.T.Cantrill KiA
73 Sqn	Hurricane II BN279 shot down Gazala-Acroma; Sgt A.S.Wilson safe
73 Sqn	Hurricane II BN375 badly damaged by Bf 109s, Gazala-Acroma; Sgt D.R.Wiseman safe
213 Sqn	Hurricane II forced to land Gazala-Acroma, 1015-1025, by MC.202

German Claims				
6./JG 27	Uffz Otto Schwekutsch	P-40 o.Zg.	Fort Acroma	1320
3./JG 27	Oblt Hans-Joachim Marseille	2 P-40s	SW & NE El Adem	1610-1613
8./JG 53	Hptm Helmut Belser	P-40	5km SW El Adem	1611
III./JG 53	unspecified	3 Hurricanes*		

*These were disallowed as they were double claims with the MC.202s

German Casualties	
7./JG 27	Bf 109F-4 trop WNr 8725 combat with P-40, crash-landed SE Acroma; Lt Wilhelm Scheiter MiA, but returned
3./LG 1	Ju 88 A-4 Wnr 140706 L1+XL shot down by AA at 2121, crashed 70m NE Tobruk; Lt Günther Alisch and three MiA

Italian Claims					
91ª Sq, 10°Gr, 4°St CT	Magg Paolo Maddalena	MC.202 MM7814	2 P-40s	10km W Acroma	0910-
91ª Sq, 10°Gr, 4°St CT	u/i pilots	MC.202	P-40	10km W Acroma	0910-
90ª Sq, 10°Gr, 4°St CT	Cap Ranieri Piccolomini	MC.202	P-40	10km W Acroma	0910-
90ª Sq, 10°Gr, 4°St CT	Ten Mario Squarcina	MC.202	P-40	10km W Acroma	0910-
AA at Barce		Martin Maryland			2330

Monday, 8 June 1942

The Commonwealth squadrons were largely switched back to Bir Hacheim this day, the German 90th Light Division having now joined the besieging forces. One of the first units in the air was 73 Squadron again, followed by 33 and 274 Squadrons which carried out a sweep over the Knightsbridge area where they were attacked by four Bf 109s and two MC.202s. Plt Off Kallio of 33 Squadron claimed damage to a Bf 109 but his own aircraft was slightly damaged and that of Plt Off Merritt was more seriously hit. Over Bir Hacheim, meanwhile, Flg Off Selby of 73 Squadron claimed a Bf 109 shot down and a second was claimed damaged. At 0655 eight Bf 109s of II./JG 27 on a Freie Jagd over Bir Hacheim reported combat with 25-30 British fighters, two being claimed shot down at 0703-0705, and a third some 20 minutes later. Between 0630-0800 no less than 54 Bf 109s were in the air.

Around 0815 ten Kittyhawks of 260 Squadron, six of 2 SAAF Squadron and nine Tomahawks each from 4 SAAF and 5 SAAF Squadrons (virtually the whole of 233 Wing) took off, and these carried out an offensive sweep over Bir Hacheim, being almost constantly attacked by Bf 109s and Macchis. Four Messerschmitts of II./JG 27 engaged 260 Squadron, Fw Walchhofer making a 'Schnauze auf Schnauze' attack (literally, head-on) on Flt Sgt Edwards' aircraft, but his Bf 109 was hit and he crash-landed in Axis territory with a damaged engine, but in doing so touched a mine which destroyed his aircraft and killed him. The South African pilots claimed damage to five Messerschmitts and one Macchi, while Lt McMasters of 2 SAAF baled out after his controls had been shot away. No German claims were made beyond the initial three, but an early patrol was flown by seven MC.202s of 9° Gruppo during which four P-40s were claimed, a later sweep by seven Macchis of 10° Gruppo resulting in claims for another four.

Four MC.200s of 13° Gruppo on an early sortie claimed three armoured cars destroyed in the El Agerasc area. They were followed at midday by four more which strafed in the El Mteilim area, making further claims. These were followed by five 8° Gruppo aircraft in the early afternoon, which strafed vehicles in the El Cheimar-El Mteilim area. The MC.200 pilots saw the 4° Stormo MC.202s in combat and were able to confirm six of their claims. The only losses suffered during these operations were two MC.200s which force-landed after being hit by AA. The pilot of one was the commanding officer of 93ª Squadriglia, Cap Riccardo Marcovich, who became a PoW. During the first half of the afternoon 10° Gruppo pilots were again in action, claiming another three P-40s. During a free sweep by nine MC.202s of 6° Gruppo in the Bir Hacheim-Bir el Harmat area a little later, their pilots engaged a reported 20 P-40s and Hurricanes, claiming one probable, but lost one Macchi shot down; the pilot of this also became a PoW.

The Luftwaffe again put up a large formation between 1100-1230 when 39 Bf 109s escorted Ju 87s to Bir Hacheim. Four aircraft of I./JG 27 on a Freie Jagd had two fleeting combats with British fighters following one of which Uffz Pfeiffer crash-landed near Tmimi in the lines of the Bologna Division – but, as it turned out, due to engine trouble rather than combat damage.

There were many engagements recorded by WDAF units throughout the afternoon, but, although many were registered as involving Bf 109s, such clashes as included German fighters during the rest of the day led to no definite claims or losses. Given the high level of activity reported by the Italians, it is clear that many of these engagements were with MC.202s rather than with Messerschmitts. One claim made around 1600 was for a Bf 109 shot down by Flt Lt Sabourin and Sgt James of 145 Squadron, this being recorded as the first confirmed victory for Spitfires in North Africa. At 1115 Flg Off J.H.Brown of 208 Squadron had undertaken a TacR sortie in a Tomahawk over Bir Hacheim. He reported being attacked by two Bf 109s which he evaded. Ten miles to the east, flying at only a few feet above the ground, he was again attacked, apparently by the same pair of fighters, and this time his aircraft was hit. He managed to reach Sidi Rezegh where he crash-landed.

450 Squadron carried out an escort mission to fighter-bombers at 1122, strafing ground targets during the flight back to base, but Sgt James did not return. 112 Squadron lost one Kittyhawk during the day when Sgt White crash-landed. Taking off at 1152, six Baltimores of 223 Squadron attacked Barce, but during the raid one bomber blew up over the target, probably due to a direct Flak hit. This also damaged a second aircraft, killing one member of the crew; on landing the aircraft was classified as damaged beyond repair, and was scrapped.

At 1325 six Kittyhawks of 250 Squadron escorted fighter-bombers of 3 RAAF Squadron and tank-busters of 6 Squadron. Intense Flak shot down two of the latter, one pilot force-landing and being picked up by 8th Army armoured cars; the pilot of the second baled out, wounded. One of the escorting Kittyhawks was also hit and force-landed. Sixteen Tomahawks, drawn equally from 4 SAAF and 5 SAAF Squadrons, together with four 2 SAAF Squadron Kittyhawks, again swept over Bir Hacheim, reporting meeting 21 Bf 109s at 15.30. Luftwaffe fighters were indeed out in force again during the afternoon, 44 of them once more escorting Stukas over Bir Hacheim. However, it was almost certainly Macchis which the South Africans encountered on this occasion. Lt Kemsley of 5 SAAF force-landed 12 miles south of El Adem, returning safely next day. Lt Kaufmann of 4 SAAF received a hit in the back of the cockpit canopy by a cannon shell, his aircraft being badly damaged.

33 and 274 Squadrons again carried out a sweep at 1604, six Hurricanes of the former unit and 12 Hurribombers of the latter, attacking MT near Bu Amud. MC.202s were reported to have attacked the top flight of 33, Sgt Menzies' aircraft being hit and force-landing. Plt Off Keefer of 274 Squadron claimed an MC.202 shot down which was probably that flown by Ten Palazzeschi of 6° Gruppo, with one also being claimed damaged.

Despite all the activity on this date, III./JG 27 recorded that their total claims for the day amounted to three camels killed near Tobruk! Within JG 27 Maj Eduard Neumann, on the strength of his extensive desert experience, was promoted to become Kommodore of the Geschwader in place of Oberstleutnant Bernhard Woldenga, who was promoted to become Fliegerführer Balkans. With the promotion, the post of Kommandeur of I.Gruppe was now filled by Hptm Gerhard Homuth; he in turn was replaced as Staffelkapitän of 3.Staffel by Oblt Hans-Joachim Marseille. On the Allied side of the lines 213 Squadron now moved forward to Gambut West from LG.12 to commence operations with WDAF.

The 6 Squadron tank-busters had got properly into their stride during the day, Wg Cdr Porteous leading an attack during which one unidentified tank was claimed destroyed and several other vehicles damaged. On the unit's second operation of the day, however, two of its Hurricanes were shot down and a third damaged – all falling victims to Flak; one pilot baled out but was hit by splinters and was removed to hospital. However, the unit would remain active throughout the rest of the month, operating from

LG.75, Sidi Haneish, Fuka, LG.106 and then LG.91 as the retreat continued. Regular strikes on both tanks and troop convoys were reported.

British Claims

213 Sqn	Flg Off F.A.W.J.Wilson	Hurricane IIc BN136 'S'	Bf 109	LG.21	0645-0755
33 Sqn	Plt Off O.C.Kallio	Hurricane IIb BG929 'P'	Bf 109 Damaged	Knightsbridge area	0700
73 Sqn	Plt Off H.W.Coussens	Hurricane IIc BN280	Bf 109 Damaged	15m W Bir Hacheim	0730
73 Sqn	Flg Off J.B.Selby	Hurricane IIc BE568	Bf 109F	15m W Bir Hacheim	0730
260 Sqn	Flt Sgt J.F.Edwards	Kittyhawk Ia 'M'	Bf 109F	Bir Hacheim area	0820-0930
2 SAAF Sqn	Flt Lt C.J.Laubscher	Kittyhawk I AL134 'H'	Bf 109E Damaged	Bir Hacheim	0845
5 SAAF Sqn	Capt L.C.Botha	Tomahawk IIb AK519 'A'	Bf 109 Damaged	NE Bir Hacheim	0900
5 SAAF Sqn	Maj J.E.Frost	Tomahawk IIb AN422 'B'	Bf 109F Damaged	NE Bir Hacheim	0900
5 SAAF Sqn	Lt J.V.Lindbergh	Tomahawk IIb AN309 'O'	Bf 109F Damaged	Bir Hacheim	0900
5 SAAF Sqn	2/Lt F.L.Stevens	Tomahawk IIb AN370 'I'	Bf 109F Damaged	NE Bir Hacheim	0900
4 SAAF Sqn	Lt G.H.Kaufmann	Tomahawk IIa	Bf 109E Damaged	Bir Hacheim	1530
5 SAAF Sqn	Lt J.V.Lindbergh	Tomahawk IIb AN309 'O'	Bf 109F Damaged	Bir Hacheim	1530
145 Sqn	Sgt H.G.James	Spitfire Vb AB324 'L' }	Bf 109	10 m SW Tobruk	1600-1650
145 Sqn	Flt Lt J.J.P.Sabourin	Spitfire Vb AB321 'N' }			
274 Sqn	Sgt G.J.Craggs	Hurricane IIc	MC.202 Damaged	10m E Bir Hacheim	1604-

British Casualties

6 Sqn	Hurricane BN861 hit by Flak and abandoned; Flg Off A.E.Morrison-Bell safe
6 Sqn	Hurricane shot down by Flak 4m W El Adem; Flt Lt A.J. Simpson baled out but KiA
33 Sqn	Hurricane IIb Z5270 forced to land by MC.202 nr Bu Amud 1600; Sgt P. Menzies safe
33 Sqn	Hurricane IIb BG884 'B' badly damaged by Bf 109 Knightsbridge area 0700; Plt Off A.G.Merritt safe
33 Sqn	Hurricane IIb BN929 'P' damaged Cat II by Bf 109 Knightsbridge 0700; Plt Off O.C.Kallio safe
208 Sqn	Tomahawk IIa AN334 damaged by Bf 109s and crash-landed nr Sidi Rezegh at 1215; Flg Off J.H.Brown safe
208 Sqn	Tomahawk IIa AK460 left 0700, damaged by Flak nr Knightsbridge Cat I; Flg Off R.L.Macgregor safe
112 Sqn	Kittyhawk I AL211 force-landed after strafe; Sgt D.J.B.White
250 Sqn	Kittyhawk I AK919 'B' shot down by Flak W Bir Hacheim 1435; Sgt F.C.De Salvo Hall safe
450 Sqn	Kittyhawk I AL146 MiA from ground attack nr Bir Hacheim, after escort about 1200; Sgt J.E.James MiA
2 SAAF Sqn	Kittyhawk I AK923 'V' shot down by MC.202s over Bir Hacheim 0840; Lt H.S.McMaster baled out, returned
4 SAAF Sqn	Tomahawk IIa damaged Cat II by Bf 109 1530; Lt G.H.Kaufmann safe
5 SAAF Sqn	Tomahawk IIa AK533 'Y' force-landed on sweep 12m S El Adem 0900, glycol trouble; Lt K.C.Kemsley safe
40 SAAF Sqn	Tomahawk AK445 damaged by own AA 0630-0715; Capt W.A.Nel
223 Sqn	Baltimore II AG777 off 1152 to bomb Barce l.g.; blew up over target; Sgt F.J.A.Saunders and three KiA
223 Sqn	Baltimore II AG825 off 1152 to bomb Barce l.g.; DBR when AG777 blew up; one of Flt Lt N.A.Fidney's crew injured

German Claims

4./JG 27	Obfw Karl-Heinz Bendert	P-40	E Bir Hacheim	0603
4./JG 27	Obfw Alfred Schulze	P-40	SE Bir Hacheim	0605
4./JG 27	Obfw Karl-Heinz Bendert	P-40	8km SE Bir Hacheim	0625

German Casualties

6./JG 27	Bf 109F-4 trop WNr 8465 LK, force-landed in minefield S El Adem; Fw Johann Walchhofer KiA
I./JG 27	Bf 109F-4 WNr 7397 belly-landed at Tmimi, 30% damaged; Uffz Eberhard Pfeffer safe
7./JG 27	Bf 109F-4 trop WNr 8695 crash-landed at Martuba; 60% damaged, pilot safe
4./KG 100	He 111H-6 WNr 7093 6N+JG shot down by AA, crash-landed between Fuka and Sidi Barrani; Oblt Karl Heschl and 4 PoW

Italian Claims

97ª Sq, 9°Gr, 4°St CT	Ten Fernando Malvezzi	MC.202	P-40	Bir Hacheim	0640-
97ª Sq, 9°Gr, 4°St CT	Ten Fernando Malvezzi	MC.202	P-40 shared w 6 pilots	Bir Hacheim	0640-
97ª Sq, 9°Gr, 4°St CT	six u/i pilots	MC.202	2 P-40s shared	Bir Hacheim	0640-
91ª Sq, 10°Gr, 4°St CT	Magg Paolo Maddalena	MC.202	P-40	E Bir el Harmat	0905-
91ª Sq, 10°Gr, 4°St CT	M.llo Leonardo Ferrulli	MC.202	P-40	E Bir el Harmat	0905-
90ª Sq, 10°Gr, 4°St CT	Serg Magg Massimo Salvatore	MC.202	P-40	E Bir el Harmat	0905-
90ª Sq, 10°Gr, 4°St CT	M.llo Angelo Savini	MC.202	P-40	E Bir el Harmat	0905-
84ª Sq, 10°Gr, 4°St CT	Ten Luigi Giannella	MC.202 MM 7803	P-40	Bir Hacheim	1345-1510

84ª Sq, 10°Gr, 4°St CT	Serg Luciano Perdoni	MC.202 MM 7919	P-40	Bir Hacheim	1345-1510
84ª Sq, 10°Gr, 4°St CT	Cap Franco Lucchini	MC.202 MM 7797			
84ª Sq, 10°Gr, 4°St CT	Ten Paolo Berti	MC.202 MM 7937	P-40	Bir Hacheim	1345-1510
84ª Sq, 10°Gr, 4°St CT	Serg Piero Buttazzi	MC.202 MM 7933			
81ª Sq, 6°Gr, 1°St CT	Cap Guido Beggiato	MC.202	P-40 Probable	Bir el Harmat	1455-1620

Italian Casualties

78ª Sq, 13°Gr, 2°St CT	MC.200 MM 8303 hit by AA, S.Ten Raffaele Valenzano safe
93ª Sq, 8°Gr, 2°St CT	MC.200 MM 6700 hit by AA, force-landed near Mteilim 1330-1500, Cap Riccardo Marcovich PoW
81ª Sq, 6°Gr, 1°St CT	MC.202 MM 7898 shot down at Bir el Harmat 1455-1620, Ten Antonio Palazzeschi PoW

Tuesday, 9 June 1942

The Luftwaffe carried out three more large Stuka attacks on this date, 42, 33 and 36 Bf 109s escorting the Ju 87s respectively. Operations over Bir Hacheim were reaching a climax, an overwhelming mass of artillery now being trained on the fortress where conditions were becoming critical, rations, ammunition, care for the wounded, and above all, water, becoming increasingly scarce. Two Hurricanes dropped supply canisters to the French during the day, but little else could now be done.

The first sweep by WDAF was made by 16 Tomahawks of 4 SAAF and 5 SAAF Squadrons, with Kittyhawks of 260 and 2 SAAF Squadrons as top cover. One of the big attacks by 30 Stukas escorted by Bf 109s and MC.202s was intercepted, but the 233 Wing fighters could not get through to the bombers on this occasion. Lt Bidwell of 5 SAAF was shot down and wounded, ending up in Tobruk hospital and Lt van Nus of 4 SAAF had his aircraft badly damaged and overturned on landing, the Tomahawk being destroyed. One Bf 109 was claimed shot down and three more were claimed as probables by pilots of 5 SAAF, with one more shot down and one probable being claimed by those of 4 SAAF. Fourteen Bf 109s of II./JG 27 and 14 of III./JG 53 were involved in this engagement, two fighters being claimed by I.Gruppe pilots but Uffz Pfeffer was shot down and killed. One more was claimed in flames and one damaged by the JG 53 units.

Five Bf 109s of II./JG 27 escorting a Bf 110 over Bir el Gobi, met four Curtiss fighters over Mteifel, where two were claimed shot down at 0926. At 1120 seven III./JG 53 aircraft carried out a Freie Jagd over Mteifel, but here Oblt Kläger's aircraft was hit by AA and he force-landed east of Tmimi. At 1700 11 Hurricanes of 73 Squadron, covered by the newly-arrived 127 Squadron, undertook a sweep over Bir Hacheim. They were joined by more Hurricanes of 33 and 213 Squadrons. The formations were jumped by 12 Bf 109s and 14 MC.202s of 9° Gruppo, but turned into them, 213 Squadron claiming one Messerschmitt. 33 Squadron claimed a Messerschmitt probable and an MC.202 shot down. 9° Gruppo Macchi pilots claimed five P-40s and Hurricanes shot down, with three probables; one Macchi and its pilot were lost. Ten Kittyhawks of 260 Squadron carried out an interception patrol around the same time from which Sgt Clark failed to return. One claim was made by a pilot of Stab II./JG 27.

About 1920 six Kittyhawks of 3 RAAF Squadron patrolled over Bir Hacheim; six Hurricanes from 274 Squadron, covered by others from 33 Squadron, swept over the same area. Both formations met Axis fighters, the Hurricanes fighting MC.202s. Plt Off Wade and Plt Off Challis of 33 each claimed Bf 109s, and Plt Off McClarty damaged a Macchi, but was attacked himself, his aircraft being badly damaged. Sgt Eagle of 274 Squadron claimed a Bf 109 destroyed, and he and Sgt Henderson each claimed a damaged. Sixteen Bf 109s of III./JG 53, escorting 40 Ju 87s, claimed two fighters, both by Lt Müller who reported one that broke up in the air and one that blew up, but neither was confirmed due to lack of witnesses.

During the night Bombays of 216 Squadron flew in more supplies to the French, but at Bir Hacheim the end of resistance was near.

British Claims

2 SAAF Sqn	Lt J.O.de Waal	Kittyhawk AL126 'R'	Bf 109 Damaged	Bir Hacheim	0830
5 SAAF Sqn	Lt T.Finlayson	Tomahawk IIb AN427 'D'	Bf 109F Probable	W Bir Hacheim	0845
5 SAAF Sqn	Maj J.E.Frost	Tomahawk IIb AN422 'B'	Bf 109F Probable	20m NW Bir Hacheim	0845
5 SAAF Sqn	Lt R.C.Hirst	Tomahawk IIb AN309 'O'	Bf 109F	W Bir Hacheim	0845
5 SAAF Sqn	Lt H.W.G.Bidwell	Tomahawk IIb AN415 'T'	Bf 109F Probable	SE Bir Hacheim	0855
4 SAAF Sqn	Capt G.G.Bayly	Tomahawk IIb AM418 'S'	Bf 109	Bir Hacheim	0900
4 SAAF Sqn	Lt G.H.Kaufmann	Tomahawk IIb AN452 'M'	Bf 109F Damaged	Bir Hacheim	0845

British Claims

260 Sqn	unstated	Kittyhawk Ia	Bf 109		0900
213 Sqn	Plt Off W.Henderson	Hurricane IIc BN128 'K'	Bf 109F	10m NW Bir Hacheim	1750
213 Sqn	Flt Lt C.B.Temlett	Hurricane IIc BM981 'G'	Bf 109F Damaged	10m NW Bir Hacheim	1750
213 Sqn	Flg Off F.A.W.J.Wilson	Hurricane IIc BN136 'S'	MC.202 Damaged	10m NW Bir Hacheim	1750
73 Sqn	Flt Sgt E.L.Joyce	Hurricane IIc BN156 'L'	Bf 109F Probable	12m W Bir Hacheim	1750
73 Sqn	Flt Lt G.R.A.McG.Johnston	Hurricane IIc BF272	MC.202 Probable	5m E Bir Hacheim	1750
274 Sqn	Sgt W.G.Eagle	Hurricane IIc	Bf 109F	Bir Hacheim	1920-
274 Sqn	Sgt W.G.Eagle	Hurricane IIc	Bf 109F Damaged	Bir Hacheim	1920-
274 Sqn	Sgt R.W.Henderson	Hurricane IIc	Bf 109F Damaged	Bir Hacheim	1920-
33 Sqn	Plt Off B.W.Challis	Hurricane IIb BG950 'A'	Bf 109	Bir Hacheim area	1920-
33 Sqn	Plt Off D.W.McClarty	Hurricane IIb BG992 'Q'	Bf 109 Damaged	Bir Hacheim area	1920-
33 Sqn	Plt Off L.C.Wade	Hurricane IIb BP239	Bf 109	Bir Hacheim area	1920-
3 RAAF Sqn	Sqn Ldr A.W.Barr	Kittyhawk I AK992	Bf 109 Damaged	Bir Hacheim area	2010

British Casualties

260 Sqn	Kittyhawk I shot down by fighters at El Adem c0900; pilot unidentifed, but WiA
260 Sqn	Kittyhawk I shot down by fighters at El Adem c0900; Sgt H.Clark MiA
5 SAAF Sqn	Tomahawk IIb AN415 'T' shot down by Bf 109s nr Bir Hacheim at 0845, crash-landed 8m S Rotonda Mteifel; Lt H.W.G.Bidwell returned on 12th
4 SAAF Sqn	Tomahawk IIb AN377 'B' badly damaged by Bf 109s nr Bir Hacheim at 0845, overturned on landing; Lt J.van Nus safe
40 SAAF Sqn	Tomahawk ..915 damaged by Flak 0630; Lt R.W.B.Acutt
33 Sqn	Hurricane IIb BG992 'Q' badly damaged by MC.202s nr Bir Hacheim 1920; Plt Off D.W.McClarty safe

German Claims

7./JG 53	Oblt Ernst Kläger	P-40	20km NW Bir Hacheim	0735
1./JG 27	Hptm Ludwig Franzisket	P-40	SW Hagfa el Beda	0750
1./JG 27	Fw Günther Steinhausen	P-40	S Mteifel Chebir	0753
4./JG 27	Obfw Karl-Heinz Bendert	P-40	SE El Adem	0825
4./JG 27	Obfw Alfred Schulze	P-40	SE El Adem	0826
Stab II./JG 27	Uffz Willi Kientsch	P-40	NE Bir Hacheim	1905
8./JG 53	Lt Rudolf Müller	2 P-40s o.Zg n.b.	Bir Hacheim	

German Casualties

3./JG 27	Bf 109F-4 trop WNr 8647 Yellow 9 combat with P-40 20km NNW Bir Hacheim; Uffz Eberhard Pfeffer MiA
7./JG 53	Bf 109F-4 trop WNr 10179 shot down by AA, belly-landed nr Tmimi, destroyed; Oblt Ernst Kläger safe
5./KG 100	He 111H-6, WNr 7094 6N+FH, shot down by AA, crashed nr Qotaifiya; Fw Heinz Lenninger and two PoW. One MiA

Italian Claims

73ª Sq, 9°Gr, 4°St CT	S.Ten Alvaro Querci	MC.202	P-40	Bir Hacheim	1600-
73ª Sq, 9°Gr, 4°St CT	Serg Teresio Martinoli	MC.202	2 P-40s	Bir Hacheim	1600-
73ª Sq, 9°Gr, 4°St CT	Serg Mario Guerci	MC.202	P-40	Bir Hacheim	1600-
73ª Sq, 9°Gr, 4°St CT	Serg Mario Guerci	MC.202	P-40 Probable	Bir Hacheim	1600-
73ª Sq, 9°Gr, 4°St CT	Ten Vittorio Squarcia	MC.202	P-40 Probable	Bir Hacheim	1600-
73ª Sq, 9°Gr, 4°St CT	Serg Magg Salvatore Mechelli	MC.202	Hurricane	Bir Hacheim	1600-
73ª Sq, 9°Gr, 4°St CT	Serg Magg Salvatore Mechelli	MC.202	Hurricane Probable	Bir Hacheim	1600-
96ª Sq, 9°Gr, 4°St CT	Serg Bruno Biagini	MC.202	P-40	Bir Hacheim	1600-

Italian Casualties

73ª Sq, 9°Gr, 4°St CT	MC.202 MM 7831 '73-11' failed to return, Serg Magg Pasquale Rossi MiA at Bir Hacheim
94ª Sq, 8°Gr, 2°St CT	MC.200 MM 5889 damaged on landing, Serg Magg Alessandro Ruzzene safe

Wednesday, 10 June 1942

Hurricanes, covered by Spitfires of 145 Squadron, beat off one heavy raid on the forts, but two others got through as concentrated artillery shelling continued all day. At 0750 12 Hurricanes of 73 Squadron covered others of 213 Squadron on a sweep to Bir Hacheim, again with a top cover of Spitfires. The Hurricanes were jumped by five MC.202s, but turned into them three times and drove them off. Two groups of Ju 87s, escorted by Bf 109s, were then spotted, pilots of 213 Squadron claiming two Stukas and three damaged, with the escorting Spitfires of 145 Squadron claiming a Bf 109. The Luftwaffe aircraft involved included 14 Bf 109s of I./JG 27 and eight of II./JG 27, but it appears that III./JG 53 aircraft

Laden with 500kg bombs, Ju 88 L1+GK of LG 1 heads off on a bombing sortie.

were also present. Between 0735-0753 these units claimed ten Allied fighters shot down, four of them by Oblt Marseille. One Messerschmitt was shot down, Oblt Rudolf Sinner force-landing with his aircraft a complete write-off.

Once again most German claims, and indeed, the identity of Sinner's victor, were listed as P-40s, whereas the formation with which they had become engaged included only Hurricanes and Spitfires. During this engagement Flt Lt Scade of 73 Squadron was wounded and crash-landed, whereas amongst the 213 Squadron pilots Sgt Jackson was shot down, Flg Off Sowrey crash-landed and Plt Off Hancock was wounded in one arm and was chased to El Gobi, 20 miles away, where he force-landed; his aircraft was then strafed to destruction by three pursuing Bf 109s. Both Hancock and Scade would receive awards of the DFC during the following month.

At 1540 213 Squadron undertook a similar mission to that of the morning, and other Hurricanes of 33 and 274 Squadrons also flew a sweep during the afternoon. Pilots of these units reported engaging both Messerschmitts and Macchis, but no decisive combats were recorded by the Luftwaffe at this time. However, six MC.202s of 6° Gruppo patrolled over the Bir Hacheim-Bir el Harmat area 1600-1720, joined by six of 17° Gruppo. The 6° Gruppo men claimed six fighters shot down and a seventh probably, while the 17° Gruppo pilots added claims for two more. Two of the former unit's victories were credited to M.llo GianLino Baschirotto, an ace of the Spanish Civil War. Of course, all the victims were identified as P-40s! The Hurricane pilots made claims for one Bf 109 probable and five damaged; one Hurricane was shot down and a second was damaged.

During the day 127 Squadron, newly re-equipped with Hurricane IIbs, arrived in Egypt from St Jean; three experienced pilots joined the unit on its arrival, Sqn Ldr C.O.J.Pegge, DFC, as commanding officer, with Flt Lt R.Marples, DFC, and Flt Lt Finnis as flight commanders. That night the 2,000 surviving defenders of Bir Hacheim slipped out of the fortress and made for Allied lines.

British Claims

145 Sqn	Sqn Ldr C.N.Overton	Spitfire Vb ..502 'B'	Bf 109		0750-0855
213 Sqn	Flt Lt G.H.Westlake	Hurricane IIc BE340 'W'	Bf 109 Probable	10m NW Bir Hacheim	0840
213 Sqn	Flt Lt G.H.Westlake	Hurricane IIc BE340 'W'	Ju 87 Damaged	10m NW Bir Hacheim	0840
213 Sqn	Flt Sgt J.W.Edwards	Hurricane IIc BN285 'M'	Ju 87 Damaged	10m NW Bir Hacheim	0840
213 Sqn	Plt Off A.J.Hancock	Hurricane IIc BM966 'T'	Ju 87	Bir Hacheim	0840
213 Sqn	Plt Off D.R.Rehill	Hurricane IIc BN139 'U'	Ju 87 Damaged	10m NW Bir Hacheim	0840
213 Sqn	Flg Off J.A.Sowrey	Hurricane IIc BN562 'F'	Ju 87	10m NW Bir Hacheim	0840
73 Sqn	Sgt R.L.Baker	Hurricane IIc BN402	Bf 109F Probable	15m SW El Adem	0840
213 Sqn	Plt Off W.H.Thomlinson	Hurricane IIc BM981 'G'	Bf 109F Damaged	10m SW Knightsbridge	1535-1655
213 Sqn	Wt Off R.J.Wallace	Hurricane IIc BN139 'U'	Bf 109F Damaged	10m SW Knightsbridge	1535-1655

British Claims

213 Sqn	Plt Off P.P.Wilson	Hurricane IIc BM983 'C'	Bf 109F Damaged	10m SW Knightsbridge	1535-1655
73 Sqn	Plt Off L.T.Henry	Hurricane IIc BE372 'H'	Bf 109F Damaged	15m SW El Adem	1620
73 Sqn	Sqn Ldr D.H.Ward	Hurricane IIc BN131 'P'	Bf 109F Damaged	15m SW El Adem	1620

British Casualties

6 Sqn	Hurricane BN860 SOC, DBR
73 Sqn	Hurricane II BE568 shot down at Bir Hacheim 1620; Sgt A.S.Wilson safe
73 Sqn	Hurricane II BN370 shot down Bir Hacheim at 0840; Flt Lt T.P.K.Scade WiA
208 Sqn	Tomahawk IIa AK567 left 1610, damaged by Bf 109, crash-landed nr El Adem 1700; Flg Off R.L.Macgregor safe
213 Sqn	Hurricane II BM966 'T' damaged by Bf 109s over Bir Hacheim at 0830, force-landed at El Gubbi; Plt Off A.J.Hancock WiA
213 Sqn	Hurricane II BN159 'J' shot down Bir Hacheim at 0830; Sgt D.H.Jackson KiA
213 Sqn	Hurricane II BN562 'F' crash-landed, 1m S Gazala at 0830 destroyed by strafing Bf 109s; Flg Off J.A.Sowrey safe
213 Sqn	Hurricane II BN353 'D' left 1535, damaged by Bf 109, hit in cockpit and oil cooler; Sgt Menzies safe
4 SAAF Sqn	Tomahawk IIb AM410 and Tomahawk IIb AN236 collided while forming up; Capt G.G.Bayly and Lt M.P.Ironside KiFA

German Claims

3./JG 27	Oblt Hans-Joachim Marseille	2 P-40s *	5-6km NW & NE Mteifel Chebir	0735-0741
6./JG 27	Fw Fritz Gromotka	Hurricane	Sidi Rezegh	0740
2./JG 27	Lt Karl von Lieres und Wilkau	P-40	N Bir Hacheim	0743
3./JG 27	Obfw Karl Mentnich	P-40	N Bir Hacheim	0743
3./JG 27	Oblt Hans-Joachim Marseille	P-40	6km E Mteifel Chebir	0745
Stab I./JG 27	Lt Werner Schroer	P-40	5km W Bir Hacheim	0749
3./JG 27	Oblt Hans-Joachim Marseille	P-40	6km ENE Mteifel Chebir	0750
9./JG 53	Oblt Franz Götz	Spitfire	N Bir Hacheim	0750
8./JG 53	Lt Karl-Heinz Quaritsch	P-40	N Bir Hacheim	0753

*(or two Hurricanes)

German Casualties

6./JG 27	Bf 109F-4 trop WNr 8492 Yellow 2 combat with P-40 Bir Hacheim-El Adem area; force-landed 100%; Oblt Rudolf Sinner safe
III./SG 3	Ju 87D-5 WNr 2060 shot down by Hurricanes, crash-landed nr Gazala, crew safe

Italian Claims

79ª Sq, 6°Gr, 1°St CT	Cap Domenico Camarda	MC.202	P-40	N Bir Hacheim	1450-1605
79ª Sq, 6°Gr, 1°St CT	Serg Magg Amedeo Benati	MC.202	P-40	N Bir Hacheim	1450-1605
81ª Sq, 6°Gr, 1°St CT	Serg Magg Luigi Morosi	MC.202	P-40	N Bir Hacheim	1450-1605
81ª Sq, 6°Gr, 1°St CT	Serg Magg Luigi Morosi	MC.202	P-40 Probable	N Bir Hacheim	1450-1605
88ª Sq, 6°Gr, 1°St CT	M.llo GianLino Baschirotto	MC.202	2 P-40s	N Bir Hacheim	1450-1605
88ª Sq, 6°Gr, 1°St CT	Serg Magg Anano Borreo	MC.202	P-40	N Bir Hacheim	1450-1605
80ª Sq, 17°Gr, 1°St CT	Serg Magg Alvise Andrich	MC.202	P-40	N Bir Hacheim	1500-1620
80ª Sq, 17°Gr, 1°St CT	Cap Clizio Nioi	MC.202	}		
80ª Sq, 17°Gr, 1°St CT	Ten Giovanni B. Ghiglia	MC.202	} P-40	N Bir Hacheim	1500-1620
80ª Sq, 17°Gr, 1°St CT	Serg Magg Aldo Bersani	MC.202	}		

Thursday, 11 June 1942

The Vigorous convoy departed from Alexandria for Malta during the day (see Chapter Three), adding coastal escort operations to the duties of the hard-pressed desert squadrons. At 1602 four Bf 109s of I./JG 27 flew a Freie Jagd during which they intercepted a Tomahawk of 208 Squadron on a TacR sortie, flown by Flg Off Macgregor. With his aircraft hit repeatedly by cannon fire, Macgregor reached El Adem where he was finally shot down in flames by Uffz Timmermann, and crash-landed – claiming to have probably shot down one of his assailants.

Eleven Hurricanes of 274 Squadron provided top cover to 33 Squadron at 1705, their pilots spotting a large formation of Ju 87s five miles north-west of El Adem, flying west at 7,000 feet. The dive-bombers had an escort of eight I./JG 27 Bf 109s, nine from III./JG 27 and 13 from III./JG 53. These fighters all attacked the Hurricanes, three of which were hit, two crash-landing but one was badly damaged, but kept flying. The pilots of 274 Squadron claimed two Messerschmitts shot down and one damaged, and

Bomb-laden Kittyhawk Is of 260 Squadron in summer 1942. The nearest aircraft appears to be carrying a 500lb weapon, while that next to it has one of 250lb.

seem to have been successful in bringing down two Jabos of 10.(Jabo)/JG 27, one of which failed to return, the other crash-landing at Martuba, damaged beyond repair. Two Kittyhawks of 112 Squadron were lost during a ground-attack mission, both apparently succumbing to ground fire, as did an MC.200 of 8° Gruppo which was hit and force-landed during an attack on 24 Allied vehicles near Bir Hacheim.

British Claims

208 Sqn	Flg Off R.L.Macgregor	Tomahawk IIa AK567	Bf 109F probable	El Adem	1610-1700
2 SAAF Sqn	Maj J.D.W.Human	Kittyhawk I ET530 'G'	Ju 87		1705
274 Sqn	Flt Sgt J.W.Neil	Hurricane IIc	Bf 109F	5m NW El Adem	1740
274 Sqn	Plt Off R.H.N.Walsh	Hurricane IIc	Bf 109F	5m NW El Adem	1740
274 Sqn	Plt Off R.H.N.Walsh	Hurricane IIc	Bf 109F Damaged	5m NW El Adem	1740
33 Sqn	Plt Off B.W.Challis	Hurricane IIb Z4953	MC.202 Damaged	El Adem	c 1740

British Casualties

208 Sqn	Tomahawk IIa AK567 damaged by Bf 109, crash-landed nr El Adem; Flg Off R.L.Macgregor
33 Sqn	Hurricane IIb 5547 damaged Cat II by fighters about 1740, landed at base; Sgt P.Menzies safe
33 Sqn	Hurricane IIb BP239 shot down by Bf 109 El Adem area about 1740, force-landed; Plt Off L.C.Wade safe
33 Sqn	Hurricane IIb Z4953 badly damaged by Bf 109 El Adem area about 1740; Plt Off B.W.Challis safe
274 Sqn	Hurricane IIc BE864 shot down 5m SE El Adem at 1740: Plt Off C.W.P.Persse KiA
112 Sqn	Kittyhawk I AK937 lost in attack on MT at 2005; Sgt D.F.Greaves returned safe
112 Sqn	Kittyhawk I AK988 shot down on ground attack; Sgt E.B.Adye MiA

German Claims

1./JG 27	Uffz Walter Timmermann	P-40	N Sidi Rezegh	1545
7./JG 53	Lt Jürgen Harder	Hurricane	W El Adem	1625
3./JG 27	Oblt Hans-Joachim Marseille	P-40	SW El Adem	1625
3./JG 27	Oblt Hans-Joachim Marseille	Hurricane	18km NW El Adem	1635
9./JG 53	Obfw Werner Stumpf	Hurricane	W El Adem	1640

German Casualties

10.(Jabo)/JG 27	Bf 109F-4 trop WNr 8539 Green 5 combat with Hurricanes, crashed 15km E El Adem; Uffz Fritz Zeller MiA
10.(Jabo)/JG 27	Bf 109F-4/B WNr 7477 crash-landed Martuba, 75% damaged; pilot safe

Italian Casualties

93ª sq, 8°Gr, 2°St CT	MC.200 damaged by ground fire, Serg Vittorio Periotto force-landed, aircraft repaired and recovered

Friday, 12 June 1942

At 1620 12 Kittyhawks of 3 RAAF Squadron took off on a fighter-bomber mission near El Adem. Here one aircraft was shot down in flames by Flak and several other fighters were damaged. Ten more Kittyhawks from 260 Squadron escorted bombers from 0855, pilots reporting being attacked by six Bf 109s and 14 MC.202s which shot down one of the unit's aircraft, the pilot being wounded. Their opponents on this occasion were 10° Gruppo MC.202s, six pilots from this unit jointly claiming two P-40s shot down.

Eleven Hurricanes of 274 Squadron swept over the El Adem area from 1145, encountering three Ju 88s and a single Ju 87, escorted by 15 Bf 109s of III./JG 53 and two MC.202s, which were bombing transport 30 miles west of El Adem. The British pilots claimed three Bf 109s and a Macchi as probables, but one Hurricane was claimed shot down by Obfw Stumpf, a second claim failing to obtain confirmation. However, Fw Herkenhoff of the German unit was shot down and baled out, but hit the tailplane of his aircraft and was killed.

450 Squadron on its fourth mission of the day provided five Kittyhawks as top cover to a fighter sweep at 1255, during which Sgt House crash-landed. At 1855 two more Kittyhawks from this unit carried out a reconnaissance over the Trigh Capuzzo and El Adem. Plt Off Young and Flt Sgt Beste reported over the R/T that they were about to be attacked by enemy aircraft and both failed to return. They had been set upon by three Bf 109s of II./JG 27 on a Freie Jagd and were shot down by Obfw Clade and Uffz Gierster.

Ju 88A-4 of LG 1 flown by Oblt Gerd Stamp at Benina, with 250kg and 500kg bombs ready for loading in the foreground.

Fifteen minutes later eight Kittyhawks of 260 Squadron took off again on a bomber escort sortie. They were followed at 1935 by Hurricanes of 33, 73, 213, 238 and 274 Squadrons, and Spitfires of 145 Squadron, all of which were scrambled to intercept a large formation of Ju 87s and 88s, escorted by eight Bf 109s of I.Gruppe, ten of III.Gruppe and eight MC.202s of 9° Gruppo, all of which were heading for the El Adem area. 73 Squadron got to the bombers, claiming five Ju 87s and one Ju 88, plus four more of the former as probables. Most of the other Hurricane units submitted a plethora of claims, the overall result of these amounting actually to the loss by the Axis of one Ju 87 and one MC.202! The cost was three aircraft of 33 Squadron and two of 213 Squadron shot down, plus one of 73 Squadron badly damaged. Meanwhile, the Kittyhawks of 260 Squadron flew into the fight, Flg Off Waddy claiming one MC.202, but the unit losing two or three Kittyhawks. During this confused and confusing aerial conflict, the German fighters claimed five victories and the Italians one.

During the day 112 Squadron also lost one Kittyhawk whilst undertaking a fighter-bomber sortie, the pilot being reported safe with the army. A TacR Hurricane of 208 Squadron was hit by Flak and crash-landed, but South African Bofors gunners shot down a 10° Gruppo MC.202. Ready to enter action, a detachment of 127 Squadron's newly-arrived Hurricanes moved up to Sidi Barrani.

British Claims

145 Sqn	Flt Lt J.J.P.Sabourin	Spitfire Vb AB339 'M'	Bf 109	W El Adem	1000-1100
145 Sqn	Flt Lt J.J.P.Sabourin	Spitfire Vb AB339 'M'	Bf 109 Damaged	15m SE El Gazala	1000-1100
73 Sqn	Plt Off G.R.Woolston	Hurricane IIc BN363	2 Bf 109s Damaged	10m W Gambut	1025
274 Sqn	Plt Off C.D.A.Browne	Hurricane IIc	Bf 109 Probable	30m W El Adem	1135-
274 Sqn	Plt Off J.Buckley	Hurricane IIc	MC.202 Damaged	30m W El Adem	1135-
274 Sqn	Sgt R.W.Henderson	Hurricane IIc	Bf 109 Probable	30m W El Adem	1135-
274 Sqn	Sgt R.W.Henderson	Hurricane IIc	Bf 109 Damaged	30m W El Adem	1135-
274 Sqn	Plt Off R.H.Hunter	Hurricane IIc	MC.202 Probable	30m W El Adem	1135-
274 Sqn	Sgt W.E.Marsh	Hurricane IIc BG707 'Z'	Bf 109 Probable	30m W El Adem	1135-
274 Sqn	Sgt R.J.Thompson	Hurricane IIc	Bf 109 Probable	30m W El Adem	1135-
250 Sqn	Sgt H.Stewart	Kittyhawk I AL182 'C'	Ju 88 Damaged	Gambut South l.g.	1150
450 Sqn	Sqn Ldr A.D.Ferguson	Kittyhawk I AL107	Bf 110 Damaged		1255-1405
208 Sqn	Flt Lt J.C.Paish	Hurricane N2627	Ju 87 Probable		1630-1745
33 Sqn	Flt Lt D.C.Cloete	Hurricane IIb BE173 'M'	2 Bf 109s Probable	El Adem	1910-2000
33 Sqn	Lt H.Inglesby	Hurricane IIb BE168 'N'	MC.202 Probable	El Adem	1910-2000
33 Sqn	Plt Off W.A.R.MacDonald	Hurricane IIb BG968 'R'	MC.202 Probable	El Adem	1910-2000
33 Sqn	Plt Off H.S.Woods	Hurricane IIb BG960 'F'	MC.202 Probable	El Adem	1910-2000
260 Sqn	Flg Off J.L.Waddy	Kittyhawk I ET579	MC.202	El Adem	1910-2025
213 Sqn	Wt Off R.J.Wallace	Hurricane IIc BN139 'U'	Bf 109	El Adem area, SW Bir Hacheim	1935-2030
213 Sqn	Flt Lt G.H.Westlake	Hurricane IIc BN117 'X'	Bf 109	El Adem area, SW Bir Hacheim	1935-2030
274 Sqn	Sgt C.R.Parbury	Hurricane IIc	Bf 109 Probable	5m NW El Adem	1942-
274 Sqn	Sgt E.P.Presland	Hurricane IIc	MC.202 Damaged	5m NW El Adem	1942-
274 Sqn	Plt Off F.B.Samuel	Hurricane IIc	Ju 87	5m NW El Adem	1942-
274 Sqn	Plt Off W.A.G.Conrad	Hurricane IIc BG700	Bf 109F	5m NW El Adem	1942-
274 Sqn	Plt Off G.C.Keefer	Hurricane IIc BN109 'B'	Bf 109F Damaged	5m NW El Adem	1942-
274 Sqn	Sgt J.Dodds	Hurricane IIc	Bf 109F	5m NW El Adem	1942-
274 Sqn	Sgt J.Dodds	Hurricane IIc	Bf 109F Damaged`	5m NW El Adem	1942-
73 Sqn	Sgt M.S.Jones	Hurricane IIc BN570	Ju 87	W El Adem	1955
73 Sqn	Sgt M. S.Jones	Hurricane IIc BN570	Ju 87 Damaged	W El Adem	1955
73 Sqn	Sgt G.Hill	Hurricane IIc BN546	Ju 87	8m SE Acroma	1955
73 Sqn	Plt Off H.W.Coussens	Hurricane IIc BN165	Ju 87	W El Adem	1955
73 Sqn	Sgt R.L.Baker	Hurricane IIc BE482	Ju 87	8m SE Acroma	1955
73 Sqn	Flg Off R.M.Chatfield	Hurricane IIc BN560	Ju 88	Acroma	2000
73 Sqn	Sgt S.A.Goodwin	Hurricane IIc BN357	Ju 87 Probable	Acroma	2000
73 Sqn	Plt Off L.T.Henry	Hurricane IIc BN156	Ju 87	Acroma	2000
73 Sqn	Plt Off L.T.Henry	Hurricane IIc BN156	Ju 87 Probable	Acroma	2000
73 Sqn	Flg Off J.Irwin	Hurricane IIc BN363	Ju 87 Probable	8m SE Acroma	2000
73 Sqn	Sgt D.R.Wiseman	Hurricane IIc BN183	Ju 87 Probable	Acroma	2000

British Casualties

33 Sqn	Hurricane IIb Z5318 'Z' shot down by Bf 109s near El Adem 1910-2000; Flt Lt F.J.Aldridge safe
33 Sqn	Hurricane IIb BG917 'X' shot down by Bf 109s near El Adem 1910-2000; Sgt Hall PoW
33 Sqn	Hurricane IIb Z5143 'C' shot down by Bf 109s near El Adem 1910-2000; Sgt W.Cameron KiA
73 Sqn	Hurricane badly damaged; Flg Off R.Chatfield WiA nr Acroma
274 Sqn	Hurricane IIc force-landed wheels down, 1135; Plt Off Bell safe
274 Sqn	Hurricane IIc left 1942, 5m NW El Adem, damaged Cat I by Bf 109; pilot safe
208 Sqn	Hurricane Z5330 left 0630, shot down by Flak, crash-landed 10m W ALG at 0800; Flg Off D.W.Barlow
208 Sqn	Hurricane I V7821 landed to check new LG, hit mine and blew up; Flt Lt J.C.Paish inj

British Casualties

213 Sqn	Hurricane IIc BN276 left 1935, shot down by Bf 109s nr El Adem; Flg Off Edmunds MiA
213 Sqn	Hurricane IIc BN285 left 1935, shot down by Bf 109 between Knightsbridge and Acroma; Flt Sgt J.Edwards baled out
112 Sqn	Kittyhawk I AL149 'U' shot down by Flak during ground attack 5m SE El Adem; Flt Sgt S.D.Cassell safe
112 Sqn	Kittyhawk I AL185 shot down by Flak; Flg Off J.M.S.Crichton safe
260 Sqn	Kittyhawk I ET587 shot down by fighters near El Adem, 1910-2000; Sgt J.C.Wrigley KiA
260 Sqn	Kittyhawk I ET260 shot down by fighters near El Adem, 1910-2000
260 Sqn	Kittyhawk I AK810 shot down by fighters 0858-0950; Sgt R.A.Matthews baled out, safe
450 Sqn	Kittyhawk I AL170 shot down by fighters, E of El Adem area at approx 1930; Plt Off I.C.Young KiA
450 Sqn	Kittyhawk I AL165 shot down by fighters, E of El Adem area at approx 1930; Flt Sgt F.W.Beste PoW
450 Sqn	Kittyhawk I AK749 force-landed at approx 1315 after propeller hit ground while strafing; Sgt E.C.House safe
3 RAAF Sqn	Kittyhawk I AK786 hit by Flak and crash-landed nr El Alamein in minefield c 0700; Sgt H J Bray safe
3 RAAF Sqn	Kittyhawk I AL208 hit by Flak Cat II; Sgt W.D.S.Finlason safe
3 RAAF Sqn	Kittyhawk I AL187 hit by Flak, crash-landed at base with bomb on board, Cat II; Sgt R.N.B.Stevens safe

German Claims

1./JG 27	Lt Heinz-Edgar Berres	B-24	S Braila, Rumania	0538
9./JG 53	Obfw Werner Stumpf	Hurricane	E El Adem	1130
5./JG 27	Uffz Helmut Gierster	P-40	SSE El Adem	1815
5./JG 27	Obfw Emil Clade	P-40	S El Adem	1829
1./JG 27	Hptm Ludwig Franzisket	Hurricane	El Adem	1850
1./JG 27	Fw Günther Steinhausen	Hurricane	W El Adem	1903
1./JG 27	Fw Günther Steinhausen	P-40	SSW El Adem	1914

German Casualties

9./JG 53	Bf 109F-4 trop WNr 8586 Yellow 9 shot down by Hurricane 5km W El Adem; Fw Heinz Herkenhoff baled out but KiA
2./StG 3	Ju 87R-2 WNr 6101 S7+LK AA 25km SW Tobruk; Uffz Theodor Hagedorn (gunner) WiA; pilot safe
I./StG 3	Ju 87R-4 WNr 6277 S7+DB shot down by Hurricanes, crashed SE Acroma; Fw Rudolf Löper/Uffz Hermann Klingele MiA
4.(H)/12	Bf 110E-3 WNr 2446 destroyed by sabotage at Benina airfield
KGrzbV 400	Ju 52/3m WNr 5645 destroyed by sabotage at Benina airfield

Italian Claims

90ª Sq, 10°Gr, 4°St CT	Cap Ranieri Piccolomini	MC.202	P-40	SE Acroma	0915-
90ª Sq, 10°Gr, 4°St CT	S.Ten Virgilio Vanzan	MC.202 MM 7906			
90ª Sq, 10°Gr, 4°St CT	Serg Gregorio Taverna	MC.202 MM 7937			
84ª Sq, 10°Gr, 4°St CT	Cap Franco Lucchini	MC.202 MM 7797	P-40	NE El Adem	0920-1040
84ª Sq, 10°Gr, 4°St CT	Serg Piero Buttazzi	MC.202 MM 7805			
84ª Sq, 10°Gr, 4°St CT	Serg Magg Mario Veronesi	MC.202 MM 7815			
91ª Sq, 10°Gr, 4°St CT	Magg Paolo Maddalena	MC.202	Hurricane	El Adem	1745-
73ª Sq, 9° Gr, 4°St CT	Serg Mario Guerci	MC.202			

Italian Casualties

90ª Sq, 10°Gr, 4°St CT	MC.202 MM 7937 failed to return from morning sortie, Serg Gregorio Taverna MiA
90ª Sq, 10°Gr, 4°St CT	MC 202 MM 7906 '90-8' hit by AA, S.Ten Virgilio Vanzan safe back at base

Saturday, 13 June 1942

During the hours of darkness a combined raid by several SAS parties failed to find their objectives in the Benghazi-Derna-Martuba area, other than at the Benghazi K2 airfield. Here all that could be achieved was some damage to three S.79s of 284ª Squadriglia AS. At Martuba some of the commandos were intercepted and captured.

Up to this point the battle had been in the balance. The prolonged resistance at Bir Hacheim had seriously upset Rommel's timetable, and the initial setback had thrown the future of his whole offensive into jeopardy. However, 13 June was to be the decisive day as 90th Light Division once more attacked, and this time succeeded in capturing El Adem, moreover the British armour in the Knightsbridge area, inexpertly handled, suffered heavy losses and was driven backwards towards the coast. 2nd, 4th and 22nd Armoured Brigades all suffered very substantial losses, particularly of tanks. Sandstorms during the day would again hinder air operations, which continued on a restricted scale.

Hurricanes of 213 Squadron swept over the Tobruk-Gazala road at 0700, but here they were bounced

Ten Vittorio Bacchi-Andreoli crash-landed his MC.202 '71-1' MM 7859 within Axis lines on 13 June 1942.

by six Bf 109s of I./JG 27, half of a formation which had been sent out to escort a Bf 110 on a reconnaissance over the Acroma-El Adem area. Lt Friedrich Körner claimed three fighters shot down and Lt Stahlschmidt one; Körner and Stahlschmidt each claimed one Hurricane, the former also claiming two P-40s at the same time, although no losses other than those suffered by 213 Squadron have been found. From this unit Plt Off Wilson's aircraft was seen to crash into the sea. Flt Sgt Dick Halvorsen (pictured below) seems fairly certainly to have been shot down by Körner and baled out.

"Hardly had I levelled out when I turned again; I couldn't just sit there depending on the weaver tactics and the mirror. I pulled back hard but sensed a lack of response in the rudder. I gave it hard left rudder when I straightened out and there was only a slight yaw, but in the mirror I saw an angled view of the rudder and bits of fabric fluttering from it. Quickly I looked forward and up. The Jerries had pulled up out of their initial dives, swung round, and were angling in twos from one o'clock and two o'clock. I canted left and lifted the nose, lining up my reflector sight for a 700-yard burst. The shots were off but an erratic tracer hit the wingman, and I got another burst in before I turned defensively, this time to the right. It was the correct move for the two o'clock bandits, who went by me a hundred yards away diving, but in my mirror I could see one of those I'd just fired at – had I damaged the other? I wasn't about to check on that – sitting behind and above me, and flashes came from his nose. Little holes like hemstitching appeared in my right wing and I turned left, losing something in the turn because of the holed wing and damaged rudder. She was as unresponsive as a sloop in stays, a mushy tub with no steerageway – she was a dying ship. The lack of response in the last turn told me my controls or cables had just been shot away.

"The manoeuvre hadn't done any good; the fighter was sticking to me like a band-aid, like a guy riding tandem on a bicycle made for two! I flipped the guard off the emergency gate and pulled for the extra zing I needed, then flicked right and down, knowing damn well it was useless but might buy some time for the Blue cavalry to show. I looked around the sky, eastwards, but there weren't any friendlies, not even the sound of bugles! Another twist, and a cannon tracer went by and machine-gun slugs hemstitched the right wing. Just a split-second burst; he was in no hurry. But where the hell are the other two?

"Suddenly a cannon shell hit the prop, right on the nose, just behind the spinner. Then another one hit, a few feet back of the first, then another, all in a line like a draughtsman's mechanical drawing. I sat transfixed, awed by the shooting accuracy, then in a split-second realised that with the spacing the next one should hit me in the back of the neck. For that fleeting moment I felt utterly serene – something I never experienced before or since. It had to be a split-second but seemed timeless, a fractional moment I was willing to trade for eternity. I loosened the harness in that moment and hit the lever to drop my seat, at the same time kicking desperately at the left rudder praying that this time something would somehow respond. Fantastically, it did and I yawed a little – the next shell went over my shoulder, still beautifully accurate, and hit just above the windscreen and burst into the reserve petrol tank just forward of the instrument panel. That did it. The explosive shell tore the tank apart and spilled flaming gasoline into the cockpit. Everything splashed wetly and then flamed, the whole cockpit an inferno. With my right hand I clawed at the harness release, awkwardly, desperately pulling the pin. It yanked free. I had no thought of my left hand, which was clutching the spade-grip of the stick, but I saw it was on fire. So were my longs (trousers) and desert shoes, and the fire crept onto my right hand and up to my tunic. By this time I was turning the aircraft over on its back and with the harness released I fell free, closing my eyes a second and counting, fearful that damn rudder might hit me, then I pulled the ripcord. 'Did they pack it right?' A moment later I was reassured as the straps jerked at my crotch, and I looked quickly up from my swinging perch to make sure I wasn't dreaming. I saw my flaming aircraft heading downwards, then suddenly it exploded, the flames no doubt having raced through the vapour in the wing tanks and set off the belts of cannon shells in the wings. My first wild swings from the blossoming 'chute were slowing and I lifted my legs to smother some smouldering stuff on the knees of my trousers. Then I saw that in the upside-down bale-out I'd lost my shoes and socks. I looked at my hands and almost got sick and now knew better than ever why I'd called my gauntlets lucky.

"It was quiet up there at – what? – Angels 12? When I'd last looked at the altimeter it had read 13,000 on this Friday the 13th. I looked down and saw nothing but a mist of brown, and knew from experience that the promised *khamsin* (sandstorm) had arrived and was sweeping its sand across the desert. Then the quiet was broken by a rattle of gunfire and the pump-pump-pump of cannons, up around where I was. I found I was riding with my hands up – like a man surrendering – to keep the blood from rushing to them. I wasn't – or hadn't been – aware of pain moments back because the terror had been a good counter-irritant. Now another fear made me forget them. Blue Section, what was left of it, had returned to take on the Jerries – no – the damn fools were circling me, far out and around, to ward off any attack on me.

"The Jerries kept hitting and running, diving in at the Hurris, and tracers were skittering around me, and I knew that plenty of GP armour-piercing stuff was peppering the air around me. All I needed was a tracer in my parachute and that would be it. 'Get lost! Who needs you?', I mentally screamed it aloud. 'You're damn near out of gas, you bloody idiots, and you'll never get back to base!' I saw one Hurricane break away seaward chasing a Messerschmitt, and then a second 109 following a Hurri. That left one 109 and he broke away as we got nearer the deck, and the rest of Blue Section headed south-easterly. I hoped they'd make it back.

"That one 109 wasn't gone long. I saw him whirl in a tight turn, gently extend it to a flat crescent, then come towards me. Was the bastard lining me up in his sights? I saw his flaps come down a bit, slowing him, in the distance, and had visions of his mainplane hitting me amidships, cutting me in two – real negative thinking. But he came past, throttle back, his goggles back on his forehead and gave me a smile and then a thumbs-up followed by a wave – and if I could lip-read German, which I didn't understand, he seemed to be saying 'Lots of luck'. That was the way it was in the desert air war – when you had time for it. Lots of *noblesse oblige* – a little chivalry expended when you let somebody off the hook. The German pilot's final wave said, 'So long, Alphonse', and my abortive wave back, 'Auf Wiedersehen, Gaston'.

"Crazy. I began thinking of all that happened. A ringside seat from a parachute, free show to a dogfight. The kite blowing up, seconds after getting out. That last moment when the rudder functioned. I'd almost uttered the blasphemy, 'Okay, JC, you've got control!' And then a silly thought, would the plane have exploded if I'd left the gun button on safe? Casuistical dilemma. I laughed. I must be going round the bend, really nuts. I was getting into the top billows of the hot khamsin wind, feeling the needles of sand on my feet. Funny I should have worn longs today – the first day ever. They saved my legs, but good. Why hadn't the bale-out fanned the flames instead of putting them out? My hands were hurting like hell but I didn't want to look at them again. Through the murk of the khamsin I saw stabs of orange and red on the deck – artillery? – Tanks? I hadn't worn shorts because they were all mucked up with diarrhoea and we were still short-rationed in water. Today no diarrhoea – everything was 'constricted', I guess.

"Suddenly the parachute caught in the khamsin and I was jerked like a puppet northwards. Almost lost the family jewels that time, and I tried to adjust the leg straps but my hand hurt too much. My vision adjusted to the brown twilight of the khamsin and I saw that I was getting close to the ground and saw vague silhouettes. Tanks. A lot of them. All shooting. God! And I thought four cannons made a bloody racket! Knock off, chaps, I'm coming in on runway 00. I in my bare feet and I could see the ground was chewed-up shale. Touch and roll that was the only answer. All I needed for this one was flippin' leotards. My toes touched and I rolled *ballet buffe* style, but the straps of the wind-filled parachute lifted me and slammed me down again, aggravating the back injury I'd got in a flip-over crash of a Defiant night fighter back in Scotland. I tried to turn the scored wheel of the 'chute release but there was no skin on my hands so I couldn't get any purchase.

"Guns crashed all around me and there was a screeching of metal as tanks moved ponderously on their treads of steel. There were vague silhouettes in the murk, moving, and others at a dead halt, on fire. My feet were taking a hell of a beating as I whipped through the battles, and my pant legs were in ribbons. I seemed to be coming out of the centre of the action, and suddenly saw a Bren gun-carrier, here where it was clearer, stop, change direction towards me, and presently overtake me. A couple of men leapt out and ran in my direction. One hurled himself across the shrouds of the 'chute, the other racing beyond him to stamp down and take the wind out of it. He gathered it up in a rumpled mass and walked towards me, and they both looked at me, puzzled, hesitating, maybe pitying. As I got to my feet, 'You okay, mate?' one asked, the short one. It was a Scots accent and I saw that they were Scots Guards. I nodded and said, 'Release the 'chute, will you?' Then I told them how to turn the knurled snap-lock, hit it, and then the straps dropped away. The tall one looked at my hands, then said, 'Shall we take off them rubber gloves?' I looked at my hands, held shoulder-high against the blood-rush, and laughed. 'Better leave it for the MO. That's skin, mate. The doc'll have to cut it away.' The Bren gun-carrier was darting around us, its driver sensibly not stopping to provide a sitting target.

"Soon we were out of the angry, dust-whipping battle and clearing into relative sunshine, coming at last to an area where great tank-carriers sat, and busted-up tanks. An Italian Fiat CR.42 suddenly whipped out of the sky, a fast biplane that did a dipsy-do over the area, flying real low and strafing everywhere. The tall Scot got him in his sights and held him in a long burst and swinging his gun, never letting up. The Eyetie pilot dropped his bombs in the open as Scotty's bullets ripped through his wings, then chewed away at his tail assembly, and the aircraft went out of control and hit somewhere over the dunes. You could see the black cloud slowly rising. I congratulated Scotty. 'I wish we had all them bastards instead of that flippin' Rommel. He's tearing us to bits.' A moment later we clanked up to a van with a Red Cross on it. Days later I was safe, in Palestine."

In 1969 Dick Halvorsen approached the author to see if it was possible to identify the chivalrous German pilot who had shot him down on that day. A ready identification of Oberst Friedrich Körner, then serving with the West German Luftwaffe allowed a meeting to be arranged between the two veterans who swiftly became friends. Interestingly, Körner recalled noting the 'yellow gauntlets' which appeared to be dangling from Halvorsen's wrists as he floated down under his parachute…

Much later in the day at 1900, six Kittyhawks of 450 Squadron escorted eight of 112 Squadron to attack vehicles in the Sidi Rezegh area. Before reaching the target, 12 Ju 88s were seen, escorted by 12 Bf 109s of I./JG 27. At much the same time about 20 fighters from 2 SAAF, 4 SAAF and 5 SAAF Squadrons had been scrambled to intercept this formation, attacking the bombers over El Adem. As they did so they were attacked by both the Bf 109s, coming out of the sun, and a patrol of 10° Gruppo MC.202s.

Five claims were made by the German pilots, four of them by Oblt Marseille, but although they fired at several British aircraft, the Italians were not able to submit any claims, although two Macchis failed to return and a third crash-landed within Axis lines with the pilot wounded. The damage had been inflicted by the South Africans, who claimed two MC.202s and two Bf 109s shot down, plus a third Messerschmitt probable. Only one 4 SAAF Squadron Tomahawk was hit and badly damaged, belly-landing at base. However, the 239 Wing units had fallen foul of the Messerschmitts, three of 450 Squadron's aircraft being shot down, while one of 112 Squadron's Kittyhawks was also lost when attacking Axis artillery positions at this time – either a victim of I./JG 27 or of Flak.

British Claims

4 SAAF Sqn	Lt S.Cohen	Tomahawk IIb AN397 'U'	MC.202 Probable	SW Gambut Main	1900-2025
2 SAAF Sqn	Lt V.M.L.Lindsay	Kittyhawk I AL134 'H'	MC.202	El Adem	1910
2 SAAF Sqn	Lt R.D.B.Morton	Kittyhawk I AK926 'L'	} MC.202	El Adem	1910
2 SAAF Sqn	Capt E.Smith	Kittyhawk I AL223 'F'	}		
4 SAAF Sqn	Maj J.L.Hewitson	Tomahawk IIb AN525 'H'	Bf 109F	E El Adem l.g.	1930
4 SAAF Sqn	Lt G.H.Kaufmann	Tomahawk IIb AN400 'V'	} Bf 109F	5m N El Adem	1930
4 SAAF Sqn	Lt B.A.Robertshaw	Tomahawk IIb AN428 'K'	}		
4 SAAF Sqn	Lt J.van Nus	Tomahawk IIb AN452 'M'	Bf 109F Damaged	El Adem	1930

British Casualties

112 Sqn	Kittyhawk I AK949 MiA in attack on artillery positions at 1940; Plt Off F.F.J.Edwards KiA
260 Sqn	Kittyhawk I damaged Cat II in Acroma area, 1145-1225
450 Sqn	Kittyhawk I AL106 shot down by Bf 109s on escort sortie N El Adem circa 1915; Plt Off J.C.Osborne safe
450 Sqn	Kittyhawk I AL117 shot down by Bf 109s on escort sortie N El Adem circa 1915; Sgt W.J. Halliday, KiA
450 Sqn	Kittyhawk I AK958 shot down by Bf 109s on escort sortie N El Adem circa 1915; Sgt R.Stone, KiA
4 SAAF Sqn	Tomahawk IIb AN397 'U' badly damaged and belly-landed at base, Cat II; Lt S.Cohen safe
213 Sqn	Hurricane BE340 damaged by Bf 109s and abandoned nr Acroma 0700-0900; Sgt R.Halvorsen WiA
213 Sqn	Hurricane Z3507 FTR, Acroma 0700-0900; Plt Off P.P.Wilson
14 Sqn	Blenheim IV Z6044 MiA

German Claims

2./JG 27	Lt Friedrich Körner	P-40	S Fort Acroma	0640
2./JG 27	Lt Friedrich Körner	Hurricane	N Wadi Es Sahaae	0650
2./JG 27	Lt Hans-Arnold Stahlschmidt	Hurricane	Tobruk	0652
2./JG 27	Lt Friedrich Körner	P-40	Tobruk	0653
3./JG 27	Oblt Hans-Joachim Marseille	P-40	5km W El Adem	1810
3./JG 27	Oblt Hans-Joachim Marseille	P-40	3km NW El Adem	1811
3./JG 27	Oblt Hans-Joachim Marseille	P-40	2km NNE El Adem	1814
3./JG 27	Oblt Hans-Joachim Marseille	Hurricane	3km ENE El Adem	1815
1./JG 27	Lt Hans Remmer	Hurricane	NW El Adem	1820

Italian Casualties

71ª Sq, 17°Gr, 1°St CT	MC.202 MM 7751 failed to return 1730-, Cap Ferdinando Vicentini PoW
71ª Sq, 17°Gr, 1°St CT	MC.202 MM 7732 failed to return 1730-, Ten Sergio Morandi KiA
71ª Sq, 17°Gr, 1°St CT	MC.202 MM 7859 '71-1' crash-landed within Axis lines 1730-, Ten Vittorio Bacchi-Andreoli WiA
84ª Sq, 10°Gr, 4°St CT	MC.202 MM 7814 '84-5' force-landed after sortie 1535-1700, Serg Pietro Buttazzi safe
284ª Sq, 131° Gr AS	3 S.79s MM 24076, 24300, 24087 damaged at Benghazi by SAS raid

Sunday, 14 June 1942

The Commonwealth forces began an increasingly precipitate retreat from the Gazala positions, fearful of being cut off by the Afrika Korps columns sweeping up towards the coast from the El Adem area in their rear. This required WDAF to commence a series of 'leapfrogging' moves to the east but maintaining squadrons over the front at all times. Fortunately, these carefully-planned moves were achieved with a

S.Ten Federico Vallauri in front of his MC.200 '77-4' MM 6699. Vallauri took part in the strafing raid on 14 June, but failed to return from a convoy escort on 12 August.

high degree of success. The main action of the day, however, occurred over the Vigorous convoy to Malta which had now entered 'Bomb Alley' between Crete and the Libyan coast. AVM Coningham despatched Kittyhawks and Tomahawks to protect the merchant ships, joining the Beaufighters of 201 Group in this task. These particular operations are dealt with in full detail in Chapter Three, and will therefore be mentioned only in passing here.

At 1931, following a day of protracted operations over the convoy, five Bf 109s of II./JG 27 took off on a strafing sortie north of the Via Balbia. Uffz Gierster was hit by AA and baled out into the sea north of Gazala; he was not rescued. A few minutes later, 12 Kittyhawks of 3 RAAF Squadron escorted by 112 and 450 Squadrons, carried out a similar mission during which Flt Lt Chinchen was shot down by Flak; he baled out, becoming a PoW. Sgt Diden's aircraft was damaged and he crash-landed at Gambut.

2° Stormo MC.200s made three attacks on vehicles and troop concentrations on the strip between the Via Balbia and the sea from Gazala to Mrassas. Two of the Macchi strafers were lost and three damaged; one pilot failed to return, his body being found five days later. One of the pilots of 77ª Squadriglia, S.Ten Federico Vallauri, wrote to his parents: "As far as size, the strafing actions of Sunday 14th have likely been the largest and most powerful carried out by the Regia Aeronautica since the beginning of the war."

During the afternoon 50° Stormo took part in this series of attacks, 24 CR.42s strafing in the same area, claiming to have set two tank-transporters on fire. However, two of the biplanes were shot down by AA with the loss of both pilots, and a third was damaged.

British Claims

213 Sqn	Sqn Ldr M.H.Young	Hurricane IIc BN286 'O'	Bf 109F Damaged	El Adem	0949
260 Sqn	Flt Sgt J.F.Edwards	Kittyhawk Ia ET859 'T'	Bf 109F Probable	Acroma area	1144-1225
260 Sqn	Flt Sgt J.F.Edwards	Kittyhawk Ia ET859 'T'	Bf 109F Damaged	Acroma area	1144-1225
5 SAAF Sqn	Maj J.E.Frost	Tomahawk IIb AN422 'B'	Ju 87	off coast 15m E Tobruk	1215
5 SAAF Sqn	Maj J.E.Frost	Tomahawk IIb AN422 'B'	Bf 109F Damaged	off coast 15m E Tobruk	1215
5 SAAF Sqn	Lt K.C.Kemsley	Tomahawk IIb AN345 'V'	Ju 87	off coast 15m E Tobruk	1215
5 SAAF Sqn	Lt K.C.Kemsley	Tomahawk IIb AN345 'V'	Ju 87 Probable	off coast 15m E Tobruk	1215
5 SAAF Sqn	Lt K.C.Kemsley	Tomahawk IIb AN345 'V'	Bf 109F Damaged	off coast 15m E Tobruk	1215
5 SAAF Sqn	Lt L.B.van der Spuy	Tomahawk IIb AK533 'Y'	Bf 109	off coast 15m E Tobruk	1215

British Casualties

260 Sqn	Kittyhawk damaged Cat II Acroma area 1145-1225
238 Sqn	Hurricane II 'U' shot down, baled out over sea, 0810-0930; Plt Off O.F.A.Oram rescued
238 Sqn	Hurricane II 'D' shot down over sea, 0740-0930; Flt Lt M.R.Jenkins rescued?
4 SAAF	Tomahawk AN452 'M' damaged by 2 Bf 109s, 20m N Gambut at 1215, landed safely; Lt G.H.Kaufmann safe
3 RAAF Sqn	Kittyhawk I AL215 shot down by Flak SW El Adem, 2000-2040; Flt Lt G.Chinchen PoW
3 RAAF Sqn	Kittyhawk I AL208 hit by Flak and crash-landed, Gambut Main; Sgt R.Biden safe
3 RAAF Sqn	Kittyhawk I AL838 hit by Flak and damaged, landed at 2100-; Sgt W.W.Thomas safe
5 SAAF Sqn	Tomahawk IIb AN345 'V' shot down by two Bf 109s, nr Tobruk force-landed 10m W Gambut 1215; Lt K.C.Kemsley safe
5 SAAF Sqn	Tomahawk IIb AK533 'Y' shot down by Bf 109s Tobruk 1215; Lt L.B.van der Spuy baled out WiA, to Tobruk hospital and evacuated, returning to unit

German Claims

2./JG 27	Lt Friedrich Körner	2 P-40s	N Gambut	1105
9./JG 53	Oblt Franz Götz	Hurricane		1105
9./JG 53	Obfw Werner Stumpf	Hurricane		1106
2./JG 27	Lt Hans-Arnold Stahlschmidt	P-40	NNW Gambut	1108
7./JG 53	Lt Jürgen Harder	P-40		1125
8./JG 53	Hptm Helmut Belser	P-40		1145
7./JG 53	Uffz Hartmut Klötzer	P-40		1147

German Casualties

5./JG 27	Bf 109F-4 trop WNr 8510 Red 9 shot down by AA 2km NE Ain el Gazala; Uffz Helmut Gierster baled, WiA

Italian Casualties

77ª Sq, 13°Gr, 2°St CT	MC.200 MM 5236 '77-3'damaged by ground fire, landed in enemy territory 1500, M.llo Felice Sozzi PoW
78ª Sq, 13°Gr, 2°St CT	MC.200 MM 8295 damaged by ground fire 1430-1550, Serg Magg Cassio Poggi WiA returned
78ª Sq, 13°Gr, 2°St CT	MC.200 MM 5305 damaged by ground fire 1430-1550, Serg Italo Rossini safe
82ª Sq, 13°Gr, 2°St CT	MC.200 MM 5346 failed to return 1805-, Serg Magg Luigi Giannotti MiA
94ª Sq, 8° Gr, 2°St CT	MC.200 MM 5277 damaged by ground fire 1445-1615, Cap Orfeo Cecchet safe
390ª Sq, 159°Gr, 50°St Ass	CR.42 MM 7493 failed to return 1710-1840, S.Ten Paolo Guillet MiA
388ª Sq, 158°Gr, 50°St Ass	CR.42 MM 7629 failed to return 1740-1900, Serg Leo Panizzi MiA
389ª Sq, 159°Gr, 50°St Ass	CR.42 damaged by ground fire 1720-1845, Serg Magg Costante Cipitelli returned

Monday, 15 June 1942

Again, much of the action on this date was over the convoy. During the day, however, Rommel turned his forces east from Acroma, by-passing El Adem and striking for Sidi Rezegh.

The assault on the coastal highway by the Italian fighter-bombers continued from early in the morning. 2° Stormo MC.200s took up the attack again between 0750-0910, but the newly-promoted commanding

A 250 Squadron Kittyhawk III FR241 with its engine shrouded against dust with a cover which also carries the aircraft's codes, LD-A.

officer of 93ª Squadriglia, Cap Mario D'Agostini (who had claimed two victories over the Aegean during 1940) was shot down and killed by ground fire; he was awarded a Medaglia d'Oro 'In Memoriam'. A second MC.200 was also shot down, the pilot also being killed. Shortly behind the Macchis came the 50° Stormo CR.42s again, ten from 159° Gruppo attacking vehicles 0800-0945. This time Hurricanes of 274 Squadron had been scrambled after a reported 20 aircraft over Tobruk, and 15 miles east of Gazala the pilots of this unit reported engaging three CR.42s, two MC.202s and two Hs 126s at 1,000 feet, these being joined by some Bf 109s thought to be E variants. Wg Cdr Fenton shot down one CR.42 in flames into the sea, Sgt Dodds claiming an MC.202 probable and a CR.42 damaged. One CR.42 was shot down by fighters, the pilot being killed, and a second was damaged but got back to base with a punctured fuel tank.

Over El Adem mid-afternoon a claim was made for a P-40 by a 10° Gruppo MC.202 pilot. At 1832 12 Bf 109s of I./JG 27 escorted a reconnaissance Bf 110 over the Gambut-Acroma area, engaging a dozen British fighters identified as Curtiss types, north of El Alamein. Between 1901-1906 Oblt Marseille claimed four shot down, Lt Schroer adding two more. Although no details have been found to identify their opponents on this occasion, JG 27 reported that the whole combat was observed by all the 3.Staffel pilots who were able to confirm their leader's victories 88-91. At 1841, however, two Jabo Messerschmitts of III./JG 27 attacked Gambut airfield, where Uffz Panier was shot down and baled out to become a PoW. RAF records indicate that during this attack on Gambut Main three Hurricanes of 33 Squadron were damaged Cat II, one airman being killed and one wounded. Panier's victor appears to have been Flt Lt Darwin of 274 Squadron, who claimed only a damaged.

During the day the whole of III./JG 53 less the new Jabo Staffel, was ordered to return to Sicily, leaving JG 27 as the sole Jagdgeschwader in North Africa; it would take a few days for the unit to clear up and move completely. On the Allied side of the lines, 40 SAAF Squadron moved to Bir Sheferzen. Cap Carlo Maurizio Ruspoli di Poggio Suasa, a Roman prince, assumed command of 91ª Squadriglia of 10° Gruppo.

British Claims

274 Sqn	Sgt J.Dodds	Hurricane IIc	MC.202 Probable	15m E Gazala	0905-
274 Sqn	Sgt J.Dodds	Hurricane IIc	CR.42 Damaged	15m E Gazala	0905-
274 Sqn	Wg Cdr H.A Fenton	Hurricane IIc	CR.42	15m E Gazala	0905-
274 Sqn	Flt Lt C.W.Darwin	Hurricane IIc	Bf 109E Damaged	over base Gambut Main	1915

British Casualties

274 Sqn	Hurricane IIc left 0905, 15m E Gazala, damaged Cat I by MC.202; Plt Off W.A.G.Conrad safe
33 Sqn	3 Hurricane IIbs damaged Cat II by fighter-bombers, LAC Wiseman KiA, LAC Leaburn WiA
6 Sqn	Hurricane BN797 hit by Flak and crash-landed 1600-1650; Plt Off Lee safe
208 Sqn	Hurricane V7821 force-landed in minefield and blown up

German Claims

3./JG 27	Oblt Hans-Joachim Marseille	4 P-40s	4-8km N El Adem	1801-1806
Stab I./JG 27	Lt Werner Schroer	2 P-40s	NW El Adem	1806-1811

German Casualties

10.(Jabo)/JG 27	Bf 109F-4 trop WNr 10039 Green 8+ lost 30km WSW Gambut; Uffz Karl-Heinz Panier baled and PoW

Italian Claims

90ª Sq, 10°Gr, 4°St CT	Serg Magg Amleto Monterumici MC.202	P-40	El Adem	1620-

Italian Casualties

391ª Sq, 159°Gr, 50°St Ass	CR.42 MM 8846 shot down by fighters, 0800-0925, Serg Magg Giuseppe Della Valle KiA
389ª Sq, 159°Gr, 50°St Ass	CR.42 damaged, 0800-, Serg Magg Giuseppe Maturi safe
389ª Sq, 159°Gr, 50°St Ass	CR.42 damaged, 0800-, Ten Sergio Flaccomio safe
93ª Sq, 8°Gr, 2°St CT	MC.200 MM 5111 shot down by ground fire 0840, Cap Mario D'Agostini MiA, body found June 19th
93ª Sq, 8°Gr, 2°St CT	MC.200 MM 5918 hit by ground fire 0840, Serg Magg Bartolo Palumbo WiA

Tuesday, 16 June 1942

The Vigorous convoy ships, having turned about, re-entered Alexandria on this date, leaving WDAF free to return to its activities over the desert. The day saw the 21st Panzer Division drive through Sidi Rezegh and on to Belhamed. WDAF fighters flew a large number of sorties in defence of Gambut, a typical example of which was to be seen in 3 RAAF Squadron's records, which showed that Flt Lt Barr flew a record six sorties, Flg Off Spence completed five and Flt Sgt Kildey four. The tank-busters of 6 Squadron completed their 37th sorties since going into action on 6 June, during which time 31 tanks had been claimed immobilised and 28 large vehicles destroyed or badly damaged.

Six Kittyhawks of the Australian squadron were attacked by two Bf 109s, two aircraft suffering damage, but thereafter the rest of the morning was relatively quiet. The afternoon was busy and was interspersed with a number of complex engagements. Before that, however, 17° Gruppo had undertaken its last mission in Libya, seven MC.202s flying a free sweep over Acroma-El Adem-Tobruk from 0900. By now the unit had only eight serviceable fighters on hand, and 1° Stormo CT was ordered to repatriate. Aircraft and equipment was to be handed over to 4° Stormo; the schedule for the departure to Italy was to be as follows: 71ª Squadriglia to leave Martuba on 19 June, 79ª Squadriglia on 21st, 72ª Squadriglia on 23rd, 81ª Squadriglia on 25th, 80ª Squadriglia with 17° Gruppo HQ on 27th, 88ª Squadriglia with 6° Gruppo HQ on 29th. This plan was actually revised two days later when 88ª Squadriglia, reinforced with six 17° Gruppo pilots, was ordered to stay in Libya until mid-July, to take part in the forthcoming offensive.

Maj John 'Jack' Frost, commanding officer of 5 SAAF Squadron, was the SAAF's most successful fighter pilot when he was shot down and killed on 16 June.

At 1335 ten Kittyhawks of 3 RAAF Squadron again undertook a mission, two aircraft being hit by Flak and both crash-landing at base. 112 Squadron also flew fighter-bomber sorties in the afternoon, two of this unit's pilots being shot down between 1400-1500, Plt Off K.Carson being killed. Eleven Hurricanes of 274 Squadron patrolled east of Tobruk at 1435, five Bf 109s being spotted 2,500 feet below. Two Messerschmitts were claimed shot down, plus a probable and a damaged. III./JG 27 had taken off on a Freie Jagd at 1425, the unit reporting meeting 12 fighters over El Adem where Uffz Fahrenberger was shot down and baled out; he returned later. At 1450 seven Kittyhawks of 3 RAAF Squadron again carried out a fighter-bomber mission, but these were attacked by four Bf 109s, newly-promoted Sqn Ldr Barr claiming one damaged.

From 1500 onwards operations became extremely intense and involved many engagements, some of which appear to have impinged on each other. The first WDAF unit to become airborne at this time was 213 Squadron, scrambled at 1530 to patrol a line east of Tobruk. This unit was jumped by three Bf 109s, two of which were claimed shot down. Twenty-five minutes later 12 Kittyhawks of 250 Squadron with others of 112 and 3 RAAF Squadrons, took off to strafe in the Sidi Rezegh area, one pilot crash-landing east of the target area. At 1620 nine more Kittyhawks from 3 RAAF Squadron flew yet another ground-attack mission during which they were attacked by four Bf 109s. During the return flight Sgt Biden crash-landed at Gambut when his engine stopped; unfortunately, his bomb had not released and as he landed, this blew up, killing him; one other pilot also failed to return.

During this period four Bf 109s of I./JG 27 were on a Freie Jagd in the Sidi Rezegh area where at 1546 a dozen Kittyhawks were encountered, Lts Stahlschmidt and Körner each claiming one shot down. At 1602 five more Messerschmitts from III.Gruppe carried out a similar mission, engaging nine Kittyhawks and Hurricanes, Oblt Tangerding claiming one in flames and Fw Fisk one which crash-landed.

Six Kittyhawks of 250 Squadron were off at 1725 to strafe near Sidi Rezegh, but one was hit by Flak and on trying to crash-land, collided with some MT on the ground, bursting into flames. Five minutes later Plt Off Glenn of 208 Squadron took off on a TacR to El Adem from which he failed to return. Twelve Hurricanes of 73 Squadron were next off at 1735, patrolling over El Duda, where these aircraft were jumped by Bf 109s, one flight commander being shot down. 33 Squadron also scrambled Hurricanes

Hurricane II KC-G of 238 Squadron.

near El Adem during the afternoon, meeting ten Bf 109s and MC.202s. Two Hurricanes were badly damaged, one of the pilots suffering wounds.

At 1849 233 Wing started to take off in strength, four Kittyhawks of 2 SAAF, four Tomahawks of 4 SAAF and six of 5 SAAF Squadrons setting course to provide escort for Bostons west of El Adem, 2 SAAF as top cover and 4 SAAF as close cover. Bf 109s attacked during the raid, 2 SAAF losing one aircraft shot down in flames, but Lt de Villiers survived this to return that evening; a second pilot was wounded and had his aircraft badly damaged. Lt McGregor of 4 SAAF was wounded in the face and his aircraft was also damaged, but he returned safely. 5 SAAF Squadron took the brunt of the attack, losing Maj J.E.Frost, DFC, and Lt R.C.Derham.

The last mission of note was undertaken by 250 Squadron Kittyhawks which strafed south-west of Acroma from 1935, being engaged by four Bf 109s. Sgt Hall was shot down by one fighter which dived and then came up underneath his aircraft, and Plt Off Cable was involved in a 15-minute dogfight during which his Kittyhawk was very badly damaged, causing him to crash-land at base where he claimed to have damaged one Messerschmitt.

Few claims were made by Italian fighters on this date, amounting to one Boston – of which none were actually lost – and two P-40 probables. Luftwaffe fighters claimed 15 during the afternoon. Not all WDAF losses were to fighters, of course, but 13 Kittyhawks and Tomahawks had been shot down or damaged sufficiently to have to crash-land, with four more damaged; to these must be added two Hurricanes lost and two damaged, plus, apparently, a Spitfire PR IV of 2 PRU. Amongst the German pilots Marseille made four claims as did Fw Steinhausen, Lt Körner claiming two.

The Spitfires of 145 Squadron undertook 22 sorties over Gambut in the course of the day, one Ju 88 being shot down and a second damaged. In the evening 213 Squadron moved to Sidi Aziez. For the South Africans the loss of Jack Frost was a heavy blow. This veteran pilot, who had done so well in East Africa during the previous year (see *Dust Clouds in the Middle East*), had doubled his personal tally during the past few days. He had also led his young squadron with great dash and vigour; Capt L.C.Botha took his place.

On this date the order sending III./JG 53 to Comiso was revoked, but from now until 20 June the greater part of the Gruppe was temporarily based in Crete, Greece and Sicily. Meanwhile, I./JG 27 moved to Gazala.

British Claims

145 Sqn	Flg Off H.J.Phillips	Spitfire Vb ..284 'T'	Ju 88 Damaged	Gambut	1140-1300
250 Sqn	Flg Off G.W.Garton	Kittyhawk I AK925 'H'	Bf 109	Gazala	1415
274 Sqn	Sgt J.Dodds	Hurricane IIc	Bf 109	E Tobruk	1435-
274 Sqn	Sgt J.Dodds	Hurricane IIc	Bf 109E Damaged	E Tobruk	1435-
274 Sqn	Flt Lt G.C.Keefer	Hurricane IIc BE689	Bf 109	E Tobruk	1435-

British Claims

3 RAAF Sqn	Sqn Ldr A.W.Barr	Kittyhawk I AK745	Bf 109 Damaged	SW Sidi Rezegh	1450-1525
213 Sqn	Flt Lt G.H.Westlake	Hurricane IIc BN184 'W'	Bf 109F	SW Sidi Rezegh	1610
213 Sqn	Flg Off. J.L.Briggs	Hurricane II BN367	Bf 109*	E Tobruk	1610
274 Sqn	Flt Lt W.A.G.Conrad	Hurricane IIc BN676	Bf 109 Probable	E Tobruk	1610
145 Sqn	Sgt M.J.Mahady	Spitfire Vb AR284 'T'	Ju 88	SE Sidi Rezegh	1710-1745
145 Sqn	Plt Off Norman	Spitfire Vb AB412 'V'			
250 Sqn	Plt Off W.O.Cable	Kittyhawk I AK884 'F'	Bf 109 Damaged	SW Acroma	1940
260 Sqn	Flg Off J.L.Waddy	Kittyhawk I ET579	Bf 109 Damaged	SE El Adem	

*claimed damaged, confirmed destroyed later

British Casualties

112 Sqn	Kittyhawk I AL105 left 1400, MiA from ground attack nr Sidi Rezegh to AA at 1450; Plt Off K.F.Carson PoW
112 Sqn	Kittyhawk I AL175 left 1400, MiA from fighter-bomber sortie nr Sidi Rezegh; Sgt R.H.Newton safe
250 Sqn	Kittyhawk I AL139 shot down by Flak 15m E Sidi Rezegh at 1630; Sgt H.R.Hannaford safe
250 Sqn	Kittyhawk I AL179 left 1925 shot down by Bf 109s Nr El Adem; Sgt F.C.De Salvo Hall safe
250 Sqn	Kittyhawk I AL168 'F' shot down nr Sidi Rezegh by Flak at 1800; Plt Off A.R.Simpson KiA
250 Sqn	Kittyhawk I AK884 'Y' badly damaged by Bf 109 SW Acroma, crash-landed at base; Plt Off W.O.Cable safe
250 Sqn	Kittyhawk I AK785 left 1925 badly damaged by Bf 109 SW Acroma, crash-landed; Plt Off M.Rogerson safe
260 Sqn	Kittyhawk I left 1530, shot down by Bf 109 SE El Adem c1630; Sgt J.V.Carlisle baled out safe
260 Sqn	Kittyhawk I ET579 left 1530 chased back to Bir El Baheira by 3 Bf 109s; crash-landed at base c1630; Flg Off J. L.Waddy safe
3 RAAF Sqn	Kittyhawk I AL145 shot down by Bf 109 NW El Adem , 1620-1705; Sgt F.J.Ryan KiA
3 RAAF Sqn	Kittyhawk I AL159 shot down by Bf 109, crash-landed, near Gambut main, 1620-1705 with bomb still attached and it exploded; Sgt R.Biden KiA
3 RAAF Sqn	Kittyhawk I AK961 'O' damaged by Bf 109 NW El Adem, 1620-1705; Sgt J.Donald safe
3 RAAF Sqn	Kittyhawk I AK838 crash-landed at base, 1335-1415; Sgt H.J.Bray safe
3 RAAF Sqn	Kittyhawk I AK812 crash-landed at base, 1335-1415; Sgt L.L.Boardman safe
2 SAAF Sqn	Kittyhawk I AK926 'L' shot down, crash-landed near Gambut at 1615 – Cat II; Lt P.D.Bryant slt WiA
2 SAAF Sqn	Kittyhawk I AK993 'R' shot down by Bf 109, near Gambut 1615; Lt T.V.de Villiers back five hours later, slt WiA
4 SAAF Sqn	Tomahawk IIb AN300 damaged by Bf 109 at 1900 over base, but landed safely; 2/Lt G.W.McGregor WiA
5 SAAF Sqn	Tomahawk IIb AN422 'B' shot down by Bf 109s near LG. 167 Bir el Baheira at 1940; Maj J.E.Frost KiA
5 SAAF Sqn	Tomahawk IIb AK370 'I' shot down by Bf 109s near LG. 167 Bir el Baheira at 1940; Lt R.C.Derham PoW
33 Sqn	Hurricane IIb Z5453 stalled at low altitude and crashed 10m SW Sollum; Sgt N.W.Callister KiFA
33 Sqn	Hurricane IIb ..226 badly damaged by e/a El Adem area 1835-1940; Plt Off W.M. Schwartz safe
33 Sqn	Hurricane IIb ..273 badly damaged by e/a El Adem area 1835-1940; Plt Off K.C.Rolls safe
73 Sqn	Hurricane BN560 MiA, shot down El Duda; Flt Lt M.G.Robin KiA
208 Sqn	Hurricane IIa BG914 left 1730 on TacR to El Adem, failed to return; Plt Off W.Glenn

German Claims

2./JG 27	Lt Friedrich Körner	P-40	E El Adem	1520
2./JG 27	Lt Hans-Arnold Stahlschmidt	P-40	SW Gambut	1525
7./JG 27	Oblt Hermann Tangerding	P-40	5km E El Adem	1535
7./JG 27	Fw Walter Fink	P-40	10km SE El Adem	1537
5./JG 27	Fw Hans Niederhöfer	P-40	5km E El Adem	1640
5./JG 27	Obfw Emil Clade	P-40	E Bu Amud	1642
1./JG 27	Fw Günther Steinhausen	Hurricane	E El Adem	1800
3./JG 27	Oblt Hans-Joachim Marseille	Hurricane	17km SW El Adem	1802
3./JG 27	Oblt Hans-Joachim Marseille	P-40	5km E El Adem	1810
1./JG 27	Fw Günther Steinhausen	P-40	E El Adem	1810
3./JG 27	Oblt Hans-Joachim Marseille	2 P-40s	5km NNE & 10km N El Adem	1811 & 1813
1./JG 27	Fw Günther Steinhausen	P-40	SW El Adem	1814
1./JG 27	Fw Günther Steinhausen	P-40	E Gambut	1820
2./JG 27	Lt Friedrich Körner	P-40	SW Gambut	1850

German Casualties

8./JG 27	Bf 109F-4 trop Black 3 combat Sidi Rezegh area, slight damage; Uffz Hans Fahrenberger safe

Italian Claims

90ª Sq, 10°Gr, 4°St CT	S.Ten Virgilio Vanzan	MC.202	Boston	Sidi Rezegh	1730-
91ª Sq, 10°Gr, 4°St CT	Magg Paolo Maddalena	MC.202	P-40 Probable	Sidi Rezegh	1730-
10° Gr, 4°St CT	u/i pilots	MC.202	P-40 Probable	Sidi Rezegh	1730-

Wednesday, 17 June 1942

Air operations reached a crescendo when it was announced that British fighters escorting Bostons during the day were bounced by Bf 109s, and lost ten of their number. Details of only eight of these losses are available, together with the operations of the fighter-bomber squadrons on what was in many ways a most momentous day for both sides. It may be, however, that the numbers of Luftwaffe claims made were simply accepted as reflecting the WDAF casualties.

At 0930 four Tomahawks of 5 SAAF Squadron provided part of the escort to Bostons bombing east of El Adem. They were bounced by four Bf 109s of II./JG 27 on a Freie Jagd, three of the South African fighters being shot down including that flown by Capt Botha, the commanding officer of one day's standing, who was killed. Half an hour later 450 Squadron escorted Kittybombers of 3 RAAF Squadron to El Duda and El Adem. Four Bf 109s of I./JG 27 on another Freie Jagd intercepted the formation, shooting down two of the Australian fighters, one from each unit.

Eleven Hurricanes of 274 Squadron took off at 1055 to escort nine Bostons to El Duda. The fighter pilots found the bombers over Gambut, but 2,000 feet higher, which prevented them from catching up with their charges. Sgt Dodds then spotted four MC.202s over the fighters' base and the Hurricanes attacked these, two being claimed damaged while Dodds attacked one at 10,000 feet, firing a five to eight-second burst from 100 yards astern. He reported that the Macchi rolled over and dived straight into the ground, blowing up. He then saw a second Macchi on the tail of a Hurricane, with a second Hurricane on its tail. The Italian broke away and Dodds closed in on it, getting within range when ten miles east of Sidi Rezegh. He described how he fired a three-second burst from 100 yards, closing to 50 yards at which point the Macchi exploded into flames and crashed. There is little doubt that 274 Squadron was engaged with 10° Gruppo at this time, pilots of this latter unit claiming five British fighters during the morning, four P-40s and one Hurricane. However, there is no note of any casualties being suffered by the Italians on this occasion.

Distinguished by his unruly mop of hair, Glaswegian Flt Sgt James 'Hamish' Dodds sits on the wreckage of a Bf 109. Dodds claimed more victories than any other Hurricane pilot in North Africa during 1942, his final two claims being made on 17 June.

These claims, however, brought James 'Hamish' Dodds' run of successes to an end. Since December 1941 he had claimed 14 confirmed and six probable victories, the majority being against Bf 109s and MC.202s, superior in performance to his Hurricane. His tactics, according to pilots who served with him, had been, whenever a dogfight developed, to try and climb as high as possible instead of turning with the others, and when well above, to pick a target well below and go for it. The success of this Scotsman's plan seems to have been witnessed, at least on occasions. However, during this period he had remained a sergeant and had received no decoration, illustrating perhaps that his 'lone wolf' tactics were not entirely appreciated by those commanding him. The officer who had been his flight commander commented to the authors: "I never believed Dodds' claims for aircraft shot down, and I do not think many other people did either." It was not until the following January that what seemed to be a well-deserved DFM was gazetted for having apparently been one of the most successful exponents of the Hurricane in the RAF, and certainly in North Africa. Whatever the case, 274 Squadron's duties became much more concerned with ground attack thereafter, and Dodds had little more chance to add further to his list of claims.

In the meantime, four Bf 109s of II./JG 27 on a Freie Jagd had joined the fight, reporting nine Bostons and 30 escorting fighters. Oblt Schulz caught Flt Lt Conrad of 274 and shot him down east of Bu Amud, where Conrad carried out a crash-landing, being slightly wounded. Schulz, in his usual manner, came down to make certain of his 51st victory, strafing it thoroughly. This time it was to prove his undoing, for as he began his second run, he was attacked by a Kittyhawk, being shot down and killed.

260 Squadron had also been involved in escorting Bostons, becoming engaged with a number of Bf 109s. Flt Lt Edwards got a good burst into one Messerschmitt which overshot him, seeing an explosion in the engine area. He may have hit the aircraft of III./JG 53 flown by Lt Wolf Schaller, who crash-landed at Gambut as a result of combat, becoming a PoW; he would be released when Tobruk fell on 21 June. However, a claim was also submitted for a Bf 109 by Flt Lt McKay during this sortie, and a second by the pilot of a 145 Squadron Spitfire. Uncertainty is increased here by the possibility that this latter claim may have been only for a Messerschmitt damaged, which may have been confirmed later. Edwards, finding himself alone, turned south-east and set course for base at full throttle. Minutes later, flying at zero feet, he saw more Messerschmitts ahead of him – two or three above and one near the ground. The latter appeared to be turning towards him when he was within about half a mile, but he had come upon Schulz turning in for his second pass at Conrad's Hurricane. Climbing slightly, but maintaining his speed, he turned in slightly, got the deflection just right, and with a burst sent the Messerschmitt crashing into the ground. He then headed away with all speed, not having spotted Conrad's wrecked fighter. Conrad had certainly seen him, and was able to spot the squadron letters on the side of the Kittyhawk before it disappeared.

Delighted at having apparently sent down two Messerschmitts, Edwards was also concerned at the reception he would receive to such a story without witnesses on his return. He too had been suffering some of the raised eyebrows at his claims. He decided, therefore, to claim only one Bf 109 probable at low level. Despite the confirmation which Conrad was able to provide later, neither of these victories appear to have been included in his confirmed total. However, shortly after the loss of Schulz, Obfw Kientsch, who was one of those flying with him, claimed a P-40 shot down, which appears to have been that flown by Sgt Matthews of 260 Squadron.

At 1130 four Bf 109s of III./JG 53 carried out a Freie Jagd, meeting four Kittyhawks over Gambut, damage being claimed to one of them. It could be surmised that this had been one of nine 112 Squadron Kittyhawks on a fighter-bomber sortie from which Flt Sgt Drew failed to return, last being seen near Sidi Rezegh at about this time; however he had fallen to Flak. During the mid-morning period, however, Lt Schaller's aircraft was hit and damaged – possibly by 260 Squadron's Flt Sgt Edwards, or by a 145 Squadron Spitfire, as suggested above. At 1225 three Kittyhawks of 250 Squadron and 12 Hurricanes of 73 Squadron escorted Bostons over the front again. Four I./JG 27 pilots reported meeting 20 Curtiss's and ten Hurricanes between Gambut and Ras Aziez, Oblt Marseille at once diving to the attack, claiming two aircraft shot down, the second while making an evasive turn to avoid other Allied fighters behind him. He then spotted a defensive circle around a parachute, claiming two more shot down out of this. He was now in a high state of nervous tension, and was ready to stop. However, these four claims had brought his personal tally to 99 and his comrades egged him on with cries of "Und nur den Hundersten, Jochen !" Spotting a lone Hurricane flying at about 300 feet above Gambut airfield, he shot this down in flames, seeing it fall onto an AA emplacement.

The Schwarme then re-assembled and set course for home base. Marseille's five claims – identified as two P-40s and three Hurricanes – had all been made in the space of seven minutes. Four of the five can

Newly commissioned and promoted, Oblt Otto Schulz was shot down and killed on 17 June after achieving his 51st and last victory over a 274 Squadron Hurricane.

be confirmed, but all were 73 Squadron Hurricanes from which two pilots baled out, but the other two were killed. The latter included the unit's commanding officer, Sqn Ldr D.H.Ward, DFC & Bar, who had claimed victories over six or seven German aircraft since 1940. As the Messerschmitt pilots returned, Marseille saw high above two Spitfires. Climbing steeply and in a sharp turn, he claimed one of these which was observed by the other three members of the Schwarm to crash. There seems little doubt that this was an unarmed photo-reconnaissance Spitfire IV of 2 PRU in which Flt Lt Spicer was last seen over Sidi Barrani. This loss seems to have been incorrectly recorded as having occurred on the previous day, but no relevant claims were made on that date according to Luftwaffe and Regia Aeronautica records. This claim raised Marseille's total to 101 and he was immediately ordered to Berlin, leaving the desert next day in a Ju 52/3m for the capital where he was to be awarded the Swords to his Knights' Cross with Oak Leaves.

The main force of Axis fighters had now moved to Gazala, though during the afternoon Ju 52/3ms, escorted by Bf 109s, landed at El Adem which had just been abandoned by the British, bringing with them an advanced party to secure the airfield there. At 1345 Wg Cdr Mayers led 239 Wing to Gazala, Kittyhawks of 112, 250, 450 and 3 RAAF Squadrons arriving over the area without encountering either fighters or Flak. Pilots reported strafing 15 Bf 109s on the ground, 112 Squadron claiming seven aircraft damaged, including one Bf 109 and two Fi 156s; Sqn Ldr Judd of 250 Squadron claimed one

The tail of Bf 109F-4 'Red 11' of 2./JG 27 showing Lt Friedrich Körner's claims. The 25th aircraft was claimed on 17 June, and he had also claimed a number of tanks strafed.

Messerschmitt destroyed, other pilots claiming damage to two more. Flg Off Garton attacked a Bf 109 as it was attempting to take off, believing that he had shot this down, but did not see it crash.

The Allied pilots had either attacked a number of dummies, or had been very optimistic in their claims, no more than two Messerschmitts suffering damage during this attack, only one of which proved to be beyond repair. Somewhat later at 1420 three Kittyhawks of 260 Squadron carried out a further bomber escort during which one Bf 109 was claimed probably shot down by Flt Sgt Edwards. Ten minutes later 11 more of this unit's fighters were scrambled on an interception patrol, apparently encountering three III./JG 27 Bf 109s. The German pilots reported engaging four or five British fighters without apparent results. However, one Kittyhawk was damaged by fire from a Messerschmitt and the pilot crash-landed, suffering some injuries in doing so.

That evening the British fighter units were ordered to withdraw to airfields in the Sidi Aziez area. Thereafter, in the next eight days operations over the front proceeded on a much reduced scale. Col Bonner Fellers, US military observer in the Middle East, cabled the US War Department to advise that the situation in the area was less secure than at any time since the German attack on Russia. Unfortunately this message was intercepted by German intelligence, considerable satisfaction being derived from its contents. However, the cable did produce some very positive immediate results in bringing US aid to the Middle East, as will be seen in Chapter Four.

British Claims

260 Sqn	Flt Lt W.R.McKay	Kittyhawk Ia	Bf 109F		0945-1135
4 SAAF Sqn	Lt S.I.Reinders	Tomahawk IIb AN394 'N'	MC.202 Damaged	E El Adem	1020
274 Sqn	Sgt J.Dodds	Hurricane IIc	MC.202	over base	1055-
274 Sqn	Sgt J.Dodds	Hurricane IIc	MC.202	10m E Sidi Rezegh	1055-
274 Sqn	Flt Lt G.C.Keefer	Hurricane IIc BE689	MC.202 Damaged	over base	1055-
274 Sqn	Sgt S.Lerche	Hurricane IIc	MC.202 Damaged	over base	1055-
145 Sqn	Sgt F.R.Barker	Spitfire V BP848 'B'	Bf 109	South Gambut	1125-1235
73 Sqn	Flt Lt I.J.Badger	Hurricane IIc BN357	Bf 109F Damaged	Sidi Rezegh	1300
73 Sqn	Plt Off H.W.Coussens	Hurricane IIc BE401	Bf 109F Damaged	W Gambut	1300
250 Sqn	Flg Off G.W.Garton	Kittyhawk I AK925 'H'	Bf 109*	Gazala No 2 l.g.	1415
250 Sqn	Sqn Ldr M.T.Judd	Kittyhawk I	Bf 109 on ground	Gazala	1415
250 Sqn	Flt Lt A.E.Marshall	Kittyhawk I	Bf 109 Damaged	on ground Gazala	1415
250 Sqn	Sgt Seabrook	Kittyhawk I	Bf 109 Damaged	on ground Gazala	1415
112 Sqn	unstated pilots	Kittyhawk I	Bf 109 Damaged	on ground Gazala	1415
112 Sqn	unstated pilots	Kittyhawk I	2 Fi 156s Damaged	on ground Gazala	1415
112 Sqn	unstated pilots	Kittyhawk I	4 u/i e/a Damaged	on ground Gazala	1415
260 Sqn	Flt Sgt J.F.Edwards	Kittyhawk Ia 'S'	Bf 109F Probable	nr El Duda	1420-1520

*claimed as a Probable but confirmed on 14 August

British Casualties

238 Sqn	Hurricane II 'G' left 0535, damaged by AA landed safely at 0620, Cat II; Plt Off J.A.Ormerod safe
2 PRU	Spitfire IV BP916 MiA Sidi Barrani; Flt Lt F.Spicer
112 Sqn	Kittyhawk I AK586 FTR on ground attack near Sidi Rezegh last seen at 1140; Flt Sgt R.A.Drew MiA
250 Sqn	Kittyhawk I AK783 'G' badly damaged by Flak in Gambut area, crash-landed at base at 1740; Plt Off A.C.Crofton safe
260 Sqn	Kittyhawk I ET585 damaged by Bf 109 Bir el Baheira crash-landed at LG.76 on return 1630-2025; Sgt J.S.E.M.Bernier safe
260 Sqn	Kittyhawk I shot down by Bf 109, Sidi Rezegh; Sgt R.A.Matthews WiA
450 Sqn	Kittyhawk I AK934 shot down by 4 Bf 109s nr El Duda 1030; Sgt A.N.Glancy KiA
3 RAAF Sqn	Kittyhawk I AK813 shot down by 3 Bf 109s W El Adem; 1000-1030; Sgt J.H.Hooke MiA but returned safely
5 SAAF Sqn	Tomahawk IIb AN309 'O' FTR from escort, shot down by Bf 109s 12m NW Gambut at 1000; Lt K.C.Morgan KiA
5 SAAF Sqn	Tomahawk IIb AK519 'A' shot down 12m W Gambut at 1000; Capt L.C.Botha KiA
5 SAAF Sqn	Tomahawk IIb AN420 'P' shot down by Bf 109s NW Gambut at 1000; Lt C.Sommerville returned later
274 Sqn	Hurricane II BM967 shot down by Bf 109 at 1120, crash-landed; Flt Lt W.A.G.Conrad safe
274 Sqn	Hurricane II BG706 'G' shot down by Bf 109 at 1120, force-landed; Plt Off F.B.Samuel
73 Sqn	Hurricane BN277 took off at 1230, shot down 2m W Gambut; Sqn Ldr D.H.Ward KiA
73 Sqn	Hurricane BN649 took off at 1230, shot down Gambut; Plt Off G.J.Wooley KiA
73 Sqn	Hurricane BN121 took off at 1230, shot down, Gambut; Sgt Goodwin baled out

73 Sqn	Hurricane BN157 took off at 1230, shot down W Gambut; Plt Off Stone baled out, injured
208 Sqn	Hurricane IIa BG862 left 0645, shot down by Bf 109s nr Gasr el Arid at 0810, crash-landed; Plt Off P.M.Bezencenet WiA
12 SAAF Sqn	Boston III W8382 'G' off from LG.140 to fly to LG.148 to escape advancing Axis troops. Hit wires on approach to Sidi Aziez and damaged landing gear. Effort to save it, towed behind tractor down Trigh Capuzzo, but finally abandoned; believe DBF

German Claims

2./JG 27	Lt Friedrich Körner	P-40	E Sidi Rezegh	0850
2./JG 27	Lt Karl von Lieres und Wilkau	P-40	E Sidi Rezegh	0859
7./JG 27	Obfw Ludwig Bauer	P-40	SW El Adem	0908
9./JG 27	Uffz Hans-Günther Junge	P-40	8km SE Bu Amud	0910
9./JG 27	Oblt Hans-Joachim Heinecke	P-40	S Bu Amud	0913
Stab II./JG 27	Oblt Otto Schulz	Hurricane	E Bu Amud	1020
Stab II./JG 27	Obfhr Willi Kientsch	P-40	E Sidi Rezegh	1025
3./JG 27	Oblt Hans-Joachim Marseille	P-40	5km W Gambut	1202
3./JG 27	Oblt Hans-Joachim Marseille	P-40	3km W Gambut	1204
3./JG 27	Oblt Hans-Joachim Marseille	Hurricane	4km SW Gambut	1205
3./JG 27	Oblt Hans-Joachim Marseille	Hurricane	6km SW Gambut	1208
3./JG 27	Oblt Hans-Joachim Marseille	Hurricane	2km SW Gambut	1209
3./JG 27	Oblt Hans-Joachim Marseille	Spitfire	SE Sidi Omar	1212

German Casualties

Stab II./JG 27	Bf 109F-4 trop WNr 10271 Black <+- shot down in Sidi Rezegh area; Oblt Otto Schulz, Tech Off, KiA
9./JG 53	Bf 109F-4 trop WNr 10103 Yellow 6 combat; crash-landed Gambut 100%. Lt Wolf Schaller PoW, released by own troops 21 June
10.(Jabo)/JG 53	Bf 109F-4 trop WNr 8624 10% damaged while strafing at Gazala
III./JG 27	Bf 109F-4 trop WNr 10285 crash-landed at Gazala, 85% damaged
8./ZG 26	Bf 110F-2 WNr 4545 3U+DS, crashed E Derna, destroyed; Obfw Hans Swoboda/Fw Heinz Pampuch KiA
III./StG 3	Ju 87D-1 WNr 2537 30% damaged in combat nr Acroma, landed safely

Italian Claims

90ª Sq, 10°Gr, 4°St CT	M.llo Angelo Savini	MC.202	2 P-40s	Sidi Rezegh	0800-0940
91ª Sq, 10°Gr, 4°St CT	u/i pilot	MC.202	P-40	Sidi Rezegh	0800-0940
84ª Sq, 10°Gr, 4°St CT	Ten Luigi Giannella	MC.202 MM 7815	P-40 (Hurricane ?)	Sidi Rezegh	0800-0940
84ª Sq, 10°Gr, 4°St CT	Ten Luigi Giannella	MC.202 MM 7815			
84ª Sq, 10°Gr, 4°St CT	Cap Franco Lucchini	MC.202 MM 7797			
84ª Sq, 10°Gr, 4°St CT	Serg Piero Buttazzi	MC.202 MM 7919	P-40	Sidi Rezegh	0800-0940
84ª Sq, 10°Gr, 4°St CT	Serg Roberto Ugazio	MC.202 MM 7928			
90ª Sq, 10°Gr, 4°St CT	Ten Italo Alessandrini	MC.202			

Italian Casualties

82ª Sq, 13°Gr, 2°St CT	MC.200 damaged on landing after a test flight, Serg Sergio Vanello safe

Thursday, 18 June 1942

At 0730 four Bf 109s of III./JG 53 carried out a Freie Jagd over the Gambut-Gasr el Arid area, encountering numbers of British fighters, two of which their pilots claimed shot down. Plt Off Bezencenet of 208 Squadron carried out an early morning reconnaissance in a Hurricane II, being attacked by three Messerschmitts over the latter area. He was unable to fire his guns due to insufficient pneumatic pressure, and was shot down, force-landing at 200mph, his aircraft totally wrecked. He was slightly wounded by cannon shell splinters, but was picked up safely.

Two Kittyhawks of 450 Squadron flew a reconnaissance over the area from 0755, being attacked over Gambut by a lone Bf 109 which Flt Lt Williams claimed to have shot down. An hour later six more Kittyhawks flew a similar mission over Gambut, this time being attacked by two Bf 109s which inflicted damage on three of the Kittyhawks, but Flt Sgt Dyson claimed one shot down. However, the only Luftwaffe losses recorded for this date were three of I./JG 27's Bf 109Fs, damaged to varying degrees during a strafing attack on their new base at Gazala airfield. The day was also noted by the destruction by their own personnel of four Bostons, two of 12 SAAF and two of 24 SAAF Squadrons, on evacuation of these units from Bir el Baheira.

Meanwhile, 4 SAAF Squadron moved from LG.176 to LG.26; however, next day the unit would be ordered off operations to begin re-equipping with Kittyhawks. Circumstances would require the unit to be thrown back into action before the end of the month, during which period it would operate a mixed 'bag' of Tomahawks and Kittyhawks. Many squadrons were on the move during the day, making for LG.6 and LG.115.

British Claims					
450 Sqn	Flt Lt J.E.A.Williams	Kittyhawk I AK636	Bf 109	Gambut	0755-0845
450 Sqn	Flt Sgt R.D.Dyson	Kittyhawk I AL195	Bf 109	Gambut	0855-0945

British Casualties	
250 Sqn	Kittyhawk I badly damaged by Flak in Gambut area; Plt Off G.W.A.Troke safe
450 Sqn	3 Kittyhawks damaged
208 Sqn	Hurricane BD862 damaged by Bf 109 and crash-landed in desert; Plt Off P.M.Bezencenet
12 SAAF Sqn	Boston III AL669 'M' destroyed on evacuation of Bir el Baheira
12 SAAF Sqn	Boston III W8376 'N' destroyed on evacuation of Bir el Baheira
24 SAAF Sqn	Boston III Z2180 destroyed on evacuation of Bir el Baheira
24 SAAF Sqn	Boston III Z2202 destroyed on evacuation of Bir el Baheira

German Claims				
9./JG 53	Obfw Josef Kronschnabel	P-40	15km S Gambut	0710
9./JG 53	Lt Hermann Munzert	P-40	20km SW Gambut	0714

German Casualties	
1./JG 27	Bf 109F-4 trops WNrs 10146 50%, 10029 15% & 10035 30% damaged at Ain el Gazala by strafing attack
III./ZG 26	Bf 110F-2 WNr 4573, hit by AA, crash-landed at Gambut, 80% damaged
Italian Casualties	
231ª Sq, 95°Gr, 35°St	Cant.Z.1007bis MM 23761 '231-2' crash-landed at Barce,w/o, pilot Ten Salvatore Savonelli, copilot Serg Magg Antonio Zaffina and four safe

Friday, 19 June 1942

The day remained quiet in the air although there was a fair amount of unit movement taking place. III./JG 27 flew to Gazala, but lost Hptm Belser, who was killed in a take-off accident. 73 Squadron moved to LG.76 from where 233 Wing units, 2 SAAF, 4 SAAF and 260 Squadrons went to LG.115. In 274 Squadron Wally Conrad was promoted to flight commander. During the day also seven Ju 88s of I./KG 54 flew in to Derna from Sicily, led by Lt Graf von Platen. The commanding officer fell ill with dysentery on arrival but the detachment departed again on 23 June.

Saturday, 20 June 1942

At 0710 seven Bf 109s of III./JG 53 escorted Ju 87s of I./StG 3 to bomb Tobruk. On the way, however, two of the Stukas were hit by AA fire and collided, both crews being killed. A third bomber was brought down, also by AA, but in this case the crew survived to become PoWs. Tobruk had been bombed regularly during recent nights by small formations of 35° Stormo Cant.Z.1007bis. Now, however, nine such aircraft took off very early in the morning being escorted by MC.202s of 10° Gruppo to bomb this port. Other targets had also been attacked during the night, but while on a sortie to El Daba, an He 111 of 6./KG 100 had been reported missing.

A Bf 109 of II./JG 27 flew a Freie Jagd to the same area, three pilots reporting combat with six Hurribombers and 14 Kittyhawks with belly tanks at 1330. Over Gambut Oblt Vögl and Fw Steis claimed two Kittyhawks in flames. No such losses have been identified. It was on this date that Tobruk was assaulted.

During the early afternoon 10° Gruppo carried out a free sweep over Tobruk, one Macchi was hit by intense AA fire but managed to return. Nine MC.200s of 8° Gruppo and 11 of 13° Gruppo on patrol over the Bir el Gobi area between 1725-1925 had one aircraft hit by ground fire, the pilot being wounded in the throat. On three occasions during the day 158° Gruppo CR.42s attacked 8th Army troop concentrations at the crossroads between Tobruk-El Adem-Bardia, reportedly with good results. At 1745 a further Luftwaffe fighter claim was made, this time by Obfw Seidl of III./JG 53, for a P-40 south of Mersa Matruh. Again, no identification has been made. As night fell a Baltimore of 223 Squadron which had set out to bomb Tmimi, force-landed south of Mersa Matruh. The aircraft was a complete write-off, but the crew survived.

A mystery! GA-X of 112 Squadron appears to carry the serial number AK726 or 728. Only the latter number relates to a Kittyhawk which served with this squadron, but it is not recorded as having been lost in action. However, the aircraft on which this Italian soldier is posing has clearly been hit hard and a cannon shell seems to have gone through from below, bursting out through the top of the fuselage. Perhaps this aircraft was later recaptured, repaired and put back into service?

British Casualties	
250 Sqn	Kittyhawk AK640 crash-landed at Sidi Rezegh 1240-1450; Sgt G.W.A.Troke
223 Sqn	Baltimore II AG758 off from LG.116 2120 to bomb Tmimi a/f. Force-landed 9m SE Mersa Matruh, DBR; Plt Off H.B.Nicholls and two safe, one injured

German Claims				
9./JG 53	Oblt Franz Götz	Blenheim	20km SE Sollum	1030
8./JG 53	Oblt Ernst Kläger	Hurricane	20km SE Mersa Matruh	1035
4./JG 27	Fw Heinrich Steis	P-40	16km S Gambut	1237
4./JG 27	Oblt Ferdinand Vögl	P-40	16km S Gambut	1240
8./JG 53	Obfw Alfred Seidl	P-40	30km S Mersa Matruh	1745

German Casualties	
1./StG 3	Ju 87R-4 WNr 6236 S7+LH collision; Oblt Eberhard Morgenroth/Uffz Heinz Erdel KiA 2km N Tobruk
1./StG 3	Ju 87R-2 WNr 6075 S7+KH collision; Gefr Otto Schaar/Gefr Fritz Kleinfeldt KiA 2km N Tobruk
1./StG 3	Ju 87R-4 WNr 6220 S7+BH AA 30km S El Adem; Uffz Johann Danninger/Gefr Josef Mittendorfer PoW

Italian Casualties	
78ª Sq, 13°Gr, 2°St CT	MC.200 MM 5305 damaged by ground fire, Serg Gardo Ravasio WiA, returned, taken to hospital and repatriated
84ª Sq, 10°Gr, 4°St CT	MC.202 MM 7928 '84-9' damaged by AA, Serg Luciano Perdoni landed safely

Sunday, 21 June 1942

Early in the day aircraft of 8° Gruppo were again active in the Bir el Gobi area, where pilots of four MC.200s strafed a large concentration of vehicles 15 miles to the east; one of the attacking fighters was shot down by ground fire, the pilot being killed.

At 0825 eight Kittyhawks of 112 Squadron undertook an armed reconnaissance over the Bardia-Sidi Barrani area, bombing Sidi Aziez airfield. Here Flt Lt Leu had to force-land. Plt Off Johnson attempted to land to pick him up, but was then prevented from doing so by fire from Axis troops, and Leu became a PoW. Having claimed seven victories, this Australian had recently been awarded the DFC. A second Kittyhawk force-landed near Sollum, where Flg Off Crichton was rescued and returned to his unit by the army.

III./JG 27 now moved to El Adem with the Gefechtsverband Sigel. Twelve Bf 109s carried out a strafing attack on a battalion of Cameron Highlanders some five miles north of the airfield, but Lt Doyé's Messerschmitt was hit by ground fire and he crash-landed. At Gazala III./JG 53 recorded that a British bombing attack totally destroyed seven Bf 109s and badly damaged eight more.

Late in the day Tobruk surrendered, General Auchinleck having been determined that the port should not again become invested for a long period. Nonetheless, the rapid, costly and generally unexpected fall of the port and fortress which had been such a feature of Allied propaganda during the past many months, spread despondency throughout the Allied nations. Prime Minister Winston Churchill, who was at the time in Washington with President Roosevelt, was particularly upset. Roosevelt was very moved by Churchill's distress and immediately offered all possible help. This would soon bear fruit, increasing the flow of USAAF units to the area, and resulting also in the earliest possible deliveries of the latest and potent M.3 Sherman tank which had only just begun to come off the production lines for the US Army. Among the considerable numbers of Axis prisoners released with the capture of Tobruk, was Lt Wolf Schaller of III./JG 53 who now re-joined his unit.

British Casualties	
112 Sqn	Kittyhawk I AL225 'T', hit by Flak force-landed nr Sidi Aziez and captured; Flt Lt R.M.Leu PoW
112 Sqn	Kittyhawk I AK571 hit by Flak force-landed in desert nr Sollum; Flg Off J.M.S.Crichton safe
German Casualties	
7./JG 53	Bombing attack on Ain el Gazala. On ground Bf 109F-4 trops WNrs 10172 100%; 8779 90%; 10011& 10041 70%; 10143 60%; 8775 40%
Italian Casualties	
94ª Sq, 8°Gr, 2°St CT	MC.200 MM 6692 hit by ground fire, crashed to ground, Serg Giordano Casadio KiA

Luftwaffe personnel in a Kübelwagen pass an abandoned Douglas Boston III of 3 SAAF Wing on a desert airfield during the Allied retreat from Gazala in June.

Monday, 22 June 1942

The success of his recent offensive coupled with the early fall of Tobruk with its potential for quicker and more plentiful supplies, now caused Rommel to cancel his original plan. Until now it had been decided that he would halt his forces on the Egyptian frontier until the island of Malta had been invaded and occupied, thereby neutralising the island's stranglehold on the supply route to North Africa from Southern Europe. Now instead, he insisted that he would push straight on into Egypt while the British were still demoralized and in full retreat. He was confident that Alexandria, Cairo, the Nile Delta area and the Suez Canal would be within his grasp in weeks rather than months.

During the day III./JG 53 with I. and III./JG 27 moved forward to the Gambut airfields, whereas on the other side of the lines 3 RAAF and 450 Squadrons withdrew to Sidi Haneish. 80 Squadron moved its Hurricane IIcs to LG.15 to form part of a new 244 Wing with 127, 274 and 1 SAAF Squadrons.

British Casualties

112 Sqn	Kittyhawk I AL112 MiA from fighter-bomber sortie
145 Sqn	Spitfire V AR284 'T' ran out of fuel forced to land 1100-1240; Sgt Bailey safe
145 Sqn	Spitfire V AR324 'L' ran out of fuel forced to land 1100-1240; Plt Off L.A.Malins safe

German Casualties

1./StG 3	Ju 87D-1 WNr 2539 destroyed in air raid at Tmimi

In late June 1942 Sqn Ldr John Bisdee led his 601 Squadron from Malta to North Africa to undertake operations over the desert. Note the unit's 'Flying Sword' emblem on the tail. Bisdee would only make one claim here before being posted to training duties in August.

Tuesday, 23 June 1942

At 1020 four Hurricanes of 238 Squadron reconnoitred the Fort Maddalena-Sidi Omar area, but whilst they were so engaged, intense light Flak was experienced, two aircraft being shot down and a third so damaged that Flt Lt Collenette had to crash-land.

Four III./JG 27 Bf 109s escorted a single Bf 109E on a TacR during which they were engaged by four British fighters over Sidi Omar. One of these was claimed shot down by Lt Schroer, who reported that it crash-landed and somersaulted. In this case the opponents may have been from 274 Squadron, Flg Off Samuel from this unit claiming damage to a Bf 109 at around this time and in the relevant location. During the evening II./JG 27 moved to Monastir. 9° Gruppo of 4° Stormo moved from Martuba to El Adem.

British Claims

274 Sqn	Plt Off F.B.Samuel	Hurricane IIc	Bf 109 Damaged Sidi Omar 1450-

British Casualties

238 Sqn	Hurricane II BH233 'V' took off at 1020 with three others, lost to Flak nr Sidi Omar at c1100; Plt Off N.R.Holmes MiA
238 Sqn	Hurricane II 'X' took off at 1020 with three others, lost to Flak nr Sidi Omar at c1100; Flt Sgt Stein FTR
238 Sqn	Hurricane II 'T' took off at 1020 with three others, lost to Flak nr Sidi Omar at c1100; Flt Lt F.D.B.Collenette crash-landed (one of these believed to have been BG954)

German Claims				
8./JG 27	Lt Werner Schroer	P-40	10km S Sidi Omar	1449

German Casualties	
10.(Jabo)/JG 27	Bf 198F-4 trop WNr 8566 crash-landed Gambut, 80% damaged
6./KG 100	He 111H-6 WNr 7074 6N+KJ 20% damaged by AA while strafing at Sidi Barrani; Lt Bruno Stange and one WiA

Wednesday, 24 June 1942

During the early hours Sgt Hill of 73 Squadron claimed a Ju 88 shot down over Sidi Haneish, two more being claimed damaged by Plt Off Henry around the same time. Hill's victim may have been a He 111 of 6./KG 100 which was hit and damaged in the Sidi Barrani area, one member of the crew being wounded.

On this date Rommel's armoured columns crossed the Egyptian frontier and General Auchinleck took over direct command of the 8th Army from General Ritchie, who had lost heart. Despite the loss of 60,000 men, the 8th Army remained a whole and cohesive unit, mainly due to the comprehensive air cover and support which its units had received. Axis attacks were broken up again and again by the formations of Bostons and the marauding Hurri- and Kittybombers.

Kittyhawk Is of 3 RAAF Squadron prepare to set out on a sortie over the front during June.

In the morning five Kittyhawks of 3 RAAF Squadron set off on a reconnaissance over the forward area at 1105, with two Hurricanes of 33 Squadron also scrambled. Four Bf 109s of II./JG 27 on a Freie Jagd were reported to have encountered seven Hurricanes – possibly a composite group formed by the two units mentioned. The Australians recorded meeting six Messerschmitts and five fighters identified as G.50s near Maddalena, and one Kittyhawk was lost, last being seen with one of the latter aircraft on its tail. One of the 33 Squadron pair, Plt Off Inglesby, dived from 17,000 feet, but failed to return. Oblt Sinner claimed a Hurricane shot down south of Tholata, but crash-landed himself after this combat. Sqn Ldr Barr claimed a 'G.50', Sgt Boardman a Bf 109 and Sgt Kildey another Messerschmitt as a probable.

On this date Plt Off Doak of 208 Squadron commenced a TacR sortie in a Tomahawk, but was attacked by three Bf 109s, and his aircraft was severely damaged. He managed to reach LG.121 where he force-landed. This airfield was captured shortly after this and the aircraft had to be abandoned. In addition to his claim for a Hurricane, Sinner reported chasing and firing at a Curtiss fighter for a considerable time, but was unable to shoot it down. This occurred prior to his engagement with the seven aircraft described above, and probably involved Doak's Tomahawk.

More moves in the eastwards direction took place, 112 Squadron going to LG.102 and 145 Squadron to LG.13. The Regia Aeronautica also moved up closer to the front, 4° Stormo and 9° Gruppo going from Martuba to Gambut, 2° Stormo (8° and 13° Gruppi) moving to Gazala where the unit's MC.200s were mainly to be employed on convoy escort duties. Most of the future activities of these units therefore occurred over the sea lanes and will be recorded in the main in Chapter Three. Meanwhile, 88ª Squadriglia (6° Gruppo) was ordered from Martuba to Sidi Barrani where the unit was reinforced by the arrival of six pilots from the recently repatriated 17° Gruppo: Ten Marchi, Ten Talamini, Serg Magg Host, Serg Brianti, M.llo Baldelli and Serg Zavatti. 159° Gruppo's CR.42s moved from Derna to El Adem.

British Claims

73 Sqn	Plt Off L.T.Henry	Hurricane IIc BN985	Ju 88 Damaged		2355-0140
73 Sqn	Sgt G.Hill	Hurricane IIc BN546	Ju 88	Sidi Haneish	0100
73 Sqn	Plt Off L.T.Henry	Hurricane IIc BN985	Ju 88 Damaged		0120
3 RAAF Sqn	Sqn Ldr A.W.Barr	Kittyhawk I AK756	G.50	18m NE Maddalena	1200
3 RAAF Sqn	Sgt L.L.Boardman	Kittyhawk I AK961	Bf 109F	18m NE Maddalena	1200
3 RAAF Sqn	Sgt E.K.Kildey	Kittyhawk I AL101	Bf 109F Probable	18m NE Maddalena	1200

British Casualties

208 Sqn	Tomahawk IIa AN385 damaged by Bf 109s, crash-landed at LG.121 at 1210; Plt Off Doak safe. Aircraft captured soon after
208 Sqn	Hurricane IIa Z4954 damaged Cat I by Flak nr Wadi el Bardia; 2/Lt M.Levine safe
3 RAAF Sqn	Kittyhawk I AK806 'B' shot down, presumed by fighters 18m NE Maddalena; Sgt P.W.Fox MiA
33 Sqn	Hurricane IIb Z5647 took off from Sidi Haneish, dived down from 17,000ft; Plt Off H.Inglesby MiA

German Claims

6./JG 27	Oblt Rudolf Sinner	Hurricane	20km S Bir el Tholata	1000

German Casualties

6./JG 27	Bf 109F-4 trop damaged in combat, belly-landed, under 10% damaged; Oblt Rudolf Sinner safe
7./ZG 26	Bf 110E-2 WNr 4440 3U+HR damaged by AA, ditched off Mersa Matruh; pilot rescued, gunner Obgefr Gotthard Kunke drowned

Wednesday-Thursday, 24/25 June 1942

German Casualties

5./KG 100	He 111H-6 WNr 7201 6N+DH reportedly shot down by night fighter, crashed 5km SW Qasaba, Obfw Wilhelm Peve, Hptm Ewald Gustavus and two MiA

Thursday, 25 June 1942

Lt Jenisch of II./JG 27 claimed a Curtiss fighter near Sidi Barrani soon after midday; this was probably a 250 Squadron Kittyhawk which was reported shot down by a Bf 109 in the Sofafi area when escorting bombers. Around the same time a Boston of 12 SAAF Squadron was hit by Flak as it bombed Axis armoured units and spun into the ground in flames; only one member of the crew survived, becoming a prisoner. During the day 33 Squadron exchanged its Hurricane IIbs for Mark IIcs with cannons. 9° Gruppo moved eastwards to Sidi Barrani.

British Casualties

250 Sqn	Kittyhawk I AK944 MiA from escort, shot down by Bf 109 in Sofafi area 1305-1425; Plt Off R.E.Hamilton PoW
112 Sqn	Kittyhawk I AK909 'M' crashed taking off at night evacuating LG.102; Flg Off J.A.Milne inj
112 Sqn	Kittyhawk I AK770 'J' lost at night evacuating LG.102, crash-landed nr LG.104; Plt Off W.A.J.Johnson safe
12 SAAF Sqn	Boston III AL691 'W' off 1239 from Qotaifiya (LG.21) to bomb Axis armour. Hit by Flak in starboard engine over target and spun into ground in flames; Lt E.Jones and two KiA, one baled and PoW

German Claims

5./JG 27	Lt Kurt Jenisch	P-40	Sidi Barrani	1232

Italian Casualties

600ª Sq, 145°Gr T	S.81 MM 20502, failed to reach Sidi Barrani, Serg Aldo Biondi and crew MiA

Friday, 26 June 1942

Recent movements of bases had again brought units on both sides into closer proximity with each other, and the arrival of the withdrawing 8th Army units into the defended areas around El Alamein caused a resumption of heavy fighting in the air as WDAF launched a series of heavy attacks on the advancing

On this MC.202 '73-11' MM7778, the previous code '79-8' of 79ª Squadriglia of 6° Gruppo, 1° Stormo CT can still be seen.

Axis columns. Many squadrons broke their own records for sorties flown on this date, 3 RAAF Squadron for instance undertaking ten missions whereas aircraft of 112 Squadron put in no less than 69 individual sorties; 450 Squadron provided bomber escorts on eight occasions, and similar performances were achieved by many other units.

First off at 0910 were three Kittyhawks of 3 RAAF Squadron which escorted Bostons but also carried bombs themselves which were to be dropped on the same target. These aircraft were attacked by six Bf 109s and two Italian fighters, mis-identified as a MC.200 and a G.50; they appear actually to have been MC.202s of 9º Gruppo. One Kittyhawk was damaged. Close behind the Australians, a 208 Squadron Tomahawk had gone off on a TacR sortie from which it failed to return. No German fighter claims were made during these early sorties, but 9º Gruppo Macchi pilots were active throughout the morning.

At 0755 ten MC.202s of 9° Gruppo, led by Magg Larsimont-Pergameni took off on a free sweep. A formation of nine bombers, covered by 15 fighters, was sighted and engaged west of Mersa Matruh; in the following combat two P-40s were claimed destroyed plus two (or three) probables. Another free sweep sortie was carried out about noon by Ten Fernando Malvezzi with eight MC.202s of 97ª Squadriglia; over Bir el Astas six bombers identified as Marylands were encountered and attacked and one was claimed shot down, shared by Malvezzi and two wingmen. A third engagement occurred two hours later in the same area, when eight MC.202s led by Ten Emanuele Annoni met a formation of 15 P-40s, claiming three shot down and a probable. Serg Martinoli was hit and crash-landed unhurt.

274 Squadron undertook a bombing mission at 1026 from which one Hurricane failed to return, thought to have been shot down by Flak. This aircraft may, however, have fallen to a pilot of 8./JG 53, Oblt Kläger claiming a Hurricane at 1035 south-east of Mersa Matruh. At 1105 450 Squadron began a bomber escort, but over the target the unit was attacked by three Bf 109s and a Kittyhawk was seen to go down in a dive, but flattening out near the ground; however, Plt Off Jones did not return. Five more 3 RAAF Squadron Kittyhawks with others of 112 Squadron escorted Bostons to Mingar el Ahmar at 1205, but each unit lost one aircraft. The Australian loss was Sqn Ldr Barr, who was seen to be attacked by Bf 109s, one of which gained hits on his aircraft which was seen to dive away steeply, pouring flames. 'Nicky' Barr managed to bale out at 4,000 feet, suffering rather severe burns, and he became a PoW. One of the leading Allied fighter pilots in North Africa at the time, having claimed more than 12 aircraft shot down since December 1941, plus several more probables, he had risen from junior pilot officer to squadron leader in just six months.

Following these losses, three Kittyhawks of 250 Squadron joined others of 450 Squadron at 1300 for another Boston escort, attacking targets west of Mersa Matruh. The former unit was targeted by MC.202s and possibly by Bf 109s as well. Sgt Wallis and Sgt Seabrook both had their aircraft badly damaged, Seabrook landing at LG.91; Flt Lt Copeland did not return. 450 Squadron lost its second Plt Off Jones (M.J.), but he successfully baled out, returning later; several other squadron aircraft were damaged.

Four Hurricanes of 238 Squadron provided top cover to fighter-bombers at 1315, but when so engaged Sgt Lawrence-Smith's aircraft was attacked and severely damaged by a Bf 109, the pilot also being badly wounded. At the same time six Baltimores of 223 Squadron set off to attack vehicles in the Bir el Gallas area, but these bombers were attacked by 9° Gruppo MC.202s, two being badly damaged; one crash-landed west of LG.116, a second also crash-landing, but on its return to base. The first of these was claimed shot down by three Italian pilots jointly, identified by them as a Maryland.

Meanwhile, at 1150 nine Bf 109s of III./JG 27 had been escorting a Bf 110 over Mersa Matruh where the pilots engaged ten Bostons and 12 Kittyhawks, three of the escort fighters being claimed shot down, a Hurricane then being claimed a few minutes later. Six more Messerschmitts, this time from I./JG 27, took off on a Freie Jagd over the panzer columns at 1225, Lt Körner claiming one fighter shot down at 1248, four minutes after the last of the II.Gruppe claims. Claims for five Allied fighters were then made between 1312-1330 – three of them by Lt Stahlschmidt.

After a meteoric run of successes with 3 RAAF Squadron which also saw him rise to command the unit by the end of May, A.W.'Nicky' Barr was shot down on 26 June and was badly wounded, baling out to become a PoW. He would escape from a camp in Italy in 1943, later adding the award of an MC to his DFC and Bar. He is seen here being photographed as a PoW, the recent burns to his face readily visible.

At 1455 five Tomahawks of 5 SAAF Squadron with a mixed formation of six Kittyhawks and Tomahawks of 4 SAAF Squadron, escorted bombers south-west of Mersa Matruh where five Bf 109s were encountered by the former unit; Lt Popham was shot down, later being reported safe in hospital. 4 SAAF Squadron was jumped out of the sun by four Bf 109s, Maj Hewitson being shot down and baling out over Axis-held territory.

Six Kittyhawks of 3 RAAF Squadron carried out an armed reconnaissance at 1505, one aircraft being slightly damaged by two Bf 109s. At the same time two Spitfires of 145 Squadron maintained a standing reconnaissance patrol over Sidi Barrani at 12,000 feet, where they were at a fatal disadvantage when attacked, two of their number being shot down; one pilot was reported to have baled out, but neither returned. This latter pair was clearly shot down by two I./JG 27 pilots who patrolled over their airfield, having taken off at 1415, and attacked and shot down the two Spitfires at 1505-1510 over the Sidi Barrani area although Fws Pöttgen and Mrosla claimed Curtiss fighters, obviously not yet familiar with the recently-arrived Spitfires. They had been waiting impatiently for the relief Rotte when they suddenly saw two fighters approaching, somewhat lower. Pöttgen was surprised as he had not seen any aircraft take off, but he then spotted the red and blue cockades. The Spitfire pilots could not see the German pair as by chance they were directly up-sun from them. The Messerschmitts dived, and the aircraft attacked by Mrosla carried out a belly-landing in no mans' land, the pilot running off in the direction of the coast. Pöttgen's victim baled out (as reported by his unit), and was later brought in to the airfield by an Fi 156, Pöttgen having the chance to talk to him. He was described as a very tall New Zealander, who congratulated his victor, adding: "You have cheated me! Why did you come out of the sun?" He then asked if it would be possible to remain in German captivity rather than be handed over to the Italians. He was later driven to hospital, accompanied by Pöttgen, who removed a number of small splinters from his face with tweezers en route.

Four fighters of II.Gruppe, off on a Freie Jagd at 1503, encountered six Curtiss fighters at 1530, four being claimed shot down. At 1519 450 Squadron carried out its sixth mission of the day, six Kittyhawks providing top cover for Bostons. These fighters were attacked by three Bf 109s west of Charing Cross, one Kittyhawk being lost. However, British bombers attacked Sidi Barrani airfield at 1600, totally destroying seven aircraft, and killed Lt Erich Beckmann on the ground.

Twelve Hurricanes of 213 Squadron were scrambled at 1608, and when at 19,000 feet eight Bf 109s were seen below. The pilots exulted at this chance to turn the tables, and bounced the Messerschmitts "with astronomical results", five being claimed destroyed and one damaged without loss. In fact no German or Italian losses of this magnitude were recorded and it has to be assumed that the evasive actions of the Axis pilots, coupled with the unusual nature of the Hurricanes' attack gave an altogether incorrect impression. This must be classed as another of those unexplained events, for the reports of the pilots involved were so specific that how such a high level of over-claiming could occur remains baffling. Their story was as follows: The Messerschmitts crossed the Hurricanes' path right to left, and when spotted, they were already beneath B Flight which was ahead, led by the commanding officer. Unable, therefore, to see them, he ordered A Flight, which was flying above and behind, to attack first. Flt Lt Temlett reported that he selected the second aircraft from the back of the German formation, on the right, closing to a very short range of 20 yards before firing a five-second burst which struck the right mainplane from tip to root whereupon he stated, the wing crumpled and fell away, the aircraft bursting into flames and diving to the ground. Thomlinson, flying on Temlett's wing, identified the Bf 109s by their white wingtips and saw pieces fly off the one he attacked, following which he reported that it also crashed. Henderson then attacked the third Messerschmitt on the right, closed on it at which it pulled up almost vertically, allowing him to close to 75 yards and fire a two-second burst. According to him 'chunks' flew off the engine and cockpit, black smoke 'belched forth' and the fighter went down in five spiral turns before straightening out briefly at 4,000 feet. He closed again to 100 yards, fired another two-second burst at which, he reported, it crashed south-west of LG.07. Meantime Sgt Ritchie reported that his fire struck the tail of one, which disintegrated and fell off, the aircraft then going into a spiral dive to the ground. Finally, Ken Sissons selected one on the far left of the formation from 600 yards behind but 5,000 feet above. This pulled up in a steep climbing turn to the left. He turned with it, reporting that it flew right through his line of sight, a two-second burst apparently achieving hits all along the cockpit at which pieces broke off, the aircraft rolled over onto its back, pulled up, half-rolled, and dived into the ground. And yet not even damage was reported to any German fighter at this time.

At 1635 seven Bf 109s of III./JG 27 flew a Freie Jagd over the advancing columns on the ground, engaging six bombers escorted by 12 Curtiss fighters, one of which was claimed by Lt Schroer at 1710 for his third claim of the day. At 1815 eight Kittyhawks of 260 Squadron carried out a bomber escort sortie from which Sgt Carlisle failed to return. Around 1935 2 SAAF Squadron provided top cover to Bostons during which this unit was also attacked by Bf 109s, Lt Wilkinson being shot down and baling out.

The last big interception of the day occurred around 2000 when six Bf 109s of I.Gruppe and 11 of II.Gruppe escorted 20 Ju 87s of III./StG 3 over Mersa Matruh. 213 Squadron scrambled six Hurricanes at 1930, followed by six Spitfires of 145 Squadron five minutes later, two of the latter returning early with overheating engines. At 1940 more aircraft of 2 SAAF, 4 SAAF and 5 SAAF squadrons took off, and at 1950 five Hurricanes of 73 Squadron followed. Pilots of 213 Squadron attacked the Stukas, claiming three shot down and four damaged, while the South Africans added claims for three more and two damaged. The four Spitfires dived on three Bf 109s and chased them to LG.07. Sgt Spears pursued one which was going westwards, but he did not return. Meanwhile, the remaining aircraft joined in a great fight between the Hurricanes, Kittyhawks, Tomahawks, Ju 87s and Bf 109s. 73 Squadron's aircraft were bounced and two were lost, Plt Off Coussens baling out but Plt Off Fraser, wounded, got his damaged Hurricane back to base. One Staffelkapitän of 8./StG 3 was shot down, returning three days later. During the engagement the German pilots claimed nine shot down. One of these, claimed by Uffz Beckmann, had first been attacked by Lt Körner, but escaped in a steep turn. In doing so, the aircraft crossed in front of his wingman, Beckmann, who shot it down with five rounds of cannon and ten of machine-gun fire, the pilot then baling out.

During the day Axis claims against WDAF fighters amounted to 28 by the Luftwaffe plus three and three probables by the Italians. Actual losses had been at least 16 shot down or crash-landed, plus five damaged – a fairly good claim-loss ratio given the intensity of operations. It was, indeed, a much better one than that achieved by the WDAF units, whose claims for seven Bf 109s and six Ju 87s were in the main unsubstantiated. However, the real success insofar as the air effort was concerned, had been achieved on the ground. There the various bombing and strafing attacks had destroyed or seriously damaged eight Bf 109s.This time, however, it was not just losses of fairly easily replaceable aircraft, for six Luftwaffe pilots had been killed or wounded. Moreover at Sidi Barrani three MC.202 pilots of 9° Gruppo had been killed, including the Gruppo commander, Magg Larsimont-Pergameni, and a fourth wounded; those killed were the trio who had earlier in the day claimed the first Italian victories of the 26th. Also two MC.202s were destroyed on the ground and many others suffered minor damages.

During the day two Cant.Z.1007bis bombers of 191ª Squadriglia had departed Derna on a reconnaissance sortie. Over Siwa Oasis one was hit by AA fire which damaged the central engine and wounded the gunner, although the pilot successfully regained Axis territory and landed at Tobruk. Other Regia Aeronautica units were still on the move, the CR.42s of 50° Stormo and 158° Gruppo going from Derna to Sidi Barrani, with 159° Gruppo moving from El Adem to the same destination.

British Claims

73 Sqn	Flt Sgt E.L.Joyce	Hurricane IIc BP177 'L'	Ju 88	Maaten Bagush	0105
208 Sqn	Flg Off C.B.S.Montagu	Tomahawk IIa AK565	Ju 52		0600-0705
3 RAAF Sqn	Plt Off V.F.Curtis	Kittyhawk I AL10 }	Bf 109 Damaged	El Alimat area	0935
250 Sqn	Flt Lt A.E.Marshall	Kittyhawk I AK921 }			
450 Sqn	Plt Off F.R.Schaaf	Kittyhawk I AK636	Bf 109 Damaged	7m E Charing Cross	1310-1410
260 Sqn	Sqn Ldr O.V.Hanbury	Kittyhawk I	Bf 109F	LG.09	1335-1440
260 Sqn	Sqn Ldr O.V.Hanbury	Kittyhawk I	Bf 109F Probable	LG.09	1335-1440
260 Sqn	Sgt T.Parrot	Kittyhawk I	Bf 109F	LG.09	1335-1440
213 Sqn	Plt Off W.Henderson	Hurricane IIc BN537 'J'	Bf 109F	Charing Cross area, SW LG.07	1515-1620
213 Sqn	Flt Lt P.Olver	Hurricane IIc BN141	Bf 109F Damaged	Charing Cross area, SW LG.07	1515-1620
213 Sqn	Sgt J.D.Ritchie	Hurricane IIc BM972 'B'	Bf 109F	Charing Cross area, SW LG.07	1515-1620
213 Sqn	Plt Off K.N.R.Sissons	Hurricane IIc BN290 'L'	Bf 109F	Charing Cross area, SW LG.07	1515-1620
213 Sqn	Flt Lt C.B.Temlett	Hurricane IIc BN349 'D'	Bf 109F	Charing Cross area	1515-1620
213 Sqn	Plt Off W.H.Thomlinson	Hurricane IIc BN128 'K'	Bf 109F	Charing Cross area	1515-1620
112 Sqn	Flg Off W.M.Whitamore	Kittyhawk AK890	Bf 109E		1720-1815
260 Sqn	Flt Sgt J.F.Edwards	Kittyhawk Ia 'P'	Bf 109F Probable	S Mersa Matruh	1815-1930
213 Sqn	Flt Sgt W.H.Stephenson	Hurricane IIc BN128 'K'	Ju 87 Damaged	Mersa Matruh area	1930-2005
213 Sqn	Sgt J.F.C.Ballantyne	Hurricane IIc BN539 'V'	Ju 87	Mersa Matruh area	1930-2005
213 Sqn	Sgt J.F.C Ballantyne	Hurricane IIc BN539 'V'	Ju 87 Damaged	Mersa Matruh area	1930-2005
213 Sqn	Plt Off L.O.H.Boucher	Hurricane IIc BN349	Ju 87 Damaged	Mersa Matruh area	1930-2005
213 Sqn	Flt Lt G.H.Westlake	Hurricane IIc BN139 'U'	Ju 87	Mersa Matruh area	1930-2005
213 Sqn	Flg Off F.A.W.J.Wilson	Hurricane IIc BN368	Ju 87	Mersa Matruh area	1930-2005
213 Sqn	Flg Off F.A.W.J.Wilson	Hurricane IIc BN368	Ju 87Damaged	Mersa Matruh area	1930-2005
5 SAAF Sqn	Capt D.V.D.Lacey	Tomahawk IIb AK445 'A'	Ju 87	S Matruh	1950
5 SAAF Sqn	Capt D.V.D.Lacey	Tomahawk IIb AK445 'A'	2 Ju 87s Damaged	S Matruh	1950
2 SAAF Sqn	Lt R.D.B.Morton	Kittyhawk I ET530 'G'	Ju 87	5m E Matruh	1955
4 SAAF Sqn	Capt T.P.L.Murray	Tomahawk IIb AN366 'W'	Ju 87	Matruh area	2010
4 SAAF Sqn	Capt L.B.Pearce	Tomahawk IIb }	Bf 109 Damaged	Matruh area	2010
4 SAAF Sqn	Lt G.H.Kaufmann	Tomahawk IIb }			

British Casualties

208 Sqn	Tomahawk I AK565 left 0920, FTR from Tac recce on coastal railway; 2/Lt J.W.P.Somerville PoW
112 Sqn	Kittyhawk I ET526 shot down near Charing Cross at 1230-1240; Plt Off B.A.F.Cuddon baled out, returned safe
250 Sqn	Kittyhawk I AK921 shot down by MC.202s near Mersa Matruh 1330-1400; Flt Lt P.Copeland KiA
250 Sqn	Kittyhawk I badly damaged by Bf 109 or MC.202 at Mersa Matruh, 1330-1400; Sgt R.T.A.Wallis safe
250 Sqn	Kittyhawk I AK932 'R' damaged by Bf 109 or MC.202 at Mersa Matruh; safe at LG.91 1330-1400; Sgt J.A.Seabrook safe
250 Sqn	Kittyhawk I AK640, engine failure on return from sortie, crash-landed at LG.109; Sgt G.W.A. Troke safe
260 Sqn	Kittyhawk I shot down by Bf 109s S Mersa Matruh 1815-1930; Sgt J.V.Carlisle MiA
450 Sqn	Kittyhawk I AL107 shot down by Bf 109s Mersa Matruh 1130-1140; Flg Off T.E.Jones KiA

British Casualties

450 Sqn	Kittyhawk I AK750 shot down by Bf 109 E Charing Cross 1320-1345 ; Plt Off M.J.Jones baled PoW
450 Sqn	Kittyhawk I AK990 shot down by Bf 109s W Charing Cross, crash-landed 1540-1600; Plt Off K.A.Murdoch WiA PoW
450 Sqn	Kittyhawk I AK618 crashed on landing at Fuka Satellite at 2215; Plt Off F.R.Schaaf safe
3 RAAF Sqn	Kittyhawk I AL101 slt damaged by MC.202 in head-on attack at 0935; Plt Off V.F.Curtis safe
3 RAAF Sqn	Kittyhawk I ET873 'N' shot down by 2 Bf 109s at Mingar el Ahmar and abandoned 1230-1245; Sqn Ldr A.W.Barr PoW
3 RAAF Sqn	Kittyhawk I ET 911 slt damaged by 2 Bf 109s near Mingar el Ahmar c1530; Sgt G.R.Jones safe
2 SAAF Sqn	Kittyhawk I AK980 'T' damaged by Bf 109s, Charing Cross 1910-2020; Lt C.J.Wilkinson baled out slt WiA
4 SAAF Sqn	Kittyhawk I AK835 shot down by Bf 109s 53m SW Mersa Matruh 1530; Maj J.L.Hewitson PoW
5 SAAF Sqn	Tomahawk IIa AN241 shot down by Bf 109 S Mersa Matruh 1950; Lt E.W.L.Popham WiA
73 Sqn	Hurricane II BE280, Mersa Matruh at 2010; Plt Off W.Coussen baled out, safe
73 Sqn	Hurricane II badly damaged by Bf 109, Mersa Matruh; Plt Lt Fraser injured
94 Sqn	Hurricane Z4174 hit sea on approach to El Gamil
213 Sqn	Hurricane IIc BN527 left 1930, FTR from interception of Ju 87s near Mersa Matruh; Sgt W.A.Lack KiA
213 Sqn	Hurricane IIc BE702 left 1515, damaged in port wing by Bf 109, Cat I; Wt Off R.J.Wallace safe
238 Sqn	Hurricane (believed to be BN106 'H') took off 1315, badly damaged by Bf 109, Cat II; Sgt M.L.Lawrence-Smith safe
274 Sqn	Hurricane shot down by Flak W Charing Cross; Sgt R.J.Thompson KiA
145 Sqn	Spitfire V AB 322 'E' near coast 15m E Sidi Barrani 1510, crash-landed; Sgt M. J.Mahady PoW
145 Sqn	Spitfire V AR284 'T' near Sidi Barrani 1505; Sgt Bailey baled out PoW
145 Sqn	Spitfire V AB 326 'A' shot down by Bf 109 near Mersa Matruh,1850-1900; Sgt Spears
12 SAAF Sqn	Boston III crash-landed at base 0934 due to damage from MC.202
223 Sqn	Baltimore II AG748 off 1315 to attack MT. At 1345 formation attacked by fighter NW Bir el Gallas; badly damaged and crash-landed 20m W LG. 116; SOC; Sgt H.Hewitt and three safe
223 Sqn	Baltimore II AG797 off 1315 to attack MT. Damaged by fighters and crash-landed on return to LG.116; SOC; Plt Off D.G.W.Leake and three safe

German Claims

8./JG 53	Oblt Ernst Kläger	Hurricane	15m SE Mersa Matruh	1035
8./JG 27	Lt Werner Schroer	P-40	SW Mersa Matruh	1140
9./JG 27	Obfw Heinrich Rosenberg	P-40	Mersa Matruh	1141
8./JG 27	Lt Werner Schroer	Hurricane	SW Mersa Matruh	1144
2./JG 27	Lt Friedrich Körner	P-40	W Mersa Matruh	1148
7./JG 27	Fw Helmut Kabisch	P-40	Mersa Matruh	1155
1./JG 27	Hptm Ludwig Franzisket	P-40	SW Mersa Matruh	1212
2./JG 27	Lt Friedrich Körner	P-40	W Mersa Matruh	1218
2./JG 27	Lt Hans-Arnold Stahlschmidt	2 Hurricanes	SW Mersa Matruh	1220 & 1227
2./JG 27	Lt Hans-Arnold Stahlschmidt	P-40	W Mersa Matruh	1230
3./JG 27	Fw Rainer Pöttgen	P-40	E Sidi Barrani	1405
3./JG 27	Fw Bernhard Mrosla	P-40	E Sidi Barrani	1410
5./JG 27	Lt Kurt Jenisch	P-40	SW Mersa Matruh	1432
5./JG 27	Fw Siegfried Fricke	Hurricane	SW Mersa Matruh	1435
5./JG 27	Lt Kurt Jenisch	P-40	30km SW Mersa Matruh	1443
5./JG 27	Obfw Emil Clade	P-40	35km SW Mersa Matruh	1450
8./JG 27	Lt Werner Schroer	P-40	SW Mersa Matruh	1610
8./JG 53	Obfw Alfred Seidl	P-40	30km S Mersa Matruh	1746
6./JG 27	Oblt Rudolf Sinner	Hurricane	SE Mersa Matruh	1840
2./JG 27	Lt Friedrich Körner	P-40	Mersa Matruh	1842
2./JG 27	Lt Friedrich Körner	2 Spitfires	Mersa Matruh & SE	1846 & 1905
4./JG 27	Fw Heinrich Steis	P-40	S Mersa Matruh	1855
4./JG 27	Fw Franz Stigler	P-40	S Mersa Matruh	1857
4./JG 27	Oblt Ernst Börngen	P-40	SE Mersa Matruh	1903
2./JG 27	Lt Hans-Arnold Stahlschmidt	P-40	SW Mersa Matruh	1906
2./JG 27	Uffz Helmut Beckmann	Spitfire	E Mersa Matruh	1912

German Casualties

Stab/JG 27	Uffz Erich Opitz WiA by bombing at Sidi Barrani
5./JG 27	Bf 109F-4 WNr 7417 10% damaged by bombs on ground at Sidi Barrani; Lt Kurt Jenisch KiA

5./JG 27	Bf 109F-4 trop WNr 8466 crash-landed at Sidi Barrani; 10% damaged; Fw Siegfried Fricke WiA
III./JG 53	bombing raid on Sidi Barrani West at 1600; results:-
7./JG 53	Bf 109F-4 trop WNr 10020 White 4 25% damaged on ground
7./JG 53	Bf 109F-4 trop WNr 8684 50% damaged on ground; Uffz Paul Gläser WiA
9./JG 53	Bf 109F-4 trop WNr 10111 45% damaged on ground; Uffz Walter Manz WiA
9./JG 53	Bf 109F-4 trop WNr 8792 50% damaged on ground; Lt Wolf Schaller WiA
9./JG 53	Bf 109F-4 trop WNr 10036 95% damaged on ground; Lt Erich Beckmann WiA – died of wounds
9./JG 53	Bf 109F-4 trop WNr 10114 70% damaged on ground
9./JG 53	Bf 109F-4 trop WNr 10156 80% damaged on ground
10.(Jabo)/JG 53	Bf 109F-4 trop WNr 10140 60% damaged on ground by bombs at Sidi Barrani West; Lt Max Lange WiA
10.(Jabo)/JG 53	Bf 109F-4/Z WNr 7094 90% damaged on ground by bombs at Sidi Barrani
8./StG 3	Ju 87D-1 10% damaged in combat, crashed 18km SE Mersa Matruh; Hptm Patschkowski WiA
8./StG 3	Ju 87D-1 shot down in combat, crashed 18km SE Mersa Matruh; Uffz Otto Eckardt/Uffz Herbert Wagner MiA
6./StG 3	Ju 87D-1 WNr 2539 S7+EP shot down in combat, crashed nr Mersa Matruh; Lt Josef Lipsky/Gefr Otto Kinateder MiA
6./KG 100	He 111H-6 WNr 7214 6N+BJ shot down by AA, crashed Fuka-Burg el Arab; Fw Erwin Rohloff and three MiA
2./LG1	Ju 88A-4 WNr 5549 L1+CK, shot down by Hurricanes, crashed Mersa Matruh-Fuka; Uffz Adolf Mader and three MiA

Italian Claims

73ª Sq, 9°Gr, 4°St CT	Magg Ludovico Laurin	MC.202	P-40	W Mersa Matruh	0755-
73ª Sq, 9°Gr, 4°St CT	Ten Ferruccio Zarini	MC.202	P-40 Probable	W Mersa Matruh	0755-
97ª Sq, 9°Gr, 4°St CT	Magg A. Larsimont-Pergameni	MC.202	P-40 Probable	W Mersa Matruh	0755-
96ª Sq, 9°Gr, 4°St CT	Serg Bruno Biagini	MC.202	P-40	W Mersa Matruh	0755-
97ª Sq, 9°Gr, 4°St CT	Ten Fernando Malvezzi	MC.202			
97 ªSq, 9°Gr, 4°St CT	Ten Jacopo Frigerio	MC.202	Maryland	Bir el Astas	1210-
97 ªSq, 9°Gr, 4°St CT	Serg Magg Massimo Salvatore	MC.202			
73ª Sq, 9°Gr, 4°St CT	Serg Magg Salvatore Mechelli	MC.202	P-40	Bir el Astas	1400-
73ª Sq, 9°Gr, 4°St CT	Serg Teresio Martinoli	MC.202	P-40 Probable	Bir el Astas	1400-
96ª Sq, 9°Gr, 4°St CT	Ten Emanuele Annoni	MC.202	P-40 Probable	Bir el Astas	1400-

Italian Casualties

73ª Sq, 9°Gr, 4°St CT	MC.202 crash-landed, Serg Teresio Martinoli safe
9° Gr, 4°St CT	2 MC.202s (MM 7920 '73-4'and 7932 '97-8') damaged and 11 slightly damaged by bombs at Sidi Barrani 1500
73ª Sq, 9°Gr, 4°St CT	Magg Ludovico Laurin killed by bombs at Sidi Barrani 1500
97ª Sq, 9°Gr, 4°St CT	Magg Antonio Larsimont-Pergameni killed by bombs at Sidi Barrani 1500
97ª Sq, 9°Gr, 4°St CT	Serg Magg Angelo Golino killed by bombs at Sidi Barrani 1500
73ª Sq, 9°Gr, 4°St CT	S.Ten Ferruccio Zarini wounded by bombs at Sidi Barrani 1500
191ª Sq, 86°Gr, 35°St BT	Cant.Z.1007bis MM 24279 damaged by AA at Siwa, pilot Cap Aurelio Salvadori, copilot Serg Magg Gioacchino Pennacchio and four safe, gunner M.llo Lorenzo De Padova WiA

Saturday, 27 June 1942

III./JG 53 was now so low on fuel that it was able only to put up one mission by four Bf 109s which took off on a Freie Jagd over the advancing armoured columns at 0745. At 0835 Oblt Kläger shot down a Hurricane IIa of 208 Squadron flown by Lt G.T.Sedgwick who had taken off at 0815 to carry out a TacR sortie. Six Bf 109s of I./JG 27 took off at 0922, intercepting six Baltimores of 223 Squadron which had just taken off to fly from LG.116 to LG.24. The German pilots mistook them for Martin 167s (Marylands), Hptm Franzisket and Fw Steinhausen each shooting down one; a third was badly damaged, encountering the attackers but force-landing at Wadi Natrun.

At 1030 five Kittyhawks of 112 Squadron carried out a TacR mission from which Flt Lt Walker failed to return, having been shot down. He returned safely next day. Three Tomahawks of 5 SAAF Squadron escorted bombers to Charing Cross, being intercepted over Fuka by five Bf 109s of II./JG 27 which were out on a Freie Jagd. Oblt Vögl claimed one at 1100; Lt Kemsley force-landed, but reported that this was due to engine failure.

Eight Kittyhawks of 260 Squadron escorted nine Bostons to a target south of Mersa Matruh but here they were attacked by six Bf 109s of I./JG 27, Lt Stahlschmidt claiming one fighter in flames near Fuka. In return Sqn Ldr Hanbury and Sgt Parrott claimed two Messerschmitts shot down and one probably so; Uffz Beckmann of II.Gruppe reported that he was surprised by fighters when he was watching Stahlschmidt's Schwarm in combat with Hurricanes 3,000 feet below. He was hit in the shoulder and

GC 1 Alsace operated for some time in the defence of Egypt, but only on one occasion became involved with Axis fighters after moving nearer to the front during June. On 27th four of the unit's Hurricanes were shot down in combat with Bf 109s.

feet, diving steeply out of control through the fighting aircraft, but managing subsequently to land at his own airfield. When taken out of the aircraft he found that he had lost the big toe of his right foot.

Nine III./JG 27 Bf 109s undertook a Freie Jagd from 1445, reporting engaging two Hurricanes and three Curtiss fighters in the Qasaba area. Oblt Heinecke claimed a Hurricane at 1545, and Obfw Rosenberg attacked a second three minutes later. A minute thereafter Heinecke claimed an aircraft which he identified as a Swordfish. Initially, they seem to have encountered Hurricane Is of the French Alsace escadrille; two of this unit's aircraft had taken off from Maaten Bagush at 1550, Lt Lafont and Sous Lt Thirez being attacked by four Bf 109s. Thirez' aircraft was attacked twice and damaged, a shell bursting in the cockpit, injuring him in one leg. He crash-landed and was strafed by one of the Messerschmitts. At the same time Sous Lt Louchet and Lt Brisdoux were scrambled, Louchet being attacked by a Bf 109 which Brisdoux drove off his tail, the pair then returning to base. The biplane which Heinecke then claimed was an Albacore of 826 Squadron which was in the act of taking off when he attacked and shot it down.

At 1920 five Bf 109s of I.Gruppe reported engaging Hurricanes in the Fuka area again, and four were claimed shot down, two by Fw Steinhausen. Once more, the opponents were from the Alsace unit. Four of this unit's fighters had taken off at 1918, Sous Lt Louchet and Sgt Chef Mailfert providing cover for Lt Colin and Sous Lt Deville. Twelve miles south of Maaten Bagush they were attacked by five Messerschmitts, Louchet's aircraft being hit and set on fire. Wounded, he baled out, but his parachute failed to open. Mailfert then set about some of the German fighters but his aircraft was hit in the left wing. According to him, he was then "hit by our Bofors", and crash-landed, slightly wounded. He was picked up by troops of the 5th Indian Division.

Meanwhile, Colin and Deville spotted two Bf 109s approaching and Colin avoided their attack, turning onto the tail of one. Deville then lost sight of him and was attacked again by one of the Messerschmitts. Colin failed to return, his fate not being observed. Apart from those German pilots claiming Hurricanes, Lt Körner reported that he forced one down which belly-landed, but which he did not claim; this sounds like Deville's aircraft.

Shortly after this engagement, Obfw Bendert of II./JG 27 claimed two P-40s shot down south-east of Mersa Matruh. The only combat which might have involved this pilot related to a patrol undertaken by two Greek pilots of 335 Squadron, Flt Sgt Soufrilas and Flt Sgt Papandreopoulos patrolling over the Alexandria-Mersa Matruh road. They encountered four Bf 109s over Maaten Bagush, two of which attacked them, but the Hurricane pilots evaded them though Soufrilas' aircraft received a bullet through the port wing. At 1949 four more Bf 109s were off, Uffz Berben force-landing between Fuka and Mersa Matruh, though not, apparently, as a result of combat.

Hurricanes of 127 Squadron.

On this day four Spitfires of the newly-arrived 601 Squadron also flew their first sorties in company with 145 Squadron. A detachment of 127 Squadron reached LG.92 at Amiriya; up to this date the unit had been at LGs 11 and 15 at Gerawla, flying patrols but experiencing no contacts with Axis aircraft.

British Claims

260 Sqn	Sqn Ldr O.V.Hanbury	Kittyhawk I	Bf 109F	LG.09	1335-1440
260 Sqn	Sqn Ldr O.V.Hanbury	Kittyhawk I	Bf 109F Probable	LG.09	1335-1440
260 Sqn	Sgt Parrott	Kittyhawk I	Bf 109	LG.09	1335-1440
GC 1 Alsace	Sous Lt Louchet	Hurricane I Z4434	Bf 109 Probable	Maaten Bagush	1550
GC 1 Alsace	Sgt Chef Mailfert	Hurricane I Z4708	Bf 109	12m S Maaten Bagush	1920

British Casualties

GC 1 Alsace	Hurricane I Z4856 shot down by Bf 109, crash-landed, strafed; Sous Lt Thirez WiA, Maaten Bagush 1550-
GC 1 Alsace	Hurricane I Z4718 shot down by Bf 109s; Lt Louchet baled out WiA but unable to open parachute 1918-
GC 1 Alsace	Hurricane I Z4708 damaged by Bf 109, then hit by own AA; Sgt Chef Mailfert crash-landed slt WiA 1918-
GC 1 Alsace	Hurricane I Z4648 MiA in combat with Bf 109s; Lt Colin KiA 1918-
112 Sqn	Kittyhawk I AK652 shot down, forced to land nr Daba; Flt Lt J.A.Walker safe
208 Sqn	Hurricane IIa Z5412 MiA; Lt G.T.Sedgwick
223 Sqn	Baltimore II AG771 off from LG.116 to fly to LG.24; shot down soon after take-off, crashed 5m E LG.116; Flt Lt N.A.Gidney and 3 KiA
223 Sqn	Baltimore II AG774 shot down by fighters 20m SE LG.100 at 1055; Sgt P.P.W.Carruthers and 3 safe, one injured
223 Sqn	Baltimore II AG782 shot down by fighters 5m E LG.116 at 1030; Plt Off I.H.G.Davies and 3 KiA
5 SAAF Sqn	Tomahawk IIa AM392 force-landed due to engine failure at LG.15 at 1145, Cat II; Lt K.C. Kemsley
335 Sqn	Hurricane slt damaged; Flt Sgt Soufrilas
24 SAAF Sqn	Boston III Z2302 abandoned at LG.97; destroyed by Army on 5 July when recovery effort failed
826 Sqn	Albacore shot down by Bf 109 at Maaten Bagush

German Claims

8./JG 53	Oblt Ernst Kläger	Hurricane	8km S Mersa Matruh	0735
1./JG 27	Hptm Ludwig Franzisket	Martin 167	SW El Daba	0855
1./JG 27	Fw Günther Steinhausen	Martin 167	SW El Daba	0858
4./JG 27	Oblt Ferdinand Vögl	P-40	SW Fuka	1110
2./JG 27	Lt Hans-Arnold Stahlschmidt	P-40	SW Fuka	1305
9./JG 27	Oblt Hans-Joachim Heinecke	Hurricane	W Fuka	1445
8./JG 53	Obfw Heinrich Rosenberg	Hurricane	E Haggag el Qasaba	1448
8./JG 53	Oblt Hans-Joachim Heinecke	Swordfish	NE Haggag el Qotaifiya	1454
1./JG 27	Hptm Ludwig Franzisket	Hurricane	SW Fuka	1825
2./JG 27	Hptm Ernst Maack	Hurricane	Fuka West l.g.	1827
1./JG 27	Fw Günther Steinhausen	2 Hurricanes	SW Fuka	1827, 1830
4./JG 27	Obfw Karl-Heinz Bendert	2 P-40s	SE Mersa Matruh	1855 & 1900

German Casualties

2./JG 27	Bf 109F-4 trop Red 7 combat Sidi Barrani area; Uffz Helmut Beckmann crash-landed WiA, but less than 10% damaged
5./StG 3	Ju 87D-1 WNr 2459 S7+FN 10% damaged by strafing fighters at Bu Haneish; Uffz Friedrich Wolff/ Fw Heinz Renner KiA

Italian Claims

88ª Sq, 6°Gr, 1°St CT	M.llo Alfredo Bordin	MC.202	Hurricane damaged	SW Mersa Matruh 1135-1255

Italian Casualties

236ª Sq, 158°Gr, 50°St Ass	CR.42 damaged, Ten Giacomo Carra wounded

Sunday, 28 June 1942

Soon after midnight, when 28 June was but an hour old, Flg Off Selby of 73 Squadron claimed a Ju 88 shot down north of Fuka. With the arrival of daylight operations were once again on a limited scale, the main action taking place soon after midday when ten Hurricanes of 238 Squadron carried out a reconnaissance near Sidi Haneish. They were bounced by three Bf 109s of I./JG 27 which were out on a Freie Jagd; these diving almost vertically out of the sun, four Hurricanes falling to their fire. The other six reformed, but were attacked again by two of the Messerschmitts, one more Hurricane being shot down. Six claims were made by the attackers, three of them by Fw Steinhausen. On this occasion all five British pilots survived unhurt and were able to return to their unit subsequently.

II./JG 27 was unable to get any aircraft off due to lack of fuel, whereas three Messerschmitts of III./JG 27 which were scrambled to intercept British fighters attacking the road to Bir el Astas airfield, saw only an MC.202 shooting down one of the raiders. In fact this success had been shared by four pilots of 88ª Squadriglia, led by Ten Marchi, on a free sweep over Mersa Matruh between 1045-1220, but one of the Italian pilots involved had then been obliged to force-land. Their victim would seem to have been either a Tomahawk of 5 SAAF Squadron which Lt Bidwell crashed during a force-landing, or a Kittyhawk of 260 Squadron which was lost on a ferry flight.

Hurricane II BP166 KC-J of 238 Squadron.

The day also saw 1 SAAF Squadron, which had moved to LG.92, practice a new battle formation which the pilots had devised. This required three sections, each of four aircraft to fly in line astern, the sections side by side, Red Section in the centre, with Blue and Yellow Sections to each side, the No.1 aircraft of these two latter flight formating on the No.2 aircraft in Red Section, the whole formation weaving. This unnecessarily complicated and fuel-extravagant exercise was typical of the efforts being made to find some way of reducing the vulnerability of the Commonwealth fighters to the depredations of the Axis aircraft. The most practical – the classic 'Finger Four', employed by the Luftwaffe – still seemed to escape the imagination of many WDAF units – possibly for the very reason that it was used by the Germans!

Meanwhile, 4 SAAF Squadron moved to LG.105 where during the afternoon the unit completed its re-equipment with Kittyhawks. A Cant.Z.1007bis of 262ª Sq, flown by Ten Emanuele Trivella, was sent to bomb the railway line between El Daba and Burg el Arab.

British Claims					
73 Sqn	Sqn Ldr G.R.A.Johnston	Hurricane IIc BE405	Ju 88 Damaged	S Qasaba	0100-0500
73 Sqn	Flg Off J.B.Selby	Hurricane IIc BE554	Ju 88 Probable	10m N Fuka	0100-0500

British Casualties	
208 Sqn	Hurricane IIa Z5412 left 0815 for Charing Cross area, FTR; Lt G.T.Sedgwick MiA
238 Sqn	Hurricane II 'T' left 1200 for Sidi Haneish, attacked by three Bf 109s at c1220, shot down; Flt Lt F.D.B.Collenette KIA
238 Sqn	Hurricane II 'C' left 1200 for Sidi Haneish, attacked by three Bf 109s at c1220, shot down; Sgt M.P.S.Cummings KIA
238 Sqn	Hurricane II 'A' left 1200 for Sidi Haneish, attacked by three Bf 109s at c1220, shot down; Sgt W.B.Doig safe
238 Sqn	Hurricane II 'X' left 1200 for Sidi Haneish, attacked by three Bf 109s at c1220, shot down; Sgt J.W.T.Purdy safe
238 Sqn	Hurricane II 'U' left 1200 for Sidi Haneish, attacked by three Bf 109s at c1220, shot down; Sgt M.L Lawrence-Smith safe (three of these believed to be BE330, BG965 and BP281)
260 Sqn	Kittyhawk I ET574 lost on ferry flight, Flt Sgt D.C.Copping MiA; this aircraft was found in the desert in June 2012
5 SAAF Sqn	Tomahawk IIa ..460 crashed in force-landing, aircraft destroyed by fire; Lt H.W.G.Bidwell

German Claims				
1./JG 27	Fw Günther Steinhausen	Hurricane	SW Fuka	1125
1./JG 27	Fw Gerhard Keppler	Hurricane	SW Fuka	1127
1./JG 27	Fw Günther Steinhausen	2 Hurricanes	SW Fuka	1130-1131
1./JG 27	Uffz Walter Timmermann	Hurricane	SE Fuka	1137

Italian Claims					
88ª Sq, 6°Gr, 1°St CT	Ten Emilio Marchi	MC.202	P-40	W Mersa Matruh	1045-1220
88ª Sq, 6°Gr, 1°St CT	Serg Magg Mario Host	MC.202			
88ª Sq, 6°Gr, 1°St CT	M.llo Italo Baldelli	MC.202			
88ª Sq, 6°Gr, 1°St CT	S.Ten Roberto Sgorbati	MC.202			

Italian Casualties	
88ª Sq, 6°Gr, 1°St CT	MC.202 force-landed at Bir el Astas, S.Ten Roberto Sgorbati safe, aircraft recovered on July 1

Monday, 29 June 1942

In a move very similar to that of the previous day, 12 Hurricanes of 213 Squadron were sent to sweep over Mersa Matruh around midday, where, as had happened to 238 Squadron the day before, they were jumped by four fighters believed to be Messerschmitts. It seems that on this occasion they were Macchis, three pilots of 9° Gruppo each claiming a P-40 in this area at this time. On this occasion, however, only one Hurricane was hit and damaged, Flg Off Beedham force-landing at LG.06, claiming to have shot down one fighter, Flt Lt Olver claiming a second damaged. Beedham's Hurricane was abandoned due to the evacuation from the area, and was lost.

274 Squadron now moved to LG.92 for a rest from operations, while 145 Squadron moved to LG.154 and 239 Wing departed El Daba for an airfield further east. Behind them came the Luftwaffe, II. and III./JG 27, accompanied by III./JG 53, moving to Fuka on this date, I./JG 27 arriving at Fuka East next day. The day also saw the arrival of Benito Mussolini at Derna, ready to lead a triumphal entry into Cairo. By night 47° Stormo was again involved in bombing the railway line and road along the Egyptian coast, three Cant.Z.1007bis delivering 48 50kg bombs.

Hurricane IIc AK-S of 213 Squadron.

British Claims					
213 Sqn	Plt Off D.W.Beedham	Hurricane IIc BN539 'V'	Bf 109F	S Sidi Haneish	1245
213 Sqn	Flt Lt P.Olver	Hurricane IIc BN139 'U'	Bf 109F Damaged	S Sidi Haneish	1245

British Casualties	
213 Sqn	Hurricane II BN539 damaged by Bf 109s Cat II and force-landed LG.06; lost on evacuation; Plt Off D.W.Beedham safe
213 Sqn	Hurricane II BN117 'X' damaged by Bf 109s Cat I at 1245; Plt Off D.F.Chadwick safe
40 SAAF Sqn	Hurricane Z4647 swung on take-off and hit Beaufort at LG.104; Lt J.H. Heald KiFA
US Casualties	
	B-24 FTR 41-11624 'Balls of Fire', shot down on night raid; Capt Francis Nestor & 6 KiA

German Casualties	
4./LG 1	Ju 88 A-4 WNr 5672 L1+LM , shot down by Hurricanes, crashed nr El Alamein, Obfw Werner Doring & three MiA

Italian Claims				
73ª Sq, 9°Gr, 4°St CT	S.Ten Alvaro Querci	MC.202	P-40	SE Mersa Matruh 1015-1130
73ª Sq, 9°Gr, 4°St CT	Serg Teresio Martinoli	MC.202	P.40	SE Mersa Matruh 1015-1130
97ª Sq, 9°Gr, 4°St CT	Serg Bruno Biagini	MC.202	P-40	SE Mersa Matruh 1015-1130

Italian Casualties	
92ª Sq, 8°Gr, 2°St CT	MC.200 MM 5185 damaged on taking-off, S.Ten Giuseppe Calsolaro safe
191ª Sq, 86°Gr, 35°St BT	Cant.Z.1007bis MM 23758 collided with G.12 at 2020 on landing, w/o, S.Ten Achille Scaduto and five safe, one slightly wounded

Tuesday, 30 June 1942

There were no engagements during the day, which was mainly one of movement. 4° Stormo CT was ordered to move to Fuka South, and 50° Stormo Assalto arrived at Abar Nimeir (LG.15). Amongst the British units, 213 Squadron moved to LG.154. 3 RAAF Squadron received the news that Sgt Fox, missing on the 24th, was safe in hospital, and 112 Squadron celebrated the return of Plt Off Cuddon.

The Commonwealth forces were now firmly entrenched on the El Alamein line, whereas those of the Axis were seriously weakened after their long advance; both sides were extremely weary, however during the month Curtiss squadrons and 260 Squadron, together in 233 Wing, had specialised in bomber escort duties, led by Wg Cdr T.B.de la P.Beresford, DSO, DFC. During the first 23 days of the Axis offensive not one bomber had been lost to the opposing fighters. The RAF had undertaken a very successful retreat to the El Alamein area, retaining the organisation undamaged, and leaving behind the minimum possible numbers of aircraft and quantities of equipment to be captured. All Blenheims had now been withdrawn from bombing operations with the WDAF bomber formations, and the last bomber squadron operating these aircraft, 14, had gone over to night operations.

Twenty-three pilots of 134 Squadron who had arrived in Palestine with 601 Squadron's personnel, were now posted on attachment to 213 Squadron for operations (by the end of November nine of them would have been killed or would be missing). The ground staff of this unit remained in Palestine without aircraft. As demonstrated (see Chapter Four), the first USAAF aircraft had begun to arrive in the Middle East and more would soon follow in growing numbers.

The pendulum had swung as far in the adverse direction for the Commonwealth forces in the Middle East as it was ever to do. Now, with greatly shortened lines of communication, 8th Army and Western Desert Air Force would begin building up their strength once more, first to hold the Axis on the El Alamein line, and then to start the long trek back across Cyrenaica.

British Claims

73 Sqn	Sgt R.L.Baker	Hurricane IIc BN402	Ju 88 Damaged	6m E Fuka	0145

German Casualties

II./StG 3	Ju 87D-1 WNr 2476 75% damaged by air raid at Bu Haggag

Egypt, summer 1942

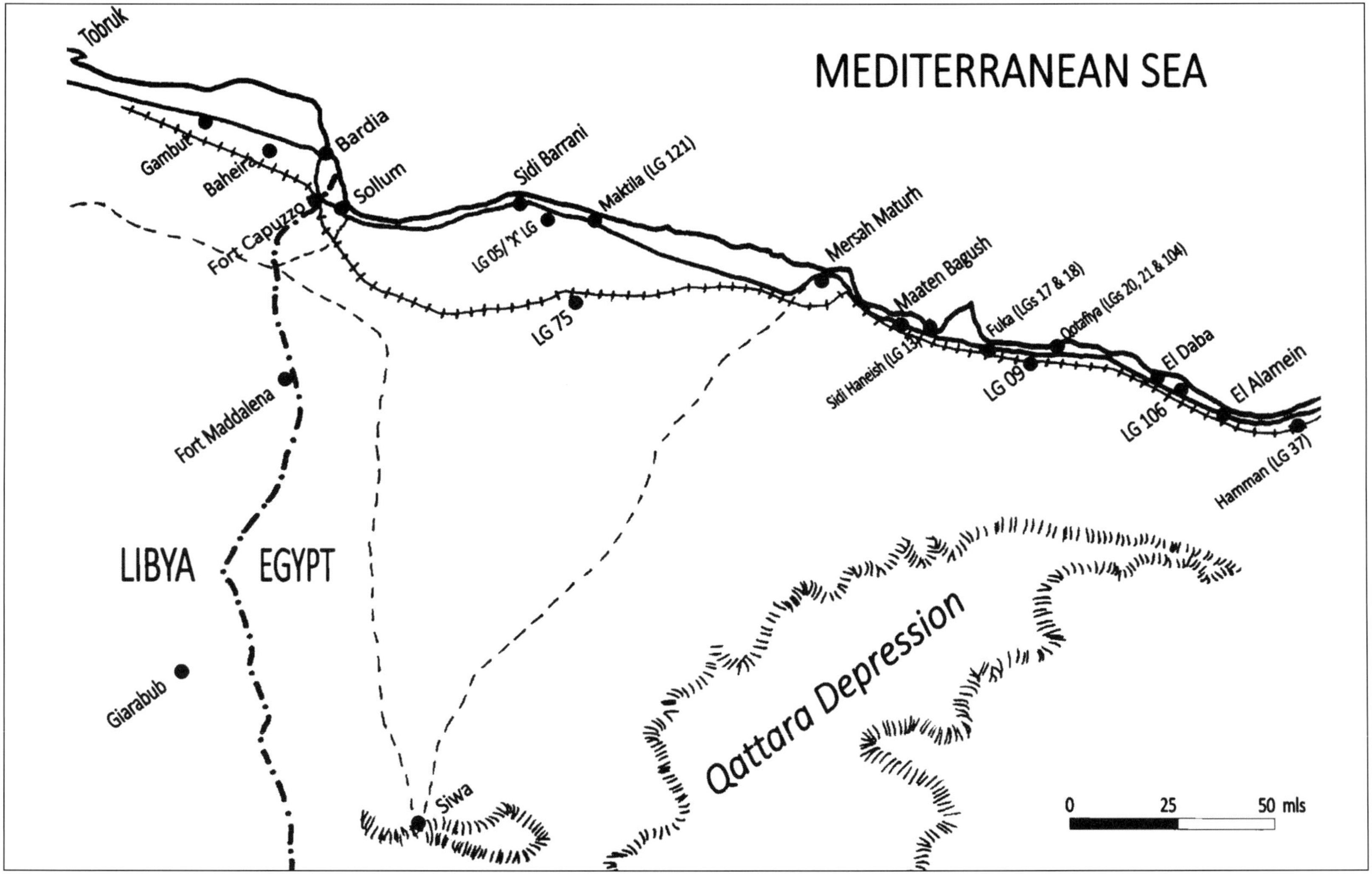

CHAPTER 3

ABOVE THE WAVES, 1 FEBRUARY – 30 JUNE 1942

It will be recalled that throughout the earlier months of the war the Royal Navy, in the person of its Commander-in-Chief, Admiral Cunningham, had constantly pressed for an increased commitment to reconnaissance, anti-submarine and other naval co-operation duties by the Royal Air Force. As early as September 1939, 201 (Naval Co-operation) Group had been established, although with very limited resources. Although efforts had been made to increase the size and strength of this group, the demands of the Western Desert battlefront and that of the Far East following the recent entry into the war of the Imperial Japanese Empire and its forces, had militated against any such growth in the short term.

Many of the functions demanded by the navy were at this time being provided by the squadrons on Malta, based as they were astride the main Axis supply routes to Tripoli and Benghazi. The success of the Crusader offensive had initially provided bases along the North African coast closer to Malta, allowing an increased level of mutual support between the island's striking force and 201 Group's units.

Unfortunately for the British, the very success of Crusader had led to a greatly renewed offensive by the Luftwaffe against Malta, and by February 1942 the island's ability to maintain its offensive capacity had been seriously reduced. Indeed, this had almost been brought to a halt and the sinking of Italian supply vessels had been substantially reduced compared with the levels achieved during the preceding summer.

At much the same time the unexpectedly sudden and successful riposte by Rommel's forces in Libya had driven 8th Army and the WDAF half way back towards the Egyptian frontier. This had meant the loss of those so recently captured and utilized airfields in the area of Benghazi and towards El Agheila. In consequence thereof, for most of 1942, 201 Group's activities were to be restricted and maintained mainly over the eastern basin of the Mediterranean Sea.

Following the British advance into Libya, the threat to the British bases around Alexandria and the Suez Canal Zone was considerably reduced. Consequently the air defence here was not reinforced to any great extent. This was aided by the recent arrival in the area of 89 Squadron with the first Beaufighters to operate outside the UK equipped with AI (Airborne Interception) radar. This offered a considerably improved potential for interception of raiders than had previously been the case with ground-directed Hurricane squadrons.

For daytime operations a small force of Hurricane Is remained based in the area together with some RN fighters. The Mark I Hurricane was still considered to have sufficient performance to deal with multi-engined Axis bombers. Also present were Beaufighter Ics of 252 and 272 Squadrons, these units operating the coastal long-range version of this formidable fighter. At times of high activity over the main front detachments of these aircraft were on occasion sent forward to support WDAF, while at times similar detachments were sent to operate from Malta, typically when efforts were being made to run through reinforcement and re-supply to the beleaguered island. Their predominant role, however, involved cover and support to the navy in the eastern basin. (For the sake of continuity, operations over the battlefront are dealt with in the chapters relating to WDAF activity, and actions over Malta have already been covered in *Malta: The Spitfire Year, 1942*. These will be cross-referenced into this chapter as appropriate to prevent a loss of continuity, but to avoid unnecessary repetition.)

It should also be mentioned that anti-submarine activities in the western section of the Mediterranean had since the outbreak of war been undertaken by flyingboats from Gibraltar, mainly operated by 202

Squadron (commanding officer Wg Cdr A.A.Case, who was just taking over the unit in February). The unit was equipped with Catalinas and with a few Sunderlands; it also received sporadic reinforcement with Sunderlands from UK-based units. During December 1941 Gibraltar had been strengthened by the arrival from England of the Lockheed Hudson patrol bombers of 233 Squadron. Initially this unit continued to maintain detachments in the UK, but the whole unit would have become Gibraltar-based by the end of March. Commanding officer at this time was Wg Cdr E.H.Clarke, AFC, who would hand over to Wg Cdr W.T.McComb during the latter month. 233 Squadron's duties also included patrol over, and escort to, convoys sailing down the Portuguese western and southern coastlines on their way to the Mediterranean.

When HMS *Ark Royal* had been sunk on 14 November 1941, whilst the ship's Fulmars of 807 Squadron had gone down with her, sufficient of the Swordfish were in the air and were able to reach Gibraltar, to allow 812 Squadron to be re-established here under Lt Cdr B.J.Prendergast, to operate alongside the resident RAF units in an anti-submarine role. Fortuitously, these Swordfish were equipped with some of the first ASV MK I radar sets to be issued, and were to make numerous attacks on surfaced U-Boats in the coming weeks. Although formally disbanded on 18 December, one of the unit's aircraft had been able to achieve the first night sinking of a U-Boat by aircraft three days later when U-451 was sunk in the Strait of Gibraltar, off Tangier. The remaining Swordfish went home to the UK aboard USS *Wasp* during that carrier's return from delivering Spitfires to Malta in April 1942 (see *Malta: The Hurricane Years* and *Malta: The Spitfire Year*).

What then was available to 201 Group and to the defence of Egypt and the Eastern Mediterranean bases at the start of February 1942?

Wings (Defensive and Naval Co-operation)

250 (Signals) Wing was essentially a fighter control unit, based at Ismailia to direct allocated fighter units in the defence of the Suez Canal area.

252 Wing was categorised as a Defensive Fighter unit; based at Seagull Camp at Mex, close by Alexandria, it looked after the defence of the port and city nearby, and to an extent parts of the Nile Delta and Suez Canal which it had taken over from 250 Wing on its arrival during the previous summer.

234 Wing was classified as a Mobile Defensive Fighter unit. Under AHQ, Egypt, control at the start of February 1942, it would be transferred to AHQ, Western Desert, on 8 February. The activities of the squadrons under its control are therefore dealt with in the main chapters until its reversion to AHQ, Egypt, control in May.

235 Wing; while many squadrons available for naval co-operation and associated duties were operated directly by 201 Group, 235 Wing had been formed in January 1942, incorporating Advanced HQ, 201 Group.

247 and 248 Wings were planned to be formed as 201 Group units, but in early February neither yet formally existed.

Regarding the various squadrons, at this time these were as follows:

a. Day Fighters

- 30 Squadron was based at LG.121, a few miles east of Sidi Barrani, operating over the Egyptian-Libyan border; command of the unit was just passing to Sqn Ldr C.F.Chater, DFC. However, on 18 February this unit with its Hurricane Is would be withdrawn to Heliopolis from where it would be transferred aboard the aircraft carrier HMS *Indomitable* to Ceylon on the 25th.

- 213 Squadron had moved to Egypt from Nicosia, Cyprus, during December, arriving at LG.229, Edcu, on 14 January. Commanded by Sqn Ldr G.V.W.Kettlewell, who had just taken over, the unit was now in the process of re-equipping with Hurricane IIcs.

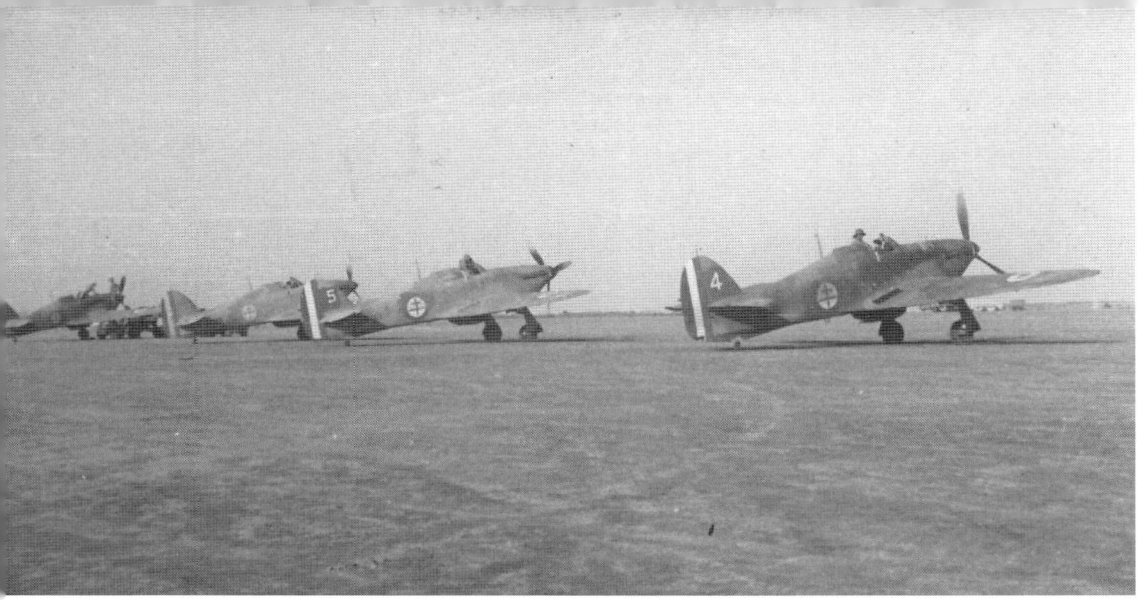

Hurricanes of GC 1 Alsace being prepared for use by their Free French pilots. The aircraft in the distance seem to be in the process of being painted with French roundels and rudder stripes to replace their RAF markings.

- 335 Squadron, composed of Greek pilots flying Hurricane Is and commanded by Sqn Ldr X.J.Varvaressos, had formed in October 1941 (see Vol 1). The unit was based at LG.20 near Alexandria, but with a detachment with 30 Squadron at LG.121.

- Groupe de Chasse N.1 'Alsace' had been formed from a nucleus of pilots who had flown on attachment to 73 Squadron as Fighter Flight 1 during the defence of Tobruk in April 1941 (see Vol 1), which had subsequently merged with Free French Flight 1 at Rayak, Syria, to create the Alsace Groupe. Here it had been equipped initially with 12 Morane 406 fighters taken over after the departure of the Vichy forces; these had previously equipped GC I/7. Re-equipped with Hurricane Is, the unit had become operational during September; in January 1942 it had moved to LG.X at Ismailia for air defence duties, led by Cdt J.Tulasne (see Vol 1, page 432).

- 261 Squadron, also equipped with Hurricane Is, was based at St Jean, Palestine, with detachments at Nicosia and Beirut. Command had just passed from Sqn Ldr E.M. 'Imshi' Mason, DFC, to Sqn Ldr D.R.Walker both of whom were veterans of the early fighting in the Western Desert. However, this unit too was about to leave for Ceylon, joining 30 Squadron aboard HMS *Indomitable*.

- 127 Squadron had taken part in the fighting over Syria during June and July 1941. It had then been absorbed into 261 Squadron which itself was about to take part in the brief actions during the Anglo-Soviet occupation of Iran. 127 Squadron was reformed, initially without aircraft, in August 1941. On 22 February 1942, now led by Sqn Ldr D.R.Walker, who transferred over from 261 Squadron at this time, the unit, newly-equipped with Hurricane Is, arrived at St Jean to take over the air defence of Haifa from 261 Squadron; it would also maintain a detachment in Cyprus.

- The Royal Naval Fighter Squadron was disbanded at Dekheila at the start of February, reverting to the three squadrons which had formed the composite unit. 803 and 806 Squadrons were each re-equipped with Fulmar IIs, the borrowed Hurricane being returned to the RAF. These two units then followed 30 and 261 Squadrons to Ceylon in early March. 805 Squadron remained at Maaten Bagush equipped with the remaining Grumman Martlets, commanded by Lt Cdr A.F.Black. However, at the same time a new RN Fulmar Flight was formed at Dekheila. It would subsequently be expanded into a full squadron – 889 – with 12 Fulmar IIs on 16 March, moving to Fuka Satellite; commanding officer of this new unit would be Lt Cdr A.R.Ramsey, DSC.

In summary, therefore, by the latter part of February the day defence of Egypt, Palestine and the Eastern Mediterranean rested in the hands of:

213 Squadron	Hurricane IIcs	at Edcu
335 Squadron	Hurricane Is	at LG.20
GC 1 Alsace	Hurricane Is	at LG.X
127 Squadron	Hurricane Is	at St Jean (detachment at Nicosia)
805 Squadron	Martlet Is	at Maaten Bagush
RN Fulmar Flight	Fulmar IIs	at Dekheila

There were, of course, also three Royal Egyptian Air Force fighter squadrons equipped with Gladiators, but these would in practice take no active part in the defence of their country.

b. Night Fighters

- 89 Squadron (Wg Cdr G.H.Stainforth, AFC) at Edcu with Beaufighter Ifs as detailed above.

c. Long-Range Coastal Fighters – these operated under 201 Group control.

- 252 Squadron (Sqn Ldr A.G.Wincott) at Edcu with Beaufighter Ics and 272 Squadron similarly equipped, but based at LG.10, Gerawala, near Maaten Bagush; this unit would return to Edcu on 14 March. With this latter unit Wg Cdr R.C.Yaxley, DSO, MC, DFC, was just handing over command to Sqn Ldr J.V.Hoggarth.

d. Bomber, Reconnaissance, Anti-Submarine and Torpedo-Dropping Aircraft

- 22 Squadron (Sqn Ldr J.A.Bateson) was posted from England to the Far East during February 1942. Equipped with Beauforts, the ground party left by sea for Ceylon while the air party commenced flying out the unit's Beauforts, but were retained on arrival at Malta, the first six aircraft arriving on the island on 19 March.

- 38 Squadron (Wg Cdr J.H. Chaplin, DFC) at Shallufa with Wellington Ics, some converted for torpedo-dropping.

- 39 Squadron (Wg Cdr A.J. Mason, DFC) at LG.86 with detachments; the unit had recently converted from Marylands to Beauforts.

A Wellington of 38 Squadron releases a torpedo during a daylight practice run.

- 203 Squadron (Wg Cdr A.F. Johnson, DFC) with Blenheim IVs and Marylands, the latter recently taken over from 39 Squadron, was operating from Gambut in the forward area at the start of the month. It would move to LG.05 on 3 February and then LG.39 three days later. Duringthe month the squadron would receive the first Lockheed Hudson III patrol bombers to reach the Middle East, but almost at once these were detached to allow a new unit – 459 Squadron, RAAF – to be formed with these aircraft at LG.39. Initially this latter unit also operated a number of Blenheim IVs.

- 220 Squadron detachment, equipped with a small number of four-engined Boeing Fortress Is, had been based at Shallufa as 90 Squadron detachment for some months, operating with 205 Group. In December 1941 it had been re-titled 220 Squadron detachment, and was now available for use by 201 Group.

One of 221 Squadron's Wellington VIIIs fitted with a variety of ASV radar aerials for shipping search.

- 221 Squadron (Wg Cdr A.M.Murdoch), a specialist unit equipped with Wellington VIIIs which were basically converted Mark Ics fitted with ASV MK II (air to surface vessel) radar. The squadron had arrived from the UK at LG.39 in January 1942 but at once despatched detachments to operate from LG.05, Luqa and St Jean, mainly for nocturnal ship-hunting work.

- 230 Squadron (Wg Cdr M.C.Collins) was equipped with Sunderland flyingboats, but now also had the balance of 2 Yugoslav Squadron attached with their few remaining Do 22 and Rogozarski Sim-XIV-H floatplanes. The main duty of this unit was anti-submarine patrol for which it was based at Aboukir.

- 13 (Hellenic) Squadron (Sqn Ldr R.Pongis), a Greek unit which had escaped from mainland Greece in April 1941, was still equipped with the Avro Ansons which its aircrews had evacuated to Egypt. It was involved mainly with anti-submarine patrol and convoy escort in the eastern reaches of the Mediterranean.

- 700 Squadron, Fleet Air Arm, was a detachment from the United Kingdom, initially responsible for all naval aircraft at the main Fleet Air Arm base at Dekheila. Operating under 201 Group control, the unit undertook some patrol work, flying Walrus amphibians. Command passed to Lt Cdr G.W.R.Nicholls on 4 February.

- 815 Squadron, Fleet Air Arm (Lt Cdr E.D.Crick) was equipped with Swordfish biplanes and operated mainly in the anti-submarine and convoy patrol role. During February it was based at St Jean D'Acre in Palestine, but operated as necessary from Nicosia, Cyprus, and from Maaten Bagush (LG.14) and Amiriya (LG.86).

- 821 and 826 Squadrons, Fleet Air Arm (Lt C.W.B.Smith, DSC) were both equipped with Albacores, undertaking patrol and bombing duties, particularly illuminating with flares targets by night for 205 Group Wellingtons to attack (operations of the latter nature are also frequently mentioned in Chapter Eleven). During March 1942 Lt Smith would hand over command of 821 Squadron to Maj A.C.Newsome, RM, and of 826 Squadron to Lt P.W.Compton.

The Luftwaffe and Regia Aeronautica both maintained quite substantial bomber forces in the Aegean Islands and in Greece, together with associated reconnaissance units. For the Italians particularly anti-shipping activity was their main 'raison d'etre'. Certainly for the British the potential of these Axis units to interfere with – and sometimes to thwart the sailing of supply convoys either way through the Eastern Mediterranean – was high, particularly those heading westwards to try and re-provision Malta.

Whilst quite successful in this role, the Axis failed to achieve much against the Egyptian base areas. They appeared to have underestimated just how important this area was to the Allied cause. Not only was the main RAF night bomber force based there, but increasingly a huge supply, maintenance, repair and training complex was established which the Axis bombers did surprisingly little to damage or disrupt. Regular efforts were made to lay mines in the canal itself, but these were usually swept rapidly and with only minor delays or problems.

This was of equal importance to all the three British services, but during 1942 as the RAF – and the WDAF in particular – expanded rapidly, this importance became ever more critical. The Regia Aeronautica force was based entirely on Rhodes at this time, and comprised:

Aeronautica dell'Egeo	Gen DA Ulisse Longo	
47° Stormo BT	24 Cant Z.1007bis	Con Mario Grotti
106° Gruppo BT		Magg Alessandro Bavassano
260ª Squadriglia BT		Cap Mario Popaiz
261ª Squadriglia BT		Cap Athos Maestri
107° Gruppo BT		Magg Renato Roveda
262ª Squadriglia BT		Cap Nicolò Falco
263ª Squadriglia BT		S.Ten Pietro Sarasso (prov.)
87° Gruppo BT	16 Cant Z.1007bis	T.Col Mario Giuliano
192ª Squadriglia BT		Cap Mario Cesari
193ª Squadriglia BT		Cap Vincenzo Guidi
41° Gruppo AS	16 S.79	T.Col Ettore Muti
204ª Squadriglia AS		Cap Gian Battista De Stefano
205ª Squadriglia AS		Cap Ettore Sondalini
154° Gruppo CT	23 CR.42, 18 G.50bis	Magg Delio Guizzon
395ª Squadriglia		Cap Bruno Trevisan
396ª Squadriglia		Cap Fernando Giocondi

On Crete and in Greece the Luftwaffe's X Fliegerkorps was commanded by General Hans-Ferdinand Geisler as follows:

Stab/LG 1	Ju 88A-5	Obstlt Friedrich-Karl Knust RK, DKG
I./LG 1	Ju 88A-5	Maj Joachim Helbig RK, EL, SW
II./LG 1	Ju 88A-5	Maj Gerhard Kollewe RK, EL
12./LG 1	Ju 88A-4 and -5	Oblt Rudolf Meier
II./KG 26	He 111H-6	Obstlt Horst Beyling DKG
1.(F)/121	Ju 88D, Bf 110E	Maj Hans von Osterhausen
1.(F)/122	Ju 88D	Oberst Fritz Köhler RK
2.(F)/123	Ju 88A & D, Bf 110E	Maj Gerhard Koppen RK
2./SAGr 125	Ar 196	Oberst Gerg Kolbe
SAGr 126	He 60, T.VIIIW, Ar 196, He 114	Maj Hermann Kaiser

Typically the Kampfgruppe each had a strength of about 30 aircraft (or slightly more). The reconnaissance units had 10-15 aircraft each, Ju 88Ds predominating over the Bf 110Es. Although the SAGr 125 Staffel had nine Arado floatplanes, the larger SAGr 126 enjoyed a considerable establishment of 13 Ar 196s, 20 He 60s and six He 114s, plus unusually seven ex-Netherlands Naval Air Force Fokker T.VIIIW floatplanes.

The tail of Ju 88A-4 L1+GP of 6./LG 1 demonstrates claims for shipping sunk; it is seen here at Catania, Sicily.

At this stage of the war most aerial transport to either the German or Italian forces tended to emanate from Sicily and Southern Italy, during periods when shipping was suffering heavy losses, and particularly when Axis supply lines were extended as a result of successful offensives. The Greece-North Africa route would become of considerably greater importance, and of concern to the Allies. It was against this background that operations by 201 Group and the small force defending the base area, continued into 1942.

Sunday, 1 February 1942

British Casualties

38 Sqn	Wellington X9735 flew into sea at night, Suez Bay

Thursday, 5 February 1942

Two S.79s of 205ª Squadriglia 41° Gruppo AS intercepted at 1645 a naval convoy sailing off Tobruk. One torpedo was released by Ten Giuseppe Cimicchi, who claimed a hit on a steamer. Ten Giulio Cesare Graziani's aircraft was hit by AA fire, which killed one crew member and wounded three; he failed to release his torpedo. On this date 41° Gruppo AS received five new S.79s from Italy, these replacing seven SM.84s and a Cant.Z.1007bis which had previously served with the unit.

Following a patrol over the Arabian Gulf, one of the Sim-XIV-H floatplanes of the Yugoslav squadron crashed on return, two members of the crew being killed.

Two notable Italian torpedo-bomber pilots were Cap Cimicchi (first from left) and Magg Buscaglia (first from right); both were decorated with Medaglia d'Oro al valor militare.

British Casualties	
230/Yugoslav Sqn	Sim-XIV-H crashed on landing and destroyed following patrol; two KiFA

Italian Casualties	
205ª Sq, 41° Gr AS	S.79 damaged by AA fire, pilot Ten Giulio Cesare Graziani safe, copilot Serg Giovanni Riso and two WiA, one KiA

Friday, 6 February 1942

British Casualties	
272 Sqn	Beaufighter T4875 FTR from attack on road transport near Martuba; Flg Off H.H.Crawford KiA; Sgt Patterson WiA returned on 25th

Italian Casualties	
607ª Sq, 149° Gr, 45° St T	S.82 MM 60613 force-landed on sea 40 miles off Libyan coast, one crew member and 15 passengers killed, aircraft lost, pilot Ten Eleuterio Troncone, copilot M.llo Raoul Bruschini, two crew and ten passengers safe

Malta: The Spitfire Year records the loss of three Blenheims to Bf 109s. The claiming Luftwaffe pilots were:

German Claims				
6./JG 53	Lt Hans Möller	Blenheim		1713
II./JG 53	Oblt Heinz-Eugen Wittmeyer	Blenheim		1715
II./JG 53	Lt Herbert Soukuo	Blenheim		1718
Also				
2./NJG 2	Fw Vinzenz Giessübel	Beaufighter	100km E Malta	

Saturday, 7 February 1942

During the early afternoon, Lt Körner of 2./JG 27 claimed to have shot down a twin-engined aircraft which he identified as a Blenheim. In the absence of the loss of such an aircraft on this date, it is possible that his victim was either a Beaufighter of 272 Squadron which failed to return from a strafing sortie, or another such aircraft on a delivery flight to Malta from the UK. Particularly given the location of the German claim, the former would seem most likely.

229 Squadron now moved from LG.111 to LG.102 at Sidi Haneish where Sqn Ldr W.A.Smith rejoined the unit. A few days later the squadron would move to El Firdan in the Canal Zone.

British Casualties	
272 Sqn	Beaufighter T4838 'F' lost – one of four strafing Barce-Apollonia road, 1340-1445; last seen near Martuba; Flt Sgt J.S.Ross/Sgt F.H.W.Hoadley MiA
OADU	Beaufighter T4889 MiA on ferry flight off Malta; presumed shot down by Bf 109s; Sgt B.B.Smith, Sgt H.K.Sprason and Wg Cdr J.F.Maffitt MiA

German Claims				
2./JG 27	Lt Friedrich Körner	Blenheim	NE Derna	1427

Sunday, 8 February 1942

Five Cant.Z.1007bis of 107° Gruppo BT (two of 262ª and three of 263ª Squadriglie) led by the 47° Stormo commander, Col Mario Grotti, took off from Gadurra at 0240-0255 to bomb Alexandria. The crews returned at 0725-0735 reporting hits on the docks and facilities in the harbour.

Monday, 9 February 1942

Five Cant.Z.1007bis of 106° Gruppo BT (two of 260ª and three of 261ª Squadriglie) led by T.Col Alessandro Bavassano, took off from Gadurra at 0315-0335 to bomb Alexandria. Four aircraft returned at 0715, crews reporting hits on the docks and a marshalling yard. The fifth bomber, flown by Ten Mario La Terza, failed to return. It was thought that the aircraft might have been shot down by night fighters, but no claim was made by British units.

Two S.79 torpedo-bombers of 41° Gruppo AS, flown by Ten Ardito Cristiani and S.Ten Dorando Cionni, attacked a British convoy sailing off Mersa Matruh at 1600. A torpedo reportedly hit an auxiliary cruiser of approximately 5,500 tons, but no British casualties were reported.

British Casualties	
272 Sqn	Beaufighter T4836 'N' FTR from attack on shipping at Sirte, 1520-1700: Sgt D.Pearcey/Sgt J.S.Crossley PoW
272 Sqn	Beaufighter T3324 'S' FTR from attack on shipping at Sirte; Sqn Ldr J.V.Hoggarth/Plt Off G.Sproutes PoW

A Cant.Z.1007bis of 261ª Squadriglia, 106° Gruppo, 47° Stormo BT. This Rhodes-based unit was very active in night bombing operations.

Italian Casualties

261ª Sq, 106°Gr, 47°St BT	Cant.Z.1007bis MM 23742 '261-4' failed to return from a night bombing mission to Alexandria, pilot Ten Mario La Terza, copilot S.Ten Giovanni Pomodoro and three MiA

Thursday, 12 February 1942

During the morning Sgt Paxton of 30 Squadron was scrambled, claiming to have shot down an aircraft which he identified as a He 111. No Luftwaffe bombers were reported lost or damaged on this date, but a Cant.Z.1007bis of 263ª Squadriglia, flown by Ten Mario Sami, had taken off from Maritza at 0900 on a reconnaissance mission along the African coast, from El Alamein to Mersa Matruh. This failed to return, and was thought probably to have been shot down by British fighters.

At 1420 the newly appointed commanding officer of the unit, Cap Alberto Insom, took off to search for the missing bomber without result. Reportedly soon after midday two Fulmars from the new RN flight intercepted a Cant Z.1007bis, but one of these fighters was shot down in flames. It would therefore appear that it was Insom's aircraft which they had encountered and that return fire from this had sent down the Fulmar flown by Sub Lt Polwin. The latter was subsequently picked up by a Walrus, but his navigator was not found.

By now the situation of Malta was parlous in the extreme, desperately short of supplies and fuel, under heavy attack and with diminishing defences and an ability to act offensively against the Axis convoys rapidly fading. In these circumstances Admiral Cunningham had reported on 6 February of his intention to sail a convoy through from the east in the near future. He warned the First Sea Lord that so few fighters now remained serviceable on the island that he doubted whether they could give adequate support to incoming ships. However, so desperate was the island's plight, and so important was its continued defence, that the operation was approved.

Still at Malta were three merchant vessels from earlier convoys and the *Breconshire*, which would sail out, covered by Force K (HMS *Penelope* and six destroyers), to rendezvous with the incoming ships which this force would then escort into harbour, while the covering force from the east would in turn escort the empty vessels to Egypt.

Thus at evening three laden supply vessels departed Alexandria – *Clan Chattan*, *Clan Campbell* and *Rowallan Castle*, with an escort of HMS *Carlisle* and six destroyers. These vessels sailed in two groups as far as Tobruk in an effort to give the impression that it was to this port that they were heading. All arrived off the coast there by nightfall.

British Claims

30 Sqn	Sgt T.G.Paxton	Hurricane I	He 111	off Matruh	0900-1000

British Casualties

RN Fulmar Flt	Fulmar II X8685 shot down in flames; Sub Lt I.J.Polwin rescued, inj; L/Air N.Davison KiA

Italian Casualties	
263ª Sq, 107°Gr, 47°St BT	Cant.Z.1007bis MM 22157 from Rhodes failed to return, pilot Ten Mario Sami, copilot M.llo Alessandro Rampazzini and five MiA

Friday, 13 February 1942

The ships outside Tobruk then formed a single convoy, turning north-west to head for the island. This timing ensured that by morning the vessels would at least be out of range of Cyrenaican-based dive-bombers. When daylight came there was no fighter cover for the main convoy which had to rely on the warships' anti-aircraft artillery for protection. At evening a bomb hit *Clan Campbell* which reduced her speed and she was ordered to turn back and put in to Tobruk instead.

During one of the attacks, Flt Lt Rydall of 272 Squadron targeted a Ju 88 which had just dive-bombed the convoy; he may have inflicted damage on an aircraft of 3./LG 1, although no formal claim appears to have been made.

British Casualties	
RNFS	fighter had engine fail, pursuing Ju 88, ditched 5m off Gambut; Sub Lt D.B.Law rescued
German Casualties	
3/./LG 1	Ju 88A-4 10% damaged in combat; landed safely at base with radio operator WiA; DoW 18 February

Saturday, 14 February 1942

With morning Admiral Vian's 15th Cruiser Squadron of three cruisers and eight destroyers joined the escort, but by the afternoon Axis aircraft were attacking intermittently both singly and in groups. Two S.79s of 284ª Sq AS, flown by Cap Oscar Pegna and Ten Paolo Lombardi, took off at 1530 to intercept the British convoy, correctly identified initially as comprising three freighters escorted by a light cruiser and four destroyers, sailing in the Eastern Mediterranean. Pegna claimed a hit on the cruiser and Lombardi claimed a steamer probably sunk.

Two more S.79 torpedo-bombers of 41° Gruppo, flown by Ten Giulio Cesare Graziani and S.Ten Saverio Mayer, attacked a British convoy sailing off El Daba at 2245. They reportedly torpedoed a steamer which was claimed sunk, with a second claimed as a probable.

During one of these attacks *Clan Chattan* was hit by a bomb and began to burn furiously. Her crew and service personnel aboard were taken off and she was then sunk. This left only *Rowallan Castle* heading for the island, with the whole force of escorting warships. Just before 1400 Force K arrived with the 'empties', and 45 minutes thereafter the first Beaufighters from Malta appeared to give cover as the two forces of warships exchanged their charges. Shortly after this, at about 1500, *Rowallan Castle* was near-missed, which disabled her engines. A long delay for repairs was considered too dangerous at this point, and Force K returned to Malta empty-handed.

Sunday, 15 February 1942

Vian's force now headed eastwards with the 'empties', but in so doing, passed the stricken *Clan Chattan*, which was sunk to prevent her capture. Meanwhile, Regia Aeronautica aircraft were again out in force. Two patrols from 41° Gruppo were in action. The first, three S.79s strong, was led by Ten Ardito Cristiani, to attack a convoy sailing westbound off Sidi Barrani; two torpedoes were released at 1504 but the result could not be ascertained due to the intervention of eight escort fighters. The gunners of the Italian aircraft claimed a Beaufighter shot down, all three torpedo-bombers returning to base. Two Beaufighter pilots of 252 Squadron claimed an aircraft shot down between them, named as either a Cant.Z.506B or an S.79, but suffered no loss themselves. However, their victim may have been a Sicily-based Cant.Z.506B of 170ª Squadriglia which was lost 35 miles south-south-east of Cape Passero, with the whole crew apart from a lone survivor, who was later rescued by another Cant.Z.506B.

A second patrol of two S.79s, flown by Cap Marino Marini and Ten Saverio Mayer, then attacked the same convoy, both releasing their torpedoes and claiming a destroyer of the Jervis type hit. Marini's bomber, hit by AA and attacked by three fighters identified as P-40s, ditched in the sea. The RAF pilots, all members of 30 Squadron and actually flying Hurricanes, claimed one S.79 *each* during this interception, reporting that one caught fire and crashed into the sea, a second crashed after a large part of one wing had been shot away, and the third went straight into the sea. The crew of the S.79, apart from engineer 1°Av Giuseppe Colucci who disappeared as the aircraft hit the sea, climbed into their dinghy. During the night they were rescued by the German submarine U-331, commanded by Kapitänleutnant Hans-Diedrich von Tiesenhausen, noted for having sunk the battleship HMS *Barham* on 25 November 1941. Cap Marini and his crew returned to Rhodes on 28 February. The extent of the overclaiming on this occasion raises the question of whether the 30 Squadron records had been written incorrectly or whether the three pilots involved had in fact jointly shot down the single aircraft actually lost.

British Claims					
252 Sqn	Flg Off A.D.Frecker/ Sgt Fuller	Beaufighter Ic T4896 'G'	Bf 110 Damaged	50m E Malta	0910-1225
252 Sqn	Flg Off A.D.Frecker/ Sgt Fuller	Beaufighter Ic T4896 'G'	He 111 Damaged	50m E Malta	0910-1225
252 Sqn	Plt Off B.F.Mooney, DFM / Sgt I.J.Phillipp DFM	Beaufighter Ic T4918			
252 Sqn	Plt Off T.J.P.Nisbet/ Sgt L.G.Lewis	Beaufighter Ic T4868 'P'	Cant.Z.506B or S.79	50m E Malta	1215-1545
252 Sqn	Sgt W.J.Smith/ Sgt R.S.Coles	Beaufighter Ic T4888 'F'			
30 Sqn	Sgt G.Bate	Hurricane I	S.79	convoy patrol	1555
30 Sqn	Sgt R.F.Marrack	Hurricane I	S.79	convoy patrol	1555
30 Sqn	Sgt G.Lawrence	Hurricane I	S.79	convoy patrol	1555

German Casualties			
2.(F)/123	Ju 88D-1 WNr 1223 4U+HK MiA NW Alexandria; Uffz Albert Mühlhaupt, Lt Hans Zenker and two KiA		
Italian Claims			
205ª Sq, 41° Gr AS	gunners aboard S.79s	Beaufighter	1515
205ª Sq, 41° Gr AS	gunners aboard Cap Marini's S.79	P-40	1545
Italian Casualties			
205ª Sq, 41° Gr AS	S.79 MM 23859 crash-landed on sea, pilot Cap Marino Marini, copilot Serg Giovanni Angelini and crew (except engineer 1° Av Giuseppe Colucci MiA) rescued by German U-Boat		
205ª Sq, 41° Gr AS	S.79 damaged by fighters, copilot M.llo Alceste Borghi WiA, pilot Ten Saverio Mayer and crew safe		
170ª Sq, 83° Gr RM	Cant.Z.506 MM 45323 lost 35m SSE of Cape Passero, pilot S.Ten Giulio Paccagnella, copilot Serg Camillo Miglioli and crew MiA but one survivor later rescued		

Monday, 16 February 1942

Immediately after their recent successes, next day the pilots of 30 Squadron received the news that they were posted to the Far East. Handing in its Hurricane Is, the unit departed a few days later on the aircraft carrier HMS *Indomitable* for Ceylon, re-equipped with Hurricane IIbs (see *Bloody Shambles, Vol 2* for this unit's further activities).

The eastbound convoy was now under fighter escort as it approached Tobruk. With the previous nightfall and throughout the day these ships were escorted by a Sunderland, three Albacores and two Ansons. With daylight these were joined by a regular fighter escort by pairs of aircraft.

Meanwhile, an Italian naval force had put to sea, ordered to attack Force K as it returned to Malta. The hostile force was spotted by a Malta-based Maryland, but this was then shot down as it returned to the island to report, and it was several hours before the crew could be picked up and de-briefed, by which time it was too late for a daytime strike to be launched. An attack was made in the early hours of 16th by Malta-based Albacores, and subsequently the destroyer *Carabiniere* was sunk by the RN submarine P.36. (For more aspects and details of the operations south of Malta on 15th and 16th, see *Malta: The Spitfire Year, 1942*.)

Wednesday, 18 February 1942

A Cant.Z.1007bis of 261ª Squadriglia flown by Serg Magg Aldo Perazzoli took off from Gadurra at 1310 on a reconnaissance mission over the Eastern Mediterranean. It was attacked by two Beaufighters not far from Alexandria, fire from which damaged the propeller of the central engine. Despite this, the pilot managed to return at 1655, reporting that one attacker had been seen falling in flames as a result of the gunners' defensive fire; 252 Squadron, which was the British unit involved, did not report any casualties, but mis-identified the Italian aircraft.

One of the Boeing Fortress Is of the 220 Squadron detachment attempted to bomb targets in Navarino Bay, but was unable to do so because of bad weather.

British Claims

252 Sqn	Flg Off Frecker/Sgt Shaw	Beaufighter Ic	S.79 Damaged

Italian Claims

261ª Sq, 106°Gr, 47°St BT	gunners of Cant.Z.1007bis '261-7'	Beaufighter	off coast of Egypt	1310-1655

Italian Casualties

261ª Sq, 106°Gr, 47°St BT	Cant.Z.1007bis '261-7' damaged by Beaufighter off coast of Egypt early afternoon, pilot Serg Magg Aldo Perazzoli, observer T.V. Giuseppe Musmeci and crew safe

Friday, 20 February 1942

British Claims

272 Sqn	Plt Off P.C.Cobley/ Sgt G.W.Williams	Beaufighter Ic 'U'	He 111 Damaged	Mersa Matruh patrol	0620-1100

British Casualties

272 Sqn	Beaufighter Ic 'U' damaged in combat with He 111, crash-landed at base 1100; Plt Off P.C.Cobley/Sgt G.W.Williams safe

Saturday-Sunday, 21/22 February 1942

Aware on the 20th that a major Axis convoy was about to depart for Tripoli, plans were made for a major interception of this. In view of Malta's current situation, the strengthened 201 Group was to play the main role on this occasion, operating in co-ordination with the island's remaining forces.

Available for this important operation were the following aircraft:

12 Blenheims	(18 and 55 Squadrons)	at Bu Amud
7 Blenheims	(14 Squadron)	at Gambut
3 torpedo-Wellingtons	(38 Squadron)	at Gambut
1 ASV Wellington	(221 Squadron)	at Gambut
6 Beauforts	(39 Squadron)	at LG.05
2 Fortresses	(220 Squadron)	at LG.05
4 Marylands 12 Blenheims	(203 Squadron)	at LG.09
1 Liberator	(108 Squadron)	at LG.09
25 Wellingtons	(205 Group)	at LG.09
6 Wellingtons	(37 Squadron)	despatched to Malta

The first sighting of the convoy, which was sailing in two groups about 85 miles apart, was made at 2230 during the night of 21/22 February by a Malta-based ASV Wellington which reported the vessels as being respectively 175 and 250 nautical miles from Malta and more than 350 miles from Bu Amud. It had been intended that the 108 Squadron Liberator would shadow the vessels throughout the day. However, it crashed on take-off and was destroyed – the first of an almost unending series of mishaps which were to plague the group's operations throughout the action.

The next sighting occurred at 0725 when the crew of a 203 Squadron Maryland reported eight merchant ships, two battleships, five cruisers, 15 destroyers and an escort of Bf 109s. At this stage the convoy was still some 220 miles from Malta and 330 from Bu Amud. It was to be shadowed throughout most of the day by a Blenheim and two Marylands, again from 203 Squadron. The persistence and accuracy of their reporting in the face of hostile fighter escorts was subsequently considered to be the most outstanding positive feature of the operation – or perhaps its sole redeeming feature.

On receipt of the first ASV Wellington's sighting, five of Malta's resident Albacores took off, but were recalled when it became clear that there had been a 100-mile error in the reckoning of the search aircraft's crew. 220 Squadron's two Fortress Is had taken off at 0700 on a rare operation for these aircraft, briefed both to attack and shadow. Unfortunately, owing to a navigational error, one of these aircraft failed to find the convoy. However, the other did so, reporting that it now appeared to include six merchant vessels of 8-12,000 tons displacement each, one battleship of the Littorio Class, two 8in gun cruisers, four 6in gun cruisers and 18 destroyers. The crew then released seven 500lb SAP bombs on the ships below, but were unable to observe the results due to intense Flak and a reported attack by two Bf 109s. These were evaded, and the aircraft returned safely to base. However, 203 Squadron recorded that the Fortress had been attacked by a Bf 110 during the run-up to bomb. This does, however, seem to resolve a long-standing research query. In *Malta: The Spitfire Year, 1942* it was recorded that Oblt Peter Habicht of 8./ZG 26 had attacked an aircraft which he identified as a 'Boeing' at 1442, which he claimed to have shot down. It was originally thought that his claim might have been made against a delivery Wellington. Despite the fact that the Fortress crew identified their assailants as Bf 109s, it now seems very likely that it was against this aircraft that Habicht's unique claim was made. Notably, 201 Group records did indeed identify the attacker as a Bf 110.

Twenty minutes behind the Fortresses, five Beauforts took off from the same airfield, intending to attack simultaneously with the high altitude aircraft. These torpedo-bombers were not refuelled at Bu Amud as had originally been planned, and thereby reached the limit of their range without seeing anything. Their crews were then obliged to return at the absolute limit of their fuel capacity.

There was then a considerable delay until Blenheims of 18 and 55 Squadrons began launching in two formations. The first of these, comprising four aircraft only because a fifth failed to start, took off at 1220, but one more then returned early with engine trouble. Again, nothing was found, the leader then cutting short the search when he considered the limit of endurance had been reached. One of this remaining trio then force-landed in the sea.

The second formation of six got off at 1335, but the leader's aircraft almost at once suffered engine trouble. After a further 25 minutes the deputy leader's W/T failed, and he led the formation back to base. Seven more Blenheims from 14 Squadron were then sent off at 1420, but no less than four of these aircraft then turned back with engine troubles. The remaining three reached the estimated position of the Axis shipping, but again found nothing. Since the first sighting, 29 aircraft had been sent out to attack, but only one of these had actually bombed the target.

British Claims

238 Sqn	Sgt G.H.Borham	Hurricane I 'N'	Ju 88	convoy patrol	1330-1530
238 Sqn	Sgt G.H.Borham	Hurricane I 'N'	Ju 88 Probable	convoy patrol	1330-1530
238 Sqn	Sgt G.H.Borham	Hurricane I 'N'	Ju 88 Damaged	convoy patrol	1330-1530

Sunday-Monday, 22/23 February 1942

With nightfall, attacks by 205 Group were planned. These were to be directed to their target by the ASV Wellington at Gambut, but this became unserviceable shortly before it was due to take off. Three more such aircraft had been available on Malta, but two of these had been destroyed or badly damaged during bombing raids, leaving only one available for this role. It took off at 2200, but before anything could be achieved, it also suffered engine trouble and had to return. Without guidance or illumination, the whole Wellington striking force failed to locate the convoy apart from one aircraft which had taken off late. The crew of this bomber did spot the convoy and bombed, but without observed results.

Meanwhile the ASV aircraft was swiftly repaired, again taking off at 2235. It found the convoy three hours later, about 77 miles east of Homs. Due to the wind direction, the distance from Malta and the time of the sighting, a strike by Swordfish and Albacores had to be cancelled and no further action could be taken; the convoy reached its destination unscathed. Even the benefit of Ultra intercepts had been of little help on this occasion – it was not one of the air forces' greatest days.

British Casualties

108 Sqn	Liberator II AL574 'O' began to take off 0230 to undertake reconnaissance; crashed and damaged beyond repair; Plt Off F.H.McDonald and crew safe
55 Sqn	Blenheim IV Z9657 'C' took off 1205 part of formation of six; 1530 engine fire and ditched in sea; Flt Sgt I.W.Jones and two seen to get into dinghy, but not picked up
148 Sqn	Wellington II Z8360 to attack convoy; port engine seized and crash-landed in enemy territory; Sgt R.Hamilton

Tuesday, 24 February 1942

A Cant.Z.1007bis of 261ª Squadriglia, again flown by Serg Magg Aldo Perazzoli, took off from Gadurra at 0655 on a reconnaissance sortie to Alexandria. It was attacked by a reported five Hurricanes over the target. The aircraft suffered considerable damage on this occasion, two crew members being wounded;

the gunners claimed one Hurricane probably hit. Perazzoli returned at 1145, crash-landing his aircraft. Next day Cap Nicola Falco took command of 262ª Squadriglia, 107° Gruppo BT.

British Claims

213 Sqn	Plt Off E.K.Ismay	Hurricane II BE569	Cant.Z.1007 Damaged	N Alexandria Bar	0930
213 Sqn	Flt Sgt R.J.Wallace	Hurricane I Z2406			

British Casualties

38 Sqn	Wellington Ic Z9108 'R' hit by Flak when minelaying off Benghazi; crew ordered to bale out in bad weather; Plt Off E.W.Knowles and two KiA, three picked up safely by army

Italian Claims

261ª Sq, 106°Gr, 47°St	BT gunners aboard Cant.Z.1007bis MM 23753 '261-8'	Hurricane Probable	mid-morning

Italian Casualties

261ª Sq, 106°Gr, 47°St BT	Cant.Z.1007bis MM 23753 '261-8' damaged by Hurricanes crash-landed 1134, pilot Serg Magg Aldo Perazzoli, copilot Serg Magg Lauro Corallini safe, two WiA

Friday, 27 February 1942

During an Axis bombing raid on Tobruk, the SS *Southern Sea* and *Harboe Jansen* were badly damaged by bombs.

British Casualties

221 Sqn	Wellington NN476 destroyed in air raid on Shandur

Saturday, 28 February 1942

British Claims

805 Sqn	Lt M.F.Fell	Martlet III	Ju 88	N Ras Abu Lehman
805 Sqn	Midspm D.G.Jenkins	Martlet III		

British Casualties

2 PRU	Hurricane MiA; Plt Off R.H.Jacobs

German Casualties

3./LG 1	Ju 88A-4 WNr 8613 L1+NL shot down in Sidi Barrani area; Oblt Adolf Kottmeier and three KiA

Monday-Tuesday, 2/3 March 1942

During the night 89 Squadron gained the first AI successes over the Alexandria area.

When first established in Egypt, 89 Squadron's night fighter Beaufighter Ics carried the squadron code letters WP and individual letter D. These did not last long, aircraft subsequently carrying just the single individual letter.

British Claims

89 Sqn	Sqn Ldr D.S.Pain	Beaufighter If X7671	He 111	crashed Magrun	0410
89 Sqn	Flg Off R.C.Fumerton	Beaufighter If X7635	He 111	Alexandria	0510

British Casualties

89 Sqn	Beaufighter If X7635 hit by return fire; Flg Off R.C.Fumerton FTR, slightly WiA

German Casualties

4./KG 26	He 111H-6 WNr 4205 1H+CM combat with Beaufighter El Kabrit, crash-landed nr Alexandria; Lt Edgar Lersch & three PoW
4./KG 26	He 111H-6 WNr 4199 1H+LM combat with Beaufighter, crash-landed nr Alexandria; Fw Roman Liebsch & two KiA, one PoW

Saturday, 7 March 1942

A detachment of four Beaufighter If night fighters was sent from Egypt to Malta to enhance the island's night defence. Over the coming weeks this detachment was to achieve very considerable success. It arrived on the same day as the first Spitfires to operate in the fighter role outside the United Kingdom, also flew in, having taken off from the aircraft carrier HMS *Eagle*. (See *Malta: The Spitfire Year, 1942* for all further details of the operations of the Malta detachment.)

In Tobruk harbour the SS *Cervia* was dive-bombed and set on fire.

Sunday, 8 March 1942

British Casualties

272 Sqn	Beaufighter ditched near convoy after engine failure; Flg Off P.Cobley/Sgt G.W.Williams and navigator picked up safely 1225

Monday, 9 March 1942

Malta Command were aware from Ultra intercepts that another Axis convoy (*Nino Bixio*, *Reginaldo Giuliani*, *Gino Allegri* and *Monreale*) was heading for North Africa. A Maryland of 69 Squadron was sent out, the crew of this spotting a convoy of four merchant ships (*Giulio Giordani*, *Ravello*, *Lerici* and *Unione*), three destroyers and three torpedo boats about 200 miles south-east of Malta. The pilot was not to know, of course, that this was not the correct convoy for which he had been sent out to search for. This one was heading north, but the one hopefully to be intercepted was going in the opposite direction. It also included four merchant vessels, escorted by five destroyers and two torpedo boats. Its importance is indicated by the fact that it enjoyed a covering force of warships which included three cruisers and five more destroyers.

This latter, more important convoy was sighted a little later by a 203 Squadron Maryland and a strike force of eight torpedo-carrying Beauforts of 39 Squadron was ordered off from Bu Amud, together with one of 220 Squadron's Fortress Is. A promised escort of Beaufighters failed to appear at the rendezvous point, and the Beaufort formation carried on alone. At 1640 this force, led by Flt Lt C.S.Taylor in L8923, intercepted the wrong convoy, 170 miles north-east of Tripoli, finding it under escort by three Ju 88s and at least one Bf 110.

One torpedo was launched at the largest merchant ship, the rest at the escorting warships, the Beauforts then making good their escape, undamaged by the Flak that was encountered.. The German fighters then gave chase, but Sgt Frank White, gunner in Flg Off Derek Bee's W6506, claimed one Ju 88 shot down, and Sgt Holland in Flg Off Tony Leaning's L9876 got a "good burst" at the Bf 110 and claimed damage. One Beaufort was slightly damaged in return. Hits were claimed on one merchant ship, one cruiser and one destroyer, the latter believed to have been sunk. In fact no damage had been inflicted on any of these vessels, and it was later thought that what the crews had seen were the explosions of the torpedoes at the end of their runs. It was subsequently considered that it was more likely to have been faulty Duplex firing pistols which probably saved many Axis vessels from destruction during the year.

More attacks were launched at night by Malta-based aircraft (see *Malta: The Spitfire Year, 1942* for additional details).

During the afternoon a Wellington of 38 Squadron, loaded with two torpedoes, took off to fly to Bu Amud from where it was to operate against the convoy. South-west of Sidi Barrani it was intercepted by a pair of Bf 109s of I./JG 27, and was shot down; the pilot undertook a crash-landing during which two members of the crew were killed. The German pilots then shot-up the downed Wellington but the survivors scrambled clear just in time to see their attackers intercept three Albacores of 826 Squadron heading for the same airfield. One of these was shot down, Sub Lt Nathan and his crew all suffering serious wounds, with a second extensively damaged (see also in Chapter Eleven).

British Claims			
39 Sqn	Flg Off Bee	Beaufort I	Ju 88
39 Sqn	Gunner Sgt Holland in Beaufort L9876 flown by Flg Off A.Leaning		Bf 110 Damaged

British Casualties	
39 Sqn	Beaufort slt damaged in combat
38 Sqn	Wellington Ic Z9099 'C' shot down, crash-landed; Wg Cdr J.H.Chaplin, DFC, and three walked to Allied territory; two KiA
826 Sqn	Albacore T9149 '4B' shot down in flames 20m S Sollum; Sub Lt R.S.Nathan and two seriously WiA
826 Sqn	Albacore badly damaged by Bf 109s near Bu Amud airfield

German Claims				
I./JG 27	Gefr Herbert Romeikat	Wellington	SW Sidi Barrani	1635
I./JG 27	Lt Friedrich Körner	Albacore	SW Sidi Barrani	1650

Tuesday, 10 March 1942

During a 0935 Freie Jagd, two Bf 109s of I./JG 27 in the Sidi Barrani area, encountered a Beaufort – which the pilots mis-identified as a Boston – and this was shot down by Oblt Keller (see more details in Chapter One).

Following the reports of the previous day's attack, Admiral Cunningham decided that a search should be made of the area, sending out the 15th Cruiser Squadron and all available destroyers from Alexandria early in the day. This operation would also allow the cruiser *Cleopatra*, which had arrived at Malta some days earlier, to join the force and accompany it back to Alexandria.

British Casualties	
39 Sqn	Beaufort N1182 shot down by Bf 109s between Bu Amud and Sidi Barrani; Sgt Elliot and two KiA

German claims				
I./JG 27	Oblt Fritz Keller	Boston	E Sidi Barrani	0935
2./LG 1	Oblt Iro Ilk and crew	Blenheim	N Derna	
I./LG 1	unstated	Blenheim	N Derna	

Wednesday, 11 March 1942

Cleopatra and one destroyer met the 15th Cruiser Squadron next morning, the whole force then heading east for Alexandria. Beaufighters soon arrived at maximum range to give cover. Two S.79s of 41° Gruppo flown by Ten Giorgio Tourn and S.Ten Saverio Mayer took off from Rhodes to attack the British naval formation sighted by German aircraft south of Crete while on its way to Alexandria. Torpedoes were released at 1603 and a hit on a cruiser was claimed. Ten Tourn's aircraft was badly damaged by AA.

A second patrol of two S.79s, led by 41° Gruppo commanding officer, T.Col Ettore Muti, with S.Ten Dorando Cionni as wingman, attacked the convoy at 1815, claiming hits on two cruisers. In fact no damage was suffered during these and other attacks. The escorting Beaufighters of 252 Squadron enjoyed considerable success, claiming six intruding bombers shot down – it appears that in fact they actually brought down no more than one, although in doing so two of the fighters were lost.

However, at 2000 the flagship *Naiad* was hit by a torpedo from U-565 and sank an hour later with the loss of 82 of her crew. Rear Admiral Vian moved his flag temporarily to *Dido*, although after arrival back at base he changed this to the newly-arrived *Cleopatra*.

British Claims					
252 Sqn	Flg Off A.D.Frecker/ Sgt Fuller	Beaufighter Ic T4896 'G'	2 He 111s	escort 15th Cruiser Sqn	1000-1455
252 Sqn	Plt Off H.H.K.Gunnis/ Sgt E.A.Waller	Beaufighter Ic T4880	Ju 88	escort 15th Cruiser Sqn	1115-1445
252 Sqn	Plt Off H.H.K.Gunnis/ Sgt E.A.Waller	Beaufighter Ic T4880	2 He 111s	escort 15th Cruiser Sqn	1115-1445
252 Sqn	Plt Off A.I.Smith/ Sgt J.P.Diaper .	Beaufighter Ic T4886	Ju 88	escort 15th Cruiser Sqn	1200-1530

British Casualties

252 Sqn	Beaufighter T4935 shot down by Bf 110; Plt Off B.F.Mooney, DFC, and Sgt J.Philipp DFM rescued by Seenot within 15 minutes
272 Sqn	Beaufighter while on escort flew into sea, tail broke off, and aircraft crashed; Sgt J.S.Forder/Plt Off R.H.Dunn KiFA

German Casualties

4./KG 26	He 111H-6 WNr 4922 1H+GN shot down into sea by Beaufighters; Fw Peter Merten and three MiA

Italian Casualties

205ª Sq, 41°Gr AS	S.79 damaged by AA, pilot Ten Giorgio Tourn and crew safe

Thursday, 12 March 1942

British Claims

252 Sqn	Plt Off H.H.K.Gunnis	Beaufighter Ic T4896 'G'	Ju 52/3m	55m from Derna	0920
252 Sqn	Plt Off H.H.K.Gunnis	Beaufighter Ic T4896 'G'	Ju 52/3m Damaged	55m from Derna	0920
238 Sqn	Sgt R.F.Southern	Hurricane I 'J'	Ju 88 Damaged	convoy patrol	1715-1845

Friday, 13 March 1942

Two S.79s torpedo-bombers of 41° Gruppo took off at 1125 to attack the British convoy off Mersa Matruh; however, the intervention of two Hurricanes and two Beaufighters prevented the crews from releasing their torpedoes.

201 Group's squadrons were extremely active at this time, providing regular daily reconnaissance flights on behalf of the navy, and also undertaking much patrol work, both in the anti-submarine and fighter escort roles. Raids were also organised and undertaken, usually in conjunction with the bombers of 205 Group, on the harbours at Benghazi, Piraeus and Patras. The Malta units, insofar as they were able to at this time, sought to attack Palermo, Tripoli, Pantelleria and Messina.

Changes were afoot, for by this time some five of 38 Squadron's Wellingtons had been modified for torpedo dropping, and five crews trained for this function. Although it was realised that there would be considerable benefit in being able to attach one of 221 Squadron's ASV Wellingtons to the unit on a permanent basis, current commitments did not allow this, although such aircraft would act in co-operation with the squadron whenever possible. Training in this role, and in shadowing, flare dropping and night formation flying was also being provided to Fleet Air Arm crews at this time.

The group was temporarily weakened on 14 March when 805 Squadron was withdrawn for refitting; ten days later 13 (Hellenic) Squadron was stood down to replace its Ansons with Blenheim IVs. Both units would soon become operational again.

British Claims

272 Sqn	Flg Off D.H.Hammond/ Sgt J.Bryson	Beaufighter Ic 'Z'	S.79 Damaged	over convoy	1322

Sunday, 15 March 1942

Planning was now well-advanced on another attempt to fight a supply convoy through to Malta. In an effort to divert Axis attention elsewhere, a bombardment of Rhodes was now put in hand. Very early on 15 March 15th Cruiser Squadron with *Dido*, *Euryalus* and six destroyers departed for this target as Operation MF8. For this action fighter cover was provided by Beaufighters of 252 Squadron, target illumination by Albacores of 821 Squadron and accompanying diversionary bombing by 205 Group.

Between 0020-0135 seven Wellingtons bombed Calato as three more raided and strafed the harbour there, four others doing the same at Maritza. Nine Blenheims of 14 Squadron tried to raid Candia, but had difficulty in finding the target in poor visibility.At 0230, while these attacks were underway, the naval guns opened fire, aiming at shipping, seaplanes and harbour installations, MT repair shops, oil storage tanks, aircraft hangars and the island's largest flour mill at Alliotti. Flares were dropped by the Albacores, but the illumination was rendered poor by low cloud, which also made observation of the fall of the shells difficult. Nonetheless, the cruisers each fired 150 rounds and the destroyers 100 each.

Operating from Nicosia, the detachment of ten Beaufighters had little to do as no attacks were directed at the British forces, all of which returned safely to Egypt next day. However, one crew reported intercepting and damaging what the pilot identified as a Bf 110 in Italian markings. This was actually a Rhodes-based Cant.Z.1007bis of 262ª Squadriglia flown by Cap Nicolò Falco, which had been sent out to reconnoitre the area between Cyprus and the Turkish coast. He sighted the British naval vessels at 0740, correctly reporting their composition and the fact that they had a fighter escort. One of these, again correctly identified as a Beaufighter, attacked, but Falco was able to evade this, his gunners claiming to have got some hits on their assailant in return; the aircraft landed safely at 0850.

British Claims				
252 Sqn	Sgt A.G.Cutten/Sgt F.Burrow	Beaufighter Ic T4840 'P'	Bf 110 Damaged	escort 15th Cruiser Sqn 0735
British Casualties				
221 Sqn	Wellington VIII one of three on shipping search FTR; Flt Sgt Abbot and crew MiA			
Italian Claims				
262a Sq, 107°Gr, 47°St	gunners in Cap Nicolò Falco Cant.Z.1007bis		Beaufighter damaged	

Tuesday, 17 March 1942

Three Marylands of 203 Squadron were out on reconnaissance when the crew of one of these spotted and reported a convoy comprised of two merchant vessels, a cruiser and seven destroyers. Against a target of such obvious importance, nine Beauforts were at once despatched, but failed to find it. One of 203 Squadron's remaining Blenheims was also out, Flt Lt Green in 'C' bombing and strafing a submarine.

British Casualties	
39 Sqn	Beaufort I W6495 crashed in force-landing at Fort Maddalena; out of fuel
272 Sqn	Beaufighter X8132 missing from escorting strike

Wednesday, 18 March 1942

During the early hours an unidentified British aircraft was reported shot down by AA over Tagiura, seen crashing into the sea. This aircraft has not been identified.

Two Cant.Z.1007bis of 47° Stormo took off from Maritza at 0640-0650 on reconnaissance missions over the Eastern Mediterranean and returned safely at 1210-1245. S.Ten Marcello Trona of 260ª Squadriglia who was flying the second aircraft, reported having sighted a British convoy sailing not far from Alexandria on a south-westerly course at 1010. A third Cant.Z.1007bis flown by S.Ten Pierluigi Lauro took off at 1330, but radio contact was lost at 1400 and the aircraft was reported as missing.

Italian Casualties	
263ª Sq, 107°Gr, 47°St BT	Cant.Z.1007bis MM 23730 failed to return, pilot S.Ten Pierluigi Lauro, copilot Ten Ottone Alenzi and four MiA

Thursday, 19 March 1942

A Beaufort IIa in transit from the UK to England was attacked and damaged by two Bf 110s.The pilot crash-landed the damaged aircraft at Hal Far, Malta, but as there were no spares available on the island for the Twin-Wasp engines of this version of the aircraft, it was not repaired.

British Casualties	
22 Sqn	Beaufort IIa AW339 damaged by Bf 110s and crash-landed at Hal Far; Plt Off J.C.White and crew safe

Friday, 20 March 1942

At 1420 a pair of S.79s of 41° Gruppo AS, flown by Cap Ettore Sondalini of 205ª Squadriglia and S.Ten Normanno White of 204ª Squadriglia (MM 24305), released two torpedoes and reportedly sunk a British warship of about 2,500 tons sailing off Tobruk. This was the first strike against Convoy MW10 which had sailed early in the day from Alexandria, taking urgently-needed supplies to Malta. During the next several days there was considerable naval and air-sea action, involving 132 Italian torpedo-carrying aircraft and 124 Luftwaffe bombers as well as major fleet activity. The greater part of the Axis air effort was made by units based in Sicily and southern Italy, although the Regia Aeronautica units based on Rhodes played an important part. Attacks by night on the bases in Crete were made by 205 Group (see Chapter Eleven), but for 201 Group there was little involvement. The full story of MW10 may be found in *Malta: The Spitfire Year, 1942*, pages 138-144, although some additional details of the activities of the Italian Rhodes-based units are included here.

Sunday, 22 March 1942

At 0630 five S.79s of 279ª Squadriglia AS took off to attack convoy MW10 which had sailed from Alexandria on 20 March. These torpedo-bombers were flown by Cap Giulio Marini, Ten Andrea Dell'Anna, S.Ten Alfredo Pulzetti, S.Ten Giuseppe Coci and Ten Gugliemo Ranieri. At 0935, at a position 34°10-19°10 (about half way between Benghazi and Malta) four S.79s intercepted the enemy ships sailing westward and released their torpedoes. Marini, Dell'Anna and Pulzetti aimed at a cruiser, which they reported was hit, while Coci claimed a hit on a destroyer. No damage was actually inflicted on the warships attacked.

Dell'Anna's S.79 was severely damaged by AA. Ranieri's S.79, which took off 20 minutes later due to engine trouble, did not reach the formation and failed to return. Called to the spot by the 279ª Squadriglia crews, four S.79s of 284ª Squadriglia AS, flown by Cap Oscar Pegna, M.llo Urbano Gentilini, Ten Orfeo Fiumani and S.Ten Giorgio Concato, reached the same convoy at 1107 and attacked. The pilots aimed at different targets and claimed, rather optimistically, direct hits on two cruisers and a freighter. Both Fiumani's and Concato's aircraft limped back to base, hit by AA. Torpedo-bombers from Sicily also took part in this long fight against the British convoy. Twelve S.79s of 132° Gruppo AS (278ª and 281ª Squadriglie) attacked and claimed some unconfirmed hits on a cruiser and a steamer. Three S.79s, flown by Ten Emilio Iuzzolino, S.Ten Giovanni Scalia and S.Ten Gaetano Marletta, failed to return, likely hit by ships' AA barrage.

Italian Casualties

279ª Sq, 131° Gr AS	S.79 MM 24094 failed to return, Ten Guglielmo Ranieri, copilot Serg Omero Meco and four MiA
279ª Sq, 131° Gr AS	S.79 severely damaged by AA, pilot Ten Andrea Dell'Anna and crew safe
284ª Sq, 131° Gr AS	2 S.79s severely damaged by AA, pilots Ten Orfeo Fiumani, Ten Giorgio Concato and crew safe
278ª Sq, 132° Gr AS	S.79 MM 24173 flew into a hill, pilot Ten Emilio Iuzzolino, copilot Serg Gualtiero Calanca and three KiA
278ª Sq, 132° Gr AS	S.79 MM 24167 force-landed on sea, crew climbed on dinghy that sunk, pilot S.Ten Gaetano Marletta, copilot M.llo Albino Scalabrin and two KiA, two rescued
278ª Sq, 132° Gr AS	S.79 MM 24308, failed to return, pilot S.Ten Giovanni Scalia, copilot Serg Magg Sergio Verderi and three MiA

An S.79 torpedo-bomber at Gadurra airfield (Rhodes).

Monday, 23 March 1942

201 Group's two Beaufighter squadrons were both operating from Gambut during this period, six of 272 Squadron's aircraft being despatched from Gambut to provide air cover for the convoy, which they had been unable to locate. The formation then spotted bombers which were under attack by Malta Spitfires, which were in hot pursuit. Flg Off Derek Hammond at once ordered Flt Lt G.L.Campbell's section to prevent their escape to the west. The trio of Beaufighters quickly caught up with two Ju 88s of 3./KGr 806 just after a third had fallen to the Spitfires.

Campbell attacked in a dive but missed his intended target which took violent evasive action. Behind him came Sgt George Tuckwell who got a clear shot at the bomber, two bursts hitting the port wing which forced the pilot to change direction back towards Malta. Tuckwell fired again and the Junkers exploded into a mass of orange flames, burning debris floating into the sea. The other bomber managed to escape in cloud; two bombers and their crews were lost in this engagement, there being no survivors from either aircraft.

The Gruppenkommandeur of I./LG 1, Maj Joachim Helbig (right) checks the readiness of Ju 88A-4 L1+BB before getting into the aircraft.

Even as these actions were taking place just off the coast, other air fights were ensuing over Rear Admiral Vian's covering force further to the east, as this withdrew back towards Alexandria. As the ships came within patrol range of Gambut, Beaufighters of the other squadron – 252 – were out to give cover, these engaging in several interceptions, mainly of 'shadowers'. On the first occasion Sgt Machin made two astern attacks on an He 111 which dived away steeply, trailing black smoke from its port engine. A little later Plt Off Ian Maclean and Sgt Abdul Ydlibi pursued another Heinkel almost to Crete, claiming to have inflicted severe damage. A Ju 88 was also engaged by Sgt Cripps who claimed to have damaged this too before it escaped into cloud. Sgt Tom Shaw's aircraft was attacked by a Bf 109 from JG 27 and suffered damage to the hydraulic system which caused Shaw to crash-land the aircraft on return to Gambut. 201 Group's activities, although not involving many such actions, met with the firm approval of the commander-in-chief, Mediterranean, who signalled "We are most grateful for the prodigious efforts put out by 201 Group which played such a large part in ensuring safety of convoy and escort under most difficult conditions."

Finally, in the late afternoon, as the warships neared their base, a patrol of three S.79s of 41° Gruppo Autonomo AS (one of 204ª Squadriglia and two of 205ª) led by T.Col Ettore Muti, sighted the vessels, awaited a favourable light, and at 1810, attacked. Although the crews believed that all torpedoes had run true, no hits were actually gained, though AA fire damaged the leader's aircraft. T.Col Muti and S.Ten Saverio Mayer each claimed to have hit a cruiser, and S.Ten Dorando Cionni probably a destroyer.

British Claims

252 Sqn	Plt Off I.Maclean/ Sgt E.V.B.Strange	Beaufighter Ic T4883	He 111 Damaged	Crete	1055-1420
252 Sqn	Sgt A.Ydlibi/Sgt E.W.Spiller	Beaufighter Ic T4839			
252 Sqn	Sgt A.G.G.Machin/ Sgt C.B.A.Nichols	Beaufighter Ic T4877 'R'	He 111 Damaged	escort 15th Cruiser Sqn	1410-1820

British Casualties

252 Sqn	Beaufighter T4866 damaged by Bf 109; Sgt T.G.Shaw/Sgt Snape crash-landed, both safe

German Casualties

3./KGr 806	Ju 88A-4 WNr 1647 M7+DL missing from shipping reconnaissance off Malta; Lt Hermann Damaske and three MiA
3./KGr 806	Ju 88A-4 WNr 1516 M7+GL missing from shipping reconnaissance off Malta; Fw Herbert Augustin and three MiA

(Both these aircraft appear in Luftwaffe records as presumed shot down and crashed into the sea off Malta; although six Ju 88s were lost in such circumstances on this date, these two accord closely with the claims made by 272 Squadron and Malta-based Spitfires)

Tuesday, 24 March 1942

With dawn Admiral Vian's escort force was still struggling to reach Alexandria when at 0755 a pair of S.79s of 41° Gruppo, one of 204ª Squadriglia (MM 24305) flown by S.Ten Antonio Monterumici and one of 205ª Squadriglia (MM 24176) flown by Ten Giorgio Tourn, sighted the warships which the Italian crews reported were under escort by a Sunderland and three fighters. Evading these, they carried out an attack without material result. It is probable that Ten Tourn's aircraft was hit by AA fire, for it force-landed in the sea during the return flight, the crew being seen to get into their life raft by those in S.Ten Monterumici's aircraft, which circled overhead for a time. Three more aircraft were sent out from Gadurra to relieve Monterumici, but the rescue service was unable to find any trace of the missing crew.

Italian Casualties

205ª Sq, 41°Gr Aut AS	S.79 MM 24176 ditched 34°55'-28°50', pilot Ten Giorgio Tourn, copilot Serg Magg Luciano Leoni and crew MiA

Friday, 27 March 1942

Two Sunderlands of 230 Squadron on anti-submarine patrol, each attacked what was taken to be the same submarine north of Bardia. The first flyingboat dropped two 250lb bombs and two depth charges without observed results. The second later dropped eight 250lb bombs, claiming to have achieved six direct hits, and this vessel was claimed destroyed. No Axis submarine was recorded as lost on this date, however.

Sunday, 29 March 1942

Two Hurricanes of 1 SAAF Squadron flying a convoy escort patrol from LG.13, intercepted and attacked an He 111, which Plt Off Galyer claimed to have shot down. Two Cant.Z.1007bis of 47° Stormo, one from 260ª Squadriglia flown by Ten Carlo Perelli-Cippo and one of 263ª Squadriglia flown by Cap Alberto Insom, left Rhodes at 0130 on a leaflet dropping mission to Alexandria. Over the target Perelli-Cippo's aircraft was damaged by AA fire but managed to return.

British Claims

1 SAAF Sqn	Plt Off J.H.Galyer	Hurricane II	He 111	60m ENE Bagush	1100

Italian Casualties

260ª Sq, 106°Gr, 47°St BT	Cant.Z.1007bis damaged by AA over Alexandria 0320, pilot Ten Carlo Perelli-Cippo and crew safe

Monday, 30 March 1942

British Casualties

272 Sqn	Beaufighter Ic 'R' damaged by MC.202 over Gulf of Sirte; Sgt K.A.Graham/Sgt Matin safe

Tuesday, 31 March 1942

At dusk two S.79s of 41° Gruppo, flown by T.Col Ettore Muti with S.Ten Dorando Cionni, released their torpedoes at a steamer sailing off El Daba; both claimed hits on the target. In *Malta: The Spitfire Year, 1942*, it was recorded that a Mosquito (W4063) was crash-landed on the island after being attacked by Bf 109s, and a Hudson (V9025) crash-landed at Luqa, the crew being killed. A claim was submitted by Obfw Rudolf Ehrenberger of 6./JG 53 for an aircraft identified as a Hampden. It seems possible that this related to the Hudson which had a somewhat closer resemblance to such an aircraft than did the Mosquito.

Wednesday, 1 April 1942

The crew of a Swordfish of 815 Squadron on a night patrol spotted a submarine on the surface. Two depth charges were dropped, exploding under the stern, following which four machine-gun attacks were made.

British Casualties	
OADU	Hudson III V9026 crashed in the desert

Thursday, 2 April 1942

At 0910 a Sunderland was attacked north of Alexandria by a Cant.Z.1007bis of 262ª Squadriglia flown by Cap Nicolò Falco, without observed results.

Saturday, 4 April 1942

By night Wellingtons of 38 Squadron carried out a torpedo attack on Axis shipping off Salamis, one of the bombers failing to return.

British Casualties	
38 Sqn	Wellington Ic DV419 'J' FTR from Salamis area; Plt Off R.Langley and four KiA

Sunday, 5 April 1942

In the early morning at 0455 five Beaufighters of 252 Squadron undertook a strike on shipping in the Benghazi area. HQ, Western Desert, then sent out a Beaufighter and a Maryland to try and destroy a four-engined aircraft reported to be present at Gialo. The crew of the Maryland returned to report that the Beaufighter had been shot down by Flak and had force-landed after destroying a twin-engined twin-finned unidentified aircraft.

Later, as night fell, two Wellingtons of 38 Squadron set off at 2106 to make a torpedo attack on shipping in the Athens area. One aircraft failed to return, the crew of the other reporting having experienced much Flak and many searchlights in the Piraeus area.

The day also saw the replacement of Grp Capt A.T.Cole, MC, DFC, in command of Advanced 201 Group HQ by Grp Capt A.P.Revington, OBE.

British Claims			
272 Sqn	unstated	Beaufighter Ic (believed to be T4839)	t/e u/i e/a destroyed on ground

British Casualties	
272 Sqn	Beaufighter Ic (believed to be T4839) FTR from attack on Gialo airfield; Flg Off Gee/Sgt Gill MiA
38 Sqn	Wellington FTR from Athens area; Plt Off R.Langley and crew MiA
German Casualties	
KGrzbV 400	Ju52/3m WNr 5809 destroyed on ground at Gialo

Monday, 6 April 1942

At 0600 two S.79 torpedo-bombers of 205ª Squadriglia, 41° Gruppo AS, took off from Rhodes on an armed reconnaissance mission to the Haifa-Port Said area. At 0820 the S.79 '205-3' flown by Ten Saverio Mayer force-landed in the sea due to engine trouble when ten miles north of Port Said. The crew of '205-5', flown by Cap Ettore Sondalini, saw Mayer's crew climbing safely into their dinghy. All five aboard were later picked up and taken PoW.

During the afternoon the Schwarme of Bf 109s from III./JG 27 on detachment at Crete, intercepted a Beaufighter of 2 PRU and shot this down.

British Casualties	
2 PRU	Beaufighter I T4705 shot down over Crete by Bf 109; Flt Lt D.H.V.Smith KiA, LAC Fisher MiA

German Claims				
7./JG 27	Lt Wilhelm Scheiter	Beaufighter	N Crete	1540

Italian Casualties	
205ª Sq, 41°Gr Aut AS	S.79 '205-3' ditched near coast of Egypt, pilot S.Ten Saverio Mayer, copilot Serg Magg Ugo Martini and crew PoW

Tuesday, 7 April 1942

At 0145 three Cant.Z.1007bis of 106° Gruppo led by Gruppo commander, Magg Alessandro Bavassano, left Rhodes on a night bombing mission to Alexandria. At 0330 they released twelve 160kg bombs, reporting having hit some harbour facilities.

A line of Cant.Z.1007bis of 263ª Squadriglia, 107° Gruppo, 47° Stormo BT at Gadurra. The undersurfaces of these bombers have been overpainted black for night operations over Egypt.

Another Cant from 263ª Squadriglia flown by S.Ten Carlo Tancioni took off at 0720 from Maritza on a reconnaissance sortie over the Eastern Mediterranean, from the Nile Delta to the Gulf of Antalya, but failed to return. Ten Eugenio Giordano took off in the lone 263ª Squadriglia aircraft which was still serviceable at this time, to search for the missing aircraft, but without result. It appears that it was a victim of AA fire.

British Claims	
AA	Cant Z.1007bis shot down into sea N Alexandria
British Casualties	
38 Sqn	Wellington Ic AD604 'U' after shipping strike on Benghazi harbour, engine caught fire in cloud and crashed nr Mersa Matruh; Flt Sgt T.A.Holdsworth and two KiA, three injured
Italian Casualties	
263ª Sq, 107°Gr, 47°St BT	Cant.Z.1007bis MM 23290 from Rhodes failed to return, pilot S.Ten Carlo Tancioni, copilot Serg Alberico Manfredini, observer S.T.V. Rolando Ronconi and three MiA

Wednesday, 8 April 1942

Another night raid on Alexandria was carried out by two Cant.Z.1007bis of 261ª Squadriglia which took off from Maritza at 0205. Both Cap Athos Maestri and Ten Renato Ottaviani reported hits on the docks.

British Claims					
89 Sqn	Flt Lt R.C.Fumerton/ Sgt Bing	Beaufighter If X7743	He 111	Nile Delta area; crew baled into sea off Alexandria	0415
89 Sqn	Flt Lt R.C.Fumerton/ Sgt Bing	Beaufighter If X7743	He 111 force-landed		

German Casualties	
4./KG 26	He 111H-6 WNr 4201 1H+CC shot down in sea by Beaufighter off Alexandria; Obfw Richard Hess and one PoW, Obfw Rudolf Henkel and one KiA
4./KG 26	He 111H-6 WNr 4577 1H+AC shot down in sea by Beaufighter off Alexandria; Obgefr Ernst Kichbiaw and three MiA

Thursday, 9 April 1942

Pilots of 213 Squadron on Fleet patrol off Alexandria were able to claim their first successes against Luftwaffe reconnaissance aircraft since their arrival in Egypt from Cyprus.

British Claims					
213 Sqn	Flt Sgt A.B.Horn	Hurricane IIc BM966 'T'	Ju 88	10m N Alexandria Bar	1040
213 Sqn	Sgt G.R.S.McKay	Hurricane IIc BE569	Ju 88 Damaged	80-90m off Edcu	1120

German Casualties	
2.(F)/123	Ju 88D-5 WNr 430001 4U+ZK shot down by Hurricane N Alexandria; Uffz Martin Kalwitta, Lt Karl von Walde and two KiA

Saturday, 11 April 1942

A Cant.Z.1007bis of 260ª Squadriglia flown by Ten Francesco Alù reported having sunk the steamship *Kawsar* (8,139 tons) with four 50kg bombs, catching her sailing north of Port Said.

British Claims					
213 Sqn	Sgt A.J.Hancock	Hurricane IIc BM966 'T'	Ju 88	15m NW Alexandria harbour	1105
213 Sqn	Wt Off R.J.Wallace	Hurricane II BN132 'U'			

German Casualties*	
2.(F)/122	Ju 88D-5 WNr 430186 F6+NK crashed in sea S Crete; Obfw Otto Lange, Lt Wolfgang Leuschner and two MiA

*Reported lost on 10 April

Monday, 13 April 1942

British Claims					
213 Sqn	Sgt W.H.Stephenson	Hurricane IIc BE553	Ju 88 Damaged	W of Alexandria Bar	1715

Tuesday, 14 April 1942

This proved to be a day of sustained action, involving both 201 Group and Malta. A fairly full account of the day's actions is included in *Malta: The Spitfire Year, 1942*. However, since there was quite a lot of confusion therein regarding the identity of the Luftwaffe pilots involved during the day, a somewhat revised coverage is provided here.

Ultra intercepts of Italian naval signals had revealed that three convoys were now at sea. From Malta the submarines *Upholder*, *Urge* and *Thrasher* of the 10th Flotilla were ordered out to try and intercept the ships known to be departing Naples; simultaneously from Bu Amud Blenheims and Marylands of 203 Squadron were briefed to search for the vessels, aided by a single ASV-equipped Wellington of 221 Squadron. The crews were fully aware that should they sight and shadow the ships to the limit of their range, they would be obliged to land on Malta to refuel – probably under attack from the omnipresent Messerschmitts which patrolled around the island.

The convoy which had put out from Naples comprised the German *Reichenfel*s and the Italian *Vettor Pisani*, escorted by two destroyers and a torpedo boat. A third transport – *Ravello* – had departed Taranto with two destroyers, whilst from Brindisi came *Reginaldo Giuliani*, with a destroyer and an MTB. East of Sicily the three groups converged into a single convoy. Freedom from air assault from Malta was confidently anticipated, given the level of attack the island had been suffering. Indeed, 70 Ju 87 and 60 Ju 88 sorties were to be made during the day against Grand Harbour and the airfields in three attacks, whilst Bf 109s maintained a continuous patrol over and around the island, while also joining Bf 110s and Ju 88s in providing cover for the ships.

Searches had begun by single ASV Wellingtons from both Malta and Bu Amud at about four hours before midnight on the previous evening, the Malta Wellington sighting a small convoy at 0030 to the north-east of Sicily, heading northwards; this, however, was not the convoy for which the search was being made. The other Wellington was forced to abandon its task owing to severe electrical storms, the crew having made no sightings.

With the arrival of daylight three reconnaissance Marylands of 203 Squadron departed Bu Amud to continue the search, joined in the task at 0930 by two of the unit's Blenheims. A few minutes later a Cant.Z.1007bis of 262ª Squadriglia on a reconnaissance over the Eastern Mediterranean ceased radio contact, the pilot, S.Ten Giuseppe Velardi, and his crew being reported missing. At 1000 one of the

Marylands flown by Flg Off J.B.Halbert, made contact with the main convoy a short distance from the east coast of Sicily, steaming southwards at an estimated ten knots. The crew reported four merchant vessels and five destroyers. The Maryland commenced shadowing and sent reports of progress until fuel shortage forced Halbert to head for Malta. Four miles from the island the aircraft was intercepted and shot down, victim it was believed of a Bf 110 or Ju 88; there were no survivors. The cause of the loss of one of 203 Squadron's Blenheims, flown by Flg Off Miles Bowker has not been definitely ascertained, but it too may have fallen victim to one of the many Luftwaffe fighters active around the convoy. When Sqn Ldr J.A.G.Coates, the unit commander, arrived in the area later, he saw hostile aircraft but was not attacked as he took over the shadowing role. He was to continue until late in the day, finally landing back at Bu Amud in the dark with his fuel virtually exhausted.

Meanwhile, an ASV-equipped Beaufort of 22 Squadron had also been sent out, having departed Bu Amud at 0700, with Flt Sgt S.E.Howroyd at the controls. He too located the convoy and reported its position, then headed for Malta. As he came in to land at Luqa, a Bf 109 appeared behind him and sprayed the aircraft with cannon fire; the pilot was killed instantly and slumped forward, the Beaufort crashing at once. The other three members of the crew all sustained wounds, Flt Sgt Joe Lee, the navigator, dying later in hospital.

The first raid on Malta had occurred at 1045, when six Ju 88s attacked Takali. Immediately thereafter three 249 Squadron Spitfires took off to provide initial protection for a departing Maryland of 69 Squadron, but these were engaged by Bf 109s. Plt Off Kelly claimed one damaged before being shot down himself. He baled out from about 800 feet, three miles west of Hal Far, but his parachute failed to open properly and he hit the water very hard, suffering severe bruising. He also became entangled in the shroud lines, and lost his dinghy whilst freeing himself; he was safely picked up (see *Malta: The Spitfire Year, 1942*, for more details of the island's fighter combats on this date).

More Spitfires were off at 1300 to cover the return of the 69 Squadron Maryland, BS762 flown by Plt Off Tom Channon, which was being pursued by a fighter. The latter was attacked and was claimed shot down into the sea, apparently the German pilot subsequently being picked up by the Axis ASR service. In view of the Maryland's narrow escape and the loss of the 203 Squadron aircraft, it was decided that 69 Squadron should suspend all such flights by these aircraft, relying upon the speed and manoeuvrability of its handful of PR Spitfires to complete the reconnaissance required.

While this little action had been underway, six torpedo-armed Beauforts of 39 Squadron and two of 22 Squadron had departed Bu Amud to strike at the convoy; they were then to fly on to Malta and land, as were the four Beaufighters of 272 Squadron supplied as escort. At the briefing it was stressed that all aircraft were to fly very low, down to 100 feet in the reconnaissance area; the Beaufighters were to locate the target for the Beauforts, then break for Malta when at the limit of their fuel. Originally it had been intended that nine Beauforts would participate in the strike but at the last moment one 39 Squadron machine developed a fault, and only eight departed, formed into three flights as follows:

X8024	Flt Lt J.M.Lander	(22 Squadron detachment)
N1100	Plt Off G.Belfield	(22 Squadron detachment)
N1169	Flt Lt R.G.W.Beveridge	
N1186	Flg Off R.B.Seddon	(47 Squadron, attached to 39 Squadron)
X8923	Flg Off S.A.R.Bee	
W6505	Flt Lt A.T.Leaning	
N1002	Flg Off S.W.Gooch	
N1166	Plt Off B.W.Way	(47 Squadron, attached to 39 Squadron)

The rather inadequate escort of four Beaufighters was led by Sqn Ldr Bill Riley, who was actually no longer officially with the squadron, and was employed as a controller at 201 Group while waiting to take command of a new Beaufighter unit; he had volunteered to lead the escort on this occasion. His No.2 was Plt Off Stephenson, Flg Off Derek Hammond leading the other section with Flt Sgt J.S.France on his wing. Due to the speed differential with the Beauforts, these four were obliged to weave overhead, increasing fuel consumption and thereby reducing their range.

By the time the strike force had reached a point 70 miles south-east of Malta the leader, Flt Lt Lander, realised that they must have overshot the convoy and turned south-west to continue the search. Twenty minutes into the new heading, Sqn Ldr Riley sighted a Bf 110 on the same course as the Beauforts, and chased it for 15 minutes without result. On turning to rejoin the formation he sighted what he took to be two more Bf 110s at 2,000 feet. He climbed to attack and claimed both shot down into the sea. Whilst one of his victims would seem to have been a Zerstörer of III./ZG 26 in which the gunner, Uffz Rudolf Leuthoff was wounded, the other was actually a Do 17Z of the same Gruppe, which was shot down. It was assumed that one of these two aircraft had been responsible for the loss of Flg Off Halbert's Maryland. Riley then chased a Ju 88 but was only able to inflict some damage before running out of ammunition. These combats led him towards the convoy, which he saw only a few miles away.

The other Beaufighter pilots attacked a Ju 88 which appeared to be shadowing the Beauforts, but the action was indecisive. On climbing to attack this aircraft (which was at about 1,000 feet) the crews also spotted the convoy: "It was at this time that the mistake was made which affected the success of the operation," so stated the subsequent official enquiry into the mission, which was about to turn into a disaster for the gallant torpedo-bomber crews, now 500 miles from their base, for neither Sqn Ldr Riley nor Flg Off Hammond ascertained whether the convoy had also been seen by those in the Beauforts before turning towards Malta. Both section leaders apparently thought that the strike force could not have failed to see the convoy and that they were manoeuvring for position to attack. In fact the Beauforts, flying much lower than their escort – at approximately 40-50 feet – had not sighted it and did not do so until about 30 minutes later, owing to the small field of vision at such a low altitude.

The Beauforts, now devoid of escort, pressed on but as they approached the convoy at wave-top height, some 15-20 Bf 109s of JG 53, six Bf 110s and a number of Ju 88s were seen patrolling overhead. The crews were alarmed at the prospect of having to evade the Messerschmitts, particularly the Bf 109s, such types not being anticipated so far out to sea – at least 120 nautical miles from Sicily; it seems likely that they were fitted with auxiliary tanks for the purpose. The fighters pounced on the torpedo-bombers as the pilots attempted to line up on their chosen targets – the two largest transports, *Reichenfels* and *Reginaldo Giuliani*.

Flt Lt Lander and Plt Off Belfield went for the rear side on the left, attacking from starboard, Leaning's section making for the same vessel from the port quarter; Beveridge's trio took the rear right-hand transport. Only five torpedoes were launched – three explosions being reported, with much smoke being seen from both ships, while a destroyer was also believed hit – the other three aircraft being forced to jettison when engaged by the escort. In fact, none of the torpedoes struck home and no damage was inflicted on any of the vessels.

As soon as the torpedoes had been released, Plt Off Bert Way's aircraft was seen to have lost contact with the others of its section; Way attempted to join up with Lander's section instead, but as he moved closer he was attacked by a Bf 109 and shot down. The crew of an escorting Cant.Z.506B floatplane of 170ª Squadriglia RM reported being attacked by three 'Blenheims', one of which was then shot down by a Messerschmitt; the Italians undoubtedly witnessed the demise of Way's aircraft and crew. It seems likely that N1166 fell to Fw Ludwig Reibel of I./JG 53, who claimed a Beaufort shot down about 60 miles south-east of Malta, and of this, his seventh victory, he reported:

> "Shortly before reaching the convoy our Gruppe noticed eleven (*sic*) low-flying Bristol Beauforts. We managed to drive them away from our convoy by attacking. I chased three Beauforts flying south-west and attacked the last one. On my second attack the aircraft was leaking fuel from its left side. On my fifth attack there was an explosion on the left side. The aircraft went into the water and crashed. I couldn't see what happened to the crew as I had to follow the other aircraft."

A desperate race to reach distant Malta now began as the remaining Beauforts stayed close above the water, taking violent evasive action. Their chances were slim, but they nearly made it. Malta was almost in sight when Flt Lt Robert Beveridge's luck ran out and his aircraft splashed into the sea. This was closely followed by another from his section, flown by Flg Off Bob Seddon, whose crippled N1186 ditched some six miles short of the island. Flg Off Derek Bee's aircraft was seen flying low over Malta, endeavouring to line up for a landing, but a Messerschmitt appeared on his tail and shot the Beaufort down into the sea; there were no survivors.

Next to go down was Plt Off Belfield's N1100, four Bf 109s being seen buzzing around this until it ditched off Zurrieq, the crew taking to their dinghy. A nearby fishing boat which went to pick them up turned back owing to the presence of the Messerschmitts. Two fishermen in another boat disregarded the fighters however, and rescued the crew. In the meantime another boat manned by L/Cpl Julian Sciberras and Paul D'Amato went out to meet the fishing boat and two of the airmen were transferred to this.

Only three Beauforts now remained, and Flt Lt John Lander's aircraft was next singled out for attack as he made his final dash for safety. His badly damaged aircraft had sustained a twisted wingtip, caused by hitting the sea when taking evasive action, and the gun turret was out of action. Dodging some of his pursuers by flying close to Dingli Cliffs, he managed to crash-land on Luqa runway, without hydraulics and with the rudder stripped of fabric over three-quarters of its length; he and his crew escaped injury. Flg Off Gooch's machine also got down, badly holed in the fuel tanks and with the hydraulic lines severed, and Flt Lt Leaning's W6505 also landed safely; paradoxically, it had escaped even a single bullet hole.

As the Beauforts had approached the island at 1645, two Hurricanes of 185 Squadron had been scrambled to go to their aid, followed ten minutes later by three more of 229 Squadron. Plt Off Philip Wigley of the former unit recalled:

> "One Beaufort was spotted too late – it was at sea level and under attack from two Bf 109s – and before the Hurricanes could reach it, it was shot down a mile short of the relative safety of Malta. 185 felt badly about the loss of the Beaufort crew so close – unfortunately, the Hurricanes had been ordered to climb after take-off and, of course with the benefit of hindsight, a sea-level patrol would have been more appropriate and the Beaufort might have been saved."

The Luftwaffe patrols had enjoyed a field day and were credited with nine victories. During the evening rescue launch HSL 128, which had been shot-up during the day, was hastily patched up and was off again in less than half an hour as it was believed that four Beaufort survivors were in their dinghy under the cliffs of Dingli; however, the craft was unable to get to the given location. In the event, only one man was still alive in the sea – Sgt McGregor, the Canadian navigator from Flg Off Seddon's aircraft. Following the ditching, the crew had managed to extricate themselves, although two had been badly wounded. However, their dinghy had been holed, and would not inflate. McGregor, whose back had been peppered with splinters, and Sgt Alex Miller, one of the gunners, decided to swim for the shore. The wounded Seddon and Sgt Tom Keegan remained with the sinking aircraft supported by their Mae Wests, in the hope that an ASR craft would spot them and pick them up. They perished, however, as did Miller when exhaustion finally overtook him. Alone, McGregor swam for five hours before finally reaching a rocky cliff edge, from where he was rescued next morning.

Meanwhile further east at 1530 another Cant.Z.1007bis of 261ª Squadriglia, flown by Ten Enrico Gotti, sighted a British freighter off Mersa Matruh escorted by four destroyers and a flyingboat identified as a Saro London. When attacked by two fighters, the Italian crew's aircraft recognition proved little better, for they identified their attackers as 'Buffaloes'. The bomber was seriously damaged but managed to make for its base; no report of such an interception has been found, but presumably this was carried out by a pair of 805 Squadron Martlets, remaining unreported.

British Claims

272 Sqn	Sqn Ldr W.Riley/ Sgt Blakely	Beaufighter Ic 'R'	2 Bf 110s	SE Malta	1215-1635
272 Sqn	Sqn Ldr W.Riley/ Sgt Blakely	Beaufighter Ic 'R'	Ju 88 Damaged	SE Malta	1215-1635
249 Sqn	Plt Off H.Kelly	Spitfire V AB342	Bf 109 Damaged		
185 Sqn	Flt Lt J.W.S.Fletcher	Hurricane II BN163	Bf 109 Damaged		
249 Sqn	Flt Lt .N.C.Macqueen	Spitfire V }	Bf 109		
249 Sqn	Plt Off R.Sergeant	Spitfire V }	2 Bf 109s Damaged		
185 Sqn	Sgt G.E.Horricks	Hurricane II Z4004	Bf 109 Damaged		
185 Sqn	Sgt G.R.Tweedale	Hurricane II	Bf 109 Damaged		
229 Sqn	Sgt R.J. Lees	Hurricane II	Bf 109 Damaged		

British Casualties

203 Sqn	Maryland AH298 shot down; Flg Off J.B.Halbert and crew KiA
203 Sqn	Blenheim IV Z7902 took off 0920 from Bu Amud, due back at 1530 MiA; Flt Lt M B Bowker & crew MiA
22 Sqn	Beaufort II AW282 'B' shot up on landing at Luqa by Bf 109; Flt Sgt S.E.Howroyd KiA, one died of wounds, two WiA

British Casualties

249 Sqn	Spitfire V AB342 shot down by Bf 109; Plt Off H.Kelly baled out, slt injured, picked up safe
39 Sqn	Beaufort N1166 shot down into sea by Bf 109; Plt Off B.W.Way and three KiA
39 Sqn	Beaufort N1169 shot down into sea by Bf 109; Flt Lt R.G.W.Beveridge and three KiA
39 Sqn	Beaufort N1186 ditched in sea after damage by Bf 109s, 6m from Malta; Flg Off R.B.Seddon and two MiA, one picked up
39 Sqn	Beaufort X8923 shot down into sea by Bf 109; Flg Off D.A.R.Bee and three KiA
22 Sqn	Beaufort N1100 ditched in sea after damage by Bf 109s; Plt Off G.Belfield and three into dinghy and picked up
39 Sqn	Beaufort X8924 badly damaged by Bf 109s, crash-landed at Luqa; Flt Lt J.M.Lander and four safe
39 Sqn	Beaufort N1002 badly damaged by Bf 109s, but landed safely; Flg Off S.W.Gooch and three safe
185 Sqn	Hurricane II HA-D damaged by Bf 109s and crash-landed at Hal Far; Sgt J.W.Yarra safe

German Claims

Stab/JG 53	Maj Günther von Maltzahn	P-40	Malta	1040
7./JG 53	Uffz Paul Gläser	Beaufort		1240
7./JG 53	Fw Rudolf Schmidt	Spitfire		1310
4./JG 27	Oblt Oskar Simon	Blenheim	40km NW Derna	1525
1./JG 53	Fw Ludwig Reibel	Beaufort	100km SE Malta	1605
2./JG 53	Oblt Klaus Quaet-Faslem	Beaufort		1645
5./JG 53	Fw Herbert Rollwage	Beaufort	3km S Krendi	1705
5./JG 53	Fw Alexander Kehlbuth	Beaufort	S Krendi	1706
5./JG 53	Fw Herbert Rollwage	Beaufort	2km S Krendi	1707

German Casualties

10./ZG 26	Do 17Z-10 WNr 3250 shot down into sea by Beaufighters; crew KiA
III./ZG 26	Bf 110E-1 WNr 3924 force-landed Marsala to engine failure; 20% damaged

Italian Casualties

262ª Sq, 107°Gr, 47°St BT	Cant.Z.1007bis MM 23729 '262-10' from Rhodes, FTR; pilot S.Ten Giuseppe Velardi, copilot Serg Magg Mario Nasi, observer S.T.V. Giuseppe Lombardo and three MiA
262ª Sq, 107°Gr, 47°St BT	Cant.Z.1007bis MM 23738 '262-1' damaged by fighters, pilot Ten Enrico Gotti slightly wounded, copilot Serg Magg Arturo Ardizzoia, observer T.V. Guglielmo Griendl and three safe

Wednesday, 15 April 1942

Three Albacores of 826 Squadron dropped flares over Martuba landing ground, assisting Wellingtons to bomb 15 fighters on the ground there. Twenty sticks of bombs were seen to fall by the naval airmen, causing one of the aircraft on the ground to explode; three large fires were also reported.

Thursday, 16 April 1942

British Claims

GC 1 Alsace	Lt Claude Raoul-Duval	Ju 88	Alexandria

British Casualties

	Unidentified Wellington FTR from anti-submarine patrol

German Casualties

1./LG 1	Ju 88A-4 WNr 5570 L1+KK, crashed into sea due to engine failure 150km N Alexandria, Oblt Karl Hohn and 3 MiA

Saturday, 18 April 1942

British Claims

213 Sqn	Flt Lt C.B.Temlett	Hurricane IIc BM983	Ju 88 Damaged	N Aboukir	1000

British Casualties

213 Sqn	Hurricane IIc BM983 'C' forced to land at Aboukir at 1010 after combat with Ju 88; Flt Sgt C.B.Temlett safe

German Casualties

1./LG 1	Ju 88A-4 WNr 5543 L1+CH damaged in combat with Hurricanes N Aboukir; ditched in sea 300km N Alexandria; Oblt Iro Ilk safe, Sdf Dr Hans Lemp and two WiA

Sunday, 19 April 1942

British Claims

213 Sqn	Sgt G.R.S.McKay	Hurricane IIc BN136	Ju 88 Damaged	Burg el Arab area	1035-1145

Tuesday, 21 April 1942

Two Beaufighters of 252 Squadron took off at 1830 to attack a ship reported to be aground off Zuertica. A merchant vessel estimated as being of 2,500 tons was located one and a half miles west of the reported spot, surrounded by two escorts and two Flak ships. Both Beaufighter pilots attacked the main vessel with cannon and machine-gun fire, but observed no results. That night Albacores of 821 Squadron attempted to attack again, but visibility proved very bad and no effective strike could be launched.

During the day the first contingent of 22 Squadron Beauforts and their crews departed to continue their delayed journey to Ceylon.

German Casualties

4./KG 100	He 111H-6 6N+EJ FTR from attack on Mersa Matruh

He 111H of KG 100 crash-landed in North Africa.

Thursday, 23 April 1942

During the day a Maryland of 203 Squadron attacked nine Ju 52/3ms over the Mediterranean, but was itself attacked and driven off by two escorting Bf 110s. A second Maryland of this unit failed to return from a sortie.

British Claims

89 Sqn	Sgt R.G. Peters	Beaufighter If X866? or 806?	Ju 88 force-landed in flames 2245 ?? night 23/24th

British Casualties

1443 Flt	Wellington MiA on ferry flight Malta to Egypt; possibly DV573

Friday, 24 April 1942

British Casualties

203 Sqn	Blenheim IV V6014 FTR from shipping reconnaissance, believed shot down by fighter; Flt Lt W.R.Hole and two MiA

German Claims

7./ZG 26	Uffz Fritz Lauff	Blenheim	1025

German Casualties

6./KG 100	He 111H-6 WNr 4856 6N+EJ shot down by AA, crashed nr Qotaifiya; Obfw Walter Rauch and three MiA

Saturday, 25 April 1942

British Claims

89 Sqn	Sgt C.C.Webb/Sgt Mathers	Beaufighter If X7717	He 111 Damaged	30m S Raltim	2215

Sunday, 26 April 1942

British Casualties

223 Sqn	Baltimore I AG729 FTR from training flight off Alexandria

Tuesday, 28 April 1942

A Cant.Z.501 of 196ª Sq RM flown by Cap Oreste Genta, during a convoy escort was attacked at 1200, 22 miles east of Anegia, by three aircraft identified as Blenheims. The pilots and the wireless operator were wounded and the aircraft damaged. Hits were claimed on one attacker, and the flying boat managed to return. It would appear that this aircraft was mis-identified as a Do 18 flyingboat by two pilots of 272 Squadron, each of which claimed such an aircraft shot down in the same location and at much the same time. The Beaufighters had taken off from Bu Amud to attack an Axis convoy and its air escort. The Edcu detachment of 89 Squadron was in action over Alexandria during the night against a reported 25 Ju 88s of I./LG1 and He 111s of KG 26.

At 1900 two Cant.Z.1007bis of 47° Stormo, one of 263ª Squadriglia flown by Cap Alberto Insom and another of 260ª Squadriglia flown by Ten Carlo Perelli-Cippo took off from Maritza on a night bombing mission to Alexandria. On the target at 2105, they dropped eight 160kg bombs and 300kg of leaflets. After the launch Cap Insom's aircraft was attacked by a fighter that inflicted some damage.

British Claims

272 Sqn	Plt Off R.E.C.Deppe/ Sgt J.M.Carlin	Beaufighter Ic 'O'	Do 18	Gulf of Sirte	1044-1540
272 Sqn	Sgt Y.C.Tedesco/ Sgt Blakely	Beaufighter Ic 'V'	Do 18	Gulf of Sirte	1050-1545
89 Sqn	Flt Lt R.M.Mackenzie/ Flg Off Craig	Beaufighter If X7743	He 111	Alexandria	2150
89 Sqn	Sqn Ldr J.A.A.Read/ Flg Off Howell	Beaufighter If X7746	2 He 111s	Alexandria	2210-2300
89 Sqn	Sgt F.F.Felton/ Sgt Sylvester	Beaufighter If X7671	Ju 88	Alexandria	2230

German Casualties

5./KG 100	He 111H-6 WNr 7056 6N+DH shot down by Beaufighter into sea off Alexandria; Fw Heinz Krempien and two KiA, one PoW
2./LG 1	Ju 88A-4 WNr 5651 L1+AA shot down into sea off Alexandria by Beaufighter; Obfw Karl Müller and one MiA, one KiA, one PoW

Italian Casualties

196ª Sq, 93°Gr RM	Cant.Z.501 MM 35543 '196-6' damaged by Blenheims 1200, pilot Cap Oreste Genta, copilot Serg Magg Aldo Brambati and one WiA
263ªSq, 107°Gr, 47°St BT	Cant.Z.1007bis damaged by night fighter 10km from Alexandria 1900-2320, Cap Alberto Insom and crew safe

Wednesday, 29 April 1942

Next morning a reconnaissance Ju 88 appeared over Alexandria, presumably seeking to identify the previous night's damage. It was intercepted by a Hurricane of 213 Squadron and shot down. A CR.42 of 153ª Squadriglia, during a convoy escort, at 0810 sighted a surfaced submarine and released two bombs that near-missed the target.

British Claims

213 Sqn	Flt Sgt A.J.Hancock	Hurricane IIc BE340	Ju 88	at sea, 5km NW Alexandria Bar	1202

German Casualties

2.(F)/123	Ju 88D-1 WNr 1357 4U+HK shot down by Hurricane into sea off Alexandria; Obfw Kurt Rohrback KiA, Fw Ernst Zahn PoW, two MiA

Thursday-Friday, 30 April/1 May 1942

During the night 89 Squadron's Beaufighters operated from El Gamil at Port Said.

British Claims

89 Sqn	Flt Lt H.G.Edwards/Sgt Phillipson	Beaufighter If	Ju 88 Damaged	N Abu Sueir	0345
89 Sqn	Flg Off V.C.Lovell/Flt Sgt Lilley	Beaufighter If	Ju 88	NW Port Said	0350

German Casualties

I./LG 1	Ju 88A-4 WNr 142035 L1+TL shot down by Beaufighter NE Port Said; Uffz Kurt Beer and three MiA

Friday, 1 May 1942

Three Beaufighters of 272 Squadron undertook an offensive sweep along the western Cyrenaican coast during which a convoy of 50 lorries was attacked on the Benghazi-Agedabia road. Six tankers, a petrol bowser and 21 trucks were claimed destroyed, but Sqn Ldr Riley forced a Ju 52/3m of KGrzbV 400 to land apparently becoming bogged down in soft sand. He then shot it up on the ground as three men jumped out of it and ran for cover; during this second attack he did not see any further visible signs of damage. This successful intruder pilot had led a flight in one of the Polish Hurricane squadrons during the Battle of Britain. This latest claim raised his tally to six, although the aircraft was in fact only damaged. A week later he would join 247 Wing preparatory to taking command of a new squadron.

At the other end of the Mediterranean on Gibraltar a Hudson squadron, 233, had just arrived from Thorney Island in the UK to undertake anti-submarine patrol work. Plt Off V.E.Camacho commenced a patrol in T93387 at 1150, almost at once spotting a U-Boat on the surface, but apparently low on buoyancy. He turned to attack, but the vessel remained on the surface for one minute after the sighting had been made before crash-diving. The conning tower disappeared 13 seconds before four 250lb depth charges, set at 25ft, were released from 870ft with 60ft spacing. These fell across the submarine's track 80-100 yards ahead of the swirl as it disappeared. Two bursts were seen, one very large and one smaller.

At 1456 Sgt Brent in AM735 also sighted a submarine on the surface during an 1159-1745 patrol, and he too attacked. Diving from 1,200ft across the conning tower and bows, he released three depth charges from 30ft, settings at 25ft and spacing 60ft. The vessel was still on the surface, decks awash, when two of the charges exploded against the starboard side by the conning tower. The U-Boat then submerged and a patch of oil of about 100 yards diameter appeared. One minute later ten feet of the bows appeared perpendicular out of the water, then slid back. The U-Boat then formed a steep angle with the surface of the sea before the bows fell forward and the vessel settled on an even keel. The crew then appeared in the conning tower with hands raised until the aircraft left at 1520. These attacks, made off Cape Tenes, had badly damaged U-573 (Kptlt Heinrich Heinsohn), leaving one dead and 43 survivors. Next day the vessel was interned at Cartagena, Spain, to where it had been able to limp.

That night two Cant.Z.1007bis of 261ª Squadriglia led by Magg Renato Roveda bombed Port Said at night. Also, three CR.42s of 161° Gruppo, led by the commanding officer T.Col Giovanni Zappetta, attacked an intruder over Rhodes.

British Claims

272 Sqn	Sqn Ldr W.Riley/ Flt Sgt Williams	Beaufighter Ic 'D'	Ju 52/3m	f/ld on beach, Gulf of Sirte	0520-1020

German Casualties

KGrzbV 400	Ju 52/3m 40% damaged by Beaufighters 40km N Agedabia; landed safe at base, one of crew KiA, one WiA

Saturday, 2 May 1942

Gibraltar's other squadron, the Catalina-equipped 202, was also successful during a U-Boat hunt when Flt Lt Powell in aircraft 'J' assisted the destroyers HMS *Wishart* and *Wrestler* in sinking U-74 (Oblt Karl Friedrich) off Cape Palos.

Sunday-Monday, 3/4 May 1942

The ground party of 46 Squadron had reached Egypt by sea about a year ago, but had never been joined by the aircrew and aircraft. These had flown off an aircraft carrier to Malta, where they had remained, being renumbered 126 Squadron. Now 46 Squadron was at last re-established with some aircraft and crews from 89 Squadron, becoming the second Middle East night-fighter unit. It had moved to Edcu on 2 May, and now gained its first victory in this role, claimed by one of the ex-89 Squadron crews.

British Claims

46 Sqn	Sgt R.G.Peters	Beaufighter If X7843	He 111K	12m NNE Aboukir	0455-0510

German Casualties

5./KG 100	He 111H-6 WNr 4995 6N+DJ shot down by Beaufighter into sea N Aboukir; Lt Rudolf Schwierer and one PoW, two KiA

46 Squadron was formed in May from an element of aircraft and crews supplied by 89 Squadron and the original groundcrew whose air party had gone instead to Malta in 1941. The 'arrow' aerials of the AI radar can be seen here clearly on V8502.

Wednesday, 6 May 1942

British Casualties

89 Sqn	Beaufighter If X7766 crashed on landing, Abu Sueir

Sunday, 10 May 1942

94 Squadron, which had suffered considerable casualties over the desert when flying first Hurricanes, and then Kittyhawks, was ordered to hand its Kittyhawks to other units in 233 Wing, and withdraw to Maryut without aircraft. It was to become involved in defensive duties and convoy patrols for the rest of the North African campaigns. At the start of June it would move to El Gamil and receive Hurricanes – initially both Mark I and Mark IIcs which it would operate for the next two years.

Monday, 11 May 1942

Six Beaufighters of 272 Squadron took off from LG.10 to protect a British naval force identified as Convoy Rivet during the afternoon. Initially a Ju 88 and an He 111 were spotted and claimed probably shot down by two of the pilots just after one of these had been seen to sink a destroyer. Sometime later all six joined in claiming to have probably shot down a Ju 88 which had attacked at 2000, sinking a further destroyer. No Luftwaffe losses were suffered on either occasion.

Two S.79s torpedo-bombers of 204[a] Squadriglia, flown by Cap Giovanni B. De Stefano and S.Ten Normanno White, took off from Rhodes at 0815 on an armed reconnaissance sortie over the Port Said area. Some merchant vessels were sighted in the area, and a torpedo was released but was stranded in shallow waters. On return they were attacked by an 89 Squadron Beaufighter that shot down White's S.79 and killed the wireless operator, Serg Magg Nicola Favero, aboard De Stefano's aircraft.

British Claims

272 Sqn	Flt Lt D.H.Hammond	Beaufighter Ic 'B'			
272 Sqn	Flg Off A.P.Stephenson	Beaufighter Ic 'U'	Ju 88 Probable	escort Convoy Rivet	1520-1900
272 Sqn	Sgt Y.C.Tedesco	Beaufighter Ic 'S'			
272 Sqn	Flt Lt D.H.Hammond	Beaufighter Ic 'B'			
272 Sqn	Plt Off E.H.Hodgson	Beaufighter Ic 'N'			
272 Sqn	Flt Lt Lingard	Beaufighter Ic 'O'	He 111	escort Convoy Rivet	1755-2005
272 Sqn	Sgt Y.C.Tedesco	Beaufighter Ic 'S'			
272 Sqn	Flg Off A.P.Stephenson	Beaufighter Ic 'B'			
272 Sqn	Sgt E.R.F.Truby	Beaufighter Ic 'V'			

89 Sqn	Plt Off M.W.Kinmonth/ Sgt Edgar	Beaufighter If X7636	S.79	30m N Damietta	1215
89 Sqn	Plt Off M.W.Kinmonth/ Sgt Edgar	Beaufighter If X7636	S.79 Probable	N Damietta	

British Casualties

38 Sqn	Wellington Ic BB484 'X' departed LG.117 at 2024 on minelaying sortie with four others, FTR; Flt Sgt Ward and crew MiA

Italian Casualties

204ª Sq, 41°Gr AS	S.79 MM 24303 shot down by Beaufighter near Port Said 1117, pilot S.Ten Normanno White, copilot M.llo Ferruccio Carli and four MiA
204ª Sq, 41°Gr AS	S.79 MM 24174 damaged by Beaufighter, pilot Cap Giovanni B. De Stefano, copilot Serg Magg Gian Maria Scotti safe, one crew KiA

Tuesday, 12 May 1942

Recently Luftwaffe Ju 52/3m transports had been flying a much-increased number of sorties between Crete and North Africa, carrying reinforcements and fuel. The famous Vladimir Peniakoff (widely known as 'Popski') with his Libyan Arab Force had been observing the frequency of these flights from behind Axis lines, and reporting them to Cairo.

Consequently an attempt was made to intercept one of these flights, six Beaufighters of 252 Squadron taking off, covered by ten Kittyhawks of 250 Squadron, the whole formation being led by Wg Cdr Howard Mayers, with Flt Lt John Waddy leading the top cover. One Beaufighter and one Kittyhawk were obliged to turn back to Gambut due to mechanical problems, but the remainder intercepted a large formation of transports shortly after 0900. Fourteen Ju 52/3ms, mainly from III./KGrzbV 1, but with a few aircraft and crews from other units, were being escorted by two Bf 110s of III./ZG 26 from Maleme. All were loaded with infantry troops, 20 to each aircraft, the formation led by Maj Stein. Soon after take-off, as with the British formation, one aircraft of each type was forced to turn back. The two formations now met some 50 miles from the African coast, the RAF fighters making a head-on attack before breaking up into individual pursuits.

Flg Off C.E.Casbolt commenced a second tour of operations in North Africa in April, now flying Kittyhawks with 250 Squadron. On 12 May he was part of a formation which intercepted Ju 52/3ms over the sea between Crete and North Africa. He claimed two of these shot down to raise his ultimate total to 13 and one shared.

In the ensuing engagement each side slightly over-estimated the results, but these were convincing, none the less. The British pilots reported the strength of the formation they attacked as comprising 16 Ju 52/3ms and three Bf 110s. 250 Squadron claimed 11 of the transports and two Bf 110s, while the Beaufighter crews claimed four; it was thought that five more aircraft had been damaged. In fact nine Ju 52/3ms were shot down and crashed either in the sea or on the shore, with two more force-landing on the beach. One of these, flown by Fw Günther Frenzel, finished only 50 yards from Derna hospital, where he was taken with four fingers shot off his right hand. A few weeks later Feldmarschall Kesselring arrived at his bedside and decorated him with the Ritterkreuz.

The lone Bf 110, piloted by Uffz Baumann, was also shot down, the pilot being rescued by a motor torpedo boat; he claimed to have shot down one of the attacking fighters which he incorrectly identified as a Hurricane. Two of the transports landed at Derna, flown by Maj Stein and Fw Zillmer. The latter's aircraft had received 20 hits by bullets, but the gunner, Uffz Graf von Polier, had shot down the Beaufighter of Sgt Cripps/Sgt Bateman with his lone MG 15 machine gun. The Beaufighter had attacked head-on, and von Polier had held his fire until it passed the tail of the Junkers before firing and hitting it in the right wing root. The wing caught fire and the aircraft touched the water with its left wing, which broke off, whereupon the fighter at once disappeared beneath the waves, two other aircraft circling over the spot. This was the only Allied loss suffered. The British pilots reported that throughout the engagement the German troops in the transports kept up a steady fire with sub-machine guns from the windows of the aircraft.

It is likely that the overclaiming which had occurred resulted from the initial attack. With all the fighters attacking together, it seems very probable that several would have fired at the same aircraft. A very interesting report of this combat was given by John Waddy which well illustrates its involved nature:

"About five or ten minutes after turning on to our patrol line I observed a number of Ju 52s approaching head-on. I gave 'Tally-ho' and immediately climbed to 1,000 feet to look for the Me 110s, as I was leading the top cover. I did one complete circuit of the Ju 52s without seeing any enemy escort, so I made a head-on attack on a Ju 52 and my first burst hit straight into the cockpit. To deliver this I dived from 1,000 feet and pulled out of the drive and went over the top. My No.2, Sgt Devlin, subsequently confirms this 52 as destroyed, as it went straight into the water. I then observed a Me 110 attacking a Beaufighter, so I made a right hand turn and delivered a rear quarter attack. My first burst hit the fuselage and the Me 110 pulled up into a steep climbing turn which I followed. I then put a burst into his port engine which caught fire but at the same time was hit by the fire from the Ju 52s over which the Me 110 had cleverly led me. Gave the Me 110 another burst and he dived into the sea. I then made a rear quarter attack on a 52 and flew to within 20 yards before pulling away. This one was straggling a little on the starboard side of the enemy formation. It caught fire and crashed into the sea.

"I then observed another Me 110 about 1,000 feet so I started to climb as it began diving. It saw me and pulled out of its dive and started a left hand climbing turn. I followed out of range and then the Me 110 whipped over to a right hand turn and dived. I made a rear quarter attack developing to dead astern and followed him to the sea. One burst set his port motor on fire, the next hit the tail and entered the rear cockpit, and the next chopped off his left tailplane. It then immediately dived into the sea. I observed a Beaufighter blow up a 52 from a rear quarter attack and I also saw one Beau dive into the water in flames. I, myself, counted eight fires plus the Beaufighter. One 'Red Cross' 52 was in the enemy formation. When I left the fight only three enemy aircraft were flying, all Ju 52s."

Flt Lt John Waddy also played an active part in the interception of Ju 52/3m transports over the Mediterranean on 12 May upon which he comments here. He is seen later in the year by which time he was flying Spitfires with 92 Squadron. The name 'Ve' beneath his tally of victories was that of his wife.

Flg Off H.H.K.Gunnis of 252 Squadron claimed his fifth victory over a Ju 52/3m on 12 May. On 28 June he was badly wounded during a strafing sortie. The navigator, Sgt Edmund Waller, took over and managed to fly the aircraft back to base and land it, for which he was awarded the DFM.

In the original *Fighters over the Desert* the text continued as follows: 'Extensive research of German records shows only one Bf 110 engaged and lost in this operation, and it would seem possible that the first aircraft, after suffering damage, escaped at sea level when Flg Off Waddy was distracted by fire from the Ju 52s, drew away from the fight, and was then again attacked by him under the impression that it was a second aircraft. John Waddy, later a minister in the New South Wales government in Australia, had helped considerably with information for that book, and was quick to respond to this suggestion. On 12 May 1969 he wrote:

> "However, I am now going to take issue with you about the battle on 12th May 1942 with the Ju 52s and the Bf 110s and as today is the 27th anniversary I couldn't think of a more appropriate day to write to you.
>
> "You know, I don't care what the records show, there were in fact two Bf 110s that day and I can see them now as clearly as I could then. First they were of different camouflage colours, one much darker than the other; secondly I personally saw both these aircraft go into the water. The first one more or less controlled but the second one completely disintegrated as it cartwheeled after I cut off its tailplane. If you care to check with my combat report you will see that, whereas a number of pilots said there were three, I stressed that I only saw two and, in fact, reported two. I might also advise that both 110s were seen to go into the water by several pilots and further my Intelligence Officer Flight Lieutenant C.A.McD.Anderson advised me later that day that the German news had in fact announced they had lost two 110s as well as several Ju 52s.
>
> "I have re-read the letter that I wrote to my wife following this particular combat and, my dear Christopher, while I don't care about records or numbers of aircraft shot down, I do know that on this particular day there were two Messerschmitt 110s and that I shot down both of them and further I saw them both hit the water as well as did some of my other pilots. Whether the second one was a stray who had joined the melee or whether Luftwaffe records are crazy, I don't know."

During the 40-odd years which have passed since that letter, no further evidence has appeared to verify Waddy's statements (including confirmation regarding the German radio broadcast apparently mentioned by 250 Squadron's Intelligence Officer). This remains one of the mysteries of the Mediterranean war.

Following news of the engagement, I./JG 27 sent out four Bf 109s which discovered five oil slicks and a number of swimming survivors. Most of the sorties for the rest of the day were flown to cover rescue operations, 62 men being picked up. Hptm Kroseburg of I.Wüstenotstaffel flew an Fi 156 over the area and dropped his life jacket to some survivors. He failed to return from this sortie and was not seen again. A total of 175 German soldiers died as a result of this attack, 47 others being rescued from the sea.

During a patrol, the crew of a Blenheim of 203 Squadron spotted a submarine at 1356, dropping four 250lb anti-submarine bombs on this. One direct hit was claimed, causing a column of water to rise 200ft into the air and a patch of oil some 50 yards in diameter and full of bubbles to be seen. They claimed to have sunk their victim, but there is no record of such a vessel being lost on this date.

British Claims

250 Sqn	Sgt G.G.Buckland	Kittyhawk I AK825	Ju 52/3m	60m N Derna	0920
250 Sqn	Sgt G.G.Buckland	Kittyhawk I AK825	Ju 52/3m Damaged	60m N Derna	0920
250 Sqn	Sgt G.G.Buckland	Kittyhawk I AK825	Bf 110 Damaged	60m N Derna	0920
250 Sqn	Plt Off C.E.Casbolt	Kittyhawk I AK583	2 Ju 52/3ms	60m N Derna	0920
250 Sqn	Sgt L.J.Devlin	Kittyhawk I AK953	2 Ju 52/3ms	60m N Derna	0920
250 Sqn	Sqn Ldr M.T.Judd	Kittyhawk I AK911	2 Ju 52/3ms	60m N Derna	0920
250 Sqn	Flg Off J.L.Waddy	Kittyhawk I AK846	2 Ju 52/3ms	60m N Derna	0920
250 Sqn	Flg Off J.L.Waddy	Kittyhawk I AK846	2 Bf 110s	60m N Derna	0920
252 Sqn	Flt Sgt R.Ivey/ Flt Sgt Pyrah	Beaufighter Ic T4831 'D'	2 Ju 52/3ms	55m from Derna	0920
252 Sqn	Flt Sgt R.Ivey/ Flt Sgt Pyrah	Beaufighter Ic T4831 'D'	Ju 52/3m Damaged	55m from Derna	0920
252 Sqn	Sqn Ldr A.G.Wincott/ Sgt J.Kilmister	Beaufighter Ic T4881 'N'	2 Ju 52/3ms	55m from Derna	0920
252 Sqn	Sqn Ldr A.G.Wincott/ Sgt J.Kilmister	Beaufighter Ic T4881 'N'	Ju 52/3m Damaged	55m from Derna	0920

British Claims

252 Sqn	Plt Off H.H.K.Gunnis/ Sgt E.A.Waller	Beaufighter Ic T4896 'G'	Ju 52/3m	55m from Derna	0920
252 Sqn	Plt Off H.H.K.Gunnis/ Sgt E.A.Waller	Beaufighter Ic T4896 'G'	Ju 52/3m Damaged	55m from Derna	0920
239 Wg	Wg Cdr H.C.Mayers	Kittyhawk I AK890	Ju 52/3m	60m N Derna	0920
239 Wg	Wg Cdr H.C.Mayers	Kittyhawk I AK890	Ju 52/3m Damaged	60m N Derna	0920

British Casualties

252 Sqn	Beaufighter IIc T5028 'H' shot down attacking Ju 52/3ms off Derna; Sgt R.A.Cripps/Sgt T.Bateman MiA
250 Sqn	Kittyhawk I badly damaged by return fire from Ju 52/3ms N Derna; Plt Off W.J.Whitside safe
39 Sqn	Beaufort N1002 DBR in air raid

German Claims

7./ZG 26	Uffz Julius Baumann	Hurricane	0840

German Casualties

7./ZG 26	Bf 110C-4 WNr 3277 shot down by P-40 70km N Derna; Uffz Julius Baumann and Bordfunker WiA
KGrzbV 50	Ju 52/3m WNr 6966 shot down and crash-landed 4km N Derna; Uffz Matthias Neureither and two WiA, one safe
III./KGrzbV 1	Ju 52/3m WNr 6433 1Z+CV shot down in sea 150km N Derna; Obfw Ernst Schiele WiA, three KiA
III./KGrzbV 1	Ju 52/3m WNr 6441 1Z+GV shot down in sea 150km N Derna; Uffz Walter Schwarz and three KiA
III./KGrzbV 1	Ju 52/3m WNr 6466 shot down in the sea 150km N Derna; Uffz Albert Rademacher and one WiA, two safe
III./KGrzbV 1	Ju 52/3m WNr 6391 50% damaged and force-landed Derna; Uffz Günther Frenzel and two WiA; one safe
KGrzbV 400	Ju 52/3m WNr 2836 KJ+AH shot down into sea 150km N Derna; Stfw Emil Matthäus and four MiA
KGrzbV 400	Ju 52/3m WNr 6936 shot down into sea 150km N Derna; Lt Wilhelm Kadel and three WiA, one safe
KGrzbV 400	Ju 52/3m WNr 3082 KJ+MF shot down into sea 150km N Derna; Obfw Otto Henning WiA, two MiA, one safe
KGrzbV 400	Ju 52/3m WNr 1372 G6+CA shot down into sea 150km N Derna; pilot u/k and one safe, two KiA
Wüstenotstaffel	Fi 156C-3 WNr 5591 crashed in sea 80km N Derna for u/k reason, Hptm Heinz Kroseberg/Uffz Walter Büchner MiA

Bf 110s of III./ZG 26 on convoy patrol.

Thursday, 14 May 1942

German Casualties

1./LG 1	Ju 88A-4 WNr 5543 L1+CH FTR from sortie to Alexandria; Uffz Helmut Schaarschmidt and three MiA

Sunday, 17 May 1942

During a patrol over Benghazi, S.Ten Giovanni Dell'Innocenti of 364ª Squadriglia, intercepted three intruders which he identified as Beauforts, claiming damage to one.

Italian Claims

364ª Sq, 150°Gr CT	S.Ten Giovanni Dell'Innocenti	MC.200	Beaufort damaged	Benghazi	1025-1140

Monday, 18 May 1942

Three Marylands of 203 Squadron were on a special search east of Malta when Flg Off Slaughter spotted ten Ju 52/3ms, escorted by three Ju 88s, at 1519. Some time later (at 1700) this pilot spotted a floatplane – probably a Cant Z.506B – which he attacked, believing that he had inflicted some damage before he himself was attacked and driven off by a Ju 88.

British Claims

203 Sqn	Flg Off I.A.Slaughter	Maryland	floatplane damaged	1700

Thursday, 21 May 1942

A Ju 88 from 1.(F)/121 was shot down by two pilots of 213 Squadron, crash-landing near Burg el Arab. A patrol of Egyptian police went to pick up the crew of four who were led by the observer, Oblt Rüthers, but were fired on by them. The police returned fire, killing one and wounding a second, the other two were caught later. 2.(F)/123 also lost a reconnaissance Ju 88 on this date, cause unrecorded.

Two Cant.Z.1007bis of 107° Gruppo took off from Maritza on a reconnaissance mission at 0700. Just after take-off the aircraft of 263ª Squadriglia flown by S.Ten Giovanni Sarica crashed, causing severe burns to all crew.

British Claims

213 Sqn	Plt Off W.Henderson	Hurricane IIc BE742	Ju 88 Damaged	20m NE Burg el Arab	1010
213 Sqn	Flg Off J.A.Sowrey	Hurricane IIc BN285 'M'	Ju 88	70-80m SE Burg el Arab	1755
213 Sqn	Sgt W.H.Stephenson	Hurricane IIc BN133 'Y'			

German Casualties

1.(F)/121	Ju 88D-1 WNr 430159 7A+AH shot down by Hurricanes and crashed nr Burg el Arab; Uffz Karl-Heinz Wever and two PoW, Oblt Friedrich-Wilhelm Rüthers KiA
2.(F)/123	Ju 88D-1 WNr 430153 4U+MK crashed nr Abu Ogg; Oblt Joachim Rolfes and one PoW, Uffz Gorontzki MiA, one KiA

Italian Casualties

263ª Sq, 107° Gr, 47° St BT	Cant.Z.1007bis MM 23420 crashed after take-off, pilot S.Ten Giovanni Sarica, copilot Serg Magg Guerrino Soncini (died two days later) and four WiA

Friday, 22 May 1942

Four Beaufighters of 252 Squadron were sent off to strafe tankers reported in the Gulf of Sirte. One crew found such a vessel but were driven off by escorting fighters. The pilots instead then attacked targets on shore along the coast on their way back. Plt Off Gibson in 'P' spotted a Ju 88 at 500 feet over the sea, making a starboard quarter attack and seeing some hits on the starboard engine. He then strafed a column of 30 MT on the road south of Sidi Barrani, claiming damage to two trucks and a bowser, one of these vehicles being set on fire.

British Claims

252 Sqn	Plt Off D.C.Gibson/ Sgt A.R.Sparey	Beaufighter Ic T5007 'P'	Ju 88 Damage	Gulf of Sirte	0510-0930

British Casualties

335 Sqn	Hurricane Z4101 ditched off El Daba

German Casualties

5./LG 1	Ju 88A-4 WNr 5603 L1+LN shot down by AA and crashed in the Abu Sueir area; Fw Bruno Scharnowski KiA, three PoW

Friday-Saturday, 22/23 May 1942

British Casualties

38 Sqn	Wellington lost

Saturday, 23 May 1942

Two Beaufighters of 272 Squadron's detachment at LG.05 undertook a search for shipping in the Gulf of Sirte at dawn. At 0750 Sgt Tuckwell in 'V' spotted a freighter of some 2,500 tons escorted by two Flak barges which he described as "of German invasion type" 12 miles west of Tolmetta. He attacked in a shallow dive from 3,090 feet, seeing pieces fly off the MV's superstructure and steam escaping, although he experienced heavy Flak fire in return. Two minutes later Sgt Tedesco attacked in 'P', but his aircraft was damaged in the port wing and fuselage. The ship was thought to have been brought to a halt.

The pair of 213 Squadron pilots who had been successful two days earlier, were again able to intercept and shoot down a Ju 88 on this date, this time their victim being a bomber aircraft from II./LG 1. The Sea Rescue Flight's Fairchild amphibian picked up four German survivors from their dinghy during the day.

Sgt W.H.Stephenson (left) and Flg Off John Sowrey of 213 Squadron shot down Ju 88s on 21 and 23 May. These successes led to them being invited to describe their experiences on the Egyptian Broadcasting Company, which they are doing here.

British Claims

213 Sqn	Flg Off J.A.Sowrey	Hurricane IIc BN128 'F'	Ju 88	15-20m NW Burg el Arab	1005
213 Sqn	Sgt W.H.Stephenson	Hurricane IIc BM981 'G'			

British Casualties

252 Sqn	Beaufighter Ic 'P' damaged by Flak; Sgt Tedesco and observer safe

German Casualties

6./LG 2	Ju 88A-4 WNr 5633 L1+BO shot down by Hurricanes, crashed off Alexandria; Oblt Otto Obernhuber and three MiA

Sunday, 24 May 1942

Plt Off Young of 203 Squadron undertook a submarine search in his Blenheim north of Sidi Barrani. At 0718 he spotted one such vessel, attacking with four 250lb anti-submarine bombs. During his run in to attack, the submarine submerged, the bombs falling where it was estimated it would have been beneath the waves. An oil patch 50 yards by 20 yards then appeared, but no bubbles were seen and it was thought that the attack had not been close enough to inflict any serious damage.

In *Malta: The Spitfire Year, 1942*, it was recorded that on this date Wellingtons of 104 Squadron operating from Malta attacked two merchant vessels, but the crews were unable to observe the results of their bombing due to the laying of a smoke screen. However, subsequent research indicates that the *Agostino Bertani* (8,324 tons) was damaged by Wellingtons and Albacores, while the 6,836-ton *Gino Allegri* was sunk by the attacks of Wellingtons and a Royal Navy submarine.

The only other action of note on this date occurred when an MC.200 of 150° Gruppo intercepted an aircraft identified as a Beaufort over Benghazi, claiming to have damaged it.

Italian Claims

150° Gr CT	unidentified pilot	MC.200	Beaufort damaged	Benghazi	1340

Tuesday, 26 May 1942

German Casualties

Trsp.X.Fl.K.	Ju 52/3m WNr 7109 badly shot-up by fighters and crash-landed Maleme airfield

Wednesday, 27 May 1942

British Casualties

252 Sqn	Beaufighter Ic T4898 departed 0540 on strafing sorties; force-landed 0555; Sgt F.E.Thwaites/Sgt J.P.Diaper safe

Thursday, 28 May 1942

A pair of ASV Wellingtons of 221 Squadron undertook a search during which a convoy was located. However, intense Flak was encountered and one of the aircraft did not return.

British Casualties

221 Sqn	Wellington VIII FTR

Friday, 29 May 1942

Six of 221 Squadron's Wellingtons searched for the unit's missing aircraft, spotting a dinghy. The SRF sent out the Fairchild and a Walrus to pick up the crew.

Over the following few days there were numerous sightings of submarines and a number of attacks were made. On this date one such was spotted by the crew of a 230 Squadron Sunderland who released four anti-submarine bombs and four depth charges, the latter falling all around the vessel which had only the conning tower above the waterline, but no evidence of damage was to be seen. A 203 Squadron Blenheim also made an attack on one which crash-dived as the aircraft approached, and had just submerged when depth charges were dropped. Two days later another of the latter unit's Blenheims, operating from LG.39, made one attack, and one operating from LG.05 made two attacks.

Monday, 1 June 1942

Yet another Blenheim from 203 Squadron's detachment attacked two submarines, but again these escaped by crash-diving. On this date 459 Squadron at last came into its own as an independent unit of the RAAF, receiving a full complement of 12 Hudsons. Sqn Ldr Hennock became a Wg Cdr. The unit was now based at LG.40.

British Claims

1 SAAF Sqn	Lt I.R.Pryde	Hurricane II Z5348 'M'	Ju 88 Damaged	on convoy patrol	0806

British Casualties

459 Sqn	Hudson III V8997 crashed at LG.40 and DBR

Tuesday, 2 June 1942

Swordfish 'L' of 815 Squadron, also detached to a forward airfield, undertook another attack on a submarine, one depth charge being seen to explode about ten feet from the target. Another of this unit's aircraft, 'P', also made an attack during the day as did one of 203 Squadron's detached aircraft. The first of these attacks had inflicted serious damage on U-652 (Oblt Georg-Werner Fraatz), and she was later sent to the bottom by torpedoes from U-81.

1 SAAF Squadron stripped Hurricane IIb BG764 AX-W to lighten it for high altitude interception. On this date 2/Lt E.E.Jory tried to engage Ju 88 at 25,000 ft – the highest SAAF engagement to date, but without success.

Wednesday, 3 June 1942

British Claims

1 SAAF Sqn	Capt P.C.R.Metelerkamp	Hurricane IIb BG764 'W'	Ju 88 Damaged	Nile Delta area	0845

Wednesday-Thursday, 3/4 June 1942

The crews of two 221 Squadron Wellingtons searched during the night, one finding a convoy onto which six torpedo-carrying aircraft of 38 Squadron were homed. One of these attacked a merchant vessel with both its torpedoes, estimating that one strike had been achieved. The other aircraft also attacked but no results were seen.

Two 39 Squadron Beauforts followed in the early hours after the convoy which had already been attacked by the Wellingtons. Sqn Ldr Gibbes targeted a merchant vessel at 0558 and a hit was observed. As the aircraft departed, the ship was seen to be stationary and there was a column of smoke or steam reaching to 100ft amidships. Later this vessel was spotted again, stationary and down at the stern, with three destroyers moving slowly around it; this was the *Reginaldo Giuliani* of 6,837 tons, which subsequently sank.

After the attack Plt Off Abram's N1024 'D' was pursued for 15 minutes by a Macchi fighter, but his aircraft suffered no damage.

Thursday, 4 June 1942

British Casualties

OADU	Beaufighter T4990 hit by Flak on ferry flight and ditched nr Lampedusa; Sgt H.Gould/Sgt D.Newbury PoW

Friday, 5 June 1942

The day saw yet another submarine attack, this time by a Blenheim of 13(Hellenic) Squadron in the Eastern Mediterranean. 80 Squadron moved from Gambut to Edcu to operate on patrols with the 'Alsace' Squadron, a detachment of 335 Squadron, and the remaining Fleet Air Arm fighter elements in North Africa.

Saturday, 6 June 1942

The almost daily sighting of submarines continued, this time one being attacked by a 203 Squadron Blenheim once again. The SRF Fairchild was also out again, searching for a crew reported in the sea near Ras el Kanayes. A dinghy was found empty near the shore and it was reported that this had been from an He 111, the crew of which had been picked up by the army. It is presumed that this was probably from one of the Ju 88s recently shot down.

Sunday-Monday, 7/8 June 1942

British Claims

89 Sqn	Sgt R.G.Peters	Beaufighter If	He 111	10m NNW Burg el Arab	2330-0050

German Casualties

4./KG 100	He 111H-6 WNr 7093 6N+JG shot down by AA, crashed nr Qotaifiya; Fw Heinz Lenninger and two PoW, one MiA

Italian Claims

AA at Barce	Martin Maryland	2330

Monday, 8 June 1942

213 Squadron left LG.12 for Gambut where it was to become operational over the Western Desert.

Tuesday, 9 June 1942

From the United Kingdom 240 Squadron, equipped with Catalina flyingboats, was slowly moving to the Indian Ocean. When transiting through the Mediterranean, the unit undertook a number of anti-submarine patrols from Gibraltar. On this date Flg Off Frank Godber was engaged in such a patrol which he had commenced at 0146 in Catalina VA726. South of Majorca he spotted the Italian submarine *Veniero* (T.V Elio Zappetta) on which he dropped a stick of eight depth-charges which exploded around the vessel, destroying it and leaving no survivors from its crew of 57.

14 Sqn	Blenheim Z9656 'G', on return from bombing Crete, crashed on landing; Flg Off D.R.W.Brooks and one inj, one KiFA

Wednesday-Thursday, 10/11 June 1942
On each of the next two days Swordfish crews of 815 Squadron undertook further attacks on submarines.

The June Convoys

Despite the dire position of 8th Army in North Africa, the situation of Malta and its defences were in such a parlous position by mid-June that it became vital that all efforts should be expended to resupply this vital island. Although the story of the convoys despatched from each end of the Mediterranean at this time has been covered in some considerable detail in *Malta: The Spitfire Year, 1942*, so important was this event to the island's garrison, to 201 Group and the Royal Navy, and ultimately to 8th Army and the Western Desert Air Force, that it has been deemed appropriate to repeat a substantial part of it here, mainly relating to the events to the east of Malta; included also are such further items of information as have become available in the meantime.

To set the scene, Air Vice-Marshal Sir Hugh Pugh Lloyd, AOC on Malta, wrote: "Petrol and food were the key items. The one was useless without the other. Food to live; petrol for the fighters in the air... once the Spitfires could not fly again it would be the end for Malta....Petrol and food had to travel along so as to reach the starvation date (August) more or less together." Moreover, the War Cabinet was fully aware of Malta's plight. The prime minister had become personally and emotionally involved as never before: "Malta cried aloud for help. The strain was at many points more than could be borne....I was prepared to run serious naval risks to save Malta, and the Admiralty were in full accord. We prepared, and kept the option in hand, to send Admiral Somerville with all his carriers and the *Warspite* through the Canal into the Mediterranean, and to carry a convoy through to Malta, hoping to bring about a general engagement with the Italian Fleet on the way."

Admiral Sir James Somerville's newly-assembled Indian Ocean Fleet included three armour-decked carriers – *Formidable*, *Indomitable* and *Illustrious* – as well as his flagship, the modernised battleship *Warspite* and a number of cruisers and destroyers. It represented all the navy could spare from other operational theatres to oppose the all-conquering Japanese forces, which were now at the door of India. Serious risks, indeed, were being considered.

The plan devised to bring relief to the island was a bold one, given the weakness of the naval forces available to support such a venture. Demands in the Pacific eventually precluded use of Somerville's fleet and further US involvement, whilst the need to maintain a substantial fleet in the North Atlantic was paramount. Force H (Gibraltar) could provide as main escort only the carriers *Eagle* and *Argus* – the latter little more than useless as an operational vessel – together with the unmodernised battleship *Malaya*. These capital ships would be supported by the cruisers *Kenya* and *Liverpool*, the anti-aircraft cruiser *Charybdis* (equipped with the first ship-borne W/T and R/T intelligence-gathering Y Unit, manned by RN and RAF parties) and eight destroyers; this assemblage was identified as Force W. To provide oiling facilities, the Royal Fleet Auxiliary oiler *Brown Ranger* would accompany the warships, complete with her personal escort of two corvettes, and this group was labelled Force Y.

The close escort (Force X), which would chaperone the convoy right through to Malta, comprised the light AA cruiser *Cairo*, five large fleet destroyers, four smaller Hunt-class vessels, four minesweepers of 17th Flotilla (due to be based at Malta to replace earlier losses) and six motor launches of 6th Flotilla, which added further minesweeping facility. The convoy to be protected by this force included two British merchant vessels, the 7,421-ton *Troilus* and the 5.602-ton *Burdwan*, the New Zealand Shipping Co's large (10,350 tons) freighter *Orari*; the Dutch *Tanimbar* (8,169 tons); the US *Chant* (5,600 tons), and a fast new American Texaco tanker, the 9,308-ton *Kentucky*. The five merchantmen carried fuel, ammunition, wheat and other foodstuffs. The whole force, which was to operate under the codename Harpoon, was to be commanded by Vice-Admiral A.T.B.Curteis. Additionally, under cover of the main convoy the speedy *Welshman* (no stranger to the island), was to proceed individually at greater pace crammed full with urgent supplies.

As many submarines as could be assembled were to aid the operation – nine were to patrol off Taranto and south of the Straits of Messina, and four others were to be stationed between Sicily and Sardinia.

Aboard Admiral Curteis' two aircraft carriers were based the following units:

Eagle	***Argus***
813F Squadron; four Sea Hurricanes	807 Squadron; two Fulmars
801 Squadron: 12 Sea Hurricanes	813 Squadron: nine Swordfish
807 Squadron: four Fulmars	824 Squadron: four Swordfish

On Malta the defenders were preparing to play their part in the forthcoming actions. Of the 213 Spitfires which had reached the island during the past three months, 52 had been shot down and a further 16 had crash-landed due to combat damage, with at least 35 written off on the ground during bombing raids; currently just 95 serviceable aircraft remained with the five fighter squadrons. For longer-range work a detachment of 14 Beaufighters from 235 Squadron of Coastal Command in the UK were available; 25 Beauforts of 217 Squadron bound for Ceylon had also been 'shanghaied', but only a dozen of these were serviceable.

To increase the night anti-shipping force, a flight of six Wellington torpedo-carriers from 38 Squadron had returned to Malta from El Adem. These joined seven Fleet Air Arm torpedo-bombers of 828/830 Squadron, three of which were equipped with ASV. To provide reconnaissance, the long-serving 69 Squadron was being brought back to strength, three PRU Spitfires which had been held on the island during their flights from England, keeping a close watch on Italian naval forces based at Taranto. These were now joined by six twin-engined Baltimores which had flown in from the Middle East during the first half of the month; the latter were to co-operate with the anti-shipping aircraft. Four of the ASV-equipped Wellington VIIIs had also been hijacked to ensure the continuation of the work undertaken for so long by the Special Duties Flight, and to keep the ports of Palermo and Naples under nocturnal surveillance. Finally, the night defence of the island remained in the hands of five AI Beaufighters of the 89 Squadron detachment.

The second string to the British bow on this occasion, convoy MW11, was forming far to the east at Alexandria, Port Said and Haifa at the same time as the Harpoon convoy assembled ready to pass through the Straits of Gibraltar. This second convoy comprised 11 merchant vessels and the operation designed to get these ships to Malta was to be codenamed Vigorous. Present were nine British vessels – *Ajax*, *Bhutan*, *Bulkoil*, *City of Calcutta*, *City of Edinburgh*, *City of Lincoln*, *City of Pretoria*, *Potaro* and *Rembrandt* – with two Dutch ships, *Aagtekerk* and *Elizabeth Bakke*.

The Mediterranean fleet had been weakened to a point where no capital vessels at all could be made available for this operation, although support could be expected from the hard-pressed WDAF throughout the first leg of the journey. Close escort was provided by a dozen destroyers (from 2nd and 5th Destroyer Flotillas), four corvettes, two minesweepers and two rescue ships. The fleet was joined by the ancient battleship *Centurion* and although she was nothing more than a sea-going hull normally used as a gunnery target ship, she had been fitted with dummy 15-inch guns in a desperate bluff to deceive the enemy!

Rear-Admiral Philip Vian's covering force comprised eight cruisers of 4th and 15th Cruiser Squadrons, including the flagship *Cleopatra*, 14 destroyers (from 7th, 12th, 14th and 22nd Destroyer Flotillas) and four MTBs to be towed by the merchant ships. Aboard the cruiser *Euryalus* as fighter direction officer was Sqn Ldr Innes Westmacott, late commander of the Malta Night Fighter Unit. On being posted to the cruiser, Westmacott discovered that she was not fitted with VHF radio, and that reception with the existing equipment was very poor; in response to his urgent pleas for up-to-date equipment, a Type RTD9 VHF unit was immediately installed.

Of immediate threat to the convoy were the Luftwaffe's specialist anti-shipping Ju 88s based on Crete – I. and II./LG 1, Stab and I./KG 54, and a back-up reconnaissance unit, 2.(F)/124. Quantities of the new LT350 'circling' torpedoes were available for use against the convoy, designed to be dropped by parachute in confined spaces ahead of approaching ships where they would perform a slow, circling run. Their subsequent use by aircraft of I./KG 54 – the first time they had been employed operationally – would, however, prove ineffective. As the ships progressed westwards they could also expect to come under attack by German and Italian aircraft based in Libya.

Friday, 12 June 1942

From this point the actions which were to follow over the western end of the Mediterranean involved almost entirely Axis aircraft operating from Sardinia and Sicily, the Fleet Air Arm carrier-based aircraft, and Malta's defending squadrons. As these operations hardly involved either 201 Group or WDAF units, readers interested in following these are again directed to *Malta: The Spitfire Year 1942*.

In an attempt to neutralize some of the Luftwaffe's potential, a number of commando raids were launched by Maj David Stirling's recently-formed Special Air Service (SAS) against airfields in Cyrenaica and Crete on the night of 13/14 June. Two parties raided airfields in the Benghazi sector, three in the vicinity of Derna, and one at Barce. The island of Crete contained two major Luftwaffe bases at Heraklion and Maleme; these, too, were visited, as well as the newly-constructed landing ground at Tymbaki and Kastelli. The raids on the Cyrenaican airfields resulted in limited successes and serious losses; a group of 16 Free Frenchmen under Lt Augustin Jordain, aided by Capt Herbert Buck and one British NCO, were betrayed and subsequently ambushed at Derna with only the two leaders escaping and no losses to the enemy. Elsewhere, Major Stirling personally led two NCOs to Benina, where it was claimed bombs placed on two Bf 110s and three Ju 53/3ms all detonated, whilst much machinery and stores were also believed to have been destroyed.

The sortie undertaken by Capt Blair 'Paddy' Mayne and three NCOs to the Berka satellite landing ground resulted in a gun-fight; only one bomb had been placed on an aircraft when the party was discovered, and one NCO was killed in the retreat. Another all-Free French party of six under Lt André Zirnheld achieved greater success at Berka Main, where 11 aircraft were claimed destroyed and many casualties inflicted on the airfield guards. A further Free French quartet visited Barce but succeeded only in blowing up petrol and supply dumps.

Perhaps the most ambitious raid was that on Heraklion airfield by a small party of four Frenchmen, led by Cmdt Bergé, and aided by Capt Lord Jellicoe – son of the famous admiral. They had been conveyed to Crete by the submarine *Triton* from Alexandria, arriving off Heraklion on the night of the 12/13th. At least 60 Ju 88s were to be seen on the airfield. The following night as the six men approached the perimeter to commence their sabotage operation, eight Ju 88s came in to land followed by a single Blenheim, which apparently made the correct landing signals, then roared across the airfield dropping bombs, and departed as swiftly as it had arrived! The Blenheim (Z9795 from 14 Squadron) flown by Australian Sgt J.H.Elliott, had filtered in with the returning Junkers, being led to the airfield without difficulty, where the flare path was in full operation. Circling aircraft were seen with their navigation lights on as Elliott dived his Blenheim down to 3,000 feet, releasing bombs from east to west of the flare path. For all the daring of this audacious raid, however, he succeeded only in severely damaging one bomber – an aircraft of 5./LG 1. Two more Blenheims followed at intervals, two others bombing Kastelli, but results of these attacks were unobserved.

The confusion caused by the Blenheim's appearance allowed the SAS party to gain access to the airfield and soon delayed-action bombs (with two-hour time fuses) were placed on the wings and tailplanes of 16 Ju 88s, and on four other aircraft including an Fi 156, as well as on a Ju 88 about to take off. More bombs were placed in four trucks and a petrol dump and in crates or aero engines. The commandos got away undetected and rejoined their Greek guide. Capt Lord Jellicoe and the guide separated from the others to seek a British agent in a nearby village, but misfortune then overtook the Frenchmen when they ran into a German patrol. Caporal Leostic (who claimed to be 18 but was in fact just 14) was killed; Caporal Chef Siebert was wounded and captured, whilst Cmdt Bergé and Sgt Muhot were both taken prisoner. Lord Jellicoe and the guide made good their escape and joined by 25 Cretan patriots, were later picked up by *Triton*. When the time bombs exploded seven of I./LG 1's Ju 88s were severely damaged, whilst two of 2.(F)/124's reconnaissance Ju 88Ds were so badly damaged that they were deemed irreparable.

The attempted raid on Maleme was called off when it was discovered that the airfield was too well guarded for infiltration, but reconnaissance showed Tymbaki to be vacant. Better success was achieved at Kastelli though, where Capt George Duncan and two NCOs succeeded in placing their explosive devices on eight aircraft, as well as on six trucks, four bomb dumps and seven petrol dumps; later, intelligence reports suggested that at least 70 military personnel had been killed in the resultant explosions. Eight New Zealanders who had evaded capture when the island fell the previous year and who had been hiding ever since, were brought out with the SAS party.

British Claims

127 Sqn	unspecified		Ju 88 Damaged	over convoy	1730-1930
73 Sqn	Sgt G.Hill	Hurricane IIc BN546	Ju 87	8 m SE Acroma	1955
GC1 Alsace	unspecified		Ju 88 Damaged	Sidi Barrani	2000

German Casualties

I./LG 1	Ju 88A04 WNr 5556 35% damaged by sabotage at Heraklion a/f
I./LG 1	Ju 88A-4 WNr 5572 35% damaged by sabotage at Heraklion a/f
I./LG 1	Ju 88A-4 WNr 5578 35% damaged by sabotage at Heraklion a/f
I./LG 1	Ju 88A-4 WNr 140007 35% damaged by sabotage at Heraklion a/f
I./LG 1	Ju 88A-4 WNr 140008 L1+YL 35% damaged by sabotage at Heraklion a/f
I./LG 1	Ju 88A-4 WNr 140025 35% damaged by sabotage at Heraklion a/f
II./LG 1	Ju 88A-4 WNr 5585 70% damaged by sabotage at Heraklion a/f
2.(F)/123	Ju 88D-5 WNr 430093 80% destroyed by sabotage at Heraklion a/f
2.(F)/123	Ju 88D-5 WNr 430054 70% destroyed by sabotage at Heraklion a/f

Despite the heroism of these actions, the Vigorous convoy seemed to be ill-fated from the start. Four of the merchant vessels, escorted by the AA cruiser *Coventry* and eight destroyers had departed 36 hours prior to the main sailing as a feint (codenamed Rembrandt) designed to draw the Italian fleet to sea early. Late next day (13 June) as these vessels headed back to Alexandria, a number of Ju 88s and 15 Ju 87s of II./StG 3 arrived overhead and commenced their dives; *Coventry* was near-missed by sticks of bombs dropped by three Ju 88s on either flank, her crew fortunate to escape injury as splinters whined overhead, but *City of Calcutta* was severely shaken. With her plates leaking, caused by the blast of another near-miss, she was ordered to make for Tobruk.

As the attack on the convoy progressed, four Hurricanes of GC 1 Alsace arrived on the scene from Fuka. The French pilots observed bombs falling on the convoy and exploding close to *City of Calcutta*, but they failed to spot the attackers in the fading light. The quartet of Hurricane pilots were soon forced by the rapidly approaching darkness to return to base, Capitaine Paul Ezanno (the leader) and Sgt Chef Pierre Leplang force-landing en route; neither pilot was hurt.

No sooner had the main convoy and the rest of the diversionary shipping rendezvoused on the 13th, than *Elizabeth Bakke* began to drop astern, unable to maintain the convoy speed of 13 knots; she was escorted back to Alexandria. Within a few more hours two of the corvettes had been obliged to drop out, while *Aagterkerk* was found to be too slow and was ordered to the closest friendly haven, which was by now Tobruk. When still some dozen miles out, the old Dutch vessel was discovered, attacked and sunk by an estimated 40 Ju 87s and Ju 88s, five of her crew being lost. Escorting destroyers put up a spirited resistance, claiming three of the Stukas shot down, although the accompanying corvette *Primula* also suffered damage during the attack. Three of II./StG 3's Stukas were indeed reported lost, including that flown by the 6 Staffelkapitän, Oblt Anton Ostler and his gunner.

Sunday, 14 June 1942

By dawn the remaining vessels were well into 'Bomb Alley' between Crete and North Africa, the convoy having been shadowed throughout the night. German aircraft dropped flares almost continuously, practically transforming night into day, but no attacks developed. With the coming of daylight, attacks were expected from both north and south, although some escort was provided by elements of the Western Desert Air Force, diverted from the desperate fighting which was underway in the Gazala area.

At 0835 Kittyhawks of 260 Squadron, from their airfield near Mersa Matruh, began a series of patrols over the ships and just over an hour later the first attack by African-based Luftwaffe aircraft was intercepted, as Ju 87s and Ju 88s approached, escorted by 19 Bf 109s of III./JG 53 – the unit which until recently had been operating from Malta. The Messerschmitts attacked at once, Lts Harder and Quaritsch each claiming a Kittyhawk shot down; Plt Off F.A.Creighton and Sgt Webster of 250 Squadron were lost. The German pilots also reported meeting Hurricanes, two of which were claimed by Oblt Götz and a third by Obfw Stumpf. The Hurricanes were from 238 Squadron, Flt Lt M.R.Jenkins and Plt Off O.F.A.Oram both being obliged to bale out. In return Flt Sgt Edwards of 260 claimed a Bf 109 probable and one damaged. He would seem to have hit the aircraft of Lt Hicke of Stab III./JG 53, who landed at base wounded, and with his aircraft slightly damaged. The British fighters, however, succeeded in keeping the bombers away from the convoy.

It was now the turn of eight Tomahawks of 5 SAAF Squadron to patrol from 1150 as the convoy passed the stretch of coast between Tobruk and El Adem. Again the Luftwaffe appeared, Ju 87s of III./StG 3 attacking under cover of ten Bf 109s from I./JG 27 and others from III./JG 53. This time the South Africans were able to get at the bombers, claiming two shot down and one probable before the escorts struck. Lt van der Spuy claimed one fighter shot down and it would seem that this was flown by III./JG 53's Lt Quaritsch, who failed to return. Van der Spuy was then shot down himself, baling out wounded. Two more Messerschmitts were claimed to have been damaged, but as the claimants turned for home, Lt Kemsley's aircraft was hard hit and he was obliged to force-land. During these morning combats which had caused the WDAF fighters six losses, Luftwaffe pilots had claimed eight.

None of the ships were hit during the Stuka attacks, thanks mainly to the fierce barrage put up by the escorts and the determination of the South African fighters; III./StG 3 reported the loss of one of its Ju 87s. By the early afternoon the convoy was getting beyond the range of single-engined fighter protection, Beaufighters and Hudsons taking over patrol duties. Unfortunately, the ships and their air escorts were not beyond the range of the German fighters which were, of course, based further to the west than were those of WDAF. Indeed, I./JG 27 and III./JG 53 swiftly moved to Derna to continue their activities. It was to a patrolling Ju 88C of I./NJG 2's Derna detachment that the first Beaufighter fell victim, however, as six such aircraft from 272 Squadron and three from 252 Squadron took up their patrol areas. T4709 'O' of the former unit, crewed by Free Frenchman Flt Sgt Jacques Gael and Sgt F.V.Amos, was seen to fall in flames at 1430, shot down by Lt Wiedow.

Operating against the Vigorous convoy on 14 June was Oblt Gerhard Brenner of LG 1, who was awarded the Ritterkreuz.

At 1635, ten Messerschmitts of I./JG 27 were off from Derna to escort Ju 87s of II./StG 3, followed by nine III./JG 53 aircraft, at about the same time as three 272 Squadron Beaufighters departed from Gambut to commence their convoy patrols. Half an hour later two more aircraft from this unit, and one from 252 Squadron, also set out to cover the convoy and to join a Hudson from 459 Squadron flown by Plt Off W. Blackstock. During the next hour two of the Beaufighters ('A' and 'S') and the Hudson were shot down, the latter by Oblt Ernst Kläger of III./JG 53 and the Beaufighters by Lt Körner and Lt Karl von Lieres of I./JG 27; none of the RAF and RAAF crews survived. It seems likely that the Beaufighter pilots put up a stiff resistance before their demise, as one of the Messerschmitts also failed to return, Lt Heinrich Hesse of 7./JG 53 baling out of 'White 6' into the sea. One Stuka (S7+GC) fell to the ships' AA fire, the crew being killed.

The other 272 Squadron machine from the second patrol, 'R' flown by Belgian Sgt Yves Tedesco – an aggressive and successful pilot with several victories to his credit – also failed to return. As twilight approached, Tedesco was warned by *Coventry*'s fighter direction officer that two twin-engined 'hostiles' were in the vicinity and almost immediately he encountered a Ju 88 emerging from cloud, but he only had time for a short burst of cannon fire; he reported seeing a streak of flame from the Junkers before it disappeared from sight again. Control then vectored him onto the second 'shadower' which he saw below, and attacked in a gentle dive; the German gunner opened fire and the Belgian replied, but at once the Beaufighter's starboard engine exploded, the flaming aircraft plummeting into the sea. It was believed, however, that the Beaufighter had been hit by AA fire from the convoy's escorts; neither Tedesco nor his navigator survived. Meanwhile, Plt Off Easton Thwaites, the pilot of the 252 Squadron aircraft, also encountered a Ju 88 and carried out two stern attacks with machine guns and cannon; the Junkers was believed to have been damaged but was lost sight of when its pilot took evasive action, then out-pacing the Beaufighter to escape.

Just before 5 SAAF got to the Stukas 15 miles off Tobruk, the latter bombed and set a cargo ship alight. Uffz Beckmann of 2./JG 27 then undertook a sortie in a Red Cross-marked FW 44 Weihe at 1615, searching for any survivors. Apparently his aircraft was spotted by the crew of a Beaufighter but they forbore to attack it.

Taking into consideration all the missions performed by Sardinia and Sicily based units, (see *Malta: The Spitfire Year, 1942*, for details), Sunday 14 June probably saw the largest and most powerful assault carried out by Regia Aeronautica aircraft since the beginning of the war. During the three hours from 1800-2100 no fewer than seven separate waves of bombers attacked, generally at a strength of about a dozen aircraft per wave. Most were Ju 88s of LG 1 and KG 54 from Crete, joined by five Cant.Z.1007bis of 47° Stormo (four of 262ª Squadriglia and one of 261ª) which had taken off from Rhodes at 1625, led by Cap Athos Maestri. At 1845 a large formation of 36 ships was sighted and bombed by these aircraft, some hits on a freighter being claimed.

The convoy was now frequently devoid of fighter escort as the Junkers made their individual dives to 3,000ft before releasing their bombs. The 6,104-ton freighter *Bhutan*, lying at the rear of the port column, received much of this attention, being struck by at least three bombs in quick succession. She sank within 20 minutes, six of her crew going down with her, although 174 others were picked up by the rescue ships *Antwerp* and *Malines*. A second freighter, *Potaro*, also sustained damage during these attacks and several other vessels were near-missed. The ancient but heavily-armed and armour-decked *Centurion* absorbed several hits, her gunners claiming four of the attackers shot down. However, four torpedo-carrying S.79s of 41° Gruppo Aut BT/AS from Derna failed to locate the convoy.

Five more 272 Squadron Beaufighters departed Gambut at 1815, led by Wg Cdr Bill Riley who had again been attached to this unit from group headquarters. As the new escorts took up their station, two Messerschmitts from III./JG 53 appeared overhead, searching for their missing comrade, Lt Hesse. Obfw Alfred Seidl at once dived on Plt Off W.H.Rogers' aircraft (T4885 'F') and shot it down so swiftly that the pilot and observer, Sgt G.L.Woolven, later reported that they thought they had been accidentally shot down by Wg Cdr Riley. This belief was reinforced when Riley returned to claim a Ju 88 shot down (raising his victory tally to at least seven). There is little doubt, however, that his victim had indeed been a German aircraft for, apart from the fact that Seidl did claim a Beaufighter shot down, two Ju 88s were reported lost to fighters or AA and three more were damaged and crash-landed on return to Crete.

The crew of the shot-down Beaufighter (Rogers and Woolven) were fortunate to survive the ditching. When their aircraft hit the sea, the observer was able to scramble clear but it rapidly sank, taking the pilot down with it. Unable to open the escape hatch, Rogers resigned himself to his fate until pressure burst open the hatch and he was shot to the surface in an air bubble! At the same time an almost empty fuel tank was ripped from the wing as the aircraft broke up and surfaced nearby allowing Woolven, who was a poor swimmer, to use it as a raft as Rogers pushed him ashore – in a swim that lasted ten hours.

Another of the bombers was claimed during this patrol by 272 Squadron's Sgt George Tuckwell for his second victory. Tuckwell had been endeavouring to maintain station over the convoy but was constantly fired on by the escorting warships, despite his being in radio contact with *Coventry*, and firing off the correct identification flares. Eventually, finding himself low on fuel, he decided to fly on to Malta but while en route he spotted a Ju 88, managed to manoeuvre onto its tail – apparently unseen – and shot it down. Tuckwell's victim was possibly an LG 1 aircraft flown by Oblt Gerhard Brenner, from which the crew took to their dinghy; of their subsequent plight, colleague Gerd Stamp recalled: "We shadowed them for several days whilst they were in their dinghy, but the sea was too high and too rough for a landing by a flyingboat. It was terrible not to be able to get them out of the water."About a week later the dinghy was recovered but of Brenner and his crew there was no sign; it was assumed that they had been washed overboard in heavy seas.

Two other Ju 88s from LG 1 crash-landed at Heraklion having sustained fighter or AA damage; Oblt Helmut Löhnert's Junkers had been heavily damaged, while I./KG 54 also suffered a further loss. Lt Herbert Knöthe's B3+ML was attacked by a fighter about 70 miles to the west of Crete (probably Wg Cdr Riley's victim); the damaged aircraft succeeded in reaching Crete, only to crash on landing at Tymbaki, where it was totally destroyed. The crew perished.

Such was the almost continuous barrage put up by the escorts during the day, particularly during the evening period, that a number of warships now had extremely depleted supplies of anti-aircraft ammunition. Doubt was seriously expressed as to whether sufficient remained to see the convoy through during the final, most dangerous leg of the journey. Worse was to come, for later in the day the pilot of a reconnaissance Spitfire from Malta spotted a major sortie into the Ionian Sea by a substantial part of the Italian fleet from Taranto. This sortie included the battleships *Vittorio Veneto* (Ammiraglio Angelo Iachino) and *Littorio* (Ammiraglio Giuseppe Fioravanzo), the latter embarking an R/T and W/T interception unit, as did the cruiser *Garibaldi*. These two ships, and the cruiser *Gorizia*, also carried

Luftwaffe fighter direction officers (FDOs). Two other cruisers and a dozen destroyers completed the force, one of the latter (*Legionario*) equipped with German 'Dete' radar apparatus. It was on the personal orders of Mussolini, who had for the first time assumed supreme command of the Italian navy, that Iachino's fleet had put to sea to challenge the British force.

The report of this foray was a sufficient deterrent to Rear Admiral Vian's small escorting force of British cruisers – they would be quite unable to match the gun power of such formidable adversaries and reluctantly, at 0200 on 15 June, the convoy was ordered to return to Alexandria. As the escort vessels turned, six German S-boats of the 3rd MTB Flotilla operating out of Derna – which had been circling the convoy awaiting opportunities to strike – attacked with the benefit of the confusion caused by 40 ships attempting an about-turn manoeuvre. While shadowing aircraft overhead continued to illuminate the scene, Lt Wüppermann in MTB S.56 seized the opportunity to fire a torpedo at the cruiser *Newcastle*, achieving a hit on her bow which forced her to reduce speed. The captain of S.55, Lt Horst Weber, hit another of the escort when *Hasty* took a torpedo amidships; the disabled destroyer was later abandoned and sent to the bottom.

Malta was at once alerted to strike at the new Italian threat and at 2345 five Wellingtons of 38 Squadron, armed with two torpedoes apiece, commenced taking off from Luqa, from where they were homed to the target area by a sixth aircraft, equipped with ASV. On the approach of these bombers the Italians at once made smoke, and only Flg Off Michael Foulis (DV544 'J') was able to complete a couple of runs at the ships; no results of the attack were observed by his crew although the crew of the ASV aircraft reported a red glow in the darkness.

British Claims

213 Sqn	Sqn Ldr M.H.Young	Hurricane IIc BN286 'O'	Bf 109F Damaged	El Adem area	0900-1015
260 Sqn	Flt Sgt J.F.Edwards	Kittyhawk Ia 'T'	Bf 109F Probable	Acroma area	1144-1225
260 Sqn	Flt Sgt J.F.Edwards	Kittyhawk Ia 'T'	Bf 109F Damaged	Acroma area	1144-1225
5 SAAF Sqn	Maj J.E.Frost	Tomahawk IIb AN422 'B'	Ju 87	S El Adem-Tobruk	1150-1255
5 SAAF Sqn	Maj J.E.Frost	Tomahawk IIb AN422 'B'	Bf 109F Damaged	S El Adem-Tobruk	1150-1255
5 SAAF Sqn	Lt K.C.Kemsley	Tomahawk IIb AN345 'V'	Ju 87	S El Adem-Tobruk	1150-1255
5 SAAF Sqn	Lt K.C.Kemsley	Tomahawk IIb AN345 'V'	Ju 87 Probable	S El Adem-Tobruk	1150-1255
5 SAAF Sqn	Lt K.C.Kemsley	Tomahawk IIb AN345 'V'	Bf 109F Damaged	S El Adem-Tobruk	1150-1255
5 SAAF Sqn	Lt L.B.van der Spuy	Tomahawk IIb ..	Bf 109	S El Adem-Tobruk	1150-1255
252 Sqn	Plt Off F.E.Thwaites/ Sgt R.S.Coles	Beaufighter Ic T4828 'D'	Ju 88 Damaged	escort convoy MW 11	1455-1850
272 Sqn	Sgt G.A.Tuckwell/ Sgt Forrest	Beaufighter Ic T7329 'W	Ju 88 Probable	escort convoy MW 11	1815-0005
227 Sqn	Sqn Ldr W.Riley	Beaufighter Ic	Ju 88	escort convoy MW11	1815-2005

British Casualties

250 Sqn	Kittyhawk I AK775 left 0955 MiA on convoy patrol; Sgt Webster baled out, rescued by corvette after 30 hours in dinghy
250 Sqn	Kittyhawk I AL151 left 0955 MiA on convoy patrol; Plt Off F.A.Creighton MiA
272 Sqn	Beaufighter T4840 'R' shot down by return fire from Ju 88 at approx 1800; Sgt Y.C.Tedesco/Sgt F.Ransom
272 Sqn	Beaufighter T4867 'S' shot down by Bf 109; Sgt E.R.F.Truby PoW/Sgt K.J.Garrett KiA
272 Sqn	Beaufighter T4885 'F' shot down by Bf 109 NE of Derna at 1915; Plt Off W.B.Rogers/Sgt G. L.Woolven both rescued
272 Sqn	Beaufighter T4709 'O' shot down by Ju 88C at 1430; Sgt J.Gael PoW/Sgt F.V.Amos KiA
272 Sqn	Beaufighter T3291 'A' took off 1615 for convoy escort, shot down; Flt Sgt A.E.Cooper /Sgt C.C.Ridgeway MiA
108 Sqn	Wellington AD624 MiA Benghazi Harbour 0025-0054
459 Sqn	Hudson IV V9022 shot down by Bf 109s on convoy escort; Plt Off W Blackstock and crew MiA
158 Sqn	Liberator II reported crash-landed short of Fayid on return from escorting convoy from Alexandria to Malta with one gunner dead. May be AL553 struck off charge on 31 July

German Claims

2./JG 27	Lt Friedrich Körner	Beaufighter	NNE Derna	1705
2./JG 27	Lt Karl von Lieres und Wilkau	Beaufighter	NNE Derna	1708
7./JG 53	Uffz Paul Gläser	Hudson	NNE Derna	
8./JG 53	Obfw Alfred Seidl	Beaufighter	110km NNE Derna	1915
Stab/NJG 2	Lt Georg Wiedow	Blenheim	NE Derna	1330
Stab I./LG 1	Oblt Gerhard Stamp	Beaufighter	NE Derna	1800

German Casualties

Stab III./JG 53	Bf 109F-4 trop WNr 8680 Black <1+I combat P-40 50km NE Tobruk landed slightly damaged; Lt Walter Hicke WiA
7./JG 53	Bf 109F-4 WNr 10163 White 6+I combat P-40 over sea 100km N Derna; Lt Heinrich Hesse picked up next day by rescue launch
8./JG 53	Bf 109F-4 WNr 10068 Black 9+I combat P-40 over sea. Crashed 3-4km NE Tobruk; Lt Karl-Heinz Quaritsch MiA
5./StG 3	Ju 87D-1 WNr 2463 S7+QC ships' AA 100km NE Derna; Uffz Julius Küpers/ Uffz Johann Kammann KiA
6./StG 3	Ju 87D S7+HN shot down by ships' AA; Oblt Anton Ostler and Obfw Wilhelm Lichtenstein KiA
7./StG 3	Ju 87 LK P-40 20km NE Tobruk; Obfw Gerhard Pantel/Uffz Hermann Riegel KiA
1./LG 1	Ju 88A-4 WNr 5542 L1+CH shot down by AA into sea 100km S Crete; empty dinghy found a week later; Oblt Gerhard Brenner (RK) and three MiA
1./LG 1	Ju 88A-4 WNr 6753 badly shot-up in combat, crash-landed Comiso 50% damaged
5./LG 1	Ju 88A-4 10% damaged in combat S Crete but landed safely at base; one of crew WiA
2./KG 54	Ju 88A-4 WNr 140216 B3+TL ditched in sea 90km S Crete

Monday, 15 June 1942

Nine of 217 Squadron's recently-arrived Beauforts were to follow before first light, but the unit's aircrew were largely 'green', with little torpedo training and virtually no operational experience. Following take-off at 0415, only five managed to form up in the dark, the other four proceeding independently. After a long and fruitless search, one of the latter, flown by Flg Off Arthur Aldridge – in DD958 'M' one of the few experienced pilots – spotted the long column of big warships in the dawn light. He headed straight in, putting his torpedo into the heavy cruiser *Trento* which came to a halt, on fire, listing and badly damaged. Apparently Italian lookouts had mistaken Aldridge's aircraft as one of their own, the guns opening up only as the Beaufort sped away, although the gunners were fully alerted by the time the main formation arrived shortly afterwards, guided in by the gunfire.

Wg Cdr Davies led the first vic of three which, despite intense AA fire, claimed two possible hits on a battleship. Flg Off Goodale's aircraft was struck by shrapnel and a small fire started, which was soon extinguished by two members of the crew. From the opposite direction Sqn Ldr R.G.Lynn led another pair also to attack one of the battleships, which was believed hit, as was an escorting destroyer. Lt Ted Strever, SAAF, went after the battleships and their escorts to the north but his aircraft (DD995) was shot-up and his air gunner, Sgt Bob Gray, wounded; a belly-landing was effected on return to Luqa. Finally,

An IMAM Ro.43 was employed for reconnaissance purposes aboard the larger warships of the Italian navy.

A Ro.43 floatplane is hoisted back aboard its parent warship.

Flg Off Bill Stevens, the unit's other experienced pilot on the mission, arrived but his torpedo, aimed at the crippled *Trento* enveloped in the smoke-screen, missed its target. Although crews believed they had achieved hits on various vessels, including both battleships, in fact no additional damage was caused. In return, Italian gunners claimed two of the Beauforts shot down.

The whole attack had been witnessed by Lt S.L.C.Maydon from the conning tower of his submarine *Umbra*. Amidst all the confusion he went in close to give the stricken cruiser the 'coup de grace', firing two more torpedoes into her considerable bulk; she rolled over and sank taking many of her crew with her, including her captain, C.V. Stanislao Esposito, as well as her Ro.43 floatplane (MM 27097).

Further strikes were on their way in the shape of a flight of seven USAAF B-24Ds and two RAF Liberator IIs of 160 Squadron from Fayid in Egypt. Following a flight of five and a half hours from Fayid, during the latter stages of which they had overflown Vian's force – to be greeted by an intense barrage of AA fire resulting in a number of aircraft being peppered with shell splinters – the B-24Ds (led by Maj Al Kalberer) and accompanied by the two RAF aircraft, arrived over the Italian warships just ahead of another small force of Beauforts from Sidi Barrani. Each of the American bombers carried a Royal Navy observer to help with identification of targets. Although a number of Ju 88s were seen at low level over the ships – obviously seeking low-flying Beauforts – Kalberer led four of the big bombers down to attack *Littorio*, while the other three of his formation went for *Gorizia*; the two RAF Liberator crews attacked from low level in an attempt to divert Italian AA gunners. Of the attack, Maj Kalberer later reported:

> "Most of the bombs crashed on the main deck of the big ship, setting fires. The second flight dropped a higher percentage on the cruiser.....It was the rare perfect bombing operation. We attained complete surprise and wasted very few bombs. The two ships stopped dead in the water, and the Ju 88s climbed after us. We dived to within ten feet of the waves and made it home untouched, except for the 'friendly' damage."

This statement would not appear to be completely accurate though, for as the bombers sped for home they were seen by two of III./JG 27's Bf 109 pilots, who had in the meantime found the missing Lt Hesse and were circling over his dinghy. Initially identifying the big, slab-sided bombers as "nine four-engined flyingboats", they attacked at 1040, Oblt Heinecke claiming one shot down into the sea 60 miles off the North African coast. In return one of the American gunners claimed a Messerschmitt shot down – the first USAAF claim to be made for an Axis aircraft in the Mediterranean area; no Luftwaffe loss was actually suffered. It would seem that Heinecke – formerly of III./JG 53 – had attacked one of the RAF Liberators, for Sgt W.J.Wilson's aircraft was hit and badly damaged, the mid-upper gunner being killed; bad weather eventually forced the Australian Wilson to crash-land his ailing machine short of Fayid, fortunately without much further damage to the aircraft or injury to the crew.

Although the bombing was accurate – the three warships being straddled by many near-misses – only one 500lb bomb actually found a target, hitting the *Littorio*'s 'A' turret, killing one member of the crew and wounding 12 others. Little damage resulted apart from shaking one of the battleship's Ro.43 spotter aircraft (MM27152) off its launching platform into the sea, with the other Ro.43 (MM27160) being damaged.

There was to be a third assault on the Italian force, for 12 Beauforts of 39 Squadron had set out from LG.05 (near Sidi Barrani) shortly after sunrise. They were led by their commanding officer, Wg Cdr Mason, in DD951, and were to be homed to the area of action by a Maryland of 203 Squadron. Two Beaufighters of 272 Squadron from Gambut accompanied them as a rather inadequate escort. Spread out in four vics of three, line abreast, the Beauforts – mainly more powerful Mark IIs but led by the CO in an older, slower Mark I – were nearing the limit of their search range without seeing any sign of their quarry, when splashes were noticed in the distance. Believing these to be bomb explosions, the formation headed in that direction, but Mason had been misled. The splashes were as a result of long-range fuel tanks being jettisoned into the sea by five Bf 109s of 9./JG 53, which were on their way to Athens/Eleusis airfield in Greece.

The Messerschmitt pilots had spotted what they believed to be 15 Beauforts and Beaufighters heading for Malta and now swept in behind the formation diagonally from the south-east. By all reports they approached with initial caution. The first the torpedo-bomber crews knew of their presence was when the Beaufort at the far left of the formation, Flt Lt C.S.Thomas' AW352, broke in half behind the dorsal turret, the front section of the aircraft plunging into the sea in flames. The remaining aircraft dived for the sea, their throttles wide open. The Messerschmitts followed, 'hosepiping' their fire at the torpedo-carriers and within seconds AW297, positioned on the right and flown by Plt Off James Abram, a former Sunderland pilot on his first torpedo operation, crashed into the water. Sgt Lionel Daffurn's DD974 was so badly damaged by three of the German fighters that he could hardly keep it in the air; with his air gunner, Sgt Pearson, wounded by splinters in both legs and in one hand and arm, Daffurn turned back and eventually managed to crash-land near Sidi Barrani.

Plt Off Grant's aircraft (DD940) was also badly hit and his observer, Sgt Williams, wounded by a cannon shell. He also turned for land as did two of the flight leaders, Flt Lts Taylor and Leaning, both of whom had used excessive fuel in evading their attackers. Meanwhile, Flg Off R.C.Hooper's aircraft (DD955) was seen to break away and head in the direction of Malta, but came down in the sea from where the pilot and two of his crew were rescued by an Axis aircraft; the missing crewman, air gunner Sgt J.Haining, was picked up separately.

One of the escorting Beaufighters, T4869 'J' piloted by another Belgian, Plt Off Roger Corbisier, had been shot down a few minutes before the Beauforts, but apparently double-claimed by two of the German pilots who each claimed a Beaufighter shot down in the same location and within a minute of each other. The rest of the 9 Staffel pilots over-estimated their success a little; they had hit seven Beauforts, shooting down two and causing two subsequently to crash-land, but claimed eight shot down including three by Hptm Belser and two each by Lt Dietrich Kasten and Obfw Alfred Seidl. At around this time, two more Bf 109s from III./JG 27 were out looking for Lt Hesse's dinghy, unaware that two others had already located it. By chance they came upon the other 272 Squadron Beaufighter – Sgt W.G.Blessing's T4829 'V' – as it headed back towards North Africa. It was shot down into the sea by Obfw Rösenberg, the Australian pilot and his observer (Sgt J.R.Williams) being lost.

Meanwhile, Wg Cdr Mason, now with only five of his force of Beauforts remaining, had at last made contact with the 203 Squadron Maryland shadowing the Italian warships. This aircraft led the torpedo-bombers in to attack the capital ships at the same time as the composite formation of Liberators released their bombs from higher level. Two of the Beauforts were hard-hit by AA fire and were forced to release their torpedoes prematurely, but the other three – flown by Wg Cdr Mason, Flg Off Jepson and Wt Off F.Morse – pressed on and made their drops, reporting a hit on the battleship *Littorio*. All had missed, however; what they had seen was the explosion of the bomb dropped by one of the B-24Ds. On completion of the attack, the five aircraft headed for Malta where Sqn Ldr Pat Gibbs successfully belly-landed his Flak-damaged aircraft (AW337), and Plt Off Dick Marshall collided with a damaged 217 Squadron machine on landing his heavily-damaged DD975. Both went up in flames, although Marshall and his crew escaped. Wg Cdr Mason was awarded an immediate DFC for his leadership, and Sqn Ldr Gibbs received an immediate Bar to his DFC.

Whilst these actions were taking place to the west, other Beaufighters were continuing to provide some cover for the convoy. One pair, flown by Plt Off Peter Cobley and Sgt Bill Knight, encountered an Ro.43 biplane spotter which they shot down, MM27186 from the cruiser *Gorizia* being lost, Cap Gastone Mezzetti and T.V. Arnaldo Pannaria failing to return. A second Ro.43, MM27127 from the cruiser *Garibaldi*, flown by Serg Ermanno Tommasini and T.V. Benedetto Ferraro, crashed into the sea when being launched, the two aboard both being killed.

Meanwhile, the convoy's escort continued to fire at friend and foe alike, and while the fighter controller aboard *Coventry* desperately tried to keep the escorting fighters out of harm's way, the situation was very confused. At one stage of the proceedings it became apparent that Cobley was being vectored onto his own shadow, and he retorted with the classic "Peter was merely chasing Cobley".

Another 272 Squadron Beaufighter, which followed at 1020, came across S.Ten Edoardo Visentin's Cant.Z.506B floatplane of 171ª Squadriglia out from Augusta since 0825, which Sgt N.J.Cleggett promptly despatched into the sea. Shortly afterwards a lone S.79 was met by this same crew and in an exchange of fire was claimed damaged. Earlier in this sortie, the Beaufighter had flown over elements of the Italian fleet and making a careful observation, Plt Off Gerry Williams (the observer) flashed "Balls!" on his Aldis lamp at the nearest cruiser, which promptly opened fire, albeit very inaccurately!

Another Cant.Z.506 of 288ª Squadriglia, flown by Ten Mario Martinelli from Taranto, was attacked by an aircraft identified as a Blenheim at 1145 but managed to drive away the attacker; the latter was almost certainly another Beaufighter. Then, about 120 miles off Benghazi, the crew sighted the wreck of Visentin's floatplane and a dinghy with two men aboard. However, an attempt to land on the rough sea to pick up these survivors ended in disaster when the aircraft was swamped by high seas, ending with the destruction of this floatplane too. All six surviving crewmen from the two aircraft were subsequently rescued by the Regia Marina destroyer *Camicia Nera*.

Following the initial attacks on the Italian fleet by 217 Squadron, during which it was believed that both battleships had been hit, Admiral Sir Henry Harwood, commander-in-chief Mediterranean (working closely with Air Marshal Sir Arthur Tedder in Alexandria), ordered Admiral Vian's Vigorous convoy again to turn westwards. Then, at 0830, a signal was received from a reconnaissance aircraft to the effect that the two battleships, with three cruisers and nine destroyers were still heading for the convoy and were now within 150 miles of intercepting. Admiral Vian was again ordered, for the third time, to reverse course.

Two hours later with the reports to hand of the claims of the American B-24 crews for hits and near misses on the Italian warships, a further signal was sent to Vian to turn westwards yet again! At 1345, when he received this signal, his ships were under heavy attack by ten Ju 87s from III./StG 3, which disabled the cruiser *Birmingham*. Vian realized the battle was lost and that any further attempt to push the convoy westwards would most probably result in the loss of all his ships and their gallant crews, so he ignored this latest order and continued withdrawing to the east. Admiral Harwood finally conceded that Vian – as the man on the spot – must do what he considered best.

To those of the convoy the sky never seemed empty of Axis bombers which continued to appear in small waves of two or three to dive at individual ships. During the early afternoon 35 Ju 87s of II./StG 3 arrived on the scene, and soon the destroyer *Airedale* was severely damaged by a number of hits and near-misses which killed 44 of her crew, and she had to be abandoned and sunk by gunfire. *Centurion* was repeatedly hit and *Arethusa* damaged, while the Australian destroyer *Nestor* was so badly holed that she had to be scuttled; three of her crew were lost. Amongst the afternoon attackers was Lt Sattler of I./LG 1, on his second sortie of the day in his Ju 88 L1+NH, who reported a near miss on the port side of a light cruiser.

272 Squadron from Gambut was again called upon to fly protective sorties as the convoy came within range, but with the loss of seven aircraft and crews in two days' fighting, only a handful of aircraft were available. The squadron diarist sadly noted: "Two of the blackest days in the Squadron's history". Hence only Plt Off E.H.Hodgson's Beaufighter was available to patrol between 1500-1900. Help was to hand, however, for 252 Squadron was ordered to make available all its Beaufighters to assist its sister unit, four pairs commencing patrols as from 1400. The ships' gunners continued to give the Beaufighters a hostile reception. When the aircraft flown by 272 Squadron's Sqn Ldr C.V.Ogden and his No.2, Flg Off Gunnis (of 252 Squadron) arrived to assist, they were almost blasted out of the sky – at which the Beaufighter leader contacted *Coventry* and informed the FDO that he was withdrawing.

As soon as the vessels came within range of single-engined fighters, such of these as could be spared were sent out to join the Beaufighters in their task. In addition to the Luftwaffe attacks. four Cant.Z.1007bis of 190ª Squadriglia led by T.Col Marrama had taken off at 1445 from Barce to bomb the convoy, one ship being claimed probably sunk.

Towards evening, four Kittyhawks from 250 Squadron arrived and these were over the convoy when six S.79s from 279ª Squadriglia AS from Derna swept in, joined by four more such aircraft from 204ª Squadriglia, 41° Gruppo AS, led by Ten Silvio Cella from Rhodes. Torpedoes were released at 1715 and a destroyer was claimed sunk. The Italian crews also reported that they had been attacked by Hurricanes and Spitfires, but it was actually the Kittyhawks which had intercepted them. Flg Off Percy Copeland claimed two shot down, while Sgt F.C.De Salvo claimed another damaged. One of the 252 Squadron Beaufighters also engaged the Savoias, Plt Off Easton Thwaites (T4831) claiming one of the torpedo-bombers probably destroyed. Ten Salvatore Annona's aircraft was lost, reportedly having been shot down by two Beaufighters, while Ten Luigi Vicariotto had to force-land his aircraft in Crete. Returning crews additionally claimed hits on two cruisers, while gunners believed that they had shot down three British fighters and probably a fourth. Following this fight, Copeland remained alone over the ships until 2000, when darkness once more fell to protect them.

It was nearly dusk when Ju 88s of I./LG 1 and I./KG 54 made their final attack and reported patrolling RAF night fighters with their navigation lights switched on. In an attempt to deceive the ships' gunners Lt Sattler, now flying L1+AL, switched on his own lights and dived onto a destroyer which he claimed suffered three direct hits on its stern, exploded and sank. The reported 'night fighters' were in fact, the Beaufighters and Kittyhawks and a single Hudson of 459 RAAF Squadron, which had continued to provide individual aircraft in support of the convoy.

The pilot of the Hudson (V9052 'D'), Plt Off W.G.Cowan-Hunt, reported attacking two Ju 88s when flying at 400 feet – one on a parallel course, the other attacking his aircraft from astern. As he took evasive action – with the Hudson almost touching the waves – the turret gunner (Sgt H.A.Jackson) returned fire, reporting strikes on the Junkers' starboard engine. Cowan-Hunt opened fire on the other aircraft with his front guns as it turned to attack and strikes were seen on its fuselage and starboard engine, which reportedly burst into flames; it was last seen losing height. Another Ju 88 was claimed shot down by 252 Squadron's Sgt R.H.Vickery (T4828), one of the Royal Navy ships apparently confirming his victory.

With these assaults on the battered convoy underway, Admiral Vian received yet another signal from Alexandria. Reports indicated the Italians had now given up the chase, and were retiring to Taranto. "Now is the golden opportunity to get the convoy to Malta" was the gist of Admiral Harwood's message, but he conceded this would be impractical should fuel and ammunition be causing anxiety. Indeed it was, the majority of the destroyers having just 20% ammunition remaining, which was considered insufficient for the passage to Malta. The operation was now officially aborted and all ships finally ordered back to Alexandria. The nightmare was not yet over, however, for as the long haul back began, the German submarine U-205 attacked and sank the cruiser *Hermione* with two torpedoes; 85 of her crew perished. Admiral Harwood later reflected: "Events proved with painful clarity that our air striking force had nothing like the necessary weight to stop the Italian fleet."

Meanwhile, reconnaissance aircraft from Malta were again searching for the Italian capital ships and their escorts, which were found once more at 1500, heading towards Taranto. On one of these sorties over the Ionian Sea Baltimore AG715 of 69 Squadron, flown by Plt Off A.H.Patrick, failed to return. On board this aircraft as an observer was the squadron's commanding officer, Wg Cdr Eric Tennant. There seems little doubt that the aircraft fell victim to one of I./NJG 2's Ju 88Cs, Oblt Albert Schulz claiming an aircraft which he identified as a Maryland for his sixth victory.

Upon the report of the new sighting, a further strike from Malta was ordered by the surviving Beauforts of 217 Squadron, but the crews failed to find anything during the subsequent five and a half hours of night flying. At dusk, five Wellingtons were sent out, ASV equipment again allowing these torpedo-bombers to find their target, but only Plt Off O.L.Hawes (DV541 'C') was able to penetrate the low cloud and smoke screen to carry out an attack. His target was the slightly damaged *Littorio*, which was struck by one of his two torpedoes, this time suffering severe damage.

This attack virtually brought to an end the June convoy operations. Although some supplies had got through from the west, the actions were essentially an Axis success, gained at relatively small cost on terms of shipping – one cruiser sunk and several vessels, including one battleship, damaged. In the air, however, losses had been quite heavy.

At the end of the day a Beaufighter on detachment at Gambut 2 landing ground was searching for a dinghy when a Do 24 flyingboat was seen and attacked. However, return fire hit the starboard engine and the side of the cockpit, causing the British aircraft to come down in the sea. The crew took to their dinghy and reached the shore safely.

British Claims

272 Sqn	Plt Off P.C.Cobley/ Sgt G.W.Williams	Beaufighter 'O'	Ro.43	convoy escort MW 11	0850-1315
272 Sqn	Sgt W.H.Knight	Beaufighter			
272 Sqn	Sgt N.J.Cleggett	Beaufighter Ic 'N'	Cant.Z.506B	convoy escort	1020-1415
252 Sqn	Plt Off E.Thwaites	Beaufighter Ic 'B'	S.79 Probable	convoy escort MW 11	1950
252 Sqn	Sgt B.H.Vickery	Beaufighter Ic T4828	Ju 88	convoy escort MW 11	1950
250 Sqn	Plt Off P.Copeland	Kittyhawk I AK955 'O'	2 S.79s	130m N Gambut	1950
250 Sqn	Sgt F.C.De Salvo Hall	Kittyhawk I AL157 'B'	S.79 Damaged	130m N Gambut	1950

British Casualties

250 Sqn	Kittyhawk I shot down by Flak SW Gambut; Sgt Hannaford safe
69 Sqn	Baltimore AG715 took off at 0650 from Luqa FTR from recce over Ionian Sea; Plt Off A.H.Patrick and two MiA
39 Sqn	Beaufort Ia DD949 damaged by fighters, crash-landed Sidi Barrani at 0900; Plt Off Grant and two safe, one WiA
39 Sqn	Beaufort Ia DD955 shot down by fighters 100m off Derna at 0830; Flg Off R.C.Hooper and three rescued
39 Sqn	Beaufort II AW297 shot down by fighters off Derna at 0830; Plt Off J.Abram and three KiA
39 Sqn	Beaufort IIa AW337 belly-landeed at Luqa, DBR by Flak; Sqn Ldr R.P.M.Gibbs and crew safe
39 Sqn	Beaufort IIa AW352 shot down by fighters off Derna at 0830; Flt Lt C.S.Thomas and three KiA
39 Sqn	Beaufort Ia DD975 crashed into DD995 of 217 Squadron on return to Luqa, damaged by Flak; Plt Off Marshall and crew safe
39 Sqn	Beaufort Ia DD974 damaged by Bf 109s, crashed on landing at Sidi Barrani; Sgt L.Daffurn and crew safe
227 Sqn	Beaufighter T4933 took off from LG. 143 at 0715 to escort convoy MW11; Plt Off D.C.Gibson/Sgt A.R.Sparey MiA
272 Sqn	Beaufighter T4829 'V' shot down by Bf 109s escorting Beauforts to Malta at approx 0730; Sgt W.G.Blessing/Sgt J.R.Williams FTR
272 Sqn	Beaufighter T4869 'J' shot down by Bf 109s escorting Beauforts to Malta at approx 0730; Plt Off R Corbisier/Sgt McLeish
272 Sqn	Beaufighter T4941 (poss 4821)
M.E.	Beaufighter X8078 MiA
108 Sqn	Wellington lost

German Claims

9./JG 53	Oblt Franz Götz	Beaufighter	110km NNE Ras el Tin	0616
9./JG 53	Lt Erich Beckmann	Beaufighter	110km NNE Ras el Tin	0617
9./JG 53	Hptm Helmut Belser	Beaufort	130km NNE Derna	0728
9./JG 53	Lt Dietrich Kasten	Beaufort	130km NNE Derna	0728
9./JG 53	Obfw Alfred Seidl	Beaufort	130km NNE Derna	0729
9./JG 53	Hptm Helmut Belser	Beaufort	130km NNE Derna	0730
9./JG 53	Uffz Fritz Göhmann	Beaufort	130km NNE Derna	0731
9./JG 53	Lt Dietrich Kasten	Beaufort	130km NNE Derna	0732
9./JG 53	Obfw Alfred Seidl	Beaufort	130km NNE Derna	0734
9./JG 53	Hptm Helmut Belser	Beaufort	130km NNE Derna	0738
9./JG 27	Obfw Heinrich Rosenberg	Beaufighter	NNE Derna	0740
1./NJG 2	Oblt Albert Schulz	Maryland		0745
9./JG 27	Oblt Hans-Joachim Heinecke	B-24	100km NNE Derna	0940
2./NJG 2	Obfw Hermann Sommer	t/e a/c		2010

German Casualties

10.(Jabo)/JG 27	Bf 109F-4 trop WNr 10039 Green 8+ lost 30km WSW Gambut; Uffz Karl-Heinz Panier baled and PoW
6./StG 3	Ju 87D-1 WNr 2482 S7+HN ships' AA 50km S Goudos; 1 baled, Oblt Anton Ostler/Obfw Wilhelm Lichtenstein KiA
Verb.Fhr.Lehrg Foggia	Ju 88A-5 shot down in combat and crashed into sea 40km S Malta

Italian Claims

204ª Sq, 41°Gr Aut AS	gunners aboard S.79s	3 e/a	Eastern Med	1740

Italian Casualties

204ª Sq, 41°Gr Aut AS	S.79 MM 24211, shot down by fighters, pilot Ten Salvatore Annona, copilot Serg Magg Aurelio Di Carlo and four MiA

Italian Casualties

171ª Sq RM	Cant.Z.506 MM 45351 failed to return, pilot S.Ten Edoardo Visentin, copilot Serg Magg Marino Abascià, observer S.Ten RE Francesco Marino and three MiA
288ª Sq RM	Cant.Z.506 MM 45397 crash-landed on sea, pilot Ten Mario Martinelli, copilot Serg Magg Giovanni Russo and four rescued
288ª Sq RM	Cant.Z.506 MM 45355 shot down by Hurricane, pilot S.Ten Ugo Cusmano, copilot Serg Magg Dino Rigacci and four rescued
144ª Sq RM	RS.14 MM 35391 failed to return, pilot Ten Antonio Carnielli, copilot Serg Albano Squarzoni and four MiA
Reparto Aereo *Eugenio di Savoia*	Ro.43 MM 27147 floatplane launched, shot down by Beaufighters, pilot Ten Mario Sodi rescued, observer T.V. Vitaliano Mastroianni MiA
Reparto Aereo *Gorizia*	Ro.43 MM 27186 floatplane launched, failed to return, pilot Cap Gastone Mezzetti, observer T.V. Arnaldo Pannaria MiA
Reparto Aereo *Giuseppe Garibaldi*	Ro.43 MM 27127 floatplane launched, crashed in sea, pilot Serg Ermanno Tommasini, observer T.V. Benedetto Ferraro KiA
Reparto Aereo *Littorio*	Ro.43 MM 27152 and Ro.43 MM 27160 floatplanes fell from catapult, ditched
Reparto Aereo *Trento*	Ro.43 MM 27097 floatplane lost with ship, M.llo Dante Biondi wounded

Tuesday, 16 June 1942

British Claims

46 Sqn	Flt Lt C.G.Clegg/ Sgt K.Tailor	Beaufighter 1f X7746	unspecified	N Alexandria	1925-2145

British Casualties

2 PRU	Spitfire IV BP916 MiA Sidi Barrani

German Casualties

5./LG 1	Ju 88A-4 WNr 140713 L1+CN shot down by AA and crashed into sea N Alexandria; Hptm Wilger Schach and three MiA
3./KG 54	Ju 88A-4 WNr 140001 B3+VL shot down by AA at 2030 and ditched in sea 80km NW Alexandria; Fw Alfred Oelsner and three MiA

Thursday, 18 June 1942

German Casualties

10./LG 1	Ju 88A-5 WNr 0303 L1+ZU collided with L1+SU and crashed into sea; Lt Walter Ebert and one KiFA; two baled out and survived
10./LG 1	Ju 88A-5 WNr 3324 L1+SU collided with L1+ZU and crashed into sea SE Kythera Island; Lt Maximillian Karlhuber and three KiFA

Friday, 19 June 1942

British Claims

80 Sqn	Plt Off R.G.Foskett	Hurricane IIc BN405	Ju 88	80m out to sea from LG.121	0735-0825

Friday-Saturday, 19/20 June 1942

All nine serviceable Cant.Z.1007bis of 86° Gruppo off to bomb Tobruk and harbour. Direct hits on two steamers were claimed.

British Claims

89 Sqn	Flg Off C.A.Crombie	Beaufighter X7719	He 111	Mersa Matruh	1250
89 Sqn	Sqn Ldr D.S.Pain	Beaufighter X7700	He 111	SW Mersa Matruh	0015

Saturday, 20 June 1942

89 Squadron Beaufighters were now operating from Fuka.

Lt Rökker of I./NJG 2 claimed to have shot down a Beaufort of 217 Squadron flying at low level over the sea near Crete. A second Beaufort was attacked by three of NJG 2's fighters in an engagement which lasted for 35 minutes, the crew of this aircraft getting 25 hits on Rökker's Ju 88.

British Claims

217 Sqn	Sgt J.Hutcheson and crew of Beaufort DD954		Ju 88 Damaged		
89 Sqn	Sqn Ldr D.S.Pain/Sgt Briggs	Beaufighter If X7700	He 111 ?	Mersa Matruh	2250; no A.I. radar

British Casualties

217 Sqn	Beaufort DD958 'WQ'; Plt Off F.Minster and crew MIA

German Claims

1./NJG 2	Lt Heinz Rökker	Beaufort	S Crete	1720

German Casualties

1./NJG 2	Ju 88C slt damaged ; Lt Heinz Rökker safe
6./KG 100	He 111H-6 WNr 7223 6N+LJ, shot down by AA, crashed El Daba, Uffz Friedrich Enste and three MiA (night 19/20)

Sunday, 21 June 1942

British Casualties

217 Sqn	Beaufort DD996 shot down by Flak, off Sfax on shipping strike
217 Sqn	Beaufort I W6502 MiA from shipping strike

Italian Casualties

175ª Sq AS	S.79 failed to return, pilot M.llo Antonino Valenti, copilot Serg Ercole Ambrogetti and crew MiA

Monday, 22 June 1942

An 815 Squadron Swordfish crew attacked a submarine, the bombs hitting the sea close by while it remained on the surface. However no results were observed.

British Casualties

272 Sqn	Beaufighter T4988 lost; NFD

German Claims

10.(Jabo)/JG 53	Oblt Walter Langemann	Beaufighter

Tuesday, 23 June 1942

Reportedly a strafing He 111 was shot down by night fighters.

British Casualties

39 Sqn	Beaufort W6518 shot down by Flak MiA from shipping strike at Punta Stilo
39 Sqn	Beaufort DD976 down by Flak MiA from shipping strike at Punta Stilo

Wednesday, 24 June 1942

British Casualties

272 Sqn	Beaufighter 'C' Sgt H.F.M.Pien/Sgt R.W.Lane damaged slightly by Bf 110 1200-1536

German Claims

8./ZG 26	Uffz Heinz Susemihl	Beaufighter	Bomba Bay	1305

German Casualties

III./ZG 26	Bf 110 hit by AA and force-landed in sea; pilot in dinghy and rescued; Ogfr Kumke drowned

Wednesday-Thursday, 24/25 June 1942

British Claims

73 Sqn	Sgt G.Hill	Hurricane IIc BN546	Ju 88	Sidi Haneish	0100

German Casualties

5./KG 100	He 111H-6 6N+DH over Fuka, shot down by fighter; Obfw Wilhelm Peve, Hptm Ewald Gustavus and two MiA

Thursday, 25 June 1942

British Casualties

272 Sqn	Beaufighter T4981 'C' strafing near Martuba at 1905 shot down by Flak; Flg Off J. E.Makgill /Flt Sgt G.J.Sumner KiA
272 Sqn	Beaufighter 'W' hit by Flak, crashed on landing; Flt Lt E.C.Lane-Sansam DFC, Sgt F.Chapman safe

Friday, 26 June 1942

Two S.79s of 41° Gruppo AS set off from Rhodes at 0650. A ship was seen and attacked off Port Said by S.Ten Giuseppe Briatore, but the torpedo missed the target. Briatore's aircraft was then attacked by an 89 Squadron Beaufighter on day patrol and was shot down.

During the second reconnaissance sortie of the day to be carried out by 47° Stormo, a Cant.Z.1007bis of 260ª Squadriglia, flown by Ten Francesco Alù, sighted and bombed a steamship at 0840, claiming some hits on this vessel. AA fire seriously damaged the central engine of the bomber, forcing the pilot to crash-land on the sea. The wreck of the missing aircraft was later spotted at map reference 34°20'- 28°10' by another of the unit's aircraft sent out to search for it. The crew of Cant (MM 23342) '260-8', flown by Cap Mario Popaiz, saw the crew clinging to the wooden fuselage of the aircraft which was still afloat. A Cant.Z.506S floatplane of Sezione Soccorso Rodi personally flown by Gen Ulisse Longo, the commander of the Aeronautica dell'Egeo, with Cap Francesco Molteni, was sent to pick up the survivors, but after having landed alongside, the floatplane was unable to take off again due to adverse sea conditions. Finally, at 1000 next day, having floated for 17 hours on the rough water, the rescue plane reached Rhodes. The wounded crew was taken to the Regina Elena hospital.

During the day Beaufighters were again active. Flt Lt Lane-Sansam, DFC, apparently none the worse for his crash-landing on the previous day, and Plt Off Deppe, strafed targets along the Buq Buq-Sidi Barrani road. Here they were attacked by two fighters, one of which got on Lane-Sansam's tail. This was driven off by Deppe, who then returned to base. Lane-Sansam and his observer, Sgt Chapman, failed to arrive, however, and were listed as missing. It would appear that they had been shot down by Oblt Franz Götz of 9./JG 53 who claimed a twin-engined aircraft at 1030 south-east of Sollum which he identified as a Blenheim. During another sortie by the unit a further aircraft was shot down by Flak. The pilot, Sqn Ldr Bill Riley, survived and returned safely next day.

Also on this date the new South African unit, 7 SAAF Squadron, arrived from Palestine at LG.85, just south of Alexandria, equipped in the main with elderly Hurricane Is. Two Italian top officers, Gen Guido Piacenza and Col Vittorio Raffaelli, were killed by Beaufighters strafing the coast road; Gen Ettore Baldassarre, commander XX Corpo d'Armata, was gravely wounded and died a few hours later. Eight Albacores of 826 Squadron undertook 26 bombing sorties during a very active night, attacking MT concentrations in the Mersa Matruh area. However, aircraft 'Q' was attacked in error by a Hurricane, the lower part of the port wing and the observer's legs being hit, at which point bombs were jettisoned and the aircraft returned to base.

British Claims

272 Sqn	Plt Off R.E.C.Deppe/ Sgt J.M.Carlin	Beaufighter Ic 'P'	Bf 109	coast at Buq Buq	1025-1240
89 Sqn	Sqn Ldr P.M.J.Evans/ Sgt Houston	Beaufighter If X7754	S.79	NE Port Said	1100

British Casualties

272 Sqn	Beaufighter T4985 'N' shot down by Bf 109 during ground attack near Sidi Barrani; Flt Lt E.C.Lane-Sansam, DFC/Sgt F.Chapman FTR
272 Sqn	Beaufighter 'P' damaged by Bf 109 after attacking another, crash-landed 1240; Plt Off R.E.C.Deppe/Sgt J.M.Carling safe
826 Sqn	Albacore 'Q' damaged in error by Hurricane; observer suffered leg wounds

German Claims

9./JG 53	Oblt Franz Götz	Blenheim	20km SE Sollum	1030

German Casualties

6./KG 100	He 111 Fuka; Fw Erwin Rohloff and three MiA NTD

Italian Casualties

205ª Sq, 41°Gr Aut AS	S.79 failed to return, pilot S.Ten Giuseppe Briatore, copilot Serg Italo Accornero and crew MiA. Accornero PoW, died in Cairo hospital on 4 July
260ªSq, 106°Gr, 47°St BT	Cant.Z.1007bis MM 23739 '260-3' hit by AA 0840, ditched in open sea, pilot Ten Francesco Alù, copilot Serg Magg Giovanni Peluso, observer T.V. Giuseppe Musmeci and three wounded and later rescued by a floatplane

During the spring and summer of 1942, Junkers Ju 86R-1 reconnaissance aircraft (referred to in British records as the Ju 86P) were supplied in small numbers to 2.(F)/123 based on Crete, supplementing that unit's Ju 88Ds. These aircraft flew several ultra-high photographic missions over British military installations in Egypt. This advanced aircraft was powered by two Jumo 207 diesel engines with two-stage superchargers, and had a pressurized cabin for its two-man crew.

Throughout June 80 and 1 SAAF Squadrons had been attempting to intercept these high-flying reconnaissance intruders which were appearing regularly over Port Said and the Delta area. Each squadron had stripped a Hurricane IIb of its armour and eight of the 12 machine guns in order to achieve sufficient performance to catch one of these pressurised aircraft. However, to date these attempts had met with no success. With 8th Army dug in along its 'last ditch' line at El Alamein, and with Rommel preparing a major offensive to penetrate that line, the ability of the Ju 86Rs to run line coverage of large parts of the British defences and rear areas at regular intervals, effectively unchallenged, was not acceptable.

In an initial bid to counter this menace, half a dozen Spitfire VI high-altitude fighters had arrived in Egypt. With its pressurised cockpit, however, this variant was just too heavy to reach the altitude at which the Ju 86Rs were operating. Engineers at 103 Maintenance Unit at Aboukir then sought to lighten two Spitfire Vs in a similar manner to that employed with the Hurricanes. All unnecessary equipment was removed, including armour and the four .303in machine guns. The engines were modified to give an increased compression ratio of 7:1, although this decreased take-off boost, and each fighter was fitted with a four-bladed propeller taken from a Spitfire VI; all protruding nuts were also cut off flush wherever possible. At least three Spitfires, BP985, BR114 and BR234, were modified in this way. They were also fitted with locally-manufactured pointed wingtips and an armament of two .50in Browning machine guns instead of the 20mm cannon.

At this point it is necessary to digress, to explain the effect of the height of the stratosphere on a Spitfire's performance. At altitudes below the stratosphere, the air temperature decreases at a steady rate as altitude increases. Once the stratosphere is reached, however, as altitude is increased the temperature remains reasonably constant over the next 10,000 feet or so. The nearer to the equator, the greater the height of the stratosphere. Cairo lies at 30° North, the stratosphere commences at about 45,000 feet and above that altitude the air temperature remains steady at about –62° C. Moving further from the equator, the stratosphere gets lower and the layer of air above it is a little less cold. Thus over London, at 52° North, the height of the stratosphere is about 36,000 feet and above it the air temperature is about –54° C.

Differences in the outside air temperature at high altitude had a marked effect on the performance of the Spitfire V. The colder the air drawn into its carburettor, the greater its density and therefore the greater the power developed by the Merlin engine. Thus a Spitfire flying over Egypt had a substantially higher service ceiling than if it was flying over the United Kingdom. Of course, all this work took time to complete. For the first time two Spitfires managed to intercept one of the elusive German aircraft, their pilots claiming to have inflicted some damage; the pilot of one of the Spitfires was Flg Off George Genders who previously had flown Hurricanes with 33 Squadron.

Saturday, 27 June 1942

Between 0020 and 0100 four Cant.Z.1007bis of 47° Stormo took off on a low level mission to bomb the coast road between Mersa Matruh and Alexandria and the railway line between El Daba and Burg el Arab. Three bombers returned at 0435-0500, the crews reporting hits on the objectives, but Cap Insom's plane was not with them. Insom had been forced to crash-land on the sea, about 60 miles from base, due to engine failure. The pilot then climbed into the dinghy with the flight engineer 1°Av Silvio Ales. Unfortunately the dinghy broke loose from the wreck, and was carried away by wind and waves, soon disappearing in the dark; it was never recovered. The three survivors then remained on the floating wreck, clinging to the tail assembly. The search for the missing plane started immediately, but without success. Finally, at about 1000, the wreckage was sighted by a Cant.Z.1007bis of 261ª Squadriglia flown by M.llo Teodorico Perusi, who was returning from a reconnaissance sortie. A Cant.Z.506S of Sezione Soccorso Rodi and a motor boat were called to the rescue, but the floatplane, flown by Ten Giuseppe Boschetti, suffered damage in landing near the wreck. Finally, the motor boat, directed by another Cant.Z.1007bis flown by Cap Athos Maestri, reached the spot and recovered the three survivors of Insom's bomber and the floatplane crew.

Four Beaufighters of 272 Squadron strafed Derna airfield during the day, damaging six Ju 52/3ms on the ground. One Beaufighter was shot down by Obfw Köster of I./NJG 2. The stripped Spitfires of 103 MU again intercepted a Ju 86P, damage once more being claimed.

British Claims

103 MU	unspecified	Spitfire V	Ju 86P Damaged	Delta area

British Casualties

272 Sqn	Beaufighter 'B' shot down; Plt Off Wood PoW/Sgt R.A.Naylor KiA

German Claims

9./JG 27	Oblt Hans-Joachim Heinecke	Swordfish	NE Haggag el Qotaifiya	1454
3./NJG 2	Obfw Alfons Köster	Beaufighter	Derna	2344

Italian Casualties

263ª Sq, 107°Gr, 47°St BT	Cant.Z.1007bis MM 24254 crash-landed in open sea, pilot Cap Alberto Insom and 1°Av Silvio Ales MiA, copilot Ten Ugo Mutti and two rescued

Sunday, 28 June 1942

Plt Off Gunnis of 252 Squadron attacked Derna airfield where he claimed to have destroyed two Ju 52/3ms on the ground. However, his Beaufighter was hit by ground fire and he received severe wounds in his legs. His observer, Sgt Edmund Waller, put tourniquets on these limbs, then taking over the controls and flying the aircraft back to base. He was awarded a DFM for this action; Gunnis had just been awarded a DFC, having brought his personal claims for aircraft shot down to five.

A Cant.Z.1007bis of 263ª Squadriglia, flown by Ten Emanuele Trivella, was sent to bomb at night the railway line between El Daba and Burg el Arab.

British Casualties

272 Sqn	Beaufighter T5030 MiA attack on Derna airfield at 1320; Flg Off F.E.Thwaites/Sgt G.Johnston PoW
252 Sqn	Beaufighter T4877 shot down by Flak, strafing Derna airfield 1100-1158; Plt Off H.H.K Gunnis/Sgt Waller crash-landed, Gunnis WiA, Waller safe

Monday, 29 June 1942

By night 47° Stormo was involved again in bombing the railway line and the road along the Egyptian coast. Three Cant.Z.1007bis delivered 48 50kg bombs.

British Claims

46 Sqn	Plt Off P.C.W.Sage	Beaufighter If X7745	Dornier ?	50m W Aboukir	2245-0020
46 Sqn	Flt Lt C.G.Clegg	Beaufighter If X7674	He 111 Probable	30m N Aboukir	2321

Monday/Tuesday, 29/30 June 1942

Two torpedo-carrying Wellingtons of 38 Squadron on a shipping search launched two torpedoes at 0140-0145. Crews reported that the first strike resulted in orange fire amidships, while the second strike on the same vessel caused a red flash further along the side.

Tuesday, 30 June 1942

87° Gruppo BT arrived at Gadurra from Lecce, led by T.Col Mario Giuliano, with six Cant.Z.1007bis; two more landed at Corinth and another on Kermion island. Ten Aniello Colasanti and Ten Santo Sciacca flew on from Corinth to Gadurra on 2 July, with S.Ten Giuseppe Ferri finally arriving from Kermion on 7 July. During the night of 30 June/1 July three Cant.Z.1007bis of 47° Stormo from Rhodes bombed roads and railway lines in the El Alamein area.

British Casualties

89 Sqn	Beaufighter X7806 belly-landed Abu Sueir
39 Sqn	Beaufort I W6506 crashed on landing LG.88; Sgt L.W.Daffurn
459 Sqn	Hudson IV V9187 FTR from anti-sub patrol

CHAPTER 4

THE YANKS ARE COMING !

June 1942 was undoubtedly one of the low points of the war for the United Kingdom and its Commonwealth. The month marked a year since the Soviet Union had been brought into the war, and six months since the Japanese assaults in the Far East had added the United States to the Allied fold. The Russians had survived the onslaught of 1941, but despite prolonged resistance during the autumn, winter and early spring that followed, were still struggling desperately to hold off the Axis forces, particularly in the south. Here the Crimea and the Caucasus were the main areas of concern, particularly to the British, who greatly feared a push into the area of the eastern Mediterranean should the Germans succeed in breaking through the Caucasus mountains into the oil-rich areas of the Middle East.

Although the US entry into the war had undoubtedly brought an increased flow of military hardware from that great arsenal, because of the vital need to stabilize the position in the Pacific – nearest to home for their population –there had as yet been no action (apart from anti-submarine and convoy escort activities in the Atlantic) against the German and Italian elements of the Axis, despite the German declaration of war immediately following the US involvement in the conflict. Indeed, there was still considerable dispute within the political and military hierarchies of the country as to which of its new enemies should be dealt with first. In the initial instance much of the new alliance had proved negative for the Middle East, occasioned by the transfer to the Soviet Union of considerable quantities of the war materials originally intended for the United Kingdom under Lend-Lease provisions. This was particularly the case in regard to aircraft.

For the British high command, the withdrawal back to Russia of elements of the Luftwaffe from Sicily and the arrival of quantities of M.3 heavy tanks in Egypt from the US which appeared to promise an enhanced level of performance by the armoured units on the Gazala line, offered an opportunity to re-supply the critically important island base of Malta. The possibility of an Axis landing and occupation here was still seen as a very possible threat. In fact such an invasion was being actively promoted and planned in Italy, not least by Feldmarshall Albert Kesselring. The latter perceived occupation of Malta as a vital prerequisite to the control of North Africa in order to secure permanently any further success which Rommel's forces there might achieve.

Against this background, as has been described (see Chapter Two) on each side of the Gazala positions, preparations for a new offensive, be it from east or west, were proceeding as rapidly as the combatants' supply routes permitted. The shorter route across the Mediterranean enjoyed by the Germans and Italians at this stage remained considerably less secure than the much longer and more tortuous one to Egypt and Libya on which the Commonwealth forces relied. Thus it was that Rommel had struck first on 26 May, although the battle remained very much in the balance for over two weeks. The decisive day proved to be 12 June when the continued faulty use of armour by the British resulted in such heavy losses (about 75% of the 300 or so tanks available) that the Commonwealth forces were forced to begin a withdrawal eastwards to prevent the encirclement of the XIII Corps infantry elements in the northern part of the area.

It was against this unpromising backdrop that the planned relief of Malta commenced on that very day. By this time the Royal Navy too was critically short of capital ships, be they battleships or aircraft carriers. Two convoys were involved in this venture, both extremely short of escorts. The effort from Gibraltar eastwards, past Sardinia, was dubbed Operation Harpoon, with that from Egypt heading west, known as Operation Vigorous. Full details relating to both these operations may be found in Chapter 6 of *Malta: The Spitfire Year, 1942*, and it is not intended to repeat those relating to Harpoon here. However, Vigorous impinged considerably on RAF Middle East and the Western Desert Air Force, so as will have been noted, some considerable information related thereto is to be found in this volume (see mainly Chapter 2 and Chapter 3). As recounted therein, by 16 June Vigorous had failed to get through and had returned to Alexandria, whereas next day the surviving elements of Harpoon reached Malta to provide just sufficient supplies to allow operations from the island to continue for the time being. On land the 8th Army was now in full retreat and Tobruk was once again under threat at least of a renewed siege.

On 17 June the US military observer in the Middle East, Col Bonner Fellers, cabled the US war department to advise that the Middle East was less secure than at any time since the German invasion of the Soviet Union 12 months earlier. Fellers was doing more than ringing alarm bells – he was seeking US aid for the British in the only way that it could swiftly be given. Heavy bombers, he pointed out, could provide effective immediate help in attacking supply shipping in the eastern Mediterranean to reduce the supply of fuel, reinforcements and provisions to the Axis in North Africa – precisely in line with the British desire to keep Malta secure.

He differed from the British high command on one critical fact, however. British strategy was based on a conception that the Middle East and India were inter-dependent. Japanese forces had passed rapidly north through Burma and only a month earlier had arrived on the Indian eastern frontier, apparently threatening British control there. If India fell, the British believed, the Middle East would inevitably fall too. This was where Fellers disagreed. If the Middle East fell, he believed India would then fall too, threatening planned US aid to China and future operations there.

This cable brought immediate results, for on 23 June Lt Gen Joseph W.Stillwell ('Vinegar Joe' to his subordinates), commander of American Army Forces in the new China-Burma-India theatre, received a message from General George C.Marshall (with copies to Maj Gen Lewis Brereton, commanding general of the US 10th Air Force in India, and Maj Gen Russell Maxwell, commanding general of US Army Forces in the Middle East). This stated in part: ".....Brereton will come at once to the Middle East with available heavy bombers with mission to assist Auchinleck. Instruct Brereton all our units in the Middle East will come under his command. Place at his disposal transport planes and personnel required. The War Department will return Brereton's force to your command at the completion of his mission...." (Stillwell would wait a long time for this assurance to bear fruit.)

Three days later Brereton departed for Egypt with 60 officers, 165 enlisted men and seven Boeing B-17E Flying Fortresses. These latter aircraft had already been in action against Japanese forces in Java and India, and were drawn from the 9th Bomb Squadron of the 7th Bombardment Group (see *Bloody Shambles, Vol 1*). The whole party arrived at Fayid on 28 June, but with the threat of Rommel's advance approaching the Delta area, they were moved back to Lydda, Palestine. Two days later Brereton was given command of the new US Army Middle East Air Force (USAMEAF), which would subsequently become the US 9th Air Force. Despite the speed of this US action, it had already been pre-empted to a degree, for even before Fellers' vital cable, USAAF aircraft had arrived and been active in the Middle East, although in this case more by chance than intention. (One is also tempted to ask did this presence actually precipitate Fellers' action ?)

During the opening days of June 1942 a detachment of 23 Consolidated B-24D Liberators (similar to the RAF's Liberator II) had arrived at Fayid led by Col Harry A.Halvorson, on their way to China from where it was planned they would undertake bombing attacks on the Japanese home islands. They had arrived in Egypt via the southern ferry route from the USA, but on arrival were diverted from their planned onward flight due to the Gazala emergency with the intention that they would undertake a single strategic mission to bomb the oilfields in Rumania, which were just about within range from Egypt for these long-ranging aircraft.

Hence between 2230-2300 on 11 June 13 B-24s took off individually for this target, all arriving a little before dawn the next day, as a result of which they had to orbit until daylight. Ten bombed the Astra Romana refinery at Ploesti, one attacked the port of Constanta and two released their bombs on unidentified targets. No serious opposition was encountered, although a pilot of 1./JG 77, which operated in Rumania from April until the end of 1942 as 1./JG 4, claimed to have intercepted a B-24 at 0538 south of Braila and shot it down. This was the seventh victory credited to Lt Heinz-Edgar Berres who we will meet again soon in the very different skies of North Africa. Despite this claim, none of the American aircraft reported being attacked, and none were hit as far as can be ascertained.

Due to the distances involved, however, on the return flight Col Halvorson's and three other crews landed at Ramadi, Iraq; three others landed in other parts of that country, one of them crash-landing on doing so. Two more reached Aleppo in Syria, but four had to come down in Turkey where they and their aircraft were interned. The attacks, made by so small a force, achieved no critical damage, but an oil depot at Ploesti was destroyed and port facilities at Constanta were hit. Months later on 15 December nine of the interned aircrew managed to steal aircraft 41-11596 and fly it to Cyprus. Some of the other crewmen were also able to escape and made their way out of Turkey by train and boat; the remainder were released by the Turkish authorities on 30 April 1943.

A USAAF B-24D Liberator of the Halvorson Detachment soon after the unit's arrival in North Africa.

US Casualties

Halvorson Detachment	B-24D 41-11586/2 'Brooklyn Rambler' force-landed in Turkey; Lt N.K.Brown Jr and six interned (Later flown to Cyprus 15 December 1942 after being stolen by crew)
Halvorson Detachment	B-24D 41-11622/5 'Town Hall' force-landed in Turkey; Lt F.W.Mesbitt Jr and six interned
Halvorson Detachment	B-24D 41-11609 'Little Eva' force-landed in Turkey; Lt H.J.E.Walker and six interned
Halvorson Detachment	B-24D 41-11597/19 'Blue Goose'; Lt E.A.Cave and six interned
Halvorson Detachment	B-24D 41-11629/25 'Jap Trap' crash-landed Habbaniya, Iraq; Lt M.T.Y.Mooty and crew safe

German Claims

1./JG 77	Lt Heinz-Edgar Berres	Bf 109F	B-24	S Braila	0538

No sooner were the scattered aircraft gathered together again, than on 14 June came another emergency – the Italian fleet had sortied in an effort to intercept the Vigorous convoy en route to Malta. Consequently seven of Halvorson's B-24s (his small unit now referred to as Halpro) were sent off to join RAF aircraft in an attack on the Italian warships (see details in Chapter Three). Although little significant damage could be inflicted on capital ships with the 500lb bombs available, some damage had been caused to the battleship *Littorio*, and more importantly, the Italian fleet had been driven back into harbour.

At this point Halvorson requested to be allowed to continue with his original mission to China, but due to the Axis advance, this was refused. Instead the detachment was ordered on 17 June to the Cairo area to report to Brig Gen Russell L.Maxwell, commanding general, US Army Forces in the Middle East (USAFIME). Two days later Maxwell formally became head of US Military North African Mission. Coming now under the initial direction of the RAF's 205 Group, the B-24s became involved primarily in a number of night bombing sorties, attacking both Benghazi and Tobruk, which by this time had fallen into Axis hands (details of all further US heavy bombing operations until the end of March 1943 are included in Chapter Eleven).

Meanwhile, on 5 July the rest of the aircraft in India arrived at Lydda, incorporating five more B-17Es of the 9th Bomb Squadron and 436th Bomb Squadron (previously known as the 88th Reconnaissance Squadron). The bombers then became engaged in the role for which Col Fellers had appealed, attacking shipping convoys carrying supplies from southern Europe. Fuller details are included in Chapter Three, which describes five attacks on shipping up to the end of July, during which an initial loss occurred (on 9th). Also during the month 21 raids were made on Benghazi and Tobruk (see Chapter Eleven).

By 19 July total US strength stood at 19 B-24Ds and nine B-17Es, although only seven of the former and three of the latter were serviceable at that date. In 36 days of operations three aircraft had been lost to enemy action, four remained interned in Turkey, and one had crash-landed and been written off. Next day Halpro and the Brereton Detachment were consolidated into the 1st Provisional Group at Lydda operating as two squadrons, initially referred to as the Halvorson and Brereton squadrons.

Rapid action had also been taken in the metropolitan US, where three groups were ordered to begin moving to North Africa as quickly as possible. The ground echelons of all three actually sailed aboard the British SS *Louis Pasteur* on 16 July, crossing the South Atlantic and following the route via Freetown and Durban, and then up the Red Sea to the Gulf of Suez which would be reached on 16 August. The air echelons got there much quicker, of course, and between 17-30 July 35 B-24Ds of the 98th Bomb Group (Heavy) were the first to arrive. One party comprising the 344th Bomb Squadron and two aircraft of the group's HQ Flight (one of them flown by the commanding officer, Col Hugo P.Rush), and second led by the commander of the 344th, Maj John R.Kane, reached Ramat David, Palestine, on 25 July; only one aircraft was lost en route.

In the early hours of 12 August the first mission by the 98th Bomb Group was flown by seven B-24s from Fayid to attack harbour facilities and a tank repair depot at Mersa Matruh. Thrown so suddenly into action, initial raids could be somewhat mystifying to the crews. Wrote Lt Henry D.Chism, a 345th Squadron bombadier who flew in an aircraft carrying the name 'Li'l De-Icer', "12 August – (First mission). We went for Besa Matruh (sic). We were at 15,000, cold as hell and black as pitch and there wasn't any moon. We couldn't find the target and the Germans were smart. They wouldn't light their searchlights and would stop their antiaircraft fire when we got close. I didn't even know they were shooting shells at us...Dropped five 1,000 pound bombs. No one in the flight saw the target." (see also Chapter Eleven.)

By 7 August the whole group had arrived, the HQ and the 345th and 415th Squadrons settling at Ramat David, with the 343rd and 344th based at St Jean d'Acre. The ground echelon arrived on the 20th. Meanwhile, operations continued with frequent attacks on convoys which had been spotted by RAF photo-reconnaissance Spitfires (see Chapter Three).

The second of these groups to reach Egypt was the 12th Bombardment Group (Medium), commanded by Col Charles Goodrich, the air echelon of 57 North American B-25C Mitchells leaving the US between 14 July and 2 August. These aircraft flew via Brazil and Ascension Island across the South Atlantic to West Africa, then following the Takoradi cross-Africa route to Sudan and Egypt. HQ, 81st and 82nd Squadrons arrived at Deversoir between 31 July-11 August; 83rd and 484th Squadrons reached Ismailia 13-17 August. The ground parties reached these bases on 18 August. Meanwhile the first operational sorties were undertaken at night on 16 August with Mersa Matruh as the target. The group then received considerable training from 3 SAAF Wing which prepared it for full involvement in the forthcoming Alam el Halfa battle at the end of the month.

The 57th Fighter Group's air echelon had left home earlier than had the 12th's, but this unit's Curtiss P-40F Warhawks – Merlin-engined versions of the WDAF's now-familiar Kittyhawk – did not, of course, possess the range to fly across the Atlantic. Instead the unit's 72 fighters left Rhode Island on 1 July aboard the aircraft carrier USS *Ranger* to sail across. When 100 miles off the West African coast these

North American B-25 Mitchells of the USAAF 12th Bomb Group (Medium). Lower left are more B-25s and an RAF Martin Baltimore, with a formation of six more Baltimores directly below. In the distance, far left, an escorting fighter can just be observed.

were flown off in groups of 18 at a time, to land ashore, refuel, and start the long series of 'hops' up the Takoradi route. Recorded Capt Lyman D.Middleditch :

> "In what seemed a very short time our last night on board ship arrived. The chefs outdid themselves this night, and the navy swing band was superb. Hitting the sack later, each of us had a different sort of anticipation of the take-off hour. The day dawned cloudy but calm. Many of us breathed a sigh of relief as our experiences of carrier take-offs was then zero. All too soon the *Ranger* began her long straight run, and Colonel Mears sat ready in the cockpit of his plane, awaiting Commander Ottenger's take-off signal. It was not long in coming and we all heaved a sigh of relief as the colonel's plane took a firm hold on the air. It could be done! In a short time the rest of our planes were in the air buzzing low about the *Ranger* in a noisy farewell, then heading off towards Africa."

Arriving ultimately at Muqueibila, Palestine, during 29-31 July, their pilots found the balance of their numbers for whom there had not been sufficient aircraft to fly, awaiting them. These fortunate fellows had travelled from the States in the relative comfort of a Pan American Airways Clipper flyingboat.

It was not until 17 August that the ground party finally arrived after their journey by sea, but already the commanding officer, Col Frank Mears, had got his men included in a training programme. This involved pilots on arrival being integrated initially into existing British and Commonwealth units for instruction and training. At first, like the bomber units, the group was dependent on the RAF for intelligence briefings, airfield facilities and servicing. This, however, allowed the newly-arrived Americans to benefit from vital experience without delay, acting at first not as individual units, but as a part of existing operational squadrons. That this appeared to work well was confirmed later by Brig Gen Auby C.Strickland, soon to be commanding general of IX Fighter Command, who stated that in his opinion the success enjoyed by US fighter units in the Middle East was due largely to the excellent training and experience received through the assistance of the British fighter command.

The third USAAF type to reach Egypt was the Curtiss P-40F Warhawk – the Merlin-engined version of the Kittyhawk. One such aircraft of the recently-arrived 65th Fighter Squadron 57th Fighter Group, is seen here at Burg el Arab during October.

For the fighters the first involvement in operations took place on 9 August, and on the 14th they experienced their first combat. "Six P-40s of the 57th Group, who have been in training with the RAF, got their first action this morning. Forming part of the cover for 12 Baltimores and 11 Bostons which attacked the El Fuka airport, the fighters ran into a swarm of Me 109s. Lt William O'Neill engaged five Me 109s himself and shot down two Huns. Though he himself was shot down into the sea, he was later rescued." (*The Brereton Diaries*) This, and further activity by this unit and the 12th Bomb Group, will be found in the main chapters relating to the activities of WDAF units.

During preparations for such operations, other training also continued. Between 5-29 August the 65th Fighter Squadron was sent to Cyprus, then moving to Muqueibila where the 64th Squadron was based when its pilots were flying with RAF units. The 66th Squadron moved to Beit Davos, Palestine, on 19 August, then to Maryut on the 27th prior to entering action. Here it was to become the group's first squadron to operate as a full unit, but flying as part of an RAF wing; the date that this happened was 31 August.

On 2 September the squadron moved to LG.97, returning to Maryut five days later, and then going to LG.184 on the 16th. On the latter date the American pilots were joined there by the group HQ and the other two squadrons. Now operating under the direct control of AOC, Western Desert, at this stage the 64th and 65th Squadrons became effectively a separate wing (British terminology) within 211 Group, RAF. In October the 66th Squadron would join the RAF's 239 Wing. Certainly with the Alam El Halfa battle of 31 August-3 September the 12th Bomb Group and 57th Fighter Group became important integral parts of Western Desert Air Force.

Generally speaking at this early stage of the war, although the USAAF pilots lacked the front-line operational experience (albeit temporarily) of their Commonwealth contemporaries, their training had been of considerably greater duration and thoroughness than had been possible with the bulk of the young and swiftly-trained pilots emanating from the Commonwealth Air Training Scheme. At this time the latter were still being rushed into action as rapidly as possible to replace the not inconsiderable levels of attrition being experienced by Middle East units. Particularly at this time, US levels of gunnery training may be considered to have been considerably better.

Next unit to begin arriving was the 79th Fighter Group. At home in the USA this unit had already received the worn training P-40s previously used by the 57th Fighter Group and left behind when that unit departed for Africa. These were now handed on to the new 325th Fighter Group (which would itself subsequently follow the aforementioned groups to the same continent – see Volume 3). Ordered to move during October, the air echelon of the 79th, 85th, 86th and 87th Squadrons, led by the commanding officer, Lt Col Peter McGoldrick, flew out via the Antilles Islands to Natal, Brazil, in Air Transport Command C-54s. From there they were flown across the South Atlantic via Ascension Island to Accra in the Gold Coast in Pan American Clippers. Accra was at this time an assembly area for Curtiss fighters which were being delivered in crates from Takoradi. From here P-40s were picked up and flown across the African reinforcement route to Heliopolis. Meanwhile, the ground party sailed on the pre-war liner *Mauritania*, arriving on 12 November after a journey of 37 days. From Kasfareet, this party then moved to LG.174 on the 19th where the unit was re-united, but with bad news.

Meanwhile, here, immediately after the air party's arrival, two senior officers – McGoldrick and one other – were detached to the 57th Fighter Group on 5 November to gain experience of desert conditions before organising training of the unit in this regard. Unfortunately, on his very first operational flight next day, McGoldrick was killed (see Chapter Eight). His place was taken by Lt Col Earl E.Bates, until then the group operations officer. As with the 57th Group, the 79th was not at once ordered onto operations, being retained for some months as the replacement fighter unit, although several of its pilots were exchanged with others from the longer-serving unit in order to provide some appropriate operational experience.

Although the arrival of the 79th Fighter Group had coincided with the El Alamein victory and the Operation Torch landings in North-West Africa, immediately following these events there were a number of important command changes. These commenced on 12 November when USAMEAF was re-titled more simply as the US 9th Air Force under Brereton's command. At the same time three sub-commands were set up in this renamed organisation, these being:

IX Bomber Command under Brig Gen Patrick C.Timberlake, established on 27 November,
IX Fighter Command under Brig Gen Aubrey C.Strickland established early December, and
IX Air Service Command under Brig Gen Elmer E.Adler, established in early February 1943

Just prior to these changes the heavy bomber elements which were to be incorporated in IX Bomber Command had moved westwards, back to the Delta from Palestine. These were now:

376th Bombardment Group (Heavy) renumbered from the 1st Provisional Group, which arrived at Abu Sueir on 9 November
98th Bombardment Group (Heavy) with HQ, 345th and 415th Squadrons at Fayid from 13 November, and with 343rd and 344th Squadrons at Kabrit from the same date.

On formation, the IX Air Service Command had only a few borrowed C-47 Dakotas (also known at that time as Skytrains), but the British, still desperately short of air transport, requested that more US aircraft of this type be made available. Consequently, immediately on receipt of this request, 316th Troop Carrier Group (36th, 37th, 44th and 47th Squadrons) in Texas and under the command of Col Jerome B.McCawley, which was being held as part of a possible Anglo-US force to operate in the Caucasus in the event of a German breakthrough there, was ordered to move to Africa. This group with 52 C-47s and with most of its personnel aboard, set off on the pan-South Atlantic flight, initially to West Africa. Here the 44th Squadron was detained at Accra for ten days, the rest of the aircraft arriving at Deversoir, Egypt, during 23-25 November; the unit would move up to El Adem on 10 December to support the forward units – a hugely valuable addition to the Allied aerial presence in North Africa.

Meanwhile, almost by default, further reinforcement for IX Bomber Command was arriving. In the UK one of the first two B-24-equipped heavy bomber groups to join the new US 8th Air Force, the 93rd, was ordered to send the air echelon of three of the unit's squadrons, the 328th, 330th and 409th, to Algeria on a 'ten day detachment' where additional long-range bombing capacity was in urgent need of enhancement. Led by another Timberlake, Col Edward J. Jr, the unit left behind its 329th Squadron, 24 of its Liberators arriving on 6 December to strengthen XII Bomber Command of the new US 12th Air Force. After some initial raids on the Bizerta area (see Volume 3), on the 15th – just before the conclusion of the notional 'ten days' – the unit was sent south-eastwards to LG.139 at Gambut Main to become a temporary part of IX Bomber Command. Having flown 22 missions for the two bomber commands during which five B-24s were lost, but ten Axis aircraft had been claimed shot down by the unit's air gunners, it was ordered back to England on 18 February 1943. It left behind Lt Col Keith K.Compton from the group HQ, who two days later was posted to take command of the 376th Bomb Group.

The last two new units to arrive with 9th Air Force before the conclusion of the fighting in North Africa were the 324th Fighter Group and the 340th Bombardment Group (Medium). The first of these, another P-40-equipped unit, arrived at Kabrit on 2 February 1943 where it was to remain until June.

However, on 8 March the unit's 314th Squadron was attached to the 57th Fighter Group for operations, and a week later the 316th Squadron similarly joined the 79th Group. On 6 March, meanwhile, the 79th had moved up to the forward area, arriving at 'Causeway' landing ground where it came under the tactical control of RAF 211 Group.

The 340th Bomb Group, commanded by Col William C.Mills, arrived at Heliopolis during the last ten days of March, the air echelon having followed the now-familiar reinforcement route across central Africa. Arriving in the midst of a storm, one B-25 of the unit's 489th Squadron crashed in poor visibility, the pilot and two members of the crew being killed after the rest had baled out.

A few days earlier on 3 March two squadrons from the 12th Bomb Group had moved to El Assa in the 12th Air Force's southern territory in the face of an Axis offensive in that area (see Volume 3). This airfield was located 80 miles from Mareth and 20 miles from the sea, thereby still being placed to operate over 8th Army to the south when called upon to do so. Aircraft from the newly-arrived 340th Group were despatched at once to reinforce the units in this location. However, no sooner had the balance of the unit arrived in Egypt, than IX Bomber Command put a hold on all operations for seven days to allow units to rest and train in readiness for the forthcoming offensive on the Mareth Line (see Chapter Nine).

MC.202 '73-8' MM 7324 was frequently flown by Serg Teresio Martinoli, who would have become the Regia Aeronautica's top-scoring fighter pilot by the end of the war.

CHAPTER 5

THE STAND ON THE EL ALAMEIN LINE

Luftwaffe Order of Battle
July 1942

Fliegerführer Afrika

Unit	Aircraft
Stab JG 27	Bf 109F-4
I./JG 27	Bf 109F-4
II./JG 27	Bf 109F-4
III./JG 27	Bf 109F-4
10.(Jabo)/JG 27	Bf 109F-4
III./JG 53	Bf 109F-4
10.(Jabo)/JG 53	Bf 109F-4
I./NJG 2	Ju 88C-2 Ju 88C-4 Ju 88C-6
III./ZG 26	Bf 110C-5 Bf 110D-0 Bf 110D-1 Bf 110D-3 Bf 110E-1 Bf 110E-2 Bf 110F-2 Bf 109E-7
10./ZG 26	Do 17Z-2
Stab StG 3	Ju 87D-3 He 111H-5 Bf 110E-3
I./StG 3	Ju 87R-2 Ju 87R-4
II./StG 3	Ju 87D-1 Ju 87D-3
III./StG 3	Ju 87D-12
4.(H)/12	Bf 110E-3 Bf 110F-3 Bf 109E-7 Bf 109F-4

2(H)/14 Personnel only

X. Fliegerkorps

Unit	Aircraft
Korpskette X.FlK	He 111H-5 He 111H-6
Stab LG 1	Ju 88A-4
I./LG 1	Ju 88A-4
II./LG 1	Ju 88A-4
12./LG 1	Ju 88A-4
II./KG 100	He 111H-6
1.(F)/121	Ju 88D-1 Ju 88D-5
1(F)/122	Ju 88D-1 Ju 88D-5 Bf 109F-4
2.(F)/123	Ju 88A-5 Ju 88D-1

2.(F)/123	Ju 88D-5 Bf 110C-7 Ju 86R-1	**Transportverbände Süd**	
		III./KGzbV 1	Ju 52/3m
		IV./KGzbV 1	Ju 52/3m
2./SAGr 125	Ar 196A-3	KGrzbV 400	Ju 52/3m
SAGr 126	He 111H-6 He 60A-1 Fokker T.VIII Ar 196A-3 Bv 138C-1	KGrzbV 600	Ju 52/3m

Wednesday, 1 July 1942

On 1 July Rommel began his assault on the new Allied line, attacking El Alamein and Deir el Shein. At 0900 six Kittyhawks of 3 RAAF Squadron with six of 450 Squadron escorted nine Bostons to Deir el Shein, fighting a running engagement with four Bf 109s of III./JG 53 which were out on a Freie Jagd. Uffz Bahnsen shot down Sgt O'Neil's aircraft which fell into the sea, the pilot baling out. He was picked up by the army and returned safely next day. During the day Beaufighters of 252 Squadron strafed Fuka Satellite airfields, claiming several aircraft destroyed on the ground (see Chapter Ten).

At 1845 six Bf 109s of III./JG 53 in another Freie Jagd intercepted two TacR Hurricanes, one of which Obfw Stumpf claimed to have shot down. This appears to have been an aircraft of 208 Squadron being used by Lt Sturgeon, a pilot of 40 SAAF Squadron. Sturgeon was attacked by two Messerschmitts and caused to crash-land, slightly wounded, but claiming to have inflicted some damage on one of his attackers.

Four Bf 109s of II./JG 27 then took off on a similar sortie at 1914, followed at 1945 by ten of I./JG 27, escorting Stukas to El Alamein. The pilots of both formations reported meeting about 11 bombers with 20 escorting fighters near El Imayid. The I.Gruppe pilots claimed four P-40s shot down, II.Gruppe adding two more. Their opponents had included 11 Kittyhawks of 3 RAAF Squadron and six of 450 Squadron, together with others of 260 Squadron, all of which were escorting Bostons south of Daba at the time. The Messerschmitts followed the Allied formation to the target and then back to within five miles or so of LG.91. 3 RAAF lost one aircraft to the German fighters, with another two by 260 Squadron.

During the day 80 and 1 SAAF Squadrons moved their Hurricanes to LG.92 and 601 Squadron, the second Spitfire unit to arrive, landed at LG.154. 33 Squadron now commenced operations after re-equipment with cannon-armed Hurricane IIcs. Meanwhile, the German fighters were now disposed as follows:

I./JG 27 III./JG 27	} Fuka	II./JG 27 III./JG 53	} Qotaifiya

4° Stormo moved to Fuka airfield. The transfer flight from Sidi el Barrani was hampered by a sand storm and Ten Mario Squarcina destroyed his MC.202 on landing. His fighter overturned and the pilot was rescued and taken to a nearby German field hospital, where Squarcina's serious wounds were treated. Two Squadriglie of 9° Gruppo were forced to land at Abar Nimeir and reached Fuka later in the day.

British Claims

450 Sqn	Flt Sgt D.H.McBurnie	Kittyhawk I AL634	Bf 109F Probable	N El Imayid	0905-1005
450 Sqn	Sgt G.J.Gleeson	Kittyhawk I AK636 'M'	Bf 109F	N El Imayid	0905-1005
40 SAAF Sqn	Lt E.I.H.Sturgeon	Hurricane I Z9577	Bf 109 Damaged		1925

British Casualties

260 Sqn	Kittyhawk I shot down by Bf 109s El Alamein area, 1905-1910
260 Sqn	Kittyhawk I shot down by Bf 109s El Alamein area, 1905-1910
112 Sqn	Kittyhawk I crash-landed at base due to damage from Bf 109
450 Sqn	Kittyhawk I AK729 shot down by Bf 109 Deir el Shein-N El Imayid, 0930-0940; Sgt G.C.W.O'Neil baled out, swam ashore, safe

450 Sqn	Kittyhawk I AL195, damaged by Bf 109 Deir el Shein-N El Imayid, 0930-0940; Sgt R.C.Davidson landed safe
3 RAAF Sqn	Kittyhawk I AK598 'H' left 1910, escort bombers to NE Daba, shot down either by fighters or Flak; Plt Off D.V.Ritchie baled out, returned next day
40 SAAF Sqn	Hurricane I Z9577, shot down by two Bf 109s 10m E El Alamein, crash-landed at 1935 ; Lt E.I.H.Sturgeon slt WiA

German Claims

8./JG 53	Obgefr Jens Bahnsen	P-40	4km N El Ruweisat	0840
9./JG 53	Obfw Werner Stumpf	Hurricane		1840
2./JG 27	Lt Friedrich Körner	P-40	W Burg el Arab	1901
2./JG 27	Lt Friedrich Körner	P-40	W Burg el Arab	1901
2./JG 27	Lt Karl von Lieres und Wilkau	P-40	E El Alamein	1902
2./JG 27	Lt Friedrich Körner	2 P-40s	W Burg el Arab	1903 & 1911
4./JG 27	Obfw Alfred Schulze	P-40	5km SW El Alamein	1903
4./JG 27	Obfw Alfred Heidel	P-40	5km SE El Alamein	1904

Italian Casualties

90ª Sq, 10°Gr, 4°St CT	MC.202 MM 7798 '90-4' destroyed in landing accident at Fuka, Ten Mario Squarcina wounded
96ª Sq, 9°Gr, 4°St CT	MC 202 destroyed in landing accident at Abar Nimeir, Serg Angelo Parodi wounded
390ª Sq, 159°Gr, 50°St Ass	CR.42 MM 8542 damaged, Serg Magg Vittorio La Noce wounded
390ª Sq, 159°Gr, 50°St Ass	CR.42 MM 8544 damaged, Ten Pietro Ferraro wounded

Thursday, 2 July 1942

Five Bf 109s of III./JG 27 on an early Freie Jagd reported meeting 20 bombers and 30 fighters west of El Daba. They then encountered what they identified as 11 Wellingtons (highly unlikely), nine Bostons and 20 fighters south-east of El Alamein, claiming three escorting fighters shot down. At much the same time five MC.202s of 10° Gruppo were undertaking a similar free sweep over the area, claiming a Boston and three P-40s with four fighters as probable. The Boston was an aircraft of 12 SAAF Squadron which was badly shot-up and crash-landed at base as a result. It seems that the Macchi pilots had attacked Hurricanes of 33 Squadron, shooting down the aircraft flown by Flt Lt Hayter. The MC.202 flown by Ten Alessandrini then overshot Hayter's stricken Hurricane, allowing the New Zealander to shoot down one of his attackers in turn. Both aircraft crash-landed within Allied territory, where the Italian pilot became a PoW.

Even earlier, 252 Squadron had strafed several Axis airfields, pilots claiming three Bf 109s destroyed on the ground at one of these. Lt Stahlschmidt of I./JG 27 and M.llo Luigi Bignami of 10° Gruppo each claimed one of these shot down, Stahlschmidt's victim being seen by many witnesses to crash into the sea; a third Beaufighter arrived back at base badly shot-up (for more details, see Chapter Ten). At 1830 eight Kittyhawks of 2 SAAF Squadron providing top cover for Bostons, were attacked by five I./JG 27 Messerschmitts which had been escorting Stukas to El Alamein, the pilots of these claiming three P-40s shot down. The South Africans lost two aircraft, one of these force-landing; a third was damaged Cat I.

7 SAAF Squadron now arrived at LG.154 to join 243 Wing, but being equipped only with early Mark Is, the unit was initially assigned merely to meteorological reconnaissance and local defence duties. The squadron had originally been provided with Mark IIbs, but on arrival these had been passed to 1 SAAF Squadron which was in dire need of replacement aircraft – hence the re-equipment with the Mark Is. Since May the squadron had been involved in training at Amiriya under its commanding officer, Maj D.Loftus.

The pilots of 92 Squadron, originally intended to be the second Spitfire unit to operate in North Africa, had been in the Middle East for some months now, but had still not received any aircraft. As a result, Sqn Ldr Wedgwood, the commanding officer, and 14 pilots were now attached to 80 Squadron to gain operational experience of desert conditions in that unit's Hurricane IIcs.

British Claims

33 Sqn	Flt Lt J.C.Hayter	Hurricane	MC.202	El Alamein area	0900-1030
112 Sqn	Sqn Ldr B.Drake	Kittyhawk I ET510	Bf 109E Probable	nr Bir Hacheim	0905-1020
260 Sqn	unspecified	Kittyhawk I	Bf 109	El Alamein area	1900-2000
260 Sqn	unspecified	Kittyhawk I	Bf 109	El Alamein area	1900-2000
260 Sqn	unspecified	Kittyhawk I	Bf 109 Damaged	El Alamein area	1900-2000
260 Sqn	unspecified	Kittyhawk I	Bf 109 Damaged	El Alamein area	1900-2000

Egyptian-Cyrenaican frontier area, July-November 1942

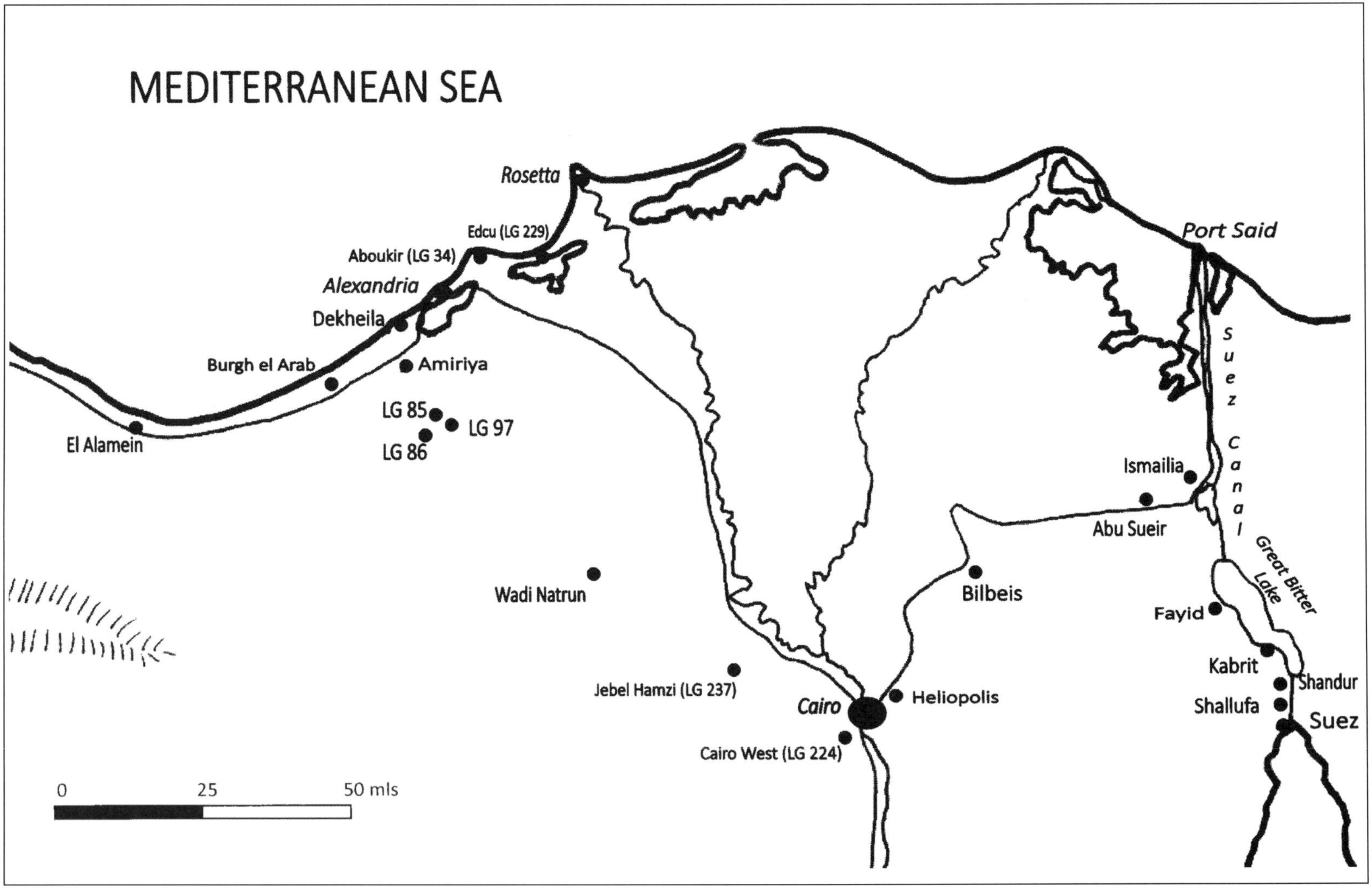

British troops inspect MC.202 '90-12' MM 7792 which had crash-landed in Allied territory on 2 July. The pilot, Ten Italo Alessandrini was unhurt and became a PoW.

British Casualties

33 Sqn	Hurricane shot down, crash-landed near El Alamein by MC.202; Flt Lt J.C.F.Hayter WiA
260 Sqn	Kittyhawk I 'X' 1900-2000 pilot baled out
260 Sqn	Kittyhawk I 'M' 1900-2000 crash-landed
2 SAAF Sqn	Kittyhawk I ET906 'R' shot down by Bf 109s on bomber escort 1830-2000; Capt J.O.de Waal WiA, baled out
2 SAAF Sqn	Kittyhawk I AK941 'K' damaged by Bf 109s, 1830-2000, force-landed nr 1 SAAF Sqn Hurricane; Lt R.A.Du Rose safe
2 SAAF Sqn	Kittyhawk I AK970 'C' damaged Cat I by two Bf 109s; Capt H.E.N.Wildsmith safe
1 SAAF Sqn	Hurricane II force-landed due to engine trouble approx 48km from LG.92; Lt T.A.Meek flown out next day; aircraft repaired and flown out later
24 SAAF Sqn	Boston III Z2298 'D' third raid of day on enemy in El Daba area; on return flew into dust storm and flew into ground nr LG.99 at 1600
12 SAAF Sqn	Boston III Z2198 left 0919, damaged by MC.202 and crash-landed on return at LG. 99; Capt Bernieux (Belgian) and crew safe

German Claims

2./JG 27	Lt Hans-Arnold Stahlschmidt	Beaufighter	N Fuka	0625
8./JG 27	Lt Werner Schroer	P-40	SE El Alamein	0700
8./JG 27	Uffz Hans Fahrenberger	P-40	SE El Alamein	0703
8./JG 27	Lt Werner Schroer	P-40	E El Alamein	0705
8./JG 53	Obgefr Jens Bahnsen	P-40	4 km N El Ruweisat	0840
2./JG 27	Lt Friedrich Körner	P-40	El Alamein	1815
2./JG 27	Lt Friedrich Körner	P-40	Burg el Arab	1820
2./JG 27	Lt Hans-Arnold Stahlschmidt	P-40	Burg el Arab	1823
9./JG 53	Obfw Werner Stumpf	Hurricane		1840

German Casualties

III./KG40	FW 200 transport mission Derna-Lecce, fuel leak caused ditching off Greece; pilot Riepold & radio op KiA

Italian Claims

90ª Sq, 10°Gr, 4°St CT	Cap Ranieri Piccolomini	MC.202	Boston	El Alamein	0810-0940
90ª Sq, 10°Gr, 4°St CT	S.Ten Virgilio Vanzan	MC.202	P-40	El Alamein	0810-0940
90ª Sq, 10°Gr, 4°St CT	S.Ten Virgilio Vanzan	MC.202	P-40 Probable	El Alamein	0810-0940
90ª Sq, 10°Gr, 4°St CT	Serg Amleto Monterumici	MC.202	P-40	El Alamein	0810-0940
90ª Sq, 10°Gr, 4°St CT	Serg Amleto Monterumici	MC.202	}		
90ª Sq, 10°Gr, 4°St CT	Serg Magg Elio Trevisan	MC.202	}		
90ª Sq, 10°Gr, 4°St CT	Ten Italo Alessandrini	MC.202 MM 7792	} P-40	El Alamein	0810-0940
90ª Sq, 10°Gr, 4°St CT	S.Ten Virgilio Vanzan	MC.202	}		
90ª Sq, 10°Gr, 4°St CT	Cap Ranieri Piccolomini	MC.202	}		

Italian Casualties

90ª Sq, 10°Gr, 4°St CT	MC.202 MM 7792 '90-12' crash-landed, Ten Italo Alessandrini PoW

Friday, 3 July 1942

At 0700 ten Kittyhawks of 4 SAAF Squadron escorted Bostons on a raid; at the same time ten Spitfires of 145 Squadron were scrambled to intercept fighters over El Alamein. Three Bf 109s of III./JG 53 on a Freie Jagd encountered the Kittyhawks over Hammam, Oblt Kläger, who had claimed 22 victories, being shot down by Lt Reinders and becoming a prisoner. The Spitfires, however, were jumped at 13,000 feet by 12 Axis fighters, Plt Off Weber's aircraft being damaged. 2 SAAF Squadron provided top cover to Bostons from 0910-1040, the Kittyhawks being continually attacked by a pair of Bf 109s; Lt Allen belly-landed three miles south of LG.85 when the engine of his aircraft was hit in the cooling system and in the right wing ammunition bay.

Around this time four Bf 109s of I./JG 27 were on a Freie Jagd when they encountered a lone fighter which Fw Steinhausen claimed to have shot down near El Alamein at 1015. Four more fighters of this unit were scrambled at 1045, engaging 12 bombers with fighter escort, Lt Kugelbauer claiming one fighter at 1120. No more Luftwaffe engagements were reported until sometime after midday, but during the later morning period the Regia Aeronautica fighters of 4° Stormo were very active.

After a couple of uneventful missions, at 1005 eight MC.202s of 91ª Squadriglia, led by Cap Carlo Maurizio Ruspoli, took off for a free sweep over the El Alamein area. Flying in pairs at 15,000 feet, the formation was attacked by fighters. At the end of the combat five P-40s were claimed by the Italian pilots. Then a formation of 16 Bostons escorted by 30 P-40s was reported and engaged, a bomber and a fighter being claimed shot down for no losses. The Hurricanes of 213 Squadron had taken off at 1047, reporting being jumped at 12,000 feet by 11 Bf 109s – which were probably in fact 10° Gruppo Macchis. Three of the unit's aircraft were shot down, two of them crash – or force-landing, but all three pilots survived; one of the attacking fighters was claimed damaged.

Maj G.J.le Mesurier, commanding officer of 1 SAAF Squadron, with Hurricane BG971 AX-V, in which he led his pilots to intercept Ju 87s on 3 July. He force-landed in this same aircraft next day.

At 1125 14 MC.202s of 10° Gruppo (seven each from 84ª and 90ª Squadriglie), led by Magg Paolo Maddalena, took off from Fuka to escort 15 CR.42s of 158° Gruppo. Flying in pairs, the new formation which was now replacing the traditional vic, was at 14,000 feet when 19 P-40s flying at lower altitude

Hurricane IIc of 33 Squadron, armed – as were most of the Hurricanes of this model at the time – with only one 20mm cannon in each wing in an effort to improve the performance of these aircraft against the Messerschmitt and Macchi fighters.

were bounced, four of these being claimed shot down after a 20-minute combat. Many others were fired at but Maddalena failed to return. In the meantime 158° Gruppo attacked vehicle concentrations in the El Qasimiya-El Ruweisat area. Here at 1210 a lone twin-engined aircraft was encountered and claimed shot down, the Italian pilots tentatively identifying it as a Beaufighter. Three of the biplanes failed to return. In the absence of RAF claims, they may have all fallen to ground fire, none of the pilots returning.

At 1110 eight Kittyhawks of 3 RAAF Squadron bombed and strafed south of Mukheisin, one aircraft being hit by Flak and crash-landing. A few minutes later eight more Kittyhawks from 2 SAAF Squadron provided top cover for Bostons, but while the formation was turning to return from the raid, a lone fighter attacked, Lt McLeod being slightly wounded and his aircraft badly damaged. During the day this unit carried bombs on its Kittyhawks for the first time. Meanwhile, at 1145 six fighter-bombers and six fighter Hurricanes of 274 Squadron took off from LG.92 to bomb gun positions. They were attacked by three MC.202s, Sgt Garwood claiming one shot down.

Twelve Hurricanes of 73 Squadron with others of 33 Squadron, departed at 1230 to patrol over El Alamein. In a fight with fighters – identified as Bf 109s – two Hurricanes of 73 Squadron and one of 33 Squadron were shot down. The 73 Squadron pilots claimed three fighters shot down and one damaged. During this middle part of the day three Macchi pilots claimed two fighters and one Boston shot down between them. At much the same time four Bf 109s of III./JG 27 on a Freie Jagd reported intercepting two formations. One of eight and one of 12 British fighters – possibly the 73/33 Squadron aircraft – claiming three of them shot down. However, 12 Hurricanes of 274 Squadron were off again from 1440 on a patrol over El Alamein, the pilots of these reporting that four MC.202s had attacked the top cover, two of which were claimed damaged. Actually another free sweep was carried out from 1315 by 16 MC.202s of 9° Gruppo, led by Cap Luigi Mariotti. Over El Hammam the pilots of these engaged a reported 12 Bostons and 22 P-40s, claiming two fighters shot down and a Boston probably so. Several others were claimed damaged.

At 1535 213 Squadron's aircraft were again scrambled over El Alamein and again were jumped by fighters – this time Bf 109s of I./JG 27 on a Freie Jagd. The German pilots claimed four shot down, the pilots of three of which were killed, the fourth wounded; only Plt Off Avise returned to base. Four Bf 109s of III./JG 27 escorted Ju 87s of I./StG 3 over the front where they were intercepted by 33 and 73 Squadrons, Obw Rosenberg claiming one of these Hurricanes shot down. Sqn Ldr Johnston claimed one Stuka shot down and one probable. Sgt Wilson claimed two, one of which he reported blew up in midair.

Other pilots added claims for two more probables and another four damaged. During these early hours of the afternoon, Hurricanes of 1 SAAF Squadron had been scrambled, one aircraft flown by Capt Rhodes being slightly damaged by a Bf 109, although the aircraft was repaired prior to its use again in the evening. Whilst on a bomber escort sortie from 1415, Capt Colman of 5 SAAF Squadron claimed a Bf 109 shot down south of El Daba. At 1720 Kittyhawks of 112 Squadron undertook a bombing mission during which one aircraft was shot down.

Another Stuka raid approached at 1835, when 12 Hurricanes of 274 Squadron scrambled to provide top cover to 1 SAAF Squadron which was intercepting the incoming raid. A large formation of Ju 87s was seen, escorted by seven Bf 109s of II./JG 27. The South Africans attacked the bombers 274 held off the escorts, managing to claim damage to one Messerschmitt in doing so. Against the Stukas, 1 SAAF got "well stuck in", claiming 13 shot down, three by Lt Collingwood and two by Capt Metelerkamp for the loss of only one aircraft. Hit by a stray bullet from one of the Ju 87s, Lt Connell had to crash-land at Burg el Arab. The escorting Messerschmitt pilots claimed two of the Hurricanes shot down, but neither of the Allied units suffered any loss to fighters. The fighting continued all the way back to the German base at Fuka, during which Lt Biden claimed a Bf 109 shot down. Of the 13 dive-bombers claimed shot down, army observers confirmed nine from the ground within 30 minutes; at least four are recorded as shot down, including that flown by Ritterkreuzträger and Staffelkapitän Oblt Josef Wenigmann, who was killed. During this very busy day the RAF had undertaken 780 sorties.

Axis unit moves were underway at this time, I. and III./JG 27 going to Mumin Busaq, joined by the Macchis of 88ª Squadriglia of 6° Gruppo. Cap Lucchini assumed provisional command of 10° Gruppo, replacing the missing Magg Maddalena.

British Claims

4 SAAF Sqn	Lt S.I.Reinders	Kittyhawk I	Bf 109F	10m SW El Alamein	0700-0810
274 Sqn	Sgt H.Garwood	Hurricane IIc BE669 'C'	MC.202	W Bir-Makhkhad	1210
213 Sqn	Sgt H.A.Aitken	Hurricane IIc BN537 'J'	Bf 109F Damaged	N El Alamein line	1058-1215
3 RAAF Sqn	Sgt J.F.H.Cashmore	Kittyhawk I AK651	Bf 109 Damaged	El Mreir	1155
73 Sqn	Sgt M.S.Jones	Hurricane IIc BE183	Bf 109	El Alamein box	1250
73 Sqn	Flt Sgt E.L.Joyce	Hurricane IIc BP177 'L'	Bf 109	El Alamein box	1250
73 Sqn	Flt Sgt E.L.Joyce	Hurricane IIc BP177 'L'	Bf 109 Damaged	El Alamein box	1250
73 Sqn	Sgt R.L.Baker	Hurricane IIc BN402	Bf 109F Damaged	El Alamein box	1250
73 Sqn	Flg Off J.F.Pain	Hurricane IIc BN566	Bf 109	El Alamein box	1250
73 Sqn	Flt Lt I.J.Badger	Hurricane IIc BN403	Bf 109 Damaged	El Alamein box	1300
73 Sqn	Flt Lt S.P.V.Bird	Hurricane IIc BP175	Bf 109F Damaged	El Alamein box	1300
73 Sqn	Sgt H.W.E.Packham	Hurricane IIc BE372 'H'	Bf 109F Probable	El Alamein box	1305
274 Sqn	Flt Sgt J.W.Neil	Hurricane IIc BP326 'T'	2 MC.202s Damaged	S Burg el Arab	1440-1600
5 SAAF Sqn	Lt E.N.Colman	Tomahawk IIb AN427 'D'	Bf 109F	20m SE El Daba	1445
73 Sqn	Flg Off J.F.Pain	Hurricane IIc BN566	Ju 87 Probable	El Alamein box	1700
73 Sqn	Flg Off J.F.Pain	Hurricane IIc BN566	Ju 87 Damaged	El Alamein box	1700
73 Sqn	Flt Lt J.B.Selby	Hurricane IIc BE554	Ju 87 Damaged	El Alamein box	1700
73 Sqn	Sgt A.S.Wilson	Hurricane IIc BN538	2 Ju 87s	El Alamein box	1700
33 Sqn	Flt Lt F.J.Aldridge	Hurricane IIc BP181	Bf 109	El Imayid	1705
73 Sqn	Plt Off E.O.Double	Hurricane IIc BE557	Ju 87 Damaged	El Alamein box	1710
73 Sqn	Sgt G.H.Farley	Hurricane IIc BN175	Ju 87 Probable	El Alamein box	1710
73 Sqn	Flt Lt G.R.A.McG.Johnston	Hurricane IIc BE415	Ju 87	El Alamein box	1710
73 Sqn	Flt Lt G.R.A.McG.Johnston	Hurricane IIc BE415	Ju 87 Probable	El Alamein box	1710
73 Sqn	Sqn Ldr G.P.H.Matthews	Hurricane IIc BP177	Ju 87 Damaged	El Alamein box	1710
274 Sqn	Flt Sgt J.W.Neil	Hurricane IIc BP326 'T'	Bf 109F Damaged	W El Alamein	1835-1935
1 SAAF Sqn	Lt A.J.Biden	Hurricane II BG762 'P'	Ju 87	6m S El Alamein	1900
1 SAAF Sqn	Lt A.J.Biden	Hurricane II BG762 'P'	Bf 109F	6m S El Alamein	1900
1 SAAF Sqn	Lt R.J.P.Collingwood	Hurricane II Z2503 'E'	3 Ju 87s	6m S El Alamein	1900
1 SAAF Sqn	Lt R.J.P.Collingwood	Hurricane II Z2503 'E'	Bf 109F Damaged	6m S El Alamein	1900
1 SAAF Sqn	Lt G.R.Connell	Hurricane II ..173 'J'	Ju 87 Damaged	6m S El Alamein	1900
1 SAAF Sqn	2/Lt J.H.Gaynor	Hurricane II BG968 'G'	2 Ju 87s	6m S El Alamein	1900
1 SAAF Sqn	Maj G.J. le Mesurier	Hurricane II BG971 'V'	Ju 87	6m S El Alamein	1900

1 SAAF Sqn	Lt A.D.Maclean	Hurricane II Z5348 'M'	Ju 87	6m S El Alamein	1900
1 SAAF Sqn	2/Lt H.Marshall	Hurricane II Z4959 'C'	Ju 87	6m S El Alamein	1900
1 SAAF Sqn	Capt P.C.R.Metelerkamp	Hurricane IIb BG764 'W'	2 Ju 87s	6m S El Alamein	1900
1 SAAF Sqn	Capt P.C.R.Metelerkamp	Hurricane IIb BG764 'W'	Ju 87 Damaged	6m S El Alamein	1900
1 SAAF Sqn	Lt T.W.Phillips	Hurricane II ..356 'A'	Ju 87 Damaged	6m S El Alamein	1900
1 SAAF Sqn	Lt I.R.Pryde	Hurricane II Z5606 'Z'	Ju 87	6m S El Alamein	1900
1 SAAF Sqn	2/Lt C.R.Sinclair	Hurricane II Z5335 'U'	Ju 87	6m S El Alamein	1900

British Casualties

274 Sqn	Hurricane IIc BG494 'Y' left 1440, damaged by MC.202 Cat II; Sgt S.Lerche safe
112 Sqn	Kittyhawk I AK920 shot down by Flak at 1740; Sgt D.J.B.White baled out and returned
260 Sqn	Kittyhawk I ET842 'X' engine cut, force-landed N LG.85 and bombs exploded
3 RAAF Sqn	Kittyhawk I AL128 hit by Flak and crash-landed N Amiriya at 1150; Plt Off R.V.P.Feiffer safe
2 SAAF Sqn	Kittyhawk I AK871 'O' damaged in cockpit by Bf 109; engine seized and belly-landed SSE LG.85 Cat II 1035; Lt A.D.Allen
2 SAAF Sqn	Kittyhawk I AK853 'E' damaged Cat II by Bf 109; 1125-1240; Lt T.M.McLeod slt WiA
4 SAAF Sqn	Kittyhawk I AK692 'I' damaged Cat I by Bf 109 Lt A.C.Paterson slt WiA
1 SAAF Sqn	Hurricane II Z4959 'C' damaged by Bf 109s 5m W El Alamein at 1410; Capt T.Rhodes landed safely with 4 bullet holes
1 SAAF Sqn	Hurricane II ..173 'J' shot down by Ju 87, crash-landed Burg el Arab, Cat II; Lt G.R.Connell safe
33 Sqn	Hurricane IIc BE643 shot down by Bf 109 El Alamein; Sgt B.O.Woollard baled out WiA
73 Sqn	Hurricane IIc BN546 shot down by Bf 109s, El Alamein 1300; Sgt G.Hill KiA
73 Sqn	Hurricane IIc BN538 shot down by Bf 109s, El Alamein 1300; Flt Sgt H.W.E.Packham safe
208 Sqn	Hurricane Z4954 slt damaged by Flak over El Alamein 1930-2025; Flt Lt C.B.S.Montagu DFC safe
213 Sqn	Hurricane IIc BM972 took off at 1100, shot down by Bf 109s, crash-landed 30m W Burg el Arab; Plt Off W R.Henderson safe
213 Sqn	Hurricane IIc BN128 took off at 1100, shot down by Bf 109s, nr El Alamein; Plt Off L.O.H.Boucher baled WiA
213 Sqn	Hurricane IIc BN569 took off at 1100, shot down by fighters; force-landed Amiriya; Plt Off J.M.Cochrane
213 Sqn	Hurricane IIc BN537 took off at 1535 shot down by Bf 109s nr El Alamein; Sgt J.D.Ritchie KiA
213 Sqn	Hurricane IIc BN597 took off at 1535, shot down by Bf 109 nr El Hammam; Sgt G.S.Bolton KiA
213 Sqn	Hurricane IIc BM981 took off at 1535, shot down by Bf 109s, El Alamein; Flt Lt C.B.Temlett KiA
213 Sqn	Hurricane IIc BN541 took off at 1535, shot down by Bf 109s, El Alamein; Plt Off K.N.R.Sissons WiA
208 Sqn	Hurricane Z4708 destroyed by enemy action
M.E.	Hurricane BN449 SOC, DBR (one of the above may have been the sixth 213 Sqn aircraft)
145 Sqn	Spitfire V damaged; Flg Off Weber

German Claims

1./JG 27	Fw Günther Steinhausen	P-40	ESE El Alamein	0915
3./JG 27	Lt Karl Kugelbauer	P-40	20km ESE El Alamein	1030
8./JG 27	Lt Werner Schroer	2 Hurricanes	S El Imayid & SE El Hammam	1440 & 1447
8./JG 27	Lt Werner Schroer	P-40	SE El Hammam	1450
2./JG 27	Lt Hans-Arnold Stahlschmidt	Hurricane	SE El Alamein	1509
2./JG 27	Lt Friedrich Körner	Hurricane	SE El Alamein	1511
2./JG 27	Lt Hans-Arnold Stahlschmidt	Hurricane	E El Alamein	1515
2./JG 27	Lt Karl von Lieres und Wilkau	Hurricane	SE El Alamein	1517
9./JG 27	Obfw Heinrich Rosenberg	Hurricane	S El Hammam	1612
4./JG 27	Obfw Alfred Schulze	2 P-40s	SW El Alamein	1806 & 1810
5./JG 27	Oblt Ernst Börngen	P-40	W El Alamein	1812

German Casualties

8./JG 53	Bf 109F-4 trop WNr 10077 Black 5+I shot down by P-40 nr El Hammam 0635; Oblt Ernst Kläger PoW
2./StG 3	Ju 87R-2 WNr 6122 S7+KK AA 10km S El Alamein; Lt Josef Wenigmann StKap and RK holder /Gefr Michael Kugler KiA
2./StG 3	Ju 87R-4 WNr 6272 S7+EK shot down by Hurricane 10km S El Alamein; Fw Peter Spies PoW/Uffz Josef Zeilbauer KiA
3./StG 3	Ju 87R-2 WNr 6199 S7+JL shot down by Hurricane S El Alamein; Oblt Rudolf Schnurawa/Fw Otto Naumann KiA
3./StG 3	Ju 87R-2 WNr 5690 shot down by Hurricanes S El Alamein; crew safe
5./StG 3	Ju 87D-1 WNr 2490 shot-up by Hurricanes S El Alamein; crash-landed on return at Bir el Abd; Uffz Friedrich Wolff safe/Fw Heinz Renner KiA

Italian Claims

91ª Sq, 10°Gr, 4°St CT	Cap Carlo Maurizio Ruspoli	MC.202	P-40	S El Alamein	1005-1130
91ª Sq, 10°Gr, 4°St CT	Serg Ferruccio Terrabuio	MC.202	P-40	S El Alamein	1005-1130
91ª Sq, 10°Gr, 4°St CT	Serg Alessandro Bladelli	MC.202	P-40	S El Alamein	1005-1130
91ª Sq, 10°Gr, 4°St CT	M.llo Leonardo Ferrulli	MC.202	P-40	S El Alamein	1005-1130
91ª Sq, 10°Gr, 4°St CT	M.llo Leonardo Ferrulli	MC.202			
91ª Sq, 10°Gr, 4°St CT	Cap Carlo Maurizio Ruspoli	MC.202	2 P-40s	S El Alamein	1005-1130
91ª Sq, 10°Gr, 4°St CT	Serg Ferruccio Terrabuio	MC.202			
91ª Sq, 10°Gr, 4°St CT	Serg Alessandro Bladelli	MC.202			
91ª Sq, 10°Gr, 4°St CT	unspecified	MC.202	Boston	S El Alamein	1005-1130
84ª Sq, 10°Gr, 4°St CT	M.llo Luigi Bignami	MC.202 MM 7803	P-40	El Ruweisat	1130-1300
84ª Sq, 10°Gr, 4°St CT	Serg Magg Mario Veronesi	MC.202 MM 7901	P-40	El Ruweisat	1130-1300
84ª Sq, 10°Gr, 4°St CT	Serg Livio Barbera	MC.202 MM 7905	P-40	El Ruweisat	1130-1300
90ª Sq, 10°Gr, 4°St CT	M.llo Angelo Savini	MC.202	P-40	El Ruweisat	1130-1300
387ª Sq, 158°Gr, 50°St Ass	Serg Magg Vittorio Albanello	CR.42	Beaufighter	2km E El Ruweisat	1210
73ª Sq, 9°Gr, 4°St CT	Cap Luigi Mariotti	MC.202			
73ª Sq, 9°Gr, 4°St CT	S.Ten Alvaro Querci	MC.202	2 P-40s + Boston	El Hammam	1315-1445
73ª Sq, 9°Gr, 4°St CT	Serg Teresio Martinoli	MC.202			

Italian Casualties

91ª Sq, 10°Gr, 4°St CT	MC.202 MM7797, crash-landed at Burg el Arab 1130-1300, Magg Paolo Maddalena MiA
236ª Sq, 158°Gr, 50°St Ass	CR.42 failed to return, Ten Mario Porta MiA
387ª Sq, 158°Gr, 50°St Ass	CR.42 MM 4307 failed to return, Serg Giacomo Laini KiA
388ª Sq, 158°Gr, 50°St Ass	CR.42 failed to return, S.Ten Giancarlo Cocchi MiA

Saturday, 4 July 1942

A new wing, 7 SAAF, had now been formed within WDAF, and on this day it began initial operations. Based at LG.89, it controlled 33, 73 and 7 SAAF Squadrons. The new wing's first sorties were undertaken by four aircraft of the latter unit over the Burg el Arab-Amiriya road at 0645 in that unit's elderly Hurricane Is. They were tasked with seeking the CR.42s which had been reported operating in this vicinity on the previous day, against which the early-model Hurricane should have been adequate – but no opposition appeared this time. In the afternoon the wing operated as such for the first time, all three squadrons undertaking a front-line patrol during which 7 SAAF Squadron found it difficult to keep up with the faster Mark IIs of the RAF squadrons.

MC.202 '84-5' frequently flown by Ten Luigi Giannella who made eight claims for aircraft shot down during service in North Africa, ending the war on a total of 12.

At 0615 two Bf 109s of I./JG 27 were scrambled, intercepting a bomber formation without result. A formation of 20 Kittyhawks was then spotted at 0730 near El Alamein, Lt Stahlschmidt claiming two of them shot down. These aircraft appear to have been from 450 Squadron which was initially escorting Bostons from 0705, one Kittyhawk being shot-up Cat II. Seven more I./JG 27 Messerschmitts escorted Stukas next, encountering nine Hurricanes near Burg el Arab, Stahlschmidt claiming one of these at 0825, There may have been a mistake in the registering of times on this occasion, for at 1015 Hurricanes of 213 Squadron were scrambled to intercept dive-bombers, but were bounced by six Bf 109s, two pilots being shot down and killed, while others claimed two Messerschmitts as probables. However, 73 Squadron, patrolling over the El Alamein area at the same time, claimed to have shot down three Bf 109s (or two probables and two damaged).

Flt Sgt D.H.McBurnie in his 450 Squadron Kittyhawk after claiming his sixth victory on 4 July.

At 0930 a free sweep was carried out over the El Alamein area by 11 MC.202s of 10° Gruppo (five from 84ª and six from 90ª Squadriglie) led by Cap Franco Lucchini. A mixed formation of about 20 P-40s, Hurricanes and Spitfires escorting 20 Bostons was reportedly engaged at 15,000 feet. Following a 30-minute fight, claims for one Boston and a probable, one Hurricane, one P-40 and two Spitfires (plus two probables) were submitted by the Italian pilots.

1 SAAF Squadron was scrambled at 1320, attacking five Bf 109s of I./JG 27 which had been about to intercept a bomber formation. Lt Waugh shot down Lt Körner, who baled out, becoming a PoW; he had been credited with 36 victories up to this date, mostly in North Africa. Seven pilots of the same German unit on a Stuka escort a little earlier had spotted a Beaufighter of 252 Squadron strafing the Sidi Barrani-Sollum road, and this had been shot down near Burg el Arab by Fw Kaiser (see Chapter Ten).

At 1400 six Kittyhawks of 450 Squadron, with others of 3 RAAF Squadron, bombed landing grounds west of El Daba. During the return flight the 450 Squadron pilots were strafing vehicles when Flt Sgt McBurnie spotted a reconnaissance Bf 110 of 4.(H)/12 which he attacked. The tail came off the aircraft when his fire hit it and it dived into the sea near its own airfield, the crew being killed.

Macchis of 10° Gruppo were again in the air at 1630 when six aircraft of 84ª Squadriglia led by Cap Lucchini and six of 90ª led by Cap Piccolomini, covered CR.42s of 50° Stormo, following which they were to undertake a free sweep over the El Alamein area. These pilots reported a formation of about 20 fighters, this time claiming two P-40s shot down and a third probably. All MC.202s landed safely at Fuka at 1830. At 1725 eight more Macchis from 88ª Squadriglia led by Cap Dante Ocarso commenced a free sweep south of El Adem during which a bomber formation identified as Marylands was intercepted, one of the bombers being claimed shot down; two escorting P-40s were thought to have probably been shot down and one damaged. During the day German Flak gunners claimed a Boston shot down, but despite these two claims, no bombers were lost by WDAF squadrons on this date.

Eight Bf 109s of I./JG 27 took off to escort Stukas at 1725, joined by eight from II.Gruppe. Hurricanes of 80 Squadron, several of them flown by attached 92 Squadron pilots, were scrambled, covered by 1 SAAF Squadron; a big fight commenced. Lt Stahlschmidt and Fw Steinhausen attacked the South African top cover, shooting down Maj le Mesurier and Lt Powell in flames. The major force-landed near El Imayid, wounded, and was taken to hospital. Powell, however, got out safely when he too crash-landed. Despite his wounds, le Mesurier claimed one Ju 87 probably destroyed with the rest of the Hurricane pilots claiming five shot down, two probables and several damaged. Flt Lt Sowrey of 80 Squadron claimed two of those thought to have been shot down, but collided with his second victim and had to bale out.

One more of this unit's Hurricanes was shot down, Plt Off Hill baling out and returning with Sowrey two days later. One was badly damaged, but returned safely. Plt Off Chisholm undertook the whole engagement with one wheel of his undercarriage hanging down. Oblt Vögl of II.Gruppe claimed one Hurricane, but this was not confirmed due to a lack of witnesses.

More Ju 87s were intercepted in the evening, this time by six Kittyhawks of 112 Squadron, which claimed two and a Bf 109 damaged. Sgt Agnew's aircraft was badly damaged. Four pilots of the escorting III./JG 53 Messerschmitts reported that 15 fighters attacked and they saw one Stuka force-land. One P-40 was claimed shot down at an unspecified time by Lt Scheiter of III./JG 27 near Emeisat, which might have been Agnew's aircraft, or a Kittyhawk of 250 Squadron which crash-landed during the day. During these evening engagements, two Bf 109s of III./JG 27 were scrambled to intercept bombers attacking Mumin Busak, Lt Schroer claiming one P-40 at 1840. Also at an unspecified time 33 Squadron lost Plt Off Merritt and his Hurricane, reportedly shot down near Angelisi by an MC.202.

Rommel now gave up his attack on the El Alamein line, ordering his troops onto the defensive after 20 of his tanks had been destroyed by British armour. XIII Corps then counter-attacked in the south, and 9th Australian Division attempted to strengthen the position in the northern sector, these moves leading to considerably bitter fighting. The Luftwaffe airfields at Mumin Busak and Sanyet Qotaifiya were attacked during the day and night by bombers and fighter-bombers at two-hour intervals during this period.

On 4 July bombs just missed the fighter units' tents and the calculator of an 88mm Flak emplacement was destroyed, some of the gun crew being killed. Allied bombing was being developed into quite a fine art; the steady formations of nine or 12 bombers which had so helped to save the day during June, were now being increased in size to 18 Bostons or Baltimores, usually escorted by three squadrons of Kittyhawks which now frequently also carried bombs to the targets themselves, and now often with a roving extra-high cover of Spitfires. Initially, 233 Wing specialised in this escort work with 239 Wing maintaining the independent fighter-bomber attacks, but as the number of bombers available increased, so both wings flew escorts, 233 Wing generally supporting the Bostons, 239 looking after the Baltimores.

During this period a new name was coined for the high-flying Bf 109s and MC.202s which continually dived and pecked at the Commonwealth formation – 'Snappers'. The Luftwaffe had a name for the Allied fighters also –'Höllenhunds' (Hellhounds). This was to be the pattern for the rest of the campaign – Kittyhawks flying bomber escorts with the added duty of fighter-bombing. The Hurricanes joining them in the latter task and also always being on readiness to intercept the Stuka formations – a job for which the Hurricane was well-suited, provided the escorting fighters were kept off their backs by the Spitfires roaming the battlefield at high altitude, watching over the formations of lesser-performance aircraft going about their missions below.

British Claims

33 Sqn	Flt Lt F.J.Aldridge	Hurricane IIc BE134 'Y'	MC.202	El Alamein	0915
33 Sqn	5 pilots	Hurricane IIcs	2 MC.202s Probable	El Alamein	0915
73 Sqn	Plt Off J.H.Fairbairn	Hurricane IIc BN357	Bf 109 Damaged	El Alamein line	1100
73 Sqn	Sgt R.L.Baker	Hurricane IIc BN402	Bf 109	El Alamein line	1105
73 Sqn	Flt Lt G.R.A.McG.Johnston	Hurricane IIc BE416	Bf 109F	El Alamein line	1105
73 Sqn	Flt Sgt E.L.Joyce	Hurricane IIc BP177 'L'	Bf 109 Damaged	El Alamein line	1110
213 Sqn	Plt Off G.R.S.McKay	Hurricane IIc BN136 'S'	Bf 109F Probable	SE El Alamein	1110
213 Sqn	Wt Off R.J.Wallace	Hurricane IIc BN378 'M'	Bf 109F Probable	SE El Alamein	1110
450 Sqn	Flt Sgt D.H.McBurnie	Kittyhawk I AK886	Bf 110		1402-1522
1 SAAF Sq	Lt L.R.S.Waugh	Hurricane IIb BG764 'W'	Bf 109F	El Alamein	1415
80/92 Sqn	Flt Sgt R.W.Blades	Hurricane IIc BE713 'H'	Ju 87	10m S El Alamein	1730-1830
80/92 Sqn	Plt Off J.M.V.Carpenter	Hurricane IIc BN389 'C'	Ju 87 Damaged	S El Alamein	1730-1830
80/92 Sqn	Plt Off W.L.Chisholm	Hurricane IIc BN291 'S'	Ju 87 Damaged	S El Alamein	1730-1830
80/92 Sqn	Plt Off. Morgan	Hurricane IIc BM991 'V'	Ju 87 Probable	S El Alamein	1730-1830
80/92 Sqn	Flt Lt J.M.Morgan	Hurricane IIc BM984 'Z'	Ju 87	S El Alamein	1730-1830
80/92 Sqn	Flt Lt J.M.Morgan	Hurricane IIc BM984 'Z'	Ju 87 Damaged	S El Alamein	1730-1830
80/92 Sqn	Plt Off D.K.Ryder	Hurricane IIc BE553	Ju 87 Probable	S El Alamein	1730-1830
80/92 Sqn	Plt Off W.A.Wales	Hurricane IIc BM974 'B'	Ju 87	S El Alamein	1730-1830
80/92 Sqn	Plt Off E.H.Hill	Hurricane IIc BE141 'J'	Ju 87 Damaged*	10m S El Alamein	1730-1830

80 Sqn	Flt Lt J.A.Sowrey	Hurricane IIc BE564 'A'	2 Ju 87s	10m S El Alamein	1730-1830
80 Sqn	Sgt J.D.Robb	Hurricane IIc BN462 'R'	Ju 87 Damaged	10m S El Alamein	1730-1830
80 Sqn	Sgt G.T.Pratley	Hurricane IIc BE542 'E'	Ju 87 Probable	10m S El Alamein	1730-1830
1 SAAF Sqn	Maj G.J.le Mesurier	Hurricane II BG971 'V'	Ju 87 Probable	El Alamein line	1735-
1 SAAF Sqn	Lt A.D.Maclean	Hurricane II Z5348 'M'	Bf 109F Probable	10m SW El Alamein	1810
1 SAAF Sqn	Capt P.C.R.Metelerkamp	Hurricane IIb BE703 'R'	Bf 109F	15m SSW El Alamein	1805
112 Sqn	Sgt D.Ibbotson	Kittyhawk I AK890	Ju 87	forward area	1915-2020
112 Sqn	Flg Off W.M.Whitamore	Kittyhawk I ET510	Ju 87		
112 Sqn	Flg Off W.M.Whitamore	Kittyhawk I ET510	Bf 109F Damaged		

*claimed on his return after being shot down

British Casualties

112 Sqn	Kittyhawk I AK852 badly damaged by Bf 109 over Daba at 1900, crashed on landing at base; Flt Sgt J.B.Agnew safe
450 Sqn	Kittyhawk I AK918 left 0705, attacked and damaged Cat II by a lone Bf 109E; Sgt E.C.House landed safely
260 Sqn	Kittyhawk I AK888 force-landed in desert, shot down by 3 Bf 109s, 0850-1000
33 Sqn	Hurricane IIc BE469 shot down by MC.202 El Alamein area at 0915; Plt Off A.G.Merritt KiA
33 Sqn	Hurricane IIc BN348 'E' damaged by MC.202 El Alamein area at 0915; Plt Off K.C.Rolls safe
33 Sqn	Hurricane IIc BN473 damaged by MC.202 El Alamein area at 0915; Plt Off H.S.Woods safe
33 Sqn	Hurricane IIc BN358 damaged by MC.202 El Alamein area at 0915; Sgt Wilson safe
80 Sqn	Hurricane IIc BE564 'A' collided with Ju 87; Flt Lt J.A.Sowrey baled out
80 Sqn	Hurricane IIc BE703 'J' shot down by Bf 109 El Imayid area, 1730-1830; Plt Off E.H.Hill safe
80 Sqn	Hurricane IIc BM974 'B' shot-up by Bf 109 El Imayid area, 1730-1830; Plt Off W.A.Wales (92 Sqn) safe
213 Sqn	Hurricane IIc BN349 'B' shot down by Bf 109, 10m W LG.122, at 1100; Plt Off W.H.Tomlinson KiA
213 Sqn	Hurricane IIc BN368 'Z' shot down by Bf 109, 10m W LG.122, at 1100; Plt Off D.R.Rehill KiA
213 Sqn	Hurricane IIc BN404 'E' damaged Cat I by Bf 109, 10m W LG.122, at 1100; Flg Off J.L.Briggs safe
1 SAAF Sqn	Hurricane II BE200 shot down by Bf 109 and crash-landed Cat II; Lt W.F.Powell returned later
1 SAAF Sqn	Hurricane II BG971 'V' Maj G.J.le Mesurier shot down by Bf 109 nr El Imayid 1825 WiA

German Claims

2./JG 27	Lt Hans-Arnold Stahlschmidt	2 P-40s	El Alamein & SE	0630-0632
2./JG 27	Lt Hans-Arnold Stahlschmidt	Hurricane	El Alamein	0825
Stab I./JG 27	Fw Emil Kaiser	Beaufighter	Burg el Arab	1100
2./JG 27	Lt Hans-Arnold Stahlschmidt	Hurricane	SW Burg el Arab	1705
1./JG 27	Fw Günther Steinhausen	Hurricane	20km SSE El Alamein	1705
4./JG 27	Oblt Ferdinand Vögl	P-40 o.Zg. n.b.	SE El Alamein	1718
7./JG 27	Lt Wilhelm Scheiter	P-40	SE Emeisat	
8./JG 27	Lt Werner Schroer	P-40	SE El Alamein	1840
Flak		Boston		1207

German Casualties

2./JG 27	Bf 109F-4 trop WNr 8696 Red 9, combat with Hurricane El Alamein area; Lt Friedrich Körner PoW
4.(H)/12	Bf 110E-2 WNr 2373 3U+BS shot down by P-40 N Turbiya; Fw Kurt Querner, Oblt Alexander Schult, Ogefr Georg Rastedt KiA
6./StG 3	Ju 87D-1 WNr 2547 combat with Hurricane 30km SE El Alamein; Lt Johannes Suckow PoW, Uffz Wilhelm Printz KiA

Italian Claims

84ª Sq, 10°Gr, 4°St CT	Ten Luigi Giannella	MC.202 MM 7815 '84-6'	Spitfire	El Alamein	0930-1030
84ª Sq, 10°Gr, 4°St CT	Serg Magg Mario Veronesi	MC.202 MM 7789 '84-5'	Spitfire	El Alamein	0930-1030
84ª Sq, 10°Gr, 4°St CT	Serg Magg Mario Veronesi	MC.202 MM 7789 '84-5'	Boston probable	El Alamein	0930-1030
90ª Sq, 10°Gr, 4°St CT	M.llo Pietro Del Turco	MC.202	Hurricane	El Alamein	0930-1030
90ª Sq, 10°Gr, 4°St CT	M.llo Angelo Savini	MC.202	Boston	El Alamein	0930-1030
90ª Sq, 10°Gr, 4°St CT	Cap Ranieri Piccolomini	MC.202	Spitfire Probable	El Alamein	0930-1030
90ª Sq, 10°Gr, 4°St CT	Ten Virgilio Vanzan	MC.202	Spitfire Probable	El Alamein	0930-1030
10°Gr, 4°St CT	11 pilots	MC.202	P-40	El Alamein	0930-1030
84ª Sq, 10°Gr, 4°St CT	Cap Franco Lucchini	MC.202 MM 7896 '84-8'	P-40	El Alamein	1600-1730
84ª Sq, 10°Gr, 4°St CT	Ten Luigi Giannella	MC.202 MM 7815 '84-6'	P-40 Probable	El Alamein	1600-1730
84ª Sq, 10°Gr, 4°St CT	Ten Paolo Berti	MC.202 MM 7803 '84-1' }	P-40	El Alamein	1600-1730
84ª Sq, 10°Gr, 4°St CT	Serg Corrado Patrizi	MC.202 MM 7789 }			
88ª Sq, 6°Gr, 1°St CT	Serg Rolando Roberti	MC.202	Maryland	S El Alamein	1715-1835

Italian Claims

88ª Sq, 6°Gr, 1°St CT	S.Ten Giuseppe Sparapani	MC.202	2 P-40s Probable	S El Alamein	1715-1835
88ª Sq, 6°Gr, 1°St CT	Ten Gino Ramarini	MC.202	P-40 Damaged	S El Alamein	1715-1835

Italian Casualties

230ª Sq, 95°Gr, 35°St BT	Cant.Z.1007bis MM 23412, destroyed at Barce on take-off, pilot Ten Gaetano Ferrante wounded, crew safe

Sunday, 5 July 1942

Seven of 450 Squadron's Kittyhawks were off at 0806 on an armed reconnaissance. Near LG.21 a lone Ju 88 of I./LG 1 was observed and this was shot down by Flt Lt Williams. About eight more of these bombers and four Bf 109s were then seen on the ground, six of the former and one Ju 87 being claimed damaged and one Messerschmitt destroyed by strafing by Sgt George O'Neil.

At 0905 213 Squadron swept over the battle area, encountering four Ju 88s and four Bf 110s. Flt Lt Westlake and Flt Sgt Stephenson each claimed a 110 and Sgt Ballantyne a Ju 88. Sqn Ldr Young and another pilot each claimed a bomber damaged. Four of III./JG 53's Bf 109s reported encountering 20 plus fighters and saw one of the Bf 110s being shot down. Nine Bf 110s of III./ZG 26 had been involved, their crews reporting being attacked by 35 Hurricanes and Curtiss's, one of their number being shot down by two fighters, indicating that the two 213 Squadron pilots had double-claimed on the same aircraft. The Bf 109s do appear to have become engaged in the action, Uffz Klaus Dyk of III./JG 53 failing to return.

Twenty minutes later nine Kittyhawks of 2 SAAF Squadron provided top cover for Bostons, the South African fighters being attacked by two Bf 109s, one of which was claimed shot down. Nine Kittyhawks from 4 SAAF Squadron were then top cover to another formation of Bostons raiding Daba Station soon after 1000. Six Bf 109s were engaged, one and one probable being claimed. Two Bf 109s of III./JG 27 which had been scrambled, encountered 12 Kittyhawks near Burg el Arab, one being claimed shot down in flames. A little later two Bf 109s of II.Gruppe on a meteorological flight met a formation of bombers, but were attacked by three Curtiss fighters, one Messerschmitt being badly damaged, but the pilot managed to land this at the unit's own airfield. Six Kittyhawks of 250 Squadron covered five of 112 Squadron which bombed and strafed LG.106. Here two Bf 109Es were identified as they took off and one of these was claimed shot down by Flt Lt Marshall of 250, a second being claimed as a probable. During this mission Sgt Ibbotson of 112 Squadron was shot down, but returned safely later.

After a free sweep at 0830, aborted due to bad weather, Cap Lucchini repeated this sortie at 1145 leading 12 MC.202s of 10° Gruppo, six each of 84ª and 90ª Squadriglie. They engaged a formation of Spitfires and P-40s and claimed seven fighters damaged, then landing back at Fuka at 1320. A few minutes later Cap Ruspoli led nine more Macchis of the same unit on a similar mission. 18 Bostons escorted by about 25 fighters were reported and two P-40s were claimed shot down. M.llo Bignami who was cruising at higher altitude, engaged nine Spitfires and claimed one shot down.

At 1035 12 Spitfires of 145 Squadron set off on patrol, during which Sgt James reported that he was short of oxygen, after which he was not seen again. 450 Squadron sent six more Kittyhawks on a bombing mission just before 1100, from which Flt Sgt Beste and Sgt Simpson failed to return – probably shot down by 10° Gruppo Macchis. They had attacked LG.106 again, claiming to have damaged five Bf 109s and a Bf 110 before being attacked by hostile aircraft. During the day a Bf 109 of III./JG 27 and an MC.202 of 6° Gruppo were destroyed on the ground during strafing attacks on Mumin Busak. 450 Squadron strafed LG.106 again at 1130, this time Bf 109s and six Bf 110s being seen. Claims were made for five Bf 109s and Bf 110s damaged, but two of the unit's Kittyhawks were lost to Flak.

At 1420 three Spitfires of 145 Squadron again took off for a sweep. At the same time 11 Bf 109s of I.Gruppe, four of II.Gruppe and four of III./JG 27 set off to escort Stukas over the forward area. At 1445 Lt Scheiter of III.Gruppe claimed a Spitfire in flames near El Alamein and five minutes later Obfw Clade of II.Gruppe claimed another, also in flames, 30 miles south-east of El Daba; after a further five minutes Hptm Franzisket of I.Gruppe also claimed one in the area of El Alamein. 145 Squadron reported meeting 15 Ju 88s and ten Bf 109s, losing Flt Lt Monk, while Sgt Burman claimed a Bf 109 damaged. It seems reasonably likely that this combat was one in which 33 Squadron also participated, as the unit fought a number of Bf 109s, one each being claimed by Flt Lt Wade and Flg Off Wooller, a third being claimed as a probable. Plt Off Challis did not return and was believed to have been shot down by a Bf 110.

Two MC.202s of 88ª Squadriglia, off at 1335 to patrol over Mumin Busak, pursued ten P-40s, claiming damage to three of them. However, S.Ten Sparapani's aircraft was damaged in the left wing. Between 1520 and 1640 12 MC.202s of 9° Gruppo (six each from 96ª and 97ª Squadriglie) were in the air and undertook the last 4° Stormo combat of the day. Over Bir el Mukheisin they reportedly engaged 15 Bostons escorted by about 20 P-40s and claimed two of the fighters shared among them, plus about a dozen damaged. Eleven CR.42s of 159° Gruppo also strafed troops and vehicles in the Gebel Kalakh area, following which one of the fighter-bombers force-landed, the pilot returning on foot.

At 1235 thee Spitfire pilots of 601 Squadron saw their first action over the desert, taking off to intercept a reconnaissance aircraft identified as an Me 210, which Sqn Ldr Bisdee claimed to have damaged. 213 Squadron carried out another sweep at 1233, encountering four MC.202s which were 1,000 feet below, and two more which were away to port. Flt Lt Westlake dived on those below, claiming one shot down and the other damaged. He may have hit Sparapani's aircraft, mentioned above, which force-landed after being damaged, to be recovered three days later.

In the evening six Bf 109s of I./JG 27 took off on a Freie Jagd, encountering 12 bombers and 20 fighters, one of which was claimed shot down near Burg el Arab by Fw Steinhausen at 1800.

During the day 7 SAAF Squadron received its first Hurricane IIbs, sufficient to equip one flight. It was planned, therefore, that these should provide cover to the Mark Is – now to be termed Mark I Specials – which were to drop Jefferis 'sticky' bombs on tanks. So what was the Jefferis bomb? Maj Gen Millis Rowland Jefferis, KBE, MC, headed a part of a specialist department in the War Office developing unusual and new forms of weapons for the army, and thereby on occasion for the other services. The Jefferis bomb was originally designed as a hand-held anti-tank weapon for the infantry, and comprised a glass sphere, filled with nitroglycerin, coated in a very strong adhesive. The weapon was intended to be placed on the side plates of a tank or other armoured vehicle by an intrepid soldier. The short fuse would then cause the bomb to explode and hopefully blow a hole in the target vehicle. Early tests showed that there were problems in getting the adhesive to stick to dirty or very dusty surfaces, which rather restricted the potential use of the weapon in the desert conditions of North Africa.

However, since the bomb was of relatively light weight, theoretically a goodly number could be carried by an aircraft such as a Hurricane. Potentially the roof of a tank or armoured car might be expected to be less heavily encrusted with dust and dirt than the sides; moreover the velocity of the weapons when air-dropped might be anticipated to explode on impact, rather than requiring a time fuse. This would make its use from an aircraft rather simpler and perhaps less dangerous than in the hand-held mode. The carriage of these weapons by 7 SAAF Squadron seems to have been the only example of its use in North Africa. Such use was also brief and there is little evidence of any widespread success. Another weapon which perhaps appeared more promising in prospect than in actuality?

Rommel's forces had spent the day probing to the south of the XIII Corps counter-attack in an effort to turn the British flank.

British Claims

450 Sqn	Flt Lt J.E.A.Williams	Kittyhawk I AK634	Ju 88	LG.21	0805-0918
213 Sqn	Sgt J.F.C.Ballantyne	Hurricane IIc BN337	Ju 88	El Alamein area	0905-1010
213 Sqn	Plt Off C.D.A.Smith	Hurricane IIc BM966 'T'	Ju 88 Damaged	El Alamein area	0905-1010
213 Sqn	Sqn Ldr M.H.Young	Hurricane IIc BN286 'O'	Ju 88 Damaged	El Alamein area	0905-1010
213 Sqn	Flt Sgt W.H.Stephenson	Hurricane IIc BN136 'S'	Bf 110	El Alamein area	0905-1010
213 Sqn	Flt Lt G.H.Westlake	Hurricane IIc BN184 'W'	Bf 110	El Alamein area	0905-1010
260 Sqn	Sgt W.R.Cundy	Kittyhawk I ET908 'G'	Bf 109 Damaged	E El Daba	0905-1010
260 Sqn	Sgt J.F.Edwards	Kittyhawk I ET623 'E'	Bf 109 Damaged	E El Daba	0905-1010
260 Sqn	Sgt L.J.Shepherd	Kittyhawk I	Bf 109 Damaged	E El Daba	0905-1010
260 Sqn	Sgt D.W.C.England	Kittyhawk I AK891 'F'	Bf 109 Damaged	E El Daba	0905-1010
33 Sqn	Plt Off W.A.R.McDonald	Hurricane IIc BE134 'Y'	Bf 109		0910-
33 Sqn	Flt Lt L.C.Wade	Hurricane IIc BP186	Bf 109		0910-
33 Sqn	Flg Off J.Wooller	Hurricane IIc BP184 'X'	Bf 110		0910-
4 SAAF Sqn	Lt S.I.Reinders	Kittyhawk I	Bf 109F	El Daba area	0910-
2 SAAF Sqn	Lt P.D.Bryant	Kittyhawk I AK776 'V' }	Bf 109	Burg el Arab	1010
2 SAAF Sqn	Lt V.R.Burdon	Kittyhawk I AK662 'Y' }			
250 Sqn	Sgt R.Wallis	Kittyhawk I AK921 }	Bf 109	W El Daba LG.106	1100
250 Sqn	Flt Lt A.E.Marshall	Kittyhawk I ET513 'A' }			
601 Sqn	Sqn Ldr J.D.Bisdee	Spitfire Vb BR232	Me 210 Damaged	Aboukir Sector	1235-1330
213 Sqn	Flt Lt G.H.Westlake	Hurricane IIc BN184 'W'	MC.202	over El Alamein line	1235-1345

British Claims

213 Sqn	Flt Lt G.H.Westlake	Hurricane IIc BN184 'W'	MC.202 Damaged	over El Alamein line	1235-1345
5 SAAF Sqn	Lt C.Sommerville	Tomahawk IIb AK547 'S'	Bf 109F Probable	El Daba	1240-
145 Sqn	Sgt D.C.Burman	Spitfire Vb ..959 'D'	Bf 109		1420-
3 RAAF Sqn	Sgt R.H.Bayly	Kittyhawk I AK653	Bf 109 Damaged	Ras Gibeisa area	1700

British Casualties

260 Sqn	Kitthhawk I AK891 'F' damaged by Bf 109 while on Boston escort 0905-1010 ; Sgt D.W.C.England safe
450 Sqn	Kittyhawk I AL114 MiA from ground attack shot down by ground fire at LG.106 1110; Flt Sgt S.Simpson KiA
450 Sqn	Kittyhawk I AL164 MiA from ground attack nr Ghazal-El Adem at 1110; Sgt F.W.Beste PoW
112 Sqn	Kittyhawk AK890 'M' of 73 OTU MiA, hit by Flak while bombing at 1100; Sgt D.Ibbotson safe
2 SAAF Sqn	Kittyhawk AK970 'C' slt damage by Bf 109 1645-1800; Capt H.E.N.Wildsmith
33 Sqn	Hurricane IIc BN385 shot down N El Alamein at 0910 by Bf 110, or hit sea while chasing it; Plt Off B.W.Challis KiA
213 Sqn	Hurricane IIc BM966 'T' left 0845, crash-landed at base 1005; Plt Off C.D.A.Smith safe
145 Sqn	Spitfire V BP851 left 1420; Flt Lt A.G.D.B.Monk PoW
145 Sqn	Spitfire V AB411 'L' left 1035, reported being short of oxygen; Sgt H.G.James KiA
131 MU	Hurricane BP138 missing in dust storm

German Claims

10.(Jabo)/JG 53	Oblt Werner Langermann	Hurricane		0845
9./JG 27	Oblt Hans-Joachim Heinecke	P-40	N Burg el Arab	0905
1./JG 27	Hptm Ludwig Franzisket	Spitfire	20km S El Alamein	1350
5./JG 27	Obfw Emil Clade	Spitfire	40km SE El Daba	1355
7./JG 27	Lt Wilhelm Scheiter	Spitfire	25km S El Alamein	1355
1./JG 27	Fw Günther Steinhausen	P-46	12-3km SW Burg el Arab	1800

German Casualties

7./JG 53	Bf 109F-4 trop WNr 8680 Black <I+I shot down El Alamein area 0840; Uffz Klaus Dyck MiA
III./JG 53	Bf 109F-4 trop WNr 10194 damaged 40% on ground by bombs Qotaifiya
III./JG 53	Bf 109F-4 trop WNr 10280 damaged 15% on ground by bombs Qotaifiya
7./JG 27	Bf 109F-4 trop WNr 8563 combat with P-40; force-landing 10km S Mumin Busak, 100%; Uffz Rudolf Moycis safe
III./JG 27	Bf 109F-4 trop WNr 8735 100% in ground attack at Mumin Busak
9./ZG 26	Bf 110E-2 WNr 4441 3U+JT shot down by Hurricanes, crashed 10km N El Alamein; Lt Walter Sedlacek/Uffz Gerhard Häseler KiA
9./ZG 26	Bf 110F-2 WNr 4577 shot down by Hurricanes W El Alamein, crash-landed at Fuka, destroyed, crew safe
2./LG 1	Ju 88A-4 WNr 5616 shot down by P-40 landing at Bir el Abd, destroyed; Oblt Friedrich Michel and three KiA
II./LG 1	Ju 88A-4 WNr 5577 15% damaged by P-40 landing at Bir el Abd, crew safe
II./LG 1	Ju 88A-4 WNr 140058 15% damaged by P-40 landing at Bir el Abd, crew safe
II./LG 1	Ju 88A-4 WNr 5599 crash-landed at Bir el Abd, 40% damaged, crew safe
I./StG 3	Ju 87R-4 WNr 6341 shot-up in combat, crash-landed at Bir el Abd, 65% damaged, crew safe
III./StG 3	Ju 87D-3 WNr 2396 shot-up in combat, force-landed at Derna, 10% damaged, crew safe
1.(F)/121	Ju 88D-1 WNr 430151 shot-up in combat, force-landed at Derna, 30% damaged, crew safe

Italian Claims

84ª Sq, 10°Gr, 4°St CT	M.llo Luigi Bignami	MC.202 MM 7815	Spitfire	El Alamein	1320-1455
10° Gr, 4° St CT	unstated	MC.202s	2 P-40s shared	El Alamein	1320-1455
88ª Sq, 6°Gr, 1°St CT	S.Ten Giuseppe Sparapani	MC.202	3 P-40s Damaged	nr Mumin Busak	1335-
9° Gr, 4° St CT	unstated	MC.202s	2 P-40s shared	Bir el Mukheisin	1520-1640

Italian Casualties

391ª Sq, 159°Gr, 50°St Ass	CR.42 force-landed, S.Ten Armando Marin walked back
88ª Sq, 6°Gr, 1°St CT	MC.202 damaged in left wing, S.Ten Giuseppe Sparapani safe; aircraft recovered on 8 July
88ª Sq, 6°Gr, 1°St CT	MC.202 MM 7886 destroyed in ground strafing at Mumin Busak
230ª Sq, 95°Gr, 35°St BT	Cant.Z.1007bis MM 23412, destroyed in take-off accident al Barce, Ten Gaetano Ferrante and crew safe

Monday, 6 July 1942

Nine Kittyhawks of 4 SAAF Squadron carried out an escort at 0855, meeting about six Bf 109s, one of which Capt Murray claimed to have shot down. Nine more Kittyhawks attacked Mumin Busak airfield during the morning, followed by 12 bombers; one Italian aircraft was burnt out on the ground. Half an hour later 11 more bombers attacked and another Italian was destroyed, the Regia Aeronautica then

Magg Roberto Fassi sits on the wing of a Macchi, having assumed command of 9° Gruppo of 4° Stormo on 6 July. In the cockpit is Cap Roberto Dagasso.

deciding that the airfield was too exposed, withdrawing 88ª Squadriglia back to Fuka.

At 1200 12 Kittyhawks of 2 SAAF Squadron provided top cover for Bostons, being attacked by two Bf 109s, Lt Allen's aircraft being badly damaged, the only casualty sustained by the unit at this time. However, two fighters had been scrambled by III./JG 27, the pilots of these claiming three victories over P-40s. Half an hour later three more of the unit's Messerschmitts were sent up, reporting meeting 15 Hurricanes, one of which was claimed. Hurricanes, reported to be Mark IId tank-busters, were escorted by 239 Wing Kittyhawks at 1220. One Kittyhawk of 450 Squadron flown by Flt Sgt Dangar was attacked for some time by a pair of Messerschmitts which inflicted slight damage on it. Four Spitfires of 601 Squadron, patrolling soon after 1300, attacked three Ju 88s escorted by five Bf 109s of III./JG 53. The British pilots spotted only three of these and were jumped by the other two, Oblt Götz shooting down two of them. During an otherwise uneventful escort to CR.42s carried out from 1255-1425 by six MC.202s of 10° Gruppo, S.Ten Barsotti had his aircraft damaged by ground fire.

During the day Lt Jackson of 40 SAAF Squadron on a TacR sortie, crash-landed after his Hurricane was hit by Flak. A Beaufighter of 252 Squadron was also shot down by Flak when attacking a convoy of lorries, the crew being killed (see Chapter Ten).

At 1500 eight of 260 Squadron's Kittyhawks provided top cover to some bombers, engaging five Bf 109s of I./JG 27 which were escorting some Ju 88s. Flt Sgt Edwards claimed one Bf 109, Fw Würschinger force-landing after his engine was hit in the cooling system, his fighter being a complete write-off. Claims for two further Messerschmitts may have been made, one of them by Sgt England. An MC.200 of 364ª Sq was scrambled from Benghazi K3 at 2000. Ten Mecatti intercepted a Liberator and claimed it damaged. Hit by return fire, he flew back to land at base. Magg Roberto Fassi arrived at Fuka during the day, assuming command of 9° Gruppo in substitution of Cap Luigi Mariotti who had provisionally held this role since the death of Magg Larsimont-Pergameni on 26 June. Mariotti now took command of 73ª Squadriglia.

British Claims

4 SAAF Sqn	Capt T.P.L.Murray	Kittyhawk I 'E'	Bf 109		0855-
260 Sqn	Flt Sgt J.F.Edwards	Kittyhawk Ia ET623 'E'	Bf 109F Damaged	E El Daba	0930-1045
601 Sqn	Plt Off A.R.Boyle	Spitfire Vb BR384	Ju 88 Damaged	El Daba area	1255-1405
145 Sqn	Sgt S.N.Duigan	Spitfire Vb ..287 'K'	Bf 109 Damaged	W El Alamein	1455-
260 Sqn	Flt Sgt J.F.Edwards	Kittyhawk Ia ET623 'E'	Bf 109F	E El Daba	1500-1610

British Claims

260 Sqn	Flt Sgt J.F.Edwards	Kittyhawk Ia ET623 'E'	Bf 109F Damaged	E El Daba	1500-1610
260 Sqn	Sqn Ldr O.V.Hanbury	Kittyhawk Ia ET575 'D'	Bf 109F	E El Daba	1500-1610
260 Sqn	Plt Off R.A.Dunbar	Kittyhawk Ia	Bf 109F	E El Daba	1500-1610

British Casualties

601 Sqn	Spitfire V BR232 left 1255, shot down by Bf 109s nr El Daba; Flt Lt W.J.E.Haggar KiA
601 Sqn	Spitfire V BR325 left 1255, shot down by Bf 109s nr El Daba; Wt Off Belcher PoW
145 Sqn	Spitfire V BP847 'E' shot down by Bf 109, crash-landed at 1635; Sgt G.W.Small safe
80 Sqn	Hurricane IIc BM987 shot down by fighters, probably an MC.202; Sgt C.W.House MiA, got back
260 Sqn	Kittyhawk I damaged Cat I
2 SAAF Sqn	Kittyhawk I AK970 'C' damaged Cat II by Bf 109 1200-1330; Lt A.D.Allen safe
4 SAAF	Kittyhawk I 'E' crash-landed to Bf 109; Capt T.P.L.Murray safe
274 Sqn	Hurricane IIc shot down by a Bf 109 crash-landed at 1230
40 SAAF Sqn	Hurricane crash-landed due to Flak at El Daba 1600; Lt C.D.Jackson PoW
450 Sqn	Kittyhawk I slight damage by Flak 0630-0735; Flt Sgt R.V.Dangar FTL safe

German Claims

9./JG 27	Obfw Heinrich Rosenberg	P-40	SW El Alamein	1140
8./JG 27	Lt Werner Schroer	2 P-40s	20 & 21km SW El Alamein	1140 & 1143
7./JG 27	Fw Helmut Kabisch	Hurricane	SSW El Alamein	1200
9./JG 53	Oblt Franz Götz	2 Spitfires		1231 & 1237

German Casualties

6./JG 27	Bf 109F-4 WNr 7404 Yellow 4 shot down by AA, force-landed nr El Alamein, 100%; Obfw Hans Würschinger safe
7./JG 27	Bf 109F-4 trop WNr 8517 destroyed in fighter-bomber attack at Mumin Busak

Italian Claims

364ª Sq, 150° Gr CT	Ten Mario Mecatti	MC.200	B-24 Damaged	near Benghazi	2015

Italian Casualties

364ª Sq, 150° Gr CT	MC.200, damaged by return fire, Ten Mario Mecatti safe
91ª Sq, 10°Gr, 4°St CT	MC.202 MM 7935 damaged by AA, S.Ten Luciano Barsotti WiA
88ª Sq, 6°Gr, 1°St CT	MC.202 MM 7709 destroyed in ground attack at Mumin Busak
73ª Sq, 9°Gr, 4°St CT	MC.202 MM 7827 '73-6' belly-landed, damaged

Tuesday, 7 July 1942

In the early hours two Bf 109s of I./JG 27 were on defensive patrol over their airfield when at 0702 Lt Stahlschmidt shot down a biplane near El Daba, which fell in flames. When *Fighters over the Desert* was originally researched the identity of this aircraft was a complete mystery. However, the background was subsequently discovered by Brian Cull and included in his book (*Spitfires over Israel*, with Shlomo Aloni and David Nicolle, Grub Street). The most appropriate way to explain the situation is by quoting:

> "Despite the successes achieved by the Beaufighters in defending central Egypt from the night bombers, by mid 1942 the British and Commonwealth ground forces were being pushed back across the Libyan-Egyptian border by Rommel's triumphant Afrika Korps; the Germans were confident of reaching Cairo by Christmas. Thus pre-occupied, Britain's lack of interest in Egypt's political turmoil was understandable. With their very existence threatened, Egyptian politicians continued to squabble amongst themselves – undecided whether to back Britain or Germany in the mighty struggle – despite the fact that German bombers frequently bombed Egyptian targets.
>
> "A minor conspiracy among a group of junior REAF officers came to light early in July – with the Germans edging ever nearer to Cairo – when four REAF pilots procured aerial photographs of British military positions with the intention of handing these over to the German authorities. It was agreed that Plt Off Ahmed Saudi Hussein, with a set of the photographs, would fly a Gladiator across the lines, which he did at first light on 7 July. However, at 0702 over El Daba the Gladiator was intercepted by two Bf 109Fs of I./JG 27 and shot down by Lt Hans-Arnold Stahlschmidt. Probably unaware of the fate of his colleague, Wt Off Muhammad Ridwan Salim set out next morning on a similar mission in a second Gladiator, reaching the German lines safely with a second set of photographs. Ridwan Salim was taken to Germany, where he was captured by the Allies in 1945, being returned to Egypt for trial. His fate is uncertain.

"When news of the defection reached Cairo, it was the REAF which promptly grounded all its own aircraft, the British seemingly unconcerned. The commander of the REAF, Brigadier Ali Muafi, resigned while two of his senior officers were transferred to the army, together with 14 junior officer pilots and 17 NCO pilots, as a disciplinary measure. The majority of the REAF personnel, however, were appalled at the treachery of their colleagues."

Cap Mariotti led 12 MC.202s of the three squadriglie of 9° Gruppo on a free sweep over the Bir el Mukheisin area between 0920-1040. At 16,000 feet they were bounced by four P-40s but managed to claim three shot down. Then Cap Ruspoli took off at 1035 leading 11 MC.202s of 10° Gruppo (five from 84ª Squadriglia and six from 91ª) on an escort mission to CR.42s attacking enemy vehicles over the front. At 15,000 feet they engaged a formation reportedly composed of 12 Bostons, ten P-40s and ten Spitfires and after a 30-minute combat they claimed a Boston, a Spit and a P-40 shot down plus a Boston probably so. At about noon Ten Virgilio Vanzan led four MC.202s of 90ª Squadriglia to cover CR.42s of 50° Stormo in the same area. This time the clash with 15 P-40s and ten Spitfires ended with no losses for either side, just four P-40s that were claimed damaged by the Italians.

In the battle area meanwhile, at midday 12 Tomahawks of 5 SAAF Squadron and eight Kittyhawks of 4 SAAF Squadron escorted 11 Bostons of 12 SAAF Squadron to bomb west of El Daba – the first of three raids on this date. The formation was attacked by MC.202s of 10° Gruppo which broke through the various layers of escorts and attacked the bombers. The lead Boston, flown by Maj S.A.Pharoah, was attacked repeatedly by Cap Carlo Ruspoli, who closed to 50 yards. His fire seriously wounded Pharoah, punctured the starboard fuel tank, the engine and the oil tank, also shooting away the elevator on that side of the aircraft. Close to unconsciousness, Pharoah turned out to sea, jettisoned the bombs, and just managed to crash-land in the forward infantry positions at El Alamein as he passed out. Medical help was fortunately close at hand, and he was removed to hospital. His victor only claimed a probable due, it seems, to the 10/10ths cloud cover which prevented him seeing the Boston go down. One Tomahawk was shot down, the pilot baling out safely. The Italian pilots claimed one P-40 and one Boston, but a second P-40, a Spitfire and the second Boston were all claimed as probables.

Four ground-attack missions were undertaken by 50° Stormo CR.42s in the Wadi Kalakh area, the first between 1150-1335 during which one aircraft force-landed, the pilot returning safely. During the third raid, 1550-1715, Ten Gaggero of 236ª Squadriglia failed to return. Escorting MC.202 pilots reported seeing a pilot bale out and land safely; he was captured by British troops. At 1505 eight Bf 109s of II./JG 27 escorted eight Ju 88s to attack vehicles, but one of the bombers was hit by AA and force-landed during the return flight. Twelve Hurricanes of 73 Squadron took off at 1555, covered by 213 Squadron, and patrolled over the forward area, where a number of CR.42s were encountered – obviously the 50° Stormo aircraft on the third mission of the day; two were claimed shot down. Four Spitfires of 601 Squadron on a sweep were attacked by a reported three Bf 109s and three MC.202s, one Spitfire being damaged. Their opponents appear to have been ten Macchis from 9° Gruppo, led by Ten Malvezzi, which claimed three fighters, identified as P-40s, shot down in the Bir el Mukheisin area during the later afternoon.

Due to the continual bombing of the Mumin Busak airfield, I./JG 27 now withdrew to Turbiya. III./ZG 26 carried out a ground-attack mission near Fuka, but one Bf 110 was hit by ground fire which wounded Uffz Scherkenbeck, causing him to force-land. Another of the unit's aircraft then landed alongside and picked up the crew. During the day a motorized 8th Army column shelled III./ZG 26's airfield at Fuka for 30 minutes, but without inflicting any material damage. However, that night SAS forces led by Maj David Stirling and Capt 'Paddy' Mayne destroyed at least ten of 50° Stormo's CR.42s on Abar Nimeir airfield, together with an MC.202 of 88ª Squadriglia and an S.81.

British Claims

145 Sqn	Plt Off L.A.Malins	Spitfire Vb AB321 'N'	Bf 109 Damaged		1145-
12 SAAF Sqn	unspecified gunners	Boston III	MC.202		1200-1300
73 Sqn	Flt Sgt E.L.Joyce	Hurricane IIc BP167 'L'	CR.42	25-30m SW El Alamein	1640
73 Sqn	Flt Lt J.B.Selby	Hurricane IIc BE554	CR.42	Maaten Bagush l.g.	1640
73 Sqn	Flt Lt J.B.Selby	Hurricane IIc BE554	u/i/e/a Probable	Maaten Bagush l.g.	1640

British Casualties

5 SAAF Sqn	Tomahawk IIb AN365 'M' shot down and abandoned 5m W Daba on bomber escort at 1245; 2/Lt B.J.Grove baled out
1 SAAF	Hurricane 'P' force-landed wheels down for glycol leak, then strafed by Bf 109 at 1200; Lt S.W.Rabie safe

British Casualties

601 Sqn	Spitfire V AB460 damaged by Bf 109 at 1125, flown to Aboukir, back on 9th July; 2/Lt A.Bartleman safe
12 SAAF Sqn	Boston III AL735 'R' attacked repeatedly by MC.202; jettisoned bombs in sea and crash-landed badly damaged in front line area; Maj S.A.Pharoah badly wounded, crew safe
12 SAAF Sqn	Boston III ..727 'J' attacked by 2 MC.202s, damaged but returned safely; Lt Jordan and crew safe
274 Sqn	Hurricane IIc BD750 'W'; on patrol 1910-2030, damaged by MC.202 Cat I; Plt Off R.H.N.Walsh safe

Egyptian Casualties

2 REAF	Gladiator shot down by Bf 109; Plt Off A.S.Hussain KiA

German Claims

2./JG 27	Lt Hans-Arnold Stahlschmidt	Gladiator	10km NE El Daba	0502

German Casualties

9./ZG 26	Bf 110F-2 WNr 4550 3U+LS, shot down by AA, crashed 65km S Fuka, destroyed; Uffz Josef Scherkenbeck WiA
I./StG 3	Ju 87R-2 WNr 6033 65% damaged in strafing attack at Abu Haggag
4/(H)/12	Bf 109E-7 WNr 3839 65% belly-landed at Fuka, 30% damaged

Italian Claims

9° Gr, 4° St CT	unspecified pilots	MC.202	3 P-40s	Bir el Mukheisin	0925-1040
91ª Sq, 10°Gr, 4°St CT	Cap Carlo M. Ruspoli	MC.202	Boston Probable	El Alamein	1035-1200
91ª Sq, 10°Gr, 4°St CT	Serg. Ferruccio Terrabuio	MC.202	Spitfire	El Alamein	1035-1200
90ª Sq, 10°Gr, 4°St CT	Serg Magg Massimo Salvatore	MC.202	P-40	El Alamein	1035-1200
10° Gr, 4° St CT	unspecified pilot	MC.202	Boston	El Alamein	1035-1200
97ª Sq, 9°Gr, 4°St CT	Ten Fernando Malvezzi	MC.202	P-40	Bir el Mukheisin	1730-1900
97ª Sq, 9°Gr, 4°St CT	Ten Antonio Canfora	MC.202	P-40	Bir el Mukheisin	1730-1900
97ª Sq, 9°Gr, 4°St CT	M.llo Dante Labanti	MC.202	P-40	Bir el Mukheisin	1730-1900

Italian Casualties

387ª Sq, 158°Gr, 50°St Ass	CR.42 force-landed 1150-1335, Serg Gino Facchini safe
236ª Sq, 158°Gr, 50°St Ass	CR.42 failed to return 1550-1715, M.llo Carlo Gaggero PoW
88ª Sq, 6°Gr, 1°St CT	MC.202 MM 7892 damaged at Fuka by SAS raid
390ª Sq, 159°Gr, 50°St Ass	CR.42 MM 8529 destroyed and CR.42 MM 8896 badly damaged by SAS raid at Abar Nimeir
387ª Sq, 158°Gr, 50°St Ass	3 CR.42s MM 8497, 8501 and 4446 destroyed by SAS raid at Abar Nimeir
389ª Sq, 159°Gr, 50°St Ass	4 CR.42s MM 8861, 8844, 8859 and 8862 damaged to various degree by SAS raid at Abar Nimeir
391ª Sq, 159°Gr, 50°St Ass	CR.42 MM 8858 damaged by SAS raid at Abar Nimeir

Wednesday, 8 July 1942

Nine MC.202s of 10° Gruppo took off from Fuka at 0900, led by Cap Piccolomini, on a free sweep over the lines. Twelve Hurribombers were encountered, escorted by 20 P-40s and 25 Spitfires. A short clash occurred where one P-40 was claimed probably shot down by the formation leader. All MC.202s landed safely at 1025. Five minutes later Magg Fassi led nine more MC.202s, this time of 9° Gruppo, to the Bir el Mukheisin area. Here 18 bombers were intercepted and one was claimed as a probable.

Hurricanes of 33, 127 and 1 SAAF Squadrons took off soon after 1100 to patrol over the forward area, where a number of Messerschmitts were seen. Six such fighters from I./JG 27 had taken off on a Freie Jagd and these jumped the 12 Hurricanes of 33 Squadron, Lt Stahlschmidt claiming to have shot down three; two pilots were killed, with a third aircraft, flown by the unit's commanding officer, badly damaged. The Germans were then attacked by the 12 Hurricanes of 127 Squadron, the pilots of which claimed two Messerschmitts shot down, both reportedly witnessed by 1 SAAF Squadron. However, no Luftwaffe losses were recorded and it is possible that the South African pilots had actually seen the two 33 Squadron aircraft crashing.

Around midday 11 Kittyhawks from 250 Squadron, ten from 112 and ten more of 3 RAAF Squadron undertook a fighter-bomber attack on LGs 20 and 21, catching four Bf 109s just taking off with a number of Ju 87s. Two other Messerschmitt pilots of III.Gruppe had set off a few minutes earlier to cover the assembly of the Stukas, and these attacked the British fighters, but one was shot down, force-landing near El Daba. Wg Cdr Mayers, leading 250 Squadron, claimed a Bf 109 shot down over LG.20, and 250 Squadron pilots claimed two Ju 87s and a Bf 109. One more Stuka was claimed damaged on the ground, but one of the unit's Kittyhawks was badly shot-up by two fighters during the return flight and the pilot wounded. This aircraft may have been attacked by Macchis of 4° Stormo, both 9° and 10° Gruppi claiming P-40s as probable victories during the morning. Another Bf 109 was claimed by Sqn Ldr Drake

Bomb-laden Kittyhawk I ET790 GA-? in which Sqn Ldr Billy Drake claimed a Bf 109 shot down over El Daba on 8 July.

of 112 Squadron, bringing 239 Wing's claims here to three Bf 109s and two Ju 87s shot down, two Bf 109s probable and one damaged. No further Luftwaffe claims were made, but two more Bf 109s were shot down during this engagement. Lt Hoffmann of I.Gruppe belly-landed, Lt Kugelbauer being hit in the chest and right arm, baled out. A bullet had also severed one strap of his parachute harness and he fell out of this when the canopy opened, falling to his death.

At 1630 12 MC.202s of 9° Gruppo, led by Cap Mariotti, were despatched to attack SAS vehicles sighted south of El Daba. Some scout cars were reportedly effectively strafed. In the evening five Bf 109s of II./JG 27 strafed a column south of Qotaifiya until Oblt Sinner recognised them as Axis troops and pulled away. Six Ju 87s also bombed their own troops in error on this date. However, 2° Stormo CT now moved up to Egypt, 13° Gruppo to Bu Amud, at Tobruk, and 8° Gruppo to Abu Haggag.

British Claims

24 SAAF Sqn	Lt T.A.van der Spuy *	Boston III	MC.202		1105-1330
2 SAAF Sqn	Capt H.E.N.Wildsmith	Kittyhawk I AL181 'W'	Bf 109 Damaged		1130-1240
127 Sqn	Plt Off J.H.Currie	Hurricane IIb BE325 'E' }	Bf 109		1200
127 Sqn	Flt Lt R.Marples	Hurricane IIb Z5235 H }			
127 Sqn	Sqn Ldr C.O.J.Pegge	Hurricane IIb BN406 B	Bf 109F		1200
112 Sqn	Sqn Ldr B.Drake	Kittyhawk I ET790	Bf 109F	LG.21	1205-1330
112 Sqn	Plt Off Johnson	Kittyhawk I ET1024	Bf 109F Damaged	LG.21	1205-1330
450 Sqn	Sgt V.J.McFarlane	Kittyhawk I ET789	Bf 109 Damaged	LG.21	1205-1325
250 Sqn	Sqn Ldr M.T.Judd	Kittyhawk I ET919	Ju 87	LG.21	1240
250 Sqn	Lt A.E.Marshall	Kittyhawk I ET916 'A'	Ju 87	LG.21	1240
250 Sqn	Plt Off G.F.Newton	Kittyhawk I AK917 'T'	Bf 109F Probable	LG.21	1240
250 Sqn	Plt Off N.T.Whitside	Kittyhawk I AK888 'D'	Bf 109F	LG.21	1240
239 Wg	Wg Cdr H.C.Mayers	Kittyhawk I ET826	Bf 109F	LG.21	1240
3 RAAF Sqn	Sgt J.Donald	Kittyhawk I ET871 'E'	Bf 109 Probable	10m SW El Alamein	1315
450 Sqn	Sgt A.W.J.Taylor	Kittyhawk I AL142	Bf 109E Damaged	6m out to sea	1807-1925

*crew Sgt Mitchell & Sgt McDermott

British Casualties

2 SAAF Sqn	Kittyhawk I AK776 'V' damaged by MC.202, crashed on landing, 1130-1240; Lt H.S.McMaster safe
33 Sqn	Hurricane IIc BN359 badly damaged Cat II by Bf 109 S Burg el Arab 1030-1140; Sqn Ldr D.C.Cloete safe
33 Sqn	Hurricane IIc BP181 shot down by Bf 109 S Burg el Arab 1030-1140; Plt Off R.E.Wigle RCAF KiA
33 Sqn	Hurricane IIc BN116 shot down by Bf 109 S Burg el Arab 1030-1140; Sgt D.A.Morris KiA
250 Sqn	Kittyhawk I AK844 left 1210, badly damaged by Bf 109 in El Daba area, landed at base at 1300; Sgt H.R.Hannaford WiA

German Claims				
2./JG 27	Lt Hans-Arnold Stahlschmidt	Hurricane	SE El Alamein	1032
2./JG 27	Lt Hans-Arnold Stahlschmidt	2 Hurricanes	S & SE Burg el Arab	1035 & 1040

German Casualties	
3./JG 27	Bf 109F-4 trop WNr 8486 Yellow 3 shot down by P-40 crashed 1km W Turbiya; Lt Karl Kugelbauer baled out KiA
3./JG 27	Bf 109F-4 trop WNr 10277 shot down by P-40, crash-landed El Daba 70%; Lt Friedrich Hoffmann safe
8./JG 27	Bf 109F-4 trop WNr 10007 force-landing Qotaifiya, after combat 100%; Fw Kurt Maraun WiA
8./JG 27	Bf 109F-4 trop WNr 8729 30% damaged in strafing attack at Qotaifiya
III./JG 53	Bf 109F-4 trop 30% damaged in strafing attack at Qotaifiya
10.(Jabo)/JG 53	Bf 109F-4 trop WNr 8624 70% damaged crash-landing at Qotaifiya
7./StG 3	Ju 87 combat with P-40 Bir el Abd; Fw Günther Ulrich KiA/Gefr Bruno Fischer WiA

Italian Claims					
90ª Sq, 10°Gr, 4°St CT	Cap Ranieri Piccolomini	MC.202	P-40 Probable	El Alamein	0900-1025
73ª Sq, 9°Gr, 4°St CT	Serg Leonardo Rinaldi	MC.202	P-40 Probable	Bir el Mukheisin	1030-1125

Italian Casualties	
99ª Sq Av Sahariana	Ca.309 MM 12389 failed to return, Ten Giovanni Pedranghelu and crew MiA

Thursday, 9 July 1942

At 0930 Magg Fassi led ten MC.202s of 9° Gruppo off again to look for SAS vehicles, which were sighted and strafed south of El Daba. Later in the day Cap Lucchini led 12 MC.202s to cover CR.42s active in the Kalakh area. Near El Alamein 12 fighter-bombers were encountered; these were protected by a strong formation of about 35 fighters. Lucchini and his pilots attacked and claimed a P-40 shared among four of them after a 15-minute combat; Ten Giuseppe Ferazzani, a pilot just arrived from Italy, was hit and wounded. In the evening eight Bf 109s of I./JG 27 were scrambled, meeting five of six B-24 Liberators of the US Halvorson Detachment which were hunting for a convoy. Fw Steinhausen shot one down north-west of Bir el Astas, the bomber falling into the sea. The American gunners claimed to have shot down two of their attackers but only one Bf 109 was damaged.

British Claims				
112 Sqn	Plt Off F.Knoll	Kittyhawk I ET527	MC.202 Damaged	1400-1455
112 Sqn	Plt Off J.M.S.Crichton	Kittyhawk I		

German Claims				
1./JG 27	Fw Günther Steinhausen	B-24	100km NW Bir el Astas	1800

Italian Claims					
84ª Sq, 10°Gr, 4°St CT	Cap Franco Lucchini	MC.202 MM 7789 '84-5'	P-40	El Alamein	1230-1400
84ª Sq, 10°Gr, 4°St CT	Serg Livio Barbera	MC.202 MM 7933 '84-10'			
84ª Sq, 10°Gr, 4°St CT	Ten Paolo Berti	MC.202 MM 7803 '84-1'			
84ª Sq, 10°Gr, 4°St CT	Serg Magg D.Santonocito	MC.202 MM 7805 '84-2'			

Italian Casualties	
90ª Sq, 10°Gr, 4°St CT	MC.202 hit in combat and damaged, Ten Giuseppe Ferazzani slightly WiA

Friday, 10 July 1942

The 9th Australian Division now launched an attack in the northern sector of the line, making some gains in doing so. This resulted in another day of heavy aerial fighting. At 0630 12 Hurricanes of 274 Squadron covered 1 SAAF Squadron on a patrol over El Alamein where they were attacked by Bf 109s of II./JG 27. Four of these were on a Freie Jagd and had just engaged in a brief encounter with eight Kittyhawks when they spotted the 21 Hurricanes about to attack some Ju 87s. Oblt Sinner, with only one gun working, shot down Sgt Craggs' aircraft which was seen to spin into the ground. The Hurricanes of the same two units took off again at 0915 to patrol over the same area, this time meeting a mixed formation of Messerschmitts and Macchis. Two Axis fighters were claimed probably destroyed and six damaged by the 274 Squadron pilots, one of whom was hit and slightly wounded.

Cap Lucchini led 12 MC.202s of 10° Gruppo at 0830 on a free sweep in the El Alamein area. A formation of about 15 P-40s was encountered and engaged; a 30-minute combat followed during which the British fighters adopted the 'defensive circle' practice, but reportedly eight P-40s were shot down. Later in the morning, at 1105, Magg Fassi led ten MC.202s of 9° Gruppo on a free sweep over the front.

Three enemy formations were met at different altitudes, composed of six Spitfires, ten Hurricanes and eight P-40s. Cap Mariotti jumped the latter and immediately claimed a P-40; a fierce combat followed during which the Italians claimed two more P-40s, three Hurricanes and two probables; five MC.202s suffered slight damage.

At 1100 the Hurricanes of 80 Squadron with the 92 Squadron detachment, took off on a front-line patrol, followed ten minutes later by eight Kittyhawks of 112 Squadron. At the same time 15 Bf 109s of II./JG 27 and two from III./JG 27 set off on a Stuka escort to 15 Ju 87s. The MC.202s of 9° Gruppo were also in the air at this time. 80 Squadron attacked the dive-bombers but were themselves intercepted by the Bf 109s which made eight claims between 1032-1040, the Italians claiming a further six. In this engagement the 80 Squadron pilots claimed three Bf 109s shot down, one Hurricane being lost and one damaged, while 112 Squadron lost two Kittyhawks.

Eleven Hurricanes of 73 Squadron also patrolled in the same area shortly meeting five CR.42s at 300 feet. The squadron was driven off them by four Bf 109s, having first claimed two of the biplanes shot down. 50° Stormo actually lost one such aircraft, however one of that unit's pilots claimed to have shot down one of the British aircraft. According to the squadron it was the Messerschmitts which caused Flt Lt Selby to force-land, however.

Italian records show that at 1100 Ten Mariano Monaldi led five CR.42s of 159° Gruppo on a ground-attack mission NE of El Alamein. Some armoured cars were hit but the CR.42s were bounced by a larger formation of enemy fighters. Despite the inferiority in numbers, the Italians reacted: S.Ten Iadanza claimed a P-40 shot down and Monaldi claimed a probable for the loss of Serg Rivolta, who was shot down to protect his leader.

Hptm Gustav Rödel became Kommandeur of II./JG 27 in May having served with this unit throughout its service in North Africa. He had previously seen action over England and Greece, and had already claimed 33 victories by early 1942. On 10 July he claimed three victories to raise his total to 45; by the start of November he had increased this tally to 73.

During the early afternoon 80/92 and 127 Squadrons again patrolled over the front line, intercepting bombers escorted by Bf 109s. Six of the latter from I./JG 27; which were escorting Ju 88s on this occasion, attacked the Hurricanes, Lt Stahlschmidt claiming three and Lt von Lieres one. Two of the 80 Squadron aircraft were shot down and one of 127 Squadron was damaged, the pilot being wounded.

Six Kittyhawks of 450 Squadron with four of 250 and others from 112 Squadron, attacked LGs.20 and 21 again the pilots claiming one aircraft destroyed on the ground and others damaged. The formation was then attacked by three Bf 109s of III./JG 27, Lt Schöfböck claiming two shot down. Three more aircraft of III./JG 27 were scrambled to meet the raid, and a third Kittyhawk was claimed. One from 450 Squadron and two from 250 Squadron were lost. However during the first of these engagements, two of 450 Squadron's pilots ('Blondie' Lindsay and Jack Phelps) force-landed. It appears that both walked back to Allied lines as they are included as members of the Boomerang Club according to its honour board which is kept at the Australian War Memorial. Next day though, the two 'missing' aircraft were recovered and flown back to base. Neither aircraft flew with 450 Squadron again.

The three Kittyhawk units undertook a further attack on LG.21 later in the afternoon, being intercepted over the sea by a formation which was at least predominantly Italian. Five MC.202s of 88ª Squadriglia had taken off on a free sweep south of El Alamein at 1620, their pilots spotting two formations identified as P-40s and Spitfires over the Gulf of Bomba, claiming four P-40s shot down and a fifth as a probable, their only casualty being damage to one Macchi which was hit in both wings. During this engagement 250 Squadron's Sgt Troke claimed two fighters shot down. Initially the first of these was a Bf 109E, and the second a Macchi which overshot when attacking him; in the event he was credited with two MC.202s. One

Kittyhawk was lost, Sgt Wallis being seen to bale out into the sea, but he was not rescued.

Eleven MC.202s of 10° Gruppo, led by Cap Piccolomini, swept over the El Alamein area between 1800-1930. A formation of 15 P-40s covered by four Spitfires was engaged; when the 20-minute clash came to an end, two P-40s and two probables were claimed by 4° Stormo pilots. Ten Kittyhawks of 2 SAAF Squadron also provided cover to 260 Squadron on a wing sweep at 1840, being attacked by a dozen fighters identified as MC.202s and Bf 109s, one of the former being claimed as a probable.

Throughout the day sections of four Spitfires of 145 Squadron had flown top cover missions on six occasions, one Bf 109 being claimed in the late afternoon/early evening period, and one probable. This, however, had been a day of almost astronomical overclaiming by both sides. JG 27's various Gruppen had claimed 16 fighters shot down, the eight mid-morning claims by II.Gruppe appearing somewhat optimistic. The Regia Aeronautica units had really 'gone to town', adding 22 and four probables to make an Axis total of 38. Actual WDAF losses, at times confused, appear to have amounted to 10 Kittyhawks and 11 Hurricanes and one Spifire shot down for a total of 22, plus perhaps five more damaged. However, the Allied units had claimed eight German and Italian fighters shot down (including two CR.42s), plus five probables and eight damaged whilst Axis fighter losses, apart from one CR.42 and six damaged MC.202s, were precisely – nil!

British Claims

250 Sqn	Sgt G.W.Troke	Kittyhawk I ET919 'B'	2 MC.202s	at sea, off LG.21	0700
123 Sqn	Flt Lt R.L Wade	Hurricane IIc BG949 'Y'	MC.202 Damaged	15m SW El Alamein	0915-1115
274 Sqn	Flt Lt W.A.G.Conrad	Hurricane IIc BF698 'J'	MC.202 Damaged	15m SW El Alamein	0915-1115
274 Sqn	Flt Sgt H.Garwood	Hurricane IIc BD750 'W'	Bf 109 Probable	15m SW El Alamein	0915-1115
274 Sqn	Flt Sgt H.Garwood	Hurricane IIc BD750 'W'	Bf 109 Damaged	15m SW El Alamein	0915-1115
274 Sqn	Sqn Ldr J.C.F.Hayter	Hurricane IIc BE487 'F'	MC.202 Probable	15m SW El Alamein	0915-1115
274 Sqn	Sgt R.W.Henderson	Hurricane IIc BE826 'G'	MC.202 Damaged	15m SW El Alamein	0915-1115
274 Sqn	Flt Lt G.C.Keefer	Hurricane IIc BN111 'D'	MC.202 Damaged	15m SW El Alamein	0915-1115
274 Sqn	Sgt B.Ott	Hurricane IIc BN107 'B'	Bf 109 Damaged	15m SW El Alamein	0915-1115
80 Sqn	Sgt W.F.Burke	Hurricane IIc BM991 'V'	2 Bf 109s	El Alamein-Ghazal area	1145
80 Sqn	Plt Off R.G.Foskett	Hurricane IIc BP542 'E'	Bf 109	El Alamein-Ghazal area	1145
80 Sqn	Sgt C.W.House	Hurricane IIc BE703 'J'	2 Bf 109s Damaged	El Alamein-Ghazal area	1145
73 Sqn	Flg Off J.F.Pain	Hurricane IIc BN566	CR.42 Damaged	El Alamein box	1220
73 Sqn	Flt Sgt E.L.Joyce	Hurricane IIc BP167 'L'	CR.42	8-10m SW El Alamein	1240
73 Sqn	Flt Sgt H.W.E.Packham	Hurricane IIc BN415	CR.42	8-10m SW El Alamein	1240
145 Sqn	Sgt F.R.Barker	Spitfire Vb AB339 'M'	Bf 109	LG.21	1710-1830
145 Sqn	Sgt F.R.Barker	Spitfire Vb AB339 'M'	Bf 109 Probable		1710-1830
145 Sqn	Plt Off H.J.Phillips	Spitfire Vb AB290 'A'	Bf 109 Probable		1710-1830
450 Sqn	Sgt A.W.J.Taylor	Kittyhawk AL142	Bf 109 Damaged	near LG.20 & 21	1807-1925
250 Sqn	Sgt D.J.Cormack	Kittyhawk I ET783 'G'	Bf 109E Damaged	LG.21	1845
250 Sqn	Plt Off Hopkinson	Kittyhawk I ET622 'R'			
2 SAAF Sqn	Lt A.Higgo	Kittyhawk I ET874 'D'	MC.202 Probable	5m E El Alamein	1925

British Casualties

112 Sqn	Kittyhawk I ET794 'C' shot down by Bf 109 NE Daba at 1850-1900; Sgt D.J.B.White baled outo into sea, returned safely
112 Sqn	Kittyhawk I AK892 'D' fighter-bomber sortie; shot down by Bf 109 NE Daba at 1850-1900; Flg Off F.Knoll KiA
250 Sqn	Kittyhawk I AK657 'V' left 1220, shot down by MC.202 S Ghazal Station; Sgt J.A.Seabrook MiA
250 Sqn	Kittyhawk I AK962 'E' left 1220, shot down by MC.202 S Ghazal Station; Sgt W.J.Mortimer KiA
250 Sqn	Kittyhawk I ET915 damaged by MC.202, 1220-1320; Plt Off J.R.Falconer-Taylor safe
250 Sqn	Kittyhawk I AK661 'N' left 1440, raid on LG.21 shot down by Bf 109 El Daba 1430-1600; Plt Off A.A.MacLeod, PoW
250 Sqn	Kittyhawk I AK917 'A' left 1440, bombing raid on LG.21, 1430-1600 shot down by Bf 109 SE El Daba; Sgt J.Power KiA
250 Sqn	Kittyhawk I ET837 of 3 RAAF Sqn, borrowed; left 1005, shot down by MC.202 NE El Daba 1845-1900; Sgt R.T.A.Wallis KiA
450 Sqn	Kittyhawk I AK606 left 1158 for ground attack on LG.21, damaged by AA, FTL; Sgt G.Lindsay safe
450 Sqn	Kittyhawk I AK740 left 1158 for ground attack on LG.21, damaged by AA, FTL; Sgt J.S.Phelps safe
450 Sqn	Kittyhawk I ET868 left 1433 for ground attack on LG.21, shot down by Bf 109, S El Daba; Sgt J.C.Osborne PoW
450 Sqn	Kittyhawk I AL142, crash-landed at base with 250lb bomb on board; Sgt A.W.J.Taylor safe
4 SAAF Sqn	Kittyhawk I AK632 'F' damaged Cat I by Bf 109 near Ghazal at 1000; Lt A.C.Paterson safe
4 SAAF Sqn	Kittyhawk I damaged near Ghazal at 1000 by Bf 109; Lt G.H.Kaufmannn safe

73 Sqn	Hurricane BN557 shot down by CR.42 nr Ghazal at 1210; Flt Lt J.B.Selby force-landed
80/92 Sqn	Hurricane BP503 took off 1330, shot down by Bf 109s El Alamein; Sgt R.S.Sykes KiA body washed ashore three days later
80/92 Sqn	Hurricane BE141 took off 1330, shot down by Bf 109s El Alamein force-landed; Plt Off W.A.Wales, WiA
80/92 Sqn	Hurricane BN352 took off 1330, shot down by Bf 109s El Alamein force-landed; Flt Sgt Hempstead, safe
80/92 Sqn	Hurricane BP511 'A' left 1905, shot down by fighters, crash-landed; Flt Sgt W.F.Kenwood (92 Sqn), safe?
80/92 Sqn	Hurricane BE713; left 1905, damaged by fighters near Daba, force-landed; Plt Off Carpenter, safe?
80/92 Sqn	Hurricane II BP228 left 1025, shot down by fighters Ghazal area; Plt Off F.C.Bradley-Smith WiA
274 Sqn	Hurricane II BG707 'Z' left 0630 shot down by Bf 109 near El Alamein; Sgt G.J.Craggs KiA
274 Sqn	Hurricane BP398 'P' left 0915 to El Alamein area, damaged by fighters; Sgt P.G.Hemmer WiA
274 Sqn	Hurricane II Z5337 'D', left 1910 slightly damaged by MC.202; Sgt R.McFarlane safe
127 Sqn	Hurricane BE325 'E' took off 1330, damaged Cat I by Bf 109 El Alamein; Flt Sgt A.R.Moulden WiA
40 SAAF	Hurricane II dusk recce, hit by Breda shell in the cockpit, badly damaged, force-landed Cat II at 1635; Lt C.W.Lambon safe
55 Sqn	Baltimore II AG795 off 0941 from LG.98 to bomb Axis MT near El Alamein. Stalled on take-off, hit ground and undercarriage collapsed; DBR; Sgt E.C.Hyde and three safe

German Claims

6./JG 27	Oblt Rudolf Sinner	Hurricane	SW El Alamein	0615
Stab II./JG 77	Oblt Gustav Rödel	Spitfire	NE El Miteiriya	1032
6./JG 27	Obfw Herbet Krenz	P-40	SE Mumin Busak	1035
4./JG 27	Oblt Ferdinand Vögl	Spitfire	N El Alamein	1035
4./JG 27	Fw Heinrich Steis	Spitfire	N El Alamein	1036
Stab II./JG 27	Oblt Gustav Rödel	Spitfire	S Mumin Busak	1037
Stab II./JG 77	Oblt Gustav Rödel	P-40	NE Miteiriya	1040
4./JG 27	Fw Franz Stigler	Spitfire	N El Alamein	1040
7./JG 27	Lt Erich Schöfböck	P-40	El Alamein	1040
2./JG 27	Lt Hans-Arnold Stahlschmidt	Hurricane	N El Alamein	1325
2./JG 27	Lt Hans-Arnold Stahlschmidt	P-40	W El Alamein	1333
2./JG 27	Lt Karl von Lieres und Wilkau	Hurricane	WSW El Alamein	1333
2./JG 27	Lt Hans-Arnold Stahlschmidt	P-40	E El Alamein	1335
9./JG 27	Obfw Heinrich Rosenberg	P-40	E El Daba	1430
7./JG 27	Lt Erich Schöfböck	2 P-40s	S & SSE El Daba	

German Casualties

1./JG 27	Bf 109F-4 trop WNr 10282 1005 destroyed by sabotage at Fuka
1.(F)/121	Ju 88 D-5 WNr 430010 destroyed by sabotage at Fuka
1.(F)/121	Ju 88 D-5 WNr 430037 30% damaged by sabotage at Fuka
4.(H)/12	Bf 110F-3 WNr 5004 destroyed by sabotage at Fuka
4.(H)/12	2 Bf 109F-4s WNr 10182 70%, 8764 40% damaged by sabotage at Fuka
II./LG 1	Ju 88A-4 WNr 140005 25% damaged in strafing attack at Bir el Abd

Italian Claims

84ª Sq, 10°Gr, 4°St CT	Cap Franco Lucchini	MC.202 MM 7901	P-40	El Alamein	0930-1040
84ª Sq, 10°Gr, 4°St CT	Ten Luigi Giannella	MC.202 MM 7815	P-40	El Alamein	0930-1040
90ª Sq, 10°Gr, 4°St CT	Ten Virgilio Vanzan	MC.202	P-40	El Alamein	0930-1040
90ª Sq, 10°Gr, 4°St CT	Serg Amleto Monterumici	MC.202	P-40	El Alamein	0930-1040
91ª Sq, 10°Gr, 4°St CT	S.Ten Elio Miotto	MC.202	P-40	El Alamein	0930-1040
91ª Sq, 10°Gr, 4°St CT	Serg Magg L.Migliorato	MC.202	P-40	El Alamein	0930-1040
91ª Sq, 10°Gr, 4°St CT	M.llo Leonardo Ferrulli	MC.202	2 P-40s	El Alamein	0930-1040
96ª Sq, 9°Gr, 4°St CT	Magg Luigi Mariotti	MC.202	P-40	El Alamein	0930-1040
391ª Sq, 159°Gr, 50°St Ass	S.Ten Francesco Iadanza	CR.42	P-40	El Alamein	1100-1220
390ª Sq, 159°Gr, 50°St Ass	Ten Mariano Monaldi	CR.42	P-40 Probable	El Alamein	1100-1220
97ª Sq, 9°Gr, 4°St CT	Ten Antonio Canfora	MC.202	Hurricane	El Alamein	1105-1240
97ª Sq, 9°Gr, 4°St CT	Ten Fernando Malvezzi	MC.202	2 P-40s	El Alamein	1105-1240
96ª Sq, 9°Gr, 4°St CT	Serg Bruno Biagini	MC.202	Hurricane	El Alamein	1105-1240
73ª Sq, 9°Gr, 4°St CT	Serg Teresio Martinoli	MC.202	P-40	El Alamein	1105-1240
9°Gr, 4°St CT	unstated	MC.202	Hurricane	El Alamein	1105-1240
9°Gr, 4°St CT	unstated	MC.202	Hurricane Probable	El Alamein	1105-1240
9°Gr, 4°St CT	unstated	MC.202	P-40 Probable	El Alamein	1105-1240

Italian Claims

88ª Sq, 6°Gr, 1°St CT	Cap Dante Ocarso	MC.202	P-40	at sea, off El Alamein	1620-1740
88ª Sq, 6°Gr, 1°St CT	S.Ten Alfredo Civetta	MC.202	P-40	at sea, off El Alamein	1620-1740
88ª Sq, 6°Gr, 1°St CT	M.llo Natalino Stabile	MC.202	P-40	at sea, off El Alamein	1620-1740
88ª Sq, 6°Gr, 1°St CT	Serg Luigi Bartesaghi	MC.202	P-40	at sea, off El Alamein	1620-1740
88ª Sq, 6°Gr, 1°St CT	Ten Renato Talamini	MC.202	P-40 Probable	at sea, off El Alamein	1620-1740
90ª Sq, 10°Gr, 4°St CT	Cap Ranieri Piccolomini	MC.202	P-40 Probable	El Alamein	1800-1930
90ª Sq, 10°Gr, 4°St CT	M.llo Angelo Savini	MC.202	P-40	El Alamein	1800-1930
91ª Sq, 10°Gr, 4°St CT	Serg Alessandro Bladelli	MC.202	P-40	El Alamein	1800-1930
10°Gr, 4°St CT	unstated	MC.202	P-40 Probable	El Alamein	1800-1930

Italian Casualties

391ª Sq, 159°Gr, 50° St Ass	CR.42 MM 8847 shot down by enemy fighters 1100-1220, Serg Pasquale Rivolta KiA
9° Gr, 4° St CT	5 MC.202s damaged in combat
88ª Sq, 6°Gr, 1°St CT	MC.202 damaged by fighters, M.llo Natalino Stabile safe

Saturday, 11 July 1942

Hurricanes of 238 Squadron on patrol over El Alamein in the early morning had a brief encounter with Bf 109s, one being claimed damaged in return for one of the unit's own aircraft similarly damaged. Just before 0800 12 Hurricanes of 73 Squadron provided cover to four of 7 SAAF Squadron on a sweep, engaging four Bf 109 Jabos of III./JG 53, Flt Lt Badger shooting down Uffz Raasch's aircraft, this pilot surviving unhurt to return to his unit; a probable was also claimed.

The biggest engagement of the day occurred when 12 Kittyhawks of 2 SAAF Squadron and 12 Tomahawks of 5 SAAF Squadron, escorted 12 Bostons on a raid south-west of El Alamein. On the way to the target a large formation was seen comprising 30 Ju 87s escorted by seven I./JG 27 Bf 109s, 12 from II.Gruppe and two from III.Gruppe. The South African fighter pilots were ordered to leave the Bostons and attack. 2 SAAF's aircraft made contact, claiming one Ju 87, two Bf 109s, plus two probables and a damaged; one Kittyhawk was shot down and one slightly damaged. However, the Tomahawks were bounced by the escorting Messerschmitts before they could attack, two being shot down and three more badly damaged. As the units made for base, Maj Human, the commanding officer of 2 SAAF Squadron, was attacked by three Bf 109s which put a single bullet into his aircraft's oil system, causing him to force-land at El Alamein. The defending German fighters reported meeting 40-45 fighters and claimed eight shot down, variously identified as P-40s, Hurricanes and Spitfires. They did, however, confirm seeing one Ju 87 force-landing. On this occasion II./JG 27 lost two aircraft to the South Africans, Oblt Börngen crash-landing his badly damaged aircraft as did Uffz Dix who became a PoW.

During the day 145 Squadron flew no less than eight escort missions to Hurricanes. Four Spitfires undertook one of these operations at 1900, covering 12 aircraft of 213 Squadron during the course of which Plt Offs Taylor and Hanley each claimed a Bf 109 shot down. A little later eight Bf 109s of III./JG 53 escorted Ju 88s of II./LG 1 on a raid, but one of the bombers was shot down by AA fire. During the day a reconnaissance Bf 110 of 4.(H)/12 was also lost, crashing south of Fuka with the loss of the crew. This may have been attacked in error by five CR.42s which then dropped bombs on German positions. CR.42s of 50° Stormo carried out three strafing mission in the Qattara area. During the1620 sortie ten fighter-bombers of 50° Stormo were covered by ten 10° Gruppo MC.202s which managed to prevent an attack by a formation of about 20 Kittyhawks and Hurricanes. An aircraft was seen crashing, reportedly shot down by an Italian pilot. Six MC.200s of 8° Gruppo strafed in the Fuka area.

During an evening patrol over Benghazi, two MC.200s of 150° Gruppo, flown by S.Ten Pietro Ferrari and M.llo Walter Bertocci, intercepted some Liberators and reportedly shot down one.

British Claims

238 Sqn	Flt Sgt G.H.Borham	Hurricane IIb 'X'	Bf 109 Damaged	El Alamein	0710
73 Sqn	Sgt M.S.Jones	Hurricane IIc BN584	Bf 109F Probable	5m E Ras el Shaqiq	0830
73 Sqn	Flt Lt I.J.Badger	Hurricane IIc BN403	Bf 109	5m E Ras el Shaqiq	0850
238 Sqn	Flt Sgt W.J.Morris	Hurricane IIb 'T'	Bf 109 Damaged	El Alamein	1400
2 SAAF Sqn	Plt Off E.R.Hanley	Spitfire Vb AR287 'K'	Bf 109		1550-1730
2 SAAF Sqn	Flg Off J.S.Taylor	Spitfire Vb AR290 'A'	Bf 109		1550-1730
2 SAAF Sqn	Lt P.D.Bryant	Kittyhawk I ET874 'D'	Bf 109F Probable		1705

The emblem painted on the rear fuselages of the fighter-bomber Bf 109s of 10.(Jabo)/JG 53.

2 SAAF Sqn	Lt A.Higgo	Kittyhawk I ET1019 'Q'	Bf 109F Probable	1705
2 SAAF Sqn	Capt R.Clifton	Kittyhawk I AK853 'E'	Ju 87	1705
2 SAAF Sqn	Maj J.D.W.Human	Kittyhawk I ET530 'G'	Ju 87	1705
2 SAAF Sqn	Lt L.C.H.Hope	Kittyhawk I ET912 'H'	Bf 109F	1705
2 SAAF Sqn	Lt H.S.McMaster	Kittyhawk I AL158 'K'	Bf 109 Damaged	1705
2 SAAF Sqn	Capt H.E.N.Wildsmith	Kittyhawk I AL103 'P'	Bf 109E c/l	1705

British Casualties

2 SAAF Sqn	Kittyhawk I ET530 'G' damaged by Bf 109s (single bullet in oil system); Maj J.D.W.Human force-landed at El Adem in 1st SA Div lines
2 SAAF Sqn	Kittyhawk I ET912 'H' 'Pinkie IV' slt damaged; Lt L.C.H.Hope safe
2 SAAF Sqn	Kittyhawk I ET1020 'B' shot down El Alamein 1700; Lt A.R.Du Rose KiA
5 SAAF Sqn	Tomahawk IIb AK382 FTR on Boston escort SW El Alamein 1700-1715; 2/Lt L.W.Rapp KiA
5 SAAF Sqn	Tomahawk IIb AK392 shot down nr Daba on Boston escort SW El Adem 1700-1715; Capt K.R.Coster, WiA, PoW
5 SAAF Sqn	Tomahawk IIb AN394 badly damaged by Bf 109 1700; Maj D.V.D.Lacey safe
5 SAAF Sqn	Tomahawk IIb AK439 damaged by Bf 109 1735 10km S El Alamein; Lt J.V.Lindbergh WiA
5 SAAF Sqn	Tomahawk IIb AN451 badly damaged by Bf 109 1700; 2/Lt A.O.Hinton slt WiA
238 Sqn	Hurricane Z5312 'A' crashed while force-landing in the desert; Plt Off W.Snider
238 Sqn	Hurricane 'P' left 0650, damaged by fighters El Alamein and crash-landed Cat II; Sqn Ldr R.G.A.Barclay safe
238 Sqn	Hurricane 'N' damaged Cat II by Bf 109 El Alamein at 0730; Plt Off O.F.A.Oram
238 Sqn	Hurricane 'U' damaged Cat II by Bf 109 El Alamein at 1400; Flt Lt P.Olver safe
69 Sqn	Baltimore AG700 MiA from recce to Tunisia

German Claims

5./JG 27	Uffz Josef Vavra	Spitfire	E El Alamein	1603
4./JG 27	Fw Heinrich Steis	Hurricane	S El Alamein	1605
8./JG 27	Lt Werner Schroer	Spitfire	SE El Alamein	1605
5./JG 27	Oblt Ernst Börngen	Spitfire	SW El Alamein	1607
4./JG 27	Fw Heinrich Steis	P-40	W El Alamein	1610
8./JG 27	Lt Werner Schroer	P-40	SW El Alamein	1610
2./JG 27	Lt Hans-Arnold Stahlschmidt	P-40	SW El Alamein	1610
1./JG 27	Uffz Walter Timmermann	P-40	S Mumin Busak	1610

German Casualties	
5./JG 27	Bf 109F-4 trop WNr 10203 Black 3 combat with P-40 SE El Daba, 60%; Oblt Ernst Börngen safe
6./JG 27	Bf 109F-4 trop WNr 8690 Yellow 6 combat with P-40 15km, E El Alamein, crash-landed 100%; Uffz Johannes Dix PoW
10.(Jabo)/JG 53	Bf 109F-4/Z WNr 7457 shot down by Hurricane; crash-landed El Daba; Uffz Günther Raasch MiA, but back
4.(H)/12	Bf 110F-2 WNr 5002 crashed 10km S Fuka; Uffz Kurt Schwerdt, Obfw Georg Behrendet, Ogefr Heinz Degelmann KiA
II./LG 1	Ju 88A-4 WNr 140009 shot down by AA, crashed nr El Alamein, Fw Heinz Bartelt and 1 MiA, 2 baled and evaded capture

Italian Claims					
364ª Sq, 150°Gr CT	S.Ten Pietro Ferrari	MC.200	B-24	near Benghazi	1830-2015
364ª Sq, 150°Gr CT	M.llo Walter Bertocci	MC.200			
10° Gr, 4° St CT	unstated	MC.202	e/a	El Qattara area	1620-

Italian Casualties	
93ª Sq, 8°Gr, 2°St CT	2 MC.200s MM 6691 and 8135 damaged at night by LRDG raid
94ª Sq, 8°Gr, 2°St CT	MC.200 MM 6719 damaged at night by LRDG raid

Sunday, 12 July 1942

Six MC.200s of 8° Gruppo took off at 0520 on an armed-reconnaissance mission. Some small trucks were attacked and two were set on fire south of Fuka. A similar mission was carried out between 1740 and 1910 by six more MC.200s led by Cap Cecchet: again some motor vehicles, supposedly from LRDG, were sighted and strafed: one was left in flames.

During the morning four Spitfires of 145 Squadron returning from a reconnaissance mission were jumped by four Bf 109s, one Spitfire being damaged. At 1835 four Bf 109s of III./JG 53 escorting two Bf 109E TacR aircraft, encountered a number of Curtiss fighters, Lt Wolf Schaller reportedly shooting one down near El Alamein though immediately after this he was shot down and killed himself. He would seem to have fallen to one of the 92 Squadron pilots flying with 80 Squadron. Half an hour later four more fighters of this unit on a Freie Jagd, reported encountering a large British formation, Fw Seidl claiming another P-40 in flames, once again in the El Alamein area.

Seven MC.202s of 88ª Squadriglia, 6° Gruppo, flew an uneventful free sweep in the El Alamein area, the last mission over Africa for the only remaining element of 1° Stormo CT left in the theatre. The unit was then ordered to repatriate and all serviceable MC.202s were handed over to 4° Stormo. Since 1 January 1° Stormo had claimed 88 aircraft shot down, 22 probables and 15 more destroyed on the ground.

British Claims					
80/92 Sqn	Sgt I.H.S.Watson	Hurricane IIc BM991'D'	Bf 109F	SW El Alamein battle area	1910-1930
80/92 Sqn	Plt Off H.MacLachlan	Hurricane IIc BN126 'P'	Bf 109F Damaged	SW El Alamein battle area	1910-1930
3 RAAF Sqn	Sgt E.A.Kildey*	Kittyhawk AK792	Fi 156	Ras el Shaqiq	

*he destroyed this aircraft by bombing whilst it was flying at low level; however, it was treated as an aircraft destroyed on the ground

British Casualties	
145 Sqn	Spitfire V AR289 'J' damaged Cat II at 1925 by a Bf 109; Plt Off J.Twitchett force-landed safe
80 Sqn	Hurricane IIc BM987 badly damaged by Bf 109s nr El Alamein at 1910-1930 Cat II; Wt Off Mitchell safe
80 Sqn	Hurricane IIc BM984 'Z' damaged by Bf 109 nr El Alamein at 1910-1930 Cat I; Sqn Ldr J.H.Wedgewood safe

German Claims				
9./JG 53	Lt Wolf Schaller	P-40	25km SSE El Alamein	1825
8./JG 53	Obfw Alfred Seidl	P-40	50km S El Alamein	1828

German Casualties	
9./JG 53	Bf 109F-4 trop WNr 10115 Yellow 10+I shot down by Hurricane 25km SSE El Alamein 1830; Lt Wolf Schaller KiA

Monday, 13 July 1942

Two Bf 109s of III./JG 27 on a defensive patrol at 1015 reported meeting 12 British fighters, Lt Schroer claiming to have shot down three Hurricanes between 1057-1105 in the Hammam area. The units and pilots involved have not been ascertained. At 1230 eight Kittyhawks of 2 SAAF Squadron provided top cover for a formation of Bostons, and at much the same time six Spitfires of 601 Squadron and Hurricanes of 80 Squadron swept over the forward area. The Spitfire pilots spotted 15 Ju 88s with an escort of Macchi fighters. Attacking this formation, they claimed to have shot down one Ju 88 and damaged a second. The Kittyhawks were attacked by two Bf 109s during their return journey, part of a force of ten III./JG 53

Flg Off W.M. 'Babe' Whitamore served fairly briefly with 112 Squadron before being moved to 601 Squadron to fly Spitfires. He achieved his first success in the former unit's Kittyhawks, in one of which he is seated. Apart from three victory crosses, this also carried an only partially readable name, which appears to be 'Chester Billy'. Whitamore claimed a Ju 87 shot down on 13 July.

aircraft providing top cover to Stukas; one Bf 109 was claimed shot down and one damaged. In this engagement Lt Rudolf Müller of 8./JG 53 was shot down and killed. Four Messerschmitts of II./JG 27 had also taken off to provide indirect cover for the Stukas, the pilots of these reporting meeting 20 Bostons and 20 Curtiss fighters, two of the latter being claimed shot down. It seems that they had encountered the patrolling Hurricanes of 80 Squadron, two of this unit's aircraft being badly damaged by Bf 109s, although both pilots returned safely to base. One Messerschmitt damaged was claimed by another of the unit's pilots.

Cap Mariotti led 11 MC.202s of 9° Gruppo which took off at 1200 to cover five CR.42s of 159° Gruppo, led by Cap Carlo Robboni, bound for an attack on El Alamein railway station. The Macchis engaged ten Hurricanes at 15,000 feet, claiming three probables. Five MC.200s of 8° Gruppo (three of 94ª Squadriglia led by Cap Cecchet and two of 93ª led by Ten Bissoli) took off at 1745 on a ground-attack mission. Serg Ottorino Lancia of 93ª Squadriglia belly-landed due to engine failure ten minutes after take-off, but walked back. The four remaining aircraft strafed vehicles north of the Qattara Spring area and left three in flames. Four CR.42s of 159° Gruppo took off from Abar Nimeir at 1750 to strafe and bomb vehicles east of El Alamein. S.Ten Plinio Borghi of 389ª Sq was hit by ground fire and wounded in the left leg, but managed to return at 1930.

At 1805 five CR.42s of 388ª Squadriglia of 50° Stormo, led by Ten Mario Bonino, set off to attack artillery batteries along the coast at Diraziya. The pilots of these reported being bounced by about 30 fighters and three of the biplanes were shot down, with a fourth damaged and the pilot wounded. The unit had been attacked by 1 SAAF Squadron which had taken off on a patrol and which dived on a reported 12 CR.42s, claiming five shot down and two probables. As they were attacking the Italian aircraft the South Africans were themselves set upon by about 15 Bf 109s which made hit-and-run attacks throughout the combat and during the flight back to base. Their attackers were in fact 14 aircraft of II./JG 27 which had taken off to escort Ju 87s and 88s on a raid, this unit's pilots claiming to have shot down four fighters, the last of these by Hptm Düllberg of the Geschwaderstab at 1848. Two claims were made by Oblt Vögl, who identified these both as Spitfires. 1 SAAF Squadron suffered the loss of two aircraft and one pilot.

During the day 450 Squadron had one Kittyhawk damaged by Flak; a Hurricane of 6 Squadron was also hit in this way, and crash-landed. At this point 213 Squadron recorded that the unit was now the highest second scorer during 'Third Libyan' with 20 confirmed, three probables and 19 damaged; the leading unit was noted to be 73 Squadron.

British Claims

601 Sqn	Sgt G.Allen-Rowlandson	Spitfire Vb BR175	Ju 88 Damaged	W El Alamein	1300
601 Sqn	Plt Off A.R.Boyle	Spitfire Vb BR384	Ju 88	W El Alamein	1300
2 SAAF Sqn	Lt V.R.Burdon	Kittyhawk I AK662 'Y'	Bf 109F Damaged		1315
2 SAAF Sqn	Lt D.A.Ruiter	Kittyhawk I ET1019 'Q'	Bf 109		1315
4 SAAF Sqn	Capt L.B.Pearce	Kittyhawk I	Bf 109F Damaged		
274 Sqn	Sgt W.E.Marsh	Hurricane IIc BG706 'G'	Bf 109F Damaged	1340-1425	
80/92 Sqn	Sgt I.H.S.Watson	Hurricane IIc BM991	Bf 109 Damaged	SW El Alamein	1845-2000
2 SAAF Sqn	Lt R.D.B.Morton	Kittyhawk I ET1019 'Q'	Ju 88 Damaged		1920
1 SAAF Sqn	Lt G.R.Connell	Hurricane II ..173 'J'	CR.42	off beach El Alamein	1955
1 SAAF Sqn	Lt G.R.Connell	Hurricane II ..173 'J'	CR.42 Probable	off beach El Alamein	1955
1 SAAF Sqn	Lt T.A.Meek	Hurricane II Z5130 'N'	CR.42	off beach El Alamein	1955
1 SAAF Sqn	Lt H.Williams	Hurricane II ..962 'K'	CR.42	El Alamein box	1955
1 SAAF Sqn	Lt Staff Hope	Hurricane II ..282 'F'	Bf 109 Probable	El Alamein box	1955
1 SAAF Sqn	Lt L.R.S.Waugh	Hurricane II BG764 'W'	CR.42	5m off coast N El Alamein	1955
1 SAAF Sqn	Lt L.R.S.Waugh	Hurricane II BG764 'W'	CR.42 Probable	off coast N El Alamein	1956
1 SAAF Sqn	Lt L.R.S.Waugh	Hurricane II BG764 'W'	CR.42	on coast N El Alamein	1957

British Casualties

450 Sqn	Kittyhawk I badly damaged by Flak; Sgt E.G.Brown safe
80 Sqn	Hurricane IIc badly damaged by Bf 109s nr El Alamein at 1845; u/i pilot safe
80 Sqn	Hurricane IIc badly damaged by Bf 109 nr El Alamein at 1845; u/i pilot safe
1 SAAF Sqn	Hurricane IIc BE703 'R' shot down by Bf 109 and crash-landed nr 2 SA Brigade at 2000; Capt T.Rhodes back later
1 SAAF Sqn	Hurricane IIc BP332 'T' shot down by Bf 109 at 2000; 2/Lt W.F.Powell KiA
6 Sqn	Hurricane BN841 hit by Flak amd crash-landed

German Claims

8./JG 27	Lt Werner Schroer	3 Hurricanes	S El Hammam	0957, 1002 & 1005
6./JG 27	Uffz Otto Monska	P-40	S El Radas	1220
6./JG 27	Oblt Rudolf Sinner	P-40	ENE El Dakar	1225
Stab II./JG 27	Oblt Hans Bosch	P-40	S Haggag el Qasaba	1835
4./JG 27	Oblt Ferdinand Vögl	2 Spitfires	SW & S El Hammam	1840 & 1842
Stab/JG 27	Hptm Ernst Düllberg	Hurricane	12km SW El Alamein	1848

German Casualties

8./JG 53	Bf 109F-4 trop WNr 10050 Black 6+I shot down by P-40 30km SW El Alamein 1230; Lt Rudolf Müller KiA
8./JG 27	Bf 109F-4 trop WNr 10178 80% damaged by bombs at Mumin Busak
8./JG 27	Bf 109F-4 trop WNr 8797 shot-up in combat, force-landed Qotaifiya 30% damaged; pilot safe
I./StG 3	Ju 87 R-4 WNr 6280 40% damaged in air raid at Bir el Abd
II./StG 3	Ju 87 D-3 WNr 2377 40% damaged in air raid at Bir el Abd

Italian Claims

73ª Sq, 9°Gr, 4°St CT	S.Ten Alvaro Querci	MC.202	P-40 Probable	El Alamein	1200-1330
73ª Sq, 9°Gr, 4°St CT	Serg Leonardo Rinaldi	MC.202	P-40 Probable	El Alamein	1200-1330
73ª Sq, 9°Gr, 4°St CT	Serg Teresio Martinoli	MC.202	P-40 Probable	El Alamein	1200-1330

Italian Casualties

388ª Sq, 158°Gr, 50°St Ass	CR.42 failed to return, Serg Magg Gianni Campolongo MiA
388ª Sq, 158°Gr, 50°St Ass	CR.42 failed to return, S.Ten Lelio Zampaglione PoW
388ª Sq, 158°Gr, 50°St Ass	CR.42 failed to return, Serg Magg Antonio Grillo MiA
389ª Sq, 159°Gr, 50°St Ass	CR.42 MM 8856 damaged in combat 1800-1930, S.Ten Plinio Borghi WiA, returned
93ª Sq, 8°Gr, 2°St CT	MC.200 MM 5179 damaged on force-landing, Serg Magg Ottorino Lancia safe

Tuesday, 14 July 1942

The first action of the day occurred when four Bf 109s of III./JG 27 carried out a Jabo attack, following which they intercepted eight British fighter-bombers, which jettisoned their bombs in the sea. Fw Waibel failed to return from this mission and no claims were made.

At 0915 12 Hurricanes of 238 Squadron were attacked over El Alamein by half a dozen MC.202s. four of which were claimed damaged by the British pilots. These were aircraft of 10° Gruppo, Cap Ruspoli leading 11 MC.202s on a free sweep over El Alamein between 0735-0935. A formation of 12 Bostons escorted by about 20 P-40s, 12 Hurricanes and six Spitfires, flying at higher altitude, was encountered. A long and confused combat followed during which five P-40s were claimed shot down, plus two probables. Four Spitfires of 601 Squadron took off on a freelance patrol at 1010, followed 20 minutes later by nine Kittyhawks of 3 RAAF Squadron which were to bomb in the Bir Malchkad area. At 1020 three Bf 109s of III./JG 27 took off on another Jabo mission, followed ten minutes later by four more on a Stuka escort, joined by six from I.Gruppe.

A little later eight Kittyhawks of 260 Squadron gave top cover to 12 Bostons at 1100. At this same time Lt Schöfböck of III.Gruppe on the Jabo mission, claimed a fighter 15 miles south of El Alamein, but Lt Tigerström, a fellow member of 7 Staffel, was shot down and force-landed within Axis lines. Three Spitfire pilots of 601 Squadron claimed a Bf 109 between them, and 3 RAAF Squadron reported meeting a lone Messerschmitt which was also claimed shot down. A little later III.Gruppe's escort Schwarme reported meeting ten Curtiss fighters, one of which Lt Schroer claimed shot down, Flt Lt McKay of 260 Squadron failing to return. A claim for a Hurricane was made at 1037 which may have related to a 6 Squadron aircraft missing from an anti-tank sweep.

127 Squadron Hurricane, BP289 EJ-X.

In the early afternoon eight Kittyhawks of 4 SAAF Squadron were top cover to Bostons, being jumped by a mixed force of Messerschmitts and Macchis, two Kittyhawks being slightly damaged. Their main opponents had again been 10° Gruppo, which were carrying out another free sweep, Cap Piccolomini leading 12 MC.202s. The pilots of these reported a formation of 12 Hurribombers covered by 20 P-40s, which they engaged in a 15-minute dogfight. One Hurribomber and one P-40 were claimed shot down. During the afternoon ten Bf 109s of I.Gruppe escorted Ju 87s, encountering a reported 20-25 fighters, one of which Lt Stahlschmidt claimed, identified as a Spitfire.

Seven CR.42s of 50° Stormo set off at 1710 to bomb enemy forces just south of El Alamein. The cover was provided by 11 MC.202s of 9° Gruppo led by Cap Mariotti. The fighter-bombers were intercepted by a formation of P-40s and Hurricanes and, despite the intervention of the escorts, which claimed two Hurricanes probably shot down, Ten Giovanni Battista Modica failed to return. He actually baled out of his aircraft after it had been damaged by ground fire over the target area, and he was picked up, with both legs broken, by Italian troops; he died in a field hospital four days later.

During the day 33 Squadron on patrol engaged Bf 109s, two being claimed shot down plus a probable. It may have been in this combat that Gefr Franz Scheffl of 10.(Jabo)/JG 53 was killed trying to force-land at Qotaifiya. 601 Squadron lost one Spitfire in unidentified circumstances – possibly Stahlschmidt's victim – and other Spitfire pilots of 145 Squadron claimed a Ju 87 probably shot down, plus one damaged. Flt Lt Conrad was posted from 274 Squadron to lead a flight in 145 Squadron on this date – another experienced Hurricane pilot being moved to the Spitfires.

British Claims

238 Sqn	Flt Sgt G.H.Borham	Hurricane IIb 'X'	3 MC.202s Damaged	El Alamein	0945
238 Sqn	Plt Off B.Nordon	Hurricane IIb 'V'	MC.202 Damaged	El Alamein	0945
601 Sqn	Sgt G.Allen-Rowlandson	Spitfire Vb BR363	}		
601 Sqn	Flt Lt M.R.B.Ingram	Spitfire Vb BR118	Bf 109	battle area/El Alamein line	1010-1105
601 Sqn	Plt Off C.R.Scollan	Spitfire Vb BR175	}		
260 Sqn	Plt Off R A.Dunbar	Kittyhawk Ia	}		
260 Sqn	Flt Lt J.M.Strawson	Kittyhawk Ia	Bf 109F Damaged	SW El Alamein	1100-1210
260 Sqn	Sgt C.E.Ody	Kittyhawk Ia	}		
3 RAAF Sqn	Sgt G.A.Neill	Kittyhawk I AL102 'R'	Bf 109F		1105
601 Sqn	Sgt F.W.Farfan	Spitfire Vb BR459	e/a Damaged		1845-2010
33 Sqn	Plt Off W.A.R.MacDonald	Hurricane IIc BE134 'Y'	Bf 109	patrol from LG.154	1930
33 Sqn	Flt Lt L.C.Wade	Hurricane IIc BP186	CR.42	patrol from LG.154	1930
33 Sqn	Flt Lt L.C.Wade	Hurricane IIc BP186	Bf 109 Damaged	patrol from LG.154	1930
33 Sqn	Flg Off J.Wooller	Hurricane IIc BN523 'R'	Bf 109	patrol from LG.154	1930
33 Sqn	Plt Off L.H.Peterson	Hurricane IIc BP184 'X'	Bf 109 Probable	patrol from LG.154	1930

British Casualties

238 Sqn	Hurricane El Alamein 0915-1025; Plt Off E.Winterbottom MiA returned next day
6 Sqn	Hurricane IId BN842 MiA from anti-tank sweep, 1710-1850; Plt Off McKee MiA
6 Sqn	Hurricane IId hit by Flak, damaged Cat II; Flg Off Welford safe
601 Sqn	Spitfire V BR459 damaged
260 Sqn	Kittyhawk I left 1100, shot down by Bf 109 SW El Alamein; Flt Lt W.R.McKay MiA
260 Sqn	Kittyhawk I left 1100, shot down by Bf 109 SW El Alamein, force-landed; Plt Off J.A.Maclean safe
260 Sqn	Kittyhawk I left 1100, shot down by Bf 109 SW El Alamein, force-landed; Sgt N.E.McKee safe
7 SAAF Sqn	Hurricane flew into ground nr Wadi Natrun poss Lt R.S.Carr KiFA

German Claims

7./JG 27	Lt Erich Schöfböck	P-40	20km S El Alamein	1000
8./JG 27	Lt Werner Schroer	P-40	SW El Alamein	1015
2./JG 27	Uffz Walter Gläser	Hurricane	20km S El Alamein	1037
2./JG 27	Lt Hans-Arnold Stahlschmidt	Spitfire	El Alamein	1829

German Casualties

1./JG 27	Bf 109F-4 trop WNr 8741 combat, crash-landing Sidi Barrani, 30% damaged; Lt Karl-Heinz von Tigerström safe
7./JG 27	Bf 109F-4 trop WNr 7391 Green 4 combat El Alamein 100%; Fw Karl Waibel MiA
10.(Jabo)/JG 53	Bf 109F-4 WNr 7300 White 12 crash-landed at Qotaifiya, 90% damaged; Gefr Franz Scheffl WiA
II./StG 3	Ju 87D-1 WNr 2549 shot-up in error by own Flak, crash-landed at Abu Haggag, 60% damaged, crew safe

Italian Claims

91ª Sq, 10°Gr, 4°St CT	Cap Carlo M.Ruspoli	MC.202	Hurricane Probable	El Alamein	0745-0935
84ª Sq, 10°Gr, 4°St CT	M.llo Luigi Bignami	MC.202 MM 7896	P-40	El Alamein	0745-0935
84ª Sq, 10°Gr, 4°St CT	Serg Magg D. Santonocito	MC.202 MM 7815	P-40	El Alamein	0745-0935
84ª Sq, 10°Gr, 4°St CT	Serg Magg Luciano Perdoni	MC.202 MM 7805	P-40	El Alamein	0745-0935
91ª Sq, 10°Gr, 4°St CT	M.llo Leonardo Ferrulli	MC.202	P-40	El Alamein	0745-0935
91ª Sq, 10°Gr, 4°St CT	unstated	MC.202	P-40 + Probable	El Alamein	0745-0935
90ª Sq, 10°Gr, 4°St CT	unstated	MC.202	Hurricane	El Alamein	1230-1410
10°Gr, 4°St CT	11 pilots	MC.202	P-40 shared	El Alamein	1230-1410
9°Gr, 4°St CT	11 pilots	MC.202	P-40 shared	El Alamein	1750-1850
73ª Sq, 9°Gr, 4°St CT	M.llo Rodolfo Stoppani	MC.202	Hurricane Probable	El Alamein	1750-1850
73ª Sq, 9°Gr, 4°St CT	Serg Mario Guerci	MC.202	Hurricane Probable	El Alamein	1750-1850

Italian Casualties

387ª Sq, 158°Gr, 50° St Ass	CR.42 6255 failed to return, Ten G.Battista Modica baled, picked up with broken legs by Italian troops, died of wounds four days later

Wednesday, 15 July 1942

Four Kittyhawks of 3 RAAF Squadron in company with 450 Squadron carried out a bombing reconnaissance west of El Alamein from 0915. From this one aircraft failed to return, reportedly shot down by Flak attacking MT. 4° Stormo MC.202s were on patrol in the early morning period. Cap Mariotti led 12 MC.202s of both 9° and 10°Gruppi on an escort to four Ju 88s over the front, between 0905-1025. They engaged a formation of a reported 15 P-40s covered by ten Spitfires patrolling at higher altitude, claiming two P-40s shot down plus three probable. Just as they landed, 12 more MC.202s, led by Cap Ruspoli, took off to carry on the escort. Ruspoli had to make an early return due to engine trouble and the experienced M.llo Bignami took his place as formation leader. They too encountered a formation of P-40s, this time estimated to be 48 strong, and claimed two shot down after a 15-minute combat; a Ju 88 was reportedly hit by British fighters. Serg Magg Trevisan was hit and forced to land in the desert. Serg Monterumici saw him getting out of the cockpit and sitting down, leaning against his aircraft. On return to Fuka Monterumici took off in the Ca.133 'hack' to recover Trevisan. He landed nearby but discovered that his comrade who had appeared to be asleep was actually dead. Trevisan's aircraft was later recovered by Piccolomini, who flew it back to Fuka.

Some at least of the Macchis were engaged with Hurricanes of 33 and 213 Squadron, the pilots of the latter unit reporting meeting six MC.202s and four Bf 109s. They claimed one Macchi shot down, two damaged and a Bf 109E damaged. Ten Bf 109s of I./JG 27 were also in the area at this time, providing top cover to Ju 87s. The pilots of this unit reported meeting 18 Hurricanes, Lt Stahlschmidt attacking one which crash-landed a few miles west of Hammam. This was almost certainly Sgt Newick, who was slightly wounded.

A crash-landed Ju 88A-4 of 1./LG 1 being inspected by Allied troops.

Soon after 1100 eight Hurricanes of 1 SAAF Squadron provided top cover for others of 238 Squadron, patrolling over the El Alamein area where Ju 88s were encountered, escorted by Messerschmitts and Macchis. Two Bf 109s with white spinners and wingtips dived on the South Africans whose Hurricanes all now sported red wingtips. The two WDAF squadrons between them claimed damage to a Ju 88, a Bf 109 and an MC.202, the pilot being killed, but two of 238 Squadron's Hurricanes were also damaged. During a midday TacR sortie a 208 Squadron Hurricane crash-landed for unspecified reasons. Twelve

MC.202s of 9° Gruppo were again in the air at 1805, led by Magg Fassi, to cover CR.42s of 50° Stormo over the lines. Six patrolled at 17,000 feet and six at 20,000. A large formation of about 30 P-40s was sighted and attacked, one P-40 being claimed shot down.

Seven 2 SAAF Squadron Kittyhawks went up on an evening sweep and encountered two Ju 87s escorted by seven Bf 109s, Lt de Villiers claiming one of the dive-bombers probably shot down. Three minutes later they met a dozen Ju 88s with a top cover of Bf 109s, one of the latter being claimed shot down. Eleven Bf 109s of II./JG 27 were escorting the Stukas, their pilots reporting meeting 30-40 Curtiss fighters, one of which Fw Steis claimed to have shot down. On this date one Ju 87 was lost in the El Alamein area, reportedly shot down by AA; the crew were killed.

During the day 5ª Squadra established Settore Aeronautico Centrale at El Chalifa, 15 miles east of Benghazi, under the command of Col Augusto Bacchiani with the primary task of co-ordinating the defence of Benghazi and operations in the area between the 19th and 25th meridians. In the late afternoon MC.200s of 13° Gruppo escorted an S.79 flown by Benito Mussolini personally on a visit to front-line units. During this he awarded Medaglie d'Argento for outstanding acts of valour in North Africa to Ten Giorgio Savoia, Ten Camillo Luglio and S.Ten Raffaele Velenzano. Also several 4° Stormo pilots were awarded decorations: notably, Cap Franco Lucchini, Ten Luigi Giannella,Ten Paolo Berti, M.llo Leonardo Ferrulli, Ten Emanuele Annoni, S.Ten Alvaro Querci and Ten Fernando Malvezzi.

British Claims

213 Sqn	Sgt H.A.Aitken	Hurricane IIc BN357	MC.202 Damaged	N sector, El Alamein line	1025-1130
213 Sqn	Plt Off L.J.Barnes	Hurricane IIc BP197	Bf 109E Damaged	N sector, El Alamein line	1025-1130
213 Sqn	Wt Off R.J.Wallace	Hurricane IIc BP338	MC.202	N sector, El Alamein line	1025-1130
213 Sqn	Wt Off R.J.Wallace	Hurricane IIc BP338	MC.202 Damaged	N sector, El Alamein line	1025-1130
33 Sqn	Flg Off J.Wooller	Hurricane IIc BE172 'T'	MC.202 Damaged	N sector, El Alamein line	1025-1130
238 Sqn	Sgt W.E.G.Cordwell	Hurricane IIb 'P'	} Ju 88 Damaged	El Alamein	1120-1230
238 Sqn	Flt Lt P.Olver	Hurricane IIb 'U'			
238 Sqn	Plt Off B.Nordon	Hurricane IIb 'V'	MC.202 Damaged	El Alamein	1120-1230
1 SAAF Sqn	Lt G.R.Connell	Hurricane II BG764 'W'	} Bf 109F Damaged	centre of El Alamein line	1205-
1 SAAF Sqn	Lt S.A.Finney	Hurricane II Z5348 'M'			
2 SAAF Sqn	Lt T.V. de Villiers	Kittyhawk I ET1019 'Q'	Ju 87 Probable	El Alamein line	1950
2 SAAF Sqn	Lt A.Higgo	Kittyhawk I AL158 'K'	Bf 109F	El Alamein line	1950

British Casualties

213 Sqn	Hurricane BP189 left 1025 damaged by MC.202 and force-landed, Cat II; Sgt J.D.Newick slt WiA
213 Sqn	Hurricane BP197 left 1025 damaged by MC.202, Cat I; Plt Off L.J.Barnes safe
238 Sqn	Hurricane 'F' damaged; Sqn Ldr R.G.A. Barclay
208 Sqn	Hurricane IIa Z2408, force-landed at 1310, Cat II; Flt Lt R.L.Macgregor
3 RAAF Sqn	Kittyhawk I ET911 left 0915, shot down by Flak W El Alamein while attacking MT; Flg Off G.A.Dougall KiA

German Claims

2./JG 27	Lt Hans-Arnold Stahlschmidt	Hurricane	n.e.17km W El Hammam	
4./JG 27	Fw Heinrich Steis	P-40	SE El Alamein	1855

German Casualties

9./JG 27	Bf 109F-4 trop WNr 8550 crash-landed Qotaifiya 60%; pilot safe
1./StG 3	Ju 87R-2 WNr 5931 S7+EH AA 20km SE El Alamein; Uffz Horst Pekar/Uffz Ludwig Kienast KiA

Italian Claims

73ª Sq, 9°Gr, 4°St CT	Ten Vittorio Squarcia	MC.202	P-40	El Alamein	0905-1025
9°Gr, 4°St CT	unspecified	MC.202	P-40 + 3 Probables	El Alamein	0905-1025
96ª Sq, 9°Gr, 4°St CT	M.llo Dante Labanti	MC.202	P-40 Probable	El Alamein	1030-1140
84ª Sq, 10°Gr, 4°St CT	Serg Magg Piero Buttazzi	MC.202 MM 7919'84-12'	P-40	El Alamein	1030-1140
90ª Sq, 10°Gr, 4°St CT	Serg Amleto Monterumici	MC.202	P-40	El Alamein	1030-1140
9°Gr, 4°St CT	unspecified	MC.202	P-40	El Alamein	1805-1930

Italian Casualties

90ª Sq, 10°Gr, 4°St CT	MC.202 MM 7900 '90-11'force-landed near El Daba and recovered, Serg Magg Elio Trevisan KiA

Thursday, 16 July 1942

Ten Hurricanes of 1 SAAF Squadron set out at 0745 to provide top cover to 238 Squadron on a patrol. Over El Alamein they spotted 15 Stukas with an escort of Bf 109s below them. Diving to the attack, 238 Squadron's pilots claimed one Ju 87 probable and seven damaged; in addition Lt Tom Phillips of 1 SAAF Squadron added a claim for a Bf 109 probable. III./JG 53, eight of whose Messerschmitts were engaged on this mission, reported that one of its fighters was damaged and crash-landed. Eight Hurricanes of 127 Squadron patrolled over the same area from 1027, covered by aircraft of 80 Squadron. Eight Bf 109s were seen a few thousand feet above and the squadron at once formed a defensive circle, but one aircraft was picked off from this and the pilot baled out, burnt, with a second damaged. Eight Bf 109s of I./JG 27 on Stuka escort reported combat with 20 fighter-bombers and Hurricanes, Lt Stahlschmidt claiming one of the latter and a second damaged – most probably the 127 Squadron aircraft.

At 1110 eight Hurribombers and four fighters of 274 Squadron took off to strafe vehicles, but during this attack two were shot down by Flak. At the same time other Hurricanes of 213 Squadron took off on a sweep. 33 Squadron was supposed to provide top cover, together with some Spitfires of 601 Squadron, but on take-off two of the Hurricanes collided, both pilots being killed. The wreckage then blocked the runway, preventing any further aircraft taking off. Consequently, 213 Squadron was bounced by one MC.202 and one Bf 109, one Hurricane being shot down.

At 1150 1 SAAF and 238 Squadrons took off again, this time with 238 as top cover. Four Bf 109s and two MC.202s were seen below but were deemed by the South Africans to be decoys, and were left alone by them. 238's pilots also spotted them, 'tally-ho'-ed, and dived straight through 1 SAAF's formation to get at them. Several South Africans then peeled off and followed them. "Shambles!" recorded the squadron diary. Sqn Ldr Barclay claimed a Bf 109 and Flt Sgt Borham a Macchi probable, but during the return flight Barclay's Hurricane was attacked and damaged.

Eight Kittyhawks of 250 Squadron on a mission at 1145 were jumped by four MC.202s, one of the British fighters being shot-up, but Sgt Cairns claimed to have shot down one of the attackers. During an afternoon sweep a Hurricane of 33 Squadron force-landed, the pilot returning on foot. All these noontime engagements had been with 10° Gruppo pilots, who claimed four Allied fighters between 1035-1200. The two confirmed claims for WDAF fighters appear to be justified since two 10° Gruppo pilots were obliged to force-land.

According to Italian records, eleven MC.202s of 10° Gruppo, led by Cap Franco Lucchini, took off at 1035 to escort CR.42s of 50° Stormo. With their mission carried out, they intercepted ten Hurribombers over Deir el Qattara flying at 1,500 feet, covered by ten P-40s at 6,000, 15 P-40s at 16,000 and six Spitfires at 20,000. A 20-minute running fight followed, during which the Italian pilots claimed four P-40s shot down, one each by Serg Magg Mario Veronesi and Ten Paolo Berti, one shared by Lucchini, Berti, Benedicti and Giannella and a fourth shared by Veronesi, Bignami, Monterumici, Piccolomini and Baroni. Lucchini's aircraft was hit and he crash-landed near Qotaifiya but managed to return to Fuka in the afternoon in a car. Baroni was hit and forced to land near El Daba; Berti and Bignami returned with slight damage to their Macchis.

In the evening 12 Tomahawks of 5 SAAF Squadron patrolled over the El Alamein area, meeting Ju 87s escorted by nine Bf 109s of III./JG 27 and six of III./JG 53. The South Africans got through to the bombers, claiming two probably shot down, but one of their aircraft was badly damaged, Lt Schroer and Obfw Rosenberg of JG 27 each claiming one victory.

At this stage the personnel of 88ª Squadriglia, 6° Gruppo, returned to Lecce in Italy in a transport aircraft. In the opposite direction, 74ª and 75ª Squadriglie of 23° Gruppo CT, led by Magg Luigi Filippi, arrived at Abu Haggag with 18 MC.202s. 70ª Squadriglia was still at Naples/Capodichino due to bad weather. As 3° Stormo CT was delayed from reaching Africa since the commanding officer, T.Col Tito Falconi, was still in Italy with 18° Gruppo, Gen Venceslao D'Aurelio, commander of the Eastern Sector, temporarily assigned 23° Gruppo to the command of 4° Stormo.

British Claims

1 SAAF Sqn	Lt T.W.Phillips	Hurricane II Z5130 'N'	Bf 109F Probable	centre El Alamein	0845
238 Sqn	Plt Off D.B.Baker	Hurricane IIb 'J'	Ju 87 Damaged	W El Alamein	0845
238 Sqn	Flt Lt D.W.Beedham	Hurricane IIb 'D'	Ju 87 Damaged	W El Alamein	0845
238 Sqn	Plt Off W.B.Hay	Hurricane IIb 'F'	Ju 87 Damaged	W El Alamein	0845
238 Sqn	Plt Off I.W.Matthews	Hurricane IIb 'S'	Ju 87 Damaged	W El Alamein	0845
238 Sqn	Flt Lt P.Olver	Hurricane IIb 'X'	Ju 87 Probable	W El Alamein	0845

British Claims

238 Sqn	Flt Lt P.Olver	Hurricane IIb 'X'	Ju 87 Damaged	W El Alamein	0845
238 Sqn	Plt Off J.D.Phelan	Hurricane IIb 'B'	Ju 87 Damaged	W El Alamein	0845
238 Sqn	Plt Off W.Snider	Hurricane IIb 'A'	Ju 87 Damaged	W El Alamein	0845
238 Sqn	Sqn Ldr R.G.A.Barclay	Hurricane IIb 'F'	Bf 109	W El Alamein	1215
238 Sqn	Flt Sgt G.H.Borham	Hurricane IIb 'X'	MC.202 Probable	W El Alamein	1215
250 Sqn	Sgt D.W.Cairns	Kittyhawk I ET513 'A'	MC.202	NW El Mreir	1215
1 SAAF Sqn	Lt L.R.S.Waugh	Hurricane II BG764 'W'	Bf 109F Probable	NW El Alamein	1215
33 Sqn	Plt Off O.C.Kallio	Hurricane IIc BE172 'T'	Ju 88 Damaged	El Alamein	1425-1525
33 Sqn	Flg Off J.Wooller	Hurricane IIc BN523 'R'	Ju 88 Damaged	El Alamein	1425-1525
33 Sqn	Flt Lt L.C.Wade	Hurricane IIc BP186	Ju 88	El Alamein	1905-2030
33 Sqn	Flt Lt L.C.Wade	Hurricane IIc BP186			
33 Sqn	Flg Sgt R.G.Davidson	Hurricane IIc BP120	Ju 88 Damaged	El Alamein	1905-2030
33 Sqn	Sgt L.H.Moher	Hurricane IIc BP184 'X'			
33 Sqn	Flg Off J.Wooller	Hurricane IIc BN523 'R'			
5 SAAF Sqn	Capt R.F.Armstrong	Tomahawk IIb AK439 'D'	Bf 109F Probable	5m W El Alamein	1915
5 SAAF Sqn	Lt H.W.G.Bidwell	Tomahawk IIb AN466 'V'	Ju 87 Probable	5m W El Alamein	1915
5 SAAF Sqn	2/Lt B.A.Kearns	Tomahawk IIb AN462 'J'	Ju 87 Probable	5m W El Alamein	1915
5 SAAF Sqn	2/Lt H.Smith	Tomahawk IIb AN461 'K'	Bf 109F Probable	5m W El Alamein	1915

British Casualties

4 SAAF	Tomahawk AK388 left 1015, missing after fight with seven Bf 109s; Plt Off H.C.Hain KiA
601 Sqn	Spitfire V BR479 collided with Hurricane on take-off, LG.154; Sgt Q. Di Persio KiFA
33 Sqn	Hurricane BP179 collided with Spitfire on take-off, LG.154; Plt Off E.W.Ollen-Brittle KiFA
33 Sqn	Hurricane IIc BP186 force-landed 15m W of base, possibly hit by Bf 109; Sgt R.I Reading safe
33 Sqn	Hurricane IIc BN523 'R', forced to land at LG.39 by bullet in radiator by Bf 109, 1915; Flg Off J.Wooller safe
73 Sqn	Hurricane IIc shot down by Bf 109s; Sgt Edwards crash-landed safe
127 Sqn	Hurricane Z5235 'H' left 1027 shot down by Bf 109s at 1100; Flt Sgt W.P.Benedict (US) baled out injured
127 Sqn	Hurricane BP323 'Z' left 1027 damaged by Bf 109 at 1100 Cat I; Lt R.E.Gray safe
213 Sqn	Hurricane BN378 shot down by MC.202 at 1135; Sgt J.F.C.Ballantyne KiA
274 Sqn	Hurricane BG884 'K' left 1045 shot down by Flak attacking MT; Sgt E.P.Presland baled out, but KiA
274 Sqn	Hurricane Z4964 'D' left 1045 shot down by Flak, crash-landed; Sgt E.Harrington
94 Sqn	Kittyhawk I ET521 lost
250 Sqn	Kittyhawk I AK824 left1145, badly damaged by MC.202 SW El Alamein; Plt Off J.E.Collier safe
5 SAAF Sqn	Tomahawk IIb AK537 'S' badly damaged by e/a W El Alamein 1915; Lt C.Somerville safe

German Claims

2./JG 27	Lt Hans-Arnold Stahlschmidt	Hurricane	SE El Alamein	1015
9./JG 27	Obfw Heinrich Rosenberg	P-40	SW El Alamein	1822
8./JG 27	Lt Werner Schroer	P-40	SW El Alamein	1830

Italian Claims

84ª Sq, 10°Gr, 4°St CT	Serg Magg Mario Veronesi	MC.202 MM 7928 '84-9'	P-40	nr Deir el Qattara	1035-1200
84ª Sq, 10°Gr, 4°St CT	Ten Paolo Berti	MC.202 MM 7803 '84-1'	P-40	nr Deir el Qattara	1035-1200
84ª Sq, 10°Gr, 4°St CT	Ten Paolo Berti	MC.202 MM 7803 '84-1'			
84ª Sq, 10°Gr, 4°St CT	Cap Franco Lucchini	MC.202 MM 7901 '84-3'	P-40	nr Deir el Qattara	1035-1200
84ª Sq, 10°Gr, 4°St CT	Ten Luigi Giannella	MC.202 MM 7805 '84-2'			
91ª Sq, 10°Gr, 4°St CT	Ten Paolo Benedicti	MC.202			
84ª Sq, 10°Gr, 4°St CT	M.llo Luigi Bignami	MC.202 MM 7896 '84-8			
84ª Sq, 10°Gr, 4°St CT	Serg Magg Mario Veronesi	MC.202 MM 7928 '84-9'			
90ª Sq, 10°Gr, 4°St CT	Cap Ranieri Piccolomini	MC.202	P-40	nr Deir el Qattara	1035-1200
90ª Sq, 10°Gr, 4°St CT	S.Ten Renato Baroni	MC.202 MM 7906 '90-8'			
90ª Sq, 10°Gr, 4°St CT	Serg Amleto Monterumici	MC.202			

Italian Casualties

90ª Sq, 10°Gr, 4°St CT	MC.202 MM 7906 '90-8' force-landed near El Daba, damaged and recovered, Serg Magg Renato Baroni WiA
84ª Sq, 10°Gr, 4°St CT	MC.202 MM 7901 '84-3' force-landed at Qotaifiya, damaged and recovered, Cap Franco Lucchini safe
84ª Sq, 10°Gr, 4°St CT	MC.202 MM 7803 '84-1' hit in combat, slightly damaged, Ten Paolo Berti safe
84ª Sq, 10°Gr, 4°St CT	MC.202 MM 7896 '84-8' hit in combat, slightly damaged, M.llo Luigi Bignami safe

Friday, 17 July 1942

Early on 12 Spitfires of 145 Squadron provided top cover for six Hurricanes of 73 and 7 SAAF Squadrons on patrol. They were jumped at 0737 by eight Bf 109s of II./JG 27 on a Freie Jagd, Oblt Sinner shooting down Sgt Rostant, who baled out with a wounded arm. Meanwhile, Cap Cecchet led ten MC.200s of 8° Gruppo to strafe motor vehicles along the road to Qattara Spring Works (0845-0940); nine trucks were reportedly hit and damaged.

Magg Luigi Filippi, encumbered by his parachute, prepares to climb into his MC.202 on which the commander's pennant is clearly visible beneath the cockpit.

Maj Erich Gerlitz was posted from II./JG 27 to become Gruppenkommandeur of III./JG 27 in May. He only made one claim with this unit – his 18th – on 17 July.

At 1115 four more of 145 Squadron's Spitfires set out to provide similar cover to fighter-bombers, this time Kittyhawks, seven of which were aircraft of 3 RAAF Squadron; their targets were in the Bir el Abd area. Between El Alamein and the target area eight Bf 109s of III./JG 53 on a Freie Jagd attacked, shooting down one Spitfire from which the pilot baled out, and inflicting severe damage on one of the Australian Kittyhawks.

A formation of Hurricanes from 80 Squadron, most flown by 92 Squadron pilots, took off to cover others from 238 Squadron on a patrol over El Alamein. Thirty Ju 87s of III./StG 3 were seen, the latter escorted by 14 Messerschmitts of I.Gruppe, nine from II.Gruppe and six from III./JG 53. These escorting fighters attacked the 80 Squadron formation, and also prevented A Flight of 238 Squadron from reaching the bombers. B Flight got through, however, forcing the Stukas to jettison their bombs and claiming two shot down, a probable and two damaged. In a 20-minute running fight several claims were made against the Messerschmitts, but only one was a confirmed victory by Plt Off Samouelle, one of the 92 Squadron pilots; however, two of the Bf 109s received damage and one Ju 87 was shot down. The German pilots claimed five victories, four of the 92 Squadron pilots being shot down, three of them killed; only Flt Lt Cocker survived to bale out, having been wounded. Two of the 238 Squadron

Hurricanes were also damaged. Towards evening, 11 Hurricanes of 274 Squadron took off at 1705, encountering more Messerschmitts and Macchis followed by 20 plus Ju 87s covered by 12 more fighters. These were flying below the Hurricanes, allowing the latter to dive on them, a Ju 87 being claimed shot down.

The first operation to be undertaken by newly-arrived 23° Gruppo occurred when Magg Luigi Filippi, the unit commander, led 12 MC.202s (seven of 75ª and five of 74ª Squadriglie) on a free sweep over the lines. North of El Alamein fighters were seen, Filippi claiming one and Serg Magg Felice Papini a probable, identified as P-40s. At about the same time Cap Ruspoli led 14 more Macchis, this time of 10° Gruppo to escort a formation of Ju 88s to this area. North of El Alamein a reported ten Hurricanes and eight Spitfires attacked the bombers but were engaged by the escorting pilots, Ruspoli claiming one of the Hurricanes.

80 and 238 Squadrons were patrolling in the same area again around 1840, spotting 15 Ju 87s with eight escorting Bf 109s of III./JG 27 and MC.202s of these two units. The escorts were indeed successful in preventing the Hurricanes getting at the bombers, Lt Schroer of III./JG 27 claiming one shot down, while the Italian pilots added the claims detailed above. 238 Squadron's commanding officer, Sqn Ldr R.G.A.Barclay, DFC, was shot down and killed; Barclay had claimed seven confirmed victories prior to his demise, five over England in 1940 and two since arriving in the desert.

During the day II./JG 53 arrived at Qotaifiya for a four-day detachment, bringing over about 20 Bf 109s.

British Claims

238 Sqn	Sqn Ldr R.G.A.Barclay	Hurricane IIb 'U'	Ju 87	El Alamein area	1325-1450
238 Sqn	Plt Off I.F.Gilbert	Hurricane IIb 'M'	Ju 87	El Alamein area	1325-1450
238 Sqn	Plt Off O.F.A.Oram	Hurricane IIb 'T'	Ju 87 Probable	El Alamein area	1325-1450
238 Sqn	Sgt H.R.Robertson	Hurricane IIb 'P'	Ju 87 Damaged	El Alamein area	1325-1450
238 Sqn	Sgt W.Waddell	Hurricane IIb 'B'	Bf 109F Damaged	El Alamein area	1325-1450
274 Sqn	Flt Lt G.C.Keefer	Hurricane IIc BE487 'F'	Bf 109F Damaged	El Alamein area	1345-1555
80/92 Sqn	Plt Off C.J.Samouelle	Hurricane IIc BN126 'P'	Bf 109F	S El Alamein	1350-1415
238 Sqn	Plt Off B.Nordon (?Sgt)	Hurricane IIb 'V'	Bf 109F Damaged	El Alamein area	1840-1930
274 Sqn	Sgt R.W.Henderson	Hurricane IIc BE669 'C'	Ju 87	S El Alamein	1850-1945
274 Sqn	Sgt W.E.Marsh	Hurricane IIc BE487 'F'	MC.202 Damaged	El Alamein area	1850-1945

British Casualties

80 Sqn	Hurricane IIc BM984 'Z' FTR, shot down by Bf 109s nr El Alamein 1350-1415; Wt Off Mitchell PoW
80 Sqn	Hurricane IIc BN542 'E' FTR, shot down by Bf 109s nr El Alamein 1350-1415; Flt Lt L.Crocker (92 Sqn) baled out, WiA
80 Sqn	Hurricane IIc BP121 'L' FTR, shot down by Bf 109s nr El Alamein 1350-1415; Sgt R.H.Groom KiA
80 Sqn	Hurricane IIc BP511 'A' FTR, shot down by Bf 109s nr El Alamein 1350-1415; Sgt I.H.S.Watson (92 Sqn) PoW
238 Sqn	Hurricane BP296 'U' left 1840, shot down by Bf 109; Sqn Ldr R.G.A.Barclay KiA
238 Sqn	Hurricane 'J' left 1840 shot down El Alamein by two MC.202s, crash-landed; Plt Off E.M.Frost severely WiA
145 Sqn	Spitfire V AR277 'Q' left 0800, shot down; Sgt J.K.Rostant, baled out safe
145 Sqn	Spitfire V AB373 'F' left 1115; Plt Off Weber baled out, WiA
3 RAAF Sqn	Kittyhawk I ET1017, badly damaged by Bf 109s, near El Imayid 1130-1230; Sgt R.N.B.Stevens safe

German Claims

6./JG 27	Oblt Rudolf Sinner	Spitfire	El Dakar	0637
Stab III./JG 53	Maj Erich Gerlitz	Spitfire	NE El Alamein	1033
9./JG 53	Obfw Werner Stumpf	P-40	NE El Alamein	1108
1./JG 27	Hptm Ludwig Franzisket	Hurricane	SW El Alamein	1312
6./JG 27	Oblt Rudolf Sinner	Hurricane	Haggag el Qasaba	1322
4./JG 27	Fw Franz Stigler	P-40	SE El Alamein	1324
2./JG 27	Lt Hans-Arnold Stahlschmidt	Hurricane	SW El Alamein	1325
6./JG 27	Oblt Rudolf Sinner	Hurricane	S Haggag el Qasaba	1327
8./JG 27	Lt Werner Schroer	P-40	W El Alamein	1825
Flak		4 a/c		

German Casualties

Stab/JG 27	Bf 109F-4 trop WNr 8746 combat, force-landed Qotaifiya 40% damaged; Fw Seidel safe
6./JG 27	Bf 109F-4 trop WNr 8607 combat with Hurricane SE Qotaifiya, 60%; Lt Hans Doyé safe
9./StG 3	Ju 87D-1 WNr 2572 combat with Hurricane El Alamein, crash-landed at base; Oblt Siegfried Göbel/ Uffz Gerhard Nalenz WiA
II./StG 3	Ju 87D-1 WNr 2477, destroyed in fighter-bomber attack at Bir el Abd

Italian Claims

75ªSq, 23°Gr, 3°St CT	Magg Luigi Filippi	MC.202	P-40	El Alamein	720-1840
74ªSq, 23°Gr, 3°St CT	Serg Magg Felice Papini	MC.202	P-40 Probable	El Alamein	1720-1840
91ª Sq, 10°Gr, 4°St CT	Cap Carlo M. Ruspoli	MC.202	Hurricane	El Alamein	1730-1900

Saturday, 18 July 1942

At dawn six MC.202s of 4° Stormo moved to Bu Amud to provide protection to Tobruk harbour. At 0645 Cap Franco Lucchini led eight Macchis of 10° Gruppo on a free sweep over the lines. At 12,000 feet they intercepted a formation of nine P-40s covered by 11 Hurricanes. The Italians chased these fighters towards the east as far as Burg el Arab; after a 15-minute combat they claimed four P-40s shot down and some others damaged.

At 0720 12 Hurricanes of 274 Squadron, covered by others of 80 Squadron, patrolled north and south over El Alamein. Two Bf 109s jumped the top cover, followed by six more and some MC.202s. Claims for five fighters damaged were submitted by the two RAF units, one aircraft of 274 Squadron being shot down by a Macchi and another of 80 Squadron receiving a bullet in the cooling system which caused the pilot to crash-land. During the course of the afternoon Flg Off Buckley of 208 Squadron had flown a TacR sortie in a Hurricane I with one other aircraft as his protective 'weaver'. However, his aircraft was seen to dive vertically into the sea for no apparent reason. In the evening ten Bf 109s of I./JG 27 provided high cover to Stukas, encountering 80 Squadron which was again flying top cover to 274 Squadron. Lt Remmer forced down Plt Off Ryder who landed on the German airfield at Mumin Busak.

70ª Squadriglia of 23° Gruppo arrived at Wadi Tamet with 11 MC.202s led by Cap Claudio Solaro. On the same day Magg Giuseppe D'Agostinis arrived at Fuka to take command of 10° Gruppo, temporarily held by Cap Lucchini.

British Claims

274 Sqn	Sqn Ldr J.C.F.Hayter	Hurricane IIc BE487 'F'	Bf 109E Damaged	El Alamein	0721-0945
274 Sqn	Plt Off R.H.Hunter	Hurricane IIc BE229 'S'	MC.202 Damaged	El Alamein	0721-0945
274 Sqn	Sgt S.Lerche	Hurricane IIc BE683 'O'	Bf 109 Damaged	El Alamein	0721-0945
80 Sqn	Flt Lt R.G.Foskett	Hurricane IIc BP235 'J'	2 Bf 109s Damaged	El Alamein	0800
450 Sqn	Sqn Ldr A.D.Ferguson	Kittyhawk I ET918	Bf 109F Damaged		1856-2015

British Casualties

80 Sqn	Hurricane IIc BN348 left 1846, forced down by Bf 109 nr El Alamein; Plt Off D.K.Ryder PoW
274 Sqn	Hurricane IIc Z5064 'Z' left 0721, shot down by MC.202,crash-landed; Flt Sgt T.B.Hamilton safe
208 Sqn	Hurricane I V7670 dived into sea from 21,000ft; Flg Off J.C. Buckley KiA (formerly a Captain in the Royal Artillery)
243 Wing	Hurricane II missing on delvery flight to 33 Squadron. Overshot destination in bad weather and strayed into Axis lines, chased and shot down by fighters; Wt Off V.J.Hibbens RAAF PoW

German Claims

1./JG 27	Lt Hans Remmer	Hurricane n.e.	Bir Mumin Busak

Italian Claims

84ª Sq, 10°Gr, 4°St CT	Cap Franco Lucchini	MC.202 MM 7803 '84-1'	P-40	El Alamein	0645-0815
84ª Sq, 10°Gr, 4°St CT	Serg Magg Piero Buttazzi	MC.202 MM 7896 '84-8'			
84ª Sq, 10°Gr, 4°St CT	Ten Luigi Giannella	MC.202 MM 7805 '84-2'	P-40	El Alamein	0645-0815
84ª Sq, 10°Gr, 4°St CT	Serg Magg Mario Veronesi	MC.202 MM 7928 '84-9'			
90ª Sq, 10°Gr, 4°St CT	M.llo Angelo Savini	MC.202	P-40	El Alamein	0645-0815
90ª Sq, 10°Gr, 4°St CT	Serg Amleto Monterumici	MC.202			
90ª Sq, 10°Gr, 4°St CT	Ten Virgilio Vanzan	MC.202	P-40	El Alamein	0645-0815
90ª Sq, 10°Gr, 4°St CT	Cap Ranieri Piccolomini	MC.202			

Sunday, 19 July 1942

On this date the Afrika Korps, which was now down to 28 serviceable tanks, received special orders to dig in the armour against air attack – a sign of how effective WDAF was proving to be in support of the army.

At 0625 eight Kittyhawks of 250 Squadron carried out an armed reconnaissance of the southern sector of the front, attacking LG.21 at the same time as a formation of Bostons, planting five 500lb and two 250lb bombs on the airfield. Flt Lt Marshall, after bombing, shot down a Ju 52/3m as it was about to land, and then strafed a Ju 87 on the ground. The rest of the squadron then came down to strafe, claiming to have shot-up two more Ju 87s, four Ju 88s, one Ju 52/3m and a Bf 110. One aircraft failed to return, believed to have been a victim of Flak.

Seven Hurricanes of 127 Squadron covered 238 Squadron patrolling over the El Alamein box fortifications at 1000. Ten Bf 109s of II./JG 27 on a Freie Jagd attacked the top cover, forcing them down to the level of 238 Squadron's aircraft which were also attacked. Flg Off Gardner of 127 was shot down in flames, baling out and being taken to hospital suffering severe burns, additionally Flt Sgt Sherwood of 127 was shot down. Plt Off Galyer of 238 Squadron claimed an MC.202 shot down, although no Italian fighter losses were recorded on this date. Five Italian fighters of 84ª Squadriglia, led by Cap Lucchini, were actually on a free sweep between 0900-1030 over El Alamein but the pilots reported no encounters. Seven Hurricanes were claimed by the German pilots, Oblts Rödel and Sinner being credited with two each. They recorded that the whole combat took place in sight of the German lines, at least three Hurricanes being reported to have belly-landed. The pilots of two Bf 109s of I./JG 27 patrolling over the same area at this time reported eight fires on the ground, II./JG 53 observed four and III./JG 53 also reported seeing eight. This discrepancy cannot be readily explained, but no other WDAF losses have been found.

An MC.200 fighter-bomber carrying a British 250lb bomb, from a captured ammunition dump.

At 1025 eight Kittyhawks of 112 Squadron strafed LG.21 in company with 11 aircraft of 450 Squadron and others of 250 Squadron. The two latter units encountered four Ju 52/3ms and a Ju 87 coming in to land, claiming all five aircraft shot down before the Australian pilots had yet released their bombs. They then strafed five Ju 87s, three Bf 109s and a Ju 88 on the ground. The pilots of 112 Squadron claimed four Ju 88s damaged on the ground. III. /JG 53 reported that one of their Bf 109s was totally destroyed during this attack.

At 1700 Cap Livio Ceccotti of 91ª Squadriglia took off from Bu Amud on a patrol over Tobruk habour. He then sighted six B-17s and attacked one but was hit by return fire and forced to belly-land at base.

260 Squadron bade farewell to their commanding officer, Sqn Ldr O.V.Hanbury, DFC, who was awarded a Bar to his decoration and posted off operations. His place was taken by Sqn Ldr G.D.L.Haysom, DFC, an ex-Battle of Britain pilot with five claims to his credit. Two Squadriglie of 18° Gruppo of 3° Stormo (83ª and 95ª) arrived at Castel Benito from Italy with their MC.200s.

British Claims

238 Sqn	Plt Off J.Galyer	Hurricane IIb	MC.202	El Alamein	0950-1055
250 Sqn	Flt Lt A E Marshall	Kittyhawk I AK886	Ju 52/3m	LG.20	1040-1208
450 Sqn	Sqn Ldr A.D.Ferguson	Kittyhawk I ET918	Ju 87	LG.21	1040-1208

450 Sqn	Sgt R.G.Brown	Kittyhawk I ET869	Ju 52/3m	LG.20	1040-1208
450 Sqn	Flt Lt R.D.Dyson	Kittyhawk I AK634			
450 Sqn	Sqn Ldr A.D.Ferguson	Kittyhawk I ET918	Ju 52/3m	LG.104	1040-1208
450 Sqn	Flt Lt F.E.Parker	Kittyhawk I ET864			
250 Sqn	Flt Lt A.E.Marshall	Kittyhawk I ET953 'P'	Ju 52/3m	LG.21	1205

British Casualties

127 Sqn	Hurricane IIb BN160 damaged by Bf 109s and abandoned SE El Alamein at 1045; Flg Off M.E.Gardner baled out severely burned
127 Sqn	Hurricane IIb BE224 shot down SE El Alamein at 1045; Flt Sgt L.D.Sherwood safe
250 Sqn	Kittyhawk I ET913 left 1035 shot down by Flak nr LG.104; Plt Off A.C.Crofton KiA

German Claims

Stab II./JG 27	Oblt Gustav Rödel	Hurricane	Chebel el Gabir	0913
6./JG 27	Oblt Rudolf Sinner	Hurricane	Bir el Themta	0915
6./JG 27	Obfw Herbert Krenz	Hurricane	SW El Alamein	0917
Stab II./JG 27	Oblt Gustav Rödel	Hurricane	Bir Garbatte	0917
5./JG 27	Obfw Emil Clade	Hurricane	Bir Ibrahim	0918
6./JG 27	Oblt Rudolf Sinner	Hurricane	S El Alamein	0919
6./JG 27	Obfw Herbert Krenz	Hurricane	Mallahed Maryut	0920

German Casualties

9./JG 53	Bf 109F-4 WNr 10111 50% damaged in air raid at Bir el Abd
I./StG 3	Ju 87R-4 WNr 6311 destroyed in air raid at Bir el Abd
4.(H)/12	Bf 109E-7 WNr 1522 destroyed in air raid at Fuka
4.(H)/12	Bf 110E-3 WNr 2466 destroyed in air raid at Fuka
TrspSt.II.F1K	Ju 52 WNr 6141 shot down in combat, crashed 15km E Fuka; Fw Friedrich Mädel and 1 KiA, 2 safe

Italian Casualties

97ª Sq, 9°Gr, 4°St CT	MC.202 MM 7819 '97-6' hit in combat by B-17, belly-landed at Bu Amud, Cap Livio Ceccotti (91ª Sq) safe

Monday, 20 July 1942

A heavy raid was made on Fuka and El Daba during the morning, LGs 17 and 18 being the selected targets. Soon after 0930 18 Bostons escorted by 233 Wing, swept in, as Kittybombers of 239 Wing bombed and strafed from a lower level. 112 and 250 Squadrons shot-up between them six Ju 88s, two MC.202s, two Bf 109s and an S.81. The Boston crews claimed to have destroyed two aircraft with their bombs. One aircraft of 112 Squadron was hit by Flak and crash-landed, the pilot returning to his unit the same evening. 450 Squadron's eight Kittybombers carried out their attack, but over the target a Bf 109 targeted Sgt Brown, who was shot down. Heavy casualties were sustained on the ground by 9° Gruppo: Cap Mariotti was badly wounded in both legs, two airmen were killed and more than a dozen injured. Mariotti was then replaced as 73ª Squadriglia commander by Ten Giulio Reiner.

The 239 Wing leader, Wg Cdr Mayers, also failed to return and it seems that he and Brown were the victims of four III./JG 53 Bf 109s which were scrambled to intercept the raid, claiming two Kittyhawks. Twelve more Kittyhawks from 4 SAAF Squadron were flying top cover to the Bostons and to other units of 233 Wing, and these were also attacked by Bf 109s, one pilot failing to return. Eight fighters from I./JG 27 had scrambled, Uffz Gläser claiming one victory over an aircraft which belly-landed; this was possibly 4 SAAF's Lt White.

Mayers was a considerable loss to 239 Wing; a dashing leader, this Australian had brought his personal total to over 11 by this time, and had been recommended for a DSO, which was gazetted soon after he was lost. Fighters combed the area searching for him. Spitfire pilots of 601 Squadron finally found his Kittyhawk which had crash-landed with little observable damage, but the cockpit was open and there was no sign of him. It is believed that he became a PoW but was killed when a Ju 52/3m in which he was being transported to Sicily, was shot down over the Mediterranean by a Spitfire.

Four Bf 109s of II./JG 27 undertook a reconnaissance at 1140, encountering Hurricanes of 33 Squadron, which they jumped. Oblt Sinner shot down Sgt Moher's aircraft in flames, the pilot getting clear but dying later in 28 Australian Field Ambulance. At 1900 four Bf 109s of II./JG 27 carried out a Freie Jagd. Entering a combat which was already underway between six other Messerschmitts of II.Gruppe and 26 British fighters, Oblt Börngen claimed a Curtiss fighter near El Alamein, but this has not been identified.

During the course of the day the flight commanders of 127 Squadron were both promoted and posted, Flt Lt R.Marples, DFC, to command 238 Squadron and Flt Lt Finnis, DFC, to command 33 Squadron. Benito Mussolini now gave up waiting for his triumphal entry into Cairo and returned to Italy. 83ª and 95ª Squadriglie of 18° Gruppo reached their base at Derna. Cap Francesco Paolo 'Romolo' Artina had to stop at Tamet because of engine trouble.

British Claims

112 Sqn	Sqn Ldr B Drake	Kittyhawk I	MC.202 Damaged	LG.18	0930
112 Sqn	Flg Off W.M.Whitamore	Kittyhawk I ET102	Bf 109 Damaged	LG.18	0930
239 Wg	Wg Cdr H.C.Mayers	Kittyhawk I	MC.202	SE Fuka	1025
250 Sqn	Plt Off R.I.Baldwin	Kittyhawk I AK960 'X'	MC.202 Damaged	Fuka	1030
250 Sqn	Flt Lt N.P.W.Hancock	Kittyhawk I ET525 'Y'	MC.202 Damaged	Fuka	1030
450 Sqn	Sgt G.Lindsey	Kittyhawk I AK886	Ju 52/3m	LG.20	1040-1208

British Casualties

33 Sqn	Hurricane IIc BE134 'Y' shot down by Bf 109 SE Bir el Khasa 1200; Sgt L.H.Moher KiA
112 Sqn	Kittyhawk I AK677 'G' damaged over El Alamein and force-landed; Sgt R.De Bourke safe
250 Sqn	Kittyhawk I badly damaged by Bf 109 El Daba area 1030; Plt Off J.E.Collier safe
250 Sqn	Kittyhawk I AN960 'X' badly damaged by MC.202 El Daba area 1030; Plt Off R.I.Baldwin safe
450 Sqn	Kittyhawk I AK872 left 0928, shot down by Bf 109s nr Fuka; Sgt R.G.Brown PoW
239 Wg	Kittyhawk I shot down by fighters 40m SE Fuka; Wg Cdr H.C.Mayers MiA
4 SAAF Sqn	Tomahawk IIb AK460 engine failed on ops, crashed nr 22nd Armoured Brigade at 0950; 2/Lt D.G.White KiA

German Claims

2./JG 27	Uffz Walter Gläser	P-40	SE Fuka	0935
8./JG 53	Uffz Kurt Zielke	P-40	El Daba	0945
8./JG 53	Lt Dietrich Kasten	P-40	El Daba	0945
6./JG 27	Oblt Rudolf Sinner	Hurricane	3km SE Bir el Khasa	1119
5./JG 27	Oblt Ernst Börngen	P-40	El Alamein	1823

German Casualties

1.(F)/121	Ju 88D-5 WNr 430037 70% damaged in air raid at Fuka

Italian Casualties

95ª Sq, 18°Gr, 3°St CT	MC.200 MM 5098 damaged on force-landing at Tripoli, Serg Leone Casadei safe
73ª Sq, 9° Gr, 4°St CT	2 MC.202s MM 7763 '73-5' and MM 7926 '73-8' damaged on the ground by bombs at Fuka
73ª Sq, 9° Gr, 4°St CT	Cap Luigi Mariotti badly wounded on the ground by bombs at Fuka, two airmen killed and some wounded

Tuesday, 21 July 1942

General Auchinleck now launched a counter-attack in force in an attempt to drive the Axis forces back to the Egyptian frontier. In the early hours four Bf 109s of II./JG 27 escorted a reconnaissance Bf 110, but during this mission Oblt Zahn turned back early as his engine was overheating, however he did not arrive at base. A month later his aircraft would be found undamaged south-east of Bir el Abd with the pilot dead at the controls; this remains one of the mysteries of the desert war, no reason for his fate ever being found. Nomadic Arabs had made a hole in his skull to allow his spirit to escape! Four Messerschmitts of I.Gruppe carried out a similar mission at 1130, Lt Stahlschmidt's aircraft being hit by AA, causing him to force-land near Sidi Abd el Rahman. Fw Gerlitzki also force-landed near his own airfield, his aircraft somersaulting; he was badly injured.

Six Spitfires of 601 Squadron carried out a freelance patrol at 0740, the pilots seeing two Bf 109s on which they dived, Flt Lt Ingram claiming to have shot one of these down. There is a possibility that this may have been Zahn's or Gerlitzki's aircraft. Twelve MC.202s of 23° Gruppo led by Magg Filippi, undertook a free sweep south of El Alamein between 0810-1010 during which eight Spitfires and four P-40s were reported to have been encountered. Ten Lolli and Serg Mandolesi of 75ª Squadriglia forced one Spitfire to crash-land and then, after the pilot had got out, they strafed it and set it on fire. The unit and pilot have not been definitely identified.

In the evening at 1845, 80 Squadron, covered by 238, patrolled over El Alamein where the Hurricanes were jumped by Bf 109s which shot down one aircraft from each unit and damaged a third. Flg Off Frank Mason claimed to have shot down one of the attackers, and Flt Sgt Morris of 238 Squadron a second. At around this time ten Kittyhawks of 4 SAAF Squadron, flying close cover to Bostons, were also attacked by Bf 109s, two aircraft being damaged; Flg Off Waddy claimed one Bf 109 damaged.

The Hurricanes of 33 and 213 Squadrons, with a top cover of four Spitfires of 145 Squadron, carried out a further patrol immediately after 80 and 238 Squadrons, the top cover also being attacked by Bf 109s, two Spitfires being shot down and a third slightly damaged. The victors of all these combats were the pilots of II./JG 27 on a Freie Jagd, who ended up carrying on a running fight with many Allied fighters over the El Alamein area. In a little over ten minutes they claimed nine victories, three of them by Oblt Rödel, although strangely they failed to identify the last three which had been against Spitfires, as other than more Hurricanes. WDAF losses during this evening battle actually amounted to ten – two Hurricanes and two Spitfires shot down, three Hurricanes, two Kittyhawks and one Spitfire damaged. It seems that one Bf 109 was shot down during the fight, Lt Förstmann of 5.Staffel returning safely later.

During the day the Regia Aeronautica was quite substantially strengthened, ten more MC.202s for 23° Gruppo arriving at Abu Haggag from Italy, bringing this unit up to full strength. From Italy too came the 101° Gruppo Tuffatori with 16 serviceable CR.42s, 12 of 238ª Squadriglia led by Cap Carlo Alberto Rizzi, and four of 208ª Squadriglia, commanded by Ten Sergio Bigoni. The unit flew in first to Castel Benito, then moved forward to Derna.

After claiming several victories over Malta with 601 Squadron, Bruce Ingram was to add many more over North Africa. One of the first of these was over a Bf 109 on 21 July.

British Claims

601 Sqn	Flt Lt M.R.B.Ingram	Spitfire Vb BR118	Bf 109	battle area	0845
4 SAAF Sqn	Flg Off J.L.Waddy	Kittyhawk I ET512 'H'	Bf 109 Probable		1840-1920
238 Sqn	Flt Sgt W.J.Morris	Hurricane IIb 'X'	Bf 109	El Alamein area	1845-1945
145 Sqn	Plt Off P.B.Laing-Meason	Spitfire Vb AR288 'C'	Bf 109 Probable		1910
80 Sqn	Flt Lt F.Mason	Hurricane IIc BN126 'P'	Bf 109	El Alamein area	1915

British Casualties

238 Sqn	Hurricane II 'M' took off 1845, shot down by Bf 109s at 1910; Flg Off C.R.Morrison-Jones MiA
80 Sqn	Hurricane IIB BN462 took off 1845, shot down by Bf 109s at 1910; Flt Sgt J.D.Robb MiA
4 SAAF Sqn	Kittyhawk AK 817 damaged by 109 and crash landed at base, 0900 approx;.Lt J.van Nus slt WiA
4 SAAF Sqn	Kittyhawk shot-up by Bf 109 and crash-landed at base, 0910-1025; Lt B.Futeran WiA
40 SAAF Sqn	Hurricane II BD827 left 1630 'weaver' to Lt S.Cohen, forced to land 5m W El Hammam; 2/Lt C.Rose WiA
274 Sqn	Hurricane II BD750 'W' left 0925, force-landed, no reason given, probably Flak; Sgt W.S.Howie safe
274 Sqn	Hurricane II BE685 'T' left 0925, force-landed, no reason given, probably Flak; Flt Sgt J.W.Neil
145 Sqn	Spitfire Vb AR288 'C' shot down by Bf 109 at 1915; Plt Off P.B.Laing-Meason baled out safe
145 Sqn	Spitfire Vb AR282 'Q' left 0950, shot down; Plt Off C.J.Frith PoW
601 Sqn	Spitfire Vb BR384 left 1840, damaged by Bf 109 10m W Burg el Arab at 1925; Sgt E.G.Shea safe

German Claims

6./JG 27	Oblt Rudolf Sinner	P-40	N Bir el Harmat	1809
Stab II./JG 27	Oblt Gustav Rödel	3 Hurricanes	SW El Alamein & NE El Daba	1810 & 1812
6./JG 27	Fw Hans Würschinger	Hurricane	E Bir el Mukheisin	1815
6./JG 27	Oblt Rudolf Sinner	Hurricane	SW El Alamein	1816
6./JG 27	Obfw Herbert Krenz	P-40	El Alamein	1818
Stab II./JG 27	Oblt Gustav Rödel	Hurricane	8km SW El Alamein	1820
5./JG 27	Obfhr Willi Kientsch	Hurricane	SE El Alamein	1820

German Casualties

1./JG 27	Bf 109F-4 trop WNr 8654 20% damaged by bombs at Turbiya
2./JG 27	Bf 109F-4 trop WNr 19188 force-landed SE Turbiya 30% damaged by AA; Fw Erich Gerlitzki injured, died 22nd
2./JG 27	Bf 109F-4 trop WNr 8478 force-landed S Sidi Abd el Rahman 30% damaged by AA; Lt Hans-Arnold Stahlschmidt safe

German Casualties

5./JG 27	Bf 109F-4 trop WNr 8759 Red 8 shot down in El Alamein area, 100%; Lt Gerhard Förstmann MiA, but returned on foot
6./JG 27	Bf 109F-4 trop WNr 8370 Yellow 5, engine failure, force-landed 50km SE Bir el Abd, 100%; Oblt Günther Zahn KiA
3./NJG 2	Ju 88C-6 WNr 260229 shot down in combat with Boston, crashed nr El Alamein; Obfw Alfons Köster and crew safe
III./StG 3	Ju 87D-1 WNr 2467 damaged in combat, force-landed at Bir el Abd, 15% damaged

Italian Claims

75ªSq, 23°Gr, 3°St CT	Ten Gualtiero Lolli	MC.202	Spitfire	S El Alamein	0840-1010
75ªSq, 23°Gr, 3°St CT	Serg Maurizio Mandolesi	MC.202			

Wednesday, 22 July 1942

Auchinleck's offensive fared badly this day, 8th Army losing 40 out of 100 tanks to a German loss of three. Air activity was again heavy, beginning when eight Kittyhawks of 112 Squadron took off on a bombing operation, being intercepted by six Bf 109s of I./JG 27 which were out on a Freie Jagd. Lt Stahlschmidt shot down Plt Off Barrow's aircraft at 0925, which blew up on hitting the ground. The Messerschmitts then continued with their patrol.

At 0900 eight Spitfires of 601 Squadron had also taken off on a freelance patrol, encountering six Bf 109s of III./JG 53 and 11 of II./JG 27 which were escorting Stukas. Oblt Götz of the former unit shot down Flt Off Hone at 0935, the latter going into a spin before baling out with a leg wound. Five minutes later the I./JG 27 formation spotted 12 Baltimores escorted by 20 Curtiss fighters, one of which Stahlschmidt claimed; Lt Futeran of 4 SAAF Squadron claimed a probable Bf 109 in return.

Ten Hurricanes of 1 SAAF Squadron, covered by others of 80 Squadron, then intercepted the Stukas, being attacked in turn by four Bf 109s, The South African pilots claimed two Bf 109s damaged. Twelve Hurricanes of 73 Squadron patrolled over the central section of the El Alamein line at 1215, spotting eight Bf 109s of I./JG 27 3,000 feet above them. The opposing fighters turned on each other, Lt Stahlschmidt claiming one, Uffz Winkler a second a few minutes later. Two Hurricanes went down and a third was damaged.

Just before 1500 Hurricanes of 80 and 1 SAAF Squadrons took off again to patrol over the coast road, followed a quarter of an hour later by 11 of 274 Squadron, six of which were carrying bombs, these attacking vehicles north of the Sidi Abd el Rahman track. The two former squadrons attacked a formation of Ju 87s escorted by Bf 109s, causing the bombers to jettison their loads and turn for home. 274 Squadron was attacked by two fighters, identified as Bf 109s, and Sgt Howie crash-landed. There were no Luftwaffe claims at this time and it is likely that this Hurricane had been shot down by a pilot of 10° Gruppo, claimed as so often as a P-40. Eight of this unit's MC.202s, led by Cap Ruspoli, had taken off at 1400 on an escort mission reporting a formation of 18 Hurribombers escorted by P-40s. Two of the latter were claimed shot down plus one more probably, one of the claims being made by Serg Magg Veronesi as his seventh individual victory.

At 1845 12 Hurricanes from 274 Squadron took off again to attack MT once more, but encountered instead a big formation of Stukas with Bf 109 escort, which they attacked. They were able only to claim a probable and a damaged, but in doing so, suffered only damage to one Hurricane. At the same time 12 MC.202s of 9° Gruppo, led by Magg Fassi, involved in a direct escort to some Ju 88s, joined some Bf 109s already engaged with a mixed formation of Hurricanes and P-40s claiming one of the former shot down. Eight Kittyhawks of 112 Squadron set off at 1900, also meeting dive-bombers and escorting fighters, probably of the same formation as had been engaged by 274 Squadron, but the results were similar – one probable and one damaged, albeit without loss.

There were more postings of note during the day, Flt Lt Walker of 112 Squadron taking over command of 250 Squadron from Sqn Ldr M.T.Judd, while Sqn Ldr Haysom, the new commanding officer of 260 Squadron, moved on promotion to lead 239 Wing in place of the missing Wg Cdr Mayers. Haysom's place was taken in 260 Squadron by Sqn Ldr P.P.Devenish from 127 Squadron. On this date 244 Wing established a training flight to instruct ten pilots at a time. Four Hurricanes were collected from Alsace Groupe to rise the establishment of the new unit to eight; Flt Lt John Sowrey became the commander, aided by three instructors. In 1 SAAF Squadron Capt Metelerkamp noted in his logbook that the Squadron was now flying in fours, rather then in the line astern or line abreast formations employed for so long. 85ª Squadriglia arrived at Derna to join the other Squadriglie of 18° Gruppo. The MC.200s of this unit would be employed as fighter-bombers and for this purpose they were fitted with bomb racks to carry 50kg bomb.

British Claims

5 SAAF Sqn	2/Lt F.L.Stevens	Tomahawk IIb ..428 'R'	Bf 109F Damaged	10m SE El Alamein	0940
5 SAAF Sqn	2/Lt F.L.Stevens	Tomahawk IIb ..428 'R'	Bf 109G Damaged	10m SE El Alamein	0945
1 SAAF Sqn	Capt P.C.R.Metelerkamp	Hurricane IIb BG764 'W'	Bf 109F Damaged	El Alamein	1000
1 SAAF Sqn	Lt J.H.Gaynor	Hurricane II ..356 'A'	Bf 109F Damaged	El Alamein	1000
274 Sqn	Flt Lt C.W.Darwin	Hurricane IIc BE229 'S'	Bf 109 Damaged		1505-1605
274 Sqn	Plt Off J.Bell	Hurricane IIc BE491 'A'	Bf 109 Probable		1505-1605
274 Sqn	Plt Off D.C.Mitchell	Hurricane IIc BE699 'G'			
274 Sqn	Flt Sgt J.W.Neil	Hurricane IIc BP326 'T'	Bf 109 Probable		1505-1605
4 SAAF Sqn	Lt B.Futeran	Kittyhawk I	Bf 109 Probable	Deir el Abyad	1740-1830
274 Sqn	Plt Off J.Bell	Hurricane IIc BE491 'A'	Ju 87 Probable		1845-1935
274 Sqn	Flg Off C.D.A.Browne	Hurricane IIc BE487 'F'	Ju 87 Damaged		1845-1935
145 Sqn	Plt Off H.V.Freckleton	Spitfire AB146 'G'	Bf 109F	North Sector	1845
112 Sqn	Sgt D.Ibbotson	Kittyhawk I AK866	Bf 109 Probable		1900-1955
112 Sqn	Flg Off W.M.Whitamore	Kittyhawk I ET515	Bf 109E Damaged	1900-1955	

British Casualties

112 Sqn	Kittyhawk I ET790 '?' left 0900 shot down by fighters during ground attack; Plt Off J.S.Barrow KiA
250 Sqn	Kittyhawk I AK903 'Z' left 1905 shot down by six fighters SW El Alamein 1845; Plt Off T.W.Prentice KiA
450 Sqn	Kittyhawk I AK805 shot down by Flak nr El Alamein at about 1800; Sgt R.C.Hughes baled PoW
73 Sqn	Hurricane BN165 left 1215, shot down at Deir el Munassib; Flt Sgt A.A.Carcary KiA
73 Sqn	Hurricane BP220 left 1215, shot down by Bf 109s Deir el Munassib; Plt Off Hall baled out, safe
73 Sqn	Hurricane damaged
274 Sqn	Hurricane IIc BG753 'U'; left 1505, shot down by MC.202 and crash-landed; Flt Sgt J.W.Howie safe
274 Sqn	Hurricane IIc BE487 'F' left 1845 damaged Cat I, landed at base 1935; Flg Off C.D.A.Browne safe
274 Sqn	Hurricane IIc BG949 'Y' left 1015 damaged by MC.202 Cat I; Flt Sgt P.G.Hemmer safe
601 Sqn	Spitfire V AB327 left 0900, shot down; Flg Off C.M.Hone baled out

German Claims

2./JG 27	Lt Hans-Arnold Stahlschmidt	2 P-40s	W & SW El Alamein	0825-0840
9./JG 53	Oblt Franz Götz	Spitfire		0900
4./JG 27	Oblt Ferdinand Vögl	P-40	SW Burg el Arab	0913
2./JG 27	Lt Hans-Arnold Stahlschmidt	Hurricane	S El Alamein	1200
2./JG 27	Uffz Max Winkler	Hurricane	NE El Hammam	1210

Italian Claims

84ª Sq, 10°Gr, 4°St CT	Serg Magg Mario Veronesi	MC.202 MM 7905	P-40	El Alamein	1400-1515
91ª Sq, 10°Gr, 4°St CT	unidentified	MC.202	P-40	El Alamein	1400-1515
91ª Sq, 10°Gr, 4°St CT	unidentified	MC.202	P-40 Probable	El Alamein	1400-1515
9° Gr, 4° St CT	unidentified	MC.202	Hurricane	El Alamein	1800-

Thursday, 23 July 1942

The British 'push' continued to make little progress, tank losses now amounting to 118 in two days – a crippling rate of attrition for the tired army. Twelve Bostons carried out an attack during the early morning, nine Kittyhawks of 4 SAAF Squadron providing top cover for the formation. Five Bf 109s of III./JG 27 were escorting Stukas, meanwhile ten more from II.Gruppe had taken off on a Freie Jagd, both formations attacking the South African fighters, claiming two shot down, although about 25 minutes apart. 4 SAAF Squadron lost one aircraft, whilst the other might have been a Tomahawk of 208 Squadron, lost on a TacR sortie on this date.

At 1020 two Spitfires of 601 Squadron took off after a reconnaissance aircraft which the pilots shot down between them, identifying their victim as an Me 210. A reconnaissance Ju 88 of 1.(F)/121 was shot down by Spitfires in the El Alamein area on this date, and clearly this was the aircraft which they had despatched – particularly because there were no Me 210s operating over the Mediterranean area at this time. It is presumed that the pilots had recently been advised of intelligence information that such aircraft might be encountered. Eight Kittyhawks of 112 Squadron took off on a fighter-bomber sortie just before midday during which two pilots crash-landed. They were both picked up safely and returned to the squadron by an army unit.

Eleven Bf 109s of II./JG 27 and four of III./JG 53 undertook another Stuka escort at 1430, the bombers being intercepted over El Alamein by ten Hurricanes of 1 SAAF Squadron, covered by eight of 127 Squadron. The Messerschmitt pilots dived in pairs onto the top cover. Flt Lt Mannix drove two off the tail of a Hurricane, claiming one damaged, but one Hurricane pilot was slightly wounded and his aircraft was damaged. Meanwhile, the South Africans reached the dive-bombers with rather more telling effect than had been the case recently, claiming five shot down, with one Messerschmitt also claimed. The German escorts finally broke through the top cover to get at the South African aircraft, shooting down two and damaging a third. One then stuck to Capt Metelerkamp's Hurricane, attacking until he force-landed.

In the evening at 1845 eight II./JG 27 Bf 109s gave cover to another Stuka raid, the Messerschmitt pilots reporting combat with ten Spitfires and 20 Curtiss fighters, four pilots of 4.Staffel each claiming one Spitfire. No comparable information is to be found in WDAF records to match these claims. This became an increasingly common occurrence during the weeks to come with this particular Staffel and its pilots. There was one further claim of note during the day when Serg Magg D'Ilio of 365ª Squadriglia, MC.200-equipped 150° Gruppo, claimed to have shot down a Liberator some 100km north-north-east of Benghazi (see also Chapter Eleven).

During the day 19 Bf 110s of III./ZG 26, led by Hptm Herzberg escorted 30 Ju 52/3m transports carrying an Italian infantry battalion to Siwa, finding the oasis already deserted by the British. 73 Squadron now moved its Hurricane IIcs to El Ballah, 3 RAAF received no less than 17 pilots as reinforcements. By night a Boston of 24 SAAF Squadron was lost when shot down in flames by Flak. At the Luftwaffe's fighter airfields II./JG 27 had one Bf 109 destroyed and 11 damaged by bombing, some aircraft of I.Gruppe also being damaged. 83ª and 95ª Squadriglie of 18° Gruppo moved to Abu Haggag.

British Claims

601 Sqn	Plt Off A.R.Boyle	Spitfire Vb BR118	Me 210		1020-1110
601 Sqn	Sgt A.A.Toller	Spitfire Vb AB468			
1 SAAF Sqn	Lt J.M.Faure	Hurricane II ..282 'F'	2 Ju 87s	El Imayid station	1505
1 SAAF Sqn	Lt S.A.Finney	Hurricane II ..893 'X'	Ju 87	El Imayid station	1505
1 SAAF Sqn	Lt J.H.Gaynor	Hurricane II Z2503 'E'	Ju 87	El Imayid station	1505
1 SAAF Sqn	Capt P.C.R.Metelerkamp	Hurricane IIb Z5348 'M'	Ju 87	El Imayid station	1505
1 SAAF Sqn	Capt P.C.R.Metelerkamp	Hurricane IIb Z5348 'M'	Ju 87 Damaged	El Imayid station	1505
1 SAAF Sqn	2/Lt R.G.Baker	Hurricane IIb BG672 'P'	Ju87	El Imayid station	1505
1 SAAF Sqn	Lt L.R.S.Waugh	Hurricane IIb BG764 'W'	Bf 109	El Imayid station	1505
127 Sqn	Flt Lt R.L.Mannix	Hurricane IIb BP298 X	Bf 109 Damaged		1505

British Casualties

112 Sqn	Kittyhawk I ET510 force-landed, AA?; Flt Lt G.W.Garton
112 Sqn	Kittyhawk I AK866 'Z' force-landed, AA?; Sgt C.D.Young
4 SAAF Sqn	Kittyhawk I AK924 shot down by Bf 109s near El Alamein at 0905 escorting Bostons; Lt G.D.M.McKenzie KiA
33 Sqn	Hurricane IIc HL704 shot down by Bf 109 1815-1935; Sgt P.Menzies safe
127 Sqn	Hurricane BP292 left 1420, damaged by Bf 109 Cat II, SE Daba, landed at base 1540; Lt H.C.Warren slt WiA
1 SAAF Sqn	Hurricane Z5348 'M' shot down and force-landed 1m S El Imayid station; Capt P.C.R.Metelerkamp safe
1 SAAF Sqn	Hurricane BG764 'W' damaged Cat II by Bf 109s; Lt L.R.S.Waugh
1 SAAF Sqn	Hurricane Z5335 'U' shot down by ground fire S El Daba; Lt F.J.Schofield PoW
1 SAAF Sqn	Hurricane BG672 'P' shot down by Bf 109 after shooting down Ju 87; 2/Lt R.G.Baker PoW, but died 27 July
1 SAAF Sqn	Hurricane BG751 'D' damaged by Flak; Lt C.R.Sinclair
24 SAAF Sqn	Boston III Z2223 off 2055 to attack LG.20 and LG.104. Damaged by heavy Flak and crashed 2310 near LG.99; Lt L.A.Nichols and three KiA (night)

US Casualties

344th/98th BG	B-24D 41-11814 'Pink Elephant' shot down, 2/Lt Robert G. McCormick and crew KiA

German Claims

8./JG 27	Uffz Viktor Gruber	P-40	SE El Alamein	0810
4./JG 27	Fw Heinrich Steis	P-40	ESE Deir el Taga	0835
4./JG 27	Fw Heinrich Steis	P-40	ESE El Alamein	1420
8./JG 53	Obfw Alfred Seidl	P-40	30km SW El Alamein	1420

8./JG 27	Obfw Alfred Seidl	P-40 o.Zg. n.b.	SW El Alamein	
4./JG 27	Obfw Karl-Heinz Bendert	Spitfire	S El Alamein	1810
4./JG 27	Oblt Ferdinand Vögl	Spitfire	SW El Alamein	1812
4./JG 27	Fw Franz Stigler	Spitfire	E El Alamein	1815

German Casualties

1.(F)/121	Ju 88D-5 WNr 1701 7A+BH shot down by Spitfires El Alamein; Oblt Heinrich Osbahr and three PoW
II./St G 3	Ju87 D-1 WNr 2470, shot-up by Hurricanes and badly damaged (90%), force-landed Daba airfield
II./St G 3	Ju87 D-1 WNr 2591 crash-landed at Qasaba, 70% damaged

Friday, 24 July 1942

The British offensive had now ground to a temporary halt, but dawn heralded another day of heavy fighting in the air. At 0830 six Bf 109s of III./JG 27 flew a Freie Jagd, during which Lt Schöfböck sighted two Bristol Bombays of 216 Squadron about to land at a temporary airfield at Deir el Mon. He attacked both, forcing them to carry out hasty emergency landings, one with an engine shot-up and stopped, and the other with a badly damaged rudder. He then undertook a second attack, strafing them on the ground and destroying both. On return to base, however, he was informed that he had destroyed two Red Cross aircraft and as a result his claim was disallowed. Schöfböck protested that he had seen roundels, not red crosses, on the fuselage, and in fact he was quite correct, the Bombays being employed on a transport mission. These were the first losses 216 Squadron had suffered to aircraft carrying out transport duties.

At 0940 the Kittyhawks of 239 Wing together with Kittyhawks and Tomahawks of 233 Wing, took off to escort 18 Bostons and 12 Baltimores to attack LGs 20 and 104 at Qotaifiya, many of the Kittyhawks also carrying bombs on this occasion. Seven Bf 109s of II./JG 27, escorting a reconnaissance Bf 110 of 4.(H)/12, ran into the formation immediately after take-off, and were joined by two aircraft of I.Gruppe which were scrambled. The Bf 110 was carrying Oblt Josef Hofbauer, the Nachtrichtenoffizier of II./JG 27. This ground officer had a strong desire to gain flying experience and combat hours in order to qualify for a decoration, so Hptm Rödel permitted him to fly occasionally with the reconnaissance pilots, and this was his 13th such flight. Despite the large escort, the aircraft was shot down by three Curtiss fighters; although seriously wounded, Hofbauer was able to bale out, but Fw Birckner, the pilot, was killed and the observer, Oblt Brauner, died two days later. Hofbauer reported that the Curtisses circled round his parachute as it floated down and waved to him.

During this combat Oblt Sinner and Uffz Schneider each claimed one fighter. Sqn Ldr Drake of 112 Squadron claimed a Bf 110 and Plt Off Loree a Ju 88, which may have been the 110 incorrectly identified, but Plt Offs Wright and Johnson were attacked by three Bf 109s, the latter being shot down and crash-landing, Wright claiming a Bf 109 shot down. Two of 5 SAAF Squadron's Tomahawks also failed to return.12 SAAF Squadron lost one Boston to Flak during this raid. On the ground one Bf 109 was totally destroyed by a direct bomb hit – it was Oblt Marseille's famous 'Yellow 14'.

Three Hurricane squadrons were involved in combats during the afternoon. 33 Squadron had moved to LG.172 from where a patrol was carried out over El Alamein. Here two pilots were shot down by Bf 109s and were believed to have been killed. 213 Squadron had also arrived at LG.172 from LG.154, its aircraft being scrambled from here at 1500. This unit too was jumped by two Bf 109s, the fire from one of which hit the port wing magazine of Plt Off McKay's aircraft. This Messerschmitt pilot then continued to attack him until he force-landed; he returned next day.

At 1430 Flt Lt C.S.B.Montagu, DFC, of 208 Squadron had taken off in a Hurricane PR I, escorted by a Mark II, to carry out a photo-reconnaissance sortie. Near El Imayid station, when diving for home with his mission completed, he was attacked by three Bf 109s and shot down. Six Bf 109s of III./JG 53 had taken off on a Freie Jagd at 1445, Uffz Zielke claiming a fighter near El Hammam at 1515 which was probably the 213 Squadron aircraft. Five minutes later seven fighters of III./JG 27 took off on a similar mission, encountering a formation of 20 Allied fighters, Lt Schöfböck and Obfw Rosenberg claiming one each; ten minutes later Rosenberg claimed a second. It seems likely that their first two claims related to the 33 Squadron aircraft and the final claim to the 208 Squadron aircraft.

Soon after 1730 Hurricanes of 80 Squadron provided top cover to others of 238 Squadron on an evening patrol. Eight Messerschmitts of II./JG 27 were scrambled to intercept this formation, bouncing the top cover. Oblt Sinner shot down Sgt Moore, one of the attached 92 Squadron pilots, who baled out, badly wounded, over Deir el Raghil; he died of his wounds two days later. Six Kittyhawks were then scrambled on an interception patrol at 1850 by 260 Squadron, six Bf 109s and MC.202s being seen. On the return flight the squadron was jumped by MC.202s of 10° Gruppo and one Kittyhawk was shot down, the pilot returning later, reporting his belief that he had been shot down by a Bf 109. However, no Luftwaffe claims were made at this time, but three P-40s were claimed as probables by Italian pilots, one of them Cap Franco Lucchini. He had led a first sortie of 14 MC.202s of 10° Gruppo in the morning, between 0845-1010, encountering about 20 fighters but emerging from the fight without claims or losses. On the second mission, 1730-1840, 21 MC.202s of both Gruppi of 4° Stormo, returning from an uneventful free sweep over El Alamein, intercepted 12 P-40s covered by 12 Spitfires. Lucchini, Veronesi and an unidentified pilot of 9° Gruppo claimed a P-40 probable apiece.

Another move on this date had seen 7 SAAF Squadron arrive at LG.173.

British Claims

112 Sqn	Sqn Ldr B.Drake	Kittyhawk I ET524	Bf 110	LGs 20 and 104	0945-1115
112 Sqn	Plt Off J.E.Loree	Kittyhawk I AK788	Ju 88	LGs 20 and 104	0945-1115
112 Sqn	Plt Off J.G.Wright	Kittyhawk I AK995	Bf 109F	LGs 20 and 104	0945-1115
601 Sqn	Flt Lt M.R.B.Ingram	Spitfire V BR132 'W'	Ju 88	10m off El Alamein	1700
80/92 Sqn	Plt Off W.L.Chisholm	Hurricane IIc BN359 'T'	Bf 109 Probable	15-20m E battle line	1915
2 SAAF	Lt H.S.McMaster	Kittyhawk I ET1019 'Q'	Bf 109F Damaged	El Alamein line	1915

British Casualties

112 Sqn	Kittyhawk I AK603 left 0945 shot down by Bf 109 crash-landed 15m SE LG.20; Plt Off W.A.J.Johnson PoW
260 Sqn	Kittyhawk I ET857 'W' left 1850 shot down by Bf 109s or MC.202s on interception; Sgt D.W.C.England safe
5 SAAF Sqn	Tomahawk IIb AK428 'R' shot down by Bf 109 on escort S Daba 1040; Lt F.L.Stevens KiA
5 SAAF Sqn	Tomahawk IIb AK547 'S' shot down by Bf 109 on escort S Daba 1040; 2/Lt B.J.Grove PoW
208 Sqn	Hurricane PR 1 P2638, left 1430, shot down near El Imayid by 3 Bf 109s; Flt Lt C.S.B.Montagu DFC KiA
33 Sqn	Hurricane IIc BP120 left 1500, shot down by Bf 109s nr El Alamein; Flt Sgt F.G.Davison KiA
33 Sqn	Hurricane IIc BN358 'H' left 1500, shot down by Bf 109s at El Alamein; Sgt J.B.Waddell, KiA
80/92 Sqn	Hurricane IIc BP241 lost E battle line 1810; Sgt A.C.Moore died of wounds 27 July
213 Sqn	Hurricane IIc BP123 left 1500, damaged by Bf 109 force-landed; Plt Off G.R.S.McKay safe
216 Sqn	Bombay L5824 forced to land and destroyed by Bf 109
216 Sqn	Bombay L5835 forced to land and destroyed by Bf 109
12 SAAF Sqn	Boston III Z2215 'C' off 0927 to attack airfields in Daba area. Damaged by Flak over LG.104 and last seen heading E under control at 30m S El Daba and one of crew seen to bale out before the aircraft crash-landed nr El Daba at 1033, but Lt W.P.Colman and three KiA

German Claims

6./JG 27	Oblt Rudolf Sinner	P-40	S Bir el Abd	0940
2.(H)/14	Fw Karl Birckner	P-40	E Bir el Abd	0940
5./JG 27	Uffz Bernd Schneider	P-40	Ain el Gazala	0946
8./JG 53	Uffz Kurt Zielke	P-40	El Hammam	1420
9./JG 27	Obfw Heinrich Rosenberg	2 Hurricanes	SSE El Alamein	1446 & 1458
7./JG 27	Lt Erich Schöfböck	P-40	SE El Alamein	1502
6./JG 27	Oblt Rudolf Sinner	Hurricane	S Deir el Raghil	1719
7./JG 27	Lt Erich Schöfböck	2 Bombays n.b.	Deir el Monas l.g.	

German Casualties

2./JG 27	Bf 109F-4 trop WNr 7382 & 7055 both 70% damaged by bombs at Qotaifiya
4./JG 27	Bf 109F-4 trop WNr 10034 40% damaged, WNr 8782 20% damaged, WNr 8432 100% all by bombs on ground at Qotaifiya
4.(H)/12	Bf 110F-2 WNr 5007 BG+GI shot down by P-40 E Bir el Abd; three baled out; Fw Karl Birckner (P), Lt Josef Hofbauer PoWs; Oblt Karl Brauner KiA

Italian Claims

84ª Sq, 10°Gr, 4°St CT	Cap Franco Lucchini	MC.202 MM 7896	P-40 Probable	El Alamein	1730-1840
84ª Sq, 10°Gr, 4°St CT	Serg Magg Mario Veronesi	MC.202 MM 7789	P-40 Probable	El Alamein	1730-1840
9°Gr, 4°St CT	unidentified	MC.202	P-40 Probable	El Alamein	1730-1840

Italian Casualties

74ª Sq, 23°Gr, 3°St CT	MC.202 MM 8377 '74-6' damaged on landing, Ten Giorgio Solaroli safe

Saturday, 25 July 1942

Early this morning eight Kittyhawks of 450 Squadron carried out an armed reconnaissance from which Sgt O'Neil failed to return; he arrived back on foot later, having been shot down by an MC.202 over the El Alamein area. Eleven Macchis of 23° Gruppo led by Cap Giorgio Tugnoli had taken off at 0720 for a free sweep south of El Alamein. Something over an hour later a large formation of hostile aircraft was engaged and three P-40s were claimed shot down, with a fourth claimed as a probable, plus others believed to have been damaged.

During the day Flt Lt Ingram of 601 Squadron claimed a Ju 88 shot down, whereas in the evening during a late Freie Jagd by 11 Bf 109s of I./JG 27, Hptm Homuth reported attacking a Hurricane west of El Daba which apparently crashed in Axis territory near his airfield. Although the identity of the aircraft has not been discovered, his report indicates that it was probably a TacR aircraft.

British Claims					
601 Sqn	Flt Lt M.R.B.Ingram	Spitfire Vb BR245 'X'	Ju 88 Damaged	W Ghazal	1215
British Casualties					
450 Sqn	Kittyhawk I shot down by MC.202 in El Alamein area; Sgt O'Neil returned on foot				
260 Sqn	Kittyhawk I left 0845, damaged by fighters, landed safely				
M.E.	Hurricane Z5606 SOC desert (30°15'-21°40') probably shot down by Bf 109 on TacR sortie				
German Claims					
Stab I./JG 27	Hptm Gerhard Homuth		Hurricane	W El Daba	1745
German Casualties					
3./JG 27	Bf 109F-4 trop WNr 10137 Yellow 14 destroyed by bombs at Turbiya				
Italian Claims					
70ª Sq, 23°Gr, 3°St CT	Cap Claudio Solaro	MC.202	P-40 Probable	S El Alamein	0820
74ª Sq, 23°Gr, 3°St CT	Cap Giorgio Tugnoli	MC.202	P-40	S El Alamein	0820
74ª Sq, 23°Gr, 3°St CT	Ten Giorgio Solaroli	MC.202	P-40	S El Alamein	0820
74ª Sq, 23°Gr, 3°St CT	Serg Magg Mario Mantelli	MC.202	P-40	S El Alamein	0820

Sunday, 26 July 1942

Auchinleck's forces now began a new counter-attack, this time inflicting heavy losses on the Italian divisions in the central and southern parts of the line. Though this attack improved the general position for 8th Army, it still failed to make a breakthrough. At this point the Luftwaffe recorded the losses sustained by its fighter forces in terms of aircraft for the period since the Gazala offensive had commenced on 26 May to the current date – 26 July. These were as follows:

Damaged 60-100% 66 Bf 109s to enemy action, 26 to other causes

Damaged 10-60% 25 Bf 109s to enemy action, 18 to other causes

Unfortunately, these figures do not specify how many of the 91 aircraft caused by Allied action, crashed totally, crash-landed only slightly damaged, etc, but does give a useful overall idea of the extent of losses. During the same period it is interesting to note, that WDAF units made 95 claims for Bf 109s which were allowed as confirmed claims, but not including probables or damaged.

British Casualties				
213 Sqn	Hurricane BP231 shot down by Bf 109s over LG.172			
German Claims				
1./NJG 2	Oblt Heinz-Horst Hissbach	Wellington	SW Crete	2250

Monday, 27 July 1942

After the quiet of the previous two days, this proved once more to be one of intense aerial activity. This began at 0625 when nine Kittyhawks of 112 Squadron took off on a mission. They were back within 20 minutes, minus two pilots, both of whom had crash-landed. One of them, Plt Off Cuddon, was later flown back to base in a Lysander. At 1000 ten Kittyhawks of 3 RAAF Squadron carried out a reconnaissance north-west of Mukheisin and bombed MT there. Sgt Cashmore became separated from the squadron and was attacked by two Bf 109s, one of which he claimed to have probably destroyed. At 1030 four Bf 109s of II./JG 27 scrambled, intercepting two Hurricanes of 208 Squadron carrying out a TacR sortie. Sqn Ldr J.W.Stewart, DFC, was weaving behind 2/Lt Lambon as his escort, but Stewart was attacked by two Messerschmitts at 1100, Fw Torfer's fire hitting his aircraft, the tail unit of which burst into flames. Obviously considering that the Hurricane was finished, Torfer returned to base, claiming a victory. However, the flames went out, leaving the aircraft severely damaged, but nonetheless Stewart was able to carry out a crash-landing from which he escaped unharmed.

33 Squadron took off at 1310, followed 15 minutes later by ten more Hurricanes of 213 Squadron which were scrambled after a raid, not realizing that five Bf 109s were still sitting overhead. B Flight was attacked, four aircraft being shot down; three pilots were killed, two of them being members of 134 Squadron on attachment to 213. Returning to base after the mission, 33 Squadron was then also jumped, one more Hurricane being shot down and a second badly shot-up. Twelve Bf 109s from I./JG 27 had taken off to escort Ju 87s at 1235, claiming five Hurricanes from 20 reportedly encountered, three of these being credited to Hptm Homuth. It was subsequently reported that 213 Squadron did not receive any warning of the presence of the Messerschmitts as these, having completed their escort duties, had followed 33 Squadron as this unit took off, not therefore being plotted on the radar as hostiles as a result. It therefore seems likely that having followed 33 in, they first attacked 213, then going for their original quarries as these were about to land. As a result of this combat it was decided that the Hurricanes were based too near the front line, 33 moving back to LG.92 and 213 to LG.154.

During the morning ten Hurricanes of 1 SAAF Squadron were scrambled, being attacked by four Bf 109s, one of the South African aircraft being badly damaged. In the evening eight aircraft from this unit covered 80 Squadron over the line, engaging nine /twelve Bf 109s of I./JG 27 which had taken off on a Freie Jagd at 1750. These attacked the rear aircraft of 1 SAAF and fierce fighting followed for the next ten minutes, the engagement becoming very confused. While manoeuvring after one Messerschmitt, Plt Off Simmons found himself behind another which was on the tail of a Hurricane, and he opened fire, the Messerschmitt at once carrying out a wing-over, whereupon he lost sight of it. Just before attacking, he saw a flash at the wing root of the Hurricane being attacked by the 109, and since Lt Hope failed to return it seems that this was his aircraft. On return to base Lt Faure reported that he had seen the aircraft fired on by Simmons, flame and crash, so the latter was credited with a Bf 109 confirmed. No Luftwaffe loss was reported, Lt Stahlschmidt claiming one Hurricane, and it seems clear that it was his aircraft that Simmons had attacked just as the German pilot was in the process of shooting down Hope. Faure, in fact, had seen the latter's aircraft falling to the ground, shrouded in flames. This is an example of how over-claiming in the heat of a complex combat can all too easily happen.

80 Squadron reported meeting 30 Ju 87s and escorting Bf 109s near Deir el Dhib, the attached 92 Squadron pilots doing all the claiming for a Ju 87 and a Bf 109, with one of each also damaged. These victories were nonetheless credited to the parent unit (80), although also to the individual pilots – but not to 92 Squadron. This brought 80 Squadron's claims total to 199½ .

I./JG 27 now encountered six Kittyhawks of 3 RAAF Squadron providing cover for others of 450 Squadron in the Deir el Dhib area where the latter unit was bombing. Plt Off Forsyth's aircraft of 450 Squadron was seen to spin and hit the ground after attacks by Bf 109s, bursting into flames on impact. Two of the 3 RAAF Squadron pilots claimed Messerschmitts damaged, but claims for two P-40s were made by I./JG 27, one of them being Lt Stahlschmidt's third of the day.

British Claims

3 RAAF Sqn	Sgt J.F.H.Cashmore	Kittyhawk I ET875 'S'	Bf 109 Probable	Mukheisin area	1035
80/92 Sqn	Flt Lt J.M.Morgan	Hurricane IIc BN126 'P'	Bf 109F	15m W El Alamein	1250-1310
80/92 Sqn	Plt Off C.J.Samouelle	Hurricane IIc BN389 'C'	Ju 87 Damaged	15m W El Alamein	1250-1310
80/92 Sqn	Sqn Ldr J.H.Wedgwood	Hurricane IIc BP379 'E'	Ju 87	15m W El Alamein	1250-1310
80/92 Sqn	Sqn Ldr J.H.Wedgwood	Hurricane IIc BP379 'E'	Bf 109F Damaged	15m W El Alamein	1250-1310
1 SAAF Sqn	Plt Off R.G.Simmons	Hurricane II ..361 'M'	Bf 109F	El Alamein line	1830
3 RAAF Sqn	Sgt J.Churchill	Kittyhawk I AK862 'B'	Bf 109 Damaged	Deir el Dhib area	1855
3 RAAF Sqn	Sgt E.K.Kildey	Kittyhawk I ET840 'P'	Bf 109 Damaged	Deir el Dhib area	1855
450 Sqn	Plt Off F.R.Schaaf	Kittyhawk I AK636	Bf 109 Damaged	Deir el Dhib area	1855

British Casualties

112 Sqn	Kittyhawk I ET527 'J' left 0645, oil pressure failure, force-landed; Plt Off B.A.F.Cuddon safe
112 Sqn	Kittyhawk I ET865 'K' left 1640, oil pressure failure, force-landed; Sgt D.F.Greaves safe
450 Sqn	Kittyhawk I AK805 shot down by 2 Bf 109s near Deir el Dhib at about 1900; Plt Off T.J.Forsyth KiA
33 Sqn	Hurricane IIc BP199 'C' left 1325, shot down by Bf 109s nr El Alamein; Sgt J. D.Leicester KiA

33 Sqn	Hurricane IIc BN342 left 1325, badly damaged by Bf 109 over LG.172; Plt Off D.W.McLarty safe
208 Sqn	Hurricane II Z5279 left 1040, shot down at 1100, and crash-landed in desert; Sqn Ldr J.W.Stewart DFC safe
213 Sqn	Hurricane IIc BN539 left 1325, shot down by Bf 109s over LG.172; Sgt J.D.Newick KiA
213 Sqn	Hurricane IIc BP231 left 1325, shot down by Bf 109s over LG.172; Plt Off T.A.McCann KiA
213 Sqn	Hurricane IIc BP197 left 1325, shot down by Bf 109s over LG.172; Flt Sgt R.Griffiths KiA
213 Sqn	Hurricane IIc BN180 left 1325, shot down; Wt Off R.J.Wallace baled out safe
1 SAAF Sqn	Hurricane Z5606 'E' left 1700, shot down by Bf 109 at 1830; Lt S.M.Hope KiA
1 SAAF Sqn	Hurricane left 0840, badly damaged by Bf 109 at 0910; Lt L.M.Marshall safe

German Claims

4./JG 27	Fw Josef Torfer	Hurricane	SW El Alamein	1000
Stab I./JG 27	Hptm Gerhard Homuth	Hurricane	SE El Hammam	1225
2./JG 27	Lt Hans-Arnold Stahlschmidt	Hurricane	S El Hammam	1226
3./JG 27	Fw Karlheinz Berben	Hurricane	5km SW El Hammam	1226
Stab I./JG 27	Hptm Gerhard Homuth	2 Hurricanes	SE El Hammam	1227 & 1228
2./JG 27	Lt Hans-Arnold Stahlschmidt	Hurricane	SW El Alamein	1730
2./JG 27	Lt hans-Arnold Stahlschmidt	P-40	W El Alamein	1742
2./JG 27	Oblt Josef Unterberger	P-40	15km S El Alamein	1745

German Casualties

StG 3	Ju 87 D-3s WNr 2612 60% damaged, WNr 2618 60%, Ju 87E-3 WNr 2473 50%, Ju 87 R-2s WNr 5686 100%, WNr 6030 100%, Ju 87R-4s WNr 6270 85%, WNr 6235 55%, WNr 6237 S7+JH 40%, Ju 87D-1s WNr 2478 90%, WNr 2576 60%, Ju 87D-3 WNr 2367 60%, El Alamein by British raiders at Qasaba
Wüstenotstaffel	Fi 156C-3 WNr 5671 shot down by AA, crashed nr Garaet el Markaz, Uffz Karl Horst PoW

Tuesday, 28 July 1942

With the end of the British counter-offensive for the time being, there was once again a settling down, a quieter period thus ensuing during which both sides rested and re-equipped. Nine Bf 109s of II./JG 27 escorted Ju 88s of I./LG 1 over Bir el Kaha, one of the bombers being seen to crash into the sea. Six Allied bombers attacked Qasaba, where one of JG 53's Messerschmitts was damaged on the ground. In the evening two of 208 Squadron's Hurricane IIas took off on a TacR, Plt Off Doak weaving behind Plt Off Clark as escort. Six Bf 109s of II./JG 27 had taken off at 1845 on a Freie Jagd, and an hour later attacked the pair. Doak saw two Messerschmitts coming and tried to warn Clark, but his R/T failed to operate, Clark being shot down by Oblt Sinner, his aircraft crashing near El Imayid station where it blew up.

Ten Egeo Broccolino of 236ª Squadriglia, 158° Gruppo, 50° Stormo Assalto, in front of his CR.42 at Sorman.

The day also saw the arrival of the first two MC.202s to be assigned to 13° Gruppo CT by 4° Stormo. A third would arrive within a few days. 6 Squadron now moved to LG.89 where it was joined by 7 SAAF Squadron to undertake a special role administered by 243 Wing which involved anti-tank sweeps, the South African pilots assisting the gun-armed tank-busters using Jefferis bombs.

British Casualties

208 Sqn	Hurricane II Z2328 shot down El Imayid at c1900; Plt Off K.Clark KiA

German Claims

6./JG 27	Oblt Rudolf Sinner	Hurricane	3km E Deir el Taga	1925

German Casualties

9./JG 53	Bf 109F-4Z WNr 7649 damaged 20% on ground by bombs at Qasaba
II./StG 3	Ju 87D-3 WNr 2391 20% and Ju 87D-1 WNr 2075 15% damaged by strafing at Qasaba

Wednesday, 29 July 1942

On this date 40 SAAF Squadron was withdrawn from operations, proceeding to LG.100 at Wadi Natrun. 6 Squadron left 239 Wing to join 7 SAAF Wing.

British Casualties

3 RAAF Sqn	Kittyhawk I ET576 left 0955 hit by Flak strafing Qattara area; crash-landed; Sgt J.Donald safe

Thursday, 30 July 1942

Tomahawks of 5 SAAF Squadron carried out a patrol over El Alamein soon after midday, but when so involved, the engine of Lt Bidwell's aircraft caught fire and he had to bale out. Six Kittyhawks of 260 Squadron then flew an interception patrol at 1840 as top cover for two Hurricanes returning from a sortie. Two Bf 109s attacked, causing one Kittyhawk to spin and recover. On the return flight an aircraft was seen to drop behind and this failed to return, the pilot crashing and being slightly injured.

German Casualties

I./NJG 2	Ju 88 C-6 WNr 36006 R4+DH destroyed by artillery fire at Qasaba

Friday, 31 July 1942

At 0740 two Bf 109s of III./JG 53 were scrambled, intercepting a Wellington near Mersa Matruh which was shot down by Lt Munzert. This was an aircraft despatched by 1 OADU for service in the Middle East. Its Australian crew, all members of 458 Squadron, had departed Gibraltar for Luqa Malta.

Plt Off H.S.W. 'Bill' Fordyce and his crew are listed in the records as being attached to 43 Group, however they were a 458 Sqn crew, making their second delivery trip to Egypt. The navigator made an error and brought them in over Daba instead of the Delta, early in the morning. Two Bf 109s intercepted them and they were shot down. Sgt G.W.S.Crompton RAAF, the tail gunner was severely wounded, but fired back until a further attack killed him. Fordyce was injured and later flown to Crete. The other survivors were transported to Europe by ship, presumably the *Nino Bixio* which was sunk by HMS *Turbolent*, and many prisoners lost their lives. Fordyce ended up in Stalag Luft III, where his peacetime profession of commercial artist was put to good use. He drew the original plans for the 'Great Escape' tunnels, and kept them in his possession postwar, until both the RAF Museum and the Australian War Memorial were made aware of the existence of such significant drawings.

At 0915 12 MC.202s of 23° Gruppo, led by Cap Giorgio Tugnoli, began a free sweep over the lines. Over Bir el Mukheisin a formation of about 20 WDAF fighters was intercepted and engaged, five P-40s being claimed shot down plus two probables, with many others believed to have been damaged. One Macchi returned slightly damaged. Their opponents appear to have been aircraft of 250 Squadron, two pilots from which shared in claiming damage to one Macchi; 260 Squadron also seem to have been involved, losing one Kittyhawk to the Italian fighters. The only other WDAF casualty on this date related to one of 24 SAAF Squadron's Bostons which was shot down by heavy Flak during the early hours of the morning, with the loss of the crew.

73 Squadron now moved to Shandur in the Delta to continue so far fruitless attempts to intercept high-flying reconnaissance Ju 86Ps (see Chapter Ten). GC III/2, as it was now termed (the Alsace fighter group) had also withdrawn to Alexandria after the Axis forces had been held. During the latter part of the month the Luftwaffe had received the first Bf 109Gs to arrive in Africa, whereas in WDAF 223 Squadron had begun being issued with a new variant of the Baltimore, the Mark III, which had a power-operated Boulton-Paul dorsal turret, armed with a pair of .303in Browning machine guns. During the last days of the month 4° Stormo received from Italy ten new pilots as reinforcements.

British Claims

250 Sqn	Wt Off L.G.Edwards	Kittyhawk I AK779 'Z'	MC.202 Damaged	4m SW El Mreir	1100-1130
250 Sqn	Flt Lt N.P.W.Hancock	Kittyhawk I ET525 'Y'			

British Casualties

1 OADU	Wellington HX580 shot down by Bf 109 at Mersa Matruh; Plt Off H.S.W.Fordyce and three PoW, one KiA
260 Sqn	Kittyhawk I AK671 left 1840, shot down by MC.202 El Alamein; Plt Off N.E.McKee WiA
24 SAAF Sqn	Boston III Z2163 'D' off 2343 to attack LG.13. Hit by heavy Flak, crashed in flames 18km SE LG.99 at 0048; Lt A.E.Corby and three KiA

250 Sqn	Kittyhawk I AK799 'Z' damaged Cat I by MC.202 near Daba, 1130; Wt Off L.G.Edwards safe
250 Sqn	Kittyhawk I AK811 'V' damaged Cat I by MC.202 near Daba, 1130; Plt Off D.W.M.Rogerson

German Claims

9./JG 53	Lt Hermann Munzert	Wellington	Mersa Matruh	0644

Italian Claims

70ª Sq, 23°Gr, 3°St CT	Cap Claudio Solaro	MC.202	P-40	Bir el Mukheisin	0915-1030
70ª Sq, 23°Gr, 3°St CT	Serg Magg Celso Zemella	MC.202	P-40	Bir el Mukheisin	0915-1030
74ª Sq, 23°Gr, 3°St CT	Cap Giorgio Tugnoli	MC.202	P-40	Bir el Mukheisin	0915-1030
74ª Sq, 23°Gr, 3°St CT	Cap Giorgio Tugnoli	MC.202	P-40 Probable	Bir el Mukheisin	0915-1030
74ª Sq, 23°Gr, 3°St CT	Serg Magg Emilio Stefani	MC.202	P-40	Bir el Mukheisin	0915-1030
74ª Sq, 23°Gr, 3°St CT	Serg Magg Mario Mantelli	MC.202	P-40	Bir el Mukheisin	0915-1030
74ª Sq, 23°Gr, 3°St CT	S.Ten Carlo Brigante-Colonna	MC.202 MM 8375	P-40 Probable	Bir el Mukheisin	0915-1030

Italian Casualties

74ª Sq, 23°Gr, 3°St CT	MC.202 MM 8375, damaged in combat, S.Ten Carlo Brigante-Colonna safe

Saturday, 1 August 1942

During the early hours, 14 Squadron lost a Blenheim to Flak during a night raid. This was to be the unit's final Blenheim casualty, for before the month was out it would be withdrawn to be re-equipped with more modern aircraft (see Chapter Ten).

Six Bf 109s of III./JG 53 scrambled twice during the day to intercept fighter-bombers, but the resulting combats did not bring any claims or losses. At 1645, however, Hurricanes of 80 Squadron, flown by attached 92 Squadron pilots, provided top cover to 127 Squadron. They suffered a bounce by three Messerschmitts of I./JG 27 which had been briefed to intercept 20 Hurricanes near El Alamein. Here Lt Stahlschmidt shot down two of the 80 Squadron aircraft. Plt Off Atkins was seen to go down in flames and was killed; Flt Sgt Reece was also shot down, dying of the wounds he suffered ten days later. Two of the Hurricane pilots claimed one Bf 109 shot down between them, but no Luftwaffe loss was recorded.

Two MC.202s of 91ª Squadriglia led by Cap Ruspoli carried out a recce mission from 1700-1815 over El Qattara depression. Some isolated motor transports were strafed.

Several changes occurred both in locations and leadership positions during the day. 601 Squadron moved its Spitfires to LG.85, while in 250 Squadron Flt Lt A.E.Marshall, DFC, DFM, ended his tour and left for the United Kingdom for a well-earned rest. He had completed two tours in North Africa, the first during the First Libyan Campaign, and had claimed 18 and one shared aerial victories, the majority of them in the desert. He was replaced by Flt Lt M.C.H.Barber. The day was also marked by the first raid to be undertaken by the US 98th Bomb Group, seven of this unit's B-24s attacking harbour facilities and a tank repair depot at Mersa Matruh (see also Chapter Four).

British Claims

80/92 Sqn	Plt Off W.L.Chisholm	Hurricane IIc BN359 'T'	Bf 109F (shared)	9m E El Alamein	1643-1810
80/92 Sqn	Plt Off I.D.Colquhoun-Thomson	Hurricane IIc BN351 'C'			

British Casualties

80/92 Sqn	Hurricane IIc BP379 shot down by Bf 109 15m E El Alamein; Plt Off R.P.Atkins (92 Sqn) KiA
80/92 Sqn	Hurricane IIc BP235 shot down by Bf 109s 15m E El Alamein; Flt Sgt M.P.Reece (92 Sqn) KiA
112 Sqn	Kittyhawk I AK744, left 0930, hit by Flak force-landed at 1055; Sgt R.C.C.Smith

German Claims

2./JG 27	Lt Hans-Arnold Stahlschmidt	2 Hurricanes	W El Alamein	1640-1645

Sunday, 2 August 1942

Two Hurricane IIs of 208 Squadron carried out a TacR mission during which the 'weaver', Plt Off Worth, was seen to bale out for no apparent reason. His parachute did not open and he was killed. Another Hurricane of 274 Squadron was reported to have been shot down by a Bf 109 off Sollum, and a Kittyhawk of 250 Squadron was shot down by Flak 70 miles south of Mersa Matruh, the pilot being captured. These aircraft may have fallen to the gunners of the Italian Trento Division which claimed two on this date.

244 Wing ORB noted a radial-engined fighter had been seen and there was concern it could be a FW190. Which it was! A small test unit, Erprobungskommando 19, had formed on 1 July at Castel Benito

to test the Bf 109 and FW 190 for their suitability for ground-attack duties. The test unit was non-operational and worked for a relatively short time until disbanded. However, its sole surviving example of the Focke-Wulf FW 190, Werke Nummer 0145614, carrying a White 1 on its fuselage sides, was discovered abandoned on the ground at Benghazi by troops advancing from El Alamein in November. It is entirely possible that one of the two original aircraft of this type supplied to the unit had been spotted in the air during the testing period. It is, perhaps, interesting to note that about a year later, in June 1943, a batch of three tropicalised Hawker Typhoons had been sent out for testing under desert conditions to Edcu. A detachment of 451 Squadron carried out these tests from LG.106, El Daba, from 13 July-20 October 1943.

On the ground the Afrika Korps panzer divisions had by now rapidly been brought back up to strength, and had some 163 tanks. However, Rommel's troops were described as too weary to re-assume the offensive yet.

British Casualties	
208 Sqn	Hurricane II Z2416 shot down on TacR E El Alamein; Plt Off P.A.Worth baled out at 50ft KiA
274 Sqn	Hurricane Z5337 shot down by Bf 109 off Sollum; details not known
250 Sqn	Kittyhawk I AK671 'D' left 0945 shot down by Flak 70m S Mersa Matruh; Plt Off R.I.Baldwin PoW
Italian Claims	
Trento Division gunners	2 aircraft

Monday, 3 August 1942

At 0815 80 and 1 SAAF Squadrons escorted a TacR Hurricane of 208 Squadron on a sortie, during which two of the South African aircraft collided, the pilot of one crash-landing, the other baling out. At evening ten Spitfires of 145 Squadron took off to patrol over the northern part of the line at 19,000 feet, followed by Hurricanes from 33 and 213 Squadrons. Eight Bf 109s of II./JG 27 were sent off on a Freie Jagd about ten minutes later, six more escorting Jabos on a raid at the same time. The German unit's pilots reported three different engagements, the first with two Spitfires, one of which was claimed by Obfw Clade, the pilot reportedly baling out. One aircraft of 145 Squadron was shot down into the sea, the pilot baling out.

The second engagement reported was with eight more Spitfires, two of which were claimed. 145 Squadron recorded meeting 12 Messerschmitts, one Spitfire being damaged as two of the British pilots claimed possible victories over two Bf 109s.(Readers should note the names of the claiming pilots from 4./JG 27 in this case for reasons which will soon become obvious.) Meanwhile, the third engagement was with a reported 24 Hurricanes, three of which were claimed, one of the pilots again being seen to bale out. 33 Squadron lost two Hurricanes, one pilot baling out and one crash-landing. An aircraft of 213 Squadron was also shot down, the pilot being killed.

Four Jabos of II./JG 27 and two of III./JG 53 bombed Hammam airfield, claiming hits on some tents. On this day 3 RAAF Squadron was rested, being released from operations for a three-week period.

British Claims					
145 Sqn	Flt Lt C.H.Saunders	Spitfire Vb BR583 'T'	Bf 109 Probable	N end line	1825-1930
145 Sqn	Sgt P.G.C.Thomas	Spitfire Vb BP986 'X'	Bf 109 Probable	N end line	1825-1930

British Casualties	
33 Sqn	Hurricane IIc BP352 slightly damaged by Bf 109 SE El Daba at 1900; Plt Off W.Friend safe
33 Sqn	Hurricane IIc BP192 shot down by Bf 109 SE El Daba at 1900; Plt Off H.Steward baled out safe
33 Sqn	Hurricane IIc BE409 'G' badly damaged by Bf 109 SE El Daba at 1900, forced to land; Sgt J.A.Kingdon WiA
213 Sqn	Hurricane IIc BP331 left 1825, spun in and crashed cause not apparent 10-15m SW Burg el Arab; Wt Off R.J.Wallace KiA
1 SAAF Sqn	Hurricane IIb BD893 'X' collided with Z5130; Lt S.A.Finney baled out
1 SAAF Sqn	Hurricane IIb Z5130 'N' collided with BD893; Lt T.A.Meek belly-landed
145 Sqn	Spitfire V BP865 left 1825, shot down by Bf 109; Plt Off A.E.Mulhall baled out (Argentinian)
145 Sqn	Spitfire V BR519 left 1825, shot down by Bf 109, damaged and crashed on landing; Sgt R.A.Cunningham safe
2 SAAF Sqn	Kittyhawk I AK714 slt damaged; Lt J.P.Kruyshaar safe

German Claims				
6./JG 27	Oblt Rudolf Sinner	2 Hurricanes	SE El Daba & Bir Ibrahim	1855 & 1900

5./JG 27	Obfw Emil Clade	Spitfire	N El Bahrein	1905
4./JG 27	Obfw Karl-Heinz Bendert	Spitfire	NW El Hammam	1912
4./JG 27	Obfw Erwin Sawallisch	Spitfire	NNW El Hammam	1915
6./JG 27	Obfw Herbert Krenz	Hurricane	NW Quabr Hanizadr	1920

Tuesday, 4 August 1942

At 0830 12 Tomahawks of 5 SAAF Squadron were provided with cover by Kittyhawks during a raid, the South Africans being attacked by two Bf 109s of 4./JG 27 which were escorting a reconnaissance Bf 110. Obfwn Bendert and Sawallisch each claimed one fighter shot down and indeed one Tomahawk was shot down, 2/Lt Johnson crash-landing, wounded in his left leg. He remained unconscious in the cockpit for three hours, but ultimately recovered, then walked for eight hours until picked up and put in hospital.

At 1325 213 Squadron patrolled over the El Alamein line as top cover to 33 Squadron, awaiting the return of a formation of Baltimores, Kittyhawks and Spitfires from a raid. Eight Bf 109s of II./JG 27, pilots including Bendert and Sawallisch again, were scrambled, this latter pair each claiming a fighter shot down near Hammam. Flt Sgt Fry of 213 Squadron was shot down, force-landing north of Hammam, the Squadron reporting that they had been bounced by MC.202s, but no Italian claims were made in the area during this day.

About two hours later three Bf 109s of III./JG 27 scrambled, attacking a reported 12 bombers and escorting fighters. Seven Kittyhawks of 260 Squadron were escorting 12 Bostons when attacked out of the sun by three Messerschmitts, one of which attacked Plt Off Gilboe when he was in a spin, causing him to bale out. 260 Squadron then recorded that the Messerschmitt which had attacked Gilboe's aircraft had been seen to be attacked itself, blowing up in mid-air. His attacker seems to have been Fw Stegmann who was credited with shooting down a P-40 but was then shot down himself, baling out to become a PoW. The only British claim at this time was made by Sgt Stewart of 145 Squadron who claimed one Messerschmitt shot down and a second damaged; he was clearly Stegmann's victor.

213 Squadron was scrambled again at 1755 and again reported being attacked by MC.202s. Sgt McKay was shot down, but survived with some burns, and Flt Sgt Gwynne's aircraft was slightly damaged. Seven Bf 109s of I./JG 27 were recorded as having become involved in a fight with three squadrons of Hurricanes, Spitfires and Kittyhawks, noting one British fighter carrying out an emergency landing, but not apparently as the result of any action by the German pilots.

33 Squadron was now also withdrawn from the forward area, moving back to Edcu, and the 92 Squadron pilots on attachment to 80 Squadron finally left that unit. The higher command expressed itself well-pleased with their performance on Hurricanes and the unit now at last received its first eight Spitfire Vs.

British Claims

80/92 Sqn	Plt Off L.G.Smith	Hurricane IIc BN291	Bf 109 Damaged	El Alamein area	0820-0945
4 SAAF Sqn	Flg Off J.L.Waddy	Kittyhawk I ET903	Bf 109 Probable	S Derna	
260 Sqn	Flt Sgt J.F.Edwards	Kittyhawk I AL140 'O'	Bf 109 Probable	SW El Alamein	1545-1655
260 Sqn	Sgt W.R.Cundy	Kittyhawk I ET861 'V'	Bf 109 Probable	SW El Alamein	1545-1655
145 Sqn	Sgt A.H.M.Stewart	Spitfire Vb ..201 'N'	Bf 109	Daba-El Alamein	1755-1905
145 Sqn	Sgt A.H.M.Stewart	Spitfire Vb ..201 'N'	Bf 109 Damaged	Daba-El Alamein	1755-1905

British Casualties

5 SAAF Sqn	Tomahawk IIa AK429 shot down by Bf 109 10m W El Alamein 0900 a/c Cat II; 2/Lt.E.H.Johnson crash-landed WiA
213 Sqn	Hurricane IIc BN117 left 1325, shot down by MC.202 N Hammam, crash-landed; Flt Sgt S.R.Fry
213 Sqn	Hurricane IIc BP338 left 1755 shot down apparently by MC.202 when on escort; Sgt R.J.McKay, suffered burns,baled out
213 Sqn	Hurricane IIc BN137 left 1755, slt damaged by MC.202; Flt Sgt W.D.Gwynne safe
208 Sqn	Hurricane II BG691 left 1235, damaged by Flak Cat II, landed 1330; Plt Off S.H.Kevill-Davies safe
238 Sqn	Hurricane II left 1620 crash-landed; Sgt Wise
260 Sqn	Kittyhawk I AK891 'F' left 1545, shot down by Bf 109 10m S El Alamein; Plt Off N.E.Gilboe baled out safe

German Claims

4./JG 27	Obfw Erwin Sawallisch	P-40	SE El Alamein	0808
4./JG 27	Obfw Karl-Heinz Bendert	P-40	SE El Alamein	0810
4./JG 27	Obfw Erwin Sawallisch	Spitfire	NW El Hammam	1328
4./JG 27	Obfw Karl-Heinz Bendert	Spitfire	NW El Hammam	1330
9./JG 27	Fw Wilhelm Stegmann	P-40	SE El Alamein	1427

German Casualties

9./JG 27	Bf 109F-4 trop WNr 7015 Black 6 shot down by Spitfires 15-20km SE El Alamein; Fw Wilhelm Stegmann baled and PoW

Italian Casualties

93ª Sq, 8°Gr, 2°St CT	MC.200 MM 8140 destroyed, MM 5918, 5288, 6696 damaged by bombs at Martuba
91ª Sq, 10°Gr, 4°St CT	MC.202 MM 7877 '91-4' damaged

Wednesday, 5 August 1942

1 SAAF Squadron took off at 1005 as top cover to 127 Squadron, followed 50 minutes later by 80 Squadron which provided top cover for the whole formation. Eight Bf 109s attacked the latter unit which lost one aircraft which crash-landed; Sgt Keeping was badly wounded and died later in the 18th Field Hospital. Plt Off Hill attacked one fighter, but this turned on him and he was shot down also, carrying out a force-landing. Sgt House was cut off from the squadron and forced out over the sea by four fighters, but managed to return safely, claiming one shot down and one damaged. The South Africans reported that near the end of the patrol a lone MC.202 dived on the squadron and this was claimed to have been damaged. It seems that there was some confusion during this engagement as to whether the Axis fighters were Messerschmitts or Macchis – or both. Twelve MC.202s of 10° Gruppo, led by Cap Lucchini and Cap Piccolomini had flown a free sweep over the El Hammam area at around this time, claiming four P-40s shot down and a fifth damaged. Meantime, two Bf 109s of 4./JG 27 had scrambled to intercept 12 bombers and 20 fighters near Alam el Halfa, Obfw Bendert claiming one fighter shot down.

Finally, at 1804 six Jabo Bf 109Es of III./JG 27 and III./JG 53, attacked the railway station at Burg el Arab, escorted by 26 fighters from all four Gruppen. However, the bombing was reported as being very inaccurate. At this stage 145 Squadron was withdrawn to Edcu for a rest and to assist in attempts to intercept high altitude reconnaissance Ju 86Rs (see Chapter Ten). 601 Squadron moved to LG.219 and 213 Squadron also moved back to the rear area for a rest on this date. The day was also marked for 4 SAAF by the first carriage of bombs by three of the unit's Kittyhawks.

British Claims

1 SAAF Sqn	Lt B.Haynes	Hurricane II BP350 'Z'	MC.202 Damaged	El Alamein line, El Imayid	1110
80 Sqn	Sgt E.Burke	Hurricane IIc BP340 'D'	Bf 109 Probable	El Alamein area	1054-1145
80 Sqn	Sgt C.W.House	Hurricane IIc BE350	Bf 109	El Alamein area	1054-1145
80 Sqn	Sgt C.W.House	Hurricane IIc BE350	Bf 109 Damaged	El Alamein area	1054-1145
80 Sqn	Sgt G.T.Pratley	Hurricane IIc BE482	2 Bf 109s Damaged	El Alamein area	1054-1145

British Casualties

260 Sqn	Kittyhawk I badly damaged by MC.202, El Alamein; Plt Off E.G.Aitchison safe
80 Sqn	Hurricane IIc BN870 shot down by Bf 109s or MC.202s nr El Alamein; Plt Off E.Hill safe
80 Sqn	Hurricane IIc BP187 shot down by Bf 109s or MC.202s nr El Alamein 1054-1145; Sgt P.D.Keeping KiA
80 Sqn	Hurricane IIc BE359 damaged Cat I in wing by MC 202 off El Alamein 1054-1145; Sgt C.W.House

German Claims

4./JG 27	Obfw Karl-Heinz Bendert	P-40	Alam el Halfa	1008

Italian Claims

84ª Sq, 10°Gr, 4°St CT	Cap Franco Lucchini	MC.202 MM 7905	P-40	El Alamein-Amiriya	0940-1120
84ª Sq, 10°Gr, 4°St CT	Ten Paolo Berti	MC.202 MM 7803	P-40	El Alamein-Amiriya	0940-1120
84ª Sq, 10°Gr, 4°St CT	Ten Luigi Giannella	MC.202 MM 7815	P-40 Probable	El Alamein-Amiriya	0940-1120
90ª Sq, 10°Gr, 4°St CT	Cap Ranieri Piccolomini	MC.202	P-40	El Alamein-Amiriya	0940-1120
90ª Sq, 10°Gr, 4°St CT	Serg Magg Natale Molteni	MC.202			
84ª Sq, 10°Gr, 4°St CT	Ten Luigi Giannella	MC.202 MM 7815			
84ª Sq, 10°Gr, 4°St CT	Serg Magg D.Santonocito	MC.202 MM 7805	P-40	El Alamein-Amiriya	0940-1120
84ª Sq, 10°Gr, 4°St CT	Serg Magg Corrado Patrizi	MC.202 MM 7919			
84ª Sq, 10°Gr, 4°St CT	Serg Livio Barbera	MC.202 MM 7789			

Thursday, 6 August 1942

Five Bf 109s of 4./JG 27 took off at 1247, reporting a fight with 30 Curtiss fighters south-west of El Alamein, Obfw Bendert claiming two and Obfw Stigler one. There is no record of such an engagement in WDAF documents, although at about the same time a single Hurricane I Special of 7 SAAF Squadron was shot down by Flak.

4./JG 27's 'White 12' prepares to take off.

Considerably later, however, 12 Hurricanes of 127 Squadron covered ten of 1 SAAF Squadron on a scramble, 16 Bf 109s being sighted, three of which were seen to dive and attack. Part of the formation comprised eight aircraft of I./JG 27 on a Freie Jagd shortly before a Jabo attack was to take place. The Hurricanes were spotted, and four of the Messerschmitts attacked near Hammam, firing at long range; the pilots of these aircraft claimed to have damaged two Hurricanes, but no claims for aircraft shot down were submitted. The German pilots had achieved much more than they realised, however, for two of 127 Squadron's Hurricanes were badly damaged and two 1 SAAF Squadron aircraft suffered similarly – one of them reportedly by an MC.202. Two MC.200s of 8° Gruppo led by the commander, Magg Mario Bacich, off on a recce sortie at 1650, strafed two armoured cars south of Abu Haggag.

British Claims

1 SAAF Sqn	Lt E.E.Jory	Hurricane II BG968 'G'	Bf 109F Damaged	El Alamein line	1835

British Casualties

2 PRU	Spitfire IV BP914 left 1400 on recce to Mersa Matruh; Plt Off W.L.V. Hallett MiA
73 Sqn	Hurricane Plt Off H.W.E.Packham KiFA
127 Sqn	Hurricane IIb badly damaged by Bf 109 nr Hammam at 1830; Plt Off J.H.Currie safe
127 Sqn	Hurricane IIb badly damaged by Bf 109 nr Hammam at 1830; Lt H.C.Warren
1 SAAF Sqn	Hurricane damaged by MC.202 at 1830; Lt J.H.Gaynor safe
1 SAAF Sqn	Hurricane II BP227 'R' damaged Cat II by Bf 109; Lt G.R.Connell safe
7 SAAF Sqn	Hurricane I Special .9291 shot down by Flak nr El Alamein 1250, Lt L.le C.Theron PoW

German Claims

4./JG 27	Obfw Franz Stigler	P-40	E Deir el Abiod	1204
4./JG 27	Obfw Karl-Heinz Bendert	P-40	E Deir el Abiod	1205
4./JG 27	Obfw Karl-Heinz Bendert	P-40	SW El Alamein	1208

Friday, 7 August 1942

Twelve Tomahawks of 5 SAAF Squadron took off at 0845 to escort Kittybombers. Over Axis territory 2/Lt Duncan's aircraft received a direct Flak hit and dived straight into the ground. Maj Lacey was also hit and turned for home, escorted by two of his pilots. Four Bf 109s of III./JG 53 were scrambled at 0905, attacking these three Tomahawks 19 miles west of their base, the Germans reporting that Gefr Dohrmann's aircraft flew into a Tomahawk, both crashing. However, the South Africans recorded that a Bf 109 opened fire on Lacey's aircraft which immediately exploded in flames, and that Lt Jack at once shot down this fighter which also fell in flames, crashing alongside its victim; in either case, both the pilots were killed and were later buried together. Jack's aircraft was slightly damaged in the encounter, but Capt Dove's was badly hit.

Around 0950 eight more Bf 109s, four each from I. and II. Gruppen, were scrambled, soon encountering 12 Hurricanes of 274 Squadron, six with bombs and six as escort, which were attacking MT before making off out to sea. The I.Gruppe pilots saw them over the sea near Ras Gibeira, and Hptm Homuth claimed two of them shot down, Lt Remmer claiming to have damaged a third. 274 Squadron reported being attacked over the sea by two Bf 109s, one of which had a blue spinner; Flt Lt Darwin and Sgt Hemmer were both shot down and baled out, but neither was rescued.

The four Messerschmitt pilots of II.Gruppe's 4.Staffel, led by Oblt Vögl, reported meeting 24 Hurricanes and 12 Curtiss fighters near Hammam, and later another formation of fighter-bombers. Nine claims were submitted by the pilots of this unit. Although the opponents of III./JG 53 and I./JG 27 and the identity of those 'shot down' have proved readily accessible to identify, no details of such losses as those now claimed can be found. The reader should note that among the pilots claiming two victories each were Bendert and Sawallisch.

The notorious 4./JG 27 Schwarm who submitted a considerable number of dubious claims during August. Left to right: Obfw Franz Stigler, Oblt Ferdinand Vögl, Obfw Erwin Sawallisch and Obfw Karl-Heinz Bendert, all seen here at Qotaifiya.

During the afternoon III./JG 53 lost one aircraft and its pilots due to engine failure. At 1618 six aircraft of II./JG 27's 5.Staffel were scrambled. On this date Lt Gen W.H.E.Gott had been appointed, at Winston Churchill's insistence, as the new commander of 8th Army despite being very tired from many months of campaigning. On this afternoon Sgt James of 216 Squadron was piloting a Bombay transport in which Gott – who had not yet been advised of this, and who was on his way to Cairo on leave – was a passenger, from Burg el Arab to LG.90. Fourteen other passengers, mainly sick or injured were aboard, together with a fitter, a rigger and a medical orderly. Instead of flying at zero altitude as was the usual practice with the Bombays, James had climbed to 500 feet due to an overheating engine.

Apparently entirely by chance the aircraft was spotted by two of the 5.Staffel aircraft intruding well into Allied territory, and was attacked at once, Uffz Schneider riddling the aircraft, causing it to land. As it touched the sand, the navigator's seat collapsed and he fell out of the cockpit, followed at the earliest opportunity by the pilot, second pilot (who had been wounded in the back), and by the wireless operator and medical orderly, as the 109s attacked again, Schneider completing the destruction of the aircraft. All but one of the passengers still in the Bombay, including 'Strafer' Gott, were killed. It was this chance event which led directly to the appointment of General Bernard Montgomery to command 8th Army in Gott's place.

British Claims

5 SAAF Sqn	Lt G.B.Jack	Tomahawk IIb AN461 'K'	Bf 109	30m W LG.97	0950
238 Sqn	Flt Lt P.Olver	Hurricane IIb BP283 'U'	Bf 109 Damaged		1010

British Casualties

127 Sqn	Hurricane II shot-up by Bf 109 and force-landed at 1035, dam Cat II; Sgt D.G.Andrews safe
274 Sqn	Hurricane II BE683 'P' bounced by 2 Bf 109s, shot down off Sollum between 1005-1110; Flt Lt C.W.W.Darwin MiA
274 Sqn	Hurricane II Z5337 'O' bounced by 2 Bf 109s, shot down nr Burg el Arab between 1005-1110; Flt Sgt P.G.Hemmer MiA
5 SAAF Sqn	Tomahawk IIa AK445 'A' damaged by Flak, collided with AN221, then shot down by Bf 109s on return flight 0930; Maj D.V.D.Lacey KiA
5 SAAF Sqn	Tomahawk IIa AN221 'G' shot down by Flak while on escort; 2/Lt A.M.Duncan KiA
5 SAAF Sqn	Tomahawk IIa AN461 'K' slt damaged by Bf 109, then shot down by Bf 109; Lt G.B.Jack WiA
5 SAAF Sqn	Tomahawk IIa AN248 damaged Cat II by Bf 109 0945; Capt D.C.Dove safe
216 Sqn	Bombay L5814 shot down; Sgt James WiA, Lt Gen Gott KiA

German Claims

9./JG 53	Obfw Josef Kronschnabel	P-40	30km S Hammam	0842
1./JG 27	Lt Hans Remmer	Hurricane n.e.	NW El Alamein	0905
4./JG 27	Oblt Ferdinand Vögl	Hurricane	SE Alam el Kadim	0912
4./JG 27	Obfw Erwin Sawallisch	Hurricane	E Alam el Kadim	0912
4./JG 27	Obfw Karl-Heinz Bendert	Hurricane	SE Alam el Kadim	0913
4./JG 27	Obfw Franz Stigler	Hurricane	E Alam el Kadim	0914
4./JG 27	Obfw Erwin Sawallisch	Hurricane	SE Alam el Kadim	0915
4./JG 27	Oblt Ferdinand Vögl	Hurricane	E Alam el Kadim	0916
4./JG 27	Obfw Franz Stigler	Hurricane	ENE Alam el Kadim	0920
4./JG 27	Obfw Karl-Heinz Bendert	Hurricane	5km NW El Alamein	0921
4./JG 27	Obfw Karl-Heinz Bendert	P-40	S El Hammam	0923
Stab I./JG 27	Hptm Gerhard Homuth	Hurricane	N & NW El Alamein	0935
Stab I./JG 27	Hptm Gerhard Homuth	P-40	N El Hammam	0937
5./JG 27	Uffz Bernhard Schneider	Bombay	S & SE Alexandria	1608

German Casualties

7./JG 53	Bf 109F-4 trop WNr 10020 White 4+I shot down by P-40 15km W El Alamein; Gefr Hermann Dohrmann KiA

Saturday, 8 August 1942

At 1452 four Bf 109s of III./JG 27 scrambled, reporting a combat with five fighters, one of which Lt Schöfböck claimed shot down near Hammam. This appears to have been a 2 SAAF Squadron Kittyhawk, shot down on an interception patrol. Somewhat later 12 Hurricanes of 274 Squadron, covered by 1 SAAF Squadron, took off on another interception, but were attacked by four more III.Gruppe Messerschmitts which had taken off at 1821 on a Freie Jagd. One Hurricane was shot down in which Flt Sgt Hamilton was killed. Flt Sgt Gordon claimed to have shot down his attacker, Obfw Rosenberg, but no German loss actually occurred. By now 92 Squadron had reached a strength of 17 Spitfires and was nearly ready to re-commence operations with these aircraft. Ready now for the Spitfire squadrons, the first five pilots graduated from 244 Wing's training flight on this date.

British Claims

145 Sqn	Flt Lt W.A.G.Conrad	Spitfire Vb BR467	Ju 88 Damaged	50m S Dekeila	000-1150
145 Sqn	Sgt R.A.Cunningham	Spitfire Vb BP847			
274 Sqn	Flt Sgt D.C.Gordon	Hurricane IIc BP444 'Z'	Bf 109F		1805-1915

British Casualties

2 SAAF Sqn	Kittyhawk I AL160 shot down by Bf 109 on interception 1545; Lt D.D.Stuart baled out WiA
274 Sqn	Hurricane II BP440 'U' shot down by Bf 109 W Burg El Arab at approx 1900; Flt Sgt T.B.Hamilton KiA

German Claims

7./JG 27	Lt Erich Schöfböck	P-40	SW El Hammam	1440
9./JG 27	Obfw Heinrich Rosenberg	P-40	W El Hammam	1855

German Casualties

Stab/JG 27	Fw 58C-1 WNr 3575 NC+CR 60% damaged by bombs at Qotaifiya
Stab/JG 27	Fi 156C-3 WNr 5407 DO+A1 damaged by bombs at Qotaifiya
4./JG 27	Bf 109F-4 trop WNr 8644 95%, WNr 8721 10% damaged by bombs on ground at Qotaifiya
6./JG 27	Bf 109F-4 trop WNr 10284 Yellow 1 30%, WNr 10279 Yellow 8 20% damaged by bombs on ground at Qotaifiya
6./JG 27	Bf 109F-4 WNr 7400 Yellow 3 95% damaged on ground by bombs at Qotaifiya
III./JG 53	Bf 109F-4 trop WNr 10194 30% damaged on ground by bombs at Qotaifiya
Kurierst. Fl.Fhr Afrika	He 111P-2 WNr 1478 destroyed on ground by bombs at Qotaifiya
Fl.Ber.Fl.Fhr Afrika	Bf 108B-1 WNr 2092 20% damaged on ground by bombs at Qotaifiya

Sunday, 9 August 1942

The day saw the first sorties flown by US pilots attached to Commonwealth squadrons from the 57th Fighter Group.

At Benghazi K3 airfield two pilots of 364ª Sq, S.Ten Fausto Filippi and Cap Mario Bellagambi, were scrambled at 1600 and 1615 to intercept a formation of Liberators. One was claimed as damaged.

British Claims

274 Sqn	Flt Sgt J.W.Neil	Hurricane IIc BP326 'T'	MC.202 Damaged	SW Burg el Arab	1500-1545

US Casualties

415th/98th BG	B-24D 41-11808 'Root of Evil' shot down, 1/Lt Paul H.Francis and copilot baled out safe, crew KiA

German Casualties

1./JG 27	Bf 109F-4 trop WNr 13142 20% and 8676 15% damaged by bombs at Turbiya

Italian Claims

364ª Sq, 150° Gr CT	Cap Mario Bellagambi MC.200	Liberator Damaged	Benghazi area	1620
364ª Sq, 150° Gr CT	S.Ten Fausto Filippi MC.200			

Monday, 10 August 1942

Twelve Kittyhawks of 4 SAAF Squadron were scrambled at 0830 to carry out a patrol, encountering four II./JG 27 Bf 109s which took off at 0909, the German pilots reporting encountering 16 British fighters south-east of El Alamein; Obfw Sawallisch and Stigler claimed two each. The South Africans reported being jumped by two Bf 109s out of the sun, one being claimed damaged. One Kittyhawk was shot down, one crash-landed and one was damaged.

Two Bf 109s of I./JG 27 then escorted a reconnaissance Bf 110, encountering a lone aircraft identified as a Blenheim at 1030 near Abu Dweis, and this Lt Remmer claimed to have shot down. The identity of this aircraft is believed to have been a Baltimore of 1437 Strategic Reconnaissance Flight, the first loss to be suffered by this unit since its formation in October 1941. Three pilots from the same German unit then scrambled at 1016 and shot down an He 111 near Mersa Matruh, the reason for this not having been discovered.

At 1038 four II.Gruppe Messerschmitts commenced a Freie Jagd, the pilots reporting meeting 16 Hurricanes and Curtiss fighters, Oblt Vögl and Obfw Bendert claiming two shot down each. Twelve Hurricanes from 80 Squadron and four Kittyhawks of 2 SAAF had a brief fight with three Bf 109s, one damaged claimed, no losses being reported. War weary 12° Gruppo retired its 12 G.50bis from convoy escort and Tripoli's protection duties.

British Claims

4 SAAF Sqn	Lt W.J.Wheeler	Kittyhawk I ET901 'U'	Bf 109F Damaged	El Alamein	0925

British Casualties

4 SAAF Sqn	Kittyhawk I AK623 took off 0830 shot down by 2 Bf 109s at 0925; Plt Off J.K.McIvor KiA
4 SAAF Sqn	Kittyhawk I ET901 'U' took off 0830, damaged by Bf 109 Burg el Arab at 0925; Lt W.J.Wheeler safe
4 SAAF Sqn	Kittyhawk I ET512 took off 0830, damaged and crash-landed on return; Lt T.B.Milne safe
1437 Flt	Baltimore AG737 left LG.28 1000, MiA; Plt Off V.J.Dumas RAAF and three MiA. Apparently crashed near El Maghra in Qattara depression

German Claims

4./JG 27	Obfw Erwin Sawallisch	P-40	N El Muhafid	0831
4./JG 27	Obfw Franz Stigler	P-40	N El Muhafid	0832
4./JG 27	Obfw Franz Stigler	Hurricane	NNE El Muhafid	0833
4./JG 27	Obfw Erwin Sawallisch	P-40	NW El Muhafid	0834
1./JG 27	Lt Hans Remmer	Blenheim	SE Abu Dweis	0930
4./JG 27	Obfw Karl-Heinz Bendert	2 P-40s	SE & SSE El Alamein	1104 & 1105
4./JG 27	Oblt Ferdinand Vögl	2 Hurricanes	SE & SSE El Alamein	1106 & 1107

German Casualties

Stab X.Fl.K.	He 111H-6 WNr 7338 P4+AA shot down in error by I./JG 27 fighters, crashed into sea 10km S Mersa Matruh: Lt Werner Muffey and one MiA, one KiA and one WiA

Tuesday, 11 August 1942

Four Bf 109s of III./JG 53 were scrambled mid-morning, joined by twelve MC.202s of 10° Gruppo (six of 84ª and six of 90ª Squadriglie), led by the Gruppo's commander Magg Giuseppe D'Agostinis. Directed by Freya, they attacked ten Curtiss fighters between Hammam and El Alamein. The Germans made no claims but Cap Piccolomini claimed one P-40 and Cap Lucchini one probable. It seems likely that they had intercepted nine Tomahawks of 5 SAAF Squadron which reported being jumped by Bf 109s and MC.202s 15 miles south-west of Burg el Arab; 2/Lt Kearns claimed a Macchi during this engagement. At 1550 4./JG 27 despatched four Bf 109s, the pilots of which reported engaging ten Hurricanes, claiming five of them. Ten Hurricanes of 1 SAAF Squadron were repeatedly subjected to 'hit and run' attacks by a reported six Bf 109s, but suffered no casualties.

Two of the South African units received new commanders at this time, Maj A.M.Colenbrander taking over 2 SAAF and Maj L.B.Pearce 5 SAAF.

British Claims

1 SAAF Sqn	Capt L.R.S.Waugh	Hurricane II b ..698 'P'	Bf 109F Damaged	15m W Burg el Arab	1120-
5 SAAF Sqn	2/Lt B.A.Kearns	Tomahawk IIb AK559 'S'	MC.202	10m SW Burg el Arab	1150
145 Sqn	Plt Off L.A.Malins	Spitfire VBR201 'N'	Ju 88 Damaged	N Wadi Natrun	1615-1736
145 Sqn	Sgt P.C.G.Thomas	Spitfire VBP986 'X'			
2 SAAF Sqn	Capt R.Clifton	Kittyhawk I	MC.202 Damaged	El Imayid area	1925

German Claims

4./JG 27	Obfw Erwin Sawallisch	Hurricane	NW El Hammam	1010
4./JG 27	Oblt Ferdinand Vögl	Hurricane	WNW El Hammam	1011
4./JG 27	Obfw Erwin Sawallisch	Hurricane	E El Hammam	1013
4./JG 27	Obfw Franz Stigler	Hurricane	S El Hammam	1013
4./JG 27	Oblt Ferdinand Vögl	Hurricane	ENE El Hammam	1017

Italian Claims

84ª Sq, 10°Gr, 4°St CT	Cap Franco Lucchini	MC.202 MM 7896	P-40 Probable	El Hammam-Burg el Arab	1032
90ª Sq, 10°Gr, 4°St CT	Cap Ranieri Piccolomini	MC.202	P-40	El Hammam-Burg el Arab	1032

Wednesday, 12 August 1942

The claims of 4./JG 27 became even more exaggerated on this date. Twelve 2 SAAF Squadron Kittyhawks undertook an armed reconnaissance of the southern area. After bombs had been released on various targets the three aircraft of the top section were jumped by two Bf 109s, Lt Moon's Kittyhawk being badly damaged, causing him to force-land at a forward landing ground. Lt McLeod also force-landed, but Lt Burls was able to claim damage to a Messerschmitt. Another aircraft was hit by Flak as the attack was underway and Lt Morrison force-landed with his aircraft on fire; he managed to get out just before it blew up.

Three of 4./JG 27's Messerschmitts had taken off early in the morning, but a fourth, piloted by Oblt Vögl, was unable to get off due to engine trouble. Obfw Bendert, Sawallisch and Stigler returned to report having encountered 40 fighter-bombers and 16 escorting Curtiss fighters, between them claiming eight Hurricanes and four P-40s. Undoubtedly they had been the attackers who had hit the three South African

Kittyhawks; equally undoubtedly, these claims were vastly overstated. At 1815 12 Hurricanes of 1 SAAF Squadron provided top cover to 80 Squadron. Ten Bf 109s of II. and III./JG 27 were seen above and these made frequent attacks without inflicting any damage. The returning Hurricane pilots reported that the German pilots appeared to be under rigid control from a lone Messerschmitt flying above.

A Cant.Z.1007bis of 230ª Sq flown by S.Ten Salvatore Morelli was despatched at 0550 on an armed reconnaissance mission to Gialo and Kufra oases. Enemy vehicles were strafed and bombed at Kufra. Hit by AA fire, the aircraft was damaged and the radio operator wounded. Soon after this reconnaissance Kufra would become the base for a series of operations which will be dealt with in Chapter Ten.

British Claims					
2 SAAF Sqn	Lt J.R.Burls	Kittyhawk I AK760 'K'	Bf 109 Damaged	El Imayid area	0735
British Casualties					
2 SAAF Sqn	Kittyhawk I AL174 'U' badly damaged by Bf 109, belly-landed; Lt W.L.O.Moon safe				
2 SAAF Sqn	Kittyhawk I AK906 'O' damaged by Bf 109, force-landed at base 0730; Lt T.M.McLeod WiA				
2 SAAF Sqn	Kittyhawk I ET874 'D' damaged by Flak and crash-landed at El Hammam station, aircraft burnt out; Lt A.Morrison safe				
208 Sqn	Tomahawk I AN446 left 1740, hit by Flak, returned to base at 1845 Cat I; Lt R.H.Rogers safe				

German Claims				
4./JG 27	Obfw Erwin Sawallisch	Hurricane	SE El Alamein	0642
4./JG 27	Obfw Karl-Heinz Bendert	Hurricane	SE El Alamein	0643
4./JG 27	Obfw Franz Stigler	Hurricane	SSE El Alamein	0644
4./JG 27	Obfw Erwin Sawallisch	Hurricane	W Alam el Kadim	0648
4./JG 27	Obfw Karl-Heinz Bendert	Hurricane	W Alam el Kadim	0650
4./JG 27	Obfw Erwin Sawallisch	Hurricane	N Alam el Kadim	0651
4./JG 27	Obfw Karl-Heinz Bendert	Hurricane	E Alam el Kadim	0652
4./JG 27	Obfw Franz Stigler	Hurricane	S Alam el Kadim	0653
4./JG 27	Obfw Erwin Sawallisch	P-40	SW Alam el Halfa	0700
4./JG 27	Obfw Karl-Heinz Bendert	P-40	SW Alam el Halfa	0702
4./JG 27	Obfw Franz Stigler	P-40	SW Alam el Halfa	0703
4./JG 27	Obfw Karl-Heinz Bendert	P-40	SW Alam el Halfa	0704
Italian Casualties				
230ª Sq, 95°Gr, 35°St BT	Cant Z.1007bis damaged by AA, S.Ten Salvatore Morelli and crew safe, radio operator WiA			

Thursday, 13 August 1942

92 Squadron became fully operational on this date – WDAF's third Spitfire unit; it now had 19 pilots and 22 aircraft. In Rome Oblt Hans-Joachim Marseille was presented with the highest Italian award, the Medaglia d'Oro, by Benito Mussolini personally.

Friday, 14 August 1942

Eleven Kittyhawks of 2 SAAF and 11 of 4 SAAF Squadron escorted 12 Baltimores to bomb LG.18 in the Daba-Fuka area. Ten minutes behind them came 12 more Kittyhawks of 260 Squadron with six attached US P-40Fs of the 57th Fighter Group, to provide top cover for 12 Bostons bombing Fuka Station. Twenty minutes behind these aircraft came eight Spitfires of 92 Squadron on their first patrol since re-equipment, their task being to cover the returning formations against any pursuing Axis fighters. At 0657 four Bf 109s of II./JG 27 were scrambled, followed seven minutes later by six more. The Messerschmitts initially attacked the Baltimores and their escorts, one Kittyhawk being claimed by Oblt Sinner, but not confirmed due to lack of witnesses. MC.202s of 4° Stormo's 9° Gruppo also took part in this interception. At 0558 Ten Antonio Canfora led six MC.202s of 97ª Squadriglia that were scrambled at Fuka to face raiders. Near El Daba they intercepted 12 bombers, identified as Marylands, covered by about 18 P-40s. At the end of the fight, one P-40 and one Maryland were claimed as probables and some others damaged.

4 SAAF Squadron reported being attacked by seven plus Bf 109s and MC.202s when flying top cover; two of the unit's aircraft were shot down, and a third was badly damaged and belly-landed at base.

The German fighters then attacked a formation identified as ten Bostons and 20 Kittyhawks, without result, finally heading for that escorted by 260 Squadron. Here Sawallisch claimed two, Sinner and Obfw

Krenz adding one each. 260 Squadron's top flight was attacked out of the sun, two Kittyhawks being shot down. This unit's next section of four was then attacked over Daba by two Bf 109s, losing sight of the bombers. Their pilots patrolled the area until they spotted the Baltimores which had just bombed LG.18 and were now being engaged by Messerschmitts; the Kittyhawk pilots at once joined in this combat. The third four were the only aircraft of the unit to actually reach the target, and here they were also attacked by Messerschmitts, one Kittyhawk force-landing. Two then returned to base, the fourth fighting a lone combat, the pilot claiming one Messerschmitt damaged. This aircraft was then attacked when flying at only 50-100 feet altitude near its home base, and force-landed ten miles north of LG.97. Lt William O'Neill of the USAAF reported engaging five Bf 109s, two of which he claimed to have shot down, before being shot down into the sea himself. At this stage the 92 Squadron Spitfires joined the action, Sqn Ldr Wedgwood opening the unit's scoring in its new guise, shooting down Lt Mix of II./JG 27 who crash-landed after his aircraft was hit in the cooling system and became a PoW.

Although O'Neill's claims were noted in contemporary USAAF documents, possibly because he was flying as part of an RAF formation and probably filled in an RAF combat report, his victories appear not to have been noted as such in subsequent US records. Later in the day 12 B-24s of the US 98th Bomb Group undertook a daylight attack on Tobruk, bombing ships in harbour from 25,000 feet. Two pilots of 13° Gruppo, Serg Davide Zanarini and Serg Galileo Petti took off from Bu Amud at 1345 attempting to intercept. Flying at 15,000 feet Zanarini claimed a Liberator shot down and a second damaged.

A conference was held during the day, attended by Wg Cdr Burnand of 240 Wing to determine what re-equipment might be possible for the hard-pressed TacR units. He was advised that Spitfires would not be forthcoming following an air ministry signal to the effect that these aircraft were considered too valuable to be used on low-level duties. Tomahawks and Hurricane IIas would continue to be the types provided to 208 and 40 SAAF Squadrons. However, all aircraft were now to be fitted with vertical/oblique cameras, with two aircraft in each flight being fitted with two or more cameras for high altitude photography.

British Claims

92 Sqn	Sqn Ldr J.H.Wedgwood	Spitfire Vc BP476	Bf 109	N El Alamein	0650-0805
260 Sqn	Sgt W.R.Cundy	Kittyhawk I ET1016 'V'	Bf 109 Probable	El Alamein	

British Casualties

260 Sqn	Kittyhawk I AL149 damaged by Hurricane near LG.97 and crash-landed; Plt Off E.G.Aitchison safe
260 Sqn	Kittyhawk I shot down by Bf 109 El Alamein; Sqn Ldr P.P.Devenish safe
260 Sqn	Kittyhawk I shot down by Bf 109 El Alamein; Wt Off O.Bowerman safe
4 SAAF Sqn	Kittyhawk I ET978 shot down on escort to Baltimores LG.97 Fuka at 0620; Lt N.W.Hancock KiA
4 SAAF Sqn	Kittyhawk I AK720 damaged by Bf 109 over Fuka at 0620, tailplane badly hit and belly-landed on return; Lt D.Woodliffe safe
4 SAAF Sqn	Kittyhawk I AK788 damaged Cat I by Bf 109 safe

US Claims

57th FG	Lt William O.Neill	P-40F	2 Bf 109s

US Casualties

57th FG	P-40F shot down into sea; Lt William O'Neill picked up safely

German Claims

4./JG 27	Obfw Erwin Sawallisch	P-40	ENE Fuka	0615
6./JG 27	Obfw Herbert Krenz	P-40	N El Hammam	0625
6./JG 27	Oblt Rudolf Sinner	P-40 o.Zg. n.b.	NW El Alamein	0625
6./JG 27	Oblt Rudolf Sinner	P-40	NW El Alamein	0625
4./JG 27	Obfw Erwin Sawallisch	P-40	NW El Alamein	0630

German Casualties

6./JG 27	Bf 109F-4 trop WNr 10074 Yellow 5 shot down by Spitfires N El Alamein, crash-landed 100%; Lt Gert Mix PoW
3./StG 3	Ju 87D-3 WNr 2630 S7+BL AA NNW Philippeville; Uffz Oskar Bennebach/Fw Karl André KiA

Italian Claims

97ª Sq, 9°Gr, 4°St CT	Ten Antonio Canfora	MC.202	P-40 Probable	El Daba	0620
97ª Sq, 9°Gr, 4°St CT	unspecified	MC.202	Maryland Probable	El Daba	0620
77ª Sq, 13°Gr, 2°St CT	Serg Magg Davide Zanarini	MC.202 MM 7893	B-24	off Tobruk	1345-1430
77ª Sq, 13°Gr, 2°St CT	Serg Magg Davide Zanarini	MC.202 MM 7893	B-24 Damaged	off Tobruk	1345-1430

Italian Casualties

84ª Sq, 10°Gr, 4°St CT	MC.202 MM 7803 '84-1'set on fire by bombs at Fuka
84ª Sq, 10°Gr, 4°St CT	MC.202 MM 7905 '84-4' damaged by bombs at Fuka
91ª Sq, 10°Gr, 4°St CT	MC.202 MM 7794 '91-2' damaged by bombs at Fuka
91ª Sq, 10°Gr, 4°St CT	MC.202 MM 7762 '91-10' damaged by bombs at Fuka

Saturday, 15 August 1942

This was a day of major changes for the Commonwealth forces in North Africa. General Auchinleck was replaced as commander-in-chief by General Sir Harold Alexander, while command of 8th Army was taken over by Lt Gen Bernard Montgomery. This complete change of command at the top was accompanied, not surprisingly, by a thorough shake-up in lower echelons as Montgomery particularly sought to change the whole ethos of his new command as rapidly as possible prior to any new offensive, or further Axis advance.

Air operations continued unchanged for the time being and Montgomery was soon to show that he fully appreciated the need for close co-operation between air and ground. The two headquarters were moved closer together and he quickly built up a working rapport with Air Vice-Marshal Coningham, although there was not to be any great personal warmth between the two, their individual lifestyles being too different for that. Montgomery was very much the abstaining, non-smoking aesthete, whereas Coningham certainly enjoyed his creature comforts.

During the early morning of this notable day, two Hurricane IIas of 208 Squadron took off on a TacR sortie on behalf of their army colleagues. But once again they were intercepted by four Bf 109s of I./JG 27 when north-east of Abu Dweis. Lt Rogers was hit, but managed to escape destruction, landing back at base with the little finger of his left hand shot off and injuries to the third finger. Lt Welgemoed force-landed near the Qattara Depression. The German pilots claimed one Hurricane shot down, but the claim did not obtain confirmation. These latest losses rendered 208 Squadron in a critical situation. Army commanders placed the highest importance on their reconnaissance work and in the light of this Tedder agreed to give precedence over the fighter units in bringing the unit up to full strength with Tomahawks and Hurricane IIbs, no further Mark IIas currently being available.

At 0933 five Bf 109E Jabos of III./JG 53 attacked vehicles and guns north-east of Alam Nagil with three more such aircraft from III./JG 27, but one of the former was shot down by a direct hit from AA, the pilot baling out south of Ruweisat and becoming a PoW. At 1155 two III./JG 53 Messerschmitts provided escort to a coastal convoy, becoming involved in a fight with Beaufighters. Full details of this engagement will be found in Chapter Ten. With the Regia Aeronautica Magg Simeone Marsan was posted to 4° Stormo, handing over temporary command of 101° Gruppo Tuffatori to Cap Carlo Alberto Rizzi.

British Casualties

208 Sqn	Hurricane IIa Z3357 damaged by Bf 109 and returned to base at 0830; Lt Rogers slt WiA, had finger shot off
208 Sqn	Hurricane IIa BV155 damaged by Bf 109, force-landed nr Qattara Depression at about 0810; Lt P.Welgemoed returned safe

German Casualties

10.(Jabo)/JG 53	Bf 109F-4/Z WNr 7540 White 4+ shot down by AA 15km SE El Alamein; Obgefr Werner Staudt PoW

Sunday, 16 August 1942

The day proved to be one of consternation for JG 27. At 0727 a pair of I.Gruppe Bf 109s was scrambled and was involved in two combats, the first at 0915 when Lt Stahlschmidt claimed one Curtiss fighter out of six over El Alamein. He then claimed a second ten minutes later from a formation of 20 in the same area. Five more Messerschmitts had been scrambled by 4./JG 27 at 0912, and it seems that these had become involved with the second formation reported by the I.Gruppe pilot. At this time 11 Tomahawks of 5 SAAF Squadron were escorting Bostons on a photo-reconnaissance mission when they were attacked, one of these fighters being shot down, Lt Trenchard baling out of the blazing aircraft and falling in no mans' land where he was captured, becoming a PoW. However, he had been badly wounded and he died next day. Three more of the unit's aircraft were damaged by Bf 109s. Eight Kittyhawks of 2 SAAF Squadron on a fighter reconnaissance were also attacked by Bf 109s, Capt Clifton baling out and landing in the sea at El Alamein, slightly wounded; another of the unit's aircraft was hit and damaged. It would appear that the two South African aircraft shot down represented Stahlschmidt's victims, and given his known expertise as a fighter pilot, the various aircraft damaged may have been hit by him or his wingman. Equally, it is possible that the 4. Staffel pilots may also have become involved in one of these engagements – probably with 5 SAAF Squadron.

Whatever may have happened at this moment, the five pilots returned to report a combat deep in enemy territory at about 0930 with five Curtiss fighters and ten Hurricanes. In the next quarter of an hour they claimed to have shot down all five Curtisses and seven of the Hurricanes. However, when Stahlschmidt landed he had a different story to tell. After his combats he had seen the aircraft of 4.Staffel shooting off their ammunition into the desert sands in the course apparently of a mock dogfight! It is, of course, just possible that he did not see clearly from long range what was going on, but this seems unlikely, and no details of any such heavy losses are to be found in British records. It has been suggested that they were practising 'shadow-shooting' to improve their marksmanship, but why they should have been doing so, and with what ammunition if they had already shot down a dozen British aircraft between them, is very difficult to explain or justify.

The authors are aware that in recent years certain people have sought to cast doubts on the explanation offered in *Fighters over the Desert* in regard to these events. Let there be no doubt as to where the information came from. In the preparation of that book, Hans Ring, then historian of the *Gemeinschafter der Jagdflieger*, had been helped and guided throughout and to a very considerable degree by Edu Neumann, in 1942 Kommodore of Jagdgeschwader 27. In his role, Neumann had, of course, been deeply involved in this matter. Ring had been reluctant to have this information included and thereby publicized. However, Neumann personally, in the interests of historical accuracy, insisted that it was recorded. It was therefore not the assessment or the judgement of the authors, but of the superior commanding officer of the German pilots involved.

The JG 27 staff was at a loss to know what to do. Until this time, as has been demonstrated, Luftwaffe claims had, allowing for the inevitable errors during heavy combat which occurred on both sides, been remarkably accurate. Here, however, was the exception to the rule – and it is such unfortunate lapses which would appear to have largely been responsible for the scepticism with which Luftwaffe claims are still treated by many people. Throughout the first three weeks of August the main duties of JG 27 had been daily escorts to convoys sailing along the coast between Tobruk and Mersa Matruh and relatively few combats had occurred. The apparent luck of 4.Staffel's 'Experte Schwarme', as it had become known, had become legendary, and had led to some shaking of heads. As their claims raised higher, certain of the pilots, notably Sinner and Börngen, had come to distrust them, and now energetically pressed for action to be taken against them.

However, when questioned, these pilots emphatically denied falsifying their claims. It was considered undesirable to report the matter to the higher command, as this would reflect badly upon the whole unit. Plans were therefore made to break up the Schwarme, posting the pilots to other Staffeln. It was also agreed to treat all future claims from them with some scepticism and to get rid of them as soon as possible. It was also suggested that all their victories to date should be forfeited, and they should start again from scratch. However, Rommel's next offensive was due shortly, and they could not be spared until after it, so it was several weeks before they were sent home to Germany. Due to the hushing-up of the incident, the pilots' claims for their combats in the desert were fully accepted by the authorities when they arrived home, and one of them even went on to be awarded the Ritterkreuz.

The only other action in the air to occur this day involved the Spitfires of 92 Squadron which provided independent top cover to two squadrons, claims being submitted for two Bf 109s damaged. From 2 SAAF Squadron Capt E.C.Saville was posted to 112 Squadron as a flight commander.

British Claims

5 SAAF Sqn	Capt D.C.Dove	Tomahawk IIb AN366 'N'	Bf 109F Damaged	12m SW El Alamein	0935
5 SAAF Sqn	Lt R.C.Hirst	Tomahawk IIb AN238 'O'	Bf 109F Damaged	12m SW El Alamein	0935
5 SAAF Sqn	2/Lt H.Smith	Tomahawk IIb AN461 'K'	Bf 109F Damaged	12m SW El Alamein	0935
92 Sqn	Flt Sgt R.Hempstead	Spitfire Vc BR494 'R'	Bf 109 Damaged	El Imayid	1130-1245
92 Sqn	Sqn Ldr J.H.Wedgwood	Spitfire Vc BG476 'J'	Bf 109F Damaged	El Imayid	1130-1245

British Casualties

2 SAAF Sqn	Kittyhawk I AL160 damaged by Bf 109 and abandoned off El Alamein
2 SAAF Sqn	Kittyhawk I ET522 'W' shot down by Bf 109s 7m SW El Alamein 0915; Capt R.Clifton baled out WiA
5 SAAF Sqn	Tomahawk IIa AN329 shot down in flames by Bf 109 12m SW El Alamein 0935; Lt C.Trenchard WiA, PoW
5 SAAF Sqn	Tomahawk IIa AN427 'D' damaged Cat I by Bf 109; Capt R.F.Armstrong safe

British Casualties

5 SAAF Sqn	Tomahawk IIa damaged Cat I by Bf 109
5 SAAF Sqn	Tomahawk IIa damaged Cat I by Bf 109

German Claims

2./JG 27	Lt Hans-Arnold Stahlschmidt	P-40	NW El Hammam	0815
2./JG 27	Lt Hans-Arnold Stahlschmidt	P-40	WSW El Alamein	0825
4./JG 27	Obfw Erwin Sawallisch	Hurricane	W Alam el Kadim	0826
4./JG 27	Oblt Ferdinand Vögl	Hurricane	Alam el Kadim	0827
4./JG 27	Obfw Karl-Heinz Bendert	P-40	S Alam el Kadim	0828
4./JG 27	Obfw Franz Stigler	P-40	S Alam el Kadim	0828
4./JG 27	Obfw Erwin Sawallisch	Hurricane	SW El Hammam	0832
4./JG 27	Oblt Ferdinand Vögl	Hurricane	SW El Hammam	0833
4./JG 27	Obfw Karl-Heinz Bendert	P-40	E Alam el Kadim	0835
4./JG 37	Oblt Ferdinand Vögl	P-40	S El Hammam	0838
4./JG 27	Obfw Franz Stigler	Hurricane	SSW El Hammam	0838
4./JG 27	Obfw Erwin Sawallisch	Hurricane	SSW El Hammam	0839
4./JG 27	Obfw Karl-Heinz Bendert	P-40	S El Hammam	0840
4./JG 27	Uffz Ferdinand Just	Hurricane	SW El Hammam	0840

Monday, 17 August 1942

Two pilots of 208 Squadron took off on a midday TacR in a Hurricane IIa and a Tomahawk. They were intercepted at low level south of Burg el Arab by four Bf 109s of III./JG 53, both being shot down and killed. Ten of 92 Squadron's Spitfires undertook an offensive sweep, four Bf 109s of II./JG 27 being encountered near El Alamein, one of which was claimed as a probable.

During the day a 24 SAAF Squadron Boston was shot down by Flak when bombing MTBs and F Boats in Mersa Matruh harbour. Maj J.P.Verster was able to crash-land the burning aircraft in the middle of a German camp east of Mersa Matruh, he and his crew managing to get out before the bomber, which was still under heavy fire, exploded. The constant hammering at Tobruk harbour had been paying dividends, however, for on this date a German report indicated that of 50 barges under Italian control, only 28 were now serviceable, and in addition of 22 operated by German crews, only nine were currently capable of use.

British Claims

92 Sqn	Plt Off R.A.Cooke	Spitfire Vb AB252 'C'	Bf 109F Probable	W Bomb line at 8,000ft 1330

208 Squadron Tomahawk AK350 shot down by Bf 109s on 17 August. The code letters RG can just be seen.

British Casualties	
208 Sqn	Hurricane II Z5468 shot down by five Bf 109s on TacR in southern area; Plt Off R.Filson-Young, KiA
208 Sqn	Tomahawk IIa AK350 shot down by five Bf 109s 20m SE El Alamein; Lt W.J.Vine KiA
24 SAAF Sqn	Boston III Z2294 'N'attacking MTBs and 'F'Boats in Mersa Matruh harbour hit by Flak and caught fire. Crash-landed in middle of German camp 4m E Mersa Matruh; Maj J.P.Verster and three got out before it exploded

German Claims				
9./JG 53	Uffz Max Nairz	P-40	S Burg el Arab	1101
9./JG 53	Lt Rolf Klippgen	P-40	S Burg el Arab	1105

Tuesday, 18 August 1942

Ten Kittyhawks of 260 Squadron carried out a reconnaissance of the coast between 1000 and 1100, being intercepted by six Bf 109s of I./JG 27. These had been scrambled, reaching altitude from where they dived out of the sun from 12,000 feet onto the British aircraft. One, flown by Plt Off Maclean, exploded on the ground, the pilot being killed, with a second badly damaged.

British Casualties	
260 Sqn	Kittyhawk I shot down by Bf 109 10m W El Alamein; Plt Off J.A.Maclean KiA
260 Sqn	Kittyhawk I badly damaged by Bf 109; Sgt N.S.Stebbings safe

German Claims				
3./JG 27	Lt Friedrich Hoffmann	P-40	15km W El Alamein	0935
Stab I./JG 27	Hptm Gerhard Homuth	P-40	W El Alamein	0938

Wednesday, 19 August 1942

There was another coastal interception for I./JG 27 when four Messerschmitts caught a lone Beaufighter of 252 Squadron which was shot down (see Chapter Ten for details). Somewhat later in the morning 12 Spitfires of 92 Squadron provided top cover for the Hurricanes of 274 Squadron and 1 SAAF Squadron. The formation ran into a force of fighters including six Bf 109s from II./JG 27 and eight MC.202s of 9° Gruppo, led by Ten Reiner, at 20,000 feet. On this occasion the Spitfire pilots considerably over-estimated the results of their attacks, claiming four Bf 109s shot down, four probables and three damaged. In fact one new Bf 109G force-landed having suffered 10% damage, but with the pilot safe, and one MC.202 was shot down, the pilot, S.Ten Gibellini, on his first combat being wounded and baling out; he died shortly afterwards as a prisoner. Ten Reiner, whose wingman he had been, was pursued for some time by

At Fuka in August 1942 may be seen in the foreground the MC.202 '73-7' MM 7823, which was usually flown by Ten Giulio Reiner. In the background is '73-10' MM 7936 which was flown by Ten Rinaldo Gibellini, who was forced down by a 92 Squadron pilot on 19 August.

a Spitfire, landing in his Macchi, riddled with holes. The German pilots claimed three Spitfires and the Italians two more. The former claims were made by two of the recently-disgraced 4.Staffel pilots. 92 Squadron suffered a single loss, Plt Off Samouelle crash-landing.

As an indication of just how detailed were the Luftwaffe's record of their fighter operations at this time, an example of this day's operations is set out below:

I./JG 27	0835 hours scrambled four Bf 109s, contact with six to ten Spitfires over Alamein, due to unfavourable position the Bf 109s did not attack.	
	0858 hours. Two Bf 109s escort for Bf 110, no combat.	
II./JG 27	0831 hours four Bf 109s scrambled	
	0833 hours four Bf 109s scrambled	
	Both sections had combat with twelve Spitfires west and south-west of Hammam at 6,000 metres. Three claims.	
	Times of landings:	
	1 Bf 109	0843
	1 Bf 109	0850
	5 Bf 109s	0930
	1 Bf 109	0937 belly-landing on own base, troubles with landing gear, but not to enemy action.
III./JG 27	0850 hours two Bf 109s cover for German convoy which left Mersa Matruh on westerly course.	
III./JG 53	0845 hours six Bf 109s scrambled, no combat.	
	1 Bf 109 landed 0900 hours	
	5 Bf 109s landed 0942 hours at Bir el Abd.	

Despite the increases in WDAF's strength recently, the Luftwaffe fighter forces were also now at their peak to date. Dispositions now being as follows:

Stab/JG 27	2 Bf 109F	at Sanyet Qotaifiya
I./JG 27	23 Bf 109F	at Turbiya
II./JG 27	24 Bf 109F	at Sanyet Qotaifiya
III./JG 27	24 Bf 109F	at Haggag Qasaba
JaboStaffel/JG 27	12 Bf 109E	at Haggag Qasaba
III./JG 53	24 Bf 109E & F	at Haggag Qasaba
10./ZG 26	7 Do 17Z	at Barce
Jagdkommando/JG 27	3 Bf 109F	at Kastelli, Crete
III./ZG 26	46 Bf 110C	at Kastelli, Crete
	165	

97 of these aircraft were currently serviceable and ready for use.

During the early afternoon of the day, however, Obfw Sawallisch of 4./JG 27 took off on a test flight from which he failed to return. Next day his naked body was washed ashore, the reason for his death officially unknown. However, it was thought possible that, accused of making false claims and fearing a possible court martial, he had deliberately dived into the sea.

At the start of August a new South African fighter wing, 7 SAAF was formed at LG.89. Maj D.H.Loftus, DFC, who had recently returned to North Africa after a period in the Union following his earlier service with 2 SAAF Squadron, was commanding 7 SAAF Squadron, which had been involved in training in the Delta area since July. He was now promoted Lt Col and given command of the new wing. After camp had been set up, the first units for the wing flew in, including 7 SAAF Squadron, 6 and 274 Squadrons. They would be followed next day by 127 Squadron, the initial purpose of the wing being to co-ordinate anti-tank operations. Following their arrival, 6 and 7 SAAF Squadrons remained at LG.89, the other two units moving to LG.88 from LG.92.

Flt Lt Samouelle of 92 Squadron claimed victories in QJ-E BR523 on 19 August before force-landing beside the Alexandria-Mersa Matruh road.

British Claims

92 Sqn	Plt Off Bradley-Smith	Spitfire Vc BR389 'P'	Bf 109	El Mreir-El Hammam	0915-1040
92 Sqn	Plt Off J.Buckley	Spitfire Vc BR134 'N'	Bf 109 Damaged	El Mreir-El Hammam	0915-1040
92 Sqn	Plt Off W.L.Chisholm	Spitfire Vc BR492 'T'	Bf 109	El Mreir-El Hammam	0915-1040
92 Sqn	Plt Off W.L.Chisholm	Spitfire Vc BR492 'T'	Bf 109 Probable	El Mreir-El Hammam	0915-1040
92 Sqn	Plt Off R.A.Cooke	Spitfire Vc BR474 'V'	Bf 109	El Mreir-El Hammam	0915-1040
92 Sqn	Plt Off G.W.Rose	Spitfire Vc BR580 'B'	Bf 109 Probable	El Mreir-El Hammam	0915-1040
92 Sqn	Flt Lt C.J.Samouelle	Spitfire Vc BR523 'E'	Bf 109 Probable	El Mreir-El Hammam	0915-1040
92 Sqn	Flt Lt C.J.Samouelle	Spitfire Vc BR523 'E'	Bf 109 Damaged	El Mreir-El Hammam	0915-1040
92 Sqn	Plt Off L.F.C.Smith	Spitfire Vc BP978 'U'	Bf 109 Probable	El Mreir-El Hammam	0915-1040
92 Sqn	Sqn Ldr J.H.Wedgwood	Spitfire Vc BR476 'J'	Bf 109	El Mreir-El Hammam	0915-1040
92 Sqn	Sqn Ldr J.H.Wedgwood	Spitfire Vc BR476 'J'	Bf 109 Damaged	El Mreir-El Hammam	0915-1040
92 Sqn	Sgt G.Titmus	Spitfire Vc BR494 'R'	Bf 109 Damaged	El Mreir-El Hammam	0915-1040

British Casualties

92 Sqn	Spitfire Vc BR523 'E' left 0915, damaged by Bf 109 El Hammam and force-landed; Fl Lt C.J. Samouelle safe

German Claims

4./JG 27	Obfw Karl-Heinz Bendert	2 Spitfires	W & WSW El Hammam	0901 & 0905
4./JG 27	Oblt Ferdinand Vögl	Spitfire	WSW El Hammam	0907

German Casualties

4./JG 27	Bf 109F-4 trop WNr 8782 crashed in sea during test flight; Obfw Erwin Sawallisch KiA
4./JG 27	Bf 109F-4 trop WNr 8596 shot-up by Spitfire W El Hammam, force-landed Qotaifiya, 10% damaged; pilot safe

Italian Claims

73ª Sq, 9°Gr, 4°St CT	Ten Giulio Reiner	MC.202 MM 7823 '73-7'	Spitfire	El Hammam	0830-
73ª Sq, 9°Gr, 4°St CT	Ten Giulio Reiner	MC.202 MM 7823 '73-7'	Spitfire Damaged	El Hammam	0830-
73ª Sq, 9°Gr, 4°St CT	Ten Mario Mecatti	MC.202	Spitfire	El Hammam	0830-
73ª Sq, 9°Gr, 4°St CT	S.Ten Rinaldo Gibellini	MC.202 MM 7936 '73-10'	Spitfire Probable	El Hammam	0830-

Italian Casualties

73ª Sq, 9°Gr, 4°St CT	MC.202 MM 7936 '73-10' shot down, S.Ten Rinaldo Gibellini baled, taken prisoner, died of wounds
73ª Sq, 9°Gr, 4°St CT	MC.202 MM 7823 '73-7' damaged in combat, landed safely, Ten Giulio Reiner safe

Thursday, 20 August 1942

The first sorties by units of the new 7 SAAF Wing were undertaken on this date, bomb-carrying Hurricane IIbs of 274 Squadron attacking dispersed MT, under cover of aircraft of 127 Squadron. On this date also, 3 RAAF Squadron returned to operation, and from 112 Squadron Plt Off Whitamore was posted to 601 Squadron to fly Spitfires. 101° Gruppo moved from Derna to Abar Nimeir.

Friday, 21 August 1942

Soon after 1000 four Kittyhawks of 250 Squadron covered others of 112 Squadron on an armed reconnaissance, Spitfires of 92 Squadron providing high cover on a sweep over the battle area. Four Bf 109s of II./JG 27 were scrambled at 1015, and 40 minutes later Uffz Schneider shot down Sgt Thompson of 92 Squadron, who was slightly wounded; Sqn Ldr Wedgwood claimed damage to one Messerschmitt as the other three dived on the Kittyhawks, damaging two of them.

At this stage the various WDAF squadrons which had been rested after the hard July battles, began returning to forward landing grounds. 145 Squadron now moved to LG.154, followed next day by 601 Squadron. This latter unit had been taken over by Sqn Ldr A.V.'Taffy' Clowes, DFC, DFM, from Sqn Ldr J.D.Bisdee, DFC. Like Bisdee, Clowes was an ex-Battle of Britain pilot who had also served in France. He had claimed 12 victories and had been squadron leader flying with 244 Wing during recent weeks; Bisdee left the unit having brought his own tally to ten.

Meanwhile 213 Squadron moved up to LG.85 where it was decided in the interest of manoeuvrability and overall performance, to remove experimentally two of the four cannons from the wings of two of the unit's Hurricanes. At LG.88 an Axis raid just before midnight hit the 127 Squadron dispersal area with three 250kg bombs. Two Hurricanes were damaged Cat II and two Cat I, with one member of the ground staff killed and six badly wounded. Two of the latter later died; three more men suffered slight wounds.

British Claims

92 Sqn	Sqn Ldr J.H.Wedgwood	Spitfire Vc BR175 'E'	Bf 109 Probable		1000-1115
250 Sqn	Flt Lt M.C.H.Barber	Kittyhawk I ET955 'K'	Bf 109 Damaged	N Gabr Kalakh	1100

British Casualties

92 Sqn	Spitfire V BR518 left 1000, shot down on sweep by Bf 109; Sgt J.L.Thompson baled out slt WiA
250 Sqn	Kittyhawk I ET525 'Y' damaged by Bf 109, N Gabr Kalakh, 1100; Flg Lt N.P.W.Hancock
250 Sqn	Kittyhawk I ET622 'R' damaged by Bf 109; N Gabr Kalakh, 1100; Flg Off J.Miluck
250 Sqn	Kittyhawk I AK613 shot down by Flak Deir el Abiod 0630; Plt Off G.F.Newton WiA
6 Sqn	Hurricane BP551 stalled and crashed near LG.89

German Claims

5./JG 27	Uffz Bernhard Schneider	Spitfire	SSE El Alamein	0955
5./JG 27	Fw Hans Niederhöfer	P-40 n.b.		

Saturday, 22 August 1942

Despite investigations, two of the suspect pilots of 4./JG 27 made more dubious claims during the early morning – possibly in the belief that to have suddenly stopped claiming would have risked incriminating them further. Three of them had scrambled at 0700, reporting combat with six Spitfires near Abu Dweis at 15,000 feet, claiming three shot down; no RAF losses were suffered. In the early afternoon ten Spitfires of 601 Squadron set off on patrol, engaging five I./JG 27 Bf 109s at 25,000 feet near Burg el Arab. Obfw Steinhausen attacked Flt Sgt Schofield's aircraft, inflicting damage. Schofield tried to get away by diving for the ground but Steinhausen kept after him, and the Spitfire belly-landed five miles south of Hammam, somersaulting; Schofield survived, but with wounds.

At 1720 two 145 Squadron Spitfires were scrambled to 27,000 feet where Flt Lt Taylor claimed damage to a Ju 88. 92 Squadron, patrolling at 20,000 feet, were attacked by Messerschmitts, identifying these as both Bf 109s and Fs, from 32,000 feet; it is highly unlikely that any of the former model were actually involved at this height, although the Spitfire pilots noted that they had never seen any Messerschmitt at this altitude before. However the German pilots did not press their attack and no claims or losses occurred. During the day 73 Squadron moved up to LG.85 to commence night operations again. On the other side of the lines, Oblt Marseille returned to I./JG 27 from his spell of leave.

British Claims

145 Sqn	Sgt G.Titmus	Spitfire Vc BR494	Bf 109 Damaged	0915-1040	
601 Sqn	Plt Off W.R.P.Sewell	Spitfire Vb BR392	Bf 109 Damaged	SW Burg el Arab	1400-1515
145 Sqn	Flt Lt J.S.Taylor	Spitfire Vb BR583 'T'	Ju 88 Damaged		1720-1845

British Casualties

601 Sqn	Spitfire V BR982 left 1400, crash-landed; Flt Sgt T.D.Schofield WiA

German Claims

4./JG 27	Obfw Karl-Heinz Bendert	2 Spitfires	S El Hammam & S Alam Uzeiligh	0728 & 0730
4./JG 27	Obfw Franz Stigler	Spitfire	SSW Alam Uzeiligh	0731
1./JG 27	Obfw Günther Steinhausen	Spitfire	7km S El Hammam	

Sunday, 23 August 1942

Two Bf 109s of III./JG 53 undertook a dawn convoy escort, engaging a reported eight Beauforts north of Sidi Barrani, one of which was claimed shot down although identified as a Beaufighter (see Chapter Ten for more details). Two hours or so later four Bf 109s of I./JG 27 and four of II.Gruppe scrambled, the former Schwarme intercepting eight Kittyhawks of 3 RAAF Squadron which were providing top cover for 450 Squadron on a reconnaissance over the Deir el Qattara area where they had bombed Axis MT. Here Lt Stahlschmidt shot down Flt Sgt Stevens' Kittyhawk in flames, the Australian pilot baling out, slightly burned; he was back with the unit by 1700. Eleven Spitfires of 92 Squadron were undertaking an offensive patrol at the same time, the II.Gruppe aircraft running into these near Burg el Arab where Plt Off Samouelle claimed one probable.

46° Gruppo BT arrived at Benghazi (K1 airfield) on this day.

British Claims

92 Sqn	Plt Off G.W.Rose	Spitfire Vc BR580	Bf 109 Damaged	offensive patrol	0800-0930
92 Sqn	Flt Lt C.J.Samouelle	Spitfire Vc BR520	Bf 109 Damaged (? Prob)	offensive patrol	0800-0930
3 RAAF Sqn	Sgt H.J.Bray	Kittyhawk I AK969 'Z'	Bf 109F Damaged	Deir el Qattara area	0855

British Casualties

3 RAAF Sqn	Kittyhawk I ET875 shot down by fighters on ground attack, crash-landed; Flt Sgt R.N.B.Stevens

German Claims

2./JG 27	Lt Hans-Arnold Stahlschmidt	P-40	S El Hammam	0803

Monday, 24 August 1942

At 1535 Sqn Ldr I.L.McG.Hallam and Flt Lt R.L.MacGregor of 208 Squadron took off on an important TacR sortie in a pair of Hurricane IIas. Neither pilot returned, but no Axis fighter claims were made for either of these aircraft shot down, nor for another of the unit's Hurricanes reported missing on a night flight. Luftwaffe bombers again appeared over the forward area by night, but on this occasion Wt Off Joyce in one of the newly-arrived night-fighting Hurricanes of 73 Squadron, stalked a Ju 88 of I./LG 1 and shot it down near Burg el Arab (see Chapter Ten).

British Claims

73 Sqn	Wt Off E.L.Joyce	Hurricane IIc BP167 'L'	Ju 88	12-16m SE LG.39	2305

British Casualties

208 Sqn	Hurricane II BE567 left 1935 on recce, failed to return; Flt Lt R.L.MacGregor MiA
208 Sqn	Hurricane II BN156 left 1935 on recce, failed to return; Sqn Ldr I.L.McG.Hallam MiA
208 Sqn	Hurricane BN759 MiA on night flight (hit by bombs? As Ju 88 bombed them)
112 Sqn	Kittyhawk I AK703 'X' damaged by Flak, force-landed; Sgt C.D.Young safe

Tuesday, 25 August 1942

Around midday three Bf 109s of III./JG 27 were scrambled, reporting intercepting six bombers and 15 escorting Kittyhawks east of Abu Dweis. The pilots claimed to have hit two Kittyhawks which nosed down in an easterly direction. From 7 SAAF Wing 12 Hurricanes of 274 Squadron provided top cover for an attack to be made on 70-80 tank transporters. These were not found and the pilots attacked armoured vehicles instead, but were jumped by at least four Bf 109s. These were aircraft of I./JG 27 which had taken off as the British aircraft appeared in the area; they split up into pairs to attack the Hurricanes, Obfw Steinhausen and Ogfr Benthin claiming one shot down each, reporting that the Hurricanes had jettisoned their bombs on some Arab tents. The second German pair claimed to have inflicted serious damage on a third Hurricane.

Plt Off Wigton's aircraft crashed two miles north of the target and he was killed. Flt Lt R.L. 'Gerry' Wade, a pilot of 123 Squadron, attached to 274 Squadron, claimed one Messerschmitt probably shot down, but he was then shot down himself and slightly wounded; he walked back to Allied lines. Surviving this, he rose to the rank of air chief marshal post war. Sgt MacFarlane was also hit and belly-landed, but he also returned that evening, claiming one Bf 109 damaged. Plt Off Simpson's aircraft was also damaged and he was slightly wounded. Meanwhile, Sgt Lerche's Hurricane was hit by Flak and he also force-landed, having been wounded. He ended up in hospital, but was back with the unit next day.

British Claims

274 Sqn	Flt Lt R.L.Wade	Hurricane IIc BP693 'P'	Bf 109 Probable	SE El Alamein	1230-1340
274 Sqn	Sgt R.MacFarlane	Hurricane IIc BN109 'M'	Bf 109 Damaged	SE El Alamein	1230-1340

British Casualties

274 Sqn	Hurricane IIc BP693 'P' left 1230, shot down by Bf 109s attacking tanks; Flt Lt Wade slt WiA
274 Sqn	Hurricane IIc BP445 'E' left 1230, damaged by Bf 109s, crash-landed in desert; Plt Off W.C.Wigston KiA
274 Sqn	Hurricane IIc BN109 'P' left 1230, damaged by Bf 109s, belly-landed in desert; Sgt R.MacFarlane safe
274 Sqn	Hurricane IIc Z4007 'V' left 1230, damaged by Bf 109 and force-landed; Plt Off Simpson slt WiA
274 Sqn	Hurricane IIc BE398 'X' left 1230, damaged by Bf 109 and crash-landed; Sgt S.Lerche safe
260 Sqn	Kittyhawk I ET1021 'H' crash-landed, badly damaged by Bf 109 10m W Abu Dweir; Plt Off G.Fallows safe

German Claims

1./JG 27	Obgfr Hans Benthin	Hurricane	SE El Alamein	1210
1./JG 27	Obfw Günther Steinhausen	Hurricane	S El Alamein	1214

Italian Casualties

94ª Sq, 8°Gr, 2°St CT	S.Ten Franco Mauri wounded by splinters at Sidi Barrani

Wednesday, 26 August 1942

5 SAAF Squadron received the news that the body of the late commanding officer, Maj L.C.Botha, had been found between Belhamed and Tobruk.

German Casualties

6./JG 27	Bf 109F-4 trop WNr 8372 destroyed in strafing attack at Mumin Busak

Thursday, 27 August 1942

Twelve Hurricanes of 1 SAAF Squadron took off at 1430 with a top cover of Spitfires, to escort a TacR Hurricane of 208 Squadron on a sortie. One Hurricane was hit by Flak and had half the tailplane shot away, Lt Salmon returning to base, escorted by Lt Williams. Four Bf 109s of II./JG 27 were scrambled to intercept, and at 1510 these dived on the ten remaining Hurricanes at 6,000 feet, Oblt Sinner shooting down 2/Lt D.de Klerk, a new pilot with the squadron. The Hurricane dived vertically into the ground in flames.

During the day two Spitfire pilots of 145 Squadron intercepted and claimed damage to a Ju 88 south of El Alamein. Somewhat later ten Spitfires of 92 Squadron provided top cover to 238 Squadron on a reconnaissance, meeting Bf 109s; Flt Lt Morgan and Sgt Hempstead each claimed a damaged.

A Baltimore from 70 OTU undertook a daylight reconnaissance mission, but when five miles north of Maghra Flak was encountered and the aircraft was shot down. Meanwhile, an Ultra intercept reported that an He 111, GH+JH, fitted with a special installation had taken off at 1657, ultimately landing at Catania (Sicily) at 0105. No Allied emissions had been picked up throughout the whole flight. Two of the four transmitters were not serviceable, the aircraft therefore enjoying only marginal serviceability. The Ultra service reported that the unit from which the aircraft came, Sonderkommando Koch, was often identified undertaking both listening and jamming activities against Allied radio communications.

British Claims

145 Sqn	Sgt Mac A.Powers	Spitfire Vb AB339 'M' }	Ju 88 Damaged	15m S El Alamein	1205-1310
145 Sqn	Sgt G.W.Small	Spitfire Vb AB146 'G' }			
92 Sqn	Flt Sgt R.Hempstead	Spitfire Vc BR515 'D'	Bf 109F Damaged		1430-1600
92 Sqn	Flt Lt J.M.Morgan	Spitfire Vc BR525 'S'	Bf 109 Damaged		1430-1600

British Casualties

1 SAAF Sqn	Hurricane IIb Z5469 'T' shot down by Bf 109; 2/Lt D.de Klerk KiA
1 SAAF Sqn	Hurricane IIb BP284 'C' damaged by Flak; Lt J.Salmon returned safe
70 OTU	Baltimore AG 718, shot down by Flak undertaking a reconnaissance sortie; Plt Off P.D.Parker and two safe, one KiA

German Claims

6./JG 27	Oblt Rudolf Sinner	Hurricane	5k NE Kharita	1410

German Casualties

III./StG 3	Ju 87D-3 WNr 2598 80% damaged in air raid at Qasaba

Friday, 28 August 1942

Four Kittyhawks of 250 Squadron took off at 0800 to escort eight from 112 Squadron, which were led by Capt Saville. At the same time 11 Spitfires of 601 Squadron set off on a freelance patrol over the battle area. The Kittyhawks reconnoitred the Deir el Abiod area and released their bombs on some MT, but were then attacked by three Bf 109s of I./JG 27, six of which had been scrambled at 0815. Two Kittyhawks were shot down and were seen burning on the ground, while one parachute was floating down, believed to have been that of Plt Off Loree; both 112 Squadron pilots became PoWs. One of the 250 Squadron aircraft was also shot down, but fell to Flak, Plt Off Newton being wounded. The Italian Ariete Division claimed three aircraft shot down by their AA, one of which was very likely Newton's aircraft. However, since the two 112 Squadron Kittyhawks fell in the same area, it is possible that these were the other two which they claimed.

British Claims

601 Sqn	Sgt G.Allen-Rowlandson	Spitfire Vb BR132 'G'	Bf 109 Probable	Burg el Arab	1715-1825

British Casualties

238 Sqn	Hurricane BE681 'G' damaged by Flak, force-landed at Burg el Arab; Flt Lt D.W.Beedham safe
208 Sqn	Hurricane IIb Z3357 left 0635, hit by Flak, landed at base 0735 Cat I; Plt Off J.D.Wilson safe
112 Sqn	Kittyhawk I AK746 shot down by Bf 109 nr Deir el Abiod 0830; Sgt L.D.P.Barlow PoW
112 Sqn	Kittyhawk I ET1017 'V' shot down Deir el Abiod 0830; Plt Off J.E.Loree PoW
250 Sqn	Kittyhawk I AK613 shot down by by Flak Deir el Abiod 0630; Plt Off G.F.Newton WiA
1437 Flt	Baltimore AG718 badly damaged by intense Flak over Lake Maghra, landed LG.100 with observer KiA; Plt Off H.D.Parker and rest of crew safe

German Claims

1./JG 27	Lt Hans Remmer	P-46	N Abu Dweis	0733
1./JG 27	Obfw Willi Stephan	P-40	N Abu Dweis	

German Casualties

6./JG 27	Bf 109F-4 WNr 8372 destroyed at Mumin Busak by strafing fighter-bombers

Italian Claims

Ariete Division gunners	3 aircraft

Saturday, 29 August 1942

At 0400 Wt Off Joyce of 73 Squadron claimed a single-engined aircraft shot down during a defensive patrol, seeing it crash and burn. A search of the area found only the wreckage of another of the unit's aircraft from which Sqn Ldr Johnston had baled out after being attacked. It was concluded that Joyce had inadvertently shot down this aircraft; fortunately, Johnston suffered only slight injuries. Two Bf 109s of I./JG 27 took off at dawn, Fw Steinhausen shooting up a motor boat a mile or so out to sea off the coast at Daba, setting it on fire. Ten minutes later Flg Off Ardley of 208 Squadron took off on a TacR sortie, but missed his escort and carried on alone over the Qattara Box, failing to return. He probably fell to German Flak, which claimed one Hurricane on this date.

Within a few more minutes 12 Hurricanes of 238 Squadron were ordered to patrol over a torpedoed destroyer off the coast, and these were attacked several times by four Bf 109s of I.Gruppe on a Freie Jagd. At first the attacks were beaten off, but then Oblt Unterberger shot down one, and Sgt West's Hurricane was seen to spin, pull out, and dive gently towards the sea. An hour later eight Kittyhawks of 260 Squadron were briefed to escort a convoy, but three of these fighters were also intercepted by Bf 109s, this time three from II.Gruppe, Fw Torfer shooting down Flt Sgt Ody 30 miles north-west of El Daba; Ody was hurt, but was picked up safely. It was still quite early in the day when four Kittybombers of 450 Squadron took off at 0903 to attack MT. Two more Bf 109s of II.Gruppe had taken off at the same time to escort a reconnaissance Bf 109E, and these attacked the Kittybombers and their escort, Uffz Schneider shooting down one. Four more Bf 109s, this time from I.Gruppe, scrambled at 0908 and also attacked, Hptm Homuth claiming a Kittyhawk. Plt Off Shillabeer and Sgt Markle were both shot down, the latter picked up next day, wounded in arms and legs, and taken to hospital.

At 1005 11 Kittyhawks of 2 SAAF Squadron and 11 Tomahawks of 5 SAAF Squadron patrolled over the forward area, meeting a reported ten plus Messerschmitts and MC.202s. Between them the South Africans claimed two MC.202s and a Bf 109 with a 'mixed bag' of probables and damaged. Lt J.A.Kourie of 2 SAAF was shot down and killed, Capt Parsonson's aircraft being hit in the cooling system; one of the 5 SAAF Tomahawks was damaged Cat I. No German fighters had actually been involved in this engagement, the South Africans having engaged 11 MC.202s of 23° Gruppo, 3° Stormo which had scrambled at 0915. At 0950 south-east of El Mukheisin the Italian pilots reported engaging about 30 P-40s and five of these were claimed shot down, plus one probable. One Macchi failed to return and one crash-landed with the pilot wounded. A third crash-landed at Abu Haggag, this pilot also suffering some injuries.

During the day the two JaboStaffeln, 10./JG 27 and 10./JG 53 were formed into an independent JaboGruppe under Oblt Langermann. The new Gruppe was joined at this time by III./ZG 1 which arrived from Germany, equipped with Bf 110s.

British Claims

73 Sqn	Wt Off E.L.Joyce	Hurricane IIc BP767	Ju 88 (Hurricane)	nr LG.90	0400
3 RAAF Sqn	Sgt G.A.Neill	Kittyhawk I ET953 'V'	Bf 109 Damaged	Qattara area	0950
2 SAAF Sqn	Lt B.R.Bennetts	Kittyhawk I AL181 'W'	MC.202	10-25m SSW El Alamein	1045
2 SAAF Sqn	Lt R.C.Hojem	Kittyhawk I ET9699 'I'	MC.202 Damaged	10-25m SSW El Alamein	1045
2 SAAF Sqn	Lt L.C.H.Hope	Kittyhawk I EV351 'U'	Bf 109 Damaged	10-25m SSW El Alamein	1045
2 SAAF Sqn	Lt L.C.H.Hope	Kittyhawk I EV351 'U'	Bf 109 Damaged	10-25m SSW El Alamein	1045
2 SAAF Sqn	Lt L.C.H.Hope	Kittyhawk I EV351 'U'	MC.202 Damaged	10-25m SSW El Alamein	1045
2 SAAF Sqn	Lt A. Morrison	Kittyhawk I EV366 'L'	Bf 109 Damaged	10-25m SSW El Alamein	1045
2 SAAF Sqn	Capt J.E.Parsonson	Kittyhawk I ET1019 'Q'	MC.202 Damaged	10-25m SSW El Alamein	1045
5 SAAF Sqn	Capt E.N.Colman	Tomahawk IIb AN366 'N'	Bf 109F Probable	S El Alamein	1100
5 SAAF Sqn	Lt J.V.Lindbergh	Tomahawk IIb AN446 'V'	Bf 109F	S El Alamein	1100
5 SAAF Sqn	Maj L.B.Pearce	Tomahawk IIb AN231 'X'	Bf 109F Probable	S El Alamein	1100
5 SAAF Sqn	2/Lt H.Smith	Tomahawk IIb AN238 'O'	MC.202	S El Alamein	1100

British Casualties

73 Sqn	Hurrricane BN538 shot down by 73 Sqn Hurricane; Sqn Ldr G.R.A.McG Johnston baled out injured
260 Sqn	Kittyhawk I shot down by Bf 109 NE El Daba; Sgt C.E.Ody WiA
450 Sqn	Kittyhawk I ET1029 presumed shot down by Bf 109s while on armed recce; Plt Off N.H.Shillabeer, KiA
450 Sqn	Kittyhawk I ET916 'W' presumed shot down by fighters while on armed recce, SE Abu Dweis; Sgt A.G.Markle, WiA
2 SAAF Sqn	Kittyhawk I AK760 'K' shot down by Bf 109s nr El Alamein; Lt J.A.Kourie KiA
2 SAAF Sqn	Kittyhawk I ET1019 'Q' damaged, bullet in coolant system; Capt J.E.Parsonson safe
238 Sqn	Hurricane BP758 'K' left 0650, spun into ground, presumed hit by AA of own ships, just after Bf 109s attacked; Sgt R.G.West KiA
208 Sqn	Hurricane II BG998 left 0935, failed to return from TacR of Qattara Depression; Flg Off W.J.E.Ardley MiA
5 SAAF Sqn	Tomahawk IIb AN231 'X' damaged by Bf 109s 14m SW El Alamein,1100; Maj L.B.Pearce safe

German Claims

2./JG 27	Oblt Josef Unterberger	Hurricane	10km N El Alamein	0650
4./JG 27	Fw Josef Torfer	P-40	45km NE El Daba	0748
5./JG 27	Uffz Bernhard Schneider	P-40	10km SSW Abu Dweis	0843
Stab I./JG 27	Hptm Gerhard Homuth	P-40	15km SE Abu Dweis	0855
Flak		Hurricane		

German Casualties

4./JG 27	Bf 109F-4 WNr 7335 White 4 shot down by Spitfire, force-landed SE El Alamein; Uffz Ferdinand Just PoW
9./JG 27	Bf 109F-4 WNr 8722 crash-landed at Qasaba due to handling error, 30% damaged, pilot safe
2.(F)/123	Ju 86R-1 WNr 5144 engine failure, crashed in Port Said area, destroyed, crew safe

Italian Claims

70ªSq, 23°Gr, 3°St CT	Cap Claudio Solaro	MC.202	P-40	SE Bir el Mukheisin	0950

70ªSq, 23°Gr, 3°St CT	Cap Claudio Solaro	MC.202	} P-40 Probable	SE Bir el Mukheisin	0950
70ªSq, 23°Gr, 3°St CT	Ten Marco Marinone	MC.202			
70ªSq, 23°Gr, 3°St CT	Serg Luigi Bandini	MC.202			
70ªSq, 23°Gr, 3°St CT	Serg Luigi Bandini	MC.202	P-40	SE Bir el Mukheisin	0950
75ªSq, 23°Gr, 3°St CT	Magg Luigi Filippi	MC.202	P-40	SE Bir el Mukheisin	0950
75ªSq, 23°Gr, 3°St CT	S.Ten Pietro Farinetti	MC.202 MM 8385	2 P-40s	SE Bir el Mukheisin	0950

Italian Casualties

75ªSq, 23°Gr, 3°St	CT MC.202 MM 8385 failed to return, S.Ten Pietro Farinetti KiA
75ªSq, 23°Gr, 3°St	CT MC.202 MM 8371 damaged in combat, crash-landed at Abu Haggag, Serg Aldo Bianchini WiA
70ªSq, 23°Gr, 3°St	CT MC.202 MM 9048 force-landed within Axis lines, w/o, S.Ten Giuseppe Spinelli-Barrile WiA
70ªSq, 23°Gr, 3°St	CT MC.202 MM 8117 damaged on landing at Tamet, S.Ten Giuseppe Melandri safe
74ªSq, 23°Gr, 3°St	CT MC.202 MM 8107 broke wing on landing at Benghazi K3, Serg Giuseppe Marchiotto safe

Sunday, 30 August 1942

A Boston of 24 SAAF Squadron which had taken off from LG.99 to bomb the Fuka-El Rahman road in the early hours was shot down when strafing; Capt Furstenburg and his crew were all killed.

There were no losses of bombers recorded by the Luftwaffe during this night, but in addition to the Boston, a Wellington crew of 70 Squadron reported twice being attacked by night fighters, their aircraft being damaged and having to be crash-landed on fire (see Chapter Eleven). The only German night fighter claim that night was for a Swordfish – a very different aircraft, but pilots from 73 Squadron claimed two Ju 88s within a period of five minutes, some hours before this latter claim was made. One has to consider the possibility that perhaps the Hurricane pilots had got it wrong again.

At 0908 nine Spitfires of 92 Squadron flew an offensive sweep over Qattara and El Daba where Plt Off Chisholm claimed a Bf 109, one damaged also being claimed. One Spitfire, flown by Plt Off Bradley-Smith, was badly damaged and crash-landed. It is likely that the unit was actually engaged with 10° Gruppo MC.202s which claimed two P-40s and a probable at around the same time, two of their Macchis force-landing in the Fuka area.

According to Italian records, at 0800 Magg D'Agostinis led 12 MC.202s of 10° Gruppo on a free sweep sortie over the El Alamein-El Qattara area. A formation of about 15 P-40s was encountered over Deir el Qattara and later another formation of 12 Spitfires and P-40s coming from the north. A 15-minute combat followed, two P-40s being claimed shot down plus a probable and some damaged. Serg Magg Migliorato during the return flight was attacked by three Spitfires which hit his aircraft in the radiator. Migliorato recalled:

> "After having shot down a P-40 in Deir el Qattara I lost contact with my formation and headed back to Fuka all alone. A few minutes later another Macchi joined me and we flew together at 5,000 metres [15,000 feet] when we were bounced by three Spitfires that opened fire from about 100 metres. My wingman evaded the attack, but my aircraft was hit in the cooling system and started trailing white smoke. I was ready to bale out when I saw the Spits leaving in a steep left upwards turn. The white trail had been my fortune because they evidently thought I was finished. So I decided to try and get back to our territory. My engine had terrible vibrations but I managed to land safely and got out of the cockpit. Then I noticed that the radiator had been torn away completely by a cannon shell. I sat under a wing hoping to be searched for. All I had was a dozen cigarettes. I stayed there for about nine hours when I sighted a German scout car in a cloud of dust. They had water and chocolate and took me on to El Daba. There I tried to call 4° Stormo at Fuka but the telephone lines were interrupted due to Allied bombing. So I spent the night in the German camp and next afternoon I managed to notify my comrades that I was still alive."

80 Squadron Hurricanes escorted a TacR aircraft over the Axis lines at 1703 with a top cover of nine 92 Squadron Spitfires. Four Bf 109s were scrambled a quarter of an hour later, attacking the formation at 1750. Fw Niederhöfer claimed one Hurricane which belly-landed, but Uffz Just was shot down by one of the Spitfires and became a PoW. 80 Squadron had lost three Hurricanes during this clash, Sqn Ldr Denison's aircraft crash-landing after being hit by a burst of cannon fire. The two other pilots failed to return, and it was thought possible that they had collided. The Messerschmitt pilots reported having seen three crashes south of El Alamein, but apparently due to lack of witnesses, Niederhöfer's claim was not

confirmed. Coming to the defence of the Hurricanes, the Spitfire pilots had claimed two shot down and one damaged. During the day Sqn Ldr G.P.H.Matthews, DFC, and several other pilots who had been posted from the UK with 74 Squadron, were posted to 145 Squadron, Matthews taking command of the unit. 40 SAAF Squadron was at last provided with a few Mark II Hurricanes to continue its TacR duties with slightly more security.

At dusk, Rommel's forces started moving up for a new offensive in the southern sector of the El Alamein front. At once they were held up for longer than anticipated in breaking through the British minefield there. The lull was over and a major battle was again in the immediate offing.

British Claims

73 Sqn	Wt Off E.L.Joyce	Hurricane IIc BP167 'L'	Ju 88	4m E LG.85	0357
73 Sqn	Sqn Ldr G.R.A.McG.Johnston	Hurricane IIc BE518	Ju 88	Amiriya district	0402
92 Sqn	Plt Off W.L.Chisholm	Spitfire Vc BR474	Bf 109	Qattara and El Daba	0908-1033
92 Sqn	Lt D.Hewitson	Spitfire Vc BR491	Bf 109 Damaged	Qattara and El Daba	0908-1033
80 Sqn	Plt Off V.B.Handyside	Hurricane IIc BN355	Bf 109F Damaged	El Alamein area	1700-1820
92 Sqn	Sqn Ldr J.H.Wedgwood	Spitfire Vc BR479	Bf 109E	top cover to 80 Sqn	1703-1823
92 Sqn	Plt Off Bradley-Smith	Spitfire Vc BR389	Bf 109	top cover to 80 Sqn	1703-1823
92 Sqn	Plt Off W.L.Chisholm	Spitfire Vc BR525			

British Casualties

80 Sqn	Hurricane IIc BN126 left on TacR 1700-1820, collided ?; Sgt J.F.J.Montgomerey
80 Sqn	Hurricane IIc BN359 left on TacR 1700-1820, collided ?; Sgt R.J.Thompson KiA
80 Sqn	Hurricane IIc left on TacR, forced to land by Bf 109 hit sand and undercarriage collapsed 1700-1820; Sqn Ldr R.W.Denison safe
92 Sqn	Spitfire V badly damaged and crash-landed at base when a wheel did not extend; Plt Off Bradley-Smith safe
24 SAAF Sqn	Boston III AL787 off from LG.99 to bomb Fuka-El Rahman road in early hours; shot down while strafing, probably by Flak; Capt J.P.Furstenburg and three KiA

German Claims

5./JG 27	Fw Hans Niederhöfer	Hurricane n.b.	S El Alamein	1650

Italian Claims

84ªSq, 10°Gr, 4°St CT	Ten Luigi Giannella	MC.202 MM 7815 '84-6'	P-40	El Alamein	0800-0935
84ªSq, 10°Gr, 4°St CT	Ten Paolo Berti	MC.202 MM 7896 '84-8'	P-40 Probable	El Alamein	0800-0935
91ªSq, 10°Gr, 4°St CT	Serg Magg Lorenzo Migliorato	MC.202 MM 7808 '91-9'	P-40	Deir el Qattara	0800-0935

Italian Casualties

91ª Sq, 10°Gr, 4°St CT	MC.202 MM 7808 '91-9' damaged and force-landed, Serg Magg Lorenzo Migliorato safe, rescued by Germans
84ª Sq, 10°Gr, 4°St CT	MC.202 MM 7905 '84-4' damaged in combat, Serg Livio Barbera safe
394ª Sq, 160°Gr Aut CT	CR.42 MM 7543, w/o, in night landing at Benghazi collided with CR.42s MM 7546 and 7548, Serg Pietro Balliano WiA

CHAPTER 6

THE BATTLE OF ALAM EL HALFA

Monday, 31 August 1942

As daylight filtered over the desert sands, Rommel's attack began, a three-pronged drive being made against the northern, central and southern parts of the front. 7 SAAF Wing had already been hit during one of the Luftwaffe's night raids; one Hurricane of 127 Squadron was set on fire at LG.86, and two more were damaged, with two 274 Squadron Hurricanes also slightly damaged. At nearby LG.86 a 55 Squadron Baltimore, fully bombed-up, was hit and burnt out.

At dawn 20 MC.202s of 10° Gruppo led by Magg D'Agostinis took off in the haze to carry out a low-level attack at three airfields in the Burg el Arab area. About ten minutes after take-off Ten Bevilacqua was forced to bale out of his aircraft due to a seized engine; he fell into the sea and swam three hours to reach the coast in friendly territory. The remaining aircraft reached their target where eight fighters made three strafing runs as the others covered. Despite an intense AA fire, the raiders claimed a number of enemy aircraft destroyed or damaged on the ground: five Lysanders, five P-40s, three Gladiators, one Albacore and one unidentified. On their return course two P-40s were met and one was effectively strafed. At 0720 Magg Fassi led ten MC.202s of 9° Gruppo on a free sweep sortie over the southern El Alamein area. Flying at 21,000ft they encountered eleven Spitfires and ten P-40s but gun stoppages prevented any engagements. At 0840 eleven MC.202s of 4° Stormo (seven of 9° Gruppo led by Ten Reiner and four of

A smiling Ten Emanuele Annoni, commander of 96ª Squadriglia (second from right); he claimed eight victories in North Africa.

10° Gruppo led by M.llo Del Turco) took off on a free sweep over the Qaret el Shirab area. Flying at 3,000ft they sighted and bounced a formation of about 25 Spitfires flying a thousand metres lower; Serg Bladelli and Serg Martinoli claimed a Spitfire each and Ten Mecatti a probable; five damaged were claimed, two by Ten Reiner, one by S.Ten Querci and two by unspecified pilots of 10° Gruppo.

Three Hurricanes of 213 Squadron carried out a dawn reconnaissance over the southern sector, four aircraft being seen near the Qattara Depression. Following this sighting, the squadron then flew to LG.20 which they strafed, claiming to have damaged a number of Bf 109s on the ground.

At 0857 six Bf 109s of I./JG 27 scrambled, briefly engaging with ten Spitfires near Hammam, but without result. They then chased a lone Boston which Lt Kaiser claimed to have shot down near Burg el Arab at 0930, the aircraft crashing in flames. He had in fact shot down a Baltimore of 1437 Strategic Reconnaissance Flight. Nine Messerschmitts of I./JG 27 and eight of III./JG 53 then took off at 1020 to escort 40 Ju 87s of II./StG 3 on a raid, accompanied by other Bf 109s and MC.202s. Back on the ground from their earlier sortie, 213 Squadron was scrambled and intercepted this formation, the bombers at once jettisoning their loads and turning for home. Three Stukas were claimed shot down but one of the claiming pilots was himself shot down and baled out, suffering from severe burns. One Stuka pilot and his gunner were killed, a second pilot becoming a PoW. I./JG 27 encountered eight Hurricanes, Oblt Marseille claiming two shot down in two minutes, reporting that one of the pilots baled out. III./JG 53 reported meeting 20 Hurricanes; Obfw Kronschnabel was seen apparently to shoot one down, but was then himself downed by AA, baling out to become a PoW. The other JG 53 pilots reported seeing one Ju 87 being shot down by a Hurricane and a second disappearing, trailing white smoke.

Fw Hans Niederhöfer of 5./JG 27 was shot down by a Spitfire on 31 August, but survived to return to his unit.

At 1116 ten Bf 109s of II./JG 27 set off on a Freie Jagd, engaging 12 Hurricanes of 1 SAAF Squadron which were flying top cover for 11 more of these fighters from 238 Squadron. Lt Gaynor claimed to have damaged two Bf 109s, but his aircraft was then hit by Oblt Sinner and he crash-landed. Plt Off Hay's 238 Squadron aircraft was hit by Flak and also crash-landed. The German pilots then encountered two Spitfires, but without result. 92 Squadron was also in action during the morning. Lt Rabie, on attachment from 1 SAAF Squadron to gain experience of the Spitfire, and Flt Sgt Hempstead each claimed an MC.202 shot down, Sqn Ldr Wedgwood claiming a fighter damaged.

At 0950, 15 CR.42s of 50° Stormo Assalto had been despatched to attack strongpoints in the Alam el Halfa area, followed at 1325 by 11 more of 101° Gruppo (six of 238ª and five of 208ª Squadriglie) over the same area. This time one was shot down, the pilot baling out and being taken prisoner; however, he had been badly wounded and died next day. Towards evening an 18° Gruppo MC.200 failed to return from a sortie providing cover for motor boats sailing to Mersa Matruh. Shot by AA, the pilot managed to reach the coast, baled out and was captured by British troops.

The second big Stuka attack of the day was made in the evening, 20 Ju 87s being escorted by 11 Bf 109s of III./JG 27, two of I.Gruppe, 11 more of II.Gruppe acting as indirect cover, 11 from III./JG 53 and some MC.202s. Six Spitfires from 601 Squadron were on patrol, and Hurricanes of 80 Squadron took off to intercept, the Spitfire pilots reporting attacking four Bf 109s and four Macchis. Flg Off Le Bas claimed one Messerschmitt, but Sgt Lusty was shot down. 80 Squadron's pilots found visibility very poor and several aircraft suffered from cannon stoppages, but they forced the Ju 87s to jettison their bombs, also claiming damage to two of them.

Oblt Marseille reported fighting a lone Spitfire which he claimed to have shot down at 1925, Oblt Rödel and Sinner of II.Gruppe each claiming one such aircraft in flames around the same time. Claims were also made for three Spitfires shot down and a fourth probably by Macchi pilots of 4° Stormo CT. Although these claims cannot be supported by more than one Spitfire loss on this date, two Kittyhawks of 450 Squadron were shot down, Sgt Reid reportedly falling to a Messerschmitt and becoming a PoW, while Sqn Ldr J.E.A.Williams force-landed when strafing and was also captured. During the II.Gruppe engagement Fw Niederhöfer's Messerschmitt was hit and he force-landed in Axis lines, probably shot down by 601 Squadron's Flg Off 'Pancho' Le Bas. Two more Bf 109s were lost during the day, reportedly both to AA fire. Oblt Tangerding, Staffelkapitän of 7./JG 27, apparently received a direct hit whilst over the target and was killed; in addition one of the JaboGruppe Bf 109Es was brought down near El Alamein, the pilot becoming a prisoner.

During the day 33 Squadron moved up to LG.85, ready for operations. In 213 Squadron the commanding officer, Sqn Ldr Young, was taken ill and during his absence Sqn Ldr George Westlake, who had until recently been a flight commander in the squadron, but who had been posted to 244 Wing on promotion, returned to lead in his stead. According to WDAF's overall loss records, it is possible that one further Spitfire (unit and pilot unidentified) may have been lost on this date. At the end of the day Grp Capt Carter notified Maj Wheeler of the US 64th Fighter Squadron that he should send forward a flight of P-40Fs to operate with 2 SAAF Squadron. At once six aircraft departed Edcu, but these were forced to turn back by a dust storm. This delayed their arrival until early the next morning.

British Claims

73 Sqn	Flt Lt G.R.A.McG.Johnston	Hurricane IIc BE518	Ju 88	Amiriya district	0402
92 Sqn	Flt Sgt R.Hempstead	Spitfire Vc BR522	MC.202		0935-1055
92 Sqn	Lt S.W.Rabie	Spitfire Vc BR390	MC.202		0935-1055
92 Sqn	Sqn Ldr J.H.Wedgwood	Spitfire Vc BR520	Bf 109 Damaged		0935-1055
80 Sqn	Flt Lt R.G.Foskett	Hurricane IIc BP337 'B'	Ju 87 Damaged	E El Alamein	1015-1135
80 Sqn	Plt Off R.O.Smith	Hurricane IIc BN291	Ju 87 Damaged	El Alamein area	1015-1135
213 Sqn	Plt Off L.J.Barnes	Hurricane IIc BP451	Ju 87	E El Alamein	1045
213 Sqn	Flt Sgt J.R.Rebstock	Hurricane IIc BP341 'Y'	Ju 87	E El Alamein	1045
213 Sqn	Flt Sgt W.H.Stephenson	Hurricane IIc BP351 'D'	Ju 87	E El Alamein	1045
1 SAAF	Sqn Lt J.H.Gaynor	Hurricane II BP663 'A' 2	Bf 109Fs Damaged	nr El Alamein	1135
601 Sqn	Flg Off M.H.Le Bas	Spitfire Vb BR392	Bf 109	El Alamein	1830-1940

British Casualties

1437 Flt	Baltimore AG752 shot down by fighters; Sgt A.C.Dyte and crew KiA
223 Sqn	Baltimore III DV887 off 0653 from LG.86 to attack vehicle concentration of 3,000 MT. Hit by heavy Flak over target and last seen heading for coast; Flt Sgt W.E.Wilson and three KiA
55 Sqn	Baltimore II AG794 bombed-up at LG.86 at 0430, but destroyed by direct bomb hit
80 Sqn	Hurricane II BN355 landed at Burg el Arab to check Flak damage; on take-off attacked by 3 Bf 109s; Sgt W.F.Burke escaped
213 Sqn	Hurricane IIc BP451 shot down by fighters E El Alamein at 1045; Plt Off L.J.Barnes baled out
213 Sqn	Hurricane IIc BP351 'D' shot down by fighters E El Alamein, force-landed nr Imayid at 1115; Flt Sgt W.H.Stephenson
1 SAAF Sqn	Hurricane II BP663 'A' damaged by Bf 109s and crash-landed Cat II at 1150; Lt J.H.Gaynor safe
145 Sqn	Spitfire Vb AB189 crash-landed at 0810; Sgt J.S.Anderson safe
238 Sqn	Hurricane BP359 'H' left 1100, hit by Flak, crash-landed at base damaged Cat I; Plt Off W.B.Hay
238 Sqn	Hurricane Z5148 'J' left 1100, crash-landed at LG.92; Plt Off J.C.Rylands safe
601 Sqn	Spitfire V BR636, left 1835, shot down by Bf 109; Sgt K.J.Lusty baled out?

German Claims

Stab I./JG 27	Lt Emil Kaiser	Boston	5km S Burg el Arab	0830
3./JG 27	Oblt Hans-Joachim Marseille	2 Hurricanes	23 & 26km SSE El Alamein	1003 &1004
6./JG 27	Oblt Rudolf Sinner	Hurricane	NE Deir el Raghil	1030
9./JG 53	Obfw Josef Kronschnabel	Hurricane	10km SSE El Alamein	1112

German Claims

3./JG 27	Oblt Hans-Joachim Marseille	Spitfire	15km E El Alamein	1825
Stab II./JG 27	Oblt Gustav Rödel	Spitfire	SSE El Alamein	1829
6./JG 27	Oblt Rudolf Sinner	Spitfire	15km S El Imayid	1830

German Casualties

5./JG 27	Bf 109F-4 WNr 7296 Black 2 shot down by Spitfire Deir el Taga, 100%; Fw Hans Niederhöfer MiA, but returned
9./JG 53	Bf 109F-4/Z WNr 7339 Yellow 5+ I shot down by AA 18km S El Alamein; Obfw Josef Kronschnabel baled PoW
7./JG 27	Bf 109F-4 WNr 7169 shot down by AA S El Alamein; Oblt Hermann Tangerding KiA
7./JG 27	Bf 109F-4 trop WNr 10283 crash-landed Qasaba, 60%; pilot safe
7./ZG 1	Bf 109E-7 WNr 4964 S9+DR shot down by AA nr El Alamein; Uffz Hans Sennholz PoW
5./StG 3	Ju 87D-1 WNr 2459 S7+FN shot down by Hurricane N Deir el Hima; Fw Otto Uhl/Uffz Anton Weilandt PoWs
6./StG 3	Ju 87D-1 WNr 2532 S7+LP shot down by Hurricane Deir el Hima; Uffz Walter Stolp/Gefr Hans Berbig KiA
II./StG 3	Ju 87D-1 WNr 2701 shot down by AA, crashed nr El Alamein
4./KG 100	He 111H-6 WNr 7456 6N+HG Alem Shaltut cause u/k; Fw Hans Spieling KiA, two MiA, one PoW
6./LG 1	Ju 88A-4 WNr 140739 L1+FP shot down by Hurricane night fighter; Hptm Wolfgang Voigt and one KiA, two PoW
6./KG 77	Ju 88A-4 WNr 140108 3Z+EN shot down by AA; Uffz Willi Rochow and three MiA

Italian Claims

73ª Sq, 9°Gr, 4°St CT	Serg Teresio Martinoli	MC.202	Spitfire	Qaret el Shirab	0840-1010
73ª Sq, 9°Gr, 4°St CT	Ten Mario Mecatti	MC.202	Spitfire Probable	Qaret el Shirab	0840-1010
91 ªSq, 10°Gr, 4°St CT	Serg A. Bladelli	MC.202	Spitfire	Qaret el Shirab	0840-1010
73ª Sq, 9°Gr, 4°St CT	Ten Giulio Reiner	MC.202	2 Spitfires Damaged	Qaret el Shirab	0840-1010
73ª Sq, 9°Gr, 4°St CT	S.Ten Alvaro Querci	MC.202	Spitfire Damaged	Qaret el Shirab	0840-1010
10° Gr, 4° St CT	unspecified	MC.202	2 Spitfires Damaged	Qaret el Shirab	0840-1010
84ªSq, 10°Gr, 4°St CT	Cap Franco Lucchini	MC.202 MM 7901 '84-3'	Spitfire	Deir el Hima	1340-1510

Italian Casualties

84ª Sq, 10°Gr, 4°St CT	MC.202 MM 7933 '84-10' force-landed at Qotaifiya 1450, Serg Livio Barbera safe
84ª Sq, 10°Gr, 4°St CT	MC.202 MM 7776 engine seized 0600, Ten Ezio Bevilacqua baled safely
83ª Sq, 18°Gr, 3°St CT	MC.200 MM 8160 shot down by AA 1615-1835, Cap Albo Ferrari baled and PoW
238ª Sq, 101°Gr, 5°St Tuff	CR.42 MM 8903 failed to return, Serg Magg Nicolò Gentile baled and PoW, died next day

Saviour of the downed fighter pilot! A Fieseler Fi 156 Storch lands in the open desert to collect the pilot of a crash-landed Bf 109. It appears that recovery personnel have already been flown in earlier.

Western Desert Air Force Order of Battle, 1 September 1942

AHQ, Western Desert – Burg el Arab (Advanced AHQ) Wadi Natrun (Rear AHQ)

Under direct control of AHQ, WD		
1 Air Ambulance Unit	Wadi Natrun	DH-86
Comm Flt	Wadi Natrun	Various
285 Wing	**Burg el Arab**	
2 PRU (Det from HQ, RAF ME)	Burg el Arab	Spitfire
208 Sqn	Burg el Arab	Hurricane, Tomahawk
1437 Strat Recce Flt	Burg el Arab	Maryland, Baltimore
60 SAAF Sqn (one flt)	Wadi Natrun	Maryland
3 SAAF Wing	**Amiriya**	
12 SAAF, 24 SAAF Sqns	Amiriya	Boston
55, 223 Sqns	Amiriya	Baltimore
81st US Sqn (attached)	Deversoir	B-25C
211 GROUP	**Amiriya**	
66th US Sqn (attached)	Amiriya	P-40F
7 SAAF Wing	**Amiriya**	
6 Sqn	Amiriya	Hurricane IId
7 SAAF Sqn	Amiriya	Hurricane I,IIb (Mark Is equipped to carry 24 x 9lb Jefferis bombs)
127, 274 Sqns	Amiriya	Hurricane IIb
233 Wing	**Amiriya**	
2 SAAF, 260 Sqns	Amiriya	Kittyhawk
4 SAAF Sqn	Amiriya	Kittyhawk, Tomahawk
5 SAAF Sqn	Amiriya	Tomahawk
239 Wing	**Amiriya**	
3 RAAF, 112, 250, 450 Sqns	Amiriya	Kittyhawk
243 Wing	**Amiriya**	
33, 213 Sqns	Amiriya	Hurricane IIc
145, 601 Sqns	Amiriya	Spitfires
244 Wing		
1 SAAF, 238 Sqns	Amiriya	
Hurricane IIb		
80 Sqn	Amiriya	Hurricane IIc
92 Sqn	Amiriya	Spitfire
Available to reinforce WDAF but not under its control		
205 GROUP	**Ismailia**	
231 Wing	Abu Sueir	
37, 70 Sqns	Abu Sueir	Wellington
236 Wing	**Jebel Hamzi**	
108, 148 Sqns	Jebel Hamzi	Wellington

238 Wing	**Kabrit**	
40, 104 Sqns	Kabrit	Wellington
201 GROUP	**Alexandria**	
252, 272 Sqns	Edcu	Beaufighter
821, 826 Sqns (FAA)	Dekheila	Albacore

Tuesday, 1 September 1942

This proved to be Marseille's day of glory, but for the Axis ground forces it was not such a success, their armoured units running into 8th Armoured Brigade in the southern part of the front where the British troops were well dug in in prepared defences with their tanks situated in hull-down positions. The Afrika Korps was also now assailed by an almost constant stream of well-protected bomber formations. The situation was described by 3 SAAF Wing as being a bomb-aimer's dream.

At 0610 two formations of 23° Gruppo Macchis, the first of eight led by Magg Filippi, and the second of ten led by Cap Solaro, took off to provide cover for the ground troops south-east of El Adem. At 0715 Filippi and his pilots spotted 24 Bostons and attacked their escorts, claiming two P-40s shot down. Almost at the same time Solaro's pilots joined the attack, claiming a Spitfire and a P-40. One Macchi was hit after its pilot had claimed damage to another P-40, and he force-landed near El Alamein, within Axis lines, badly damaging his aircraft but escaping unhurt himself. At the end of the day ten new MC.202s would be sent over from Italy and assigned to 23° Gruppo. At 1000 Ten Annoni took off with ten MC.202s of 9° Gruppo to cover a formation of CR.42s to bomb a concentration of tanks and motor vehicles west of El Alamein. After carrying out the escort, they went on a free sweep and attacked a formation of 12 Bostons escorted by 12 P-40s, scoring hits on one Boston and some P-40s. At 1010 Cap Ruspoli led over the same area seven MC.202s of 10° Gruppo. They met possibly the same formation of Bostons with their escort of P-40s and claimed one Boston and one P-40, credited to Ruspoli and Serg Magg Elio Miotto. With these victories the tally of 91ª Sq's claims reached the 100 mark. Later in the day 4° Stormo pilots had another successful combat. This time it was the turn of Magg Fassi to lead from 1640-1835 eleven MC.202s of 9° Gruppo over the area south of El Alamein. Three formations were encountered, flying at different altitudes, from 12,000 to 24,000 feet. An intense fight followed during which two Spitfires and one P-40 were claimed by the Italian pilots, plus three probables (again two Spits and a P-40).

There were several other or related engagements between a number of units during this early morning period. Six Kittyhawks of 450 Squadron had provided top cover for 18 Bostons at 0738, encountering four Bf 109s, one of which the commanding officer claimed to have shot down. Six Messerschmitts of II./JG 27 had taken off at 0736 on a Freie Jagd, the pilots of these reporting encountering two bomber formations, one of Baltimores, the other of Bostons, these being escorted by about 80 fighters. Three Curtiss fighters were claimed, but Oblt Krenz who had 11 victories to his credit, was shot down in flames by Spitfires, probably from 601 Squadron, before the German pilots had commenced their attacks on the bombers' escorts. Kittyhawks and Tomahawks of 2 SAAF and 5 SAAF Squadrons had also taken off around 0720 to escort bombers. The latter unit was attacked by a reported 12 plus Bf 109s and Macchis, and "quite a hectic dogfight" followed during which 2/Lt Brown, on his first operational sortie, disappeared, last being seen chasing a Macchi.

2 SAAF Squadron pressed on with the bombers, but over the target this unit too was attacked by at least ten Axis fighters, Capt Wildsmith making an astern attack on one MC.202 which shed large pieces. His wingman saw this fighter turn slowly onto its back and dive towards the ground. Wildsmith did not try to follow for confirmation, but returned to the bombers. He recorded: "All the cover were drawn off except Vic, Gerry (Gericke) and myself...There were 18 very worried Baltimores. Warmly thanked by leader." However, when the unit returned it was found that Lt Harold Ironside was missing. Thus in the first clash of the morning two South African fighters had been lost against Axis claims for five.

Four II./JG 27 pilots engaged eight bombers and 20 fighters at 0840, then attacking a similar formation, but all without results. Ten minutes later they took on 30 Hurricanes, again without results. The latter were probably aircraft of 238 and 1 SAAF Squadrons, 12 from each unit having taken off at 0815 with a top cover of nine Spitfires from 92 Squadron, to escort a TacR aircraft along the coastal road near El Alamein. Four Bf 109s attacked near El Alamein when the formation was on the return flight, followed by ten more. Plt Off Bradley-Smith's Spitfire was shot down and he baled out, while two more Spitfires were damaged. In return Plt Off Chisholm was able to claim one Messerschmitt shot down and one damaged, Sqn Ldr Wedgwood claiming three fighters and one Stuka damaged, other pilots adding claims for several more damaged. Amongst the Hurricanes, Lt Bailey of 1 SAAF Squadron was shot down and wounded. The South Africans then saw 9-12 Ju 88s which they were ordered to intercept, but failed to do so. Two more of the unit's pilots claimed three Messerschmitts damaged between them, but the commanding officer, Maj Metelerkamp, was badly shot-up and wounded in the arm. Flg Off Matthews of 238 Squadron was attacked by two Bf 109s and shot down south of El Imayid.

Between 0845-0900 15 Bf 109s of I.Gruppe and ten of III.Gruppe were escorting Stukas over the front when they encountered 16 British fighters. Oblt Marseille, covered by Oblt Schlang, attacked one formation in a left hand turn, his first victim being the last in the formation and the second also from this formation (apparently Bailey and Metelerkamp). His third claim was against a fighter which was attempting to attack the Stukas at low level (Matthews), but he was then attacked by six Spitfires from above. The first overshot as he was turning swiftly to port, and this he also claimed to have shot down (Bradley-Smith). He had fired a total of 80 cannon shells and 240 machine-gun bullets at this stage – but as so often, claimed his four victories as P-40s. However, during this engagement one pilot of I.Gruppe had been lost and one of II.Gruppe was shot down and captured.

At 1120 I./JG 27 again launched 12 Bf 109s on a Stuka escort, but these met two Allied bomber formations with fighter escorts. These escorts were again aircraft of 233 Wing, the Kittyhawks and Tomahawks of 2 SAAF and 5 SAAF Squadrons now joined by four P-40Fs of the US 64th Squadron which flew with the former of the South African units. From close cover, Lt Moon looked up and saw five Axis fighters above, one firing on Capt Parsonson's aircraft. Shouting a warning, Moon got behind the Bf 109, now on his leader's tail, and claimed to have shot pieces off it. However, his Kittyhawk was then hit and he baled out. Lt 'Sandy' Morrison also failed to return, Lt Stearnes of the US unit force-landing, having been wounded. The 5 SAAF Squadron formation, flying top cover, was also attacked by Bf 109s, Lt Gordon Jack being shot down and becoming a PoW, with two more Tomahawks badly damaged.

During these engagements, Marseille and two other pilots attacked the escorts of the first bomber formation which formed a defensive circle. Marseille dived into this, claiming to have shot down two of the fighters which caused the circle to break up and scatter. He then attacked the tail-end aircraft, claiming to have shot it down, followed by another and then a fifth, which he reported blew up in mid-air. This was followed by a sixth which he shot down in a steep left turn. These claims were probably made against 2 SAAF and the 64th Squadron. A new formation then appeared, flying east as his Schwarme were climbing steeply to return to base; this was probably 5 SAAF Squadron. These fighters were also attacked, Marseille's seventh victim apparently also blowing up; Schlang attacked one, but missed, and Marseille got behind it in a left turn, claiming to have shot it down from under 100 yards range. A few minutes later Lt Remmer spotted a further formation, and claimed one of these. On landing Marseille was greeted by Feldmarschall Kesselring who was visiting the unit, and was congratulated. Allied contemporary records indicate that in a dogfight around the bombers at this time, six fighters were lost for one Axis fighter claimed shot down.

Led by Maj Eric Smith, 4 SAAF Squadron provided medium cover to eight Bostons during the mid-afternoon period. Enemy fighters were reported and were seen by the bomber crews, but not by the escorts. On landing Maj Smith turned off the runway and taxied alongside it towards dispersal. As he did so, unfortunately a P-40F of the 57th Fighter Group's 66th Squadron, ran into the back of the Kittyhawk, the propeller chewing its way up the rear fuselage, killing Smith in the process. A very popular pilot who had also been the first wartime volunteer of the SAAF to become a squadron commander, he was a sad loss. Capt du Toit was at once appointed the squadron's new leader.

Meanwhile at 1400 six Kittyhawks of 3 RAAF Squadron had been scrambled to intercept hostile aircraft at 6,000 feet to the east of El Alamein, the squadron acting as top cover to four Kittyhawks of 250 Squadron and others of 112 and 450 Squadrons. Having climbed to 13,000 feet, the Australians were attacked by two Bf 109s without any result, but at 1515 more than 50 Ju 87s, escorted by 30 or more fighters, were seen. The escorts included 12 Messerschmitts of I./JG 27 and seven of III./JG 53. These fighters were engaged, Sqn Ldr Gibbes later recording:

> "A pretty big balbo…The others flew straight into the bombers and we in our capacity of top cover, flew straight into the escort. Four of us only. 109s came down on us like hail. I shot at five 109s all told

in the space of about three minutes and was forced down a few thousand feet by a couple of pretty determined attacks on me. Attacked one as it was climbing up from port beam to astern. Flicked and went down with smoke and glycol pouring from it. Two others were attacked from close range – both flicked and dived away. Don't know what happened then as was much too busy to try and look. The other two attacks I observed had no results. Probably didn't hit them. Claimed a 109F as probable, was given to me as destroyed. Makes my tally eight. All told we knocked down seven aircraft without loss to ourselves. Hell, there seemed to be a lot of 109s. We were lucky to get away with it so completely."

One Kittyhawk was hit and slightly damaged, but a pilot of 250 Squadron claimed to have destroyed a Bf 109. Five pilots of 450 Squadron attacked four Bf 109Es, two probables being claimed. One of these was probably an aircraft of III./ZG 1 in which the Kommandeur, Maj Roland Bohrt, was shot down when attacked by 15 British fighters; he would die of his wounds on 9 September. 112 Squadron also engaged six Bf 109s, one being claimed as a probable by Capt Saville following which the unit managed to break through to the Stukas, claiming four shot down. Fw Walter Fink of 7./JG 27 claimed one P-40 during this engagement, but two Messerschmitts force-landed, both apparently due to engine trouble when on a Freie Jagd.

Between 1730-1900 the rest of the day's combats occurred. Hurricanes of 33 and 213 Squadrons were scrambled to intercept bombers over Burg el Arab, meeting Ju 87s, Ju 88s and Bf 109s. Ten II.Gruppe Messerschmitts took off to escort Ju 88s at 1600, followed six minutes later by 11 more from I.Gruppe, the latter providing cover and the former indirect support. At 1820 six Kittyhawks of 3 RAAF Squadron formed part of an escort to Baltimores of 223 Squadron, and at 1830 Wg Cdr J.K.Rogers took off in a 208 Squadron Hurricane II on a Tac R sortie. III./JG 27 encountered eight Spitfires over Hammam and 12 Kittyhawks at Deir el Raghil, but no claims resulted. A Ju 88 of III./KG 77 was seen going down, the crew baling out, almost certainly one of three claimed by 213 Squadron at this time. Involved in the direct escort, I.Gruppe was engaged by 10-15 Hurricanes, Oblt Marseille claiming five of these between 1847-1853, Lt Stahlschmidt two and Lt von Lieres one. 213 Squadron lost five aircraft during this fight, although three of the pilots survived unhurt. However, Wg Cdr Rogers' 208 Squadron aircraft also failed to return. 3 RAAF Squadron reported that their formation was attacked by four Bf 109s south of Deir el Munassib without result, but one of the Baltimores being escorted was hit by Flak and blew up.

The Spitfires of 601 Squadron had flown 32 sorties by the end of the day, meeting a total of 48 Ju 87s and 34 Bf 109s. The unit's American flight commander, Flt Lt 'Crash' Curry, claimed one Bf 109 during the early morning engagement and a second between 1730 and 1900. 3 SAAF Wing had undertaken 125 sorties during the day, six of them by US B-25s. In spite of increasingly intense Flak, 75 tons of bombs were dropped, although 23 bombers were damaged to some extent by the gunfire. On one raid led by Maj D.U.Nel of 24 SAAF Squadron, a Boston and a B-25 appeared to be hit simultaneously, both having their tails blown off. Apart from the 223 Squadron Baltimore shot down, on another mission another of these aircraft from 55 Squadron was hit by Flak over Daba and crash-landed on return to LG.86.

During the day 7 SAAF Wing was able to operate in its designated anti-tank role although in a rather bizarre manner. Led by Maj Whelehan, 7 SAAF Squadron sent off three Hurricane I Specials, each carrying 24 Jefferis bombs, to attack three tanks at a specific location. These were not found, but a lone armoured car was attacked and straddled by the bombs, a direct hit being claimed. Later eight 7 SAAF Squadron Hurricane IIbs provided medium cover, led by Lt Col Loftus, to three 6 Squadron tank-busters, 127 Squadron giving top cover. This time two tanks and some MT were reported and attacked.

Losses of Allied fighters during the day had amounted to 20 aircraft against German claims for 26 and Italian for nine. 17 of these claims had been made by Joachim Marseille, and it can be seen that it is possible to identify with a fair degree of certainty, quite a high proportion of his victims – probably eight or nine shot down plus three or four more damaged. It seems that the main reason for the many doubts that have been expressed in the past regarding the veracity of his claims, arises from his poor aircraft recognition (or inaccurate recording of the types claimed). This was a weak point with many of the German pilots – and indeed of the Italians. In all three of his big combats on this date he claimed Curtiss fighters, whereas in the first and the third his victims included, or were fully composed of Hurricanes.

Despite the high losses incurred by the Allied fighters during the day, the Axis fighters failed completely to stop any of the bomber formations getting through or inflicting any serious damage on them. Such losses as there had been were all caused by the Flak defences. That night Rommel wrote that very heavy continuous air attacks by day and night had caused considerable losses in personnel and material, and had had a detrimental effect on the morale of his troops. The war diary of the Afrika Korps noted: "The enemy air forces carried out extremely widespread and successful operations throughout the day. The Deutsche Afrika Korps was attacked at least seven times by bomber formations of 12 or more aircraft. The Luftwaffe and Flak could not prevent these attacks. Seven enemy aircraft were shot down in the DAK zone. Losses, especially of vehicles, were considerable. Command became difficult at times owing to the loss of several signals vehicles of the Korps Signal Detachment, and frequent interruptions in telephone communications."

British Claims

145 Sqn	Plt Off E.H.Bicksler	Spitfire Vb AR321 'N'	Bf 109 Probable		0710-0830
145 Sqn	Sqn Ldr G.P.H.Matthews	Spitfire Vb BR235 'B'	Bf 109 Damaged		0710-0830
450 Sqn	Sqn Ldr A.D.Ferguson	Kittyhawk I EV169	Bf 109F		0738-0848
601 Sqn	Flt Lt J.H.Curry	Spitfire Vc BP988	Bf 109		0745-0930
2 SAAF Sqn	Capt H.E.N.Wildsmith	Kittyhawk I ET900 'T'	Bf 109F Probable	El Alamein area	0800
92 Sqn	Plt Off W.L.Chisholm	Spitfire Vc BR525 'S'	Bf 109	El Alamein	0830-1000
1 SAAF Sqn	Lt G.R.Connell	Hurricane II ..290 'E'	Bf 109F Damaged	El Alamein area	0905
1 SAAF Sqn	Lt T.W.Phillips	Hurricane II HV317 'N'	2 Bf 109s Damaged	El Alamein area	0905
92 Sqn	Plt Off W.L.Chisholm	Spitfire Vc BR525 'S'	Bf 109	8m S Hammam	0915
92 Sqn	Plt Off G.W.Rose	Spitfire Vc BR580 'B'	Bf 109 Damaged	S Hammam	0915
92 Sqn	Flt Lt C.J.Samouelle	Spitfire Vc BR479 'E'	2 Bf 109s Damaged	S Hammam	0915
92 Sqn	Sqn Ldr J.H.Wedgwood	Spitfire Vc BR476 'J'	3 Bf 109s Damaged	S Hammam	0915
92 Sqn	Sqn Ldr J.H.Wedgwood	Spitfire Vc BR475 'J'	Ju 87 Damaged	S Hammam	0915
213 Sqn	Plt Off C.D.A.Smith	Hurricane IIc BN137 'A'	Bf 109F Damaged	S El Alamein	0915-1015
2 SAAF Sqn	Lt W.L.O.Moon	Kittyhawk I EV351 'U'	Bf 109F Damaged	El Alamein area	1150
450 Sqn	Sgt G.Lindsey	Kittyhawk I EV158	Bf 109E Probable		1355-1527
450 Sqn	Flt Sgt V.J.McFarlane	Kittyhawk I AK907	Bf 109E Probable		1355-1527
450 Sqn	Flt Lt J.E.A.Williams	Kittyhawk I EV367	Bf 109E Damaged	1355-1527	
92 Sqn	Lt J.M.Faure	Spitfire Vc BR491 'Q'	Bf 109F	El Alamein	1440-1550
92 Sqn	Sqn Ldr J.H.Wedgwood	Spitfire Vc BR475 'J'	Bf 109 Damaged	El Alamein	1440-1550
92 Sqn	Flt Lt C.J.Samouelle	Spitfire Vc BR479 'E'	Bf 109 Damaged	El Alamein	1440-1550
601 Sqn	Sgt D.V.Watts	Spitfire Vc BR245 'X'	Bf 109 Probable	El Hammam	1445-1540
250 Sqn	Sgt H.Stewart	Kittyhawk I EV362 'Y'	Bf 109	E El Alamein	1500
112 Sqn	Sqn Ldr B.Drake	Kittyhawk I EV365	2 Ju 87s	Qzut el Abd area	1510
112 Sqn	Plt Off T.Livingstone	Kittyhawk I ET795	Ju 87 Damaged	Qzut el Abd area	1510
112 Sqn	Plt Off H.Phillips	Kittyhawk I EV162	Ju 87	Qzut el Abd area	1510
112 Sqn	Capt E.C.Saville	Kittyhawk I EV368	Ju 87	Qzut el Abd area	1510
112 Sqn	Capt E.C.Saville	Kittyhawk I EV368	Bf 109 Probable	Deir el Munassib area	1510
3 RAAF Sqn	Sqn Ldr R.H.Gibbes	Kittyhawk I ET953 'V'	Bf 109F	S El Alamein	1515
601 Sqn	Flt Lt J.H.Curry	Spitfire Vc BP988 'N'	Bf 109		1730-1900
213 Sqn	Plt Off J.E.Avise	Hurricane IIc BP342	Ju 88	S El Alamein	1800-1905
213 Sqn	Sgt A.Garrod	Hurricane IIc BN273	Ju 88 Damaged	S El Alamein	1800-1905
213 Sqn	Flg Of A.U.Houle	Hurricane IIc BP341 'Y'	Ju 88	S El Alamein	1800-1905
213 Sqn	Sgt W.J.Steele	Hurricane IIc BP592 'F'	Ju 88 Damaged	S El Alamein	1800-1905
213 Sqn	Plt Off G.P.Waite	Hurricane IIc BP219 'H'	Ju 88	S El Alamein	1800-1905

British Casualties

145 Sqn	Spitfire Vb AR321; damaged Cat II by Bf 109, crashed on landing at 0830; Plt Off E.H.Bicksler safe
2 SAAF Sqn	Kittyhawk I ET575 MiA, presumed shot down by Bf 109s nr El Alamein at 0806; 2/Lt H.E.Ironside KiA
2 SAAF Sqn	Kittyhawk I EV351 'U' shot down SW El Alamein; Lt W.L.O.Moon baled out 1155 and returned
2 SAAF Sqn	Kittyhawk I EV366 'L' damaged by Bf 109 and abandoned 13m SE El Alamein 1200; Lt A.Morrison PoW
4 SAAF Sqn	Kittyhawk I ET903 hit by P-40F while taxying at LG.97 at about 1600; Maj E.Smith K
5 SAAF Sqn	Tomahawk IIb AK559 'S' shot down 18m SE El Alamein 0820; 2/Lt W.H.H.Brown KiA
5 SAAF Sqn	Tomahawk IIb AM390 'F' shot down by fighters 5m S Alam el Halfa 1200; Lt G.B.Jack PoW
5 SAAF Sqn	Tomahawk IIb AN399 'T' damaged by Bf 109; Lt D.W.Murdoch
5 SAAF Sqn	Tomahawk IIb AK489 'B' damaged by Bf 109; Lt B.A.Kearns back safe
3 RAAF Sqn	Kittyhawk I AK776 slt damaged by Bf 109 at 1515; Sgt T.G.Wood safe

British Casualties

213 Sqn	Hurricane IIc BP499 shot down by Bf 109 at 1830; Sgt F.G.Potter MiA, found and buried by 10th Hussars
213 Sqn	Hurricane IIc BP409 shot down by Bf 109 at 1830; Flg Off R.F.Wollaston KiA
213 Sqn	Hurricane IIc BN273 damaged by Bf 109 and abandoned at 1830; Flt Sgt A.Garrood baled out
213 Sqn	Hurricane IIc BP342 damaged by Bf 109 on sweep and crash-landed at 1830; Plt Off J.E.Avise safe
213 Sqn	Hurricane IIc HL704 damaged by Bf 109s and crash-landed at 1830; Flt Sgt P.D.Ross safe
238 Sqn	Hurricane Z5666 'P' shot down SE El Imayid at 0930-0940; Flg Off I.W.Matthews
33 Sqn	Hurricane IIc BN544 'F' force-landed due to Flak; Sgt M.A.Perkins safe
208 Sqn	Hurricane II HL566 left at 1830 on TacR sortie; Wg Cdr J.K.Rogers MiA
1 SAAF Sqn	Hurricane IIb BH283 'R' left 0835, damaged Cat II by Bf 109 0915, landed 0950; Maj P.C.R.Metelerkamp slt WiA
1 SAAF Sqn	Hurricane IIb left 0835, damaged by Bf 109 at 0905, belly-landed N Burg el Arab; Lt D.G.Bailey WiA
335 Sqn	Hurricane Z4327 ditched off Alexandria
92 Sqn	Spitfire V BR474 'D' shot down on TacR by Bf 109 El Alamein at 0915; Plt Off F.C.Bradley-Smith baled out safely
92 Sqn	Spitfire V BR145 damaged by Bf 109 at El Alamein at 0915, landed at base Cat II; Lt C.R.Sinclair safe
92 Sqn	Spitfire V BR476 'J' hit by leader of Bf 109s in starboard wing, Cat I; Sqn Ldr J.H.Wedgwood
601 Sqn	Spitfire V BR245 left 1725, forced to land El Hammam area at 1845; Sgt A.H.Sowerby safe
55 Sqn	Baltimore II AG828 'H' off 0707 to bomb armour W Deir el Raghil. Badly damaged by Flak over El Daba, crash-landed at LG.86 on return; DBR; Flt Sgt R.C.Payne and three safe
223 Sqn	Baltimore III AG843 off 1756 to attack MT at El Alamein. Shot down by Flak over target at 1850; Sgt P.W.Carruthers and three KiA
24 SAAF Sqn	Boston III AL674 off to attack MT at El Alamein. Tail blown off by Flak 15m S target at 1821. Observer, Lt A.B.Sluter baled out and PoW; Lt J.A.Pocock and two KiA

US Casualties

82nd BS/12th BG	B-25C off with SAAF for battle area. Shot down in flames by Flak with tail assembly blown off; Capt H.P.Croteau and two crew from 83rd Bomb Squadron PoW, three KiA
57th FG	P-40F force-landed LG.172; Lt H.M.Stearns, attached 2 SAAF Sqn, WiA

*Allied fighter casualties listed as 9 Hurricanes, 4 Kittyhawks, 4 Tomahawks, 2 Spitfires, 2 Beaufighters and one USAAF P-40

German Claims

6./JG 27	Oblt Rudolf Sinner	2 P-40s	ENE & E Deir el Taga	0659 & 0705
Stab II./JG 27	Oblt Gustav Rödel	P-40	S Sana Hut	0705
3./JG 27	Oblt Hans-Joachim Marseille	4 P-40s	SSE Imayid	0826-0839
3./JG 27	Oblt Hans-Joachim Marseille	8 P-40s	SE & E Alam el Halfa	1055-1105
1./JG 27	Lt Hans Remmer	P-40	SE El Alamein	1112
7./JG 27	Fw Walter Fink	Spitfire	N Amiriya	1415
1./JG 27	Obfw Günther Steinhausen	Hurricane	Alam el Halfa	1746
3./JG 27	Oblt Hans-Joachim Marseille	2 P-40s	S Imayid	1747 &1748
2./JG 27	Lt Hans-Arnold Stahlschmidt	Hurricane	SE El Alamein	1748
3./JG 27	Oblt Hans-Joachim Marseille	2 P-40s	SE & SSE Imayid	1749 &1750
2./JG 27	Lt Hans-Arnold Stahlschmidt	Hurricane	7km SE El Alamein	1750
3./JG 27	Oblt Hans-Joachim Marseille	P-40	7km SSW Imayid	1753
2./JG 27	Lt Karl von Lieres und Wilkau	Hurricane	SE El Alamein	1754

German Casualties

1./JG 27	Bf 109F-4 trop WNr 8585 Yellow 3, combat with Spitfire SE El Alamein; Fw Karl-Heinz Berben MiA
6./JG 27	Bf 109F-4 trop WNr 8703 Yellow 12 combat 20km S El Hammam, 100%; Obfw Herbert Krenz WiA
7./JG 27	Bf 109F-4 WNr 7279 White 5 shot down by Hurricane 20km S El Alamein; Fw Fritz Gahr KG
III./ZG 1	Bf 109E-7 WNr 6305 S9+AD combat with P-40 E El Alamein, crash-landed; Maj Roland Bohrt WiA; died of wounds 9th
7./KG77	Ju 88A-4 WNr 8526 3Z+KR shot down in combat with Hurricanes in Imayid area; Obfw Josef Moritz and three MiA

Italian Claims

70ª Sq, 23°Gr, 3°St CT	M.llo Balilla Albani	MC.202	P-40	SE El Alamein	0610-0740
70ª Sq, 23°Gr, 3°St CT	Serg Magg Celso Zemella	MC.202	Spitfire	SE El Alamein	0610-0740
70ª Sq, 23°Gr, 3°St CT	Ten Marco Marinone	MC.202	P-40 Probable	SE El Alamein	0610-0740
75ª Sq, 23°Gr, 3°St CT	Magg Luigi Filippi	MC.202	P-40	SE El Alamein	0715
75ª Sq, 23°Gr, 3°St CT	Cap Mario Pinna	MC.202	P-40	SE El Alamein	0715
91ª Sq, 10°Gr, 4°St CT	Cap Carlo M. Ruspoli	MC.202	Boston	El Alamein	1010-1150

91ª Sq, 10°Gr, 4°St CT	Serg Magg Elio Miotto	MC.202	P-40	El Alamein	1010-1150
96ª Sq, 9°Gr, 4°St CT	Cap Roberto Fassi	MC.202	Spitfire	Deir el Agram	1640-1835
97ª Sq, 9°Gr, 4°St CT	Ten Fernando Malvezzi	MC.202	Spitfire	Deir el Agram	1640-1835
97ª Sq, 9°Gr, 4°St CT	Ten Jacopo Frigerio	MC.202	P-40	Deir el Agram	1640-1835
9°Gr, 4°St CT	unstated	MC.202	3 e/a Probable	Deir el Agram	1640-1835
Italian Casualties					
70ªSq, 23°Gr, 3°St CT	MC.202 MM 9060 '70-11' damaged in combat and force-landed, Ten Marco Marinone safe				

Wednesday, 2 September 1942

Early in the morning 4° Stormo was back in action. At 0610 Magg D'Agostinis led 18 MC.202s of 10° Gruppo over Bir Mseilik area. A formation of twelve Spitfires was intercepted and subsequently two large formations of Bostons, Spitfires and P-40s were met. The combat developed into many individual dogfights, lasting about 15 minutes. Six Spitfires and one Boston were claimed for the loss of M.llo Pietro Del Turco.

Ten Spitfires of 92 Squadron took off on an offensive sweep at 0720, meeting MC.202s of 10º Gruppo in the El Alamein area. Lts Rabie and Faure, the 1 SAAF Squadron attackers, claimed an MC.202 and a Bf 109 respectively, one of the Italian pilots being shot down. Rabie was then shot down, baling out from 15,000 feet, and Flt Sgt Mount also failed to return; Rabie arrived back with the squadron during the afternoon. The Italian pilots were clearly delighted with their success, claiming six Spitfires shot down as well as a Boston, claimed by Cap Franco Lucchini, who also claimed one of the Spitfires; there is no record of a Boston being lost on this date, however. The combat appears to have been witnessed by eight Messerschmitt pilots of III./JG 53, who were escorting Stukas and reported seeing a British bomber formation with a strong escort, including four Spitfires as top cover. They recorded that as they watched, one Spitfire crashed.

Six Bf 109s of III./JG 27 took off on a Freie Jagd at 0930, and a quarter of an hour later eight from I.Gruppe set off to undertake a defensive patrol over the front line. They were followed four minutes later by 16 more Messerschmitts from II.Gruppe on a Stuka escort. 33 Squadron scrambled at 0940 on patrol, while at 1000 a formation of 15 Bostons and three B-25s were despatched with a heavy escort. Five Kittyhawks of 2 SAAF Squadron and seven P-40Fs of the 64th Squadron provided close cover, seven Kittyhawks of 260 Squadron were top cover and the Tomahawks of 5 SAAF Squadron were medium cover. II./JG 27's aircraft attacked this formation as the German pilots were on their way to the Stukas' target. They achieved no definite success and returned to the dive-bombers. These were then attacked by the Hurricanes of 33 Squadron, but 12 Messerschmitts intercepted these, breaking up their formation and preventing them reaching the bombers. One Hurricane was shot down by Obfw Bendert. At 1016 I.Gruppe engaged the bombers' escorts, Oblt Marseille claiming three fighters in the El Imayid area; one Kittyhawk of 2 SAAF Squadron was shot down, the pilot baling out, and one of the US Warhawks was damaged and the pilot was wounded, carrying out a crash-landing at LG.172. III.Gruppe then also joined the combat but lost Lt Scheiter who became a prisoner. 260 Squadron reported being attacked by a single Bf 109 which was claimed shot down by Wt Off Bernier, another claim for a Messerschmitt being made by 2/Lt H.Smith of 5 SAAF Squadron.

Just after noon 12 MC.200s of 18º Gruppo led by T.Col Tito Falconi, and escorted by 17 MC.202s of 23º Gruppo, attacked vehicles in the El Hammam area with British 250lb bombs which had been found in various captured dumps. On return one MC.200 was destroyed in a landing accident, the badly injured pilot later dying.

At the same time 13 Bf 109s of I./JG 27 escorted Ju 88s, two of which were shot down by AA fire. At 1425 eight III.Gruppe aircraft covered 14 Ju 87s of II./StG 3 over the lines where they were intercepted by 12 Hurricanes of 127 Squadron and 12 of 274 Squadron, both units reaching the Stukas and forcing them to jettison their bombs, the pilots of these two units making a multitude of claims, including six Ju 87 shot down (all but one by pilots of 127 Squadron), three probables and three damaged, plus two Bf 109s shot down and four damaged. During the fight Plt Off Rebman's aircraft was damaged, Uffz Krainik of III.Gruppe claiming one fighter shot down, while the pilots of this unit reported seeing three Stukas force-landed; another 127 Squadron pilot, Flt Sgt Reynolds, had to force-land due to engine failure.

Soon after 1500 nine Spitfires of 92 Squadron covered Hurricanes of 80 and 238 Squadrons on a TacR mission which was intercepted by some Bf 109s, the Spitfire pilot claiming two of these shot down. They may have been engaged with Macchis, 18 MC.202s of 23º Gruppo. Led by Magg Filippi, patrolling over the Axis armoured columns between 1545-1730, they engaged large formations of P-40s and Spitfires, two of the former being claimed shot down with others believed to have been hit. Cap Solaro, the 70ª Squadriglia commanding officer, ran out of fuel and landed at the Luftwaffe airfield at Sanyet Qotaifiya, returning next day.

Three I./JG 27 Bf 109s escorted a reconnaissance aircraft at 1558, also reporting a large formation of Curtiss fighters, two of which Marseille claimed around 1620 (again as the 'phantom' P-46s). 5 SAAF Squadron on a bomber escort at this time, lost two Tomahawks, both reported as shot down either by Bf 109s or MC.202s. At 1700 12 Hurricanes of 274 Squadron provided top cover to a trio of 6 Squadron tank-busters, eight of 7 SAAF Squadron giving medium cover. Their target was again to be three tanks in the Lake Maghra area, but once more these were not found, 6 Squadron claiming a single armoured car. One of the Hurricane IIds was hit by Flak, landing back at base damaged Cat II. Meanwhile, however, 274 Squadron had been hit by six Bf 109s of I./JG 27 on a Freie Jagd at 1710. Two of their Hurricanes were shot down by Hptm Homuth and Lt Stahlschmidt. The latter's victim belly-landed and he strafed and destroyed it on the ground. Both pilots survived and each claimed to have shot down a Messerschmitt before going down themselves; there were, however, no such losses of German fighters at this time.

Eleven more Bf 109s of II.Gruppe took off on another Freie Jagd at 1720, just as eight Spitfires of 601 Squadron and Hurricanes of 33 Squadron were scrambling, the two formations clashing at 1800. Obfw Clade shot down Flt Sgt Schofield of 601 Squadron, who baled out and was taken to hospital with burns. Of the ten British fighters lost during the day, five of the pilots were reported safe. The Axis forces had made little progress and had suffered heavy casualties. As a result Rommel had now decided to abandon the offensive and begin a gradual withdrawal. With evening he complained bitterly to Kesselring about the precision formations of bombers attacking his forces which the Luftwaffe appeared unable to stop.

At night 3° Stormo commander T.Col Falconi took off from Abu Smeit in an MC.200 of 83ª Squadriglia to try and intercept a raider. At 2305 he fired two long bursts but was unable to observe the result.

To give an idea of the magnitude of the air supply effort now being made by the Luftwaffe, the Matruh aerodrome control report on movements provided figures for this particular day as shown below. This information is extracted from Ultra CX/MSS 1370/T15 Africa Air Transport QT821.

2 Bf 109	landed	0705
62 Ju 52	landed	0750
48 Ju 52	took off	0810 for Comiso
Gotha 242 No 595	landed	1210
Me 110 3U+VR	landed	1230, took off 1330
3 a/c JS, PS, KS	landed between 0705 to 1200, took off 0900 to 1325	
He 111 R1+DA	landed 1108, took off 1400	
He 111 CC+UN	landed 1225, took off 1405	

British Claims

73 Sqn	Flt Sgt R.Chandler	Hurricane IIc BP398	Ju 88 Damaged	5-7m NE LG.85	0205
92 Sqn	Lt J.M.Faure	Spitfire Vc BR479 'E'	Bf 109F	El Alamein	0720-0845
92 Sqn	Lt S.W.Rabie	Spitfire Vc BR475 'A'	MC.202	El Alamein	0720-0845
92 Sqn	Flt Sgt R.Hempstead	Spitfire Vc BR573 'T'	Bf 109 Damaged	El Hammam	0720-0845
92 Sqn	Flt Lt J.M.Morgan	Spitfire Vc BR525 'S'	2 Bf 109Fs Damaged	El Hammam	0720-0845
145 Sqn	Plt Off E.H.Bicksler	Spitfire Vb AR290 'A'	Bf 109 Probable		0740-0845
5 SAAF Sqn	2/Lt H.Smith	Tomahawk IIb AK449 'U'	Bf 109F	25m SE El Alamein	0820
260 Sqn	Wt Off J.S.Bernier	Kittyhawk IIa	Bf 109		1000-1058
274 Sqn	Sgt F.A.Carter	Hurricane IIc BG966 'N'	Ju 87 Probable	15m S El Alamein	1445-1540
274 Sqn	Sgt F.A.Carter	Hurricane IIc BG966 'N'	Ju 87 Damaged	15m S El Alamein	1445-1540
274 Sqn	Flg Off J.R.C.Graves	Hurricane IIc BP763 'V'	Bf 109 Damaged	15m S El Alamein	1445-1540
274 Sqn	Plt Off R.W.Henderson	Hurricane IIc BE669 'C'	Ju 87 Damaged	15m S El Alamein	1445-1540
274 Sqn	Flt Sgt J.W.Neil	Hurricane IIc BP326 'T'	Ju 87	15m S El Alamein	1445-1540
274 Sqn	Flt Sgt J.W.Neil	Hurricane IIc BP326 'T'	Ju 87 Probable	15m S El Alamein	1445-1540
7 SAAF Wg	Lt Col D.H.Loftus	Hurricane IIc	Ju 87 Damaged	15m S El Alamein	1445-1540
7 SAAF Wg	Lt Col D.H.Loftus	Hurricane IIc	Bf 109F Damaged	15m S El Alamein	1445-1540
127 Sqn	Flt Lt R.C.Lawrence	Hurricane IIb BN160 'J'	2 Ju 87s		1510

127 Sqn	Sqn Ldr C.O.J.Pegge	Hurricane IIb BN406 'B'	Ju 87		1510
127 Sqn	Wt Off B.Raises	Hurricane IIb BP294 'Y'	Ju 87		1510
127 Sqn	Wt Off B.Raises	Hurricane IIb BP294 'Y'	Ju 87 Probable		1510
127 Sqn	Plt Off A.L.Rebman	Hurricane IIb BP300	Ju 87		1510
127 Sqn	Plt Off A.L.Rebman	Hurricane IIb BP300	Bf 109F Damaged		1510
127 Sqn	Plt Off B.R.Terry	Hurricane IIb Z5586 'S'	Ju 87 Probable		1510
127 Sqn	Flt Sgt A.R.Moulden	Hurricane IIb BP224 'F'	Ju 87 Damaged		1510
127 Sqn	Sgt A.C.Pauley	Hurricane IIb BP751	Ju 87 Damaged		1510
127 Sqn	Sgt I.R.Campbell	Hurricane IIb Z3759 'R'	Ju 87 Damaged		1510
127 Sqn	Sgt F.A.LePoer-Trench	Hurricane IIb BP286 'T'	Ju 87 Damaged		1510
92 Sqn	Flt Lt J.M.Morgan	Spitfire Vc BR525 'S'	Bf 109F	W El Alamein	1515-1635
92 Sqn	Sqn Ldr J.H.Wedgwood	Spitfire Vc BR476 'J'	Bf 109F	W El Alamein	1515-1635
274 Sqn	Sgt F.A.Carter	Hurricane IIc BG966 'N'	Bf 109		1700-1820
274 Sqn	Flt Sgt J.W.Neil	Hurricane BP742 'X'	Bf 109 Damaged		1700-1820
274 Sqn	Sgt B.Ott	Hurricane BP667 'B'	Bf 109		1700-1820
33 Sqn	Flt Lt L.C.Wade	Hurricane IIc HL661 'J'	Bf 109	patrol from LG.85	1720-1830
601 Sqn	Flg Off M.H.Le Bas	Spitfire Vc BR113	Bf 109 Damaged	El Hammam	1720-1835
601 Sqn	Plt Off W.R.P.Sewell	Spitfire Vc BR478	Bf 109		1720-1840

British Casualties

33 Sqn	Hurricane IIc BN908 'V' scrambled at 0935, shot down by Bf 109 10m SW El Alamein; Plt Off G.R.Dibbs KiA
127 Sqn	Hurricane IIc BM979 'C' force-landed at 1510, engine failure after an attack by Bf 109, Cat II; Flt Sgt A.O.Reynolds safe
127 Sqn	Hurricane IIc BP300 damaged by Bf 109 at 1510, Cat II; Plt Off A.L.Rebman safe
127 Sqn	Hurricane IIc Z5586 'Z' damaged by Bf 109 at 1510, Cat I; Plt Off B.R.Terry
127 Sqn	Hurricane IIc Z3759 'R' damaged by Ju 87 gunner at 1510, Cat I; Sgt I.R.Campbell
238 Sqn	Hurricane IIc 'K' shot down by fighters c1545; Sgt J.J.Webb safe
238 Sqn	Hurricane IIc BE681 'Z' shot down by fighters or glycol leak c1545, force-landed; Plt Off D.L.G.Turvey safe
274 Sqn	Hurricane IIc BG966 'N' took off at 1720, shot down; Sgt F.A.Carter
274 Sqn	Hurricane IIc BP667 'B' took off at 1720, shot down; Sgt B.Ott
92 Sqn	Spitfire V BR515 'D' took off at 0720, shot down by Bf 109 El Alamein; Flt Sgt L.B.Mount KiA
92 Sqn	Spitfire V BR475 'A' took off at 0720, shot down by Bf 109s; Lt S.W.Rabie baled out, back in afternoon
601 Sqn	Spitfire V BR118 took off at 1725, damaged by enemy aircraft at 1800; Flt Sgt T.D.Schofield baled out
2 SAAF Sqn	Kittyhawk I AL181 on bomber escort shot down by Bf 109s 20m E El Alamein; Lt D.D.Stuart baled out at 0845
5 SAAF Sqn	Tomahawk IIb AK349 took off at 1630, shot down, crash-landed 20m SE El Alamein; Lt J.V.Lindbergh slt injured
5 SAAF Sqn	Tomahawk IIb AN238 'O' took off at 1630, shot down by fighters 5m SE Alam el Halfa; Lt E.H.D.Carman WiA

US Casualties

57th FG	P-40F crash-landed nr LG.172; Lt McMariel, attached to 2 SAAF Sqn, slt injured

German Claims

3./JG 27	Oblt Hans-Joachim Marseille	2 P-46s	25-30km SE Imayid	0916 & 0918
4./JG 27	Obfw Karl-Heinz Bendert	Spitfire	12km SSW Imayid	0922
3./JG 27	Oblt Hans-Joachim Marseille	Spitfire	10km S Imayid	0924
8./JG 27	Uffz Erich Krainik	P-40	SSE El Alamein	
3./JG 27	Oblt Hans-Joachim Marseille	2 P-46s	20-18km SE El Alamein	1518 & 1521
Stab I./JG 27	Hptm Gerhard Homuth	P-46	SW El Hammam	1610
2./JG 27	Lt Hans-Arnold Stahlschmidt	P-46	SW El Hammam	1612
5./JG 27	Obfw Emil Clade	Spitfire	SSW El Hammam	1705

German Casualties

10.(Jabo)/JG 27	Bf 109F-4 WNr 7258 Green 9 shot down by Flak nr Nelmachras Lake; Uffz Helmut Fiebelkorn MiA, but returned
8./JG 27	Bf 109F-4/B WNr 7329 Black 9 combat with P-40 S El Alamein; Lt Wilhelm Scheiter KG
4./StG 3	Ju 87D-3 WNr 2604 hit in combat with Hurricane Alam el Kadin; Uffz Fritz Strassburger WiA; pilot safe
5./StG 3	Ju 87D-3 WNr 2373 hit in combat with Hurricane Alam el Kadin, crash-landed nr Qasaba; Obfw Fritz Reuter WiA, returned
4.(H)/12	Bf 110F-3 WNr 5010 shot-up in combat with fighters, belly-landed at Bir el Abd airfield on return, crew safe
8./ZG 1	Bf 109E-7 WNr 4140, ran into belly-landed Bf 110 while taking off at Bir el Abd; Uff Johannes Rauhut KiA
5./KG 77	Ju 88A-4 WNr 142164 3Z+KN shot down by AA El Alamein area; Lt Josef Herzinger and one KiA, two baled out and PoW

Re-arming a P-40F of the 57th Fighter Group. A 500lb bomb is fastened into place as armourers add small anti-personnel bombs to racks beneath the wings.

German Casualties

Stab II./KG 77	Ju 88A-4 WNr 140764 hit by AA El Alamein area; observer Uffz Herbert Just baled out and PoW, ditched off Crete, crew rescued
II./St G 3	Ju 87D-1 WNr 2545 hit in combat with Hurricanes over Alam el Kadim, 15% damaged; crew safe
II./St G 3	Ju 87D-1 WNr 2545 shot down in combat with Hurricanes over Alam el Kadim; crew safe
Sd St Go 242	Go 242A-1 WNr 0597 crash-landed at Tobruk, 70% damaged

Italian Claims

84ª Sq, 10°Gr, 4°St CT	Cap Franco Lucchini	MC.202 MM 7901 '84-3'	Boston	El Alamein	0610-0745
84ª Sq, 10°Gr, 4°St CT	Cap Franco Lucchini	MC.202 MM 7901 '84-3'	Spitfire	El Alamein	0610-0745
91ª Sq, 10°Gr, 4°St CT	Cap Carlo M.Ruspoli	MC.202	Spitfire	El Alamein	0610-0745
91ª Sq, 10°Gr, 4°St CT	Magg Giuseppe D'Agostinis	MC.202	Spitfire	El Alamein	0610-0745
91ª Sq, 10°Gr, 4°St CT	S.Ten Luciano Barsotti	MC.202	Spitfire	El Alamein	0610-0745
91ª Sq, 10°Gr, 4°St CT	M.llo Leonardo Ferrulli	MC.202	Spitfire	El Alamein	0610-0745
90ª Sq, 10°Gr, 4°St CT	Cap Ranieri Piccolomini	MC.202	Spitfire	El Alamein	0610-0745
90ª Sq, 10°Gr, 4°St CT	Ten Luigi Padovani	MC.202	Spitfire	El Alamein	0610-0745
74ª Sq, 23°Gr, 3°St CT	Cap Giorgio Tugnoli	MC.202	P-40	S El Alamein	1445-1730
70ª Sq, 23°Gr, 3°St CT	Ten Antonio Maccanti	MC.202	P-40	S El Alamein	1445-1730

Italian Casualties

90ªSq, 10°Gr, 4°St CT	MC.202 MM 7785 failed to return 0610-, M.llo Pietro Del Turco MiA
85ªSq, 18°Gr, 3°St CT	MC.200 MM 8799 crashed to ground on landing, Ten Guglielmo Neumayer KiA
95ªSq, 18°Gr, 3°St CT	MC.200 MM 8149 damaged in landing accident, Cap Romolo Artina WiFA

Thursday, 3 September 1942

8th Army now launched a counter-offensive in the Alam el Halfa area, forcing the Axis columns into a faster retreat than Rommel had planned. This attack, by the New Zealand Division, became bogged down in soft sand and failed in its attempt to cut off the main German armoured forces before they could reach their previous positions. It did, however, succeed in sending them back towards the latter a little faster than intended.

During the day the light and medium bombers flew more than 200 sorties, the only casualties being two Bostons which collided due to a Flak burst, although both managed to get back to base in a damaged condition. The escorting fighters again suffered heavily in achieving this. It was a day, nonetheless, which showed how great Allied air superiority was beginning to become, since 126 of the 139 sorties made by German fighters were Freie Jagd missions, aimed at interrupting the WDAF bomber formations, but achieving no worthwhile success in doing so.

At 0800 three Kittyhawks of 4 SAAF Squadron, eight from 260, four from 2 SAAF and eight P-40Fs of the 64th Squadron, escorted 15 Bostons and three B-25s on a raid, as eight Spitfires of 145 Squadron scrambled over Burg el Arab to provide roving high cover for the whole formation. At the same time 12 Hurricanes of 274 Squadron covered ten of 127 Squadron to intercept German transport aircraft. The Hurricanes flew to Burg el Arab, searching for the reported Ju 52/3ms, but finding none there, were ordered to patrol 20 miles south of El Alamein. They were then attacked by six or more Bf 109Es and Fs; one of these was claimed damaged, but one of 274 Squadron's aircraft was hit in the starboard wing by a cannon shell and damaged Cat I. The attacker may have been a TacR aircraft of 2.(H)/14, given the identification of the E models, as a pilot of this unit claimed a victory during the day.

Fourteen Bf 109s of I./JG 27 undertook a Freie Jagd, six of them engaging Spitfires and Kittyhawks without result while the other eight attacked the bombers and their escorts over Hammam. The pilots of the Hurricanes now spotted the fight and headed for it, but were jumped by six Messerschmitts. 145 Squadron reported encountering a total of 17 fighters – Bf 109s, MC.200s and MC.202s, the latter reportedly with red spinners; this would appear to be a mistaken identification of friendly aircraft, since in North Africa both Bf 109s and MC.202s generally had the spinners painted white, whereas WDAF fighters had red spinners. An MC.202 and two Bf 109s were claimed, all as probables. Flt Sgt MacArthur Powers baled out, being hit by flying bullets and wounded several times. During the action at this time 260 Squadron lost Wt Off Bernier, and Lt Ryneke of 2 SAAF Squadron force-landed after his aircraft was hit in the engine. One 57th Fighter Group P-40F was also shot down, the pilot being wounded. Plt Off Scudday of 4 SAAF Squadron claimed to have shot two Bf 109s off Lt Leppan's tail.

Oblt Marseille and Lt Stahlschmidt each claimed three aircraft shot down during this early morning engagement, the hectic nature and confusion of which were well-captured in a letter home written by Stahlschmidt:

> "Today I have experienced my hardest combat. But at the same time it has been my most wonderful experience of comradeship in the air. We had a combat in the morning, at first with 40 Hurricanes and Curtisses, later some 20 Spitfires appearing from above. We were eight Messerschmitts in the midst of an incredible whirling mass of enemy fighters. I flew my 109 for my life, but although the superior strength of the enemy was overwhelming, not one of us shirked our duty, all turning like madmen. I worked with every gram of my energy, and by the time we finished I was foaming at the mouth and utterly exhausted. Again and again we had enemy fighters on our tails. I was forced to dive three or four times, but I pulled up again and rushed into the turmoil. Once I seemed to have no escape; I had flown my 109 to the limit of its performance, but a Spitfire still sat behind me. At the last moment Marseille shot it down, 50 metres from my 109. I dived and pulled up. Seconds later I saw a Spitfire behind Marseille. I took aim at the Spitfire, I have never aimed so carefully, and the enemy dived down burning. At the end of the combat only Marseille and I were left in the dogfight. Each of us had three victories. At home we climbed out of our planes and were thoroughly exhausted. Marseille had bullet holes in his 109, and I had 11 machine-gun hits in mine. We embraced each other, but were unable to speak. It was an unforgettable event."

Eight Kittyhawks of 112 Squadron flew top cover to Baltimores at 1045, led by Capt Saville. Eleven Bf 109s of II./JG 27 on a Freie Jagd spotted the 12 bombers and their escort over Deir el Raghil at about 1115 and attacked. Nine fighters which they identified as Spitfires, dived on them unexpectedly, but these were probably 112's aircraft, Hptm Rödel claiming one shot down. Flt Sgt Ibbotson was attacked as he turned and claimed one 109 shot down, but his own aircraft was damaged. 6 Squadron enjoyed more success on this date when six of its tank-busters were sent off at 1125, escorted by eight Hurricanes of 7 SAAF Squadron and 12 of 127 Squadron. Tasked with attacking 12 tanks, the pilots of the Mark IIds claimed three PzKw III panzers, two unidentified tanks, one armoured car and a three-ton lorry.

Seven Bf 109s of III./JG 53 escorted Jabos at 1225, fighting 20 British fighters near El Alamein. Twelve Macchis suddenly appeared and made a spirited attack, but without success. Six more Kittyhawks of 3 RAAF Squadron and five of 450 Squadron escorted 18 Baltimores to Deir el Raghil at 1355, but were attacked by 16 Bf 109s and 13 MC.202s, Sgt Thomas of 3 RAAF being severely wounded and his aircraft badly damaged, but he reached base where he crash-landed. Flt Sgt Dyson and Sgt Hannaford of 450 Squadron each claimed to have probably shot down a Messerschmitt, but Hannaford was also wounded and his aircraft damaged, crash-landing at base like Thomas.

MC.202s of 10° Gruppo were involved in actions between 1140-1320. Magg D'Agostinis led 13 fighters on a free sweep mission over the El Alamein area; a formation of 12 Hurricanes, covered by ten P-40s, was engaged and two 'Hurribombers' were claimed. At the end of this combat another formation was encountered comprising 12 Bostons escorted by ten P-40s and eight Spitfires. A long fight followed and two P-40s were claimed plus one Boston probable, for no losses. Following an uneventful morning sortie, 19 MC.202s of 23° Gruppo had taken off again at 1240 to patrol over the front line. A large formation of 18 twin-engined bombers, identified as Bostons, escorted by about 35 P-40s, was reported and three of the fighters were claimed, plus two probables. Attacks were made on several others and one more was claimed damaged. One Macchi was damaged and force-landed south of El Alamein.

Around this time seven Bf 109s of II./JG 27 carried out a Freie Jagd, first engaging ten Curtiss fighters, followed by 15 more Curtiss or Hurricanes, and 15 Spitfires. Oblt Sinner claimed one in each engagement. Three Kittyhawks of 4 SAAF Squadron again provided top cover to 15 Bostons and six B-25s, 260 and the 66th US Squadron flying close and medium covers. Six plus enemy aircraft were reported and three were seen, Plt Off Joerns failing to return, his aircraft last being seen going down pouring black smoke. He was reported safe in hospital next day.

At 1510 six Spitfires of 145 Squadron were scrambled again, with Hurricanes of 33 and 213 Squadrons. During their patrol 13 Bf 109s and MC.202s were engaged, the Spitfire pilots claiming one Messerschmitt shot down, two probables and one damaged, but lost Sgt Anderson who crash-landed at El Kanabish. 33 Squadron lost Flt Sgt Belleau, who baled out. Eight Bf 109s of I.Gruppe took off at 1548 on another Freie Jagd, followed by two more four minutes later. Their pilots engaged in three combats with various formations of Curtiss, Hurricanes and Spitfires, the first at 1608 when Oblt Marseille claimed two fighters over El Imayid and Lt Stahlschmidt one. Fifteen minutes later Stahlschmidt claimed a second, the Messerschmitts then continuing their patrol until 1642.

In the meantime 11 Hurricanes of 274 Squadron, each loaded with two 250lb bombs with extension rods to their fuses, took off to attack a column estimated to comprise 1,000 MT. They were covered by seven 7 SAAF Squadron Hurricane IIbs and 12 of 127 Squadron, flying to Lake Maghra, and then north-east of point where 200 MT were attacked, one direct hit and two near misses being seen. 274 and 7 SAAF Squadrons then turned for home, but 127 Squadron lost sight of them. At that moment three Bf 109s dived on them, hitting the South African unit hard. Lts Small and Meikle were shot down together, one parachute being seen; Lt Pearce was also seen to bale out and Lt Kirby to belly-land, getting out of his aircraft. Those attacking the 7 SAAF Squadron Hurricanes were Marseille, Obfw Steinhausen and Lt Remmer who claimed these four aircraft.

Six Bf 109s of III./JG 27 flew a later Freie Jagd at 1620, attacking bombers and their escorts near Hammam, Uffz Gruber claiming one Curtiss fighter shot down. On their last sortie of the day the Tomahawks of 5 SAAF Squadron seem to have been the recipients of this attack, one of their aircraft being shot down and one badly damaged. Eleven Spitfires of 92 Squadron commenced a patrol at 1720, one claim for a Bf 109 damaged being made. At 1758 two Messerschmitts of II./JG 27 had escorted a reconnaissance Bf 110, their pilots reporting engaging three Hurricanes near Alam el Mseilik, claiming to have hit one inconclusively.

It is instructive to note the number of bombing sorties which had been flown by WDAF units during the day – 92 by Baltimores, 90 by Bostons and 12 by B-25s. These had been escorted by 156 Kittyhawk sorties, 21 by Tomahawks and 60 by P-40Fs. Additionally, of course, had been the considerable number of Spitfire and Hurricane sorties connected with the actions on the ground generally.

At the close of the day Capt J.R.R.Wells was posted from 7 SAAF Squadron to take command of 274 Squadron, where Sqn Ldr Hayter, DFC , had completed his tour. Promoted major with this posting, Wells had become the first SAAF officer to be given command of an RAF squadron.

British Claims

73 Sqn	Plt Off E.L.Joyce	Hurricane II c BP167 'L'	Bf 110 Damaged	5m W LG.39	0435-0440
5 SAAF Sqn	Lt D.W.Murdoch	Tomahawk IIb AN399 'T'	Bf 109F Damaged	25m S El Alamein	0730
145 Sqn	Sgt G.W.Small	Spitfire Vb BP987	Bf 109 Probable	El Hammam	0740-0845

145 Sqn	Sqn Ldr G.P.H.Matthews	Spitfire Vb BR235 'B'	MC.202 Probable	El Hammam	0740-0845
260 Sqn	Flt Sgt J.F.Edwards	Kittyhawk IIa FL233 'T'	Bf 109F Damaged	El Hammam	0800-0900
274 Sqn	Plt Off D.C.Mitchell	Hurricane IIc BG949 'Y'	Bf 109E Damaged	NE bulge in bombline	0800-0905
4 SAAF Sqn	Plt Off F.Scudday	Kittyhawk I ..880 'Z'	2 Bf 109Fs		0825
112 Sqn	Flt Sgt D.Ibbotson	Kittyhawk I EV365	Bf 109F	W Deir el Raghil	1040-1150
92 Sqn	Flt Lt C.J.Samouelle	Spitfire Vc BR479 'E'	Bf 109 Damaged	patrol central sector	1047-1208
450 Sqn	Flt Sgt R.D.Dyson	Kittyhawk I EV158	Bf 109E Probable	1352-1509	
450 Sqn	Sgt H.R.Hannaford	Kittyhawk I EV367	Bf 109E Probable		1352-1509
3 RAAF Sqn	Sgt G.G.Scribner	Kittyhawk I AL167 'F'	MC.202 Probable	Deir el Raghil	1430
145 Sqn	Sgt S.N.Duigan	Spitfire Vb BP984	Bf 109 Probable	1510-1640	
145 Sqn	Flt Sgt E.A.Ker	Spitfire Vb AR290	Bf 109 Damaged		1510-1640
145 Sqn	Plt Off L.A.Malins	Spitfire Vb AR286 'R'	Bf 109		1510-1640
145 Sqn	Flt Lt C.H.Saunders	Spitfire Vb BP987	Bf 109 Probable	1510-1640	
5 SAAF Sqn	Capt E.N.Colman	Tomahawk IIb AN366 'N'	Bf 109F Damaged	15-20m SE El Alamein	1630
80 Sqn	Plt Off L.Buchan	Hurricane IIc BP358 'X'	MC.202 Damaged		1725-1900

British Casualties

112 Sqn	Kittyhawk I EV365 'A' damaged Cat I; Sgt D.Ibbotson safe
260 Sqn	Kittyhawk II FL226 shot down by Bf 109 10-15m SW El Hammam 0800-0900; Wt Off J.S.E.M.Bernier KiA
450 Sqn	Kittyhawk I EV367 left 1352, shot down by two MC.202s S Bir el Ibrahim; Sgt H.R.Hannaford
2 SAAF Sqn	Kittyhawk I ET900 'T' damaged by Flak, force-landed 1700; Lt L.Ryneke back on 6th
4 SAAF Sqn	Kittyhawk I EV352 shot down by fighter at 1515 and force-landed Cat II; Plt Off J.C.Joerns, RAF (US) safe
5 SAAF Sqn	Tomahawk IIb AN342 shot down by Bf 109 SE El Alamein at 1700; Lt C.Somerville crash-landed; back next day delivering ex-208 Sqn Tomahawk
5 SAAF Sqn	Tomahawk IIb AK453 damaged by Bf 109 Cat II at 1700, landed at base; Lt E.W.L.Popham safe
3 RAAF Sqn	Kittyhawk I EV167 crash-landed; Sgt W.W.Thomas badly WiA
33 Sqn	Hurricane IIc crash-landed; Sgt Anderson
33 Sqn	Hurricane IIc BE334 'Z' left 1510, shot down by Bf 109 S Imayid; Flt Sgt M.J.H.M.Belleau baled out safe
7 SAAF Sqn	Hurricane IIb shot down by Bf 109, crash-landed 33m S El Alamein; Lt H.E.Kirby WiA in leg, but returned
7 SAAF Sqn	Hurricane IIb Z5312 shot down by Bf 109; Lt W.B.Pearce baled out S El Alamein, slt WiA
7 SAAF Sqn	Hurricane IIb BE678 shot down by Bf 109; Lt B.W.Small baled out, PoW
7 SAAF Sqn	Hurricane IIb BP918 shot down by Bf 109, force-landed; Lt A.W.Meikle slt WiA; walked back on 5th
145 Sqn	Spitfire V AB349 'V' shot down by Bf 109 0740-0845; Sgt MacA.Powers Jr baled out, WiA
145 Sqn	Spitfire V AB277 'P' , took off 1510, shot down by Bf 109, crash-landed El Kannabish; Sgt J.S.Anderson safe
24 SAAF Sqn	Boston III Z2156 'V' off 1410 to attack Axis MT at El Alamein; Boston AL723 blown by Flak burst into this, the lead aircraft, propeller chewed large piece off Z2156's wing; wing of AL723 impaled fuselage of Z2156 just behind the mid gunner's position and nearly cut off the tail. Still managed to return and land, but DBR; Maj D.U.Nel and crew safe
24 SAAF Sqn	Boston III AL723 'Z' collided with Z2156 and damaged DBR, but returned; Lt F.A.L.de Marrillav and two safe, one injured

US Casualties

57th FG	P-40F operating with 5 SAAF Sqn, shot down by Bf 109; pilot WiA

German Claims

3./JG 27	Oblt Hans-Joachim Marseille	P-46	25km SW El Hammam	0720
2./JG 27	Lt Hans-Arnold Stahlschmidt	P-40	SW El Hammam	0722
3./JG 27	Oblt Hans-Joachim Marseille	Spitfire	27km SW El Hammam	0723
2./JG 27	Lt Hans-Arnold Stahlschmidt	Spitfire	SW El Hammam	0724
3./JG 27	Oblt Hans-Joachim Marseille	Spitfire	30km SW El Hammam	0728
2./JG 27	Lt Hans-Arnold Stahlschmidt	P-40	SW El Hammam	0729
Stab II./JG 27	Hptm Gusav Rödel	P-40	Deir el Raghil	1020
6./JG 27	Oblt Rudolf Sinner	P-40	S El Hammam	1425
6./JG 27	Oblt Rudolf Sinner	Spitfire	S Bir Ibrahim	1435
3./JG 27	Oblt Hans-Joachim Marseille	P-46	El Imayid	1508
3./JG 27	Oblt Hans-Joachim Marseille	P-40	2km SW El Imayid	1510
2./JG 27	Lt Hans-Arnold Stahlschmidt	Hurricane	SW El Imayid	1512
2./JG 27	Lt Hans-Arnold Stahlschmidt	P-40	S El Imayid	1526
3./JG 27	Oblt Hans-Joachim Marseille	P-46	40km SSE El Alamein	1542
1./JG 27	Obfw Günther Steinhausen	Hurricane	N Manga el Rhala	1543

German Claims

1./JG 27	Lt Hans Remmer	Hurricane	N El Masra	1543
1./JG 27	Obfw Günther Steinhausen	Hurricane	N Manga el Rhala	1546
8./JG 27	Uffz Viktor Gruber	P-40	S El Hammam	1550

Italian Claims

84ª Sq, 10°Gr, 4°St CT	Cap Franco Lucchini	MC.202 MM 7901 '84-3'	Hurricane	El Alamein	1140-1320
84ª Sq, 10°Gr, 4°St CT	7 pilots	MC.202			
90ª Sq, 10°Gr, 4°St CT	Ten Luigi Padovani	MC.202	Hurricane	El Alamein	1140-1320
90ª Sq, 10°Gr, 4°St CT	Serg Magg G.B.Ceoletta	MC.202	P-40	El Alamein	1140-1320
91ª Sq, 10°Gr, 4°St CT	Magg G. D'Agostinis	MC.202	P-40	El Alamein	1140-1320
84ª Sq, 10°Gr, 4°St CT	Ten Luigi Giannella	MC.202 MM 7815 '84-6'	Boston Probable	El Alamein	1140-1320
70ª Sq, 23°Gr, 3°St CT	Cap Claudio Solaro	MC.202	P-40	El Alamein	1240-1425
70ª Sq, 23°Gr, 3°St CT	Serg Carlo Papa	MC.202	P-40 Probable	El Alamein	1240-1425
74ª Sq, 23°Gr, 3°St CT	Ten Giorgio Solaroli	MC.202	P-40 Probable	El Alamein	1240-1425
75ª Sq, 23°Gr, 3°St CT	Serg Luigi Bozzolan	MC.202	P-40	30km S El Alamein	1240-1425
75ª Sq, 23°Gr, 3°St CT	Serg Aldo Orsucci	MC.202	P-40	30km S El Alamein	1240-1425
75ª Sq, 23°Gr, 3°St CT	Magg Luigi Filippi	MC.202	P-40 Damaged	30km S El Alamein	1240-1425

Italian Casualties

70ª Sq, 23°Gr, 3°St CT	MC.202 damaged in combat 1240-1425, force-landed S of El Alamein, Serg Carlo Papa safe

Friday, 4 September 1942

Seven CR.42s of 101° Gruppo, led by 5° Stormo's commander T.Col Guido Nobili, carried out a rather uncommon night sortie, from 0345 to 0600, to dive-bomb enemy concentrations in the Alam el Halfa area. The target was located through some light signals placed by Italian troops 5km from the front. Despite the lack of night flight training, 13 MC.200s of 8° Gruppo also took part in this operation, strafing a concentration of troops between 0430 and 0600 in the El Mreis area.

The day was to be a busy one for 23° Gruppo CT which undertook three sorties in support of the ground forces. The first of these was between 0705-0845; at 0715 a formation of Bostons and P-40s was reported 50km east of Taga, three of the fighters being claimed shot down plus two probables. However, as the engagement ended, Cap Solaroli was hit, with wounds to his head and one of his feet. He force-landed in a minefield and was subsequently rescued by a patrol from the 8° Regiment Bersaglieri. The main opponents appear to have been seven Kittyhawks of 260 Squadron which were escorting 15 Bostons and three B-25s, being attacked by a reported two or three MC.202s. One was claimed shot down, but no British losses were listed on this occasion. US P-40Fs were also involved during this engagement, claiming a Bf 109 probable.

Two hours later six Spitfires of 601 Squadron escorted two formations of Bostons, nine MC.202s and 12 Bf 109s reportedly coming down out of the sun as the bombers were withdrawing. Again the Italian fighters were from 23° Gruppo which recorded engaging Spitfires and P-40s, this time claiming to have inflicted damage to five Spitfires and a P-40. Pilots of 601 Squadron claimed four fighters damaged, all identified as Messerschmitts. At 1340 33 and 213 Squadrons were scrambled during a sandstorm, being scattered top four different landing grounds on return. Flt Sgt Belec of 33 Squadron claimed a Bf 109 by collision, baling out himself. Six Bf 109s of III./JG 27 took off on a Freie Jagd at 1405, attacking 35 fighters, one of which Uffz Stückler claimed at 1450 (or ? 1250). The third operation of the day for 23° Gruppo, by 19 MC.202s from 1710-1830 proved uneventful.

7 SAAF Wing was again active. Six Hurricane Is with 24 Jefferis bombs apiece set out to attack four tanks, three trucks and an eight-wheeled armoured car. They were covered by 12 Hurricanes of 274 Squadron and 12 more of 127 Squadron as top cover. The 7 SAAF Squadron aircraft bombed and strafed, Maj Whelehan and Lt Geere each claiming direct hits on a tank. During the return flight Lts Geere and Taylor both lost their way in dust haze and landed at the wrong airfield, returning next day. Maj Whelehan and Lt Kelly force-landed, but both were safe, although Whelehan's aircraft had been damaged by debris from the bombing, while Kelly reported that he had been hit by Flak. However, Lt Kirby and 274 Squadron's Sgt Ott were both attacked by Bf 109s, Ott being shot down and baling out, slightly wounded. Kirby's aircraft was shot-up, causing him to force-land; he too suffered slight wounds.

4 SAAF Squadron reported that the number of serviceable Kittyhawks available to it was now down to three from a total of 21 during August. Five aircraft had been lost to the enemy, but 17 had been

crashed "through absolute carelessness on the part of the pilots". It was decided that drastic action would in future be taken against pilots making unnecessary crash-landings. They would be made to sit in the cockpit in full kit until the aircraft was repaired, or to walk round the airfield in flying kit, if the aircraft was too badly damaged to be repaired locally.

British Claims

213 Sqn	Flg Off A.U.Houle	Hurricane IIc BP128	Bf 109F Damaged	central sector	0715-0830
260 Sqn	Sgt N.S.Stebbings	Kittyhawk IIa	MC.202 Probable		0730-0840
601 Sqn	Plt Off A.R.Boyle	Spitfire Vc BR113	Bf 109 Probable		1105-1225
601 Sqn	Flt Lt M.R.B.Ingram	Spitfire Vc BP959 'Y'	Bf 109 Damaged		1105-1225
601 Sqn	Plt Off C.R.Scollan	Spitfire Vc BR136 'H'	Bf 109		1105-1225
601 Sqn	Plt Off R.J.F.Sherk	Spitfire Vc BR132 'W'	Bf 109 Damaged	1105-1225	
33 Sqn	Flt Sgt J.W.E.Belec	Hurricane IIc BN348 'E'	Bf 109 (collision)	S El Alamein	1345-

US Claims

66th FS/57th FG	2/Lt Thomas T. Williams	P-40F '95'	Bf 109 Probable		0730-0830

British Casualties

33 Sqn	Hurricane IIc BN348 'E' left 1200 collided with Bf 109 W El Hammam; Flt Sgt J.W.E.Belec safe
7 SAAF Sqn	Hurricane I Special hit by splinters in low attack, crash-landed; Maj T.B.Whelehan back next day
7 SAAF Sqn	Hurricane I Special hit by Flak and crash-landed, damaged Cat II; Lt O.J.Kelly slt WiA, back next day

German Claims

8./JG 27	Uffz Alfred Stückler	P-46	W El Hammam	1150

Italian Claims

74ª Sq, 23°Gr, 3°St CT	Cap Giorgio Tugnoli	MC.202	P-40	50km E El Taga 0605-0745
74ª Sq, 23°Gr, 3°St CT	Serg Magg Felice Papini	MC.202	P-40	50km E El Taga 0605-0745
74ª Sq, 23°Gr, 3°St CT	Serg Magg Mario Mantelli	MC.202	P-40 Probable	50km E El Taga 0605-0745
74ª Sq, 23°Gr, 3°St CT	Ten Giorgio Solaroli	MC.202 MM 8095	2 P-40s	50km E El Taga 0605-0745
70ª Sq, 23°Gr, 3°St CT	Serg William Dusi	MC.202	P-40	50km E El Taga 0605-0745
70ª Sq, 23°Gr, 3°St CT	S.Ten Giuseppe Melandri	MC.202	P-40 Probable	50km E El Taga 0605-0745

Italian Casualties

74ª Sq, 23°Gr, 3°St CT	MC.202 MM 8095 '74-9' damaged in combat, crash-landed, Ten Giorgio Solaroli WiA

Saturday, 5 September 1942

Rommel's forces completed their withdrawal during the day, having gained only two British minefields as a consequence of the Battle of Alam el Halfa. Seven Bf 109s of II./JG 27 took off on a Freie Jagd at 0700, eight Spitfires of 145 Squadron being scrambled five minutes later to intercept them. However the British aircraft were bounced by five of the Messerschmitts, Uffz Schneider shooting down one Spitfire. Sgt Stewart baled out, wounded in the leg, whilst the aircraft of Sgts Thomas and Small were both badly damaged, Thomas crash-landing at base as a result.

At 1015 six Hurricane IIds of 6 Squadron took off to attack a reported nine or more tanks. Six Mark IIbs of 7 SAAF Squadron gave medium cover and 12 of 127 Squadron were above. The formation was ordered back due to the presence of hostile fighters, but 127 Squadron was attacked by some 20 or more and Plt Off Rebman was shot down, crash-landing; he was picked up safely by an army unit. He had probably fallen foul of the 15 MC.202s of 23° Gruppo which were providing

Marseille's rudder shows claims for 136 victories, the last of these on 5 September.

protection to Italian armoured forces. The pilots of these reported meeting a large formation of Spitfires and P-40s, claiming four P-40s shot down.

At 1100 39 Bf 109s took off on a Stuka escort, their numbers including 24 from I.Gruppe and 19 from II.Gruppe. After the bombers had completed their mission, the fighters went off on a Freie Jagd, six from I.Gruppe engaging five Spitfires and 10-15 Kittyhawks. II.Gruppe then spotted Spitfires already in combat with Messerschmitts near Hammam, and then saw 40 Curtiss fighters, apparently carrying bombs; these were seen between Ruweisat and El Taga. Between 1148 and 1200 the I.Gruppe pilots claimed four Spitfires and two 'P-46s', Hptm Rödel of Stab II.Gruppe additionally claiming three P-40 fighter-bombers. Six Spitfires of 145 Squadron, eight Kittyhawks of 112 Squadron and others of 450 Squadron had been scrambled at 1125 to patrol over the central sector of the front, but here they were jumped by four Bf 109s which the Spitfire pilots claimed to have fought up to 17,000 feet when the Messerschmitts then departed, but 12 more then attacked. During this fight two Spitfires were shot down, the pilots both baling out, and a third was damaged. 112 Squadron was also attacked by four Bf 109s, one of their Kittyhawks being shot down, while one more Kittyhawk of 450 Squadron was badly damaged.

One of the highest-claiming fighter pilots in North Africa was Lt Hans-Arnold 'Fifi' Stahlschmidt of 2./JG 27, who claimed his 57th and 58th victories on 5 September. Two days later he was shot down and killed by Spitfires.

Elsewhere during the day 1 SAAF Squadron lost one Hurricane when 2/Lt James' engine cut returning from a sortie at 1510, and he crash-landed. An hour later Oblt Burger of II./JG 27, one of 40 pilots engaged in a Stuka escort, baled out when his engine seized, but he was killed when his parachute failed to open. The 66th Fighter Squadron of the 57th Fighter Group was now attached to 239 Wing to operate with Kittyhawks of 112, 250, 450 and 3 RAAF Squadrons; the 64th Squadron remained with 233 Wing.

British Claims

112 Sqn	Capt E.C.Saville	Kittyhawk I EV368 'H'	Bf 109 Damaged		1125-1235
450 Sqn	Flt Sgt D.N.McQueen	Kittyhawk I AL157	Bf 109F Damaged	S El Daba	1131-1222
450 Sqn	Sgt E.P.Oakley	Kittyhawk I EV158	Bf 109F Damaged	S El Daba	1131-1222
145 Sqn	Plt Off L.A.Malins	Spitfire Vb BP986 'X'	Ju 88 Damaged	Ras el Kanayis	1500-1625

British Casualties

112 Sqn	Kittyhawk I AK701 'F' shot down by Bf 109; Sgt H.G.E.Thomas PoW
450 Sqn	Kittyhawk I EV158 badly damaged by Bf 109 S El Daba; Sgt E.P.Oakley safe
213 Sqn	Hurricane IIc BP219 'H' left 0715, shot up by Bf 109, damaged Cat II; Plt Off A.J.Thrift safe
127 Sqn	Hurricane IIb shot down by MC.202 N Lake Maghra; Plt Off A.L.Rebman crash-landed, safe
1 SAAF Sqn	Hurricane 2/Lt D.O.James crash-landed on return from sortie, 1510
145 Sqn	Spitfire V AB468 left 0700, shot down by Bf 109s 15m S Imayid 0735; Sgt A.H.Stewart baled out, WiA
145 Sqn	Spitfire V AR286 left 0700, shot down by Bf 109s 15m S Imayid 0735; Sgt P.G.C.Thomas crash-landed due to damage
76/454 Sqn	Halifax II W1144 'Q' from Fayid to attack Heraklion l.g. Attacked by Bf 109 and possibly also hit by Flak and caught fire. Flt Lt J.Bryan and one KiA; four PoWs, two having been WiA
10/227 Sqn	Halifax II W7670 'C' seen going down with an outer engine on fire, and crashed S Castelli Padiada on return; Sqn Ldr A.H.Hacking and five KiA
267 Sqn	Hudson VI EW944 swung on take-off at Kabrit and undercarriage collapsed

German Claims

5./JG 27	Uffz Bernhard Schneider	Spitfire	SW El Hammam	0642
3./JG 27	Oblt Hans-Joachim Marseille	2 Spitfires	SE El Alamein	1048 & 1049

2./JG 27	Lt Hans-Arnold Stahlschmidt	Spitfire	SW Imayid	1049
3./JG 27	Oblt Hans-Joachim Marseille	Spitfire	SSE Imayid	1051
2./JG 27	Lt Hans-Arnold Stahlschmidt	P-46	SE Imayid	1052
Stab II./JG 27	Hptm Gustav Rödel	3 P-40s	SSW El Alamein	1053, 1057 & 1100
3./JG 27	Oblt Hans-Joachim Marseille	P-46	SSE Imayid	1100

German Casualties

5./JG 27	Bf 109F-4 trop WNr 8718 Red 2 Feindflug. Engine damage. Oblt Wolfgang Burger baled out 30km SW El Alamein, parachute did not open; KiA
II./StG 3	Ju 87D-3 WNr 2614 shot-up by AA, 20% damaged, force-landed at Qasaba, crew safe

Italian Claims

74ª Sq, 23°Gr, 3°St CT	Cap Giorgio Tugnoli	MC.202 }	P-40	S El Alamein	0930
70ª Sq, 23°Gr, 3°St CT	Serg Magg Celso Zemella	MC.202 }			
74ª Sq, 23°Gr, 3°St CT	Serg Magg Emilio Stefani	MC.202	P-40 Probable	S El Alamein	0930
75ª Sq, 23°Gr, 3°St CT	Ten Ezio Monti	MC.202	P-40	S El Alamein	0930
75ª Sq, 23°Gr, 3°St CT	Ten Milano Pausi	MC.202	P-40	S El Alamein	0930
75ª Sq, 23°Gr, 3°St CT	Serg Aldo Orsucci	MC.202	P-40	S El Alamein	0930

Italian Casualties

70ª Sq, 23°Gr, 3° St CT	MC.202 MM 9059 force-landed within Italian lines, Cap Claudio Solaro safe

Sunday, 6 September 1942

At dawn Magg Filippi led 18 MC.202s of 23° Gruppo to provide cover for Italian troops in the area south of El Alamein. No opposition was encountered, and although one pilot force-landed due to engine trouble, he was unhurt and his aircraft was recovered. Thereafter the rest of September was to see little flying for the unit due mainly to fuel shortage. Only three sorties – all uneventful convoy escorts – would be undertaken during the rest of the month.

CR.42 '21-1' MM 9184 of 15° Stormo Assalto. This unit entered operations in mid-September 1942.

For WDAF the situation was to be very different. On this date 12 Hurricanes of 274 Squadron took off on fighter-bomber sorties at 0830, with a medium cover of 7 SAAF Squadron's Hurricane IIbs and 12 from 127 Squadron, as usual as top cover. Four Bf 109s of I./JG 27 took off a few minutes later on a Freie Jagd, followed four minutes thereafter by four more which had been ordered to scramble. Twenty minutes later the Messerschmitts dived on the cover squadrons of 7 SAAF Wing's Hurricanes, wreaking great havoc, claiming eight fighters shot down between 0857-0911 – all identified as Spitfires or P-40s. The first claim, made on behalf of Obfw Steinhausen, was his 40th victory.

Two pilots of 127 Squadron were shot down, both baling out, one of them becoming a PoW. It was 7 SAAF Squadron which bore the brunt of the Messerschmitts' attack, however, and only one of their six aircraft returned. Their commanding officer, the veteran Maj Whelehan, was shot down and killed, whereas one of the flight commanders, Capt Stanford, baled out, seriously wounded. The other three pilots were all shot down, one returning next day, having crash-landed, but one of them had been killed. The only pilot to return, Lt Botha, reported that he had shot at and hit a Bf 109, but was unable to ascertain with what effect. One of the 274 Squadron aircraft was also damaged and crash-landed, but the pilot reported that his Hurricane had been hit and damaged by Flak, not by the Messerschmitts. Two of the 127 Squadron pilots, Flt Lt Mannix and Sgt Malone, each managed to shoot down a Bf 109. From one of these the pilot survived to become a PoW, but the other was that flown by Obfw Günther

Steinhausen, who was killed. It is uncertain which of the British pilots brought down this brilliant exponent of the Messerschmitt, who was posthumously commissioned and awarded the Ritterkreuz.

Sixteen Bf 109s of II./JG 27 escorted Stukas at 1230, meeting a reported 18 Spitfires over Hammam; Fw Krumlauf baled out on the return flight due to engine trouble, returning safely. At 1730 a further Stuka attack was launched, nine I./JG 27 Bf 109s providing the escort on this occasion, with eight from III./JG 53 flying a Freie Jagd ahead of the formation and 14 more aircraft of II./JG 27 giving indirect escort. Eight Kittyhawks of 260 Squadron were scrambled as top cover to an interception patrol, Tomahawks of 5 SAAF Squadron also taking off, together, it would appear, with P-40Fs of the 64th Squadron. II.Gruppe pilots reported meeting 12 Curtiss fighters and 11 American fighters. I.Gruppe made the first interception of the defending fighters at 1703. During the next 20 minutes or so Oblt Marseille claimed four victories and Stahlschmidt one, II.Gruppe's Oblt Sinner adding one more and Obfw Stumpf of III./JG 53 a seventh. Sinner identified his target as an Airacobra, although he was uncertain about this. He saw a blue and white circle on the fuselage which some of the pilots thought might be a Star of David. Intelligence decided that it was American.

260 Squadron took the initial brunt of this attack, one Kittyhawk being shot down with a second badly damaged. 5 SAAF Squadron's Tomahawks initially managed to get through to the Stukas, claiming two shot down, three probables and two damaged. Lt Joubert's Tomahawk was then attacked by a Bf 109, catching fire in the air; he crash-landed and the aircraft then blew up. Joubert survived to return next day, but two more pilots were killed, and three aircraft were damaged, one pilot being slightly wounded. The squadron was uncertain whether their aircraft had fallen victims to Messerschmitts or Flak, but there can be little doubt but that the former had been responsible. Back at 233 Wing's base, following this debacle, Wg Cdr Beresford completed his tour, handing over to Wg Cdr W.G.Wells.

15° Stormo moved from Castel Benito to Benghazi, K1 (Berka) airfield, joined by the ground echelon in an S.81. Serg Chendi stalled on landing and crashed, sustaining serious injuries.

British Claims

127 Sqn	Sgt W.J.Malone	Hurricane IIb BP294 'Y'	Bf 109 Probable	0825-0935	
127 Sqn	Flt Lt R.L.Mannix	Hurricane IIb BE329 'X'	Bf 109		0825-0935
450 Sqn	Sgt G.Lindsey	Kittyhawk I EV160	Bf 109F Damaged	S El Daba	1131-1223
260 Sqn	Flt Sgt J.F.Edwards	Kittyhawk IIa FL233 'T'	Bf 109F Probable	nr El Alamein	1730-1850
5 SAAF Sqn	Lt T.Finlayson	Tomahawk IIb AN427 'D'	Ju 87	10m S El Alamein	1810
5 SAAF Sqn	Lt A.D.Hinton	Tomahawk IIb AN402 'E'	Ju 87	10m S El Alamein	1810
5 SAAF Sqn	Lt R.T.Rogers	Tomahawk IIb AK401 'F	Ju 87 Damaged	10m S El Alamein	1810
5 SAAF Sqn	2/Lt H.Smith	Tomahawk IIb AK439 'B'	Ju 87	10m S El Alamein	1810
5 SAAF Sqn	2/Lt H.Smith	Tomahawk IIb AK439 'B'	Ju 87 Probable	10m S El Alamein	1810
5 SAAF Sqn	Lt K.C.Whyte	Tomahawk IIb AN231 'X'	Ju 87 Probable	10m S El Alamein	1810
5 SAAF Sqn	Lt K.C.Whyte	Tomahawk IIb AN231 'X'	Bf 109F Damaged	10m S El Alamein	1810
5 SAAF Sqn	Lt A.C.Joubert	Tomahawk IIb AN424 'A'	Ju 87 Probable	10m S El Alamein	1815
103 MU	Flg Off G.E.C.Genders	Spitfire V ..234	Ju 86P	Aboukir area, 60m out to sea	

British Casualties

260 Sqn	Kittyhawk II FL241 'D' left 1750, shot down by Bf 109 SE El Alamein; Plt Off R.A.Dunbar KiA
260 Sqn	Kittyhawk II FL242 left 1750 badly damaged by Bf 109 SE El Alamein; Sgt L.J.Sheppart safe
145 Sqn	Spitfire V AB146 shot down by Bf 109 10m S Imayid 0740; Flt Lt V.P.Cannam baled out
145 Sqn	Spitfire V AR290, shot down by Bf 109 Hammam 0740; Plt Off E.H.Bicksler baled out
145 Sqn	Spitfire V BP984 damaged by Bf 109 Hammam 0740; Sgt G.V.Small
5 SAAF Sqn	Tomahawk IIb AM424 'A' shot down by Bf 109 15m from El Alamein, 1820; Lt A.C.Joubert slt WiA, returned on 7th
5 SAAF Sqn	Tomahawk IIb AN366 'N' shot down by Bf 109 12m SW El Alamein, 1810; Capt E.N.Colman KiA
5 SAAF Sqn	Tomahawk IIb AK439 'B' damaged Cat I by Bf 109 SW El Alamein, 1810; 2/Lt H.Smith safe
5 SAAF Sqn	Tomahawk IIb AN231 'X' damaged by Bf 109, SW El Alamein, 1810; Lt K.C.Whyte slt WiA
5 SAAF Sqn	Tomahawk IIb AN446 'V' shot down by Bf 109 15m from El Alameim; Lt W.F.Turnbull KiA
5 SAAF Sqn	Tomahawk IIb AN436 'S' damaged by Bf 109; Lt J.W.Atkinson safe
7 SAAF Sqn	Hurricane II BD785 shot down by Bf 109 10m SW El Alamein; Maj T.B.Whelehan KiA
7 SAAF Sqn	Hurricane II BE694 shot down by Bf 109; Capt W.P.Stanford seriously WiA and baled out
7 SAAF Sqn	Hurricane II engine cut and crash-landed; Lt R.P.Burl safe
7 SAAF Sqn	Hurricane II BP750 shot down by Bf 109 15m from El Alamein; 2/Lt A.G.Turner safe

7 SAAF Sqn	Hurricane II BE553 shot down by Bf 109 15m from El Alamein; Lt J.H.Haire KiA
274 Sqn	Hurricane IIc BN111 damaged by Flak attacking MT and crash-landed El Alamein; Plt Off M.C.Elhanney safe
127 Sqn	Hurricane IIb BP294 'Y' left 0825 damaged by Bf 109 and abandoned; Sgt W.J.Malone baled out safe
127 Sqn	Hurricane II BP333 left 0825 damaged by Bf 109s and abandoned; Flg Off R.J.Crot (US) baled and PoW
6 Sqn	Hurricane BN843 stalled and abandoned over Shandur ranges
M.E.	Hurricane BE694 shot down by Bf 109 on escort mission nr El Alamein
M.E.	Hurricane BE678 SOC due to enemy action

US Claims

66th FS/57th FG	Capt Raymond A.Llewellyn	P-40F	Bf 109 Damaged	1810

German Claims

1./JG 27	Fw Günther Steinhausen	P-40	SW El Alamein	0757
2./JG 27	Lt Karl von Lieres und Wilkau	Spitfire	SE El Alamein	0803
2./JG 27	Uffz Heinrich Becker	Spitfire	SSE El Alamein	0804
1./JG 27	Fw Gerhard Keppler	P-40	SE El Alamein	0805
2./JG 27	Lt Karl von Lieres und Wilkau	P-40	SE El Alamein	0805
2./JG 27	Lt Karl von Lieres und Wilkau	Spitfire	SE El Alamein	0807
2./JG 27	Lt Karl von Lieres und Wilkau	P-40	SSE El Alamein	0809
2./JG 27	Uffz Max Winkler	P-40	SSE El Alamein	0811
3./JG 27	Oblt Hans-Joachim Marseille	3 P-46s	SE & SW El Alamein	1703-1716
9./JG 53	Obfw Werner Stumpf	P-40	5km NE El Alamein	1718
3./JG 27	Oblt Hans-Joachim Marseille	Spitfire	SSW El Alamein	1720
2./JG 27	Lt Hans-Arnold Stahlschmidt	P-40	SE El Hammam	1725
6./JG 27	Oblt Rudolf Sinner	US fighter	S Imayid	1725
2./JG 27	Uffz Gustav Sturm*	US P-46	SW El Alamein	

*unconfirmed

German Casualties

1./JG 27	Bf 109G-4 trop WNr 13272 White 5 combat with Hurricane SE El Alamein about 0800; Fw Günther Steinhausen MiA
1./JG 27	Bf 109F-4 trop WNr 8551 White 10 combat with Hurricane SE El Alamein about 0800; Obgfr Hans Benthin KG
3./StG 3	Ju 87 D-3 WNr 2662 S7+EL shot down by AA 25km S El Alamein; two baled – Uffz Heinz Lotz/Uffz Ferdinand Sandtner PoW

Italian Casualties

94ª Sq, 8°Gr, 2°St CT	MC.200 MM 8139 belly-landed after test flight, Cap Orfeo Cecchet safe
54ª Sq, 47°Gr, 15°St Ass	CR.42 MM 8993 '54-12' destroyed at Benghazi K1, Serg Jago Chendi WiA
85ªSq, 18°Gr, 3°St CT	MC.200 MM 8157 engine cut, Serg Francesco Casini baled and landed safely
75ªSq, 23°Gr, 3°St CT	MC.202 MM 8379 belly-landed, Serg Magg Vannetto Cavicchioli safe

Monday, 7 September 1942

I./JG 27 suffered another severe loss next day when four Bf 109s which had taken off on a Freie Jagd at 1450 were intercepted by seven Spitfires of 601 Squadron, 25 miles south-west of El Alamein. The latter were providing high cover to Hurricanes of 33 and 213 Squadrons which were escorting a TacR aircraft, when their pilots spotted a small force of Axis fighters and attacked them. Flt Lt Curry and Plt Off Frecklington each claimed a Bf 109 shot down, and each also claimed one damaged; at the same time Flt Lt Bruce Ingram claimed a probable and Plt Off Scherk an MC.202 damaged. These pilots can have had little idea of the calibre of the pilots they had shot down, one of whom, Lt von Lieres, force-landed. The other was Lt Hans-Arnold 'Fifi' Stahlschmidt. Friend of Marseille and the third-ranking ace of the whole desert campaign, Stahlschmidt had been credited with 59 victories and had received the Ritterkreuz; some 18 months later came the posthumous award of the Eichenlaube and promotion to Oberleutnant. Coming after the loss of Steinhausen, this was a heavy blow to the unit. In his last letter home, Stahlschmidt had written: "I don't know what fate awaits me. Perhaps things are going otherwise than our thoughts and wishes desire. But, if it should happen, then I know that I have done my duty with all my heart." At the time of his death he had flown the greatest number of operational sorties of any German pilot in North Africa – over 400.

At 1810 four Kittyhawks of 4 SAAF Squadron provided medium cover to 2 SAAF, 5 SAAF, 260 and the 64th and 66th Squadrons on a Stuka interception. 2 SAAF Squadron lagged behind, cruising at only 170mph instead of about 190, and as a result the formation arrived ten minutes after the Ju 87s had left

Spitfire Vc BR392 UF-P of 601 Squadron in which Flt Lt Bruce Ingram claimed a Bf 109 shot down on 7 September.

the target area. The wing was ordered back to base, whereupon the P-40Fs of the two American units pulled up in front of the other squadrons and turned, causing them to split up. At this moment Bf 109s of I./JG 27 which had been providing indirect support to the Stukas, attacked the formation ten miles south of El Alamein. Maj du Toit of 4 SAAF Squadron claimed to have shot one down, but received a cannon shell in the tail of his aircraft which caused damage to the elevators.

In another Kittyhawk Lt Douglas was hit and tried to bale out, but he was only at 200 feet and his parachute did not open. He was reported also to have shot down a Bf 109, but it appears that this was not officially credited to him. 260 Squadron lost one pilot also, and two Tomahawks of 5 SAAF Squadron were badly damaged, although both pilots survived unhurt. During this engagement four claims were made by I./JG 27, one by Hptm Homuth for a P-40, two for Marseille for two 'P-46s', and another of the latter as a shared Gruppe victory. Marseille particularly seemed to be in the habit of claiming P-46s, usually when the older Tomahawks were present.

During the day two Albacores of 826 Squadron were attacked by a pair of Bf 109s, but without result. The British aircrews reported that they thought the German pilots were inexperienced. No report of this engagement has been found in Luftwaffe records. At 2300 Flt Lt Selby of 73 Squadron took off on a night-intruder sortie, strafing Maaten Bagush airfield just as a bomber was landing; he claimed to have damaged this. Having recovered from his illness, Sqn Ldr Mike Judd returned to 250 Squadron to resume command.

British Claims

4 SAAF Sqn	Maj S.F.du Toit	Kittyhawk I ET901 'O'	Bf 109F	El Alamein	1040
601 Sqn	Flt Lt J.H.Curry	Spitfire Vc BR478 'B'	Bf 109	central sector of line	1440-1555
601 Sqn	Flt Lt J.H.Curry	Spitfire Vc BR478 'B'	Bf 109 Damaged		1440-1555
601 Sqn	Plt Off L.J.Frecklington	Spitfire Vc BR253	Bf 109 Damaged	central sector of line	1440-1555
601 Sqn	Plt Off L.J.Frecklington	Spitfire Vc BR253	Bf 109	NE Burg el Arab	1440-1555
601 Sqn	Flt Lt M.R.B.Ingram	Spitfire Vc BR392 'P'	Bf 109 Probable	central sector of line	1440-1555
601 Sqn	Plt Off R.J.F.Sherk	Spitfire Vc BP959 'Y'	MC.202 Damaged	central sector of line	1440-1555
73 Sqn	Flt J.B.Selby	Hurricane IIc BN410	U/ie/a Probable	Maaten Bagush a/f	2400
73 Sqn	Flt J.B.Selby	Hurricane IIc BN410	U/ie/a Damaged	Maaten Bagush a/f	2400

British Casualties

260 Sqn	Kittyhawk I AL134 lost; Plt Off R.A.Dunbar
3 RAAF Sqn	Kittyhawk I ET844 lost
4 SAAF Sqn	Kittyhawk I ET522 (??) damaged by fighters and abandoned 10m S El Alamein
4 SAAF Sqn	Kittyhawk I AK880 'Z' shot down by Bf 109 1840 24m SW El Alamein; Lt B.R.Douglas KiA baled out but parachute did not open
4 SAAF Sqn	Kittyhawk I ET987 'O' damaged Cat I SW El Alamein 1840; Maj S.F.du Toit
5 SAAF Sqn	Tomahawk IIb AN394 left 1810, damaged Cat II by Bf 109, crash-landed at base; Lt R.O.McCarthy safe
5 SAAF Sqn	Tomahawk IIb AN399 'T' left 1810, shot down and crash-landed 12-15m S Amiriya, damaged Cat II; Lt P.F.Cowen safe
208 Sqn	Hurricane II Z4950 left 1430, dived into ground near Cairo; Sgt M.R.Hayworth KiFA

92 Sqn	Spitfire Vc BR573 'T' left 1004, spun into ground near LG.173; Plt Off W.M.Menzies KiFA			
German Claims				
Stab I./JG 27	Hptm Gerhard Homuth	P-40	SE El Alamein	1742
3./JG 27	Oblt Hans-Joachim Marseille	P-46	SE El Alamein	1743
3./JG 27	Oblt Hans-Joachim Marseille	P-46	10km SW El Hammam	1745
I./JG 27	Gruppe	P-46	SW El Hammam	1752
German Casualties				
2./JG 27	Bf 109F-4 trop WNr 8704 Red 4 combat with Spitfire SE El Alamein; Lt Hans-Arnold Stahlschmidt MiA			
2./JG 27	Bf 109F-4 trop WNr 8534 combat with Spitfire. Force-landed nr Gebiet in El Alamein area; Lt Karl von Lieres und Wilkau safe			

Tuesday, 8 September 1942

As a result of the serious losses suffered during the past four days, I./JG 27 was rested for a day. Soon after 1300 ten Bf 109s of II.Gruppe, four of III.Gruppe and 14 of III./JG 53 carried out an escort for Stukas. Eight Kittyhawks of 450 Squadron and eight of 3 RAAF Squadron were scrambled to intercept, with Spitfires from 145 Squadron as high cover. The Allied fighters soon met 20 Ju 87s and the same number of Bf 109s and MC.202s. II.Gruppe reported engaging two formations of fighters, Uffz Jürgens claiming to have damaged one which poured smoke. III.Gruppe, flying high cover, encountered a formation identified as Spitfires, two of which were claimed shot down by Lt Schroer, meanwhile III./JG 53 met three different formations, Obfw Stumpf claiming one Spitfire. The pilots of 3 RAAF Squadron became heavily engaged, claiming a Bf 109 and a Ju 87, plus a number of probables and damaged. In addition Sgt Taylor of 450 Squadron claimed a Bf 109 probable and Flt Lt Sabourin of 145 Squadron a Messerschmitt. Sgt Freer of 3 RAAF was shot down and force-landed, slightly wounded, and one Spitfire was lost.

Bf 109F of 8./JG 27 Kapitän, Lt Werner Schroer at Qasaba with 32 victories indicated, meaning that this photograph was taken circa 8 September.

British Claims					
450 Sqn	Sgt A.W.J.Taylor	Kittyhawk I EV169	Bf 109F Probable		1319-1433
145 Sqn	Flt Lt J.J.P.Sabourin	Spitfire Vb BP986 'X'	Bf 109	10m S Sidi Abd el Rahman	1320-1440
3 RAAF Sqn	Flt Sgt L.L.Boardman	Kittyhawk I EV322 'I'	Bf 109F Probable	Qattara area	1350
3 RAAF Sqn	Flt Sgt L.L.Boardman	Kittyhawk I EV322 'I'	Bf 109E Damaged	Qattara area	1350
3 RAAF Sqn	Sgt J.Donald	Kittyhawk I EV361 'C'	Bf 109F Damaged	Qattara area	1350
3 RAAF Sqn	Sgt G.A.Neill	Kittyhawk I AL167 'F'	Bf 109F	Qattara area	1350
3 RAAF Sqn	Sgt G.A.Neill	Kittyhawk I AL167 'F'	Ju 87	Qattara area	1350
3 RAAF Sqn	Sgt G.A.Neill	Kittyhawk I AL167 'F'	Bf 109F Probable	Qattara area	1350

British Claims

3 RAAF Sqn	Sgt G.A.Neill	Kittyhawk I AL167 'F'	Bf 109F Damaged	Qattara area	1350
3 RAAF Sqn	Sgt G.G.Scribner	Kittyhawk I AK778 'J'	Bf 109F	Qattara area	1350
3 RAAF Sqn	Sgt G.G.Scribner	Kittyhawk I AK778 'J'	Bf 109E Damaged	Qattara area	1350
3 RAAF Sqn	Sgt G.G.Scribner	Kittyhawk I AK778 'J'	MC.202 Damaged	Qattara area	1350
33 Sqn	Flt Lt L.C.Wade	Hurricane IIc HL721 'C'	MC.202 Damaged		

British Casualties

3 RAAF Sqn	Kittyhawk I AK625 damaged by Bf 109s and force-landed in minefield; Sgt K.H.Freer safe

German Claims

9./JG 53	Obfw Werner Stumpf	Spitfire	20km SSE El Alamein	1230
8./JG 27	Lt Werner Schroer	2 Spitfires	Deir el Tarfa	1245 & 1250

Wednesday, 9 September 1942

At Shandur 7 SAAF Squadron, which had recently suffered such heavy losses, had also been withdrawn from operations with 7 SAAF Wing and was now to begin training on Hurricane IIds to become the second tank-buster unit. From the same wing, 274 Squadron moved to LG.229 at Edcu.

British Casualties

112 Sqn	Kittyhawk I EV368 'A' forced to land; Plt Off H.L.Phillips safe

Thursday, 10 September 1942

238 Squadron received Hurricane IIcs fitted with only two cannon each, to replace their Mark IIbs, which were passed to 335 Squadron.

Friday, 11 September 1942

Nine Bf 109s of I./JG 27 flew indirect escort for Stukas at 0750, attacking a formation of nearly 20 fighter-bombers which jettisoned their bombs in Allied territory. Oblt Marseille claimed two 'P-46s' shot down. Hurricanes of 33 and 213 Squadrons had been scrambled to intercept the Stukas at 0755, joined by Spitfires of 145 and 601 Squadrons. Flt Lt Lance Wade of 33 claimed one Ju 87 while Flg Off Phillips claimed a probable.

Twelve MC.202s of 10° Gruppo (six of 90ª Squadriglia led by Cap Piccolomini and six of 91ª led by Cap Ruspoli) were scrambled at 0930 and vectored to the El Imayid area. Two formations were intercepted, one at 6,000 feet of 15 P-40s carrying bombs and one of ten Spitfires flying at 12,000 feet. A third formation of eight Spitfires bounced the Macchis diving from 18,000 feet. The following combat lasted about 20 minutes, as far as 36 miles west of El Alamein. The Italian attack forced the P-40s to jettison their bombs into the sea while the 90ª Squadriglia claimed three P-40s and a Spitfire, plus one Spitfire as a probable. In return the Gruppo had five of its fighters hit and damaged to some extent; two pilots were wounded and at least one MC.202 force-landed as a consequence of the damage suffered.

At 1005 eight Spitfires of 601 Squadron and four of 145 Squadron again provided cover to 33 Squadron, this time the unit's Hurricanes escorting a TacR aircraft over the front. The formation was attacked by Axis fighters south of El Alamein, Sqn Ldr Matthews and Flt Lt Saunders of 145 Squadron each claiming an MC.202, two other pilots each claiming damage to two Macchis. 601 Squadron's Flt Lt Curry claimed a Bf 109 as a probable and a Macchi damaged, with a further claim for a Macchi damaged also submitted. The WDAF formation appears to have been engaged with Macchis of 10° Gruppo. Amongst the Allied units, Sgt Douglas of 33 Squadron crash-landed in flames, whereas Flt Sgt Downing's 601 Squadron Spitfire was damaged as was Flt Lt Wade's Hurricane.

At the same time as this engagement took place, four Bf 109s of III./JG 27, fitted with long-range fuel tanks, undertook an intruder mission to the south-west of Cairo, targeting an airfield at Fayoum Road. Here two of the pilots attacked Bostons on the ground, each claiming to have left one in flames, while Uffz Gruber shot down a Harvard trainer in the same area.

Two Hurricanes of 127 Squadron were scrambled at 1045 to intercept two aircraft reportedly strafing LG.221 which the pilots identified as Bf 109Es with long-range tanks. They both attacked and damaged one of these, Fw Fink baling out of his Messerschmitt after it had been hit in the oil cooler, and he became a PoW. The other German pilots returned to base, reporting that they had been attacked by ten Spitfires! This seems to have been a typical case of far multiplying the size of the opposition (see further details in Chapter Ten).

Sgt Alwyn Stephens had undertaken his conversion to Kittyhawks and was awaiting posting to a squadron at 239 Wing HQ. He recorded:

> "I started on my Italian grammar again, when some kites shot us up, coming very low over the Mess tent. Then we heard the popping of a Kitty engine cutting, ran out, and saw a column of smoke on the 'drome, and assumed a kite had gone in. Then we saw that four Me 109s had come over the Mess, shot-up the drome, destroying a Boston and a Wellington and holing several aircraft. Then they shot-up the wireless station and went down to Mene. I ran to my tent and got my camera out and took a photo of the smoke column. They also shot a Harvard down with a Sqn Ldr in it! He made a safe crash-landing. I returned to my tent and put my camera away, and on coming out saw the Me's returning. Over the Mess two Hurricanes jumped them and shot one down. Some of our chaps went out and brought back a parachute, cannon shells and odds and ends. The pilot was taken by the army. He baled out and was slightly wounded."

4 SAAF Squadron was ordered from LG.97 to Edcu during the day. On their first scramble from this base at 1810, three 'snappers' were reported but no enemy aircraft were encountered. Following his release from hospital, Sqn Ldr Young resumed command of 213 Squadron. In the Regia Aeronautica Cap Edoardo Molinari was posted to 2° Gruppo CT, handing over command of 83ª Squadriglia to Ten Guglielmo Specker.

British Claims

33 Sqn	Plt Off H.J.Phillips	Hurricane IIc BN831 'F'	Bf 109 Probable	El Alamein	0755-0850
33 Sqn	Flt Lt L.C.Wade	Hurricane IIc HL661 'J'	Ju 87	El Alamein	0800-0900
213 Sqn	Sgt D.C.Usher	Hurricane IIc BP592 'F'	MC.202 Damaged	El Alamein line	0800-0900
145 Sqn	Flt Lt C.H.Saunders	Spitfire Vb AR287 'K'	MC.202	Burg el Arab	0805-0905
601 Sqn	Flt Lt J.H.Curry	Spitfire Vc BR481 'K'	Bf 109 Probable	S El Alamein	1020-1120
601 Sqn	Flt Lt J.H.Curry	Spitfire Vc BR481 'K'	MC.202 Damaged	S El Alamein	1020-1120
601 Sqn	Flt Sgt E.G.Shea	Spitfire Vc BP988 'N'	MC.202 Damaged	S El Alamein	1020-1120
145 Sqn	Flg Off R.G.Bates	Spitfire Vb BP847 'Z'	2 MC.202s Damaged		1020-1130
145 Sqn	Flg Off P.B.Laing-Meason	Spitfire Vb AB186	2 MC.202s Damaged		1020-1130
145 Sqn	Sqn Ldr G.P.H.Matthews	Spitfire Vb AR287 'K'	MC.202	N end of line	1020-1130
127 Sqn	Sgt I.R.Campbell	Hurricane II b Z3759 'R' }	Bf 109	8m N LG.221	1100
127 Sqn	Flt Lt R.C.Lawrence	Hurricane II b BN160 'J' }			

British Casualties

33 Sqn	Hurricane IIc BP474 'N' left 1000, shot down by fighters nr El Alamein; Sgt W.E.Douglas WiA
33 Sqn	Hurricane IIc HL661 'J' left 0800, damaged; Flt Lt L.C.Wade safe
213 Sqn	Hurricane IIc BP394 damaged by MC.202 at 0830 Cat I; Flt Sgt H.A.Aitken safe
601 Sqn	Spitfire Vc BR113 damaged by MC.202; Flt Sgt R.Downing safe
?? Auster	

German Claims

3./JG 27	Oblt Hans-Joachim Marseille	P-46	15km SE El Alamein	0740
3./JG 27	Oblt Hans-Joachim Marseille	P-46	5km WSW Imayid	0742
8./JG 27	Uffz Viktor Gruber	NAA 64	Fayoum Road l.g.	1010

German Casualties

7./JG 27	Bf 109F-4 WNr 7421 White 5 shot down by Hurricane 20km W Saqqara Pyramids, Cairo area; Fw Walter Fink PoW

Italian Claims

90ª Sq, 10°Gr, 4°St CT	Cap Ranieri Piccolomini	MC.202	P-40	SW El Alamein	0930-1045
91ª Sq, 10°Gr, 4°St CT	Ten Orlando Mandolini	MC.202	Spitfire	SW El Alamein	0930-1045
91ª Sq, 10°Gr, 4°St CT	S.Ten Luciano Barsotti	MC.202 MM 7907	P-40	SW El Alamein	0930-1045
91ª Sq, 10°Gr, 4°St CT	Serg Guerriero Silvestri	MC.202	P-40	SW El Alamein	0930-1045
90ª Sq, 10°Gr, 4°St CT	Ten Luigi Padovani	MC.202 MM 7894 }	Spitfire Probable	SW El Alamein	0930-1045
90ª Sq, 10°Gr, 4°St CT	Ten Sforza Libera	MC.202 MM 7801 }			
90ª Sq, 10°Gr, 4°St CT	Serg Magg Bruno Bortoletti	MC.202 }			
90ª Sq, 10°Gr, 4°St CT	M.llo Angelo Savini	MC.202 }			

Italian Casualties

90ª Sq, 10°Gr, 4°St CT	MC.202 MM 7894 damaged in combat, Ten Luigi Padovani WiA
91ª Sq, 10°Gr, 4°St CT	MC.202 MM 7907 '91-7' hit in combat, S.Ten Luciano Barsotti slightly wounded
90ª Sq, 10°Gr, 4°St CT	MC.202 hit in combat, force-landed at Hisiyet, Serg Magg Bruno Bortoletti safe
90ª Sq, 10°Gr, 4°St CT	MC.202 MM 7801 '90-10' hit in combat, Ten Sforza Libera safe
90ª Sq, 10°Gr, 4°St CT	MC.202 hit in combat, M.llo Angelo Savini safe
78ª Sq, 13°Gr, 2°St CT	MC.200 MM 5305 crashed, u/k cause, 1710-, Ten Edoardo Mulattiero baled and wounded, later repatriated

Saturday, 12 September 1942

Six Kittyhawks of 112 Squadron with ten from 450 Squadron took off at 1005 to patrol over the line. Fourteen Bf 109s of III./JG 53 provided direct cover to 25 Ju 87s of III./StG 3, which the Kittyhawks intercepted over El Alamein. Between them the two squadrons claimed two Stukas shot down plus three probables and seven damaged, one pilot also claiming a Bf 109E. Two fighters identified as Spitfires were claimed by the German pilots. An hour later five Spitfires of 145 Squadron were scrambled, a Bf 109 being claimed probably shot down and one damaged.

Identified photos of Kittyhawks in the air are fairly rare. OK-M of 450 Squadron is being flown here by the unit's New Zealand flight commander, Flt Lt J.E.A.Williams. On 12 September he claimed two Ju 87s shot down (one a probable) and a third damaged.

British Claims

450 Sqn	Sgt E.P.Oakley	Kittyhawk I ET869	Bf 109E	SW Maghra	1004-1345
450 Sqn	Flt Lt J.E.A.Williams	Kittyhawk I EV363	Ju 87	SW Maghra	1004-1345
450 Sqn	Flt Lt J.E.A.Williams	Kittyhawk I EV363	Ju 87 Probable	SW Maghra	1004-1345
450 Sqn	Flt Lt J.E.A.Williams	Kittyhawk I EV363	Ju 87 Damaged	SW Maghra	1004-1345
145 Sqn	Flt Lt J.S.Taylor	Spitfire Vb BP986 'X' }	Bf 109 Probable		1105-1210
145 Sqn	Sgt P.G.C.Thomas	Spitfire Vb AB147 'Y' }			
145 Sqn	Flt Lt J.S.Taylor	Spitfire Vb BP986 'X'	Bf 109 Damaged		1105-1210
112 Sqn	Sgt D.F.Greaves	Kittyhawk I EV360 'F'	Ju 87 Probable	El Alamein area	1005-1220
112 Sqn	Sgt D.F.Greaves	Kittyhawk I EV360 'F'	Ju 87 Damaged	El Alamein area	1005-1220
112 Sqn	Sgt W.D.Hogg	Kittyhawk I ET789 'C'	Ju 87 Damaged	El Alamein area	1005-1220
112 Sqn	Sgt W.Money	Kittyhawk I AK694	Ju 87 Damaged	El Alamein area	1005-1220
112 Sqn	Sgt W.E.Pollock	Kittyhawk I AK716	Ju 87	El Alamein area	1005-1220
112 Sqn	Sgt W.E.Pollock	Kittyhawk I AK716	Ju 87 Damaged	El Alamein area	1005-1220

112 Sqn	Capt E.C.Saville	Kittyhawk I EV136 'Q'	Ju 87 Probable	El Alamein area	1005-1220
112 Sqn	Capt E.C.Saville	Kittyhawk I EV136 'Q'	Ju 87 Damaged	El Alamein area	1005-1220
112 Sqn	Capt E.C.Saville	Kittyhawk I EV136 'Q'	Bf 109 Damaged	El Alamein area	1005-1220

German Claims

9./JG 53	Obfw Werner Stumpf	Spitfire	60km SSE El Alamein	1020
9./JG 53	Uffz Max Nairz	Spitfire	60km SSE El Alamein	1030

German Casualties

8./StG 3	Ju 87D-3 hit in combat by P-40 Deir el Raghil, 10% damaged; Obfw Karl Konsorke WiA; pilot safe
8./StG 3	Ju 87D-3 hit in combat by P-40 Deir el Raghil, 10% damaged; Uffz Rudi Michaelis WiA; pilot safe

Sunday, 13 September 1942

Fifteen III./JG 27 Bf 109s provided top cover to another Stuka raid at 0750, reporting meeting eight Hurricanes, ten Kittyhawks and some Spitfires near El Alamein. Lt Herfried Körner's Messerschmitt was hit in the cooling system and he force-landed in Axis territory. Two claims for Bf 109s probably shot down at this time were made, one by Plt Off Sherk of 601 Squadron, the other by Flt Sgt Boardman of 3 RAAF Squadron; according to German records, Körner's combat had been with Spitfires, so Sherk's claim does appear to have been the more likely – though it could well have been both pilots attacking the same aircraft.

At 1740 12 Messerschmitts of I.Gruppe, 11 of III./JG 27 and 14 of III./JG 53 escorted Stukas on a further raid. Sqn Ldr Drake, leading Kittyhawks from his own and the other 239 Wing squadrons, spotted Bf 109s apparently bombing in the El Alamein area and he claimed one of these shot down. Other 112 Squadron pilots claimed a probable and two damaged. Sgt Morrison was shot down by a Bf 109, crash-landing with his aircraft on fire; he got out safely before it burnt out. Uffz König fought with a lone Kittyhawk (probably Drake) and was shot down, force-landing near Daba. Lt Schroer of III./JG 27 and Uffz Klötzer of III./JG 53 each claimed one Allied fighter in flames, Schroer's victim reportedly being another lone aircraft. 4 SAAF Squadron now returned from Edcu to LG.97.

Plt Off Andy Taylor of 450 Squadron in his Kittyhawk, named after his wife. Note the solar helmet hanging from the conveniently protruding muzzle of one of the aircraft's .50in machine guns.

British Claims

601 Sqn	Plt Off R.J.F.Sherk	Spitfire Vc BR253	Bf 109 Probable		0750-0900
3 RAAF	Sqn Flt Sgt L.L.Boardman	Kittyhawk I EV322 'I'	Bf 109 Probable	20m SW El Alamein	0845
112 Sqn	Sqn Ldr B.Drake	Kittyhawk I EV168	Bf 109F		1740-1900
112 Sqn	Flt Sgt D.Ibbotson	Kittyhawk I EV315	Bf 109 Probable	El Alamein area	1740-1900
112 Sqn	unstated	Kittyhawk I	2 Bf 109Fs Damaged	El Alamein area	1740-1900

British Casualties

112 Sqn	Kittyhawk I AK716 damaged by Bf 109s and crash-landed; destroyed by fire at 1850; Sgt J.H.Morrison safe

German Claims

7./JG 53	Uffz Hartmut Klötzer	P-40	SE El Alamein	1716
8./JG 27	Lt Werner Schroer	P-40	7km SW El Alamein	1725

German Casualties

3./JG 27	Bf 109F-4 WNr 7334 combat with P-40; force-landed 5km E El Daba, 60% damaged; Uffz Karl Könning safe
6./JG 27	Bf 109F-4 WNr 7655 combat with Spitfire, belly-landed near Abu Dweis, 40% damaged; Lt Herfried Körner safe
II./StG 3	Ju 87D-1 WNr 2574 70% damaged by bombs at Qasaba airfield

Monday, 14 September 1942

Eight Kittyhawks of 3 RAAF Squadron scrambled at 1035, six Bf 109s being spotted 4,000 feet below and to the west of Qattara. Attacking from this favourable position, two of the Australian pilots claimed one Messerschmitt probably shot down between them, but this was later confirmed. 213 Squadron was now suffering some problems of indiscriminate crash-landing such as 4 SAAF Squadron had recently experienced. Sqn Ldr Young called his pilots together and threatened similar punishments for future offenders.

British Claims

3 RAAF Sqn	Flt Lt G.C.Coward	Kittyhawk I EV361 'C'	Bf 109	Daba area	1100
3 RAAF Sqn	Sgt G.R.Jones	Kittyhawk I EV323 'X'			

German Casualties

4./StG 3	Ju 87D-3 WNr 2623 crashed near Qasaba following a mid-air collision with a Ju 87; Lt Jakob König/Uffz Franz Huber KiA
5./StG 3	Ju 87D-3 WNr 2578 crashed near Qasaba following a mid-air collision with a Ju 87; Uffz Josef Jaumann KiA

Italian Casualties

54ª Sq, 47°Gr, 15°St Ass	CR.42 MM 8910 '54-5' crashed probably hit by AA, Serg Ettore Mura KiA

Tuesday, 15 September 1942

Once more, 15 Bf 109s of III./JG 27 provided indirect escort for a Stuka raid at 1220, pilots reporting combats with 20 Curtiss fighters and eight Spitfires near El Alamein. Seven Kittyhawks of 260 Squadron had scrambled to intercept at 1235 with other units which have not been identified. During this interception Lt Schroer claimed three P-40s and Oblt Althof one. In return Flt Sgt J.F.Edwards claimed one Messerschmitt as a probable. Another Stuka raid was met at 1715, this time escorted by 18 Bf 109s of I.Gruppe, 15 of II.Gruppe and ten of III.Gruppe. Ten Kittyhawks of 250 Squadron, ten of 450 Squadron, eight of 3 RAAF Squadron and eight of 112 Squadron were scrambled this time, attacking the German formation ten miles south-west of El Alamein. The two Australian squadrons sighted eight Bf 109s above and seven more 'up-sun', a general dogfight beginning. More Messerschmitts then joined the fight, but 112 and 250 Squadrons then dived in with a height advantage and the Axis fighters were driven off.

Between themselves, the 239 Wing units claimed two Bf 109s shot down (both identified as Es), three probables and three damaged, but lost six Kittyhawks with two more badly damaged. From this fight six pilots failed to return and a seventh was slightly wounded; three of those missing were later reported to have become PoWs. One of the latter, Plt Off Thorpe, had been seen going down with the Kittyhawk's mainplane shot away. The 112 Squadron aircraft flown by Sgt Young was seen to be hit by a white Flak burst and to crash-land, bursting into flames. It is very possible, however, that this Kittyhawk had in fact been hit by a burst of cannon fire from a Bf 109 below it.

During the fight the pilots of 3 RAAF Squadron had seen a Bf 109 and a Kittyhawk crash and a Bf 109 colliding with another aircraft. The latter were undoubtedly both Messerschmitts, Lt Hoffmann of 3./JG 27 ramming the aircraft flown by Uffz Prein of 5.Staffel, one wing breaking off his own aircraft. He baled out, but hit the tail unit, breaking his legs. Prein crashed and was killed, Hoffmann dying five weeks later in hospital. However, in the course of this large and confused combat, the German pilots went well over the top in their claims, reporting 21 Allied fighters shot down! Ten of these were claimed as P-46s, seven of them by Oblt Marseille. Another ten were listed as P-40s, Uffz Krainik claiming four of these, Lt Schroer two and one Spitfire. Apart from the two Messerschmitts which had collided, Hptm Gustav Rödel's aircraft was also shot down, crash-landing south-west of El Alamein without harm to the pilot.

British Claims

260 Sqn	Flt Sgt J.F.Edwards	Kittyhawk II FL238 'E'	Bf 109 Probable	El Alamein area	1235-1340
450 Sqn	Sgt J.D.Gleeson	Kittyhawk I EV324	Bf 109E	10m SW El Adem	1727-1835
450 Sqn	Flg Off H.F.Marting	Kittyhawk I EV160	Bf 109E	10m SW El Adem	1727-1835
450 Sqn	Flg Off H.F.Marting	Kittyhawk I EV160	Bf 109F Damaged	10m SW El Adem	1727-1835
3 RAAF Sqn	Plt Off E.H.T.Alderson	Kittyhawk I EV361 'C'	Bf 109F Damaged	15-20m SW El Alamein	1800
3 RAAF Sqn	Plt Off G.E.S.Clabburn	Kittyhawk I ET824 'K'	Bf 109F Probable	10m SE El Alamein	1800
3 RAAF Sqn	Plt Off E.K.Kildey	Kittyhawk I EV346 'U'	Bf 109F Damaged	10m SE El Alamein	1800
250 Sqn	Sgt D.J.Cormack	Kittyhawk I ET977 'C'	Bf 109 Probable	2m SW El Alamein	1800

British Casualties

112 Sqn	Kittyhawk I AK694 shot down by own AA, crash-landed, DBR; Sgt C.D.Young WiA
250 Sqn	Kittyhawk I AK641 shot down by Bf 109s W El Alamein 1800; Sgt A.J.Strong PoW
250 Sqn	Kittyhawk I ET1024 shot down by Bf 109s SW El Alamein 1800; Plt Off C.R.Thorpe (US) PoW
450 Sqn	Kittyhawk I ET869 shot down by Bf 109 10m SW El Alamein; Sgt P.A.Ewing PoW
3 RAAF Sqn	Kittyhawk I EV322 'I' FTR, presumed shot down by Bf 109s SW El Alamein 1800; Sgt G.G.Scribner KiA
3 RAAF Sqn	Kittyhawk I EV345 FTR, presumed shot down by Bf 109s SW El Alamein 1800; Plt Off J.Donald PoW
3 RAAF Sqn	Kittyhawk I EV346 'U' badly damaged by Bf 109s SW El Alamein 1800; Plt Off E.K.Kildey safe
3 RAAF Sqn	Kittyhawk I AK867 badly damaged by Bf 109s SW El Alamein 1800; Sgt K.Bee WiA

German Claims

9./JG 27	Oblt Willi Althof	P-40	W El Alamein	1140
8./JG 27	Lt Werner Schroer	3 P-40s	W & S El Alamein	1140, 1143, 1145
8./JG 27	Lt Werner Schroer	2 P-40s	NE Deir el Tarfa	1645 & 1655
8./JG 27	Uffz Erich Krainik	P-40	S El Hammam	1651
3./JG 27	Oblt Hans-Joachim Marseille	3 P-46s	25-28km SW El Alamein	1651-1654
Stab I./JG 27	Hptm Gerhard Homuth	P-46	SW El Alamein	1654
7./JG 27	Uffz Viktor Gruber	P-40	El Alamein area	1655
2./JG 27	Lt Karl von Lieres und Wilkau	P-46	SW El Alamein	1657
3./JG 27	Oblt Hans-Joachim Marseille	4 P-46s	18-26km SW El Alamein	1657-1702
5./JG 27	Oblt Ernst Börngen	P-40	S El Alamein	1702
8./JG 27	Uffz Erich Krainik	P-40	El Alamein area	1702
8./JG 27	Lt Werner Schroer	Spitfire	El Alamein area	1703
2./JG 27	Lt Karl von Lieres und Wilkau	P-46	SW El Alamein	1703
8./JG 27	Uffz Alfred Stückler	P-40	El Alamein area	1705
8./JG 27	Uffz Erich Krainik	2 P-40s	S & ESE El Alamein	

German Casualties

3./JG 27	Bf 109F-4 trop WNr 10059 Yellow 12 combat; collided with Bf 109, crashed 25km SW El Alamein; Lt Friedrich Hoffmann baled out and WiA, died 12 October
5./JG 27	Bf 109F-4 trop WNr 8665 Red 4 collided with Bf 109; crashed 25km SW El Alamein; Uffz Heinrich Prein KiA
Stab II./JG 27	Bf 109F-4 WNr 7347 combat with P-40, belly-landed SW El Alamein, 100% Hptm Gustav Rödel safe

Wednesday, 16 September 1942

The hunt for LRDG vehicles went on early morning, when two Cant.Z.1007bis of 190ª Squadriglia, flown by Cap Leo Vecellio-Reane and Ten Edison Franco, flying at low altitude over the desert, sighted and bombed 20 light trucks. Two more Cant.Zs, flown by Ten Amato Caccavale and Ten Aldo Ulmi, carried out the same mission in the afternoon, bombing some motor transports concealed west of the Gialo oasis. Some columns of black smoke were observed. During the afternoon some CR.42s of 15° Stormo were despatched to search and strafe the LRDG vehicles south of Regima. M.llo Tavernelli of 53ª Squadriglia failed to return. Magg Roberto Fassi led at 0825 16 MC.202s of 9° Gruppo on a free sweep sortie over the area east of El Alamein. Flying at 19,500 feet the Italian fighters engaged a large formation of P-40s and were later jumped by about 20 Spitfires flying 1,500 feet higher.

At 0936 another Stuka attack was launched on the Allied lines, 15 Bf 109s of III./JG 27 providing close escort. Eight Spitfires of 145 Squadron and others from 601 Squadron, were scrambled, followed by Kittyhawks from 112, 450 and 3 RAAF Squadrons. Three of the six aircraft sent off by the last of these units, returned at once with various troubles, the other three covering those of 450 Squadron, while eight of 112 Squadron sat above the formation as high cover. The Spitfires attacked over 12 Bf 109s and MC.202s, one of each being claimed. 112 Squadron's pilots saw two MC.202s diving on the Australians, the Italians pulling up in front of the squadron, allowing Flt Lt Garton to claim one as a probable. 3 RAAF Squadron was twice attacked by Bf 109s, Sgt Wood being shot-up and wounded; he returned to base straight away. Lt Schroer and Lt Schöfböck each claimed one Kittyhawk, with one Spitfire claimed by M.llo Mechelli and another probably so by M.llo Perno; Serg Martinoli claimed a P-40 probable, and four MC.202s returned slightly damaged.

213 Squadron's Hurricanes provided top cover to 33 Squadron, escorting a TacR aircraft over the lines at 1450, where they were attacked by four Bf 109s of II./JG 27 which had been scrambled at 1523. Sqn Ldr Young alone fought two, claiming damage to one but suffering hits on his own aircraft. Lt Jürgens claimed one fighter, but as he had no witness, his claim was not confirmed.

At 1799 12 Bf 109s of III.Gruppe again provided escort for Stukas; this time six of 145 Squadron's Spitfires were scrambled with 601 Squadron, with 12 Kittyhawks of 4 SAAF Squadron also taking off. Uffz von Arnswald fought a lone Spitfire which he claimed shot down and Flt Lt Sabourin of 145 Squadron was seen to crash, his aircraft exploding on hitting the ground. 4 SAAF Squadron was jumped by a single Messerschmitt, Lt Dummett going into a spin, but recovering; Obfw Bauer claimed one Kittyhawk shot down. The day also saw the promotion of Hans-Joachim Marseille to Hauptmann – the youngest officer of this rank in the Luftwaffe at the time.

Flt Lt J.J.P.Sabourin, a French Canadian, flew Tomahawks with 112 Squadron on his first tour, and then Spitfires with 145 Squadron on his second. On 16 September he was shot down and killed by Uffz von Arnswald of III./JG 27.

British Claims

145 Sqn	Flt Lt J.J.P.Sabourin	Spitfire Vb BP986 'X'	Bf 109	El Alamein	0950-1050
145 Sqn	Sgt F.R.Barker	Spitfire Vb AB339 'M'	Bf 109 Damaged	El Alamein	0950-1050
145 Sqn	Sgt J.A.Greaves	Spitfire Vb AB207	Bf 109 Damaged	El Alamein	0950-1050
145 Sqn	Flt Sgt E.A.Ker	Spitfire Vb AR287	MC.202	El Alamein	0950-1050
145 Sqn	Flt Sgt E.A.Ker	Spitfire Vb AR287	Bf 109 Damaged	El Alamein	0950-1050
601 Sqn	Lt A.Bartleman	Spitfire Vc BR132	Bf 109 Damaged	El Alamein	1000-1045
112 Sqn	Flt Lt G.W.Garton	Kittyhawk I EV136	MC.202 Probable	Dir el Hima area	1000-1045
213 Sqn	Sqn Ldr M.H.Young	Hurricane IIc BP450	Bf 109F Damaged	El Alamein line	1450-1635
145 Sqn	Flt Sgt E.A.Ker	Spitfire Vb AR287	Bf 109 Damaged	El Alamein	1725-1820
145 Sqn	Flg Off P.B.Laing-Meason	Spitfire Vb AB136	MC.202 Damaged	El Alamein	1725-1820

British Casualties

33 Sqn	Hurricane IIc badly damaged by MC.202; Flt Lt L.C.Wade safe
213 Sqn	Hurricane IIc BP450 'O' damaged by Bf 109 El Alamein at 1540, Cat II; Sqn Ldr M.H.Young safe
213 Sqn	Hurricane IIc BN184 'W' damaged by Bf 109 or Flak El Alamein at 1540, Cat I; Flt Sgt W.D.Gwynne
145 Sqn	Spitfire V BP847 'Z' left 1725, shot down by Bf 109; Flt Lt J.J.P.Sabourin KiA
3 RAAF Sqn	Kittyhawk I damaged by Bf 109 force-landed at base; Sgt T.G.Wood WiA

German Claims

7./JG 27	Lt Erich Schöfböck	P-40	S El Alamein	0923
8./JG 27	Lt Werner Schroer	P-40	S El Alamein	0925

5./JG 27	Uffz Hans Jürgens	P-40 o.Zg. n.b.	3 km NW Deir el Tarfa	1438
7./JG 27	Obfw Ludwig Bauer	P-40	S El Alamein	1645
9./JG 27	Uffz Bernhard von Arnswald	Spitfire	SW El Alamein	1707

Italian Claims

73ª Sq, 9°Gr, 4°St CT	M.llo Salvatore Mechelli	MC.202	Spitfire	E El Alamein	0825-0955
73ª Sq, 9°Gr, 4°St CT	M.llo Paolo Perno	MC.202	Spitfire Probable	E El Alamein	0825-0955
73ª Sq, 9°Gr, 4°St CT	Serg Teresio Martinoli	MC.202	P-40 Probable	E El Alamein	0825-0955

Italian Casualties

92ª Sq, 8°Gr, 2° St CT	MC.200 MM 8137 damaged on take-off accident, S.Ten Costantino Petrosellini safe
53ª Sq, 46°Gr, 15° St Ass	CR.42 failed to return, M.llo Adriano Tavernelli MiA
9° Gr, 4° St Ct	MC.202s slightly damaged

Thursday, 17 September 1942

A Cant.Z.1007bis of 231ª Sq, piloted by Magg Zigiotti, took off at 0855 to bomb enemy troops and vehicles besieging the oasis of Gialo, followed by another Cant.Z.1007bis, flown by Cap Casadio, in the early afternoon. A third bomber, this time of 230ª Sq, was despatched from Derna to carry out the same mission. The aircraft, flown by Ten Marco Sommi-Picenardi, failed to return, probably shot down by ground fire.The attack on Gialo was carried out also by CR.42s of 15° Stormo Assalto, which lost two fighter-bombers in this action.

80 Squadron moved from LG.42 to El Bassa; moreover, all three squadrons of the 57th Fighter Group were now re-united at LG.174, coming under the command of the AOC, Western Desert. However, at this stage the group itself remained in reserve, although the three squadrons were still being filtered into the RAF wings for operations as appropriate. A Bf 109 of III./ZG 1 was shot down by AA south-west of Hammam during the day, the pilot being killed when his aircraft lost its wings and crashed.

British Casualties

3 RAAF Sqn	Kittyhawk I EV169 crashed on take-off at LG.91

German Casualties

7./ZG 1	Bf 109E-7 WNr 4835 S9+CR shot down by AA and crashed 50km SW El Hammam; Uffz Max Müller MiA

Italian Casualties

230ª Sq, 95°Gr, 35°St BT	Cant.Z.1007bis MM 23391 '230-8' hit by AA, pilot Ten Marco Sommi-Picenardi, copilot Serg Magg Paolo D'Andrea and crew KiA
53ª Sq, 46°Gr, 15°St Ass	CR.42 crashed at Gialo, Serg Primo Ghinelli KiA
53ª Sq, 46°Gr, 15°St Ass	CR.42 shot down at Gialo, S.Ten Vasco Cinti safe, returned to Agedabia

Friday, 18 September 1942

33 Squadron took off at 0915 for a TacR mission, covered by 213 Squadron. Four Bf 109s of I./JG 27 were scrambled to intercept, attacking the formation when south-west of El Alamein. Fw Keppler claimed one victory and Sgt Brookes of 213 baled out, although it was reported that he had been hit by Flak; he landed in no mans' land, and there was a race between a British tank and a German armoured car to get to him first; fortunately for him, the tank won. Plt Off Jowsey of 33 Squadron had the tail of his aircraft shot-up and that of Sgt McNamara was hit and damaged in the left wing.

The troop concentrations around Gialo were again bombed during the day by nine Cant.Z.1007bis of 35° Stormo. This unit continued these sorties during the next few days. CR.42s of 15° Stormo moved from K1 (Benghazi) to Agedabia and went on with their ground-attack missions targeting the troops surrounding Gialo. Also 23 CR.42s of 159° Gruppo, accompanied by three S.82s, arrived at Benghazi K3 to take part in these operations. Magg Simeone Marsan led 16 MC.202s of 9° Gruppo (eight each of 73ª and 96ª Squadriglie) on a free sweep south of El Alamein from 1530 to 1710. The formation encountered ten Spitfires at 22,500 feet, ten more flying 6,000 feet lower. Three Spitfires were claimed by the Italian fighters at the end of the combat.

At 1655 six Spitfires of 145 Squadron with others of 601 Squadron met eight fighters identified as Bf 109s over Burg el Arab, the pilots claiming two probables and two damaged. It is likely that their opponents were actually MC.202s of 9° Gruppo. During the day 260 Squadron received a new flight commander, Flt Lt.K.N.T.Lee, DFC, another Battle of Britain veteran. From 92 Squadron Lt Johannes

Fuka, 19 September. Hptm 'Jochen' Marseille (second from left in front row) visits 4° Stormo. Close to him, with sunglasses, is Ten Annoni, whose MC.202 the German pilot was about to test fly, but badly damaged a few minutes later.

Hptm Marseille in the cockpit of Annoni's '96-10' MM 7821.

Faure returned to 1 SAAF Squadron having gained valuable experience of flying and operating the Spitfire during his attachment.

Next day a rather curious episode occurred at Fuka involving 4° Stormo. Its pilots received the welcome visit of newly promoted Hptm Hans-Joachim Marseille, at that time already very popular among Axis airmen. He was greeted by T.Col François, the Stormo's commander, and then Marseille asked for a test flight in an MC.202. François called Ten Annoni who gave to the German ace his own mount, the '96-10', providing him with a short description of the flight controls, which differed, in some way, from those of the Bf 109. Marseille took off and did some manoeuvres over the airfield; when ready to land, he lowered the undercarriage but in so doing inadvertently shifted the switch lever to the 'off' position and the engine cut immediately. Marseille reacted rapidly by retracting the wheels and proceeding to belly-land, but the Macchi sustained serious damage. This time an Italian casualty was not due to a Commonwealth pilot but to the most famous Axis ace in North Africa!

British Claims					
145 Sqn	Flt Sgt E.A.Ker	Spitfire Vb AR287 'K'	Bf 109 Probable	Burg el Arab	1655-1820
145 Sqn	Flt Lt J.S.Taylor	Spitfire Vb AB147 'Y'	Bf 109 Damaged	Burg el Arab	1655-1820
145 Sqn	Sgt P.G.C.Thomas	Spitfire Vb BP986 'X'	Bf 109 Probable	Burg el Arab	1655-1820
601 Sqn	Flt Lt M.R.B.Ingram	Spitfire Vc AR289 'P'	Bf 109 Damaged	Burg el Arab	1700-1800

British Casualties	
33 Sqn	Hurricane IIc BM971 'Y' left 0915, badly damaged by Bf 109 SW El Alamein; Plt Off M.E.Jowsey safe
33 Sqn	Hurricane IIc HL516 left 0915, badly damaged by Bf 109 SW El Alamein; Sgt M.H.McNamara safe
112 Sqn	Kittyhawk I ET789 damaged by Bf 109 and crash-landed; Sgt D.Hogg
145 Sqn	Spitfire V AB136 left 0945 on TacR and force-landed; Plt Off P.B.Laing-Meason safe
213 Sqn	Hurricane IIc BP196 'B' damaged by Flak and crash-landed; Sgt K.G.Brookes safe

German Claims			
1./JG 27	Fw Gerhard Keppler	Hurricane	SW El Alamein

German Casualties	
10.(Jabo)/JG 27	Bf 109F-4 trop WNr 10275 damaged by AA; force-landed 30%
10.(Jabo)/JG 27	Bf 109F-4/B WNr 7565 damaged by AA, force-landed at Mumin Busak, 30% damaged
12./LG 1	Ju 88A-4 L1+EW shot up by AA at Gialo oasis, 70% damaged, Fw Heinz Sievert KiA, one WiA

Italian Claims					
73ª Sq, 9°Gr, 4°St CT	Magg Simeone Marsan	MC.202			
73ª Sq, 9°Gr, 4°St CT	Ten Giulio Reiner	MC.202			
73ª Sq, 9°Gr, 4°St CT	Ten Giuseppe Oblach	MC.202	Spitfire	El Alamein	1530-1710
73ª Sq, 9°Gr, 4°St CT	Ten Vittorio Squarcia	MC.202			
73ª Sq, 9°Gr, 4°St CT	M.llo Salvatore Mechelli	MC.202			
73ª Sq, 9°Gr, 4°St CT	Serg Teresio Martinoli	MC.202	Spitfire	El Alamein	1530-1710
73ª Sq, 9°Gr, 4°St CT	M.llo Paolo Perno	MC.202			
73ª Sq, 9°Gr, 4°St CT	Serg Armando Angelini	MC.202	Spitfire	El Alamein	1530-1710
73ª Sq, 9°Gr, 4°St CT	Serg Leonardo Rinaldi	MC.202			

Italian Casualties	
96ª Sq, 9°Gr, 4°St CT	MC.202 MM 7821 '96-10' belly-landed at Fuka, Hptm Hans-Joachim Marseille unharmed

Sunday, 20 September 1942

Eight Kittyhawks of 250 Squadron took off at 0930, climbing to 11,000 feet to escort fighter-bombers of 112 Squadron on a mission. At the same time Hurricanes of 33 Squadron took off to escort TacR Hurricanes of 208 Squadron. Four Bf 109s of II./JG 27 were scrambled, attacking the Kittyhawks as they finished bombing. One Bf 109 flown by Fw Krummlauf was seen going down to attack 112 Squadron, but was itself attacked by Flg Off Whitside and Sgt Warman, who then broke away. Flg Off Tribken took up the attack, causing Krummlauf to crash-land. He was taken prisoner, the three 250 Squadron pilots all attending his interrogation. Lt Börngen's Messerschmitt was hit in the cockpit, but he returned, although wounded. Initially, Tribken was awarded one victory, the other two pilots a second shared between them. Meanwhile, 33 Squadron reported little Flak and few enemy aircraft, but nonetheless Flt Lt A.P.V.Strachan of 208 Squadron flying a Hurricane IIc borrowed from 33, was seen to break away below after flying through some heavy Flak, and did not return.

Bf 109F WNr 8635 in which Fw Alfred Krumlauf was shot down near El Hammam on 20 September; the pilot became a PoW.

Four Bf 109s of III./JG 53 were scrambled at 1000 and reported attacking a lone fighter near Abu Dweis, Obfw Alfred Seidl shooting this down. It would appear that Strachen's aircraft was damaged by Flak, causing him to head for base, but that he was then attacked after he had left his escorts. In the afternoon 16 Bf 109s of III./JG 27 provided direct escort for Stukas as 14 from II.Gruppe flew indirect support. 12 Kittyhawks of 4 SAAF Squadron were scrambled to intercept, being able to jump some Messerschmitts, one of which was claimed by Flg Off Waddy, two other pilots claiming a probable each, others claiming two damaged. Three Kittyhawks were shot down, one flown by an RAF pilot who became a PoW. One of these aircraft was shot down by Lt Schroer, whose personal tally now reached 40.

During the day 335 Squadron completed re-equipment with Hurricane IIbs, all the Mark Is and IIas having been replaced by the 11 aircraft passed over by 238 Squadron, and with ten more from 59 RSU.

British Claims

250 Sqn	Plt Off C.W.Tribken	Kittyhawk I AK959 'E'	Bf 109F	9m SW El Hammam	1005
250 Sqn	Sgt D.B.Warman	Kittyhawk I ET950 }	Bf 109E	S sector of front line	1030
250 Sqn	Flg Off W.J.Whitside	Kittyhawk I ET905 }			
4 SAAF Sqn	Lt L.J.de la Harpe	Kittyhawk I EV350 'E'	Bf 109F Damaged	El Alamein	1700
4 SAAF Sqn	Lt A.C.Peterson	Kittyhawk I EV347 'K'	Bf 109F Probable	El Alamein	1700
4 SAAF Sqn	Lt J.Stewart	Kittyhawk I ET1018 'F'	Bf 109F Probable	El Alamein	1700
4 SAAF Sqn	Flg Off J.L.Waddy	Kittyhawk I EV321 'G'	Bf 109F	El Alamein	1700
4 SAAF Sqn	Lt D.Woodliffe	Kittyhawk I ET869 'B'	Bf 109F Probable	El Alamein	1700

British Casualties

208 Sqn	Hurricane IIc borrowed from 33 Sqn, shot down by Flak at El Mreir; Flt Lt A.P.V.Strachan MiA
208 Sqn	Hurricane IIc HL567, weaver to Strachan, crash-landed S El Hammam Cat II; Capt J.Becourt-Foch safe
4 SAAF Sqn	Kittyhawk I ET971 presumed shot down by fighters E El Alamein 1715; Plt Off J.D.Howard PoW
4 SAAF Sqn	Kittyhawk I EV316 eng hit by explosive shell and seized; force-landed in Allied lines Cat II; Lt T.B.Milne returned on 21st
4 SAAF Sqn	Kittyhawk I EV347 'K' damaged Cat I by Bf 109 El Alamein; Lt A.C.Paterson slt WiA
4 SAAF Sqn	Kittyhawk I AK795 'L' shot down, crash-landed 7m W El Alamein 1715; Lt R.B.McKechnie slt WiA

German Claims

8./JG 53	Obfw Alfred Seidl	P-40	S Deir el Tarfa	0910
5./JG 27	Uffz Bernhard Schneider	P-40	ESE Deir el Tarfa	1620
8./JG 27	Uffz Heinz Keller	P-40	8km SW El Alamein	1625
8./JG 27	Lt Werner Schroer	P-40	8km SW El Alamein	1633

German Casualties

4./JG 27	Bf 109F-4 trop WNr 8635 White 3 combat with P-40, belly-landed 15km SW El Hammam, 100%; Fw Alfred Krumlauf PoW
5./JG 27	Bf 109F-4 trop combat, hit in cockpit; Oblt Ernst Börngen WiA

Monday, 21 September 1942

Six Spitfires of 601 Squadron flew top cover to Hurricanes of 33 and 213 Squadrons escorting two TacR aircraft. Four Bf 109s of I./JG 27 were scrambled, but were jumped by four of 601 Squadron's Spitfires over Abu Dweis, Sgt Downing shooting down Uffz von Arnswald, who was killed. In the evening eight Spitfires of 92 Squadron on patrol ran into 12 Bf 109s of III./JG 27 and ten of III./JG 53, with about 25 MC.202s of 4° Stormo, all escorting Stukas over El Alamein. The British pilots fought these for ten minutes until the Axis fighters broke away and returned to base. Lt Schroer claimed one Spitfire shot down, but no loss was actually suffered.

British Claims

601 Sqn	Flt Sgt R.Downing	Spitfire Vc BR132 'W'	Bf 109	SW Abu Dweis	0945-1100
274 Sqn	Sgt F.A.Carter	Hurricane IIc BP438 'P' }	Ju 88 Damaged	NW Cairo-SW Lake Maghra-SSW Daba	1210-1340
274 Sqn	Plt Off D.C.Mitchell	Hurricane IIc BE490 'W' }			

German Claims

8./JG 27	Lt Werner Schroer	Spitfire	N El Hammam	1630

German Casualties

9./JG 27	Bf 109F-4 trop WNr 101078 Yellow 5 shot down by Spitfires, crashed 15km SE Abu Dweis; Uffz Bernhard von Arnswald KiA

Tuesday, 22 September 1942

German Casualties

9./JG 53	Bf 109F-4/Z WNr 10102 100% destroyed on ground by bombs at Qotaifiya
9./JG 53	Bf 109F-4/Z WNr 7263 75% damaged on ground by bombs at Qotaifiya

Wednesday, 23 September 1942

At 1100 six Bf 109s of III./JG 27 escorted Jabos, reporting an engagement with eight Spitfires over El Hammam, pilots reporting that a Spitfire was seen to crash-land south-west of the airfield. However, no claim was made and no loss has been found. In the evening at 1825 Serg Magg Botticelli of 78ª Squadriglia, 13 ° Gruppo CT, undertaking a test flight in an MC.202, reported intercepting a formation of seven four-engined bombers south of Martuba, claiming to have hit the last aircraft. Next day while testing an MC.200, Botticelli suffered trouble with the synchronising mechanism of his aircraft's guns, the propeller being hit by a bullet which caused the aircraft to crash to the ground, killing him.

British Claims

450 Sqn	Sgt R.J.Prowse	Kittyhawk I EV339	Bf 109F Damaged	Burg el Arab	1030-1200

German Casualties

II./StG 3	Ju 87D-3 WNr 2640 100% destroyed on ground by bombs at Qotaifiya

Italian Claims

78ª Sq, 13°Gr, 2°St CT	Serg Magg Collatino Botticelli	MC.200	four-engined bomber Damaged	40km S Bu Amud	1825

Thursday, 24 September 1942

British Casualties

24 SAAF Sqn	Boston III Z2248 caught fire in air and abandoned nr LG.208

British Casualties

274 Sqn	Hurricane BD827 SOC as lost to enemy action
M.E.	Hurricane Z4171 SOC

German Casualties

I./StG 3	Ju 87D-3 WNr 2687 100% and Ju 87D-3 WNr 2664 80% damaged on ground by bombs at Qasaba
	DFS 230 WNr 227524 10% damaged by bombs at Qasaba
II./StG 3	Ju 87D-3 WNr 2647 65% damaged on ground by bombs at Qasaba

Friday, 25 September 1942

On this date 4 SAAF Squadron was withdrawn from operations for a rest. By now, the unit recorded, claims had been made for 39 and one shared confirmed victories, 12 probables and 27 damaged. The cost had been 11 killed in action plus four in accidents, four confirmed as PoWs, five missing and four wounded; five of the squadron's pilots had been awarded DFCs.

Saturday, 26 September 1942

At 0925 eight Spitfires of 92 Squadron provided top cover to the Hurricanes of 33 and 213 Squadrons which were escorting two TacR aircraft. Five Bf 109s of I./JG 27 attacked the formation near Daba. Hptm Marseille claimed one aircraft from the lower formation, identified as a Spitfire but apparently a 213 Squadron Hurricane, in which Plt Off Luxton carried out a crash-landing. Marseille then attacked the Spitfires, claiming three shot down in three minutes. Two Spitfires were lost, two more of 92 Squadron's pilots claiming Bf 109s shot down, although none were reported lost. I./JG 27 was in the air again when nine Bf 109s took off at 1617 to escort Stukas bombing south of El Hammam. Combat with six Spitfires was reported, and it would appear that 145 Squadron was involved since a pilot of this unit claimed damage to a Bf 109 at this time. Marseille again claimed three shot down, reporting that the pilot of the third fought in a most masterly fashion. However, on this occasion, unlike the morning engagements, no British losses were to be found.

145 Squadron had just moved to LG.92, joining 92 and 601 Squadrons in 244 Wing. During September the French unit, GC III/2 Alsace as it had become known, had departed for the United Kingdom where

One of 92 Squadron's flight commanders in September was John Morgan, seen here in Spitfire QJ-S soon after his fourth victory on 26th of that month.

it was to become 341 Squadron. The unit's Hurricanes were now handed on to 417 Squadron which had at last becoming established at Shandur. Here it would take part in the defence of the Suez area, and indeed would claim its first success on this very day (see Chapter Ten).

At night T.Col Nobili led six CR.42s of 101° Gruppo on a ground-attack sortie, to bomb and strafe the El Hammam railway station. The target was reached and claimed badly damaged. During the return flight German Flak fired some rounds at the CR.42s, near Daba, fortunately missing them.

British Claims					
92 Sqn	Flt Sgt R.W.Blades	Spitfire Vc BR522 'K'	Bf 109 Damaged	nr Daba	0925-1040
92 Sqn	Plt Off J.C.Carpenter	Spitfire Vc BR479 'E'	Bf 109 Probable	10m SSW Daba	0925-1000
92 Sqn	Flt Lt J.M.Morgan	Spitfire Vc BR525 'S'	Bf 109	nr Daba	0925-1000
92 Sqn	Plt Off G.W.Rose	Spitfire Vc BR580 'B'	Bf 109	nr Daba	0925-1000
145 Sqn	Flt Sgt F.R.Barker	Spitfire Vb AB339 'M'	Bf 109 Damaged	Burg el Arab	1610-1715

British Casualties	
92 Sqn	Spitfire Vc BR478 'U' left 0925 shot down by Bf 109 on sweep nr Daba; Wt Off W.F.Kenwood MiA
92 Sqn	Spitfire Vc BR494 'R' left 0925 shot down by Bf 109 on sweep nr Daba, crash-landed; Plt Off D.Turvey safe
213 Sqn	Hurricane IIc BN186 left 0930, damaged by Bf 109s and crash-landed nr Ghuzil; Plt Off C.Luxton

German Claims				
3./JG 27	Hptm Hans-Joachim Marseille	P-40	12km SW El Alamein	0910
3./JG 27	Oblt Joseph Schlang	Spitfire	10km SW El Alamein	0912
3./JG 27	Hptm Hans-Joachim Marseille	3 Spitfires	14-15km SW El Alamein	0913-0916
3./JG 27	Hptm Hans-Joachim Marseille	3 Spitfires	SW Imayid & 10km S El Hammam	1656-1710

Sunday, 27 September 1942

On this date 238 and 1 SAAF Squadrons moved forward to LG.154 following their rests from operations. 450 Squadron commenced re-equipment with Kittyhawk IIIs, the balance of the unit's Mark Is being divided between 112, 250 and 3 RAAF Squadrons.

During the morning five Bf 109s of III./JG53, fitted with belly tanks, were led by Lt Harder on an intruder mission to Cairo. An attack was made on the Fayoum Road (LG.221) airfield. During their sortie they encountered and shot down a Boston of 24 SAAF Squadron. This unit lost two of its bombers during night attacks on Luftwaffe forward airfields, and although both were reported shot down by Flak, it would appear possibly to have been one of these which had been attacked. It may, however, have been Boston AL791, listed as lost the next day, but regarding which very little information is available (see Chapter Eleven).

British Casualties	
24 SAAF Sqn	Boston III Z2288 one of nine off 2140-2215 for attacks on LG.101 and LG.13. One of three attacking LG.101 damaged by Flak and SOC on return (Night)
24 SAAF Sqn	Boston III AL785 'S' one of nine off by night and one of four attacking LG.13; shot down by Flak over target; Lt G.Cohen and one KiA, two PoW (Night)

German Claims				
7./JG 53	Lt Jürgen Harder	Boston	NW Cairo	1945

German Casualties	
7./JG 53	Bf 109F-4/Z WNr 7006 White 13+I shot down by AA nr Cairo; Uffz Adolf Jennerich baled out, PoW
Italian Casualties	
230ª Sq, 95°Gr, 35°St BT	Cant.Z.1007bis MM 23446 '230-2' crashed to ground for u/k causes 9km from Villaggio Maddalena, pilot S.Ten Salvatore Morelli, copilot Serg Gastone Bacchi and three KiA
238ª Sq, 101°Gr, 5°St Tuff	CR.42 MM 8890 crashed at Abar Nimeir, u/k reason, S.Ten Luigi De Regis KiA

Monday, 28 September 1942

Flt Lt Morgan and Plt Off Chisholm of 92 Squadron were scrambled at 1720 to intercept a Ju 88. They ran into 20 Bf 109s and a dogfight ensued. Seven more Spitfires took off at 1745, engaging another formation of Messerschmitts. Meanwhile, Morgan and Chisholm claimed to have jointly shot down one Bf 109, while in the second encounter, one more was claimed by Flt Lt Samouelle. At the same time a Hurricane PR IIa of 208 Squadron, flown by Plt Off Fookes, had departed for a photo-reconnaissance sortie over Deir el Munassib, but he was shot down in flames near Burg el Arab by Uffz Klötzer of III./JG 53, who claimed this aircraft as a Spitfire. Klötzer had been part of a formation of 12 III./JG 53 fighters, the pilots of which had reported engaging eight Spitfires – clearly the second 92 Squadron group. Klötzer appears to have strayed away from the other Messerschmitts before this encounter took place, as his claim was timed at 1712. Because he had no witness of this combat, it seems that he did not receive confirmation.

British Claims					
92 Sqn	Plt Off W.L.Chisholm	Spitfire Vc BR475 'J'	Bf 109	Burg el Arab	1720-1825
92 Sqn	Flt Lt J.M.Morgan	Spitfire Vc BR525 'S'			
92 Sqn	Plt Off J.C.Carpenter	Spitfire Vc BR479 'E'	Bf 109 Damaged	Burg el Arab	1745-1850
92 Sqn	Flt Lt C.J.Samouelle	Spitfire Vc BR520 'L'	Bf 109	Burg el Arab	1745-1850
British Casualties					
208 Sqn	Hurricane PR IIa BE709 left 1745, shot down by fighters nr Burg el Arab; Plt Off R.Fookes KiA				
German Claims					
7./JG 53	Uffz Hartmut Klötzer	Spitfire		15km S Daba	1712
Italian Casualties					
82ª Sq, 13°Gr, 2°St CT	MC.200 MM 8296 damaged on landing, Ten Camillo Luglio safe				

Tuesday, 29 September 1942

At 1340 Sqn Ldr Matthews of 145 Squadron with Flt Lt Curry and Plt Off Sherk of 601 Squadron, set off to try and intercept an Axis train on the railway line west of Mersa Matruh. They failed to find this target, but spotted instead a Ju 52/3m flying westwards from Charing Cross at 200 feet. Matthews attacked this aircraft which immediately attempted to land, but it was then fired on by Curry and Sherk, its port wing striking the ground. However, it is possible that during the engagement Sherk's Spitfire was hit by return fire, and he force-landed at the eastern end of the Qattara Depression on return.

Fourteen Bf 109s of III./JG 27 and ten of III./JG 53 escorted Stukas at 1450, their pilots reporting an engagement with 20-30 Kittyhawks and Spitfires, one pilot from each unit claiming a victory over these fighters, but once more, no WDAF losses or claims have been found relating to this incursion.

British Claims					
601 Sqn	Flt Lt J.H.Curry	Spitfire Vc BR469			
601 Sqn	Plt Off R.J.F.Sherk	Spitfire Vc BR392	Ju 52/3m	W Charing Cross	1340-1615
145 Sqn	Sqn Ldr G.P.H.Matthews	Spitfire Vb ..978 'Z'			
British Casualties					
601 Sqn	Spitfire Vc BR392 left 1335, force-landed Qattara Depression, hit by return fire from Ju 52/3m; Plt Off R.J.F.Sherk PoW				
238 Sqn	Hurricane 'Z' probably hit by Flak and crash-landed; Sgt R.W.Cairns safe				
German Claims					
8./JG 27	Uffz Erich Krainik	Spitfire		SSW El Alamein	
8./JG 53	Obfw Alfred Seidl	P-40		30km SSE El Alamein	1630
German Casualties					
1-(Flg)Kp/Ln-Rgt 40	Ju 52/3m WNr 5460 NQ+AV shot down by Spitfires, crash-landed near Mersa Matruh, Obfw Kulpe and two safe, one KiA				
Italian Casualties					
238ª Sq, 101°Gr, 5°St Tuff	CR.42 MM 8883 damaged, Serg Magg Alvise Dell'Avanzo safe				

Wednesday, 30 September 1942

Seven Spitfires of 601 Squadron provided cover for Hurricanes of 33 and 238 Squadrons during the morning. The Hurricanes were recalled after a short time, the Spitfires patrolling over El Alamein instead. Four Bf 109s of III./JG 53 were scrambled and reported attacking Spitfires north-west of Maghra. The two small formations obviously clashed, each side claiming to have damaged one opposing fighter. It appears that the German claim was ultimately confirmed, Obfw Seidl being credited with a victory.

At 1050 eight Messerschmitts of I.Gruppe and 15 of III./JG 27 provided escort to Stukas. The latter unit reported a combat with four Allied fighters over Abu Dweis, Lt Schroer claiming one Spitfire over El Alamein. Twelve Kittyhawks of 112 Squadron had been scrambled at 1105 with 250 Squadron, patrolling over El Alamein. No contact was reported, and the units were recalled, but on the way back to base Sgt Morrison's aircraft caught fire and he crash-landed, exiting his aircraft rapidly as it burnt out completely. During these mid-morning sorties Hptm Marseille was flying a new Bf 109G when it too caught fire due to an oil pipe fracture. He managed to get the aircraft back over Axis lines, but here he was forced to bale out. As he fell, he hit the tailplane which probably knocked him unconscious since his parachute did not open. So died the brilliant sunbird, 'Die Stern von Afrika' (The Star of Africa), victor of more than double the number of combats of any other pilot in the desert.

As has been shown, Marseille undoubtedly did overclaim occasionally during his last two months in combat. His sheer success had clearly given him such complete confidence in his own ability that he had developed an 'if I fire at it, it must go down,' mentality. However, there can be little doubt that two thirds or three quarters of his claims had definitely crashed, force-landed, or at the least suffered heavy damage, giving this controversial young pilot a score of some 100 or more Allied aircraft. This was an incredible achievement by any standards and clearly his brilliant shooting justifies the description of "the unrivalled virtuoso of the fighter pilots" used to describe him by Generalmajor Adolf Galland, Inspector of the Day Fighters. Marseille's total of confirmed claims at the time of his death was 158, 151 of them over North Africa. September 1942 had been a very bad month for I./JG 27, three of the unit's most successful pilots having been killed in it.

At 1743 eight Bf 109s of III./JG 53 undertook a sortie during which their pilots reportedly became involved in a combat with about 20 Spitfires and Hurricanes. Obfw Seidl's aircraft was hit and he baled out. However, it seems his victor's fire had also struck him, for he was dead by the time he reached the ground. The Allied squadrons involved have not been ascertained, but it is possible that this may actually have been the combat in which 33, 238 and 601 Squadrons had taken part, reported as the earlier engagement with the same German unit.

During the latter part of the month the units of JaboGruppe Afrika – III./ZG 1 and the JaboStaffeln of JGs 27 and 53, were withdrawn to form a new unit, Schlachtgeschwader 2, comprising initially two Gruppen.

British Claims

601 Sqn	Flg Off W.M.Whitamore	Spitfire Vc AB345 'J'	Bf 109 Damaged	NW Maghra	0948
145 Sqn	Flt Sgt J.S.Anderson	Spitfire VB AB502 'B'	Bf 109 Damaged		1745-1840

British Casualties

112 Sqn	Kittyhawk I ET795 'C' caught fire in air and crash-landed El Hanwariya; Sgt J.H.Morrison safe

German Claims

8./JG 53	Obfw Alfred Seidl	Spitfire	20km E Abu Dweis	0848
8./JG 27	Lt Werner Schroer	Spitfire	SSW El Alamein	1030

German Casualties

3./JG 27	Bf 109G-2 trop WNr 14256 crashed Sidi Abd el Rahman, Hptm Hans-Joachim Marseille baled out and KiA

Thursday, 1 O ctober 1942

Soon after 1730 19 Ju 87s of III./StG 3, escorted by 16 Bf 109s of II./JG 27, ten of III.Gruppe and eight of III./JG 53, carried out a raid in the El Taga area. As has been seen, most Stuka raids had been getting through to their targets recently, their fighter escorts proving as effective as those being given to the WDAF bomber formations. On this occasion, however, the Kittyhawks of 112 and 250 Squadrons intercepted and broke through to the dive-bombers, claiming six shot down (three by Flt Lt Barber) plus four probables and two damaged. One Bf 109 was also claimed as a probable and one damaged. This was also achieved without loss to the WDAF units, although one claim for a fighter was submitted by III./JG 27. At least two Ju 87s were lost with their crews. During the day a pair of Bf 109s of 4.(H)/12 managed to get as far as Alexandria, flown by Fw Ernst Depke and Uffz Budzinski. Here, however, Depke's aircraft was shot down by the AA defences.

In 73 Squadron Sqn Ldr G.R.A.M.'Robin' Johnston handed over command of the unit to Sqn Ldr J.B.Selby, who had for some time been one of the flight commanders. Meanwhile, at Benghazi Feldmarschall Kesselring paid a visit to the Flak units, holding a conference with the local commanders in an effort to improve the effectiveness of the defence against enemy aircraft.

British Claims

112 Sqn	Plt Off L.H.Curphey	Kittyhawk I EV339	Ju 87	El Taga	1730-1845

British Claims

112 Sqn	Sqn Ldr B.Drake	Kittyhawk I EV168 '?'	Ju 87	El Taga	1730-1845
112 Sqn	Flt Lt G.W.Garton	Kittyhawk I EV136 'Q'			
112 Sqn	Sqn Ldr B.Drake	Kittyhawk I EV168 '?'	Ju 87 Probable	El Taga	1730-1845
112 Sqn	Flt Lt G.W.Garton	Kittyhawk I EV136 'Q'	Ju 87 Probable	El Taga	1730-1845
112 Sqn	Sgt M.H.Lamont	Kittyhawk I AL178 'C'	Ju 87 Damaged	El Taga	1730-1845
112 Sqn	Flg Off T.Livingstone	Kittyhawk I EV319 'G'	Ju 87 Probable	El Taga	1730-1845
112 Sqn	Flt Sgt R.C.C.Smith	Kittyhawk I ET919 'T'	Bf 109F Probable	El Taga	1730-1845
112 Sqn	Plt Off J.G.Wright	Kittyhawk I EV318 'L'	Bf 109F Damaged	El Taga	1730-1845
250 Sqn	Flt Lt M.C.H.Barber	Kittyhawk I AK707 'I'	3 Ju 87s	El Taga-Lake Maghra	1800
250 Sqn	Flg Off M.A.Calver	Kittyhawk I EV356 'K'	Bf 109 Probable	El Taga-Lake Maghra	1800
250 Sqn	Plt Off D.J.Cormack	Kittyhawk I ET977 'C'	Ju 87	El Taga-Lake Maghra	1800
250 Sqn	Flg Off E.Y.Miluck	Kittyhawk I ET953 'P'	Bf 109 Damaged	El Taga-Lake Maghra	1800

German Claims

7./JG 27	Lt Erich Schöfböck	Spitfire	30km S El Alamein	1712

German Casualties

7./StG 3	Ju 87D-1 WNr 2561 shot down by P-40 Gebel Kalakh; Uffz Konrad Leidheiser KiA; Uffz Georg Claus WiA
7./StG 3	Ju 87D-1 WNr 2034 shot down by P-40 Deir Abu Hiqueif; Uffz Albert Lischke/Ogefr Günther Konrad KiA
III./StG 3	Ju 87D-1 WNr 2548 hit in combat with P-40 S Qotaifija, 10% damaged; crew safe
4.(H)/12	Bf 109 Fw Ernst Depke shot down by AA, MiA

German Claims

7./JG 27	Lt Erich Schöfböck	Spitfire	30km S El Alamein	1712

Friday, 2 October 1942

Eight Bf 109s of III./JG 27 provided top cover for Stukas, taking off at 0830. They were joined by 21 MC.202s of 23° Gruppo, now back in action. Both sets of pilots reported large formations of British fighters intercepting. Ten Kittyhawks of 3 RAAF Squadron and six of 112 Squadron had been scrambled over El Alamein at 0850, reporting 20 enemy aircraft at 20,000 feet to the south. A lone Bf 109 was then seen approaching from the west and this was at once attacked and claimed shot down by Flt Lt Plinston. The only other WDAF claim to be made at this time was for another Messerschmitt by Flt Sgt Shea of 601 Squadron. In the combat at this time the Italian pilots claimed one Spitfire shot down, one probable and one damaged, but lost one aircraft from which the pilot baled out, becoming a PoW. 8./JG 27 also claimed two Spitfires. At 1010, as the Kittyhawks were landing, four more from 112 Squadron took off on a practice flight. Sgt Rae's aircraft suddenly burst into flames and crashed; the pilot was thrown clear, but was killed instantly.

Two 92 Squadron Spitfires took off at 1145 intercepting a reconnaissance Ju 88 which was chased out to sea and hit repeatedly until it crashed. In the afternoon at 1610 16 Bf 109s of III./JG 27 again provided escort for Ju 87s, once more engagements with defending fighters being reported during which three P-40s were claimed shot down. 112 and 3 RAAF Squadrons had again been scrambled to intercept this formation, six aircraft of the former unit and 12 of the latter taking off and meeting the Axis aircraft south of Deir el Dhib. 112 Squadron reported seeing seven aircraft and then being attacked by two sets of Messerschmitts, one of which was shot down, the pilot baling out; a probable was also claimed by 3 RAAF Squadron. 13 MC.202s, led by Cap Livio Ceccotti were also involved in this escort, but this time the pilots of 10° Gruppo, which claimed two Spitfires shot down, lost the Macchi flown by Ceccotti.

112 Squadron scrambled five more Kittyhawks at 1725, this time with others of 250 Squadron, and attacked Bf 109 Jabos of III./ZG 1 bombing in the Maghra area. Capt Saville claimed two shot down and two pilots of this Luftwaffe unit were indeed downed, one being killed and the other picked up safely by an Fi 156. A few minutes later six Spitfires of 601 Squadron scrambled, meeting 14 Axis fighters. Sgt Allen-Rowlandson's aircraft was hit and he crash-landed at base due to the damage inflicted. This had been a rather confused day since not all the records and times matched up as neatly as might have been hoped.

During the day I./JG 27 buried Hptm Marseille. At the funeral service Eduard Neumann, the Geschwader Kommodore, said: "A restless heart is now resting, but we fly on. May the spirit of Marseille inspire all new of JG 27." However, the pilots felt that the death of their leading Experte was a symbol of the changing fortunes of the Axis in North Africa, and morale fell low. The whole Gruppe was therefore

These three pilots were all active in early October 1942. Geoff Garton (centre) would later take command of 112 Squadron, where his two flight commanders would be Capt Eric Saville (left) and Dennis Usher (right). They are seen here with Kittyhawk III FR472 coded GA-1, a few weeks later.

withdrawn from operations. A formation was flown over the grave, and all pilots were given a few days' rest, after which the Gruppe moved to Pachino in Sicily, arriving there on the 8th (although a few pilots stayed at Fuka and on Crete with the 'Alert Schwarme'). From Sicily the Gruppe would fly a number of missions escorting Ju 88s over Malta, claiming seven Spitfires and losing two Bf 109s (see *Malta: The Spitfire Year, 1942*). The unit was not to return to Africa until late in the month, this leaving only three Gruppen to oppose the build-up in operations which now began prior to the forthcoming Allied offensive.

British Claims

601 Sqn	Flt Sgt E.G.Shea	Spitfire Vc AB253	Bf 109	El Alamein area	0850-0945
3 RAAF Sqn	Flt Lt G.H.F.Plinston	Kittyhawk I EV346 'O'	Bf 109		0950
92 Sqn	Plt Off E.Hill	Spitfire Vc BR491 'Q'			
92 Sqn	Lt S.W.Rabie	Spitfire Vc BR479 'E'	Ju 88	Alexandria area	1145-1250
112 Sqn	Flg Off J.M.S.Crichton	Kittyhawk I EV315 'P'	Bf 109 Damaged	centre of front line	1620-1755
112 Sqn	Sgt J.M.MacAuley	Kittyhawk I EV360 'F'	Bf 109	centre of front line	1620-1755
3 RAAF Sqn	Sgt G.A.Neill	Kittyhawk I ET116 'B'	Bf 109F Probable	1650	
112 Sqn	Flg Off T.Livingstone	Kittyhawk I EV318 'L'	Bf 109F Damaged	Maghra area	1725-
112 Sqn	Plt Off H.Phillips	Kittyhawk I AK847	Bf 109F Damaged	Maghra area	1730-1920
112 Sqn	Capt E.C.Saville	Kittyhawk I EV339 'A'	2 Bf 109s		1730-1920

British Casualties

112 Sqn	Kittyhawk I AL192 burst into flames and crashed; Sgt G.Rae KiA
601 Sqn	Spitfire V BR113 damaged and crash-landed at base; Sgt G.Allen-Rowlandson

German Claims

8./JG 27	Uffz Hans-Joachim Rohrlack	Spitfire	SSE El Alamein	0825
8./JG 27	Uffz Erich Krainik	Spitfire	SSW El Alamein	
8./JG 27	Lt Werner Schroer	P-40	NNE Deir el Tarfa	1540
8./JG 27	Fw Viktor Gruber	P-40	NE Deir el Tarfa	1555
7./JG 27	Lt Erich Schöfböck	P-40	S El Alamein	1605

German Casualties

8./ZG 1	Bf 109E-7 WNr 0775 shot down by P-40s 40km SW El Alamein; Lt Walter Burger KiA
8./ZG 1	Bf 109E-7 WNr 6130 shot down by P-40s SW El Alamein; Lt Norbert Schmidt WiA, picked up by Fi 156
I./SchG 2	Bf 109F-4 WNr 13004, damaged in combat, belly-landed at Bir el Abd, 40% damaged; pilot safe

Italian Claims

70ª Sq, 23°Gr, 3°St CT	Cap Claudio Solaro	MC.202	Spitfire	S El Alamein	0725-0900
70ª Sq, 23°Gr, 3°St CT	S.Ten Giuseppe Melandri	MC.202	Spitfire Probable	S El Alamein	0725-0900
70ª Sq, 23°Gr, 3°St CT	M.llo Balilla Albani	MC.202	Spitfire Damaged	S El Alamein	0725-0900
84ª Sq, 10°Gr, 4°St CT	Ten Luigi Giannella	MC.202 MM7815	Spitfire	El Alamein area	1515-1630
91ª Sq, 10°Gr, 4°St CT	M.llo Lorenzo Migliorato	MC.202	Spitfire	El Alamein area	1515-1630

Italian Casualties

91ª Sq, 10°Gr, 4°St CT	MC.202 MM 7767 '91-1' failed to return, Cap Livio Ceccotti MiA
74ª Sq, 23°Gr, 3°St CT	MC.202 MM 9500 failed to return, Ten Riccardo Bignamini PoW

Saturday, 3 October 1942

British Claims

601 Sqn	Flt Lt J.H.Curry	Spitfire Vc BR583 'L'	Ju 88 Damaged	1155-1235

German Casualties

9./ZG 26	Bf 110F-2 W Nr 5036 3U+UT shot down in error by own fighter, crashed into sea; Fw Ludwig Orthwerth/Gefr Heinz Pannenberg WiA

After a period on defensive duties in Egypt, the first Greek fighter squadron, 335, moved up to join WDAF at the start of October. The pilot is believed to be Wg Cdr Constantine Platsis.

Monday, 5 October 1942

Twelve Hurricanes of 238 Squadron escorted three of 6 Squadron's tank-busters on a mission at 0900, with 1 SAAF Squadron as top cover. The formation was attacked by Bf 109s, Sgt Robertson's aircraft being hit and damaged, he being wounded. No Axis claims were recorded. At 1500 a ruinous flood devastated the camp of 5° Stormo at Abar Nimeir, curtailing operations for several days.

British Casualties

238 Sqn	Hurricane BP453 'J' left 0900 damaged by Bf 109, landed at base at 1045; Sgt K.R.Robertson WiA

Italian Casualties

192ªSq, 87°Gr, 30°St BT	Cant.Z.1007bis crashed in the sea near base for unknown reason at 1850; pilot S.Ten Walter Sensi, copilot Serg Magg Giovanni Previti and four KiA

Tuesday, 6 October 1942

It was 12 Hurricanes of 238 Squadron which were again involved in a mission on this date, strafing Daba airfield at 1600; Sgt Inde's aircraft hit the ground with a wingtip and crashed, the pilot surviving to become a PoW. Three of 55 Squadron's Baltimores were hit by Flak during the day, and all crash-landed, one blowing up. Very heavy rain began to fall during the day and when fighter-bombers attacked Axis landing grounds, personnel there were forced to jump into slit tranches which had become overflowing ponds. 150° Gruppo scrambled a number of MC.200s on this date, four pilots jointly claiming one Allied fighter, identified as a P-40, shot down. KG 77 moved from Comiso to Gerbini with 50 Ju 88s.

Obfw Werner Stumpf of III./JG 53 was one of the unit's more successful pilots. He claimed three victories during the Gruppe's first period in Libya in 1941 (see Vol 1), adding ten more after the return there in May. He was shot down and killed by AA over El Alamein on 13 October.

British Casualties

238 Sqn	Hurricane BL615 'T' left 1600, hit ground while strafing nr Daba and crashed; Sgt H.A.Indge PoW ?
55 Sqn	Baltimore II AG769 'B' off 1655 as one of 12 to attack fuel dump 3m E El Daba railway station; hit over target by intense Flak and lost starboard propeller and revolutions of port engine. Pilot ordered bale-out and three crew PoW. Plt Off R.D.M.Evers (pilot) could not because of jammed hatch. Belly-landed under fire between lines and hid under wing until rescued by 2nd South African AFVs. Attempt at night to recover a/c by tank transporter, but fire too intense and a/c subsequently destroyed
55 Sqn	Baltimore II AG807 'P' on same mission as AG769 , crippled by Flak over target. With port engine out pilot reached Allied lines and ordered crew to bale out. Only two heard and went; Flt Lt D.H.Hannah belly-landed just short of El Alamein. He and two safe, but one of crew KiA on landing from bale-out
55 Sqn	Baltimore II AG811 'Z' on same mission as AG769, crippled by Flak over target, crash-landed and aircraft blew up; Flt Lt A.Ward and three KiA

Italian Claims

365ª Sq, 150°Gr Aut CT	S.Ten Bruno Serotini	MC.200	P-40
365ª Sq, 150°Gr Aut CT	S.Ten Ettore Caregnato	MC.200	
364ª Sq, 150°Gr Aut CT	M.llo Walter Bertocci	MC.200	
364ª Sq, 150°Gr Aut CT	Serg Magg Pietro Secchi	MC.200	

Wednesday, 7 October 1942

Two Bf 109s of III./JG 27 were scrambled at 1117, attacking a reported 30 fighters south of El Hammam, where one Kittyhawk was claimed shot down. Twelve aircraft of 112 Squadron carried out an armed reconnaissance, the bombing being finished before Plt Off Wiley force-landed and was removed to hospital; he may have been the victim of this claim by Uffz Rohrlack. The latter then also claimed an unidentified radial-engined aircraft, but this was not confirmed, although apparently witnessed by his Röttenflieger, Uffz Fischer. What this aircraft might have been has not been ascertained.

Eight Spitfires of 92 Squadron carried out a patrol from 1155, but these were intercepted half way through the flight by two Messerschmitts of III./JG 27 which had been scrambled. Flt Lt Samouelle and Plt Off Chisholm each claimed one shot down. It appears, however, that they had both attacked the same aircraft, which force-landed after being hit in the cooling system, the pilot becoming a prisoner. 3 RAAF Squadron reported being attacked by an aircraft with yellow cowling and wingtips which pilots thought might have been an FW 190. It is interesting to speculate whether this might have been the unknown radial-engined aircraft claimed by Rohrlack. This may possibly have been a test aircraft of Erprobüngskommando 19 which is known to have been in North Africa at around this time.

On this date 335, the Greek squadron, undertook its first operational sortie over the front line, taking part in a sweep over El Alamein as top cover to 33 Squadron. 5 SAAF Squadron lost one of its most aggressive pilots when 2/Lt H.'Hack-'em-Down' Smith was posted to 92 Squadron to fly Spitfires. The US contingent now included the 64th and 65th Fighter Squadrons flying with 233 Wing and the 66th with 239 Wing at LG.91. The 12th Bombardment Group (Medium) was operating with the Baltimores of 232 Wing from LG.88; this wing had also been joined by 21 SAAF Squadron, now also operating Baltimores.

British Claims					
92 Sqn	Plt Off W.L.Chisholm	Spitfire Vc BR525 'S'	Bf 109	Arab Gulf	1155-1315
92 Sqn	Flt Lt C.J.Samouelle	Spitfire Vc BR520 'L'	Bf 109	Arab Gulf	1155-1315
British Casualties					
112 Sqn	Kittyhawk I ET919 'C' damaged by Flak and crash-landed El Imayid; Plt Off G.W.Wiley broke leg				
2 SAAF Sqn	Kittyhawk I 'U' canopy blown off by Flak; Capt H.E.N.Wildsmith				
German Claims					
7./JG 27	Uffz Hans-Joachim Rohrlack		P-40	30km S El Hammam	1055
German Casualties					
9./JG 27	Bf 109F-4 WNr 7074 Yellow 7 combat, engine hit, crash-landed 10km S El Adem, 100%; Uffz Hermann Flendt PoW				
4.(H)/12	Bf 109 collided with Ju 52/3m at Maleme on take-off; Lt Edgar Meyer KiA				

Thursday, 8 October 1942

1 SAAF Squadron lost two Hurricanes, Lt Williams crashing in mist in Axis territory, becoming a PoW; meanwhile Lt Lanham, flying over a sector of the opposing lines held by the Italian Folgore Parachute Division, received a 7mm bullet in his aircraft's glycol system and crash-landed 20 miles south of El Alamein, hitching a lift to 92 Squadron's airfield, which was the nearest. In 13° Gruppo CT, Cap Paolo Zanini, promoted major, handed over command of 78ª Squadriglia to Ten Camillo Luglio.

British Casualties	
1 SAAF Sqn	Hurricane IIc HM121 'E' shot down by small-arms fire, crash-landed 25m S El Alamein; Lt J.R.Lanham returned next day
1 SAAF Sqn	Hurricane IIc HL836 'R' flew into ground in mist SW El Alamein; Lt H.C.Williams PoW
Italian Casualties	
196ªSq RM	Cant.Z.501 MM 35851 crash-landed at Tocra, w/o, pilot Ten Attilio Spinelli and crew safe

Friday, 9 October 1942

Allied reconnaissance now found the Daba airfields under water and those at Fuka scarcely useable due to the recent rains. This seemed an opportunity too good to miss, and in an effort to destroy much of the Axis air forces on the ground, an all-out effort was mounted, 500 sorties being flown during the day compared to 102 by German fighters seeking to defend their bases and similar efforts by the Regia Aeronautica. Seven heavy bombing attacks were launched and many fighter-bomber strikes were carried out.

This was a particularly intense day for the Regia Aeronautica fighters. Ten MC.202s of 9° Gruppo (six of 73ª Squadriglia led by Ten Giulio Reiner and four of 96ª led by Ten Emanuele Annoni), took off at 0900 to escort a formation of German Ju 87s. Near Qotaifiya, nine of them engaged a formation of Bostons, escorted by Kittyhawks and Spitfires. Reiner attacked the bombers whilst Annoni took care of the Kittyhawks. A 20-minute combat followed, reportedly very successful for the Italian pilots: one Boston, three Spitfires and eight P-40s were claimed, plus four P-40s and one Spitfire probably shot down and some others damaged.

Five MC.202s of 23° Gruppo, led by Magg Filippi, were scrambled at 1150 from Abu Haggag. Twenty km south of Daba they met a formation of 18 'Bostons' (as the British twin-engined bombers were invariably identified by the Italians) and fighters. A fight occurred during which Filippi claimed a P-40 and Ten Brigante-Colonna a Spitfire probable. At the same time three MC.202s of 91ª Squadriglia were scrambled from Fuka and M.llo Leonardo Ferrulli claimed a 'P-46'.

At 1215 4° Stormo pilots were again scrambled: eight MC.202s of 96ª Squadriglia led by Ten Annoni took off from Fuka heading to Daba. A formation of 20 Bostons, escorted by Kittyhawks and Spitfires, was engaged; Annoni claimed a Spitfire, with a 'P-46' reportedly shot down by S.Ten Alberto Giampaoli for no Italian losses. In the afternoon, at 1530, it was the turn of 84ª Squadriglia to be scrambled: eight MC.202s led by Ten Luigi Giannella intercepted over Qotaifiya a formation of 42 Bostons and later another formation of twelve 'Hurribombers' flying at very low altitude. Giannella, an ace with nine victories already in the bag, claimed a P-40 and a Spitfire probable; Serg Domenico Santonocito strafed two Spitfires. The same enemy formations were also engaged by nine MC.202s of 97ª Squadriglia which took off at 1545 led by Ten Jacopo Frigerio. In this combat a Hurribomber and another probable were claimed by M.llo Gianni Bianchelli, while a P-40 was credited to S.Ten Leonardo Boselli. An MC.202 returned badly damaged. At 1555 seven MC.202s of 91ª Squadriglia led by Cap Carlo Maurizio Ruspoli took off and joined this combat during which Ruspoli claimed a Spitfire; S.Ten Alvaro Bondi, possibly hit in the tail, baled out owing to severe vibrations and landed safely.

The last scramble of the day occurred at 1600 when nine MC.202s of 23° Gruppo led by Cap Mario Pinna took off from Abu Haggag but no enemy was encountered.

The Luftwaffe carried out their initial sorties at 1000, when six Bf 109s of II./JG 27, 12 from III.Gruppe and eight from III./JG 53 took off to escort a Stuka raid. These units were just forming up when 20 Allied fighters swept in to strafe, followed by a second, larger, formation. Five minutes later the bombers appeared. Ten Bf 109s of the Fuka Detachment had already taken off on a Freie Jagd and two more were at once scrambled so that all 38 Messerschmitts in the air were able to concentrate on the raiders, the Stuka mission being abandoned. At the same time MC.202s of 9° and 10° Gruppi were also scrambled, as we have seen. Within a few minutes 23 victories had been claimed, the German units seven fighters and one bomber, the Italians 11 fighters and one bomber, plus four more fighters as probables.

Flying on attachment to 239 Wing, 1/Lt W.J.Mount of the US 57th Fighter Group made the first claim for a USAAF victory on 9 October.

Spitfire Vb BR476 QJ-J was frequently flown by the commanding officer of 92 Squadron, Sqn Ldr Jefferson Wedgwood, often without the cockpit hood present in order to allow for better visibility. He flew this aircraft on 9 October when he claimed two Bf 109s shot down near Daba.

A pair of Bf 109Fs of 7./JG 53.

Twelve Kittyhawks of 4 SAAF Squadron, seven of 2 SAAF Squadron, 12 of 112 Squadron, 12 of 250 Squadron and P-40Fs of the US 66th Squadron escorted 18 Bostons and six Baltimores to attack LG.104, nine Spitfires of 92 Squadron and seven of 601 Squadron providing top cover to these units and to Hurricanes strafing Daba. Receiving a report that the latter were under attack, the 601 Squadron pilots dived on Axis fighters so engaged and drove them off. Allied claims during this initial attack would amount to seven shot down and five damaged. 4 SAAF Squadron claimed one but lost one Kittyhawk; 250 and 2 SAAF Squadrons, operating together, claimed one and three damaged, two of the South African Kittyhawks being badly damaged.

Twelve Kittyhawks of 3 RAAF Squadron covered 12 more of 450 Squadron to strafe LG.21 after the airfield had been bombed. Plt Off Chisholm of 3 RAAF was attacked out of the sun by five Bf 109s, but Plt Off Ritchie claimed one shot down which he reported fell into the sea after he had shot its tail off. The first official USAAF claim for a squadron operating in its own right, not as part of an RAF unit, occurred when 13 aircraft of the 64th Squadron were attacked by ten Axis fighters after the American pilots had strafed LG.104. 1/Lt William J.Mount chased one of these out to sea, reporting that he had shot its tail off. Since this claim is virtually identical to that submitted by Plt Off Ritchie, and since only one Bf 109 was reported lost over the sea, it is very likely that these pilots had double-claimed on the same aircraft. 450 Squadron, meanwhile, reported strafing four Bf 109s or Ju 87s, a Ju 88 and a Ju 52/3m, but lost one pilot.

Although the Germans and the Italians claimed Bostons shot down during this engagement, the only WDAF loss of such an aircraft did not occur until the late afternoon when a 223 Squadron Baltimore was reported to have been hit almost certainly by Flak over Qotaifiya (LG.104). It was not seen again, its final fate remaining uncertain, but probably not due to the fighters of either Axis air force. However, one of the escorting unit, 5 SAAF Squadron, lost two Tomahawks whilst claiming a Bf 109 and a probable.

At 1210 12 Kittyhawks of 250 Squadron with other aircraft of 239 Wing escorted 12 Baltimores and six B-25s over LGs. 21 and 104, nine Spitfires of 92 Squadron providing top cover. After the bombing 20 Bf 109s and MC.202s attacked the formation, one Kittyhawk being shot down and three damaged. One Spitfire of 92 Squadron was also lost. Seven Bf 109s of II.Gruppe were scrambled as were five MC.202s of 23° Gruppo, plus others of 9° and 10° Gruppi. This time the Germans claimed four fighters, the Italians four more plus a probable. At 1330 18 more bombers attacked the area, followed by 30 more at 1345. Another 17 which arrived at 1415, hit the operations room of III./JG 53 which was destroyed. Fw Lüer, a member of the Fuka Detachment, was scrambled alone, claiming a Hurricane near Daba. Another raid was mounted at 1620, this time 50 bombers appearing over Daba at 1700. 239 Wing escorted 24 Baltimores with nine Spitfires of 92 Squadron and others of 601 Squadron providing high cover, led by Wg Cdr R.C.Love, DFC. Bf 109s attacked the Spitfires. Three of them then dived on six Kittyhawks of 250 Squadron which were providing top cover to the Baltimores, one Kittyhawk being shot down, but one Bf 109 being claimed from which the pilot was seen to bale out.

This raid was followed by a strafing attack by the Hurricanes of 33, 213, 238 and 1 SAAF Squadrons, led by Wg Cdr Darwen at 1620. The Hurricanes came in from the sea, swept over the escarpment, the road, LG.104 and the railway, making off to the south towards the Qattara Depression before turning for base. One aircraft of 33 Squadron was shot down by a Bf 109 and landed in the sea off Daba; one more was last seen over LG.104 with its engine on fire; in addition Wg Cdr Darwen's aircraft was seen to hit the ground and crash after his attack; two more pilots of this squadron failed to return, and one of 213 Squadron's aircraft was picked off in flames while straggling. A further Hurricane was attacked, the wingtip was seen to hit the ground and it crashed; four more 213 Squadron Hurricanes were damaged, one of 238 Squadron being shot down, apparently by Flak, the pilot becoming a PoW. Darwen was later picked up safely by a patrol of the 11th Hussars and brought back.

It seems to be on this occasion that Darwen, a career officer who had managed to bring quite a lot of personal kit with him to North Africa, had been hunting jerboas with his small terrier, wearing full 'Hunting Pink' costume. Having no time to change when the afternoon attack by 243 Wing was ordered, he had flown so clothed. During the attacks he had gone so low that his propeller hit the ground, causing him to have to crash-land. When picked up, the aristocratic young Hussar officer commented that it was the first time since he had arrived in North Africa that he had seen an RAF officer properly dressed.

During these afternoon and evening raids, 11 more fighters were claimed by the Luftwaffe, four and a probable by the Italians. The last bombing raid was made at 1730. The success of these attacks, known thereafter to the WDAF as the 'Daba Prang' is questionable having regard to the size of the effort and the quantum of the losses on each side. The Allied air forces claimed to have destroyed at least 50 aircraft on the ground and to have shot down ten Bf 109s; the Luftwaffe reported that ten aircraft were destroyed on the ground and 20 damaged. III./JG 53 had suffered the heaviest losses, 13 of the unit's Bf 109s being amongst those heavily damaged. However, only one man was killed on the ground and a few were slightly wounded.

In the air Bf 109 losses amounted to four aircraft, probably three of these to opposing aircraft with only one MC.202 lost, although four more were damaged. The defenders' claims were equally exaggerated in such conditions. Amounting to 54 or 55 aircraft believed shot down, 23 by German fighters, 20 by Italians and 12 by Flak. Several of the German claims were for aircraft identified as P-39s – probably USAAF P-40Fs, while Italian claims included several for the 'phantom' P-46s. WDAF as far as can be ascertained given the intensity of operations, had lost 15-17 aircraft with eleven more damaged. This total included ten Hurricanes shot down and five damaged, four Kittyhawks and one Tomahawk, with six more damaged, one Spitfire and one Baltimore.

British Claims

92 Sqn	Flt Lt C.J.Samouelle	Spitfire Vc BR479 'E'	Bf 109E	W Fuka	0940-1100
92 Sqn	Sqn Ldr J.H.Wedgwood	Spitfire Vc BR476 'J'	Bf 109	W Fuka	0940-1100
92 Sqn	Sqn Ldr J.H.Wedgwood	Spitfire Vc BR476 'J'	Bf 109	3m E Daba	0940-1100
250 Sqn	Flt Sgt A.E.Roberts	Kittyhawk III FR898	Bf 109F	Fuka	1020
3 RAAF Sqn	Plt Off D.V.Ritchie	Kittyhawk I EV346 'O'	Bf 109	Daba	1020
2 SAAF Sqn	Lt H.J.Lourens	Kittyhawk I	Bf 109 Damaged	LG.104	1025
2 SAAF Sqn	Capt J.E.Parsonson	Kittyhawk I	Bf 109F Damaged	LG.104	1025
2 SAAF Sqn	Capt J.E.Parsonson	Kittyhawk I	MC.202 Damaged	LG.104	1025
4 SAAF Sqn	Lt R.W.Rowan	Kittyhawk I ET864 'C'	MC.202 Damaged	LG.104	1035
250 Sqn	Sgt A.A.W.Orr	Kittyhawk III FR287	Bf 109E	Daba	1320
5 SAAF Sqn	Capt R.F.Armstrong	Tomahawk IIb AN291 'N'	Bf 109F	N Daba	1400
5 SAAF Sqn	Lt H.W.G.Bidwell	Tomahawk IIb AK401 'F'	Bf 109F Probable	N Daba	1400
250 Sqn	Plt Off D.W.Cairns	Kittyhawk III FR285 'Y'	Bf 109	Daba	1700

British Claims

92 Sqn	Flt Sgt R.Hempstead	Spitfire Vc BR522 'K'	Bf 109 Probable	Daba area	1705
92 Sqn	Flt Lt J.M.Morgan	Spitfire Vc BR525 'S'			
92 Sqn	Plt Off W.L.Chisholm	Spitfire Vc BR476 'J'	Bf 109 Damaged	NW Daba	1705
92 Sqn	Flt Lt C.J.Samouelle	Spitfire Vc BR519 'D'	Bf 109 Probable	NW Daba	1705
601 Sqn	Flg Off W.M.Whitamore	Spitfire Vc BR136 'L'	Bf 109F	S Daba	1725

British Casualties

33 Sqn	Hurricane IIc BP548 'S' shot down by Bf 109; Flt Sgt N.R.Learmonth KiA
33 Sqn	Hurricane IIc BP454 'L' damaged by Bf 109s and ditched off El Daba; Sgt J.A.Kingdon PoW
33 Sqn	Hurricane IIc BP546 'J' FTR from sweep shot down by Flak nr El Daba; Flg Off D.W.McLarty PoW
33 Sqn	Hurricane IIc HL621 'M' FTR from sweep nr El Daba; Sgt H.J.Bastian PoW
213 Sqn	Hurricane IIc BP581 left 1625 damaged by Bf 109 or Flak, force-landed; Wg Cdr J.Darwen safe
213 Sqn	Hurricane IIc BP355 shot down by Bf 109s nr El Alamein at 1700; Plt Off C.F.A.Cantin MiA
213 Sqn	Hurricane IIc BP462 shot down by Flak nr LG.09 at 1715; Plt Off B.J.McClelland KiA
213 Sqn	Hurricane BP401 damaged by Flak, bullet through wing into cockpit Cat I, landed; Sqn Ldr M.H.Young safe
213 Sqn	Hurricane BP345 damaged by Flak, in the tail Cat I, landed; Sgt D.C.Usher safe
213 Sqn	Hurricane BP415 damaged by Bf 109 or Flak, cannon shell in wing spar Cat II, landed; Flt Lt N.Cameron safe
213 Sqn	Hurricane BE395 damaged by Flak, Cat I; Flt Sgt J.T.Field safe
238 Sqn	Hurricane II HL849 'H' left 1625, hit by Flak nr LG.21, crash-landed; Flg Off J.Galyer PoW
1 SAAF Sqn	Hurricane II damaged by Flak, El Daba
335 Sqn	Hurricane BP661 collided and abandoned 3m SW Dekheila
335 Sqn	Hurricane Z5379 crashed in force-landing, Lake Maryut
92 Sqn	Spitfire V BR479 'E' left 1203, FTR from escort to Daba; Plt Off T.Harvey MiA
250 Sqn	Kittyhawk III FL898 off 1210, shot down by MC.202, while on bomber escort to El Daba; Plt Off D.W.M.Rogerson PoW
250 Sqn	Kittyhawk III FR292 off 1620, shot down by Bf 109s on bomber escort, S El Alamein; Sgt G.R.Rodney PoW
250 Sqn	Kittyhawk III FR287 off 1210, badly damaged by MC.202 at 1320; Sgt A.Orr WiA
250 Sqn	Kittyhawk III FR238 off 1210, damaged by MC.202s, crash-landed at base 1345; Flg Off C.W.Tribken safe
250 Sqn	Kittyhawk III left 1620, badly damaged by Bf 109s, crash-landed at base; Flg Off E.Y.Miluck
450 Sqn	Kittyhawk III FR239 shot down by Flak LG.104; Sgt R.O.Holloway PoW
2 SAAF Sqn	Kittyhawk I ET1019 'Q' damaged Cat II by Flak, LG.104, 1015; pilot not identified
2 SAAF Sqn	Kittyhawk I EV356 badly damaged by Flak, LG.104, 1015; pilot not identified
4 SAAF Sqn	Kittyhawk I EV321 'G' shot down W Daba 1010, possibly by MC.202s; 2/Lt A.R.Schulz PoW
5 SAAF Sqn	Tomahawk IIb AM377 'Y' shot down by Bf 109 in sea N Sidi Abd el Rahman 1430; Lt J.V.Thornley PoW
5 SAAF Sqn	Tomahawk IIb AK410 'X' damaged by Flak and belly-landed NE Burg el Arab; Lt D.W.Murdoch safe
223 Sqn	Baltimore II AG975 took off 1605 from LG.86 to bomb Qotaifiya II l.g. (LG.104). Almost certainly hit by Flak over target; minutes later broke formation and last seen near coast; Sgt B.V.Ekbery and three PoW

US Claims

64th FS/57th FG	1/Lt George D.Mobbs	P-40F '23'	Bf 109 Damaged	LG.104	1020
64th FS/57th FG	1/Lt William J.Mount	P-40F '27'	Bf 109	LG.104	1020
66th FS/57th FG	Capt James G.Curl	P-40F '91'	MC.202 Damaged	6m SE El Alamein	1400

German Claims

7./JG 53	Lt Jürgen Harder	2 P-40s		0915 & 0925
Stab II./JG 27	Hptm Gustav Rödel	P-39	N Turbiya	0923
6./JG 27	Uffz Otto Monska	P-40	NW El Daba	0925
8./JG 27	Lt Werner Schroer	Boston	NE El Daba	0925
Stab II./JG 27	Hptm Erich Woitke	P-39	SE El Daba	0925
Stab II./JG 27	Hptm Gustav Rödel	P-39	NNE El Daba	0927
Stab II./JG 27	Hptm Gustav Rödel	Spitfire	NW Sanyet Qotaifiya	0935
4./JG 27	Fw Alfred Heidel	Spitfire	SE El Daba	1205
6./JG 27	Fw Fritz Lüer	P-40	NE El Daba	1215
5./JG 27	Oblt Ernst Börngen	Spitfire	N Sanyet Qotaifiya	1220
8./JG 53	Uffz Jens Bahnsen	P-40	NW Sanyet Qotaifiya	1315
7./JG 53	Fw Horst Olzmann	P-40		1524
8./JG 27	Lt Werner Schroer	Spitfire	NW El Daba	1615

4./JG 27	Fw Heinrich Steis	Spitfire	NW Bir Mumin Busak	1618
6./JG 27	Fw Fritz Lüer	Hurricane	SE Sanyet Qotaifiya	1620
8./JG 27	Lt Werner Schroer	Hurricane	SE Bir el Abd	1620
7./JG 53	Lt Jürgen Harder	2 P-40s		1620 & 1623
5./JG 27	Uffz Bernhard Schneider	P-40	SSE Bir Mumin Busak	1625
8./JG 27	Uffz Erich Krainik	Hurricane	N El Daba	
7./JG 27	Lt Erich Schöfböck	P-40	NE El Daba	
9./JG 53	Lt Rolf Klippgen	2 P-40s	40km & 45km SSE Fuka	1630 & 1831
7./JG 27	Lt Erich Schöfböck	P-40	SE El Alamein	1635
8./JG 53	Uffz Jens Bahnsen	P-40		1735

German Casualties

7./JG 53	Bf 109F-4 trop WNr 10142 destroyed on ground by bombs at Qotaifiya
8./JG 53	Bf 109F-4/Z WNr 7195 10% damaged on ground by bombs at Qotaifiya
8./JG 53	Bf 109F-4/Z WNr 8606 20% damaged on ground by bombs at Qotaifiya
III./JG 53	Bf 109F-4/Z WNr 7256 10% damaged on ground by bombs at Qotaifiya
III./JG 53	Bf 109F-4 trop WNr 8354 15% damaged on ground by bombs at Qotaifiya
III./JG 53	Bf 109F-4 trop WNr 8605 70% damaged on ground by bombs at Qotaifiya
III./JG 53	7 Bf 109F-4s damaged on ground by bombs at Qotaifiya
4./JG 27	Bf 109F-4 trop WNr 10340 20% damaged by bombs at Qotaifiya
6./JG 27	Bf 109F-4 trop WNr 8598 White 9 shot down by P-40 Fuka-Qotaifiya, 100% Obfw Hans Würschunger KiA
6./JG 27	Bf 109F-4 trop WNr 8658 Yellow 1 40% damaged by bombs at Qotaifiya
6./JG 27	Bf 109F-4 WNr 7413 20% damaged by bombs at Qotaifiya
6./JG 27	Bf 109F-4 trop WNr 10336 15% damaged by bombs at Qotaifiya
7./JG 27	Bf 109E-4 trop WNr 13283 30% damaged by bombs at Fuka
7./JG 27	Bf 109F-4 trop WNr 8572 crashed at Fuka due to combat; pilot baled, safe
7./JG 27	Bf 109F-4 trop WNr 13019 White 6 combat with P-40 20-25km SE El Alamein; Fw Werner Fingerhuth baled, PoW
7./JG 27	Bf 109F-4 WNr 7412 destroyed by bombs at Fuka
7./JG 27	Bf 109F-4 trop WNr 8674 75% damaged by bombs at Fuka
7./JG 27	Bf 109F-4 trop WNr 8648 combat; crash-landed Bir el Abd, 100% pilot safe
Wüstennotst. 7	Fi 156C-3 WNr 5620 40% damaged in strafing attack at Qotaifiya
III./ZG 1	Bf 109E-7 WNr 6222 35% damaged in strafing attack at Bir el Abd
4.(H)/12	Bf 109F-4 WNr 7441 destroyed in strafing attack at Bir el Abd
4.(H)/12	Bf 109F-4 WNr 7057 40% damaged by bombs at Fuka
1.(F)/121	Ju 88D-1 WNr 430305 destroyed by bombs at Fuka
1.(F)/121	Ju 88D-1 WNr 430184 35% damaged by bombs at Fuka

Italian Claims

73ª Sq, 9°Gr, 4°St CT	Ten Giulio Reiner	MC.202	Boston	Qotaifiya	0915
73ª Sq, 9°Gr, 4°St CT	Ten Giulio Reiner	MC.202	P-40	Qotaifiya	0915
73ª Sq, 9°Gr, 4°St CT	Ten Giulio Reiner	MC.202	P-40 Probable	Qotaifiya	0915
73ª Sq, 9°Gr, 4°St CT	Ten Giulio Reiner	MC.202	Boston Damaged	Qotaifiya	0915
73ª Sq, 9°Gr, 4°St CT	Ten Vittorio Squarcia	MC.202	Spitfire	Qotaifiya	0915
73ª Sq, 9°Gr, 4°St CT	Ten Vittorio Squarcia	MC.202	P-40 Probable	Qotaifiya	0915
73ª Sq, 9°Gr, 4°St CT	Serg Magg A.Angelini	MC.202	P-40	Qotaifiya	0915
73ª Sq, 9°Gr, 4°St CT	Ten Giuseppe Oblach	MC.202	P-40	Qotaifiya	0915
73ª Sq, 9°Gr, 4°St CT	Ten Giuseppe Oblach	MC.202	P-40 Probable	Qotaifiya	0915
73ª Sq, 9°Gr, 4°St CT	Serg Teresio Martinoli	MC.202	Spitfire	Qotaifiya	0915
73ª Sq, 9°Gr, 4°St CT	unspecified	MC.202	Spitfire Probable	Qotaifiya	0915
73ª Sq, 9°Gr, 4°St CT	M.llo Paolo Perno	MC.202	Spitfire	Qotaifiya	0915
96ª Sq, 9°Gr, 4°St CT	Ten Emanuele Annoni	MC.202	P-40	Qotaifiya	0915
96ª Sq, 9°Gr, 4°St CT	Ten Emanuele Annoni	MC.202	P-40 Probable	Qotaifiya	0915
96ª Sq, 9°Gr, 4°St CT	Ten Enrico Moretto	MC.202	P-40	Qotaifiya	0915
96ª Sq, 9°Gr, 4°St CT	Serg Magg Bruno Biagini	MC.202	P-40	Qotaifiya	0915
96ª Sq, 9°Gr, 4°St CT	Serg Magg Giuseppe Zardini	MC.202	2 P-40s	Qotaifiya	0915
75ª Sq, 23°Gr, 3°St CT	Magg Luigi Filippi	MC.202	P-40	S El Daba	1150-1300
74ª Sq, 23°Gr, 3°St CT	S.Ten C.Brigante-Colonna	MC.202	Spitfire Probable	S El Daba	1150-1300

Italian Claims

91ª Sq, 10°Gr, 4°St CT	M.llo Leonardo Ferrulli	MC.202	P-46	S Qotaifiya	1155-1305
96ª Sq, 9°Gr, 4°St CT	Ten Emanuele Annoni	MC.202	Spitfire	El Daba	1215
96ª Sq, 9°Gr, 4°St CT	S.Ten Alberto Giampaoli	MC.202	P-46	El Daba	1215
84ª Sq, 10°Gr, 4°St CT	Ten Luigi Giannella	MC.202 MM 7815	P-40 (or Spitfire)	S Qotaifiya	1515-1650
84ª Sq, 10°Gr, 4°St CT	Ten Luigi Giannella	MC.202 MM 7815	Spitfire Probable	S Qotaifiya	1515-1650
84ª Sq, 10°Gr, 4°St CT	Serg Magg D.Santonocito	MC.202 MM 7928	2 Spitfires Damaged	S Qotaifiya	1515-1650
97ª Sq, 9°Gr, 4°St CT	M.llo Giovanni Bianchelli	MC.202	Hurricane	El Daba	1600-
97ª Sq, 9°Gr, 4°St CT	M.llo Giovanni Bianchelli	MC.202	Hurricane Probable	El Daba	1600-
97ª Sq, 9°Gr, 4°St CT S.	Ten Leonardo Boselli	MC.202	P-40	El Daba	1600-
91ª Sq, 10°Gr, 4°St CT	Cap Carlo M. Ruspoli	MC.202	Spitfire	El Daba	1600-1615

Italian Casualties

73ª Sq, 9°Gr, 4°St CT	MC.202 damaged, Ten Giulio Reiner safe
73ª Sq, 9°Gr, 4°St CT	MC.202 damaged, Ten Giuseppe Oblach safe
73ª Sq, 9°Gr, 4°St CT	MC.202 damaged, Serg Magg Armando Angelini safe
73ª Sq, 9°Gr, 4°St CT	MC.202 damaged, Serg Teresio Martinoli safe
97ª Sq, 9°Gr, 4°St CT	MC.202 MM 7807 '97-1' damaged on ground by bombs
97ª Sq, 9°Gr, 4°St CT	MC.202 MM 7913 '97-3' damaged on ground by bombs
91ª Sq, 10°Gr, 4°St CT	MC.202 MM 7902 '91-5' shot down, S.Ten Alvaro Bondi baled and safe

Saturday, 10 October 1942

Six Bf 109s of III./JG 53 scrambled at 1135, engaging a lone fighter (unidentified) which was probably a TacR or PRU machine seeking to check on the results of the previous day's raids; Uffz Bahnsen claimed to have shot this down. Four Spitfires from 92 Squadron took part in an evening 'rhubarb' at 1658, attacking ground targets in the Fuka area. Three Messerschmitts of III./JG 53 were scrambled again, reporting meeting three fighters over the sea, one of which Bahnsen, in the air again, claimed, Flg Off Hill being shot down in flames. It seems that on this occasion the German pilot experienced some trouble in getting confirmation for his claim. However, another of the Spitfires crash-landed on the surface of the sea on returning from the sortie. Ten Bruno Serotini claimed a P-40 (or Spitfire according to other sources). I. and III./JG 27 moved from North Africa to Comiso with 25 Bf 109s.

British Casualties

92 Sqn	Spitfire Vc BR491 'Q' crashed in sea off El Daba returning from ground attack 1745; Wt Off L.Edwards
92 Sqn	Spitfire Vc BR437 'R' shot down in flames; Flg Off E.H.Hill KiA
250 Sqn	Kittyhawk III badly damaged by Bf 109; Flg Off Milluck safe
M.E.	Hurricane BM993 SOC, DBR

German Claims

8./JG 53	Uffz Jens Bahnsen	Spitfire	15km S El Daba	1035
8./JG 53	Uffz Jens Bahnsen	P-40 n.b.		1638

German Casualties

I./SchG 2	Bf 109F-4 WNr 7378 shot down by AA and crashed nr El Ruweisat, pilot safe

Italian Claims

363ª Sq, 150°Gr Aut CT	Ten Bruno Serotini MC.200	P-40

Sunday, 11 October 1942

At 1450 two Spitfires of 601 Squadron were scrambled, climbing to 25,000 feet. Here their pilots spotted six Bf 109s 7,000 feet below and they attacked these, Flt Lt Curry claiming one probably shot down. 13° Gruppo moved from Abu Haggag to Abu Amud.

British Claims

601 Sqn	Flt Lt J.H.Curry	Spitfire Vc BR583	Bf 109 Probable	Burg el Arab	1450-1550

German Casualties

III./ZG 1	Bf 109E-7 WNr 1406 shot down by AA and crashed W Salt Lake, pilot safe

Monday, 12 October 1942

Thirteen MC.202s of 10° Gruppo provided top cover to a formation of German Ju 87s over the lines. No fighters were met but Ten Barsotti did not return, probably due to a failure of his oxygen mask. Thirteen Bf 109s of II./JG 27 escorted Stukas at 1522, two peeling off on their own and returning later, reporting combat with 12 Spitfires near Hammam. The leader of this Rotte, Oblt Vögl, who had been leading 4.Staffel in August, claimed that he had shot down one Spitfire at which the others had veered away so that the rest of the German formation did not see them. This was the last claim Vögl was to make in North Africa.

80 Squadron now moved from El Bassa to LG.85, joining 127, 274 and 335 Squadrons in a re-formed 7 SAAF Hurribomber Wing. 6 Squadron had now left this wing to become an independent special anti-tank unit, as had 7 SAAF Squadron.

German Claims				
4./JG 27	Oblt Ferdinand Vögl	Spitfire	SSW Ogon	1455
Italian Casualties				
91ª Sq, 10°Gr, 4°St CT	MC.202 MM 7910 '91-8' failed to return, Ten Luciano Barsotti MiA			

Kittyhawk I of 250 Squadron crash-landed within Axis lines. The ammunition bays are open in both wings, indicating that the guns have probably been disarmed.

Tuesday, 13 October 1942

Five Bf 109s of II./Gruppe, eight of III./JG 27 and 15 of III./JG 53 set off at 1000 to escort a Stuka raid. Twelve Kittyhawks of 4 SAAF Squadron took off on a wing scramble ten minutes later joining 12 P-40Fs of the 57th Fighter Group which were undertaking a fighter sweep. The Americans spotted a dozen Ju 87s ten miles south of El Alamein at 1025 but these were seen to be under attack by the South African squadron whose pilots reported encountering nine Ju 87s and eight of the Messerschmitts, claiming two of the dive-bombers shot down, two probables and two damaged. Two Kittyhawks were damaged by the escorting fighters, which claimed several of the defenders shot down.

At that stage at least 20 Messerschmitts engaged the US aircraft at 15,000 feet in a 20-minute dogfight. 1/Lt George Mobbs of the 64th Squadron and 1/Lt Arnold Jaqua of the 65th each claimed one Bf 109 shot down, the latter pilot claiming a second damaged. However, 1/Lt Robert Nichols of the latter unit failed to return. Hptm Rödel claimed a P-39 which was probably the US P-40F, while Obfw Werner Stumpf claimed one P-40 and two Spitfires. The only Spitfire lost on this date was a PRU aircraft which may have wandered into the fight at this point. However, Stumpf was then shot down and killed, Uffz Augst being shot down and crash-landing. One of JG 27's Bf 109s was also shot down, reportedly by AA, Lt Erich Schöfböck reported missing. In the late afternoon, at 1720, ten Bf 109s of III./JG 27 and ten of III./JG 53 carried out a Freie Jagd during which they were intercepted by ten Kittyhawks of 3 RAAF Squadron and P-40Fs of the 57th Fighter Group. Oblt Althof of JG 27 and Lt Harder of JG 53 each claimed one shot down, one of the Australian aircraft being damaged.

During the day Flt Lt Olver of 238 Squadron was posted to 213 Squadron as a supernumerary squadron leader to gain experience of command and leadership.

British Claims

4 SAAF Sqn	Maj S.F.du Toit	Kittyhawk I ET897 'O'	Ju 87	S El Alamein	1040
4 SAAF Sqn	Lt H.B.Johnson	Kittyhawk I AL177 'B'	2 Ju 87s Damaged	S El Alamein	1040
4 SAAF Sqn	Lt J.G.MacKay	Kittyhawk I AL156 'P'	Ju 87 Probable	S El Alamein	1040
4 SAAF Sqn	Lt J.G.MacKay	Kittyhawk I AL156 'P'	MC.202 Damaged	S El Alamein	1040
4 SAAF Sqn	Flg Off F.Scudday	Kittyhawk I ET864 'C'	Ju 87 Damaged	S El Alamein	1040
4 SAAF Sqn	Lt I.D.Sparg	Kittyhawk I ET1018 'F'	Ju 87 Probable	S El Alamein	1040
4 SAAF Sqn	Capt W.J.Wheeler	Kittyhawk I EV347 'K'	Ju 87	S El Alamein	1040
4 SAAF Sqn	Capt W.J.Wheeler	Kittyhawk I EV347 'K'	Bf 109F Damaged	S El Alamein	1040

British Casualties

2 PRU	Spitfire IV BP934 MiA
238 Sqn	Hurricane II HL884 'X' left 0940 on TacR escort, hit by Flak, damaged Cat I, landed safely; Flt Sgt F.B.Gillis safe
4 SAAF Sqn	Kittyhawk I ET684 'C' hit by Flak and belly-landed Cat II; Plt Off F.Scudday, RAF (US) safe
4 SAAF Sqn	Kittyhawk I AK765 'D' badly damaged by e/a but back; 2/Lt J.D.Robertson slt WiA
3 RAAF Sqn	Kittyhawk III AL 103 left 1705, attacked by ten Bf 109s, damaged, landed safely; Plt Off A.B. Taylor safe
274 Sqn	Hurricane IIc BP514 collided with BP326 and crashed
274 Sqn	Hurricane IIc BP326 collided with BP514 and crash-landed

US Claims

64th FS/57th FG	1/Lt George D.Mobbs	P-40F '23'	Bf 109	10m S El Alamein	1025-1045
65th FS/57th FG	Lt Arnold D.Jaqua	P-40F '47'	Bf 109	10m S El Alamein	1035
65th FS/57th FG	Lt Arnold D.Jaqua	P-40F '47'	Bf 109 Damaged	10m S El Alamein	1035
66th FS/57th FG	1/Lt Albert O.Zipser	P-40F '86'	Bf 109F Damaged	2m S El Alamein	1755

US Casualties

65th FS/57th FG	P-40F '53', shot down S El Alamein, 1/Lt Robert N.Nichols MiA

German Claims

7./JG 53	Lt Jürgen Harder	P-40		0935
Stab II./JG 27	Hptm Gustav Rödel	P-39	SSW El Alamein	0939
9./JG 53	Obfw Werner Stumpf	P-40		0940
9./JG 53	Obfw Werner Stumpf	2 Spitfires		0942 & 0945
9./JG 27	Oblt Willi Althof	P-40	S El Hammam	1647
7./JG 53	Fw Horst Olzmann	P-40		1655
7./JG 53	Lt Jürgen Harder	P-40		1755

German Casualties

8./JG 53	Bf 109F-4 trop WNr 13061 crash-landed from combat with P-40, 100%; Uffz Hannes Augst safe
9./JG 53	Bf 109F-4 trop WNr 10175 Yellow 7+I shot down AA; Obfw Werner Stumpf KiA
7./JG 27	Bf 109F-4 trop WNr 8697 White 4 combat 10km S El Alamein; Lt Erich Schöfböck MiA
I./StG 3	Ju 87D-3 WNr 2668 shot down by P-40, force-landed at El Daba, crew safe

Wednesday, 14 October 1942

At 1030 12 Hurricanes of 1 SAAF Squadron provided top cover for 33 Squadron to escort two TacR aircraft over the front. Five Bf 109s and MC.202s attacked, joined by three more. One Messerschmitt was seen going down and it had to be decided which of three pilots was responsible. All protested that it should be credited to the others and eventually it was decided that it should be shared between them all. This unit was now flying Hurricane IIc aircraft with cannons. Later in the day, around midday, 11 Kittyhawks of 2 SAAF Squadron covered aircraft of 4 SAAF Squadron on a dive-bombing attack west of Daba. Four Bf 109s attacked, one of which was claimed shot down by Lt Bryant. It appears that this was a combat reported by III./JG 27, five of this unit's Bf 109s having taken off at 1155 to intercept 20 fighters over Daba. Obfw Rosenberg was shot down and baled out, but hit the tailplane of his aircraft, breaking both legs; he had claimed 12 victories up to this time.

During the day 4 SAAF Squadron received a visit from the AOC, who at the end of his inspection asked if there were any questions. One mechanic at once replied: "What about more food, Sir?" "You South Africans seem to eat half as much again as we do!" replied the AOC; quick as a flash came the response, "Well Sir, we're twice as big as you are!"

During a night patrol Sgt Beard spotted a Ju 88 and chased this out to sea. Closing to 50 yards as both aircraft were flying just above the water, he saw strikes on the fuselage of the bomber, but at that moment his propeller clipped the top of the waves and he was lucky to pull up, although in doing so he lost sight of his target. His R/T was not working and he had to make his way back to the coast without guidance. Eventually, he spotted an Allied landing ground when his aircraft had become very short of fuel, and therefore belly-landed close by.

British Claims

1 SAAF Sqn	Lt D.T.Gilson	Hurricane IIc ..666 'K'	} Bf 109F (shared)		1100
1 SAAF Sqn	Lt H.F.Smith	Hurricane IIc HL892 'H'	Bf 109F		1100
1 SAAF Sqn	Capt S.de K.Viljoen	Hurricane IIc ..798 'T'	}		
2 SAAF Sqn	Lt P.D.Bryant	Kittyhawk I ET972 'P'	Bf 109	W Daba	1215
73 Sqn	Flg Off D.R.Beard	Hurricane IIc HL847	Ju 88 Damaged	N Daba	1940-0020

British Casualties

127 Sqn	Hurricane IIb BP227 engine cut and crashed in force-landing S Dekheila
267 Sqn	Hudson VI EW961 hit by bomb during a raid on Kufra

German Casualties

9./JG 27	Bf 109F-4 trop WNr 10008 combat; Obfw Heinrich Rosenberg baled WiA over El Daba
6./KG 100	He 111 Kufra Oasis, force-landed; Lt Harald Bydlo and two PoW

Thursday, 15 October 1942

Heavy sandstorms stopped flying for the next three days. 8° Gruppo CT moved to Bu Amud.

British Casualties

450 Sqn	Kittyhawk III badly damaged by Flak; Sgt Fourneau safe

Italian Casualties

90ª Sq, 10°Gr, 4°St CT	MC.202 MM 7795 '90-6'collided in landing with MC.202 MM 7930 '90-2', a/c damaged, Serg Carlo Ferriani WiA

Saturday, 17 October 1942

British Casualties

73 Sqn	Hurricane destroyed by exploding train in El Alamein station; Flt Sgt J.C.McPherson KiA
103 MU	Hurricane HL842 missing on delivery flight between Aboukir and Wadi Natrun

Italian Casualties

77ª Sq, 13°Gr, 2°St CT	MC.202 MM 7893 force-landed through engine failure, w/o, Serg Sergio Vanello (82ª Sq) WiA

Sunday, 18 October 1942
Sqn Ldr A.D.Ferguson left 450 Squadron which was now based at LG.175; he departed for the UK. His place was taken by Flt Lt J.E.A.Williams who was promoted to command. An Italian floatplane of 612ª Squadriglia Soccorso recovered a German fighter pilot slightly wounded 35km S of Capo Scaramia.

Monday, 19 October 1942
On this date Gen SA Mario Bernasconi took over command of 5ª Squadra Aerea. At 1250 Ten Giuseppe Oblach led eight MC.202s of 73ª Squadriglia on a scramble from Fuka. Four Spitfires were met over El Alamein and one was claimed damaged; a Macchi returned badly hit.

WDAF now opened the air offensive that had been planned prior to the pending 8th Army assault on the ground. At 1230 seven Spitfires of 601 Squadron provided independent top cover to Kittyhawks bombing LG.104. Six Bf 109s and some MC.202s were seen and attacked, four probables being claimed. Twelve Kittyhawks of 2 SAAF Squadron carried out the dive-bombing, seven attacking. As they came out of their dives they were met by Bf 109s, the wing being shot clean off Lt Gunyon's aircraft and he baled out into the sea. One Spitfire was also damaged beyond repair.

Five Bf 109s of III./JG 27 and seven of III./JG 53 were scrambled at 1300, Oblt Althof and Uffz Krainik of III./JG 27 each claiming one fighter shot down. Later in the afternoon another victory was claimed by Lt Harder of JG 53, but during one of these engagements Uffz Augst of the latter unit was shot down for the second time in seven days and crashed in the sea, being picked up by the rescue service. During the day the Hurricanes of 33 and 213 Squadrons patrolled 15 miles east of El Alamein, meeting Bf 109s, one of which was damaged by Plt Off C.Smith of the latter unit; one Hurricane was reported lost.

British Claims

213 Sqn	Plt Off C.D.A.Smith	Hurricane IIc BP237	Bf 109 Damaged	10m SE El Alamein	1025
601 Sqn	Plt Off A.R.Boyle	Spitfire Vc BR135	Bf 109 Probable	LG.104	1230-1355
601 Sqn	Plt Off D.Ibbotson	Spitfire Vc BR253	Bf 109 Damaged	LG.104	1230-1355
601 Sqn	Flt Lt M.R.B.Ingram	Spitfire Vc EP303	Bf 109 Probable	LG.104	
601 Sqn	Plt Off J.H.Nicholls	Spitfire Vc AR289 'P'	MC.202 Probable	LG.104	1230-1355
601 Sqn	Flg Off W.M.Whitamore	Spitfire Vc BP852 'K'	Bf 109 Probable	LG.104	1230-1355
250 Sqn	Plt Off G.W.Troke	Kittyhawk III FR284	Bf 109G Damaged	Daba, LG.21	1320-1450

British Casualties

2 SAAF Sqn	Kittyhawk I AK654 damaged by Bf 109s and abandoned off LG.104; Lt N.M.M. Gunyon KiA; baled out over sea at Daba Point 1320; Bf 109s seen circling his parachute
92 Sqn	Spitfire V BR522 'K' crashed on return from operations at 1145; Flt Sgt R.Hempstead KiA

German Claims

9./JG 27	Oblt Willi Althof	Spitfire	E El Daba	1223
8./JG 27	Uffz Erich Krainik	Spitfire	NE El Daba	
7./JG 53	Lt Jürgen Harder	P-40	7km N El Daba	1516

German Casualties

8./JG 53	Bf 109F-4 trop WNr 13341 shot down over sea by P-40, N Qotaifiya; Uffz Hannnes Augst baled, safe
9./JG 53	Bf 109F-4/Z WNr 7504 Yellow 9+I 30% damaged by bombs on ground at Qotaifiya
7./JG 27	Bf 109F-4 trop WNr 8720 combat with P-40, force-landed El Daba, 60%; pilot safe

Italian Claims

73ª Sq, 9°Gr, 4°St CT	unstated	MC.202	Spitfire Damaged	El Alamein	1320

Italian Casualties

73ª Sq, 9°Gr, 4°St CT	MC.202 damaged by Spitfires, pilot safe

Monday-Tuesday, 19/20 October 1942
One Hurricane and two bombers claimed by German Flak.

Tuesday, 20 October 1942
Hurricanes of 73 Squadron undertook a night strafing attack on the Axis airfields, but from one such sortie Flt Sgt G.McD.MacKinnon failed to return. Two other pilots who had accompanied him reported seeing his Hurricane illuminated by searchlights and heavy Flak bursting around it near LG.20.

Gen Mario Bernasconi, newly-promoted to commander of 5ª Squadra Aerea, inspects the damage suffered by MC.202 '75-12' MM 8373 during a sortie flown by Ten Bozzolan on 20 October.

With daylight the WDAF again struck at the Axis airfields at Daba. For the Regia Aeronautica, the first scramble occurred at 0815, when six MC.202s of 91ª Squadriglia and one of 73ª Squadriglia took off from Fuka. Cap Ruspoli and his pilots encountered 27 aircraft, identified as 'Bostons' and 'Hudsons', covered by a large number of P-40s and Spitfires. The escort was engaged and two P-40s were claimed by Ruspoli and Serg Silvestri. One Macchi returned badly damaged. At 0820 another scramble was undertaken by seven MC.202s of 70ª Squadriglia led by Cap Solaro. Hostile aircraft were again engaged, Solaro claiming two P-40s and Serg Dusi a Spitfire, although Ten Giorgio Santamaria failed to return. Twelve Kittyhawks of 450 Squadron had been providing top cover to Baltimores and B-25s, the US 65th and 3 RAAF Squadrons giving close and medium cover. Over Fuka one Macchi attacked 450 Squadron, but Flg Off Marting claimed to have shot this down. Three more then attacked and two Kittyhawks were damaged.

The Italians had undertaken an uneventful scramble at 0900, but at 0920 Serg Locatelli claimed a P-40. Another scramble at 0940 again achieved no encounters. Meanwhile, Bf 109s had now taken off, including two of II./JG 27 and two of III./JG 53, followed by six of III./JG 27. Oblt Börngen of II.Gruppe and Hptm Düllberg of III./JG 27 each claimed one Kittyhawk, but Lt Feldkötter of JG 53 was shot down, baling out over the sea but being drowned. At 0915 it was the turn of Cap Lucchini to lead four MC.202s of 84ª Squadriglia and one of 91ª to face 25 Hurribombers raiding Fuka, covered by 20 P-40s. One Hurribomber and two P-40s were claimed by Ten Mandolini, Cap Lucchini and Ten Berti, for no losses.

Seven Kittyhawks of 260 Squadron escorted 12 of 4 SAAF Squadron over Daba at 0935. Eight of the South Africans were to dive-bomb LG.21, an additional section providing top cover. Having bombed, the pilots turned out to sea to reform but a call warned them that one Kittyhawk was under attack. Lt Robottom dived on one Bf 109, firing two bursts and chasing it low over the water, firing again and hitting it in the fuselage. He then lost sight of it, but it was seen by the rest of the squadron to crash into the sea. However, 2/Lt Johnson's aircraft was hit, apparently by a Bf 109, and he crash-landed in the El Alamein defences, slightly wounded.

260 Squadron was jumped by ten fighters, Sgt Meredith claiming one shot down into the sea, and Flt Lt Davis hit a second which he reported disintegrated, the pilot baling out. Davis was then attacked by an MC.202 which chased him back to El Alamein, making continual attacks and damaging his aircraft badly. Two other Kittyhawks, flown by Flg Off Thagard and Flt Sgt Barker were also badly damaged, while Sgt Stebbings failed to return. A repeat attack was made at 1040, this time targeting LG.104 "with orders to fight in preference to bombing". Twelve Kittyhawks, this time from 2 SAAF Squadron led by Capt Parsonson with the Tomahawks of 5 SAAF Squadron as cover, flew out to sea before turning in towards Daba from the west, diving in line-astern on the target. As they did so, fighters were seen taking off and Parsonson led the Kittyhawks down to bomb the nearest target – a supply dump – before turning to face the defenders which Parsonson thought were Macchis as they dived past, although others reported them to be Messerschmitts. Lt Bryant and his wingman attacked two, but Bryant then saw one diving on his No.2. Making a sharp turn, he attacked as it pulled up in a steep climb, seeing his fire hitting the underside at close range, and it dived into the sea, witnessed by Lt Blignault.

During the return flight Capt Wildsmith spotted two fighters to port and climbing steeply to the left, he turned onto the tail of the closest. A long burst hit the rear fuselage and the fighter made a gentle turn and went straight down. With only one gun still firing, Wildsmith did not follow him down. However, Parsonson did so, reporting that it was smoking so badly that it must have been on fire. He too was not then able to follow further, and initially Wildsmith's claim was treated as a probable, although it was later confirmed as destroyed. 5 SAAF Squadron's Tomahawks as top cover were attacked by at least nine Axis fighters from the west. Lt Bidwell, who was in the lead, thought the attacking fighters looked a lot more like 12 plus, but got in one burst during a 20-minute dogfight before heading for base.

At 1100 came the fifth scramble of the morning for the Axis fighters;13 MC.202s (seven of 70ª Squadriglia, 23° Gruppo, led by Magg Filippi and six of 10° Gruppo led by Cap Lucchini) intercepted a large formation of bombers and fighters. Five Bf 109s of III./JG 53 also took off at this time, followed by six from II./JG 27. The former unit engaged eight Spitfires, but Uffz Hans Freytag was shot down, baling out with severe wounds within ten minutes of taking off, while a second Messerschmitt was damaged and force-landed. Meanwhile the Macchi pilots claimed seven fighters and two bombers shot down with two further fighters claimed as probables. During this late morning period pilots of 5./JG 27 claimed five more P-40s, and Lt Bahnsen of 8./JG 53 claimed a Hurricane.

Twelve Kittyhawks of 112 Squadron (top cover), ten from 3 RAAF Squadron (medium cover) and others from 250 Squadron (close cover) escorted 24 Baltimores and B-25s over Fuka where they were attacked by 16 Bf 109s and MC.202s. Sgt Greaves of 112 Squadron did not return, but a probable Bf 109 and an MC.202 damaged were claimed. 3 RAAF Squadron's pilots spotted a twin-engined Italian bomber which three pilots attacked, claiming multiple hits before it landed near Abu Haggag. The identity of this aircraft has not been discovered. In the meantime three fighters attacked the rest of the squadron, two Kittyhawks being shot down as was a third from 250 Squadron.

Ten Bf 109s of II./JG 27 scrambled at 1159, followed five minutes later by two from III./JG 53. The pilots of these claimed a further three P-40s. During the morning Flg Off Philipps of 145 Squadron, when sweeping over Daba claimed a Bf 109 from which the pilot baled out. The Italians undertook two further scrambles at 1235 and 1340 without meeting anything, but at 1445 during the eighth scramble of the day, twelve MC.202s led by Cap Tugnoli again engaged a large formation of fighters and bombers, this time five fighters (plus a probable) and two bombers being claimed; one Macchi failed to return.

Twelve Hurricanes of 238 Squadron escorted two TacR aircraft on a mission at 1430, but nine Bf 109s of III./JG 27 and six of III./JG 53 were scrambled, these also engaging a big formation. The JG 27 pilots claimed three victories, Lt Harder of JG 53 claiming one more. Plt Off Ormerod's Hurricane was damaged when two Bf 109s attacked the unit, but he claimed one Messerschmitt shot down. During the day 11 Kittyhawks and Tomahawks had been lost and six more damaged. Additionally, one Hurricane had been lost and one damaged. Against 11 losses the Axis had made some 63 claims, 11 by German fighters, 42 and three probables by Italian fighters and six by the Flak defences. Allowing for mis-identifications, Allied claims had been remarkably accurate on this occasion, 11 Axis fighters being claimed shot down plus one more probable. The apparently massive Italian fighter 'victories' broke down as follows:

9° Gruppo	six P-40s, six Spitfires and one Boston
10° Gruppo	nine P-40s, one Spitfire and one probable, one Hurricane and one Boston
23° Gruppo	eleven P-40s and two probables, three Spitfires and three Bostons.

Obviously, in the confused and crowded circumstances appertaining here again, the claims for 26 Curtiss fighters, together with six more claimed by the German fighter pilots does represent a three times mark-up of claims over losses – but this is not notably worse than the level of over-claiming relating on a number of occasions to Allied units. However, it does need to be pointed out that no Spitfires were actually lost on this date and only one bomber – and that apparently to Flak!

Recognition remained the other problem. It is interesting to note here that whereas the WDAF claims included eight Bf 109s against a loss of five, they also included three Macchis against a loss of five, total claims against fighters were about correct. Allied pilots seem to have mixed up Macchis and Messerschmitts nearly as frequently as the Germans and Italians mistook Hurricanes for Kittyhawks or either for Spitfires. Since it was prestigious to shoot down Spitfires or Bf 109s, this coupled with optimism helped further in making the always difficult task of recognition even more so.

British Claims

450 Sqn	Flg Off H.F.Marting	Kittyhawk III FR251	MC.202	Fuka	0831-1014
260 Sqn	Flt Lt C.C.H.Davis	Kittyhawk IIa FL326	Bf 109	off Daba	0935-1110
260 Sqn	Sgt J.G.Meredith	Kittyhawk IIa	Bf 109	off Daba	0935-1110
4 SAAF Sqn	Lt R.Robottom	Kittyhawk I EV158 'J'	Bf 109F		1030
145 Sqn	Plt Off H.J.Phillips	Spitfire Vb EP618 'P'	Bf 109	Daba	1035-1145
145 Sqn	Flt Lt J.S.Taylor	Spitfire Vb EP327 'R'	Bf 109 Damaged	Daba	1035-1145
2 SAAF Sqn	Lt P.D.Bryant	Kittyhawk I ET968 'Y'	Bf 109F	LG.104	1115
2 SAAF Sqn	Capt H.E.N.Wildsmith	Kittyhawk I EV348 'U'	Bf 109F	LG.104	1115
112 Sqn	Sgt J.M.MacAuley	Kittyhawk III FR245 'B'	MC.202 Damaged	Fuka-El Alamein	1140-1315
238 Sqn	Plt Off J.A.Ormerod	Hurricane IIc HL620 'C'	Bf 109	escort TacR	1430-1550
601 Sqn	Flt Lt J.H.Curry	Spitfire Vc BP852 'K'	Bf 109	Daba-Fuka area	1535-1635
112 Sqn	Flt Sgt R.C.C.Smith	Kittyhawk III FR263 'X'	Bf 109 Probable	LG.21-El Alamein	1540-1655
2 SAAF Sqn	Lt L.Dawson-Squibb	Kittyhawk I ET969 'I'	Bf 109F Damaged	Fuka l.g.	1615
2 SAAF Sqn	Capt H.E.N.Wildsmith	Kittyhawk I EV348 'U'	MC.202	Fuka l..g.	1615
5 SAAF Sqn	Lt S.V.Coleman	Tomahawk IIb AK401 'F'	MC.202 (collision)	48km W Daba	1615-1630

British Casualties

112 Sqn	Kittyhawk III FR248 shot down nr LG.21, ditched in sea; Sgt D.F.Greaves PoW
250 Sqn	Kittyhawk III FR265 'F' left 1130, presumed shot down by MC.202s nr Fuka at 1230; Flt Sgt A.E.Roberts PoW
250 Sqn	Kittyhawk III FR284 left 1545, shot down by Bf 109s while escorting Bostons to Fuka; Sgt R.C.Taylor KiA
260 Sqn	Kittyhawk IIa left 0935, shot down by Bf 109 nr Daba; Sgt N.D.Stebbings PoW
260 Sqn	Kittyhawk IIa FL326 left 0935, badly damaged by Flak nr LG.21; not repaired; Flt Lt C.C.H.Davis safe
260 Sqn	Kittyhawk IIa left 0935, damaged by Bf 109 nr Daba; Flg Off V.J.Thagard safe
260 Sqn	Kittyhawk IIa left 0935, badly damaged by Bf 109 nr Daba; Flt Sgt W.D.Barker safe
450 Sqn	Kittyhawk III FR250 badly damaged by MC.202s over Fuka; Flt Lt D.H.Clarke safe
450 Sqn	Kittyhawk III FR300 badly damaged by MC.202s over Fuka; Sgt A.H.Gregory safe
3 RAAF Sqn	Kittyhawk ET954 left 1100, shot down by two Bf 109s and crash-landed, Sgt T.G.Wood PoW
3 RAAF Sqn	Kittyhawk EV315 left 1100, ditched off LG.18, engine failure returning from Daba, Flt G.H.F.Plinston safe
3 RAAF Sqn	Kittyhawk EV361 'C' left 1100, presumed shot down by fighters Daba at 1225; Plt Off E.H.T.Alderson KiA
2 SAAF Sqn	Kittyhawk I AK868 'X' shot down at 1600 and fell in Allied lines; 2/Lt P.H.M.Jackson KiA, buried by 1st NMR
4 SAAF Sqn	Kittyhawk I AK765 shot down by fighters nr Fuka at 1630; 2/Lt J.G.McKay PoW
4 SAAF Sqn	Kittyhawk I AK824 shot down by Bf 109 and crash-landed in El Alamein line at 1030 Cat II; 2/Lt M.B.Johnson safe
4 SAAF Sqn	Kittyhawk I ET897 left 1500, damaged by Bf 109 and by Flak nr Daba at 1630 Cat II; Maj S.F.du Toit safe
5 SAAF Sqn	Tomahawk IIb AK401 'F' collided with MC.202 48 km W Daba; both fell in flames,1615-1630; Lt S.V.Coleman KiA
73 Sqn	Hurricane BE554 MiA to Flak nr LG.20; Sgt G.M.MacKinnon MiA
238 Sqn	Hurricane HL620 'C' escort TacR 1430-1550, damaged by Bf 109 Cat II; Plt Off J.A.Ormerod safe

British Casualties

21 SAAF Sqn	Baltimore III AG912 'O' off 1518 as one of 15 and 3 Bostons of 12 SAAF Sqn to attack Axis a/c at Fuka Main (LG.17); shot down by heavy Flak while crossing front line and spun into ground at 1612; Capt J.G.Potgieter and one PoW, two KiA

US Claims

434th BS/12th BG	B-25C turret gunner Sgt L.N.Burger	Bf 109	Fuka	1225
82nd BS/12th BG	B-25C turret gunner S/Sgt G.A.Kielbasa	Bf 109	Fuka	1225

German Claims

5./JG 27	Oblt Ernst Börngen	P-40	ENE El Daba	0920
Stab III./JG 27	Hptm Ernst Düllberg	P-46	E El Daba	0925
8./JG 53	Uffz Jens Bahnsen	P-40	15km SSW Fuka	1125
5./JG 27	Uffz Josef Vavra	P-40	NW Ghala	1132
5./JG 27	Lt Willi Kientsch	P-40	SE Bir el Abd	1140
7./JG 53	Lt Jürgen Harder	Hurricane	5km SE Abu Dweis	1410
8./JG 27	Lt Werner Schroer	P-40	SW Deir el Tarfa	1412
9./JG 27	Oblt Hans-Joachim Heinecke	2 P-40s	ESE Deir el Tarfa	1415 & 1416
5./JG 27	Fw Bernhard Schneider	P-40	SSE El Daba	1530
5./JG 27	Uffz Hans Jürgens	P-40	SW El Alamein	1540
Flak		6 a/c by day		

German Casualties

5./JG 27	Bf 109F-4 trop WNr 8557 combat with P-40, collided on landing El Dacam 100%; Uffz Hans Jürgens safe
7./JG 53	Bf 109F-4 trop WNr 7250 White 11+I shot down by Spitfire 30km SE Qotaifiya; Uffz Hans Freytag WiA
8./JG 53	Bf 109F-4 trop WNr 13218 Black 5+I shot down over sea by P-40 12-15km N Qotaifiya; Lt Friedrich Feldkötter baled out but KiA
8./JG 27	Bf 109F-4 trop WNr 8387 Black 6 combat Turbiya, 100%; Lt Wolfgang Lang WiA
9./JG 27	Bf 109F-4 trop WNr 8271 combat Qasaba, 10% damaged
III./ZG 1	Bf 109E-7 WNr 4014 shot down by AA, crash-landed in the desert, pilot safe
1.(F)/121	2 Ju 88 D-1 WNr 430297 50% damaged and WNr 430158 25% damaged by bombs at Fuka

Italian Claims

91ª Sq, 10°Gr, 4°St CT	Cap Carlo M. Ruspoli	MC.202	P-40	Fuka	0815-0930
91ª Sq, 10°Gr, 4°St CT	Serg Guerriero Silvestri	MC.202	P-40	Fuka	0815-0930
70ª Sq, 23°Gr, 3°St CT	Cap Claudio Solaro	MC.202	2 P-40s	El Daba	0820-0950
70ª Sq, 23°Gr, 3°St CT	Serg William Dusi	MC.202	Spitfire	El Daba	0820-0950
84ª Sq, 10°Gr, 4°St CT	Cap Franco Lucchini	MC.202 MM 7901	P-40	Fuka	0915-1020
84ª Sq, 10°Gr, 4°St CT	Ten Paolo Berti	MC.202 MM 7896	P-40	Fuka	0915-1020
91ª Sq, 10°Gr, 4°St CT	Ten Orlando Mandolini	MC.202	Hurricane	Fuka	0915-1020
70ª Sq, 23°Gr, 3°St CT	Serg Franco Locatelli	MC.202	P-40 (shared?)	Fuka	0920-1025
75ª Sq, 23°Gr, 3°St CT	Serg Francesco Cuscunà	MC.202	P-40	Fuka	1000-1120
97ª Sq, 9°Gr, 4°St CT	Ten Fernando Malvezzi	MC.202 MM 7828	Spitfire	El Alamein	1005-1120
97ª Sq, 9°Gr, 4°St CT	Ten Flavio Fratini	MC.202 MM 7761	2 Spitfires	El Alamein	1005-1120
84ª Sq, 10°Gr, 4°St CT	Ten Luigi Giannella	MC.202 MM 7901	Spitfire Probable	Fuka	1025-1100
97ª Sq, 9°Gr, 4°St CT	Ten Jacopo Frigerio	MC.202	P-40	Fuka	1055-1220
97ª Sq, 9°Gr, 4°St CT	S.Ten Leonardo Boselli	MC.202	P-40	Fuka	1055-1220
97ª Sq, 9°Gr, 4°St CT	M.llo Gianni Bianchelli	MC.202	Spitfire	Fuka	1055-1220
97ª Sq, 9°Gr, 4°St CT	Ten Giovanni Barcaro	MC.202	P-40	Fuka	1055-1220
73ª Sq, 9°Gr, 4°St CT	Ten Giuseppe Oblach	MC.202	2 P-40s	Fuka	1055-1220
91ª Sq, 10°Gr, 4°St CT	Cap Carlo M. Ruspoli	MC.202	2 P-40s	Fuka	1100-1230
91ª Sq, 10°Gr, 4°St CT	M.llo Leonardo Ferrulli	MC.202	2 P-40s	Fuka	1100-1230
91ª Sq, 10°Gr, 4°St CT	Serg Alessandro Bladelli	MC.202	P-40	Fuka	1100-1230
70ª Sq, 23°Gr, 3°St CT	S.Ten Luigi Bandini	MC.202	P-40	El Daba	1100-1230
70ª Sq, 23°Gr, 3°St CT	Serg Magg Celso Zemella	MC.202	P-40	El Daba	1100-1230
70ª Sq, 23°Gr, 3°St CT	Ten Antonio Maccanti	MC.202	P-40 Probable	El Daba	1100-1230
74ª Sq, 23°Gr, 3°St CT	Serg Magg Felice Papini	MC.202	Boston	S El Alamein	1100-1230
74ª Sq, 23°Gr, 3°St CT	Serg Magg Emilio Stefani	MC.202	Spitfire	S El Alamein	1100-1230
74ª Sq, 23°Gr, 3°St CT	Ten Carlo Moruzzi	MC.202	P-40 Probable	S El Alamein	1100-1230

74ª Sq, 23°Gr, 3°St CT	Ten Giorgio Solaroli	MC.202	Spitfire	S El Alamein	1100-1230
75ª Sq, 23°Gr, 3°St CT	Serg Maurizio Mandolesi	MC.202			
74ª Sq, 23°Gr, 3°St CT	Cap Giorgio Tugnoli	MC.202	P-40	El Alamein	1445-1620
75ª Sq, 23°Gr, 3°St CT	Cap Mario Pinna	MC.202	2 P-40s	El Alamein	1445-1620
75ª Sq, 23°Gr, 3°St CT	Serg Maurizio Mandolesi	MC.202	P-40	El Alamein	1445-1620
75ª Sq, 23°Gr, 3°St CT	Serg Aldo Orsucci	MC.202	P-40	El Alamein	1445-1620
75ª Sq, 23°Gr, 3°St CT	Serg Luigi Bozzolan	MC.202 MM8373	Boston	El Alamein	1445-1620
95ª Sq, 18°Gr, 3°St CT	Ten F. Bordoni-Bisleri	MC.202	Boston	El Alamein	1445-1620
91ª Sq, 10°Gr, 4°St CT	Ten Orlando Mandolini	MC.202	Spitfire	Fuka	1515-1630
97ª Sq, 9°Gr, 4°St CT	Ten Giovanni Barcaro	MC.202	P-40	Fuka	1515-1630
97ª Sq, 9°Gr, 4°St CT	Ten Antonio Canfora	MC.202	2 Spitfires	Fuka	1515-1630
97ª Sq, 9°Gr, 4°St CT	Ten Antonio Canfora	MC.202	Boston	Fuka	1515-1630
97ª Sq, 9°Gr, 4°St CT	Ten Giovanni Barcaro	MC.202			
91ª Sq, 10°Gr, 4°St CT	Ten Orlando Mandolini	MC.202			
96ª Sq, 10°Gr, 4°St CT	M.llo Antonio Sacchi	MC.202	Boston	Fuka	1515-1630
97ª Sq, 10°Gr, 4°St CT	Serg Magg A.Bombardini	MC.202			
96ª Sq, 10°Gr, 4°St CT	M.llo Manlio Olivetti	MC.202			
96ª Sq, 10°Gr, 4°St CT	M.llo Fiorenzo Milella	MC.202			

Italian Casualties

70ª Sq, 23°Gr, 3°St CT	MC.202 MM 9050 '70-7' failed to return 0820-0950, Ten Giorgio Santamaria-Niccolini MiA
75ª Sq, 23°Gr, 3°St CT	MC.202 MM 8370 failed to return 1445-1620, Ten Milano Pausi MiA
75ª Sq, 23°Gr, 3°St CT	MC.202 MM 8373 '75-12' damaged in combat 1445-1620, Serg Luigi Bozzolan safe
84ª Sq, 10°Gr, 4°St CT	MC.202 MM 7905 '84-4' damaged in combat, force-landed 1130, Cap Franco Lucchini safe
97ª Sq, 9°Gr, 4°St CT	MC.202 MM 7761 '97-4' hit in combat, force-landed, Ten Flavio Fratini WiA
97ª Sq, 9°Gr, 4°St CT	MC.202 MM 7828 '97-10' hit in combat, force-landed, Ten Fernando Malvezzi slightly wounded
91ª Sq, 10°Gr, 4°St CT	MC.202 MM 7873 '91-12' hit in combat, belly-landed, Ten Enrico Moretto safe
84ª Sq, 10°Gr, 4°St CT	MC.202 MM 7720 '84-1' damaged by bombs at Fuka
73ª Sq, 9°Gr, 4°St CT	MC.202 MM 7925 '73-6' damaged by bombs at Fuka with Ten Ferruccio Zarini on board, KiA
73ª Sq, 9°Gr, 4°St CT	MC.202 MM 7926 '73-8' damaged by bombs at Fuka with Serg Paride Lorenzoni on board, WiA
90ª Sq, 10°Gr, 4°St CT	3 MC.202s MM 7906 '90-8', MM 7802 '90-9', MM 7801 '90-10' damaged by bombs at Fuka

Wednesday, 21 October 1942

Heavy clouds somewhat limited operations. However, at 0723 four Bf 109s of II./JG 27 scrambled, their pilots reporting meeting nine fighters and a single claim may have been made. At 0930 213 Squadron gave top cover to 33 Squadron escorting a TacR aircraft. Nine II.Gruppe Bf 109s were scrambled this time, three pilots attacking the 213 Squadron formation, one Hurricane being shot down by Lt Kientsch.

Nine Spitfires of 145 Squadron took off at 1215 on a 'de-lousing' mission ahead of 18 B-25s escorted by 12 Kittyhawks of 112 Squadron as top cover, to bomb LG.21; six 250 Squadron aircraft also involved in this escort, carried 500lb bombs. The Spitfire pilots encountered two pairs of Messerschmitts, Plt Off Barker claiming hits on one of these which span at very low altitude and crashed. Claims were also made for three Messerschmitts as probables, but one Spitfire failed to return. 112 Squadron passed nine fighters which banked over their airfield, and one Kittyhawk failed to return. 250 Squadron meanwhile was attacked over Gazala by 15 Bf 109s and MC.202s, one of this

One of the RAF's 'resident' Americans, of whom there were a goodly number, Flt Lt J.H. 'Crash' Curry was one of the more successful Spitfire pilots with 601 Squadron. On 21 October he claimed an MC.202 as his seventh victory (one of which had been shared).

This MC.202 '91-5' MM 7838 was shot down on 21 October. The pilot, Cap Ezio Bevilacqua, was killed.

unit's Kittyhawks also being lost, although the pilot returned safely on foot on the 24th.

Eight Bf 109s of III./JG 53 had scrambled at 1231, but the Regia Aeronautica was again the WDAF units' main opponents during this engagement. Between 1140-1300 nine MC.202s of 23° Gruppo had engaged British fighters, one P-40 and three probables plus a Spitfire as a probable being claimed. Macchi pilots of 9° and 10° Gruppi claimed four Spitfires and a probable. One 10° Gruppo aircraft was shot down, the pilot being killed. At this time also, Lt Harder of III./JG 53 claimed a P-40, but one Messerschmitt of II./JG 27 was lost in combat with Kittyhawks. It seems that a second escorted formation of bombers became involved whilst this engagement was still underway, 12 Kittyhawks of 260 Squadron providing top cover to six Bostons and 12 Baltimores at 1320, attacking LG.104. The Kittyhawk pilots reported that 15 Bf 109s and MC.202s appeared 500 feet above, but Flt Sgt Edwards was able to claim one Macchi shot down, the pilot baling out, with Flg Off Fallows claiming a probable. Spitfires of 601 Squadron had followed ten minutes later on an offensive sweep over the Daba-Fuka area; seeing the fight underway beneath them, they dived down, Flt Lt Curry also claiming a Macchi shot down. Given these circumstances it is quite likely that he had attacked the same aircraft as had Edwards.

The Italian airfield at Abu Haggag was attacked just after sunset, four MC.200s being destroyed and five damaged, with nine MC.202s also damaged to various degrees. At Qotaifiya a Bf 109 of III./JG 53 was also damaged on the ground. On this date 7 SAAF Squadron returned to operational readiness, now equipped with Hurricane IIds to operate in the tank-buster role with 6 Squadron again.

British Claims

145 Sqn	Plt Off F.R. Barker	Spitfire Vb AB339 'M'	Bf 109E	Daba-Fuka area	1215-1325
145 Sqn	Flt Lt V.P.Cannam	Spitfire Vb EP692	} Bf 109 Probable		1215-1325
145 Sq	Plt Off P.B.Laing-Meason	Spitfire Vb AR287			

145 Sqn	Plt Off L.A.Malins	Spitfire Vb BR389 'Z'	Bf 109 Probable	1215-1325	
145 Sqn	Sqn Ldr G.P.H.Matthews	Spitfire Vb EP618 'P'	Bf 109 Probable	1215-1325	
3 RAAF Sqn	Sqn Ldr R.H.Gibbes	Kittyhawk III FR305 'V'	Bf 109E Damaged	LG.21	1245
3 RAAF Sqn	Sgt A.J.Richardson	Kittyhawk I EV306 'O'	Bf 109E Damaged	LG.21	1250
260 Sqn	Flt Sgt J.F.Edwards	Kittyhawk IIa FL322 'V'	MC.202	LG.104	1320-1455
260 Sqn	Flg Off G.Fallows	Kittyhawk IIa	Bf 109 Probable	LG.104	1320-1455
260 Sqn	Sgt E.G.Hill	Kittyhawk IIa	Bf 109 Damaged	LG.104	1320-1455
260 Sqn	Flt Sgt W.E.Stewart	Kittyhawk IIa	Bf 109F Damaged	LG.104	1320-1455
260 Sqn	Sgt B.H.Thomas	Kittyhawk IIa	Bf 109F Damaged	LG.104	1320-1455
601 Sqn	Flt Lt J.H.Curry	Spitfire Vc AB345 'J'	MC.202	Daba-Fuka area	1330-1435

British Casualties

112 Sqn	Kittyhawk III FR236 'G' shot down nr Gazala; Sgt W.D.Hogg PoW
250 Sqn	Kittyhawk III FR240 'K' left 1240, shot down by Bf 109s over LG.21, crash-landed; Plt Off J.R.Falconer-Taylor walked back
213 Sqn	Hurricane IIc BP455 left 0920, damaged by Bf 109 and crash-landed nr El Alamein DBR; Plt Off W.H.Stephenson PoW
145 Sqn	Spitfire V AB207 left 1215, shot down by Bf 109 Daba-Fuka area; Sgt R.A.Cunningham KiA

German Claims

5./JG 27	Lt Willi Kientsch	P-40	SE El Daba	0850
7./JG 53	Lt Jürgen Harder	P-40	25km NW El Alamein	1157
6./JG 27	Lt Herfried Körner	P-40	SE El Daba	1240

German Casualties

7./JG 53	Bf 109F-4 trop WNr 8495 20% damaged on ground by bombs at Qotaifiya
9./JG 27	Bf 109F-4 trop WNr 8611 combat with P-40, force-landed Turbiya, 70%
4.(H)/12	Bf 109F-4 WNr 7223, crash-landed at Bir el Abd

Italian Claims

74ª Sq, 23°Gr, 3°St CT	Serg Dante Pancaldi	MC.202	P-40	Fuka	1140-1255
74ª Sq, 23°Gr, 3°St CT	Serg Magg Mario Mantelli	MC.202	Spitfire Probable	Fuka	1140-1255
75ª Sq, 23°Gr, 3°St CT	M.llo Gino Giannelli	MC.202	P-40 Probable	Fuka	1140-1255
75ª Sq, 23°Gr, 3°St CT	Serg Magg V. Cavicchioli	MC.202	P-40 Probable	Fuka	1140-1255
75ª Sq, 23°Gr, 3°St CT	Serg Luigi Bozzolan	MC.202	P-40 Probable	Fuka	1140-1255
91ª Sq, 10°Gr, 4°St CT	Ten Ezio Bevilacqua	MC.202 MM 7838	2 Spitfires	Fuka	1140-1255
84ª Sq, 10°Gr, 4°St CT	Serg Magg Luciano Perdoni	MC.202 '90-5'	Spitfire	Fuka	1140-1255
96ª Sq, 9°Gr, 4°St CT	Ten Enrico Moretto	MC.202	Spitfire		
96ª Sq, 9°Gr, 4°St CT	Ten Anselmo Maggini	MC.202	Spitfire Probable		

Italian Casualties

91ª Sq, 10°Gr, 4°St CT	MC.202 MM 7838 '91-5' shot down, Cap Ezio Bevilacqua KiA
97ª Sq, 9°Gr, 4°St CT	MC.202 MM 7939 '97-12' hit in combat, belly-landed, M.llo Fiorenzo Milella (96ª Sq) WiA
83ª Sq, 18°Gr, 3°St CT	MC.200 damaged on landing, Ten Carlo Tommasi safe
18°Gr, 3°St CT	4 MC.200s destroyed (MM 8841, 8187, 8132, 8172) and 5 MC.200s (including MM 8163, 8613, 8158, 8149) damaged by bombs at Abu Haggag
23°Gr, 3°St CT	MC.202 MM 8386 destroyed (74ª Sq) and 8 MC.202s damaged by bombs at Abu Haggag

Thursday, 22 October 1942

Three more raids were made on the Daba airfields during the day as WDAF fighters also began patrolling over the Axis landing grounds on a regular basis. The first attack was made on LG.20 by 18 Bostons, 233 Wing again providing the escort which included 12 Kittyhawks of 4 SAAF Squadron, departing at 0945. Eighteen Bf 109s of II./JG 27 and seven of III.Gruppe scrambled at around 1025, two Kittyhawks being shot down; Lt Lane of 4 SAAF Squadron failed to return.

At 1045 18 B-25s escorted by six Kittyhawks of 450 Squadron as close cover, ten of 3 RAAF Squadron as medium cover and others of 250 Squadron as top cover, set out to attack LG.104. Fifteen minutes later Spitfires from 145 Squadron, Kittyhawks of 112 Squadron and P-40Fs from the US 66th Squadron flew a 'de-lousing' mission over Daba in support of the bombers. Seven Bf 109s of II./JG 27 and four of III./JG 53 scrambled at 1117, followed a few minutes later by six from III./JG 27. 3 RAAF Squadron reported very heavy Flak over the target, nearly all the B-25s being hit. One did not return and this was thought to have fallen to Flak, but Hptm Rödel of II.Gruppe claimed a Mitchell and it seems likely that

Macchi '97-12' MM 7939 was damaged in combat on 21 October, but the pilot M.llo Milella, survived unhurt.

one of the bombers fell out of formation due to Flak damage and was then caught and shot down by this pilot. The Australians also reported seeing a Kittyhawk suffer a double Flak hit after which the pilot baled out. Two Bf 109s attacked after the bombing and Plt Off Neill was seen to go down, streaming glycol. Two aircraft of 450 Squadron were also shot down, thought to have collided under fire from Axis fighters. However, Sqn Ldr Judd and Plt Off Cairns of 250 Squadron saw two fighters which they attacked in a climb, each claiming one shot down, Cairns' victim being seen to bale out.

145 Squadron now appeared on the scene, but the Spitfires were attacked by ten fighters, Sgt Thomas being shot down. Flt Lt Taylor claimed a probable, two other pilots each claiming a fighter identified as a G.50 as a probable. There were at this time no aircraft of this type operating over the El Alamein area and no MC.200s seem to have been involved in this engagement, so the identity of these aircraft remains a mystery. 112 Squadron's pilots reported seeing four Bf 109s below them and dived to the attack, claiming one shot down, one probable and two damaged. During this engagement the Luftwaffe fighters also claimed three Allied aircraft shot down for the loss of two or three Bf 109s; Lt Bindert baled out, having been wounded. One more aircraft crash-landed at Turbiya and one force-landed at Qotaifiya, both fighters badly damaged. III./JG 53 also lost one aircraft destroyed and one damaged on the ground at Qotaifiya by bombs.

Meanwhile, a wing sweep carried out from 1215 by nine Spitfires of 92 Squadron and 12 Kittyhawks of 260 Squadron, encountered six Bf 109s of III./JG 27 which had been scrambled to meet this incursion, Uffz Krainik claiming one Curtiss fighter (P-46!) shot down. Sqn Ldr Wedgwood and Flg Off Waddy, DFC, who had just joined 92 Squadron after claiming 11 and one shared victories flying Tomahawks and Kittyhawks, each claimed one fighter shot down, as did Flt Sgt Edwards of 260 Squadron. Ten Axis fighters were reported altogether, and during the fight two of 260 Squadron's aircraft were damaged. During the early afternoon P-40Fs of the 66th Squadron, 57th Fighter Group set off on a fighter sweep during which one Messerschmitt was claimed as a probable. On this date, therefore, WDAF pilots had claimed seven Axis fighters shot down against actual losses of four.

Once more the 5ª Squadra Aerea Macchis had been heavily involved throughout the mid-morning-midday period, 9° and 10° Gruppi claiming six fighters shot down, all identified as Spitfires on this occasion. One MC.202 was lost, the pilot killed. At mid-morning 15 MC.202s of both Gruppi of 4° Stormo were scrambled to intercept a formation of 18 Bostons, escorted by about 25 Spitfires, heading to Fuka. In the clash that followed the British bombers were forced to jettison their bombs in the desert and three Spitfires were claimed, one each by Ten Mecatti and Ten Vanzan and another shared by Cap Piccolomini, Ten Libera, S.Ten Dell'Antonio and Serg Magg Molteni. Two MC.202s suffered minor damage. At 1135 eleven MC.202s of 4° Stormo, led by Cap Piccolomini, were again scrambled to face about 40 Spitfires, split in two formations at 16,000 and 20,000 feet. The Italian pilots climbed to 23,000 feet and bounced the higher formation of British fighters. M.llo Antonio Sacchi claimed a Spitfire but was shot down and baled out slightly wounded; Ten Giulio Reiner and Serg Teresio Martinoli claimed a Spitfire each. A few minutes later eight MC.202s of 10° Gruppo led by Ten Orlando Mandolini encountered the Spitfires and Serg Ferruccio Terrabuio claimed one.

1 SAAF Squadron had now moved to LG.172 during the day, ready to resume operations forthwith. The first sorties were made at once, escorting Hurricanes of 238 Squadron which were providing cover to a TacR aircraft. During the night Commonwealth assault infantry moved ahead of the Allied lines and dug in. They were to remain hidden throughout the whole of the following day, as air operations against the unsuspecting Axis continued. All serviceable aircraft of 3° Stormo were ordered to move from Abu Haggag, heavily bombed the day before, to Abu Smeit, just four miles away.

British Claims

250 Sqn	Plt Off D.W.Cairns	Kittyhawk III FR288	Bf 109F	Daba, LG.104	1045-1215
250 Sqn	Sqn Ldr M.T.Judd	Kittyhawk III FR291 'B'	Bf 109F	Daba, LG.104	1045-1215
145 Sqn	Plt Off H.J.Phillips	Spitfire Vb EP618 'P'	G.50 Probable	LG.104	1100-1210
145 Sqn	Flt Lt C.H.Saunders	Spitfire Vb AB502 'B'	Bf 109 Damaged	LG.104	1100-1210
145 Sqn	Flt Lt J.S.Taylor	Spitfire Vb EP327 'R'	Bf 109 Probable	LG.104	1100-1210
145 Sqn	Plt Off A.F.Wilson	Spitfire Vb BP981 'N'	G.50 Probable	LG.104	1100-1210
260 Sqn	Sgt J.C.Colley	Kittyhawk IIa	Bf 109F Damaged	Daba l.g.	1206-1336
260 Sqn	Flt Sgt J.F.Edwards	Kittyhawk IIa FL233 'O'	Bf 109F	Daba l.g.	1206-1336
260 Sqn	Sgt G.G.Rattle	Kittyhawk IIa	Bf 109F Probable	Daba l.g.	1206-1336
260 Sqn	Sgt G.G.Rattle	Kittyhawk IIa	Bf 109F Damaged	Daba l.g.	1206-1336
601 Sqn	Flg Off W.M.Whitamore	Spitfire Vc BR136 'H'	Bf 109	Daba area	1210-1320
92 Sqn	Flg Off J.L.Waddy	Spitfire Vb EP193 'U'	Bf 109	forward area	1255
92 Sqn	Sqn Ldr J.H.Wedgwood	Spitfire Vc BR476 'J'	Bf 109	forward area	1255
112 Sqn	Plt Off L.H.Curphey	Kittyhawk III FR195	Bf 109 Damaged	Daba l.g.	1445-1545
112 Sqn	Sqn Ldr B.Drake	Kittyhawk III FR293 '?'	Bf 109 Probable	Daba l.g.	1445-1545
112 Sqn	Capt E.C.Saville	Kittyhawk III FR214 'A'	Bf 109 Damaged	Daba l.g.	1445-1545
112 Sqn	Flt Lt R.R.Smith	Kittyhawk III FR217 'C'	Bf 109	Daba l.g.	1445-1545

US Claims

66th FS/57th FG	2/Lt Richard W.Kimball	P-40F '84'	Bf 109 Probable	Fuka	1445-1555

British Casualties

450 Sqn	Kittyhawk III FR249 bomber escort, shot down by fighters nr Daba at 1145; Sgt G.Lindsay PoW
450 Sqn	Kittyhawk III FR298 bomber escort, shot down by fighters nr Daba at 1145; Sgt J.D.Evans PoW
260 Sqn	Kittyhawk IIa badly damaged by Bf 109 NE El Alamein; Sgt G.G.Rattle safe
260 Sqn	Kittyhawk IIa damaged by Bf 109 NE El Alamein; Sgt J.C.Colley safe
3 RAAF Sqn	Kittyhawk I ET1016 'B' left 1045 shot down by fighters nr Daba 1145; Plt Off G.A.Neill DFM, MiA
4 SAAF Sqn	Kittyhawk I ET964 'W' shot down by fighters at 1045; Lt J. de la H.Lane KiA
145 Sqn	Spitfire V BP986 'X' left 1100, shot down by Bf 109 LG.104; Sgt C.P.Taylor

US Casualties

83rd BS/12th BG	B-25C '52' shot down over target, 1/Lt J.L.Cleary and three PoW, one MiA

German Claims

9./JG 27	Oblt Hans-Joachim Heinecke	P-40	NNE El Daba	0942
5./JG 27	Uffz Hans Jürgens	P-40	WNW El Alamein	0950
7./JG 53	Lt Jürgen Harder	P-40	20km SE Qotaifiya	1027
7./JG 27	Fw Viktor Gruber	P-46	W Turbiya	1030
8./JG 53	Uffz Jens Bahnsen	P-40	SSE Qotaifiya	1040
Stab II./JG 27	Hptm Gustav Rödel	B-25	SW El Alamein	1045
8./JG 27	Uffz Erich Krainik	P-46	N El Alamein	
Flak		3 a/c by day		

German Casualties

Stab II./JG 27	Bf 109G-2 trop WNr 10583 White 1 combat with P-40, crashed nr Bir el Abd; Lt Erich Bindert baled, hurt
9./JG 53	Bf 109F-4/Z WNr 7582 destroyed on ground by bombs at Qotaifiya
9./JG 53	Bf 109F-4/Z WNr 7407 20% damaged on ground by bombs at Qotaifiya
7./JG 27	Bf 109F-4 trop WNr 10162 combat, force-landed Qotaifiya 60%
8./JG 27	Bf 109F-4 WNr 7220 combat, crash-landed Turbiya 65%
1./SchG 2	Bf 109F-4 WNr 8637 White 11 shot down by AA, crashed 10km S El Alamein; Fw Bernhard May PoW
1./SchG 2	Bf 109F-4 WNr 7111 White 9 shot down by AA, crashed 10km S El Alamein; Uffz Rudi Tacke MiA
4.(H)/12	Bf 109F-4 WNr 7569 crash-landed at Bir el Abd, 45% damaged, pilot safe

Italian Claims

73ª Sq, 9°Gr, 4°St CT	Ten Mario Mecatti	MC.202	Spitfire	E Fuka	1020-1105
90ª Sq, 10°Gr, 4°St CT	Ten Virgilio Vanzan	MC.202	Spitfire	E Fuka	1020-1105
90ª Sq, 10°Gr, 4°St CT	Ten Sforza Libera	MC.202	} Spitfire	E Fuka	1020-1105
90ª Sq, 10°Gr, 4°St CT	Cap Ranieri Piccolomini	MC.202			
90ª Sq, 10°Gr, 4°St CT	Ten Piero Dell'Antonio	MC.202			
90ª Sq, 10°Gr, 4°St CT	Serg Magg Natale Molteni	MC.202			
73ª Sq, 9°Gr, 4°St CT	Ten Giulio Reiner	MC.202	Spitfire Probable	Fuka	1140-1230
73ª Sq, 9°Gr, 4°St CT	Ten Giulio Reiner	MC.202	Spitfire Damaged	Fuka	1140-1230
73ª Sq, 9°Gr, 4°St CT	Serg Teresio Martinoli	MC.202	Spitfire	Fuka	1140-1230
96ª Sq, 9°Gr, 4°St CT	M.llo Antonio Sacchi	MC.202 MM 7786	Spitfire	Fuka	1140-1230
91ª Sq, 10°Gr, 4°St CT	Serg Ferruccio Terrabuio	MC.202	Spitfire	Fuka	1415-1515

Italian Casualties

97ª Sq, 9°Gr, 4°St CT	MC.202 MM 7786 '97-2' shot down, M.llo Antonio Sacchi KiA

Friday, 23 October 1942

The first mission was flown at 0705 when 11 Kittyhawks of 450 Squadron set off with others of 3 RAAF Squadron on a wing fighter-bomber attack on LGs. 20 and 104 at Daba. From this raid Flg Off Marting failed to return and Sgt Prowse crash-landed – though in his case due to engine failure. At 0836 ten Bf 109s of II./JG 27 scrambled, followed four minutes later by five from III./ JG 27 and six from III./JG 53. 5 SAAF Squadron Tomahawks had departed at 0805 to patrol over Daba, II.Gruppe pilots reporting meeting 12 Allied fighters north-east of El Alamein, one of which was claimed shot down at 0855, but one Messerschmitt was damaged, Uffz Jürgens force-landing. The other German units met a reported 20 fighters in the same area, where Lt Schroer claimed two more at 0900. Three more II.Gruppe aircraft took off at 0911, these pilots also reporting 20-30 fighters near Daba. Fw Schneider claimed one of these shot down at 0923, the pilot baling out. The South African pilots claimed two Bf 109s shot down and two damaged, but lost 2/Lt Nolte shot down and killed by two Bf 109s in the Sidi Abd el Rahman area at about 0840.

2 SAAF Squadron Kittyhawks escorted Kittybombers to the area from 0930, encountering MC.202s during this sortie which damaged two of the squadron's aircraft Cat I. Six Kittyhawks of 450 Squadron then swept over Daba between 1000-1200, being intercepted by eight Bf 109s of II.Gruppe over that unit's airfield where the Australian pilots claimed two shot down; Gefr Schmidt-Rex force-landed at Daba after the engine of his aircraft had been hit. Around midday 12 Kittyhawks of 260 Squadron covered 5 SAAF Squadron on a sweep over Daba, nine Spitfires of 145 Squadron and nine of 601 Squadron flying high cover. Four fighters attacked the Spitfires over Daba, Flt Lt Curry claiming one damaged. Two claims for Bf 109s were also submitted by Sqn Ldr Matthews and Flt Sgt MacArthur Powers at this time. However, Wt Off Tomlinson of 260 Squadron failed to return and Sgt Colley force-landed. Twelve Messerschmitts of II.Gruppe, four of III.Gruppe and one of III./JG 53 had been scrambled this time, but were only able to claim one possible victory which was not confirmed.

Italian units were again very active during this morning period, 23° Gruppo claiming one P-40, one probable and four damaged between 0905-1000; during mid-morning 9° Gruppo claimed three P-40s, two Spitfires and an Airacobra (probably a P-40F). 2 SAAF Squadron aircraft took off on a Kittybomber raid at 1330 during which Lt de Villiers attacked a Bf 109 low over LG.21. It seems that this landed, and although he reported that it was burning on the ground, he was allowed only a damaged in respect of it. At 1355 Cap Lucchini led a formation of eleven MC.202s of 10° Gruppo (five of 84ª and six of 90ª Squadriglie) to intercept raiders heading to Fuka. 20 P-40s and 20 Spitfires were met and engaged,

Lucchini and Ten De Seta (who was flying 97ª Squadriglia aircraft, '97-5') claiming one P-40 plus a probable, for the loss of Serg Ugazio, who baled out of his damaged Macchi.

At 1500 Hurricanes of 33 and 213 Squadrons took off, covered by Kittyhawks of 260 Squadron and Tomahawks of 5 SAAF Squadron, with Spitfires of 145 and 601 Squadrons above. Four Bf 109s of II./JG 27 had taken off at the same time to escort Jabo aircraft, but they engaged the Allied fighters over Daba at about 1600, at around the same time as MC.202s of 10° Gruppo became engaged. Attacking the lower squadron, Oblt Sommer claimed a Spitfire while two Macchi pilots shared a P-40. A reported 18 Bf 109s were encountered at 17,000 feet, with MC.202s also present. Sgt Lionel Sheppard of 260 Squadron:

Lionel Sheppard began operations with 260 Squadron as a Sgt; he was later commissioned and awarded a DFC. He describes here his experiences on 23 October.

"In the afternoon we did another patrol over Daba but the ME 109s and Macchi 202s were up in strength and in amongst us. Everything happens quickly in a dogfight. Turning to face the attack suddenly there is one right in front of me, a Macchi 202. So I get after it, get in a good burst and that was the end of him. Officially my first outright 'kill'. I then got after another, a ME 109 this time, but he dived away and I followed. The Kittyhawk was much heavier than the ME109, and faster when diving and as he turned towards the left, heading back presumably to Fuka, I was able to cut inside him and give him a good burst. He pulled up I believe with the intention of jumping out but, suddenly, there was a 'ping' and I realised I had picked up a bullet from somewhere and oil began leaking over my windscreen so I was unable to see the end result of my attack, although there is no doubt in my mind that I scored a second kill.

"I made out to sea and was out about five miles down on the deck skimming the waves and out of ammunition, when a third enemy aircraft turned up. Every few seconds he would have a little burst and I would see the water jumping up all around the aircraft, but he knew that he needed to go lower to get me, and if he did he would become a submarine and near to the line, he pushed off.

"The engine finally gave up the ghost and I turned in along the coast, executing a belly-landing on the beach, wheels up, about eight miles east of El Alamein just as the engine caught fire. I had the good fortune to land on the beach right by a casualty clearing station, and an Australian pulled me out of the cockpit and put a bottle of gin in my hand. He obviously thought I needed it more than him! As I appeared to be all right with no obvious damage, I was taken to the Senior Officers Mess for tea and had a great deal of fuss made of me. Later I was given a lift up to the main road in the hope of hitching a lift back to the squadron."

Two more of his unit's aircraft were damaged, with a 33 Squadron Hurricane shot down, the pilot baling out; he returned safely later. The stage was now set for the final action in the Western Desert; large Allied reinforcements had now been received so that Montgomery's forces for the first time considerably outnumbered those of the Axis in overall strength of all arms, and supplies of the new and superior Sherman tank had arrived, greatly enhancing the power of the armoured divisions. These new vehicles had been provided urgently from the USA by the good offices of President Franklin D.Roosevelt, following the fall of Tobruk. Many had been taken from the US Army's own divisions which had just begun receiving them.

The air forces were at their zenith in strength and experience, the Allies being able to call on 605 fighters, 254 light and medium bombers, and 61 heavy bombers compared to the Axis totals of 247 fighters, 72 dive-bombers and 171 medium bombers. Many of the latter were Italian, and overall serviceability was not as high as in the WDAF. At this moment the whole future of the war hung in the balance, with the British at El Alamein and the Russians at Stalingrad prepared to go firmly onto the offensive. The pendulum of fate was about to swing in favour of the Allies.

British Claims

5 SAAF Sqn	Capt R.F.Armstrong	Tomahawk IIb AN291 'N'	Bf 109G	8m NE Sidi Abd el Rahman	0900
5 SAAF Sqn	Lt R.C.Hirst	Tomahawk IIb AN225 'O'	Bf 109G	8m NE Sidi Abd el Rahman	0900
5 SAAF Sqn	Lt A.C.Joubert	Tomahawk IIb AK434 'H'	Bf 109G Damaged	8m NE Sidi Abd el Rahman	0900
5 SAAF Sqn	Lt P.F.Cowen	Tomahawk IIb AM382 'V'	Bf 109G Damaged	8m NE Sidi Abd el Rahman	0915
33 Sqn	Plt Off L.H.Peterson	Hurricane IIc BP130 'R'	Bf 109	sweep, N El Alamein	0945
450 Sqn	Sgt J.D.Gleeson	Kittyhawk III FR212	Bf 109F	Daba area	1100-1215
450 Sqn	Flt Lt F.R.Schaaf	Kittyhawk III FR270	Bf 109F	Daba area	1100-1215
145 Sqn	Sqn Ldr G.P.H.Matthews	Spitfire Vb BR477	Bf 109	sweep to Daba	1200-1315
145 Sqn	Flt Sgt MacA.Powers	Spitfire Vb EP618 'P'	Bf 109	sweep to Daba	1200-1315
601 Sqn	Flg Off W.M.Whitamore	Spitfire Vc BR136 'H'	MC.202	N Daba	1200-1315
2 SAAF Sqn	Lt T.V.de Villiers	Kittyhawk	BF 109 Damaged	LG.20	1415
601 Sqn	Plt Off D.E.Llewellyn	Spitfire Vc BR136 'H'	Bf 109F	N Daba	1455-1610
601 Sqn	Flt Lt J.H.Curry	Spitfire Vc BR583	Bf 109 Damaged	N Daba	1455-1610
260 Sqn	Sgt L.J.Sheppard	Kittyhawk IIa	MC.202	Daba area	1505-1605

British Casualties

33 Sqn	Hurricane IIc HL907 FTR from sweep Daba, shot down by Bf 109 at 0930; Sgt S.L.Pointon baled out
73 Sqn	Hurricane BP167 shot down by own AA at night; Sgt R.Harris
94 Sqn	Hurricane BE197 SOC, enemy action
260 Sqn	Kittyhawk IIa FL238 'E' shot down by Bf 109s over Daba,1200-1315; Plt Off L.P.Mink safe
260 Sqn	Kittyhawk IIa FL314 shot down by Bf 109s over Daba, 1200-1315; Wt Off E.K.Tomlinson KiA
260 Sqn	Kittyhawk IIa badly damaged by MC.202 nr Daba, crash-landed 1200-1315; Sgt J.C.Colley safe
260 Sqn	Kittyhawk IIa FL233 'T' badly damaged by MC.202 nr Daba, 1600; Flg Off E.G.Aitchison safe
260 Sqn	Kittyhawk IIa badly damaged by MC.202s Daba, forced to land 1600; Sgt L.J.Sheppard safe
260 Sqn	Kittyhawk IIa 'X' badly damaged by MC.202s, 1600; Plt Off J.H.Thornhill safe
450 Sqn	Kittyhawk III FR309 shot down by a lone Bf 109 nr Daba; Flg Off H.F.Marting PoW escaped
2 SAAF Sqn	2 Kittyhawk Is slt damaged by MC.202s
5 SAAF Sqn	Tomahawk IIb AK405 shot down by 2 Bf 109s 0840 5m from El Alamein; 2/Lt I.H.Nolte KiA

German Claims

5./JG 27	Lt Willi Kientsch	P-40	NE El Alamein	0755
8./JG 27	Lt Werner Schroer	2 P-46s	NE & SE El Alamein	0800 & 0830
5./JG 27	Fw Bernhard Schneider	P-40	NW El Alamein	0823
4./JG 27	Oblt Paul Sommer	Spitfire	E El Daba	1500

German Casualties

5./JG 27	Bf 109F-4 trop WNr 10058 shot-up in combat, force-landed 100%; pilot safe
5./JG 27	Bf 109F-4 WNr 7208 force-landed El Daba 40% damaged; Gefr Schmidt-Rex safe
7./JG 53	Bf 109F-4/Z WNr 7374 20% damaged on ground by bombs at Qotaifiya
8./JG 53	Bf 109F-4 trop WNr 8606 50% damaged on ground by bombs at Qotaifiya

Italian Claims

74ª Sq, 23°Gr, 3°St CT	Ten Giorgio Solaroli	MC.202	P-40 Probable	NE El Daba	0905-1000
75ª Sq, 23°Gr, 3°St CT	M.llo Gino Giannelli	MC.202	P-40	NE El Daba	0905-1000
70ª Sq, 23°Gr, 3°St CT	Cap Claudio Solaro	MC.202	2 P-40s Damaged	NE El Daba	0905-1000
70ª Sq, 23°Gr, 3°St CT	Serg Magg Celso Zemella	MC.202	P-40 Damaged	NE El Daba	0905-1000

70ª Sq, 23°Gr, 3°St CT	Ten Marco Marinone	MC.202	P-40 Damaged	NE El Daba	0905-1000
73ª Sq, 9°Gr, 4°St CT	Serg Magg A.Angelini	MC.202	P-40		
73ª Sq, 9°Gr, 4°St CT	Serg Magg L.Rinaldi	MC.202	P-40		
73ª Sq, 9°Gr, 4°St CT	Ten Giulio Reiner	MC.202	Spitfire	El Daba	mid morning
73ª Sq, 9°Gr, 4°St CT	Ten Giulio Reiner	MC.202	Spitfire Probable	El Daba	mid morning
73ª Sq, 9°Gr, 4°St CT	Ten Mario Mecatti	MC.202	P-40	El Daba	mid morning
73ª Sq, 9°Gr, 4°St CT	Ten Vittorio Squarcia	MC.202	Spitfire	El Daba	mid morning
73ª Sq, 9°Gr, 4°St CT	Serg Teresio Martinoli	MC.202	Airacobra	El Daba	mid morning
84ª Sq, 10°Gr, 4°St CT	Cap Franco Lucchini	MC.202 MM 7919 }	P-40	Fuka	1355-1545
84ª Sq, 10°Gr, 4°St CT	Ten Francesco De Seta	MC.202 MM 7916 }			
84ª Sq, 9°Gr, 4°St CT	Serg Magg Corrado Patrizi	MC.202 MM7933	P-40 Probable	Fuka	1355-1545

Italian Casualties

84ª Sq, 10°Gr, 4°St CT	MC.202 MM 7808 '91-9' hit and destroyed, Serg Roberto Ugazio baled and WiA, returned next day
208ª Sq, 101°Gr, 5°St Tuff	CR.42 damaged by AA crash-landed near El Daba, Serg Magg Giuseppe Salvioli safe

The Alamein Line, October 1942

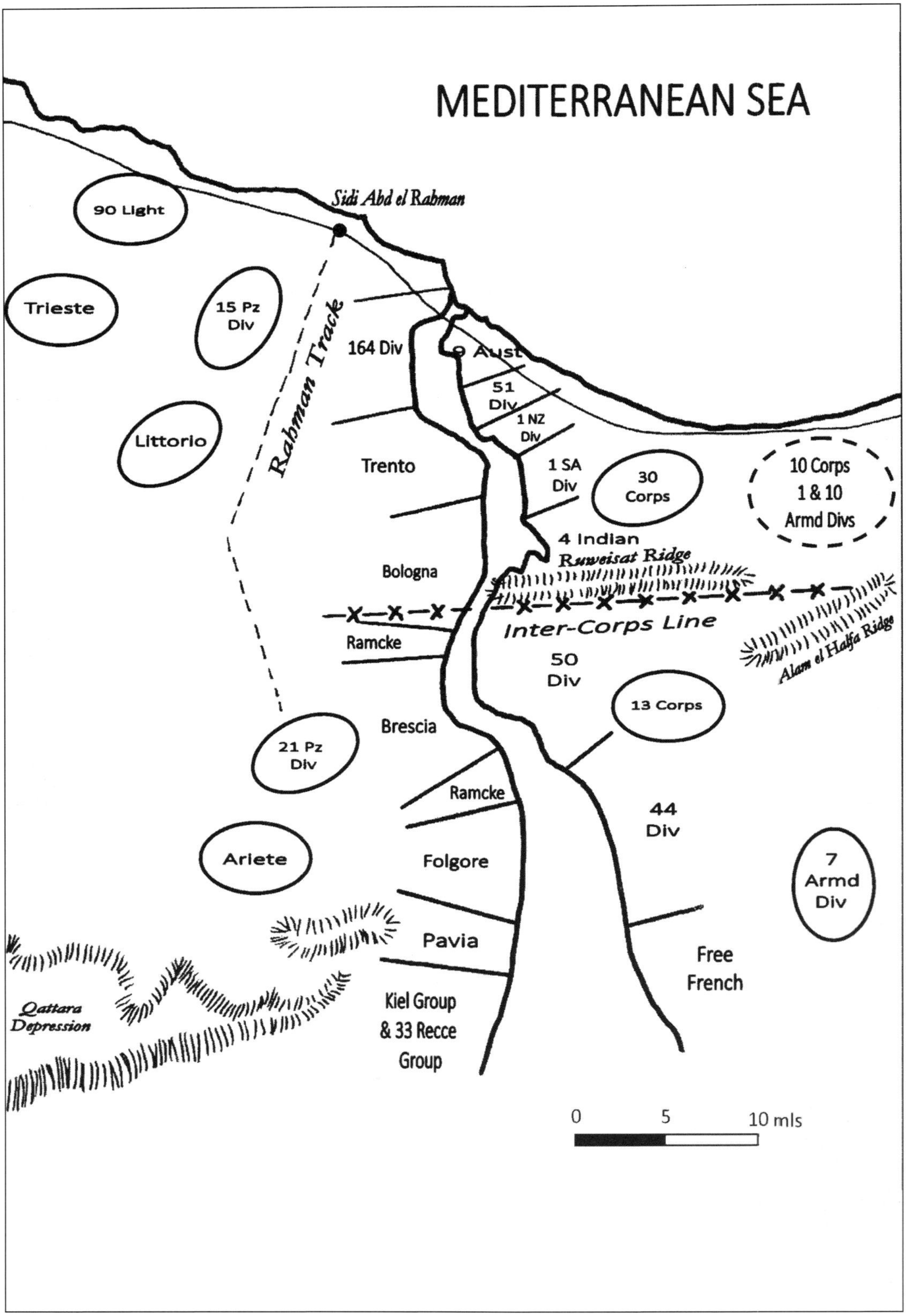

CHAPTER 7

THE BATTLE OF EL ALAMEIN

At 2140 hours on the night of 23 October 1942 more than 1,000 British guns opened the greatest barrage since World War I on the narrow front between the Qattara Depression in the south and the Mediterranean Sea at El Alamein in the north. Twenty minutes later the assaulting infantry climbed out of their trenches and moved forward towards the west; the Battle of El Alamein had commenced. In the air 73 Squadron was first into the fray, carrying out many strafing sorties during the hours of darkness. Two paths were cleared through the Allied minefields, as 1st and 10th Armoured Divisions moved up. The initial attempt to break out proved abortive, however, as did that of 7th Armoured Division near Himeimat in the south. As ever, the Axis anti-tank defences proved dauntingly difficult to overcome.

Saturday, 24 October 1942

Dawn came just before 0700, Hurricanes of 33 Squadron, covered by 1 SAAF Squadron, taking off on an early patrol. Nine Bf 109s of II./JG 27 were scrambled, approaching the rear of the 1 SAAF formation from out to sea. Seeing them, Lt Lanham closed in on Capt Bredenkamp in a turn, and cut off the tail of the latter's aircraft with his propeller; Bredenkamp's aircraft dived vertically out of control, the pilot baling out as Lanham carried out a force-landing. Fw Steis, obviously under the impression that he had caused one of the Hurricanes to crash, claimed a victory.

The aircraft in which Cap Franco Lucchini claimed a victory on 24 October 1942. He had claimed 21 individual victories by the end of the war.

Hurricane IId 'tank-buster' of 6 Squadron, showing off its main armament of a pair of 37mm cannons.

During the attack Lt Pryde saw a Bf 109 firing at a Hurricane and shot at it, hitting it on the fuselage and tail. He was then jumped by two more Bf 109s and did not notice what had happened to his target. Two pilots had been watching Bredenkamp's parachute descending to 4,000 feet, but they reported that 12 minutes after he had baled out, they saw a parachute at 10,000 feet. After 212 Group had checked that no combat had taken place in the area at the time, and that Pryde's engagement had occurred at 12,000 feet, the latter was credited with a Bf 109 destroyed. Despite this, no Luftwaffe losses appear to have occurred at this time. However, during the day an MC.202 of 23ª Gruppo was hit in combat, the pilot being wounded.

At 0850 Bostons of 24 SAAF Squadron carried out a raid during which they were intercepted by four Bf 109s of III./JG 27 on a Freie Jagd. Two Bostons collided and one, damaged, was forced to leave the formation, whereupon it was shot down by fighters. Another of the unit's aircraft was shot down, reportedly by Flak, crashing and blowing up, with a third damaged. During the day 12 SAAF Squadron also reported the loss of two Bostons to Flak and a third damaged, while 223 Squadron also recorded that Flak was the cause of the loss of a Baltimore which fell in flames attacking tanks and vehicles. Despite only one bomber having fallen to fighters, three were claimed by German fighter pilots, all during this morning period. It was the first time in many weeks that such heavy bomber losses had been suffered. On this date, however, WDAF fighter losses proved to be quite light.

Nevertheless, apart from Steis's early claim, seven more claims for fighters were made by pilots of JG 27, mostly during the morning engagements; additionally 9° and 10° Gruppi claimed three P-40s and two B-25s between 1000-1115 for the loss of one MC.202 crash-landed. Cap Lucchini had led nine MC.202s, three of 84ª and six of 96ª Squadriglie, on a free sweep east of El Alamein at 0900. A formation of 25 B-25s, covered by about 40 P-40s, was intercepted, and at the end of a combat lasting 20 minutes one Mitchell and two P-40s were claimed, plus several others damaged. Two Macchis returned early after the pilots had experienced heavy vibrations in the tailplanes of their aircraft. The remaining seven as soon as they landed were refuelled and took off again, led by Ten Annoni. The Mitchells and their escort were once more engaged and Serg Biagini claimed one more bomber and another fighter shot down. Eight Bf 109s of II./JG 27 carried out a Freie Jagd at 1100, meeting 18 bombers and 30 escorting Curtiss fighters, Hptm Rödel claiming three of the latter between 1143 -1150.

At 1645 nine Spitfires of 601 Squadron took off to patrol over the Daba-El Alamein area. Half an hour later six Bf 109s of II.Gruppe and five of III./JG 27 set off on a Freie Jagd mission, and at 1725 Hurricanes of 33 and 1 SAAF Squadrons were off again for their fourth patrol of the day. These various formations clashed, 601 Squadron losing Wt Off Bowerman who was seen to spin during a turn. Flt Lt Ayerst of 33 Squadron claimed a Bf 109, Lt Kientsch of II.Gruppe and Lt Schroer of III.Gruppe each claiming an Allied fighter. Oblt Unger of III./ZG 1 was shot down by AA five miles north of Himeimat, his Bf 109E crashing. During the day the TacR aircraft of 40 SAAF Squadron returned to operations, and 335 Squadron moved to LG.37. In 4 SAAF Squadron a welcome reinforcement was the arrival of Lt D.Golding, DFC, to commence a second tour with his old unit.

British Claims

1 SAAF Sqn	Lt I.R.Pryde	Hurricane IIc HL885 'Z'	Bf 109F	W Sidi Abd el Rahman	0725
250 Sqn	Plt Off H.Stewart	Kittyhawk III FR282 'V'	MC.202 Damaged	Daba area	1000-1115
601 Sqn	Plt Off B.R.Terry	Spitfire Vc BR134	MC.202 Damaged	Daba area	1330-1450
33 Sqn	Flt Lt P.V.Ayerst	Hurricane IIc BP130 'R'	Bf 109	N sector, El Alamein line	1730-1840

British Casualties

1 SAAF Sqn	Hurricane IIc HL911 'D' collided with HL807; 2/Lt J.M.Bredenkamp baled out into Allied lines, a/c fell in Axis positions
1 SAAF Sqn	Hurricane IIc HL807 'E' collided with HL911; Lt J.R.Lanham crash-landed nr El Alamein, a/c repairable
1 SAAF Sqn	Hurricane IIc HL885 'Z' damaged by Bf 109s at 0725; Lt B.Rose-Christie safe
5 SAAF Sqn	Tomahawk IIb engine cut and force-landed 10m SE Burg el Arab; Lt A.W.Merrick safe
7 SAAF Sqn	Hurricane IId BN967 damaged by Flak during anti-tank strafe; slt damaged, undercarriage collapsed on landing; Lt O.J.Kelly safe
223 Sqn	Baltimore III AG854 'Q' attacking vehicles and tanks W Sidi Abd el Rahman track; hit by heavy Flak and shot down in flames S target; Flt Sgt A.G.De Clerck and 3 KiA
12 SAAF Sqn	Boston III Z2291 'E' badly damaged by Flak over target and crashed 20km W El Alamein 0943; Lt A.C.E.Glendinning and three PoW
12 SAAF Sqn	Boston IIIa 31-19402 leading formation hit by Flak over target at 1440 and fell out of formation with port engine on fire. Crew of three baled out safely; pilot, Capt R.H.F.Howarth thrown clear when port wing broke off; crashed 26km W El Alamein
12 SAAF Sqn	Boston III damaged
24 SAAF Sqn	Boston III Z2237 'Z' off 0849 to attack 15th Panzer Div at El Alamein; collided over target with Boston and forced out of formation; attacked and shot down by fighters at 0930 Lt H.H.Roberts and one KiA, two safe
24 SAAF Sqn	Boston III AL727 'S' heavy and accurate Flak over target; crashed near beach, blowing up on impact. Lt B.Nichols and one KiA; two survived, WiA
24 SAAF Sqn	Boston III damaged
94 Sqn	Hurricane BP389 stalled and crashed in spin 9m W El Gamil
601 Sqn	Spitfire V BR583 left 1635, shot down by MC.202, spun into ground nr Daba; Wt Off O.R.Bowerman KiA
15 SAAF Sqn	Bisley BA335 crashed in flames, Kufra Oasis

US Casualties

83rd BS/12nd BG	B-25D 41-29685 '31', took off 1530, collided with another B-25 and crashed; 1/Lt T.E.Witt and four KiA
83rd BS/12nd BG	B-25C 41-12875 '37', damaged by Flak, crashed 15m S Burg el Arab; Col Low and crew rescued, one WiA

German Claims

4./JG 27	Fw Heinrich Steis	Spitfire	WSW El Alamein	0645
8./JG 27	Lt Werner Schroer	P-40	NE El Alamein	0825
4./JG 27	Fw Alfred Heidel	DB-7	SW El Alamein	0844
9./JG 27	Obfw Johannes Scheit	DB-7	15km NW El Alamein	0845
8./JG 27	Uffz Erich Krainik	DB-7	SW El Alamein	
Stab II./JG 27	Hptm Gustav Rödel	3 P-40s	SW, WSW & SE El Alamein	0943, 0945 & 0950
5./JG 27	Lt Willi Kientsch	P-40	SE El Alamein	1640
8./JG 27	Lt Werner Schroer	Hurricane	SW El Alamein	1645

German Casualties

7./JG 27	Bf 109F-4 trop combat El Alamein area, 100%; Oblt Willi Althof WiA
8./JG 27	Bf 109F-4 WNr 7568 damaged and force-landed 25km S Mosque Sidi Abd el Rahman, 100%; pilot MiA, but returned
7./ZG 1	Bf 109E-7 WNr 2682 S9+AR shot down by AA 3km N Himeimat; Oblt Rolf Unger MiA
III./ZG 1	BF 109E-7 3393 crash-landed at Bir el Abd; pilot safe

Italian Claims

84ª Sq, 10°Gr, 4°St CT	Cap Franco Lucchini	MC.202 MM 7919 '84-12'	P-40	W El Alamein	0900-1010
84ª Sq, 10°Gr, 4°St CT	Ten Paolo Berti	MC.202 MM 7805 '84-2'			
84ª Sq, 10°Gr, 4°St CT	S.Ten Francesco De Seta	MC.202 MM 7907 '91-7'			

Italian Claims						
96ª Sq, 9°Gr, 4°St CT	Ten Emanuele Annoni	MC.202	}	P-40	W El Alamein	0900-1015
96ª Sq, 9°Gr, 4°St CT	S.Ten Alberto Giampaoli	MC.202				
96ª Sq, 9°Gr, 4°St CT	Ten Anselmo Maggini	MC.202				
4° St CT	6 previous pilots			B-25	W El Alamein	0900-1015
96ª Sq, 9°Gr, 4°St CT	Serg Magg Bruno Biagini	MC.202		B-25	W El Alamein	1030-
96ª Sq, 9°Gr, 4°St CT	Serg Magg Bruno Biagini	MC.202		P-40	W El Alamein	1030-

Italian Casualties	
84ª Sq, 10°Gr, 4°St CT	MC.202 MM 7919 '84-12' hit in combat and crash-landed, Cap Franco Lucchini WiA
75ª Sq, 23°Gr, 3°St CT	MC.202 hit in combat, Ten Mario Pallotta WiA

Sunday, 25 October 1942

WDAF was again heavily committed, breaking up attempts by the Axis to concentrate their forces on the ground for counter-attacks. The light bombers were out all through the day, maintaining an almost constant stream of bombing attacks. Six MC.202s of 4° Stormo, led by Cap Piccolomini, were scrambled at 0815 from Fuka. Jumped by ten Spitfires flying much higher, they managed to evade the attack, claiming some hits on four of the British fighters. Seven Bf 109s of II./JG 27 took off at 0830 on a Freie Jagd, engaging eight Spitfires near El Alamein, followed by 18 bombers with escorts. Hptm Düllberg claimed one fighter at 0941, but Lt Boden was shot down and killed, Obfw Scheit was shot down and baled out, and Uffz Schelper's aircraft somersaulted on landing.

Escorting one bombing raid by 12 Bostons and six Baltimores on LG.21, the 57th Fighter Group's 64th Squadron provided nine P-40Fs and three P-40Ks as escort. Six or more Messerschmitts attacked, the US pilots enjoying considerable success, claims being submitted on return for three shot down and three damaged, all without loss. The unit would go out again at 1230, this time the eight aircraft involved all carrying 500lb bombs; 12 more of the Group's aircraft provided cover. After bombing LG.20, the 64th's aircraft were attacked by five or so fighters, Lt Middleditch spotting two on the tail of another of the unit's aircraft, one of which he claimed to have shot down into the sea, witnessed by three other pilots.

At 1030 four Spitfires of 601 Squadron swept over Daba, their pilots spotting ten Bf 109s comprised of six in a lower flight and four forming top cover. They attacked the latter, claiming a probable and a damaged. Plt Off Ibbotson then saw three more below them at 25,000 feet, claiming one of these damaged also. These pilots reported on return that they had seen a crashed B-25 carrying the number '36' on the fin.

Then at 1210 Cap Ruspoli led a patrol of 10° Gruppo MC.202s to intercept some raiders, soon joined by five Macchis of 73ª Squadriglia led by Ten Reiner. Together, they engaged 21 Bostons with the customary escort of P-40s and Spitfires. Two P-40s and two Spitfires were claimed, without losses on the Italian side.

Four Bf 109s of III./JG 53 flew a Freie Jagd at 1233, encountering two Spitfires near El Alamein; Uffz Wanneck force-landed near Daba Station. There was a fair amount of fighting during this period of the day, 260 Squadron Kittyhawk pilots claiming an MC.202 and one damaged, while pilots of 145 Squadron claimed a Bf 109, a probable and a damaged.

Wrote Lionel Sheppard:

> "Bomber Escort – Top Cover squadron and again, I was leading the middle flight. A few minutes before the bombers reached the target area, I saw three Macchi 202s moving into position to attack. As we turned in to attack there was a bit of a mix-up between ourselves and I ended up flying No.4 in the box to the three Macchis. I do not know what happened to my No.2, or to the other pair in the flight, but my attention was on the Macchis who had now lost interest in the bombers. Lining up on the leader was simply a matter of getting him in the ring sight and giving him a good burst, but as he went down it alerted the remaining two who went off again at a rate of knots and, although I got a good burst in at the second, I could not be absolutely sure that I had got him. However, as the two Macchis dived away, I managed a burst at the third but when you fire an especially large number of rounds of ammunition you lose some speed and so I had no hope of catching up with them again, although in my heart I felt I had got the second and possibly damaged the third. I also realised that I was on my own and well over the enemy lines. It is quite strange when one minute the sky is full of aircraft – bombers, enemy aircraft and our own, the fighters milling around to get some advantage – and then suddenly, the sky is empty and you are the only one there, but for how long?"

There were a couple more clashes during the afternoon, 3 RAAF Squadron submitting a claim for a damaged Macchi at 1420, and two or more hours later Flt Lt Morgan of 92 Squadron claimed a further Bf 109.

Attempts were made during the day by the 4th, 7th and 10th Armoured Divisions to break out through the Axis minefields and defences. But these were abandoned after heavy losses were suffered to German anti-tank guns. 1st Armoured Division pushed west in the Kidney Ridge area, 9th Australian Division attacking in the north. Only in the latter area was a small amount of success achieved by nightfall.

British Claims

145 Sqn	Flt Lt C.H.Saunders	Spitfire Vb EP692	Bf 109	El Alamein	0805-0930
145 Sqn	Flg Off I.H.R.Shand	Spitfire Vb BP978 'Z'	Bf 109 Damaged	El Alamein	0805-0930
145 Sqn	Flg Off I.H.R.Shand	Spitfire Vb BP97 'Z'	Bf 109 Probable	El Alamein	0805-0930
145 Sqn	Sgt J.A.Greaves	Spitfire Vb AB168 'L'	2 Bf 109s Probable	El Alamein	0825-0925
260 Sqn	Sgt D.W.C.England	Kittyhawk IIa	MC.202 Damaged		0900-1020
260 Sqn	Sgt L.J.Sheppard	Kittyhawk IIa	MC.202		0900-1020
601 Sqn	Plt Off A.R.Boyle	Spitfire Vc EP303	s/e fighter Probable	Daba area	0930-1025
601 Sqn	Plt Off D.Ibbotson	Spitfire Vc AR289 'P'	Bf 109 Damaged	SE Daba	0930-1025
601 Sqn	Flt Lt M.R.B.Ingram	Spitfire Vc EP303	Bf 109 Damaged	forward positions	1200-1320
3 RAAF Sqn	Plt Off B.G.Harris	Kittyhawk I AL205 'S'	MC.202 Damaged	Fuka	1420
92 Sqn	Flt Lt J.M.Morgan	Spitfire Vb EP399 'S'	Bf 109	E Daba	1630-1745
73 Sqn	Plt Off R.Chandler	Hurricane IIc HL118	He 111 Damaged	Sidi Haneish	1835-1935

British Casualties

3 RAAF Sqn	Kittyhawk EV319 'X' shot down by MC.202 nr Fuka, around 1400; Sgt A.J.Richardson PoW
274 Sqn	Hurricane IIc BP742 crashed on landing at LG.37, DBR

US Claims

64th FS/57th FG	1/Lt William S.Beck	P-40F '16'	Bf 109	LG.21	0910
64th FS/57th FG	Capt Glade B.Bilby	P-40F '11'	Bf 109	LG.21	0910
64th FS/57th FG	Capt Glade B.Bilby	P-40F '11'	Bf 109 Damaged	LG.21	0910
64th FS/57th FG	Lt Ernest O.Hartman	P-40F '17'	Bf 109 Damaged	LG.21	0910
64th FS/57th FG	Maj Clermont E.Wheeler	P-40F '01'	Bf 109 Damaged	LG.21	0910
64th FS/57th FG	Maj Clermont E.Wheeler	P-40F '01'	Bf 109	LG.21	0910
64th FS/57th FG	Lt Lyman Middleditch Jr	P-40F '17'	Bf 109	LG.20	1300

German Claims

Stab III./JG 27	Hptm Ernst Düllberg	P-46	NW El Alamein	0840
8./JG 27	Uffz Erich Krainik	P-40	SE El Alamein	

German Casualties

7./JG 53	Bf 109F-4/Z WNr 7093 crash-landed E El Daba 80% damaged after combat; Uffz Rudolf Wannek injured
7./JG 27	Bf 109F-4 trop WNr 13279 crash-landed Turbiya, 80%; Uffz Ernst Schelper safe
9./JG 27	Bf 109F-4 trop WNr 8669 shot down by P-40, crashed E Turbiya; Lt Werner Boden KiA
9./JG 27	Bf 109F-4 trop WNr 8764 shot-up, force-landed 100% destroyed; Obfw Johannes Scheit safe
III./ZG 1	Bf 109E-7 WNr 6301 shot down by AA; pilot safe
I./StG 3	Ju 87D-3 WNr 2672 hit by AA, 80% damaged, force-landed near El Daba; crew safe
I./StG 3	2 Ju 87D-3s WNr 2728 65% damaged and 2784 30% damaged, crash-landed at Qasaba; crew safe

Italian Claims

91ª Sq, 10°Gr, 4°St CT	Serg Feruccio Terrabuio	MC.202 MM 7933	Spitfire	15km SE Fuka	1210-1340
91ª Sq, 10°Gr, 4°St CT	Serg Alessandro Bladelli	MC.202			
73ª Sq, 9°Gr, 4°St CT	Ten Giuseppe Oblach	MC.202			
73ª Sq, 9°Gr, 4°St CT	Ten Mario Mecatti	MC.202			
73ª Sq, 9°Gr, 4°St CT	Ten Giulio Reiner	MC.202	Spitfire	15km SE Fuka	1230-1340
73ª Sq, 9°Gr, 4°St CT	Ten Giulio Reiner	MC.202	Boston Probable	15km SE Fuka	1230-1340
73ª Sq, 9°Gr, 4°St CT	Ten Giuseppe Oblach	MC.202	P-40	15km SE Fuka	1230-1340
73ª Sq, 9°Gr, 4°St CT	Ten Mario Mecatti	MC.202	P-40	15km SE Fuka	1230-1340

Monday, 26 October 1942

THE GERMAN FIGHTERS BEGIN AN 'ALL CHANGE'

Just as the El Alamein battle got underway, the Luftwaffe planned to exchange the fighter units in Africa with others elsewhere following the serious effects on morale that recent losses in JG 27, and particularly in I.Gruppe, had occasioned. These began on this date with the departure back to Sicily of III./JG 53 which had been in North Africa (for the second time) since May. During that period the unit had claimed 106 victories. It was to be replaced immediately by elements of JG 77 which in due course was to take over all North African fighter duties from JG 27 as well. At first I.Gruppe was to move to Bir el Abd from Sicily on the 27th, while III.Gruppe would move over a day earlier, beginning to fly in to Tobruk on this date.

The claims made by some of the leading pilots of I./JG 77 before arriving in North Africa during October were impressive as demonstrated by the rudders of their aircraft. Those shown here were all already at least recipients of the Ritterkreuz . A) Hptmn Heinz Bär, Gruppenkommandeur; his rudder indicating 113 victories; B) Oblt Friedrich Geisshardt, Staffelkapitän of 3./JG 77; his rudder indicating 84 victories; C) Oblt Siegfried Freytag, Staffelkapitän of 1./JG 77, and his rudder showing 57 victories.

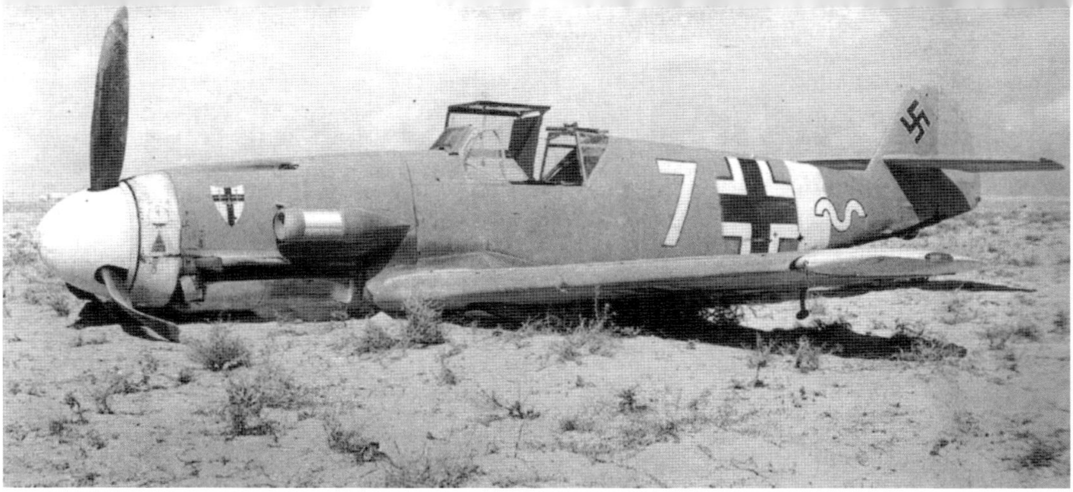

A pristine Bf 109F of 7./JG 27, shot down by Kittyhawks on 26 October. Lt Helmuth Fenzl became a PoW.

I.Gruppe had been based in Sicily since July, operating over Malta where it had claimed 102 victories – by a coincidence almost exactly the same as III./JG 53 had achieved during its absence from Sicily. A highly experienced unit, the Gruppe had just become fully re-equipped with Bf 109Gs which III./JG 53 was only now about to begin receiving. The Kommandeur was a famous and highly-skilled pilot, Hptm Heinz Bär who had been awarded the Schwerte und Eichenlaub to the Ritterkreuz, and who had a current victory tally of 117.

Two of the three Staffelkapitäne were also Ritterkreuzträger. Commanding 1.Staffel was Oblt Siegfried Freytag who was credited with almost 80 victories. He had been particularly successful over Malta where he had claimed some 20 victories, becoming known in the German popular press as 'Die Stern von Malta' (The Star of Malta). 2.Staffel was led by Oblt Herbert Thurz; however, he was in hospital and the unit was temporarily in the hands of Oblt Franz-Heinz Lange. Commanding 3.Staffel was Oblt Friedrich Geisshardt, another Ritterkreuzträger with 91 victories; he had also been awarded the Eichenlaube. This unit moved to Bir el Abd at once and began operations next day, flying initially with I./JG 27, whose ground crews looked after

Hptmn Ernst Düllberg became Kommandeur of III./JG 27 in October. He had previously served with II Gruppe and the Geschwaderstab and with his new unit he made one claim on 26 October.

Hptmn Kurt Walter, Kommandeur of III./StG 3, was credited with sinking the cruiser HMS *Coventry* on 14 September. His Ju 87 was shot down at low altitude on 26 October near El Alamein by Flg Off Bert Houle of 213 Squadron. He and his gunner baled out, but his parachute failed to open and he was killed.

the unit's aircraft in the first instance. The pilots of this premier unit arrived intending to show the pilots of JG 27 'how it was done', but soon found themselves in an increasingly difficult position, with everything against them.

Meanwhile, III.Gruppe arrived at Tobruk on the 26th, moving to Tanyet-Harun next day from where it was to operate. This unit came direct from action on the Eastern Front and had enjoyed no less a distinguished career before reaching North Africa than had I.Gruppe. Its Kommandeur was Hptm Kurt 'Kuddel' Ubben, yet another Ritterkreuzträger mit Eichenlaube, who had claimed 91 victories by this time. His unit was in the main equipped with Bf 109Gs, but still had a few F models left on strength which it was to continue to carry for some time. Ubben's three Staffelkapitäne were:

7. Staffel – Hptm Wolfdieter Huy, also Ritterkreuz mit Eichenlaube with 39 victories and a number of ships sunk;
8. Staffel – Oblt Emil Omert. Ritterkreuzträger with 53 victories, and
9. Staffel – Lt Horst Marotzke, 37 victories.

The Kommodore of JG 77 and his Geschwaderstab would follow on 1 November. The Kommodore was none other than Maj Joachim Müncheberg who had led 7./JG 26 in North Africa during the early months of 1941 (See Volume 1); he had by now been awarded the Schwerte und Eichenlaube to his Ritterkreuz, having recently raised his personal tally to over 100.

Meanwhile on the Battlefront

Even as these changes were taking place, on the ground the Axis forces counter-attacked on Kidney Ridge throughout the day. They made little impact and suffered severe casualties. The WDAF continued to hinder concentration for these attacks, enabling Montgomery to regroup his forces for a new assault. Throughout the day bombers attacked a convoy making for Benghazi which included a tanker and two merchant vessels, all with supplies of fuel and ammunition so urgently needed by both the Afrika Korps and the Luftwaffe (see Chapter Ten for full details of these operations).

Twelve Kittyhawks of 3 RAAF Squadron escorted others of 450 Squadron on an early raid at 0700, being jumped over El Alamein by nine Bf 109s of II./JG 27 which had taken off at 0714 on a Freie Jagd. Lt Kientsch attacked Flt Sgt Bullwinkel's aircraft in a turn, the latter baling out and breaking his leg. One probable was claimed in return. At 0900 12 Kittyhawks of 112 Squadron escorted bombers, four Bf 109s of III./JG 27 scrambling to intercept. Two of these dived on six Kittyhawks, claiming one, but losing one of their number. Sqn Ldr Drake and Plt Off Wright each claimed a Messerschmitt shot down, but two of the pilots of this unit failed to return, one dying of his injuries.

Around the same time ten Hurricanes of 274 Squadron, covered by 127 Squadron, set off on a raid just as eight Spitfires of 92 Squadron took off on an offensive sweep over Daba. An hour later 12 Kittyhawks of 260 Squadron provided top cover to 12 Bostons and six Baltimores which raided Fuka with 12 2 SAAF Squadron Kittyhawks as medium cover. A quarter of an hour later six more Kittyhawks, this time from 450 Squadron, took off for an offensive patrol, then at 1030 nine Spitfires of 601 Squadron set off to 'de-louse' the returning bomber formations. Into this mass of Allied aircraft six Bf 109s of II.Gruppe and five of III./JG 27 had taken off at 1000 with two of III./JG 53 on a Freie Jagd. They engaged the bomber formation in the Fuka-Daba area and attacked, II.Gruppe breaking through to the bombers on this occasion, forcing them to jettison their cargoes. Lt Harder of III./JG 53 claimed to have shot down one Kittyhawk while each of the other Gruppen claimed to have hit one. Maj Spencer of 24 SAAF Squadron claimed that he had managed to hit a Bf 109 with the front guns of his Boston as it broke through the escort, his rear gunner then also achieving hits and reporting that he saw the Messerschmitt go down in flames.

In the meantime the Hurricanes of 274 Squadron were attacked by six Bf 109s, Flg Off Graves being shot down. Flg Off Waddy of 92 Squadron claimed one Bf 109 shot down at this time. Around the bombers 2 SAAF Squadron fought ten Axis fighters, Capt Parsonson engaging one which he claimed to have totally destroyed with one burst, and Lt Burls claimed an MC.202, other claims being made for probables and damaged. Jack Parsonson:

"On one of these Fuka raids I shot down my first enemy aircraft, a ME 109. He was travelling at right angles to our line of flight and I gave him full deflection. To my amazement when he arrived dead ahead he ran into my fire. He went straight down to crash near the aerodrome. I stupidly followed after him without thinking about his number two. Gerry Gericke, my number two, said to me when we got back, 'Didn't you see his number two?' 'No,' I replied. 'Good thing for you I followed him down and chased him off your tail as he was getting ready to clobber you.' Thanks to Gerry I was not hacked that time."

260 Squadron's pilots spotted five MC.202s, two of these being claimed shot down, but one of the successful pilots, Flg Off Meredith, was shot down himself, probably by Ten Bordoni-Bisleri of 18° Gruppo, surviving the crash. At this time Bordoni-Bisleri was frequently borrowing aircraft from 23° Gruppo since his own Gruppo was still equipped with MC.200s. On the return flight, 260 Squadron was attacked by Bf 109s, Flt Sgt Ody failing to return, while a second Kittyhawk was badly damaged by Flak north of the Qattara Depression. Two more Kittyhawks were badly damaged during the earlier fight with the Macchis. 601 Squadron's Spitfires, hurrying to the combat, encountered a lone MC.202 which Flt Lt Curry claimed to have shot down. Six more Axis fighters were then seen, all flying singly, but only one claim for a Macchi damaged resulted. 450 Squadron's six pilots meanwhile, encountered a Ju 88 which they attacked and caused to force-land.

Six Bf 109s of II.Gruppe and five of III./JG 27 took off at 1330 on a Freie Jagd, the II.Gruppe pilots reporting meeting 12 bombers and their escorts south-west of El Alamein, claiming a B-25 shot down. The other Gruppe then engaged Spitfires near Tarfa, but in this combat Uffz Krainik was shot down, Lt Schroer claiming one Curtiss fighter at 1410.

At 1445 Hurricanes of 127 and 7 SAAF Squadrons set off, one of the latter unit's Mark IId tank-busters being hit by Flak and force-landing; Sgt Stoddart of 127 Squadron crashed and was killed, but reportedly this was not as the result of enemy action. Twelve Kittyhawks of 260 Squadron and twelve of 4 SAAF Squadron next escorted 12 Bostons and six Baltimores to bomb LG.21 at 1615, the former unit flying as top cover. Nine Bf 109s of II.Gruppe and two of III./JG 27 had just taken off at 1700 on a Freie Jagd when this formation approached, four of the Messerschmitt pilots attacking 260 Squadron and six going for 4 SAAF, the remaining aircraft seeking to attack the bombers. Hptm Rödel claimed one fighter, but another II.Gruppe aircraft was hit and belly-landed. The III.Gruppe pilots fought three Kittyhawks, then also attacked the bombers, Lt Werfft claiming a Boston shot down north-east of the mosque at Daba – although no loss of such an aircraft was recorded. The defending Kittyhawk pilots of the two squadrons between them claimed two Bf 109s shot down, two probables and two damaged, but two of 260 Squadron's aircraft were hit, one crash-landing and one force-landing.

213 Squadron flew a decoy patrol at 1735 to draw away opposition to a raid by other units. However, these Hurricane pilots met a formation of Ju 87s making for base. The light was failing fast, but Flg Off Bert Houle managed to claim two. Plus a probable and two damaged. Two Stukas were lost by StG 3, one of the Geschwaderstab and one by the Stab of III.Gruppe. In this latter aircraft

Flg Off J.G.'Gary' Wright served with 112 Squadron from July 1942 until the spring of 1943. On 26 October he pursued a Bf 109 over the lines, claming to have shot this down, but in doing so his own Kittyhawk was hit by Flak, obliging him to crash-land with some violence which rendered him unconscious.

Hptm Kurt Walter, the Gruppenkommandeur and a Ritterkreuzträger, was killed when his parachute failed to open. On one of the early afternoon bombing raids an escorting 5 SAAF Squadron Tomahawk had been shot down, the pilot being killed, and a TacR Hurricane of 208 Squadron was shot down by Flak during the day, crash-landing. A Bf 109 of the newly-formed I./SchG 2 was also reported shot down in combat, the pilot being killed.

57th Fighter Group P-40s were again very active during the day, mainly providing cover for the bombers. After seven such operations had been flown, at 1415 eight aircraft of the 65th Squadron were ordered to patrol, over Burg el Arab. Here they were vectored onto four MC.202s over the coast near Sidi Abd el Rahman, all of which were claimed shot down, two of them by Capt Thomas Clark, whose own aircraft was hit in the left wing during the combat. As the American pilots departed the area, they reported seeing four large fires burning on the ground.

Throughout this particularly active day, the Regia Aeronautica fighters had been almost continually in action. Their efforts had, to a considerable extent, been directed towards the protection of the shipping attempting so desperately to reach the North African ports. These resulted almost exclusively in encounters with twin-engined or four-engined aircraft, and the claims related to these actions are dealt with in Chapter Ten. However several engagements had also taken place in the battle area and these are dealt with here. During the early morning period – 0850-1030 – 9°, 10° and 23° Gruppi had claimed a P-40, a Spitfire and a Boston, plus a couple of probables in the Fuka-El Alamein area. Seven MC.202s of 4° Stormo led by Ten Reiner were scrambled at 0935 to intercept a formation of 18 Bostons heading to Fuka covered by a large number of P-40s and Spitfires. At 15,000 feet the two formations clashed and S.Ten Daffara managed to shoot down one bomber of the first patrol, Reiner claiming a Spitfire and Ten Giorgio Bertolaso a probable; Ten Vittorio Squarcia chased a P-40, forcing it to belly-land south of Daba. The British pilot, Flg Off Meredith was later taken PoW. Serg Bladelli scored some hits on four Bostons and a P-40 but then his Macchi was hit forcing him to limp back to Fuka North. Serg Monterumici was hit in the cockpit and forced to belly-land in the desert. He recalled:

> "On that day I scrambled to intercept 18 Bostons, escorted by approximately 30 Curtiss P-40s and about ten Spitfires, heading to our airfield. I attacked the bombers before they could deliver their charge on our aircraft on the ground, while the escorting fighters were still far enough off, giving me a chance to disengage. In reality, on that occasion our adversaries employed larger calibre guns, still unknown to us, and opened fire unexpectedly at a 1,500 foot range. A burst hit my cockpit, shattering the canopy and blistering my face with glass chips. I quickly rolled away to evade this difficult situation but as soon as I gained speed the windscreen smashed, hurting my forehead. I was left with no protection in the violent airflow and I felt like my head was coming off. I reduced speed but the enemy fighter was again getting on my tail. I had no more altitude to lose and, trying to dodge a burst, I touched the ground with the propeller, crash-landing at excessive speed. In the sandy desert plain, my plane kept on dragging, engaged in a never-ending run, while in those seemingly endless moments I was saying: 'I'm still alive, I'm still alive, I'm still alive...'
>
> "When at last the plane came to rest, I climbed out of my cockpit, bleeding; then, fearful that the damaged aircraft could catch fire, I went further away, and made my way northbound, with the help of a small compass that I carried with me. After a few hours walk, the real troubles started: a large minefield, marked with many pegs, was just in front of me, apparently endless. I made a detour, because I couldn't stop: I had just a half-filled water-bottle and the flies, attracted by the blood that was still dripping from the wounds on my face, kept on annoying me. After some time, I heard an aircraft engine noise far away: it was a Storch, piloted (as I was told afterwards) by my Stormo CO T.Col Armando François and by Ten Vittorino Daffara. Unfortunately they didn't notice me, although I waved my life-vest for a long time, trying to draw their attention.
>
> "I carefully resumed my march among the mines, hoping to meet with someone or something. Some time later, I came across the wreck of a shot-down aircraft. I approached to see what type it was: it was a P-40 whose pilot was lying on a wing with his head on his hands and a parachute not so far way. The body was intact but sort of mummified. Not very far away there was another aircraft, this time a Spitfire, whose pilot was sitting still on his 'chute near to the tailwheel, with his back leaning against the fuselage, holding his knees with his arms. He looked as if he was sleeping, but he too had been already transformed into a statue. I gently knocked my knuckles against his cheek-bone and a sort of dried wood sound replied. I then thought to myself: 'This will be also my

destiny, but... never mind, let's continue until there's energy to do so...'

"After many more hours of walking, I noticed what I hoped so much to see: a thin dust cloud moving towards me. I started again to wave my life-vest, but I wasn't able to make clear what it really was: was it just the wind raising some sand or something moving in my direction? As a matter of fact, my eyes were filled with clotted blood, while the right part of my face, from the nose to the cheek, was a just a congealed wound. It was 7 o'clock p.m. already, the sunset was soon to come and by then I'd been walking for ten hours. The dust cloud kept on getting closer and at last I managed to recognise a motorbike. The driver was Ten Carlo Tommasi, of 3° Stormo, wandering around in the desert looking for souvenirs to be brought back to his villa in Naples..."

Monterumici was taken to a field hospital and later repatriated. Seven MC.202s of 84ª Squadriglia led by Ten Giannella scrambled from 1300 to 1340, without encountering the enemy. The same patrol took off again at 1445 and this time intercepted seven 'P-46s' which were strafing Abu Haggag airfield. Serg Magg Santonocito claimed two damaged. A third scramble occurred at 1600, led again by Giannella. A formation of 21 Bostons, covered as usual by P-40s and Spitfires, was intercepted: the bombers were attacked and one was effectively strafed but the escort intervened immediately and in the ensuing combat Ten Francesco De Seta shot down a P-40, M.llo Luigi Bignami claiming a probable. A MC.202 from 23° Gruppo crashed due to engine trouble, the pilot baling out safely.

During the darkness of the evening, two Hurricane pilots of 73 Squadron on an intruder sortie to LG.12, found about a dozen Ju 87s orbiting the airfield which had its landing lights switched on. Sgt Gadd claimed to have shot down one and damaged two more. Flt Sgt Marsh claimed a fourth damaged.

British Claims

3 RAAF Sqn	Sgt J.F.H.Cashmore	Kittyhawk I AK653 'W'	Bf 109E Probable	Alamein	0730
112 Sqn	Sqn Ldr B.Drake	Kittyhawk III FR293 '?'	Bf 109	N El Alamein area	0900-0950
112 Sqn	Plt Off J.G.Wright	Kittyhawk III FR279 'J'	Bf 109	N El Alamein area	0900-0950
92 Sqn	Flg Off J.L.Waddy	Spitfire Vb EP401 'O'	Bf 109	Daba area	0930-1100
260 Sqn	Flg Off E.G.Aitchison	Kittyhawk IIa	MC.202	Fuka l.g.	1000-1148
260 Sqn	Flg Off J.G.Meredith	Kittyhawk IIa	MC.202	Fuka l.g.	1000-1148
3 RAAF Sqn	Flt Sgt R.N.Stevens	Kittyhawk I AK653 'X'	MC.202 Probable	Fuka l.g	1050
450 Sqn	Sqn Ldr J.E.A.Williams and four pilots	Kittyhawk III	Ju 88 Damaged		1017-1250
601 Sqn	Plt Off A.R.Boyle	Spitfire Vc EP682	MC.202 Damaged		1030-1130
601 Sqn	Flt Lt J.H.Curry	Spitfire Vc AB345 'J'	MC.202		1030-1130
5 SAAF Sqn	Capt L.B.van der Spuy	Tomahawk IIb AN226 'C'	MC.202 Probable	Fuka	1040
2 SAAF Sqn	2/Lt A.F.Allen-White	Kittyhawk I AK658 'V'	Bf 109F Damaged	Fuka Main l.g.	1050
2 SAAF Sqn	Lt A.P.Blignault	Kittyhawk I EV356 'A'	Bf 109F Probable	Fuka Main l.g.	1050
2 SAAF Sqn	Lt J.R.Burls	Kittyhawk I ET972 'P'	MC.202	Fuka Main l.g.	1050
2 SAAF Sqn	Lt H.J.Lourens	Kittyhawk I EV330 'S'	MC.202 Damaged	Fuka Main l.g.	1050
2 SAAF Sqn	Capt J.E.Parsonson	Kittyhawk I EV326 'F'	Bf 109	Fuka Main l.g.	1050
601 Sqn	Plt Off C.R.Scollan	Spitfire Vc BR469 'B'	Bf 109 Damaged	W El Alamein	1330-1435
260 Sqn	Sgt G.G.Rattle	Kittyhawk IIa FL337	Bf 109F Damaged	E Fuka	1615-1800
260 Sqn	Sgt B.H.Thomas	Kittyhawk IIa	Bf 109F	E Fuka	1615-1800
260 Sqn	Flt Lt W.R.Cundy	Kittyhawk IIa FL288	Bf 109F	E Fuka	1615-1800
260 Sqn	Flt Sgt J.F.Edwards	Kittyhawk IIa FL221 'F'	Bf 109F Probable	E Fuka	1615-1800
260 Sqn	Flg Off N.E.Gilboe	Kittyhawk IIa	Bf 109F Probable	E Fuka	1615-1800
4 SAAF Sqn	Lt A.C.Peterson	Kittyhawk I ET564 'Q'	Bf 109F Probable		1705
4 SAAF Sqn	Lt R.W.Rowan	Kittyhawk I AK711 'T'	Bf 109 Damaged		1705
4 SAAF Sqn	Lt D.F.Symonds	Kittyhawk I AK629 'E'	Bf 109F Damaged		1705
213 Sqn	Plt Off G.Carrick	Hurricane IIc BP592	Ju 87 Probable	W Daba	1810-1925
213 Sqn	Wg Cdr J.Darwen	Hurricane IIc HL960	Ju 87 Damaged	W Daba	1810-1925
213 Sqn	Flg Off A.U.Houle	Hurricane IIc HL887	2 Ju 87s	W Daba on the coast	1810-1925
213 Sqn	Flg Off A.U.Houle	Hurricane IIc HL887	Ju 87 Probable	W Daba	1810-1925
213 Sqn	Flg Off A.U.Houle	Hurricane IIc HL887	2 Ju 87s Damaged	W Daba	1810-1925
73 Sqn	Sgt D.Gadd	Hurricane IIc HV342	Ju 87	LG.12	1830-2115

British Claims

73 Sqn	Sgt D.Gadd	Hurricane IIc HV342	2 Ju 87s Damaged	LG.12	1830-2115
73 Sqn	Flt Sgt R.D.Marsh	Hurricane IIc HV664	Ju 87 Damaged	LG.12	1830-2115

British Casualties

112 Sqn	Kittyhawk III FR263 'X' FTR from bomber escort; Flg Off K.A.Gardener, died of wounds
112 Sqn	Kittyhawk III FR279 'J' crash-landed nr front line; Plt Off J.G.Wright MiA
260 Sqn	Kittyhawk IIa shot down by MC.202 SW Daba, 1000-1148; Flg Off J.G.Meredith PoW
260 Sqn	Kittyhawk IIa badly damaged, Flak N Qattara Depression, 1000-1148; Flg Off E.G.Aitchison safe
260 Sqn	Kittyhawk IIa badly damaged by MC.202 SW Daba, 1000-1148; Sgt W.D.Barker safe
260 Sqn	Kittyhawk IIa shot down by Bf 109 SW Daba, 1000-1148; Flt Sgt C.E.Ody MiA
260 Sqn	Kittyhawk IIa FL337 shot down by Bf 109 SW LG.21-E Fuka, 1615-1800; Sgt G.G.Rattle WiA
260 Sqn	Kittyhawk IIa badly damaged E Fuka 1615-1800, force-landed; Plt Off Hopkinson
3 RAAF Sqn	Kittyhawk I EV317 damaged by fighters and abandoned nr El Alamein; Flt Sgt J.Bullwinkel baled out
2 SAAF Sqn	Kittyhawk I damaged by Bf 109s; Lt L.C.H.Hope
4 SAAF Sqn	Kittyhawk I AK961 damaged by Flak Cat I; Lt I.T.S.Tapson
5 SAAF Sqn	Tomahawk IIb AN462 'J' FTR from escort, shot down S Sidi el Rahman; Lt A.D.Hinton KiA
7 SAAF Sqn	Hurricane IId BN971 damaged by Flak while attacking tanks and crash-landed nr Lake Maghra, 56m S El Alamein, Cat III; Lt A.B.Alexander slt WiA, picked up by armoured cars and returned
274 Sqn	Hurricane IIc HL774 shot down by Bf 109s; Flg Off Graves
208 Sqn	Hurricane IIb BP166 left 1715, hit by Flak, crash-landed at 1715 Cat II; Flt Lt D.W.Barlow
127 Sqn	Hurricane IIb; Sgt Stoddart crashed and K

US Claims

65th FS/57th FG	Capt Thomas W.Clark	P-40F '54'	2 MC.202s	S El Daba	1425-1530
65th FS/57th FG	1/Lt Robert L.Metcalf	P-40F '43'	MC.202	S El Daba	1425-1530
65th FS/57th FG	1/Lt Roy E.Whittaker	P-40F '43'	MC.202	S El Daba	1425-1530

German Claims

5./JG 27	Lt Willy Kientsch	P-40	SW El Alamein	0640
8./JG 27	Uffz Erich Krainik	P-40	El Alamein area	
7./JG 53	Lt Jürgen Harder	P-40	10km NE Fuka	0957
8./JG 27	Lt Werner Schroer	P-40	W El Alamein	1310
4./JG 27	Fw Alfred Heidel	B-25	SW El Alamein	1314
9./JG 27	Lt Dr Peter Werfft	Boston	NE El Daba mosque	1600
Stab II./JG 27	Hptm Gustav Rödel	Spitfire	SW Sanyet Qotaifiya	1608

German Casualties

7./JG 27	Bf 109F-4 trop WNr 13136 White 7 combat with P-40 El Alamein area, 100%; Lt Helmut Fenzl PoW
8./JG 27	Bf 109F-4 trop WNr 8727 Black 7 combat with Spitfire, Deir el Tarfa; Uffz Erich Krainik MiA
4./SchG 2	Bf 109F-4 WNr 8569 combat 15km NW El Alamein; Uffz Heinz Schäfer MiA
1./SchG 2	Bf 109F-4 WNr 7584 shot down in combat S El Daba; Oblt Wolf Zipper (Stkpt) WiA
I./SchG 2	Bf 109F-4 shot down in combat W El Alamein; pilot baled out safely
Stab/StG 3	Ju 87D-3 WNr 2639 S7+BA combat with Hurricane El Alamein; Oblt Karl Lindorfer WiA
Stab III./StG 3	Ju 87D-1 WNr 2562 shot down by Hurricane 8km E El Daba; two baled out
I./StG 3	Ju 87D-1 WNr 2461 hit in combat N El Daba, 30% damaged, crew safe
I./StG 3	Ju 87D-3 WNr 2717 hit in combat N El Daba, 80% damaged, crash-landed, crew safe
I./StG 3	Ju 87D-3 WNr 2709, 95% damaged, crash-landed at Qasaba, crew safe
III./StG 3	Ju 87D-1 WNr 2590, 60% damaged, crash-landed at Qasaba, crew safe
8./StG 3	Ju 87D-1 WNr 2105, 20% damaged, crash-landed at Qasaba, gunner Gefr Detlef Weigt inj

Italian Claims

75ª Sq, 23°Gr, 3°St CT	Cap Mario Pinna	MC.202	Boston Probable	S El Alamein	0850-1030
75ª Sq, 23°Gr, 3°St CT	Serg Francesco Cuscunà	MC.202	Boston Damaged	S El Alamein	0850-1030
75ª Sq, 23°Gr, 3°St CT	Serg Antonio Franciosi	MC.202	P-40 Probable	S El Alamein	0850-1030
95ª Sq, 18°Gr, 3°St CT	Ten Franco Bordoni-Bisleri	MC.202	P-40	S El Alamein	0850-1030
91ª Sq, 10°Gr, 4°St CT	S.Ten Vittorino Daffara	MC.202	Boston	S Fuka	0935-1030
73ª Sq, 9°Gr, 4°St CT	Ten Giulio Reiner	MC.202	Spitfire	S Fuka	0935-1030
91ª Sq, 10°Gr, 4°St CT	S.Ten Giorgio Bertolaso	MC.202	Spitfire Probable	S Fuka	0935-1030
73ª Sq, 9°Gr, 4°St CT	Ten Vittorio Squarcia	MC.202	P-40	S Fuka	0935-1030

84ª Sq, 10°Gr, 4°St CT	Serg Magg D.Santonocito	MC.202 MM 7928	2 P-46 Damaged	Abu Haggag	1445-1520
84ª Sq, 10°Gr, 4°St CT	S.Ten Francesco De Seta	MC.202 MM 7914	P-40	El Alamein	1600-1710
84ª Sq, 10°Gr, 4°St CT	M.llo Luigi Bignami	MC.202 MM 7916	P-40 Probable	El Alamein	1600-1710

Italian Casualties

70ª Sq, 23°Gr, 3°St CT	MC.202 MM 9058 '70-10' crashed to ground with engine trouble, Serg Magg Celso Zemella baled out, safe
84ª Sq, 10°Gr, 4°St CT	MC.202 MM 7933 '84-10' hit in combat, crash-landed, Serg Amleto Monterumici (90ª Sq) WiA, returned
91ª Sq, 10°Gr, 4°St CT	MC.202 MM 7805 '84-2' hit in combat, landed at Fuka, Serg Alessandro Bladelli safe

Western Desert Air Force
Relevant Orders of Battle, 27 October 1942

HQ, RAF, Middle East

60 SAAF Sqn (Det)	Maryland
162 Sqn	Lodestar, Wellington
1411Met Flt	Gladiator
2 PRU	Spitfire, Hurricane, Beaufighter

Air HQ, Levant

1413 Met Flt	Gladiator
1438 Flt	Blenheim
2 PRU (Det)	Hurricane
213 GROUP	
451 Sqn	Hurricane

Air HQ, Egypt

234 Wing	
889 Sqn (FAA)	Fulmar, Hurricane
250 Wing	
89 Sqn	Beaufighter
94 Sqn	Hurricane, Spitfire
252 Wing	
46 Sqn	Beaufighter
417 Sqn	Hurricane, Spitfire
201 GROUP	
15 SAAF Sqn	Bisley
47 Sqn	Beaufort
203 Sqn	Blenheim, Baltimore, Maryland
230 Sqn	Sunderland, Dornier 22
252, 272 Sqns	Beaufighter
459 Sqn	Hudson
701 Sqn (FAA)	Walrus
821 Sqn (FAA)	Albacore
815 Sqn (FAA)	Swordfish
1 GRU	Wellington
Sea Rescue Dlt	Wellington, Fairchild Ambulance

Air HQ, Egypt

235 Wing	
13 (Hellenic) Sqn	Blenheim
47 Sqn (Det)	Wellesley
459 Sqn (Det)	Hudson
247 Wing	
203 Sqn (Det)	Maryland, Baltimore, Blenheim
248 Wing	
38, 221, 458 Sqns	Wellington
39 Sqn	Beaufort
203 GROUP	
15 SAAF Sqn (Det)	Blenheim
1412 Met Flt	Gladiator
205 GROUP	
Special Liberator Flt	Liberator
231 Wing	
37, 70 Sqns	Wellington
236 Wing	
108, 148 Sqns	Wellington
238 Wing	
40, 104 Sqns	
242 Wing	
147, 160 Sqns	Liberator
245 Wing	
14 Sqn	Marauder, Boston
227 Sqn (Det), 462 Sqn	Halifax
216 GROUP	
117 Sqn	Hudson
173 Sqn	Various
216 Sqn	Lodestar, Hudson, Bombay
267 Sqn	Various
283 Wing	
163 Sqn	Hudson
US 1st Bombardment Group (Provisional)	
9th Sqn	B-17E
Halverson Sqn	B-24D
US 98th Bombardment Group	
343rd, 344th , 345th , 415th Sqns	B-24D

Air HQ, Western Desert	
1 Air Ambulance Unit	DH-86
3 SAAF Wing	
12 SAAF, 24 SAAF Sqns	Boston
21 SAAF Sqn	Baltimore
232 Wing	
55, 223 Sqns	Baltimore
US 12th Bombardment Group	
81st, 82nd,83rd, 434th Sqns	B-25
285 Wing	
40 SAAF, 208 Sqns	Hurricane
1437 Strat Recce Flt	Baltimore
2 PRU (Det)	Various
211 GROUP	
6, 7 SAAF Sqns	Hurricane IId
233 Wing	
2 SAAF, 4 SAAF, 260 Sqns	Kittyhawk
5 SAAF Sqn	Tomahawk
239 Wing	
3 RAAF, 112, 250, 450 Sqns	Kittyhawk
244 Wing	
92, 145, 601 Sqns	Spitfire
73 Sqn	Hurricane
US 57th FIGHTER GROUP	
64th, 65th, 66th Sqns	P-40F
212 GROUP	
7 SAAF Wing	
80, 127, 274, 335 Sqns	Hurricane
243 Wing	
1 SAAF, 33, 213, 238 Sqns	Hurricane

Tuesday, 27 October 1942

On this date the 21st Panzer Division moved north, joining 15th Panzer Division in an assault on 1st Armoured Division at Kidney Ridge. Here, however, the Rifle Brigade put up a determined defence of a position known as 'Snipe', holding out all day with six-pounder anti-tank guns, with WDAF bombers being directed to their support throughout the day, undertaking many raids to break up the German tank concentrations. Although 1st Armoured failed to advance to relieve the Snipe defenders, the panzers were nonetheless repulsed with heavy losses.

Early in the night the El Hammam railway junction was again attacked by seven CR.42s of 101° Gruppo, led by Cap Edmondo Massi. They took off at intervals between 0030 and 0135, reaching the target separately. M.llo Roberto Costantini failed to return from this action, the others landing back between 0215 and 0340.

During 1942 CR.42s were employed mainly as fighter-bombers.

Following the successful sorties reported by 73 Squadron during the previous evening, Flt Sgt Marsh returned before dawn to claim two more Ju 87s damaged, on this occasion as they were landing at Sidi Haneish. At 0730 four Spitfires of 92 Squadron climbed to 17,000 feet over Daba and El Alamein on patrol, at the same time as nine Bf 109s of II./JG 27 took off to escort Jabos and to carry out a Freie Jagd. Their pilots reported that they were attacked out of the sun by eight Spitfires, three Messerschmitts being shot down, all belly-landing in Axis territory, south of El Alamein; 92 Squadron recorded claims for two shot down and a third damaged in this first really successful bounce of the Luftwaffe fighters.

Twelve Kittyhawks of 112 Squadron set off on a bomber escort at 0830, but these were jumped by three MC.202s near Fuka. Sgt Martin was shot down, later being reported safe, but the squadron turned the tables on their attackers, claiming all three shot down. One 9° Gruppo Macchi was actually lost in this engagement, the Italian pilots claiming three P-46s and one Spitfire. One of the former was claimed on behalf of S.Ten Caregnato who was the pilot lost. In the Daba area as nine Spitfires of 145 Squadron were escorting bombers, two Axis fighters were seen, one Bf 109 attacking Sqn Ldr Matthews head-on, the latter firing back and apparently achieving hits whereupon the Messerschmitt spun past Flt

One of the most successful Spitfire pilots of 1942 in the desert was Flg Off W.L.'Red' Chisholm of 92 Squadron, seen here with his aircraft shortly before the end of his tour in early 1943. On 27 October he made his seventh claim, on this occasion for a Bf 109. He would later add one more to run his total to eight, two of which were shared.

Sgt Anderson who also claimed to have hit it as it approached; it then dived into the ground. Three Bf 109s of III./JG 53 were scrambled at 0903, attacking bombers without result. This was the last mission for this unit in the desert, as that evening it withdrew to Sicily. The day also saw the return to North Africa of I./JG 27, which at once resumed operations.

An hour later eight Kittyhawks of 4 SAAF Squadron provided top cover for 18 Bostons and Baltimores; at the same time six Bf 109s of II.Gruppe and six of III./JG 27 commenced a Freie Jagd, intercepting the bombers and their escorts, reported as 30-40 Curtiss fighters and four Spitfires. Hptm Rödel claimed a Spitfire at 1023 and a Curtiss at 1042, Obfw Sheit of III.Gruppe claiming another Curtiss at 1053. 4 SAAF Squadron reported being attacked by six MC.202s, one aircraft being damaged and the pilot slightly wounded. Twelve Kittyhawks of 3 RAAF Squadron flew top cover to 18 Baltimores at 1215, one MC.202 being seen to take off from LG.104 and climb to intercept the bombers. Flt Sgt Stevens claimed to have shot this aircraft down in flames. Apparently this was the Macchi flown by Ten Maggini of 96ª Squadriglia, who had scrambled from Fuka, but who was missing following an engagement from which a 'P46' was credited to him.

Six 66th Squadron P-40Fs strafed LG.68 soon after midday, diving on the airfield from 1,800 feet. One Italian fighter was claimed destroyed on the ground in flames by Capt Llewellyn, while Lt Kipser claimed a second and Lt T.Williams a third. As they returned to base, the American pilots encountered MC.202s, Llewellyn claiming one of these probably destroyed, but two Warhawks suffered slight damage. Seven MC.202s of 23° Gruppo, led by Cap Giorgio Tugnoli, were scrambled from Abu Haggag at 1145 to intercept an enemy formation; near El Alamein they engaged a number of P-40s claiming one shot down and three probables. Seven more MC.202s of 23° Gruppo, led by Cap Mario Pinna, took off at 1455 to escort 17 Ju 87s and 42 CR.42s of 50° and 5° Stormo. Near Daba a formation of P-40s was intercepted and engaged, two P-40s being claimed.

At 1510 four Spitfires of 601 Squadron escorted Kittybombers over Daba, but their pilots then spotted at least 30 fighters which were escorting 30 CR.42s of 50° Stormo to strafe positions at El Alamein, attacking many vehicles and armoured cars by dive-bombing. Just after these biplanes had completed their dives, they were attacked by a formation of fighters and combat commenced. Following several earlier missions, in the air at this time were eight bomb-carrying P-40Fs of the US 65th Squadron, escorted by eight more of the 64th Squadron. According to the Luftwaffe, the Axis formation included Ju 87s, and also placed the number of CR.42s involved at 43 (the Allied units involved put the size of the biplane formation at 20-24!). Apart from the MC.202s, ten Bf 109s of II./JG 27 and eight of III./JG 27 had also taken off at 1540 to take part in the escort. To add to the confusion, the Hurricanes of 33 Squadron were scrambled at 1545 to intercept the raid, covered by 213 Squadron. These pilots reported that the biplanes were flying in four vics each of six aircraft, the vics following each other in line astern, and that they were just entering their dives at this point. The Germans reported that as the formation

A 66th Fighter Squadron, 57th Fighter Group P-40F which features an insignia on the tail supporting the name applied to the aircraft which is 'The Falcon'.

Lt Lyman Middleditch Jr of the 64th Squadron, 57th Fighter Group enjoyed a very successful engagement on 27 October during which he claimed three Bf 109s shot down.

was assembling (or re-assembling) aircraft identified as 'Curtiss, Airacobras and four Spitfires' attacked; once more the reference to Airacobras seems to have been a give-away that US P-40Fs were involved. Hptm Rödel claimed one 'Airacobra/P-39' at 1605, two minutes after Oblt Börngen had claimed a Spitfire to which he added a Hurricane a few minutes later. Lt Schroer meanwhile, claimed three fighters, all of which he reported crash-landed.

Meantime, the American pilots were enjoying a very successful engagement. The pilots of the 65th Squadron released their bombs on LG.20, having spotted about six Bf 109s. They then saw more than 20 CR.42s coming in from out to sea, heading south-west. These were intercepted and following a confused engagement claims were made for three shot down, three probables and three damaged. During the fight Capt Sneed's aircraft was attacked by a Bf 109 and was quite badly damaged, although he managed to return safely.

Meanwhile, six more P-40s, this time from the 66th Squadron, had been sent out to strafe MT on the coast road west of Mersa Matruh which their pilots had been unable to locate. Flying at ten feet, they spotted a lone CR.42 at about the same height which had apparently just taken off. Pulling up together, four of the pilots opened fire simultaneously at which the biplane turned sharply and landed, then being destroyed by a further burst. The pilot was seen to leap out, but was fired on by Lt Taylor and fell to the ground.

At the same time the pilots of the 64th Squadron who were providing escort for the 65th Squadron fighter-bombers, observed a reported 20 Ju 87s approaching from the west without close escorts. Nonetheless, four Messerschmitts then appeared from the east and six more from out to sea. Some of these were engaged and Lt Middleditch became the star of the day: "got in bursts on one Me, saw smoke come out, dove down on another e/a, missed this one, stayed near the deck trying to control the plane and saw the first e/a hit the deck. Was attacked by three e/a. Turned into them, one by one, and let them have good bursts. Hit first one and saw it hit the sea. Other two kept attacking. Got close bursts on second e/a in mid-section. E/a half rolled and went into sea. Last one kept attacking." By now Middleditch had only two guns firing, so continued to turn into "e/a until it 'pooped off'". The last two aircraft were confirmed to have been shot down by Capt Burman. By then out of ammunition, he returned safely.

However the Hurricanes had also entered the fray, pilots of 213 Squadron claiming one more CR.42, plus two probables and two damaged, although one British aircraft was lost. It was probably against the Hurricanes that Lt Schroer gained his own big success (claimed as P-40s), for apart from the 127 Squadron aircraft, Sqn Ldr R.M.Lloyd, the 243 Wing sweep leader and one member of 33 Squadron's top flight were both shot down and two more Hurricanes in the lower flight were damaged. By this time the other

33 Squadron pilots had spotted 40 or more Stukas, claiming one shot down and one probable before they were driven off. These dive-bombers had taken off at 1555, escorted by 22 Bf 109s of the just-returned I./JG 27. The pilots of the latter reported combat with nine Spitfires, Hptm Homuth claiming one shot down (possibly one of the Hurricanes).

Actual losses during this very busy combat included two Bf 109s, one flown by Obfw Lüer of II.Gruppe who was killed, and one of III.Gruppe which force-landed at Daba. The hard-pressed CR.42 pilots claimed that they had managed to shoot down two P-40s, but their own losses amounted to four aircraft; one pilot was missing, but two force-landed and were soon known to be safe, while another was picked up by an Italian-flown Fi 156 Storch next day.

According to Italian records, 30 CR.42s led by T.Col Ferruccio Vosilla, 50° Stormo commander, strafed enemy positions at El Alamein from 1410-1600. They were joined in this operation by 12 CR.42s of 5° Stormo, led by Magg Carlo Alberto Rizzi. Many vehicles and armoured cars were dive-bombed. Just after the dive, despite the intervention of the MC.202s of 23° Gruppo, they were jumped by a formation of P-40s and a long fight ensued, where the biplanes apparently achieved some success: two P-40s were credited to Ten Piero Vodret and S.Ten Francesco Iadanza of 391ª Squadriglia. Also Magg Rizzi, Cap Massi and S.Ten Zaganelli scored some hits on the attacking fighters, while M.llo Urbano Suzzi of 238ª Squadriglia was shot down and crashed into the sea in flames. Three CR.42s were forced to crash-land in Axis controlled territory, and eight returned damaged.

During the day two Bf 109Gs of III./JG 77 were being flown to Africa from Crete. Upon reaching the coast Obfw Helmut Kaiser spotted six British fighters strafing traffic along the Via Balbia, reporting that he then shot down the rear aircraft with one burst – his 45th victory. He then followed the formation and shot down a second, but during this attack he failed to see another aircraft which was below his fighter and which managed to put a full burst into his engine and oil cooler. Thus hit, his Messerschmitt went down pouring black smoke to make a belly-landing near Mersa Matruh. His wingman flew on to Bir el Abd and reported him dead, but two days later Kaiser walked in, having achieved JG 77's first success in the new theatre of operations.

During the evening 92 Squadron carried out a patrol in the course of which Plt Off Chisholm's aircraft gave problems with its undercarriage, resulting in his having to land on one main wheel. With nightfall 73 Squadron aircraft were out again, Sgt Beard claiming a Ju 88 shot down 25 miles west of El Alamein.

British Claims

73 Sqn	Flt Sgt R.D.Marsh	Hurricane IIc HV342	2 Ju 87s Damaged	Sidi Haneish	0430-0645
92 Sqn	Plt Off W.L.Chisholm	Spitfire Vc BR576 'T'	Bf 109	Daba-El Alamein	0730-0845
92 Sqn	Flg Off A.Glendinning	Spitfire Vb EP397	Bf 109	Daba-El Alamein	0730-0845
92 Sqn	Flg Off J.L.Waddy	Spitfire Vb EP401 'O'	Bf 109 Damaged	Daba-El Alamein	0730-0845
250 Sqn	Plt Off N.G.Russell	Kittyhawk III FR241 'R'	MC.202 Damaged	Fuka l.g.	0822-1002
145 Sqn	Sqn Ldr G.P.H.Matthews	Spitfire Vb BR477	Bf 109	Daba	0830-1000
145 Sqn	Flt Sgt Anderson	Spitfire Vb AB168			
112 Sqn	Plt Off D.A.Bruce	Kittyhawk III FR281	MC.202	Fuka	0830-1015
112 Sqn	Plt Off L.H.Curphey	Kittyhawk III FR195	MC.202	Fuka	0830-1015
112 Sqn	Sqn Ldr B.Drake	Kittyhawk III FR293	MC.202	Fuka	0830-1015
601 Sqn	Sgt D.V.Watts	Spitfire Vc EP455	Bf 109	off coast nr LG.20	0905-1025
3 RAAF Sqn	Flt Sgt R.N.B.Stevens	Kittyhawk I AK653 'X'	MC.202 Probable	Fuka l.g.	1015
33 Sqn	Flt Sgt J.W.E.Belec	Hurricane IIc HL626 'L'	Ju 87 Probable	W El Alamein	1540-1635
33 Sqn	Flt Lt O.C.Kallio	Hurricane IIc HL654 'Q'	Ju 87	W El Alamein	1545-1645
33 Sqn	Flt Lt O.C.Kallio	Hurricane IIc HL654 'Q'	Ju 87 Damaged	W El Alamein	1545-1645
33 Sqn	Plt Off L.H.Peterson	Hurricane IIc BP130 'R'	Ju 87	W El Alamein	1545-1645
213 Sqn	Plt Off C.Luxton	Hurricane IIc HL613	CR.42 Damaged	W El Alamein	1545-1640
213 Sqn	Sgt D.J.McKay	Hurricane IIc BP507	CR.42 Damaged	E LG.105-W El Alamein	1545-1640
213 Sqn	Plt Off G.R.S.McKay	Hurricane IIc BM354	CR.42	W El Alamein	1545-1640
213 Sqn	Plt Off C.D.A.Smith	Hurricane IIc BP237	CR.42 Probable	W El Alamein	1545-1640
213 Sqn	Sgt W.G.Sweney	Hurricane IIc HL680	CR.42 Probable	W El Alamein	1545-1640
73 Sqn	Sgt D.R.Beard	Hurricane IIc HL972	Ju 87	25m W El Alamein	2300-2359

British Casualties

33 Sqn	Hurricane IIc BP398 'H' shot down by fighters W El Alamein; Sqn Ldr R.M.Lloyd MiA

British Casualties

33 Sqn	Hurricane IIc HV398 shot down by fighters W El Alamein; Plt Off Gardner KiA
33 Sqn	Hurricane IIc left 1545, badly damaged; Sgt F.J.Bateson safe
33 Sqn	Hurricane IIc left 1545, badly damaged; Sgt M.D.Marcus safe
335 Sqn	Hurricane II Z2503 crashed force-landing at LG.172
213 Sqn	Hurricane IIc HL987 left 1545, shot down by MC.202 or CR.42 nr El Alamein; Flt Sgt S.G.Brookes PoW
112 Sqn	Kittyhawk III FR262 'Z' FTR from fighter-bomber sortie to Fuka, crash-landed; Sgt A.F.G.Martin DoW
3 RAAF Sqn	Kittyhawk I EV168 left 0830, shot down by MC.202 nr Fuka; Sgt J.Churchill PoW
4 SAAF Sqn	Kittyhawk I AL177 'B' damaged by MC.202, belly-landed at base on return Cat II; Lt R.W.Humphrey WiA
21 SAAF Sqn	Baltimore III AH141 'M' off 1211 one of 12 and six Bostons to attack Axis forces at El Alamein; hit by Flak over Sidi Abd el Rahman area and crashed 20km W El Alamein; Capt T.Rhodes and three KiA

US Claims

66th FS/57th FG	Capt Raymond A.Llewellyn	P-40F '71'	Italian fighter destroyed on LG.68		
66th FS/57th FG	Lt Alberto Zipser	P-40F	Italian fighter destroyed on LG.68		
66th FS/57th FG	2/Lt Thomas T.Williams	P-40F	Italian fighter destroyed on LG.68		
66th FS/57th FG	Capt Raymond A.Llewellyn	P-40F '71'	MC.202 Probable	12m S LG.68	1220-1355
66th FS/57th FG	1/Lt William B.Campbell	P-40F '77'	CR.42 (shared)	W Matruh	1500-1715
66th FS/57th FG	1/Lt William E.Taylor	P-40F '74'			
66th FS/57th FG	1/Lt Thomas M.Tilley	P-40F '75'			
66th FS/57th FG	Capt William J.Yates	P-40F '70'			
65th FS/57th FG	Capt Thomas W.Clark	P-40F '41'	CR.42 Damaged	LG.20	1510-1635
65th FS/57th FG	Lt Harry H.Stanford	P-40F '43'	CR.42 Probable	LG.20	1510-1635
65th FS/57th FG	1/Lt Roy E.Whittaker	P-40F '54'	CR.42	LG.20	1510-1635
65th FS/57th FG	1/Lt Roy E.Whittaker	P-40F '54'	CR.42 Probable	LG.20	1510-1635
65th FS/57th FG	1/Lt Roy E.Whittaker	P-40F '54'	CR.42 Damaged	LG.20	1510-1635
65th FS/57th FG	1/Lt Gilbert O.Wymond Jr	P-40F '48'	2 CR.42s	LG.20	1510-1635
65th FS/57th FG	1/Lt Gilbert O.Wymond Jr	P-40F '48'	CR.42 Probable	LG.20	1510-1635
65th FS/57th FG	1/Lt Gilbert O.Wymond Jr	P-40F '48'	CR.42 Damaged	LG.20	1510-1635
64th FS/57th FG	1/Lt Lyman Middleditch Jr	P-40F '13'	3 Bf 109s	LG.20	1550

US Casualties

83rd BS/12th BG	B-25C '62' damaged by Flak, force-landed; Capt J.T.McKee and crew safe, one WiA

German Claims

Stab II./JG 27	Hptm Gustav Rödel	Spitfire	SSW El Hammam	0923
Stab II./JG 27	Hptm Gustav Rödel	P-40	SSW El Alamein	0942
9./JG 27	Obfw Johannes Scheit	P-40	S El Alamein	0953
5./JG 27	Oblt Ernst Börngen	Spitfire	N Turbiya	1503
Stab II./JG 27	Hptm Gustav Rödel	P-39	N El Daba	1505
5./JG 27	Oblt Ernst Börngen	Hurricane	NW El Alamein	1532
Stab I./JG 27	Hptm Gerhard Homuth	Spitfire	S Bir Mumin Busak	
8./JG 27	Lt Werner Schroer	3 P-40s	NW, NE Qotaifiya, NE El Daba	
8./JG 77	Obfw Herbert Kaiser	2 P-40s	Via Balbia & 15km S Via Balbia	

German Casualties

4./JG 27	Bf 109F-4 WNr 7345 combat, force-landed 50%; Fw Bernhard Schneider safe
4./JG 27	Bf 109F-4 trop WNr 8345 combat; crash-landed Qotaifiya 60%; Fw Alfred Heidel safe
5./JG 27	Bf 109G-2 trop WNr 10336 combat, crash-landed 40%; Fw Josef Vavra safe
6./JG 27	Bf 109F-4 WNr 7151 Yellow 10, combat, crashed in sea 15km NE El Daba Obfw Fritz Lüer MiA
6./JG 27	Bf 109F-4 WNr 7413 20% damaged by bombs at Qotaifiya
8./JG 27	Bf 109F-4 WNr 7489 combat, force-landed El Daba, 80%. pilot safe
8./JG 77	Bf 109G-2 WNr 10640 combat with P-40, 95% damaged, crash-landed in Qasaba area; Obfw Herbert Kaiser MiA, returned
8./KG 54	Ju 88A-4 WNr 140334 M7+DS hit by fighters at El Alamein, force-landed at Qasaba; Bordfunker Obgefr Karl Kroggel KiA
2./StG 3	Ju 87D-3 WNr 2387 shot up by AA, 30% damaged, crash-landed at El Daba; Uffz Adolf Ebner KiA, gunner safe

Italian Claims

96ª Sq, 9°Gr, 4°St CT	Ten Emanuele Annoni	MC.202	2 P-46s	over Fuka	0900-

96ª Sq, 9°Gr, 4°St CT	Ten Enrico Moretto	MC.202	Spitfire	over Fuka	0900-
96ª Sq, 9°Gr, 4°St CT	Ten Enrico Moretto	MC.202	P-46	over Fuka	0900-
96ª Sq, 9°Gr, 4°St CT	S.Ten Ettore Caregnato	MC.202 MM 9046	P-46	over Fuka	0900-
96ª Sq, 9°Gr, 4°St CT	Ten Anselmo Maggini	MC.202 MM 7829	P-46	over Fuka	mid-morning
74ª Sq, 23°Gr, 3°St CT	Serg Magg Felice Papini	MC.202	P-40	nr El Alamein	1145-1245
75ª Sq, 23°Gr, 3°St CT	Ten Ezio Monti	MC.202			
75ª Sq, 23°Gr, 3°St CT	Serg Vannetto Cavicchioli	MC.202	P-40 Probable	nr El Alamein	1145-1245
70ª Sq, 23°Gr, 3°St CT	Ten Marco Marinone	MC.202	P-40 Probable	nr El Alamein	1145-1245
70ª Sq, 23°Gr, 3°St CT	S.Ten Giuseppe Melandri	MC.202	P-40 Probable	nr El Alamein	1145-1245
74ª Sq, 23°Gr, 3°St CT	Ten Giorgio Solaroli	MC.202			
75ª Sq, 23°Gr, 3°St CT	Cap Mario Pinna	MC.202	P-40	near El Daba	1435-1600
75ª Sq, 23°Gr, 3°St CT	Serg Maurizio Mandolesi	MC.202			
70ª Sq, 23°Gr, 3°St CT	Serg William Dusi	MC.202	P-40	near El Daba	1435-1600
391ª Sq, 159°Gr, 50°St Ass	Ten Piero Vodret	CR.42 MM8921	P-40	El Alamein	1515
391ª Sq, 159°Gr, 50°St Ass	S.Ten Francesco Iadanza	CR.42	P-40	El Alamein	1515

Italian Casualties

96ª Sq, 9°Gr, 4°St CT	MC.202 MM 9046 failed to return, S.Ten Ettore Caregnato MiA
96ª Sq, 9°Gr, 4°St CT	MC.202 MM 7829 failed to return, Ten Anselmo Maggini MiA
238ª Sq, 101°Gr, 5°St Tuff	CR.42 MM 8936 shot down into the sea, Serg Magg Urbano Suzzi MiA
389ª Sq, 159°Gr, 50°St Ass	CR.42 MM 8856 hit in combat, force-landed and later recovered, Ten Mario Aimi safe
389ª Sq, 159°Gr, 50°St Ass	CR.42 MM 8851 force-landed near El Daba, recovered, Serg Magg Costante Cipitelli safe
387ª Sq, 158°Gr, 50°St Ass	CR.42 MM 8491 caught fire after force-landing 60km SE El Daba, Cap Giordano Bruno Rossoni WiA, rescued next day by a Fi 156 Storch flown by Magg Simeone Marsan of 4° Stormo

Wednesday, 28 October 1942

The panzer divisions again attempted to form up for a sustained attack, but the Allied artillery and bombers kept pounding them, the bombers finally striking so heavily in the evening that the attack could not be launched. During the day also Ju 87s were once more forced to jettison their bombs on their own troops. Montgomery now abandoned the thrust in the Kidney Ridge area, withdrawing 24th Armoured Brigade into reserve and renewing the attack along the coast by the Australian infantry. At the same time

Bf 109E Jabo (fighter-bomber) of 7./ZG 1.

7th Armoured Division was ordered north to be ready should a breakthrough be achieved. Realising that the north now represented the decisive area, Rommel brought all the German forces remaining in the south, up to this part of the line, leaving the Italians to hold the quieter sections of the front. Further attempts were made to supply him with fuel, but another tanker and a supply ship were sunk during the day (see Chapter Ten).

Two Spitfires of 145 Squadron flew a freelance patrol over Daba at 0710, two Bf 109s being spotted over El Alamein; Sgt Anderson attacked one which made off, but Flg Off Phillips failed to return. Four 92 Squadron Spitfires then took off on a similar mission at 0900. 27 Bf 109s of I./JG 27 and I./JG 77 set off on a Freie Jagd at 0914, meeting 30 Allied fighters near El Alamein, claiming to have shot down two; Flt Sgt Blades of 92 Squadron was shot-up and crash-landed within Allied lines, other pilots of the Squadron claiming a probable and a damaged against the Messerschmitts.

During the day two formations of Hurricanes took off. In the first, 12 aircraft of 127 Squadron with a top cover from 80 Squadron, escorted two TacR Hurricanes of 208 Squadron on an artillery shoot. These aircraft were attacked by two formations of Axis fighters, one of 18 and the other of ten aircraft; one Hurricane was damaged. Other Hurricanes of 1 SAAF Squadron, escorted during the morning by 33 Squadron, carried out a patrol during which eight Messerschmitts attacked the latter unit and forced its aircraft to lose height. The Germans then attacked the South Africans from up-sun, Maj le Mesurier's aircraft being hit in six places. As he turned, he blacked out and went into a spin. Recovering from this, he was able to regain base. One fighter (identified as a Spitfire) was claimed during the morning by Hptm Huy of 7./JG 77.

At 0945 four more Spitfires from 92 Squadron patrolled above a formation of 12 Baltimores and six B-25s, escorted by Kittyhawks and a dozen P-40s of the US 66th Squadron to bomb LG.20. Six aircraft of 3 RAAF Squadron were flying top cover to the bombers. Six Bf 109s of II./JG 27 took off at 1010 to patrol over their own airfield, attacking the fighters which were escorting the bombers, Oblt Sommer shooting down the Spitfire flown by Flt Lt Cocker of 92 Squadron. A second aircraft was damaged, Flt Sgt Novak crash-landing his Spitfire on the way back to the unit's base. It was reported that the bombers had seriously damaged four Bf 109s on the ground. Following the bombing, Sqn Ldr Gibbes of 3 RAAF Squadron attacked three Messerschmitts: "Escort to Mitchells to bomb LG.20 in the morning. We were top cover. Three 109s tried to attack. Managed to get a squirt at one as it climbed up. I hit the bugger behind the one which I aimed at and he went down streaming glycol. Later confirmed by the Yanks, 66 Squadron. Makes my ninth confirmed – the squadron's 200th."

The American pilots saw three Messerschmitts attack and one of these was watched going down in a slow dive, pouring white smoke. Just before the bombing another three attacked and one of these was claimed as a probable by Lt Overcash; it appears that this was later confirmed.

Ten Kittyhawks of 260 Squadron escorted bombers at 1410, attacking four Bf 109s, one of which was claimed probably shot down by two pilots. Eleven of this unit's aircraft were off again at 1640, this time in the fighter-bomber role, escorted by aircraft of 2 SAAF Squadron. After bombing, this formation was attacked by eight fighters, 18 Bf 109s of I./JG 27 and I./JG 77 having taken off at 1645 on a Freie Jagd. Flt Sgt Edwards of 260 Squadron claimed a Bf 109 and a probable, Lt Hilton-Barber of 2 SAAF Squadron also claiming one which he reported disintegrated in mid-air. An MC.202 was claimed by Lt Dawson-Squibb, which he reported seeing spin into the ground. Other claims by these units for a probable and a damaged were also made.

In a mid-afternoon escort to nine Bostons and nine Baltimores, Bf 109s were again escorted by US P-40s. This time the 64th Squadron's Lt Glade Bilby pursued one Messerschmitt which, after he had hit it several times, struck the ground, crashing into a vehicle. It proved to be another good day for the Americans. At 1615 a dozen 66th Squadron aircraft took off with 12 more of 450 Squadron to escort 12 Baltimores and six B-25s on yet another raid. As the formation turned for home after undertaking the bombing, six Axis fighters were reported and in rapid succession three were claimed shot down. Recorded 2/Lt Thomas Boulware: "I was on my way back from a bomber escort when we were sent back by Command on a 270 degree course for south-west of Alamein to look for bandits. We patrolled up along the bomb line without finding them and then went south to join a fight which we saw in Square 8529 between 20 plus P-40s and ten plus 109s, plus 202s. There were four Mes....over the coast. Much later in the fight I saw Capt Llewellyn and Lt Adams chase two Mes down and saw the one Capt Llewellyn was chasing hit the ground. I dived on the other that was behind Capt Llewellyn and before I reached him they pulled out of their dive and the Me turned to the left and then turned right and came up in front of me. I pulled up into him and fired. He was at about 250 yards because my tracers were just converging. My lead was too much but I held it there and he flew through my shots. I saw the tracers hit him, starting in the nose and when they reached his cockpit I stalled and went on my back. Capt Llewellyn was pulling up and saw the Me turn over on his back and go down and hit the ground. I claim one Me 109F destroyed." Lt Mayer of I./JG 27 was shot down near the Sidi Abd el Rahman mosque, with another of this unit's aircraft force-landed, the pilot surviving unhurt.

In the course of the day the Hurricanes of 335 Squadron carried out a strafing attack on the Italian general headquarters to commemorate the second anniversary of the Italian invasion of Greece, but Flak was heavy. Plt Off Kartalamakis failed to return and Plt Off Xydis crash-landed in Allied territory due to a glycol leak caused by Flak damage. Plt Off Panagopoulos' aircraft was also hit in the engine but he got back safely.

Once again, despite the number of bomber sorties flown, the Axis fighters failed to get through to attack them. However, a Baltimore of 223 Squadron was hit by Flak and went down, bursting into flames on hitting the ground.

British Claims

92 Sqn	Sgt H.Patterson	Spitfire Vb EP407 'H'	Bf 109 Damaged	10-15m W Alamein	0900-1025
92 Sqn	Lt S.W.Rabie	Spitfire Vc BR243 'D'	Bf 109	5m W El Hammam	0900-1025
92 Sqn	Flg Off J.Buckley	Spitfire Vb EP441 'R'	Bf 109 Damaged	N Ghazal	0945-1110
3 RAAF Sqn	Sqn Ldr R.H.Gibbes	Kittyhawk III FR305 'V'	Bf 109F	LG.20	1015
450 Sqn	Sgt A.W.J.Taylor	Kittyhawk III FR196	Bf 109E Damaged	6m S El Imayid	1401-1504
260 Sqn	Sgt L.J.Sheppard	Kittyhawk IIa	Bf 109 Probable	Sidi Abd el Rahman area	1410-1525
260 Sqn	Flt Sgt V.J.Thagard	Kittyhawk IIa			
260 Sqn	Flt Sgt J.F.Edwards	Kittyhawk IIa FL221 'F'	Bf 109F	E El Daba	1640-1800
260 Sqn	Flt Sgt J.F.Edwards	Kittyhawk IIa FL221 'F'	Bf 109F Probable	E El Daba	1640-1800
260 Sqn	Flg Off N.E.Gilboe	Kittyhawk IIa	Bf 109F Probable		1640-1800
260 Sqn	Sgt E.G.Hill	Kittyhawk IIa	Bf 109F Damaged		1640-1800
2 SAAF Sqn	Lt L.Dawson-Squibb	Kittyhawk I EV326 'F'	MC.202	Ghazal station	1715
2 SAAF Sqn	Lt G.Hilton-Barber	Kittyhawk I ET972 'P'	Bf 109F	Ghazal station	1715
2 SAAF Sqn	2/Lt J.R.Wight	Kittyhawk I AL186 'G'	Bf 109 Damaged	Ghazal station	1715

British Casualties

127 Sqn	Hurricane IIb BE372 left 0900, badly damaged by Bf 109 El Alamein area, landed at base 1015; Plt Off J.W.Hicks safe
1 SAAF Sqn	Hurricane IIc damaged by Bf 109 at 1000; Maj G.J.le Mesurier
335 Sqn	Hurricane II HL834 MiA from ground attack; Plt Off Kartalamakis FTR
335 Sqn	Hurricane II BP136 crash-landed; Plt Off Xydis
335 Sqn	Hurricane II damaged; Plt Off Panagopolous
145 Sqn	Spitfire V EP643 'V' left 0710, FTR presumed shot down by Bf 10 over Daba; Plt Off H.J.Phillips MiA
92 Sqn	Spitfire Vc BP983 'K' left 0900 shot down by Bf 109 El Alamein area, crash-landed; Flt Sgt R.W.Blades safe
92 Sqn	Spitfire Vb EP613 'S' left 0945, shot down by Bf 109 nr LG.21; Flt Lt L.Cocker KiA
92 Sqn	Spitfire Vc BR523 'E' shot down by Bf 109, crash-landed at 1050; Flt Sgt W.F.Novak safe
223 Sqn	Baltimore III AG959 to bomb LG.20; hit by Flak E Qotaifiya II and down smoking, bursting into flames on impact; Flg Off J.Marriner and one KiA, two PoW

US Claims

66th FS/57th FG	2/Lt Robert J.Overcash	P-40F '84'	Bf 109F	0945-1110
64th FS/57th FG	Capt Glade B.Bilby	P-40F '31'	Bf 109	1555
66th FS/57th FG	1/Lt Robert M.Adams	P-40F '78'	Bf 109F	1715-1730
66th FS/57th FG	2/Lt Thomas McC.Boulware	P-40F '86'	Bf 109F	1715-1730
66th FS/57th FG	Capt Raymond A.Llewellyn	P-40F '82'	Bf 109F	1715-1730

German Claims

4./JG 27	Oblt Paul Sommer	Spitfire	N El Alamein	0940
7./JG 77	Hptm Wolf-Dietrich Huy	Spitfire	El Alamein	

German Casualties

3./JG 27	Bf 109G-2 trop WNr 10588 Yellow 6 combat, crashed SW Sidi-Abd el Rahman mosque; Lt Albert Mayer MiA
3./JG 27	Bf 109G-2 trop WNr 10529 combat SW El Alamein, force-landed 80%; Oblt Josef Schlang safe
2.(F)/123	Ju 88D-1 WNr 430365 destroyed by own forces at Derna

Thursday, 29 October 1942

The 90th Light Division now moved north to stop the attacking Australians at which point Montgomery now decided on a new plan under the codename Supercharge. Giving up the idea of breaking out in the north, he continued to maintain the pressure there, but at the same time the New Zealand Division prepared to open up a gap in the centre for the armour to burst through that part of the line held by the Italians, to the south of the three 'crack' German divisions which would be held in the north.

Wg Cdr Love, with Sqn Ldr Wedgwood of 92 Squadron as his No.2, led a two squadron patrol of 244 Wing Spitfires at 0955. At 15,000 feet near El Alamein they met a formation of Ju 87s escorted by 22 Bf 109s of I./JG 27, I./JG 77 and III./JG 77, plus 11 more from II./JG 27 as close escort. The Spitfire pilots attacked, three Messerschmitts being claimed shot down while Wg Cdr Love claimed an MC.202 damaged. The StabRotte of II./JG 27 had carried out a Freie Jagd ahead of the main force, reporting meeting 20 fighters, one of which Hptm Rödel claimed shot down at 1005.

At 1100 11 Hurricanes of 335 Squadron escorted others of 274 Squadron, encountering three Bf 109s, one of which Plt Off Anagnostopoulos claimed to have damaged. A lone Bf 109 of II./JG 27 took off on a test flight at 1130, the pilot, Fw Schneider, attacking a fighter-bomber squadron near El Alamein at 1150, claiming to have shot down one P-40. 2 SAAF Squadron was providing cover to Kittybombers to Daba Station at this time, where one of the unit's aircraft was damaged Cat II. After the bombing, these aircraft patrolled over the forward area. Here four Bf 109s were seen to dive on Lt Wilmot who was lagging, shooting down his aircraft in flames. Eight Bf 109s of III./JG 27 took off on a Freie Jagd at 1247, followed at 1300 by 23 from I./JG 27, I./JG 77 and III./JG 77 on a similar mission. At the same time nine Spitfires of 601 Squadron swept over the line. The first Luftwaffe formation reported attacking 30 Curtiss fighters and 15 Spitfires over the Panzerarmee, Lt Schroer claiming one Spitfire at 1325. The other Messerschmitts encountered 40-50 fighters and claimed to have hit two Spitfires, but Hptm Huy, the newly-arrived Staffelkapitän from III./JG 77, was shot down and baled out to become a PoW. 601 Squadron saw four Bf 109s, one of which Plt Off Nicholls shot down, the pilot baling out (this was obviously Huy). The Squadron re-formed and attacked eight more Messerschmitts without result. 92 Squadron was also engaged again at this time, Plt Off Samouelle making a claim for a Bf 109 damaged; this was upgraded to a destroyed two days later; possibly interrogation of the captured Huy led to the decision to do this.

Six Kittyhawks of 250 Squadron took off at 1420, strafing Mersa Matruh airfield, claiming to have destroyed two He 111s and a Ju 88 on the ground here and damaged two more Ju 88s. At 1654 12 Messerschmitts of I./JG 27 and JG 77, ten from II.Gruppe and eight from III./JG 27 escorted Stukas, reporting engaging 50 British fighters over the target. Hptm Franzisket of I.Gruppe was shot down and baled out, breaking his leg. He had probably been the target of Flt Lt Taylor of 145 Squadron, nine Spitfires from this unit being scrambled over El Alamein and being attacked by Bf 109s at this time. Taylor's victim was seen to turn on its side and fall into the sea.

Towards the end of what had been a very busy and eventful month for the Regia Aeronautica units, several moves were undertaken on this date. 4° Stormo CT now departed Fuka for Martuba, while 50° Stormo Assalto also arrived at Martuba from Abar Nimeir. However, 191ª Squadriglia BT ordered its Cant Z.1007bis from Mersa Matruh further west to Barce. On this date, a 23° Gruppo MC.202 was damaged during a force-landing, the pilot being slightly hurt. This may have been the aircraft claimed damaged by Wg Cdr Love during the morning, there having been no other claims against Italian aircraft during the day. By night Cap Massi led seven CR.42s of 101° Gruppo to dive-bomb enemy landing craft. Just three fighter-bombers reached the target releasing six 50kg bombs. No results were observed. Magg Rizzi returned to Italy, handing over temporary command of 101° Gruppo Tuffatori, with 18 serviceable CR.42s, to Cap Massi.

British Claims

92 Sqn	Wg Cdr R.C.Love	Spitfire Vc BR520 'L'	MC.202 Damaged	5m W El Alamein	0955-1105
92 Sqn	Flt Lt J.M.Morgan	Spitfire Vb EP399 'S'	Bf 109	5m W El Alamein	0955-1105
92 Sqn	Flg Off J.L.Waddy	Spitfire Vb EP441 'R'	Bf 109	5m W El Alamein	0955-1105
92 Sqn	Sqn Ldr J.H.Wedgwood	Spitfire Vc BR476 'J'	Bf 109	15m W El Alamein	0955-1105
335 Sqn	Plt Off Anagnostopoulos	Hurricane IIb BP279	Bf 109 Damaged	El Alamein area	1100-1230
601 Sqn	Plt Off J.H.Nicholls	Spitfire Vc BR472	Bf 109	El Alamein area	1300-1405
92 Sqn	Flt Lt C.J.Samouelle	Spitfire Vc BR521 'E'	Bf 109*	El Alamein	1300-1415

145 Sqn	Flt Lt J.S.Taylor	Spitfire Vb EP327 'R'	Bf 109	El Alamein	1635-1800

*claimed as Damaged; confirmed Destroyed on 31st

British Casualties

260 Sqn	Kittyhawk IIa FL223 FTR, presumed shot down by Bf 109s nr El Alamein
2 SAAF Sqn	Kittyhawk I EV166 shot down by Bf 109 at Daba at 1145; Lt J.G.H.Wilmot KiA
2 SAAF Sqn	Kittyhawk I AK568 'V' damaged by Bf 109 Cat II at Daba at 1145

US Casualties

83rd BS/12th BG	B-25C '11' hit by Flak, crashed at LG.88; 2/Lt F.E.Whitker and three WiA, 2/Lt F.E.Mehmann KiA

German Claims

Stab II./JG 27	Hptm Gustav Rödel	P-40	Deir el Bein	0905
5./JG 27	Fw Bernhard Schneider	P-40	NE Deir el Tarfa	1052
8./JG 27	Lt Werner Schroer	Spitfire	S El Alamein	1225

German Casualties

1./JG 27	Bf 109G-2 trop WNr 10616 shot down by Spitfire; crashed 10km E Qotaifiya; Hptm Ludwig Franzisket baled but injured
5./JG 27	Bf 109G-2 trop WNr 14263 40% damaged by bombs at Qotaifiya
7./JG 77	Bf 109G-2 WNr 13533 White 1 shot down by Spitfire. El Alamein; Hptm Wolfdieter Huy baled, PoW
Fl Ber Fl FHr Afrika	He 111 H-6 WNr 4822 destroyed in strafing attack at Mersa Matruh airfield

Italian Casualties

74ª Sq, 23°Gr, 3°St CT	MC.202 MM 8344 '74-7' damaged on force-landing near Fuka, Serg Magg Luigi Margutti slightly wounded
96ª Sq, 9°Gr, 4°St CT	MC.202 MM 7895 '96-9' badly damaged by bombs at Fuka

Friday, 30 October 1942

33 and 238 Squadrons patrolled at 0850, encountering 15 Ju 87s. The British pilots flew through the army's AA barrage in order to get at them, but 33 lost the dive-bombers in the shell bursts. The top flight then caught sight of them again and attacked, although the guns of half of the aircraft jammed at the crucial moment. One probable and two damaged were claimed but one Hurricane was lost. 238 Squadron's dozen aircraft which were flying above at 7,000 feet, claimed one more probable and one damaged, which was not a particularly auspicious start. Meanwhile, ten Bf 109s of III./JG 27 had taken off at 0925 to provide indirect escort to the Stukas, and five minutes later ten more from I./JG 77 had set off to fly a Freie Jagd ahead of the bombers. It seems that P-40Fs of the 64th Squadron, 57th Fighter Group were present in the area at this time.

I./JG 77 encountered four fighters over their own airfield at Bir el Abd, two of these being claimed shot down near El Alamein, but Lt Niese of this unit was shot down by four Curtiss fighters – almost certainly the US aircraft, pilots of which claimed one Messerschmitt shot down, one probable and three damaged; Niese survived unhurt. About 15 minutes later Lt Schroer of III.Gruppe reported encountering three fighters which he identified as Airacobras, claiming one shot down at 1020. During these early engagements, Ten Bordoni-Bisleri of 18° Gruppo claimed one P-40 shot down in the Daba area.

Eight P-40s of the 64th Squadron, loaded with bombs and escorted by 12 more of the Group's aircraft from the 65th Squadron, had set off at 0930, briefed to attack some buildings near LG.20. After the bombing six Bf 109s engaged the fighter-bombers, but one Messerschmitt was claimed shot down, one probably so and four damaged. One of the latter claims was made by Lt Ryerson, who saw his target spin, but he was then attacked by two more fighters and the tail of his aircraft was hit and suffered severe damage, while the engine was also hit by one shell and a further bullet hit his hand. He managed to make a successful crash-landing at base.

Somewhat later six MC.202s of 23° Gruppo (two of 74ª and four of 75ª Squadriglie), led by Cap Giorgio Tugnoli, took off to escort Ju 87s; a formation of bombers and P-40s was met and Tugnoli claimed a P-40 probable. At 1005 nine MC.202s of 23° Gruppo led by Magg Filippi were scrambled. A number of British bombers and fighters were again met and attacked. Serg Magg Papini claimed one P-40 and Filippi two damaged, with a Boston probable credited to Ten Specker, a 18° Gruppo pilot.

Twelve Kittyhawks of 2 SAAF Squadron flew top cover to 18 Bostons from 1110, being attacked by two Bf 109s. Lt Hope claimed to have shot one down into the sea. Later in the afternoon, during another bomber escort, 4 SAAF Squadron's aircraft were attacked in error by US P-40Fs, two being damaged. At 1358 four Kittyhawks of 450 Squadron made a ground-attack sortie, encountering a Ju 52/3m transport as they headed out; the pilots claimed to have shot this down between them. During the day pilots of this unit claimed to have inflicted damage on three Bf 109Fs, a Bf 109E and a Ju 52/3m, all when they were on the ground. That night Australian infantry attacked the German strongpoint known as Thompson's Post, breaking through to the coast road.

4° Stormo CT and 159° Gruppo Assalto were ordered to move to Martuba. Five pilots of 4° Stormo, led by Ten Mandolini, ferried five war-weary MC.202s to Bu Amud. There they received the order to fly them to Martuba. Whilst on a truck heading to their parked aircraft, the pilots were strafed by Beaufighters attacking the airfield. Mandolini suffered serious wounds and was taken to Tobruk hospital; M.llo Mechelli and Serg Magg Migliorato were also injured. In the meantime at Fuka 4° Stormo handed over its few remaining serviceable MC.202s to 3° Stormo and prepared to retreat. Both air and ground echelons moved on motor transports towards Martuba, which was reached on 1 November.

British Claims

238 Sqn	Flt Lt K.A.MacKay	Hurricane IIc BP538 'H'	Ju 87 Damaged	E El Alamein	0855-1015
238 Sqn	Sqn Ldr R.Marples	Hurricane IIc HL609 'F'	Ju 87 Probable	E El Alamein	0855-1015
33 Sqn	Flt Sgt J.W.E.Belec	Hurricane IIc BP354 'E'	Ju 87 Damaged	El Alamein area	0900-1005
33 Sqn	Plt Off J.G.B.Campbell	Hurricane IIc BN471	Ju 87 Damaged	El Alamein area	0900-1005
33 Sqn	Sgt W.C.Francis	Hurricane IIc HL625	Ju 87 Probable	El Alamein area	0900-1005
2 SAAF Sqn	Lt L.C.H.Hope	Kittyhawk I EV349 'K'	Bf 109	LG.18, 1m off Gala	1110
450 Sqn	Plt Off T.E.N.Crouch	Kittyhawk III FL879	} Ju 52/3m	5m S Charing Cross	1358-1635
450 Sqn	Sgt M.A.Jenkins	Kittyhawk III FR252			
450 Sqn	Sgt A.G.Markle	Kittyhawk III FR273			
450 Sqn	Sgt H.B.Reid	Kittyhawk III FR274			

British Casualties

33 Sqn	Hurricane IIc ..330 left 0900, shot down over El Alamein, possibly by own AA; Plt Off L.H.Peterson KiA
4 SAAF Sqn	Kittyhawk I AK709 damaged by USAAF P-40; Lt A.C.Paterson safe

US Claims

64th FS/57th FG	Capt Richard E.Ryan	P-40F '27'	Bf 109 Probable	1005
64th FS/57th FG	Maj Clermont E.Wheeler	P-40F '10'	Bf 109s Damaged	1005
64th FS/57th FG	2/Lt Robert J. Byrne	P-40F '13'	Bf 109	1005
64th FS/57th FG	1/Lt Gordon L.Ryerson	P-40F '32'	Bf 109 Damaged	1005
64th FS/57th FG	1/Lt William S.Beck	P-40F '16'	2 Bf 109s Damaged	1005

US Casualties

64th FS/57th FG	P-40F '32' damaged in combat and crash-landed at LG. 174; 1 /Lt Gordon L.Ryerson

German Claims

8./JG 27	Lt Werner Schroer	P-39	SSE El Daba	0920
1./JG 77	Oblt Siegfried Freytag	P-40	El Alamein	
1./JG 77	Obfw Georg Ludwig	P-40	El Alamein	

German Casualties

1./JG 27	Bf 109G-2 trop WNr 10562 40% damaged in strafing by fighter-bombers Tanyet-Harun
3./JG 77	Bf 109G-2 trop WNr 10505 combat with P-40 Bir el Abd; Lt Erhard Niese baled, safe
IV./KGzb V 1	Ju 52/3m WNr 6591 destroyed on the ground at El Adem airfield; Obfw Georg Probst WiA, Uffz Gerhard Schneider KiA, two safe
Srst DFS 230 Ob Süd	Ju 87R-4 WNr 6275 shot down in combat near Qasaba, crew safe
KGr zbV 400	Ju 52/3m WNr 3167 shot down by P-40s, crashed 20km S Mersa Matruh; Oblt Dietrich Steinhausen WiA, three safe

Italian Claims

95ª Sq, 18°Gr, 3°St CT	Ten Franco Bordoni-Bisleri	MC.202	P-40	El Daba	0745-0930
74ª Sq, 23°Gr, 3°St CT	Cap Giorgio Tugnoli	MC.202	P-40 Probable	El Alamein	0830-
74ª Sq, 23°Gr, 3°St CT	Serg Magg Felice Papini	MC.202	P-40	El Alamein	1005-1035
75ª Sq, 23°Gr, 3°St CT	Magg Luigi Filippi	MC.202	2 P-40s Damaged	El Alamein	1005-1035
83ª Sq, 18°Gr, 3°St CT	Ten Guglielmo Specker	MC.202	Boston Probable	El Alamein	1005-1035

Italian Casualties

191ª Sq, 86°Gr, 35°St BT	2 Cant.Z.1007bis MM 24259 and 24273 destroyed by strafing at Barce 1400
191ª Sq, 86°Gr, 35°St BT	2 Cant.Z.1007bis MM 24279 and 23757 damaged by strafing at Barce 1400
91ª Sq, 10° Gr, 4° St CT	Ten Orlando Mandolini wounded on ground by strafing at Bu Amud

91ª Sq, 10° Gr, 4° St CT	Serg Magg Lorenzo Migliorato wounded on ground by strafing at Bu Amud
73ª Sq, 9° Gr, 4° St CT	M.llo Salvatore Mechelli wounded on ground by strafing at Bu Amud

Saturday, 31 October 1942

Afrika Korps counter-attacks against the Australian advance failed to make any headway, and 7th Armoured Division arrived from the south in an attempt to take advantage of the gains that had been made. Further Allied success had been achieved when a further small Axis supply convoy had been destroyed by Wellingtons and Beauforts (see Chapter Ten).

Eleven Kittyhawks of 250 Squadron covered others from 112 Squadron on a reconnaissance at 0720. Nineteen Bf 109s of I./JG 27 and III./JG 77 set off at 0742 to escort Stukas on their way to bomb 9th Australian Division on the right of the line. They were followed at 0750 by ten from III./JG 27 as indirect support. The formation was then joined by 14 MC.202s of 3° Stormo, led by Cap Mario Pinna. Six of these, followed by six Bf 109s attacked 250 Squadron. 112 Squadron, having bombed a group of tents, were vectored onto the Axis formation, attacking them as the bombers began their dives. Sqn Ldr Drake and Flt Lt Smith each claimed one Ju 87, while four Bf 109s, an MC.202 and another Ju 87 were all claimed as probables. The close escort Bf 109 pilots claimed to have damaged two fighters, but Lt Werfft of III./JG 27 force-landed and Uffz Löffler was hit and wounded, although he managed to regain base.

Flt Lt John Williams of 450 Squadron with his Kittyhawk claimed two Ju 87s as 'probables' on 12 September, but these were later upgraded to confirmed destroyed. He had just assumed command of 450 Squadron when on 31 October he was shot down during a low-level strafing operation. He was taken prisoner, but was later to be one of those who took part in the Great Escape from Stalag Luft III and who was subsequently shot by the Gestapo on 29 March 1944 after recapture.

Twelve Kittyhawks of 250 Squadron provided medium cover to 18 B-25s attacking Fuka at 1005, and 20 minutes later 12 260 Squadron Kittyhawks were scrambled on an interception patrol. At 1030 eight Bf 109s of III./JG 27 took off as direct escort to Stukas followed five minutes later by six from II./JG 27, and then three from I./JG 77. At 1050 Uffz Philipp of III./JG 77 took up a Messerschmitt on a test flight. From this force, four Bf 109s and three MC.202s of 3° Stormo attacked 250 Squadron over Fuka. Sgt Stephens engaged the latter which caused sufficient damage to his aircraft to cause him to force-land at LG.37; 260 Squadron meanwhile, encountered four more Bf 109s, two of which were claimed shot down for the loss of one Kittyhawk.

5 SAAF Squadron's Tomahawks were scrambled at 1040 to provide some cover for the Australian troops, but the unit was bounced by six Bf 109s. Capt Armstrong ordered a turn-about, but as the fighters went into a tight turn it seems that two of them collided, one crashing with the death of the pilot the other force-landing. During these engagements II./JG 27 claimed three P-40s shot down, two of them by Hptm Rödel. However, one Bf 109 of III.Gruppe was shot down, Uffz Moycis returning later, and Fw Steis of II.Gruppe force-landed. Uffz Philipp on his test flight, encountered seven Curtiss fighters and was shot down at 1053, becoming a PoW.

Twelve Spitfires of 601 Squadron took off at 1105 on a 'general beat-up' of LGs. 13 and 14, meeting a Ju 52/3m which was shot down by the pilots jointly. At 1145 12 Kittyhawks of 3 RAAF Squadron bombed and strafed in the northern area, encountering Bf 109s one of which was claimed as probably destroyed. Four Kittyhawks of 450 Squadron were sent off at 1340 on a long-range strafe, joined by 12 from 112 Squadron. Four Bf 109s of I./JG 77 flying top cover to Stukas, intercepted the formation, one of the Australian aircraft being shot down and one of 112 Squadron's machines being damaged. During the raid Sqn Ldr J.E.A.Williams, DFC, 450 Squadron's commanding officer, force-landed, apparently to Flak damage, and was taken prisoner. This New Zealander had been credited with five victories in the desert before he was brought down. He was later one of those shot trying to escape from Stalag Luft III on 29 March 1944.

At midday seven 64th Squadron P-40s provided bottom cover and 12 of 65th Squadron top cover to 18 Baltimores, the latter bombing from 7,000 feet at 1243. Hostile fighters were encountered and 2/Lt Kimball claimed one shot down between Fuka and El Daba:

"I first saw the Me at 12 o'clock coming down in a shallow dive, turning to his left. I was out of his sight under his nose. As he continued his turn I turned to the right and we then turned into each other. He then turned away in the direction I was turning and this put me directly on his tail. I opened up with a one-second burst. This got his glycol and I was so close to him that it completely covered my windscreen and I had to throttle back to keep from running into him. I then fired three more long bursts at him and my guns stopped. I levelled off at 2,000 feet just above the clouds and recharged my guns. As I was a target on the clouds I dropped through them to find the Me running close to the deck just below me to the right. I then swung out and made a ¾ attack from the rear and fired another burst which caused his engine to stop. He then lost all but ten feet of altitude. I pulled beside him and motioned to him to go down. He didn't so I turned into him and as soon as I started he slammed into the ground hitting a pile of dirt, overturning, and bursting into flames."

On another mission on this date other 57th Fighter Group pilots from the 66th Squadron claimed two more Bf 109s shot down and two damaged.

112 Squadron, with 3 RAAF Squadron as top cover, scrambled again at 1630 to bomb and strafe the area around Daba and Fuka, but again the unit met Ju 87s escorted by Bf 109s. Flt Sgt Brown claimed two Ju 87s and Sgt Wild one; Sgt Money claimed one of the escorting Messerschmitts as did Flg Off Crichton. Plt Off Bruce failed to return, but was later reported to be safe in hospital. The escorting 3 RAAF pilots also got into the fight, claiming a Ju 87 and a Bf 109 as probables, two pilots each claiming two Stukas damaged. 1./SchG 2 Bf 109 pilot, Uffz Mürmann, was reported to have been shot down and killed during this engagement.

Twelve Spitfires of 601 Squadron had taken off ten minutes after the 239 Wing Kittyhawks on another strafing sortie. During this, Plt Off Llewellyn's aircraft was hit by Flak and he crash-landed near the Qattara Depression. Plt Off B.R.Terry landed alongside and flew him back to base in his Spitfire. During the early afternoon one P-40 was claimed shot down by Obfw Kaiser of III./JG 77.

On this date Sqn Ldr Mannix, another ex-127 Squadron pilot, replaced Sqn Ldr J.F.F.Finnis, DFC, as commanding officer of 33 Squadron. The 57th Fighter Group noted that at the end of the month its three squadrons had claimed 27 confirmed victories, six probables and 15 damaged for the loss of two pilots.

At dusk S.Ten Antonio Caravaggio led five CR.42s of 101° Gruppo to dive-bomb the railway line and the coastal road from El Alamein to El Hammam. During the day 159° Gruppo Assalto moved to Derna El Fteiah and 101° Gruppo moved to Abu Smeit. 8° Gruppo, meanwhile, carried on its customary convoy escort sorties. The Regia Aeronautica at the end of a memorable month for its MC.202 pilots, reported that between 20-31 October,15 Macchis had been lost in air combat (Allied pilots claimed 22) and that four MC.202s, four MC.200s and two Cant.Z.1007bis had been destroyed on the ground, four, six and two respectively having been damaged; a number of CR.42s had similarly been destroyed or damaged.

British Claims

112 Sqn	Sgt D.E.Brown	Kittyhawk III FR302 'T'	Bf 109 Probable		0720-0845
112 Sqn	Plt Off B.A.F.Cuddon	Kittyhawk III FR263 'X'	Bf 109F Probable	N El Alamein	0720-0845
112 Sqn	Plt Off L.H.Curphey	Kittyhawk III FR195 'F'	Bf 109F Probable	N El Alamein	0720-0845
112 Sqn	Sqn Ldr B.Drake	Kittyhawk III FR293 '?'	Ju 87	N El Alamein	0720-0845
112 Sqn	Sgt M.H.Lamont	Kittyhawk III FR281 'D'	Bf 109F Probable	N El Alamein	0720-0845

112 Sqn	Sgt W.Money	Kittyhawk III FR264 'W'	Bf 109	N El Alamein	0720-0845
112 Sqn	Flt Sgt R.H.Newton	Kittyhawk III FR279 'J'	Ju 87 Probable	N El Alamein	0720-0845
112 Sqn	Plt Off H.Phillips	Kittyhawk III FR215 'V'	MC.202 Probable	N El Alamein	0720-0845
112 Sqn	Flt Lt R.R.Smith	Kittyhawk III FR217 'C'	Ju 87	N El Alamein	0720-0845
250 Sqn	Flg Off W.J.Whitside	Kittyhawk III FL877	Bf 109F Probable	N El Alamein	0830
250 Sqn	Flt Lt R.Taylor	Kittyhawk III FR306 'O'	MC.202 Probable	N El Alamein	0830
250 Sqn	Flt Off G.W.Troke	Kittyhawk III FR275 'E'	Bf 109F Damaged	Fuka, LG.17	1005-1125
260 Sqn	Flt Lt W.R.Cundy	Kittyhawk IIa FL229	Bf 109	12m S El Daba	1024-1204
260 Sqn	Flt Lt W.R.Cundy	Kittyhawk IIa FL229 }	Bf 109	12m S El Daba	1024-1204
260 Sqn	Sgt B.H.Thomas	Kittyhawk IIa }			
601 Sqn	12 pilots	Spitfire Vc	Ju 52/3m	LG.12 & LG.13 areas	1105-1320
450 Sqn	Sgt D.W.P.Borthwick	Kittyhawk III FR300	Bf 109F Probable	Barrani road	1349-1646
3 RAAF Sqn	Sgt R.H.Bayley	Kittyhawk I AL217 'B'	Bf 109F Probable	Ghazal station	1442
112 Sqn	Flt Sgt W.D.Brown	Kittyhawk III FR211 'E'	2 Ju 87s	nr Daba	1630-1750
112 Sqn	Flg Off J.M.S.Crichton	Kittyhawk III FR216 'P'	Bf 109F	nr Daba	1630-1750
112 Sqn	Sgt D.S.Watson	Kittyhawk III FR217 'C'	Bf 109F Damaged	nr Daba	1630-1750
112 Sqn	Sgt R.A.Wild	Kittyhawk III FR215 'V'	Ju 87	nr Daba	1630-1750
112 Sqn	Sgt R.A.Wild	Kittyhawk III FR215 'V'	Bf 109F Damaged	nr Daba	1630-1750
3 RAAF Sqn	Sgt N.R.Caldwell	Kittyhawk I ET899 'Y'	2 Ju 87s Damaged	Daba-Fuka area	1710
3 RAAF Sqn	Sgt J.F.H.Cashmore	Kittyhawk I EV346 'O'	2 Ju 87s Damaged	Daba-Fuka area	1710
3 RAAF Sqn	Plt Off D.V.Ritchie	Kittyhawk I AL154 'N'	Ju 87 Probable	Daba-Fuka area	1710

British Casualties

112 Sqn	Kittyhawk III FR281 'D' FTR from armed recce; Plt Off D.A.Bruce MiA
112 Sqn	Kittyhawk III damaged; Sgt Pollock
250 Sqn	Kittyhawk III FR306 left 1005, damaged by MC.202 Fuka area, crash-landed at LG.37; Sgt A.C.Stephens safe
250 Sqn	Kittyhawk III FR241 'R' left 1005, damaged by MC.202 Fuka; Plt Off N.G.Russell safe
260 Sqn	Kittyhawk IIa shot down by Bf 109 N Abu Dweis 1024-1204; Sgt R.G.Mockridge died
260 Sqn	Kittyhawk IIa badly damaged by Flak nr El Daba, 1024-1204; Sgt D.W.C.England safe
450 Sqn	Kittyhawk III FL879 FTR on ground attack, shot down by Bf 109; Sgt F.B.Reid KiA
450 Sqn	Kittyhawk III FR270 force-landed in the desert during ground-attack sortie; Sqn Ldr J.E.A.Williams PoW
5 SAAF Sqn	Tomahawk IIb AM471 'A' collided with AM474 during op at 1120 nr El Alamein; Lt E.W.L.Popham crashed in Axis territory and KiFA
5 SAAF Sqn	Tomahawk IIb AM474 'Z' force-landed at El Imayid station after collision; Lt B.A.Kearns
601 Sqn	Spitfire V BR132 left 1640, hit by Flak and force-landed in desert; Plt Off D.E.Llewellyn safe

US Claims

66th FS/57th FG	1/Lt Joe D.Bell	P-40F	Bf 109F	El Alameim	1145-1245
66th FS/57th FG	1/Lt Harry J.Hayden	P-40F	Bf 109F Damaged	Fuka-El Daba	1000-1120
66th FS/57th FG	2/Lt Richard W.Kimball	P-40F '85'	Bf 109F	Fuka-El Daba	1000-1120
66th FS/57th FG	Capt Raymond A.Llewellyn	P-40F	Bf 109F	Fuka-El Daba	1000-1120
66th FS/57th FG	Capt William J.Yates	P-40F	Bf 109F Damaged	El Alameim	1145-1245
66th FS/57th FG	1/Lt Robert A.Hoke	P-40F	Bf 109F Damaged	Fuka-El Daba	1000-1120

US Casualties

57th FG	2 P-40s FTR

German Claims

Stab II./JG 27	Hptm Gustav Rödel	2 P-40s	SW Sanyet Qotaifiya	0952 & 0955
7./JG 27	Uffz Hans Philipp	P-40	N Abu-Dweis	0953
8./JG 77	Obfw Herbert Kaiser	P-40		1305

German Casualties

2./JG 27	Bf 109G-2 trop WNr 10606 combat nr Bir el Abd, 50% damaged; pilot safe
2./JG 27	Bf 109G-2 trop WNr 10580 10% damaged by bombs at Tanyet-Harun
4./JG 27	Bf 109G-2 trop WNr 14264 combat, force-landed Bir el Abd, 30%; Fw Heinrich Steis safe
9./JG 27	Bf 109F-4 trop WNr 8470 combat SW El Alamein, 100%; Lt Dr Peter Werfft MiA, but returned
8./JG 27	Bf 109F-4 trop WNr 10075 combat SW El Alamein, 100%; Uffz Hans Löffler WiA
III./ZG 1	Bf 109E-7 WNr 4157 S9+ ED shot down by P-40 Alam el Halfa; Uffz Friedrich Mürmann KiA
1./StG 3	Ju 87D-3 WNr 2657 S7+HH AA 15km SE Ain el Gazala; Uffz Bodo Jansen WiA, gunner safe

German Casualties

9./StG 3	Ju 87D-3 WNr 2719 combat with P-40 15km W El Alamein; Obfw Erich Borm KiA; pilot safe
9./StG 3	Ju 87D-3 combat with P-40 15km W El Alamein; Uffz Rudolf Geisler WiA; pilot safe
KGr zbV 400	Ju 52/3m WNr 6867 M3+FA shot down in combat and crashed 40km SE Mersa Matruh; pilot and one safe, two WiA

Italian Casualties

82ª Sq, 13°Gr, 2°St CT	MC.200 MM 5128 unserviceable, set on fire
391ª Sq, 159° Gr, 50° St Ass	CR.42 force-landed near Sollum, badly damaged, Cap Valentino Festa unhurt
208ª Sq, 101° Gr, 5° St Tuff	CR.42 destroyed, Ten Giacomo Fileppo KiFA

Sunday, 1 November 1942

At dawn 12 Kittyhawks of 112 Squadron with P-40Fs of the US 66th Squadron, flew an armed reconnaissance during which a tented encampment was bombed. Following this, some 30 Ju 87s of I. and III./StG 3 were encountered. These were heavily escorted by 11 Bf 109s from I./JG 27 and III./JG 77, eight from II./JG 27 and seven from I./JG 77, joined by ten MC.202s of 23° Gruppo. The Stukas were forced to jettison their bombs on their own troops again as 112 Squadron closed with them. In quick succession seven were claimed shot down, two by Sgt De Bourke, plus six probables and two damaged.

The defending Messerschmitts were not able to do a lot to ameliorate the situation on this occasion. I./JG 27's pilots reported meeting 25-30 Curtiss fighters, some it was noted, with sharks' teeth on their noses; II.Gruppe reported six Spitfires, ten Curtiss and 20 Airacobras (presumably the US P-40Fs). Pilots of the former unit claimed hits on three aircraft, but only Oblt Unterberger claimed to have shot one down, apparently the pilot baling out. Hptm Rödel of II.Gruppe claimed one, with Lt Berres and Hptm Bär of I./JG 77 one each (identified as Spitfires). In fact 112 Squadron suffered two casualties, one of them the successful Sgt De Bourke, who was wounded but managed to get back to base. StG 3 suffered five losses amongst its Ju 87s.

Ju 87D WNr S7+KS of 8./StG 3 shot down on 1 November. Uffz Otto Eckhardt and his gunner, Uffz Herbert Wagner survived with wounds to become PoWs.

Nine Spitfires of 92 Squadron patrolled over the front from 1010, but were attacked by 11 Bf 109s from I./JG 27 which had taken off at 1048 to give indirect escort and top cover to more Stukas. The German pilots claimed to have hit two fighters which then disappeared in cloud, Fw Keppler being credited with one shot down. One Spitfire was hit, Plt Off Sly crash-landing.

At 1410 12 Kittyhawks of 250 Squadron set off to strafe the Marsa Matruh road. These were jumped by two MC.202s of the 18° Gruppo CT, flown by Ten Bordoni-Bisleri and S.Ten Caetani, which had been attracted by the smoke of burning vehicles under attack by the British aircraft. The Italian pilots reported spotting two flights, one of nine and one of six Kittyhawks. They targeted the latter and claimed two shot down and a third probably in a low level dogfight. A Kittyhawk of 450 Squadron was also shot down in the Mersa Matruh area during the day, and may have been engaged in the same combat.

Eight Kittyhawks of 4 SAAF Squadron and four from 260 Squadron took off at 1600 on another ground-attack sortie, escorted by six more 260 Squadron aircraft. Three Bf 109s of III./JG 27 were scrambled to intercept, but Flt Sgt Edwards shot down the Messerschmitt flown by Uffz Jürgens, who

Just prior to arrival in North Africa two of I./JG 77's new Bf 109G-2s are seen here. In the foreground is the aircraft of the GruppenAdjutant, Lt Heinz-Edgar Berres.

force-landed. Around the same time pilots of the US 64th Squadron were engaged in a combat, claiming one MC.202 shot down.

In the northern sector of the front a counter-attack on the Australians forced them to move south of the railway, allowing a pocket of German troops which had been encircled, to escape. However, during one strafing attack by Spitfires, the headquarters of the Panzerarmee had been attacked, the General der Panzer Truppe, Georg von Stumme, commander of the German armour, being killed. On this day III./ZG 1 was renamed II./SchG 2.

British Claims

112 Sqn	Wt Off J.B.Agnew	Kittyhawk III FR289 'Z'	Ju 87	El Alamein area	0615-0745
112 Sqn	Wt Off J.B.Agnew	Kittyhawk III FR289 'Z'	Ju 87 Probable	El Alamein area	0615-0745
112 Sqn	Wt Off J.B.Agnew	Kittyhawk III FR289 'Z'	2 Ju 87s Damaged	El Alamein area	0615-0745
112 Sqn	Plt Off G.F.Allison	Kittyhawk III FR215 'V'	2 Ju 87s Probable	El Alamein area	0615-0745
112 Sqn	Sgt R.De Bourke	Kittyhawk III FR264 'W'	Ju 87	El Alamein area	0615-0745
112 Sqn	Sgt R.De Bourke	Kittyhawk III FR264 'W'	Ju 87 Probable	El Alamein area	0615-0745
112 Sqn	Flt Lt G.W.Garton	Kittyhawk III FR213 'Q'	Ju 87	El Alamein area	0615-0745
112 Sqn	Sgt T.A.Marsden	Kittyhawk III FR302 'T'	Ju 87 Probable	El Alamein area	0615-0745
112 Sqn	Flt Sgt R.C.C.Smith	Kittyhawk III FR263 'X'	Ju 87	El Alamein area	0615-0745
112 Sqn	Flt Sgt R.C.C.Smith	Kittyhawk III FR263 'X'	Ju 87 Probable	El Alamein area	0615-0745
112 Sqn	Sgt D.S.Watson	Kittyhawk III FR279 'J'	Ju 87	El Alamein area	0615-0745
112 Sqn	Sgt R.A.Wild	Kittyhawk III FR768	Ju 87	El Alamein area	0615-0745
112 Sqn	Sgt R.A.Wild	Kittyhawk III FR789	Ju 87 Probable	El Alamein area	0615-0745
260 Sqn	Flt Sgt J.F.Edwards	Kittyhawk IIa FL305 'B'	Bf 109	S El Daba	1600-1710

British Casualties

112 Sqn	Kittyhawk III FR264 'W' left 0615, shot down by Bf 109s; Sgt R.De Bourke WiA
112 Sqn	Kittyhawk III FR289 'Z' left 0615, force-landed in battle area; Wt Off J.B.Agnew safe
250 Sqn	Kittyhawk III FR260 shot down by MC.202s and belly-landed, 1410-1645; Sgt W.K.Martin KiA
250 Sqn	Kittyhawk III damaged Cat II by MC.202, crash-landed at LG.37, 1410-1645; Sgt H.K.O'Brian safe
92 Sqn	Spitfire Vb AR 321 left at 1010, forced to land at 1135; Plt Off E.Sly safe

US Claims

64th FS/57th FG	1/Lt William S.Beck	P-40K '13'	MC.202	
64th FS/57th FG	2/Lt Robert J. Byrne	P-40K '10'	Bf 109 Damaged	1545

German Claims

Stab II./JG 27	Hptm Gustav Rödel	Spitfire	S Sidi Abd el Rahman	0705
Stab I./JG 77	Lt Heinz-Edgar Berres	P-40	S El Bahrein	0715
Stab I./JG 27	Oblt Josef Unterberger	P-40	SSW El Alamein	0717
1./JG 77	Uffz Horst Schlick	P-40		
1./JG 27	Fw Gerhard Keppler	Spitfire		1058

German Casualties

4./JG 27	Bf 109F-4 WNr 7580 10% damaged by bombs at Qotaifiya
4./JG 27	Bf 109F-4 WNr 7413 20% damaged by bombs at Qotaifiya
5./JG 27	Bf 109F-4 WNr 7607 20% damaged by bombs at Qotaifiya
5./JG 27	Bf 109F-4 trop WNr 13032 combat; force-landed S El Daba, 100%; Uffz Hans Jürgens safe
9./JG 27	Bf 109F-4 WNr 7328 crash-landed Turbiya, 45%; Uffz Albert Mödl safe
8./JG 77	Bf 109G-2 trop WNr 10491 destroyed by bombs at Tanyet Harun
8./JG 77	Bf 109G-2 trop WNr 10625 destroyed by bombs at Tanyet Harun
2.(F)/123	Ju 88D-1 WNr 430270 4U+EK MiA Alexandria; Uffz Alfred Kleinschmidt and three MiA
1./StG 3	Ju 87D-1 WNr 2074 S7+LH combat with P-40 20km S El Alamein; one baled; Oblt Walter Unterrainer/Fw Otto Heinz KiA
3./StG 3	Ju 87D-3 WNr 2636 S7+NL combat with P-40 20km S El Alamein; one baled; Uffz Johann Krieger WiA; Uffz Gustav Riegel KiA
7./StG 3	Ju 87D-1 WNr 2583 S7+FR combat with P-40 30km SW El Alamein; Uffz Fritz Satzenhofer/Gefr Viktor Schmidt KiA
7./StG 3	Ju 87D-3 combat with P-40 10km S El Alamein; Fw Jens Petersen WiA; pilot safe
8./StG 3	Ju 87D-3 WNr 2396 combat with P-40 E El Daba; Uffz Otto Eckardt/Uffz Herbert Wagner WiA

Italian Claims

95ª Sq, 18°Gr, 3°St CT	Ten Franco Bordoni-Bisleri	MC.202	P-40	30km SW Mersa Matruh	1445-1615
95ª Sq, 18°Gr, 3°St CT	S.Ten Roberto Caetani	MC.202	P-40	30km SW Mersa Matruh	1445-1615
95ª Sq, 18°Gr, 3°St CT	Ten Franco Bordoni-Bisleri	MC.202	} P-40 Probable	30km SW Mersa Matruh	1445-1615
95ª Sq, 18°Gr, 3°St CT	S.Ten Roberto Caetani	MC.202	}		

Italian Casualties

74ª Sq, 23°Gr, 3°St CT	MC.202 damaged in combat S El Alamein, Ten Cesare Tommasini safe

Monday, 2 November 1942

Operation Supercharge went into action, the New Zealand Division breaking through. However, an anti-tank screen held up 1st Armoured Division as it tried to pass through the same gap, heavy losses being suffered amongst the Allied armour. Armoured cars managed to get through south of Kidney Ridge, and despite fierce Axis attacks, Commonwealth forces reached the Sidi Abd el Rahman track during the day. By evening Rommel had come to the conclusion that withdrawal was vital if he was to prevent his army beginning to break up. It proved to be a day of sustained aerial activity again, beginning at 0600 when nine Spitfires of 601 Squadron took off to patrol over Daba. These were engaged by Bf 109s of I./JG 27, one Spitfire being shot down and one damaged.

At 0630 12 Hurricanes of 127 Squadron, covering others of 80 Squadron, commenced another patrol over the northern sector. Bf 109s of I./JG 27 had taken off at 0625, reporting 20 fighters south-west of Fuka. Four of the German fighters attacked head-on, but on this occasion no Hurricanes were lost, although one did suffer some damage. However, it appears that it was these Luftwaffe fighters which had caused the earlier casualties to 601 Squadron. The 57th Fighter Group was also active, undertaking a dawn strafe during which the American pilots claimed seven aircraft destroyed on the ground. On this date, however, two P-40Fs were lost, both pilots failing to return, although one was later reported to have become a PoW.

At 0710 six Bf 109s of III./JG 77 set off on a patrol during which three formations of Spitfires and Kittyhawks were prevented from strafing vehicles. Nine 92 Squadron pilots on a morning patrol in this area spotted two of the Bf 109s below and dived on them, Plt Off Carpenter shooting one down in flames, the pilot baling out. This was probably Uffz Heinrich Stöckmann of 9.Staffel, who became a PoW. Soon after 0900 nine Messerschmitts of I./JG 77 took off on a Freie Jagd, pilots reporting meeting 28 fighters,

Ju 87B of I./StG 3.

two of which were claimed shot down. However, two of this Gruppe's pilots were also brought down, both pilots baling out. Nine Spitfires of 601 Squadron had taken off at 0910 on patrol, followed five minutes later by 11 Hurricanes of 335 Squadron which were providing top cover to others of 274 Squadron. Eight Bf 109s attacked 601 Squadron whose pilots claimed three shot down and a probable, two of the pilots being seen to bale out. One Messerschmitt attacked 274 Squadron but was driven off but at that point four more appeared, one of which dived down to attack. Flt Sgt Soufrilas of 335 Squadron claimed this shot down, again with the pilot being seen to bale out. This was the first victory to be claimed by the Greek unit.

Capt J.Becourt-Foch of 208 Squadron then took off in a Hurricane IIb at 1000 on a TacR sortie, but he was hit by Flak and wounded in the shoulder, carrying out a belly-landing. Two Bf 109s of II./JG 27 strafed armoured cars and trucks 20 miles south-west of Qotaifiya, but apparently these were Axis vehicles. One fighter was hit in the coolant radiator by return fire, subsequently landing at base on one wheel. Twelve Hurricanes of 238 Squadron undertook an anti-Stuka patrol at 1150 with 33 Squadron as top cover. Ju 87s, escorted by fighters which included 12 from I./JG 27 which had taken off at 1218, were intercepted, Capt Phillips claiming one Stuka and Flg Off Gilbert a second as a probable. However, the latter's aircraft was hit by Flak and he force-landed, although he returned safely later; Sgt Allen was shot down and killed. I.Gruppe reported meeting three squadrons of fighters (the third may have been 92 Squadron), making several claims. 92 Squadron, while undertaking one patrol during the day, spotted Hurricanes under attack by Messerschmitts and went to their aid, one Bf 109 being claimed shot down and one probable.

At 1240 12 Hurricanes of 274 Squadron with others of 335 Squadron, swept over the battle area, three Bf 109s being seen below them. The pilots of the former unit dived on them, two being claimed for the loss of two pilots, both of whom failed to return, although one was safely back next day. Ten Kittyhawks of 3 RAAF Squadron then flew close escort for 18 Baltimores and B-25s at 1455 to bomb the Sidi Abd el Rahman track. After the bombing the formation was attacked by six Bf 109s and one Kittyhawk was hit, Sgt Holder force-landing. Sqn Ldr Gibbes then led seven aircraft to attack Ju 87s, but they were engaged by six Messerschmitts with five more appearing 3,000 feet above and another 12 beyond these. There was much firing, but the combat was too confused for the Australians to make any claims.

Then at 1545 the Hurricanes of 1 SAAF Squadron took off with 213 Squadron as top cover, the 24 Allied pilots meeting 25 Ju 87s with 12 Bf 109s as close cover and about ten more above them. The Stukas were just going down to bomb when attacked, many of them being seen to have Italian markings. The South African pilots claimed three shot down, one probable and two damaged, plus one Bf 109 damaged. For 213 Squadron claims were made for three, three probables, two damaged and one probable Bf 109.

Eleven Bf 109s of I./JG 27 and ten from III./JG 77 had taken off at 1535 to escort the Stukas, and the pilots of these reported attacking ten fighters before the bombing and 25-40 afterwards. At 1600 nine Spitfires of 601 Squadron took off again on a sweep, meeting six MC.202s which were about to attack some Hurricanes, one of these being claimed damaged. Four Bf 109s of III./JG 27 were off at 1617 to give indirect support to the Stukas, these claiming one Spitfire at 1653.

Meanwhile, at 1630 12 Hurricanes of 274 Squadron, again with 335 Squadron, swept over the area, spotting six Axis aircraft; one Bf 109 was claimed as a probable. At around this time Plt Off Eshelby of 208 Squadron had undertaken a TacR sortie over the northern part of the front, but he failed to return, possibly shot down by III./JG 27.

During the morning Flt Sgt MacArthur Powers, an American pilot in 145 Squadron, had claimed a Bf 109 damaged but on another sortie two Kittyhawks of 450 Squadron had been shot down, though both pilots survived. It will have been noted that amongst the claims made by the German pilots on this date was one by Hptm Heinz Bär of I./JG 77; this was his second in North Africa but represented his 118th claim of the war to date. Probably as a result of the Axis retreat which was just beginning, the Luftwaffe's detailed fighter operations book was no longer maintained after 2 November. On 30 October I./JG 53 had been detached from Sicily to Tobruk from where one claim was made on 2nd for a Beaufort shot down (see Chapter Ten). On 6 November the unit would be moved to Benghazi where four days later Uffz Erich Juhls would be killed in a collision with a Ju 52/3m at Berka West; on the 12th the detachment would end without any other notable events.

Within WDAF units on this day, Flt Lt M.C.H.Barber was promoted and posted from 250 Squadron to command 450. From 3 RAAF Squadron Flt Lt G.H.F.Plinston went to 250 Squadron to take Barber's place. Plinston had flown in France in 1939-40 where he had claimed five victories; he had then been off operations until late 1942. He had achieved one further victory with the Australians since his arrival. His new squadron, 250, was just making its first use of Merlin-engined Mark II Kittyhawks (similar to USAAF's P-40F) which featured a greater ceiling and a faster rate of climb.

British Claims

92 Sqn	Plt Off J.M.V.Carpenter	Spitfire Vc BR521 'E'	Bf 109	N El Alamein	0715-0820
145 Sqn	Flt Sgt MacA.Powers	Spitfire Vb BR390 'M'	Bf 109 Damaged	Rhazel Shaqiq	0825-0950
601 Sqn	Lt A.Bartleman	Spitfire Vc BR253	Bf 109 Probable	forward area	0910-1025
601 Sqn	Lt B.R.Bennetts	Spitfire Vc BP959	2 Bf 109s	forward area	0910-1025
601 Sqn	Plt Off D.Ibbotson	Spitfire Vc AB286	Bf 109	forward area	0910-1025
601 Sqn	Flg Off J.H.Nicholls	Spitfire Vc EP334	MC.202 Damaged	forward area	0910-1025
335 Sqn	Flt Sgt D.Soufrilas	Hurricane IIb BE689	Bf 109 Damaged	N El Alamein	0915-1030
238 Sqn	Flg Off I.F.Gilbert	Hurricane IIc BM974 'U'	Ju 87 Probable	El Alamein area	1150-1310
238 Sqn	Flt Sgt W.J.Morris	Hurricane IIc HL698 'Y'	Ju 87 Damaged	El Alamein area	1150-1310
238 Sqn	Capt T.W.Phillips	Hurricane IIc HL622 'P'	Ju 87	El Alamein area	1150-1310
92 Sqn	Flt Lt C.J.Samouelle	Spitfire Vc BR521 'E'	Bf 109		1205-1330
92 Sqn	Sqn Ldr J.H.Wedgwood	Spitfire Vc BR476 'J'	Bf 109 Probable	1205-1330	
274 Sqn	Plt Off P.Brickhill	Hurricane IIc BP763 'V'	Bf 109 Damaged	battle area	1240-1350
274 Sqn	Wt Off J.W.Neil	Hurricane IIc BP742 'X'	Bf 109 Damaged	battle area	1240-1350
213 Sqn	Plt Off H.A.Aitken	Hurricane IIc BP583	Ju 87 Damaged		1540-1625
213 Sqn	Flt Lt S.P.V.Bird	Hurricane IIc HV309	Bf 109 Probable	1540-1625	
213 Sqn	Plt Off G.Carrick	Hurricane IIc BP592 'F'	Ju 87		1540-1625
213 Sqn	Sgt R.W.Jones	Hurricane IIc BP599	Ju 87 Probable	1540-1625	
213 Sqn	Plt Off C.Luxton	Hurricane IIc HL613	Ju 87 Probable	W El Alamein	1540-1625
213 Sqn	Sqn Ldr P.Olver	Hurricane IIc BP401	Ju 87		1540-1625
213 Sqn	Sqn Ldr P.Olver	Hurricane IIc BP401	Ju 87 Probable		1540-1625
213 Sqn	Sqn Ldr P.Olver	Hurricane IIc BP401	Ju 87 Damaged		1540-1625
213 Sqn	Sgt D.C.Usher	Hurricane IIc BP345	Ju 87		1540-1625
601 Sqn	Flg Off J.H.Nicholls	Spitfire Vc EP334	MC.202 Damaged		1600-1700
1 SAAF Sqn	Capt J.M.Faure	Hurricane IIc HL892 'H'	Ju 87	15m W El Alamein	1605
1 SAAF Sqn	Capt J.M.Faure	Hurricane IIc HL892 'H'	Ju 87 Probable	15m W El Alamein	1605
1 SAAF Sqn	Lt I.R.Pryde	Hurricane IIc HL797 'C'	Ju 87	15m W El Alamein	1605
1 SAAF Sqn	Lt I.R.Pryde	Hurricane IIc HL797 'C'	Bf 109F Damaged	15m W El Alamein	1605

1 SAAF Sqn	2/Lt McC.E.S.Robinson	Hurricane IIc HV314 'R'	Ju 87	15m W El Alamein	1605
1 SAAF Sqn	Capt S. de K.Viljoen	Hurricane IIc HL845 'N'			
1 SAAF Sqn	Lt H.F.Smith	Hurricane IIc HL833 'I'	2 Ju 87s Damaged	15m W El Alamein	1605
274 Sqn	Sgt W.M.Bruckshaw	Hurricane IIc HL703 'H'	Bf 109 Probable	12m S El Alamein	1630-1730

British Casualties

127 Sqn	Hurricane IIc BN 160 left 0630, damaged by Bf 109 in head-on attack, returned to base; Flt Lt R.C.Lawrence safe
213 Sqn	Hurricane IIc BN134 left 0730, damaged by Bf 109 10-20m W El Alamein; Plt Off R.P.Baines safe
238 Sqn	Hurricane II HL888 'N', left 1150, shot down by Bf 109; Sgt W.T.Allen KiA
238 Sqn	Hurricane II BN974 'U', left 1150, shot down by Bf 109, crash-landed?; Flg Off I.F.Gilbert safe
238 Sqn	Hurricane II 'P' crash-landed due to Flak; Capt T.Phillips
208 Sqn	Hurricane BP604 left 1550, FTR from afternoon Tac Recce; Plt Off R.H.D.Eshelby MiA
208 Sqn	Hurricane HL657 left 0855, shot down by Flak at 1000, crash-landed; Capt J.Becourt-Foch WiA
274 Sqn	Hurricane IIc BE705 'D' left 1240, shot down by Bf 109, S El Alamein; Flt Sgt W.S.Howie KiA
274 Sqn	Hurricane IIc BP438 'J' left 1240, shot down by Bf 109, S El Alamein; Sgt J.J.Robertson returned next day
1 SAAF Sqn	Hurricane IIc HL885 'Z' damaged Cat I by Bf 109 at 1605; Lt B.Rose-Christie safe
601 Sqn	Spitfire V EP455 MiA, left 0605, presumed shot down by Bf 109s nr Daba; Plt Off G.Allen-Rowlandson baled out
601 Sqn	Spitfire V EP682 left 0605, slt damaged; Flg Off M.H.le Bas safe
3 RAAF Sqn	Kittyhawk I AK643 left 1445, shot down by Bf 109s, now believed to have collided with Uffz Schlick; Sgt J.S.Holder PoW
55 Sqn	Baltimore III AH109 off 0846 one of 12 and 5 B-25s to attack MT nr Daba. Hit by Flak over target and crashed in flames at 0901; Sqn Ldr P.D.C.Thomas. DFC, and four KiA (including Senior Intelligence Officer of 232 Group, Lt J.M.Simpson, SAAF)
223 Sqn	Baltimore III AG852 off 0816 to bomb Ghazal station. Hit by lt Flak while bombing and crashed nr target 0925; Wt Off A.C.Maclure and three KiA

US Casualties

64th FS/57th FG	P-40F '31', 0600, Capt M.E.Lancaster MiA
65th FS/57th FG	P-40F, 0600, 2/Lt Harold C.Rideout PoW
66th FS/57th FG	P-40F 1200-1355, combat with Bf 109, landed safely, 2/Lt William M.Ottaway WiA

German Claims

1./JG 27	Lt Hans Remmer	P-40	SE Fuka	0540
1./JG 27	Uffz Hans Hambeck	P-40	SE Fuka	0540
1./JG 27	Uffz Werner Döring	P-40	SE Fuka	0541
3./JG 27	Obfw Karl Mentnich	Spitfire	SE Sanyet Qotaifiya	0556
3./JG 27	Uffz Sigismund Dietz	Spitfire	15km SW Sidi Abd el Rahman	1200
Stab I./JG 27	Hptm Gerhard Homuth	P-46	SE Mumin Busak	1206
1./JG 77	Uffz Horst Schlick	P-40	SW El Alamein	
Stab I./JG 77	Hptm Heinz Bär	Spitfire	SW El Alamein	1450
1./JG 77	Uffz Wulf Focke	Spitfire	SW El Alamein	
2./JG 27	Oblt Josef Janssen	P-46	SW El Alamein	1517
9./JG 27	Lt Peter Werfft	Spitfire	25km SE El Alamein	1553

German Casualties

1./JG 77	Bf 109G-2 trop WNr 10480 combat with Spitfire. Crashed nr Bir el Abd lg.; Lt Bruno Kolthoff baled, safe
1./JG 77	Bf 109G-2 trop WNr 10549 combat with P-40, collided in the air. Crashed Bir el Abd; Uffz Hirst Schlick baled, safe
9./JG 77	Bf 109G-2 trop WNr 10665 Yellow 7 combat with Spitfire El Alamein area; Uffz Heinz Stöckmann baled out, PoW
Wüstennotst	Fi 156C-3 WNr 1013 destroyed by artillery fire at Bir el Habid

Italian Casualties

3°St CT	2 MC.202s (one was MM 9115) burned and 2 MC.202s damaged by bombing at Abu Smeit
101° Gr Tuff	CR.42 damaged by bombing at Abu Smeit

Tuesday, 3 November 1942

During the day WDAF battered away at the anti-tank screen which was preventing the large-scale breakout of X Corps. At midday, however, efforts were switched to the Axis columns which were beginning to move away westwards down the coast road. 8th Army still failed to fight its way through, and there was a brief lull in the fighting on the ground. In the meantime Adolf Hitler countermanded Rommel's order to withdraw, in his typical manner ordering the Afrika Korps to stand firm and fight for every inch of ground. Notwithstanding this instruction, a slight general withdrawal nonetheless took

This MC.202 '85-4' was usually flown by S.Ten Giuseppe 'Peppo' Re, whose nickname is clearly visible behind the cockpit.

Ten Re became completely lost on 3 November, ultimately ditching MC.202 MM 7782 near the coast of Rhodes.

place during the night which followed.

Raids had begun at 0630 when 12 Hurricanes of 238 Squadron, covered by 33 Squadron, set off to patrol over the Sidi Abd el Rahman area. They were followed ten minutes later by nine Spitfires of 145 Squadron. The pilots of the Hurricanes spotted 22 Ju 87s escorted by 12 Bf 109s at 11,000 feet, and attacked, causing the Stukas to jettison their bombs yet again. The Spitfire pilots then also spotted the bombers, but also saw 15 Bf 109s on their own level and six more overhead. Sqn Ldr Matthews, the 145 Squadron commanding officer, was shot down into the sea, apparently by Fw Schneider of II./JG 27; Matthews was rescued from the water, unhurt. Meanwhile, other members of his squadron claimed a Bf 109 and a Ju 87 shot down. A further Ju 87 was claimed by 238 Squadron and 33 Squadron also claimed one, adding two probables and three damaged. One Hurricane was hit and damaged, the pilot being wounded.

Kittyhawks of 450 Squadron undertook an escort to Baltimores and B-25s over Daba and Ghazal from 0900. During the return flight six of the fighters were detached to intercept a pair of Bf 109Gs 20 miles south-east of Daba, but as these were attacked, eight more arrived, Sgt Officer being shot down and baling out, while a second Kittyhawk was damaged. Officer's victor is believed to have been Oblt Fritz Geisshardt of I./JG 77, claiming his 92nd victory – his first in Africa.

WDAF's Hurricane units enjoyed their last series of engagements with Luftwaffe dive-bombers at the start of November. Flt Lt Russell Foskett of 80 Squadron was one of those so involved, claiming two Ju 87s shot down on 3rd of that month.

Around 1230 12 Hurricanes of 127 Squadron took off to provide cover for 80 Squadron on an interception mission. More than 25 Ju 87s with an escort of 15 Bf 109s were seen over the northern sector of the front, flying at 10,000 feet, just as the Hurricanes reached 7,000 feet. The British pilots continued to climb and attacked the bombers, but 127 Squadron then became involved in a general dogfight with the escorts. 80 Squadron's pilots were barely interfered with and were able to claim six Stukas shot down with seven more probables and three damaged. Flt Lt Foskett, who had claimed two of the probables (which have been confirmed subsequently, after he walked back), force-landed due to an oil pipe fracture. Meanwhile, the 127 Squadron pilots managed to claim two probables before the escorting Bf 109s got amongst them and cut the unit to pieces, seven aircraft failing to return from which just two of the pilots survived.

1 SAAF Squadron's Hurricanes flew several strafing sorties during the day, Lt James failing to return from one at 1330. Six Kittyhawks of 3 RAAF Squadron flew top cover to 18 B-25s at 1540, 12 Bf 109s attacking the formation and shooting down Sgt A.N.Jones. Half an hour later Hurricanes of 213 and 1 SAAF Squadrons set off on a wing strafing mission against transport targets. Two aircraft of the former unit and one from the latter all failed to return. 213 Squadron's Plt Off Luxton got back next day, reporting that he had been hit by Flak and force-landed among Australian troops; meanwhile Plt Off Aitken of the same unit had his aircraft damaged by an explosion amongst the vehicles he had been attacking and crash-landed near the Australians. Douglas Bailey, the South African, did not return. He was a veteran of the fighting in Burma and China during the previous year.

Eight Spitfires of 145 Squadron patrolled the area west of Daba at 20,000 feet mid-afternoon, spotting Axis fighters in the sun 2,000 feet higher. Despite their more favourable position, these failed to inflict any damage on the British fighters, the pilots of which claimed two Bf 109s shot down, plus a probable.

At about the same time P-40Fs of the 57th Fighter Group were also engaged by Messerschmitts. Shortly after this engagement 12 Hurricanes of 335 Squadron provided cover for others of 274 Squadron on a strafing mission from which Plt Off Anagnostopoulos failed to return. At the same time Hurricanes of 33 Squadron strafed vehicles in the Daba area, Plt Off Maxwell being hit both by Flak and a Bf 109, force-landing at LG.37, while Sgt Henfrey failed to return. During the day Sgt Rennie of this unit did not return from a cannon test over the sea.

Throughout the day Kittyhawks of 2 SAAF Squadron flew five missions. On the first, a dawn armed reconnaissance, heavy Flak was encountered and Lt 'Swazi' Stewart crash-landed, being removed to hospital. On the final sortie of the day nine Kittybombers were covered by Tomahawks of 5 SAAF Squadron, and on this occasion Capt Jack Parsonson force-landed:

> "In the afternoon I led the Wing in a hastily scrambled show, 5 Squadron were top cover. We took off at about five o'clock and were sent to the southern end of the line with orders to strafe the rapidly disintegrating enemy line. When we passed over the line in the south we were heavily engaged by anti-aircraft fire from Italian positions. However, over the line we dived down on tremendous targets of nose-to-tail enemy transport columns. We broke formation and attacked targets individually. I found a line of stationary trucks. The troops were lined up to receive their evening rations when I arrived over a low hump in the ground. I opened up with my six .50" Browning guns into the line of troops and was horrified at the carnage. I turned and shot at their transport which was in a long line on the road. Several trucks burst into flames. I was flying only a few feet above the ground. The soldiers fired madly at my aeroplane and I soon realized I'd been hit through the glycol and did not have many more seconds of flying left. I flew away from the column I had been attacking as I felt they would most likely be unkind. I forced-landed a couple of miles south, took my water bottle from the small compartment in the side of the Kitty and set off towards the front."

After a long walk by night, guided by the stars, Parsonson was spotted:

> "Suddenly, another mirage...thus time it was an armoured car with half a dozen troops on it, and this time it did not disappear! It drove towards me and all the weapons were trained on me when it stopped. 'It's probably a damned Itie, Sir'. I shouted to them hoarsely in the approved film style 'Water, Water for the love of God. Water...' 'Must be one of ours, Sir'. These chaps were then kindness itself. They helped me to sit against the wheel of the armoured car and gave me a little water. They told me that I was mighty lucky they were there at all as they should have gone forward with the rest of the battle, but that they were a little raw and had been detailed to do a training run down into the desert. They belonged to the 44th Recce Squadron, SAAF, which was nearby. I spent the night with them and two days later was back at LG.97, where everything was upside down with the Wing preparing to go forward."

One further casualty during the day was a Boston of 12 SAAF Squadron which was shot down in flames by Flak while attacking Axis ground forces. Following what had been a very successful day for the German fighters, their units were nonetheless caught up in the general Axis withdrawal. The slower vehicles of JGs 27 and 77 started the moves, destination being Stherasat, near Sidi Barrani, Menastir and Gambut. II./JG 27 was now down to a strength of only three serviceable aircraft and, handing their airfield over to JG 77, moved to Gambut where an interception commando (Auffangkommando) was set up, all aircraft that could take to the air being flown there from Qotaifiya and Turbiya to be serviced and repaired. Three MC.202s of 18° Gruppo, led by Ten Specker, were scrambled to find some vehicles in the desert, to identify them as German. On the return flight S.Ten Giuseppe 'Peppo' Re of 85ª Squadriglia had a sudden illness and lost his way, ditching his MC.202 near the coast of Rhodes.

British Claims

33 Sqn	Flt Sgt M.J.H.M.Belleau	Hurricane IIc HL621 'M'	Ju 87 Probable	El Alamein area	0625-0735
33 Sqn	Plt Off J.G.B.Campbell	Hurricane IIc	Ju 87 Damaged	El Alamein area	0625-0735
33 Sqn	Sgt L.H.Cowley	Hurricane IIc HL737	Ju 87 Probable	El Alamein area	0625-0735
33 Sqn	Flg Off M.E.Jowsey	Hurricane IIc BN501 'R'	Ju 87 Damaged	El Alamein area	0625-0735
33 Sqn	Flt Lt O.C.Kallio	Hurricane IIc HL654 'Q'	Ju 87	El Alamein area	0625-0735

33 Sqn	Sgt M.H.McNamara	Hurricane IIc BP588 'X'	Ju 87 Damaged	El Alamein area	0625-0735
238 Sqn	Sgt W.E.G.Cordwell	Hurricane IIc 'S'	Ju 87	Sidi el Rahman	0630-0735
145 Sqn	Sgt J.A.Greaves	Spitfire Vb AB189 'L'	Bf 109	Sidi el Rahman	0640-0745
145 Sqn	Flt Sgt A.H.M.Stewart	Spitfire Vb BR486 'S'	Ju 87	Sidi el Rahman	0640-0745
450 Sqn	Sgt G.C.W.O'Neil	Kittyhawk III FR303	Bf 109G	20m SE Daba	0859-1045
145 Sqn	Plt Off L.A.Malins	Spitfire Vb BR389 'Z'	}		
145 Sqn	Flt Sgt MacA.Powers	Spitfire Vb BR363 'V'	} Bf 109	10m SE Daba	1000-1110
145 Sqn	Sgt F.A.Stillman	Spitfire Vb BR481 'S'	}		
145 Sqn	Flt Lt J.S.Taylor	Spitfire Vb EP327 'R'	}		
80 Sqn	Flt Lt R.G.Foskett	Hurricane IIc BP337 'B'	2 Ju 87s	E El Alamein	1300
80 Sqn	Flg Off J.H.S.Haigh	Hurricane IIc BN361 'K'	2 Ju 87	E El Alamein	1300
80 Sqn	Flg Off J.H.S.Haigh	Hurricane IIc BN361 'K'	Ju 87 Probable	E El Alamein	1300
80 Sqn	Plt Off N.MacLachlan	Hurricane IIc HL632 'O'	Ju 87	E El Alamein	1300
80 Sqn	Sgt L.B.McKay	Hurricane IIc BP450 'V'	} Ju 87	E El Alamein	1300
80 Sqn	Plt Off B.L.McMahon	Hurricane IIc BP586 'U'	}		
80 Sqn	Plt Off B.L.McMahon	Hurricane IIc BP586 'U'	Ju 87	E El Alamein	1300
80 Sqn	Sgt G.T.Pratley	Hurricane IIc BD547 'H'	Ju 87	E El Alamein	1300
80 Sqn	Sgt G.T.Pratley	Hurricane IIc BD547 'H'	Ju 87 Probable	E El Alamein	1300
80 Sqn	Sgt G.T.Pratley	Hurricane IIc BD547 'H'	Ju 87 Damaged	E El Alamein	1300
80 Sqn	Sgt J.W. Garland	Hurricane IIc BP340 'D'	Ju 87 Damaged	E El Alamein	1300
80 Sqn	Sgt C.W.House	Hurricane IIc HL841 'C'	Ju 87	E El Alamein	1300
80 Sqn	Sgt C.W.House	Hurricane IIc HL841 'C'	Ju 87 Probable	E El Alamein	1300
80 Sqn	Plt Off N.MacLachlan	Hurricane IIc HL632 'O'	Ju 87 Probable	E El Alamein	1300
80 Sqn	Flt Sgt T.R.Broomhall	Hurricane IIc BM895 'W'	2 Ju 87s Damaged	E El Alamein	1300
80 Sqn	Flg Off K.M.Simpson	Hurricane IIc BP358 'X'	Ju 87 Probable	E El Alamein	1300
80 Sqn	Sgt C.B.Stewart	Hurricane IIc BM976 'M'	Ju 87 Probable	E El Alamein	1300
127 Sqn	Flt Sgt A.R.Moulden	Hurricane IIc HM140	Ju 87 Probable	Sidi el Rahman area	1300
127 Sqn	Sgt F.A.LePoer-Trench	Hurricane IIc HL683	Ju 87 Probable	Sidi el Rahman area	1300
127 Sqn	Sgt W.J.Willshaw	Hurricane IIc BG904	Ju 87 Probable	Sidi el Rahman area	1300
127 Sqn	unidentified	Hurricane IIc	Bf 109G	Sidi el Rahman area	1300
145 Sqn	Sgt J.A.Greaves	Spitfire Vb AB168 'L'	Bf 109	6m SE Fuka	1600-1715
145 Sqn	Sgt J.A.Greaves	Spitfire Vb AB168 'L'	Bf 109 Damaged	6m SE Fuka	1600-1715
145 Sqn	Flg Off I.H.R.Shand	Spitfire Vb EP692	Bf 109 Probable	6m SE Fuka	1600-1715

British Casualties

33 Sqn	Hurricane IIc ..853 left 0625, badly damaged by Bf 109 Sidi el Rahman; Sgt A.N.Ellis WiA
33 Sqn	Hurricane IIc left 1635, damaged by Flak nr El Adem; Flt Lt J.F.Allen safe
33 Sqn	Hurricane IIc BP161 'P' left 1635, shot down by Bf 109 W Daba; Sgt F.Henfry MiA
33 Sqn	Hurricane IIc BP 471, left 1635, force-landed LG.37 due to Bf 109 attack; Plt Off G.S.M.Maxwell safe
33 Sqn	Hurricane IIc BP358 missing from cannon test, shot down by Bf 109 NE Fuka; Sgt R.G.Rennie KiA
73 Sqn	Hurricane IIc shot down by Flak nr Fuka; Flt Lt K.M.Miller KiA
80 Sqn	Hurricane IIc BP337 'B' left 1235, damaged by Bf 109 and crash-landed in desert 1300; Flt Lt R.G.Foskett returned
127 Sqn	Hurricane II BN406 shot down by Bf 109s between Sidi el Rahman-El Alamein, 1300; Fl Lt R.C.Lawrence MiA
127 Sqn	Hurricane II BP292 shot down by Bf 109s between Sidi el Rahman-El Alamein, 1300; force-landed near Thompson's Post and capture; Sgt R.R.Mayze MiA
127 Sqn	Hurricane II BP289 shot down by Bf 109s between Sidi el Rahman-El Alamein, 1300; Sgt D.G.Andrews baled and PoW, left arm shot off before he jumped
127 Sqn	Hurricane II HM130 shot down by Bf 109s between Sidi el Rahman-El Alamein, 1300; Plt Off A.D.Melville KiA
127 Sqn	Hurricane IIc HL629 shot down by Bf 109s between Sidi el Rahman-El Alamein, 1300; Plt Off A.R.Rebman KiA
127 Sqn	Hurricane IIc HL773 shot down by Bf 109s between Sidi el Rahman-El Alamein, 1300; Sgt N.G.Thomas safe, after landing on a minefield and while running to cover setting off some mines!
127 Sqn	Hurricane IIc HM140 damaged by Bf 109s between Sidi el Rahman-El Alamein, 1300; Flt Sgt A.R.Moulden safe
127 Sqn	Hurricane IIc BG904 shot down by Bf 109s between Sidi el Rahman-El Alamein, 1300; Flt Sgt B.Willshaw safe
213 Sqn	Hurricane IIc BP583 damaged by debris from exploding vehicles, ditched in Gulf of Sollum; Plt Off H.A.Aitken, returned
213 Sqn	Hurricane IIc HL613 hit by Flak and crash-landed nr Daba; Plt Off C.Luxton returned

British Casualties

335 Sqn	Hurricane II BP279 lost in ground-attack operation; Plt Off Anagnostopoulos FTR
1 SAAF Sqn	Hurricane IIc HL828 'L' missing from strafing, shot down 9m from Daba, 1410; Lt D.O.James KiA
1 SAAF Sqn	Hurricane IIc HL722 'J' shot down by Flak into sea off Ras Abu el Guruf 1635; Lt D.G.Bailey KiA
1 SAAF Sqn	Hurricane IIc HL797 'C' damaged Cat II by Flak SE Daba 1635; Lt M.E.S.Robinson safe
1 SAAF Sqn	Hurricane IIc HL892 'H' damaged Cat II by Flak SE Daba 1635; Lt H.F.Smith
1 SAAF Sqn	Hurricane IIc HV314 'R' damaged Cat I by Flak SE Daba 1635; Capt W.R.Thompson
145 Sqn	Spitfire V BR477 left 0640,shot down in sea by Bf 109s; Sqn Ldr G.P.H.Matthews baled out, picked up safely
145 Sqn	Spitfire V EP254 shot down by Bf 109; Plt Off S.N.Duigan PoW
450 Sqn	Kittyhawk III FR218 left 0900, hit by Bf 109s and abandoned 20m SE Daba; Sgt G.J.Officer PoW
450 Sqn	Kittyhawk III FL881 badly damaged by Bf 109 SW Daba, force-landed at LG.37; Sgt H.L.Gregory safe
3 RAAF Sqn	Kittyhawk EV355 left 1540, shot down in sea by Bf 109s; Sgt A.N.Jones PoW
2 SAAF Sqn	Kittyhawk I AK662 'Y' damaged by ground fire, crash-landed Cat III; Lt B.H.Stewart bruised and concussed
2 SAAF Sqn	Kittyhawk I EV326 'F' shot down by Flak 30m S El Alamein 1630; Capt J.E.Parsonson safe, walked back on 5th
4 SAAF Sqn	Kittyhawk I ET975 damaged by Flak; Cat II, strafing W Fuka; Maj S.F.du Toit safe
4 SAAF Sqn	Kittyhawk I AK709 damaged by Flak, strafing W Fuka; Lt E.L.J.Hazeldine safe
4 SAAF Sqn	Kittyhawk I EV364 damaged by Flak, strafing W Fuka; Lt M.B.Johnson WiA
5 SAAF Sqn	Tomahawk IIb 'S' hit by Flak and force-landed at Burg el Arab Cat III; Lt H.W.G.Bidwell safe
5 SAAF Sqn	Tomahawk IIb damaged Cat II by Flak
5 SAAF Sqn	Tomahawk IIb damaged Cat II by Flak
	(one of these Tomahawks believed to have been AK447)
12 SAAF Sqn	Boston III AL270 'U' off 0740 to attack Axis ground forces at El Alamein. Hit by Flak over target, burst into flames and spun into ground and exploded; pilot Lt W.B.Dalglish baled out WiA, but died on 7th as PoW, three crew KiA

US Claims

66th FS/57th FG	1/Lt William B.Campbell	P-40F	Bf 109	S El Daba	0900-1045
64th FS/57th FG	2/Lt William E.Jenks	P-40 '15'	Bf 109	S El Daba	1615
65th FS/57th FG	Capt Marshall M.Sneed	P-40	Bf 109	El Daba	1615
65th FS/57th FG	Capt T.W Clark	P-40	Bf 109 Damaged	El Daba	1615
65th FS/57th FG	2/Lt H.H.Stanford	P-40	Bf 109 Damaged	El Daba	1615

US Casualties

66th FS/57th FG	P-40F, shot down by Bf 109, crash-landed S Daba at 1045; 1/Lt W.B.Campbell returned

German Claims

5./JG 27	Fw Bernhard Schneider	Spitfire	SW El Alamein	0630-0730
I./JG 77	Lt Rudiger Belling	Spitfire		
3./JG 77	Oblt Friedrich Geisshardt	P-40		
I./JG 77	Fw Ottokar Pohl	P-40		
7./StG 3	Uffz Alfred Lachner (gunner)	P-40	El Alamein	1205
5./JG 27	Fw Bernhard Schneider	Spitfire	S Bir Mumin Busak	1208
Stab I./JG 77	Hptm Heinz Bär	2 P-40s	SE El Alamein	1208 & 1210
9./JG 77	Obfw Herbert Kaiser	P-40		1210
1./JG 27	Lt Karl-Heinz von Tigerström	Hurricane	S Sidi Abd el Rahman	1210
2./JG 27	Lt Konrad Fels	P-40	SW El Alamein	1212
2./JG 27	Lt Karl Wünsch	Spitfire	SW El Alamein	1214
I./JG 77	Obfw Schumann	P-40	SW El Alamein	1215
Stab III./JG 77	Hptm Kurt Ubben	P-40	SW El Daba	1410
Stab III./JG 77	Obfw Heinrich Hackler	P-40		
1./JG 27	Uffz Georg Schanz	P-40	NE Fuka	1525
Stab I./JG 77	Hptm Heinz Bär	P-40	NW Qotaifiya	1555
Stab I./JG 77	Lt Heinz-Edgar Berres	P-40	NW Qotaifiya	1557
Stab I./JG 77	Hptm Heinz Bär	P-40	NW Qotaifiya	1559
Stab I./JG 77	Hptm Heinz Bär	P-40	NW El Alamein	1612
8./JG 77	Flg Ewald Kraas	Spitfire	NW El Alamein	
Flak		3 e/a		

German Casualties

Stab/JG 27	Bf 108B WNr 2092 T1+EN blown up at Qotaifiya

2./JG 27	Bf 109G-2 trop combat 30km SE Fuka, force-landed 100%; Uffz Ernst Niekammer WiA
3./JG 27	Bf 109G-2 trop combat, crash-landed; Uffz Heinrich Wiese safe
5./JG 27	Bf 109F-4 trop WNr 8579 blown up at Mersa Matruh
III./JG 77	Bf 109G-2 trops, WNrs 10657 & 10661 blown up at Tanyet Harun
Stab I./JG 77	Bf 109G-2 trop WNr 10568 combat, crashed nr Bir el Abd l.g; Lt Heinz-Edgar Berres baled, safe
1./JG 77	Bf 109G-2 trop WNrs 10549, 10533 & 10528 bomb damaged on ground at Bir el Abd
8./StG 3	Ju 87D-3 WNr 2787 combat with Hurricane 15km SE El Daba; Obfw Richard Brühl WiA, gunner safe
9./StG 3	Ju 87D-3 WNr 2632 S7+DR combat with Hurricane W Qotaifiya; 2 baled: Obfw Erich Opitz MiA, gunner returned on foot
Wüstennotst	Fi 156 C-3 WNr 5696 destroyed in strafing attack at Qotaifiya
1.(F)/121	Ju 88D-1 WNr 430357 destroyed by own forces at Fuka
Italian Casualties	
85ª Sq, 18°Gr, 3°St CT	MC.202 MM 7782 ditched off Rhodes, S.Ten Giuseppe Re safe

Wednesday, 4 November 1942

This proved to be the day of the general breakthrough, 51st Division and 4th Indian Division clearing the anti-tank screen, thereby allowing 1st Armoured Division to get through. This latter unit, supported by WDAF, then became involved in fighting at Tek el Aqqaqir. Further south the New Zealanders and 7th Armoured Division broke through and X Corps set off after the retreating Afrika Korps. XIII Corps was now left behind to round up the Italian divisions in the south which had been abandoned without transport or supplies. Rommel now ordered a general withdrawal to Fuka.

Throughout the day Hurricanes, Tomahawks, Kittyhawks, Warhawks, Spitfires, Beaufighters, Bostons, Baltimores and B-25s kept up continual bombardment and strafing attacks on the mass of vehicles retreating along the coast road, the series of hairpin bends climbing the coastal escarpment at Fuka and Mersa Matruh proving to be particular death-traps for the Axis. Typical of what was happening generally, III./JG 27 lost ten of the unit's vehicles destroyed and four men killed on this road during the day.

Early on the scene were six Hurricanes of 238, six of 1 SAAF and 12 of 33 Squadrons which took off around 0615 to strafe west of Daba. Six Bf 109s intercepted 33 Squadron's aircraft, two of which were shot down. Lt Pryde of 1 SAAF Squadron was also shot down, baling out over the sea; moreover, Lt Faure was hit by light Flak, force-landing 30 miles inside Axis territory where he was safely picked up by a patrol of the Royal Dragoon Guards, returning two days later. 238 Squadron also suffered two losses, one missing and one pilot baled out due to Flak damage. Eight Kittyhawks of 4 SAAF Squadron had been out even earlier, undertaking an armed reconnaissance over Fuka. Lt Leppan was attacked by four Bf 109s, his aircraft being hit several times, after which he force-landed at Burg el Arab, unhurt. Lt Steyn of this unit also force-landed.

Twelve 260 Squadron Kittyhawks provided escort to bombers but also encountered four Bf 109s with one of which Flg Off Gilboe collided, both aircraft crashing. This engagement may actually have been with MC.202s of 3° Stormo which had scrambled from Abu Smeit after Bostons and Curtiss fighters early in the morning. Ten Bordoni-Bisleri claimed to have shot down one fighter which had just shot down Cap Pinna, 75ª Squadriglia commander, and it is possible that, attacked by Bordoni, Gilboe had collided with his own victim. According to Italian records, Pinna and his wingman Serg Magg Cuscunà were scrambled at 0600, engaging an enemy formation. In the ensuing dogfight Pinna's MC.202s collided with a Kittyhawk and burst into flames. The Italian pilot, although badly burned, managed to bale out and landed within Axis lines. Recovered by Folgore parachute division, he was then loaded on a German Storch and removed to Mersa Matruh hospital. Cuscunà landed at 0715 claiming to have effectively damaged two P-40s.

From 1045 eight 145 Squadron Spitfires patrolled near Fuka, where three Bf 109s were seen below. Two pilots each claimed one shot down. Two more MC.202s were claimed as probables at this time by pilots of 250 Squadron. In the midst of all these battlefield-related engagements, III./JG 27 reported intercepting B-24 Liberators making a daylight attack on targets near Benghazi. Oblt Schroer claimed one east of the city and Uffz Stückler one south of Sollum. Lt Schmidt was shot down and killed over Benghazi whilst attacking the big bombers, probably by return fire from them. Pilots of JG 77 claimed 12 victories during the day, plus one unconfirmed.

Sixteen P-40s of the 64th and 65th Squadrons, 57th Fighter Group, provided cover for 18 Bostons and Baltimores from 1215. Shortly after bombing was completed, two Axis fighters attacked the bombers,

Lt Armin Köhler of I./JG 77 poses with an aircraft of JG 53 before leaving Sicily for North Africa.

but were driven off. A little later two Bf 109s repeated the attack, but one was fired on by three 64th Squadron pilots in turn, going down in flames after the third attack which was made by 2/Lt Merena, who claimed its destruction. More of the Group's aircraft, this time from the 66th Squadron, were out during the day, pilots claiming two more Messerschmitts shot down, although on this occasion 2/Lt Robert Adams' aircraft was shot down and he became a PoW.

Twelve Kittyhawks of 260 Squadron escorted a dozen more from 2 SAAF Squadron to attack MT near Galal at 1415. The South Africans saw an Fi 156 flying very low, dropping bombs in front of this until Lt de Villiers shot it down in flames. The top cover then spotted a Ju 88 at 10,000 feet and this was shot down by Flt Lt Ron Cundy:

> "After leaving the target area and flying west at 10,000 feet I saw a Ju 88 at about 500 feet flying west just off the coast. I peeled off followed by the remainder of my section and carried out a port-quarter attack putting the rear gunner out of action. Travelling at excessive speed I quickly overshot but pulled up and then attacked from the staboard quarter. Pieces flew off the starboard engine, which caught fire. The Ju 88 plunged into the sea with an enormous splash. Pilots of 2 SAAF Squadron saw the Ju 88 go down so confirmed the victory."

An hour later 4 SAAF Squadron despatched eight Kittyhawks on a dive-bombing sortie, but when on their way to the target, the pilots were ordered to jettison their bombs and intercept a formation of 15 Ju 87s with a fighter escort. Lt Golding claimed two Stukas shot down and a Bf 109 damaged, while other pilots added one more Messerschmitt destroyed and three fighters damaged. However, two Kittyhawks were shot down one pilot becoming a PoW while the other belly-landed successfully, returning next day. 238 Squadron flew a second mission at 1535, 12 Hurricanes patrolling west of El Alamein where they met Bf 109s. Flt Lt Peter Ayerst claimed one shot down and one damaged, but he and Sgt Blackford were both shot down, Blackford being injured. On a TacR sortie to Tel el Eisa, a very experienced pilot, Capt W.J.A.Webb, DFC, was shot down by Flak and killed. During the day four Spitfires arrived for 1 SAAF Squadron and this became the first of the Hurricane units to begin converting to these aircraft – much to the delight of the pilots.

British Claims

112 Sqn	Sgt W.D.Brown	Kittyhawk III FR266 'H'	Bf 109 Damaged	Galal-Fuka	0745-0920
260 Sqn	Flg Off N.E.Gilboe	Kittyhawk IIa FL351 'C'	MC.202(?Bf 109) by collision	Galal-Fuka	0810-0940
250 Sqn	Plt Off N.G.Russell	Kittyhawk III FR241 'R'	MC.202 Probable	Fuka	0820
250 Sqn	Plt Off C.W.Tribken	Kittyhawk III FR253 'C'	MC.202 Probable	Fuka	0820
145 Sqn	Flt Sgt MacA.Powers	Spitfire Vb EP309 'Q'	Bf 109	10m S Fuka	1045-1205
145 Sqn	Plt Off A.F.Wilson	Spitfire Vb BR363 'V'	Bf 109	10m S Fuka	1045-1205
260 Sqn	Flt Lt W.R.Cundy	Kittyhawk IIa FL274	Ju 88	into sea	1415-1538
2 SAAF Sqn	Lt T.V.de Villiers	Kittyhawk I AL186 'G'	Fi 156	NW Galal	1500
238 Sqn	Flt Lt P.V.Ayerst	Hurricane IIc 'G'	Bf 109	12m W El Alamein	1535-1620
238 Sqn	Flt Lt P.V.Ayerst	Hurricane IIc 'G'	Bf 109 Damaged	12m W El Alamein	1535-1620
4 SAAF Sqn	Lt S.Cohen	Kittyhawk I ET944 'A'	Bf 109F Damaged		1545
4 SAAF Sqn	Maj S.F.du Toit	Kittyhawk I EV362 'Y'	MC.202 Damaged		1545
4 SAAF Sqn	Lt D.W.Golding	Kittyhawk I ET901 'W'	2 Ju 87s		1545
4 SAAF Sqn	Lt D.W.Golding	Kittyhawk I ET901 'W'	Bf 109F Damaged		1545
4 SAAF Sqn	Lt E.L.J.Hazeldine	Kittyhawk I EV166 'O'	Bf 109F		1545

British Casualties

33 Sqn	Hurricane IIc BN501 'R' shot down by Bf 109s WDaba; Plt Off H.Steward KiA
33 Sqn	Hurricane IIc BP354 'E' shot down by Bf 109s W Daba; Plt Off H.J.Turner died of wounds
238 Sqn	Hurricane II HL890 'H' left 0615, shot down by Flak at Galal; Flg Off W.B. Hay, baled out and paddled ashore, safe
238 Sqn	Hurricane II HL906 'A' left 0615, shot down by Flak at Galal; Wt Off F.E.Wise MiA
238 Sqn	Hurricane II 'G' left 1535, shot down by Bf 109 12m W El Alamein; Flt Lt P.V.Ayerst baled out safe
238 Sqn	Hurricane II 'T' left 1535, shot down by Bf 109 12m W El Alamein, crash-landed; Sgt D.T.Blackford WiA
1 SAAF Sqn	Hurricane IIc HL606 'F' shot down by Flak, belly-landed in enemy lines S Daba 0700; Capt J.M.Faure safe, escaped from PoW, picked up by KDG patrol and back on 6th
1 SAAF Sqn	Hurricane IIc HL890 'A' shot down by Bf 109 16m WSW Daba 0700; Lt I.R.R.Pryde KiA
1 SAAF Sqn	Hurricane IIc damaged, but returned
M.E.	Hurricane II HL731 shot down by Flak into sea nr LG.20; unit unspecified
260 Sqn	Kittyhawk IIa FL351 'C' collided with MC.202 over Ras el Abd; Plt Off N.E.Gilboe PoW
4 SAAF Sqn	Kittyhawk I AK711 'T' presumed shot down by Bf 109s, but Flak S Ghazal; 2/Lt J.J.Steyn PoW
4 SAAF Sqn	Kittyhawk I ET789 'W'damaged by Bf 109s and crash-landed nr Burg el Arab, Cat II; Lt J.V.A.Leppan safe
4 SAAF Sqn	Kittyhawk I AK633 shot down and belly-landed Cat II nr Ghazal; 2/Lt C.M.Dibb returned on 5th
4 SAAF Sqn	Kittyhawk II ET1018 shot down by Bf 109 SSW Daba 1535; 2/Lt I.D.Sparg PoW
4 SAAF Sqn	Kittyhawk I ET244 damaged by Flak or Bf 109; Lt S.Cohen safe
40 SAAF Sqn	Hurricane IIc hit by Flak near Tel el Aisa, force-landed in a minefield, hit a mine, blew up at 1630, Capt W.J.A.Webb KiA

US Claims

66th FS/57th FG	Capt Raymond A.Llewellin	P-40F	Bf 109	W Ghazal	0645-0835
66th FS/57th FG	Capt Raymond A.Llewellin	P-40F	Bf 109 Damaged	W Ghazhal	0645-0835
66th FS/57th FG	2/Lt Thomas T.Williams	P-40F	Bf 109F	W Ghazhal	0645-0835
66th FS/57th FG	1/Lt Albert O.Zipser	P-40F	Bf 109F		1015-1145
64th FS/57th FG	2/Lt Steven C.Merena	P-40K '35'	Bf 109		1255
65th FS/57th FG	1/Lt Roy E.Whittaker	P-40F	MC.202 or Bf 109		1255
65th FS/57th FG	1/Lt Roy E.Whittaker	P-40	Bf 109 Damaged		1255
65th FS/57th FG	1/Lt Edwin R.Weaver	P-40	Bf 109 Damaged		1255

US Casualties

66th FS/57th FG	P-40F, shot down 1m W Ghazal about 0800, 2/ Lt Robert M.Adams baled out and PoW

German Claims

4.(H)/12	Uffz Friedrich Stannek	Hurricane	5km N El Daba	0540
4.(H)/12	Uffz Friedrich Stannek	P-40	10km NE Turbiya	0550
8./JG 77	Fw Eduard Isken	2 Hurricanes	Sanyet Qotaifiya area	0600 & 0601
3./JG 77	Lt Armin Köhler	P-40	W El Daba	0615-0720
3./JG 77	Oblt Friedrich Geisshardt	2 P-40s	W El Daba	0615-0720
I./JG 77	unstated	P-40		0615-0720

German Claims

8./JG 77	Obfw Herbert Kaiser	Hurricane		0710
9./JG 77	Stfw Georg Seckel	P-40	5km NW El Alamein	1455
8./JG 77	Fhj Uffz Hans-Werner Renzow	P-40	40km S El Daba	
8./JG 77	Flg Ewald Kraas	Spitfire n.b.	El Alamein	
3./JG 77	Oblt Friedrich Geisshardt	2 P-40s	SW El Alamein	1415-1520
3./JG 77	Lt Armin Köhler	P-40	SW El Alamein	1415-1520

German Casualties

Stab II./JG 27	Bf 108B-2 WNr 2061 destroyed by bombs at Qotaifiya
4./JG 27	Bf 109F-4 trop WNr 8586 & Bf 109G-2 trop WNr 14257 blown up at Qotaifiya
5./JG 27	Bf 109F-4 trop WNr 10005 & Bf 109G-2 trop WNr 10578 blown up at Qotaifiya
5./JG 27	Bf 109F-4 WNr 7580 & Bf 109F-4 trop WNr 13211 blown up at Qotaifiya
Stab/JG 77	Bf 109G-2 trop WNr 10508 crash-landed Bir el Abd after combat, destroyed; pilot safe
Stab/JG 77	Bf 109G-2 trop WNr 10501 blown up at Bir el Abd
1./JG 77	Bf 109G-2 trop WNr 10567 crash-landed at Bir el Abd and blown up
1./JG 77	Bf 109G-2 trop WNrs 10533 White 3, 10548 and 10528 destroyed in strafing attack at Bir el Abd
8./JG 77	Bf 109G-2 trop WNr 10642 Black 3 combat with Spitfire El Alamein area; Flg Ewald Kraas baled, WiA PoW
8./JG 77	Bf 109G-2 trop combat with Spitfire, landed Gambut, 10% damaged; Lt Heinz Lüdemann WiA
3./SchG 2	Bf 109F-4 WNr 13310 shot down by Spitfires 15km S El Daba; Obfw Hans Lampater baled but chute did not open, KiA
Wüstennotst	2 Fi 156 C-3s WNr 7379 and 5620 destroyed by own forces at Bir el Abd
KG zbV 800	Ju 52/3m WNr 6931 8T+FL destroyed in mid-air collision 200km N Tobruk; Uffz Kurt Schuck and three KiA
KG zbV 800	Ju 52/3m WNr 6471 8T+HH destroyed in mid-air collision 200km N Tobruk; Fw Erich Lehmann and three KiA

Italian Claims

75ª Sq, 23°Gr, 3°St CT	Serg Magg Francesco Cuscunà	MC.202	2 P-40s Damaged	over the lines	0600-0715
95ª Sq, 18°Gr, 3°St CT	Ten Franco Bordoni-Bisleri	MC.202	P-40	El Daba	0635-0730

Italian Casualties

75ª Sq, 23°Gr, 3°St CT	MC.202 MM 8081 '75-1' shot down 0600-, Cap Mario Pinna baled, taken to hospital seriously WiA
75ª Sq, 23°Gr, 3°St CT	MC.202 hit in combat with P-40s 0600-0715, Serg Magg Cuscunà landed safely
191ª Sq, 86°Gr, 35° St BT	2 Cant.Z.1007bis MM 24279 and 23757, damaged on Oct 30th, set to fire at Barce
238ª Sq, 101° Gr, 5° St Tuff	CR.42, damaged at Sidi Barrani, Serg Magg Vittorio Milletti

Thursday, 5 November 1942

The German armour fought a delaying action at Fuka as British forces made a very slow start in the pursuit of the Axis forces. 8th Armoured Brigade caught up with XX Korps near Galal, but the New Zealanders and 7th Armoured Division were held up south of Fuka by a dummy minefield and by shortage of fuel. 1st Armoured Division was ordered to Bir el Khalda and Charing Cross, but made a slow start here as well. By the end of the day Rommel had withdrawn his mobile forces from Fuka.

In the air the day began with an attack by 11 Hurribombers of 274 Squadron, covered by 33 Squadron, at 0715. Flt Sgt Burman of the former unit spotted two Fi 156s and dived on one, his fire causing one wing to break off completely as the little aircraft dived into the sea.

Eleven Kittyhawks of 112 Squadron then patrolled over Fuka at around 0930, but these were jumped by six Bf 109s. Sqn Ldr Drake and his pilots turned into them, claiming four shot down and two damaged without suffering any loss. At 1019 80 Squadron took off on a bombing sortie, but the unit's Hurricanes were attacked by seven Bf 109s and Plt Off Wilson was shot down, baling out into captivity. During a Freie Jagd sortie around midday Oblt Geisshardt of I./JG 77 claimed two Curtiss fighters shot down, and Lt Köhler added one after a long fight.

Kittyhawks from 250 and 450 Squadrons set off at 1130, fitted with long-range tanks to allow them to undertake a long patrol over Fuka. During this six Bf 109s and MC.202s were engaged. Flt Sgt Chap of 250 Squadron attacked one Messerschmitt which was on Plt Off Troke's tail, which he claimed as a probable. Nine Spitfires from 145 Squadron followed an hour later to carry out a reconnaissance over Sidi Haneish. Bf 109s were seen and pursued, but one pilot failed to return – probably shot down by an MC.202, the pilot of which made the only claim for a Spitfire on this date.

At 1310 12 Hurribombers of 274 Squadron were off again, this time escorted by 12 from 127 Squadron; the 274 Squadron pilots strafed near Fuka, but six Bf 109s, on this occasion flying in line

Having risen to command 260 Squadron by April 1942, Sqn Ldr O.V.Hanbury returned to commence a second tour at the helm of this unit on 5 November.

astern, dived on them, shooting down Wt Off Neil who baled out of his spinning aircraft into the sea. The 127 Squadron pilots claimed one of the attackers shot down, reporting that the Messerschmitts carried black crosses on white squares on their fuselages. Eight Kittyhawks of 260 Squadron flew top cover to 18 Bostons at 1400.Two Messerschmitts attacked the middle cover fighters, causing 260 to dive to the rescue, but in doing so the unit lost one aircraft. A little later Baltimores set out to continue the attack, but two 223 Squadron aircraft collided over the target when surrounded by Flak bursts, and both crashed with the loss of their crews.

During this early afternoon period two or three Hurricanes were claimed by III./JG 77, but during the day this Gruppe suffered the loss of two aircraft, both pilots being wounded – probably in combat with the 112 Squadron Kittyhawks. During the day 260 Squadron welcomed back its previous commanding officer, Sqn Ldr 'Pedro' Hanbury, DFC & Bar, who now returned for a further operational tour in command.

The Regia Aeronautica 2° and 3° Stormi CT and 5° Stormo Assalto retreated from Egypt to Bu Amud with all serviceable MC.200s, MC.202s and CR.42s; ten serviceable MC.200s were now handed over to 13° Gruppo by 8° Gruppo. Not far from Bu Amud the Comando Settore Est was provisionally located, commanded by Col Michele Grandinetti. A Cant.Z.1007bis of 190ª Sq flown by Ten Guido Generali took off from Barce at 1245 to bomb a fuel depot 25 miles east of the Gialo-Kufra trail. Generali flew at an altitude of 3,000 feet dropping six bombs and observed good results.

During the day, III./ KG 40 flew in 13 FW 200s together with 11 He 111 II./KG 4 from Lecce to Tobruk, all carrying supplies of petrol.

British Claims

274 Sqn	Flt Sgt D.C.Burman	Hurrricane IIc HL795 'V'	Fi 156		0715-0825
3 RAAF Sqn	Flt Sgt R.N.B.Stevens	Kittyhawk I ER957 'K'	Bf 109F Damaged	Daba-Fuka area	0740
112 Sqn	Plt Off L.H.Curphey	Kittyhawk III FR195 'F'	Bf 109	W Fuka	0925-1055
112 Sqn	Sqn Ldr B.Drake	Kittyhawk III FR293 '?'	Bf 109	W Fuka	0925-1055
112 Sqn	Sqn Ldr B.Drake	Kittyhawk III FR293 '?'	Bf 109 Damaged	W Fuka	0925-1055
112 Sqn	Flg Off T.Livingstone	Kittyhawk III FR266 'H' }	Bf 109	W Fuka	0925-1055
112 Sqn	Flt Sgt L.C.Shaver	Kittyhawk III FR281 'D' }			

British Claims					
112 Sqn	Flt Lt R.R.Smith	Kittyhawk III FR217 'C'	Bf 109	W Fuka	0925-1055
112 Sqn	Flt Lt R.R.Smith	Kittyhawk III FR217 'C'	Bf 109 Damaged	W Fuka	0925-1055
250 Sqn	Flt Sgt N.R.Chap	Kittyhawk III FR268 'R'	MC.202 Probable	Fuka	1230
127 Sqn	Flg Off J.H.M.MacKinnon	Hurricane IIb BP320	Bf 109	W Fuka	1310-1410

British Casualties	
145 Sqn	Spitfire V BR451 'S' left 1230, shot down by Bf 109; Sgt F.A.Stillman MiA
80 Sqn	Hurricane IIc BM985 'W' left 1010, shot down by Bf 109 S Fuka; Plt Off G.P.Wilson (US) PoW
274 Sqn	Hurricane IIc BH287 'X' left 1310, shot down by six Bf 109 W Fuka; Wt Off Neil safe
260 Sqn	Kittyhawk IIa FL350 left 1400, shot down by Bf 109s when on bomber escort; Sgt G.W.Harttung KiA
223 Sqn	Baltimore III AG941 off 1414 to bomb Axis troops S Maaten Bagush. Collided with AG966 during bombing; both down out of control and exploded on hitting ground; Flt Sgt A.J.Newman PoW, three crew KiA
223 Sqn	Baltimore III AG966 collided with AG941 as above; Flg Off B.A.Kirkham and two KiA, one PoW

German Claims				
3./JG 77	Oblt Friedrich Geisshardt	2 P-40s	N Fuka	1045-1145
3./JG 77	Lt Armin Köhler	P-40	N Fuka	1045-1145

German Casualties	
I./SchG 2	Bf 109F-4 WNr 10029 crash-landed, 70% damaged; pilot safe
II./SchG 2	Bf 109E-7 WNr 3587 crash-landed, 65% damaged; pilot safe
7./KG 100	He 111H-6 WNr 7706 D1+FH, presumed shot down by AA; Oblt Kurt Degner KiA, three MiA
4.(H)/12	2 Bf 110E-3s WNr 2394 and 2448 destroyed by bombs at Fuka
2./JG 27	Bf 109G-2 trop combat with P-40 crashed 2km SE Harun; Lt Karl Wünsch WiA
3./JG 27	Bf 109G-2 trop combat with P-40 crashed 10km E Fuka; Oblt Josef Schlang baled, WiA

Italian Claims					
70ª Sq, 23°Gr, 3°St CT	Ten Antonio Maccanti	MC.202	Spitfire	Abu Haggag-Bir el Astas	1020-1100

Italian Casualties	
85ª Sq, 18°Gr, 3°St CT	MC.202 MM 7779 abandoned at Cassaha, would be captured and evaluated by British Intelligence

Thursday-Friday, 5/6 November 1942

Two Cant.Z.1007bis (one of 190ª and one of 231ª Squadriglie) bombed the El Alamein-Daba road at night.

German Casualties	
7./KG 100	u/k Fuka; Oblt Kurt-Georg Degner KiA, three MiA

Friday, 6 November 1942

Nature now took a hand in favour of the Axis; as heavy rain during the day bogged down both Allied armour and aircraft. This allowed the retreating columns on the coast road to make a good start in their escape. By now the Allied ground forces had reached Fuka and the fighter units had begun moving forward to Daba. 7th Armoured Division managed to catch up with 21st Panzer Division during the day, but was too short of fuel to engage decisively, while 1st Armoured Division was delayed due to lack of the same commodity.

55 Squadron lost one Baltimore during the day, last seen as the unit split up to make individual attacks on the road near Mersa Matruh. It was almost certainly a victim of Flak, the crew failing to survive. On moving to LG.21 at Daba, 92 Squadron found many abandoned Axis aircraft including three almost perfect Bf 109Gs.

During the month a second USAAF fighter group, the 79th, began arriving at Cairo and five of the more experienced pilots, including the commanding officer, Lt Col P.McGoldrick, had been sent forward at once on attachment to the 57th Fighter Group to gain relevant local experience. Now on the 6th, McGoldrick's aircraft was hit as he made a strafing run on a convoy, and he force-landed. In doing so, however, his Warhawk struck a mine which blew up, killing him. Lt Col Earl E.Bates replaced him at the head of the newly-arrived unit.

II./JG 27 had worked so quickly on their aircraft at Gambut that it was now possible to move forward to Menastir with 17 fighters to provide some cover for the withdrawing units over the Halfaya Pass. I./JG 77 moved to Bir el Astas during the day, III.Gruppe moving to Sidi Barrani, leaving one Schwarme of

Possibly a 'proving' exercise, but certainly an attack on German panzers (captured or otherwise) by Hurricane IIds of 6 Squadron, to demonstrate the effectiveness of the big 37mm cannons carried under each wing.

8.Staffel at Stherasat. Only small bodies of ground personnel remained at Qasaba, Qotaifiya and Turbiya to demolish unflyable aircraft and bury as much material as possible. To achieve this they remained even after Allied troops had broken through on the coast road. While at Qotaifiya one morning, a reported 50 Kittyhawks attacked, some of which were shot down by light Flak. One aircraft, having been hit, was fired on by a man with a machine gun who put a full burst into the fuselage, whereupon it crash-landed right alongside JG 27's tents. A tall Canadian pilot got out, but was immediately mobbed by a crowd of Italian troops, who set about him and proceeded to rifle the contents of his pockets. Hptm Börngen rescued him from the mob, passing him on to a PoW camp. Two hours before the arrival of the first British tanks, Börngen led his men away from Qotaifiya, leaving behind 30 burning Bf 109s.

Among the Italian units, 8° Gruppo (92ª and 93ª Squadriglie) now moved to Benghazi K3, with 94ª Squadriglia going to Bu Amud. However, during the transfer flight from Sidi Barrani, one MC.200 force-landed, probably hit by Flak; the pilot was wounded. Amongst the Luftwaffe units, III./ KG 40 again flew into Tobruk, eight FW 200 taking part on this occasion.

British Casualties	
55 Sqn	Baltimore III AG898 'T' off 1405; one of three to attack MT on road W Mersa Matruh but not seen after formation broke up to make attacks; Plt Off R.C.Payne and three KiA
US Casualties	
79th FG	P-40 hit while strafing, force-landed and struck a mine; Lt Col Peter McGoldrick KiA
Italian Casualties	
94ª Sq, 8°Gr, 2° St CT	MC.200 MM 8139 force-landed near Mersa Matruh; Serg Edoardo Pisano wounded
94ª Sq, 8°Gr, 2° St CT	MC.200 MM 6680 abandoned at Bir el Astas

Saturday, 7 November 1942

10th Armoured Division was ordered to proceed along the coast road to Mersa Matruh, but like the others, made slow progress as the German armour was again fighting a rearguard action. 145 and 601 Squadrons moved forward to LG.21 and at 0845 12 Spitfires from the latter unit patrolled over the Mersa Matruh-Sidi Barrani road where nine Ju 87s, three Ju 88s, and nine Bf 109s were seen at 7,000 feet and were attacked. The bombers fled as the Messerschmitts put up a fight, but on getting past these, the Spitfires pursued the bombers, intercepting them again west of Charing Cross. During these encounters four Messerschmitts and three Stukas were claimed shot down at a cost of two Spitfires crash-landed with the pilots unhurt.

Ritterkreuzträger Hptm Bernhard Hamester, led 8./StG 3 until the end of 1942 when he was posted to command III Gruppe of this unit.

A dozen Kittyhawks of 112 Squadron flew a reconnaissance in the Sidi Barrani-Sollum area from 1315 from which one pilot failed to return. They were followed at 1500 by 12 more Kittyhawks from 250 Squadron which set off to strafe that same length of road where four Ju 52/3ms were encountered at low level in the process of flying in fuel from Crete. Three of these transports were claimed shot down in flames and the fourth crash-landed. During the flight back to base the unit then met some Ju 87s and their escort, attacking these and claiming a Bf 109 probable and two MC.202s damaged. However, one Kittyhawk was shot down in flames and a second failed to return. Ten Bordoni-Bisleri and M.llo Longhi of 18° Gruppo had been taking off from Bu Amud, where their unit had arrived during the previous day, when they saw the smoke of the three burning Ju 52/3s, following which they spotted eight Kittyhawks at low level, diving down to attack them. During the dive Bordoni lost the cockpit canopy from his aircraft, but nonetheless managed to shoot down one fighter which was confirmed by an army unit which saw it going down, shedding pieces. This was his 12th victory, and in the event was to be his last in North Africa.

More Ju 52/3ms were encountered during the day, this time by US pilots of the 66th Squadron, four of them claiming two shot down. During the day, however, 1/Lt Gordon Ryerson of the 64th Squadron was shot down and killed.

There was further considerable movements within WDAF during the day, 2 SAAF and 4 SAAF Squadrons leaving LG.97, the former unit going to LG.75 and the latter to LG.12 at Sidi Haneish. 40 SAAF Squadron moved to Maaten Bagush. Three Cant.Z.1007bis of 95° Gruppo bombed again at night the El Alamein-El Daba road.

British Claims

601 Sqn	Lt A.Bartleman	Spitfire Vc BR283	Ju 87	Matruh-Sidi Barrani road	0845-1030
601 Sqn	Lt B.R.Bennetts	Spitfire Vc BR192 }	Ju 87	Matruh-Sidi Barrani road	0845-1030
601 Sqn	Flt Lt M.R.B.Ingram	Spitfire Vc BR361 }			
601 Sqn	Plt Off D.Ibbotson	Spitfire Vc BR135	Ju 87	Matruh-Sidi Barrani road	0845-1030
601 Sqn	Plt Off D.Ibbotson	Spitfire Vc BR135	Bf 109	Matruh-Sidi Barrani road	0845-1030
601 Sqn	Flt Lt M.R.B.Ingram	Spitfire Vc BR361 'P'	Bf 109	Matruh-Sidi Barrani road	0845-1030
601 Sqn	Plt Off D.E.Llewellyn	Spitfire Vc BP852 'K'	Bf 109	Matruh-Sidi Barrani road	0845-1030
601 Sqn	Lt B.R.Bennetts	Spitfire Vc BR192 }	Bf 109	Matruh-Sidi Barrani road	0845-1030
601 Sqn	Flg Off W.M.Whitamore	Spitfire Vc BR136 'H' }			
601 Sqn	Flg Off W.M.Whitamore	Spitfire Vc BR136 'H'	Bf 109 Damaged	Matruh-Sidi Barrani road	0845-1030
250 Sqn	Flt Sgt N.R.Chap	Kittyhawk III FR268 'M'	Ju 52/3m	Matruh-Sidi Barrani road	0845-1030
250 Sqn	Sgt A.F.Nitz	Kittyhawk III FR253 'C'	2 Ju 52/3ms	Matruh-Sidi Barrani road	0845-1030

250 Sqn	Plt Off G.W.Troke	Kittyhawk III FR275 'E'	Ju 52/3m	Sollum	1600
250 Sqn	Plt Off G.W.Troke	Kittyhawk III FR275 'E'	Bf 109 Probable	E Sollum	1615
250 Sqn	Flt Sgt H.K.O'Brien	Kittyhawk III FR307	MC.202 Damaged	E Sollum	1615
250 Sqn	Plt Off N.G.Russell	Kittyhawk III FR241 'R'	MC.202 Damaged	E Sollum	1615

British Casualties

112 Sqn	Kittyhawk III FR215 'V' left 1315, shot down nr Fuka; Sgt R.Webb KiA
112 Sqn	Kittyhawk III FL878 lost
250 Sqn	Kittyhawk III FR268 'M' shot down by Bf 109 or MC.202 nr Sollum 1615; Flt Sgt N.R.Chap KiA
250 Sqn	Kittyhawk III AL177 shot down by Bf 109 or MC.202 nr Sollum 1615; Flg Off H.Calver KiA
250 Sqn	Kittyhawk III FR207 badly damaged by Bf 109 Sollum-Barrani 1620; Flt Sgt H.K.O'Brien safe
601 Sqn	Spitfire V BP852 left 0845, shot down by Bf 109, W Charing Cross; Plt Off D.E.Llewellyn crash-landed
601 Sqn	Spitfire V BR135 left 0845, shot down by Bf 109, W Charing Cross; Plt Off D.Ibbotson crash-landed

US Claims

66th FS/57th FG	1/Lt Gerald A.Brandon	P-40F	Ju 52/3m (shared)
66th FS/57th FG	1/Lt Delbert V.Mitchell	P-40F	
66th FS/57th FG	1/Lt John J.Stefanik	P-40F	Ju 52/3m (shared)
66th FS/57th FG	Capt William J.Yates	P-40F	

US Casualties

64th FS/57th FG	P-40F, 1/Lt Gordon L. Ryerson KiA

German Claims

Stab III./JG 77	Hptm Kurt Ubben	P-40	1620
8./JG 77	Lt Emil Omert	P-40	

German Casualties

4./JG 27	Bf 109F-4 trop WNr 8760 combat with P-40, crashed W Mersa Matruh 100%; Fw Alfred Heidel baled out and WiA
2./StG 3	Ju 87D-1 WNr 2075 S7+CH combat with Spitfire 10km W Sidi Barrani; Uffz Herbert Werner/Uffz Erich Männel WiA
7./StG 3	Ju 87D-3 WNr 2725 combat with Spitfire W Mersa Matruh; Uffz Hans Ortner/Gefr Willi Schäkel WiA
IV./KG zbV 1	Ju 52/3m WNr 6961 shot down by P-40, crashed 20km SW Sidi Barrani; pilot and one safe, one WiA, one KiA
IV./KG zbV 1	Ju 52/3m WNr 6856 shot down by P-40, crashed near Stherasat; crew safe
IV./KG zbV 1	Ju 52/3m WNr 6467 shot down by P-40, crashed near Stherasat; Obfw Georg Möhrke and two WiA, one safe
I./SchG 2	Bf 109F-4 WNr 10167 destroyed by own forces at Gambut

Italian Claims

95ª Sq, 18°Gr, 3°St CT	Ten Franco Bordoni-Bisleri	MC.202	P-40	N Sidi Barrani	1330

Sunday, 8 November 1942

Two MC.202s of 77ª Squadriglia, flown by Ten Savoia and S.Ten Zuccarini, undertook an early patrol over the Sollum-Sidi Barrani area between 0515-0700. Here they reported intercepting a formation of about 20 'P-46s' (as Kittyhawks were frequently identified, which probably indicated that they were Mark IIas or P-40Fs with Merlin engines). One probable was claimed by Zuccarini. During the day 15 new Macchis, ferried from Italy by pilots of 6° Gruppo (81ª and 88ª Squadriglie), landed at Martuba to restore the equipment of 4° Stormo, in order to allow the unit to resume operations. Next day they would be joined by five more, ferried by 79ª Squadriglia pilots.

213 Squadron moved from LG.172 to LG.20, and British troops reached Mersa Matruh. At the same time tanks attacked Gambut but were driven off by Stukas and Flak guns employed in the anti-tank role. During a strafing attack in the face of very heavy Flak, Sgt Markle of 450 Squadron was shot down at around 1500, crash-landing. However, the important and exciting news of the day for 8th Army and WDAF was that Anglo-American forces had landed in strength in French colonial North-West Africa and would be threatening the Axis from the rear as well from now on.

British Claims

92 Sqn	Lt D.Hewitson	Spitfire Vb EP315 'X'	Bf 109 Damaged	recce of forward area	1030-1225

British Casualties

450 Sqn	Kittyhawk III FR273 'F' left 1415, shot down by Flak at Buq Buq; Sgt A.G.Markle PoW
5 SAAF Sqn	Tomahawk IIb AN468 lost

German Claims

4.(H)/12	Uffz Friedrich Stannek	Spitfire	S Bir el Astas	1020

German Casualties

III./JG 77	Bf 109G-2 trop WNr 10652 blown up at Sidi Barrani
8./JG 77	Bf 109G-2 trop WNr 10639 Black 6 blown up at Sidi Barrani (force-landed the day before by Lt Heinz Lüdemann)
Verb Kdo (S) 2	4 DFS 230s WNr 227608, 227604, 227598 and 227600 destroyed by own forces

Italian Claims

77ª Sq, 13°Gr, 2°St CT	S.Ten Gian Mario Zuccarini	MC.202	P-46 Probable	Sidi Barrani	0800

Monday, 9 November 1942

Once again the German armoured units engaged in a rearguard action during the day despite only having some 30 tanks still serviceable from the 270 with which they had started the El Alamein battle. The Italians now had virtually none, although a new Italian armoured division was on its way to the front. During the morning Bf 109s of I./JG 77 intercepted a formation of 15 Bostons escorted by 20 Curtiss fighters east of Halfaya; Oblt Geisshardt claimed one of the latter shot down. Another 13 Kittyhawks from 3 RAAF Squadron bombed vehicles on the Halfaya Pass from 1400, and here two yellow-nosed Bf 109s attacked them. Flt Lt Kildey claimed one shot down which he reported crashed on the escarpment; Sqn Ldr Gibbes claimed the other damaged.

At 1445 450 Squadron, which had just moved to LG.115, escorted Bostons and Baltimores to attack the Sidi Barrani-Sollum road with seven Spitfires of 92 Squadron following a few minutes later to strafe in the same area. Messerschmitts of JG 77 attacked both squadrons, Maj Müncheberg seeing the Spitfires strafing east of Buq Buq and shooting down Flt Sgt Blade's aircraft in flames. Eight more of the unit's fighters attacked 450 Squadron, shooting down Sgt Borthwick, his aircraft being seen to crash and burst into flames; four other Kittyhawks were slightly damaged. Although wounded, Borthwick got out of the wreckage of his fighter and crawled on hands and knees for four days in Axis territory until he was finally picked up by the forward troops of the advancing 8th Army. During their fight Flt Lt 'Nobby' Clarke and Sgt Oakley each claimed a Bf 109 probably shot down, Clarke also claiming one damaged.

During the day Lt Trevor Cook of 40 SAAF Squadron was providing escort to Lt R.H.van der Poel on a TacR when they became involved in an action which led to the award of a DFC to Cook. His citation recorded: "...this officer was engaged with another pilot, on a reconnaissance over the Sollum area when they were attacked by two enemy fighters. Lieutenant Cook immediately turned to engage the hostile aircraft and with great skill and determination he fought them for 25 minutes before returning to base. As a result of this courageous action his fellow pilot was able to continue his reconnaissance and bring back valuable information."

By night four Cant.Z.1007bis of 35° Stormo bombed the coastal road east of Mersa Matruh.

British Claims

4 SAAF Sqn	Lt G.H.Kaufmann	Kittyhawk I EV362 'Y'	Bf 109F	LG.104	1035
250 Sqn	Plt Off G.W.Troke	Kittyhawk III FR275 'E'	MC.202 Damaged	Sollum road and pass	1150-1350
3 RAAF Sqn	Plt Off G.E.S.Clabburn	Kittyhawk IIa FL291 'A'	Bf 109F Damaged	Capuzzo	1455
3 RAAF Sqn	Flt Lt E.K.Kildey	Kirttyhawk IIa FL323 'V'	Bf 109F	Capuzzo	1455
450 Sqn	Flt Lt D.H.Clarke	Kittyhawk III FR237	Bf 109 Probable	Sidi Barrani-Sollum road	1445-1625
450 Sqn	Flt Lt D.H.Clarke	Kittyhawk III FR237	Bf 109 Damaged	Sidi Barrani-Sollum road	1445-1625
450 Sqn	Sgt E.P.Oakley	Kirttyhawk III FL881	Bf 109E Probable	Sidi Barrani-Sollum road	1445-1625
92 Sqn	Flt Lt C.J.Samouelle	Spitfire Vc BR521 'E'	Bf 109 Damaged	E Buq Buq	1500-1655
2 SAAF Sqn	Lt A.P.Blignault	Kittyhawk I EV356 'A'	Bf 109F Damaged	E Tobruk	1530

British Casualties

92 Sqn	Spitfire Vb EP616 shot down by Bf 109s nr Sidi Barrani 1600; Flt Sgt R.W.Blade KiA
92 Sqn	Spitfire Vb EP397 hit landmine on landing at LG.13 at 0730; Flt Sgt R.Clapson safe
450 Sqn	Kittyhawk III FR210 shot down by Bf 109s while escorting Baltimores S Sidi Barrani; Sgt D.W.P.Borthwick WiA
450 Sqn	Kittyhawk III FR259 badly damaged by Bf 109 S Sidi Barrani; Sgt B.V.Crist safe
450 Sqn	4 Kittyhawk IIIs slightly damaged
40 SAAF Sqn	Hurricane IIc HL679 attacked by five Bf 109s at Buq Buq, hit in wing by shell; Lt T.Cook safe

German Claims

3./JG 77	Oblt Friedrich Geisshardt	P-40	E Halfaya Pass	0955-1115
Stab III./JG 77	Obfw Heinrich Hackler	P-40	10km E Sollum	1446
Stab I./JG 77	Hptm Heinz Bär	P-40	E Sollum	1450

Stab/JG 77	Maj Joachim Müncheberg	Spitfire	E Buq Buq	1507
Stab/JG 77	Hptm Erwin Bacsilla	P-40		

German Casualties

III./JG 77	Bf 109G-2 trop WNr 10634 blown up Sidi Barrani
KGr zbV 300	Ju 52/3m WNr 3247 destroyed near Sidi Barrani, crew safe
KGr zbV 300	Ju 52/3m WNr 7618 destroyed near Sidi Barrani, pilot safe, three WiA
Verb Kdo (S) 2	He 126B-1 WNr 4240 destroyed at Sollum by own forces
Verb Kdo (S) 2	Ju 87R-4 WNr 6310 destroyed at Sollum by own forces
Verb Kdo (S) 2	Ju 87R-4 WNr 6265 destroyed at Halfaya Pass by own forces

Italian Casualties

131°Gr AS	S.79 MM 21636 force-landed near Misurata, damaged, crew safe
160°Gr CT	MC.200 MM 5799 damaged on take-off, Ten Luigi Deggiovanni safe

Tuesday, 10 November 1942

Two CR.42s of 238ª Squadriglia led by Ten Carlo Graziani bombed and strafed British vehicles in the Bu Amud area during the day; one of these aircraft was hit and damaged by AA fire. Six Spitfires of 601 Squadron took off at 1020 on a TacR mission. They were jumped by Bf 109s of I./JG 77 and Plt Off Scollan was shot down in flames and killed by Oblt Geisshardt for his 100th victory. Twelve Kittyhawks of 2 SAAF Squadron, covered by 260 Squadron, undertook a sweep to Tobruk. Here four Bf 109s were encountered which were identified by the South Africans as being E versions. Capt Charles Laubscher:

Capt J.E.'Jack' Parsonson of 2 SAAF Squadron was shot down on 10 November, and describes here that experience and others leading to his escape and return to his unit.

> "Flying as top cover for wing sweep over Tobruk. West of Sollum two 109Es flew below the formation, leader section turned after them but they evaded the attack. Went down on one but could not turn with him due to the speed built up in my dive, so pulled up again. Saw the second 109E heading west low down. Put my section into line astern and went after him, but this time I throttled back in my dive. As I was coming in on his tail he saw me and pulled his emergency boost and literally jumped forward into a climb. I opened my throttle wide and caught him in the climb. He turned and I had a deflection shot at him. He half rolled and I rolled with him firing as I was on my back. He went into a spiral dive and I followed him down, firing as he came into my sights. I suddenly saw the ground coming up fast and pulled out hard. Blacked out completely, and waited for the impact. As I 'greyed-in' I found that I was flying straight and level between two big sand dune ridges, below the level of the ridge tips – must have cleared the floor of the valley by not more than 20-30 feet at the bottom of the pull-out. Looking behind me saw the column of smoke and flames where the 109E had gone in."

Laubscher's victim appears to have been Lt Konrad Fels of 2./JG 77. Meanwhile, more Messerschmitts had appeared and Capt Parsonson was heard to call "There are nine following me". It may be recalled that Jack Parsonson had been shot down a week earlier and had just returned to the squadron:

> "It was a week since I had last flown and we took off and formed up as top cover over 260 Squadron. I thought how good it was to feel the familiar controls of a Kitty in my hands again.

Cap Claudio Solaro about to climb into MC.202 '70-5'.

The engine was performing smoothly and I looked up to the left to see Charles (Laubscher) with his yellow section holding good position and then to the right at Paddy (Hope)'s section. What splendid fellows they all were and I felt happy they were there with us. The formation of 24 aeroplanes with 260 Squadron below us, formed up into the usual finger fours and we set off for Tobruk. Far below were the Gambut, Sidi Omar and Bir Hacheim air bases which were still in German hands.

"About half way to Tobruk six 109s flying at 12 o'clock high closed round to six o'clock. We watched them carefully, then one detached and dived on Paddy's section. Passing behind and below Paddy, it was the typical decoy attack and it was going very fast; Paddy could not hope to catch it. To my surprise, Paddy yelled 'Tally Ho!' and dived after him. About eight or ten 109s now arrived above us and moved to six o'clock before diving to attack 260. The original four attacked the leader section – all that remained of 2 Squadron – and we turned sharply to meet them. Two of my section disappeared into the melee below. I thought to myself 'Gerry' Gericke and I will stay up here as top cover. In the next violent turn Gerry spun and I was alone in a desperate struggle with four 109s.

"It now ceased to be fun and as I turned to face them again I knew I was in for the fight of my life. Far below a mass of aircraft were whirling in a dogfight, and there was nothing I could do but meet these four and turn into their attacks, firing as the opportunity presented itself. I knew that more 109s had joined the four and kept turning into them to keep them off my tail. The fight had begun at 17,000 feet and we were losing height all the time. With so many of them some inevitably got behind me and from about 8,000 feet they began to hit me.

"Gaping holes appeared in the mainplanes on both sides of the cockpit. I was down to a few hundred feet when a cannon shell slammed past my right shoulder into the instrument panel, shattering the oil tank behind it. Everything became covered in oil so I raised my goggles and peered over the side. The engine seized and I had to get out fast. More shells hit my aircraft and I put her down immediately, I was doing about 180 when I touched ground the first time and the old Kitty skimmed like a flat stone thrown across water. On the fourth touch, the aircraft ploughed along the ground and came to a sudden stop. I tore off the straps and got out as fast as possible. Looking up I saw the enemy turn down on me with guns blazing. I ducked under the engine and the shells hit the ground all around. 'The bloody thing will burn any second' I thought. It did. In fact the sound of my own ammunition exploding was alarming.

"I looked round desperately for some cover, and away to the left – about 60 yards or so – was a round stone, roofless sort of hut with a narrow entrance facing me. I ran fast across the intervening ground and threw myself into it, scrabbling with my hands on the hard soil in an effort to dig in.

Hopeless, so I pressed myself against one side. Shells burst all around the little place and against the walls outside. I thought 'Hell, they really want to kill me, they're not satisfied with shooting me down'. After a while the shooting ceased and I looked cautiously over the wall to see what was happening. There were eight 109s circling like hawks. I crouched down again and waited for a short time before hearing a gharry approaching. I drew my revolver and peered over the top. What looked like a two-ton truck fully laden with armed troops was coming up fast. As it stopped a few yards away I realized the futility of my revolver so I put it back in the holster and raised my hands. A very decent young German lieutenant came towards me and looked at me carefully, 'You must be very tired' he said, and I realized that I was feeling totally exhausted. 'Well, for you the war is over. Here. Would you like to have this egg? Make a hole in each end and suck it.' I did so and it was most refreshing. He gave me a cigarette and told me to climb aboard the gharry.

"We went to Sollum, where I was transferred to another truck under the command of a sergeant major. We travelled for some distance into the desert and then the truck stopped. The sergeant major got off, pulled down his trousers and adjusted his underpants. Suddenly he leapt up and down in a screaming rage, shouting and swearing. He tidied himself and climbed back on the truck while the thought went through my mind 'What manner of men have I fallen amongst?' It was dark when we reached a large encampment, and I was told I could sleep under the lorry, and sleep I did. We were near Fort Capuzzo, which was on the boundary between Egypt and Cyrenaica."

Ju 87D of II./StG 3 abandoned by its unit and captured by advancing Allied troops.

Six I./JG 77 pilots reported meeting a lone Curtiss fighter, the pilot putting up a resolute fight for half an hour until he finally belly-landed, this victory being credited to Hptm Bär; this would appear to have been Jack Parsonson's aircraft. On a TacR sortie during the day Lt Beith of 40 SAAF Squadron failed to return, his fate not being recorded. The day also saw the arrival of 4 SAAF Squadron at LG.75 where it joined 2 SAAF. 127 Squadron moved from LG.37 to LG.20.

Eight MC.202s of 23° Gruppo, led by Cap Claudio Solaro, escorted fighter-bombers strafing Sidi Barrani. On return to Bu Amud, Solaro belly-landed damaging his aircraft. 4° Stormo retreated from Martuba, which was now too close to the front, to Benghazi K3 and then to Arae Philaenorum.

British Claims

40 SAAF Sqn	Lt R.D.Steinbach	Hurricane BV160	e/a Damaged	LG.158	1415
2 SAAF Sqn	Capt C.J.Laubscher	Kittyhawk I ET977 'Z'	Bf 109	30m W Sollum	1530
2 SAAF Sqn	Lt A.P.Blignault	Kittyhawk I EV356 'A'	Bf 109F Damaged	30m W Sollum	1530

British Casualties

601 Sqn	Spitfire Vc EP451 shot down by Bf 109 at 1120; Plt Off C.R.Scollan KiA
2 SAAF Sqn	Kittyhawk I EV325 'T' shot down by Bf 109s ansd crash-landed 10m S Sollum 1530-1600; Capt J.E.Parsonson PoW, escaped and returned on 17th
40 SAAF Sqn	Hurricane FTR; Lt C.M.Beith MiA

German Claims

2./JG 77	Lt Iring Englisch	Hurricane		0645
3./JG 77	Oblt Friedrich Geisshardt	Spitfire	SW Sollum - Sidi Barrani	0945-1100
1./JG 77	Oblt Siegfried Freytag	Spitfire		

German Claims

I./JG 77	Obfw Georg Ludwig	Spitfire		
I./JG 77	Uffz Horst Schlick	Spitfire		
Stab I./JG 77	Hptm Heinz Bär	2 P-40s	E Sollum	1434 & 1438

German Casualties

2./JG 77	Bf 109G-2 trop WNr 10543 Black 10 shot down by P-40 Sollum area; Lt Konrad Fels MiA
4.(H)/12	Bf 109F-4 WNr 13271 crash-landed at Menastir 80% damaged; Obfw Wilhelm Ritter inj
III./ZG 26	Bf 110F-3 WNr 5027 destroyed by own forces at Berka airfield
III./KGzbV 1	Ju 52/3m WNr 6082 destroyed by own forces at Berka-West
3./JG 53	Bf 109G-2 WNr 10632 Yellow 2 ran into wreck of Ju 52 on take-off at Berka-West; Uffz Erich Juhls KiA

Italian Casualties

70ª Sq, 23°Gr, 3°St CT	MC.202 damaged on landing, Cap Claudio Solaro unscathed
238ª Sq, 101°Gr, 5°St Tuff	CR.42 hit by AA

Wednesday, 11 November 1942

Jack Parsonson continued:

"Early next morning my captors allowed me to go a short distance away for my morning constitutional. As I stood up it seemed as though a large swarm of small birds was flying fast over the German column. I realised that we were being attacked by four British tanks which made their appearance on the skyline to the south of us. The sound of small birds whistling over us was small-arms automatic fire from the tanks. There was total, though controlled, consternation and I was hustled on to the lorry with my captors. This whistling sound of bullets was new to me and I felt we were very vulnerable indeed. However, all the vehicles made off at high speed while an 88mm gun battery went into action immediately and halted the tanks long enough to enable us to escape. We travelled a short distance with shells bursting around the vehicles but causing no discernible damage, then the 105mm battery, with which I was travelling, went into action to allow the 88mm battery to disengage and withdraw through us and set up further ahead. This leap frogging went on for quite a while.

"While this running battle was in progress I saw 15 Stukas pass overhead going in the direction of our troops to the east. A squadron of Kittyhawks came into view and it was obvious they were on the trail of the Stukas. Soon came the sounds of aerial battle and the Stukas did not appear again. I was sure they had all been shot down. Later I learned that this was indeed the case and that the squadron was our own No.2!"

Grp Capt Guy Carter commanded 358 Wing and then 211 Group. In his personal Hurricane he was the first Allied pilot to land back in Libya following the victory at El Alamein.

After several attempts, Jack Parsonson managed to escape by night from a truck in which he was being held captive. He was then looked after by Bedouins for some days, finally making contact with the head of the 8th Army's advancing columns, rejoining his unit towards the end of November.

8th Army reached Halfaya on this date, the Luftwaffe making its last big attempt to slow the advancing Allied armour during the day. Parsonson had been quite correct – 11 Kittyhawks of 2 SAAF Squadron on a dawn reconnaissance over Gambut had spotted 15 Ju 87s of I./StG 3 with an escort of six Bf 109s.

Capt Wildsmith led his fighters away from the enemy formation, then making a sudden attack on the bombers. The Messerschmitts at once attacked, shooting down Lts Allen-White and Theron. By doing so, however, they left the Stukas unprotected and the rest of the squadron waded in, claiming eight shot down and four probables. At 0705 16 57th Fighter Group P-40s had set off on a strafing mission against landing grounds near Gambut. Here three Bf 109s were seen in the air and five Ju 87s in the process of landing. Maj Wheeler attacked one of the latter which turned over and burst into flames, confirmed by two other pilots. Capt Ryan hit two Stukas landing on the same airfield, both reportedly exploding, again witnessed by the same two pilots. At the same time one aircraft was strafed on the ground by Lt Bourguignan, and burst into flames – once more seen by the useful pair of witnesses, Capt Burman and Lt Merena. At least 24 Bf 109s and Ju 87s were counted on the airfield, together with 18 or more Messerschmitts, Stukas and CR.42s at a nearby field, and a considerable amount of MT moving west. It seems that actual losses during these two engagements amounted to eight Ju 87s including that flown by the Kommandeur, Oblt Martin Mossdorf, a Ritterkreuzträger, who became a PoW; one Staffelkapitän was also lost. Oblt Hans-Georg Migeod (Staffelkapitän 2./StG 3):

"Early next morning (11th) an attack was ordered on a certain strong column advancing. Objection of the Gruppe Kommandeur regarding the uncertainty of location of a moving target reconnoitred the evening before was overruled at a higher level. Spirits at the briefing near to cold fury... – 15 Ju 87s were got together, orders to start at 0420 hours, pitch dark, take off in formation and without position lamps so as to be in the air quickly and to avoid unnecessary curiosity of Arab scouts, flight positions must be kept by means of faintly visible exhaust flames. At an altitude of about 1,500 metres (4,500 feet) the eastern horizon becomes silvery, and out of the darkness below a formation of two Me 109s glides up; what an enormous fighter protection – in the nice old days of El Alamein we had been spoilt by a thumb-rule of one fighter for two of us. Some poetical mind voices his mood on the wireless: 'One swallow does not make a summer' 'Shut up', the Kommandeur restores radio silence. Meanwhile we are floating in the early light and its rays begin to touch the ground far below us now. We are nosing unpleasantly against a low sun, and our so-called cousins will definitely come up from the other side to bid a good morning. We seem to be some 15km from the target, and I try to find some details worthy of our attention. How will our old man direct the approach and how will I station my few planes behind his?

"But these tactical reflections mean nothing because suddenly out of the sun, between us and the faraway coast, a party of Kittyhawks appear, and they instantly start to pour on us like warm rain. Our Me 109s may remain masters of their situation but they are not much help to us now. The whole mass of aeroplanes break up into incoherent dogfights, and away with those deadweight bombs we were carrying. The centrifugal force of tight turns jams the cartridge belts of my rear double-barrel machine gun. I am curving around with one of the fellows to get behind him, when from the periphery of our circle I feel two hits into the motor bloc in front of me, and a Kittyhawk is swerving up in front. The engine smells and blows a white trail, the motor starts to run roughly. Soon my prop stretches its three blades, the engine stops and I am already nosing down. There we are. To find a tolerable landing is not difficult here and at 300 metres I start to glide down. What a sudden silence, although behind and above the fight roars and rattles on distinctly and loudly.

"Into this relative calm cuts the voice of my gunner: 'Turn, Leutnant, turn'. How to achieve this with our low speed! Behind, out of the corner of my eye, I see the enemy in a run-up on us from above. Should the first tracer fly I will push the plane down and risk a crash-landing, an ugly feeling; I continue the landing approach. But no, no flashes, he does not press the button – pulls up above us while my undercarriage is rumbling over the camel thorn bushes – he dives down again, pulls away waving his victorious wings.

"In 1974 I emigrated to South Africa....After a while I came to know F.J.M.(Jack) Meaker, old fighter pilot and squadron leader...One good day in 1976, he comes up and says, he had now traced my conqueror of 11th November 1942. The German-English co-edition *Fighters over the Desert* contains a rather complete register of Who-Shot-Down-Whom-Where-and-When-in-North-Africa. It is his old buddy D.B.Hauptfleisch (Huffie). Yes, and when we met each other, there resulted a big party on his farm, and the happily un-widowed ladies with us. We compared notes and established that we were the two pilots involved. Finally I had met the man who 34 years earlier had proved to be a thorough gentleman."

At 0915 eight Kittyhawks of 2 SAAF Squadron were off again, this time as top cover for a wing fighter-bomber attack on Tobruk and LG.145 by 11 aircraft of 4 SAAF Squadron, 12 from 260 Squadron and Tomahawks from 5 SAAF Squadron. South of Sollum ten Bf 109s attacked 260 and 2 SAAF, two members of the latter unit being shot down in flames. A running fight to Gambut then took place, two more Kittyhawks being badly shot-up and crash-landing at base. Immediately after the bombing two of 260 Squadron's aircraft were shot down, one of them force-landing at LG.08.

Meanwhile, Flt Lt Cundy had spotted an Fi 156 at 500 feet and shot this down. 4 SAAF Squadron was attacked by six Bf 109s which had been escorting Ju 52/3ms, Maj du Toit being shot-up and force-landing although Lt Dummett was able to claim one of the transports and a Bf 109 shot down. Just after leaving the Gambut area six of 260 Squadron's pilots saw an aircraft which they took to be a Ju 88 which they shot down between them. A 'hack' Do 17Z of Stab/StG 3 was attacked between Gambut and Tobruk and this force-landed; this was very probably the aircraft which they had despatched. Ron Cundy:

> "…we took off carrying 500 pound bombs and headed for detailed targets at LG.145 or LG.156 near Tobruk. Sqn Ldr Hanbury decided instead to bomb Gambut No.1 on which there were about 50 aircraft. Bombing was good and at least two fires were started. Immediately after bombing, Hanbury and his section were jumped by two 109s. Taking evasive action he was able to get a burst at one without observing any result. Two other pilots of his section, Sgts Williams and Hill turned away from the attack, a fatal move. Williams' aircraft was damaged and he force-landed at LG.08 Mersa Matruh. Hill was shot down and became a PoW.
>
> "A Fieseler Storch suddenly appeared about 500 feet below and I attacked it head-on. Strikes in and around the cockpit were observed and then it hit the deck (on return to base I claimed a probable, which was later confirmed as destroyed). I then sighted a Ju 88 flying west at ground level. Six of us …attacked it but we had struck a very skilful pilot who managed to evade many of our attacks. Eventually numbers and persistence prevailed and we saw him crash near Tobruk with his port engine on fire. We were each credited with one sixth destroyed. Altogether a good morning's work."

James 'Eddie' Edwards of 260 Squadron, one of the most successful Allied fighter pilots of the desert war (centre) was promoted direct from Flt Sgt to Flt Lt during December, and was awarded both a DFC and a DFM. He is seen here during September with members of his flight, left to right Sgt Lionel Sheppard, Flg Off W.Ron Cundy, Flg Off G.Fallows and Flg Off Nelson Gilboe. Cundy had also enjoyed several successes, culminating on 11 November.

It seems likely that, during this hectic morning with its series of engagements, the ten Messerschmitts which had attacked Cundy's unit had been from II./JG 27, while those attacking 4 SAAF Squadron were from JG 77. Not far behind the 233 Wing formation, 12 Kittyhawks of 112 Squadron, which had just moved with 450 Squadron to LG.76, set off at 1035 on a long-range sweep over El Adem Tobruk-Gambut. Two pilots claimed Ju 52/3ms shot down and Sqn Ldr Drake claimed damage to a Bf 109. 112 Squadron had been provided with cover by 12 66th Squadron P-40s, which had taken off at 1030. Arriving over the patrol area, pilots spotted aircraft taking off from LG.159, going down to engage. Two Bf 109s and two Ju 52/3ms were claimed shot down, all falling on or near the airfield. A third Ju 52/3m was pursued by Lt Gilbertson and forced down to the south-west; the crew were strafed as they ran from the aircraft. A Kittyhawk of 450 Squadron was seen apparently recently belly-landed, while just before attacking the transport aircraft, one of the Americans heard the pilot of one of the 112 Squadron aircraft reporting that his aircraft had been hit in the glycol and that he was heading east.

Other Messerschmitts of JG 77 were certainly active during the day, two pilots claiming to have shot down B-24s over the Halfaya Pass. Amongst WDAF's other units 80 and 335 Squadrons now moved to LG.13.Stab/JG 77, I./JG 77 and III./JG 77 went to Martuba. 3° Stormo and 13° Gruppo retreated to Nofilia.

British Claims

2 SAAF Sqn	Maj A.M.Colenbrander	Kittyhawk I AL153 'L'	2 Ju 87s Probable	SW Sollum	0710
2 SAAF Sqn	Maj D.B.Hauptfleisch	Kittyhawk I AL186 'G'	Ju 87	SW Sollum	0710
2 SAAF Sqn	Lt R.C.Hojem	Kittyhawk I EV162 'I'	2 Ju 87s	SW Sollum	0710
2 SAAF Sqn	Lt R.C.Hojem	Kittyhawk I EV162 'I'	Ju 87 Probable	SW Sollum	0710
2 SAAF Sqn	Lt V.M.L.Lindsay	Kittyhawk I EV356 'A'	Ju 87	SW Sollum	0710
2 SAAF Sqn	Lt V.M.L.Lindsay	Kittyhawk I EV356 'A'	Ju 87	SW Sollum	0710
2 SAAF Sqn	Lt W.L.O.Moon	Kittyhawk I EV349 'K'			
2 SAAF Sqn	Lt W.L.O.Moon	Kittyhawk I EV349 'K'	Ju 87	SW Sollum	0710
2 SAAF Sqn	Squadron	Kittyhawk I	Ju 87 Probable	SW Sollum	0710
2 SAAF Sqn	Lt D.A.Ruiter	Kittyhawk I AL162 'S'	Ju 87	SW Sollum	0710
2 SAAF Sqn	Capt H.E.N.Wildsmith	Kittyhawk I EV348 'U'	Ju 87	SW Sollum	0710
2 SAAF Sqn	Lt R.D.B.Morton		Bf 109 Damaged		
4 SAAF Sqn	Maj S.F.du Toit	Kittyhawk I EV362 'Y'	Bf 109G		0915-1135
4 SAAF Sqn	Lt N.R.Dummett	Kittyhawk I AL189 'H'	Bf 109E	10m W LG.145	0915-1135
4 SAAF Sqn	Lt N.R.Dummett	Kittyhawk I AL189 'H'	Ju 52/3m	10m W LG.145	0915-1135
260 Sqn	Sgt J.C.Colley	Kittyhawk IIa	Ju 88	Gambut No.1, nr Tobruk	0915-1100
260 Sqn	Flt Lt W.R.Cundy	Kittyhawk IIa FL316			
260 Sqn	Flt Lt C.C.H.Davis	Kittyhawk IIa			
260 Sqn	Flt Sgt N.E.McKee	Kittyhawk IIa			
260 Sqn	Flt Sgt W.E.Stewart	Kittyhawk IIa			
260 Sqn	Sgt B.H.Thomas	Kittyhawk IIa			
260 Sqn	Flt Lt W.R.Cundy	Kittyhawk Iia FR316	Fi 156	Gambut No.1, nr Tobruk	0915-1100
112 Sqn	Sqn Ldr B.Drake	Kittyhawk III FR293 '?'	Bf 109E Damaged	El Adem-Tobruk-Gambut	1035-1235
112 Sqn	Flt Lt G.W.Garton	Kittyhawk III FR213 'Q'	Ju 52/3m	Gambut	1035-1235
112 Sqn	Sgt D.S.Watson	Kittyhawk III FR281 'D'	Ju 52/3m	Gambut	1035-1235

British Casualties

2 SAAF Sqn	Kittyhawk I ET527 'B' shot down into sea by Bf 109 SW Sollum 0735; Lt A.F.Allen-White returned
2 SAAF Sqn	Kittyhawk I AK782 'D' shot down by Bf 109, crash-landed 28m SW Bardia; 2/Lt D.C.Theron picked up
2 SAAF Sqn	Kittyhawk I ET977 'Z' slt damaged by Bf 109; Lt T.V.de Villiers safe
2 SAAF Sqn	Kittyhawk I EV356 'A' shot down by Bf 109 12m S Sollum 1030 ; Lt V.R.Burden KiA
2 SAAF Sqn	Kittyhawk I AL162 'S' shot down by Bf 109 12m S Sollum 1030; Lt H.S.McMaster KiA
2 SAAF Sqn	Kittyhawk I AL147 'V' damaged by Bf 109, crash-landed 2m short base, Cat II; Lt J.H.Burls safe
2 SAAF Sqn	Kittyhawk I EV348 'U' damaged by Bf 109, crash-landed at base Cat II; Lt L.C.H.Hope slt WiA
2 SAAF Sqn	Kittyhawk I EV324 'Q' slt damaged by two Bf 109s; Lt P.D.Bryant safe
4 SAAF Sqn	Kittyhawk I EV362 'Y' badly damaged by Bf 109s, force-landed at 1130 LG.155 Cat II; Maj S.F. du Toit safe
260 Sqn	Kittyhawk IIa 'X' shot down by Bf 109s S Sollum 0915-1000; Flt Sgt E.G.Hill PoW
260 Sqn	Kittyhawk IIa FL234 'A' damaged by Bf 109s, and force-landed LG.08, Mersa Matruh 0915-1100; Sgt R.S.Williams safe

US Claims

64th FS/57th FG	Capt Richard E.Ryan	P-40F '37'	2 Ju 87s	near Gambut	0705-0840
64th FS/57th FG	Maj Clermont E.Wheeler	P-40F '14'	Ju 87	near Gambut	0705-0840
64th FS/57th FG	Lt Bourguignon	P-40F	e/a destroyed on ground at Gambut		0705-0840
66th FS/57th FG	1/Lt John T.Gilbertson	P-40F '96'	Ju 52/3m	SW of LG.159	1030-1240
66th FS/57th FG	2/Lt Frank E.Hertzberg	P-40F '84'	Ju 52/3m	near LG.159	1030-1240
66th FS/57th FG	1/Lt Delbert V.Mitchell	P-40F '82'	Bf 109	near LG.159	1030-1240
66th FS/57th FG	1/Lt Delbert V.Mitchell	P-40F '82'	Ju 52/3m	near LG.159	1030-1240
66th FS/57th FG	1/Lt Albert O.Zipser	P-40F '86'	Bf 109	near LG.159	1030-1240

US Casualties

64th FS/57th FG P-40F '14' 0750 failed to return; Maj Clermont E.Wheeler PoW

German Claims

1./JG 77	Oblt Siegfried Freytag	2 P-40s	Sollum/Bir el Acra	
1./JG 77	Obfw Georg Ludwig	P-40	Sollum/Bir el Acra	
1./JG 77	Fw Siegfried Ott	P-40	Sollum/Bir el Acra	
1./JG 77	Uffz Horst Schlick	P-40	Sollum/Bir el Acra	
5./JG 27	Fw Bernhard Schneider	P-40	SSW Sollum	0908
5./JG 27	Obfw Emil Clade	P-40	SSE Sollum	0912
4./JG 27	Uffz Josef Brandl	2 P-40s	SE Sollum	0912 & 0925
5./JG 27	Oblt Ernst Börngen	P-40	S Sollum	0927
Stab I./JG 77	Hptm Heinz Bär	P-40	SE Gambut	0930
Stab I./JG 77	Lt Heinz-Edgar Berres	P-40	NE Bir el Acra	0931
5./JG 27	Uffz Ernst Klopp	P-40	ESE Sollum	0932
3./JG 77	Lt Eberhard Niese	P-40	SE Gambut	0935
Stab I./JG 77	Hptm Heinz Bär	P-40	SE Gambut	0938
III./JG 77	unstated	2 u/i claims (possibly B-24s)		

German Casualties

III./JG 77	Bf 109G-2 trop WNr 10649 blown up Bir el Arca
1./JG 77	Bf 109G-2 trop WNr 10607 crash-landed at Martuba and blown up
2./JG 77	Bf 109G-2 trop WNr 14250 blown up at Gambut
2./JG 77	Bf 109G-2 trop WNrs 10542 & 10539 blown up at Martuba
1.(F)/121	Ju 88D-1 WNr 430268 shot down by P-40, crashed at Bu Amud; Fw Herbert Wegeber and one KiA; Lt Erich Meyer WiA, died 29 Nov in Naples hospital; one other WiA
3./SchG 2	Bf 109 F-4 WNr 7565 shot down and crashed 10km E Tobruk; Gefr Wolfgang Schipper KiA
Stab/StG 3	Do 17Z-3 WNr 2901 S7+FA combat SE Tobruk; Obfw Georg Brodowski WiA, died 13th; plus four WiA, one KiA
2./StG 3	Ju 87D-3 WNr 2348 S7+HK combat with P-40 30km S Sollum; Uffz Johann Malle/Uffz Franz Beyer PoW
3./StG 3	Ju 87D-3 WNr 2674 S7+KL combat with P-40 SW Sollum; Oblt Heinz-Georg Migeod/Gefr Josef Meyer PoW
3./StG 3	Ju 87D-3 combat with P-40 SW Sollum; Fw Friedrich Poth/Uffz Anton Herrmann WiA
I./StG 3	Ju 87D-3 WNr 2565 S7+MB combat with P-40 SW Sollum; Oblt Martin Mossdorf/Uffz August Brandt PoW
StG 3	Ju 87 Lt Hans Töpler WiA
III./KGzbV 1	Ju 52/3m WNr 7221 shot down by P-40 10km W Gambut, one WiA, three safe
III./KGzbV 1	Ju 52/3m WNr 6675 shot down by P-40 10km W Gambut, three WiA, Uffz Friedrich Vögel KiA
III./KGzbV 1	Ju 52/3m WNr 6305 shot down by P-40 10km W Gambut, two WiA, two safe
I./SchG 2	Bf 109F-4 WNr 8549 destroyed by own forces at Gambut
II./SchG 2	2 Bf 109E-7s WNrs 5187 and 3564 destroyed by own forces at Gambut
II./SchG 2	Bf 109E-7 WNr 6007 destroyed by own forces at Qasaba
II./SchG 2	Bf 109E-7 WNr 2051 destroyed by own forces at Bir el Abd
II./KG zbV 1	2 Ju 52/3ms WNrs 7064 and 7595 destroyed by own forces at Derna
KGr zbV 800	Ju 52/3m WNr 6833 destroyed by own forces at Martuba
KGr zbV 800	Ju 52/3m WNr 9005 destroyed by own forces at Tobruk
III./KG 4	He 111H-6 WNr 4508 5J+DD destroyed by own forces at Tobruk
III./StG 3	Ju 87D-3 WNr 2659 destroyed by own forces at Martuba
III./StG 3	Ju 87D-3 WNr 2566 destroyed by own forces at Gambut
III./ZG 26	Bf 110F-2 WNr 5053 destroyed by own forces at Tobruk
Sd St Go 242	He 111H-6 WNr 4634 destroyed by own forces at Tobruk

Verb St (S).2	Ju 87 WNr 6261 destroyed by own forces at Tobruk
Verb St (S).2	Ju 87 WNr 6280 towing aircraft destroyed by own forces at Tobruk
Verb St (S).2	He 126 WNr 3237 towing aircraft destroyed by own forces at Tobruk
Verb St (S).2	Go 242 WNr 401 destroyed by own forces at Tobruk
Verb St (S).2	DFS 230 WNr 227603 destroyed by own forces at Tobruk
Verb St (S).2	He 126 WNr 4197 towing aircraft destroyed by own forces at Bomba
Verb St (S).2	DFS 230 WNr 227596 destroyed by own forces at Bomba
Verb St (S).2	He 126 WNr 3480 towing aircraft destroyed by own forces at Derna
Italian Casualties	
82ª Sq, 13°Gr, 2°St CT	MC.200 MM 5096 damaged on landing accident at Benghazi K3, Cap Guglielmo Arrabito safe
387ª Sq, 158°Gr, 50°St Ass	CR.42 MM 8938 destroyed at Martuba
190ª Sq, 86°Gr, 35°St BT	Cant.Z.1007 MM 23411 ditched 40km W Benghazi, Ten Guido Generali's crew rescued unscathed
281ª Sq, 132°Gr AS	S.79 shot down by AA at Bougie, pilot S.Ten Ramiro Angelucci, copilot M.llo Aberto Fedi and four MiA

Thursday, 12 November 1942

On this date there were more movements of WDAF units, 33 Squadron from LG.101 to LG.20, and 145 Squadron to LG.155. At 0945 12 Kittyhawks of 450 Squadron covered 3 RAAF Squadron during a strafing attack on the road between Gazala and Tobruk where four Bf 109s were met, Flt Lt Schaaf claiming one of these probably shot down.

Further big changes took place for the Luftwaffe fighters as well, Stab, I. and III./JG 27 being ordered to leave Africa. The Kommodore, Eduard Neumann, flew out in the unit's 'hack' Do 17 at once; I.Gruppe was directed to return to Germany with III.Gruppe going to Crete and Greece, leaving during the next few days in Ju 52/3ms and S.82s. All the remaining Bf 109s were handed to II.Gruppe and to JG 77. A few pilots from the departing units stayed on in II.Gruppe for a few more weeks as this unit now moved to Berka, accompanied by Stab, I. and III. until they were ready to go. During their 18 months in the desert, I./JG 27 had claimed 588 victories. III.Gruppe, in their shorter spell in the area had claimed 160, and the Geschwaderstab had claimed just one.

On this same date Grp Capt Guy Carter, DSO, AFC, commander of the Allied fighters in North Africa, touched down in Libya in his personal Hurricane, as the first WDAF pilot to do so since the last retreat when he had been the last to leave. Amongst the Italian units, 12 CR.42s of 159° Gruppo Assalto moved to Arae Philaenorum. During the transfer flight, Serg Magg Dario Baltolu of 391ª Sq crashed for no apparent reason.

This CR.42 of 388ª Squadriglia, 158° Gruppo, 50° Stormo Assalto overturned on landing.

Western Cyrenaica, November-December 1942

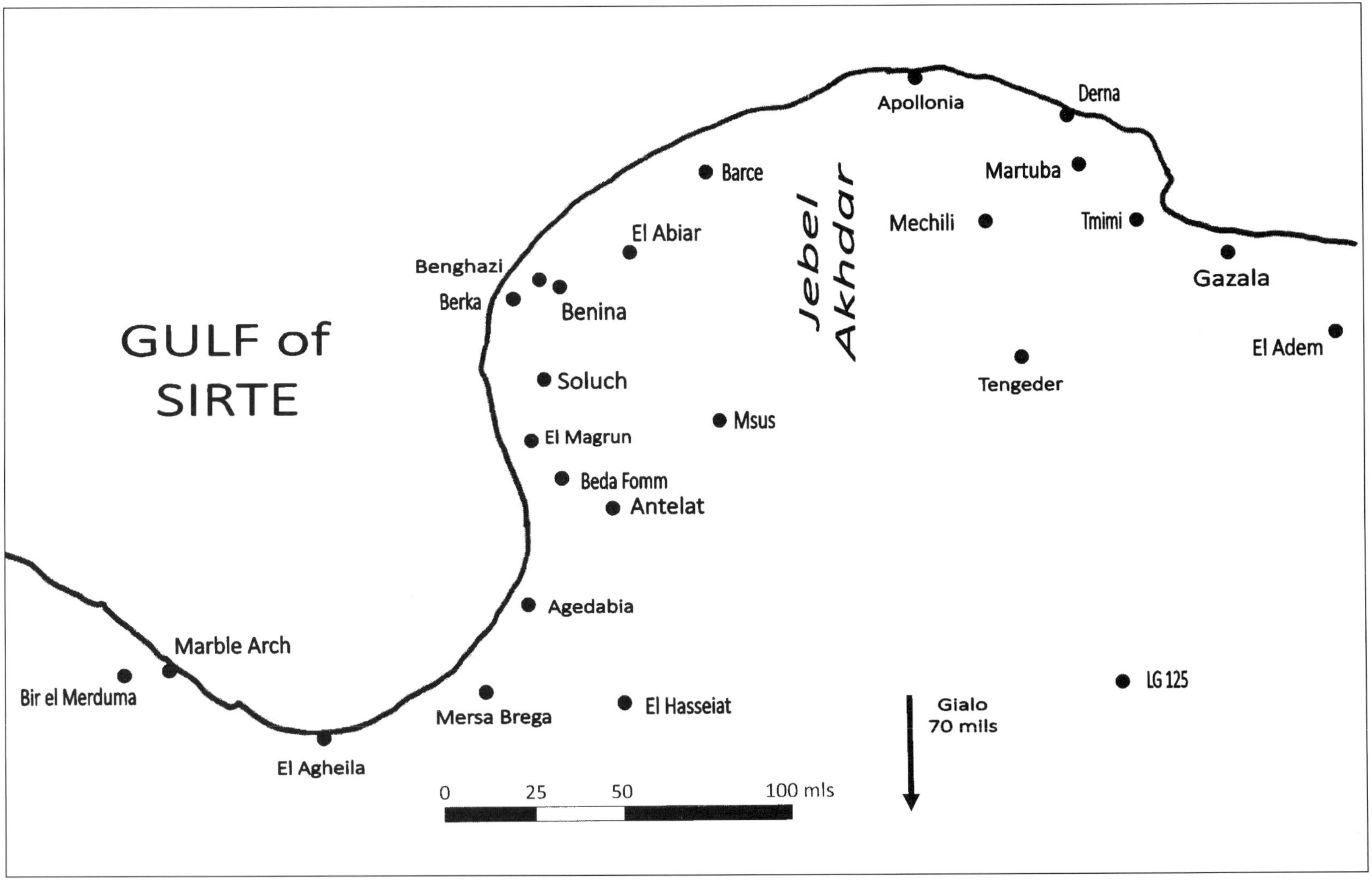

British Claims

450 Sqn	Flt Lt F.R.Schaaf	Kittyhawk III FR212	Bf 109 Probable	0929-1200

British Casualties

260 Sqn	Kittyhawk IIa badly damaged by Flak in Tobruk area; Flt Lt W.R.Cundy safe

Italian Casualties

391ª Sq, 159°Gr, 50°St Ass	CR.42 MM 8853 crashed near Marsa Brega, Serg Magg Dario Baltolu KiA
388ª Sq, 158°Gr, 50°St Ass	CR.42 MM 5656 lost, M.llo Vincenzo Delli Colli KiA
388ª Sq, 158°Gr, 50°St Ass	CR.42 MM 8940 damaged on Nov 8th at Arae Philaenorum, set on fire by own troops
390ª Sq, 159°Gr, 50°St Ass	CR.42s MM 5600 and 8857, already damaged, set on fire by own troops at Martuba

Friday, 13 November 1942

As 8th Army reached Tobruk and WDAF fighters commenced moving to Sidi Aziez, plans had rapidly been developed to establish a secret base deep in Axis territory from which the retreating columns heading westwards might be attacked. For this purpose 243 Wing under the command of Wg Cdr J.Darwen, DFC, was ready to move by this date. The wing consisted of 18 Hurricanes of 238 Squadron commanded by Sqn Ldr R.Marples and 18 of 213 Squadron commanded by Sqn Ldr P.Olver; essential ground personnel from wing and squadrons amounted to about 105. These and vital equipment had been flown to LG.105 on the previous day in 12 Hudsons, stores and rations being dumped here. During the morning the Hurricanes were flown in, all arriving safely apart from two of 238 Squadron which force-landed en route. On arrival all pilots assisted in refuelling their aircraft, allowing the first operation to be commenced at 1345. Wg Cdr Darwen led 12 aircraft of 238 and 15 of 213 on a combined strafe of the coast road from Agedabia to Agheila.

On 13 November the Hurricanes of 243 Wing moved to LG.125, an airstrip deep in the desert and well behind Axis lines, from where attacks could be made on the retreating columns of transport on the coast road. Here a Hurricane IIc of 213 Squadron, fitted with long-range tanks, and a Lockheed Hudson VI transport arrive at this destination.

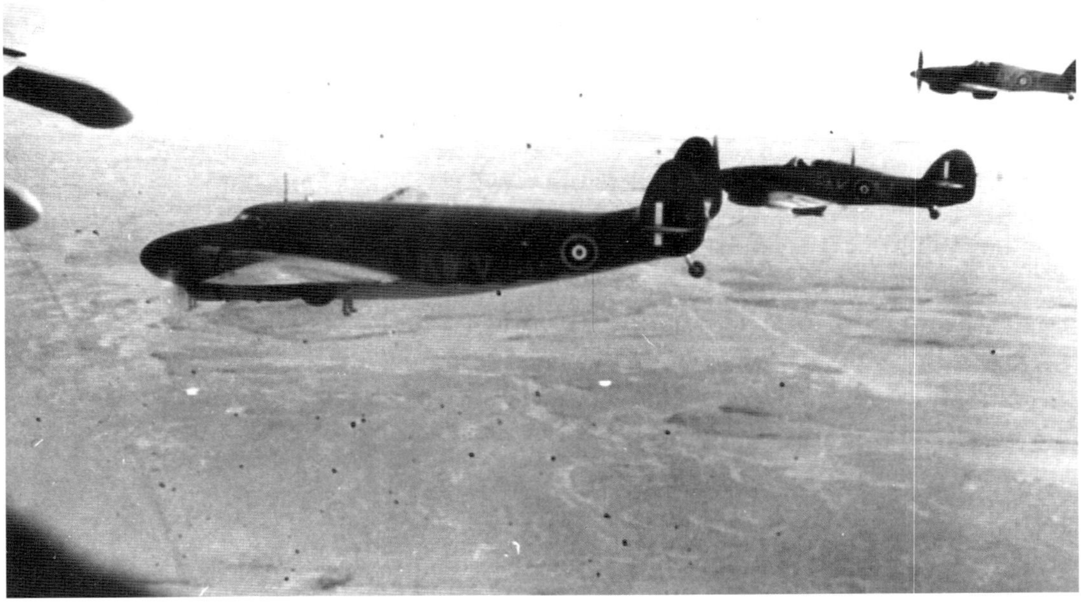

Hurricanes of 213 Squadron escort a Lockheed Lodestar transport, believed to be serving with 117 Squadron, flying supplies into LG.125.

Operating in independent sections of four, the wing hit the road at equidistant points covering it thoroughly. Darwen led his section west of Agheila, Olver's formation covered the road from there to Agedabia and Marples' aircraft dealt with the section north of Agedabia to Magrun. The essential element of surprise was wholly achieved, and it was believed that very effective results were obtained. There was considerable movement of both German and Italian troops and on return 213 Squadron claimed ten vehicles completely destroyed and 44 considered to be knocked out. 238 Squadron claimed 13 destroyed and 26 in the second category. When flying south of Agheila 213 Squadron's Plt Off McKay spotted an Fi 156 Storch flying south at 60 feet. Turning after this, he gave it a one-second burst from 20 yards range. Strikes were seen along the cockpit and it plunged straight down and burst into flames on the ground. Two pilots failed to return; Plt Off Waite's Hurricane was seen to hit the ground and burst into flames while Plt Off Campbell's aircraft was also seen to hit the ground. The low flying necessary for the success of the operation also resulted in the starboard mainplane of Sqn Ldr Olver's aircraft striking a telegraph pole, sustaining damage which needed considerable skill to return to base as the machine was inclined to stall even at 180mph and had to be landed at 160.

Further east, 12 Kittyhawks of 2 SAAF Squadron strafed the Gazala-Tmimi coast road, but while so involved Maj Colenbrander's aircraft was hit by Flak and crashed into the sea in the Gulf of Bomba. Within 233 Wing 5 SAAF Squadron moved to Gambut Main, 73 Squadron going to Gambut West to provide night defence. In the face of the Allied advance Stab, I. and III./JG 77 moved to Berka, and II./JG 27 arrived at Magrun; it would move on to Berka next day. Over Gazala MC.202 pilots of 9° Gruppo claimed three Allied fighters shot down, identifying these as P-46s.

British Claims

213 Sqn	Plt Off G.R.S.McKay	Hurricane IIc HL613	Fi 156	S Agheila	1345-1545

British Casualties

213 Sqn	Hurricane IIc HL725 FTR from ground attack nr El Agheila; Plt Off D.J.Campbell PoW
213 Sqn	Hurricane IIc HL309 FTR from ground attack nr El Agheila; Plt Off G.A.Waite PoW
2 SAAF Sqn	Kittyhawk I EV360 shot down by Flak off Bomba 1500; Maj A.M.Colenbrander KiA

German Casualties

III./KG 4	3 He 111H-6s WNr 7409, 7628, 7895 destroyed by own forces at Derna

Italian Claims

96ª Sq, 9°Gr, 4°St CT	Ten Emanuele Annoni	MC.202	P-46	Ain El Gazala

97ª Sq, 9°Gr, 4°St CT	Ten Jacopo Frigerio	MC.202	P-46	Ain el Gazala
97ª Sq, 9°Gr, 4°St CT	Ten Giovanni Barcaro	MC.202	P-46	Ain el Gazala
Italian Casualties				
92ª Sq, 8°Gr, 2°St CT	MC.200 MM 6676 unserviceable, set on fire at Derna			

Saturday, 14 November 1942

The first operation by 243 Wing was an attack on the landing grounds at Agedabia by 12 aircraft of 213 Squadron. As the formation was approaching the target from the east, an S.79 was seen orbiting above the easternmost airfield at 400 feet. Flt Lt Neil Cameron gave it an eight-second burst and the central engine caught fire, the aircraft appearing to crash into the ground. This was from 174ª Squadriglia on a flight from Benghazi to Misurata which was attacked by a fighter identified as a Beaufighter. The S.79 managed nonetheless to reach its destination with the central engine damaged.

Not many aircraft were to be observed parked at this first landing ground, but six CR.42s were seen on the tarmac and a further three situated line-abreast, one of which was beginning to taxi. Sqn Ldr Olver sprayed this trio, claiming a direct hit on one which blew up so violently that his own aircraft was engulfed in flames that shot-up from it; the other two Fiats, already damaged by Olver's fire, were destroyed in the blast. Olver flew on over the town, strafing troops on the main square, then reaching the landing ground on the west of the road where he claimed to have damaged a Ju 87. Meanwhile, another CR.42 was claimed destroyed by Plt Offs Furneaux and Smith. Subsequently the road was strafed for ten miles south, 32 vehicles being shot-up. On returning to base, due to cloud darkening the sand, 213 Squadron was unable to identify the dark belt which had been given as an aid to navigation, and consequently proceeded too far to the north. Six pilots eventually landed 50 miles north-north-west of LG.125, whilst the other six flew back to Gambut, five of these arriving back at LG.125 just before dark, one ending up at LG.101.

When it became obvious that 213 Squadron's aircraft had not returned, search patrols were sent out. Two were flown by 238 Squadron pilots and one by Wg Cdr Darwen and Flg Off Bert Houle. The missing pilots were located by one of the 238 Squadron flights but almost simultaneously four of the pilots returned from Gambut together with one of those who had landed out in the desert, whose gravity tank had been filled from the long-range tanks of the others. After finding a South African armoured car column which was moving up to occupy Martuba airfield, these had given him his correct position, enabling him to return safely.

Meanwhile, between 1040-1245, 12 of 238 Squadron's pilots had strafed the road north of Agedabia, claiming 21 vehicles destroyed with five more shot-up. The road was found still to be fairly busy, the majority of the transport being of Italian origin, but filled with German troops. Some trucks were towing 88mm guns and there was some small-arms fire. Significantly, however, two Bf 109s were seen at 3,000 feet, apparently undertaking a standing patrol. These 'shadowed' the squadron for about 15 miles south-west, but the attacks they made seemed to be half-hearted and they turned away when the Hurricanes targeted them. The possibility of further such patrols and attacks indicated that the primary effect of surprise had now passed. No opposition was encountered, however, when 238 Squadron returned for a second attack between 1420-1635, nine MT being claimed totally destroyed and six damaged on the road east of Agedabia.

Earlier in the day No.2 Armoured Car Company, RAF Regiment, under Sqn Ldr Cassona, arrived to defend against any land attack on their base. A screen of observers was then set up 35 miles from LG.125. This, during the next few days, reported one four-engined aircraft approaching, and later nine bombers, but although Hurricanes were scrambled to intercept, nothing materialised. The Wing ALO also arrived well in advance of the ground party. The arrival in time of the latter had been adversely affected by the urgency with which the entire operation had been instituted, as some 330 miles of very rough going had to be covered. Luftwaffe fighters were on the move again during the day. Leaving two Schwarme of I./JG 77 at Magrun, the remainder all flew to Arco Philaenorum. Amongst WDAF units, 601 Squadron moved to Gambut West. By the end of the day the Benghazi K1 airfield was completely evacuated by Regia Aeronautica.

British Claims					
213 Sqn	Flt Lt N.Cameron	Hurricane IIc HV548	S.79	15m E Agedabia	0930-
213 Sqn	Sqn Ldr P.Olver	Hurricane IIc	3 CR.42s on ground	Agedabia	
213 Sqn	Sqn Ldr P.Olver	Hurricane IIc	Ju 87 Damaged on ground	Agedabia	

British Claims

213 Sqn	Plt Off R.H.Furneaux	Hurricane IIc	CR.42 on ground	Agedabia
213 Sqn	Plt Off C.D.A.Smith	Hurricane IIc		

British Casualties

203 Sqn	Maryland AH280 FTR

German Claims

I./JG 77	Lt Ferdinand Jahn	Hurricane	1110
II./ZG 1	unstated	2 P.40s	

German Casualties

2./JG 77	Bf 109G-2 trop WNr 14248 crash-landed Berka and blown up

Italian Casualties

82ª Sq, 13°Gr, 2°St CT	MC.200 MM 5096 unserviceable, set on fire
174ª Sq, 133°Gr AS	S.79 MM 24344 damaged on landing at Misurata, w/o, S.Ten Ottone Sponza and crew safe
174ª Sq, 133°Gr AS	S.79 MM 24491 damaged on landing at Misurata, S.Ten Mario Baroni and crew safe
174ª Sq, 133°Gr AS	S.79 MM 21812 damaged in combat, Ten Antonio Nicoletti and crew safe

Sunday, 15 November 1942

At 0625 12 Hurricanes of 238 Squadron strafed El Agheila landing ground where Flt Lt Ayerst claimed a Ju 52/3m destroyed on the ground. Sgt Morris claimed a second and a Bf 109 was claimed damaged. The road was then strafed, 24 vehicles being claimed destroyed and 14 damaged. Sgt Cordwell's aircraft was seen to crash-land, apparently due to coolant trouble; he had climbed out of his cockpit and waved before the formation lost sight of him. As he was ten miles south of the road it was hoped that he might be able to evade capture and return.

At 0910 two aircraft of 213 Squadron flew to the remainder of the unit who had spent the night in the desert. Here the gravity tanks were filled from the long-range tanks of the relief aircraft, allowing all to return to base to continue operations. Previously, at 0900, Wg Cdr Darwen had led 213 Squadron's other six aircraft which were at LG.125, to strafe Gialo airfield. En route Darwen spotted a transport column apparently comprised of five vehicles towing four field guns, all of which were attacked and immobilized, two being totally destroyed. However, this expended the entire Hurricanes' ammunition, which necessitated a return to base, to their considerable regret, since a further four armoured cars had just been spotted. Darwen was keen to send out the RAF armoured cars to mop up and take prisoners, but as the distance was about 60 miles and the ground here was rough, this was not considered possible; nevertheless Darwen remained confident that the balance of the column could be destroyed from the air. He therefore organized a shuttle service which resulted in the destruction of the entire column, this later being confirmed when 14 vehicles, one armoured car and four guns were seen derelict and destroyed by fire.

Meanwhile Sqn Ldr Marples had led four of 238 Squadron's aircraft off at 1030 to resume the strafe, the column by then having dispersed into two different groups, both of which were stationary. Four more of the unit's aircraft went out at 1100, pressing home the attack to complete the annihilation of the column. At the same time individual aircraft of 213 Squadron had returned to base from where at 1135 six, led by Flg Off Houle, strafed Gialo. Approaching from the south, the leader selected a clearing where four Cant Z.1007bis were dispersed, one of which he claimed to have destroyed and one badly damaged; a Ju 88 was claimed by Sqn Ldr Young, who reported that personnel were working on this aircraft when he attacked, and that it blew up violently. He also claimed the destruction of two more aircraft which he believed to have been CR.42s. One S.79 was claimed by Plt Off Carrick and a second by two pilots jointly. A column entering Gialo from the east was also strafed with claims for two MT destroyed and three damaged.

Just prior to dusk the ground party reached LG.125 just as the warning mentioned above of nine bombers approaching from the west was given by the observer screen. Vehicles were rapidly dispersed and four Hurricanes of 213 Squadron were scrambled – but nothing appeared. It was, however, felt to be an augury that the lack of opposition had, perhaps, run its course. Particularly amongst the ground party there was much regret that they were not to become involved, the decision being taken to terminate operations next day. In the meantime six Kittyhawks of 112 Squadron flew a 'rhubarb' west of Cirene where a lone He 111 was seen. Sqn Ldr Drake climbed to 14,000 feet and attacked, the aircraft bursting into flames and crashing to the ground.

450 Squadron now moved to Gazala and Martuba, while 1 SAAF Squadron carried out some interesting tests between a captured Bf 109F and a tropicalized Spitfire V. It was found that at low level the 109 climbed better, but the Spitfire had better manoeuvrability and downward vision. Three victories were claimed by the Luftwaffe during the day, all against B-24s. The 11 fighters involved included one flown by Fw Gustav Sturm of 2./JG 27, who had not yet departed. However, his claim was treated as a probable, which failed to add to I.Gruppe's African total. However, the guns of six of the Messerschmitts jammed and only two confirmed claims could be made by the other pilots who were members of III./JG 77. One Messerschmitt was shot down by the bombers' gunners, Fhj Uffz Renzow baling out after making one of the claims. The Regia Aeronautica's 8° Gruppo moved to Ghindel (En Nofilia) airfield during the day.

British Claims					
112 Sqn	Sqn Ldr B.Drake	Kittyhawk III FR293	He 111	W Cirene	1430-1610
British Casualties					
238 Sqn	Hurricane II HL911 'P' crash-landed when attacking El Agheila airfield at c0830; Sgt W.E.G.Cordwell PoW?				
US Claims					
345th BS/98th BG gunners aboard		B-24D	Bf 109 + one Damaged		
415th BS/98th BG waist gunner		B-24D '810 C'	Bf 109 Probable		1635
343th BS/98th BG gunners aboard		B-24D '921 W'	Bf 109 Damaged	50m S Benghazi	1628
US Casualties					
512th BS/376th BG	B-24D 41-11592 '37 T' 'Draggin' Lady', damaged by fighters, crashed; 1/Lt J.R.Wilcox and crew rescued by British				
German Claims					
2./JG 27	Fw Gustav Sturm	B-24 HSS	S El Agheila		
9./JG 77	Fhj Uffz Hans-Werner Renzow	B-24	60km N Benghazi		
III./JG 77	Lt Horst Martzke	B-24	60km N Benghazi	1536	
German Casualties					
2./JG 77	Bf 109G-2 trop WNr 10541 combat, crash-landed; pilot safe				
9./KG 4	He 111H-6 WNr 4993 5J+CD shot down by P-40, 40km NE Barce; Fw Sigfried Elsner and two MiA, one WiA				
7./ZG 26	Bf 110F-3 WNr 5001 hit by AA at Tobruk, Ogfr Heinz Krüger/Gfr Anton Schut KiA				
III./ZG 26	2 Bf 110F-2s WNrs 5017 and 5049 destroyed by own forces				
I./SchG 2	Bf 109F-4 WNr 8542 destroyed by own forces at Martuba				
II./SchG 2	6 Bf 109E-7s WNrs 6203, 6227, 2080, 2640, 0958, 1976 destroyed by own forces at Martuba				
Italian Casualties					
93ª Sq, 8°Gr, 2°St CT	MC.200 MM 8146 userviceable, set on fire				

Monday, 16 November 1942

For 243 Wing's final effort before withdrawal, ten Hurricanes of 213 Squadron took off at 0830, again attacking Gialo airfield. Nothing was to be seen, however, except the wreck of the Ju 88 destroyed the previous day and a single armoured car, which Wg Cdr Darwen destroyed; some machine-gun and Breda fire was encountered. Thirty miles north-west of Gialo a large stationary column of about 500 vehicles was spotted and attacked. Some of the vehicles had red strips laid across their bonnets as if to create the impression that they were carrying casualties, and these were not attacked. However 16 other MT were claimed destroyed and 11 damaged.

At the same time 11 of 238 Squadron's aircraft had attacked the coast road near Agheila where movement was considerably heavier and both Flak and small-arms fire was encountered. This finale to the operation proved to be one of the most successful; twenty-eight MT were claimed destroyed and 14 damaged. A Ju 88, believed to be a night fighter version, and three Bf 109s were seen at 5,000 feet, these making no attempt to attack. It was thought that these aircraft had been placed there with the specific duty of tracking the Hurricanes back to their base. As the British aircraft departed, 15 fires were seen blazing. At 1230 the two squadrons were airborne to escort eight Hudsons which had arrived to transport personnel and equipment which were not proceeding with the ground party, back to El Adem which was safely reached at 1420. The termination of this imaginative and successful operation marked the virtual end of the use of the Hurricane as a day fighter in Libya.

Heavy thunderstorms limited activity elsewhere, but at 1620 Lt Schröer of III./JG 27 claimed a Kittyhawk shot down south of Tecis, his 61st and last claim for a victory in North Africa, making him the second highest-claiming pilot of the campaign there. His victim may have been Lt Joe Bell of the

57th Fighter Group who was lost on this date and became a PoW. From 112 Squadron Flt Lt Geoff Garton was posted to 239 Wing headquarters on promotion, becoming squadron leader flying. Having set out on a mission, 450 Squadron's Kittyhawks were forced to turn back due to the adverse weather. On this day 3° Stormo was ordered to move to Tauorga.

British Claims					
94 Sqn	Sgt G.Grove	Hurricane IIc BP392	Ju 88	Damietta	1118-1205
94 Sqn	Sgt W.D.Imrie	Hurricane IIc BP387 'J'			
British Casualties					
4 SAAF Sqn	Kittyhawk I slt damage by Flak; Lt D.H.Quillian safe				
5 SAAF Sqn	Tomahawk IIb AM410 2/Lt A.J.Lawrence on first op lost in bad weather; last seen in cloud NE				
German Claims					
8./JG 27	Oblt Werner Schroer	P-40		S Tecis	1520
German Casualties					
II./JG 27	Bf 109F-4 trop WNr 10254 destroyed after force-landing at Sidi Magrun				
Verb Kdo (S).2	He 111H-6 WNr 7835 destroyed in strafing attack at Sidi Magrun				
III./ZG 26	2 Bf 110F-3s WNrs 5042 and 5108; Bf 110F-2 WNr 5070 destroyed by own forces				

Tuesday, 17 November 1942

By this date the WDAF fighters were established in the Gazala area. Here the 66th Squadron was ordered to leave 239 Wing and re-join the 57th Fighter Group at Martuba, where it was joined by 112 Squadron to bring the group to a similar four-squadron strength as 233 and 239 Wings. The combined unit thus formed was to undertake its first operation as a cohesive entity three days later.

During the day considerable Axis effort was put to seeking to evacuate all possible personnel and supplies by air from Benghazi, employing all available transport aircraft. The first successful attempt to interfere with this traffic was made by 250 Squadron which sent a dozen Kittyhawks to patrol over the port at 1135. Approaching Benina airfield, He 111 bombers and Ju 52/3ms were seen in the circuit or in the process of landing, with other aircraft parked on the ground. Six of the Heinkels and one Junkers were claimed shot down, the latter by Flt Lt Plinston, who reported that the trimotor he attacked crashed onto a hangar which went up in flames. The squadron then went down to strafe, two more He 111s and two S.81s being claimed destroyed and a Ju 52/3m damaged.

The He 111s were aircraft of III./KG 4, pressed into service as transports. 13 of them were arriving at Benina from Lecce, one crashing on landing and one being damaged. One Kette was attacked by a reported 20 fighters and two were shot down, a third being badly damaged; one of the former fell in flames. One more Heinkel was destroyed on the ground by the strafing and another eight were damaged. Another He 111, this one from 6./KG 26, was also lost flying between Sicily and Benghazi, and may have been a part of the formation. In one of the He 111s on the ground, Gefr Wegner claimed to have shot down a 'Spitfire' using the machine gun in the aircraft's dorsal defensive position. The Italian aircraft claimed by Flt Lt Hancock were in fact S.82s, five of which were destroyed on the ground here during the day. Kittyhawks of 450 Squadron attacked Barce where more aircraft were found on the ground, a Ju 52/3m, an He 111 and a Bf 110 all being claimed destroyed here.

An hour after the Benina attack, nine Kittyhawks of 3 RAAF Squadron and 12 of 112 Squadron arrived over the area, the former unit patrolling the Magrun-Benghazi road with the latter set to strafe. Three Bf 109s of II./JG 27 attacked, Sgt Pollock of 112 Squadron force-landing as Plt Off Upward of 3 RAAF Squadron and Fw Büter of 5./JG 27 collided, both aircraft going down. However, the two Kittyhawk formation leaders, Sqn Ldr Bobby Gibbes and Flt Lt R.R.Smith, claimed a Messerschmitt shot down between them, two more of II.Gruppe's aircraft being brought down in the area 'blown up'. Gibbes:

> "Went out under cloud to west of Msus, then climbed to 6,000 feet and proceeded to Magrun. Just before reaching drome, saw three 109s climbing up east on about our level. Went round after them but they climbed away. Then spotted a 109 climbing up with one wheel down. Went after it. My first burst went behind it, but my second hit it OK. Knocked a bit off it. It dived away pouring black smoke. Ritchie dived after it and followed until it went in. 112 were, as it turned out, the first to shoot at it and knocked one wheel down. They confirmed that the attacks Plt Off Ritchie carried

out were not necessary as it was going in anyway, after my attack. Looks as if I share it with 112. (Later, I decided to share the half with Ritchie, giving us ¼ each.)"

Three hours later 450 Squadron strafed in the Barce area again, but Sgt Marrow failed to return, crash-landing unhurt. 73 Squadron moved to El Adem.

Following the victory at El Alamein which had greatly reduced the number of tanks available to the PanzerArmee Afrika, a detachment of Henschel Hs 129B anti-tank aircraft were hastily prepared for service in the desert. So far these aircraft had operated only on the Eastern Front, but the overwhelming numerical superiority of the 8th Army's armour required urgent action. On 2 November, therefore, 4.(Panzer) Staffel of Schlachtgeschwader 2, commanded by Hptm Bruno Meyer, was despatched from Poland to Greece, and then on to Crete. The initial five Henschels, escorted by two Bf 110s, flew from Crete to Tobruk on 7 November, but here their unfamiliar outlines led them to face a barrage of Axis Flak as they approached. Next day came the news of the Anglo-American landings in French North-West Africa.

4.(Pz)/SchG 2 was established at El Adem, where it received an early visit from Erwin Rommel. The first days were fraught with problems. The French-built Gnôme-Rhône engines suffered badly from desert conditions; moreover the specialist tungsten-cored shells for the aircraft's MK101 cannon, promised to be available on arrival, were not in fact delivered for several days. Meyer refused to allow his pilots to attack Allied tanks until such armament had arrived. Bruno Meyer later recalled:

"We carried out our first operation under quite normal and favourable conditions on 17 November 1942. I led a formation of three Hs 129s in a freelance sweep near Bir el Abiod, destroying two British armoured cars which were escorting about 400 German and Italian prisoners-of-war on their march into captivity. The ex-prisoners managed to get back to our lines after a two-day march through the desert.

"On the return flight we encountered for the first time British Crusader tanks at a road junction. We were making our way home at very low level – actually, we were flying below the level of the surrounding features – when, ahead and above us, we surprised the southernmost spearhead of the British tank force. They were refuelling, and some 30 tanks had moved up close to each other in a rather disorderly fashion, so that the refuelling operation could be sped up by trailing hoses over the tanks in all directions. A tanker column was about 600 feet behind the tanks.

"The officers were laying on the first tank studying maps, while the other members of the crews were standing upon the tanks and as we topped over them at very low level, they actually waved us a greeting. Obviously they had mistakenly identified our aircraft as British Beaufighters, and we roared over them as low as ten feet, just rocking our wings rather than attacking them straight away! Our joy to get Western enemies before our guns after so many months of fighting on the Eastern Front was so great that we gave vent to our feelings and could not refrain from demonstrating to the British exactly how a text book attack should be carried out.

"Looking back on it now it all seems so farcical; there we were practically performing aerobatics while the British stood and waved at us. But as we banked away and pulled into a climb, the British crews must have finally seen the black and white crosses of our national markings for they suddenly disappeared into their tanks, the turrets began to rotate and the barrels reared up and opened fire. We received a really hot reception, but we attacked the tanks with our cannon, scoring hits on five of them and setting some of the tanker column alight.

"On another occasion, we found that busting armoured cars, which usually operated in the desert in the role of fast reconnaissance vehicles, was a very simple matter. We came in from the side in a shallow dive attack at right angles to the vehicle's longitudinal axis, firing into the sand so that the shells ricocheted, hitting and penetrating the thinly-armoured underside. Since these armoured cars were usually filled with fuel for their long-distance desert raids, they invariably came to a dead stop as a blazing wreck after the first strafing pass and it sometimes happened that they exploded as we passed over them and we found ourselves flying through a cloud of the vehicle's metal debris. Naturally, this attack technique did not require the use of the precious tungsten-carbide ammunition, for we found that the aircraft's 15mm cannon did the job perfectly.

"While making our freelance sweeps, we almost always had contact with enemy fighters. Fortunately, success was denied them. This was mainly due to our excellent camouflage scheme.

Completely ignorant of the light conditions prevailing in the North African area, during our stay in Poland we had painted our aircraft in a yellow and brown scheme which we lightly oversprayed with violet. The result was that we could operate unscathed at low level without needing fighter escort. The effectiveness of the camouflage was such that quite often when flying in a loose formation I lost contact with my wingman after a slight change of course, and contact could not be restored until we had recourse to our R/T."

Thereafter adverse weather conditions rendered the aircraft unserviceable, and these operations described by Hptm Meyer which lasted for less than a week proved to be the only effective flights which were to be made by the unit in Africa. The troubles which beset the aircraft are exhaustively detailed in Martin Pegg's excellent *Hs 129 Panzerjäger* (Classic Publications, 1996). In brief, no more sorties were flown, while eventually only one damaged aircraft managed to reach Tunis. Three aircraft were destroyed during a bombing raid on Castel Benito on 13 January 1943, the rest being captured in unserviceable condition on this and other airfields.

British Claims

250 Sqn	Flt Lt N.P.W.Hancock	Kittyhawk III FR285 'Y'	He 111	Benina	1135-1335
250 Sqn	Flt Lt N.P.W.Hancock	Kittyhawk III FR285 'Y'	He 111 on ground	Benina	1135-1335
250 Sqn	Flt Lt N.P.W.Hancock	Kittyhawk III FR285 'Y'	2 S.81s on ground	Benina	1135-1335
250 Sqn	Flt Sgt N.C.Holmes	Kittyhawk III FL899 'B'	He 111	Benina	1135-1335
250 Sqn	Sgt A.F.Nitz	P-40K 42-45795 'G'	He 111	Benina	1135-1335
250 Sqn	Sgt A.A.W.Orr	Kittyhawk III FR331 'F' }	He 111	Benina	1135-1335
250 Sqn	Plt Off G.W.Troke	Kittyhawk III FR275 'E' }			
250 Sqn	Flt Lt G.H.F.Plinston	Kittyhawk III FR884 'A'	Ju 52/3m	Benina	1135-1335
250 Sqn	Plt Off H.Stewart	Kittyhawk III FR333 'Z'	He 111	Benina	1135-1335
250 Sqn	Flt Lt R.Taylor	Kittyhawk III FR244 'X'	He 111	Benina	1135-1335
250 Sqn	Flt Lt R.Taylor	Kittyhawk III FR244 'X'	He 111 on ground	Benina	1135-1335
250 Sqn	Plt Off K.N.Kopperud	Kittyhawk III FL899	Ju 52/3m Damaged	on ground Benina	1135-1335
112 Sqn	Flt Lt R.R.Smith	Kittyhawk III FR217 }	Bf 109F/G	Magrun-Benghazi road	1405
3 RAAF Sqn	Sqn Ldr R.H.Gibbes	Kittyhawk IIa FL323 'V' }			
3 RAAF Sqn	Flg Off J.W.Upward	Kittyhawk IIa FL306	Bf 109F/G (collision)	Magrun-Benghazi road	1405
450 Sqn	Flt Lt F.R. Schaaf	Kittyhawk III FR242	He 111 on ground	Barce	1506-1725
450 Sqn	Sgt A.W.J.Taylor	Kittyhawk III FR346	Ju 52/3m on ground	Barce	1506-1725
450 Sqn	Squadron	Kittyhawk IIIs	Bf 110 on ground	Barce	1506-1725
2 SAAF Sqn	Lt P.D.Bryant	Kittyhawk I 'K'	Ju 88 on ground	Magrun	

British Casualties

3 RAAF Sqn	Kittyhawk IIa FL306 collided with Bf 109 over Magrun; Flg Off J.W.Upward KiA
450 Sqn	Kittyhawk III FR330 FTR from attack on Barce l.g; Sgt Marrow safe
112 Sqn	Kittyhawk III FR245 'B' force-landed 40m W Msus; Sgt W.E.Pollock safe
250 Sqn	Kittyhawk III FL884 'A' left 1145, landed at base damaged Cat I at 1345; Flg Lt G.H.F.Plinston safe
250 Sqn	P-40K 42-45795 'G' left 1145, landed at base damaged Cat I at 1345; Sgt A.F.Nitz safe
250 Sqn	Kittyhawk III FR333 'Z' left 1145, landed at base damaged Cat I at 1345; Plt Off H.Stewart safe
250 Sqn	Kittyhawk III FR296 left 1145, landed at base damaged Cat I at 1345; Plt Off J.W.A.Stone safe

German Claims

5./JG 27	Fw Gerhard Büter	P-40	ESE Sidi Ahmed el Magrun	1315

German Casualties

5./JG 27	Bf 109G-2 trop WNr 10570 combat with P-40, collision in the air, crashed SE Magrun; Fw Gerhard Büter KiA
6./KG 26	He 111H-6 WNr 4569 1H+AP missing from Sicily-Benghazi; Obgefr Franz Fritz and one KiA, two WiA
9./KG 4	He 111H-6 WNr 7894 5J+AT shot down by P-40 near Benina, two safe and two WiA
9./KG 4	He 111H-6 WNr 7608 5J+FT shot down by P-40 near Benina; Uffz Theodor Simon and two WiA, two KiA
9./KG 4	He 111H-6 WNr 7885 5J+KR shot down by P-40 near Benina, two safe and two WiA
I./KG zbV 1	Ju 52/3m WNr 6549 shot down by P-40 near Barce, two safe and two WiA
I./KG zbV 1	Ju 52/3m WNr 7612 shot down by P-40 near Barce, crew safe
6./JG 27	Bf 109G-2 trop destroyed by own forces at Sidi Magrun
4./JG 27	Bf 109F-4 WNr 7633 destroyed by own forces at Sidi Magrun

I./SchG 2	Bf 109F-4 WNr 7629 destroyed by own forces at Sidi Magrun
Italian Casualties	
44° St T	5 S.82s MM 60604, 60791, 60762, 60745, 60603 destroyed on ground at Benina

Wednesday, 18 November 1942

The slaughter of the transports continued, six attacks being made on Benghazi airfield. Due to lack of fuel the Luftwaffe was able only to intercept two of them. At 0700 Hurricanes of 33 Squadron undertook a long-range strafe of the road south of Benghazi, shooting-up a Ju 88 on the ground and shooting down a Ju 52/3m. While strafing, the Hurricanes were attacked by six Bf 109s of II./JG 27, Sqn Ldr Mannix's aircraft being shot down, apparently by Lt Kientsch who claimed a P-40 at 0820. A dozen more Hurricanes from 213 Squadron then attacked Agedabia town and airfield a little over two hours later, four of these fighters being shot down by Flak. At about the same time six Kittyhawks of 3 RAAF Squadron strafed Magrun airfield where Flg Off Ritchie attacked a Ju 52/3m as it was taking off, the aircraft beginning to burn; it was then attacked by Plt Off Dent and burst into flames. Sqn Ldr Gibbes shot-up a Bf 109 on the ground and two He 111s were also strafed. Kittyhawks of 450 Squadron escorted a convoy from 1011, an He 111 being seen and attacked, but not observed to crash. Plt Off Crouch was attacked by a hostile aircraft and Sgt Gleeson force-landed at Derna.

A Regia Aeronautica S.82 loaded with weapons and ammunition. The national markings have been over-painted in a dark colour to reduce the aircraft's visibility in the air.

At 1115 two Kittyhawks of 4 SAAF Squadron patrolled over the Barce-Benghazi-Magrun area with three 2 SAAF Squadron aircraft and six of 260 Squadron. The South African pilots saw 20 Ju 52/3ms south of Benghazi and attacked, claiming nine shot down between the two squadrons. Lt Reinders, after claiming one, was hit in the face and force-landed at Martuba. Lt de Villiers was shot down, reportedly by a Bf 110, but returned to the unit on the 21st. The crew of a Ju 88 escorting the transports, claimed to have shot down a Spitfire, and allowing for the usual recognition problems, this was probably de Villiers' victor. Having claimed two of the transports, Lt Morton also claimed to have probably shot down a Bf 110. The Luftwaffe reported that two Ju 52/3ms crashed and three force-landed.

In the meantime, 260 Squadron's pilots had spotted six or seven Ju 52/3ms on Berka landing ground and 30-40 on Magrun. As they strafed, two took off; Flt Lt Davis and Sgt Curno hit one which landed again, obviously damaged, and Flt Sgt Barber shot down the other in flames. Two Bf 109s then attacked, Plt Off Mink being shot down at 1327; two P-40s were claimed around this time by pilots of II./JG 27 and III./JG 77. One of these may have been a P-40F of the US 66th Squadron in which 1/Lt Joe Bell failed to return; he was subsequently reported to have become a prisoner. This unit lost a second aircraft during the day, 1/Lt Arlie W.Claxton apparently falling victim to Flak.

Luftwaffe records indicate that one Ju 52/3m of III./KGzbV 1 and one Savoia transport were shot down at Magrun, so it would appear that the latter was the victim of 3 RAAF or 260 Squadron, and not a Ju 52/3m as claimed. From conversations with an Italian pilot present at the time, it seems more likely that the S.82 was shot down by the Australian unit. Regia Aeronautica records show that two such aircraft were lost by 146° Gruppo Trasporti at this airfield on this date. Both are recorded as strafed. But in each case the pilot or copilot was wounded, indicating that at least one of these aircraft was probably in the process of landing or taking off.

Eight 250 Squadron Kittyhawks took off at 1325 for the same area, strafing three He 111s, two Ju 52/3ms and a single Ca.311. At 1515 six more from 3 RAAF Squadron again attacked Flt Lt Boardman strafing a Ju 52/3m which caught fire and a Bf 109, Plt Off Taylor setting a Ju 52/3m and an unidentified aircraft alight, while two more Bf 109s were fired on.

During this day also Hptm Johann-Georg Drescher, Kommandeur of JaboGruppe Afrika, was wounded on Magrun airfield during a strafe by Beaufighters. At the time of these attacks II./JG 27 had 30 Bf 109F-4 and G-6 fighters available (including six brand new aircraft from Germany), and 36 pilots on strength, but had been able to do so little. The reason that they did no more was down entirely to the critical shortage of fuel. Once the Allied attacks had ceased, the German fighters withdrew to Arco Philaenorum (Marble Arch) and to Merduna 1, a strip in the desert 25 miles to the south of this main base. On the Allied side of the lines, 80 Squadron now moved to Bu Amud, and 335 Squadron to LG.121.

British Claims

33 Sqn	Flt Lt J.F.Allan	Hurricane IIc HV316 'D'	1/3 Ju 52/3m	S Benghazi	0650-0935
33 Sqn	Flt Sgt M.A.Perkins	Hurricane IIc HL721 'C'	1/3 Ju 52/3m	S Benghazi	0650-0935
33 Sqn	Plt Off K.C.Rolls	Hurricane IIc HL314 'K'	1/3 Ju 52/3m	S Benghazi	0650-0935
260 Sqn	Flt Sgt W.D.Barber	Kittyhawk IIa	Ju 52/3m	Magrun l.g.	1130-1430
260 Sqn	Flt Lt C.C.H.Davis	Kittyhawk IIa	Ju 52/3m Damaged*	Magrun l.g.	1130-1430
250 Sqn	unspecified pilots	Kittyhawk IIIs	3 He 111s, 2 Ju 52/3ms, Ca.311	on ground	
450 Sqn	Plt Off T.E.N.Crouch	Kittyhawk III FR267	Ju 88 Probable	36m from Derna	1011-1230
4 SAAF Sqn	Lt S.I.Reinders	Kittyhawk I EV342 'O'	Ju 52/3m	20m S Benghazi	1230
2 SAAF Sqn	Lt T.V.de Villiers	Kittyhawk I ET977 'Z'	2 Ju 52/3ms	20m S Benghazi	1245
4 SAAF Sqn	Capt D.W.Golding	Kittyhawk I EV347 'K'	Ju 52/3m	Brina l.g.	1245
4 SAAF Sqn	Capt D.W.Golding	Kittyhawk I EV347 'K' }	Ju 52/3m	20m S Benghazi	1245
2 SAAF Sqn	Lt V.M.L.Lindsay	Kittyhawk I EV162 'I' }			
2 SAAF Sqn	Lt V.M.L.Lindsay	Kittyhawk I EV162 'I'	2 Ju 52/3ms	20m S Benghazi	1245
2 SAAF Sqn	Lt R.D.B.Morton	Kittyhawk I EV349 'K'	2 Ju 52/3ms	20m S Benghazi	1245
2 SAAF Sqn	Lt R.D.B.Morton	Kittyhawk I EV349 'K'	Bf 110 Probable	20m S Benghazi	1245
3 RAAF Sqn	Plt Off D.V.Ritchie	Kittyhawk IIa FL345 }	Ju 52/3m	Magrun	1015-1330
3 RAAF Sqn	Plt Off R.C.Dent	Kittyhawk IIa FL358 }			
3 RAAF Sqn	Sqn Ldr R.H.M.Gibbes	Kittyhawk IIa FL323	Bf 109 on ground	Magrun	1015-1330
3 RAAF Sqn	Flg Off H.J.Bray	Kittyhawk IIa FL348	He111 damaged on ground		1015-1330
3 RAAF Sqn	Flt Lt Boardman	Kittyhawk IIa FL292	Ju 52/3m on ground		1515-
3 RAAF Sqn	Flt Lt Boardman	Kittyhawk IIa FL292	Bf 109 on ground		1515-
3 RAAF Sqn	Plt Off A.B.Taylor	Kittyhawk IIa FL309	Ju 52/3m on ground		1515-
3 RAAF Sqn	Plt Off A.B.Taylor	Kittyhawk IIa FL309	u/i e/a on ground		1515-
112 Sqn	Sqn Ldr B.Drake	Kittyhawk III FR293	Bf 110	Gazala	1539-1610
112 Sqn	Sqn Ldr B.Drake	Kittyhawk III FR293	Bf 110 Damaged	Gazala area	1539-1610

*confirmed on 18 Dec

British Casualties

33 Sqn	Hurricane IIc ..154 shot down S of Benghazi 0820; Sqn Ldr R.L.Mannix MiA

213 Sqn	Hurricane IIc HL991 left 1030, shot down by Flak at Agedabia; Flg Off R.P.Baines
213 Sqn	Hurricane IIc BP239 left 1030, shot down by Flak at Agedabia; Flg Off C.Luxton
213 Sqn	Hurricane IIc HL634 left 1030, shot down by Flak at Agedabia; Flt Sgt H.M.Compton – returned on 24th
213 Sqn	Hurricane IIc HL941 left 1030, shot down by Flak at Agedabia; Flt Sgt J.R.Rebstock
450 Sqn	Kittyhawk III FR212 combat with Ju88 force-landed at Derna; Sgt J.D.Gleeson safe
2 SAAF Sqn	Kittyhawk I ET977 'Z' shot down by Bf 110, crash-landed 2m E Benina; Lt T.V.de Villiers picked up by armoured cars, safe
4 SAAF Sqn	Kittyhawk I EV342 'O' hit and pilot WiA by Ju 88, force-landed Martuba; Lt S.I.Reinders WiA
3 RAAF Sqn	Kittyhawk IIa FL335 crash-landed at base, Flak damage; Sgt A.Righetti safe
260 Sqn	Kittyhawk III shot down by Bf 109; Plt Off L.P.Mink
US Casualties	
66th FS/57th FG	P-40F, 1/Lt Joe D.Bell PoW
66th FS/57th FG	P-40F, hit by Italian Flak, force-landed; 1/Lt Arlie W.Claxton WiA, rescued by British armoured car

German Claims				
5./JG 27	Lt Willi Kientsch	P-40	ENE Sidi Ahmed el Magrun	0920
4./JG 27	Uffz Josef Brandl	P-40	S Sidi Ahmed el Magrun	1227
Stab III./JG 77	Obfw Heinrich Hackler	P-40	10km NE Sidi Ahmed el Magrun	
10./ZG 26	unstated	P-40	S Benghazi	

German Casualties	
III./JG 77	Bf 109G-2 trop WNrs 10641 & 10667 destroyed by ground strafe at Magrun
III./ZG 1	Me 210A-1 WNr 0036 2N+GS shot down by AA NE Apollonia; Oblt Heinz Redlich & Fw Friedrich Hamburger KiA
III./ZG 1	Me 210A-1 WNr 0057 2N+DT 10% damaged by Spitfire NE Apollonia; pilot safe; Uffz Hans Ziesch WiA
IV./KG zbV 1	Ju 52/3m WNr 7115 shot down by P-40 while landing at Sidi Magrum, crashed 2km N of airfield; three safe, one KiA
II./KG zbV 1	Ju 52/3m WNr 3283 1Z+AP shot down by P-40, crashed 20km S Benghazi; Lt Rudolf Fritz and three KiA
II./KG zbV 1	Ju 52/3m WNr 7282 1Z+AN shot down by P-40 crash-landed at Sidi Magrum; Lt Hans Dörrie and one WiA, two safe
II./KG zbV 1	Ju 52/3m WNr 6481 1Z+EN hit in combat during flight Sidi Magrum-Maleme, 10% damaged; three safe one WiA
II./KG zbV 1	Ju 52/3m WNr 2911 1Z+JS hit in combat with P-40 near Sidi Magrum, 10% damaged; two safe, one KiA, one WiA
I./KG zbV 1	Ju 52/3m WNr 7374 shot down by P-40 near Sidi Magrum; Fw Joachim Satow and two WiA, one safe
I./KG zbV 1	Ju 52/3m WNr 6358 hit in combat with P-40 50km N Benghazi, 10% damaged; three safe one WiA
KGr zbV Wittstock	Ju 52/3m WNr 3176 shot up by P-40 crash-landed at Sidi Magrum; three safe, one WiA
KGr zbV 400	Ju 52/3m WNr 3024 shot down by P-40, crashed 20km S Benghazi; three safe, one KiA
KGr zbV 600	Ju 52/3m WNr 4033 shot down by P-40 near Sidi Magrum; three safe, one KiA
KGr zbV 800	Ju 52/3m WNr 5069 8T+LB shot down by P-40, crashed 20km S Benghazi; three safe, one KiA
KGr zbV 800	Ju 52/3m WNr 6976 8T+GL shot down by P-40, crashed 20km S Benghazi; Fw Heinrich Reitmeier and one WiA, two KiA
Stab I./LG 1	Ju 88A-4 WNr 140055 L1+BB damaged on ground at Magrun 50%; radio operator Uffz Günther Reinhard KiA
2./LG 1	Ju 88A-4 WNr 140119 L1+BH damaged on ground at Magrun 50%; radio operator Obfw Erich Wedekind KiA
II./LG 1	Ju 88A-4 WNr 140068 destroyed on ground at Magrun
II./LG 1	Ju 88A-4 WNr 140168 50% damaged on ground at Magrun
1.(F)/121	Ju 88D-1 WNr 430161 destroyed on ground by bombs at Magrun
III./StG 3	Ju 87D-3 WNr 2922 destroyed by explosion of own bomb at Nofilia
Italian Casualties	
609ª Sq, 146°Gr T	S.82 MM 60639 '608-7'strafed at Sidi Magrum, pilot Ten Antonio Gosi and one crew WiA
609ª Sq, 146°Gr T	S.82 MM 60615 '609-6'strafed at Sidi Magrum, copilot Serg Magg Felice Manganelli WiA

Thursday, 19 November 1942

British armour entered Benghazi and at once the fighter units began moving to Martuba from where they could provide air cover for the final great Malta convoy which was to break the siege at last. Eleven Kittyhawks of 250 Squadron took off to strafe Magrun again at 1300, but returned due to bad weather. The top section was ordered to intercept two Ju 88s north of Martuba which turned out to be aircraft of 10./ZG 26, one of which was shot down ten miles out to sea.

At 1520 five aircraft of 112 Squadron were scrambled, Sqn Ldr Drake taking off first, followed by Plt Off Wright. Drake claimed a Bf 110 and a damaged while Wright claimed a probable Me 210. An Me 210 of III./ZG 1 was reportedly attacked by two fighters north-east of Apollonia on the 18th, the gunner being wounded; this actually relates to the 'Ju 88' claim of 450 Squadron. A Bf 110 of 7./ZG 26 was also lost and was probably Drake's victim; 10./ZG 26 lost another Ju 88C.

As part of the general movement of units, 127 Squadron now flew to LG.08, but 92 Squadron bade farewell to the very successful Flg Off John Waddy, DFC, who now returned to Australia as one of the leading Allied fighter pilots of the desert war. On this date Magg Gino Lodi, commander of 18° Gruppo, Cap Giorgio Tugnoli, commander of 74ª Squadriglia and Ten Franco Bordoni-Bisleri of 95ª Squadriglia were seriously injured in a car accident on the Tauorga-Tripoli road. They were sent home to Italy aboard a hospital ship. Cap Giulio Cesare Giuntella assumed command of 18° Gruppo on an acting basis and Ten Carlo Moruzzi that of 74ª Squadriglia. It would be six months before Bordoni was fit to return to duty.

British Claims					
250 Sqn	Plt Off J.E.Collier	Kittyhawk III FR884 'A' }	Ju 88	10m off Martuba	1430
250 Sqn	Plt Off G.W.Troke	Kittyhawk III FR899 'T' }			
112 Sqn	Plt Off J.G.Wright	Kittyhawk III FR264	Me 210 Probable	Gazala area	1530-1640
112 Sqn	Sqn Ldr B.Drake	Kittyhawk III FR293 '?'	Bf 110	Gazala	1539-1610
112 Sqn	Sqn Ldr B.Drake	Kittyhawk III FR293 '?'	Bf 110 Damaged	Gazala area	1539-1610
4 SAAF Sqn	Lt G.H.Kaufmann	Kittyhawk I EV362 'Y'	Bf 109F	Fuka	1630

German Casualties	
10./ZG 26	Ju 88C-6 WNr 360059 3U+LU shot down N Martuba by P-40; Lt Theodor Schuster and two MiA
10./ZG 26	Ju 88C-6 WNr 360249 crashed during an enemy strafing attack at Arco Philaenorum; Fw Hugo Brückner WiA, two KiA
7./ZG 26	Bf 110F-2 WNr 5071 shot down by P-40, crash-landed SW Apollonia; Oblt Hans Kollowrat/Uffz Herbert Gries PoWs
II./KG zbV 1	Ju 52/3m WNr 7292 1Z+AN destroyed by own forces at Sidi Magrum
KGr zbV Wittstock	Ju 52/3m WNr 3010 destroyed by own forces at Sidi Magrum
Italian Casualties	
21ª Sq, 46°Gr, 15° St	CR.42 MM 8952 damaged on landing, S.Ten Angelo Mazzei safe
54ª Sq, 46°Gr, 15° St	CR.42 MM 8977 hit by ground fire, crash-landed, Ten Raffaele Giusto safe
145°Gr T	S.81 MM 20381 crash-landed near Homs, pilot Ten Max Grossi, copilot M.llo Cesare Calligaris and one WiA
3°St CT	Magg Gino Lodi, Cap Giorgio Tugnoli and Ten Bordoni-Bisleri injured in a car crash

Friday, 20 November 1942

During a convoy patrol at 0930 Flt Lt Davis' 260 Squadron Kittyhawk caught fire and he baled out. 33 and 213 Squadrons now moved to El Adem where the former unit was taken over by Sqn Ldr S.C.Norris, DFC, following the loss of Sqn Ldr Mannix. After the previous day's moves, the Luftwaffe had available for fighter duties, fuel permitting:

4.(H)/12	Arco Philaenorum	7 Bf 109Fs
Stab/JG 77	Arco Philaenorum	4 Bf 109Gs
I./JG 77	Arco Philaenorum	18 Bf 109Gs
III./JG 77	Arco Philaenorum	17 Bf 109Gs
II./JG 27	Nofilia	35 Bf 109Fs and Gs
		81, of which 43 were currently serviceable

Saturday, 21 November 1942

At 1600 two Kittyhawks of 4 SAAF Squadron were scrambled after a lone Ju 88 of 10./LG 1 which was bombing their airfield. The pilots caught and attacked the bomber, but although they believed they had damaged it, no claim was made. An interception was made by a pair of Warhawks from the 64th Squadron of the 57th Fighter Group, these pilots claiming to have damaged it between them. It seems that it was finally despatched by pilots of 260 Squadron, falling near Derna. The Kommandeur of IV./LG 1, Maj Erwin Schulz, was one of those lost aboard this aircraft. In 2 SAAF Squadron on this date one of the flight commanders, Capt Wildsmith, was promoted to command the unit.

US Claims					
64th FS/57th FG	2/Lt William M.Ottaway	P-40F '26' }	Ju 88 Damaged	LG.3	1545-1615
64th FS/57th FG	2/Lt Robert J. Overcash	P-40F '35' }			

German Casualties	
Stab IV./LG 1	Ju 88A-4 WNr 5631 L1+AF shot down by P-40 in Derna area; Lt Heinz Paech, Maj Erwin Schulz (Grkdr) KiA, two MiA

Sunday, 22 November 1942

At 0900 six Kittyhawks of 450 Squadron encountered a Ju 88 when undertaking a convoy patrol which was claimed shot down. During their return flight these aircraft passed through a heavy rainstorm after which Sgt Payne was not seen again. Sqn Ldr G.H.F.Plinston was posted from 250 Squadron to replace Sqn Ldr Clowes as commanding officer of 601 Squadron. 160° Gruppo left Castel Benito for Italy, having been ordered to repatriate.

British Claims					
450 Sqn	Flt Lt J.R.Schaaf	Kittyhawk III FR242	Ju 88	5m W Apollonia	0858-1101
450 Sqn	Plt Off R.W.Winn	Kittyhawk III FR274			

Tuesday, 24 November 1942

German Casualties	
1./SchG 2	Bf 109F-4 WNr 7426 take-off collision with S.79 at Arco Philaenorum; Oblt Wolf Zipper (Stkpt) KiA

Wednesday, 25 November 1942

More RAF command changes followed, Sqn Ldr Marples leaving 238 Squadron to take over 145 Squadron, Capt Phillips being given command of the former unit on an acting basis. It is interesting to note the number of experienced Hurricane unit commanders who were now joining Spitfire squadrons as the advance left the units with these older aircraft behind on defensive duties over lines of communication, ports and rear areas. These units had taken many severe beatings and had shown already that they were less able to stand up to the Bf 109s and MC.202s than the Kittyhawks. Recently they had been held back mainly for anti-Stuka interceptions, the ground-attack missions being taken over to an increasing extent by the Curtiss fighters. Meanwhile, 601 Squadron moved to Msus and 213 Squadron to Martuba 1. 40 SAAF Squadron lost a Hurricane flown by Lt Campbell on a TacR sortie.

British Casualties	
40 SAAF Sqn	Hurricane FTR hit by Flak Mersa Brega-Agheila; Lt P.Campbell MiA
Italian Casualties	
70ª Sq, 23°Gr, 3°St CT	MC.202 damaged on landing at Wadi Tamet, S.Ten Giuseppe Melandri safe

Thursday, 26 November 1942

Another Hurricane was lost by 40 SAAF Squadron when Lt Freemantle was shot down and belly-landed following an attack by Bf 109s; pilots of Stab III./JG 77 claimed two P-40s during the early morning. 73 Squadron moved to Magrun, led by Flt Lt R.V.Ellis, DFC, but maintained a detachment at Bu Amud. The MC.200s of 8° Gruppo CT strafed Allied vehicles south of El Akmar, but intense AA hit S. Ten Ruffini's aircraft, causing him to bale out six miles west of El Agheila. A second MC.200 suffered an engine failure during this sortie and belly-landed at Arae Philaenorum.

British Casualties			
40 SAAF Sqn	Hurricane HL954 shot down by Bf 109s near Agheila, crash-landed 0825; Lt J.E.Freemantle		
German Claims			
Stab III./JG 77	Lt Lothar Baumann	P-40	0718
Stab III./JG 77	Lt Helmut Hänsel	P-40	0720
Italian Casualties			
93ª Sq, 8°Gr, 2°St CT	MC.200 MM 8148 hit in combat, S.Ten Lorenzo Ruffini baled and safe		
93ª Sq, 8°Gr, 2°St CT	MC.200 MM 7662 belly-landed at Arae Philaenorum, Serg Nino Randich safe		
601ª Sq, 148°Gr T G.12	MM 60649 '601-7' damaged and abandoned		

Friday, 27 November 1942

At 0730 ten of 1 SAAF Squadron's new Spitfires took off on patrol. At 0815 eight Bf 109s of JG 77 were seen in pairs and these at once attacked the South Africans. Maj Müncheberg shot a wing off Lt Marshall's aircraft and he was seen to spin and hit the ground. The unit put up another ten aircraft at 1530, these climbing to 12,000 feet, but then dived down to 8,000. Fourteen Bf 109s, this time from II./JG 27, were spotted 1,000 feet higher, the squadron then climbing onto the tails of the Messerschmitts. However, a trap was suspected and sure enough, six more came through a gap in the clouds 3,000 feet above, attacking the Spitfires as their pilots were firing at the main body of fighters. Capt Faure hit one Messerschmitt which he reported crash-landed, and Maj Metelerkamp claimed a second which he saw hit the ground in flames. Fw Schneider then shot down Capt Thompson at 1615, the Spitfire going straight down streaming white smoke and exploded. Capt Bredenkamp disappeared, an aircraft being seen burning on the ground.

Maj Peter Metelerkamp recovered from wounds inflicted on him during combat in the Alam el Halfa fighting at the start of September, rejoining 1 SAAF Squadron in November as the unit re-equipped with Spitfires. He claimed the first victory for the unit in one of these on 27 November.

During the fight three Bf 109s were also claimed damaged, but it was discovered on return to base that there had been many cannon stoppages, only ten rounds of 20mm ammunition having been expended against 6,300 rounds of .303in machine-gun bullets. It was also felt that the pilots were still suffering from 'Hurricane complex', and were consequently fighting defensively. Indeed, with the limited consumption of cannon ammunition, it would appear that the aircraft reported as being Messerschmitts shot down, had in fact been the two lost Spitfires, for no Luftwaffe losses were listed. The 8° Gruppo MC.200s were active again during the day, eight of these fighters taking off at 1035 to strafe vehicles SE El Agheila. MC.202s of 13° Gruppo (77ª and 78ª Squadriglie) moved to Tauorga.

British Claims

1 SAAF Sqn	Lt J.H.Gaynor	Spitfire Vb ER171 'V'	2 Bf 109Gs Damaged	Agedabia-Marsa el Brega	0815
1 SAAF Sqn	Maj P.C.R.Metelerkamp	Spitfire Vb EP690 'A'	Bf 109G Damaged	Agedabia-Marsa el Brega	0815
1 SAAF Sqn	Maj P.C.R.Metelerkamp	Spitfire Vb EP690 'A'	Bf 109G	Agedabia-Marsa el Brega	1618
1 SAAF Sqn	Capt J.M.Faure	Spitfire V .EP204 'F'	Bf 109G	Agedabia-Marsa el Brega	1618

British Casualties

1 SAAF Sqn	Spitfire V EP793 'E' shot down by Bf 109 Agedabia-Marsa el Brega at 1615; Capt E.R.Thompson KiA
1 SAAF Sqn	Spitfire V EP897 'L' shot down by Bf 109s Agedabia-Marsa el Brega at 1615; Capt J.M.Bredenkamp KiA
1 SAAF Sqn	Spitfire V EP117 'W' spun in at start of engagement at 0815, cause not known; Lt L.M.Marshall KiA
1 SAAF Sqn	Spitfire V EP655 'Q' damaged Cat II by Bf 109s Agedabia-Marsa el Brega at 0815; Lt G.G.Paterson safe

German Claims

Stab/JG 77	Maj Joachim Müncheberg	Spitfire	5km E Bir el Gina	0732
Stab/JG 77	Hptm Erwin Bacsilla	Spitfire	10km SW Agedabia	0800
5./JG 27	Fw Bernhard Schneider	Spitfire	12km SW Agedabia	1515
5./JG 27	Lt Willy Kientsch	Spitfire	15km SW Agedabia	1525

Saturday, 28 November 1942

33 Squadron moved to Benina. Flt Lt N.P.W.Hancock replaced Sqn Ldr M.T.Judd as commanding officer of 250 Squadron, the latter having fallen sick. Eight MC.200s of 8° Gruppo again strafed vehicles south-east of Agedabia during the early morning.

Italian Casualties

96ª Sq, 9°Gr, 4°St CT	MC.202 MM 7924 '96-3' badly damaged by bombs at El Adem

Sunday, 29 November 1942

Nine MC.200s of 8° Gruppo strafed a column of about 50 vehicles in the Wadi el Faregh area between 0650-0855. Two pilots belly-landed with engine troubles.

British Claims

73 Sqn	Flg Off R.V.Smith	Hurricane IIc HV441	Bf 110 Damaged	Benghazi, 5m S Magrun	0635

Italian Casualties

92ª Sq, 8°Gr, 2°St CT	MC.200 MM 8327 force-landed 30km SE Arae Philaenorum, Serg Magg Nadio Monti safe
93ª Sq, 8°Gr, 2°St CT	MC.200 MM 8833 belly-landed 8km SE Arae Philaenorum, Serg Lotario Bertoni safe

Benghazi from the air. Note the wrecked Italian aircraft in the water in the foreground.

Monday, 30 November 1942

Nine MC.200s of 8° Gruppo again strafed vehicles in the Wadi el Faregh area, 0920-1110; two aircraft then force-landing with one pilot slightly wounded. Around midday ten Spitfires of 601 Squadron provided escort for two TacR Hurricanes from 40 SAAF Squadron over the battle area. Two Bf 109s were reported seen in the Marsa Brega area and both these were claimed shot down. No losses of such aircraft have been discovered, but a TacR Bf 110 of 4.(H)/12 was listed as shot down in combat with the pilot wounded.

As November drew to a close the Axis forces had begun to make a stand on the line at El Agheila, much as they had done in January 1942. Here they were to bring 8th Army's advance to a halt until mid-December, as supplies were brought up to allow an assault to be launched against these new positions. This also allowed for some re-organisation within WDAF, the decision, as already mentioned, having been taken that the Hurricane fighter units should no longer move forward when the advance resumed. Although the tactical reconnaissance units would continue to operate over the forward area, 33, 80, 127, 213, 238 and 335 Squadrons would remain behind, involved in training or coastal patrol duties. The main offensive elements of WDAF would remain the Kittyhawks and US P-40s, covered by the growing number of Spitfires. During the day 5 SAAF Squadron was on the move again, rejoining 2 SAAF and 4 SAAF Squadrons at Antelat. On the Axis side of the lines 3./JG 77 moved one Schwarm to Tripoli.

British Claims

73 Sqn	Flg Off S.P.Davis	Hurricane IIc BP186	Ju 88	10m W Tocra	0550
601 Sqn	Flg Off J.H.Nicholls	Spitfire Vc EP827	Bf 109	Marsa Brega area	1230-1300
601 Sqn	Flg Off K.D.Williams	Spitfire Vc BR136	Bf 109	Marsa Brega area	1230-1300

German Casualties

4.(H)/12	Bf 109F-4 WNr 8591 80% damaged in combat over El Agheila;,Obfw Günther Matthes WiA
4.(H)/12	Bf 109F-4 WNr 7502 25% damaged in combat with Spitfires over El Agheila; pilot safe
4.(H)/12	Bf 109F-4 WNr 8715 20% damaged in combat with Spitfires over El Agheila; pilot safe

Italian Casualties

607ª Sq, 146°Gr, 44°St T	S.82 607-9 badly damaged at Arae Philaenorum, w/o, Ten Pasquale Sciambra safe

Tuesday, 1 December 1942

Between 0650-0830 eight MC.200s of 8° Gruppo covered by MC.202s from the 4° Stormo strafed in the El Akmar area. Later (1420-1615) four more MC.200s attacked and bombed in the same area. On this occasion 11 Kittyhawks of 2 SAAF Squadron were carrying out a patrol over the Agedabia-Marsa Brega area, flying at 4,500 feet. Bombs were then seen exploding over to the right of the formation, following which the four Macchis were spotted flying 500 feet below. These were chased out to sea, two being shot down, a third claimed damaged. The Italian pilots claimed one of the attackers shot down in return, although the South Africans actually suffered no casualties. Charles Laubscher recalled:

> "My last combat occurred on 1 December when we spotted four aircraft bombing while on an offensive patrol over the Agedabia-Marsa Brega area south of Benghazi. We overhauled them rapidly and identified them as Macchi 200s – I attacked the leader and set him smoking but had to break away to avoid an attack by another Italian. I saw my No.3 attack the one I'd just damaged, obtaining a good hit. The Macchi pulled up in front of me in a left turn and I again hit him with a deflection shot. I then swung in behind him and fired from dead astern. Almost simultaneously the pilot baled out, releasing his 'chute immediately. It fouled for a second, then pulled clear but I think he must have caught my last burst."

In fact, Serg Magg Nadio Monti and S.Ten Giuseppe Calsolaro of 92ª Sq were shot down. Despite his wounds, Calsolaro managed to bale out, fell into the sea, swam to the coast and was later picked up by Italian troops. Cap Sansone had his MC.200 badly damaged and was consequently unable to drop one of his two clusters of four 15kg bombs; after landing his aircraft was written off.

The Kittyhawk pilots then reported that a pair of Bf 109s, spotted at a height of 10,000 feet, joined the engagement, one of these being claimed by Lt Hojem. No Luftwaffe fighter activity is reported on this date and the fighters encountered by the Kittyhawks were actually two MC.202s flown by Ten Giuseppe Oblach of 73ª Sq and his wingman

Three 4° Stormo pilots, from the left S.Ten Querci, Ten Reiner and S.Ten Oblach.

S.Ten Omero Alesi, which were flying rather higher and at some distance from the rest of the escort. Oblach, being credited with a P-40 shot down before he disappeared, had obviously become Hojem's victim. With a tally of seven individual claims, he was posthumously decorated with a Medaglia d'Oro 'in Memoriam'.

During the day the 158° Gruppo and 50° Stormo Assalto headquarters were ordered to repatriate to Italy. Serviceable aircraft and pilots were handed over to 159° Gruppo. Cap Mario Rigatti assumed command of 74ª Squadriglia, but this unit, like the whole 23° Gruppo, greatly reduced its activity up to year's end; the few serviceable MC.202s were handed over to 18° Gruppo and only 70ª Squadriglia carried out some token operations, patrolling over Tripoli harbour. This date also saw the despatch of one Schwarm of 2./JG 77 to Gabes.

British Claims

2 SAAF Sqn	Capt C.J.Laubscher	Kittyhawk I ET822 'R'	MC.200	10m NE Marsa el Brega	1645
2 SAAF Sqn	Capt J.E.Parsonson	Kittyhawk I ET904 'F'			
2 SAAF Sqn	Lt J.R.Wight	Kittyhawk I AK947 'P'	MC.200	Agedabia-Brega	1645
2 SAAF Sqn	Lt D.L.Quin	Kittyhawk I AK888 'N'	MC.200 Damaged	Agedabia-Brega	1645
2 SAAF Sqn	Lt R.C.Hojem	Kittyhawk I EV162 'I'	Bf 109F	Agedabia-Brega	1645

US Casualties

65th FS/57th FG	P-40, Lt Harold C.Rideout PoW

Italian Claims

73ª Sq, 9°Gr, 4°St CT	Ten Giuseppe Oblach	MC.202 MM 9085	P-40	El Brega	unstated
92ª Sq, 8°Gr, 2°St CT	Ten Costantino Petrosellini	MC.200	P-40	El Agheila	unstated

Italian Casualties

92ª Sq, 8°Gr, 2°St CT	MC.200 MM 8186 shot down, S.Ten Giuseppe Calsolaro wounded, baled. Picked up by Italian troops
92ª Sq, 8°Gr, 2°St CT	MC.200 MM 8147 failed to return, Serg Magg Nadio Monti MiA
92ª Sq, 8°Gr, 2°St CT	MC.200 badly damaged in combat, later written off, Cap Vincenzo Sansone safe
73ª Sq, 9°Gr, 4°St CT	MC.202 MM 9085 failed to return, Ten Giuseppe Oblach MiA

Lockheed Hudson VIs were gradually supplementing and supplanting the Bombays and other transport aircraft by the latter part of 1942. This aircraft was serving with 216 Squadron, carrying the unit code LO.

Wednesday, 2 December 1942

Sqn Ldr Wedgwood, to date the most successful of the Western Desert Spitfire pilots, who had claimed nine victories since his arrival, departed 92 Squadron, tour expired. He handed over to one of the flight commanders, J.M.Morgan, who had six claims to his credit. The latter's flight was taken over by W.L.Chisholm, a Canadian. During the night of 2nd/3rd Flt Lt E.L.'Nipper' Joyce, late of 73 Squadron but now with the 243 Wing Training Flight shot down a Ju 88 in flames eight miles east of Martuba. LG 1 suffered the loss of three bombers during this night, including one carrying the Geschwader Kommodore, Oberstlt von Benda on a special sortie to Tobruk. It was an aircraft of 3.Staffel which seems to have fallen to Joyce's fire, however.

British Claims				
243 Wg Training Flt	Flt Lt E.L.Joyce	Hurricane I	Ju 88	Sidi Haneish area

German Casualties	
3./LG 1	Ju 88A-4 WNr 140332 L1+DL crash-landed in Derna area after combat with fighter; Lt Benno Farkac and three PoW
St./LG 1	Ju 88A-4 WNr 8610 L1+BA missing Tobruk area to AA; Hptm Erwin Sy, Obstlt Franz von Benda and two MiA
4./JG 27	Bf 109G-2 trop WNr 10644 White 7 shot down by AA 60km SW Agedabia; Lt Werner Schaefer MiA
5./JG 27	Bf 109F-4 trop WNr 8733 combat 100%; pilot safe
1./SchG 2	Bf 109F-4 WNr 13363 shot down by AA and crashed near Wadi Faregh; Lt Cyrrus baled out safely

Thursday, 3 December 1942

At 0830 12 Kittyhawks of 4 SAAF Squadron were patrolling in the Agedabia-Marsa Brega area when an equal number of Bf 109s were encountered. Two of these were claimed probably shot down by the South African pilots while one claim seems to have been made in return by the Germans. In neither case was any loss or casualty actually recorded. 70ª Squadriglia of 23° Gruppo was ordered to move to Castel Benito to provide protection for Tripoli. Ten Giorgio Solaroli of 74ª Squadriglia, 23° Gruppo, was posted to assume command of 95ª Squadriglia, 18° Gruppo, replacing Cap Vittorio Bariletta. The 89° Gruppo BT was now ordered to repatriate to Gioia del Colle in mainland Italy.

British Claims					
4 SAAF Sqn	Capt D.W.Golding	Kittyhawk I EV136 'L'	Bf 109 Probable	15m SW Marsa Brega	0930
4 SAAF Sqn	Lt E.L.J.Hazeldine	Kittyhawk I ET824 'F'	Bf 109G Probable	Agedabia-Marsa Brega	0930

German Claims		
III./JG 77	unstated	P-40

Friday, 4 December 1942

German Casualties	
6./JG 27	Bf 109F-4 trop WNr 8273 combat with P-40. Crash-landed Arco Philaenorum, 30% damaged

Saturday, 5 December 1942

At 1500 11 Spitfires of 601 Squadron took off from the unit's new base on a sweep and reconnaissance over the Marble Arch area at 16,000 ft. On the return flight six Bf 109s were seen ahead and two more below. One section dived on the latter, Plt Off Ibbotson claiming one shot down, but then had to break away due to the approach of two more Messerschmitts which attempted to attack him. As this engagement was taking place 11 Kittyhawks from 4 SAAF Squadron commenced a patrol in the same area. Near Marsa Brega three Bf 109s were attacked, claims being made for a probable and two damaged. Lt McKechnie's aircraft developed engine trouble and he force-landed; he returned to base two days later. During the day II./JG 77 began arriving at Zazur in Libya from Italy, thereby bringing JG 77 to its full establishment of three Gruppen. Kommandeur was Hptm Anton Mader, a Ritterkreuzträger already credited with over 50 victories; the two Staffeln which arrived at this time – 4 and 6 – were commanded respectively by Oblt Lutz-Wilhelm Burckhardt, RK and 53 victories, and Oblt Joachim Deicke, 13 victories. This Gruppe had claimed some 1,300 aircraft shot down over the Soviet Union.

British Claims					
601 Sqn	Plt Off D.Ibbotson	Spitfire Vc BR361 'P'	Bf 109	Marble Arch l.g	1500-1625
4 SAAF Sqn	Lt H.Crosley	Kittyhawk I AK776 'V'	Bf 109 Damaged		1630

4 SAAF Sqn	Capt D.W.Golding	Kittyhawk I EV136 'L'	Bf 109F Damaged	1630
4 SAAF Sqn	Lt C.Southwood	Kittyhawk I AK967 'I'	Bf 109F Probable	1630

Sunday, 6 December 1942

Following the arrival of II./JG 77 at Zarzur the day before, JG 27's pilots began leaving between 12-18 December. The last ground crew left Zarzur for Tripoli on 12th, reportedly dancing for joy at going. In Africa the unit had claimed 1,166 victories; by the end of 1942 the claims made throughout the war amounted to 1,799, made up as follows:

Stab	34
I.Gruppe	684
II.Gruppe	558
III.Gruppe	523

Overall pilot losses in Africa had been:
37 killed (20 in air combat, 2 by AA)
25 missing (23 in air combat, 2 by AA)
27 captured (26 in air combat, 1 by AA)
24 seriously wounded (18 in air combat, 1 by AA)

Sqn Ldr H.P.Cochrane, DFC, who had flown with 112 Squadron during 1940-41 now returned to operations as commanding officer of 238 Squadron, which was now based at Martuba.

German Claims

6./JG 27	Lt Hans Lewes	P-40	10km E El Gefera	0820
4.(H)/12	Fw Friedrich Stannecke	P-51		

On a recently-occupied airfield the tailplane of a burnt-out Luftwaffe aircraft provides evidence of another type flying in to bring supplies. This appears to be the remains of an FW 200, details of the presence of which has not been discovered. The pristine Hurricane in the background is believed to have been painted overall blue, HL681 being an unarmed reconnaissance aircraft of 2 PRU.

Monday, 7 December 1942

Eight Spitfires of 145 Squadron patrolled over the Marsa Brega area between 0730-0830, meeting two Bf 109s of I./JG 77 which were attacked without result. During the return flight the unit was vectored onto two more aircraft which were TacR Bf 109s of 4.(H)/12 flying at 14,000 feet. Plt Off Laing-Meason dived on these, shooting down one flown by Fw Reiber; this crash-landed 20 miles inside the Allied lines, the pilot becoming a PoW. Laing-Meason also claimed the second Messerschmitt probably destroyed.

601 Squadron sent off 12 Spitfires to protect 'de-lousing' Kittybombers in the Marble Arch and Agheila areas. Four Bf 109s were seen west of El Agheila, Flg Off Samuel claiming one which he reported hit the ground five miles to the south; Plt Off Ibbotson then claimed one which he saw go into the sea five or six miles north-east of Agheila. His own aircraft was then hit in the wing by a Bf 109 and in the engine by Flak; he crash-landed. At 1530 92 Squadron was up patrolling over El Agheila when more Bf 109s were seen. On this occasion Plt Off Joerns was shot down and baled out, although Sqn Ldr Morgan claimed damage to one of the attackers.

During this rather confused day I./JG 77 reported intercepting two fighter-bomber raids during which two Spitfires and two P-40s were claimed shot down plus a bomber identified as a Baltimore. This latter seems without doubt to have been a Maryland of 60 SAAF Squadron lost on this date with its crew. Meanwhile 601 Squadron's Plt Off Ibbotson had been captured by Rommel's staff who were nearby. He was presented to the general himself. Nonetheless, that night he managed to escape and returned to base with the help of friendly Arabs, as he had done on a previous occasion.

British Claims

145 Sqn	Flg Off P.B.Laing-Meason	Spitfire Vb EP895	Bf 109	Marsa Brega	0705-0830
145 Sqn	Flg Off P.B.Laing-Meason	Spitfire Vb EP985	Bf 109 Probable	Marsa Brega	0705-0930
601 Sqn	Plt Off D.Ibbotson	Spitfire Vc AB147	Bf 109	5-6m NE El Agheila	1305-1445
601 Sqn	Flg Off F.B.Samuel	Spitfire Vc ER272	Bf 109	5m S El Agheila	1305-1405
601 Sqn	Sgt W.D.Steele	Spitfire Vc ER461	Bf 109 Damaged	El Agheila area	1445
92 Sqn	Sqn Ldr J.M.Morgan	Spitfire Vb EP338	Bf 109 Damaged	El Agheila	1530-1715

British Casualties

60 SAAF Sqn	Maryland and crew MiA, wreckage later found; Lt L.E.Brooks and two KiA
601 Sqn	Spitfire AB147 left 1305, damaged by Bf 109 and Flak, crash-landed 5m S El Agheila; Plt Off D.Ibbotson safe
92 Sqn	Spitfire Vb EP779 left 1530, shot down by Bf 109 El Agheila at 1600; Plt Off J.Joerns baled out

German Claims

4.(H)/12	FW Friedrich Stanneck	P-51	W Hamat	0700
Stab I./JG 77	Lt Heinz-Edgar Berres	Baltimore	W El Haseiat	1440
Stab I./JG 77	Hptm Heinz Bär	2 P-40s	W El Agheila	1450 & 1452
2./JG 77	Obfw Walter Brandt	Spitfire		1503
III./JG 77	unstated (poss Stfw Seckel)	Spitfire	W El Agheila	

German Casualties

4 .(H)/12	Bf 109F-4 WNr 8468 Black 13, lost in combat with Spitfires at El Agheila; Fw Kurt Reiber PoW
II./SchG 2	Bf 109E-7 WNr 6347, badly shot-up in error by Italian Flak E Sirte and crash-landed; pilot safe

Tuesday, 8 December 1942

Tomahawks of 5 SAAF Squadron escorted a TacR aircraft over the area between 0900 and 1045, one aircraft being shot down by a Bf 109, Lt van Niekerk crash-landing within Allied lines with the engine on fire. He had probably fallen to Hptm Bär, the I./JG 77 Gruppenkommandeur. 601 Squadron was again active, 12 Spitfires taking off at 1055 on another Kittybomber 'de-lousing' operation in the Marsa Brega area. As the pilots watched, the Kittyhawks were attacked and split up by a single Bf 109 flown by Fw Häcker of I./JG 77. This was at once shot down by Flt Lt Ingram, Häcker being badly burned in the crash and dying next day. A second Bf 109 was seen and claimed as a probable by Plt Off Nicholls.

A dozen P-40Ks from the 57th Fighter Group of 64th Squadron, three of them actually flown by pilots attached from the 85th Squadron, 79th Fighter Group, took off from Belandah No 2 to undertake a fighter-bomber attack on Marble Arch airfield, escorted by 12 P-40Fs of the 65th Squadron. Three Bf 109s were seen taking off as the P-40s approached and these attacked vigorously as soon as they reached sufficient altitude; more quickly followed. During the fight which ensued, 64th Squadron pilots claimed five Bf 109s shot down and five more damaged (one of the latter the first claim for the 79th Fighter

Group). Two of the confirmed claims were made by 1/Lt George Mobbs and two by 2/Lt Steven Merena. However Mobbs' aircraft was damaged during his first engagement and he sought to return to base, leading one of the Messerschmitts after him. Four more of these aircraft then attacked him, but nonetheless, he managed to get back to base where he crash-landed, having also been wounded.

Meanwhile, the top cover squadron also engaged Messerschmitts, Lt Jaqua firing on one which went down out of control emitting black and white smoke, and was seen by two of the unit's flight commanders to crash. Turning to avoid an attack by another Bf 109, Jaqua got in a good burst and this too was seen to hit the ground by the same pair of captains. On this occasion one of the 65th Squadron's aircraft was lost, 1/Lt William Taylor being reported missing.

One of the claiming pilot, George Mobbs, later recalled:

> "I was flying P-40K No. 11 on that mission. I had gotten good shots at two different Me 109s during the fight. Because of the intensity of the fight I hadn't observed the final results of the first one (which Merena confirmed). The second one was in a downward spiral, and I tried to watch it down. This lack of caution led to my problem. Suddenly, holes appeared in my left wing. It seemed to take a long time for me to realise what was happening. I started a tight turn and moved into a position to retaliate, but when I pulled the trigger nothing happened. My guns wouldn't fire. I also realised I was now alone.
>
> "I started trying to make headway towards our lines, hoping to get to friendly territory in case I had to go down. It was difficult to make progress. As soon as I would head toward home I was attacked. I then observed that there were two above, two on my left and two above to my right. Two from one side would make a pass and I would turn into them, and then the two from the other side would make a pass. In an attempt to make better progress I thought I would turn into them only to the point that I could see the cannon hole in the Me 109's nose spinner – maybe then they wouldn't be leading me enough, and I could make more progress toward home. Somewhere in there I took a hit in the left fuselage and a fragment in my left thigh.
>
> "Although I have a clear recollection of the thoughts I had as to how to thwart their efforts to shoot me down, the sequence of those efforts is vague in my memory. I know that somewhere in there I thought my chances were so slim that when turning into them I contemplated trying to ram one of the enemy fighters. I felt that the German anti-aircraft helped me in my plight because in shooting at me they were also getting close to the Me 109s. Eventually they broke off, either because they were out of ammunition or low on fuel, or both. I made it back to our strip and belly-landed – a very rough belly-landing. My trim tabs were ineffective, probably damaged by gunfire, and I was exhausted.
>
> "If you look closely at the Me 109 you will note that there is a hole in the spinner for the cannon. There is also a protrusion (sand filter) on the left side of the engine cowling about the size of an old-fashioned stovepipe. These are two images that I saw frequently in my dreams after that day."

233 Wing was now withdrawn to Martuba to be re-organised as 7 SAAF Wing which would become an entirely South African unit. While so involved 5 SAAF Squadron would at last be re-equipped with Kittyhawks, bringing to a close the use of the Tomahawk as a fighter aircraft. The wing's units would not return to operations until 22 February 1943. On this same date the 8° Gruppo CT was also ordered to cease active flying and return with its MC.200s to Italy. Amongst the other Italian units 159° Gruppo moved to Misurata, whereas a patrol of five CR.42s under the leadership of Ten Pietro Ferraro was detached to Hon to face the threat posed by Free French forces heading north towards southern Tunisia.

British Claims

601 Sqn	Flt Lt M.R.B.Ingram	Spitfire Vc ER280 'T'	Bf 109	Marsa Brega area	1055-1225
601 Sqn	Flg Off J.H.Nicholls	Spitfire Vc EP827	Bf 109 Probable	Marsa Brega area	1055-1225
73 Sqn	Plt Off M.W.Smyth	Hurricane IIc HV299	Ju 88	20m NNW Benghazi	1745

British Casualties

5 SAAF Sqn	Tomahawk IIb AK483 set on fire in combat and crash-landed; Lt F.T. van Niekerk returned next day
92 Sqn	Spitfire Vb EP779 left 1530, shot down by Bf 109 El Agheila at 1600; Plt Off J.Joerns baled out
M.E.	Hurricane II HL882 SOC as lost on operations

US Claims

65th FS/57th FG	1/Lt Arnold D.Jaqua	P-40F '56'	2 Bf 109s	Marble Arch	1125

US Claims

64th FS/57th FG	1/Lt William S.Barnes	P-40K '35'	Bf 109	Marble Arch	1125
64th FS/57th FG	2/Lt Robert K.Douglas	P-40K '16'	Bf 109 Damaged	Marble Arch	1125
64th FS/57th FG	2/Lt Steven C.Merena	P-40K '25'	2 Bf 109s	Marble Arch	1125
64th FS/57th FG	2/Lt Steven C.Merena	P-40K '25'	2 Bf 109s Damaged	Marble Arch	1125
64th FS/57th FG	1/Lt George D.Mobbs	P-40K '11'	2 Bf 109s	Marble Arch	1125
64th FS/57th FG	Capt Richard E.Ryan	P-40K '20'	Bf 109 Damaged	Marble Arch	1125
85th FS/79th FG	Lt Samuel L.Say	P-40K '19'	Bf 109 Damaged	Marble Arch	1125

US Casualties

65th FS/57th FG	P-40F '54' shot down 1025-1230; Lt William E.Taylor MiA
64th FS/57th FG	P-40K '11' badly damaged in combat and crash-landed at base; 1/Lt George D.Mobbs slt WiA

German Claims

Stab I./JG 77	Hptm Heinz Bär	2 P-40s	1040 & 1055
1./JG 77	Uffz Horst Schlick	P-40	
1./JG 77	unstated	P-40	

German Casualties

2./JG 77	Bf 109G-2 trop WNr 10520 blown up at Arco Philaenorum
3./JG 77	Bf 109G-2 trop WNr 14251 Yellow 3 combat with P-40, crash-landed Arco Philaenorum 100%; Fw Gerhard Häcker injured, died 9th
3./JG 77	Bf 109G-2 trop Yellow 7 crash-landed Arco Philaenorum; Uffz Gustav von Helms safe
8./JG 77	Bf 109G-2 WNr 13823 combat; crashed into sea N Arco Philaenorum; Uffz Alfred Kiefer KiA
5./LG 1	Ju 88A-4 WNr 141038 lost 12km N Benghazi, combat with Hurricane; Hptm Karl-Heinz Schomann and one WiA
7./KG 76	Ju 88A-4 WNr 142251 F1+CT lost 100km NW Benghazi; Stfw Willi Frölich and three MiA

Thursday, 10 December 1942

At 1515 12 Spitfires of 601 Squadron took off to sweep over Marble Arch. They were followed five minutes later by Kittyhawks of 112 Squadron which were providing top cover to P-40Fs of the 57th Fighter Group north of El Agheila. Seven Bf 109s of JG 77 were scrambled, joined by Maj Müncheberg, the Geschwader Kommodore. The pilots of these aircraft spotted 601 Squadron's aircraft strafing Marble Arch airfield, chasing these out to sea. The British pilots reported seeing two Messerschmitts followed by ten more; one probable was claimed but one Spitfire failed to return. At this point the Germans spotted the fighter-bombers approaching from the direction of Marsa Brega and attacked these, Müncheberg personally claiming one shot down eight miles north-west of El Agheila; one more being claimed by Lt Marotzke.

The 112 Squadron pilots reported being attacked by 20-25 Bf 109s and MC.202s, two Messerschmitts and one Macchi being claimed shot down as the US pilots also became engaged, claiming one Bf 109 shot down plus two probables and five damaged. However, two P-40s were lost and the Kittyhawk flown by the 112 Squadron formation leader, Flt Lt R.R.Smith, was badly damaged.

Marble Arch had indeed been the target for the 57th Fighter Group, 12 P-40Ks of the 64th Squadron also providing escort to 12 more aircraft of the 65th Squadron which were carrying bombs. Approaching the target at 13,000 feet at 1000 hours, four 'snappers' were seen and at once engaged. One Messerschmitt was claimed shot down by 1/Lt Overcash, while other pilots claimed a probable and three damaged. During the afternoon the 66th Squadron was also in action, pilots claiming one Messerschmitt probable and two damaged (one by an attached 79th Fighter Group pilot), but three P-40s were lost, Capts Raymond Llewellyn and Leo Margolian both becoming PoWs with 2/Lt Robert Guillebeau – attached from the 79th's 86th Squadron – shot down and killed.

During one of these fights Müncheberg's Bf 109 was damaged and he was obliged to crash-land at Marble Arch (Arco Philaenorum) with the aircraft suffering 35% damage. A second Messerschmitt was also lost, crashing near El Agheila, but the pilot survived unhurt. By this date Luftwaffe fighter strength was down to:

4.(H)/12	Arco	7 Bf 109s – 2 serviceable
Stab/JG 77	Arco/Tamet	3 Bf 109s – 1 serviceable
I./JG 77	Arco/Tamet	17 Bf 109s – 10 serviceable
II./JG 77	Zarzur	? Bf 109s – ? serviceable
III./JG 77	Arco/Tamet	22 Bf 109s – 5 serviceable
8./ZG 26	Tripoli	11 Bf 110s – 2 serviceable

Regia Aeronautica strength was also reducing and during the day 8° Gruppo's personnel were repatriated in S.82s, all remaining serviceable MC.200s being handed over to 13° Gruppo. At this time 10° Gruppo of 4° Stormo was also ordered to repatriate, after having handed over its serviceable MC.202s to its sister unit, 9° Gruppo. Now just a small bunch of 10° Gruppo pilots remained in Libya, to provide protection for Castel Benito together with their colleagues of 9° Gruppo.

British Claims					
601 Sqn	Lt B.R.Bennetts	Spitfire Vc ER283	Bf 109 Damaged	Marble Arch l.g.	1515-1630
601 Sqn	Flg Off J.H.Nicholls	Spitfire V EP827	Bf 109	Marble Arch l.g.	1515-1630
112 Sqn	Flt Sgt L.C.Shaver	Kittyhawk III FR213 'Q'	Bf 109	N El Agheila	1520-1640
112 Sqn	Flt Lt R.R.Smith	Kittyhawk III FL880 'Z'	Bf 109	N El Agheila	1520-1640
112 Sqn	Flt Lt R.R.Smith	Kittyhawk III FL880 'Z'	MC.202	N El Agheila	1520-1640
British Casualties					
601 Sqn	Spitfire V ER461 left 1515, shot down by Bf 109 Marble Arch; Wt Off B.Raises MiA				
112 Sqn	Kittyhawk III FL880 badly damaged in combat; Flt Lt R.R.Smith safe				
US Claims					
64th FS/57th FG	Capt Robert A.Barnum	P-40K '17'	Bf 109 Damaged	Marble Arch	1200
64th FS/57th FG	1/Lt Chester L.Kropidlowski	P-40K '15'	Bf 109 Damaged	Marble Arch	1200
64th FS/57th FG	1/Lt Robert J.Overcash	P-40K '22'	Bf 109	Marble Arch	1200
64th FS/57th FG	1/Lt Robert J.Overcash	P-40K '22'	Bf 109 Damaged	Marble Arch	1200
64th FS/57th FG	Capt Richard E.Ryan	P-40K '20'	Bf 109 Probable	Marble Arch	1200
66th FS/57th FG	2/Lt William B.Williams	P-40F	Bf 109 Probable	Marble Arch	1520-1640
66th FS/57th FG	1/Lt John T.Gilbertson	P-40F	Bf 109 Damaged	Marble Arch	1520-1640
86th FS/79th FG	Maj Tarleton H.Watkins	P-40F	Bf 109 Damaged		
US Casualties					
65th FS/57th FG	P-40F shot down at Marble Arch at 1200; Capt Leo B.Morgolian PoW				
66th FS/57th FG	P-40F shot down; Capt Raymond A.Llewellyn PoW				
86th FS/79th FG	P-40 shot down by e/a Marble Arch area; 2/Lt Robert Guillebeau KiA				
German Claims					
8./JG 77	Lt Emil Omert	P-40			1030
2./JG 77	Obfw Walter Brandt	P-40			1130
2./JG 77	Uffz Hans Jakobi	Spitfire		NW El Agheila	1502
Stab/JG 77	Maj Joachim Müncheberg	P-40		10km NW El Agheila	1505
2./JG 77	Obfw Walter Brandt	P-40		NW El Agheila	1505
Stab I./JG 77	Hptm Heinz Bär	2 P-40s		NW El Agheila	1510 & 1515
9./JG 77	Lt Horst Marotzke	P-40			1515
	Obfw Georg Ludwig	P-40			
German Casualties					
Stab/JG 77	Bf 109G-2 trop WNr 10725 combat, engine damaged crash-landed Arco Philaenorum, 35% damaged; Maj Joachim Müncheberg safe				
III./JG 77	Bf 109G-2 trop WNr 10618 combat, crashed nr El Agheila; pilot safe				

Friday, 11 December 1942

At 0925 112 Squadron and the US 66th Squadron were off again, bombing a tented camp. They were at once attacked by six or more Messerschmitts and Macchis, Sqn Ldr Billy Drake claiming one of each shot down; he reported that the Italian fighter spun "voluntarily" straight into the sea; there were in fact no losses of Italian aircraft on this date. He was then pursued by seven Bf 109s, crash-landing amongst the vehicles of the 11th Hussars; he returned to base that afternoon in a borrowed Hurricane. Meanwhile pilots of III./JG 77 had got amongst the US fighters, two of which were shot down.

At 1510 12 of 112 Squadron's aircraft were off again, led by Flt Lt Smith on an escort to a pair of TacR Hurricanes. An estimated four-six fighters were encountered and a dogfight commenced during which one Messerschmitt was claimed shot down, two probably so and three damaged. However, two Kittyhawks failed to return, one shot down near Marble Arch, the other force-landing in a damaged condition in the forward area near Magrun with the pilot slightly injured; the engine of this aircraft was later recovered for repair. One Messerschmitt was lost during the day's combats, Lt Horst Marotzke being killed. It is not certain whether this 30+ victory pilot, holder of the Deutsches Kreuz, had fallen during the morning or the afternoon engagement.

British Claims

112 Sqn	Sqn Ldr B.Drake	Kittyhawk III FR293 '?'	Bf 109		0925-1105
112 Sqn	Sqn Ldr B.Drake	Kittyhawk III FR293 '?'	MC.202		0925-1105
112 Sqn	Sgt W.D.Brown	Kittyhawk III FR255 'J'	Bf 109 Probable		1510-1700
112 Sqn	Sgt W.D.Brown	Kittyhawk III FR255 'J'	Bf 109 Damaged		1510-1700
112 Sqn	Plt Off D.A.Bruce	Kittyhawk III FL890 'D'	Bf 109 Probable	Marble Arch area	1510-1700
112 Sqn	Flg Off J.M.S.Crichton	Kittyhawk III FR216 'P'	Bf 109	Marble Arch	1510-1700
112 Sqn	Flg Off J.M.S.Crichton	Kittyhawk III FR216 'P'	Bf 109 Damaged	Marble Arch	1510-1700

British Casualties

112 Sqn	Kittyhawk III FR293 '?' damaged in combat, crash-landed; Sqn Ldr B.Drake returned later in a Hurricane
112 Sqn	Kittyhawk III FR255 'J' damaged and force-landed in forward area; recovered later; Sgt W.D.Brown slt injured
112 Sqn	Kittyhawk III FR217 'C' shot down in Marble Arch area; Plt Off B.A.F.Cudden MiA

US Casualties

66thFS/57th FG	P-40 shot down; 2/Lt Harry D.Duncan MiA

German Claims

7./JG 77	Uffz Werner Drehmann	P-40		0920
Stab III./JG 77	Hptm Kurt Ubben	P-40	W Marsa Brega	0940
7./JG 77	Obfw Wilhelm Baumgartner	P-40	10km NNE Arco Philaenorum	1525
Stab I./JG 77	Hptm Heinz Bär	P-40	E Ras Umm er Garanigh	1532
Stab I./JG 77	Lt Heinz-Edgar Berres	P-40	E Ras Umm er Garanigh	1532
8./JG 77	Fw Eduard Isken	P-40		
III./JG 77	unstated	P-40		
Flak		P-40		

German Casualties

9./JG 77	Bf 109G-2 WNr 13347 Yellow 1 combat N Arco Philaenorum: Lt Horst Marotzke KiA
III./StG 3	Fi 156C-6 WNr 5078 60% damaged by bombs at Nofilia

Saturday, 12 December 1942

Pilots of some of the recently-arrived Spitfires of 1 SAAF Squadron were scrambled to intercept some Ju 88s during the day, but arrived on the scene just in time to see one being shot down by AA fire.

German Casualties

7./KG 76	Ju 88A-4 WNr 140363 F1+ER lost 50km SSE Agedabia; Lt Waldemar Schmitt and three MiA

Sunday, 13 December 1942

Spitfires of 1 SAAF Squadron were again involved with bombers when at 0915 four pilots from this unit commenced a freelance patrol during which Ju 88s were spotted at an altitude of 100 feet over Marsa Brega. The South African pilots attacked, but Maj Metelerkamp's aircraft was at once hit by return fire and began streaming glycol. He ordered the other three to continue their pursuit, but he was not seen again. Lt O'Farrell claimed one probably destroyed, but the trio then lost sight of the bombers and went down to strafe some trucks instead.

Half an hour later six more of the unit's Spitfires provided escort for two TacR Hurricanes of 40 SAAF Squadron which flew along the coastal area. Over El Agheila one of the Hurricane pilots became lost in cloud, but the rest of the formation continued to Marble Arch. Here three fighters were seen behind and 1,000 feet above, and these dived on the SAAF aircraft, followed by five more. During the heavy fighting which ensued, three Spitfires were damaged and a fourth was shot down; the remaining Hurricane also failed to return. Lt Shepherd emerged from cloud cover to see nine more Messerschmitts taking off. He evaded them by flying in and out of cloud, but finally he found himself in the open and was attacked by the whole pack. "My engine started to smoke…then flames. As I went down, side-slipping, I could feel cannon shells hitting the armour plate behind me." One shell burst in the cockpit, wounding one of his feet and ripping his watch off his wrist. The Hurricane then crashed into a salt marsh and he was thrown out of the cockpit by the impact – the engine had been torn off by now and landed behind the wrecked airframe. Shepherd paddled ashore, bound up his foot in strips of underclothing and began to walk. He was picked up by an armoured car patrol. Those 1 SAAF Squadron pilots returning reported also experiencing heavy Flak.

Around lunchtime 57th Fighter Group P-40s were over the area, strafing and bombing Axis units withdrawing from El Agheila, becoming engaged with Bf 109s of which two were claimed shot down and a third damaged. One US aircraft was shot down, the pilot being killed, while a second P-40, flown by Maj Watkins, was damaged and crash-landed on return.

During the afternoon 112 Squadron sent out 12 Kittyhawks on a bombing sortie, but en route the formation was alerted to a possible 'Stuka Party' south of El Agheila and at once course was altered to the south-east to intercept. The unit actually ran into an estimated 10-15 Axis fighters, claims being submitted for four Bf 109s shot down and two damaged without loss. This apparently successful engagement raised the squadron's total of claims for aircraft destroyed to 198.

Fifteen minutes later, ten Kittyhawks of 3 RAAF Squadron on an armed reconnaissance over the Marble Arch-Nofilia area were attacked by a reported eight Bf 109s and an MC.202, one Kittyhawk crash-landing after the pilot had been wounded in the arm. A further Kittyhawk was damaged by an Axis fighter during the day, this one being an aircraft of 260 Squadron.

The number of WDAF aircraft shot down or damaged during the day exceeded quite considerably the number of Axis claims which appear to have been made, although at least three of them may have been the victims of Flak gunners. Six Bf 109s had been claimed shot down during three various combats, but German losses appear to have been restricted to just one aircraft of this type. In the circumstances the question has to be posed – did 112 Squadron in its pilots' desire to intercept Stukas that had been reported, inadvertently attack an Allied formation in error?

With nightfall, a Ju 88 was claimed shot down near Benghazi by a 73 Squadron Hurricane pilot. Magg Gustavo Garretto assumed command of 18° Gruppo. II./JG 77 arrived at Tripoli from Sicily, subsequently transferring to Castel Benito.

British Claims

1 SAAF Sqn	Lt G.H.O'Farrell	Spitfire Vc EP758 'U'	Ju 88 Probable	Marsa Brega	0950
1 SAAF Sqn	Lt D.S.Rogan	Spitfire Vc ER178 'P'	Bf 109G Damaged	5m W Marble Arch	1345
112 Sqn	Flg Off L.H.Curphey	Kittyhawk III FR195 'F'	Bf 109	S Agheila	1555-1700
112 Sqn	Sgt R.De Bourke	Kittyhawk III FR213 'Q'	Bf 109	S Agheila	1555-1700
112 Sqn	Sqn Ldr B.Drake	Kittyhawk III FR338 '?' }	Bf 109	S Agheila	1555-1700
112 Sqn	Sgt A.Shaw	Kittyhawk III FR264 'W' }			
112 Sqn	Sgt J.G.R.Lecours	Kittyhawk III FR320 'J'	Bf 109	S Agheila	1555-1700
112 Sqn	Sgt J.G.R.Lecours	Kittyhawk III FR320 'J'	Bf 109F Damaged	S Agheila	1555-1700
112 Sqn	Sgt J.M.MacAuley	Kittyhawk III FR127 'B'	Bf 109F Damaged	S Agheila	1555-1700
73 Sqn	Flt Sgt D.M.Logan	Hurricane IIc HV441	Ju 88	3m W Benghazi	1940

British Casualties

260 Sqn	Kittyhawk IIa left 1230 badly damaged by Bf 109 El Agheila; Plt Off R.S.Kent safe
3 RAAF Sqn	Kittyhawk crash-landed; Sgt F.H.Cashmore WiA
112 Sqn	Kittyhawk III FR326 damaged in combat, forced to land; Sgt M.H.Lamont safe
40 SAAF Sqn	Hurricane shot down by Bf 109s on TacR to Marble Arch area, Lt N.C.S. Shepherd returned slt WiA
1 SAAF Sqn	Spitfire V ER168 'R' hit in glycol by fire from Ju 88 24m from El Agheila; crashed in sea at 0930; Maj P.C.R.Metelerkamp KiA
1 SAAF Sqn	Spitfire V EP896 'O' damaged by lt Flak at 0940 while strafing; Lt W.P.Wickner WiA
1 SAAF Sqn	Spitfire V ER178 'P' badly damaged by Flak Marble Arch, Cat II; Lt D.S.Rogan safe
1 SAAF Sqn	Spitfire V ER344 'K' shot down by Bf 109s NW Marble Arch; 2/Lt R.R.Scott KiA
1 SAAF Sqn	Spitfire V ER278 'Y' damaged Cat II by Bf 109, NW Marble Arch at 1345; Capt J.H.Slater safe
1 SAAF Sqn	Spitfire V EP649 'B' damaged Cat II by Bf 109; NW Marble Arch at 1345; Lt H.F.Smith safe

US Claims

66th FS/57th FG	1/Lt John T.Gilbertson	P-40 '96'	Bf 109F	2m SE Agheila	1245-1350
66th FS/57th FG	2/Lt Thomas T.Williams	P-40 '83'	Bf 109F	2m SE Agheila	1245-1350
66th FS/57th FG	2/Lt Thomas T.Williams	P-40 '83'	Bf 109F Damaged	2m SE Agheila	1245-1350
86th FS/79th FG	1/Lt Frederic A.Borsodi	P-40 '91'	Bf 109F Damaged	2m SE Agheila	1245-1350

US Casualties

66th FS/57th FG	P-40F, 2/Lt Herbert M.Cohn KiA
57th FG	P-40F, damaged in combat, belly-landed at home base; Maj Tarleton H.Watkins safe

German Claims

2./JG 77	Obfw Walter Schumann	P-40		1230
1./JG 77	unstated	Spitfire	W Arco Philaenorum	
1./JG 77	Uffz Horst Schlick	Spitfire	W Arco Philaenorum	
Stab I./JG 77	Lt Heinz-Edgar Berres	Spitfire	W Arco Philaenorum	1250
Stab/JG 77	Hptm Erwin Bacsilla	Spitfire		
Stab III./JG 77	Hptm Kurt Ubben	P-40	E Nofilia	1300
9./JG 77	Fw Herbert Hohenberger	P-46		1315
2./JG 77	Obfw Walter Brandt	P-40		1537
Stab I./JG 77	Obfw Kurt Niederhagen	Spitfire		1555
I./JG 77	unstated	P-40		

German Casualties

2./JG 77	Bf 109G-2 trop WNr 10698 Black 1 shot down by Spitfire S El Agheila, 100%; Uffz Hans Jacobi safe

Monday, 14 December 1942

Ten Kittyhawks of 260 Squadron carried out a bombing sortie from 1145, but were intercepted over Marsa Brega by eight Bf 109s of I./JG 77. Pilots of this latter unit shot down two Kittyhawks, claiming three.

Continuing to attack the columns departing El Agheila, 57th Fighter Group P-40s were active during the afternoon. Four aircraft of the 64th Squadron, escorted by four of the 65th, took off with 12 Kittyhawks of 112 Squadron carrying bombs. Attacking the road near Ras el Auli, they were intercepted by Maj Müncheberg who had taken off with seven Bf 109s of III./JG 77, 2/Lt Chester Kropidlowski being lost. Müncheberg claimed one shot down 12 miles south-west of Agheila from which the pilot baled out.

About half an hour behind the first formation, a dozen 64th Squadron aircraft, four of them flown by 79th Fighter Group pilots, undertook a similar mission. Lt Steven Merena's aircraft, P-40K '20', was seen to be hit and he baled out, later being reported a prisoner, although it appears that one Messerschmitt shot down was credited to him 'in absentia'. About a quarter of an hour after his first claim, Müncheberg claimed another P-40 from which the pilot also baled out, although on this occasion he observed that the parachute did not appear to open fully. It seems fairly clear that Müncheberg's victims had been Kropidlowski and Merena, although given his report of the second parachute having partially failed and the proximity of the two claims, it may have been in the opposite order in which he had shot them down.

During the day a Baltimore of 1437 Strategic Reconnaissance Flight was attacked over Buerat by a fighter and returned with the port engine pouring white smoke. The Axis radio claimed that when last seen, the aircraft was diving towards the sea with smoke pouring from the engine. It appears that this aircraft had been attacked by two MC.202s of 95ª Squadriglia, 18° Gruppo, flown by Ten Solaroli and M.llo Pietro Salvatico, who identified it as a Boston, Salvatico claiming to have shot it down off the coast north-east of Tamet. This proved to be the only 3° Stormo claim for the month of December.

British Claims

260 Sqn	Sqn Ldr O.V.Hanbury	Kittyhawk IIa	Bf 109 Damaged		1145-1305

British Casualties

260 Sqn	Kittyhawk IIa shot down by Bf 109s El Agheila, 1145-1305; Plt Off L.V.Flury WiA
260 Sqn	Kittyhawk IIa shot down by Bf 109s El Agheila, 1145-1305; Flt Lt E.G.Aitchison safe
208 Sqn	Hurricane Z5148 crashed while force-landing in the desert
1437 Strat Recce Flt	Baltimore Damaged

US Claims

64th FS/57thFG	2/Lt Steven C.Merena	P-40K '20'	Bf 109		1600
66th FS/57thFG	2/Lt William W.Campbell	P-40F	Bf 109 Damaged		1600
66th FS/57thFG	Capt William J.Yates	P-40F	Bf 109 Damaged		1600
65th FS/57thFG	2/Lt Robert J.Goldberg	P-40F	} Bf 109	SW Agheila	1600-1705
65th FS/57thFG	2/Lt Frank E.Hertzberg	P-40F	}		
65th FS/57thFG	2/Lt William F.McGill	P-40F	}		
65th FS/57thFG	Capt Marshall Sneed	P-40F	}		

US Casualties

64th FS/57thFG	P-40K '36', lost to Bf 109s S Ras el Asli 1505-1705; 2/Lt Chester L.Kroplodowski MiA
64th FS/57thFG	P-40K '20', lost to Bf 109s; 2/Lt Steven C.Merena PoW

German Claims

Stab I./JG 77	Hptm Heinz Bär	2 P-40s	W Agheila	1120 & 1125
Stab I./JG 77	Lt Heinz-Edgar Berres	P-40	W Agheila	1122
Stab/JG 77	Maj Joachim Müncheberg	2 P-40s	15 and 20km SW El Agheila	1508 & 1525
I./JG 77	unspecified	4 P-40s		

German Casualties

III./KG zbV 1	Ju 52/3mWNr 6834 hit by landing S.82 while parked at Castel Benito, destroyed
10. /KG 54	Ju 88A-5 WNr 8270 B3+FX force-landed 20km SSE Tripoli, 50% damaged; Fw Hans Müller and one KiA, two WiA

Italian Claims

95ª Sq, 18°Gr, 3°St CT	M.llo Pietro Salvatico MC.202	Boston	25-30km off coast N Sirte	1000-1100

Italian Casualties

148°Gr T	G.12 MM 60668 'I-ALIP' destroyed in collision at Castel Benito with Ju 52, pilot Ten Giuseppe Bacchini and four wounded

Tuesday, 15 December 1942

Twelve Kittyhawks of 250 Squadron bombed transport on the Agheila-Marble Arch road early in the morning, these being intercepted by eight fighters identified as Bf 109Es, which attacked singly or in pairs in the Ain El Braghi area. Sgt Hutt got on the tail of one and claimed to have inflicted damage, but it was later reported by 8th Army observers to have crashed. A claim for a Bf 109 was also made by a P-40F pilot of the 86th Squadron, 79th Fighter Group (attached to the 57th Fighter Group), but only one Messerschmitt was lost on this date, a Bf 109G of 1./JG 77 crash-landing west of El Agheila following combat with Curtiss fighters, Fw Ott being captured.

At 1110 260 Squadron sent out 11 Kittyhawks on a bombing sortie, but these were attacked by 12 Bf 109s which shot down two and damaged a third. One of the pilots became a PoW. It seems that their attackers were from III./JG 77, led by Maj Müncheberg, who claimed one victory over an aircraft identified as an American P-40, reporting that this crash-landed on the sea shore near Ras el Ali, the pilot becoming a prisoner. Since this was precisely the area where the engagement recorded by 260 Squadron took place, it is more likely that this unit's Sgt McKee was his victim on this occasion. The confusion of identification was possibly caused by the fact that at this time 260 Squadron was operating Mark IIa Kittyhawks which were effectively identical to the P-40Fs used by the American units. The day also saw the move of Stab, I. and III./JG 77 to Wadi Tamet. From here III.Gruppe would move to Tauorga on the 17th, followed next day by I.Gruppe and on the 19th by the Geschwader Stab. On the 18th, meanwhile, II.Gruppe arrived at Zarzur.

British Claims

250 Sqn	Sgt L.G.R.Hutt	Kittyhawk III FL904 'C'	Bf 109E	Ain el Braghi	1040

British Casualties

260 Sqn	Kittyhawk IIa FL298 'L' shot down by Bf 109s nr Marble Arch; Sgt J.Takvor, safe
260 Sqn	Kittyhawk IIa shot down by Bf 109s Ras el Ali; Sgt N.E.McKee, PoW
260 Sqn	Kittyhawk IIa damaged Ras el Ali; unidentified pilot safe

US Claims

86th FS/79th FG	1/Lt Frederic A.Borsodi	P-40F	Bf 109		1415-1540

US Casualties

66th FS/57th FG	P-40 shot-up by Bf 109, 1/Lt John T.Gilbertson

German Claims

Stab III./JG 77	Hptm Kurt Ubben	P-40		1055
Stab/JG 77	Maj Joachim Müncheberg	P-40	Ras el Ali	1058

German Casualties

1./JG 77	Bf 109G-2 trop WNr 10532 White 4, combat with P-40 10km W El Agheila; crash-landing, Fw Siegfried Ott PoW
III./StG 3	Ju 87D-1 WNr 2028 and Ju 87D-3 WNr 2924 destroyed by own forces at Nofilia

Wednesday, 16 December 1942

250 Squadron once again set out on an early patrol in the Marble Arch area, the 11 pilots so engaged spotting a lone Ju 88 5,000 feet below. This was attacked and probably destroyed by Sqn Ldr Hancock.

British Claims

250 Sqn	Sqn Ldr N.P.W.Hancock	Kittyhawk III FR323	Ju 88 Probable	10m E Nofilia	1000
260 Sqn	Plt Off J.F.Edwards	Kittyhawk II ..901	Bf 109 Damaged	Marble Arch area	1110-1250

British Casualties

24 SAAF Sqn	Boston III Z2279 'C'off to attack retreating Axis forces in Agedabia area; badly damaged by Flak and belly-landed near Marble Arch at 1415; Capt W.C.Caldwell and one safe, one KiA and one died two days later damaged by Flak and belly-landed in desert

Thursday, 17 December 1942

German Casualties

1./JG 77	Bf 109G-2 trop WNr 14247 25% damaged by bombs at Wadi Tamet
1.(F)/121	Ju 88D-5 WNr 430176 destroyed by bombs at Wadi Tamet

Ex Battle of Britain pilot Sqn Ldr 'Jeff' Wedgwood led 92 Squadron out to Egypt during February 1942. He remained with the unit until December, claiming one Ju 87 when flying a Hurricane, and then eight victories on Spitfires. He was killed on 17 December when a Halifax in which he was returning to the UK at the end of his tour, crashed on Malta.

Friday, 18 December 1942

By now Marble Arch had fallen into British hands and on this date 450 Squadron moved to this forward base. From Italy 5./JG 77 flew over to join the rest of II.Gruppe, the last remaining part of the Geschwader to arrive. The unit was led by Hptm Anton 'Toni' Hackl, a Ritterkreuzträger mit Eichenlaube, who had to date claimed 112 victories.

Italian Casualties

83ª Sq, 18°Gr, 3°St CT	MC.202 MM 7775 collided with German fighter taking off at Tamet, destroyed

Saturday, 19 December 1942

Four Beaufighters of 46 Squadron undertook a reconnaissance along the Tripolitanian coast from 0720 (see also Chapter Ten), followed five minutes later by 12 Kittyhawks of 250 Squadron on a strafing sortie. The Beaufighters also began strafing, but were intercepted by I./JG 77 Bf 109s, the pilots of which claimed two shot down; one was actually lost, and is believed to have been the Gruppe's 1,000th victory. However a claim was also made for a Beaufighter by four pilots of 9° Gruppo. The following Kittyhawks also suffered a loss, Flt Sgt Robinson crash-landing after his aircraft had been hit by Flak; he became a PoW.

British Claims

450 Sqn	Flg Off G.H.Norton	Kittyhawk III FR237		Bf 109F Damaged	over sea	1305-1505
40 SAAF Sqn	Lt A.P. Lategan	Hurricane II BP286	}	Bf 109 Damaged	S. Sirte	1620
40 SAAF Sqn	Lt J.J.Orpen	Hurricane II BP980				

British Casualties

250 Sqn	Kittyhawk III FR333 'Z' crash-landed due to Flak damage nr Tamet; Flt Sgt G.L.Robinson PoW
260 Sqn	Kittyhawk III FR113 left 1340, shot down by Flak; Sgt J.Takvor baled out into sea off Libya, MiA
450 Sqn	Kittyhawk damaged Cat 1 by Bf 190; Sgt Marrows safe

German Claims

Flak	3 bombers and 1 Spitfire

Sunday, 20 December 1942

Twelve Kittyhawks of 260 Squadron took off at 0725 to strafe targets west of Tamet. When 20-30 miles west of Sirte the pilots of these aircraft were intercepted by four Bf 109s from the newly-arrived 5./JG 77, pilots of this unit claiming five shot down. Three fell at once, two crash-landing subsequently. Only one claim for a Messerschmitt damaged could be made in response. Recorded Sgt Lionel Sheppard:

> "On 20th we did a long-range recce west of Wadi Tamet towards Buerat, turning north then to come up and strafe the road. After reforming, we turned for home with Pedro (Hanbury) leading the squadron and Thagard leading the top flight of which I was a pair leader. We saw four ME 109s, obviously from one of the enemy forward landing grounds, climbing up to the north. It did not need a telegram for us to know that they were climbing for height to have a go at us, knowing we would have very little ammunition left after the strafing run we had made further west.
>
> "When flying as a squadron, the top cover flies fairly close to the lead flight, although possibly a thousand feet higher, but for some reason we were well behind Pedro, possibly due to Thagard's inexperience for which he paid dearly because both he and his number two, and a third member of the top cover were shot down.
>
> "We had changed from flying the three four's formation to the two sixes, three pairs in the lead and three pairs in the top. The four ME 109s attacked from the port side from above, and Thagard should have called a turnabout to the left. This would have meant turning in to meet the attack head on, and as I was flying on the right of the formation, it would have given both myself and my number two a chance to get a good shot in at the Hun as they came in from the left.
>
> "Unfortunately, he called a turnabout to the right which put the 109s right down on the tails of Thagard and his number two and the left hand pair. Immediately after the turnabout was called, I called my number two, Tuck, and told him to follow me in turning left into the attack, and I managed to get a burst in at one of the 109s. That burst probably saved a life because the one 109 broke off, but we did lose Thagard, McClure and Adams.
>
> "By this time the lead flight had turned to come back and give us some support, but fighting in the air is a matter of seconds. One minute there were ten aircraft, four of them and six of us; the next I was on my own avoiding one ME that came up under me and shot the underside of my port wing away. I can see him now coming up under me with the centre of the spinner through which the 20mm cannon fires were going 'puff, puff, puff'. Steep turn to the right, bottom rudder over almost onto my back, and managed a short burst at him. Then full throttle at a rate of knots and down onto the deck as I found both the altimeter and ASI (air speed indicator) were out of action, but coming along with me was Tuck, my number two. You must remember that as we were possibly out of ammunition, there was no point in hanging around, so it was 'Home James and don't spare the horses'. It is no good lining up for a shot suspecting there is possibly no ammunition to find that nothing happens.
>
> "With no ASI or altimeter, I knew I would have a problem landing, especially as I had no knowledge of what damage might have been done to the flaps and undercarriage. I told Tuck on the R/T to make a normal approach for landing and I would formate on him, but not to land in case I had a problem as I had no wish to prang him on landing. I also called up ground control and asked for a clear run in case the undercart went, but I managed to get down with no problems, and Tuck made another circuit and came in after me. It had been a two hours and twenty minutes 'op', not one of our best shows with three lost and one damaged, but for my part a good landing – they are all good if you walk away from them."

British Claims

260 Sqn	Sgt D.W.C.England	Kittyhawk IIa	Bf 109F Damaged	20-30m W Sirte	0725-0945

British Casualties

260 Sqn	Kittyhawk III shot down in flames by Bf 109 20-30m W Sirte 0725-0945; Plt Off V.J.Thagard
260 Sqn	Kittyhawk III FR134 shot down 20-30m W Sirte 0725-0945; Flt Sgt L.P.McClure MiA
260 Sqn	Kittyhawk III shot down 20-30m W Sirte 0725-0945; Sgt Adams MiA
260 Sqn	Kittyhawk III force-landed, damaged Cat II, 20-30m W Sirte 0725-0945; Sgt L.J.Sheppard safe
260 Sqn	Kittyhawk III damaged Cat II and crash-landed, 20-30m W Sirte 0725-0945; Sgt J.C.Colley safe

German Claims

5./JG 77	Oblt Anton Hackl	2 P-40s	0745 & 0747
5./JG 77	Oblt Burchard Böker	2 P-40s	0748 & 0802
5./JG 77	Lt Franz Hrdlicka	P-40	0750
8./ZG 26	unstated	Boston	1255

Monday, 21 December 1942

Two TacR Hurricanes were escorted by 12 of 3 RAAF Squadron's Kittyhawks from 0750, the formation being attacked when ten miles south-east of Sirte by four or five Bf 109s, one Kittyhawk being shot down. Six of the Australian unit's aircraft were off again at 1305 to attack the airfield at Hon. Two Ju 52/3ms, two S.79s or S.81s, a Ju 88, a Ju 87, a Bf 110, a CR.42, and Hs 126 and two gliders were seen on the ground here and seven of these were claimed to have been set alight, with damage being inflicted on three more. Two Kittyhawks were shot down by machine-gun fire from the ground, the gunners here claiming one aircraft shot down which they identified as a Spitfire. The 3 RAAF Squadron commander, Sqn Ldr Bobby Gibbes:

"I led six Kittyhawks on a reconnaissance of Hon, an Italian aerodrome, 150 miles south of Sirte and 188 miles from Marble Arch on a bearing of 237 degrees. The Long Range Desert Group intended to take it and wanted to know fortifications, combat strength etc. We were then to fly deeper into the desert on further reconnaissance. I had not been briefed to attack any ground targets but merely to get the sought-after information. Our aircraft were fitted with long-range tanks.

"On sighting the Hon aerodrome, which was on the northern edge of a small town, I noticed a number of aircraft parked around the perimeter of the field. Realizing that we would have an element of surprise, I couldn't resist such a target, and without jettisoning our drop tanks, as I intended continuing with the reconnaissance after the diversion, I led my flight down on a swift run across the aerodrome. Not a shot was fired and contrary to general prudent practice, I decided to risk a second run across the aerodrome. On this second attack, we encountered light flak which intensified as we flew away from the field. On these attacks, we had knocked out most of the aircraft, and as I led away trying to reform my flight, I saw to my extreme dismay and annoyance, Squadron Leader Watt, who had recently arrived from Australia to take over my command, lead in with his number two for a third attack. Two other pilots, seeing these aircraft lead in again, turned and followed, despite my orders for all aircraft to pull away from the area and form up. The result was inevitable. Two of the four aircraft were shot down.

"Sgt 'Stuka' Bee's aircraft was set on fire by the aerodrome defence gunfire and at the same time, Plt Off Rex Bayly called up to say that his motor had been hit and that he was carrying out a forced-landing. As Sgt Bee had a lot of speed from his dive and was flaming badly, I advised him to climb up and bail out, instead of trying to belly-land his aircraft at high speed. He mightn't have heard me, or perhaps was badly wounded or even dead, as his speed had not decreased when he hit the ground. His aircraft rolled up into a ball, an inferno of flames. He didn't have a chance. I circled and watched the Italians, showing great courage, send out an ambulance in an attempt to save him, but the outcome was obvious. It was later confirmed that he had been killed.

"In the meantime, Rex Bayly crash-landed his aircraft nearly a mile from the aerodrome, and on coming to a stop, called up on his radio to say that he was OK. His aircraft did not burn. I asked him what the area was like for a landing to pick him up, and ordered the other three aircraft to keep me covered and to stop any ground forces coming out after him. He told me that the area was impossible, and asked me to leave him, but I flew down to look for myself. I found a suitable area about three miles further out and advised Bayly that I was landing, and to get weaving out to me.

"I was nervous about this landing, in case shrapnel might have damaged my tyres, as on my first run through the aerodrome, my initial burst set an aircraft on fire. I had then flown across the aerodrome and fired from low level, and at close range at a Savoia 79. It must have been loaded with ammunition as it blew up, hurling debris 500 feet into the air. I was too close to it to do anything about avoiding the blast and flew straight through the centre of the explosion at nought feet. On passing through, my aircraft dropped its nose, despite pulling my stick back, and for a terrifying moment, I thought that my tailplane had been blown off. On clearing the concussion area, I regained control, missing the ground by a matter of only a few feet. Quite a number of small holes had been punched right through my wings from below, but my aircraft appeared to be quite serviceable.

"I touched down rather carefully in order to check that my tyres had not been punctured, and then taxied by a devious route for about a mile or more until I was stopped from getting closer to Bayly by a deep wadi. Realising that I would have a long wait, and being in a state of sheer funk, I proceeded to take off my belly tank to lighten the aircraft. The weight of the partially full tank, created great difficulty, and I needed all my strength in pulling it from below the aircraft and dragging it clear. I was not sure that I would be able to find my way back to the area where I had landed, so I stepped out the maximum run into wind from my present position. In all, I had just 300 yards before the ground dipped away into a wadi. I tied my handkerchief onto a small camel's thorn bush to mark the point of aim, and the limit of my available take-off run, and then returned to my aircraft, CV-V, and waited. My squadron's aircraft continued to circle overhead, carrying out an occasional dive towards the town in order to discourage any attempt to pick us up. After what seemed like an age, sitting within gun range of Hon, Bayly at last appeared, puffing, and sweating profusely. He still managed a smile and a greeting.

"I tossed away my parachute and Bayly climbed into the cockpit. I climbed in after him and using him as a seat, I proceeded to start my motor. It was with great relief that we heard the engine fire, and opening my throttle beyond all normal limits, I stood on the brakes until I had obtained full power, and then released them, and, as we surged forward, I extended a little flap. My handkerchief rushed up at an alarming rate, and we had not reached flying speed as we passed over it and down the slope of the wadi. Hauling the stick back a small fraction, I managed to ease the aircraft into the air, but we hit the other side of the wadi with a terrific thud. We were flung back into the air, still not really flying, and to my horror, I saw my port wheel rolling back below the trailing edge of the wing, in the dust stream. The next ridge loomed up and it looked as if it was to be curtains for me, as I could never clear it. I deliberately dropped my starboard wing to take the bounce on my remaining wheel, and eased the stick back just enough to avoid flicking. To my great relief we cleared the ridge and were flying.

"Retracting my undercart and the small amount of take-off flap, we climbed up. I was shaking like a leaf and tried to talk to Bayly, but noise would not permit. The remaining three aircraft formed up alongside me and we headed for home, praying the while that we would not be intercepted by enemy fighters, who should by now, have been alerted. Luck remained with us, and we didn't see any enemy aircraft. On nearing Marble Arch, I asked Sqn Ldr Watt to fly beneath my aircraft to confirm that I really had lost a wheel and had not imagined it. He confirmed that my wheel had gone, but that the starboard wheel and undercart appeared to be intact. I then had to make up my mind as to whether to carry out a belly-landing, thus damaging my aircraft further, or to try to attempt a one-wheel landing, which I thought I could do. We were at the time very short of aircraft and every machine counted. The latter, of course, could be dangerous, so before making a final decision, I wrote a message on my map asking Bayly if he minded if I carried out a one-wheel landing. He read my message and nodded his agreement.

"Calling up our ground control, I asked them to have an ambulance standing by, and told them that I intended coming in cross wind with my port wing up wind. Control queried my decision but accepted it. I made a landing on my starboard wheel, keeping my wing up with aileron and, as I lost speed, I turned the aircraft slowly to the left throwing the weight out. When I neared a complete wing stall, I kicked on hard port rudder and the aircraft remained balanced until it had lost almost all speed. The port oleo leg suddenly touched the ground, and the machine completed a ground loop. The port flap was slightly damaged as was the wingtip. The propeller and the rest of the aircraft sustained no further damage. The port undercart was changed, the flap repaired, the holes patched up and the aircraft was flying again on the 27th of the month, only six days after Hon."

The Hon raid and the rescue were the main matters mentioned in the citation of a subsequent award of the DSO to this intrepid pilot. Many years later he was given a copy of a communiqué for this date by an Italian air force friend which, when translated, recorded; "Enemy air activity; from 1310 hours five Spitfires effected incursion Hon airport. Two S.79s and one S.81 and three Ca.309s destroyed, one Ca.309 out of service. Personnel unhurt."

British Claims					
3 RAAF Sqn	Sgt I.H.Roediger	Kittyhawk IIa FL346 'Z'	Bf 109E/F Damaged	10m SE Sirte	0830
3 RAAF Sqn	Sqn Ldr R.H.M.Gibbes	Kittyhawk IIa FL323	2 S.79s on ground	Hon	1305-1610
3 RAAF Sqn	Flt Lt R.J.Watt	Kittyhawk IIa FL346	Ju 88 on ground	Hon	1305-
3 RAAF Sqn	Plt Off R.H.Bayly	Kittyhawk IIa FL327	Ju 52/3m on ground	Hon	1305-
3 RAAF Sqn	Plt Off R.H.Bayly	Kittyhawk IIa FL327	Ju 52/3m damaged on ground	Hon	1305-1610
3 RAAF Sqn	Plt Off A.B.Taylor	Kittyhawk IIa FL331	Bf 110 on ground	Hon	1305-1610
3 RAAF Sqn	Plt Off A.N.Austin	Kittyhawk IIa FL377	Ju 87 on ground	Hon	1305-1610
3 RAAF Sqn	Plt Off A.N.Austin	Kittyhawk IIa FL377	Hs 126 damaged on ground	Hon	1305-1610
3 RAAF Sqn	Flt Sgt K.C.Bee	Kittyhawk IIa FL286	glider on ground	Hon	1305-
3 RAAF Sqn	Flt Sgt K.C.Bee	Kittyhawk IIa FL286	CR.42 damaged on ground	Hon	1305-

British Casualties	
3 RAAF Sqn	Kittyhawk IIa FL273 shot down 10m SE Sirte 0750-1010; Plt Off W.D.Finlason MiA
3 RAAF Sqn	Kittyhawk IIa FL327 shot down by Flak 1305-1610; Plt Off R.H.Bayly picked up by Sqn Ldr R.H.M.Gibbes
3 RAAF Sqn	Kittyhawk IIa FL286 shot down by Flak 1305-1610; Flt Sgt K.C.Bee KiA

German Claims			
Stab III./JG 77	Hptm Kurt Ubben	P-40	SE Sirte
III./JG 77	Obfw Heinrich Hackler	P-40	SE Sirte
8./JG 77	Lt Emil Omert	P-40 n.b.	SE Sirte

Italian Claims		
AA at Hon	Spitfire	1310

Italian Casualties	
Aviazione Sahariana	2 S.79s, 1 S.81, 3 Ca.309 Ghiblis destroyed and one Ca.309 badly damaged on ground by strafing at 1310 at Hon

Wednesday, 23 December 1942

In 260 Squadron Plt Off J.F.Edwards, newly-commissioned, was now promoted to flight commander – flight sergeant to flight lieutenant in under a month! Next day Maj J.E.Parsonson was posted from his position as a flight commander in 2 SAAF Squadron to command 5 SAAF Squadron:

> "5 Squadron was the only squadron in the Wing still equipped with the Curtiss Tomahawk and the thought of flying them in operations did not make me happy at all. I had only about 16 or 17 hours on the Tomahawk and did not like them much – two of the guns were synchronised to fire through the airscrew as in the Mohawk – when the welcome orders came for us to fly them to Heliopolis, just outside Cairo, and change them for Kittyhawks.
>
> "Rumour had it that we were to be re-equipped with the much-improved Kitty III. We were all very pleased with this thought and on 5 January we flew from Martuba to Heliopolis, refuelling at El Adem and Mersa Matruh en route. On arrival we were rather disappointed to learn that our Kitty IIIs turned out to be old Kitty Is which had been specially reconditioned for us. However, though some pilots seemed to miss their Tomahawks, I was very happy to change to the Kittyhawk in which I had faith and liked its heavy firepower.
>
> ".....the three South African fighter squadrons were to be re-organised as a South African Wing under command of 7 SAAF Wing Headquarters. At this time 7 Wg HQ, with Doug Loftus as commanding officer, had 7 SAAF Squadron, a couple of RAF squadrons and a Greek squadron under command. They had been very active on the El Alamein line. Now 233 Wing HQ and our friends of 260 Squadron would leave us and we would form a purely South African fighter wing. This was the first wholly South African fighter wing in our history and we were very excited at the prospect."

Amongst the Regia Aeronautica units, 13° Gruppo CT now moved to Villaggio Crispi airfield. This unit had been reformed on 10 December when all the remaining MC.200s on hand with 8° Gruppo were passed to it, 8° Gruppo's personnel then being flown home to Italy.

Thursday, 24 December 1942

Six Kittyhawks of 250 Squadron took off at 0735 on Christmas Eve to reconnoitre Hon airfield following the attack on the 21st. Four S.79s, two gliders and an Fi 156 were spotted on the ground. At 1125 therefore, six more aircraft took off to strafe, but during this attack one Kittyhawk was shot down by Flak. Flt Lt D.H.'Nobby' Clarke landed to pick up Sgt Palethorpe, but in so doing, damaged his own aircraft on take-off and had to make a force-landing on arrival at base. Neither of the occupants were seriously hurt on this second such rescue in four days. During the day, however, 92 Squadron learned of the loss of their ex-commanding officer, Sqn Ldr Wedgwood. Recorded Neville Duke in his diary:

> "Sqn Ldr Wedgwood has been killed at night on Malta in a Halifax with a Polish crew. One of the cruellest blows of fate. He had been through two tours of operations and was on his way home to his well-earned rest. Those whom the gods adore….."

British Casualties	
250 Sqn	Kittyhawk III FR296 'I' shot down by Flak and crash-landed; Sgt P.L.V.Palethorpe picked up by Flt Lt Clarke
250 Sqn	Kittyhawk damaged taking off after rescue of Sgt P.L.V.Palethorpe; he and Flt Lt Clarke safe

Friday-Tuesday, 25/29 December 1942

Nothing of particular note occurred over the next five days. On the 25th Stab, I. and III./JG 77 moved to Bir Dufan airfield, and two days later Sqn Ldr Peter Olver, who had recently been awarded the DFC, was posted from 213 Squadron to command 1 SAAF Squadron following the loss of Maj Peter Metelerkamp. On the 27th Ten Mariano Monaldi of 390ª Squadriglia arrived at Hon with a detachment of five CR.42s. He was followed three days later by Ten Carlo Barone of 159° Gruppo Assalto, who led in three more CR.42s.

The wreck of a CR.42 MM 8544 fighter-bomber of 390ª Squadriglia, 159° Gruppo, 50° Stormo.

Wednesday, 30 December 1942

The last combats of 1942 were fought on 30th, ending the year in a blaze of success for the Kittyhawks. First off were eight aircraft from 450 Squadron at 0921 to patrol over the forward area. Six miles east of Bir Zidan four Bf 109s attacked, one of which was claimed damaged.

Eight new Kittyhawk IIIs of 260 Squadron followed at 1220 on an interception patrol over the same area. Here six Bf 109s were seen below, two of which dived down to strafe Allied troops who were putting up an AA screen. Passing through the shell bursts this was creating, the Kittyhawk pilots claimed all six shot down. It seems that the Messerschmitts were ground-attack aircraft of I./SG 2 with an escort from II./JG 77, the German pilots reporting being attacked by ten Spitfires. It appears that in making their diving attacks, the 260 Squadron pilots had overestimated their success, only one aircraft from each Luftwaffe unit actually being lost; two pilots firing at the same target in such circumstances not being unusual.

Following a very successful engagement on 30 December when claims were made for eight German fighters shot down, Flt Lt J.F.Edwards lines up with Flg Off Geoff Fallows, Plt Off Doug England, Plt Off Lionel Sheppard, Plt Off J.H.R.Thornhill and Flt Sgt Brown.

The I./SG 2 aircraft were probably attacked by Flt Lt Edwards, Plt Offs Thornhill and Sheppard, and Flt Sgt Brown, while the escorting II./JG 77 aircraft were targeted by Flg Off Fallows and Plt Off England. Lionel Sheppard (newly-commissioned):

> "Before we got back to base after the show, the army had confirmed five ME 109s shot down on our side of the lines and Bobby Brown had claimed a sixth but was only given a damaged because no one actually saw it hit the deck so Eddie Edwards, Fallows, Doug England, Thornhill and myself each got one. We had arrived on the scene at about 5-6,000 feet so with throttles through the gate, mixtures on rich, we were really travelling at a very good speed when we hit the ME 109s. The remaining four broke for home but from the dive we had the speed and we were quite sure that none of them got away. I got a very good burst in at two more 109s and in all possibility shot them down, but there was really no time to stop and look, and then we found ourselves spread all over the sky, were called to reform, finished our patrol and returned to base.
>
> "None of the other patrols that day had any joy. I think the Hun decided to call it a day…It also gave a boost to the squadron because we were still suffering a bit from the bad day we had on 20 December when we lost Thagard, McClure and Adams…"

He was wrong about further patrols, however. 3 RAAF Squadron apparently had a disappointing start in the morning when Sgt Roediger intercepted a He 111 at 26,000 feet and chased it to ground level. Unfortunately for him, his reflector sight fused and he was able only to claim damage. It seems, however, that his aim had been good, for the bomber, an aircraft of 5./KG 100, was in fact brought down.

At 1350 seven more of this unit's Kittyhawks patrolled over Bir el Zidan, refuelling at Alem el Gzina so that they were able to remain over the area until 1730. During their presence they were attacked by 15 Bf 109s from II./JG 77, but against these the Australians were able to claim three shot down and a fourth probably. Again there had been some over-claiming, but nonetheless two more German fighters had been destroyed, one pilot being killed and one taken prisoner. Above all, the day's successes had been achieved without a single loss. Bobby Gibbes:

"Flew to Alem el Gzina in the afternoon, refuelled and sweep over forward areas, Tamet, etc. Six of us all told. Out patrolling for 35 minutes. Saw bombing so led over and started to chase bombers heading west about five miles from us. Saw about 15 109s which split up, six heading into the sun and the remainder climbing up into the north. A single 109 came out of the sun. Turned onto it and went over us. Turned left and headed east. The other five came out of the sun and pulled away when they saw their rabbit hadn't been good bait. Only carried out one attack which we turned into. Danny, with six aircraft, ran into our friends about five minutes after we got away. The 109s used different tactics, split up and came down in twos and threes and a free for all followed. Boardman, Righetti, got one each. Watt got one 109 and a probable. All without loss and a good effort."

Some of the confusion around the claiming seems to have arisen from confirmation received from the army at the front, which appears to have referred both to the 260 Squadron and the 3 RAAF Squadron engagements. Lionel Sheppard provided an interesting insight into the strengths and weaknesses of the various versions of the Curtiss fighters in use at this time – particularly as 260 Squadron was now operating both Mark IIa (P-40F Warhawks) and Mark III Kittyhawks: "When I did top cover or fighter-bomber sweep, I used a Warhawk, but when it was a strafe and dive-bombing show, I took a Kittyhawk III. On a sweep the Warhawk gave me the advantage of height, but on the straight strafe and dive-bombing at lower levels, I preferred the Mark III."

British Claims					
450 Sqn	Plt Off R.W.Winn	Kittyhawk III FR123	Bf 109 Damaged	6m E Zidan	0921-1335
3 RAAF Sqn	Sgt I.H.Roediger	Kittyhawk IIa FL295 'B'	He 111 Damaged	E Nofilia	1000
260 Sqn	Sgt R.S.N.Brown	Kittyhawk IIa }	Bf 109G	Bir el Zidan	1220-1410
260 Sqn	Flt Lt J.F.Edwards	Kittyhawk III FR350 'B' }			
260 Sqn	Flt Lt J.F.Edwards	Kittyhawk III FR350 'B'	Bf 109G	Bir el Zidan	1220-1410
260 Sqn	Plt Off D.W.C.England	Kittyhawk III	Bf 109G	Bir el Zidan	1220-1410
260 Sqn	Flg Off G.Fallows	Kittyhawk III	Bf 109G	Bir el Zidan	1220-1410
260 Sqn	Plt Off L.J.Sheppard	Kittyhawk III	Bf 109G	Bir el Zidan	1220-1410
260 Sqn	Plt Off J.H. Thornhill	Kittyhawk III	Bf 109G	Bir el Zidan	1220-1410
3 RAAF Sqn	Flt Lt L.L.Boardman	Kittyhawk IIa FL292 'T'	Bf 109F/G	Bir el Zidan	1610
3 RAAF Sqn	Sgt A.Righetti	Kittyhawk IIa FL277 'I'	Bf 109F/G	Bir el Zidan	1610
3 RAAF Sqn	Flt Lt R.J.Watt	Kittyhawk IIa FL334 'L'	Bf 109F/G	Bir el Zidan	1610
3 RAAF Sqn	Flt Lt R.J.Watt	Kittyhawk IIa FL334 'L'	Bf 109F/G Probable	Bir el Zidan	1610

German Casualties	
4./JG 77	Bf 109G-2 trop WNr 10716 White 3 combat with Spitfire Bir el Zidan; Fw Erich Gassel KiA
5./JG 77	Bf 109G-2 trop WNr 10724 White 2 combat with Spitfire Bir el Zidan, 50km SSW Buerat; Oblt Burchard Böker
5./JG 77	Bf 109G-2 WNr 13882 Black 7 combat with Spitfire Bir el Zidan, 50km SSW Buerat; Uffz Günter Mielenz PoW
1./SchG 2	Bf 109F-4 WNr 8787 shot down by P-40 and crashed near Bir el Zidan; Lt Edgar Cerne KiA
5./KG 100	He 111H-14 6N+AN lost at Arco Philaenorum

Italian Claims		
AA at Pisida	P-38 (Lt Thomas Morris, 49th FS)	1030

Thursday, 31 December 1942

Five MC.200s of 13° Gruppo attacked 8th Army vehicles south-west of Bir el Zidan, one aircraft being damaged and carrying out a force-landing. The MC.200s were escorted by all serviceable MC.202s of 18° Gruppo, 14 aircraft, led by Cap Giuntella. At 0805 five MC.202s of 70ª Sq led by Ten Antonio Maccanti were scrambled from Castel Benito but no interception occurred; S.Ten Giuseppe Melandri force-landed owing to engine failure. During the day the whole of 239 Wing moved to Gzina.

Italian Casualties	
70ª Sq, 23°Gr, 3°St CT	MC.202 damaged in force-landing, S.Ten Giuseppe Melandri slightly wounded
77ª Sq, 13°Gr, 2°St CT	MC.200 MM 8805 damaged in force-landing at Gars Garabulli, S.Ten Gregorio Cinti safe

Tripolitania, January 1943

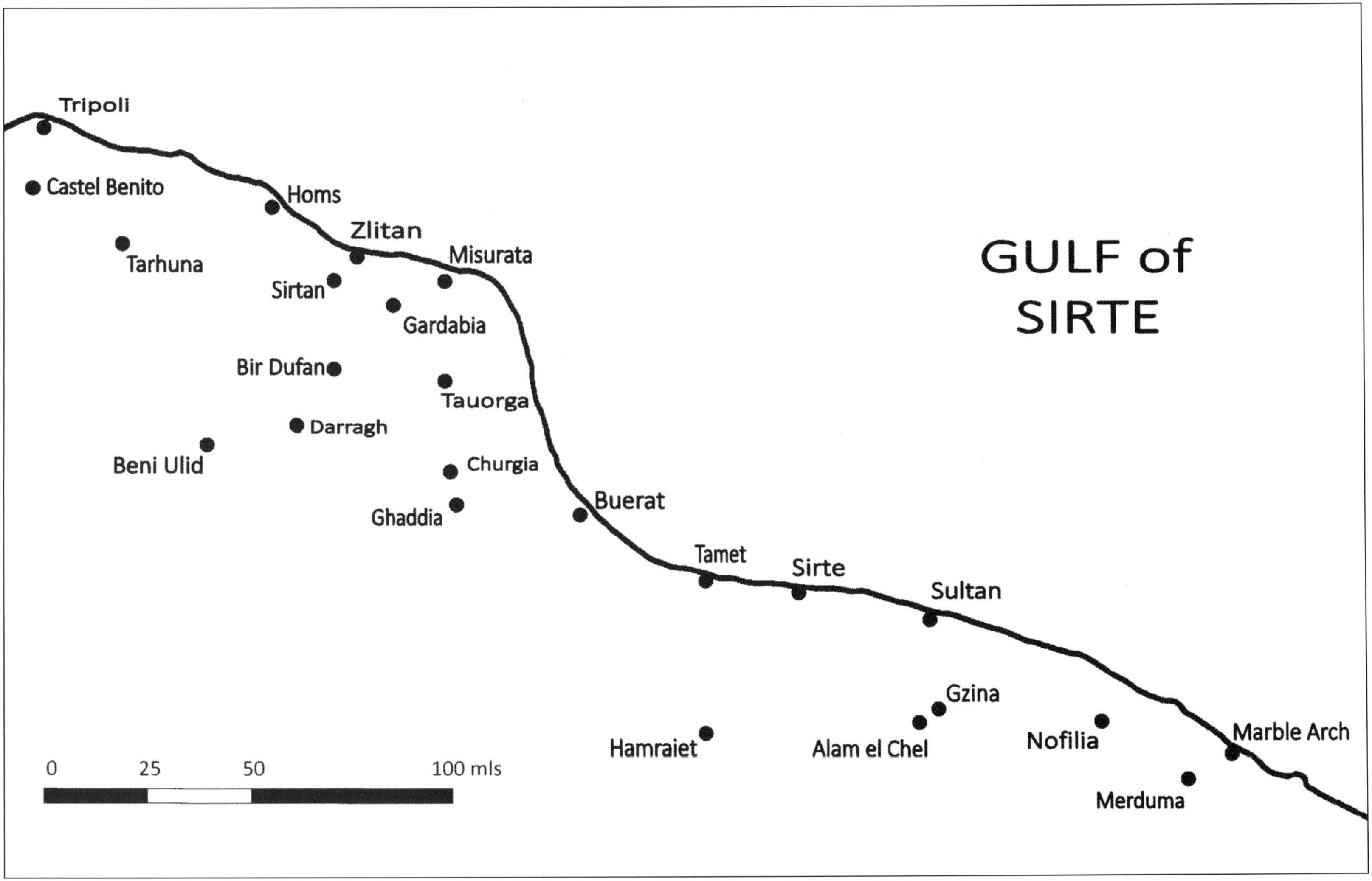

CHAPTER 8

PURSUIT INTO TRIPOLITANIA

The start of 1943 found both the 8th Army and WDAF as far forward into Western Libya as they, or their predecessors, had been able to reach during the previous two and a half years. Having left nearly all the Hurricanes behind, the Kittyhawk squadrons of 239 Wing were now rapidly re-equipping with Mark III aircraft, although the Mark IIas remained with those units which had been employing them recently. The South African units of 7 SAAF Wing continued to use the older Mark Is, although many of these had been reconditioned before being supplied. Apart from the tactical reconnaissance units, the only Hurricanes in the front line were those of 73 Squadron, now operating almost entirely by night over the forward area. Apart from its interceptor role, the unit was now also undertaking nocturnal ground-attack sorties. The commanding officer at this time was Sqn Ldr J.B.Selby, DFC, and the unit was now joined by Flt Lt C.F.Ambrose, DFC, another experienced pilot on his second North African tour, who arrived to lead a flight.

Amongst the reconnaissance units, the specialist photographic and mapping unit, 60 SAAF Squadron, was at this time down to a single Baltimore, caused by four of the unit's aircraft having force-landed due to engine failures during the preceding month. Another version of the Baltimore had begun reaching the squadrons, commencing with delivery to 223 Squadron of examples of the Mark IIIa aircraft which featured an electrically-powered dorsal turret armed with a pair of .5in Brownings – a significant improvement in defensive armament. Until the light bombers could move forward to airfields closer to the front, any need for heavier or more accurately dropped bombs was being fulfilled by the four Wellington squadrons with 205 Group – 37, 38, 70 and 104 Squadrons (see Chapter Eleven). The first of the light bombers to move forward would be those of 55 Squadron which would start to arrive at Derna on 2 January.

The opening days of January saw numerous forward moves by WDAF units as more landing grounds were taken over from the still slowly retreating Axis, and new ones were levelled and equipped. On the first day of the new year 601 and 1 SAAF Squadrons moved to El Chel, with 40 SAAF Squadron moving to Alem el Gzina, where one flight of 3 RAAF Squadron was now also based. 250, 260 and 450 Squadrons, now also with 239 Wing, moved to Chel No.2, an airstrip located 19 miles south-west of Sirte. Next day 73 Squadron also arrived at Alam el Chel from Merduna. To provide enhanced photographic reconnaissance for the army, 2 PRU now despatched one flight of Spitfire IVs to LG.219, and one to Magrun. RAF personnel were saddened by the news that Air Chief Marshal Tedder was departing RAF Middle East for other duties after his long stay as air commander-in-chief. His place was to be taken by Air Chief Marshal Sir W.Sholto Douglas, KCB, MC, DFC, previous commander-in-chief of the RAF Fighter Command in the UK.

By this time the Luftwaffe fighter units had also been consolidating their presence, Stab, I. and III. Gruppen now being based at Bir Dufan while II.Gruppe remained at Zarzur. However, all Regia Aeronautica units not of direct usefulness were being repatriated to Italy or moved to Tunisia during the month, ultimately leaving only 13° Gruppo in Libya.

Indeed the Regia Aeronautica now disbanded Settore Aeronautico Centrale (Central Air Sector) and all the units under its authority were assigned to Settore Aeronautico Est (Eastern Air Sector).

Friday, 1 January 1943

At 1040 12 Kittyhawks of 3 RAAF Squadron took off from Gzina to escort two 40 SAAF Squadron TacR Hurricanes from the same base on a sortie over the Tauorga-Churgia road. The Australian pilots climbed to 7,000 feet and flew out to sea, then turning over the coast south of Gioda. As they approached the coast, two Bf 109s were seen taking off from Tauorga airfield, four more scrambling from another strip. Shortly after this sighting, five of these fighters attacked the top cover Kittyhawks, two of which were shot down. Their attackers were aircraft of II./JG 77, whose pilots claimed four shot down, two of them by the redoubtable Toni Hackl. Claims were made against the German fighters for a number probably shot down or damaged, but no casualties were actually suffered by the Luftwaffe.

British Claims					
3 RAAF Sqn	Flg Off D.V.Ritchie	Kittyhawk IIa FL297 'E'	Bf 109F/G Damaged	nr Wadi Cheridan	1150
3 RAAF Sqn	Flg Off D.V.Ritchie	Kittyhawk IIa FL297 'E'	Bf 109F/G Probable	nr Wadi Cheridan	1150
3 RAAF Sqn	Sgt I.H.Roediger	Kittyhawk IIa FL283 'D'	Bf 109F/G Probable	nr Wadi Cheridan	1150

British Casualties	
3 RAAF Sqn	Kittyhawk IIa FL283 'D' MiA; Sgt I.H.Roediger slt WiA but safe with army
3 RAAF Sqn	Kittyhawk IIa FL297 'E' MiA; Flg Off D.V.Ritchie safe, returned on 3rd

German Claims				
5./JG 77	Lt Franz Hrdlika	P-40	8m SW Zarzur airfield	1055
5./JG 77	Hptm Anton Hackl	2 P-40s	12 & 10m SSE Zarzur airfield	1100 & 1107
6./JG 77	Lt Johann Badum	P-40	Buerat area	

Italian Casualties	
223ª Sq, 56°Gr T	S.81 failed to return, pilot S.Ten Ezio Novia, copilot Serg Magg Vincenzo Di Clemente and crew MiA

Saturday, 2 January 1943

Eleven Kittyhawks of 260 Squadron took off at 1025 for an offensive sweep over Churgia landing ground. Over the target the top cover was engaged by five Bf 109s of II./JG 77, some ten more of which took off, a general dogfight developing. Sqn Ldr Hanbury and Flt Lt Edwards each claimed a Bf 109 shot down, a third being claimed damaged, whilst Uffz Donath of 5.Staffel shot down two Kittyhawks. Claims on both sides were accurate on this occasion; Hanbury's victim blew up and crashed – probably Uffz Winter of 4.Staffel, and Edwards also saw his target crash. Two Kittyhawks were indeed shot down, but both pilots survived. Mid-afternoon 250 Squadron sent a dozen Kittyhawks to escort two of 40 SAAF Squadron's Hurricanes over the same area, but these were also engaged by II./JG 77 aircraft, the engagement being fought through heavy clouds at around 6,000 feet. The German pilots claimed four P-40s shot down with a fifth unconfirmed, while one more was claimed by Serg Magg Gorrini of 18° Gruppo; on this occasion three Kittyhawks went down. The returning 250 Squadron pilots claimed two probables and one damaged; their claims were justified for one II. Gruppe aircraft was brought down with an aircraft of 3./JG 77 damaged 20% in combat.

In a very early sortie from the new base at Derna, a 55 Squadron Baltimore was hit by Flak, causing it to force-land at Ras el Tin. From airfields back in Cyrenaica, 36 Baltimores, 11 B-25s of the 12th Bomb Group, and 12 B-24s of the 376th Bomb Group undertook a heavy raid on Crete. During the return flight two of the B-25s were forced to ditch in the Mediterranean (see also Chapter Ten).

British Claims					
260 Sqn	Flt Lt J.F.Edwards	Kittyhawk III FR350	Bf 109	SW Hesain	1025-1215
260 Sqn	Sqn Ldr O.V.Hanbury	Kittyhawk III	Bf 109	Churgia	
260 Sqn	Flg Off M.F.Perkins	Kittyhawk III	Bf 109 Damaged	Churgia	
250 Sqn	Plt Off J.E.Collier	Kittyhawk III FL899 'B'	Bf 109F/G Probable	Churgia l.g.	1600
250 Sqn	Flt Sgt C.L.Graham	Kittyhawk III FR307	Bf 109 Probable	Churgia	1600
250 Sqn	Flt Sgt C.L.Graham	Kittyhawk III FR307	Bf 109 Damaged	Churgia	1600

British Casualties	
260 Sqn	Kittyhawk III shot down; Flt Sgt A.M.Arkle PoW
260 Sqn	Kittyhawk III FR111 damaged Cat II and force-landed; Sgt Tuck safe, returned later
250 Sqn	Kittyhawk III FR244 'X' left 1510, shot down by Bf 109s, Churgia area 1600; Sgt F.H.Baron MiA
250 Sqn	Kittyhawk III FR321 'R' left 1510, shot down by Bf 109s, Churgia area 1600; Plt Off S.Holland PoW
250 Sqn	Kittyhawk III FR307 left 1510, shot down by Bf 109s, Churgia area 1600; Flt Sgt C.L.Graham slt WiA but safe
55 Sqn	Baltimore AH115 hit by Flak, caught fire during force-landing at Ras el Tin

US Claims

81st BS/12th BG	S/Sgt William L.Collins, gunner	B-25C '97'	Bf 109	Crete
81st BS/12th BG	S/Sgt John S.Dvorschak, gunner	B-25C '22'	Bf 109 Damaged	Crete

US Casualties

81st BS/12th BG	B-25C '20' ditched in sea on return from raid on Crete, Capt R.D.Heinish and five rescued
81st BS/12th BG	B-25C '39' ditched in sea on return from raid on Crete, Lt J.Holmes and five rescued

German Claims

5./JG 77	Hptm Anton Hackl	2 P-40s	SW Buerat	1022 & 1027
4./JG 77	Uffz Bruno Weidlich	P-40	17km SE El Hescia	1505
5./JG 77	Uffz Bernhard Gräff	P-40	43km WNW Buerat	1505
4./JG 77	Fw Ernst-Wilhelm Reinert	P-40	70km WSW Buerat	1507
5./JG 77	Hptm Anton Hackl	P-40	5km NW Buerat	1515

German Casualties

3./JG 77	Bf 109G-2 trop WNr 10526 Yellow 7 TN+EB LK, damaged 20% in combat
4./JG 77	Bf 109G-2 trop WNr 10 751 crashed 12m SW El Hescia in combat with P-40; Uffz Heinz Winter KiA
5./JG 77	Bf 109G-2 WNr 13 870 Black 5 destroyed in combat P-40
6./JG 77	Bf 109G-2 WNr 13889 crash-landed after combat P-40 and destroyed

Italian Claims

85ª Sq, 18° Gr, 3° St CT	Serg Magg Luigi Gorrini	MC.202	P-40	Churgia

Tuesday, 5 January 1943

By this date units of WDAF were pouring into airfields at Hamraiet. Several of 244 Wing's squadrons were already at Hamraiet North when the first P-40Fs of the 57th Fighter Group began arriving. No sooner had the Americans landed than 24 Luftwaffe fighter-bombers swept in to attack. This raid was soon followed by others, three or four attacks a day being made for the next three days. One strafe by eight Bf 109s caught New Zealand troops clearing the airfield of stones and other debris. Caught in the open without cover, ten men were killed and 25 wounded. The airfield defences claimed to have shot down four of the Messerschmitts, but actual losses amounted to one aircraft.

German Casualties

6./JG 77	Bf 109G-2 WNr 13 873 shot down by Flak and crash-landed Zarzur

Wednesday, 6 January 1943

Next day another Bf 109 from 2./SG 2 was shot down, the pilot being captured. The attacks on this latter date resulted in one 1 SAAF Squadron Spitfire being damaged by a bomb. During one of the raids at this time a member of the 57th Fighter Group groundcrew personnel, Staff Sgt Louis Lederman, claimed to have shot down one Bf 109 with a captured German machine gun.

British Casualties

1 SAAF Sqn base at Hamraiet Main raided; one Spitfire V badly damaged by bomb from Bf 109

German Casualties

2./SchG 2	Bf 109F-4 WNr 8424 Black 5 shot down by AA 25km S Buerat; Uffz Werner Lange PoW

Italian Casualties

390ª Sq, 159°Gr, 50°St Ass	Serg Magg Giuseppe Benini KiFA in a German Fi 156

Thursday, 7 January 1943

At Hamraiet Main airfield Bf 109s swept in to strafe for the third day in succession, another three such raids being made on this date. During one of these Neville Duke led 11 Spitfires of 92 Squadron in a scramble to 12,000 feet where at 1245 five Messerschmitts from II./JG 77 were engaged. "These are certainly not the demoralised pilots who moved out of Daba in November," recorded the squadron diary, noting that for the first time since El Alamein the 109s were prepared to stay and fight. Indeed 92 Squadron came out of the action significantly the worse. Sqn Ldr Morgan claimed one Messerschmitt shot down into the sea and a second damaged, Flg Off Nomis claiming a probable. However, two Spitfires were shot down, one pilot baling out, but the other being lost. The German pilots claimed three shot down for no loss on this occasion.

As part of the Italian plan for the reduction of their air force in Africa, the 50° Stormo Assalto and the 15° Stormo Assalto, all equipped with CR.42s, departed North Africa on this date.

From the north B-17s of the US 12th Air Force were despatched to bomb Tripoli during the day (see also Volume 3) escorted by P-38s of the 14th Fighter Group. Over the target Bf 109s of III./JG 77 intercepted, two P-38s being claimed shot down; Lt J.G.H.Lentz of the 94th Squadron was reported missing. (The two claims made by the German pilots were listed, apparently incorrectly, on 8 January.)

British Claims					
92 Sqn	Sqn Ldr J.M.Morgan	Spitfire Vb EP338 'S'	Bf 109	20m NW Hamraiet	1250-1335
92 Sqn	Sqn Ldr J.M.Morgan	Spitfire Vb EP338 'S'	Bf 109 Damaged	20m NW Hamraiet	1250-1335
92 Sqn	Flg Off L.S.Nomis	Spitfire Vb EP473 'P'	Bf 109 Probable	20m NW Hamraiet	1250-1335
British Casualties					
92 Sqn	Spitfire V ER279 scrambled at 1245, shot down by Bf 109s; Flt Sgt T.R.Broomhall MiA				
92 Sqn	Spitfire V ER221 scrambled at 1250, shot down by Bf 109s; Sgt H.Patterson baled out				
US Casualties					
94th FS/1st FG	P-38 shot down in south area; Lt J.C.H.Lentz				

German Claims				
5./JG 77	Hptm Anton Hackl	Spitfire	7km SW Sirte	1145
4./JG 77	Fw Ernst-Wilhelm Reinert	Spitfire	10km SE Buerat	1203
4./JG 77	Lt Lutz-Wilhelm Burkhardt	Spitfire	2km SSE Buerat	1205
Italian Claims				
AA at Pisida	US a/c, pilot captured			1110
Italian Casualties				
77ª Sq, 13°Gr, 2°St CT	MC.200 MM 8295 damaged on landing, S.Ten Guido La Ferla WiA			

Friday, 8 January 1943

Hamraiet was again the centre of activity, the first action occurring after eight Spitfires of 145 Squadron had taken off at 0815 on patrol. Bomb-laden Bf 109s were seen approaching the airfield, and Flt Lt Bert Houle attacked one of these from astern, whereupon it shed several pieces and dived into the ground. It is believed that this aircraft was 'Yellow 7' of 3./JG 77 flown by Fw Behrendt. Houle's own aircraft was damaged during the sortie by Allied AA fire.

92 Squadron, which was still based further back, had flown up to be on readiness at Hamraiet and was now scrambled at 1050. A large force of Bf 109s and MC.202s which were providing cover for some Ju 87s were engaged at 13,000 feet, two Macchis being claimed shot down and a third as a probable. Flg Off Duke and Flt Sgt Sales dived on their two Macchis which were flying 3,000 feet below them and chased them to the ground. Duke went down vertically before he managed to get several strikes on his victim which crashed in flames and broke up. Regia Aeronautica reports indicate that 16 MC.202s of 18° Gruppo were involved in escorting strafing aircraft over the front, claiming one Spitfire shot down for the loss of one Macchi. It would appear, therefore, that Duke and Sales had both attacked the same aircraft, flown by Serg Pettazzoni.

Having already completed a full tour on Tomahawks in 1941, Flg Off Neville Duke joined 92 Squadron (with which he had served previously in England) to commence a further tour. He is climbing into the cockpit of his Spitfire just prior to claiming an MC.202 on 8 January 1943.

Six Spitfires from 601 Squadron were scrambled to cover the airfield at 1615, and were vectored onto at least eight Bf 109s 30 miles south of Buerat. Eight more Messerschmitts then attacked from out of the sun and one of these was claimed shot down. Ten minutes later five 92 Squadron aircraft with one from 601 and two from 1 SAAF Squadron, scrambled towards Tamet, and were vectored onto a Bf 109 ten miles west of the area at 15,000 feet. Flg Off Nomis engaged this in a dogfight, finally claiming to have shot it down into the sea. Meanwhile, two more pairs of Bf 109s and a lone aircraft were seen and the formation split up. One pilot from 601 Squadron and one from 92 Squadron failed to return. An army unit reported that one of four Spitfires was seen to turn back and attack eight Messerschmitts and fight them for 15 minutes before spinning into the ground. Although there was some confusion regarding recorded times, pilots of JG 77 claimed three Spitfires during the afternoon, but themselves suffered no further losses.

21 SAAF Squadron now moved forward from Soluch to Chel II with Baltimores. 47° Gruppo Assalto with 23 CR.42s and 64° Gruppo OA with 16 Ca.313s and a single Ca.312 departed for Italy.

British Claims

145 Sqn	Flt Lt A.U.Houle	Spitfire Vb AB324	Bf 109	S Hamraiet	1000-1110
92 Sqn	Flt Sgt J.C.Sales	Spitfire Vc BR521 'E'	MC.202	Bir el Zidan	1050-1225
92 Sqn	Lt H.F.Smith	Spitfire V AR494 'D'	MC.202 Probable	Bir el Zidan	1050-1223
92 Sqn	Plt Off W.L.Chisholm	Spitfire Vb ER345 'T'	MC.202 Probable	Bir el Zidan	1050-1223
92 Sqn	Flg Off N.F.Duke	Spitfire Vb ER220 'R'	MC.202	Bir el Zidan	1100
92 Sqn	Flg Off L.S.Nomis	Spitfire Vb EP788 'C'	Bf 109	Tamet area	1525-1755
601 Sqn	Flt Sgt E.G.Shea	Spitfire Vc BR472	Bf 109	30m S Buerat	1615-1725

British Casualties

92 Sqn	Spitfire V ER593 left at 1625, shot down by Bf 109s, S of Buerat; Plt Off G.W.Rose MiA
601 Sqn	Spitfire V ER162 left at 1615, shot down by Bf 109 S of Buerat; Flg Off F.B.Samuel MiA
601 Sqn	Spitfire V possibly also MiA
145 Sqn	Spitfire Vb left 1000, damaged by Allied AA; Flt Lt A.U.Houle safe

German Claims

Stab I./JG 77	Lt Heinz-Edgar Berres	Spitfire	ENE Dor Umm er Rami	1307
1./JG 77	Obfw Georg Ludwig	Spitfire		
5./JG 77	Hptm Anton Hackl	Spitfire	20km E Bir Dufan	1625
9./JG 77	* Obfw Herbert Kaiser	P-38		
9./JG 77	* Obfw Arno Potzel	P-38		

*claims believed actually to relate to previous day – 7 January

German Casualties

3./JG 77	Bf 109G-2 trop WNr 10575 Yellow 7, combat with Spitfire; crashed S Hamraiet; Fw Friedel Behrend PoW

Italian Claims

95ª Sq, 18°Gr, 3°St CT	Ten Giorgio Solaroli	MC.202	Spitfire	Bir Zidan	1015-
18° Gr, 3° St CT	unstated	MC.202	Spitfire Damaged	Bir Zidan	1015-

Italian Casualties

74ª Sq, 23°Gr, 3°St CT	MC.202 MM 7877 failed to return, Serg Giorgio Pettazzoni (temporarily posted to 95ª Sq) MiA

Saturday, 9 January 1943

During a quieter day, 92 and 601 Squadrons moved up to Hamraiet. Ten MC.202s drawn from 3° and 4° Stormi CT were scrambled from Castel Benito, intercepting a reported five Bostons, one of which was claimed shot down jointly by a pilot from each unit. The identity of the bomber unit involved has not been ascertained. Thirteen Cant Z.1007bis of 95° Gruppo BT were repatriated to Italy with the 35° Stormo headquarters.

British Casualties

260 Sqn	Kittyhawk III FR134

Italian Claims

70ª Sq, 23°Gr, 3°St CT	Serg Magg Celso Zemella	MC.202	Boston	Tripoli	1210-1230
84ª Sq, 10°Gr, 4°St CT	S.Ten Francesco De Seta	MC.202			

Sunday, 10 January 1943

Twelve Spitfires from 601 Squadron scrambled at 0835, climbing to 20,000 feet over Buerat. Here eight Bf 109s were seen flying south-east, these splitting into two Schwarme of four aircraft. One section of Spitfires attacked each Schwarm and Sgt Watts fired at one Messerschmitt, claiming to have damaged it. He was then attacked himself, and crash-landed south of Tamet. Pilots of III./JG 77 seem to have claimed four Spitfires in this area during this engagement. Some hours later Hptm Kurt Ubben, this Gruppe's Kommandeur, claimed a P-38 shot down in the same area. The contradictions of this day's claims have not been fully resolved. However, at 1410 eight 145 Squadron Spitfires scrambled, intercepting a reconnaissance Ju 88 of 1.(F)/121 which was attacked by all eight pilots, being driven down from 25,000 feet to ground level where it force-landed, the crew being captured.

British Claims					
601 Sqn	Sgt D.V.Watts	Spitfire Vc ER465	Bf 109 Damaged	Buerat area	0835-0950
145 Sqn	unspecified	Spitfire Vb	Ju 88		1435
British Casualties					
601 Sqn	Spitfire V ER465 crash-landed due to combat; Sgt D.V.Watts safe				

German Claims				
9./JG 77	Fw Herbert Hohenberger	Spitfire	Feriana airfield	0730
7./JG 77	Uffz Werner Drehmann	Spitfire	S Wadi Tamet	
Stab III./JG 77	Hptm Kurt Ubben	P-38	W Wadi Tamet	0840
German Casualties				
1.(F)/121	Ju 88D-1 WNr 430384 crash-landed at Bu Ngen after combat with Spitfires; Lt Gerhard Reinecke, Fw Otto Jäschke and three PoW			

Monday, 11 January 1943

The day proved much busier than of late. At 0935 12 P-40Fs of the US 66th Squadron provided top cover to 12 Kittyhawks of 112 Squadron which were acting as close cover to a pair of TacR Hurricanes. When in the Buerat area, the formation was attacked by 15 or more Axis fighters, reported to include Bf 109Fs and Gs, and at least one MC.202 (although none of these aircraft were operating during the morning). A long fight followed during which one Bf 109 was seen to crash and burn, but Lt William Williams failed to return. A second Warhawk was observed to belly-land near the coast, Lt Reutersham seemingly wounded as he was seen being assisted by troops; he had in fact been picked up by the personnel of 151 Ambulance Corps.

Meanwhile Lt Gibson was engaged by three Bf 109Gs for 15 minutes, finally being attacked head-on by one of these. He fired from 400 down to 150 yards and saw the Messerschmitt go down in flames:

> "After approximately one hour and thirty minutes of flying, I became engaged with an Me 109G that attacked our flight from behind and above. The Me made one pass, undershot, and gained his altitude again. When I turned to try and rejoin my flight, or any friendly a/c in the vicinity, I found that they had all disappeared. I had not received the message to break off combat, due to radio difficulty. There were, however, two other Me 109Gs in the area that joined with the first one in the attack against me. My only manoeuvre was to keep turning so as to give them deflection shots only. After 15 minutes of dog-fighting, one finally came at me head-on. When I opened my guns and hit him, I thought that my shots had been ineffective, until I turned 180 degrees and saw him going down in flames. By this time I had dropped to 3,500 feet. After the next attacker dived at me, he pulled up in front of my ship, trying to gain altitude. I hit him with a long burst in the fuselage. He immediately did a wingover and disappeared. The first Me circled for several minutes above me and then headed west."

The 12 Kittyhawks from 112 Squadron which had also taken off at 0945, departed Misurata, reaching the Ghernbia road area. Here six hostile aircraft appeared and Flak opened fire, one Kittyhawk being shot down and a second force-landing due to damage. At 0940 ten Spitfires from 92 Squadron scrambled, the pilots spotting a lone Bf 109 which was fired at by four or five of them, Flt Sgt Probert being credited with a probable. During these early morning engagements pilots of 4./JG 77 claimed two Spitfires and two P-40s shot down; it appears that the US P-40s were probably misidentified as Spitfires on this occasion.

Kittyhawk IIIs of 450 Squadron lined up at Castel Benito in early 1943.

At 1545 eight Spitfires from 601 Squadron scrambled, and at 14,000 feet three Bf 109s were seen and chased. Reforming, the squadron then spotted Axis aircraft over the sea near Tamet, coming in to attack Buerat from about 12,000 feet; these intruders were identified as 12 Bf 109s and 12 MC.202s. Several Spitfire pilots saw strikes on aircraft, and one parachute was spotted, but the only claim was made by Flg Off Gilbert for a Bf 109 probably destroyed.

Twelve P-40Fs of the 64th Fighter Squadron and 12 of the 65th had also taken off at 1525 for a fighter sweep over the lines, the pilots of these sighting Axis aircraft south-west of Buerat. Lt Byrne was twice attacked, but managed to get a good burst into one of his assailants, but he was hit and wounded, returning to base with 23 bullet holes in his aircraft. As aircraft returned to land, six pilots were ordered to scramble over base at 8,000 feet. They were then directed to Tamet at 12,000 feet where they attacked four MC.202s. One of these was claimed by 1/Lt Beck to have rolled onto its back and crashed into the sea, while other pilots claimed two more damaged. Lt Brandon's aircraft was hit in the coolant system by one bullet, obliging him to force-land ten miles from base; he walked back safely that evening.

Meanwhile the 65th Squadron aircraft also became engaged with enemy fighters, Lt Whittaker claiming one Messerschmitt shot down and Lt Costanzo another just as it was lining up on a Warhawk; other claims were also made for several aircraft damaged, but Lt Weaver's Warhawk was hit by two cannon shells and he crash-landed. Around this time II./JG 77 pilots made claims for no less than nine P-40s over the Buerat area. Four of these were made by Toni Hackl and two by Fw Reinert, who had already submitted two claims during the morning fighting.

At 1540 a big Italian formation approached Tamet, comprising 17 MC.200s and 202s of the 13° Gruppo, led by Magg Lorenzo Viale, escorted by 23 MC.202s of the 18° and 23° Gruppi, led by T.Col Tito Falconi with the 18°'s new commanding officer, Magg Gustavo Garretto (later to become a Generale in the post-war Italian air force) and the 23°'s commander, Magg Luigi Filippi. Nine Spitfires of 92 Squadron were scrambled at 1530 to intercept, led by Flg Off Neville Duke (whose birthday it was). Climbing to 13,000 feet over Tamet, the Spitfire pilots then spotted five MC.202s and dived on them. Four of the Italians dived and one climbed, Duke giving chase to the latter; after a burst struck the aircraft behind the cockpit, it rolled over and the pilot, S.Ten Telleschi, baled out. Duke and Sgt McMahon then flew about for a few minutes before seeing another Macchi below, on which they dived out of the sun. Duke followed it and fired until it crash-landed; this aircraft was flown by Magg Garretto, who became a prisoner, Telleschi being reported as missing. Next day Magg Domenico Camarda took over command of 18° Gruppo.

The pilots of the other MC.202s claimed to have shot down five Spitfires and one probable, plus nine more damaged during this combat which they reported involved 25-30 Spitfires. Those claiming victories included Serg Luigi Gorrini of 18° Gruppo. M.llo Felice Longhi sustained damages to his fighter but managed to return. Meanwhile, 13° Gruppo strafed Tamet landing ground with some success, four aircraft being claimed burnt and nine damaged. Serg Torre was apparently hit by AA and was wounded; he force-landed his MC.200 some distance away and was able to reach Axis lines two days later with the help of some Arabs. At Tamet three Baltimores of 1437 Strategic Reconnaissance Flight were badly damaged, one Hurricane of 73 Squadron, which had just arrived, was burnt out, and a Lysander was destroyed. 2 PRU arrived later in the day, fortuitously missing this attack.

British Claims					
92 Sqn	Flt Sgt R.H.Probert	Spitfire Vb ER224 'U'	Bf 109 Probable	Gheddahia	0940-1100
601 Sqn	Flg Off I.F.Gilbert	Spitfire Vc BR134	Bf 109 Probable	Hamraiet	1545-1700
92 Sqn	Flg Off N.F.Duke	Spitfire Vb EP338 'S'	MC.202	NNW Tamet	1630-1715
92 Sqn	Flg Off N.F.Duke	Spitfire Vb EP338 'S'	MC.202	WSW Buerat	1630-1715

British Casualties	
112 Sqn	Kittyhawk III FR216 shot down Buerat area; Flg Off J.M.S.Crichton PoW
1437 Strat Recce Flt	3 Baltimores badly damaged on the ground at Tamet; one Hurricane of 73 Squadron and one Lysander also

US Claims					
66th FS/57th FG	2/Lt Robert E.Gibson	P-40K '92'	Bf 109G	Buerat-Gheddahia	1030
66th FS/57th FG	2/Lt Robert E.Gibson	P-40K '92'	Bf 109G Damaged	Buerat-Gheddahia	1030
87th FS/79th FG	Lt Lee V.Gossick	P-40F '41'	Bf 109 Damaged	Buerat-Gheddahia	1540
65th FS/57th FG	2/Lt Charles F.Costanzo	P-40F '60'	Bf 109	Buerat-Gheddahia	1540
65th FS/57th FG	1/Lt Roy E.Whittaker	P-40F '45'	Bf 109	Buerat-Gheddahia	1540
87th FS/79th FG	Lt Jessie F.Jory	P-40F '44'	Bf 109 Damaged	Buerat-Gheddahia	1540
64th FS/57th FG	1/Lt William S.Beck	P-40K '13'	MC.202	Tamet	1545
64th FS/57th FG	1/Lt William J.Mount	P-40K '32'	MC.202 Damaged	Tamet	1545
64th FS/57th FG	1/Lt Thomas M.Tilley	P-40K '11'	MC.202 Damaged	Tamet	1545
64th FS/57th FG	2/Lt Robert J.Byrne	P-40K '10'	MC.202 Damaged	10m W Hamraiet	1545

US Casualties	
66th FS/57th FG	P-40F '93' shot down at Tamet 1545, 1/ Lt William B.Williams MiA
64th FS/57th FG	P-40K '26', forced to land by MC.202 at Tamet 1545, 1/ Lt Gerald A.Brandon returned 'Late Arrival Club'
66th FS/57th FG	P-40F '73', Lt James H.Reutersham returned 'Late Arrival Club'
64th FS/57th FG	P-40F '40' crash-landed at base, Lt Edwin R.Weaver
64th FS/57th FG	P-40K '10' damaged by Bf 109 10m W Hamraiet, 2/Lt Robert J.Byrne WiA

German Claims				
4./JG 77	Uffz Bruno Weidlich	Spitfire	25km S Zarzur	0920
4./JG 77	Fw Ernst-Wilhelm Reinert	Spitfire	26km S Hdjem	0921
4./JG 77	Fw Ernst-Wilhelm Reinert	Spitfire	48km SW Zarzur	0924
5./JG 77	Fw Paul August	P-40	22km SSW Buerat	0926
4./JG 77	Fw Ernst-Wilhelm Reinert	P-40	40km SSW Zarzur	0927
4./JG 77	Oblt Heinrich Osswald	P-40	20km NE Zidjen	1444
4./JG 77	Fw Ernst-Wilhelm Reinert	P-40	38km E Zidjen	1455
4./JG 77	Fw Ernst-Wilhelm Reinert	P-40	26km ENE Zidjen	1456
4./JG 77	Uffz Bruno Weidlich	P-40	15km NE Zidjen	1500
5./JG 77	Hptm Anton Hackl	4 P-40s		
6./JG 77	Lt Johann Badum	P-40		
II./JG 77	unstated pilots	6 P-40s		

German Casualties	
6./JG 77	Bf 109G-1 WNr 13 892 damaged in combat 10% NW Zliten

Italian Claims					
95ª Sq, 18°Gr, 3°St CT	Ten Giorgio Solaroli	MC.202	Spitfire	Tamet	1455-
95ª Sq, 18°Gr, 3°St CT	M.llo Felice Longhi	MC.202 MM7894	Spitfire	Tamet	1455-
95ª Sq, 18°Gr, 3°St CT	M.llo Pietro Salvatico	MC.202	Spitfire	Tamet	1455-
95ª Sq, 18°Gr, 3°St CT	Ten Roberto Caetani	MC.202	Spitfire Probable	Tamet	1455-

85ª Sq, 18°Gr, 3°St CT	Ten Mario Melis	MC.202	Spitfire	Tamet	1455-
85ª Sq, 18°Gr, 3°St CT	Serg Magg Luigi Gorrini	MC.202	Spitfire	Tamet	1455-
Italian Casualties					
83ª Sq, 18° Gr, 3° St CT	MC.202 shot down, Magg Gustavo Garretto PoW				
95ª Sq, 18°Gr, 3°St CT	MC.202 MM 7908 failed to return, S.Ten Ferruccio Telleschi MiA				
95ª Sq, 18°Gr, 3°St CT	MC.202 MM 7894 damaged in combat, M.llo Felice Longhi safe				
78ª Sq, 13°Gr, 2°St CT	MC.200 MM 8324 shot down, Serg Giuseppe Torre walked back on 13th				
u/unit	2 CR .42s destroyed by bombs at Sorman				

Tuesday, 12 January 1943

Italian aircraft were again reported approaching Tamet early, and at 0800 eight Spitfires of 1 SAAF Squadron took off to provide top cover for eight more of 145 Squadron. Over Tamet the South Africans became involved in a dogfight with some Bf 109s. Lt Rogan saw four Spitfires with an aircraft lined up behind them; he was just about to formate on this when it opened fire and he recognised it as a Messerschmitt. He fired at this from 250 yards, seeing strikes on the belly whereupon it reared up and fell away towards the sea; Rogan claimed a probable. Both his own and Lt van der Merwe's Spitfires were damaged during this fight, and Lt Paterson did not return. The latter was back at 1300 however, reporting that his cockpit had filled with glycol fumes just before the fight and he had passed out, the Spitfire going down to crash which he survived unhurt.

Meantime, the eight 145 Squadron aircraft were gaining height, but two Spitfires suffered technical trouble and were forced to return to base. The other six reached 10,000 feet over Tamet and orbited up-sun. Eight MC.200s of 13° Gruppo were then seen approaching from the north-west in three vics, covered by Bf 109s; these had just finished strafing the airfield. The Italian pilots saw the Spitfires and broke formation, diving for the sea; the British fighters at once gave chase. At zero feet Sqn Ldr Marples fired a short burst at one Macchi from astern and saw strikes, followed by an explosion and black smoke. After a second burst, the aircraft crashed into the sea one mile from the coast. Marples' own engine then cut and he force-landed in the water; two soldiers watching from the shore swam out and helped get him to land safely. Meanwhile Flg Off Hesketh fired on two Macchis which were flying in line abreast, seeing strikes on both and large pieces falling off; both were reportedly seen to crash into the sea five miles from Tamet. Flt Lt Taylor saw the undercarriage and flaps of the MC.200 which he attacked come down and the aircraft force-landed on the water. Sgt Usher, while diving on the Macchis, saw a Bf 109 shoot past, firing at a Spitfire; he got on the tail, seeing his shells cause pieces to fly off the mainplanes. The 109 pulled up steeply and Usher followed, still firing. The Messerschmitt then shuddered, stalled and went down vertically, at which point he lost sight of it, although he thought he had shot off an aileron. Hesketh and Taylor both saw an aircraft crash into the sea in flames, and Usher was awarded a destroyed although in fact no loss of this nature actually occurred. Ten Giorgio Savoia of 13° Gruppo claimed one Allied fighter shot down, identified as a P-40, but two MC.200s, flown by S.Ten Plinio Pellegrini and Serg Sergio Vanello, were lost.

During the day the Western Desert Air Force began the preliminary phase of a planned attack on the Axis Buerat line, light and medium bombers again beginning to appear over the front. 21 SAAF Squadron had recently arrived at Soluch, and 12 SAAF Squadron now moved to El Gzina for these operations. 250 Squadron moved its Kittyhawks to one of the Hamraiet strips and at 1440 took off on a sweep over Churgia and Tauorga landing grounds, covered by 12 Kittyhawks from 260 Squadron. On the way back, when 15 miles from base, these latter aircraft were bounced by four Bf 109s and Plt Off Thornhill's fighter was badly shot-up by one Messerschmitt which had got on his tail. Two claims for P-40s were made by pilots of 2./JG 77 at this time.

From the north, 12 B-17s of the 97th Bomb Group, escorted by P-38s, attacked Tripoli's Castel Benito airfield, gaining many hits on two hangars, returning crews claiming to have destroyed at least 20 aircraft on the ground. They had actually destroyed six and damaged at least 26, some casualties amongst ground personnel also being reported. MC.202s of 96ª and 97ª Squadriglie were scrambled and chased the formation, claiming two of the American bombers shot down, bringing 4° Stormo its 500th victory. One B-17 was badly hit, but managed to limp back to Biskra, landing long after the rest of the formation. The crews reported that 30 MC.202s had attacked for 20 minutes and they claimed to have shot down 14 of these plus three more probably. In fact all the fighters returned, though five of them were slightly damaged. It seems that other units were involved in the interception, for one MC.200 pilot was wounded and a Bf 109 of 6./JG 77 was reportedly shot down by P-38s 27 miles west of Tripoli, one of the unit's successful pilots, Lt Johann Badum, being killed. (This engagement will also be referred to in Volume 3.)

British Claims

145 Sqn	Flg Off C.R.Hesketh	Spitfire Vb ER650 'G'	2 MC.200s	at sea, 5m NW Tamet l.g.	0805-0920
145 Sqn	Sqn Ldr R.Marples	Spitfire Vb ER166	MC.200	1m at sea, N Tamet l.g	0805-0900
145 Sqn	Flt Lt J.S.Taylor	Spitfire Vb EP880	MC.200	1m at sea, N Tamet lg	0805-0900
145 Sqn	Sgt D.C.Usher	Spitfire Vb ER313	Bf 109	N Tamet lg	0805-0900
1 SAAF Sqn	Lt D.S.Rogan	Spitfire V ER468 'L'	Bf 109G Probable		0820

British Casualties

1 SAAF Sqn	Spitfire V EP655 'O' Lt C.G.Paterson unconscious due to glycol fumes, crashed 10km SSE Sirte; returned same day
1 SAAF Sqn	Spitfire Vb damaged by Bf 109; Lt S.W. van der Merwe
1 SAAF Sqn	Spitfire Vb ER468 'L' damaged; Lt D.S.Rogan
145 Sqn	Spitfire V ER166 Sqn Ldr R.Marples force-landed due to engine failure
260 Sqn	Kittyhawk III badly damaged by Bf 109 15m W Hamreiat; Plt Off Thornhill safe

US Claims

97th BG	gunners claim 14 fighters destroyed and three probables

US Casualties

97th BG	B-17 badly damaged

German Claims

2./JG 77	Obfw Walter Brandt	P-40	1510
2./JG 77	Uffz Hans Jakobi	P-40	1511
II./JG 77	unstated	P-40	

German Casualties

6./JG 77	Bf 109G-2 trop WNr 10727 Yellow 6 + -, shot down by P-38s 45km W Tripoli; Lt Johann Badum KiA
IV./KG zbV 1	Ju 52/3m WNr 5888 40% damaged by bombs at Castel Benito

Italian Claims

77ª Sq, 13°Gr, 2°St CT	Ten Giorgio Savoia	MC.200	P-40	W Tamet	0635-0810
9°Gr, 4° St CT	u/i pilots	MC.202	2 B-17s	Castel Benito	1430

Italian Casualties

82ª Sq, 13°Gr, 2°St CT	MC.200 MM 5127 failed to return 0635-, Serg Sergio Vanello MiA
78ª Sq, 13°Gr, 2°St CT	MC.200 MM 8138 failed to return 0635-, S.Ten Plinio Pellegrini MiA
77ª Sq, 13°Gr, 2°St CT	MC.200 MM 8304 destroyed in landing accident, Serg Stanislao Scabini WiA
77ª Sq, 13°Gr, 2°St CT	MC.200 hit in combat, M.llo Fiore Mastropietro WiA
various units	6 MC.200s destroyed, 20 MC.200s, 4 SM.82s, 1 S.79, 1 BR.20, 1 CR.42 damaged by bombs at Castel Benito, 1430

Wednesday, 13 January 1943

The offensive against the Buerat line by WDAF now got fully underway. Early in the morning almost the whole available WDAF air power took to the air, starting at 0750 when 239 Wing set off to strafe the Churgia road and landing ground. Ten minutes later 18 Baltimores of 21 SAAF Squadron headed for Bir Dufan landing ground, and half an hour later, ten Warhawks each from the 65th and 66th Fighter Squadrons plus 12 Kittyhawks of 112 Squadron, left to escort these bombers, 65th as top cover, 112 Squadron at medium position and 66th Squadron providing close escort. At 0923 12 Spitfires of 92 Squadron were to follow to 'de-louse' the formation as it turned for home.

239 Wing arrived over Churgia and went in to strafe, although claims were restricted to a single Bf 109 and a Fi 156 on the ground there. The wing then flew out at low level but with the loss of one 450 Squadron aircraft which was thought to have hit the ground when leaving the target area. Two more of this unit's aircraft were badly damaged and a fourth was slightly so. The missing pilot, Sgt O'Neil, arrived back on foot two days later.

As the next formation approached Bir Dufan, JG 77 rose in force to defend the airfield, led by Maj Müncheberg, who shot down one of the South African Baltimores, the pilot of which baled out. One Baltimore was seen to go down over Axis territory apparently under control, with a second crash-landing east of Alem el Chel after being damaged by a Bf 109; a third was attacked by three Bf 109s before reaching the target, the top turret gunner being killed and much damage inflicted. The aircraft completed its bombing run and then made for Allied lines, crash-landing at Tamet North. The German pilots also

Merlin-engined Kittyhawk IIas of 3 RAAF Squadron. Such a line-up was probably in preparation for a visit by some of the 'Big Brass'.

claimed a large number of the escort. The 65th Squadron as top cover encountered ten Messerschmitts when flying along the coast road, Capt Clark and Lt Wymond each claiming one shot down, but they noticed the pilot of a 112 Squadron Kittyhawk baling out. This latter unit had met both Bf 109s and MC.202s operating in pairs, one pilot claiming a Bf 109 as a probable which was subsequently confirmed by another. Flg Off Curphey baled out and two more pilots crash-landed.

The 66th Squadron reported seeing more than 20 Axis fighters which they identified as Bf 109Es, Fs and Gs, and MC.202s, and several claims were made for aircraft damaged. Two of this unit's pilots failed to return, 2/Lt McMillan being lost but Lt John C.Kelly baling out apparently behind Axis lines.

> "Kelly was attacked by an unidentified enemy fighter. His Prestone (glycol) system went out, spraying Prestone over his cockpit. He tried to come down, but at 4,000 feet his a/c caught fire. He baled out and landed in a salt marsh near the coast behind enemy lines at about 0945 hours. He made a hard landing and was badly bruised. After disentangling himself from his 'chute, he walked about one mile from his plane and lay down. He saw what appeared to be an enemy patrol at the plane. He remained concealed until 1300 hours and then started to make his way north towards the coast. When near the coast, he saw what appeared to be an Italian infantry patrol, so he turned back. ...he saw what he thought were Arab tents, but on investigation these turned out to be a belly-landed Macchi 202, with two men nearby. These men later turned out to be members of a reconnaissance patrol of the Highland Division. Shortly afterwards, other members of the patrol came up, and he recognised them by their uniforms. He waved his pilot 'chute as a white flag, and then sat down to wait for them. After identifying him, they brought him back to our lines. He returned to his squadron next day." [Extract from the unit diary.]

The Spitfires of 92 Squadron then appeared on the scene and engaged several Messerschmitts and Macchis, but nearly all pilots suffered gun stoppages and only a single claim could be made. As a result of these operations WDAF pilots had made only three claims for aircraft shot down which were confirmed. JG 77 lost one shot down and two damaged of which one force-landed.

During the day Wg Cdr I.R.Gleed, DSO, DFC, who had arrived from England, was attached to 145 Squadron to gain experience of North African conditions prior to taking over 244 Wing. 'Widge' Gleed, author of *Arise to Conquer*, a wartime publication regarding his experiences in France and the Battle of Britain with 87 Squadron during 1940, was a short, but very aggressive pilot who had subsequently led one of the RAF wings flying on the cross-Channel sweeps during 1941. At this time he had claimed some 12 individual victories and three shared.

British Claims					
112 Sqn	Sgt R.A.Wild	Kittyhawk III FR324	Bf 109F	0840-1015	
92 Sqn	Flt Lt C.J.Samouelle	Spitfire Vc BR521	Bf 109 Probable	Churgia	0923-1048

British Casualties	
112 Sqn	Kittyhawk III FR214 'A' ; Flg Off R.G.Sayer shot down
112 Sqn	Kittyhawk III FR320 'J' ; Sgt D.S.Watson shot down
112 Sqn	Kittyhawk III FR195 'F'; Flg Off L.H.Curphey shot down
450 Sqn	Kittyhawk III FR328 left 0745, Sgt G.C.W.O'Neil evaded
450 Sqn	Kittyhawk III FR339 left 0750, badly damaged by Flak at Misurata; Sgt M.C.Harrison safe
450 Sqn	Kittyhawk III FR291 left 0750, badly damaged by Flak; Sgt G.H.Cameron safe
450 Sqn	Kittyhawk FR125 left 0750, damaged Cat I by Flak; Flt Sgt V.J.McFarlane safe
21 SAAF Sqn	Baltimore AL842 MiA
21 SAAF Sqn	Baltimore AG873 damaged by Bf 109s and crashed at Tamet N
21 SAAF Sqn	Baltimore

US Claims					
65th FS/57th FG	1/Lt Gilbert O.Wymond Jr	P-40F '48'	Bf 109	Churgia-Tauorga	0920
65th FS/57th FG	Capt Thomas W.Clark	P-40F '01'	Bf 109	Churgia-Tauorga	0920
86th FS/79th FG	1/Lt Richard P.Morrissey	P-40F '77'	Bf 109 Damaged	Churgia-Tauorga	0945
66th FS/57th FG	1/Lt Robert E.Hoke	P-40F '98'	Bf 109E Damaged	Churgia-Tauorga	1008
66th FS/57th FG	2/Lt Robert E.Gibson	P-40K '71'	Bf 109E Damaged	Churgia-Tauorga	1016

US Casualties	
66th FS/57th FG	P-40F '87', 2/ Lt Cecil M.McMillan Jr MiA
66th FS/57th FG	P-40F '76' shot down, Lt John C.Kelly baled out, picked up by British
65th FS/57th FG	P-40F 'shot down, crash-landed, 1/Lt Edward H.Ellington safe, returned

German Claims				
3./JG 77	Oblt Ernst Laube	P-40	Zarzur	0758
2./JG 77	Uffz Ernst Gronitz	P-40		0835
2./JG 77	Obfw Walter Brandt	P-40		0837
Stab/JG 77	Maj Joachim Müncheberg	Baltimore	15km NE Bir Dufan	0845

(there are possibly 7 more unspecified German claims)

German Casualties	
7./JG 77	Bf 109G-2 trop WNr 10646 White 3 shot down by P-40 Bir Dufan; Fw Heinz Furth MiA
8./JG 77	Bf 109G-2 trop WNr 10595 25% damaged in combat P-40s and force-landed Tauorga; Fw Michel safe
9./JG 77	Bf 109G-2 trop WNr 10739 Yellow 5 25% damaged in combat P-40s N Bir Dufan; Uffz Luicke safe
KGr zbV 800	Ju 52/3m WNr 6714 60% damaged by bombs at Castel Benito

Thursday, 14 January 1943

Fighting over the Buerat area intensified, proving very costly for the WDAF. First off at 0825 were a dozen 450 Squadron Kittyhawks which patrolled over the forward area. Two Bf 109s were encountered and six pilots attacked these, all reporting strikes, although no claims resulted. At 1050 36 P-40Fs from all three squadrons of the 57th Fighter Group provided escort for 18 bombers to Gheddahia, ten Spitfires of 1 SAAF Squadron being scrambled five minutes later to give top cover to this formation. When 12 miles south-west of Tamet six Bf 109s were seen below, diving on the Americans, and were at once attacked. As had happened to 92 Squadron on the previous day, many Spitfires suffered cannon stoppages, although on this occasion one Messerschmitt was claimed shot down and two probably so. As Lt Vialls dived on another, he saw a P-40F attack it and it disintegrated.

Among the Americans claims were made for two Bf 109s and an MC.202. The latter was claimed by Capt Yates of the 66th at 1120: "Leading top cover had just set course about 320 degrees and were just south-west of Tamet when Commando called and said that six plus Bogies were heading our way; also said that friends were in the area. As the enemy fighters circled behind at our level, the Spitfires jumped them, and we turned about. I met a Macchi 202 head-on and fired at about 150 yards; it exploded in my face, the right wing came off, and it went down in flames." Ten minutes later Maj Glade Bilby of the 64th

Squadron reported: "We were engaged before reaching the target. I got in bursts on an Me 109 and saw it crash-land 12 miles inland south of Buerat over our lines. Lt Crowell turned into a Me 109, got in good bursts, and spun off. The Me made a split S and I gave same e/a another burst. Lt Crowell had recovered from the spin and saw the e/a hit the deck and burst into flames." The two pilots received joint credit for this success.

During the raid 21 SAAF Squadron lost another Baltimore; it was believed that this had been hit by heavy Flak and was seen going down under attack by a Bf 109. The pilot and one gunner were later reported safe, the other gunner having been killed and the observer wounded.

At 1120 239 Wing began taking off to escort another raid, this one by 18 Bostons. The escort was even bigger on this occasion, including a dozen Kittyhawks each from 250, 260, 450 and 3 RAAF Squadrons. The formation flew out to sea, then turned south to attack Bir Dufan airfield again. Bf 109s and MC.202s, some 20 fighters in all, began a series of attacks; some Messerschmitts were reported to have yellow spinners. The Kittyhawks were hit very hard indeed; five pilots of 3 RAAF Squadron, including the commanding officer, Sqn Ldr Bobby Gibbes, failed to return as did four of 450 Squadron and two of 250 Squadron. However, at least three of the pilots survived unhurt and returned later, including Gibbes. Numerous claims for probables and damaged fighters were submitted by the returning Allied pilots, but these included only one that was to receive confirmation. Bobby Gibbes recorded in this diary:

> "I saw one of my squadron Kittyhawks losing height below the formation being attacked by three 109s. I ordered 450 to send a section down to assist, but nobody went. Again, I repeated my urgent order, but evidently they could not hear me as no aircraft went to the help of the Kitty. I had no option other than to leave the bombers and to do what I could for the aircraft below which was taking a frightful hammering. I had a height advantage, and because of it, a lot of speed. I caught the lead 109 at about 500 feet, just as the Kittyhawk was about to go in, and at close range from astern, gave it a burst. It rolled onto its back and dived vertically down, and it would not have been able to recover from that low altitude, and must have gone straight in. I had been too late to save the Kitty, so I started to climb up at high boost after the bomber formation. Due to my initial speed, it took some little time before the other two 109s were able to catch up and attack.
>
> "We had long before learned a procedure for avoiding 109 attacks from astern, and would fly with our controls slightly off balance with a little left or right rudder, correcting with opposite aileron control. This would result in our aircraft skidding slightly to one side of its flight path, and bullets aimed from astern would miss, due to our non-apparent side movement. We would watch the attack coming in and would wait until we saw the smoke from its guns before taking further avoiding action. Normally, this meant a violent forward ram of the stick and a hard turn away. We would watch the attacking aircraft which would not be able to turn with us, and as it overshot, we would pull back behind it, and fire a burst at it as it sped away. We would then be able to continue on course while awaiting any further attack.
>
> "On this occasion, I had avoided several attacks and was gaining height rapidly beneath the formation. At this juncture, one of the pilots above suddenly saw my aircraft flying below with the 109s after it, and screamed out, 'look out down below'. As it happened, I was watching the lead 109 closing on a further attack, but for the moment had lost sight of the second aircraft. The urgent call made me panic, and thinking that I was in danger from this aircraft, I turned further than I had intended, and too late, I saw that the second aircraft was well out of effective range, but I had committed myself to a 360 degree turn, which carried me through the first aircraft's zone of fire. A 20 millimetre shell ploughed into my engine which started to vibrate badly, so realizing that I had 'had it', I rolled onto my back and dived steeply for the ground, about 6 or 7,000 feet below. I hoped to put the aircraft down before the 109s could catch me.
>
> "My near vertical dive did not distance me much from the two enemy aircraft, and on pulling out just above the ground, I saw that the 109s were closing again. I was only a few feet above the desert and I cut my switches, but was still travelling at high speed. I was afraid that if I turned away from the coming attack, my body would not be protected by the armour plate behind my seat, or that a shell strike on an elevator or aileron could spell 'curtains'. I had to let the German pilots know that I was finished as a potential enemy, so I pushed my aircraft onto the ground. I was still indicating over 300 miles an hour when I hit, and I must have bounced for three or four miles before

my machine started to settle in a long slide on its belly. The two 109s did not continue with their attack but pulled out to one side. Before coming to rest, I climbed out onto the wing on the downward side from the Messerschmitts, hoping to get protection from the engine if they did come in and strafe. Both of the pilots passed me on the starboard side after I came to rest, and either waved or saluted. I had been shot down by gentlemen."

Meanwhile 250 Squadron met six Messerschmitts south-east of the target, Flt Lt Troke turning his flight into them which caused them to break away. The bombers made their run despite the Axis fighters, but the rest of 250 Squadron was broken up. Plt Off Russell fought for 125 minutes with several Messerschmitts, his aircraft being hit seven times before he was able to return alone at zero feet with a head wound. Flg Off Newton stayed with the bombers, making six attacks on Bf 109s, claiming one badly damaged. During the approach to the target area six of 260 Squadron's aircraft had to return early with various problems, accompanied by two wingmen; the remaining four aircraft were twice attacked by a pair of Bf 109s, whilst after the bombing 12 more were engaged. Although all the pilots fired, no claims resulted.

601 Squadron scrambled ten Spitfires at 1500 to 'de-louse' another Kittyhawk formation when this was west of Gheddahia. Here six or more Bf 109s were seen at 15,000 feet, harassing the Curtiss fighters; one of these was claimed damaged. Finally at 1640 3 RAAF Squadron sent eight Kittyhawks on an armed reconnaissance over the Gheddahia area, once again Bf 109s appearing. In the dogfight which followed the aircraft became separated. Three pilots saw a Messerschmitt on the tail of one Kittyhawk and Plt Off Austin failed to return; Plt Off Bayly claimed one shot down. At the end of the day WDAF had lost at least 13 Kittyhawks plus one more badly damaged. In response claims had been made for seven Bf 109s and one MC.202 shot down, plus the usual tally of four probables and 11 damaged.

JG 77 had enjoyed a field day, claims totalling 16 P-40s, two Spitfires and two B-25s, the Regia Aeronautica's 18° Gruppo adding a claim for a Spitfire probably shot down by Ten Solaroli and one damaged by M.llo Longhi. The German unit's casualties amounted to three Bf 109s shot down and one damaged 70%, plus one more slightly damaged on the ground at Bir Dufan by bombs. In the cases of the three lost aircraft, all were thought to have been shot down by Spitfires, which clearly was not the case. The worst loss of the day for JG 77 was Obfw Walter Brandt of 2.Staffel, victor of 37 combats. He was badly wounded, losing a leg; he was awarded the Ritterkreuz two months later and subsequently recovered sufficiently to return to combat with an artificial leg on home defence duties. The Italians suffered no casualties on this occasion.

Obfw Walter Brandt, having claimed ten victories over Malta, added seven more in Africa, the last on 14 January raising his personal tally to 37. On this latter date, however, he was shot down and badly wounded, losing one leg. He would return to active duty with an artificial limb later in the war, adding claims for 20 more aircraft by the close of hostilities.

British Claims

1 SAAF Sqn	Lt H.F.Smith	Spitfire V ..649 'B'	Bf 109F Probable	2m SW Tamet	1115
1 SAAF Sqn	Lt D.T.Gilson	Spitfire V ..903 'S'	Bf 109F Damaged	12m SW Tamet	1118
1 SAAF Sqn	Lt McC.E.S.Robinson	Spitfire V ..960 'H'	Bf 109F	2m SW Tamet	1118
450 Sqn	Flt Lt A.Glendinning	Kittyhawk III FL902	Bf 109F Damaged	Bir Dufan l.g.	1120-2335

450 Sqn	Flt Lt A.Glendinning	Kittyhawk III FL902	MC.202 Damaged	Bir Dufan l.g.	1130-1335
450 Sqn	Sgt J.L.Cummins	Kittyhawk III FR337	Bf 109F Damaged	Bir Dufan North area	1130-1335
450 Sqn	Sgt E.C.House	Kittyhawk III FR346	Bf 109F Damaged	Bir Dufan l.g.	1130-1335
450 Sqn	Flt Sgt V.J.McFarlane	Kittyhawk III FR125	Bf 109F	Bir Dufan l.g.	1130-1335
450 Sqn	Plt Off R.W.Winn	Kittyhawk III FR123	Bf 109 Damaged	Bir Dufan l.g.	1130-1306
450 Sqn	Plt Off R.W.Winn	Kittyhawk III FR123	MC.202 Damaged	Bir Dufan l.g.	1130-1335
3 RAAF Sqn	Flt Sgt R.N.B.Stevens	Kittyhawk IIa FL270 'Y'	Bf 109F/G Probable	Bir Dufan l.g.	1245
3 RAAF Sqn	Sgt J.H.Hooke	Kittyhawk IIa FL294 'H'	Bf 109F/G Probable	Bir Dufan l.g.	1200
250 Sqn	Flt Sgt N.C.Holmes	Kittyhawk III FR342 'X'	Bf 109 Probable	15m SE Bir Dufan	1200
250 Sqn	Flg Off G.F.Newton	Kittyhawk III FR261	Bf 109G Damaged	15m SE Bir Dufan	1200
601 Sqn	Flt Lt D.F.Westenra	Spitfire Vc ER280	Bf 109 Damaged	NW Gheddahia	1500-16005
3 RAAF Sqn	Sgt R.H.Bayly	Kittyhawk IIa FL270 'Y'	Bf 109F/G	Gheddahia area	1640-1705

British Casualties

250 Sqn	Kittyhawk III FR305 left 1120, shot down by Bf 109s nr Churgia 1200; Sgt B.C.H.Kirkman MiA
250 Sqn	Kittyhawk III FR301 'R' left 1120, shot down by Bf 109s nr Churgia 1200; Sgt D.M.Webster
250 Sqn	Kittyhawk III FR323 'Y' left 1120 badly damaged by Bf 109 nr Churgia 1200; Plt Off N.G.Russell WiA
250 Sqn	Kittyhawk III FR342 'X' left 1120 damaged by Bf 109 force-landed at Tamet at 1215; Flt Sgt N.C.Holmes safe
450 Sqn	Kittyhawk III FR279 'P' left 1130 shot down near Bir Dufan; Sgt G.H.Cameron KiA
450 Sqn	Kittyhawk III FR329 'W' left 1130 shot down near Bir Dufan; Sgt L.A.Frost evaded
450 Sqn	Kittyhawk III FR345 'D' left 1130 shot down near Bir Dufan; Flt Sgt A.D.Nicolson evaded
450 Sqn	Kittyhawk III FR415 'K' left 1130 shot down near Bir Dufan; Sgt M.C.Harrison KiA
3 RAAF Sqn	Kittyhawk IIa FL323 'V' left 1135 shot down near Bir Dufan; Sqn Ldr R.H.M.Gibbes evaded
3 RAAF Sqn	Kittyhawk IIa FL330 left 1135 shot down near Bir Dufan; Plt Off L.J.Weatherburn PoW
3 RAAF Sqn	Kittyhawk IIa FL345 'X' left 1135 shot down near Bir Dufan; Flg Off A.H.Tonkin KiA
3 RAAF Sqn	Kittyhawk IIa FL346 left 1135 shot down near Bir Dufan; Flg Off W.G.Diehm KiA
3 RAAF Sqn	Kittyhawk IIa FL363 left 1135 shot down near Bir Dufan; Sgt N.R.Caldwell PoW rescued
3 RAAF Sqn	Kittyhawk IIa FL277 'Q' left 16.40 shot down by Bf 109 near Gheddahia; Flg Off A.Austin KiA

US Claims

65th FS/57th FG	1/Lt Lee V.Gossick	P-40F '44'	Bf 109 Damaged	Gheddahia	1100-1205
66th FS/57th FG	Capt William J.Yates	P-40F '80'	MC.202	Cheridan-Gheddahia	1120
64th FS/57th FG	Maj Glade B.Bilby	P-40K '27'	Bf 109	Gheddahia	1130
64th FS/57th FG	Maj Glade B.Bilby	P-40K '27 }	Bf 109	Gheddahia	1130
64th FS/57th FG	2/Lt Glenn L.Crowell	P-40K '34' }			
65th FS/57th FG	1/Lt Richard W.Kimball	P-40F	Bf 109	Gheddahia	1510

US Casualties

85th FS/79th FG	P-40 '25' crash-landed about 1100; Lt William G.Abbott

German Claims

Stab I./JG 77	Hptm Heinz Bär	P-40		0839
2./JG 77	Obfw Walter Brandt	P-40		1020
Stab I./JG 77	Hptm Heinz Bär	2 B-25s	N Tamet	1043 & 1044
Stab I./JG 77	Lt Heinz-Edgar Berres	B-25	N Tamet	1045
1./JG 77	Fw Horst Schlick	P-40		
I./JG 77	unstated pilots	3 P-40s		
7./JG 77	Obfw Johann Pichler	P-40	NW Bir el Gheddahia	1110
9./JG 77	Lt Wolfgang Ernst	P-40	W Bir el Gheddahia	1110
Stab/JG 77	Maj Joachim Müncheberg	P-40	25km SE Bir Dufan	1112
Stab/III./JG 77	Hptm Kurt Ubben	P-40	SW Zliten	1115
Stab/JG 77	Maj Joachim Müncheberg	2 P-40s	Bir Dufan airfield	1117 & 1124
9./JG 77	Lt Wolfgang Ernst	P-40		1120
8./JG 77	Oblt Emil Omert	P-40		1125
7./JG 77	Obfw Johann Pichler	P-40		1126
Stab I./JG 77	Hptm Heinz Bär	2 P-40s		1432 & 1437
Stab/III./JG 77	Hptm Kurt Ubben	P-40		1625
5./JG 77	Hptm Anton Hackl	2 P-40s		
Stab II./JG 77	Uffz Erich Müller	2 P-40s		

German Claims

II./JG 77	unstated pilots	2 P-40s

German Casualties

2./JG 77	Bf 109G-2 trop WNr 10744 Black 4, combat with P-40 50km SW Buerat; Obfw Walter Brandt baled, WiA
2./JG 77	Bf 109G-2 trop WNr 10731 Black 11, combat with Spitfire, 45km S Buerat; Uffz Hans Jacobi PoW
3./JG 77	Bf 109G-2 trop WNr 10517 Yellow 5, combat with Spitfire 45km SE Buerat; Uffz Hans Hempfling MiA
3./JG 77	Bf 109G-2 trop WNr 10553 hit in combat 70% damaged E Zarzur
3./JG 77	Bf 109G-2 WNr 13770 15% damaged by bombs at Bir Dufan
4.(H)/12	Bf 109F-4 WNr 8805 shot down in combat and crash-landed in the desert; Fw Josef Budzinski returned on foot
III./StG 3	Ju 87D-1 WNr 2593 hit in combat, crash-landed at Bir Dufan, 30% damaged; crew safe

Italian Claims

81ª Sq, 6°Gr, 1°St CT	Ten Cesare De Panizza	MC.202	P-38	Maknassay-Mezzouma
95ª Sq, 18°Gr, 3°St CT	Ten Giorgio Solaroli	MC.202	Spitfire Probable	10km S Bir Dufan
95ª Sq, 18°Gr, 3°St CT	M.llo Felice Longhi	MC.202	Spitfire Damaged	10km S Bir Dufan

Friday, 15 January 1943

Following two very costly days in the air, 8th Army's assault on the Buerat line began on 15th, 7th Armoured Division and 51st Highland Division opening the attack. Rather than fight a major battle here, Rommel at once began withdrawing his forces to a line at Homs/Tarhuna.

Early in the afternoon 12 MC.202s of 4° Stormo were scrambled to intercept 12 B-17s from the US 12th Air Force which were raiding Tripoli again. One (or three according to other sources) was claimed shot down, four members of the crew baling out and falling into the sea. One Macchi was also shot down, Serg Magg Andraghetti being lost. He was the last 4° Stormo pilot to be killed in North Africa. In a further raid IX Bomber Command B-24s bombed the harbour at Tripoli, claiming hits on vessels and on the shore areas near the harbour. The Italian freighter *Agostino Bertani* of 8,329 tons was hit and sunk. One bomber was lost to fighters. RAF Liberators, under the operational control of US Command, hit a road junction at Tripoli. During the night Tripoli was attacked again, this time one B-24 being claimed shot down by the AA defences.

More Italian units were departing at this time, 2° Stormo headquarters having moved to Zavia on the previous day ready for repatriation; 159° Gruppo would leave on the 16th. Amongst WDAF units, 2 SAAF and 4 SAAF Squadrons moved to El Hamraiet where they would soon be joined by 5 SAAF Squadron. The two RAF Baltimore squadrons of 232 Wing were taken off operations, flying back to Derna to LG.86 for a period of training.

Following the temporary loss of Bobby Gibbes, Flt Lt R.J.Watt took over temporary command of 3 RAAF Squadron pending his return. In 112 Squadron Sqn Ldr Billy Drake, DSO, DFC & Bar who had led the squadron for several months claiming 15 victories during this period, ended his tour, being replaced by Sqn Ldr G.W.Garton, DFC.

US Claims

343rd BS/98th BG	gunners aboard B-24Ds '776/O', '761/R' and '896/T'	Bf 109	Tripoli	1150-1155
409th BS/93rd BG	gunners aboard B-24D 41-23689 'U'	Bf 109 Probable	Tripoli	1318-1322
328th BS/93rd BG	gunners aboard B-24D 41-23990	Bf 109	Tripoli	1318-1322
328th BS/93rd BG	gunners aboard B-24D 41-23990	Bf 109 Damaged	Tripoli	1318-1322

US Casualties

409th BS/93rd BG	B-24D 41-23724 'Flying Cock', damaged by Flak, pilot Lt Llewellin Brown landed safely at Berka, four crew baled out 30m E Tripoli and were lost

German Casualties

8./StG 3	Ju 87D-3 WNr 2622 S7+CS shot down at Buerat; Uffz Ernst Epple/Uffz Fritz Strehse KiA
Erp/KG 30	Ju 88A-4 WNr 140019 destroyed by own forces at Bir Dufan

Italian Claims

9°Gr, 4° St CT	unidentified pilots	MC.202	B-17	Tripoli	1215-130
AA at Tripoli			B-24	Tripoli	night

Italian Casualties

97ª Sq, 9°Gr, 4°St CT	MC.202 failed to return from a mission over Tripoli, Serg Magg Anselmo Andraghetti MiA

Saturday, 16 January 1943

The Afrika Korps was now in full retreat from Buerat with 8th Army units in close pursuit as the Axis troops made for the Tunisian frontier. 601 Squadron despatched 12 Spitfires to escort 65th Squadron P-40Fs to Gheddahia at 0955. Over Buerat 12 Bf 109s attacked but were driven off. Soon after midday 12 more of the unit's Spitfires escorted the 66th Squadron to Sedada where eight Bf 109s were seen and engaged. Sgt Tolle claimed hits on the engine of one with cannon shells and on the wings of another with machine-gun bullets. He was credited with a probable. During an attack on Sedada a Ju 87 of III./StG 3 was shot down by AA, the pilot baling out to become a prisoner; the gunner was killed. However, one of 73 Squadron's night-operating Hurricanes was also lost to Axis Flak over Tauorga.

Two MC.202s of 83ª Squadriglia were scrambled at 0930 to intercept a formation of Spitfires. An enemy fighter was claimed, but Ten Tommasi's aircraft was hit in the cockpit and the pilot was wounded and forced to crash-land. He was then rescued and taken back to base by an armoured car. During the afternoon 3° Stormo moved to Castel Benito to replace 4° Stormo which was leaving for Italy, in the defence of Tripoli; 15° Stormo Assalto headquarters and 46° Gruppo moved from Sorman to Zuara.

British Claims

601 Sqn	Flg Off W.M.Whitamore	Spitfire Vc ER212	Bf 109 Damaged	Buerat	0955-1120
601 Sqn	Sgt A.A.Toller	Spitfire Vc BR472	Bf 109 Probable	S Sedada	1335-1440
601 Sqn	Sgt D.V.Watts	Spitfire Vc EP869	Bf 109 Damaged	S Sedada	1335-1440

A patrol of MC.202s of 23° Gruppo ready to take off. Cap Solaro was piloting the leading aircraft.

British Casualties

73 Sqn	Hurricane IIc HV516 shot down by Flak at Tauorga; Flg Off S.P.Davies (or Davis) KiA

German Casualties

8./StG 3	Ju 87D-1 WNr 2564 S7+DS AA 8km SSE Sedada, pilot baled; Uffz Gerhard Bode PoW; Uffz Horst Aktories KiA

Italian Claims

83ª Sq, 18°Gr, 3°St CT	Ten Carlo Tommasi	MC.202	Spitfire Probable	Tauorga	0930-
83ª Sq, 18°Gr, 3°St CT	unstated	MC.202			

Italian Casualties

77ª Sq, 13°Gr, 2°St	MC.200 MM 8835 damaged on landing at Sorman, S.Ten Gregorio Cinti slightly wounded
83ª Sq, 18°Gr, 3°St CT	MC.202, force-landed, Ten Carlo Tommasi slightly wounded

Sunday, 17 January 1943

With the withdrawal continuing, the Axis fighter were pulled further back, or departed. Stab and III./JG 77 moved to join II.Gruppe which had now gone to El Asaba, while I.Gruppe went to Castel Benito which the Stab would also use for actual operations.

The last sortie in Libya by 4° Stormo occurred on this date when some pilots took part in an uneventful interception of 12 B-17s raiding Tripoli. Then both ground and air echelons of this long-serving unit departed for home, flying every available aircraft: MC.202s, MC.200s, S.79s, S.82s and even a Ca.309 Ghibli and a SAI touring plane. According to Italian records, during this second North African tour 4° Stormo pilots took part in 133 aerial combats, claiming 289 enemy aircraft shot down (501 since the start of hostilities). The remaining MC.202s were passed to 3° Stormo and 13° Gruppo, the latter receiving seven of these fighters from this source. Eight more followed next day. 3° Stormo immediately went into action, the newly arrived MC.202s of this unit being scrambled at 1640 to intercept a formation of Liberators flying at 25,000 feet to bomb Tripoli's harbour. At that height the MC.202s were much less effective than at lower level and the pilots failed to press home their attacks effectively. The intense return fire hit some fighters, among them those of Solaro and Solaroli.

Italian Casualties

70ª Sq, 23°Gr, 3°St CT	MC.202 damaged in combat, Cap Claudio Solaro safe
95ª Sq, 18°Gr, 3°St CT	MC.202 damaged in combat, Ten Giorgio Solaroli safe

Monday, 18 January 1943

After the relative inaction of the previous day, WDAF was again involved in several engagements on 18th, flying many sorties in support of the advancing 8th Army. Early in the day 12 Kittyhawks of 250 Squadron with others of 260 and 3 RAAF Squadrons, took off to attack motor transport along the Beni Ulid-Tarhuna road. Here 20 plus Axis fighters were reported and the 239 Wing leader, Wg Cdr 'Billy' Burton, who was leading the 3 RAAF Squadron top cover on this occasion, claimed a Bf 109 shot down – one of six which were attacked. The wing had now begun operating from Sedada, the squadrons flying in over a three-day period.

Twelve 450 Squadron aircraft flew an armed reconnaissance over the Tarhuna area during the early afternoon, attacking MT, but from this operation Sgt Gregory failed to return; he had been shot down by Flak and was to get back safely on foot on the 22nd. At 1655 250 Squadron provided six Kittyhawks as medium cover to 11 from 450 Squadron, again hunting MT in the Tarhuna area. Over the target four Bf 109s were encountered; one 450 Squadron aircraft failed to return and one from 250 Squadron was badly damaged.

Aircraft from Algeria again crossed into the southern area during the afternoon, 13 B-17s of the 97th Bomb Group escorted by 33 P-38s of the 1st Fighter Group, flying down to attack the tempting concentrations of aircraft on the ground at Castel Benito. Between 15-20 Messerschmitts and Macchis intercepted over the target and as the formation made for home. The 27th Fighter Squadron turned into the attackers, Capt Walch and Lt Shahan each claiming an MC.202 shot down while six other pilots claimed to have damaged aircraft. Final credits for the group were four destroyed, one probable and seven damaged. However, Lt Burton Weil was shot down at 1517. Two P-38s were claimed by pilots of 4./JG 77.

Nine MC.202s of the 3° Stormo, flying aircraft handed over by 4° Stormo, made a head-on attack on the left-hand aircraft of the leading vic of B-17s. Ten Guglielmo Specker of the 83ª Squadriglia, 18° Gruppo, pulled up high after this initial attack and saw the bomber begin to fall behind, dropping from

An MC.202 of 83ª Squadriglia, 18° Gruppo, 3° Stormo under repair in the open. This unit had exchanged its MC.200s for the newer aircraft during the closing weeks of 1942.

On 18 January 1943, four 3° Stormo pilots were awarded the German Eiserne Kreuz II.Klasse. From the left are: Ten Solaroli di Briona, Ten Specker, Cap Solaro and Ten Marinone.

20,000 feet to 10,000. As it was going down he attacked twice more, firing 370 rounds of 12.7mm ammunition into the stricken aircraft, from which the crew began to bale out. Specker followed it down as it completed a full 360 degree turn before reaching the ground; the wing struck first, folding up to the first engine, at which point the bomber blew up. Specker landed to find that only three of the original nine MC.202s were still serviceable. Three more pilots from 18° Gruppo also claimed a B-17 between them, but these may all have attacked the same bomber as Specker; nine crew members were captured next day. During the fight the gunners of the 87th had put in a much more modest claim for one fighter destroyed and one probable. However, no Axis fighters were shot down during this engagement (details of this raid will also be included in Volume 3.) During the day Obfw Otto Schultz of II./JG 51 claimed two B-17s, but neither of these claims were confirmed. It is possible that this unit had attacked the 97th Bomb Group formation as it crossed southern Tunisia on its return to Biskra (see Volume 3).

Later in the day more four-engined bombers, identified by the Italians as Lancasters, but possibly 9th Air Force B-24s, approached from the north and bombed Castel Benito again. The three remaining serviceable MC.202s of 3° Stormo took off, but two had to return early due to technical trouble. Ten Specker in the remaining fighter chased six bombers as they left the area, but when he tried to attack one, found that there was no pressure in the bottles of compressed air which actuated his guns, and he had to break off and return to base.

With nightfall B-25s, SAAF Bostons and Baltimores attacked Castel Benito once more, one 12 SAAF Squadron Boston force-landing south of Sirte. Following these further raids I./JG 77 moved to Ben Gardane. This proved to be a very rough strip with many loose stones on the surface which caused a high level of damage to propellers during take-offs and landings. Eight MC.202s of 3° Stormo and one S.82 were reported destroyed by the Allied raids.

During the day two TacR Hurricanes of 40 SAAF Squadron on a sortie from Sedada, became lost, Lt Black ultimately having to force-land due to fuel shortage. The 57th Fighter Group, meanwhile, was on the move again, going forward to Darragh West.

British Claims

239 Wing	Wg Cdr H.F.Burton	Kittyhawk IIa FL347	Bf 109	Tarhuna	0840-

British Casualties

250 Sqn	Kittyhawk III badly damaged by Bf 109 Tarhuna area; Sgt P.L.V.Palethorpe safe
450 Sqn	Kittyhawk III FL894 'D' left 1600 shot down by Bf 109 Tarhuna area; Sgt R.J.Prowse WiA
450 Sqn	Kittyhawk III FR129 'F' left 1430 shot down by Flak at Tarhuna; Sgt A.H.Gregory safe
12 SAAF Sqn	Boston III force-landed

US Claims

27th FS/1st FG	Capt Walch	P-38	MC.202		
27th FS/1st FG	Lt Shahan	P-38	MC.202		
343rd BS/98th BG	tail gunner aboard B-24D '803/E'		Bf 109 Probable	Tripoli	1340- 2140
343rd BS/98th BG	gunners aboard B-24D '659/V'		Bf 109 Probable	Tripoli	1340- 2140
343rd BS/98th BG	waist gunners aboard B-24D '913/N'		FW 190	Tripoli	1340- 2140

US Casualties

27th FS/1st FG	P-38 shot down in southern area; Lt Burton Weil PoW
64th FS/57th FG	P-40K '11' hit by Flak; Capt Robert A.Barnum returned
340th BS/97th BG	B-17F 41-24385 lost to fighters in Tripoli area; Lt Russel S.Wilkin and crew PoW
344rd BS/98th BG	B-24 41-11786 'C' damaged by Flak, chased by fighters, crashed 47m S Malta; 1/Lt Herman W.Lewis and nine MiA

German Claims

4./JG 77	Fw Ernst-Wilhelm Reinert	P-38	28km SSW Azizia	1417
III./JG 77	Obfw Heinrich Hackler	P-38		1422
7./JG 77	Obfw Johann Pichler	B-17		1424
4./JG 77	Uffz Bruno Weidlich	P-38	15km SW Gar el Hag	1427
Flak		B-17	Bir Ngen	

German Casualties

Stab I./JG 77	Fi 156C trop Black << destroyed by bombs at Castel Benito
2./JG 77	Bf 109G-2 trop WNr 10671 destroyed by bombs at Castel Benito
2./JG 77	Bf 109G-1 WNr 13834 30% damaged by bombs at Castel Benito

3./JG 77	Bf 109G-2 trop WNr 10738 destroyed by bombs at Castel Benito
Wustennotst	Fi 156 C-3 WNr 5140 destroyed by bombs at Castel Benito
8./JG 77	Bf 109G-2 trop WNr 10580 Black 7 shot down nr Tarhuna; Uffz Richard Förster baled, injured
I./SchG 2	2 BF 109 F-4s crash-landed at Bir Dufan: WNr 8374 15% damaged, WNr 7588 60% damaged
I./SchG 2	BF 109 F-2 WNr 12732 crash-landed at Bir Dufan, destroyed, pilot safe
I./SchG 2	BF 109 F-4 WNr 8777 crash-landed at Zarzur, destroyed, pilot safe

Italian Claims

83ª Sq, 18°Gr, 3°St CT	Ten Guglielmo Specker	MC.202	B-17	60km S Zuara
95ª Sq, 18°Gr, 3°St CT	M.llo Felice Longhi	MC.202		
85ª Sq, 18°Gr, 3°St CT	Cap Giulio C.Giuntella	MC.202	B-17	60km S Zuara
85ª Sq, 18°Gr, 3°St CT	Serg Domenico Balduzzo	MC.202		
AA at Tripoli			four-engined bomber night	

Italian Casualties

211ª Sq, 50°Gr BT	Cant.Z.1007bis failed to return, pilot S.Ten Antonino Sansone, copilot M.llo Mario Arrighetti and crew MiA
81ª Sq, 6°Gr, 1°St CT	MC.202 MM 9549 damaged in landing accident, Ten Cesare De Panizza WiA
83ª Sq, 18°Gr, 3°St CT	MC.202 MM 9564 and MM 7415 destroyed by bombs at Castel Benito
95ª Sq, 18°Gr, 3°St CT	MC.202 MM 7894 destroyed by bombs at Castel Benito
74ª Sq, 23°Gr, 3°St CT	MC.202 MM 8094 destroyed by bombs at Castel Benito
70ª Sq, 18°Gr, 3°St CT	MC.202 MM 9057 destroyed by bombs at Castel Benito
95ª Sq, 18°Gr, 3°St CT	MC.202 MM 8381 and MM 8377 damaged by bombs at Castel Benito and then set on fire
74ª Sq, 23°Gr, 3°St CT	MC.202 MM 8117 damaged by bombs at Castel Benito and then set on fire
u/unit	S.82 destroyed by bombs at Castel Benito and four more slightly damaged

Tuesday, 19 January 1943

The 51st Highland Division captured Homs and WDAF squadrons were rapidly on the move again. 112 and 250 Squadrons went to Bir Dufan Main, and 1 SAAF Squadron to Wadi Sirru. At 0750 23 Kittyhawks from 450 Squadron flew a reconnaissance over the Tarhuna area where intense Flak so damaged Flt Sgt Taylor's aircraft that he had to come down in 'no mans' land, a second Kittyhawk was badly damaged. Taylor returned to the squadron next day. 40 SAAF Squadron moved from Sedada to Darragh West and from here Lts Nicholson and Brokensha flew a TacR during which both pilots were shot down.

Just after midday 239 Wing took off in force, 3 RAAF Squadron leading, followed by two dozen aircraft from 260 and 450 Squadrons, targets south of Tarhuna being bombed. Flak was again heavy and one 260 Squadron pilot had to crash-land. During the afternoon B-24s were intercepted near Castel Benito, pilots of 4./JG 77 claiming two shot down, a third being claimed by Serg Dusi of 23° Gruppo CT south of Zuara. The 376th Bomb Group lost one such bomber. A fighter identified as a P-40 was also claimed by the Germans in the Tarhuna area at much the same time. This may have been one of the missing TacR Hurricanes.

3° Stormo's pilots moved from Castel Benito to Medenine (Tunisia). One of the last 4° Stormo's pilots departing for Italy, Ten Enrico Moretto of 96ª Squadriglia, flying an S.81 'hack' from Tripoli to Castelvetrano with two fitters and all the unit's documentation aboard, failed to reach Sicily and was reported as MiA. 2° Stormo staff left Libya for Castelvetrano on transport aircraft.

British Claims

73 Sqn	Sgt D.H.Thomas	Hurricane IIc HL769	Ju 87 Damaged	N Castel Benito	2325-0150

British Casualties

260 Sqn	Kittyhawk III Sgt G.D.Tuck crash-landed due to Flak
450 Sqn	Kittyhawk III FR114 left 0750, shot down by Flak Tarhuna area; Flt Sgt A.W.J.Taylor
450 Sqn	Kittyhawk III shot down by Flak Tarhuna area; Plt Off Winn safe
40 SAAF Sqn	Hurricane Lt Nicholson FTR
40 SAAF Sqn	Hurricane Lt Brokensha FTR

US Casualties

344th BS/376th BG	B-24 41-11786 shot down, pilot 1/Lt Daron Harden, co-pilot 1/Lt Herman W.Lewis and entire crew KiA
328th BS/93rd BG	B-24 41-23672 'Double Trouble', shot down by Flak, 1/Lt Benjamin F.Riggs and seven MiA, two PoW

German Claims

4./JG 77	Fw Ernst-Wilhelm Reinert	B-24	10km SE Castel Benito	1605
4./JG 77	Uffz Rudolf Flindt	B-24	10km SE Castel Benito	1605

German Claims

5./JG 77	Hptm Anton Hackl	P-40	5km NE Tarhuna	1610

German Casualties

9./JG 77	Bf 109G-2 trop WNr 10758 destroyed on the ground by bombs at Malacha
III./JG 77	Bf 109G-2 destroyed on the ground by bombs at Malacha
I./SchG 2	BF 109 F-4 WNr 13150 crash-landed at Asabaa, destroyed; pilot safe

Italian Claims

70ª Sq, 23°Gr, 3°St CT	Serg William Dusi MC.202	B-24	20km S Zuara

Italian Casualties

4° St CT	S.81 'hack' failed to reach Sicily, Ten Enrico Moretto and crew MiA

Wednesday, 20 January 1943

Ten P-40Fs of the 65th Squadron flew out north-west at 1144, passing beyond Azizia, which was their target. Turning, the aircraft then went back across to bomb MT. After making their bombing runs the American fighters were engaged by four Bf 109s of II./JG 77, at one of which Lt Whittaker fired several long bursts. He saw smoke and one leg of the undercarriage fall down as the aircraft turned onto its back; he claimed this shot down and a second damaged. Lt Kimball reported:

> "I was in the lead section on a dive-bombing show against MT on the road near Castel Benito. As we dived on the target, four Me's were observed patrolling the road below us. After dropping our bombs, I headed for an Me climbing up at right angles to my line of flight. He saw me and turned into me but before he could get a shot at me I had put a long burst into him from ¾ front. I made a turn after passing him and saw him spiral off into a dive and hit the deck, bursting into flames."

Capt Sneed also sought to attack the four Messerschmitts:

> "I fired 60 rounds out of two guns with the other four failing. Did not see signs of hit on first plane. Continued to circle and engaged another firing a long burst from astern. Pieces flew off as I went by. I had to pull up and to the right to miss the 109. Lt Kimball saw the pilot bale out... One Me 109 from astern attack knocked Lt Kimball out of the air as we were heading home."

At least one of these claims must have been for Lt Kurt Pressler's Messerschmitt, the only one apparently lost in this combat; the pilot was wounded.

Lt Kimball was then attacked from astern by Lt Reinert, and was shot down; Reinert in fact claimed two P-40s, one at 1130 and another four minutes later. During the day 450 Squadron had three aircraft shot down by Axis light Flak when engaged in ground-strafing sorties. 601 Squadron moved forward to Darragh North.

In the opposite direction, eight MC.200s of 13° Gruppo which had taken off at 0845, strafed and dropped small-calibre bombs on British tanks in the Tarhuna area. All returned safely, but Serg Magg Rovero Abbarchi badly damaged his MC.200 in a landing accident.

US Claims

65th FS/57th FG	Capt Marshall Sneed	P-40F '44'	Bf 109	Gorina-Azizia	1220
65th FS/57th FG	2/Lt Richard W.Kimball	P-40F '53'	Bf 109 Damaged	Gorina-Azizia	1220
65th FS/57th FG	1/Lt Robert L.Metcalf	P-40F '50'	Bf 109 Damaged	Gorina-Azizia	1220
65th FS/57th FG	1/Lt Roy E.Whittaker	P-40F '43'	Bf 109 Probable	Gorina-Azizia	1220
65th FS/57th FG	1/Lt Roy E.Whittaker	P-40F '43'	Bf 109 Damaged	Gorina-Azizia	1220

US Casualties

65thFS/57th FG	P-40F '53' shot down, 2/Lt Kimball baled out, rescued by British tank unit, consequently was first American pilot into Tripoli

German Claims

4./JG 77	Fw Ernst-Wilhelm Reinert	2 P-40s	12 & 3km E Tarhuna	1130 & 1134

German Casualties

1./JG 77	Bf 109G-2 trop WNr 10544 destroyed by bombs at Ben Gardane
2./JG 77	Bf 109G-3 trop WNr 10521 destroyed by bombs at Ben Gardane
3./JG 77	Bf 109G-2 trop WNr 10664 blown up at Castel Benito
4./JG 77	Bf 109G-2 trop WNr 10784 shot down by P-40 NW Azizia; Lt Kurt Pressler WiA

I./SchG 2	BF 109 F-1 WNr 6603 crash-landed at Ben Gardane, 85% damaged; pilot safe
4.(H)/12	BF 109 F-4 WNr 7614 destroyed by own forces at Ben Gardane
Kurierst Afrika	Ju 52/3m WNr 7175 destroyed by own forces at Ben Gardane
Italian Casualties	
77ª Sq, 13°Gr, 2°St CT	MC.200 MM 6887 destroyed on landing accident, Serg Magg Rovero Abbarchi safe

Thursday, 21 January 1943

51st Highland Division broke through the last Axis defences at Corradini and reached a point only 40 miles east of Tripoli. This push brought a renewal of activity in the air, beginning when 11 Kittyhawks from 250 Squadron and 12 from 260 Squadron, all led by Wg Cdr Burton, set course for Castel Benito. The aircraft of the latter unit each carried six 40lb bombs and a long-range tank. Nine Axis fighters were seen near Castelverde, and at Sidi Bilial these made their first attack, coming in from the rear. At Castel Benito 260 Squadron bombed from 2,000 feet and the opposing fighters came in again as the Kittyhawks flew past Tripoli, many individual combats ensuing. Plt Off Stone of 250 Squadron claimed a Bf 109 as probably destroyed, but two of the unit's aircraft were shot down in flames, although both pilots survived. They both returned three days later, confirming that Stone's 109 definitely crashed.

When over Sidi Bilial landing ground again, four MC.202s were spotted and these were attacked at 1,500 feet by 260 Squadron, one being claimed destroyed. Two fighters identified as Bf 109s then attacked the formation and one Kittyhawk was seen to belly-land. The Italian fighters were from 13° Gruppo, five Macchis having taken off on an armed reconnaissance over the lines at 0805. Attacked by the 260 Squadron Kittyhawks, their pilots claimed one shot down and one damaged, but one MC.202 suffered severe damage.

Meanwhile ten Spitfires of 1 SAAF Squadron took off at 0930 to patrol as far as Tarhuna at 8,000 feet. Cloud forced them down to 6,000, and near Castelverde at 1000 hours, three MC.202s were spotted, 1,000 feet above. This trio, again from 13° Gruppo, had taken off on a second reconnaissance patrol, undertaken between 0900-1015. Attacked by what they thought were P-40s, the Italian pilots claimed one probable for the loss of one MC.202 flown by S.Ten Sagramoso, while a second crash-landed, Serg Battista being wounded. Upon sighting this trio, the commanding officer's section of the South African unit turned to port, climbed and attacked, two being claimed shot down with the third as a probable. The squadron recorded that it had gone through a bad patch since the loss of the previous commander, Peter Metelerkamp on 13 December, but the feeling was that Sqn Ldr Olver had really pulled the unit together again, these victories restoring confidence considerably.

After four months flying Hurricanes with 33 Squadron, Flg Off Milton Jowsey moved to 92 Squadron at the start of 1943. On 21 January 1943 he claimed a Ju 87 shot down as his first victory.

At 0955 11 Kittyhawks of 3 RAAF Squadron provided cover for others from 250 Squadron to attack the Zuara-Tripoli road, but when over enemy-held territory, Sgt Goulder's aircraft was reportedly hit by Flak and he carried out a crash-landing. Twelve Spitfires from 92 Squadron, led by Wg Cdr John Darwen, took off at 1255 to patrol over the Tripoli-Castel Benito area at 18,000 feet. Near the latter location Ju

87s, which were thought to be Italian-flown, were seen bombing Allied troops and the squadron went down to attack the Stukas which were actually aircraft of the Luftwaffe's StG 3. Having dived to 1,000 feet, Flg Off Duke had got ahead of the rest of the Spitfires. He opened fire on one Ju 87, then swung his fire onto another, hitting the starboard wing root. This aircraft burst into flames, spiralled down, and exploded on hitting the ground. This was Duke's 12th victory. Two others were claimed shot down and two probably so, although Luftwaffe records indicate only the one loss from which the crew baled out but were killed. However, it appears that a second Ju 87D crashed between Azizia and Castel Benito, a third crash-landing south-west of the latter aircraft, the crews of both these bombers returning unhurt. This had been the last operational sortie in North Africa for Flt Lt C.J. 'Sammy' Samouelle, DFC, whose tour now ended. In his 12 months with the squadron he had risen from sergeant to flight commander, claiming seven confirmed, six probables and six damaged. His place as flight commander was taken by Neville Duke.

Flt Lt Samouelle served with 92 Squadron from February 1942 to 21 January 1943. On this latter day, the last of his tour, he shot down a Ju 87D of III./StG 3 as his seventh confirmed victory.

Twelve P-40Ks of the 64th Squadron, 57th Fighter Group, with two pilots of the 85th Squadron, 79th Fighter Group, took off at 1230 on a ground-strafing mission to Castel Benito. They strafed the north end of the field from east to west from an altitude of 25 to 50 feet. Lt J.S.Wilson shot-up a Ju 52/3m and the aircraft started to burn. Capt G.D Mobbs sprayed two CR.42s and one large aircraft on the ramp; he also hit some barrels of oil that started to burn. Lt R.K.Douglas shot-up a Ju 52/3m in one of the hangars, and also hit a large aircraft toward the south end of the field. One P-40 was damaged by light-arms fire and required a wing change. All aircraft returned safely to base at 1340. P-38s of the 1st Fighter Group again appeared over the far south of Tunisia on this date, 20 aircraft of the 71st Squadron sweeping over the area and claiming the destruction of 65 vehicles on the Gabes-Medenine-Ben Gardane road (see also Volume 3).

More Kittyhawks were in the air at 1421 when 12 450 Squadron aircraft strafed anything that moved on the Zuara-Tripoli road. On the way back to base they attacked Castel Benito where at least 50 aircraft were seen; three of which were left in flames, seven more being claimed damaged. Kittyhawks again attacked Castel Benito at 1545, this time with poor results, as nine Spitfires from 145 Squadron which were led by Wg Cdr Gleed, patrolled over the airfield at 8,000 feet. On the Spitfires' third run over the area an Fi 156 was seen taking off and Gleed dived down, whereupon it landed hurriedly; he was prevented from destroying it by a concentrated display of Flak. At 1600 the Spitfire pilots saw more Kittyhawks attack and this time a He 111 was set on fire. At 1705 12 Kittyhawks from 112 Squadron attacked the airfield, claiming to have destroyed two MC.202s and damaged a third.

During the afternoon one other combat took place, but the identity of the WDAF unit involved has not been discovered. S.Ten Zuccarini of 13° Gruppo took off alone in an MC.200 at 1320 to cover the road from Sorman to Medenine. He reported being attacked by about 15 P-40s, fire from which hit and damaged his aircraft, causing him to crash-land, the Macchi being destroyed. He survived unhurt, however. Bombers were also active during the day, 12 Bostons of 12 SAAF Squadron attacking the Ben Gardane-Zelten road, one aircraft being lost. Ready for further night operations, 73 Squadron now moved up to Bir Dufan. It had been a much better day for WDAF.

British Claims

260 Sqn	Flt Sgt W.E.Stewart	Kittyhawk III	MC.202	nr Sidi Billial l.g.	0840-1015
250 Sqn	Plt Off J.W.A.Stone	Kittyhawk III FR355 'T'	Bf 109	10m S Castel Benito	0930
1 SAAF Sqn	Capt J.H.Gaynor	Spitfire V ..682 'F'	MC.202	Castel Benito-Tarhuna	1045
1 SAAF Sqn	Sqn Ldr P.Olver	Spitfire V ..318 'A'	MC.202	Castel Benito-Tarhuna	1045
1 SAAF Sqn	Lt D.S.Rogan	Spitfire V ..116 'N'	MC.202 Probable	Castel Benito-Tarhuna	1045
92 Sqn	Flg Off B.Baker	Spitfire Vb ER224 'V'	Ju 87 Probable	SE Castel Benito	1255-1430
92 Sqn	Flg Off M.E.Jowsey	Spitfire Vb AR494 'D'	Ju 87	S Castel Benito	1255-1430
92 Sqn	Flt Lt C.J.Samouelle	Spitfire Vb ER328	Ju 87	S Castel Benito	1255-1430
92 Sqn	Sgt H.Patterson	Spitfire Vb EP894 'Y'	Ju 87 Probable	W Castel Benito	1255-1430
92 Sqn	Flg Off N.F.Duke	Spitfire Vb ER220 'R'	Ju 87	S Castel Benito	1400

British Casualties

3 RAAF Sqn	Kittyhawk IIa FL262 belly-landed in enemy territory due to Flak; Sgt K.Goulder
250 Sqn	Kittyhawk III FR344 left 0840, collided; Flg Off F.L.Latham baled and returned safe
250 Sqn	Kittyhawk III P-40K 42-45794 left 0840, collided; Sgt A.F.Nitz baled and returned safe
250 Sqn	Kittyhawk III FR331 'F' left 1520, badly damaged by Flak at Castel Benito; Flt Sgt A.W.A.Orr safe
250 Sqn	Kittyhawk III FR327 left 1520, badly damaged by Flak at Castel Benito; Wt Off F.V.Pledge safe
73 Sqn	Hurricane IIc HL972
12 SAAF Sqn	Boston III FTR

US Claims

64th FS/57th FG	Ju 52 destroyed, Ju 52 damaged, 2 CR.42s damaged, one large plane damaged on the ground at Castel Benito

German Casualties

7./StG 3	Ju 87D-3 WNr 2726 S7+DR shot down by Spitfire 30km SSW Tripoli; two baled; Uffz Karl Stammberger/Uffz Josef Grosinger KiA
III./StG 3	Ju 87D-3 WNr 2990 shot down by Spitfire, crashed 30km SSW Tripoli; crew safe
III./StG 3	Ju 87D-3 WNr 2526 shot down by Spitfire, crashed SW Castel Benito; crew safe
Fl Ber FlK Tunis	Fi 156C-3 destroyed by own forces at Castel Benito

Italian Claims

77ª Sq, 13°Gr, 2°St CT	Ten Giorgio Savoia	MC.202	P-40	over enemy lines	0805-0850
82ª Sq, 13°Gr, 2°St CT	Cap Guglielmo Arrabito	MC.202			
78ª Sq, 13°Gr, 2°St CT	S.Ten Ernesto Sagramoso	MC.202 MM 7955	P-40 Probable	Tarhuna	0900-1015
78ª Sq, 13°Gr, 2°St CT	Serg Giovanni Battista	MC.202 MM 9390			

Italian Casualties

78ª Sq, 13°Gr, 2°St CT	MC.202 MM 7955 shot down in combat 0900-, S.Ten Ernesto Sagramoso MiA
78ª Sq, 13°Gr, 2°St CT	MC.202 MM 9390 hit in combat 0900-, crash-landed, Serg Giovanni Battista WiA
77ª Sq, 13°Gr, 2°St CT	MC.200 MM 8336 hit in combat, crash-landed 1420, S.Ten Gian Mario Zuccarini safe
18ª Sq, 27°Gr, 8°St BT	SM.84 failed to return, Cap Vittorio Dallio and crew MiA
18ª Sq, 27°Gr, 8°St BT	SM.84 failed to return, S.Ten Mario Sanvilli and crew MiA
18ª Sq, 27°Gr, 8°St BT	SM.84 failed to return, Ten Antonio Di Nardo and crew MiA

Friday, 22 January 1943

The last German troops evacuated Tripoli during the day, and as the 8th Army pushed on forward fighting flared again in the air. Four Kittyhawks of 260 Squadron were off very early at 0600 on a sortie to strafe and bomb various targets. A landing ground believed to be Medenine South was attacked, more than 40 aircraft being spotted on the ground there, Flt Sgt Thomas shooting-up a He 111.

About two hours later 24 Kittyhawks from 450 and 3 RAAF Squadrons took off on an armed reconnaissance in the Pisida-Zuara area, where bombs were dropped. On leaving the area the Australian pilots encountered 11 MC.202s from 13° Gruppo over the coast. These, led by Magg Lorenzo Viale, were escorting two S.79s which were carrying the commander of 5ª Squadra, Gen Bernasconi, and senior officers on board from Sorman to Gabes (0715-0810), the Gruppo also being in the process of moving to the latter base. The Kittyhawks attacked at once, two 3 RAAF Squadron pilots each claiming to have damaged an S.79 (the Australians thought that three of these aircraft were present, rather than the two which were involved). Sqn Ldr Gibbes (now back with the unit) attacked one Macchi which broke away sharply and was seen making for land at low speed, while Flt Sgt Hankey shot the cockpit hood off another which went down in an inverted spin, a large splash being seen in the sea. Plt Off Winn of 450

Squadron also shot down one Macchi and Flt Sgt McQueen became the third pilot to claim to have inflicted damage to one of the bombers. In fact all three MC.202s were shot down, two of them crash-landing, the pilots suffering some wounds. Ten Savoia was severely wounded and belly-landed; he was rescued by a German column and was flown to Sicily in a transport aircraft, but died in Palermo hospital on 12 March. He was posthumously promoted Capitano and decorated with a Medaglia d'Oro in Memoriam. The surviving 13° Gruppo pilots claimed three P-40s shot down and it is possible that one was also claimed by the gunners in one of the S.79s, both of which arrived safely in Tunisia.

During this engagement 450 Squadron's Sgt Stanley was seen to crash-land at 150mph with smoke trailing from his aircraft, which broke up; nevertheless, he survived and returned safely to his unit two days later. Two of the 3 RAAF Squadron aircraft collided during the fight, one pilot being killed, the other managing to land his damaged aircraft back at base. This dramatic clash proved to be the last combat in Africa for 2° Stormo CT.

On a later operation in the early afternoon the same two Australian units strafed the coast road near Zuara, but were attacked by four Bf 109s. Sgt Righetti, who was lagging, was shot down and baled out, with Flg Off Russell's aircraft damaged and he was slightly wounded. Flt Lt Ritchie fired at a Messerschmitt and believed that he had hit it, but made no claim. There seems little doubt that the two aircraft hit were those targeted by Maj Müncheberg, who claimed one P-40 from which the pilot baled out and a second ten minutes later south of Sorman, which he reported belly-landed, the port wing breaking off.

At 1627 the Australians were once more in the air, this time attacking shipping near Zuara. Five Bf 109s were observed approaching a landing ground and these were jumped out of the sun by 450 Squadron, pilots of this unit claiming three shot down and one damaged. One pilot of 5./JG 77 was shot down and killed in this area, with a second 30% damaged. During the day Stab and II./JG 77 moved to Zuara, while on the Allied side of the lines 60 SAAF Squadron flew in to Darragh from Marble Arch. 40 SAAF Squadron received the very welcome news that it was soon to be re-equipped with Spitfire Vs for its TacR work.

British Claims

450 Sqn	Flt Sgt D.N.McQueen	Kittyhawk III FR419	3 eng e/a		0752-1030
450 Sqn	Plt Off R.W.Winn	Kittyhawk III FR341	MC.202		0752-1032
3 RAAF Sqn	Sqn Ldr R.H.Gibbes	Kittyhawk IIa FL334 'L'	MC.202	Pisida-Zuara	0920
3 RAAF Sqn	Flt Sgt E.Hankey	Kittyhawk IIa FL2921	MC.202	Pisida-Zuara	0920
450 Sqn	Flt Lt A.Glendinning	Kittyhawk III FR254 }	Bf 109F	Zuara	1627-1822
450 Sqn	Flt Lt G.B.Johns	Kittyhawk III FL894 }			
450 Sqn	Sgt K.Marrows	Kittyhawk III FR196	Bf 109F Damaged	Zuara	1627-1822
450 Sqn	Flt Lt F.R.Schaaf	Kittyhawk III FR341	Bf 109F	Zuara	1627-1828
450 Sqn	Flt Lt F.R.Schaaf	Kittyhawk III FR341 }	Bf 109F	Zuara	1627-1822
450 Sqn	Flt Sgt D.G.Minchin	Kittyhawk III FR416 }			

British Casualties

3 RAAF Sqn	Kittyhawk IIa FL235 crashed due to collision; Sgt A.Willis
3 RAAF Sqn	Kittyhawk IIa FL356 damaged in collision; Sgt Jones
3 RAAF Sqn	Kittyhawk IIa FL367 shot down; Sgt Righetti baled out
3 RAAF Sqn	Kittyhawk IIa damaged; Flg Off Russell slt WiA
450 Sqn	Kittyhawk III FR318 left 0752, crash-landed and broke up due to Flak Pisida area; Sgt J.Stonely MiA. returned on 24th

German Claims

Stab/JG 77	Maj Joachim Müncheberg	P-40	10km SE Zuara	1255
Stab/JG 77	Maj Joachim Müncheberg	P-40	30km S Sorman	1305
Stab I./JG 77	Hptm Heinz Bär	2 P-38s		1515 & 1516

German Casualties

5./JG 77	Bf 109G-2 WNr 10693 shot down 7 miles W Zuara; Uffz Werner Hennig KiA
7./JG 77	Bf 109G-2 WNr 10735 30% damaged by enemy fire near Asabaa
III./JG 77	Bf 109G-2 WNr 10659 destroyed on ground by bombs at Castel Benito
I./SchG 2	Bf 109F-4 Black 8 destroyed by own forces at Malacha
III./SchG 2	2 Bf 109E-7 WNrs 3434 and 6096 destroyed by own forces at Malacha
I./SchG 2	Bf 109F-4 WNr 10051 crash-landed at Ben Gardane, 35% damaged

Italian Claims					
78ª Sq, 13°Gr, 2°St CT	Ten Camillo Luglio	MC.202	2 P-40s	Sorman-Gabes	0725-0810
78ª Sq, 13°Gr, 2°St CT	S.Ten Felice Figus	MC.200	P-40	Sorman-Gabes	0725-0810
S.79s	gunners		P-40	Sorman-Gabes	0725-0810

Italian Casualties	
77ª Sq, 13°Gr, 2°St CT	MC.202 MM 7922 hit in combat crash-landed, Magg Lorenzo Viale WiA
77ª Sq, 13°Gr, 2°St CT	MC.202 MM 7929 hit in combat crash-landed, Ten Giorgio Savoia WiA, died 12 March
77ª Sq, 13°Gr, 2°St CT	MC.202 MM 9118 hit in combat crash-landed, Serg Magg Rovero Abbarchi WiA
77ª Sq, 13°Gr, 2°St CT	MC.202 MM 9543 unserviceable, set on fire at Sorman

Saturday, 23 January 1943

Tripoli fell into Allied hands at last, though the harbour was found to be heavily demolished, both by the actions of the Axis before they left, and by the bombing of the RAF and USAAF. Having achieved the immediate objective, operations by WDAF were considerably curtailed as the squadrons prepared to begin the move to the newly-occupied Castel Benito airfield complex. For the moment the main activity would be focussed on central and southern Tunisia (see Volume 3).

German Claims			
Stab I./JG 77	Hptm Heinz Bär	P-40	1140

German Casualties	
4.(H)/12	BF 109 F-4 WNr 7456 destroyed by bombs at Castel Benito
4.(H)/12	BF 109 F-4 WNr 13255 destroyed by own forces at Castel Benito

Sunday, 24 January 1943

Soon after 1500 239 Wing took off, all four squadrons flying a fighter-bomber mission to strafe Ben Gardane landing ground – the first attack by the Kittyhawks on a target on Tunisian soil. Here 15 Bf 109s of I./JG 77 were machine-gunned on the ground, four being badly damaged; after leaving the target a Ju 88 was seen flying west and was attacked by two pilots of 450 Squadron and was shot down. One Kittyhawk was lost and a second badly damaged.

Following this raid the wing moved to Castel Benito, joined by 40 SAAF Squadron aircraft; 2 PRU moved to Bir Dufan. I./JG 77 withdrew to Gabes South. The Italians, with 3° Stormo now using Medenine, also suffered from a severe bombing attack which destroyed three MC.202s and damaged two others. Next day 13° Gruppo passed its remaining six serviceable Macchis to 3° Stormo as it prepared to leave for Italy. The unit's unserviceable MC.200s were left with repair workshops at Gabes. By the end of the month all the unit's personnel would have been transported home by air. Ten Mario Melis and Serg Carlo Gardan of 85ª Squadriglia escorted an S.79 carrying Gen Ugo Cavallero, head of staff of Italian forces, from Medenine to Sfax.

British Claims				
450 Sqn	Flt Lt A.Glendinning	Kittyhawk III FR419	Ju 88 (shared)	1200-1245
450 Sqn	Flt Sgt D.N.McQueen	Kittyhawk III FL893		

British Casualties	
450 Sqn	Kittyhawk III FR341 left 1530, seen leaving target trailing white smoke; Plt Off R.Winn MiA, 1200-1245
450 Sqn	Kittyhawk III FR285 left 1530, badly damaged by Flak; Flt Sgt A.D.Nicholson safe, 1200-1245 (one of these aircraft was FR341)
US Casualties	
86th FS/ 79th FG	P-40 '74' damaged by Flak near Zuara, belly-landed, 2/Lt Robert T.Minett returned

German Casualties	
1./JG 77	Bf 109G-2 trop WNr 10743 White 8 damaged 40% by bombs at Ben Gardane
1./JG 77	3 Bf 109G-2 trops damaged by bombs at Ben Gardane
1.(F)/121	Ju 88D-1 WNr 430154 shot down in combat and crashed N Sabratha; crew safe
Italian Casualties	
95ª Sq, 18° Gr, 3°St CT	3 MC.202s destroyed by bombs at Medenine
95ª Sq, 18° Gr, 3°St CT	2 MC.202s damaged by bombs at Medenine

The wreck of an MC.202 of 79ª Squadriglia, 6° Gruppo, 1° Stormo. Operated from Pantelleria, the unit resumed operations in North Africa at the end of 1942.

Monday, 25 January 1943

601 Squadron was provided with the first Spitfire Vs fitted to carry bombs to be employed in North Africa.

German Claims				
Stab I./JG 77	Hptm Heinz Bär	2 P-40s		1235 & 1238
Flak		P-40	Zuara	

Tuesday, 26 January 1943

Command of 145 Squadron passed from Sqn Ldr Roy Marples to Lance Wade. During the day one of 40 SAAF Squadron's TacR Hurricanes failed to get back from a sortie. The pilot, Lt van der Poel, returned on foot four days later. Whilst attempting to scramble from Matmata, two Bf 109s of 7./JG 77 collided, one pilot being killed and the other injured.

British Casualties	
40 SAAF Sqn	Hurricane FTR; Lt van der Poel MiA
German Casualties	
7./JG 77	Bf 109G-2 WNr 14210, Oblt Ludwig Theopold, and Bf 109G-2 trop WNr 10802, Lt Ernst Buhrow collide during scramble and both aircraft destroyed; Theopold KiFA and Buhrow injured

Wednesday, 27 January 1943

At 1520 ten Kittyhawks of 3 RAAF Squadron took off to attack a pair of ships off the coast north of Ben Gardane. Six-eight aircraft were seen low over the water east of Zuara and the Australian pilots climbed into the clouds and jettisoned their bombs. Various pilots fired at Bf 109s but no claims were made although one Messerschmitt was reported to have suffered damage to its left aileron. One Kittyhawk failed to return. One claim for a P-40 in the Zuara area was made by Oblt Laube of 3./JG 77 at 1454; during the same general time span Hptm Heinz Bär, the I.Gruppe Kommandeur, claimed three and Hptm Kurt Ubben one – some of the latter may have been operating from bases to the north and west, and may not have been WDAF units (see Volume 3).

Twelve MC.202s of 3° Stormo took off from Medenine on a strafing mission; Serg Garavaldi force-landed and was picked up by a German Fi 156. Ten Tommasi's aircraft overtuned on landing and he sustained serious injuries to his back; he was evacuated to Italy two days later.

British Casualties

3 RAAF Sqn	Kittyhawk IIa FL392 left 1520, shot down over sea off Ben Gardane; Sqn Ldr R.J.Watt MiA

German Claims

Stab I./JG 77	Hptm Heinz Bär	3 P-40s		1448, 1501 & 1505
3./JG 77	Oblt Ernst Laube	P-40	2km NW Zuara	1454
Stab III./JG 77	Oblt Kurt Ubben	P-40		

German Casualties

9./JG 77	Bf 109G-2 trop WNr 10850 30% damaged in combat E El Hamet; pilot safe

Italian Casualties

83ª Sq, 18°Gr, 3°St CT	MC.202 overturned on landing at Medenine, Ten Carlo Tommasi badly wounded
74ª Sq, 23°Gr, 3°St CT	MC.202 crash-landed in desert, Serg Rolando Garavaldi safe

Thursday, 28 January 1943

German Claims*

Stab/JG 77	Maj Joachim Müncheberg	P-40	5km SE Tarhuna	1740
1./JG 77	Fw Horst Schlick	P-38		
I./JG 77	unstated	P-38		
I./JG 77	unstated	B-25		

*For full details see Volume 3.

Friday, 29 January 1943

I./JG 77 now moved to Matmata, where it joined III.Gruppe.

British Casualties

260 Sqn	Kittyhawk I ET581

Saturday, 30 January 1943

7 SAAF Wing now began moving forward ready to resume operations. Initially their new base was going to be in the Darragh complex, near Bir Dufan. 2 PRU despatched a flight forward to Castel Benito, but at the start of the next month this unit was re-named 680 Squadron as part of a general re-numbering of photo-reconnaissance units which all became squadrons. For these duties 60 SAAF Squadron was now provided with two De Havilland Mosquitos.

Sunday, 31 January 1943

German Claims*

8./JG 77	Oblt Emil Omert	2 P-40s	1243 & 1248
8./JG 77	Obfw Eduard Isken	P-38	1244
9./JG 77	Lt Wolfgang Ernst	P-40	1255

*For full details see Volume 3.

German Casualties

8./JG 77	Bf 109G-2 trop WNr 10 637 Black 8 shot down Limaguess area; Lt Friedrich Grunewald baled, safe

February 1943

The biggest change of nomenclature was the renaming of the Afrika Korps to become I Italian Army. This was commanded by Generale Giovanni Messe, who took over command from Rommel. The latter should have become leader of Armee Gruppe Afrika, but at this moment he was to return to Germany due to ill health, and possibly due to the supposedly derogatory remarks he had been making regarding the quality and performance of Italian troops. The events leading up to this period and those occurring to the north in Tunisia which now brought a considerable lull further south as 8th Army moved into positions to the south of the Mareth Line, will be fully detailed in Volume 3. Suffice to say here that for WDAF at this time it proved a good opportunity to gain some respite and begin preparing for the next major assault which all knew must come soon.

Movements continued on both sides of the line, most notably I. and III./JG 77 to Gabes on 1 February and then on to Fatnassa on the 3rd to operate in the main to the north and west for the immediate time being. 239 Wing was delighted to receive a visit from the British prime minister on the 4th. Winston

Churchill was to see each of the squadrons, now all based at Castel Benito, for which purpose he was to remain with the wing for a couple of days. Making the best of the large numbers of abandoned aircraft at their new location, 3 RAAF Squadron managed to get a Caproni Ghibli serviceable for use as a squadron 'hack', and 112 Squadron managed similarly in repairing an S.81.

Monday, 1 February 1943

By this date 3 RAAF Squadron had arrived at Castel Benito. 680 Squadron moved to LG.219 with 17 Spitfires, three Beaufighters, four Hurricanes and an Electra, however several detachments would be sent to other airfields including Castel Benito.

Wednesday, 3 February 1943

During the day before Churchill's visit, 250 Squadron despatched a dozen Kittyhawks at 1605 to attack shipping near the coast. When returning a floatplane identified as an He 115 was spotted moored in Pisida harbour. This was strafed by Flt Lt 'Nobby' Clarke and left smoking. Next day this squadron received a new commanding officer when Sqn Ldr Hancock completed his tour; Flt Lt G.B.Johns was posted in from 450 Squadron with a commensurate promotion.

German Claims

8./JG 77	Obfw Eduard Isken	P-40	1647

Thursday, 4 February 1943

Two MC.202s of 18° Gruppo, flown by Ten Giorgio Solaroli and M.llo Felice Longhi, were scrambled at 1415 to intercept a formation of bombers heading for Gabes airfield. Longhi's aircraft failed to start, so Solaroli took off alone. He encountered an isolated twin-engined bomber, identified as a Marauder, and attacked it repeatedly, claiming to have shot it down.

Italian Claims

95ª Sq, 18° Gr, 3° St CT	Ten Giorgio Solaroli	B-26	W El Hamma	1415-1515

Friday, 5 February 1943

The Kittyhawks of 239 Wing were again active, a dozen 250 Squadron aircraft making a fighter-bomber attack on transport vehicles west of Ben Gardane between 1400-1430. After the bombing, the top cover was attacked by nine Bf 109s. Flt Lt Pennick fired seven bursts at one of these and it went down vertically from 7,000 feet, giving the appearance that the pilot had been hit; Pennick then attacked two more and claimed one damaged. Flt Sgt Orr engaged two Messerschmitts, attacking one head-on at 5,000 feet; he claimed this as a probable after bullets appeared to enter the engine and the aircraft broke away in a shallow dive, pouring white smoke. He then claimed hits on the wing root, believing that he had caused damage. Intense Flak was encountered and Sgt Palethorpe's aircraft was badly damaged. During this encounter Uffz Weidlich of 4./JG 77 claimed one P-40 shot down near Ben Gardane.

Another 12 Kittyhawks, this time from 112 Squadron, took off at 1515 to attack MT and guns at Ras Agadir. Engaged in a dogfight with Bf 109s here, pilots claimed one probable and one damaged but lost Sgt Lecours, with a second aircraft damaged. 4./JG 77's Fw Reinert claimed two P-40s at this time, but one of Stab II./JG 77's Bf 109Gs was 40% damaged when north-west of Ras Agadir in combat with P-40s.

British Claims

250 Sqn	Flt Sgt A.A.W.Orr	Kittyhawk III FL892 'F'	Bf 109G Probable	W Ben Gardane	1330-1505
250 Sqn	Flt Sgt A.A.W.Orr	Kittyhawk III FL892 'F'	Bf 109G Damaged	W Ben Gardane	1330-1505
250 Sqn	Flt Lt H.G.S.Pennick	Kittyhawk III FR348	Bf 109G	W Ben Gardane	1330-1505
250 Sqn	Flt Lt H.G.S.Pennick	Kittyhawk III FR348	Bf 109G Damaged	W Ben Gardane	1330-1505
112 Sqn	Sgt R.De Bourke	Kittyhawk IIIFR130	Bf 109 Probable	Ras Agadir	1515-1650
112 Sqn	Sgt R.De Bourke	Kittyhawk IIIFR130	Bf 109 Damaged	Ras Agadir	1515-1650

British Casualties

250 Sqn	Kittyhawk FL887 damaged Cat II by Flak, W Ben Gardane area 1330-1505; Sgt P.L.V.Palethorpe safe
112 Sqn	Kittyhawk FL730 FTR Ras Agadir 1515-1650 ; Sgt J.G.R.Lecours MiA,

112 Sqn	Kittyhawk FR317 damaged Cat II, Ras Agadir 1515-1650; Flg Off T.Livingston safe			
German Claims				
4./JG 77	Uffz Bruno Weidlich	P-40	15km NW Ben Gardane	1327
4./JG 77	Fw Ernst-Wilhelm Reinert	P-40	15km NW Ben Gardane	1503
4./JG 77	Fw Ernst-Wilhelm Reinert	P-40	8km E Ben Gardane	1507
German Casualties				
Stab II./JG 77	Bf 109G-2 trop WNr 10812 40% damaged NW Ras Agadir in combat with P-40			

From 1 SAAF Squadron Sqn Ldr Peter Olver was posted to 244 Wing as OC Flying, in place of Sqn Ldr Young. Olver's place with the South Africans was now taken by Maj Moodie. This unit and 92 Squadron moved to Castel Benito at this time; Allied aircraft now to be seen on the airfields there reportedly included Hurricanes, Spitfires, Kittyhawks, Liberators, C-47s, Beaufighters, P-38s, Fairchilds, Walrus, O-49s (!), Mosquitos, Bombays, Wellingtons and B-17s. To supplement this 'aircraft spotters' paradise' was an even greater selection of abandoned Axis aircraft, noted as including He 111s, S.79s, CR.42s, MC.200s, MC.202s, Bf 109Es, Bf 109Fs, G.50bis, Hs 126s, Hs 129s, Ju 88s, Ju 52/3ms, Fi 156s, Capronis (various), Ba 88s, Ca trainers, Bf 110s, FW 58s, Do 217s (though probably Do 17Zs of III./ZG 26) and a Caudron Goeland.

Italian troops and local arabs inspect a crash-landed Kittyhawk I of 4 SAAF Squadron. The aircraft seems to have suffered a cannon shell strike on the forward section of the cockpit windscreen.

Sunday, 7 February 1943

260 Squadron moved to Sorman where 112 Squadron had arrived on the previous day, rejoining 239 Wing after its attachment to the 57th Fighter Group.

German Casualties	
2./SchG 2	Bf 109F-4 WNr 6678 Black 3 shot down by AA W Zelten; Uffz Walter Freund PoW

Monday, 8 February 1943

145 Squadron sent 12 Spitfires from Wadi Sirru to Castel Benito for local defence. Four of these were later scrambled after a Ju 88 which three of the pilots saw at 25,000 feet. Two of them caught up with it and Flt Lt Taylor attacked, firing three bursts from 250 yards which caused the port engine to begin burning. As only one of his cannons was working by this time, he was forced to break off when the ammunition for this ran out. He last saw his quarry at 10,000 feet, diving to the west. II./KG 77 reported the loss of a Ju 88 east of Tripoli, which may have been the aircraft attacked by Taylor. However, 2.(F)/122 lost a reconnaissance Me 210 – an aircraft new to the Mediterranean area – between Misurata and Tripoli.

18° Gruppo moved from Gabes to El Hamma airfield, establishing with 23° Gruppo 3° Stormo's full strength (see Volume 3).

British Claims					
450 Sqn	Sqn Ldr M.C.H.Barber	Kittyhawk III FR123	Bf 109 Damaged		0800-0953
145 Sqn	Flt Lt J.S.Taylor	Spitfire Vb EP579	Ju 88 Damaged	patrol Tripoli area	1155-1330

British Casualties	
260 Sqn	Kittyhawk III badly damaged by Flak; Sgt Potts safe

German Casualties	
II./KG 77	Ju 88 FTR E Tripoli
2.(F)/122	Me 210A-1 WNr 0130 F6+YK FTR from Misurata-Tripoli area; Uffz Kurt Schulz/Gefr Johannes Franke MiA

Tuesday, 9 February 1943

12 SAAF Squadron moved with its Bostons to Sertain West, 21 SAAF Squadron going to Sertain Main with its Baltimores. This was the first time the squadrons had each had their own airfield without being located a considerable distance apart.

German Claims		
1./JG 77	Fw Horst Schlick	P-38

Thursday, 11 February 1943

7 SAAF Wing began arriving at Zuara ready to resume operations, the wing still being led by Lt Col Doug Loftus. Initially, however, the airfield was found to be unserviceable and work began to clear and repair it.

Monday, 15 February 1943

239 Wing's squadrons were now all moving to El Assa where they were joined by 73 Squadron. Their chief opponents were also on the move again, Stab and II./JG 77 reaching La Fauconnerie this day where these units would be joined by I. and II.Gruppen somewhat later. When that happened, II.Gruppe would start using Gabes as a forward strip.

Regia Aeronautica disbanded 'Aeronautica della Tunisia' (which had been established on 21 November 1942) and established two new commands under the existing 5ª Squadra Aerea: Settore Nord (North Sector) divided by the 35° parallel, under the command of Col Augusto Bacchiani, and Settore Sud (South Sector) commanded by Col Carlo Drago. Settore Nord took charge of El Aouina, Gammart, Enfidaville, Sfax and Bizerta-Sidi Ahmed airfields, and Settore Sud of the remaining airfields located in southern Tunisia.

Tuesday, 16 February 1943

Following the quiet spell in the south, 8th Army now occupied Ben Gardane and Medenine airfields. It was here that the first aerial action over the front for some days recommenced as Kittyhawks of 450 Squadron which had taken off at 0800, provided top cover for 112 and 3 RAAF Squadrons attacking Axis defences on the Medenine West landing ground in support of the troops. After the bombing six Bf 109s and three MC.202s attacked, nine Allied pilots firing at these although only one claim resulted. The Regia Aeronautica recorded that 13 Macchis of 3° Stormo had taken part in this operation, escorting German aircraft to bomb. One British aircraft was claimed as a probable; one MC.202 then crash-landed, but this was due to engine failure.

British Claims					
450 Sqn	Sgt K.Marrows	Kittyhawk III FR417	Bf 109 Probable	Medenine W area	0800-0930
Italian Claims					
95ª Sq, 18°Gr, 3° St CT	Ten Giorgio Solaroli	MC.202	P-40 Probable	Ben Gardane area	0715-0830
Italian Casualties					
85ª Sq, 18°Gr, 3° St CT	MC.202 crash-landed near Mareth, Cap Mario Dellai KiA				

Wednesday, 17 February 1943

145 and 601 Squadrons moved to Castel Benito and 73 and 250 Squadron arrived at El Assa.

3./SChG 2	Bf 109 F-4 WNr 8553 Yellow 3, shot down by AA NW Medenine; Uffz Heinz Schröter MiA, later returned on foot

Thursday, 18 February 1942

In consequence mainly of events further north which will be more fully described and explained in Volume 3, on this date a new combined and co-ordinated command structure was instituted at all levels with immediate effect. Commander-in-Chief Mediterranean became Admiral Sir Andrew Cunningham, and General Sir Harold Alexander was appointed commander of the Allied Army Group, comprising 1st and 8th Armies, the US II Corps and the French XIX Corps. Insofar as the air forces were concerned, Air Chief Marshal Sir Arthur Tedder was appointed Mediterranean air commander, his headquarters assuming control of all units of the US 9th and 12th Air Forces (the desert and Tunisia respectively), and the RAF's three commands – Eastern (Tunisia), Middle East (desert), Malta and Gibraltar. Tedder was to have three subordinate commands, North-West African Air Force, under Major General Carl Spaatz, USAAF Middle East Air Command under Air Chief Marshal Sir W.Sholto Douglas, and Malta Air Command under Air Marshal Sir Keith Park. Throughout all commands wherever possible American commanders were given British deputies and vice versa.

At this stage the commands relative to the units being dealt with in this volume were as follows: North-West African Tactical Air Force, which was under WDAF's own current commander, Air Vice-Marshal Sir Arthur Coningham. His command now included not only WDAF (now to be known simply as Desert Air Force), but also 1st Army fighters and fighter-bombers (242 Group), US XII Air Support Command, a new Tactical Bomber Force and a Night Fighter Force. Only the activities of the first of these led by its new commander, Air Vice-Marshal Harry Broadhurst, affects us at this stage. However, a final component of NWATAF was North-West African Coastal Air Force under Air Vice-Marshal Sir Hugh Pugh Lloyd, involving coastal and rear area defence units while the RAF heavy bombers of 205 Group and the US IX Bomber Command B-24s, all still based in Egypt, remain a part of this narrative. Coningham's first order in his new role was to the effect that the fighters of 242 Group and XII ASC should concentrate on offensive patrols like WDAF, instead of the defensive missions they had been flying.

The commanding officer of 23° Gruppo, Magg Giorgio Tugnoli (second from left), with some of his pilots: from right Cap Pinna, Cap Rigatti and Serg Magg Zaccaria.

Within Desert Air Force on this date also, Wg Cdr Gleed now took over command of 244 Spitfire Wing from John Darwen. 417 Squadron, the only RCAF unit in the Middle East, now re-equipped with 18 Spitfire Vbs and three Vcs, arrived at Castel Benito to relieve the units there of defensive duties.

Saturday, 20 February 1943

Magg Luigi Filippi, 23° Gruppo CO, travelling by car to Gafsa, met a US outpost and was shot by a soldier. His body was never recovered. Cap Giorgio Tugnoli assumed the Gruppo's command.

Sunday, 21 February 1943

The Regia Aeronautica Order of Battle of 5ª Squadra as of this date was:

Settore Nord	157° Gruppo	384ª Sq	MC.200s	Tunis
	6° Gruppo	81ª Sq	MC.202s	Sfax
	88ª Squadriglia		MC.202s	Gammart
	151° Gruppo	368ª Sq	G.50bis	Sfax
Settore Sud	3° Stormo	six Sq	MC.202s and MC.200s El Hamma	
16° Gruppo	three Sq	MC.202s	K.34 and K.41	

This would ultimately provide a total strength of 55 MC.202s, 25 MC.200s, 12 G.50bis. The 30 MC.202s of 16° Gruppo CT would arrive at K.34 and K.41 near El Hammam from Italy within the next few days.

The activities of Settore Nord will be dealt with in Volume 3, whereas those appertaining to Settore Sud usually continue to be related herein. Like the units of JG 77, however, Settore Sud's activity was at this time occurring over southern Tunisia, but to both north and south of the Mareth area. Operations will normally therefore be divided as appropriate between the two volumes (i.e. when they involve engagements with US aircraft to the north, details will be found in Volume 3, but when involved with DAF aircraft from the south, inclusion in this volume continues).

German Casualties

4.(H)/12	Bf 109G-2 WNr 10764 Black 15 shot down by AA 35km SE Medenine; Fw Josef Harl PoW
6./KG 30	Ju 88A-4 WNr 1765 4D+DP; Fw Martin Scholz and three MiA

Monday, 22 February 1943

The Spitfires of 145 Squadron were scrambled after a Ju 88, Flt Lt Taylor and Sgt Breheny both attacking. Breheny gained hits but then blacked out and Taylor's cannons jammed; they could only claim the intruder as damaged. However, 2.(F)/122 reported the loss of another Me 210 over Tripoli with II./KG 30 losing three Ju 88s here. The day also saw the return to action of the SAAF Kittyhawks when aircraft of 5 SAAF Squadron undertook a reconnaissance over Gabes. Further reinforcements arrived in the shape of 6 Squadron which had now received back its tank-busting Hurricane IIds which had been overhauled following the El Alamein battles; the unit moved to Benghazi. On the same day one of 145 Squadron's long-serving flight commanders, Flt Lt A.U.'Bert' Houle, ended his tour and moved to join 73 OTU as an instructor.

Yet more strength returned next day when the 57th Fighter Group, having had no operations since 26 January, flew in to Zuara. With the arrival of the Americans, the South Africans of 7 SAAF Wing moved to Neffatia, while the Spitfires of 1 SAAF Squadron sent a detachment to Hazbub. The unit reported next day that 417 Squadron had not arrived at Castel Benito to join 244 Wing.

British Claims

451 Sqn	Plt Off W.P.G.Longbottom	Hurricane IIc BN290 'T'	Ju 88 Damaged	1008-1025
451 Sqn	Plt Off J.D.Wallis	Hurricane IIc BP342		
145 Sqn	Flt Lt J.S.Taylor	Spitfire Vb ER552	Ju 88 Damaged	1025-1150
145 Sqn	Flt Sgt R.T.Breheny	Spitfire Vb EP193		

German Casualties

2.(F)/122	Me 210A-1 WNr 0210 F6+ZK FTR from Misurata-Zuara area; Fw Walter Spitzner/ Uffz Waldemar Küch KiA
4./KG 30	Ju 88A-4 WNr 141142 4D+JM lost on mission to Tripoli; Uffz Franz Hrncirik and three MiA

Thursday, 25 February 1943

British Casualties

2 SAAF Sqn	bombed and strafed at Neffatia; Kittyhawk I ET515 badly damaged and two Kittyhawks damaged Cat I
4 SAAF Sqn	bombed and strafed at Neffatia; several Kittyhawks damaged Cat I

German Casualties

SChGr2	Bf 109F-4 WNr 13010 destroyed by bombs at Gabes airfield

Friday, 26 February 1943

This was the busiest day of the month for WDAF as a new air offensive against the Mareth Line began. Attacks were concentrated on the defences in the line itself and on the supply routes to it. Throughout the day Kittyhawks and Warhawks kept up a concerted fighter-bomber attack on Axis airfields as Spitfires roamed overhead, trying to provide an umbrella over the strafers – sadly, an umbrella which leaked rather often on this date, it must be said.

The first attack was undertaken by 239 Wing, 12 Kittyhawks from 250 Squadron and 11 from 450 Squadron, all carrying bombs, taking off at 0740, covered by 11 more Kittyhawks from 3 RAAF Squadron to attack Gabes West. Twenty minutes later 12 bomb-laden aircraft from 4 SAAF Squadron took off for the same target. Six of the top cover aircraft from 3 RAAF Squadron engaged 15 Bf 109s east of the target, Sgt McLeod claiming damage to one which was seen pouring black smoke. Heavy Flak was experienced over the target and two Kittyhawks were damaged, Sgt Eaton crashing on landing when his undercarriage collapsed.

After the airfield was bombed, A Flight of 250 Squadron was attacked by about seven Bf 109s, Flg Off Collier and his No.2, Flt Sgt Nitz, being shot down by pilots of III./JG 77. Both pilots force or crash-landed and were back before the end of the day, both making claims. Two more Kittyhawks were slightly damaged. 450 Squadron became involved in a general dogfight with 12 Bf 109s; Flg Off Regan attacked one at point-blank range and reported that it dived into the sea. A probable and a damaged were also claimed. However, two of the unit's Kittyhawks failed to return and one more was hit by Flak. A few

Yet another American – and the most successful of all – Sqn Ldr L.C.Wade. He had just crash-landed this Spitfire V on 26 February 1943 after it had been hit by 'friendly' AA fire while he was trying to intercept an Axis raid on the airfield. Unfortunately, on this occasion he was not flying one of his own 145 Squadron aircraft, but had taken off in the 244 Wing Leader's personal aircraft, IR-G – the initials of Wg Cdr Ian R.Gleed.

minutes later the South Africans arrived and were able to bomb the target unmolested. On the way back four Messerschmitts were encountered and one aircraft of 4 SAAF Squadron was shot down, the pilot crash-landing; he survived unhurt and returned in the afternoon. One German fighter was claimed shot down in return. An hour later 12 more Kittyhawks from 260 Squadron bombed Gabes West, also attacking a Ju 88 which had just landed there and was still taxying. Sgt Cundy was last seen flying west apparently under control, but he did not return. At this point the Germans retaliated, two formations each of four Bf 109s strafing Hazbub airfield at 1100. Four Spitfires of 145 Squadron were scrambled and gave chase to two of the Messerschmitts. Flt Lt Taylor caught these over Bordj Touaz, fired four bursts at one at which the starboard wing folded back and the aircraft crashed from 5,000 feet and exploded. The second 109 now turned in, but Taylor fired at this too, seeing the cockpit hood fly off. He then ran out of ammunition and was only able to claim damage in this case.

The Luftwaffe returned to make a second attack at 1310, this time 12 Spitfires getting off to intercept the bomb-laden Messerschmitts. Flg Off Shand, with six more Spitfires following, attacked three Bf 109s, hitting one with two bursts whereupon it rolled over and the pilot baled out, the aircraft hitting the ground and exploding. Flt Sgt McKinnon broke away and attacked two more from above and behind and hit one, but did not see any result. He then saw a Bf 109 in a vertical dive from 10,000 feet with the pilot baling out, the aircraft also hitting the ground and blowing up; this was subsequently credited to him. Two more Bf 109s were pursued, Plt Off Barker reporting strikes on one as it pulled up to avoid colliding with two Hurricanes; it then dived fast for home.

Flt Lt Taylor, meanwhile, chased several fighters to 4-5,000 feet, hitting one from which black smoke emitted, but with no apparent results. He was then attacked by two more, but evaded these. During one of these attacks on Hazbub, Sqn Ldr Wade's Spitfire was hit by a cannon shell and he had to make a belly-landing. Just before this particular attack had commenced, 11 Kittyhawks from 4 SAAF Squadron had provided top cover to other 7 SAAF Wing fighter-bombers, but were attacked by Bf 109s. Lt Tapson fought three, claiming damage to two, and Lt Paterson attacked one which was on Tapson's tail. He was then attacked himself and wounded. He later crash-landed on his own airfield, but two of the squadron's other pilots failed to return.

At midday eight MC.202s of 3° Stormo escorted Ju 87s over the Ksar Rhilane area; heavy AA was encountered and one Macchi was shot down, Ten Specker baling out safely. A second was hit and crash-landed, Magg Camarda returning on foot next day.

239 Wing was off again at 1445, ten aircraft from 450 Squadron covering 12 from 250 and 11 from 3 RAAF Squadrons to bomb Bordj Touaz (Gabes South) airfield. As the wing approached, eight or nine Bf 109s were seen taking off and 3 RAAF at once engaged them in a dogfight. Wg Cdr Burton claimed one shot down at 200 feet, which crashed and burnt; Wt Off Stevens claimed a second which he reported crashed eight miles south-east of the airfield; he also claimed a second badly damaged. Flt Lt Susans attacked a Messerschmitt on the tail of another Kittyhawk, and this was seen going down apparently out of control, a probable being claimed. Sgt Beer, having believed that he had damaged one, had to force-land when his own aircraft was hit; he returned safely next day. One other Kittyhawk was also hit and damaged. 250 Squadron followed the Australians in and reported seeing one of the Bf 109s claimed by the latter crash into a hill. This unit then met more than a dozen Messerschmitts, one claim for a probable resulting, although another Kittyhawk crash-landed in the line, the pilot of this also getting back next day. The top cover was not engaged by the German fighters, but Flt Lt Glendinning saw one at 3,000 feet below him and dived on it, attacking from 50 yards range, seeing it going down vertically pouring black smoke and glycol; his claim for one destroyed was confirmed.

Twenty-five minutes after 239 Wing had taken off, P-40Fs of the 57th Fighter Group departed on a similar mission, 11 aircraft of the 65th Squadron and 12 of the 64th taking part. As they approached the target, the Americans were attacked by four Bf 109s which approached from the north-west. Capt Clark fired a long burst at one and reported that it crashed in flames.

Between 1600-1630 Kittyhawks from 7 SAAF Wing took to the air, 12 from 2 SAAF Squadron on their sixth operation of the day, escorting ten from 5 SAAF Squadron to dive-bomb Gabes West. The pilots of the latter unit saw eight aircraft on the ground here, claiming a direct hit on one large aircraft and probably hitting four more. After the bombing six Bf 109s attacked the 2 SAAF Squadron top cover, Lt Platt being shot down. One parachute was observed to go down, but Lt Dold of 5 SAAF Squadron was lost and an aircraft of 2 SAAF was badly shot-up during the fight. Lt Rogers of 5 SAAF Squadron saw a Bf 109 on the tail of a 2 SAAF aircraft and made a head-on attack, firing at the fighter which went

Wg Cdr Ian Gleed in his Spitfire IR-G, soon repaired after its mishap on 26 February. The Felix-the-Cat character below the cockpit was a repeat of a similar emblem carried on his Hurricane in the United Kingdom earlier in the war.

down vertically, a column of black smoke being seen from the ground; he was credited with one destroyed. Another 5 SAAF Squadron aircraft was also hit and crash-landed.

601 Squadron had just completed the move to Hazbub Main when at 1700 four of the unit's Spitfires were scrambled to intercept another incoming raid. At 1710 five Bf 109s dived on the airfield out of the sun, dropping anti-personnel bombs which caused four casualties amongst the ground crews. In attempting to intercept these attacks, the squadron aircraft were jumped by eight more Messerschmitts. Flt Sgt Gwynne reported shooting the tail off one of these which was seen to hit the ground. Flg Off Whitamore also claimed a probable but his own aircraft was badly damaged. Gwynne's victim has proved fairly easy to identify, for Lt Hugo Hauck of III./JG 77 was reported to have been shot down by a Spitfire north-west of Medenine whilst escorting fighter-bombers; he became a prisoner.

During this hectic day pilots of JG 77 claimed a massive 21 P-40s shot down plus one unconfirmed and one Spitfire. However, WDAF losses had totalled 15 shot down or crash-landed, plus eight more damaged. What is perhaps more surprising is that amongst all these losses, only three Allied pilots had lost their lives with three surviving as prisoners; all the rest were back within days if not hours. Clearly, there had been the level of double-claiming and over-optimism that tends to occur in such busy skies. Eleven claims for Bf 109s destroyed were confirmed, most appearing to have been well-founded. However, II./JG 77's losses amounted to five shot down or crash-landed, plus one more 10% damaged. Nonetheless, two of these pilots had been killed, one wounded and one captured, leaving only one unharmed and ready to fly again soon. JG 77's Lt Armin Köhler had not been one of those to claim any success on this date. He recorded in his diary: "Accompany bombers to south-west of Medenine. Search patrol off Medenine. My formation intercept seven Kittyhawks. At the start of the attack and after firing only a few rounds, the breech mechanism of my cannon breaks into pieces. There was a terrific crack and my cockpit filled with smoke. Immediately hauled away. My Gruppe had considerable success. The Kittyhawks came mostly from (the direction of) Djerba Island." It had indeed been a good day for the Geschwader as a whole, for further north Hptm Bär had made five claims, Fw Reinert four, and four other pilots had two claims each (see Volume 3).

16° Gruppo of 54° Stormo CT moved at full strength to Gabes with 30 MC.202s ready to start operations. Gruppo commander was Magg Francesco 'Ciccio' Sforza, while three Squadriglie (167ª, 168ª and 169ª) were respectively led by Ten Giovanni D'Amelia, Cap Giovanni Pagliari and Cap Vittorio Merlo.

British Claims

450 Sqn	Plt Off A.J.Blackburn	Kittyhawk III FR421	Bf 109 Damaged	Gabes West l.g.	0741-0915
450 Sqn	Flg Off G.H.Norton	Kittyhawk III FL895	Bf 109 Probable	Gabes West l.g.	0741-0920
450 Sqn	Flg Off F.X.J.Regan	Kittyhawk III FR254	Bf 109	Gabes West l.g.	0741-0920
3 RAAF Sqn	Sgt M.McLeod	Kittyhawk IIa FL302 'Q'	Bf 109F/G Damaged	3m SW Zaret	0835
250 Sqn	Flg Off J.E.Collier	Kittyhawk III FR302 'B'	Bf 109 Damaged	Gabes West l.g	0900
250 Sqn	Flt Sgt A.F.Nitz	Kittyhawk III FL887 'I'	Bf 109	Gabes West l.g.	0900
4 SAAF Sqn	Lt G.H.Kaufmann	Kittyhawk I ET244 'A'	Bf 109	Djerba	0900
145 Sqn	Flt Lt J.S.Taylor	Spitfire Vb EP704	Bf 109	Castel Benito area	1045-1140
145 Sqn	Flt Lt J.S.Taylor	Spitfire Vb EP704	Bf 109 Damaged	Castel Benito area	1045-1140
4 SAAF Sqn	Lt I.T.S.Tapson	Spitfire Vc EV369 'Z'	2 Bf 109s Damaged	6m N and 12m E Gabes	1305-1505
145 Sqn	Plt Off F.R.Barker	Spitfire Vb EP543	Bf 109 Damaged	Castel Benito area	1310-1350
145 Sqn	Flt Sgt H.McKinnon	Spitfire Vb ER606	Bf 109	Castel Benito area	1310-1350
145 Sqn	Flg Off I.H.R.Shand	Spitfire Vb ER608	Bf 109	Castel Benito area	1310-1350
145 Sqn	Flt Lt J.S.Taylor	Spitfire Vb EP704	Bf 109 Damaged	Castel Benito area	1310-1420
450 Sqn	Flt Lt A.Glendinning	Kittyhawk III FR269	Bf 109F	Bordj Touaz l.g.	1443-1614
250 Sqn	Flt Lt G.W.Troke	Kittyhawk III FR120 'E'	Bf 109 Probable	Gabes South l.g.	1445-1535
239 Wg	Wg Cdr H.F.Burton	Kittyhawk IIa FL347	Bf 109	Bordj Touaz	1445-
3 RAAF Sqn	Wt Off R.N.B.Stevens	Kittyhawk IIa FL265 'V'	Bf 109F/G	Bordj Touaz l.g.	1525
3 RAAF Sqn	Sgt L.G.Beer	Kittyhawk IIa FL356 'X'	Bf 109F/G Damaged	Bordj Touaz l.g.	1530
3 RAAF Sqn	Flt Lt R.T.Susans	Kittyhawk IIa FL301 'I'	Bf 109F/G Probable	Bordj Touaz l.g.	1530
5 SAAF Sqn	Lt R.T.Rogers	Kittyhawk I ET867 'I'	Bf 109F	N Mareth Line	1635-1735
601 Sqn	Flt Sgt W.D.Gwynne	Spitfire Vc ER270	Bf 109	Hazbub Main l.g.	1700-1725
601 Sqn	Flg Off W.M.Whitamore	Spitfire Vc ER212	Bf 109 Probable	Hazbub Main l.g.	1700-1810
2 SAAF Sqn	Lt E.T.Newby	Kittyhawk I AK947 'P'	Bf 109F Probable	Gabes	1700

British Casualties

4 SAAF Sqn	Kittyhawk I AK651 damaged by Bf 109s, crash-landed with engine one fire; Lt K.J.Wernberg back safe in p.m.
250 Sqn	Kittyhawk III FR302 'B' left 0740, shot down by Bf 109 in Gabes area, force-landed Ben Gardane area; Flg Off J.E.Collier back safe later
250 Sqn	Kittyhawk III FR887 'I' left 0740, shot down by Bf 109s in Gabes area; Flt Sgt A.F.Nitz safe
250 Sqn	Kittyhawk III FR327 left 1445 shot down by Bf 109s in Gabes area; Sgt J.G.Turner safe
250 Sqn	Kittyhawk III FL892 left 1050, damaged Cat I; Sgt J.P.Maloney safe
3 RAAF Sqn	Kittyhawk IIa FL317 damaged by Flak 0830; Sqn Ldr B.A.Eaton safe
3 RAAF Sqn	Kittyhawk IIa FL302 'Q' damaged by Flak; Sgt M.McLeod safe
450 Sqn	Kittyhawk III FR125 shot down by Bf 109s Gabes West; Sgt F.J.Silk MiA
450 Sqn	Kittyhawk III FR346 shot down by Bf 109s Gabes West; Sgt J.Stonely MiA
450 Sqn	Kittyhawk III FL712 damaged Cat I; Sgt R.Rowe
260 Sqn	Kittyhawk III MiA W Gabes; Sgt N.E.Cundy MiA
4 SAAF Sqn	Kittyhawk I AK908 'P' FTR; Lt C.Southwood PoW
4 SAAF Sqn	Kittyhawk I AK929 'E' damaged by Bf 109s, crash-landed; Lt D.F.Symonds returned next day
4 SAAF Sqn	Kittyhawk I ET824 'F' damaged by Bf 109s and belly-landed; Lt A.C.Paterson WiA
4 SAAF Sqn	Kittyhawk I EV369 'Z' damaged Cat I by Bf 109s; Lt I.T.S.Tapson safe
3 RAAF Sqn	Kittyhawk IIa FL356 left 1445 damaged and force-landed; Sgt L.G.Beer returned next day
3 RAAF Sqn	Kittyhawk IIa FL270 1445, damaged; Sgt R.J.MacKenzie safe
2 SAAF Sqn	Kittyhawk I AK888 'N' shot down by Bf 109s nr Zelten, 1700; Lt T.J.Platt PoW
2 SAAF Sqn	Kittyhawk I AK573 'Q' badly damaged Cat II by fighters; Lt D.V.Ducasse safe
5 SAAF Sqn	Kittyhawk I AK951 probably shot down by Flak 1730; Lt G.A.L.Dold PoW
5 SAAF Sqn	Kittyhawk I AK801 damaged Cat II and crash-landed
145 Sqn	Spitfire V ER549 hit by cannon shell and crash-landed; Sqn Ldr L.C.Wade safe
601 Sqn	Spitfire V ER212 left 1700, badly damaged in combat, landed 1810; Flg Off W.M.Whitamore safe

US Claims

65th FS/57th FG	Capt Thomas W.Clark	P-40F '41'	Bf 109	Bordj Touaz	1545

German Claims

9./JG 77	Lt Wolfgang Ernst	P-40	NE Mareth	0840

8./JG 77	Uffz Ernst Mruck	P-40	Mareth	0840
8./JG 77	Oblt Emil Omert	P-40	Mareth	0845
Flak		P-40	7km W Gabes	1005
Stab I./JG 77	Hptm Heinz Bär	Spitfire		1055
4./JG 77	Uffz Bruno Weidlich	P-40	25km NW Gabes	1353
4./JG 77	Uffz Rudolf Flindt	P-40	15km NNW Gabes	1355
4./JG 77	Fw Ernst-Wilhelm Reinert	P-40	15km NE Gabes	1356
4./JG 77	Fw Ernst-Wilhelm Reinert	P-40	15km SE Gabes	1358
4./JG 77	Uffz Bruno Weidlich	P-40	25km ESE Gabes	1359
2./JG 77	Lt Iring Englisch	P-40		1400
4./JG 77	Uffz Rudolf Flindt	P-40	8km NE Zarat	1401
6./JG 77	Fw Pförtner	P-40		1402
4./JG 77	Fw Ernst-Wilhelm Reinert	P-40	18km NE Zarat	1403
Stab I./JG 77	Lt Heinz-Edgar Berres	P-40	NW Medenine	1403
Stab I./JG 77	Hptm Heinz Bär	2 P-40s	NW Medenine	1405 & 1415
5./JG 77	Uffz Donath	P-40		1406
4./JG 77	Fw Ernst-Wilhelm Reinert	P-40	15km SW Adjnia	1408
8./JG 77	Oblt Emil Omert	P-40	SE Mareth	1545
Stab I./JG 77	Lt Heinz-Edgar Berres	P-40	S Gabes	1702
Stab I./JG 77	Hptm Heinz Bär	2 P-40s		1703 &1708
3./JG 77	Oblt Ernst Laube	P-40	N Tojane	1714
1./JG 77	Fw Horst Schlick	2 P-40s		1718
8./JG 77	Fw Herbert Schwarz	P-40		

German Casualties

Stab/JG 77	Bf 109G-2 trop WNr 10537 White < 3 shot down by P-40 on take-off Matmata; Oblt Horst Huck KiA
2./JG 77	Bf 109G-2 trop WNr 10779 damaged 10% by enemy fire
4./JG 77	Bf 109G-2 trop WNr 10762 Yellow 3 + - force-landing 20% damaged; Uffz Alfred Keinath safe
8./JG 77	Bf 109G-2 trop WNr 10794 Black 7 shot down by P-40; Obfw Robert Helmer KiA
9./JG 77	Bf 109G-2 trop WNr 10712 crash-landed Matmata 30% damaged in combat; Lt Wolfgang Ernst WiA
9./JG 77	Bf 109G-2 trop WNr 10756 Yellow 8 shot down in combat with Spitfire, NW Medenine; Lt Hugo Hauck baled, PoW

Italian Casualties

18°Gr, 3°St CT	MC.202 crash-landed nr Ksar Rhilane, Magg Domenico Camarda walked back two days later
83ª Sq, 18°Gr, 3°St CT	MC.202 shot down, Ten Guglielmo Specker baled out and safe

Saturday, 27 February 1943

Fighter-bomber attacks continued as on the previous day; at 0700 12 Kittyhawks from 260 Squadron set off to attack El Hamma landing ground. They were prevented from doing so, attacking Bordj Touaz instead, bombing from 2,000 feet. A direct hit on a Bf 109 was reportedly achieved, but one Kittyhawk was hit by Flak and burst into flames, crashing at once.

Several attacks were made by 57th Fighter Group P-40s during the day, most aircraft carrying wing bombs. Twelve 65th Squadron aircraft went off at 1005, providing cover for 66th Squadron fighter-bombers. Going in to strafe Gabes West airfield, intense and accurate Flak was reported as three Bf 109s attacked. These were believed to have shot down Capt Marshall Sneed's aircraft, the pilot being killed, and Lt Kimball was thought to have been brought down by the ground fire; he survived to become a PoW. During the attack ten or twelve MT were strafed and most claimed to have been left in flames, while a patrol bowser was also set on fire. Other pilots shot-up a Ju 88 and six Bofors guns in an emplacement.

At 1030 eight Bf 109s attacked Hazbub, and it was probably these aircraft which eight Spitfire pilots of 601 Squadron spotted strafing while engaged in a patrol over the front. On turning to intercept, the squadron was then bounced by six more. Sgt Lusty had got behind one of the Jabos below, but was in turn attacked by one of the newcomers, his Spitfire being badly damaged. He returned to base where he crash-landed and was slightly injured. Flt Lt Nicholls was also attacked and his aircraft badly damaged. However, Wt Off Garden fired at his attacker and shot pieces off its cockpit hood.

Soon after midday II./JG 77 reported attacking Curtiss fighters, four of which were claimed shot down. Shortly after 1230 239 Wing put in another raid, 12 Kittyhawks from 260 Squadron providing top cover as 11 from 112 Squadron gave medium cover for 12 bomb-carriers from 450 Squadron to attack targets in the El Hamma area. North of Gabes the formation turned south and crossed the coast. Here the top cover, flying at 12-13,000 feet, was bounced by two Bf 109s, followed by two more. Sgt McParland was shot-up and wounded, but got his badly damaged aircraft back to base. Sgt Stoker was attacked by four or five and fought them off, but his aircraft also suffered considerable damage. He returned to base where he too belly-landed. 112 Squadron also became involved in the dogfight, claiming one probable for the loss of one pilot. 450 Squadron's aircraft were just diving to bomb when four Bf 109s attacked. Flg Off Norton spotted one of these on the tail of a Kittyhawk and dived on this, firing into the fuselage. The cockpit hood fell off and flames poured out of the cockpit, this aircraft being confirmed as destroyed. One more Kittyhawk was badly damaged.

WDAF commander, Air Marshal Sir Arthur Coningham, visits one of his units.

On another mission 11 Kittyhawks of 4 SAAF Squadron dive-bombed El Hammam airfield, Lt Dummett's aircraft being hit as the result of which he belly-landed at base. Capt Laubscher's aircraft was also hit and he force-landed, returning safely to the squadron later. Eight Kittyhawks had been shot down or damaged sufficiently to cause them to crash-land or force-land, with at least three more damaged but returning safely. Four nonetheless were deemed to be due to Flak, and on this occasion II./JG 77 claimed four, representing the losses suffered remarkably accurately. Two more claims were for Spitfires, and two of these were hit, one crash-landing on return, the other being badly damaged.

During the day's attacks on El Hammam four MC.202s were destroyed on the ground and five more were slightly damaged. Other Macchis of 3° Stormo had been in action, seven pilots intercepting Kittyhawks at around 0900, only claiming some as probably damaged. Five more were scrambled during the early afternoon, claiming one Kittyhawk forced to land. At El Hammam Italian AA gunners claimed to have shot down one further Kittyhawk during the day.

British Claims

601 Sqn	Sgt K.Lusty	Spitfire Vc ER558	Bf 109 Damaged	SW Hazbub Main l.g.	1035-1115
112 Sqn	Flg Off J.G.Wright	Kittyhawk III	Bf 109 Probable	El Hamma l.g.	1245-1430
450 Sqn	Flg Off G.H.Norton	Kittyhawk III FR123	Bf 109F	El Hamma area	1248-1452

British Casualties

112 Sqn	Kittyhawk III FR130 'Z' left 1245, shot down nr El Hamma; Sgt T.A.Marsden FTR
260 Sqn	Kittyhawk IIa FL322 shot down by Flak, Bordj Touaz; Flg Off R.S.Kent KiA
260 Sqn	Kittyhawk III badly damaged by Bf 109 in El Hamma area; Sgt McParland WiA
260 Sqn	Kittyhawk III badly damaged by Bf 109 in El Hamma area; Sgt Stohr safe
450 Sqn	Kittyhawk III FL885 badly damaged by Bf 109 nr Gabes West; Sgt F.C.Sanders safe
4 SAAF Sqn	Kittyhawk I EV423 'K' damaged by Flak, force-landed in Gabes area, Cat III; Capt D.C.Laubscher slt inj, returned 2 March
4 SAAF Sqn	Kittyhawk I ET1019 'J' damaged by Flak, belly-landed at base Cat II; Lt N.R.Dummett safe
5 SAAF Sqn	Kittyhawk I ET955 'V' damaged by Flak Cat II, 0630; Lt P.F.Cowen safe
601 Sqn	Spitfire V ER558 scrambled at 1035, badly damaged and crash-landed at base on return at 1115; Sgt K.J.Lusty safe
601 Sqn	Spitfire V ER464 scrambled at 1035, badly damaged, Flt Lt J.H.Nicholls safe

US Casualties

65th FS/57th FG	P-40F, shot down by Bf 109s at Gabes West a/d 1005-1230, Capt Marshall Sneed, MiA
65th FS/57th FG	P-40F, shot down by Flak at Gabes West a/d 1005-1230, 1/Lt Richard K.Kimball PoW

German Claims

4./JG 77	Fw Ernst-Wilhelm Reinert	2 P-40s	18km ESE Gabes	1132 & 1135
4./JG 77	Lt Manfred Rippe	P-40	22km SE Gabes	1136
4./JG 77	Uffz Rudolf Flindt	P-40	33km SE Gabes	1139
4./JG 77	Uffz Bruno Weidlich	Spitfire	25km NW Gabes	1347
7./JG 77	Lt Walter Kiessling	Spitfire	SW Matmata	1400
I./JG 77	unstated	P-40		

German Casualties

2./SchG 2	Bf 109F-4 WNr 8699 Black 7 shot down by P-40 5km S Medenine; Uffz Egon Schlüter KiA
5./JG 77	Bf 109G-2 WNr 13 886 combat force-landed Gabes, 50% damaged; pilot safe

Italian Claims

18° Gr, 3° St CT	unstated	MC.202	Kittyhawk	El Hamma area early afternoon

Italian Casualties

3° Stormo CT	4 MC.202s destroyed on ground at El Hammam

Sunday, 28 February 1943

Little of note occurred in the air on the last day of the month. However, 417 Squadron moved to Mellaha to the east of Tripoli for the air defence of the port. In 7 SAAF Wing Maj H.E.N.Wildsmith, commanding officer of 2 SAAF Squadron, ended his tour and was replaced by the wing's sweep leader, Maj R.F.Armstrong. 680 Squadron recorded that it now had available for photographic reconnaissance work, 14 Spitfire IVs, two Spitfire VIs and five Hurricanes.

Monday, 1 March 1943

Five Spitfires of 92 Squadron scrambled at 1108 on a local patrol, from which they were vectored onto three MC.202s, part of a force of nine of these fighters which were escorting five MC.200s to strafe vehicles south of Ksar Rhilane. Flt Lt Duke attacked:

> "I dived after enemy aircraft out of sun, and closed astern to about 300 yards, when I was observed by the port enemy aircraft which broke away to port. I attacked the starboard Macchi 202 which went up in a climbing left hand turn. I observed cannon strikes in the engine, and behind the cockpit. The e/a went down in a spiral dive and the pilot baled out. I engaged the second Macchi in a dogfight and after several short bursts with machine guns (my cannons having stopped) I observed hits in fuselage. The e/a turned on its back and went down. The pilot baled out (saw both parachutes going down almost together side-by-side). Enemy aircraft showed keenness to engage in dogfight. The third got away although one of the boys had a shot at him."

The Italian pilots were involved in the first operation of 16° Gruppo in Tunisia. Nine MC.202s led by Cap Vittorio Merlo, took off at 1030 to escort MC.200 fighter-bombers on a strafing mission against motor transport in the Ksar Rhilane area. Engaged by Spitfires, Serg Magg Ettore Dotta claimed one shot down, possibly shared with S.Ten Giuseppe Robetto, and Cap Merlo and S.Ten Virgilio Modotti were shot down and baled out into Axis territory. Modotti, although wounded, managed to walk back to base while Merlo, wounded in the head by a splinter during the combat, was almost unconscious as he left the aircraft but hit the fin which broke three of his ribs. He was then rescued by a Bersaglieri patrol and taken to a field hospital. Cap Corrado Ceccacci replaced him as 169ª Squadriglia commander.

Six more Spitfires from 145 Squadron then covered Kittyhawks on a sortie north of the Mareth Line at 1405, nine Bf 109s being encountered. Flt Lt Taylor attacked one from behind at 7,000 feet and hit the fuselage, the pilot baling out; the Messerschmitt blew up on hitting the ground. Sqn Ldr Wade saw four Bf 109s 2,000 feet below him when he was at 5,000 feet, and fired at one from which pieces flew off as it began to go down. He left this to chase the others and later claimed it as a probable, but it was subsequently confirmed as shot down. Wt Off Ker attacked three Messerschmitts which he saw below him, hitting one, but seeing no apparent results. He then saw a parachute and a fire on the ground and was awarded one destroyed. A tactical reconnaissance Bf 109 of 2.(H)/14 flown by Lt Wilhelm Metz was lost in the Goff el Aroussa area on this date, and may have been one of the aircraft claimed during this engagement.

At about 1650 Axis artillery began shelling Hazbub Main landing ground and all 601 Squadron's Spitfires were hastily got off the ground, eight going to El Assa and four to Zuara. Flt Sgt Reynolds was taking off when a shell burst under his aircraft and he crashed three miles away from the airfield and was badly injured. The squadron was then ordered to Ben Gardane. At 1820 the landing ground at Medenine, which was occupied by 92 and 145 Squadrons, was also shelled and these units were forced to evacuate in a similar hurry, most aircraft going to Castel Benito. Two Spitfires were damaged by the shelling, one crash-landing at Zuara as one 145 Squadron aircraft made the flight with two pilots aboard. Both units joined 601 Squadron at Ben Gardane next morning.

By this time the third USAAF fighter group had become ready for operational experience for some of its pilots. The unit in question was the 324th Fighter Group (314th, 315th and 316th Squadrons) which now sent units forward to gain some initial experience 'under the wings' of the established units. Thus the 314th Squadron was now attached to the 57th Fighter Group with the 316th Squadron joining the 79th Fighter Group. At this stage Erwin Rommel, sick and dispirited, left Africa for the last time. His forces would fight on in his absence against rapidly increasing odds and in a steadily more parlous position for another two and a half months.

British Claims					
92 Sqn	Flt Lt N.F.Duke	Spitfire Vb ER821 'R'	2 MC.202s	NE Medenine	1130
145 Sqn	Wt Off E.A.Ker	Spitfire Vb EP648	Bf 109	N end Mareth line	1405-1515
145 Sqn	Flt Lt J.S.Taylor	Spitfire Vb ER199	Bf 109	N end Mareth line	1405-1515
145 Sqn	Sqn Ldr L.C.Wade	Spitfire Vb ER650	Bf 109	N end Mareth line	1405-1515
British Casualties					
601 Sqn	Spitfire V ER611 destroyed by artillery fire taking off at 1715; Flt Sgt A.O.Reynolds crashed and badly injured				
92 and 145 Sqns	2 Spitfires damaged by artillery fire; one crash-landed				
German Casualties					
4.(H)/12	Bf 109 lost Goff el Aroussa; Lt Wilhelm Metz MiA				
Italian Claims					
168ª Sq, 16°Gr, 54°St CT	Serg Magg Ettore Dotta	MC.202	Spitfire	Tunisia	
Italian Casualties					
169ª Sq, 16°Gr, 54°St CT	MC.202 MM 9418 shot down, Cap Vittorio Merlo baled near Ksar Rhilane, WiA				
169ª Sq, 16°Gr, 54°St CT	MC.202 MM 9434 shot down, S.Ten Virgilio Modotti WiA, walked back				

Tuesday, 2 March 1943

5 SAAF Squadron now flew its first sorties in the fighter-bomber role, attacking a heavy gun which had been shelling Hazbub. Earlier, when the unit had been equipped with Tomahawks, these had not been fitted for the carriage of bombs other than small anti-personnel missiles. Two MC.202s of 3° Stormo undertook a recce mission at 1420-1530; Ten Antonio Naglia failed to return.

German Claims				
8./JG 77	Obfw Heinrich Hackler		P-40 n.b.	
Italian Claims				
168ª Sq, 16°Gr, 54°St CT	Serg Magg Ettore Dotta	MC.202	Spitfire	Tunisia
Italian Casualties				
18°Gr, 3°St CT	MC.202 shot down, Ten Antonio Naglia PoW			

Wednesday, 3 March 1943

A dawn reconnaissance was flown over the Gabes-Mareth road by two Hurricanes of 73 Squadron which took off at 0415. These were intercepted by Bf 109s, Flt Sgt Wright being shot down and taken prisoner. Ten minutes before the surviving Hurricane landed, ten Kittyhawks of 2 SAAF Squadron commenced a sortie accompanied by aircraft of 4 SAAF Squadron, an armed reconnaissance being flown along the road to Oudref. Pilots were forming up after bombing when 12 Bf 109s appeared, six attacking each squadron. 2 SAAF Squadron was badly broken up and a free-for-all ensued which turned to the South Africans' advantage. Lt 'Blikkies' Blignault was attacked as he came out of his bombing dive, a

Messerschmitt trying to get behind him. He turned into this and fired, causing it to pull up. This allowed him to fire three more long bursts into its underside, causing it to burst into flames below and behind the cockpit. Lt 'Bush' Moon got on the tail of another which he identified as an E version firing two bursts from 150 yards. He reported that this aircraft then lost height rapidly, headed for the coast, and crashed into the sea two miles out. Moon then turned back and made a head-on attack on another fighter which flashed past him, trailing black and white smoke. This and two other Messerschmitts were claimed damaged with the South Africans suffering only damage to one aircraft in return.

The identity of their opponents has not been ascertained, although it appears that Hptm Bär of I./JG 77 claimed two P-40s shot down at around this time. However, the squadron recorded the comment "... there might have been a different story to tell, had the enemy pilots been more experienced, for these, in the words of our lads, were keen but clueless". It was felt that the attack had been made from below, preventing the German pilots employing their favourite dive/zoom tactics.

Close behind the South Africans, three Spitfires of 92 Squadron took off to cover others from 145 Squadron north of Gabes. As they were leaving the ground one of the former unit's aircraft collided head-on with that flown by Flg Off Laing-Meason of 145. Neither pilot was seriously injured, and the two remaining 92 Squadron pilots continued with the sortie, climbing to 22,000 feet. Near Gabes 145 Squadron encountered MC.202s, one being claimed damaged. As the Spitfires returned to base, the top cover section spotted a lone Bf 109 near the Mareth Line, flying at about 10,000 feet. Flt Lt Duke at once dived on this, closed to 250 yards and fired, reporting: "The enemy aircraft turned sharply in a climbing turn to the left. I observed strikes with cannon in the fuselage and wings. After the second burst the e/a went down vertically with smoke coming from the fuselage. Flt Sgt H.Patterson confirms seeing it crash."

During a sortie around 1715, two 40 SAAF Squadron Hurricanes led the Kittyhawks of 2 SAAF Squadron to dive-bomb 500 MT reported moving south of Matmata, 5 SAAF Squadron providing top cover. The target was found after a considerable search, but the vehicles had by then been widely dispersed and results were poor. In searching, Lt Tony Mullany of 4 SAAF Squadron was seen to be lagging behind, possibly, it was thought, due to engine trouble. He was lost sight of, and was shot down by a Bf 109, becoming a PoW.

During the day I./JG 77's airfield at Fatnassa had been bombed three times, attackers coming from both north and south. Having flown an escort to Stukas during the morning, Armin Köhler recorded:

> "Shortly after noon attack by four-engined aircraft. 3. and 1.Staffeln as well as the Italians were out of luck. 3 lost two aircraft with several wounded and one killed. 1 had one man killed. The next attack, by twin-engined aircraft, fell on us as did the third attack by Mitchells. A few planes were slightly damaged by splinters. Unfortunately here Obergefreiter Merz was killed. Fw Köppen, a pilot of 1 Staffel, died. This was followed by the death of Feldwebel Hossfeld. This day played havoc with my nerves."

The Italian K.41 landing ground was very badly hit, two MC.200s being destroyed and 11 more, plus two MC.202s, damaged. However, 5ª Squadra was active during the day. At 1415 two MC.202s of 168ª Squadriglia took off to intercept a patrol of P-40s; two were claimed by Serg Magg Ettore Dotta. At 1430 nine MC.202s of 3° Stormo were off on a recce mission over the Foum Tataouin-Remtsa area. Ten Mario Pianazza crash-landed near Matmata due to engine failure, returning safely next day. Two MC.202s of 167ª Sq were scambled at 1755 and engaged a formation of about 25 Spitfires. A Spitfire was claimed by S.Ten Giuseppe Robetto and another by his wingman, believed to Serg Magg Diego Rodoz, who returned with a damaged aircraft. One MC.202 of 23° Gruppo was lost during the day, going down in flames with Serg Dante Pancaldi baling out slightly wounded.

British Claims

2 SAAF Sqn	Lt A.P.Blignault	Kittyhawk I ET899 'Y'	Bf 109F		0730
2 SAAF Sqn	Lt L.Dawson-Squibb	Kittyhawk I ET516 'I'	Bf 109E Damaged		
2 SAAF Sqn	Lt G.Hilton-Barber	Kittyhawk I ET513 'S'	Bf 109E Damaged		0730
2 SAAF Sqn	Lt W.L.O.Moon	Kittyhawk I ET951 'R'	Bf 109E	Z.34 8m off coast	0730
2 SAAF Sqn	Lt W.L.O.Moon	Kittyhawk I ET951 'R'	Bf 109F Damaged	Z.34 8m off coast	0730
92 Sqn	Flt Lt N.F.Duke	Spitfire Vb ER821 'R'	Bf 109F	Pisida	0800
80 Sqn	Plt Off W.Burke	Hurricane IIc BP475	Ju 88 Damaged	5m NE Tobruk harbour	1605-1655

British Claims

145 Sqn	Plt Off M.L.Lawrence-Smith	Spitfire Vb ER306	MC.202 Damaged	Gabes	1720-1820 (or 1425-1535)

British Casualties

2 SAAF Sqn	Kittyhawk I AK947 'P' damaged Cat II in combat; Lt D.C.Theron safe
4 SAAF Sqn	Kittyhawk I AK967 'I' shot down by Bf 109; Lt A.J.Mullany PoW
5 SAAF Sqn	Kittyhawk I EV364 hit by Flak, Cat II; Lt P.F.Cowen safe
5 SAAF Sqn	Kittyhawk I AL209 or AK578 damaged Cat II and crash-landed; Lt P.J.S.Louw safe
92 & 145 Sqns	one Spitfire V from each unit collided head-on; Flg Off P.B.Laing-Mason
73 Sqn	Hurricane IIc HL931 shot down by Bf 109 Gabes-Sfax area; Flt Sgt J.D.A.Wright PoW

US Claims

65th FS/57th FG	1/Lt Gilbert O.Wymond Jr	P-40F '46'	Bf 109 Probable	El Hamma	1345
65th FS/57th FG	1/Lt Gilbert O.Wymond Jr	P-40F '46'	Bf 109 Damaged	El Hamma	1345

German Claims

Stab I./JG 77	Hptm Heinz Bär	2 P-40s	0740 & 0745

German Casualties

1./JG 77	Fw Edgar Köppen KiA by bombs at Oudref
1./JG 77	Bf 109G-2 trop WNr 10550 damaged 60% by bombs at Oudref
1./JG 77	Bf 109G-2 trop WNr 10774 damaged 75% by bombs at Oudref
3./JG 77	Bf 109G-2 trop WNr 10620 damaged 60% by bombs at Oudref
9./JG 77	Bf 109G-2 trop WNr 10732 shot down in combat, crash-landed NW Mareth; Uffz Wilhelm Skreba safe
8./JG 77	Bf 109G-2 trop WNr 10813 crash-landed due to engine trouble; Oblt Emil Omert safe

Italian Claims

168ª Sq, 16°Gr, 54°St CT	Serg Magg Ettore Dotta	MC.202	2 P-40s	Gabes area
167ª Sq, 16°Gr, 54°St CT	S.Ten Giuseppe Robetto	MC.202	Spitfire	El Hamma area
167ª Sq, 16°Gr, 54°St CT	Serg Magg Diego Rodoz	MC.202	Spitfire	El Hamma area

Italian Casualties

167ª Sq, 16°Gr, 54°St CT	MC.202 damaged in combat, Serg Magg Diego Rodoz safe
75ª Sq, 23°Gr, 3°St CT	MC.202 crash-landed near Matmata, Ten Mario Pianazza walked back the day after
74ª Sq, 23°Gr, 3°St CT	MC.202 went on fire, Serg Dante Pancaldi baled slightly wounded

Thursday, 4 March 1943

Fighter-bomber attacks continued to be made on the Mareth area, six Kittyhawks of 260 Squadron escorting aircraft of 250 and 3 RAAF Squadrons on a mission at 1130. Sgt Mills' aircraft was hit by Flak, following which he lost his way, belly-landing at Bianchi. Eleven P-40Fs of the 64th Squadron then escorted 12 from the 66th Squadron on a similar mission, but six Bf 109s attacked the cover squadron from above and behind. Lt Overcash engaged one and fought it for ten minutes, nearly ramming it on three occasions. Finally a red flash was seen from the left side of the German fighter and the pilot baled out. Two claims were also made for Messerschmitts damaged, but one of the claiming pilots, Lt Alan Smith, was wounded when his Warhawk was hit and damaged. Overcash's opponent would appear to have been Uffz Bruno Weidlich of II./JG 77, who baled out, wounded during a fight with a reported 25 Allied fighters about 25-30 miles south-west of Gabes.

At 1715 eight Spitfires of 92 Squadron patrolled over the Mareth Line at 8,000 feet, led by Flt Lt Duke. Two Bf 109s were spotted apparently engaged in escorting three or four bomb-carrying Jabo Messerschmitts which were attacking Hazbub landing ground. Duke:

> "I chased the leading Me 109F and fired from port quarter and observed strikes. I fired a second burst from astern and fairly long range. The enemy aircraft exploded in the fuselage and went down. The pilot baled out and the e/a crashed near Medenine. I turned above the second e/a and closed astern, the e/a dived steeply to ground level. I chased him for some while and observed strikes on the aircraft. This e/a was seen to explode on the ground after I broke away, by Sgt M.Askey. No evasive action was taken by this e/a apart from a straight dive – I experienced extremely accurate fire from our own AA."

On 8 March he would add to his diary:

"The pilot of the 109 I shot down on 4 March and baled out came to see who had shot him down. He was 24, an NCO with the Iron Cross. Seemed a pretty good type."

During the day RAF pilots noted three Axis columns moving eastwards from Mareth towards the British lines in the Medenine area.

British Claims					
92 Sqn	Flt Lt N.F.Duke	Spitfire Vb ER821 'R'	2 Bf 109Fs	Pisida	1735
British Casualties					
260 Sqn	Kittyhawk III badly damaged by Flak, Mareth area and crash-landed; Sgt Mills safe				
7 SAAF Wg	Kittyhawk I 'L' damaged by Flak, Lt Col D.H.Loftus safe				
2 SAAF Sqn	Kittyhawk I ET1021 'H' tailplane hit by Breda Flak; Capt D.B.Hauptfleisch safe				
US Claims					
64th FS/57th FG	1/Lt Robert J.Overcash	P-40K-1 '35'	Bf 109		1515
64th FS/57th FG	2/Lt William E.Jenks	P-40K-1 '16'	Bf 109 Damaged		1515
64th FS/57th FG	1/Lt Alan H.Smith	P-40K-1 '33'	Bf 109 Damaged		1515
US Casualties					
64th FS/57th FG	P-40K, damaged; Lt Alan H.Smith WiA				

German Claims		
8./JG 77	Obfw Heinrich Hackler	P-40 n.b.
8./JG 77	Uffz Helmut Rosenberg	P-40 n.b.

German Casualties	
2./SchG 2	Bf 109F-4 WNr 8752 Black 6 hit by AA, crashed 22km E Medenine; Uffz Herbert Müller PoW
1./SchG 2	Bf 109F-4 WNr 7083 shot down by AA, crashed SE Mareth; pilot safe
4./JG 77	Bf 109G-2 trop WNr 10816 shot down in combat with Spitfires and P-40s SW Gabes; Uffz Bruno Weidlich baled out WiA
8./JG 77	Bf 109G-2 WNr 14527 Black 2 collided in air with Yellow 4; Fw Herbert Schwarz KiFA
9./JG 77	Bf 109G-2 trop WNr 10857 Yellow 4 collided in air with Black 2; Uffz Werner Killer PoW

Friday, 5 March 1943

Two Hurricanes of 73 Squadron again flew a dawn sortie, taking off at 0430 on an armed reconnaissance north of Mareth, to Bir Zeltan and Tojane. Both pilots failed to return, one later being reported a prisoner. At 0645 four 92 Squadron Spitfires took off to provide an independent roaming top cover to other Spitfires of 1 SAAF Squadron. However, they were suddenly attacked out of some clouds by seven Bf 109s of I./JG 77 and a 15-minute dogfight followed during which Flg Off 'Happy' McMahon was shot down and killed.

Eight Spitfires from 601 Squadron flew to Hazbub Main for readiness, and at 1215 four of these scrambled to patrol over the forward area. A lone Bf 109 was then seen going west very fast. The confident German pilot then climbed above the Spitfires and then dived on them out of the sun. The British pilots turned towards him as he passed straight by, pulled around and a few minutes later attacked Flt Sgt Tilston, who was forced to bale out. There may have been a second loss, for Neville Duke recorded: "601 were tangled with 20 plus 109s at midday and two of 601 were shot down. Both pilots baled out." Although recorded times do not accord, it is considered likely that Tilston had been shot down by Hptm Bär of I./JG 77, who claimed two Spitfires during the day. By his own admission, at this time Bär was sure of his own ability and possessed a feeling of complete invulnerability.

During 601 Squadron's last scramble of the day from Hazbub, one aircraft got caught in the slipstream of the others and crashed, the pilot being injured. The other three arrived west of Medenine at 13,000 feet, seeing more than 12 Bf 109s and MC.202s 2,000 feet higher. The British pilots climbed to 19,000 feet and then attacked an MC.202 and a Bf 109, Flt Lt Nicholls claiming damage to the Italian aircraft.

Towards the end of his tour of operations, Flt Lt J.H.Nicholls of 601 Squadron is photographed with a new Spitfire IX, flanked by Sgts Pearth and Warren.

British Claims					
601 Sqn	Flt Lt J.H.Nicholls	Spitfire Vc ER181	MC.202 Damaged	W Medenine	1220-1320

British Casualties	
92 Sqn	Spitfire V ER646 scrambled at 0645, shot down by Bf 109s; Flg Off B.L.McMahon KiA
601 Sqn	Spitfire V BR284 scrambled at 1215, shot down by Bf 109s; Flt Sgt J.Tilston baled out
73 Sqn	Hurricane IIc HM142 shot down by Bf 109 SW Gabes; Wt Off R.C.Dolan MiA
73 Sqn	Hurricane IIc HV547 shot down by Bf 109 SW Gabes; Flt Sgt D.M.Logan PoW

German Claims				
Stab I./JG 77	Hptm Heinz Bär	Spitfire	NE Medenine	0758
3./JG 77	Oblt Ernst Laube	Spitfire	8km NE Medenine	0800
Stab I./JG 77	Hptm Heinz Bär	Spitfire		0820

Saturday, 6 March 1943

Generale Messe now launched I Italian Army in a three-pronged attack down the Mareth-Medenine road (the columns that had been spotted by DAF pilots on the previous day). 10th, 15th and 21st Panzer Divisions with 100,000 men, 700 guns and 200 tanks drove from Tojane and Hallouf to begin the attack at 0900. 8th Army were ready and on this occasion were able to employ the Afrika Korps' favoured tactics against them, having positioned a powerful screen of anti-tank guns in a well dug-in hull-down position, supported by their own tanks and artillery. All three Axis columns came up against a solid front at Medenine, manned by 201st Guards Brigade, 131st Lorried Infantry Brigade and 2nd New Zealand Division, falling fowl of a massive concentration of guns of all types. The attack was halted at midday after heavy losses had been inflicted on the Axis forces; after regrouping, they attacked again at 1530 but this thrust was also stopped and the German units then began retiring to Mareth, leaving 52 tanks – more than a quarter of available strength – destroyed or damaged on the battlefield.

Bad weather prevented DAF from taking much part in the proceedings, but a few missions were flown. FW 190s of III./SKG 10 and Me 210s of III./ZG 1 had been moved south to aid in this attack, both types appearing over the front in some strength during the next few days.

Twelve Spitfires from 145 Squadron were off early at 0650 to cover Kittyhawks attacking the German columns north of Medenine, where six Bf 109s were seen below; two of these were claimed damaged. On a second mission, eight Spitfires from this unit patrolled over the forward troops, seeing nine plus MC.202s below. Sqn Ldr Wade then spotted a Bf 109 and got on its tail but his cannons failed to operate. He attacked with machine guns only and it belly-landed in Axis-held territory. Deciding that it could easily be repaired, he claimed it only as damaged on his return. In the meantime Sgt Usher dived on three MC.202s, but then saw three Ju 87s and claimed damage to two of these. Plt Off Lawrence-Smith and his wingman chased two Macchis, but broke off south-east of Gabes, giving chase instead to two Bf 109s spotted bombing a road. Lawrence-Smith hit one which turned on its back and dived into the sea.

At 1315 40 SAAF Squadron moved to Neffatia, but just after the arrival of the unit's aircraft, the airfield was strafed by 12 Bf 109s and then bombed by 18 Me 210s which achieved complete surprise. Armin Köhler was involved in this attack:

> "This morning we intended to join with the army in an attack, but the weather was bad. At midday we make a start. We escort a formation of (Me) 210s and FW 190s to the airfield at Neffatia, east of Medenine. Carry out a sequence of attacks with the 109s also joining in as fighter-bombers. It is marvellous to see German aircraft once again in the sky over Africa. It will certainly be a surprise for the British. Our force is so well and so strongly protected that the Spitfires looking on do not come down. But the Flak over the airfield was the heaviest I have seen for a long time."

Ten Spitfires, six from 1 SAAF Squadron and four from 601 Squadron, took off on patrol at 1535, two returning early. Ten miles north of Medenine the formation was flying beneath cloud at 8,000 feet when three Bf 109s dived out of the overcast, apparently in a bombing dive. 601 Squadron's section was sent down after them, but 28 Ju 87s of III./StG 3 in vics of three and with many escorting Messerschmitts were then seen. Maj 'Snowie' Moodie led his 1 SAAF section down onto them, firing into the belly of a Stuka. As he pulled away, his wingman, Lt Tyrell, also fired at it and the Ju 87 went down in a flash of fire, hitting the ground and exploding. Tyrell then attacked another which fell on its back and went down pouring black smoke; he claimed this as probably destroyed. The German unit reported that one bomber force-landed with a wounded pilot. One more claim for a damaged was made against the dive-bombers, but other pilots suffered cannon stoppages; it was also nearly dark by this time, and the attack was not pressed further.

Returning from a late patrol at 1650, pilots from 145 Squadron spotted 15-20 Me 210s, one of which was claimed damaged in the gathering gloom. During the day two Spitfires of 601 Squadron flew a reconnaissance of Gabes-El Hamma landing ground. On returning Flt Sgt Toller's aircraft was attacked in error by a Kittyhawk and he crash-landed.

From Sfax 6° Gruppo moved to Gabes to join the Regia Aeronautica's southern command, Settore Sud, bringing with it eight MC.202s; at this date 3° Stormo CT had just 12 of these aircraft, and 16° Gruppo had 19 for a total of 39 in the area. Between 1135 and 1320, in rather cloudy weather, seven MC.202s of 16° Gruppo patrolled over the Italian columns advancing in the Medenine area. Ten Spitfires were engaged and one was claimed by S.Ten Robetto, shared with S.Ten Rovina but Serg Magg Torivio Guacciolo failed to return. A probable was claimed in the same area by Ten Solaroli, commander of 95ª Squadriglia.

British Claims

145 Sqn	Sgt J.H.D.Herberte	Spitfire Vb EP648	Bf 109 Damaged	N Medenine	0550-0805
145 Sqn	Plt Off G.W.Small	Spitfire Vb ER139	Bf 109 Damaged	N Medenine	0655-0755
145 Sqn	Sqn Ldr L.C.Wade	Spitfire Vb ER486	Bf 109 Damaged (force-landed)		1255-1405
145 Sqn	Sgt D.C.Usher	Spitfire Vb ER703	2 Ju 87s Damaged		1300-1355
145 Sqn	Plt Off M.L.Lawrence-Smith	Spitfire Vb ER306	Bf 109	4m N coast	1300-1420
1 SAAF Sqn	Lt D.L.Quin	Spitfire V .. 321 'E'	Ju 87 Damaged	10m NW Medenine	1605
1 SAAF Sqn	Lt A.F.Tyrell	Spitfire V BR390 'B'	Ju 87	10m NW Medenine	1605
145 Sqn	Flt Sgt R.T.Breheny	Spitfire Vb ER199	Me 210 Damaged	Tunisia	1655-1820
145 Sqn	Flt Sgt R.T.Breheny	Spitfire Vb ER199	Ju 87 Probable	Tunisia	1655-1820

British Casualties

601 Sqn	Spitfire V ER312 left 1400, shot down – possibly by a Kittyhawk, crash-landed at 1515; Flg Off A.A.Toller safe
601 Sqn	Spitfire V ER317 left 0850 for Gabes-El Hamma area, FTR; Flg Sgt J.E.Robinson MiA
250 Sqn	Kittyhawk III FR313 left 0640 on bombing mission, force-landed at 0645; Flt Sgt A.F.Nitz safe
2 SAAF Sqn	Kittyhawk I damaged on the ground by bombing

German Claims

Stab I./JG 77	Hptm Heinz Bär	2 Spitfires	0926 & 0928

German Casualties

9./StG 3	Ju 87D-3 WNr 2959 S7+BD combat with Spitfire NW Medenine, 80% damaged; Hptm Fritz Eyer/Obfw Robert Standtke WiA
8./JG 77	Bf 109G-2 trop WNr 10767 shot down by Spitfire, 90% damaged in force-landing at Mareth; Uffz Max Dehnhardt safe

Italian Claims

95ª Sq, 18°Gr, 3°St CT	Ten Giorgio Solaroli	MC.202	Spitfire Probable	Mareth Line	1130-
167ª Sq, 16°Gr, 54°St CT	S.Ten Giuseppe Robetto	MC.202	Spitfire	Mareth Line	
167ª Sq, 16°Gr, 54°St CT	S.Ten Giacomo Rovina	MC.202			

Italian Casualties

167ª Sq, 16°Gr, 54°St CT	MC.202 failed to return, Serg Magg Torivio Guacciolo MiA

Sunday, 7 March 1943

First off at 0920 were six Spitfires of 145 Squadron on patrol; at 14,000 feet and ten miles north of Medenine, the pilots saw about six aircraft identified as MC.200s beneath them. The Spitfires peeled off in pairs and Sgt Usher attacked one, firing three bursts which caused his victim to crash into a salt marsh. Sgt Stott attacked another which dived away, but he then blacked out. On recovery he saw a column of smoke from the ground and claimed a probable. Six of 145 Squadron's aircraft were off again at 1100, led by Wg Cdr Gleed. They were followed at 1155 by six more from 1 SAAF Squadron to patrol north-west of Medenine; at 1155 six from 92 Squadron followed to patrol over the forward troops.

145 Squadron engaged a formation of 12 Bf 109s and MC.202s, Flt Lt Taylor chasing one Macchi out to sea, firing until it landed on the water where it sank about 10-15 miles north of Mareth. Whilst engaging a Macchi, Wg Cdr Gleed was attacked by four more and called for help. The pilots of 1 SAAF Squadron had spotted the same mixed Axis formation and came to Gleed's aid, attacking ten of the Axis fighters which broke away to left and right. Lts Moodie and Fouche pursued a pair, the former claiming to have probably damaged one MC.202, but both were then pursued by a very determinedly-flown Bf 109G. At this point Fouche heard Gleed's call and attacked his four Italian assailants, claiming damage to one. Other South African Spitfires were rushing to the area, Lt Brebner attacking one at which he fired two bursts, seeing it go down vertically, pouring smoke. One more was claimed damaged after which the

On his return to operations with 92 Squadron, Neville Duke enjoyed a run of successes. On 7 March 1943 he had raised his personal total to 19 (two of them shared) by claiming two Messerschmitts shot down on that date.

Spitfire Vc ER228 ZX-S in which Flt Lt John Taylor of 145 Squadron claimed an MC.202 shot down over the Mareth area on 7 March 1943.

squadron reformed to return to base. As they approached home they spotted 12 bombers attacking Neffatia airfield which they identified as Ju 88s, one of which was claimed damaged before most pilots experienced the familiar trouble with their cannons. It is likely that the bombers were III./ZG 1's Me 210s, back for a second attack on Neffatia following the previous day's success. The type was new to North Africa and of similar general arrangement to the Ju 88. Certainly one such aircraft force-landed following combat, the pilot being killed.

Meanwhile, the 92 Squadron aircraft, over Medenine at 18,000 feet, spotted three Bf 109s below and dived on them, splitting them up. Flt Lt Duke: "I closed on the port 109, and observed strikes on the fuselage as the e/a turned; with second burst e/a seemed to lurch violently. The aircraft went down in a wide spiral dive, as if the pilot was hit, and crashed. The e/a did not explode on the ground." Two more targets were claimed as probables and two shot down; in addition Flt Lt 'Red' Chisholm also claimed an MC.202 and a second damaged. As these fights were in progress six Kittyhawks from 3 RAAF Squadron left at 1145 on an armed reconnaissance west of Medenine where at 15,000 feet nine Axis fighters were encountered. Sgt Goulder fired at a Bf 109 which poured black smoke, flicked over and dived away; he was credited with this as destroyed, adding a claim for a second damaged. Other pilots claimed a probable and two more damaged. During this encounter Obfw Reinert of II./JG 77 claimed one Spitfire at 1218, with another being claimed by Fw Hosmann of I.Gruppe. Several formations of MC.202s were in the air and all were engaged. Six patrolling over Medenine reported being attacked by Spitfires, claiming one destroyed and some damaged. A further dozen Macchis in the same area split into two sections, six being attacked by Curtiss fighters of which they claimed one and two damaged, the other six reported meeting both Spitfires and P-40s, claiming three damaged but one MC.202 suffering heavy damage.

Seventeen more Macchis of 16° Gruppo led by Cap Giovanni Pagliari, attacked Neffatia landing ground as Allied aircraft were taking off, claiming seven Spitfires (or nine according to a different source) and a 'Lockheed' destroyed and five more damaged for the loss of two of their own number, the one flown by Serg Alberto Calistri, which failed to return and another badly damaged, the pilot surviving unhurt. Six MC.202s of 6° Gruppo led by Ten Adelmo Ferrazza patrolled over the Medenine area between 1130-1240, where ten Spitfires were engaged, one being claimed by M.llo Dino Forlani. At about the same time and area another patrol of six MC.202s of 16° Gruppo encountered a number of P-40s; one was claimed shot down by Ten Elio Martire.

Three 92 Squadron Spitfires scrambled at 1410, running into 20 Bf 109s near Neffatia. Neville Duke:

> "I led four aircraft on a scramble from Hazbub at 10,000 feet and engaged five plus Me 109Fs above us. The e/a dived east and I followed firing bursts at one 109 on which I observed strikes. At 6,000

feet over Neffatia aerodrome I was engaged with numerous 109s. I closed to 100 yards astern of e/a and observed top of tail, hood and large pieces of fuselage disintegrate. The e/a caught fire, and the pilot baled out."

Flg Off Ted Sly claimed a probable and Flt Sgt Patterson one damaged. Around this time 12 Kittyhawks from 112 Squadron escorted by others from 250 Squadron on an armed reconnaissance over the front, met more than six Bf 109s over Mareth. One Kittyhawk was badly damaged by a Bf 109.

During the afternoon fighting Lt Berres of I./JG 77 claimed a Spitfire south-east of Medenine at 1444 and Obfw Reinert made his second claim of the day ten minutes earlier. Several other claims were registered and Armin Köhler's diary provides another vivid account of the actions in which he was engaged:

"We make an early morning flight up to the front line and engage Spitfires in a dogfight south-east of Medenine. I manage an effective burst on one Spitfire but we are unable to distinguish the hits. We reform over Mareth and once more make for Medenine. Suddenly eight Spitfires attack us from astern. Leutnant Krieger is shot down but manages to reach his own lines. Feldwebel Hosmann drives the Spitfire off him. Because of the enemy attack from overhead, hits could not be observed. In the end Oberfeldwebel Meschke and I have three Spitfires after us. I try to get above them but to no avail. They climb much better than us. We make off towards base.

"In the afternoon again we carry out a fighter-bomber attack east of Medenine. Thereafter Freie Jagd. We climb parallel to the coast in the direction of Gabes. Look! To seaward and away to the west – 40 Kittyhawks swinging in towards land behind the Mareth Line and disappearing below the cloud base towards the mountains. I attack again but with no success. Overhead a further 20 Kittyhawks provide cover for the lower formation. Hosmann, who has lost touch with me, has attacked the higher formation and shot one down. It went through the cloud in a spin and crashed. But no one to confirm the claim. Bad luck!" Next day Köhler was to add: "Hosmann's claim of yesterday is confirmed by Kiebitz."

From the north II./JG 51 also appeared over the southern area on this date when four Bf 109s escorting bombers engaged 20 Spitfires about 25 miles south-west of Medenine (see also Volume 3). One Spitfire was claimed shot down but two Messerschmitts were lost. A Jabo Bf 109 of I./SG 2 was also shot down near Berka during the day, the pilot being captured. 5 SAAF Squadron noted that one of the pilots shot down by the Spitfires during the last attack of the afternoon on the airfield by four Bf 109s, had been captured nearby and was entertained by the South African pilots in their mess. He was described as having longish blonde hair and being a very committed supporter of the Nazi Party. He claimed that he had been fired at while on his parachute. Another of the captured German pilots was entertained by 92 Squadron but he escaped that night; he was subsequently recaptured. On this date 40 SAAF Squadron undertook its first TacR operations with its new Spitfires from Neffatia.

British Claims

92 Sqn	Flt Sgt H.Patterson	Spitfire Vb ER470	Bf 109 Damaged		0710-0815
92 Sqn	Flt Lt N.F.Duke	Spitfire Vb ER821 'R'	Bf 109F	nr Medenine	0710-0815
145 Sqn	Sgt W.F.Dorman	Spitfire Vb EP704	Bf 109 Damaged	S Medenine	0745-0855
145 Sqn	Sgt E.A.Stott	Spitfire Vb ER306	MC.200 Probable		0920-1035
145 Sqn	Sgt D.C.Usher	Spitfire Vb ER703	MC.200	0920-1035	
145 Sqn	Sgt J.E.Parker	Spitfire Vb EP193	Bf 109 Damaged	5-10m SE Gabes	1100-1225
145 Sqn	Flt Lt J.S.Taylor	Spitfire Vb EP199	MC.202	10-15m N Mareth	1100-1235
244 Wg	Wg Cdr I.R.Gleed	Spitfire Vb AB502 IR-G	Bf 109 Damaged	4m SE Mareth	1100-1230
92 Sqn	Plt Off W.L.Chisholm	Spitfire Vb ER821 'R'	MC.202	Tunisia	1155-1255
92 Sqn	Plt Off W.L.Chisholm	Spitfire Vb ER821 'R'	MC.202 Damaged	Tunisia	1155-1255
92 Sqn	Plt Off W.L.Chisholm	Spitfire Vb ER821 'R'	Bf 109 Probable	Tunisia	1155-1255
92 Sqn	Flt Lt P.H.Humphreys	Spitfire Vb ER224	Bf 109		1155-1255
92 Sqn	Flt Sgt J.C.Sales	Spitfire Vb EP777	Bf 109 Probable		1155-1255
1 SAAF Sqn	Lt D.M.Brebner	Spitfire V ER473 'M'	MC.202 Probable	NW Medenine	1210
1 SAAF Sqn	Lt H.van N.Fouche	Spitfire V ..281 'G'	MC.202 Damaged	NW Medenine	1210

1 SAAF Sqn	Lt J.R.Lanham	Spitfire V ER882 'F'	Ju 88 Damaged	W Medenine	1210
1 SAAF Sqn	Lt S.W.van der Merwe	Spitfire V ER576 'C'			
1 SAAF Sqn	Lt D.L.Quin	Spitfire V AR398 'Y'	MC.202 Probable	NW Medenine	
3 RAAF Sqn	Wt Off P.M.Nash	Kittyhawk IIa FL284 'C'	Bf 109F/G Probable	W Medenine	1225
3 RAAF Sqn	Sgt K.Goulder	Kittyhawk IIa FL288 'B'	Bf 109F/G	W Medenine	1230
3 RAAF Sqn	Wt Off R.N.B.Stevens	Kittyhawk IIa FL301 'I'	Bf 109F/G Damaged	W Medenine	1230
92 Sqn	Flg Off E.Sly	Spitfire Vb ER543	Bf 109 Probable		1325-1525
145 Sqn	Flt Lt J.S.Taylor	Spitfire Vb ER228	Bf 109	SW Medenine	1415-1530
92 Sqn	Flt Sgt H.Patterson	Spitfire Vb ER470	Bf 109 Damaged		1425-1525
92 Sqn	Flt Lt N.F.Duke	Spitfire Vb BR519 'T'	Bf 109F	nr Neffatia	1450
92 Sqn	Flg Off M.E.Jowsey	Spitfire Vb ER613	Bf 109 Probable		1600-1710

British Casualties

112 Sqn	Kittyhawk III badly damaged by Bf 109
2 SAAF Sqn	Kittyhawk AK883 crash-landed on operations 1505-1605; Lt E.T.Newby safe

German Claims

II./JG 51	Fw Alfred Rauch	Spitfire	60km SW Medenine	1213
4./JG 77	Obfw Ernst-Wilhelm Reinert	Spitfire	12km SE Medenine	1218
2./JG 77	Fw Karl Hosmann	Spitfire o.Zg.		1220
Stab I./JG 77	Hptm Heinz Bär	P-40		1227
4./JG 77	Fw Maximilian Volke	Spitfire	38km SE Medenine	1235
Stab I./JG 77	Lt Heinz-Edgar Berres	Spitfire	SE Medenine	1444
1./JG 77	Fw Horst Schlick	Spitfire		
4./JG 77	Obfw Ernst-Wilhelm Reinert	Spitfire	15km SE Medenine	1454
4./JG 77	Uffz Harry Donath	Spitfire	12km S Medenine	1502
2./JG 77	Fw Karl Hosmann	P-40	Mareth	1515

German Casualties

1./JG 77	Bf 109G-2 trop WNr 10833 combat with Spitfire, force-landing Matmata 40% damaged; Lt Karl-Heinz Krieger safe
5./JG 51	Bf 109G-4 trop WNr 15049 Black 5 shot down by Spitfires Medenine; Lt Heinz Föhl MiA
5./JG 51	Bf 109G-4 trop WNr 15004 Black 7 shot down by Spitfire SW Medenine; Uffz Werner Heidenreich baled, returned later
2./SchG 2	Bf 109F-4 WNr 7269 Black 3 shot down by Spitfires near Berka; Lt Heinz Schiedat PoW
4./KG 30	Ju 88A-4 WNr 140430 4D+KM lost on mission to Tripoli, Obfw Heribert Bauer and two MiA, one KiA
7./ZG 1	Me 210A-1 WNr 2314 2N+BD shot down by Spitfires 50km N Gabes; Uffz Johannes Häring WiA, one KiA, two safe

Italian Claims

167ª Sq, 16°Gr, 54°St CT	S.Ten Giuseppe Robetto	MC.202	Spitfire	Neffatia	0630-0900
169ª Sq, 16°Gr, 54°St CT	Serg Magg Ettore Dotta	MC.202			
168ª Sq, 16°Gr, 54°St CT	S.Ten Gian Maria Morittu	MC.202	Spitfire	Neffatia	0630-0900
168ª Sq, 16°Gr, 54°St CT	Ten Giovanni D'Amelia	MC.202	Spitfire	Neffatia	0630-0900
168ª Sq, 16°Gr, 54°St CT	Ten Alfonso Lattanzi	MC.202	Spitfire	Neffatia	0630-0900
168ª Sq, 16°Gr, 54°St CT	Ten Alfonso Lattanzi	MC.202	Spitfire Probable	Neffatia	0630-0900
168ª Sq, 16°Gr, 54°St CT	S.Ten Gian Maria Morittu	MC.202	2 Spitfires	Neffatia	0630-0900
167ª Sq, 16°Gr, 54° St CT	S.Ten Giacomo Rovina	MC.202	Spitfire Probable	Neffatia	0630-0900
16° Gr, 54° St Ct	unspecified	MC.202	Spitfire	Neffatia	0630-0900
16° Gr, 54° St Ct	unspecified	MC.202	Spitfire Probable	Neffatia	0630-0900
16° Gr, 54° St Ct	unspecified	MC.202	P-38	Neffatia	0630-0900
79ª Sq, 6°Gr, 1°St CT	M.llo Dino Forlani	MC.202	Spitfire	Medenine	1130-1240
168ª Sq, 16°Gr, 54°St CT	Ten Elio Martire	MC.202	P-40	Medenine	1135-1255

Italian Casualties

168ª Sq, 16°Gr, 54 °St CT	MC.202 MM 9623 failed to return, Serg Alberto Calistri MiA 0630-0900
16°Gr, 54 °St CT	MC.202 badly damaged in combat, pilot safe

Monday, 8 March 1943

The day proved much quieter for the DAF following the withdrawal of the German columns from the Medenine area. At 1115, however, 12 Kittyhawks of 5 SAAF Squadron took off on an armed reconnaissance. When bombing and strafing targets of opportunity, some ten Bf 109s appeared. Capt Morrison dropped his bomb, then attacked these, firing at several. Losing his wingman, he was engaged by six of the Messerschmitts, one of which dived past in front of him from the right. He fired at this, seeing hits. The German fighter turned right and he fired a long burst of about seven seconds and the aircraft dived very steeply, disappearing into a wadi pouring black smoke. I./SG 2 reported the loss of a Bf 109 which force-landed in the Zarat area, seemingly as a result of AA damage; the pilot escaped capture and returned to his unit two days later.

During the day Flt Lt Humphreys and Plt Off Wilson of 92 Squadron encountered the first FW 190s to be seen by any DAF Spitfire pilots in North Africa. Both of them suffered cannon-jamming problems and no claims resulted. Four Spitfires of 145 Squadron were scrambled from Hazbub, Sqn Ldr Wade claiming damage to a Bf 109. Sgt Denis Usher of this unit was commissioned on this date. Armin Köhler was by now becoming heartily sick of the Spitfires, confiding to his diary: "We make another early morning sortie but without success. The Spitfires are already overhead waiting for us. Very poor visibility due to the sun in the east and several cloud layers and shadows. The Spitfires have complete advantage. As expected, they try to pass over us but we do not permit this."

By now the squadrons of 239 Wing were all forward at Neffatia Main, whereas 5 Squadron had arrived at Sorman with its tank-busters. Next day the 57th Fighter Group would arrive at Ben Gardane. On 9 March the weather was very bad, greatly restricting operations.

British Claims					
92 Sqn	Lt H.Smith	Spitfire Vb AR494	MC.202 Probable	Zidan	1050-1225
5 SAAF Sqn	Capt R.L.Morrison	Kittyhawk I ..421 'C'	Bf 109 Probable		1130
145 Sqn	Sqn Ldr L.C.Wade	Spitfire Vb ES252	Bf 109 Damaged	Foum-Tataouin area	1545-1650

British Casualties	
2 SAAF Sqn	Kittyhawk I AK780 damaged on operations; Lt J.A.Bilbert safe
5 SAAF Sqn	Kittyhawk I AK650 damaged by Flak and crash-landed near base, Cat II; Lt H.E.Sansom safe

German Claims				
7./JG 77	Oblt Georg Seckel	P-40	S Mareth	1132

German Casualties	
1./SchG 2	Bf 109F-4 WNr 7342 White 8 shot down by AA near Zarat; Fw Josef Enzensberger MiA, returned later on foot
4.(H)./12	Bf 109G.2 WNr 10611 White 10 shot down in combat and crash-landed in the desert; Lt Ernst Hertrich MiA, returned later on foot
1./SchG 2	Bf 109F-4 WNr 8686 crash-landed at La Fauconnerie, pilot safe
8./JG 77	Bf 109G-2 trop slightly damaged in combat; Uffz Karl-Heinz Böttner WiA
III./StG 3	Ju 87D-3 WNr 2663 destroyed by explosion of own bomb at Mezzouna-Nord

Wednesday, 10 March 1943

General Leclerc's Free French forces were now advancing from south of the Sahara towards the area of Ksar Rhilane after a long and difficult journey. From the northern Tunisian front, the German commander, Jurgen von Arnim, despatched a force of vehicles, supported by fighter-bombers and dive-bombers, to intercept and to prevent the French from arriving on the western flank of 8th Army. To protect the French from this threat, 6 Squadron's tank-busting Hurricanes were ordered to attack, two separate assaults being made on this date. The first of these resulted in claims for 20 vehicles, 12 of which were put out of action. The second resulted in claims for a tank and an armoured car hit. Kittyhawks also strafed the Axis column, claiming petrol bowsers and other vehicles destroyed.

Five Spitfires from 601 Squadron covered the Hurricanes on a sortie at 1005 but became split up in thick cloud into two sections, one of two and the other of three aircraft. The latter trio encountered a TacR Bf 109 of 4.(H)/12 which was shot down north of Gafsa. Between 1545-1600 Kittyhawks of 112, 250 and 260 Squadrons took off to strafe Axis positions north-west of the Foum-Tataouin area. Here the 24 aircraft of the two latter units went down to strafe as those of 112 Squadron remained above to give cover. At this point 12-15 Ju 87s of III./StG 3 were seen, escorted by 20-30 Bf 109s of JG 77. The strafing aircraft engaged in general dogfights, but no claims were made. One 260 Squadron aircraft was hit by Breda fire, Flt Sgt Collet being badly wounded and belly-landing his aircraft at Neffatia South on return; he subsequently died of his wounds.

Meanwhile, the covering Kittyhawks of 112 Squadron had borne the brunt of the fighting and on return Plt Off Guess claimed to have shot down two Bf 109s, the unit's 200th and 201st victories. Flg Off Livingstone claimed a Ju 87. However, there was no jubilation for topping the 200 mark for no less than six Kittyhawks failed to return, including that flown by the flight commander, Flt Lt R.R.Smith, DFC, and a seventh was very badly damaged. Maj Müncheberg made the first claim and the third, recording that the pilot of the latter was a Canadian captain who was taken prisoner – clearly this was Smith, who was indeed a Canadian. One Messerschmitt was shot down in the same area, Lt Lüdemann being killed – probably one of those claimed by Guess.

During the day 71 sorties were flown by the MC.202s, many of them strafing missions in the course of which ten vehicles were claimed destroyed. 145 and 1 SAAF Squadrons now moved to Bu Grara, 21 SAAF Squadron flying up to Zuara. Here the unit would be joined two days later by 12 SAAF and 24 SAAF Squadrons with their Bostons.

British Claims					
601 Sqn	Plt Off R.V.Baxter	Spitfire Vc BR175	Bf 109	N Gafsa	1005-1125
601 Sqn	Flt Sgt W.D.Steele	Spitfire Vc ER133			
112 Sqn	Plt Off R.D.Guess	Kittyhawk III FR424	2 Bf 109Fs	40m NW Foum Tataouin	1545-1730
112 Sqn	Flg Off T.Livingstone	Kittyhawk III FL882	Ju 87	40m NW Foum Tataouin	1545-1730
112 Sqn	unstated	Kittyhawk III	Bf 109 Damaged	40m NW Foum Tataouin	1545-1730

British Casualties	
112 Sqn	Kittyhawk III FR131 shot down nr Foum Tataouin; Plt Off R.C.C.Smith KiA
112 Sqn	Kittyhawk III FR275 shot down nr Foum Tataouin; Flt Sgt R.De Bourke KiA
112 Sqn	Kittyhawk III FR295 shot down nr Foum Tataouin; Flg Off D.A.Bruce KiA
112 Sqn	Kittyhawk III FR361 shot down nr Foum Tataouin; Sgt J.H.Oliver KiA
112 Sqn	P-40 245798 shot down nr Foum Tataouin; Flg Off G.W.Wiley PoW; killed after Stalag Luft III breakout 30 March 1944
112 Sqn	Kittyhawk III FR325 shot down nr Foum Tataouin; Flg Lt R.R.Smith DFC, PoW
112 Sqn	Kittyhawk III FR691 "wrecked by enemy action in the air"
260 Sqn	Kittyhawk III badly damaged by Flak, Ksar Rhilane; Sgt Collet died of wounds

German Claims				
Stab/JG 77	Maj Joachim Müncheberg	P-40	S Ksar Rhilane	1633 &1648
Stab I./JG 77	Hptm Heinz Bär	P-40	SW Medenine	1633
3./JG 77	Lt Heinz-Edgar Berres	P-40	SSW Medenine	1634
2./JG 77	Fw Karl Hosmann	2 P-40s	SW Medenine	1635 & 1640
2./JG 77	Obfw Heinz Meschke	P-40	SW Medenine	1636
4./JG 77	Fw Maximilian Volke	2 P-40s	60km SW Gabes	1637 & 1645
Stab II./JG 77	Lt Günther Schimmelpfennig	P-40	90km SW Gabes	1638
Stab/JG 77	Maj Joachim Müncheberg	P-40	N Foum Tataouin	1648

German Casualties	
4.(H)/12	Bf 109G-2 WNr 10663 Black 2 shot down by Spitfire N Gafsa; Fw Werner Schmidt KiA
I./SchG 2	Bf 109F-4 WNr 7109 shot down by AA near Medenine, pilot safe
6./JG 77	Bf 109G-6 trop WNr 16316 crash-landed after combat, engine damage, 75% damaged S Matmata; Fw Franz Nägele safe
8./JG 77	Bf 109G-2 trop WNr 10819 White 1 shot down by P-40 N Ksar Rhilane; Lt Heinz Lüdemann KiA

Thursday, 11 March 1943

2nd New Zealand Division now began moving in great secrecy to Ben Gardane in preparation for the next 8th Army offensive. Otherwise no action of any note occurred over the southern front during the day. 19 MC.202s patrolled over the lines from 1315-1445. A formation of about 20 bombers escorted by 25 fighters was engaged, an unidentified twin-engined aircraft and a Spitfire were claimed shot down, plus two more Spitfires as probables.

US Casualties	
66th FS/57th FG	Capt Delbert V.Mitchell KiA, land mine

Italian Claims					
79ª Sq, 6°Gr, 1°St CT	M.llo Dino Forlani	MC.202	Spitfire	Medenine	
16° Gr, 54°St	unspecified	MC.202	twin-engined e/a	over lines	1315-1445
16° Gr, 54°St	unspecified	MC.202	2 Spitfires probable	over lines	1315-1445

Friday, 12 March 1943

Having arrived at Zuara during the day, the South African light bombers were immediately active, 14 Bostons of 12 SAAF Squadron and four of 24 SAAF undertaking a low level raid over the front. Flak was intense and three of the former unit's aircraft were badly damaged, all landing short at Neffatia Main on their return. Allied AA was by now proving as effective, two of I./SG 2's Bf 109s being shot down during the day, one crashing at Bir el Hafra with a second down at Thelepte, well in the northern area, the pilot becoming a prisoner (see Volume 3).

In 244 Wing the commanding officer of 601 Squadron, Sqn Ldr G.H.Plinston, was notified of the award of the DFC. In 92 Squadron Flt Lt W.L.'Red' Chisholm, DFC & Bar, ended his tour after claiming eight victories with the unit since mid 1942. His place as a flight commander was taken by Flt Lt E.A.G.C.Bruce. On this date the first two members of a special new unit arrived to join 145 Squadron on attachment. This unit was the Polish Fighting Team, which was composed wholly of hand-picked and highly-experienced Polish fighter pilots, all of whom were volunteers. They came to fly the first Spitfire IXs which were about to be issued to DAF units. The team was a truly elite formation, a most unusual departure from normal RAF practice which generally frowned upon such special units. It was commanded by Wg Cdr T.H.Rolski and led in the air by Sqn Ldr S.F.Skalski; it included among its 16 members, most of whom arrived in a C-47 next day, Flt Lt K.Pniak, Flt Lt W.S.Krol, Flt Lt E.Horbaczewski, Flg Off K.Sporny, Flg Off B.Arct, Flg Off W.Drecki, Flg Off L.Martel, Plt Off M.M.Woszlowski. Wt Off M.Popek and half a dozen others. The team was to be attached to 145 Squadron for operations and for administrative purposes.

British Casualties	
12 SAAF Sqn	3 Bostons badly damaged by Flak

Saturday, 13 March 1943

At 1105 six Spitfires of 601 Squadron were scrambled west of Medenine, meeting MC.202s; one was claimed as a probable and two damaged. The 57th Fighter Group then despatched 34 P-40s on a sweep over the Gabes area at 1430; the formation comprised 12 aircraft from each of the 65th and 66th Squadrons and ten from the 64th, included were several pilots attached from the newly-arrived 314th Squadron of the 324th Fighter Group. Six Spitfires of 92 Squadron followed a few minutes later to supply top cover. Heavy Flak was experienced as the formation crossed the coastline near Gabes, and here the Americans were attacked by Bf 109s from Stab, I. and II./JG 77 and a big dogfight ensued, the German pilots claiming five or six of the P-40s shot down. Three MC.202s were also scrambled, their pilots claiming one Spitfire shot down. 1/ Lt Deniston recalled: "Near Gabes at 18,000 ft we were attacked by 15+ Me 109s and Macchi 202s. God! What a fight followed. I got in a fair burst. Lost from my formation, I flew all over the place – airplanes swirling thick as flies. I saw one hit the water below. We have four pilots missing, none from our squadron. It was the longest and fiercest fight I've ever been in. Lasted at least 20 minutes. Maj Worley of the 314th shot down but is safe."

The Warhawk pilots fought a hectic battle during which five Bf 109s were claimed shot down plus two probables and three damaged. Lt Brandon of the 64th Squadron called for his section to break but Lt Douglas flew straight on, apparently not having heard the message. He was seen to be attacked by a Bf 109, but his subsequent fate was not observed. Brandon then spotted a P-40 high above which was also being attacked; he thought that this was probably Lt Jenks. As he watched, this aircraft was also targeted and dived away, pouring smoke. As this squadron returned along the coast some eight or more Messerschmitts were seen above, engaged in a big dogfight. Jenks, Douglas and Capt Simpson of the 324th Squadron all failed to return, one more crash-landing at base.

The Group's Executive Officer, Maj Archie Knight, was flying in Capt Clark's medium cover section when they were attacked by five Bf 109s. Clark and Knight turned into these and claimed damage to three of them, all being seen to peel off and dive away pouring black smoke (which sounds remarkably like exhaust smoke from Daimler-Benz engines suddenly opened to full throttle). During this encounter Knight's aircraft was hit in the spinner and the coolant system, glycol and oil spraying out over the aircraft, and he lost sight of Clark. He decided that he was now too far west of the lines to make it back alone, so continued with the rest of the US formation. After flying around, trying to clear the oil from his windscreen, he spotted a P-40 with a Messerschmitt on its tail. He dived on this and sent it down into the sea with a few short bursts.

Pulling up from this attack, his Warhawk fell into a spin, on recovery from which he was too low to bale out. He managed to crash-land in a salt marsh just to the west of the German lines, about a mile north of the nearest artillery position and about 500 yards from the sea. Axis troops sought to reach him but were forced to take cover from British forces controlling the area with fire from some high cliffs to the east. The Germans then resorted to machine-gunning and shelling the grounded aircraft and pilot, but Knight managed to remain a poor target by hiding in a shallow foxhole which he dug with his scout knife, although a splinter from a nearby shell burst knicked one of his fingers. At dusk he made for the sea and minus only his parachute, he began swimming for safer territory, carrying his wrist watch in his mouth. With the aid of his 'Mae West' life jacket he was able to wade and swim for several miles across a small bay. He finally reached the shore and climbed to higher ground, walking about ten miles until he reached a British gun position around midnight. He returned to his unit late the next day.

During this action five of the Group's aircraft had been shot down, one pilot being killed and two captured, while the other two returned safely later. JG 77 lost two aircraft and their pilots. Apparently one more P-40 was lost during the day on a separate mission, another attached 324th Fighter Group pilot being killed.

Three MC.202s of 16° Gruppo were scrambled at 1430. A large formation of bombers, escorted by fighters, was reportedly intercepted, S.Ten Robetto claiming a Spitfire shot down. During the day the three squadrons of P-40Fs of the 79th Fighter Group, the second fighter unit to join the US 9th Air Force in Libya, moved up to Causeway landing ground on the way to the front.

British Claims					
601 Sqn	Plt Off R.V.Baxter	Spitfire Vc ES115	MC.202 Damaged	W Medenine	1105-1200
601 Sqn	Flt Sgt A.D.Cripps	Spitfire Vc ER303	MC.202 Damaged	W Medenine	1105-1200
601 Sqn	Flg Off W.R.P.Sewell	Spitfire Vc ER776	MC.202 Probable	W Medenine	1105-1200
92 Sqn	Flg Off K.Simpson	Spitfire Vb ER613	Bf 109		1425-1535
92 Sqn	Flg Off B.Baker	Spitfire Vb ER492	Bf 109 Damaged	Tunisia	1448-1543
92 Sqn	Flg Off T.Savage	Spitfire Vb ER739	Bf 109 Damaged		1448-1543
US Claims					
57th FG HQ	Maj Archie J.Knight	P-40F '57'	Bf 109	N Gabes	1405-1555
57th FG HQ	Maj Archie J.Knight	P-40F '57'	2 Bf 109s Damaged	N Gabes	1405-1555
66th FS/57th FG	1/Lt Thomas M.Boulware	P-40F '80'	Bf 109	Gabes area	1410-1545
66th FS/57th FG	1/Lt John T.Gilbertson	P-40F/K	Bf 109F	battle area	1415-1545
66th FS/57th FG	1/Lt John J.Stefanik	P-40F/K	Bf 109F Probable	battle area	1415-1545
66th FS/57th FG	2/Lt John E.Teichrow	P-40F/K	Bf 109F Damaged	battle area	1415-1545
66th FS/57th FG	1/Lt Thomas T.Williams	P-40F/K	Bf 109F	battle area	1415-1545
65th FS/57th FG	2/Lt William J.Randall	P-40F '59'	Bf 109 Damaged	N Gabes	1500
65th FS/57th FG	1/Lt Edward H.Ellington	P-40F '53'	Bf 109 Probable	N Gabes	1500
64th FS/57th FG	1/ Lt William S.Beck	P-40K '19'	Bf 109	Gabes area	1505

US Casualties	
57th FG HQ	P-40F '57' shot down behind Axis lines near coast; Maj Archie J.Knight Group Ops Officer, evaded until night. Then swam and waded in sea to British lines
64th FS/57th FG	P-40K-1 '28' shot down; 2/Lt William E.Jenks KiA
64th FS/57th FG	P-40K-1 '16' failed to return; 2/Lt Robert K.Douglas PoW
314th FS/324th FG att 57th FG	P-40 shot down; Maj Worley safe, returned
314th FS/324th FG att 57th FG	P-40K-1 '20Y' failed to return; Capt John D.Simpson Jr PoW
315th FS/324th FG att 57th FG	P-40K-1 shot down; F/O Nicholas R.Colletti KiA

German Claims				
4./JG 77	Obfw Ernst-Wilhelm Reinert	2 P-40s	20km SW Gabes	1442 & 1447
II./JG 77	Lt Fritz Kolb	P-40		1455
II./JG 77	Obfw Josef Otto	P-40		1500
Stab/JG 77	Maj Joachim Müncheberg	P-40	Matmata airfield	1504

German Casualties	
3./JG 77	Bf 109G-2 trop WNr 10734 Yellow 7 combat with P-40 40km ESE Gabes over sea; Uffz Rudolf Homann MiA
5./JG 77	Bf 109G-6 trop WNr 16361 shot down combat with P-40 S Gabes; Uffz Harry Donath WiA, died 24 April 1943

Italian Claims				
167ª Sq, 16°Gr, 54°St CT	S.Ten Giuseppe Robetto	MC.202	Spitfire	southern front

Sunday, 14 March 1943

The 79th Fighter Group now undertook its first operational mission, 12 P-40Fs of the 85th Squadron and 12 of the 87th escorting 11 B-25s over the Mareth Line.

Ready for the forthcoming assault on the line, 6 Squadron moved its Hurricane IIds up to Senem, with 55 Squadron moving to Ben Gardane to resume bombing operations. 6 Squadron was joined at Senem by the forward flight of 680 Squadron from Castel Benito. Throughout the day heavy rain in the Gabes area rendered most of the Axis fighter airfields unserviceable. This bad weather was to continue for the next five days, greatly restricting operations.

German Casualties	
1./SchG 2	Bf 109F-4 WNr 10141 hit by AA, crash-landed at La Fauconnerie, 60% damaged, pilot safe

Monday, 15 March 1943

Two squadrons of B-25s from the 12th Bomb Group had, it will be recalled, been detached from 9th Air Force to operate on the US II Corps front in Tunisia in early February. Now the group's other two squadrons flew from Tripolitania to join them there. However, on this date 223 Squadron joined 55 Squadron at Ben Gardane North, bringing all DAF's light bomber units of 232 and 3 SAAF Wings back together on operations once more. In 450 Squadron Sqn Ldr M.C.H.Barber now completed his tour, Flt Lt J.P.Bartle being promoted to replace him. Flt Lt A.Glendinning was also tour-expired and left to become a controller. His place was taken by Flg Off E.A.Aitchison, posted in from 260 Squadron.

German Casualties	
III./StG 3	Ju 87D-1 WNr 2596 damaged by bombs at Mezzouna-Nord

Tuesday, 16 March 1943

Thirteen MC.202s from the 3° Stormo took off at 1130 to cover troops operating on the Mareth Line. An intense combat occurred during which Ten Solaroli claimed a Spitfire probable. Solaroli recalled that this 40-minute engagement was the longest in his fighter pilot career.

US Claims					
85th FS/79th FG	2/Lt Carl L.Simpson	P-40F 'X32'	Bf 109 Damaged	Mareth area	1225
Italian Claims					
95ª Sq, 18°Gr, 3°St CT	Ten Giorgio Solaroli	MC.202	Spitfire Probable	Mareth lines	1130-

Wednesday, 17 March 1943

At 1010 13 MC.202s of 3° Stormo took off to escort a formation of German Stukas over the Mareth Line. Ten Pianazza baled out of his MC.202 probably owing to engine trouble but in doing so hit the tailplane and landed unconscious and seriously injured. He was dragged by the wind in his parachute for a considerable distance, being rescued by some troops and taken to a field hospital. Pianazza was flown home to Italy next day.

Six Spitfires of 601 Squadron scrambled to patrol over the forward area at 1120. Reaching 10,000 feet over Medenine, a dogfight between about 30 Axis aircraft and other Spitfires was seen, the squadron joining in, one section attacking five Bf 109s, one of which was claimed damaged; the other trio attacked eight Ju 87s which had just completed their bombing dives. Wt Off Gordon attacked one which rolled over and went down vertically, pouring black smoke; he claimed this as a probable. Lt Bennetts also attacked one but was jumped by two Bf 109s and failed to return. A parachute was seen going down and a Spitfire to crash. Bennetts was later reported safe, but badly hurt.

Twelve 92 Squadron Spitfires scrambled at 1243, intercepting 12 Jabos escorted by at least six more Bf 109s and three MC.202s. Claims were submitted for two damaged, but Plt Off Paul Brickhill's aircraft was hit in the mainplane, probably by fire from Lt Berres' Messerschmitt; with his own ammunition exploding, Brickhill baled out at once to become a prisoner. Following the end of the war, Brickhill was to write *Escape to Danger*, *The Great Escape*, *The Dam Busters*, and ultimately in 1954, *Reach for the*

Sky, the biography of Douglas Bader.

During the afternoon a conference of DAF squadron commanders was held. Returning from this, Wg Cdr Gleed and Sqn Ldr Olver, commanding officer and sweep leader of 244 Wing respectively, broke away to practice dogfighting. While they were thus engaged, 'snappers' were reported and two Bf 109s were spotted, the two Spitfire pilots at once giving chase. Gleed claimed one shot down which reportedly crashed on a beach close by. This may well have been an aircraft of 2./JG 77 which crash-landed near Fatnassa as the result of combat, suffering 35% damage. On this date also, the Polish Fighting Team commenced operational duties.

British Claims					
601 Sqn	entire section	Spitfire Vcs	Bf 109 Damaged	Medenine	1120-1150
601 Sqn	Wt Off D.C.Gordon	Spitfire Vc ER985	Ju 87 Probable	Medenine	1120-1150
92 Sqn	Flt Lt E.A.G.C.Bruce	Spitfire Vb ER818	Bf 109 Damaged	Tunisia	1243-1343
92 Sqn	Flt Lt P.H.Humphreys	Spitfire Vb EP886	Bf 109 Damaged		1243-1343
244 Wg	Wg Cdr I.R.Gleed	Spitfire VB AB502 IR-G	Bf 109G		

British Casualties	
601 Sqn	Spitfire V EP309 left 1120, shot down by Bf 109s while attacking Ju 87s; Lt B.R.Bennetts WiA
92 Sqn	Spitfire V AB136 left 1243, shot down by Bf 109s; Plt Off P.Brickhill baled out

German Claims				
3./JG 77	Lt Hans-Edgar Berres	Spitfire	SW Mareth	1323

German Casualties	
2./JG 77	Bf 109G-2 trop WNr 10860 combat with Spitfires, crash-landed Fatnassa 35% damaged; pilot safe
4.(H)/12	Bf 109G-2 shot down in combat and crash-landed near Mareth; pilot safe
Italian Casualties	
75ª Sq, 23°Gr, 3°St CT	MC.202 crashed to ground, Ten Mario Pianazza baled and WiA

Thursday, 18 March 1943

At 0700 Capt J.J.Orr of 680 Squadron took off from LG.219 to photograph the Piraeus area of southern Greece, refuelling at Gambut en route; he failed to return. Lt Berres of 3./JG 77 claimed to have shot down a Spitfire at 1318 east of Mareth. The distances involved and the times recorded render it fairly unlikely that the two events were related, although the possibility exists.

British Casualties	
680 Sqn	Spitfire IV BR433; Capt J.J.Orr

German Claims				
3./JG 77	Lt Hans-Edgar Berres	Spitfire	SE Mareth	1318

Friday, 19 March 1943

Weather prevented most operations again on this date; I./JG 77 was not only mired-in at Fatnassa, but was suffering regular bombing attacks at night from British aircraft, much to the discomfiture of the personnel. During the morning another PR Spitfire of 680 Squadron which was being flown by Flt Lt Atkinson over Sfax was chased by a Bf 109, but escaped by diving into cloud. A reconnaissance Bf 109 of 4.(H)/12 was less fortunate, the pilot force-landing near Gabes after being hit by AA, becoming a prisoner. During the night of 19th/20th the New Zealand Division at Ksar Rhilane was ordered to press forward fast around the southern flank of the Axis Mareth defences, and to make for the Tebaga Gap next day. According to Italian records, a P-40, with British roundels and a Cross of Lorraine on the fuselage, crashed after a low level attack on K.41 landing ground, about 40km NW of Gabes.

German Casualties	
4.(H)/12	Bf 109G-2 WNr 10672 Black 6 shot down by AA N Gafsa; Uffz Antonius Ulcer baled and PoW

The Mareth area, March 1943

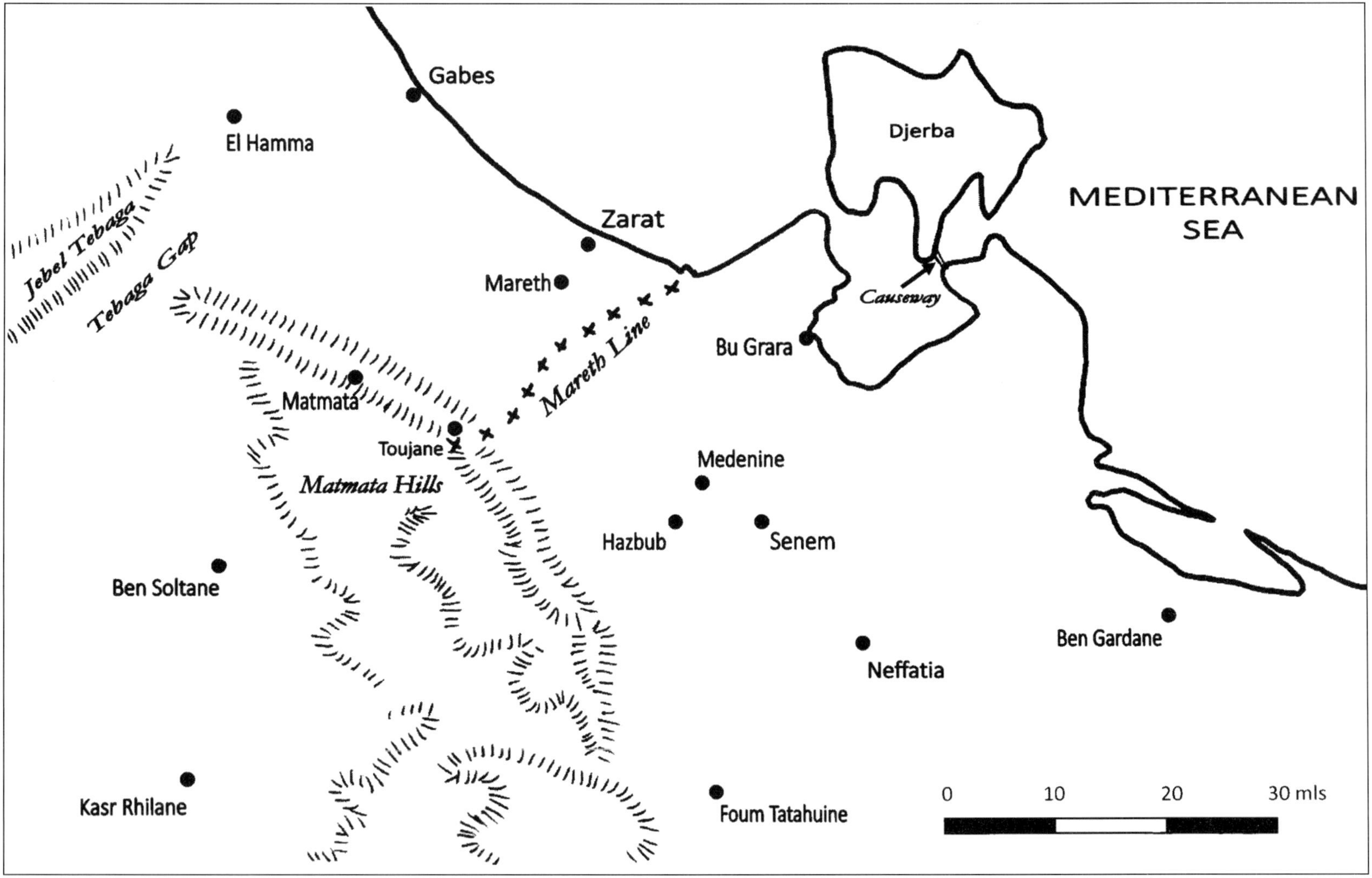

CHAPTER 9

THE MARETH LINE

Saturday, 20 March 1943

Realising the threat posed by the New Zealanders' outflanking thrust, Generale Messe rushed units of the 164th Light Division from reserve towards Tebaga, and 2nd Panzer Division at Gabes was ordered to be ready to follow if necessary.

In the morning 12 Spitfires from 1 SAAF Squadron were scrambled. Climbing to 18,000 feet, pilots saw two formations, each of 12 Axis aircraft flying in pairs. The upper formation comprised Bf 109s and MC.202s, the lower, stepped down 500 feet, were FW 190s; all were flying north-westwards. The South Africans dived immediately, completely disorganising the Axis formations. At once, the Focke Wulf pilots opened their throttles, rapidly outdistancing the Spitfires. Lt Lanham hit one and claimed to have seen it crash and burst into flames, three other pilots claiming a probable apiece. Strangely, no operations by North African-based FW 190 units have been recorded for this date which coincide with these, DAF's first claims against such aircraft.

Throughout the day raids by formations of 18 Bostons went out to attack the German fighter airfields and strongpoints in the line. Flak was heavy and two were shot down by Flak while six others were holed, one of them seriously. The first loss came during the second attack which was made against anti-tank gun positions, the second was suffered during the fourth sortie when strongpoints on the Wadi ez Zerkin were attacked under cover of a fighter escort of 33 aircraft. Hit in one engine, Lt D.R.Davies' Boston burst into flames and crashed. Davies, who was the brother of the commanding officer of 60 SAAF Squadron, was killed as was his observer. The two gunners, both members of the RAF, baled out but drifted into the sea where one was drowned; the sole survivor became a PoW.

The steady raids bore fruit during the day. Fatnassa had suffered a very heavy night attack and now received two more raids by the day. By evening every aircraft of I./JG 77's 1.Staffel had been destroyed on the ground. The Italians reported that near Ksar Rhilane 15 MC.202s of 3° Stormo escorted a Ju 88 on reconnaissance over the New Zealanders' vehicles between 1240-1400, but were engaged by about 25 Spitfires, one being claimed shot down by M.llo Longhi plus a probable, for the loss of the Macchi flown by Serg Amici-Grossi. At 1430 a bombing raid on K.41 landing ground slightly damaged two MC.202s, but reinforcements for the Regia Aeronautica were now forthcoming, nine replacement MC.202s arriving at K.41 during the day for 16° Gruppo.

During the day Flt Lt J.S.Taylor, DFC was posted from 145 Squadron to take command of 601 Squadron where Sqn Ldr Plinston's tour had ended. In Taylor's stead with 145, Flg Off I.H.Shand was promoted to command his flight. 1 SAAF Squadron received a visit from fellow South African, Grp Capt Petrus Hugo from 242 Group, who gave a lecture on the fighting in the north.

Just before darkness fell the New Zealanders were bombed in error by USAAF aircraft, but at 2030 8th Army began an artillery barrage on the Mareth Line. First hit were the positions of the Italian Young Fascists on the Wadi Zigzaou. A few minutes later 50th Division opened the frontal assault on the line. Meanwhile, at 1955 two Hurricanes of 73 Squadron which had just arrived at Neffatia Main, flew a night intruder sortie over Sfax. A Ju 88 was seen approaching from the south-west, and this was claimed to have been damaged.

Wg Cdr Ian Gleed, 244 Wing Leader, flies over the eastern Tunisian coastline in IR-G, which on the port side of the fuselage carries a wing commander's pennant. He is accompanied by two more Spitfires from 601 Squadron.

British Claims

1 SAAF Sqn	Lt J.R.Lanham	Spitfire V ..188 'F'	FW 190		1335
1 SAAF Sqn	Lt B.Rose-Christie	Spitfire V ..476 'W'	FW 190 Probable		1335
1 SAAF Sqn	Lt W.D.Wikner	Spitfire V ..193 'V'	FW 190 Probable		1335
1 SAAF Sqn	Lt W.M.Langerman	Spitfire V ..758 'U'	FW 190 Probable		1335
73 Sqn	Flg Off R.J.D.Henderson	Hurricane IIc HL601	Ju 88 Damaged	5m S Sfax	1955-2230

British Casualties

145 Sqn	Spitfire V ER869 left 1620 as top cover to Kittyhawks, FTR; Sgt E.A.Doley returned later
24 SAAF Sqn	Boston III shot down by Flak on second operation of day; seen to crash and burn; Lt G.E.Sale and two RAF gunners safe, observer KiA
24 SAAF Sqn	Boston III shot down by Flak on fourth operation of day. Hit in one engine by Flak and burst into flames; Lt D.R.Davies and observer KiA. Two RAF gunners baled out, drifted into sea; one drowned, one PoW
24 SAAF Sqn	Boston III badly damaged by Flak
24 SAAF Sqn	5 Boston IIIs holed by Flak

German Claims

3./JG 77	unstated	P-40

German Casualties

2.(F)/122	Ju 88D-1 WNr 430498 F6+BK lost from Sicily; Uffz Heinrich Surkamp and three MiA
III./ZG 1	Me 210A-1 WNr 0256 hit by AA, 30% damaged, force-landed at Sfax

Italian Claims

95ª Sq, 18°Gr, 3°St CT	M.llo Felice Longhi	MC.202	Spitfire	Ksar Rhilane	1240-1400
95ª Sq, 18°Gr, 3°St CT	M.llo Felice Longhi	MC.202	Spitfire Probable	Ksar Rhilane	1240-1400

Italian Casualties

70ª Sq, 23°Gr, 3°St CT	MC.202 shot down in flames, Serg Alberto Amici-Grossi KiA
16° Gr, 54° St CT	2 MC.202s slightly damaged on ground at K.41 by bombs

Sunday, 21 March 1943

During the night 8th Army troops crossed Wadi Zigzaou but more water than expected proved to be in it. A bridgehead to the other side was formed, but in the face of murderous fire. To the west the New Zealanders pressed on towards the southern edge of the Matmata Hills and during the day Kittyhawks and Hurricane IIds were called in to break up a group of 40 tanks threatening their advance. To support the new offensive the Allied air forces in the north and centre, particularly units of XII ASC, now put the pressure on to draw off the Luftwaffe with the result that the German fighter losses suddenly began to rise steeply. Fatnassa remained the target for many Allied bombing attacks. Details of the XII ASC operations will be dealt with in the main in Volume 3, but the rest of March until the breach of the Mareth Line brought DAF units much more into the same general area as those mentioned here. Differentiating between the activities of the two Allied air arms and those of the Axis units opposing them, becomes, at times, more difficult to resolve. This factor will be taken account of wherever possible within the two volumes, although there may be some information which is repeated in each in order to allow the reader to fully appreciate and understand the whole picture.

Armin Köhler's diary remained a good indicator of the strain now affecting both he and his fellow pilots in JG 77, caught increasingly in a vice by enemies in front and behind:

> "Enemy attacks until 0530. About 0900 18 Boeings made their attack. Fires started at the Italian jetty. The 88mm Flak position has seven dead and several wounded. Another heavy gun protects our side. An Italian 20mm gun position received a direct hit. An hour later comes a second attack. German 88mm Flak opens fire. About 1600 another air raid alarm. 54 four-engined bombers with 49 fighters attack our ill-fated airfield. There is no escape from the bombs. One must only trust to luck. The effect on the nerves is indescribable. Every single man, from airman to Staffel Officer is utterly exhausted by the incessant bombing. In addition, not a wink of sleep. An hour later came the fourth attack of the day. That was the beginning of spring in Tunisia!"

Most of these raids had come from the north and some of the bombs dropped in the Gabes area were directed at the Italian landing grounds K.41 and K.34 where one MC.202 was destroyed and 10 damaged.

At 1735 Wg Cdr Gleed led 1 SAAF Squadron on a scramble to 15,000 feet over Mareth where Maj Moodie's Spitfire was slightly damaged by Flak. Twelve more Spitfires from 145 Squadron encountered Bf 109s over Mareth during the day, Sqn Ldr Wade claiming a probable over the sea. Ten formations of Bostons, Baltimores and B-25s, each of them 18 strong had been out during the day, hammering roads and concentrating on transport vehicles. A Baltimore of 223 Squadron was hit by Flak during one raid and belly-landed on its return to base.

During the day the 85th Squadron, 79th Fighter Group, lost a Warhawk when engaged on a bomber escort, possibly shot down by a pilot of II./JG 51; a second aircraft from the same US unit was shot down by Flak, the pilot surviving unhurt. 450 Squadron moved to Medenine Main airfield on this date, joining 260 Squadron which had arrived there on the previous day.

British Claims

145 Sqn	Sqn Ldr L.C.Wade	Spitfire Vb ES252	Bf 109 Probable	in sea, 15m N Zarat	1100-1200

British Casualties

260 Sqn	Kittyhawk III ET855 shot down by Bf 109 SE Gabes; Sgt Orr MiA
2 SAAF Sqn	Kittyhawk I EV320 damaged; Lt J.S.Gericke safe
223 Sqn	Baltimore hit by Flak and crash-landed
12 SAAF Sqn	Boston III AL734 shot down by Flak and belly-landed in the desert

US Claims

85th FS/79th FG	Capt John O. Cimaglia	P-40F 'X20'	MC.202 Damaged	Gulf of Gabes	1305

US Casualties

85th FS/79th FG	P-40 failed to return after combat with e/a near Mareth; 1/Lt Melvin K.Davis
79th FG	P-40 shot down by Flak, pilot returned

US Casualties

66th FS/57th FG	P-40F '96' FTR, Lt Adrian K.Stahl safe with NZ troops

German Claims

II./JG 77	Oblt Siegfried Freytag	Spirfire	10km SE Maknassy	1147
4./JG 51	Oblt Karl Rammelt	Spitfire	5km SE Gabes	1306
II./JG 51	Hptm Hartmann Grasser	Spitfire	3km SE Gabes	1307
4./JG 51	Obfw Otto Schultz	Spitfire	35km ESE Gabes	1420
4./JG 51	Obfw Rudolf Nielinger	Spitfire n.b.	SE Gabes	
4./JG 51	Oblt Karl Rammelt	B-17 n.b.	10km SW Gabes	1630

German Casualties

1./SchG 2	Bf 109F-4 WNr 8620 badly shot-up by AA, crash-landed at Gabes

Italian Casualties

16° Gr, 54° St CT	one MC.202 destroyed and ten damaged on ground by bombs at K.41 and K.34 landing grounds

Monday, 22 March 1943

After dark on the previous evening, 40 Valentine tanks of an infantry support brigade had been manoeuvred across the Wadi Zigzaou to reinforce the hard-pressed bridgehead. Heavy rain on the 22nd in the Mareth area again reduced air activity as I Italian Army counter-attacked, Messe throwing 15th Panzer Division into the attack here against 50th Division. Meanwhile, 21st Panzer Division was committed to the fighting now being waged in the approach to the Tebaga Gap by the 164th Light Division and the 2nd New Zealand Division. DAF was to be mainly occupied during the day with attacks on concentrations of Axis armoured vehicles near Zarat.

Twelve Spitfires of 601 Squadron were scrambled at 0945 to patrol over the Gabes area. Ten or more hostile aircraft were then reported over Mareth, six pilots flying at 12,000 feet spotting four Bf 109s above. They continued climbing and the Messerschmitts were engaged at about 15,000 feet, Sqn Ldr Taylor claiming hits on one from which he saw a piece of panel fall off the starboard wing before it dived away into cloud, apparently out of control. Plt Off Desmond Ibbotson hit the fuselage of another and it was last seen at 4,000 feet, gliding over the mountains with its engine stopped and white smoke pouring out; both these claims were credited as probables.

Six Polish-manned Spitfires from 145 Squadron and six of 601 Squadron were then scrambled at 1250, when at the same time 12 more 145 Squadron aircraft also took off. The latter formation encountered seven plus Bf 109s in the Mareth area, one of which was claimed damaged. The first formation then also met seven Messerschmitts, Wt Off Majchrzyk's Spitfire suffering slight damage. At 1315 12 Kittyhawks of 250 Squadron took off to escort a dozen from 112 Squadron which bombed vehicles in the El Hamma area; over the target six Bf 109s attacked and one Kittyhawk was shot down by Maj Müncheberg. One probable was claimed in return.

Following this engagement, six more 145 Squadron Spitfires were scrambled, Kittyhawks, Spitfires and Bf 109s being spotted north of Mareth, locked in combat. The new arrivals dived to the attack, Sqn Ldr Wade claiming one Messerschmitt shot down which crashed on fire; a second was claimed damaged. Plt Off Hanley dived on two Bf 109s which were attacking a Kittyhawk and hit one as it was on top of a roll, following which it dived inverted into the sea. Plt Off Belec also hit one, smoke and flames coming from the front of the cockpit as it dived away; he was credited with a probable. It seems likely that the squadron had engaged II./JG 77 which reported that at 1615 Oblt Osswald and his wingman, Lt Kolb, were shot down into the sea by Spitfires south-east of Gabes.

In the meantime at 1325 6 Squadron despatched 13 Hurricane IIds to attack tanks south of El Hamma, nine of which were claimed destroyed. However, the tank-busters were intercepted by II./JG 77 Bf 109s and three were shot down. Two of the pilots survived unhurt, but the third, an American in the RAF, was wounded. Six more Hurricanes went off at 1620 after the same targets; on this occasion one aircraft was hit by Flak and force-landed in the hills north-west of El Hamma. Flg Off Morgan narrowly escaped capture by Italian troops and returned later. Six 145 Squadron Spitfires on yet another scramble at 1616, once again came upon Kittyhawks and Bf 109s in a dogfight. Plt Off Usher dived on two Messerschmitts from 10,000 feet, attacking one which went into a shallow dive and hit the sea north of Zarat.

Both the 57th and 79th Fighter Groups were active during the day, undertaking fighter-bombing and bomber escort sorties. At 1545 a dozen 87th Fighter Squadron P-40Fs rendezvoused with 12 Baltimores and six Bostons over Zarzis, then flying direct to the target. Immediately after the bombing had taken place nine Axis fighters attacked, Lt Wright opening the claiming with an MC.202 damaged. Then in the Mareth area 1/Lt Asa Adair claimed a Bf 109 shot down – the 87th Squadron's first confirmed victory; Adair then claimed damage to a second, two more pilots claiming a probable between them. The formation returned unscathed. Shortly behind this mission, 12 more P-40Fs of the 85th Squadron escorted 18 Baltimores of 3 SAAF Wing to the same area. Although 20 plus hostile fighters were observed, there was only some brief skirmishing before the raid was completed. However, Lt Bohlack's aircraft was hit; the crew of a 24 SAAF Squadron Boston reported seeing this Warhawk being shot down over Mareth.

In time for the new offensive, two of the 12th Bomb Group's B-25 squadrons had returned to the south. Now, after two abortive missions, 18 Mitchells were despatched close behind the South African bombers, their target being MT concentrations near Zarat. They rendezvoused with 24 P-40Fs, again from the 79th Fighter Group; these were aircraft of the 86th and 87th Squadrons, plus three attached aircraft of the 316th Squadron, 324th Fighter Group. Over the target 1633-1634, bombs were dropped from 8,000 feet. Flak was described as being very intense and accurate, 13 of the bombers being holed. Mitchell '93' reportedly received a direct hit in the left engine over the target, subsequently crashing while trying to reach a satellite airfield near Zarzis; here it spun in from 1,500 feet when two miles out, Capt Ingram and his crew all being killed. However, at around the same time and in the same area a B-25 was claimed shot down by Oblt Rübell of 5./JG 51 and it seems that he had pursued and attacked the already damaged aircraft.

Pilots from the 79th Group reported seeing Ingram's Mitchell hit by Flak, four of them following it away from the target area and seeing it crash and burn, four Axis fighters also being spotted. Over the target meanwhile 15 Bf 109s had jumped the top cover and a general dogfight had ensued. Lt Miller fired at one Messerschmitt, seeing pieces fly off it, and he claimed it as a probable; he was credited with having damaged it.

With nightfall, General Montgomery, believing that he had drawn most of the I Italian Army reserves into the Mareth Line, now decided to switch the main focus of his attack to the Tebaga Gap where the New Zealanders had become held up. He therefore ordered 1st Armoured Division to follow in their path and reinforce them with all speed. Airfields employed by the Regia Aeronautica were in such bad condition at this stage that their further use was considered temporarily impracticable.

British Claims

145 Sqn	Plt Off F.R.Barker	Spitfire Vb EP440	Bf 109 Damaged	Tunisia	1250-1310
601 Sqn	Flg Off D.Ibbotson	Spitfire Vc ER563	Bf 109 Probable	Mareth	1255-1330
601 Sqn	Sqn Ldr J.S.Taylor	Spitfire Vc ER966	Bf 109 Damaged	Mareth	1255-1330
145 Sqn	Plt Off J.W.E.Belec	Spitfire V ER550	Bf 109 Probable		1555-1630
145 Sqn	Plt Off E.Hanley	Spitfire V ES239	Bf 109		1555-1630
145 Sqn	Sgt J.H.D.Herberte	Spitfire V ER486	Bf 109 Damaged		1555-1630
145 Sqn	Sqn Ldr L.C.Wade	Spitfire V ES252	Bf 109	300-400yds from water	1555-1630
145 Sqn	Plt Off D.C.Usher	Spitfire V EP440	Bf 109	5m N Zarat	1615-1645

British Casualties

6 Sqn	Hurricane IId shot down by Bf 109 nr El Hamma; Flg Off D.W.Jones WiA
6 Sqn	Hurricane IId shot down by Bf 109 nr El Hamma; Flt Lt A.P.Q.Bluett safe
6 Sqn	Hurricane IId shot down by Bf 109 nr El Hamma; Plt Off J.M.Freeland safe
6 Sqn	Hurricane IId shot down by Flak NW El Hamma; Flg Off J.A.M.Morgan safe
	(These four aircraft were HV577, HV595, HV671 and HW271)
250 Sqn	Kittyhawk III FL724 left 1315, shot down by Bf 109, forced to land in El Hamma area;
	Flt Sgt J.P.Maloney WiA
40 SAAF Sqn	Hurricane FTR; Lt Lloyd MiA
145 Sqn	Spitfire ER920 left 1350, slt damaged, landed at 1430; Wt Off Majchrzyk safe
601 Sqn	Spitfire V ER776 scrambled at 1400 to cover Polish Flight, crash-landed; Wt Off M.A.Perkins safe
601 Sqn	Spitfire V ES115 scrambled at 1400 to cover Polish Flight, crash-landed; Flt Sgt D.C.Gordon

US Claims

87th FS/79th FG	1/Lt Asa A.Adair	P-40F '77'	Bf 109	NW Mareth	1610
87th FS/79th FG	1/Lt Asa A.Adair	P-40F '77'	Bf 109 Damaged	NW Mareth	1610

US Claims

87th FS/79th FG	Lt Fred A. Wright Jr	P-40F '75'	MC.202 Damaged	NW Mareth	1610
87th FS/79th FG	Lt Robert Ligett	P-40F '84'	Bf 109 Probable	NW Mareth	1610
87th FS/79th FG	Lt Paul G.McArthur	P-40F '83'			
87th FS/79th FG	2/Lt Kensley M.Miller	P-40F	Bf 109 Damaged		1635

US Casualties

12th BG	B-25C '93' hit by Flak, crash-landed, Capt Virgil Ingram Jr and five KiA
12th BG	12 B-25Cs slightly damaged by Flak
85th FS/79th FG	P-40, hit by Flak, crash-landed, Lt Charles K. Bolack returned

German Claims

II./JG 51	Hptm Hartmann Grasser	Spitfire	12km S Gabes	1410
Stab/JG 77	Maj Joachim Müncheberg	P-40	75km SSW Gabes	1427
Stab II./JG 77	Oblt Siegfried Freytag	Spitfire	12km N Zarat	
5./JG 51	Oblt Günther Rübell	B-25	35km NNE Medenine	1650

German Casualties

1./SchG 2	Bf 109F-4 WNr 10098 White 3 shot down by AA Negona; Lt Wilhelm Vetter MiA
4./JG 77	Bf 109G-6 trop WNr 16424 shot down by Spitfires 1615; Oblt Heinrich Osswald KiA
4./JG 77	Bf 109G-4 trop WNr 15022 NH+RV shot down SE Gabes by Spitfires 1615; Lt Fritz Kolb MiA
7./JG 77	Bf 109G-2 trop WNr 10662 White 6 shot down NW Mezzouna airfield; Lt Walter Kiessling KiA
II./JG 77	Bf 109G-6 WNr 16325 shot-up in combat with Spitfires, force-landed at Gabes, 40% damaged; pilot safe
I./SchG 2	Bf 109F-4 WNr 10258 shot down near Djel Guelia; pilot baled and safe
III./StG 3	3 Ju 87D-3s WNr 1011 20%, 1001 10%, 2992 15% damaged by bombs at Mezzouna
III./StG 3	Ju 87D-1 WNr 2528 15% damaged by bombs at Mezzouna
III./StG 3	2 DFS 230s WN 225380 15% and 221344 60% damaged by bombs at Mezzouna

Tuesday, 23 March 1943

During the day the 79th Fighter Group was again engaged over Mareth, Lt Maxwell of the 86th Squadron claiming a Bf 109 with pilots of the group's other squadrons claiming one probable and two damaged. A Baltimore of 223 Squadron was hit by Flak on one sortie and belly-landed on the way back to base. Italian pilots of 3° Stormo led by Ten Solaroli claimed to have shot down two Spitfires and damaged seven more over the Mareth Line when 12 of them intercepted a British formation during the early morning.

450 Squadron took off at 1416 to cover Kittyhawks of 260 and 3 RAAF Squadrons to strafe south-west of El Hamma, Spitfires providing extra top cover. Sgt Rowe's aircraft was hit by heavy Flak and he force-landed; picked up by Arabs, he returned safely later. A highlight of the day was marked by the despatch of 12 pilots from 244 Wing led by Wg Cdr Gleed, who flew from Bu Grara, near Djerba Island, to Algiers in a Hudson to collect the first Spitfire IXs for DAF. On their return six were handed to the Polish Fighting Team and four to 92 Squadron. The other two were held back as replacements. Neville Duke:

> "Of the Spitfire V, the Mark Vc had the advantage of being able to carry a greater quantity of 20mm ammunition with its belt feed mechanism, compared with the Vb with the drum feed system. Each mark was equipped with four .303in machine guns and two 20mm cannons, but I recall occasions when I deleted two of the machine guns and other items of equipment in an attempt to improve the performance of the Mark V. We felt we lacked climb and altitude performance compared with the 109. The Vc had the Hamilton (or De Havilland) Hydromatic airscrew and was considered superior to the Rotol airscrew on the Vb, although instances of overspeeding occurred.
>
> "Whilst we were reasonably effective with the Mark V, the advent of the Mark IX was a revelation and a source of very great joy. For the first time one felt on at least equal terms with anything the enemy had to offer and the improvement in speed, climb and altitude performance over the Mark V was a wonderful thing to experience.
>
> "We then operated a mixed formation of Vs and IXs with the Vs leading (because of their lower performance) and the IXs flying a high top cover and ranging freely at a higher speed. The IXs were perhaps 3-5,000 feet higher in a fluid four formation and whilst keeping in contact and down sun of the lower formation for the purposes of cover and support, were an independent unit. If I remember correctly, we used to patrol in the IXs at medium altitude at about 240mph indicated airspeed."

Fighting in the Mareth Line continued throughout the day, but the 50th Division was quietly and gradually withdrawn. By evening 1st Armoured Division had reached the Tebaga Gap and was preparing to attack here. With the Regia Aeronautica, T.Col Giovanni Zappetta assumed command of 54° Stormo CT, replacing T.Col Carlo Calosso.

British Casualties					
450 Sqn	Kittyhawk III shot down by Flak SW El Hamma; Sgt Rowe safe				
223 Sqn	Baltimore crash-landed due to Flak				
US Claims					
86th FS/79th FG	1/Lt George S.Maxwell	P-40F '64'	Bf 109E	Zarat area	1025
2nd FS/52nd FG	Capt Theodore R.Sweetland	Spitfire V	Bf 109 (collision)		
US Casualties					
2nd FS/52nd FG	SpitfireV lost in collision with Bf 109 (Müncheberg); Capt Sweetland				

German Claims				
Stab/JG 77	Maj Joachim Müncheberg	Spitfire	40km SSW Maknassy	0950
Stab/JG 77	Lt Gerhard Strasen	Spitfire	SSW Maknassy	0952
Stab I./JG 77	Obfw Kurt Niederhagen	2 Spitfires		1030 & 1032
Stab I./JG 77	Hptm Heinz Bär	B-25		1043
2./JG 77	Lt Willi Hennersdorf	Spitfire		1615
German Casualties				
Stab JG 77	Bf 109G-6 WNr 16381 flew into debris of shot down Spitfire and crashed 45km ESE Gafsa; Maj Müncheberg KiA			
1./JG 77	Bf 109G-2 trop WNr 10743 White 8 combat with P-40 5km E Maknassy; Uffz Johann Penall KiA			
7./JG 77	Bf 109G-2 trop WNr 10638 White 9 shot down Maknassy; Fw Hildebrandt safe			
4./JG 51	Bf 109G-4 trop WNr 15064 White 6 shot-up by Spitfire while landing at Gabes, 20% damaged; Obfw Rudolf Nielinger safe			
5./JG 51	Bf 109G-4 trop WNr 10900 Black 5 shot down by P-40s Djerba area; Uffz Willi Müller KiA			
I./SchG 2	Bf 109F-4 WNr 5508 shot down by AA near Wadi Keddab; pilot safe			
I./SchG 2	Bf 109F-4 WNr 7632 shot down by AA near Wadi Keddab; pilot safe			
I./SchG 2	Bf 109F-4 WNr 7331 hit by AA near Zhemsi, landed safely			

Italian Claims					
95ª Sq, 18°Gr, 3°St CT	Ten Giorgio Solaroli	MC.202	Spitfire	Mareth lines	0845-
70ª Sq, 23°Gr, 3°St CT	Serg Magg Celso Zemella	MC.202	Spitfire	Mareth lines	0845-

Wednesday, 24 March 1943

Throughout the day massive air attacks were directed against the Axis units opposing the New Zealand Division's assault on the Tebaga Gap; 21st Panzer, 164th Light and the Italian La Spezia Divisions were particularly hard-hit during a three-hour aerial assault. Realising that Montgomery had changed the focus of his attack, Messe ordered 15th Panzer Division to break off its counter-attacks on the Wadi Zigzaou and move to a central position in reserve so that it could be thrown in whichever direction proved necessary.

At 0800 12 Spitfires from 1 SAAF Squadron scrambled, six Bf 109s and MC.202s being seen in the circuit over Gabes Main airfield. Four Spitfires went after them but failed to catch them. Two of the Allied fighters then spiralled down over the airfield to strafe, but very intense Flak was encountered and Lt Simmons was shot down. Six more Spitfires, this time from 145 Squadron, scrambled at 0930 and were attacked south of El Hamma by eight Bf 109s; one was claimed damaged. Another 12 of this unit's fighters then patrolled south of El Hamma, the top flight of five meeting 12-15 Messerschmitts at 17,000 feet. The lower flight failed to hear the warning over the R/T and the Messerschmitts broke away, not unscathed, however, as Flt Lt Shand attacked one and saw an explosion on the starboard wing, pieces flying off. It went down and he lost sight of it, but a big flash then appeared on the ground, followed by a column of smoke. On the basis of this sighting, he was credited with a confirmed victory.

Twelve Kittyhawks from 450 Squadron strafed vehicles in the El Hamma region from 1008, two of these aircraft being hit by Flak and making belly-landings, a third returning to base badly damaged. A few minutes later 12 Hurricane IIds of 6 Squadron attacked tanks in the same area, Sgt Harris being shot down and killed while Wt Off Mercer force-landed at 200mph with a badly damaged wing. Eleven MC.202 pilots of 16° Gruppo patrolled over Mareth from 0900 -1035, engaging Allied fighters identified as Spitfires or P-40s, but possibly Hurricanes. Serg Magg Ettore Dotta claimed two shot down shared with other unspecified pilots.

Seven more 6 Squadron Hurricanes again set out to attack tanks in the El Hamma area at 1705 but two of these were shot down by Bf 109s. At 2100 seven Hurricane IIcs of 73 Squadron undertook an intruder patrol over Sfax, Plt Off Chandler intercepting a Ju 88 of III./KG 77 over Gabes. He fired two bursts at close range, blowing off half the starboard wing and the bomber crashed; the pilot was killed but two of the crew were taken prisoner (see Chapter Ten for details). Eighteen Allied bombers raided K.41 airfield again at 1000. One MC.202 was destroyed and five damaged. During a further raid at 1600 a four-engined bomber was claimed shot down by AA.

British Claims

145 Sqn	Sgt W.F.Dorman	Spitfire Vb AB145	Bf 109 Damaged	S El Hamma	0930-1035
145 Sqn	Wt Off H.McKinnon	Spitfire Vb AB252	Bf 109 Damaged		1340-1455
145 Sqn	Flt Lt I.H.R.Shand	Spitfire Vb ER946	Bf 109		1340-1455

British Casualties

450 Sqn	Kittyhawk III FR269 shot down by Flak at El Hamma; Sqn Ldr Bartle crash-landed, safe
450 Sqn	Kittyhawk III Sgt Day crash-landed
450 Sqn	Kittyhawk III badly damaged by Flak at El Hamma; Flt Sgt B.V.Crist WiA
1 SAAF Sqn	Spitfire V shot down by Flak while being pursued by Bf 109s; Flg Off R.G.Simmons WiA, PoW
6 Sqn	Hurricane IId badly damaged by Flak in El Hamma area; Plt Off J.R.Carswell safe
6 Sqn	Hurricane IId shot down by Flak; Sgt Harris KiA
6 Sqn	Hurricane IId badly damaged by Flak; Wt Off R.J.Mercer safe
6 Sqn	Hurricane IId shot down by Bf 109; Flg Off J.C.W.Walter safe
6 Sqn	Hurricane IId shot down by Bf 109s; Plt Off F.A.Day WiA
	(Three of these aircraft were HV856, HW177 and HW298)

German Claims

5./JG 77	Lt Peemüller	Spitfire	10km ESE Gabes	0835
2./JG 77	Lt Armin Köhler	B-25	NW Fatnassa	0955
3./JG 77	Lt Heinz-Edgar Berres	P-40	NW Fatnassa	0955
2./JG 77	Lt Armin Kohler	P-40	NW Fatnassa	0957
3./JG 77	Lt Heinz-Edgar Berres	B-25	NW Fatnassa	0958
9./JG 77	Uffz Ewald Bleul	P-40		1000
3./JG 77	Lt Heinz-Edgar Berres	P-40	NW Fatnassa	1006
Stab I./JG 77	Hptm Heinz Bär	2 P-40s	NW Fatnassa	1010 & 1012
II./JG 77	unstated	P-40		
5./JG 51	Uffz Götz Bergmann	Spitfire	70km S Matmata	1440

German Casualties

2./JG 77	Bf 109G-2 trop WNr 10750 Black 5 LK 30km SE Fatnassa Nord; Uffz Richard Wolfmeier baled, WiA
8./JG 77	Bf 109G-2 WNr 14525 Black 7 shot down by Spitfire Maknassy area; Uffz Max Dehnhardt PoW
9./JG 77	Bf 109G-2 trop WNr 10800 Yellow 5 shot down by P-40 90km WNW Bou Thadi; Lt Ferdinand Jahn KiA
6./JG 77	Bf 109G-6 WNr 16356 shot up in combat near Gabes, force-landed, 50% damaged; pilot safe
III./ZG 1	Me 210A-1 WNr 0251 30% damaged in combat, force-landed at Gabes; crew safe
I./SchG 2	Bf 109F-4 WNr 7654 shot down by AA and crashed S Gabes; pilot safe

Italian Claims

169ª Sq, 16°Gr, 54°St CT	Serg Magg Ettore Dotta	MC.202	2 Spitfires	Mareth Line	0900-1030
16° Gr, 54° St CT	unidentified pilot	MC.202			

Thursday, 25 March 1943

Throughout the day attacks on Axis forces in the El Hamma area continued. It was now planned that when the 8th Army attempt to break through the Tebaga Gap was made, DAF would provide close battlefield support for the first time. Consequently, selected pilots were ordered to prepare to go up to the front to direct the fighter-bombers from the ground onto observed targets.

At 1048 eight Spitfires of 92 Squadron took off on patrol, a Ju 88 being intercepted and fired at by several pilots, Flt Lt Duke managing to inflict some damage before it got away. "My approach was observed by enemy aircraft which dived away steeply going south. The e/a dived at very high speed. With the first burst I observed strikes on the port engine which threw out smoke. Accurate return fire from rear gunner in lower gun position. The e/a dived over Tebaga at nought feet." At 1120 12 Bostons and six Baltimores of 3 SAAF Wing were escorted to attack Tebaga North landing ground by 239 Wing, 3 RAAF Squadron providing medium cover. Twelve Kittyhawks of 260 Squadron were supposed to provide medium cover with 12 Spitfires of 145 Squadron as extra top cover. 260 Squadron, however, arrived late at the rendezvous and missed the bombers but headed for the target nonetheless, hoping to meet them on the way. They missed the landing ground at Tebaga, so strafed the Gafsa road instead where Sgt Carver met an Fi 156 which he shot at and claimed damaged. Meanwhile, the main formation was attacked by two Bf 109s, one being claimed damaged by 145 Squadron. The other Messerschmitt pressed home its attack right through the bombers, managing to get into the Baltimore 'box' of 21 SAAF Squadron. The gunners claimed to have shot this aircraft down, reporting seeing it crash into the sea.

6 Squadron was again after tanks at El Hamma, and at 1245 ten Hurricanes took off for this area; only four returned. Six were shot down, but by a miracle not one pilot was lost and all returned safely later. Warhawks of the 79th Fighter Group also strafed during the day, but lost one 85th Squadron aircraft, the pilot becoming a prisoner.

At 1445 1 SAAF Squadron scrambled six Spitfires which climbed to 18,000 feet, then being vectored onto 15 Me 210s flying in five vics at 2,000 feet. The Zerstörers had a close escort estimated to be 36 Bf 109s, six in line abreast to the starboard, six to port, six ahead and ten astern, with four more flying medium cover at 4,000 feet and another four above them as high cover; the whole formation was heading east. The South Africans attacked at once, Lt Robinson firing at one Me 210 which broke away; he chased this, shooting it down in flames; he also claimed damage to one of the Bf 109s. At this turn of events, the rest of the Me 210s jettisoned their bombs over the Axis lines and retreated. As they did so, the Bf 109s attacked the Spitfires; Lt Tyrell warned his section leader of aircraft on their tails, but he failed to return.

1 SAAF Squadron had a second engagement during the evening when 11 of the unit's Spitfires scrambled at 1725, encountering 20 Jabo Bf 109s and MC.202s eight miles south-south-west of Gabes when these were flying 3,000 feet above the South Africans. The Spitfires climbed and turned to attack, but 11 MC.202s were then spotted at a higher altitude, both Axis formations then attacking the Spitfires together. The Italian formation broke up into pairs, as the Bf 109s dived, fired and climbed away. The Macchis combined aerobatics with their attacks, two pilots reporting seeing some of these fighters firing from the inverted position at the top of loops before half-rolling away. One Macchi and two Bf 109s were claimed shot down, being seen to go down together in a smoking cluster, hitting the ground simultaneously. Another MC.202 was claimed by Lt Brebner, which he saw hit the ground two miles to the north of the other victims. Lt Drummond attacked a Macchi as it was firing at a Spitfire. He pursued this, but the Spitfire which had been under attack, flown by Lt H.Smith, pulled up sharply and the Italian aircraft crashed into it; one parachute was seen, but it was believed to have been the Italian pilot who escaped.

According to Italian records 14 MC.202s of 16° Gruppo led by Cap Giovanni Pagliari patrolled over the front lines from 1640-1810. The pilots reported encountering a formation of Spitfires, three of which were claimed shot down by the Italians plus two probables. Serg Rocco Gherdovich was shot down by opposing fighters, being the only loss on this occasion. Subsequent South African accounts indicate that the Italian pilot may have rammed Lt Smith's Spitfire deliberately, both aircraft thereby blowing up. Apparently the Italian pilot baled out just before the impact and two parachutes were seen by other participants in the clash, but so far it has been impossible to clarify this episode further. Both the pilots involved in the collision actually lost their lives, but none of the surviving Italians provided any report regarding a possible ramming.

The Regia Aeronautica was now very short of fighters in Africa; in the south 3° Stormo comprising one gruppo with the remaining MC.202s of 23° Gruppo (about one squadriglia in strength) and two squadriglie comprising the survivors of 6° and 18° Gruppi. Airmen not needed for keeping these remaining aircraft airworthy were formed into the Reggimento Duca d'Aosta for the defence of airfields against paratroops and commandos. One battalion – the Loreto – was based in the Enfidaville area in the north; the other, equipped for anti-paratroop operations, was near Sfax.

The Gruppen of JG 77 had now begun leaving the Gabes area for La Fauconnerie due to the constant air attacks. I.Gruppe remained at Fatnassa for the time being, however, but in increasingly impossible conditions. Armin Köhler:

> "The enemy is now coming over in daylight. In the midst of a scramble we do not get off the ground in time. After 3.Staffel gets into the air, the bombs start to drop, right in the midst of our planes

getting ready to take off. I hardly dared to look out of the trench to see the damage. Already they were fetching Unteroffizier Köller, blood streaming from him. A bomb detonated in front of his plane, which went up in flames. He had splinter wounds in his head, arms and legs. Kühdorf's plane was also damaged. The usual bombing attacks throughout the night."

British Claims

92 Sqn	Flt Lt N.F.Duke	Spitfire Vb ER689 'J'	Ju 88 Damaged	15m W Gabes	1100
21 SAAF Sqn	Bomber gunners in	Baltimores	Bf 109		1120-1200
145 Sqn	Sgt J.A.Greeves	Spitfire Vb ER486	Bf 109 Damaged	Tebaga North l.g.	1120-1235
260 Sqn	Flg Off M.F.Perkins	Kittyhawk III	Fi 156 Damaged		1120-1250
1 SAAF Sqn	Lt McC.E.S.Robinson	Spitfire V ..116 'N'	Me 210		1510
1 SAAF Sqn	Lt McC.E.S.Robinson	Spitfire V ..116 'N'	Bf 109F Damaged		1510
1 SAAF Sqn	Lt D.M.Brebner	Spitfire V ER941 'E'	MC.202	8m SSE Gabes	1740
1 SAAF Sqn	Lt G.H.O'Farrell	Spitfire V ..211 'Z'	Bf 109F	8m SSE Gabes	1740
1 SAAF Sqn	Lt H.F.Smith	Spitfire VBR390 'B'	MC.202 (collision)	8m SSE Gabes	1745
1 SAAF Sqn	Lt J.van Nus	Spitfire V .590 'M'	Bf 109F	8m SSE Gabes	1740
1 SAAF Sqn	Lt S.W.van der Merwe	Spitfire V ..576 'C'	MC.202	8m SSE Gabes	1740

British Casualties

6 Sqn	Hurricane IId shot down by Flak, El Hamma; Flg Off M.E.Zillessen safe
6 Sqn	Hurricane IId shot down by Flak, El Hamma area; Flg Off T.I.Petersen safe
6 Sqn	Hurricane IId shot down by Flak, El Hamma area; Flg Off D.S.Lee safe
6 Sqn	Hurricane IId shot down by Flak, El Hamma area; Plt Off A.J.Radcliffe safe
6 Sqn	Hurricane IId shot down by Flak, El Hamma area; Plt Off J.B.Paton safe
6 Sqn	Hurricane IId shot down by Flak, El Hamma area; Flt Sgt H.E.Orchard safe
1 SAAF Sqn	Spitfire V ER280 engine failure or Flak hit; crash-landed 24m S Gabes 1000; Lt D.R.H.McLoughlin broke back
1 SAAF Sqn	Spitfire V EP303 'S' shot down 33m SE Gabes, by Bf 109 or return fire from Me 210; Lt A.F.Tyrell KiA
1 SAAF Sqn	Spitfire V BR390 'B' rammed by MC.202 over Gabes-El Hamma area. Lt E.D.Drummond in 'V' had been attacking the Macchi; Lt H.F.Smith KiA

US Casualties

85th FS/79th FG	P-40 Lt Franklin T.Johnson hit by ground fire while strafing near Gabes; PoW

German Claims

Stab I./JG 77	Hptm Heinz Bär	Boston	1209
Stab I./JG 77	Obfw Kurt Niederhagen	Boston	1211

German Casualties

2./JG 77	Bf 109G-2 trop WNr 10733 90% damaged by bombs at Fatnassa; Uffz Herbert Köller WiA
2./JG 77	Bf 109G-2 trop damaged by bombs at Fatnassa; Stfw Karl Kühdorf WiA
6./JG 51	Bf 109G-4 trop WNr 15130 Yellow 9 shot down by fighter SE El Hamma; Obgefr Rudolf Müller MiA, returned
3./KG 54	Ju 88A-4 WNr 2561 B3+EL, missing from Gafsa raid; Uffz Hans Beckmann and three MiA
8./KG 77	Ju 88A-4 WNr 142389 3Z+DD missing from Sfax raid; Fw Helmut Essl and three MiA

Italian Claims

167ª Sq, 16°Gr, 54°St CT	S.Ten Giuseppe Robetto	MC.202	Spitfire	front lines	1725
167ª Sq, 16°Gr, 54° St CT	S.Ten Gian Maria Morittu	MC.202	Spitfire	front lines	1725
16° Gr, 54° St CT	unspecified	MC.202	Spitfire	front lines	1725

Italian Casualties

168ª Sq, 16°Gr, 54°St CT	MC.202, Serg Rocco Gherdovich MiA

Friday, 26 March 1943

The day began quietly enough on the ground and in the air. At 1015 four Polish-flown Spitfire IXs and eight Mark Vs of 145 Squadron scrambled to carry out a patrol. Flt Sgt Allington's Spitfire was hit by Flak and he returned early. The top cover Mark IXs became parted from the rest of the formation and consequently when the British pilots, who were at 17,000 feet south of El Hamma, saw four aircraft 2,000 feet above they took them to be the Poles and dived on eight Bf 109s at 15,000 feet, confident that they were protected from attack from above. Three pilots claimed to have damaged Messerschmitts, but Flt Lt Shand blacked out on pulling out of his dive, recovering to find himself alone amongst eight Bf 109s. With his Spitfire hit four times and badly damaged, he evaded his assailants by spinning from 14,000 to

7,000 feet. A second Spitfire was also badly hit in one wing and a third failed to return. Their attack seems, nonetheless to have been more effective than they thought, for in this engagement Uffz Alfred Keinath of II./JG 77 was shot down and wounded.

The 8th Army units at the entrance to the funnel-shaped gap between the Gebels Tebaga and Melab were now ready to spring their attack. During the afternoon a big bombing raid was made on Axis strongpoints here by six Baltimores from 21 SAAF Squadron, 12 Bostons from each of 12 SAAF and 24 SAAF Squadrons, 12 Baltimores of 232 Wing and 12 B-25s from the US 12th Bomb Group. One 21 SAAF Squadron Baltimore was lost, last seen leaving the target area at 2,000 feet; a message was heard on the radio: 'have force-landed'. A second Baltimore force-landed on a beach near Zuara due to engine failure.

By mid-afternoon 18 squadrons of fighter-bombers were ready on their airfields to support the initial attack, which was to be made at 1530. At about 1445 11 Kittyhawks from 3 RAAF Squadron and ten from 250 Squadron escorted 11 Hurricane IIds of 6 Squadron to attack any tanks near the Gap. The Hurricanes went down to search. But no tanks were to be found and two of the fighters were shot down; both pilots survived unhurt, returning later. 250 Squadron then bombed defensive positions, but three Kittyhawks were hit by Flak, two pilots failing to return with the third wounded. One of the former, Sgt West, was seen to go down and force-land; he got back next day, slightly wounded. 3 RAAF Squadron, providing top cover, was also targeted by the Flak, Sqn Ldr Brian Eaton force-landing, as did Sgt Goulder who came down at Neffatia Main with a damaged airscrew; Eaton returned safely next day. Following this sortie 6 Squadron was rested. Although actual pilot losses had been fairly light, 16 Hurricanes had been lost in just five days of operations.

At 1600 the New Zealanders, supported by 8th Armoured Brigade, attacked. A few minutes later the second wave of fighter-bombers went in, targeting a concentration of 88mm guns south of El Hamma which were holding up the advance. Eleven Kittyhawks of 260 Squadron led in the squadrons of the 79th Fighter Group which had been joined by the 316th Squadron of the 324th Fighter Group, up at the front to gain experience. The Americans were very hard hit; four pilots were lost, two of whom were later reported to be prisoners. Maj Delaney, commanding officer of the 316th Squadron, was wounded in the leg and belly-landed at an Allied landing ground; Lt Hoaglund of the 85th Squadron crash-landed in no mans' land after the engine of his P-40 was hit by ground fire. He was picked up by the New Zealand infantry. Capt Borsodi of this unit was also hit by Flak and baled out into the Allied artillery barrage. He survived both experiences to be safely returned to his unit by the New Zealanders. 260 Squadron landed at Causeway landing ground to re-arm and refuel, then took off for a second strafing attack. Flt Lt Fallows was seen to fire at a truck which blew up, but he then force-landed. It was thought that his aircraft had been hit by flying debris.

At 1620 the Kittyhawks of 7 SAAF Wing took off to follow up the earlier attacks, strafing and bombing gun emplacements; Capt Lindbergh of 5 SAAF Squadron failed to return, his grave later being found; three more of the unit's aircraft were badly damaged by Flak, a fourth suffering less severe damage. Following these attacks which had kept the German anti-tank gunners quiet, 1st Armoured Division poured through the hole torn in the Axis defences by the fighter-bomber attacks and the New Zealand infantry, the tanks passing through unscathed. As darkness fell they made camp, but as soon as the moon rose at 2315, they pressed on again at once.

Throughout these massed attacks the Luftwaffe and Regia Aeronautica had been able to do almost nothing to interfere. The continual raids on the airfields and the regular fighter sweeps by XII ASC squadrons had sapped their strength to an alarming degree. Even on this day the bombing continued on those elements of JG 77 still around Gabes. Köhler's diary continues the grim tale:

> "Today we again had four attacks. My Staffel had three planes out of action, one of them totally useless. Yet we had two aircraft at immediate notice and why they did not take off I have no idea. One is at one's wits end and when one has been in Africa for a time, one does not readily fly into a rage. But the early warning too was being neglected, so that men didn't even have time to reach safety. Not even a man with nerves of steel can endure sitting strapped inside a plane with bombers over the airfield. What our CO's reactions were on that day is best left unsaid. It is now evening and they are back again already."

Fourteen MC.202s of 16° Gruppo patrolled over the lines in the Tebaga area. A Liberator was reportedly attacked by S.Ten Robetto of 167ª Squadriglia, but the result was not observed.

British Claims

145 Sqn	Wt Off J.S.Anderson	Spitfire Vb ES252	Bf 109 Damaged	S El Hamma	1015-1105
145 Sqn	Flt Lt E.A.Ker	Spitfire Vb ES209	Bf 109 Damaged		1015-1105
145 Sqn	Flt Lt I.H.R.Shand	Spitfire Vb ER946	Bf 109 Damaged	S El Hamma	1015-1105
601 Sqn	Wt Off W.D.Gwynne	Spitfire Vc ER270	Ju 88 Damaged	El Marau l.g.	1020-1125

British Casualties

6 Sqn	Hurricane IId shot down by Flak, Tebaga-Melab; Plt Off F.F.A.Robey safe
6 Sqn	Hurricane IId shot down by Flak, Tebaga-Melab; Flt Sgt E.V.Hastings safe (one of these was HW652)
145 Sqn	Spitfire ER876 scrambled at 1015, shot down by Bf 109s; Sgt J.H.D.Herberte MiA
145 Sqn	Spitfire damaged by Flak and returned early; Flt Sgt Allington
145 Sqn	Spitfire ER946 left 1015, badly damaged by Bf 109s, landed at 1105; Flt Lt I.H.R.Shand safe
145 Sqn	Spitfire ER486 scrambled at 1015, badly damaged by Bf 109s; Flt Sgt D.J.McKay safe
250 Sqn	P-40K 42-45796 left 1445, shot down by Flak; Sgt R.B.Browning MiA
250 Sqn	Kittyhawk III FR342 left 1445, shot down by Flak, force-landed; Flt Sgt W.G.H.West WiA
250 Sqn	Kittyhawk III FR313 left 1445 damaged by Flak; Flt Lt R.B.Cole WiA
260 Sqn	Kittyhawk III shot down by Flak near El Hamma; Flt Lt Fallows PoW
450 Sqn	Kittyhawk III shot down by ground fire; Plt Off A.Blackburn safe
3 RAAF Sqn	Kittyhawk III FR457
2 SAAF Sqn	Kittyhawk I EV346 'K' damaged by ground fire Cat I, El Hamma 1630-1845; Maj R.F.Armstrong safe
2 SAAF Sqn	Kittyhawk I ET519 'P' damaged by ground fire Cat I, El Hamma 1630-1845; Capt L.C.H.Hope safe
2 SAAF Sqn	Kittyhawk I AL140 'Z' damaged by ground fire Cat I, El Hamma 1630-1845; Lt J.S.Gericke safe
2 SAAF Sqn	Kittyhawk I AK630' S' damaged by ground fire, El Hamma 1630-1845; Lt D.C.Theron safe
4 SAAF Sqn	Kittyhawk I ET851 probably shot down by ground fire; Lt I.T.S.Tapson PoW
4 SAAF Sqn	Kittyhawk I damaged by ground fire Cat I; Maj S.F.du Toit safe
4 SAAF Sqn	Kittyhawk I damaged by ground fire Cat I; Lt S.Cohen safe
4 SAAF Sqn	Kittyhawk I damaged by ground fire Cat I; Lt W.V.Brunton safe
4 SAAF Sqn	Kittyhawk I damaged by ground fire Cat I; Lt J.R.Robertson safe
5 SAAF Sqn	Kittyhawk I EV430 shot down; Capt J.V.Lindbergh KiA
5 SAAF Sqn	Kittyhawk I AK615 'F' damaged Cat II by Flak; Lt D.C.N.Broome safe
5 SAAF Sqn	Kittyhawk I AL120 damaged Cat II by Flak; Lt D.N.Boyd WiA
5 SAAF Sqn	Kittyhawk I ET902 damaged Cat II by Flak; Lt W.Boyle safe
5 SAAF Sqn	Kittyhawk I damaged by Flak
21 SAAF Sqn	Baltimore FTR
21 SAAF Sqn	Baltimore force-landed

US Casualties

86th FS/79th FG	P-40F 'X50' hit by ground fire while strafing near El Hamma; 1/Lt David H.Brown MiA
86th FS/79th FG	P-40F 'X52' hit by ground fire while strafing near El Hamma; 2/Lt Arthur J.Weldon MiA
86th FS/79th FG	P-40F 'X54' hit by ground fire while strafing near El Hamma; 2/ Lt Robert Spurgin III PoW
87th FS/79th FG	P-40F hit by ground fire while strafing; 1/Lt Robert E.Liggett PoW
85th FS/79th FG	P-40 crash-landed; Lt John G.Hoagland
316th FS/324th FG	P-40 crash-landed; Maj Fred Delaney WiA
314th FS/324th FG	P-40; 2/Lt Lee L.Musgrove KiA
314th FS/324th FG	P-40F '52' crash-landed at Solene l.g.; Lt Goldberger
314th FS/324th FG	P-40F '49' crash-landed near Marble Arch l.g.; Lt Metcalf WiA
86th FS/79th FG	P-40F 'X43'; Capt Frederic A.Borsodi baled out, returned
64th FS/57th FG	P-40F; 1/Lt William S.Barnes PoW
66th FS/57th FG	P-40F '86'; 1/Lt Thomas T.Williams PoW, but escaped and returned 10 April
66th FS/57th FG	P-40F '84' hit by Flak; 1/Lt Dale R.Deniston returned
65th FS/57th FG w 314th FS	P-40F 'Y32' hit by Flak; 1/Lt Walter M.Reed baled out, picked up by NZ troops

German Claims

4./JG 77	Obfw Ernst-Wilhelm Reinert	Spitfire	SE Mareth	1036
5./JG 77	Fw Alexander Preinfalk	Spitfire	10km NE El Hamma	1037
5./JG 77	Lt Franz Hrdlicka	Spitfire	28km SSE El Hamma	1050

German Casualties

1./JG 77	Bf 109G-2 trop WNr 14537 25% damaged by bombs at Fatnassa

2./JG 77	Bf 109G-2 trop WNr 10779 destroyed by bombs at Fatnassa
3./JG 77	Bf 109G-2 trop WNr 14514 40% damaged by bombs at Fatnassa
3./JG 77	Bf 109G-2 WNr 13789 35% damaged by bombs at Fatnassa
4./JG 77	Bf 109G-6 trop WNr 16421 White 5+- combat with Spitfires S El Hamma; Uffz Alfred Keinath baled, WiA

Saturday, 27 March 1943

As the British armour poured through the Tebaga Gap, the threat of being outflanked became acute for the Axis troops still in the Mareth Line; by desperately fighting, the Germans managed to hold 1st Armoured Division long enough at El Hamma to allow the Mareth defenders to escape, and during the night of 27th/28th they were to abandon these positions entirely. An attack on the Fondouk Pass by the American 34th Infantry Division (see Volume 3) timed to coincide with the 8th Army's offensive, faded out under heavy Axis artillery fire.

Twelve Spitfires of 92 Squadron escorted Kittyhawks of 4 SAAF and 5 SAAF Squadrons at 0825 to attack roads leading to El Hamma to slow down Axis reinforcements. One Spitfire was hit by Flak as were four of the South African aircraft, others being badly damaged. At 1155 six Spitfires of 145 Squadron scrambled, spotting ten Ju 88s at 10,000 feet. The British fighters were 4,000 feet higher and dived to attack, causing the bombers to jettison their bombs on their own lines. Five straggled behind the formation and were caught, Plt Off Usher chasing one in a dive until it went into a spiral with one engine on fire and crashed. Flt Sgt Allington attacked another from astern, setting the tail on fire and this bomber then went down in a steep dive and crashed. He attacked another, claiming damage to this as did two other pilots. One failed to return, however, Sgt Breheny last being heard saying that he was force-landing.

Another eight Spitfires, again from 92 Squadron, were scrambled at 1610, but after getting into the air a lone Bf 109 flew straight through one section, shooting down Flt Sgt Sales. The sheer audacity of this attack indicates that the protagonist was possibly II./JG 77's Oblt Freytag who was one of those claiming success over Allied fighters on this date. At 1750 12 Spitfires from 1 SAAF Squadron scrambled and were vectored 30 miles west-north-west of Gabes onto an Axis formation identified as eight Me 210s in two groups of four, flying at 10,000 feet. The Spitfires were at 20,000 feet and one section went down after the first four, two more sections following to attack the second Schwarm. The bombers jettisoned their bombs and broke up in disorder; two Bf 109s were seen, but these disappeared. One Me 210 was claimed by Lt Rogan and three or four more were claimed damaged. Lt Quin's aircraft was hit by return fire and he was led by Lt Gilson to territory occupied by the New Zealanders, where he baled out. There is a possibility that the formation attacked by the South Africans was actually – or partially – comprised of Henschel Hs 129s of 8.(Pz)/SG 2 which lost three of these twin-engined anti-tank aircraft operating in the El Hamma area on this date, although reportedly all were the victims of Allied AA fire.

During the afternoon 21 MC.202s of 16° Gruppo patrolled the area S of El Hamma where a large formation of Spitfires and P-40s was encountered; three Spitfires were claimed damaged for the loss of one Macchi. 16° Gruppo now moved from K.34 to Sfax. At last the final aircraft of JG 77 left Fatnassa during the day. Wrote Köhler: "We flee with the remaining serviceable aircraft of the battered I.Gruppe of JG 77 to join II. and III. Gruppen. It is extremely hazy and I am making my first landing at La Fauconnerie, where the Geschwader Stab is, then in the afternoon I.Gruppe flies on to Bu Thadi to join Hauptmann Ubben's III.Gruppe. Oberleutnant Omert is standing in for the Hauptmann. Our ground crews are already en route for Sfax, our destination too, but the airfield is not yet ready."

British Claims

145 Sqn	Sgt W.F.Dorman	Spitfire Vb ER306	Ju 88 Damaged	Gabes area	1520-1605
145 Sqn	Flt Lt C.R.Hesketh	Spitfire Vb ER650	2 Ju 88s Damaged	Gabes area	1520-1605
145 Sqn	Plt Off D.C.Usher	Spitfire Vb ES130	Ju 88		1520-1605
1 SAAF Sqn	Lt W.M.Langerman	Spitfire V 'M'	Me 210 Damaged	30m WNW Gabes	1815
1 SAAF Sqn	Lt D.S.Rogan	Spitfire V AB320 'L'	Me 210	30m WNW Gabes	1815
1 SAAF Sqn	Lt B.Rose-Christie	Spitfire V ER941 'E'	Me 210 Damaged	30m WNW Gabes	1815
1 SAAF Sqn	Capt S.de K.Viljoen	Spitfire V ES150 'S'	Me 210 Damaged	30m WNW Gabes	1815

British Casualties

92 Sqn	Spitfire V ES121 left 1610; Flt Sgt J.C.Sales
92 Sqn	Spitfire V damaged by Flak; Flg Off Bradley-Smith

British Casualties

145 Sqn	Spitfire V ER199 left 1520, FTR; Sgt R.T.Breheny MiA
1 SAAF Sqn	Spitfire V EP827 damaged by Flak or return fire from Me 210; Lt D.L.Quin crash-landed inverted and broke back; rescued by troops and subsequently recovered, returning to duty
7 SAAF Wg	Kittyhawk I ET950 damaged by Flak; Maj T.P.L.Murray belly-landed on return
4 SAAF Sqn	Kittyhawk I EV158 shot down near El Hamma; Lt A.F.Symonds PoW
4 SAAF Sqn	Kittyhawk I AK741 crashed near landing ground on return; Lt P.L.Shepheard KiA
4 SAAF Sqn	Kittyhawk I ET244 damaged by Flak and belly-landed on return, Cat II; Lt B.A.Bird safe
4 SAAF Sqn	3 more Kittyhawk Is damaged Cat I by Flak
5 SAAF Sqn	Kittyhawk I AK766 crashed on Gabes-El Hamma road; Lt R.M.Hilligan KiA
5 SAAF Sqn	Kittyhawk I ET962 damaged Cat II by ground fire; Lt J.H.Davy safe
5 SAAF Sqn	Kittyhawk I ET1025 damaged Cat II by light Flak; Lt E.H.Johnson safe

German Casualties

4./JG 77	Bf 109G-6 trop WNr 16460 White 8 shot down in combat, El Hamma; Oble Heinz Dudeck MiA, returned
8.(Pz)/SG 2	Hs 129B-2 WNr 0259 shot down by AA 20km SW El Hamma; Uffz Hans-Joachim Hesse KiA
8.(Pz)/SG 2	Hs 129B-2 WNr 0352 65% damaged in combat El Hamma; pilot safe
8.(Pz)/SG 2	Hs 129B-2 WNr 0388 hit by AA crash-landed NW El Hamma, destroyed; Uffz Karl Krauss WiA
III./SKG 10	FW 190A-4 WNr 2318 destroyed by own forces at Gabes West airfield
2./KG 54	Ju 88A-4 WNr 140465 shot-up in combat with 5 Spitfires near Gabes and force-landed at Sfax, aircraft burnt out; Lt Gerhard Faber
	Sdf Leonhard Linden (war.correspondent of Propaganda kompanie) and two safe
4./KG 54	Ju 88A-4 WNr 142460 B3+FM shot down by Spitfires 50km SW El Hamma; Uffz Albert Leiginer and one MiA, two KiA
5./KG 54	Ju 88A-4 WNr 140246 B3+NP shot down by Spitfires 50km SW El Hamma; three safe, one KiA

Italian Casualties

169ª Sq, 16°Gr, 54°St CT	MC.202, Serg Magg Vladimiro Bucco KiA

Sunday, 28 March 1943

Wg Cdr Gleed led a formation of Spitfires from 244 Wing over the Axis lines; at 1015 six Mark Vs from 145 Squadron took off, covered by six Polish Mark IXs to reconnoitre Zitouna landing ground. Five minutes later six Spitfires from 601 Squadron followed to accompany them, flying at zero feet over the sea and climbing to 5,000 feet on reaching the coast at which point the 145 Squadron aircraft went up to 8,000 feet. 601 Squadron then spotted two Ju 88s of II./KG 30 taking off from Gafsa with a Bf 109, and these were attacked. Flt Lt Nicholls and Flt Sgt Evans shot down one Ju 88 near Sfax and Flt Sgt Steele shot down the Bf 109. Wt Off Gwynne attacked the other bomber and hit it, but did not see it crash.

Meanwhile the other Spitfire pilots saw seven Ju 88s flying north-west over Sfax at zero feet and two Spitfire IXs went down to intercept, Sqn Ldr Skalski diving on two which were flying in line astern, attacking the leading aircraft. He hit the wing at which the bomber heeled over and crashed into some buildings, following which he strafed the main street. Flg Off Horbaczewski attacked the second of the

One of Poland's greatest fighter pilots, Flt Lt Stanislaw Skalski sits in a Spitfire IX in North Africa, early 1943.

bombers and reported that this also crashed. III./KG 77 reported the loss of a Ju 88 on this date, the pilot surviving to return later. Fourteen MC.202s of 16° Gruppo patrolled the area over El Hamma-Gabes from 1110-1140. Here they were bounced by a large formation of Spitfires and P-40s, but the Italian pilots managed to evade these. From 1220 to 1500 eight Macchis escorted German Ju 87s to dive-bomb in the El Hamma area.

During the course of the day the New Zealand Division outflanked El Hamma and moved towards Gabes, capturing both towns before nightfall. However, Axis forces retreated with all haste to the Wadi Akarit, once again avoiding being cut off. Allied fighter-bombers continued to provide support, two Kittyhawks of 5 SAAF Squadron being hit by Flak when involved. JG 77 recorded a number of promotions on this date following the loss of Maj Müncheberg on the 23rd (see Volume 3). Heinz Bär became a Major with Siegfried Freytag and Emil Omert both becoming Hauptmann.

British Claims

145 Sqn	Flt Lt E.Horbaczewski	Spitfire IX EN267	Ju 88	Sfax	1015-1120
145 Sqn	Sqn Ldr S.F.Skalski	Spitfire IX EN459	Ju 88	NW quarter of Sfax	1015-1120
601 Sqn	Flt Sgt R.E.Evans	Spitfire Vc ER303	} Ju 88	El Marau l.g.	1020-1125
601 Sqn	Flt Lt J.H.Nicholls	Spitfire Vc EP401			
601 Sqn	Flt Sgt W.D.Steele	Spitfire Vc EP822	Bf 109	El Marau l.g.	1020-1125

British Casualties

2 SAAF Sqn	Kittyhawk I sent into a spin by Flak, but recovered; Capt L.C.H.Hope safe
5 SAAF Sqn	Kittyhawk I damaged by Flak; Lt E.H.Johnson safe
5 SAAF Sqn	Kittyhawk I damaged by Flak; Lt D.C.N.Broome safe

German Claims

4./JG 77	Uffz Fritz Werner	P-38	15km NNE Maknassy	1412

German Casualties

I./SchG 2	Bf 109F-4 WNr 8686 shot down in combat S Sfax; Lt Jörn Schmelzer baled out safe
5./KG 30	Ju 88A-4 WNr 142385 4D+PN missing from Gafsa-Maknassy mission; Uffz Ernst Herrmann and three MiA
6./KG 30	Ju 88A-4 WNr 140424 shot down by Spitfires during take-off, crashed 3km SW Sfax; Lt Helmut Besirske and two WiA
8./KG 30	Ju 88A-4 WNr 142421 3Z+ES shot down in combat; Fw Franz Fellinger and three MiA, returned later

Monday, 29 March 1943

The remains of I Italian Army began digging in along the Wadi Akarit position on this date, as from the west the US II Corps now advanced on Maknassy. Ten Spitfires from 145 Squadron, including four Mark IXs, began a mission at 1000 patrolling north of Gabes. The pilots of the higher-performance aircraft spotted a Ju 88 south of Zitouna; two pilots attacked, the bomber's petrol tank exploding and the crew baling out, although one of the Spitfires was damaged by return fire before they did so.

The lower flight of Mark Vs attacked eight or ten Bf 109s and two MC.202s which were intercepted at 12,000 feet, 25 miles north of Gabes. Wt Off Anderson attacked one MC.202 head-on, seeing it dive steeply, followed by fire and black smoke on the ground. The Mark IXs then joined the engagement which broke up into individual dogfights. Sqn Ldr Wade attacked a Messerschmitt which went into a spin from 7,000 feet. He then chased after three more at 5,000 feet, got behind one and after a short burst, it blew up. A parachute was seen in the area of the first of his two engagements and he was credited with two shot down. Meanwhile Wt Off Ker found an MC.202 500 feet above him and climbed to attack from 100 yards range, the Italian aircraft blowing up when he fired. Plt Off Barker attacked another Macchi from astern, closing from 300 to 25 yards; he believed the pilot had baled out, but he had to pull up to avoid colliding and was able only to claim his opponent damaged.

The Italian fighters were heavily engaged on this date, MC.202s being scrambled continually due to heavy attacks on their airfields. Fifteen pilots of 1° and 3° Stormi, led by Cap Giorgio Tugnoli, reported engaging Spitfires and P-40s over Gabes, claiming three Spitfires and one P-40 destroyed and others damaged. Ten Giorgio Solaroli, who claimed a Spitfire, was later hit by friendly fire, most probably coming from his wingman S.Ten Remo Lugari. Solaroli force-landed and destroyed his aircraft, luckily emerging almost unhurt; he managed to walk back to base by late evening, where he found an almost desperate Lugari. Solaroli recalled this episode in his diary:

"Shot down for the second time! But this time by my Number two! At 10 o'clock I take off with three MC.202s on a patrol over the lines. 1° Stormo has sent about ten planes to cover us, and they are already in the air. At 4,000 metres [12,000 feet], before arriving over the lines, the carousel begins. You can see Spits and P-40s all around. The radio is useless, you can rely only on your eyes. The sky could be clear but for the trails of white and red tracer bullets. Engaged by a formation of Spitfires, 1° Stormo starts the fight. I turn 180° to get the sun behind me. The second pair doesn't follow me, diving rather prematurely to evade an attack.

"Together with my wingman S.Ten Lugari I'm just levelling when two Spits, surprised by my move, pass just in front of me. They start to dive and I follow the second, who is slightly behind his leader: 4,000 metres at full speed, diving and shooting. I see the ground approaching and I pull the stick with all my strength. For a few seconds I lose my vision and then I find myself at 3,000 metres climbing almost vertically. I level and look around: no one near, a big fire and a column of black smoke mark the end of a Spit. Towards the sea I sight four P-40s at about my altitude. I climb a little to get a favourable position to attack when I realize that a 'white spinner' (therefore a friend) is coming towards me: I imagine that Lugari, left behind after my long dive, is trying to reach his position at my side.

"All of a sudden a burst hits my fighter: I roll immediately on my back to evade the attacker. I notice that glycol and oil temperatures are rapidly increasing and out of the corner of my eye I sight a long trail of white smoke: my radiators have been hit. I decide to force-land and I spot a suitable area in front of a large Red Cross tent: in case of bad luck the hospitalization would be immediate! Undercarriage up, flaps down, engine cut, left hand pushed against the dashboard, I finally touch the ground with a rather violent impact. After a long slide on its belly my aircraft stops in a cloud of smoke. I get out of the cockpit very quickly to escape a possible fire.... It takes some hours to get back to my base, riding three different vehicles. When I reach the camp Col Falconi greets me very relieved. Later on, as soon as I'm alone, Lugari comes to me and confesses that he fired that burst. I understand his mistake and, to overcome this awkward situation, we drink a glass of cognac together..."

Another raid damaged eight German aircraft at Sfax where two attackers were claimed shot down by AA. Seven Spitfires of 92 Squadron were scrambled at 1125, but were attacked out of the sun by six Bf 109s when north of Gabes. The Spitfire pilots turned the situation to their advantage, Flt Lt Duke and Flg Off Savage each claiming one shot down. Duke's victim exploded on the ground near a German Red Cross hospital; it was his 20th victory: "I dived on one 109G and closed to about 300 yards astern. I fired six bursts and e/a took no evasive action although I observed strikes after nearly every burst on wing root and fuselage. The e/a eventually turned over and crashed on the ground near the coast road. The enemy aircraft had blackish-green camouflage and two cannons under the wings. Flg Off T.'Doc' Savage also got a 109 and the pilot baled out."

Around midday six Kittyhawks of 2 SAAF Squadron on patrol, strafed vehicles and then spotted 24 single-engined fighters on a landing ground; these were MC.202s and the base was Achichina. The South Africans went down to strafe, Capt Hauptfleisch setting one on fire and damaging a second; Lt Martin also damaged one, but his own aircraft was then hit in the coolant system by Flak and he ditched in the sea. Other 7 SAAF Wing aircraft were called over the R/T to join in the attack, all three squadrons strafing the airfield repeatedly, some of the Kittyhawks also dropping bombs. Lt Briscoe of 5 SAAF Squadron belly-landed on a beach north of Gabes after his aircraft was hit by Flak; he returned next day. By the time the attacks ceased, five MC.202s had been destroyed and 12 damaged with Serg Giuseppe Marchiotto of 74^a Sq dead.

During an early sortie three Bf 109 pilots of II./JG 77 reported engaging four Curtiss fighters, three of which were claimed shot down. It is possible that their opponents had been P-40Fs of the 79th Fighter Group which lost three aircraft strafing vehicles in the Wadi Akarit area, many of the latter claimed destroyed by the rest of the American formation. One of those shot down was killed and one captured, the third pilot returning safely later.

Twelve Kittybombers of 250 Squadron left at 1455 to attack Cekhira harbour. Two Bf 109s made an abortive attack on them, but heavy Flak was encountered, one failing to return and a second force-landing five miles south of Gabes. Six Spitfires of 1 SAAF Squadron were then scrambled at 1500. At 12,000 feet they saw a single Bf 109 in front of them at the same level, flying north-west, and this was attacked by two pilots and shot down. Three more Messerschmitts then appeared near the coast and Lt Brebner shot one of these down, seeing it bounce on the surface of the water. Another six Spitfires from 601 Squadron took off at 1700 to patrol over Zitouna; these encountered four Bf 109s at 15,000 feet over Gabes, the German fighters orbiting some 15 miles north of El Hamma. Two pilots each claimed one of these damaged.

Several losses were suffered by the Luftwaffe fighter units during the day but by now it becomes much more difficult and uncertain to identify which Allied units they had been engaged with – either DAF or XII ASC. Several of these more likely to have been engaged with aircraft of the former are listed here, but this day's lists should be read in conjunction and compared with those in Volume 3 when it appears. Lt Köhler was deeply depressed by a raid on La Fauconnerie. He confided to his diary: "Now fate has caught up with us here as well, after we had left the hell of Fatnassa behind us."

British Claims

145 Sqn	Wt Off J.S.Anderson	Spitfire Vb ER650	MC.202	25m N Gabes	1000-1115
145 Sqn	Plt Off M.L.Lawrence-Smith	Spitfire Vb EN156 }	Ju 88	S Zitouna	1000-1115
145 Sqn	Plt Off F.R.Barker	Spitfire IX EN239 }			
145 Sqn	Plt Off F.R.Barker	Spitfire IX EN239	MC.202 Damaged	Gabes area	1000-1115
145 Sqn	Flt Lt (Wt Off?) E.A.Ker	Spitfire IX EN243	MC.202 Damaged	Gabes area	1000-1115
145 Sqn	Sqn Ldr L.C.Wade	Spitfire IX EN269	2 Bf 109s		1000-1115
92 Sqn	Flg Off Bradley-Smith	Spitfire Vc ES199	Bf 109 Damaged		1125-1225
92 Sqn	Flg Off T.Savage	Spitfire Vb ER235	Bf 109		1125-1225
92 Sqn	Flt Lt N.F.Duke	Spitfire Vc ES121 'R'	Bf 109G	25m N Gabes	1200
260 Sqn	Flt Lt J.F.Edwards	Kittyhawk III FR436	2 FW 190s Damaged	Gabes-Sfax area	1430-1535
1 SAAF Sqn	Lt D.M.Brebner	Spitfire V ..590 'M'	Bf 109F		1520
1 SAAF Sqn	Capt J.H.Gaynor	Spitfire V ..193 'V'	Bf 109F Damaged		1520
1 SAAF Sqn	Capt J.H.Gaynor	Spitfire V ..193 'V' }	Bf 109F		1520
1 SAAF Sqn	Lt W.D.Wikner	Spitfire V ..607 'O' }			
601 Sqn	Flt Lt J.H.Nicholls	Spitfire Vc EP980	Bf 109 Damaged	15m N El Hamma l.g.	1700-1815
601 Sqn	Flt Sgt W.G.Sweney	Spitfire Vc ER303	Bf 109 Damaged	15m N El Hamma l.g.	1700-1815

British Casualties

145 Sqn	Spitfire Vb EN156 damaged by return fire; Plt Off Lawrence-Smith safe
250 Sqn	Kittyhawk III FR278 shot down by Flak Cekhira area; Sgt F.Waywell MiA
250 Sqn	Kittyhawk III FR313 damaged by Flak 5m S Gabes; Flt Lt H.G.S.Pennick safe
260 Sqn	Kittyhawk IIa FL278 shot down by Flak, Sfax-Gabes road; Sgt W.B.Sanble KiA
2 SAAF Sqn	Kittyhawk I ET1021 'H' ditched in sea, rescue launch bombed and strafed by Kittyhawks, which missed; Lt Martin rescued
4 SAAF Sqn	Kittyhawk I damaged Cat II by Flak
4 SAAF Sqn	Kittyhawk I damaged Cat I by Flak
4 SAAF Sqn	Kittyhawk I damaged Cat I by Flak
5 SAAF Sqn	Kittyhawk I ET793 shot down by ground fire while strafing, crash-landed on beach N Gabes; Lt J.A.Briscoe, returned on 30th

US Casualties

87th FS/79th FG	P-40F 'X82' shot down in combat near Mahares; Capt Kenneth D.Boggs KiA
86th FS/79th FG	P-40F 'X58' hit by ground fire when strafing near Mahares; Lt Harlan E.Highfield PoW
65th FS/57th FG	P-40F '47' hit by Flak, ditched 2m E Gabes, 1/Lt Arnold D.Jaqua, safe
82nd BS/12th BG	B-25C, pilot 1/Lt Roger W. Jamison and four MiA

German Claims

4./JG 77	Fw Werner Fischer	P-40	15km SW La Fauconnerie	0920
4./JG 77	Obfw Ernst-Wilhelm Reinert	2 P-40s	SW La Fauconnerie	0922 & 0926
4./JG 51	Oblt Karl Rammelt	P-40	10km NE Cekhira, low	1845
6./JG 77	Staffel	P-40	NE Cekhira	1855
8./JG 77	Obfw Heinrich Hackler	P-40	25km S Maknassy	1910

German Casualties

4./JG 77	Bf 109G-6 trop WNr 16373 shot down by P-40 1km S La Fauconnerie; Lt Günter Schimmelpfening KiA

German Casualties

4./JG 77	Bf 109G-6 trop WNr 16449 White 4 + - combat with P-40, belly-landed La Fauconnerie 70% damaged; Fw Siegfried Grimm safe
4./JG 77	Bf 109G-4 trop WNr 15100 crash-landed La Fauconnerie 20% damaged after combat; pilot safe
8./JG 77	Bf 109G-2 trop WNr 10707 Black 9 shot down 5km S La Fauconnerie; Uffz Rolf Fischer KiA
8./JG 77	Bf 109G-2 trop WNr 10765 belly-landed near Faid after combat, 70% damaged; pilot safe
9./JG 77	Bf 109G-2 trop WNr 10490 Yellow 11 shot down near La Fauconnerie; Uffz Ewald Bleul KiA
6./JG 51	Bf 109G-4 WNr 15018 Yellow 3 shot down by P-40 60km N Gabes; pilot baled out safe
6./JG 51	Bf 109G-4 WNr 15163 shot down by P-40 N Gabes; pilot safe
6./JG 51	Bf 109G-4 WNr 15131 Yellow 5 in combat with P-40 N Gabes, belly-landed at La Smala; pilot safe
III./SKG 10	FW 190A-4 WNr 2512 shot down in combat with fighters near El Hamma, crash-landed; pilot safe
III./SKG 10	FW 190A-5 WNr 5903 30% damaged in combat with fighters near El Hamma, landed safely
1.(F)/121	Ju 88D-1 WNr 430546 shot down by fighters near El Hamma; Lt Ernst Lamms and two KiA, one WiA
III./ZG 26	Bf 110G-2 WNr 5246 95% damaged by bombs at Sfax
III./ZG 1	7 Me 210A-1s damaged by bombs at Sfax: WNr 8157 95%, 8162 85%, 8167 80%, 8161 90%, 2301 15%, 8172 15%, 2318 10%

Italian Claims

95ª Sq, 18°Gr, 3°St CT	Ten Giorgio Solaroli	MC.202	Spitfire	Gabes	1000-
1° and 3° Stormo	unspecified pilots	MC.202	2 Spitfires and a P-40	Gabes	1000-

Italian Casualties

95ª Sq, 18°Gr, 3°St CT	MC.202, Ten Giorgio Solaroli crash-landed, probably hit by friendly fire, safe
74ª Sq, 23°Gr, 3°St CT	Serg Giuseppe Marchiotto killed by bombs

Tuesday, 30 March 1943

The New Zealanders made their first contact with outposts of the new Axis Wadi Akarit line. In the early afternoon 12 92 Squadron Spitfires provided top cover for Kittyhawks on an armed reconnaissance. Twelve Me 210s, escorted by 18 Bf 109s, were seen, the Zerstörers being forced to drop their bombs within their own lines again. Claims were made for one probable victory and two damaged.

Six Spitfires from 601 Squadron took off to escort bombers to Sfax going out at zero feet and climbing to 3,000 feet over the target area. Eight or nine Bf 109s and some MC.202s were seen popping in and out of clouds, Sqn Ldr Taylor attacking one Macchi, hitting the tail and fuselage; the fighter dived away very close to the ground. Two other pilots also claimed damage to three Italian fighters. On the ground one MC.202, one MC.200 and one Fiat G.50bis were destroyed, while three G.50bis and an MC.200 were badly damaged. Flak was very heavy, however, and one 55 Squadron Baltimore was shot down during this raid, a second bomber having one engine put out of action as five other aircraft suffered some damage.

Five MC.202s of 16° Gruppo were scrambled from 1510-1600: Serg Odino Soligo, who took off as the bombs were falling, had his Macchi hit by splinters but he managed to crash-land within the perimeter of the airfield. Eight more Macchis, led by Ten Alfonso Lattanzi were scrambled at 1700 when a formation of Spitfires was intercepted; four of these were claimed shot down, plus one probable. S.Ten Giovanni Battista Zucconi, newly-arrived from Italy, force-landed after the engine of his fighter was hit; he came down within Axis territory.

British Claims

92 Sqn	Flt Lt P.H.Humphreys	Spitfire Vb ER818	Me 210 Damaged		1400-1515
92 Sqn	Flg Off K.Simpson	Spitfire IX EN147	Bf 109 Damaged		1400-1515
92 Sqn	Flg Off E.Sly	Spitfire IX EN143	Bf 109 Probable		1400-1515
601 Sqn	Flt Sgt A.D.Cripps	Spitfire Vc ER985	MC.202 Damaged	Sfax l.g.	1630-1750
601 Sqn	Flg Off D.E.Llewellyn	Spitfire Vc EP870	MC.202 Damaged	Sfax l.g.	1630-1750
601 Sqn	Sqn Ldr J.S.Taylor	Spitfire Vc ER966	MC.202 Damaged	Sfax l.g.	1640-1750

British Casualties

55 Sqn	Baltimore shot down
55 Sqn	Baltimore badly damaged
55 Sqn	5 Baltimores slightly damaged

German Claims

4./JG 77	Obfw Ernst Wilhelm Reinert	Boston	22km NNW Maknassy	0910
4./JG 77	Obfw Ernst Wilhelm Reinert	Boston	40km SE Sbeitla	0915
II./JG 77	Hptm Siegfried Freytag	P-40	20km NE La Fauconnerie	0950

German Casualties

4./JG 77	Bf 109G-4 trop WNr 15161 crash-landed 35km NW Maknassy, combat with Spitfire, 60% damaged; Fw Werner Fischer KiA
6./JG 77	Bf 109G-6 trop WNr 16344 crash-landed La Fauconnerie, 35% damaged after combat; pilot safe
III./ZG 1	Me 210A-1 WNr 8175 10% damaged by bombs at Sfax

Italian Claims

167ª Sq, 16°Gr, 54°St CT	S.Ten Giuseppe Robetto	MC.202	Spitfire	Sfax	1700-1820
167ª Sq, 16°Gr, 54°St CT	Serg Magg Diego Rodoz	MC.202	Spitfire	Sfax	1700-1820
168ª Sq, 16°Gr, 54°St CT	S.Ten Gian Maria Morittu	MC.202	Spitfire	Sfax	1700-1820
168ª Sq, 16°Gr, 54°St CT	Ten Alfonso Lattanzi	MC.202	Spitfire	Sfax	1700-1820
168ª Sq, 16°Gr, 54°St CT	Ten Alfonso Lattanzi	MC.202	Spitfire probable	Sfax	1700-1820

Italian Casualties

167ª Sq, 16°Gr, 54°St CT	MC.202 hit by splinters, force-landed; Serg Odino Soligo safe
76ª Sq, 7°Gr, 54°St CT	MC.202 hit in engine, force-landed; S.Ten Giovanni Battista Zucconi safe

Wednesday, 31 March 1943

With the end of the month and of the fighting for the Mareth Line, aerial activity now swung back to the northern and central sectors, where new offensives were being prepared. DAF welcomed the arrival at El Assa of a new B-25 Group, the 340th. This unit sent a number of aircraft and crews up to be attached to the 12th Bomb Group to gain experience. Eighteen B-25s of the latter unit raided aircraft on the ground at Sfax El Maou during the morning, escorted by 23 P-40Fs of the 79th Fighter Group. Seventeen actually undertook the attack at 1125. Eighty-eight 300lb US demolition bombs and 136 250lb British general purpose bombs were dropped from 10,200 feet, falling amongst dispersed aircraft, two large and two small fires being observed as a result. Again, Flak was intense and accurate, 15 of the bombers being holed to some extent, two of which were forced to land in the sea, although both crews were rescued. One more aircraft with one engine knocked out, force-landed at an airfield near Zarzis and one with its undercarriage damaged, crashed while landing at El Azza.

During the day the Regia Aeronautica did not launch any missions due to the large number of aircraft out of commission. However, a very heavy attack on Sfax of which no advanced warning was forthcoming, caused two MC.202 pilots to scramble as the bombs were falling. Five Macchis were destroyed on the ground and twelve were damaged. With DAF 4 SAAF Squadron noted the return of Capt D.W.Golding, DFC, who had been one of the unit's most successful pilots during the desert campaigns. He had now finished his rest from operations and was ready to begin his second operational tour.

By the end of March 1943 the whole of Libya was finally in Allied hands. Already the advance into southern Tunisia was underway, and 8th Army units would soon link hands with elements of US II Corps advancing from western Tunisia, thereby creating a single Allied front pressing the Axis inexorably into the remaining north-east of the country. In such circumstances the operations of the various Allied air forces impinged increasingly into each other's territory with the elements of the North-West African Tactical Air Forces particularly becoming effectively a single body supporting the armies across the whole front. The joint activities which now became virtually the norm during the final six weeks of fighting in North Africa will therefore now form the latter section of Volume 3 in this series.

British Casualties

260 Sqn	Kittyhawk III FL719
5 SAAF Sqn	Kittyhawk I 'N' damaged by ground fire while strafing Gabes-Sfax road; Lt G.W.Scheikkard safe

US Casualties

66th FS/57th FG	P-40F '81', hit by heavy Flak, crashed and exploded in orchard in target area; 1/Lt Harry J.Hayden III KiA
65th FS/57th FG	P-40F '47', hit by Flak, ditched in sea 2m E Gabes, 1/Lt Arnold D.Jacqua, KiA
434th BS/12th BG	B-25C 42-53392 damaged by Flak, force-landed at sea, pilot 1/Lt James P.Keeshen and five rescued

US Casualties

434th BS/12th BG	B-25C 42-53248 damaged by Flak, force-landed at sea, pilot 1/Lt Perry R.Horton and four rescued
12th BG	B-25C damaged by Flak and force-landed on return
12th BG	B-25C damaged by Flak and crashed on return
12th BG	11 B-25Cs slightly damaged by Flak

German Claims

5./JG 77	Fw Alexander Preinfalk	P-40	23km SE El Guettar	1841
9./JG 77	Obfw Walter Leibnig	P-40	1km N Gebel Chouri	1851

Italian Casualties

54° St CT	5 MC.202s destroyed and 12 damaged on ground

CHAPTER 10

ABOVE THE WAVES, 1 JULY 1942 – 31 MARCH 1943

For 201 Group the result of the precipitate withdrawal to the line at El Alamein was to push the unit and its various squadrons, 235 Wing included, back eastwards into the smallest area of operations to which it had been restricted since the war had begun. Interdiction of the supply convoys from Italy to Libya could no longer be prosecuted from the Cyrenaican airfields which were now all in Axis hands, such activities devolving almost entirely on Malta's aircraft, coupled as before with her flotillas of destroyers and submarines.

Despite the arrival of the June convoy from the west, limited as it was, maintenance of the base here remained of the highest possible priority. However, both distance and the dangers of the notorious 'Bomb Alley' between Crete and the Cyrenaican coastline, rendered further aid from the eastern end of the Mediterranean virtually impossible. For the time being, 201 Group's squadrons were limited in the main to anti-submarine patrolling over the Eastern Mediterranean, with the fighters of AHQ, Egypt's 250 and 252 Wings continuing to provide protection for the base areas and the Egyptian coast almost as far westwards as the front line itself. Indeed, at the start of the month of July the previously very active 235 Wing, having fallen back steadily during June, moved to the Levant, to take up base at Qassassin. Here it became responsible for directing the anti-submarine activities in support of convoys sailing between Alexandria-Haifa-Beirut-Tripoli (Syria) and Famagusta (Cyprus).

This had been occasioned also by a shortage of airfields which arose from the number of units of all types now pushed back into Egypt. WDAF fighters and light bombers were allocated airfields in the Amiriya area supported by the maintenance bases in the Canal Zone and Cairo, whereas the mediums and heavy bombers were forced to move back into Palestine, as were the naval co-operation units.

By 7 July 235 Wing would have settled at Ramat David where it would now control:

700 Squadron, Fleet Air Arm	at Beirut with Walrus
13(Hellenic) Squadron	at Gaza with Bisleys
Free French Nancy Flight	at Rayak with Bisleys
47 Squadron Air Echelon	at St Jean with Wellesleys

together with such detachments from other units in 201 Group as might be necessary. These would chiefly be drawn from 221 (ASV Wellington) and 203 (Maryland and Blenheim) Squadrons.

Initially, the most active units would be those directed by 252 Wing, still at Seagull Camp, Mex, which now had available to it:

5 Squadron, Royal Egyptian Air Force	Heliopolis
GC 1 Alsace, Free French	Edcu (subsequently renamed GCIII/2)
889 Squadron, Fleet Air Arm	Dekheila
335 (Greek) Squadron	Edcu
252 Squadron	Edcu
272 Squadron	Edcu
46 Squadron detachment (two Beaufighters)	Edcu
two Spitfires at 103 MU	Aboukir

Wednesday, 1 July 1942

One thing which 252 Wing's units could do of a more offensive nature was to despatch Beaufighters from Edcu to attack the nearest Axis coastal airfields to the west of the Alamein positions. Thus it was at 1325 on the first day of July that two such aircraft from 272 Squadron and three from 252 Squadron flew westwards to attack LG.05. Here an estimated 20 aircraft were seen on the ground, including Bf 109s, Bf 110s, and possibly, it was reported, Ju 87s. The attacking pilots shot-up two Bf 109s which they thought they had probably damaged, also claiming five MT destroyed and a tank strafed. Somewhat later, six more Beaufighters, three from each unit, made a repeat attack on what the crews thought was LG.05 (although there was some doubt), claiming to have inflicted considerable damage on MT on the coast road, and on a CR.42, two Bf 109s and an S.79.

Ten Mario Bonino of 388ª Squadriglia took off at 0650 on a recce mission; on return to Abar Nimeir he met in his CR.42 five Beaufighters which were strafing the coastal road and scored some hits on one. By night two Cant.Z.1007bis, one each of 261ª and 262ª Squadriglie bombed Dekheila airfield. By this date the recently-arrived 87° Gruppo BT, also based on Rhodes, was ready to commence operations with 15 serviceable bombers of this type available. The unit was commanded by T.Col Mario Giuliano, while his two Squadriglie commanders were Cap Mario Cesari (192ª) and Cap Vincenzo Guidi (193ª). At this time also, 104° Gruppo AS led by Magg Virginio Reinero joined the Aeronautica dell'Egeo with 15 S.79s; Squadriglie commanders were Cap Gabriele Casini (252ª) and Cap Attilio Solimena (253ª).

Thursday, 2 July 1942

Three 252 Squadron Beaufighters took off at 0527, followed at 0540 by three more of 272 Squadron. The initial trio were tasked with strafing aircraft on Fuka main and satellite airfields, the latter being ordered to strafe LG.109. Going in in formation, the 252 Squadron aircraft reportedly attacked and probably destroyed three Bf 109s on the main airfield where 12-15 such fighters were seen on the ground. However, only one Beaufighter returned to base, the pilot reporting that he had also seen one of the 272 Squadron aircraft destroying a Bf 109 on the ground. As this aircraft left the area, it was met from above by a Messerschmitt which made at least 12 attacks on it. The Beaufighter survived these, but was extensively damaged and on return was written off as Cat III.

Meanwhile, the 272 Squadron aircraft had swung out to sea and approached from the north, but were intercepted by three Bf 109s and two Bf 110s, and a running fight ensuing. One British aircraft was hit and damaged Cat I, but the other two escaped unscathed. One crew reported having seen what they thought was a Beaufighter crashing in flames into the sea about one mile north of LG.104 at 0640. On this occasion two Bf 109s of I./JG 27 were scrambled, attacking the Beaufighters which made off low over the sea. A 10° Gruppo CT MC.202 also joined the chase, the pilot of this, M.llo Bignami, and JG 27's Lt Stahlschmidt each claiming one shot down, one Beaufighter being seen by many witnesses on the ground to crash into the sea.

At 0930 a Cant.Z.1007bis of 263ª Squadriglia, flown by Ten Trivella, was despatched to reconnoitre the area south of Rhodes. He returned 40 minutes later owing to engine trouble but crashed to the ground on landing. All crew were injured, and later taken to the Regina Elena hospital at Rhodes. Trivella and Av Sc Ariosto Franchi died thereafter.

British Casualties

252 Sqn	Beaufighter Ic T4888 MiA, shot down by fighters while attacking Fuka LG.16; Flt Lt A.S. Malcolm/Plt Off K.Sharp KiA
252 Sqn	Beaufighter Ic shot down by fighters while attacking Fuka LG.16; Plt Off Abdulgani Ydlibi, F/Sgt E.W.Spiller KiA
252 Sqn	Beaufighter Ic damaged while attacking Fuka aerodrome, crash-landed at base
109 Sqn	Wellington AD605 MiA on Special Duties flight
38 Sqn	Wellington DV575 SOC, Tobruk operation

German Claims

2./JG 27	Lt Hans-Arnold Stahlschmidt	Beaufighter	N Fuka	0625

German Casualties

6./KG 100	He 111H-6 10% damaged in combat with Hurricane nr Alexandria, returned safe but pilot, Lt Harald Bydlo, WiA

Italian Claims

84ª Sq, 10°Gr, 4°St CT	M.llo Luigi Bignami	MC.202 MM 7828 '84-9'	Beaufighter	40km N Fuka	0515-0600

Italian Casualties

263ª Sq, 107°Gr, 47°St BT	Cant.Z.1007bis MM 23731 crashed to ground on landing, pilot Ten Emanuele Trivella and fitter Av Sc Ariosto Franchi killed, copilot Ten Werther Manduchi and two WiA

Friday, 3 July 1942

On Rhodes a new unit was formed as the Sezione Autonoma, with four S.82s equipped for long-range bombing. During the night three Cant.Z.1007bis of 47° Stormo bombed Ismailia airfield, while the first nocturnal attack was undertaken by 87° Gruppo which despatched six Cant.Z.1007bis to bomb airfields in the Suez Canal area.

252 Wing recorded that six unidentified aircraft approached Alexandria at 0300, dropping HE and incendiaries on Amiriya without damage or casualties. The AA defences fired 412 heavy shells and 136 rounds of lighter ammunition; one balloon was damaged by shrapnel from this firing. The two 46 Squadron Beaufighters patrolled, but made no contact. At 0740 a pair of 272 Squadron Beaufighters went off to attack LG.05 again with 15-20 Bf 109s reportedly seen on the ground and this time four were claimed to have been destroyed and six badly damaged. On a nearby landing ground a trimotor identified as an S.79 was also attacked and left smoking.

Since all coastal shipping in the Mersa Matruh and Sidi Barrani areas was likely to be Axis, 252 and 272 Squadrons were given permission to attack any vessels seen here. These two units were much involved in strafing at this time, typically two 272 Squadron aircraft attacking vehicles to the east of Sidi Barrani during the afternoon of this day. Return attacks were not infrequent, and during the day three CR.42s were reported to have dropped bombs and strafed in the area where the 401 AMES radar station was located.

Two strikes were launched against shipping off Zante, Greece. The first, by 12 Beauforts, found nothing, but a second formation carried out an attack which proved unsuccessful, two aircraft failing to return; both crews were lost.

At 0755 a pair of S.79s of 41° Gruppo AS made a torpedo attack on a convoy sailing off Port Said. Cap Giovanni B. De Stefano, 204ª Squadriglia commander, flying S.79 MM 24100, claimed a hit on a freighter of 5,000 tons, and Ten Emilio Pucci of 205ª Squadriglia torpedoed and sank the *Stureborg*, a steamer of 1,584 tons. Remarkably, on this occasion the Italians reported that the lowly-regarded parachute-and-cable devices were fired from the ships, apparently without result. In later years, the war over, Count Emilio Pucci di Barsento, a Florentine nobleman, would found and manage a successful fashion company bearing his name.

British Casualties

39 Sqn	Beaufort I AW240 'A', off at 1830, attacked shipping S Zante, Greece; FTR Sgt R.G.Mercer and crew MiA
217 Sqn	Beaufort L9893, off at 1830, attacked shipping S Zante, Greece; FTR; Sgt J.Hutcheson and three MiA
272 Sqn	Beaufighter IC T4980 'F' damaged by Bf 109 while strafing LG.104, port engine shot out; Plt Off E.H.Hodgson/Sgt W.J.Antonia safe

Saturday, 4 July 1942

Two S.79s of 252ª Squadriglia, 104° Gruppo, flown by Ten Enrico Miranda and Ten Guglielmo Michelotti when off the Palestine coast at 0720, sighted a small convoy of two merchant vessels escorted by three destroyers: a 5,000-ton steamer was attacked and sunk. Two Cant.Z.1007bis of 231ª Squadriglia, during a convoy escort started from Barce at 0650, sighted an enemy submarine; S.Ten Mario Sechi dropped two bombs but no results were observed.

Submarines continued to hunt for Allied shipping along the eastern sea coast, regular sightings being made. One such target was attacked on the 4th by one of 47 Squadron Air Echelon's elderly Wellesleys, and next day two more were assaulted by 13(Hellenic) Squadron's Blenheims, one of which the Greek crew claimed to have damaged.

British Casualties

252 Sqn	Beaufighter T5029 presumed shot down by Bf 109; Sgt B.H.Vickery/Sgt Watling PoW

German Claims

Stab I./JG 27	Fw Emil Kaiser	Beaufighter	Burg el Arab	1100

Saturday-Sunday, 4/5 July 1942

Nine Cant.Z.1007bis, three of 47° Stormo and six of 87° Gruppo, set off for a night attack on Port Said, Ismailia and El Qantara airfield. The last aircraft, flown by T.Col Giuliano aborted take-off and was destroyed by fire, the crew managing to escape safely. The others returned at 0540.

At 2342 a raid approached Alexandria, bombs gutting a warehouse and killing several Egyptian workers. Beaufighters of 46 Squadron intercepted, two aircraft identified as Ju 88s being shot down during the early hours of the 5th. These appear to have been S.82s of 147° and 149° Gruppi, two of which failed to return from a raid on this port. Meanwhile 15-20 more bombers attacked in the Port Said/Suez Bay area. Here eight Beaufighters of 89 Squadron had been scrambled, achieving some considerable success. Claims initially were for three shot down and a fourth damaged, but it appears that the latter may subsequently have been confirmed. Flt Lt Waddingham and his observer, Flg Off Cumbers, claimed a Ju 88 in flames which exploded on hitting the sea; moreover, Sgts Pring and Phillips claimed an He 111 which blew up, some wreckage hitting and damaging their Beaufighter.

Sometime later the commanding officer, Wg Cdr Stainforth, shot down another bomber which dived into the ground in flames, two miles north of Bulgas; initially identified as another He 111, two of the crew survived as PoWs, proving it to have been a Ju 88 of 4./LG 1. In fact all three of the aircraft brought down were of this type. Finally, Flg Off Harding and Sgt Horspool claimed an aircraft which they tentatively identified as a Dornier. This may possibly have been a Cant.Z.1007bis of 87° Gruppo which failed to return from a sortie to Ismailia, the recognition as a Dornier being due to the twin tail of this aircraft. Claimed initially as damaged, this subsequently appears to have been confirmed as destroyed.

British Claims

46 Sqn	Plt Off P.C.W.Sage/ Sgt K.Taylor	Beaufighter If	Ju 88	nr Lake Burullus	0305
89 Sqn	Flt Lt J.Waddingham / Plt Off A.B.Cumbers	Beaufighter If X7719	Ju 88	NE Port Said	0310
46 Sqn	Flt Lt C.G.Clegg/ Flt Sgt J.Cockburn	Beaufighter If X7746	Ju 88	10m N Edcu	0345-0515
89 Sqn	Sgt A.M.O.Pring/ Sgt C.T.Phillips	Beaufighter If R2266	He 111		0350
89 Sqn	Wg Cdr G.H.Stainforth/ Plt Off P.T.Lawson	Beaufighter If X7704	Ju 88	2m NE Bilqas, nr Basandila SW Damietta	0415-0420
89 Sqn	Flg Off F.Harding/ Sgt Horspool	Beaufighter If X7700	Do17 (two rudders)	15m off coast	0440

German Casualties

3./LG 1	Ju 88A-4 WNr 140003 L1+HL shot down by night fighter in Suez area; Obfw Karl Fuhrmann and three MiA
4./LG 1	Ju 88A-4 WNr 140153 L1+CM shot down by AA in Suez area; Obfw Horst Grigutsch KiA, three PoW
5./LG 1	Ju 88A-4 WNr 140033 L1+LN shot down by AA in Suez area; Oblt Werner Busse and one PoW, two KiA

Italian Casualties

603ª Sq, 147°Gr T	S.82, failed to return from a night-bombing mission to Alexandria, pilot Cap Mario Cocco, copilot M.llo Francesco Prandini and three MiA
608ª Sq, 149°Gr T	S.82 failed to return from a night-bombing mission to Alexandria, pilot Ten Vincenzo Sciucca, copilot Serg Pindaro Falconi and three MiA
192ª Sq, 87°Gr, 30°St BT	Cant.Z.1007bis MM 24245, '192-5' failed to return from a night mission to Ismailia, pilot Ten Santo Sciacca, copilot M.llo Edoardo Pesaresi and three MiA
193ª Sq, 87°Gr, 30°St BT	Cant.Z.1007bis destroyed at Gadurra, pilot T.Col Mario Giuliano, copilot Serg Magg Carlo Rago and three safe

Sunday-Monday, 5/6 July 1942

British Casualties

38 Sqn	Wellington Ic HF920 'W' off 2200 on minelaying sortie, FTR; Sqn Ldr Day and crew MiA

Monday-Tuesday, 6/7 July 1942

Raiders were over Alexandria again during the night, 46 Squadron's Flt Lt Clegg shooting down one which dived steeply, bursting into flames and hitting the ground. He then engaged another over Wadi Natrun, this bomber taking no evasive action. There was a large explosion and pieces flew off. AHQ confirmed that he had shot down two He 111s, both aircraft of 4./KG 100. During the night a night fighter Ju 88C of I./NJG 2 was also lost by the Luftwaffe, reportedly shot down by a Beaufighter whilst intercepting 205 Group Wellingtons. No claims by either of the night-fighter units for such a victory has been found, however (see also Chapter Eleven).

British Claims

46 Sqn	Flt Lt C.G.Clegg/ Sgt K.Taylor	Beaufighter If X7638	He 111	Cairo	0106-0420
46 Sqn	Flt Lt C.G.Clegg/ Sgt K.Taylor	Beaufighter If X7638	He 111	Wadi Natrun	0106-0420

British Casualties

252 Sqn	Beaufighter Ic T4883 shot down by Flak nr Capuzzo; Plt Off W.J.Smith/Flt Sgt R.S.Coles KiA

German Casualties

I./NJG 2	Ju 88C-6 WNr 360191 R4+DK shot down by Beaufighter at night while intercepting 205 Grp Wellingtons; Lt Georg Wiedow and two KiA
4./KG 100	He 111H-6 WNr 7229 6N+GB lost to night fighter over Suez; Fw Ernst Jacobi and three MiA
4./KG 100	He 111H-6 WNr 7340 6N+LG lost to night fighter in Suez area; Lt Hans Völker KiA, one MiA, two PoW
2.(F)/123	Ju 88A-5 WNr 0530 shot down in error by own Flak and crashed in sea nr Crete; crew saved

Italian Casualties

252ª Sq, 104°Gr AS	S.79 '252-8' landed into sea 3km SE of Rhodes, pilot Cap Bruno Chiozzi, copilot M.llo Renzo Prampolini and three rescued, aircraft severely damaged but recovered

Tuesday, 7 July 1942

British Casualties

15 SAAF Sqn	Bisley BA314 crashed after take-off from LG.99; Capt B.J.Hutchinson safe
15 SAAF Sqn	Bisley BA325 crash-landed at LG.97; Lt O.C.Venn safe

Wednesday, 8 July 1942

13(Hellenic) Squadron now began moving from St Jean to Gaza – a move which would take several days. Next day the Sea Rescue Flight moved to LG X.

British Casualties

459 Sqn	Hudson III V9030 crashed on landing at LG.228
217 Sqn	Beaufort Ia DD981 DBR by bombs during raid on Luqa
217 Sqn	Beaufort Ia DD954 DBR by bombs during raid on Luqa
217 Sqn	Beaufort Ia DD958 DBR by bombs during raid on Luqa

Wednesday-Thursday, 8/9 July 1942

British Claims

46 Sqn	Flt Lt R.M.MacKenzie/ Plt Off A.L.Craig	Beaufighter If	He 111	nr Alexandria	0210-0325
89 Sqn	Flg Off C.A.Crombie	Beaufighter V8224	He 111 Probable	S Amiriya	0231
46 Sqn	Sgt R.G.Peters/ Sgt F.Halliday	Beaufighter	He 111	S Amiriya	0243

German Casualties

6./KG 100	He 111H-6 WNr 7407 6N+BJ shot down by night fighter in Abu Ogos area; Fw Heinz Preugschat PoW, two KiA, one MiA
4./KG 100	He 111H-6 WNr 7419 6N+HG shot down 4m W El Hamrion by night fighter in Abu Ogos area; Fw Anton Hönniger and three PoW

Thursday, 9 July 1942

At 1640 four Beaufighters, drawn equally from 252 and 272 Squadrons, intercepted 20-25 Ju 52/3ms, two Bf 110s and a Ju 88 40 miles north of Tobruk, flying at 100 feet. The British pilots attacked from the south-east, but were violently opposed by the escorts and were obliged to leave quickly, not having time to see the results of their assault. They certainly failed to repeat the success of 12 May, and one Beaufighter was shot down by one of the Bf 110s. During the day seven Beauforts of 217 Squadron took off for a torpedo attack, but one crashed on take-off, another returning unserviceable. The remaining five failed to find their target. A further two Beauforts were destroyed on the ground during an air raid on Malta.

The day also saw the launch of Operation Chocolate. Due to the Axis having denied the coastal airfields west of El Alamein to Albacores interdicting the Crete-Tobruk shipping route, the Strategic Reconnaissance Flight undertook a number of sorties to seek possible alternatives. Crews reported that LG.126 might be a possibility. The position of this landing ground, three hours flying time from LG.100, would require on-site supplies of 1,500 gallons of 100 octane petrol and 60 gallons of Shell 100 oil in order to operate a force of ten aircraft. It would also be necessary for a fitter, a rigger and a W/T operator with the necessary tools, spares and Glim lamps for the flarepath, to be present. 216 Squadron's Bombay transports carried only enough fuel of their own to get there and back. The difference in cruising speeds between these aircraft and the Albacores was such that it was deemed necessary for the two types to go in separate formations.

HQ, ME, provided six Bombays and two Strategic Reconnaissance Marylands, one to lead each formation. Rendezvous for the start of the operation was at LG.100 at 1430 hours. On arrival the Bombays lined up on the leeward side of the landing ground, the Albacores then being parked two each side of the refuelling aircraft. Refuelling was carried out using Zwichy pumps, carried by the Bombays. The flarepath was then laid out – a task which took some hours after the Albacores had departed at 1445. The biplanes then flew along the southern side of the northern escarpment of the Qattara Depression to Bir Fuad, and then direct to LG.126. The Bombays followed 15 minutes later. Both formations met in the vicinity of LG.126, but could not find it. They all landed instead on a suitable piece of desert where they refuelled as arranged, completing this task before dark.

The Albacores then took off at 0140 to attack an Axis convoy. One suffered engine trouble and returned directly to Dekheila. The others sighted flares all over the sea. Only four actually located targets, the crews of these claiming two possible hits on a 5,000-ton merchant vessel and near misses on others. Four searched until they had to jettison their bombs, and the rest took the opportunity to bomb Tobruk. All but one then reached Dekheila safely, the latter landing nearby.

During the night a convoy of eight trucks passed close by the temporary landing ground, but saw nothing. Following the departure of the Albacores, all traces of the event which had taken place were loaded into the Bombays and flown back to LG.100. It had proved to be a very useful exercise from which much was learned, although in practice it would not be used again in this form.

British Claims

252 Sqn	Flt Lt P.C.Cobley/Sgt G.W.Williams	Beaufighter Ic 'J'	Ju 52/3m	nr Tobruk	1820
252 Sqn	Sgt N.J.Cleggett/Plt Off G.H.Williams	Beaufighter Ic 'P'	Ju 52/3m	nr Tobruk	1820

British Casualties

252 Sqn	Beaufighter T4831 'D' shot down by Bf 110 while attacking Ju 52/3ms between Crete-Tobruk; Plt Off T.G.Shaw/Sgt I.R. Snape KiA
217 Sqn	Beaufort DD954 destroyed on the ground during air raid on Malta
217 Sqn	Beaufort DD958 destroyed on the ground during air raid on Malta

Friday, 10 July 1942

A submarine was again attacked by a 47 Squadron Air Echelon Wellesley. Next day one of 700 Squadron's Walrus crews launched an attack on a submarine reported by HMS *Protea* and *Southern Seas* to the east of Cyprus at 1655. *Protea* dropped a pattern of depth charges, following which the Walrus attacked with two more from 40ft. Five men on the deck of this vessel were subsequently rescued by *Protea*, together with other survivors, and the submarine sank at 1708. Their victim had been the Italian *Ondina*.

British Casualties

89 Sqn	Beaufighter X7717 lost

459 Sqn	Hudson IIIa FH300 MiA from convoy attack off Tobruk
459 Sqn	Hudson III V9027 crashed in sea off Edcu

Saturday, 11 July 1942

At 0915 six 272 Squadron Beaufighters and three from 252 Squadron undertook a patrol 60 miles north of Tobruk – again hoping to intercept transport aircraft. 25-30 Ju 52/3ms were seen approaching, all flying in tight vic formations. The lower flight of Beaufighters went in first for a head-on attack. The top cover, seeing no escorts present, joined in. There was, however, an escort of one Bf 110, one Ju 88 and one He 111; there was also considerable return fire through the fuselage portholes from the troops aboard.

Sqn Ldr Ogden initially claimed one shot down and one damaged, then attacked again, claiming damage to three more. He was at that stage attacked out of the sun by the Bf 110, his aircraft being hit and damaged. Sqn Ldr Riley, leader of the top cover four, had attacked several Ju 52/3ms, but saw the fighter on Ogden's tail and chased it off. Plt Off Hodgson reported sending one transport into the sea in flames, and the pilots of 252 Squadron claimed one destroyed, one probable and one damaged. Two of this unit's Beaufighters were damaged by return fire, one crash-landing at base with the other force-landing at LG.39. In fact Luftwaffe losses on this occasion appear to have been limited to a single Ju 52/3m lost and two damaged.

British Claims

272 Sqn	Plt Off E.H.Hodgson/ Sgt W.J.Antonia	Beaufighter Ic T4980'F'	Ju 52/3m	Crete-Tobruk	0630-1140
272 Sqn	Sqn Ldr C.V.Ogden/ Sgt M.C.Thomas	Beaufighter Ic T5031'A'	Ju 52/3m	Crete-Tobruk	0630-1140
272 Sqn	Sqn Ldr C.V.Ogden/ Sgt M.C.Thomas	Beaufighter Ic T5031'A'	4 Ju 52/3ms Damaged	Crete-Tobruk	0630-1149
252 Sqn	Flg Off A.D.Frecker/ Plt Off K.P.Hunnings	Beaufighter Ic T4979	Ju 52/3m	Crete-Tobruk	0635-1115
252 Sqn	Flg Off I.Maclean/ Sgt E.V.B.Strange	Beaufighter Ic T5040	Ju 52/3m Probable	Crete-Tobruk	0635-1115
252 Sqn	Flg Off I.Maclean/ Sgt E.V.B.Strange	Beaufighter Ic T5040	Ju 52/3m Damaged	Crete-Tobruk	0635-1115
252 Sqn	Sgt G.D.S.Rignall/ Sgt J.Kilmister	Beaufighter Ic T4881 'D'	Ju 52/3m Damaged	Crete-Tobruk	0635-1115
272 Sqn	Sgt K.A.Graham/ Sgt L.J.Powdrill	Beaufighter Ic T3290 'B'	Ju 52/3m Damaged	Crete-Tobruk	0635-1115

British Casualties

272 Sqn	Beaufighter Ic T5031 'A' damaged by Bf 110; Sqn Ldr C.V.Ogden/Sgt M.C.Thomas safe
252 Sqn	Beaufighter Ic T4881'D' damaged by return fire from Ju 52/3ms; crash-landed on return; Sgt G.D.S.Rignall/Sgt J.Kilmister safe
252 Sqn	Beaufighter Ic T4880 'O' damaged by return fire from Ju 52/3ms; force-landed at LG.39; Sqn Ldr W.Riley/Sgt J.Martin safe
248 Sqn	Beaufighter Ic T5142 MiA (may have been on loan to 252 Sqn on this date)

German Casualties

IV./KGzbV 1	Ju 52/3m WNr 5576 damaged 15% by Beaufighters on transit flight Crete to Tobruk, crash-landed Tobruk a/f; Oblt Richard Ziller and one WiA, one KiA, one safe
IV./KGzbV 1	Ju 52/3m WNr 3090 damaged 10% by Beaufighters on transit flight Crete to Tobruk; crash-landed Tobruk a/f; Uffz Otto Ständer WiA, three safe
Ln.Rgt.Afrika	Ju 52/3m WNr 6438 BA+OV shot down by Beaufighters, crashed in sea off Derna; Obfw Heinrich Bock and three MiA

Sunday, 12 July 1942

Ten Ugo Drago, of 363ª Squadriglia, during a patrol over Benghazi (1820-1930) intercepted and fired 600 rounds at a Beaufort, claiming it damaged.

British Casualties

217 Sqn	Beaufort Ia DD988 destroyed on ground at Malta

Italian Claims					
363ª Sq, 150°Gr CT	Ten Ugo Drago	MC.200	Beaufort Damaged	near Benghazi	1820-1930

Monday, 13 July 1942

Two Cant.Z.1007bis of 262ª Squadriglia were carrying out a reconnaissance mission over the Port Said-Aboukir area when the aircraft flown by Ten Mario De Angelis ditched due to engine failure, not far from the Egyptian coast. He and his crew were taken prisoner.

S.Ten Giovanni Dell'Innocenti claimed to have damaged a Beaufort over Benghazi on 13 July, flying an MC.200 (see Chapter Eleven).

British Casualties	
217 Sqn	Beaufort DD988 destroyed on the ground during an air raid on Malta
Italian Casualties	
262ª Sq, 107°Gr, 47°St BT	Cant.Z.1007bis MM 21668 '262-5' ditched near Egyptian coast, pilot Ten Mario De Angelis, copilot Serg Enrico Balucci, observer T.V. Silvano Cereser and three PoW

Wednesday, 15 July 1942

British Casualties	
13 OTU	Blenheim BA542 on transit, left Luqa 0425 and failed to arrive in Egypt; Flt Sgt P.P.Adams & two MiA

Thursday, 16 July 1942

272 Squadron's Beaufighters were out after transport aircraft again, eight taking off at 0725. As they got underway, two collided and crashed into the sea. Plt Off Deppe and Sgt Corbin were picked up, but Wg Cdr Riley and Sgt Martin were not found. In the event, no Ju 52/3ms appeared. The loss of Bill Riley, DFC, was a hard blow. An extremely experienced fighter pilot who had claimed ten individual or shared victories, he had been waiting to take command of a new Beaufighter unit due to be formed. Pilots of his calibre were not easy to replace.

British Casualties	
272 Sqn	Beaufighter Ic 'O'collided; Sqn Ldr W.Riley/ Flt Sgt J.Martin MiA
272 Sqn	Beaufighter Ic 'J' collided, engine cut and ditched; Plt Off R.E.C. Deppe/Sgt Corbin rescued

Friday, 17 July 1942

Between 0850-1900 MC.200s of 8° Gruppo covered a convoy north of Mersa Matruh. The vessels were spotted by a Maryland crew who identified them as a merchant ship with a schooner astern. A strike by five 39 Squadron Beauforts was despatched, led by Sqn Ldr Taylor in W6488 'P' – an old Mark I aircraft – to attack these off Mersa Matruh in the evening. Times differ slightly, but the Italian fighter pilots reported that seven 'Bristol-type' torpedo-bombers attempted to attack but failed to achieve any hits. One of the attackers was claimed probably shot down by Serg Magg Ernesto Pavan, while Ten Lorenzo Ruffini of 93ª Squadriglia fired on several. The Beaufort crews reported that the convoy appeared to be escorted by one torpedo boat, one Do 215 (sic), three Macchis, two Bf 109s and a Bf 110. Five torpedoes were dropped without result and four Beauforts were slightly damaged.

British Claims		
39 Sqn	Gunner in Beaufort I N1153	MC.200

British Casualties	
39 Sqn	Beaufort Ia DD952 'U' damaged; Sgt G.Clingings KiA, Lt D.Tilley and rest of crew safe
39 Sqn	Beaufort Ia DD946 'Z'; damaged; navigator WiA, Wt Off Dawson and rest of crew safe
39 Sqn	Beaufort I N1153 'K' damaged; Plt Off Hanway and crew safe
39 Sqn	Beaufort Ia DD950 'O' damaged; Plt Off Grant and crew safe

Italian Claims

92ªSq, 8°Gr, 2°St CT	Serg Magg Ernesto Pavan	MC.200	Blenheim Probable	over convoy	1715

Saturday, 18 July 1942

Serg Luigi Boieri of 77ª Squadriglia encountered Beaufighters while escorting a convoy east of Tobruk. He claimed one of these shot down in flames after a long chase, seeing it crashing into the sea 30km north-west of Bardia. Boieri then ran out of fuel and landed at Menastir; his aircraft was refuelled, allowing him to return to base. Serg Vittorio Periotto of 93ª Squadriglia crash-landed due to engine trouble following a patrol over Mersa Matruh and was injured.

Italian Claims

77ª Sq, 13°Gr, 2°St CT	Serg Luigi Boieri	MC.200	Beaufighter	30km N Bardia 1010

Italian Casualties

93ª Sq, 8°Gr, 2°St CT	MC.200 MM 6502 force-landed and damaged, Serg Vittorio Periotto slightly injured

Monday, 20 July 1942

Two Beaufighters of 272 Squadron and one of 252 Squadron attacked a convoy comprising one tanker, two schooners and three barges, escorted by an E-Boat, a Bf 109 and a CR.42. The Beaufighters struck in turn, leaving two barges on fire and one schooner smoking. Much light Flak was encountered and one Beaufighter was hit, the observer being wounded.

459 Squadron was now tasked with attacking F-Boats (tank landing craft) which were now being operated by the Germans on the Tobruk-Mersa Matruh stretch of coast. For these duties the squadron moved from Abu Sueir to Edcu from where the first two such operations were experimentally undertaken – jointly with Beaufighters.

Meanwhile, a reconnaissance Maryland of 203 Squadron failed to return from a sortie, and was probably the aircraft claimed shot down by a Bf 110 pilot, which he identified as a Blenheim.

British Casualties

203 Sqn	Maryland failed to return; Sgt D.S.Murphy, Flt Sgt F.W.Martin, Flt Sgt E.B.Moorhouse MiA

German Claims

9./ZG 26	Obfw Walter Weiss	Blenheim

Tuesday, 21 July 1942

Two Beaufighters of 252 Squadron on a shipping reconnaissance in the Tobruk-Sidi Barrani area, piloted by Plt Off Maclean and Sgt Nettleship, reported encountering a Cant.Z.1007bis which they claimed to have shot down. Apparently there were no losses of Cant.Z.1007s on this day.

British Claims

252 Sqn	Plt Off I.Maclean/ Sgt E.V.B.Strange	Beaufighter Ic T4987	Cant.Z.1007	nr Taifa Rocks	0827-1305

German Casualties

2.(F)/123	Ju 88D-1 WNr 430143 4U+AK shot down by AA in Damietta area; Lt Erich Birkenmeier and two KiA, one PoW

Wednesday, 22 July 1942

HMS *Malines*, a vessel of 3,000 tons, arrived at Port Said on this date, but here she was attacked by two torpedo-carrying S.79s which gained a hit on the vessel, badly damaging her. She was then towed into harbour and beached. Two Martlets of 805 Squadron had been on patrol at the time, but these failed to intercept. *Malines* had been the victim of two S.79 torpedo-bombers of 205ª Squadriglia, flown by S.Ten Dorando Cionni and S.Ten Ferruccio Coloni, which left Rhodes at 0535 on an armed reconnaissance mission over the eastern Mediterranean. At 0930, off Port Said, they sighted a convoy on a westerly course, which comprised a steamer, a small tanker and eight patrol boats. Both S.79s released their torpedoes at the freighter that was hit and reportedly sunk. The Italian aircraft suffered damage by AA fire and two crew members were wounded.

British Casualties	
221 Sqn	Wellington VIII ditched due to port engine failure; Flg Off Frame and crew rapidly rescued from dinghy
German Casualties	
2.(F)/123	Ju 88D-2 WNr 430063 4U+BK FTR from recce Haifa-Alexandria Rosette; Uffz Alexander Würth and three MiA
2.(F)/123	Ju 88D-1 WNr 1155 4U+CK FTR from sea search for 4U+BK; Lt Ernst Lischke and three MiA
Italian Casualties	
205ª Sq, 41°Gr Aut AS	S.79 damaged by ships' AA fire, pilot S.Ten Dorando Cionni, copilot Serg Magg Giovanni Morgagni and two safe, one WiA
205ª Sq, 41°Gr Aut AS	S.79 damaged by ships' AA fire, pilot S.Ten Ferruccio Coloni WiA, copilot Serg Gino Mazzanti and crew safe

Thursday, 23 July 1942

A reconnaissance Ju 88 was intercepted between Burg el Arab and Dekheila by two Spitfires of 601 Squadron (see also Chapter Five). Plt Off Boyle and Sgt Toller thought it might have been an Me 210 and shot it down, the aircraft crashing in flames near El Alamein.

British Claims				
601 Sqn	Plt Off A.R.Boyle	Spitfire Vb BR118	} Me 210	1020-1110
601 Sqn	Sgt A.A.Toller	Spitfire Vb AB468		

German Casualties	
1(F)/121	Ju 88D-5 WNr 1701 7A+BH shot down by Spitfires and crashed near El Alamein; Oblt Heinrich Ostahr and three PoWs

Friday, 24 July 1942

The crew of a Blenheim of 13(Hellenic) Squadron escorting convoy LW29 from Beirut-Haifa to Alexandria, spotted a submarine on the surface and dropped depth charges without apparent effect. At night a further attack was made on this submarine by a 221 Squadron Wellington in co-operation with destroyers.

Hudsons of 459 Squadron undertaking their third sortie hunting for F-Boats off Tobruk, encountered Bf 110s of III./ZG 26 which were escorting Ju 52/3ms arriving there from Crete. One of the Australian aircraft was shot down by one of the Bf 110s, which was itself hit by return fire, wounding the gunner and slightly damaging the aircraft. No F-Boats were seen. The loss of three 86 Squadron aircraft on this date was occasioned by their high visibility, since all were still painted in the UK camouflage scheme, which featured black undersides for night operations.

Two Spitfires of 601 Squadron were scrambled after a Ju 88 over Aboukir at 28,000 feet (see also Chapter Five). One pilot gave up the chase, but the other caught the German aircraft and gained hits on its tail; it was last seen losing height with one engine and wing on fire. Such an aircraft of 2.(F)/123 was reported as having been shot down by a Beaufighter, crashing north of Port Said. Such a claim was made by Plt Off A.I.Smith of 272 Squadron when five of the unit's Beaufighters were undertaking an escort to an anti-shipping sweep. No vessels were seen, but a lone Ju 88 was spotted and despatched. However, the Junkers may already have been damaged by the Spitfire earlier.

British Claims					
601 Sqn	Flt Lt M.R.B.Ingram	Spitfire Vb	Ju 88 Probable		
272 Sqn	Plt Off A.I.Smith/ Sgt J.P.Diaper	Beaufighter Ic 'P'	Ju 88	N Tobruk	1024

British Casualties	
459 Sqn	Hudson III V9052 shot down by Bf 110s nr Tobruk
69 Sqn	Maryland AH397 crashed on landing at Luqa
86 Sqn	Beaufort AW308 'H' shot down by Flak during shipping strike off Cephallonia, Greece; Plt Off D.L.Furphey and crew PoW
86 Sqn	Beaufort AW355 'G' shot down by Flak during shipping strike off Cephallonia, Greece; Sqn Ldr J.R.Hyde and crew KiA
86 Sqn	Beaufort AW356 'Z'shot down by Flak during shipping strike off Cephallonia, Greece; Plt Off Thompson and crew
39 Sqn	Beaufort Ia DD9512 DBR by bombs during air raid on Luqa
815 Sqn	Swordfish V4365 lost near Mersa Matruh; Sub Lt O.Dixon and two KiA

German Claims			
7./ZG 26	Uffz Helmut Neitzke	Hudson	0838

German Casualties	
III./ZG 26	Bf 110 3U+HR 10% damaged by Hudson, 30km N Tobruk; pilot Uffz Neitzke safe/ Uffz Erwin Spahn WiA
2.(F)/123	Ju 88D-1 WNr 1071 4U+EK shot down N Port Said by Beaufighter; Uffz Hans-Peter Fierke, Lt Willy Karras & two KiA

By evening one of 221 Squadron's ASV Wellingtons, accompanied by four more of the unit's aircraft loaded with bombs and four torpedo-carrying Wellingtons of 38 Squadron, sortied after a convoy north-east of Derna. Two of the torpedo-carriers attacked and estimated that one hit had been achieved, a merchant vessel being left apparently static in the water.

In late July a new unit was formed as the Free French Nancy Flight, equipped with Blenheims. It was at once placed under the control of 201 Group. 221 Squadron was reinforced by the arrival from England of two Liberators of 120 Squadron.

Saturday, 25 July 1942

Operating under 252 Wing control, two Spitfires of 601 Squadron were again scrambled after a Ju 88 approaching Alexandria (see also Chapter Five). They intercepted and claimed to have damaged it, last seeing it at 10,000 feet in a dive west of Ghazul. Somewhat later in the morning another was attacked and also claimed damaged.

Under 250 Wing control two 805 Squadron Martlets were patrolling near Port Said when two S.79s of 104° Gruppo Autonomo AS were seen and intercepted, both catching fire and diving into the sea when attacked. Four members of one crew were picked up and made prisoners, although a fifth man was drowned; there were no survivors from the other aircraft. This was the first success for the naval pilots of this unit since the Crusader operations many months before.

Three 252 Squadron Beaufighters and three of 272 Squadron undertook an offensive coastal reconnaissance from 1134. At 1215 two barges were seen and 252 Squadron attacked these, setting one on fire and causing smoke to rise from the other. These three aircraft were then chased and attacked by two Bf 110s and all three were damaged, one badly. The 272 Squadron crews reported that the first barge attacked by 252's aircraft "seemed to blow up". These pilots then attacked the second, but saw no obvious results.

By night a 38 Squadron Wellington crew launched torpedoes at the stern of a merchant vessel, claiming hits on this with both torpedoes. At this time owing to a shortage of torpedoes in the command, several of 39 Squadron's sorties from Egypt during the last week of July, were bomb-armed. However, no results were achieved with this type of armament.

British Claims					
601 Sqn	unspecified	Spitfire Vb	Ju 88 Damaged		
601 Sqn	unspecified	Spitfire Vb	Ju 88 Damaged		
805 Sqn	Lt Cdr T.P.Goode	Martlet	S.79	El Maghra	1215
805 Sqn	Sub Lt C.E.Lowis	Martlet	S.79	El Maghra	1215

British Casualties	
252 Sqn	Beaufighter badly damaged by Flak
252 Sqn	2 Beaufighters damaged by Flak
230 Sqn	Sunderland I L8056 'Y' off 1600 on patrol of Nile Delta, FTR; Flt Lt E.H.Brown and 11 crew MiA

Italian Casualties	
252ª Sq, 104°Gr Aut AS	S.79 '252-9' failed to return from a recce mission in East Med, pilot Cap Egidio De Rosa, copilot M.llo Leo Lorenzani and three PoW
253ª Sq, 104°Gr Aut AS	S.79 '253-4' failed to return from a recce mission in East Med, pilot Ten Guido Bresciani, copilot Serg Magg Emilio Casco and three MiA

Sunday, 26 July 1942

At 1530 a Spitfire on a test flight from 103 MU at Aboukir, was vectored onto an intruder which Plt Off Wilson claimed to have shot down 15 miles north-east of Daba. He reported seeing a white sheet of flame after which the starboard wing broke away. Thereon, the Ju 88 turned on its back and went into a spin before crashing into the sea 12-15 miles off El Alamein. Three were seen to bale out. This appears to have been an aircraft of Wekusta 26 which crashed into the sea during a reconnaissance sortie.

Six Beaufighters of 252 Squadron set off on a shipping reconnaissance, but three were forced to turn back. The other three spotted six barges and a Flakship four miles north of Sidi Barrani, going west. One aircraft attacked, the pilot reporting hits. However, intense Flak damaged the aircraft seriously and killed the observer. One of the other pilots put a long burst into one barge, which he considered had hit it below the waterline.

British Claims					
103 MU	Plt Off A.F.Wilson	Spitfire V BP582	Ju 88	Aboukir area	1520

British Casualties	
252 Sqn	Beaufighter seriously damaged by Flak; observer KiA
German Casualties	
Wekusta 26	Ju 88D-1 WNr 1125 5M+E shot down, crashed in sea; Lt August Sticht and three MiA

Monday, 27 July 1942

Three 272 Squadron Beaufighters were sent out to attack small fishing vessels west of Taifa Rocks. These were not found, but a large armed trawler and an E-Boat with an escort provided by two Bf 109s, were seen. One Beaufighter was driven off by the Messerschmitts, but the second continued to patrol, the crew spotting a trimotor which they identified as an S.81 flying west along the coast. Sgt Tuckwell attacked this and expended all his ammunition, seeing one engine smoking. Presumably after his observer had been able to reload the cannon magazines, Tuckwell then made an attack on a lorry on the coast road, which turned over.

With evening, Shandur was raided where a 221 Squadron ASV Wellington was destroyed on the ground. Nine Beaufighters were airborne, and He 111s were claimed shot down by Wt Off Thomas of 46 Squadron and Plt Off Young of 89 Squadron. Only one such aircraft was lost by 4./KG 100, but a Ju 88 of 5./LG 1 was also reported shot down by a Beaufighter in the Suez area, one member of the crew of this aircraft becoming a prisoner. A third claim was also made for a Ju 88 probable by Flg Off Crombie. In the return direction two Wellingtons of 38 Squadron carried out an attack on a large four-masted ship, reporting a direct hit with torpedoes. The vessel was believed to have already been a wreck, however. The crew of a Hudson of 459 Squadron was successful in sinking a 200-ton Italian barge, MFP348, west of Sidi Barrani.

British Claims					
272 Sqn	Sgt G.A.Tuckwell/ Sgt K.F.Hubbard	Beaufighter Ic 'A'	S.81 Damaged		1125-1410
46 Sqn	Wt Off G.W.C.Thomas/ Sgt O'Toole	Beaufighter If X7628	He 111	Gebel Gatrani	2055-2230
89 Sqn	Plt Off J.W.N.Young/ Flg Off Hunter	Beaufighter If V8220 'C'	He 111	N Tel el Kebir	2210
89 Sqn	Flg Off C.A.Crombie/ Sgt R.C.Moss	Beaufighter If V8224	Ju 88 Probable		

British Casualties	
221 Sqn	Wellington Z8713 destroyed in air raid on Shandur

German Casualties	
4./KG 100	He 111H-6 WNr 7159 6N+FG shot down by Beaufighter in Suez area; Uffz Richard Schiela and three MiA
12./LG 1	Ju 88A-4 WNr 142023 L1+JW ditched 2km offshore near Apollonia; Oblt Fritz Riedel and 1 WiA, two safe
II./LG 1	Ju 88 MiA in Suez area

Tuesday, 28 July 1942

During the afternoon 203 Squadron lost a Maryland on maritime reconnaissance between Greece and Crete, this aircraft being shot down at 1600 by the pilot of a Bf 110. Four Beaufighters of 272 Squadron and four Hudsons of 459 Squadron attacked two F-Boats near Mersa Matruh, the crews of the latter aircraft gaining their first success against these targets, diving from 800 feet to deck level to release depth charges on them. One was observed to be beached, but one Hudson was seen to crash into the sea with one engine on fire – probably hit by Flak – and two members of the crew were seen in the water. The Beaufighters attacked the barges, but when one was seen heading for the downed Hudson crew, the pilot did not open fire. A single MC.202 appeared, but was driven off. As these activities appeared potentially too costly for the Hudsons, the unit's aircraft would subsequently go out singly, each aircraft carrying ten 100 lb bombs instead of depth charges.

At 2230 five Cant.Z.1007bis bombers of 87° Gruppo approached Alexandria, but these were prevented by an overcast from identifying their targets of El Amiriya airfield and nearby railway lines. Plt Off Sage of 46 Squadron intercepted and shot down one of the Italian aircraft, that flown by S.Ten Ferri failing to return. When Sage attempted to attack a second, the pilot switched on his navigation lights. Fearing that he might be about to attack a friendly aircraft, the Beaufighter pilot broke away, but soon after this, the bomber released its cargo.

British Claims

46 Sqn	Plt Off P.C.W.Sage/ Flt Sgt J.Cockburn	Beaufighter If X7709	Cant.Z.1007bis	40-50m NW Rosetta	2150-2255

British Casualties

459 Sqn	Hudson IIIa FH292 hit by Flak from convoy off Mersa Matruh and ditched
459 Sqn	Hudson IIIa damaged by Flak
203 Sqn	Maryland AH413 'D' took off 1307 to recce south-west of Crete; Flg Off L Harvey and 3 MiA
86 Sqn	Beaufort AW296 shot down by Flak during shipping strike off Sapienza, Greece; Plt Off Dawson and crew MiA
217 Sqn	Beaufort L9820 shot down by Flak during shipping strike off Sapienza, Greece; 2/Lt Strever and crew MiA
221 Sqn	Wellington VIII Z8713 destroyed in air raid on Shandur

German Claims

7./ZG 26	Lt Hans Müller-Nalbach	Maryland	1536

German Casualties

5./LG 1	Ju 88A-4 WNr 142041 L1+DN shot down by Beaufighter in Suez area; Fw Gerhard Eberling and two KiA, one PoW

Italian Casualties

192ª Sq, 87°Gr, 30°St BT	Cant.Z.1007bis MM 24261 failed to return from a night mission to Alexandria, 1900-, pilot S.Ten Giuseppe Ferri, copilot Serg Magg Vittorio Esposito and three MiA

Wednesday, 29 July 1942

The Greek crew of a 13(Hellenic) Squadron Blenheim again attacked a submarine.

Thursday, 30 July 1942

Italian Claims

83ª Sq, 18°Gr, 3°St CT	M.llo Paolo Franchi	MC.200	twin-engined a/c Probable	Mersa Matruh	0805

Thursday-Friday, 30/31 July 1942

Four Cant.Z.1007bis of 193ª Sq took off at 0140 on a night bombing mission to Alexandria, all returning safely.

British Casualties

38 Sqn	Wellington Ic 'V' FTR from minelaying sortie; Sgt Sampson and crew MiA

Friday-Saturday, 31 July/1 August 1942

47° Stormo BT undertook its final mission from Rhodes before returning to Italy. Three Cant.Z.1007bis of 106° Gruppo took off from Maritza at 0030 to bomb airfield facilities at Aboukir. Two of the bombers of 261ª Squadriglia failed to return, falling victim to the night fighters of 46 Squadron, as did a KG 100 He 111. 252 Wing recorded that six Italian aircraft approached Alexandria, but did not make landfall. Three 46 Squadron Beaufighters were up. At 0337 Plt Off Holme-Sumner shot down one Z.1007bis north of Aboukir. Another was confirmed as shot down by Flt Lt Mackenzie at 0345 four miles north of the same airfield. Holme-Sumner then attacked a third, which was claimed damaged. Mackenzie's victim blew up and at first appeared to have been a Heinkel, but inspection of the wreckage showed it to have been one of the Italian aircraft. Plt Off Holme-Sumner's victim proved to be the other Cant, wreckage of this also being found.

Meanwhile, at about 0230 hours, a very heavy blitz took place, chiefly directed at the tented camp at Heliopolis where 950 men were living. It started with a bombing run across the main station aerodrome, during which two or three aircraft were set on fire. This lit up the aircraft dispersal in the tented camp and the bombs were dropped there. Unfortunately one bomb of a stick fell near a three-ton lorry which Tysoe, Howard, Taylor and Murphy, all airmen on 92, were sheltering behind and they were all killed, and nine wounded. Here Wt Off Thomas claimed a Ju 88 shot down which seems to have actually been an He 111 of 4./KG 100; a Ju 88 of 4./LG 1 was reported lost to a Beaufighter on 1 August, crashing east of Cairo.

British Claims					
46 Sqn	Wt Off G.W.C.Thomas/ Sgt Jackson	Beaufighter If X7745	Ju 88	Cairo area	0210-0325
46 Sqn	Plt Off B.D.Holme-Sumner/ Sgt C.Naylor	Beaufighter If X7707	Cant.Z.1007bis	off Aboukir Point	0328
46 Sqn	Flt Lt R.M.Mackenzie/ Plt Off A.L.Craig	Beaufighter If X7837	He 111 or Cant	40m N Aboukir	0337
46 Sqn	Plt Off B.D.Holme-Sumner/ Sgt C.Naylor	Beaufighter If X7707	e/a	90m NW Aboukir	0400

British Casualties	
14 Sqn	Blenheim IV Z9614 off 0320 to bomb LG.18 (one of three); hit by Flak and crash-landed nr Fuka; Sgt A.E.Ellis and two PoW – Sgt M.German subsequently lost when ship carrying him to Europe was torpedoed
German Casualties	
4./KG 100	He 111H-6 WNr 7440 6N+BG shot down in Heliopolis area by Beaufighter night fighter; Fw Willi Amrath and two MiA, one PoW
4./LG 1	Ju 88A-4 WNr 140736 L1+JM shot down by Beaufighter, crashed E Cairo; Oblt Hans-Dieter Häffner and 1 MiA, two PoW
Italian Casualties	
261ª Sq, 106°Gr, 47°St BT	Cant.Z.1007bis failed to return from a night-bombing mission to Aboukir, pilot Cap Athos Maestri and three MiA, copilot Serg Magg Celso di Marco PoW
261ª Sq,106° GR, 47° St BT	Cant.Z.1007bis failed to return from a night-bombing mission to Aboukir, pilot Ten Marcello Trona, copilot M.llo Renato Piotti and three MiA

Saturday, 1 August 1942

Two MC.200s of 92ª Squadriglia, led by M.llo Agostini, took off from Abu Haggag at 0615 to escort a convoy leaving for Italy. As a matter of fact the convoy was stopped in the harbour but the fighters engaged a formation of Beaufighters. One was claimed damaged.

British Casualties	
252 Sqn	Beaufighter T5039 damaged by Flak off Mersa Matruh after attacking barges near Tobruk; crash-landed near Sidi Barrani; Plt Off A.G.G.Machin/Sgt C.B.A.Nichols KiA

Italian Claims				
92ªSq, 8°Gr, 2°St CT	M.llo Guerrero Agostini	MC.200	Beaufighter damaged	0705

Sunday, 2 August 1942

47° Stormo BT was now ordered to repatriate to Forlì. Four Cant.Z.1007bis remained serviceable and these were handed over to 87° Gruppo. At the end of the 11 months based on Rhodes, 47° Stormo had claimed three enemy aircraft shot down, five freighters sunk and ten damaged. The offensive capabilities of Rhodes-based bombers had been reduced during 1942. Increasingly, the Cant.Z.1007bis had become mainly devoted to reconnaissance duties, leaving the task of attacking British vessels to the S.79 torpedo-bombers of 41° Gruppo AS and, since July, of 104° Gruppo AS.

Four Hudsons of 459 Squadron were out during the morning searching for F-Boats, three crews having no success in finding any. The fourth was piloted by Flt Lt I.F.D'A.Rose, who had until recently been flying Kittyhawks with 450 Squadron, and he was able to make a surprise dive attack on one of these vessels at 0600, gaining three direct hits which sent it to the bottom.

Sunday-Monday, 2/3 August 1942

Two 46 Squadron Beaufighters patrolled, Sqn Ldr Read claiming an He 111 shot down into the sea in flames 20 miles north-north-east of El Alamein at 0440. Nonetheless, eight bombers managed to attack Amiriya fighter airfield, dropping 40 HE bombs; one Kittyhawk was destroyed and one damaged Cat II. During the night five Albacores of 826 Squadron undertook a sweep five miles off the coast from Bardia. One returned early with engine trouble, but the other four reached Bardia harbour where bombs were dropped on various targets.

British Claims

46 Sqn	Sqn Ldr J.A.A.Read/ Flg Off W.G.Howell	Beaufighter If .7778	He 111	10-20m NE Alamein	0410-0525

British Casualties

	Kittyhawk destroyed on the ground by bombs at Amiriya
	Kittyhawk damaged Cat II by bombs at Amiriya

German Casualties

4./KG 100	He 111H-6 WNr 7224 6N+DJ shot down, crashed nrAlexandria; Fw Siegfried Schwerzel, Hptm Günter Ingenohl and two MiA

Monday, 3 August 1942

Wellington Z 8778 of RAF Sea Rescue Flight took off at 1000 hours on 3 August 1942 from LG.X in answer to a request from Flying Control AHQ, Egypt, to search for a missing Wellington aircraft of 104 Squadron which had signalled at about 0500 hours that it was force-landing in position 30.51N, 29.52E. The captain was instructed to carry out a search of the reported position to a depth of 30 miles. It was pointed out that the area traversed the main Cairo-Alexandria road and also contained a large number of aerodromes. At 1245 a snap D/F bearing by Gianaclis was 135 deg. At 1300 hours a W/T signal from Z 8778 read "search had up to that time been unsuccessful, but continuing". At 1642 a further attempt was made to contact Z 8778 but was not successful. The aircraft had a safe endurance of eight hours – perhaps over ten hours. Extensive searches were made over the next two days but were unsuccessful.

British Casualties

Sea Rescue Flight	Wellington Z8778 took off at 10.00, last heard from at 13.00; Flg Off J.T.Dick and six MiA

Tuesday, 4 August 1942

MC.200s of 2° Stormo CT were on convoy escort from 0540 to 1920. The pair of 8° Gruppo led by S.Ten Franco Mauri, flying between 0800 and 1015, intercepted a Beaufighter and scored some hits on it. The following pair of 13° Gruppo met four Beaufighters; Serg Galileo Petti chased the last aircraft of the formation and claimed it damaged. Later on, Magg Viale intercepted five Beaufighters and damaged two. Somewhat later Ten Luglio's aircraft was hit by friendly fire from the ships he was escorting, his MC.200 being damaged. Nonetheless, the Beaufighter strikes were successful on this date, an Italian ferry barge being strafed and sunk five miles east of Sollum, while MZ 723 was despatched in similar manner.

Off the Palestinian coast near Jaffa, an aircraft of 203 Squadron joined the destroyers HMS *Sikh*, *Zulu*, *Croome* and *Tetcott* in sinking U-372. A Swordfish crew of 815 Squadron attacked another submarine which they had spotted on the surface.

British Casualties

252 Sqn	Beaufighter T5033 shot down on sweep in Gulf of Sollum at 1049 to 3 MC.200s; Flt Sgt E.Babiak /Sgt A.W.T. Lancaster PoW

Italian Claims

94ª Sq, 8°Gr, 2°St CT	S.Ten Franco Mauri	MC.200	Beaufighter Damaged	Tobruk	0955
78ª Sq, 13°Gr, 2°St CT	Serg Galileo Petti	MC.200	Beaufighter Damaged	Tobruk	0840-1040
13°Gr, 2°St CT	Magg Lorenzo Viale	MC.200	2 Beaufighters Damaged	Tobruk	

Italian Casualties

82ª Sq, 13°Gr, 2°St CT	MC.200 MM 8296 hit by AA of escorted ships, Ten Camillo Luglio safe

Wednesday, 5 August 1942

Two Cant.Z.1007bis of 193ª Squadriglia carried out a reconnaissance mission. A British convoy was found and HMS *Fareham* was attacked 20 miles north-north-east of Port Said. A Hurricane of 94 Squadron had been scrambled at 1250, the pilot seeing one of the Italian aircraft shot down into the sea by a Royal Navy minesweeper. Five survivors were picked up by *Fareham*.

British Casualties	
459 Sqn	Hudson IIIa FH302 off at 0225 on a shipping strike, FTR; Flt Sgt W.L.Staines and three MiA
Italian Casualties	
193ª Sq, 87°Gr BT	Cant.Z.1007bis hit by AA, ditched in sea, pilot S.Ten Tullio Casini, copilot Serg Magg Carlo Rago, observer G.M. Aldo Giambartolomei and three PoW

Thursday, 6 August 1942

British Casualties	
2 PRU	Spitfire IV BP914 departed 1400 for Mersa Matruh, FTR; Plt Off W.L.V.Hallett KiA

Friday, 7 August 1942

From 0530 to 1355 MC.200s of 8° Gruppo provided escort to five landing crafts sailing to Mersa Matruh. Cap Cecchet carried out a first sortie at 0515 to spot the convoy: one of the landing craft was seen in flames, surrounded by ten sailors floating on their life vests. Once landed at Sidi Barrani, Cecchet warned the Eastern Sector Command, asking to send a German Ju 52 to drop a dinghy to the survivors. At about 0630 three MC.200s of 94ª Squadriglia, led by S.Ten Nunzio Defraia, thwarted the attack of five Beaufighters, scoring some hits on one. The others evaded easily thanks to their superior speed. A second patrol of three MC.200s led by S.Ten Lorenzo Ruffini intercepted four Beaufighters at 1120 and one, shared between Serg Magg Palumbo and Serg Magg Plodari, was claimed damaged, seen flying away trailing black smoke from the port engine. With nightfall, however, Albacore crews were successful in sinking MZ 712 and 738 off Taifa Rocks and Mersa Matruh.

Italian Claims					
94ª Sq, 8°Gr, 2°St CT	S.Ten Nunzio Defraia	MC.200	Beaufighter Damaged	off coast	0630
93ª Sq, 8°Gr, 2°St CT	Serg Magg Bartolo Palumbo	MC.200	} Beaufighter Damaged	off coast	1120
93ª Sq, 8°Gr, 2°St CT	Serg Magg Mario Plodari	MC.200	}		
Italian Casualties					
92ª Sq, 8°Gr, 2°St CT	MC.200 damaged in combat by Beaufighters' return fire				

Saturday, 8 August 1942

335 Squadron moved from Edcu to Dekheila and 272 Squadron received a new flight commander, Flt Lt Anthony Watson, DFC, a very experienced fighter Blenheim and Beaufighter pilot who had seen service in Iraq during the previous year (see *Dust Clouds in the Middle East*). 252 Squadron was now preparing to send a detachment of six aircraft to Malta since a very important new convoy was about to try and run the gauntlet through the western Mediterranean to the island. This would, of course, be the critical Operation Pedestal convoy which on this occasion 201 Group could do little to aid. The full story of this particular convoy may be found in *Malta: The Spitfire Year, 1942*. However, for the next few days the activities of most Luftwaffe Ju 88s were directed mainly at the western Mediterranean, particularly those of LG 1. Consequently, it was mainly Regia Aeronautica aircraft which were to be seen during this period.

Sunday, 9 August 1942

British Casualties	
203 Sqn	Maryland AH312 FTR

Monday, 10 August 1942

Three Beaufighters of 252 Squadron enjoyed a rather unusual success, intercepting a reconnaissance Ju 88 from 2.(F)/123, which they encountered at 200ft when flying from LG.229 to Yeraskipas. They gave chase and Flg Off Reed shot it down into the sea. A little later the Beaufighter crews' frequent adversaries, the MC.200s of 2° Stormo, reported encountering and damaging one such aircraft during a convoy escort carried out by 8° Gruppo when S.Ten Lorenzo Ruffini of 93ª Squadriglia claimed damage to one of the big RAF fighters. Also on this date a 700 Squadron Walrus attacked a submarine.

British Claims

252 Sqn	Flg Off K.J.A.Reed/ Sgt G.D.Nash	Beaufighter If X7633	Ju 88	Edcu-Paphos, Cyprus	1105-1305

German Claims

1./JG 27	Lt Hans Remmer	Blenheim	SE Abu Dweis	0930

(Possibly this was the Maryland listed missing on the previous day)

German Casualties

2.(F)/123	Ju 88D-1 WNr 430254 4U+DK shot down by Beaufighter off Cyprus; Lt Ernst Lang and three KiA

Italian Claims

93ª Sq, 8°Gr, 2°St CT	S.Ten Lorenzo Ruffini	MC.200	Beaufighter Damaged	off Tobruk	1355

Tuesday, 11 August 1942

Eight 826 Squadron Albacores, each loaded with six 250lb bombs, attacked five or six F-Boats in Mersa Matruh harbour, at least one big fire being seen.

Wednesday, 12 August 1942

MC.200s of 2° Stormo spent all daylight on convoy escort. At about 0930 a 13° Gruppo pilot witnessed the torpedoing of the ship *Ogaden*, sailing between Benghazi and Tobruk, by a British submarine, HMS *Porpoise*, commanded by Capt Leslie W.A. Bennington. The 4,546-ton steamer, carrying aboard some British PoWs, sank quickly. A few sailors and passengers survived and were rescued by the Italian torpedo-boat *Montanari*. S.Ten Federico Vallauri failed to return from one such convoy escort; the search for the missing pilots started immediately without result. Vallauri's body was found twelve days later north-west of Gambut, near the wreck of his MC.200. Albacore crews were once again successful, sinking MZ 701 off the coast of Mersda el Asi.

Italian Casualties

77ª Sq, 13°Gr, 2°St CT	MC.200 MM 6699 '77-4' failed to return from a convoy escort, 0945-, S.Ten Federico Vallauri MiA

Thursday, 13 August 1942

A Hudson crew sighted an F-Boat, attacking this with eight bombs. Three hits were claimed and a terrific flash amidships was reported. However, one of the unit's aircraft was lost during the day in another such attack. By now 248 Wing was about ready to commence operations as a unit, initially moving to Shallufa and taking control of 38 and 221 Squadrons, 5 METS and 1,2 and 3 Mobile Torpedo Units. 458 Squadron was due to join the wing with effect from 1 September. Meanwhile the wing's 37 ground gunners took over the ground defence of Shallufa from 238 Wing's gunners.

British Claims

252 Sqn	Plt Off R.D.Jaggard/ Sgt F.G.Drewry	Beaufighter Ic T4840	Ju 88 Damaged	Cyprus-Edcu	1710-1845

British Casualties

459 Sqn	Hudson IIIa FW294 MiA from shipping strike off Libyan coast; Flak at Ras Azzaz at 0901

Friday, 14 August 1942

At 1130 four Beaufighters of 272 Squadron with others of 252 Squadron provided escort for Blenheims on a shipping strike. A number of Ju 52/3ms were encountered and two were claimed shot down. During the escort of an Axis convoy sailing along the coast W of Sidi Barrani, the MC.200 flown by Ten Giorgio Zichella crashed for unknown causes, killing the pilot.

British Claims

272 Sqn	Sgt N.J.Cleggett/ Sgt G.H.Williams	Beaufighter Ic 'C'	Ju 52/3m	off Sidi Barrani	1130-1556

British Claims

272 Sqn	Sgt G.A.Tuckwell/ Sgt K.F.Hubbard	Beaufighter Ic 'F'	Ju 52/3m	off Sidi Barrani	1130-1556
252 Sqn	Plt Off R.D.Jaggard/ Sgt F.G.Drewry	Beaufighter Ic T4840	Ju 52/3m Damaged	anti-shipping sweep from Edcu	1130-1554

British Casualties

272 Sqn	Beaufighter Ic 'C' damaged by Flak, brake lines cut; crashed on landing; Sgt N.J.Cleggett/Plt Off G.H.Williams safe
272 Sqn	Beaufighter Ic 'F' damaged by return fire from Ju 52/3m off Sidi Barrani, crash-landed at base 2550; Sgt G.A. Tuckwell/Sgt K.F.Hubbard safe

German Casualties

III./KGzbV 1	Ju 52/3m WNr 6074 shot down by Beaufighter, crashed in Sollum Bay; Fw Anton Stockhammer and three KiA
III./KGzbV 1	Ju 52/3m WNr 6810 shot down by Beaufighter, crashed in Sollum Bay; Fw Ernst Stein and one KiA, two WiA
IV./KGzbV 1	Ju 52/3m WNr 6027 ditched in sea off Cape Karasalos; crew safe

Italian Casualties

95ª Sq, 18°Gr, 3°St CT	MC.200 MM 8184 crashed for unknown causes during a convoy escort, Ten Giorgio Zichella MiA

Saturday, 15 August 1942

At 1145 three Beaufighters of 272 Squadron and two of 252 Squadron escorted six Bisleys of 15 SAAF Squadron on a coastal strike to attack 16 F-Boats between Sidi Barrani and Mersa Matruh; 14-16 of these barges were seen sailing in rows of six and eight, covered by one Bf 109 and two MC.202s. In fact two Bf 109s of III./JG 53 took off at 1155 to escort the convoy, accompanied by two MC.200s of 8° Gruppo, and attacked the British formation which they identified as 12 Beaufighters. One fighter attacked the Beaufighter flown by Sgt Knight of 272 Squadron, but turned off and targeted the Bisleys. The gunners of the bombers believed that they had shot this fighter down. Plt Off Cobley then saw a Bf 109F and attacked it, but the Messerschmitt banked sharply and turned onto the tail of his aircraft and opened fire. Shells hit the British aircraft in the wings, tail and fuselage, smashing the observer's perspex dome above the fuselage. Cobley took evasive action, but an incendiary bullet hit the observer's kit, setting it on fire, and this set fire to the Very cartridge. As a result of this, thick yellow smoke gushed out of the Beaufighter, and as it dived, balls of flame came pouring out. All fuel tanks were hit and both crew members were wounded, but they eventually got the fire out and managed to fly back to base. By this time the Bf 109 had also departed, the pilot claiming the apparently blazing Beaufighter as destroyed. This is a classic example of how a legitimate claim that would have been confirmed in any air force in the world was not, in fact, correct.

Meanwhile the Bisleys had made a beam attack, all 24 bombs released being seen to drop in close proximity, five hits being claimed. Later observation indicated that three F-Boats appeared no longer to be present. During this engagement the Bisley crews claimed one MC.202 shot down as described above, although no Italian fighters were actually lost. However, one of the Macchi pilots also claimed a twin-engined aircraft which he identified as a Blenheim, his companion firing on another. It seems likely that they had engaged the Bisleys on this occasion.

British Claims

15 SAAF Sqn	Bisley gunners	MC.202	over convoy

British Casualties

272 Sqn	Beaufighter T5036 'D' seriously damaged by Bf 109 5-10m W Ishailia Rocks at 1340, on fire and crash-landed at base, Cat II; Plt Off P.C.Cobley WiA, Sgt G.W.Williams safe
252 Sqn	Beaufighter damaged

German Claims

9./JG 53	Lt Hermann Munzert	Beaufighter	N Sidi Barrani	1245

Italian Claims

93ª Sq, 8°Gr, 2°St CT	Serg Magg Ottorino Lancia	MC.200	Blenheim	off Tobruk	1240
93ª Sq, 8°Gr, 2°St CT	Serg Magg Bartolo Palumbo	MC.200	Blenheim Damaged	off Tobruk	1240

Sunday, 16 August 1942

Three Wellingtons of 221 Squadron found and illuminated a convoy off the Libyan coast by night. Ten 38 Squadron Wellingtons were despatched, reporting that the flare dropping and homing procedures were successfully employed. Four ships were seen, but the striking force found visibility very limited due to thick cloud; some therefore dropped their bombs on gun flashes seen below. One direct hit with a 1,000lb bomb was claimed by one crew who released their weapon at 4,000ft. A huge explosion was seen which rocked the aircraft violently. During the return flight bombs were also dropped on a gun position at Ras el Daba which was firing. The crew of 38 Squadron's A Flight reported seeing a mushroom-shaped cloud after the reported explosion. Meanwhile, nine Albacores of 826 Squadron bombed F-Boats at Mersa Matruh.

British Claims

145 Sqn	Flt Lt J S Taylor	Spitfire Vc BR522 'N'	Ju 88 Damaged	30m S Cairo	1600
145 Sqn	Plt Off Bates	Spitfire Vc BP986 'X'			
145 Sqn	Flt Lt J.S.Taylor	Spitfire VB BR583 'T'	Ju 88 Damaged		1720-1845

British Casualties

459 Sqn	Hudson IV V9172 MiA

Italian Casualties

94ª Sq, 8°Gr, 2°St CT	MC.200 MM 6798 ran out of fuel after convoy escort, belly-landed, Serg Giovanni Pistore safe

Monday, 17 August 1942

The sole remaining Blenheim bomber unit, 14 Squadron, was now withdrawn to LG.224 to commence conversion to Martin Marauders with which it was to become a torpedo-bomber and reconnaissance unit. At the same time the remains of 39 Squadron moved to Malta where it was reformed under the same number, incorporating with its own Beauforts those of the remnants of 86 and 217 Squadrons already at Luqa. Another departure was 805 Squadron with its Martlets which now left Fayid for Mombasa in East Africa where it was to become an operational training unit. 46 Squadron despatched a detachment of Beaufighters to LG.224.

Since 1 August 459 Squadron's attacks on F-Boats on the Tobruk-Mersa Matruh route had gained rapidly in success, 85 out of 112 sorties being against these targets. Fifteen of these vessels had been claimed sunk and three damaged, causing the Germans to withdraw their use. The cost had not been light, four more Hudsons having been lost during this two and a half week period, while several others had returned heavily damaged. With the departure of their prey, however, the crews of these aircraft would soon revert to the rather more mundane duties of anti-submarine patrols and searches for Axis convoys.

Tuesday, 18 August 1942

British Casualties

86 Sqn	Beaufort AW280, damaged by Flak during shipping strike off Pantelleria
459 Sqn	Hudson IIIa MiA

Italian Casualties

253ª Sq, 104°Gr Aut AS	S.79 failed to return from a mission to the eastern Mediterranean, 0645-, pilot Ten Vittorio Marotta, copilot Serg Magg Benito Pieri and crew PoW (off Haifa to ships' AA)

Wednesday, 19 August 1942

Four Bf 109s of I./JG 27 were scrambled to intercept Beaufighters which were carrying out a sweep near Sidi Barrani. A single 252 Squadron aircraft was spotted and was shot down.

British Casualties

252 Sqn	Beaufighter T4840; shot down by Bf 109 east of Mersa Matruh; Sgt R.P.Williams/Sgt F.J.Craven KiA

German Claims

2./JG 27	Uffz Max Winkler	Beaufighter	30km E Mersa Matruh	0703

Thursday, 20 August 1942

Over the Delta area radar tracked a Ju 86R crossing the coast near Port Said at 40,000 feet. Cruising at 200mph, it flew down the entire length of the Suez Canal photographing shipping, military bases and airfields along the waterway. Then it headed north-west to photograph the fighter landing ground near Alexandria, before passing over the naval base and heading out to sea. Five Spitfires went after the intruder and two fired bursts at it from well below its altitude, but neither pilot claimed hits. Closest was Sgt Duigan of 145 Squadron, flying a stripped Spitfire, who got to within ten yards of a Ju 86P at 40,000 feet, but his guns froze after only one shot had been fired and again the German aircraft escaped.

During an escort to a convoy, which comprised the German steamer *Dora* and the tanker *Poza Rica*, heading to Taranto, eight fighters of 161° Gruppo, led by Ten Adriano Porcù, intercepted a formation of about twelve twin-engined British torpedo-bombers. In the fight that followed four aircraft, identified as Beauforts, were claimed shot down with two being seen flying away pouring black smoke. No hits were achieved by the British aircraft as the torpedoes had been set to run too deep. Wg Cdr Pat Gibbs reported that the losses suffered were all to single-engined fighters as the convoy had been surprised and did not have a chance to put up much Flak.

British Casualties

272 Sqn	Beaufighter T7677 left on patrol 0805, MiA 80m NW Sidi Barrani to enemy aircraft; Flt Sgt W.H.P.Knight /Sgt A.Wale MiA
227 Sqn	Beaufighter X8039 ditched 5m S Kalafrana; Flg Off J.P.Eyre safe, Sgt G.D.Leslie KiA
227 Sqn	Beaufighter T4934 shot down by Flak attacking convoy off Calabria; Sgt D.G.Brisco POW, Sgt D.Paterson PoW
86 Sqn	Beaufort AW341 'F', shot down by Flak during shipping strike off Punta Stilo; Plt Off Roper and crew
39 Sqn	Beaufort II AW245 'T' shot down; Plt Off R.L.Condon and crew PoW

Italian Claims

164ª Sq, 161°Gr Aut CT	Ten Adriano Porcù	G.50bis	4 Beauforts	convoy escort Ionian Sea
161°Gr Aut CT	7 pilots	G.50bis		

Friday, 21 August 1942

A lone Cant.Z.1007 of 192ª Squadriglia flown by Ten Aldo Villanis, left at 1130 to reconnoitre Cyprus. Over Larnaca it was intercepted and shot down by two Hurricanes of 451 Squadron. A second Cant was sent out to search for survivors, but found nothing. That night a Ju 88 of III./LG 1 was shot down by a 46 Squadron Beaufighter.

A Wellington of 221 Squadron (HF857 flown by Sgt Clark) on special ASV anti-submarine patrol duties was escorting HMS *Coventry* from Beirut to Port Said, when a U-Boat was sighted on the surface at 1610. Clark attacked with depth charges from 20 feet, one hitting directly above the conning tower, the others on each side. The stern was blown out of the water and the submarine slid beneath the waves. It surfaced again and attacked the Wellington with the deck guns. Clark ordered the front, tail and side gunners to respond, and the hostile fire was silenced. The vessel then remained on the surface, circling as though out of control, slowly sinking lower and lower in the water. It remained on the surface for an hour, finally disappearing quietly, and horizontally.

At 1809 a 145 Squadron Spitfire intercepted a Ju 88, the rear gunner of which kept on firing as the aircraft, its port engine on fire, was last seen 40 miles south of Alexandria at 1824. At 2245 Wg Cdr Reid in a 46 Squadron Beaufighter intercepted a Ju 88 of 6./LG 1 over the Arabian Gulf, shooting this down into the sea with the port engine on flames.

British Claims

451 Sqn	Plt Off D.Le S.Fisher	Hurricane I	Cant.Z.1007bis	Larnaca	1400
451 Sqn	Plt Off W.L.Terry	Hurricane I			
46 Sqn	Wg Cdr G.A.Reid/ Sgt H.E.Jackson	Beaufighter If X7779	Ju 88	15-20m NW Burg el Arab	2241

British Casualties

39 Sqn	Beaufort AW353; 2/Lt W.B.Wolfe MiA near Corfu
248 Sqn	Beaufighter T5140 damaged by Flak and ditched 12m W Corfu while escorting 6 Beauforts; Flg Off G.P.Stanton PoW, Flg Off C.Bryson PoW, but died as PoW
248 Sqn	Beaufighter T5164 damaged by Flak and ditched 12m W Corfu while escorting 6 Beauforts

German Casualties

6./LG 1	Ju 88A-4 WNr 140742 L1+HP shot down by Beaufighter while raiding Mireibet, crashed nr Alexandria; Uffz Erich Röhlke and 2 MiA, 1 PoW

Italian Casualties

192ª Sq, 87°Gr, 30°St BT	Cant.Z.1007bis MM 24537 failed to return from a reconnaissance mission to Cyprus, pilot Ten Aldo Villanis, copilot Serg Magg Giovanni Clemente and four PoW

Saturday, 22 August 1942

Three Albacores of 826 Squadron illuminated Mersa Matruh harbour for nine more such aircraft of 821 Squadron. One aircraft crashed on return, pilot and observer unhurt. On this date Capt Toomy, USAAF, and his crew were temporarily attached to 221 Squadron with their B-24. At this time this latter unit moved to Shallufa, maintaining detachments with 235 Wing at St Jean and with 247 Wing at LG.226. However, the detachment of the unit on Malta was now posted to 69 Squadron, becoming an additional flight of that unit.

British Casualties

826 Sqn	Albacore crashed on return from attack on Mersa Matruh; crew safe

Sunday, 23 August 1942

Beaufighters of 252 Squadron on patrol off Derna, intercepted and shot down an S.82 of III./KGzbV 1. Survivors were seen scrambling into the water from the fuselage door. During the day 18 Cant.Z.1007bis of 90° Gruppo, led by 30° Stormo commanding officer, Col Umberto Fiori, arrived at Gadurra from Lecce. The Gruppo commander was T.Col Renzo della Pura Honorati, and the two Squadriglie (194ª and 195ª) were led by Cap Corradino Vecchi and Cap Terzo Mazzotti.

Three Beaufighters of 46 Squadron patrolled between 2237-0055. One made contact with an unidentified aircraft at 2315, finding an aircraft dropping flares 30 miles south of LG.90. Believing this to be an He 111, the pilot shot it down in flames and it crashed, four crew baling out. However, it proved to be a USAAF B-25 Mitchell, identified in error as hostile by the controller. At a subsequent inquiry it was held that no blame attached to either the squadron or the pilot. Meanwhile, at 2325 a Ju 88 of 4./LG 1 was shot down by Sqn Ldr Pain of 89 Squadron 15 miles east of Zugazig; two baled out and became PoWs.

British Claims

252 Sqn	Flg Off D.M.Garbutt/ Sgt M.A.Lea	Beaufighter Ic T5080 'K'	S.82	20m NW Derna	0805-1305
252 Sqn	Flg Off I.Maclean/ Sgt E.V.B.Strange	Beaufighter Ic T5032 'D'			
89 Sqn	Sqn Ldr D.S.Pain/ Sgt Briggs	Beaufighter If X7719	Ju 88	SW LG.229	2310
46 Sqn	Plt Off J.A.White/ Sgt K.F.C.Inskip	Beaufighter If (Turned out to be a USAAF B-25, shot down in error)	He 111	30m S LG.90	2315

US Casualties

81st BS/12th BG	B-25C 41-12862 '40' shot down by a Beaufighter in error; 1/Lt S.L.Powell Jr and three baled out safely, two KiA
81st BS/12th BG	B-25C 41-12853 failed to return from night mission to Tobruk; Capt Richard W.Carlisle and four KiA

German Claims

8./JG 53	Uffz Jens Bahnsen	Beaufighter	N Sidi Barrani	0620

German Casualties

4./LG 1	Ju 88A-4 WNr 140068 L1+HM shot down by Beaufighter, crashed S Alexandria; Uffz Heinrich Herold and one MiA, two PoW
III./KGzbV 1	S.82 WNr 0126 1Z+BD shot down by Beaufighter, crashed NW Derna; Fw Günther Streblow and four MiA

Monday, 24 August 1942

The stripped Spitfires at 103 MU gained their first success against the high-flying pressurised Ju 86Rs on this date. Flg Off Reynolds chased the reconnaissance aircraft out to sea near Alexandria after it had first been spotted north of Cairo. Climbing to 40,000 feet, he got within range but climbed a further 2,000 feet before closing to 50 yards and opening fire, reporting that he thought he had achieved hits on the starboard engine. At this point he lost control, the Spitfire falling 10,000 feet before he could steady it and return to base and landing with only five gallons of fuel left. Here he was informed that the Ju 86R had crashed; Luftwaffe records do not confirm this, however. After this engagement the three Ju 86Rs still in the Middle East operated at an even greater altitude. Following this initial action, the high altitude Spitfires underwent further modification to reduce their weight. The radios and radio masts were removed, as was the 56lb battery. This was replaced with an 8lb one which provided just enough power to light the gunsight. The fuel load was also reduced by 30 gallons.

Under a revised tactical plan for high altitude interceptions, a stripped Spitfire became known as the 'striker'. Accompanying it during the interception would be another modified Spitfire carrying a radio, called the 'marker'. The pilot of this latter aircraft was in radio contact with the ground controller, and he followed the latter's intercept vectors to bring him as close as possible to the enemy aircraft, The pilot of the striker was to maintain position several thousand feet above and to one side of the marker, until he caught sight of the Junkers. Then he could move in to engage it. If he could inflict damage with his limited armament, he might force the Junkers to descend so that the marker could attack also.

With evening a raid on Wadi Natrun by one Ju 88 of 3./LG 1 was plotted by 252 Wing which directed a 211 Group Hurricane of 73 Squadron to the intruder 20 miles north of Burg el Arab where it was shot down by Wt Off Joyce (see also Chapter Five).

British Claims

73 Sqn	Wt Off E.L.Joyce	Hurricane IIC BP167 'L'	Ju 88	10-12m SE LG.39
103 MU	Flg Off G.W.H.Reynolds	Spitfire V	Ju 86P	Aboukir area

British Casualties

39 Sqn	Beaufort AW290 shot down by Flak during a shipping strike off Corfu

German Casualties

4./KG 77	Ju 88A-4 WNr 3666 3Z+HM shot down by Beaufighter, crashed into eastern Med; Obfw Erich Seefeld and three MiA
3./LG 1	Ju 88A-4 WNr 140093 L1+NL shot down by Hurricanes S Alexandria; Oblt Walter Machazek and one MiA, two PoW

Italian Casualties

601ª Sq, 147° Gr T	S.82 MM 60611 '601-7' failed to reach Lecce from Benghazi, pilot Ten Francesco Zavattarelli, copilot M.llo Vittorio Andreani and three MiA

Tuesday, 25 August 1942

Six Bisleys of 15 SAAF Squadron were ordered to attack MT on the Sidi Barrani-Mersa Matruh road, but no targets were seen here. Instead, an attack was made on LG.121 where direct hits were claimed on a Ca.133 and a Ju 52/3m on the ground. A separate big strafing attack on MT was accompanied by Beaufighters of 252 and 272 Squadrons, while another of the South African Bisley crews attacked a submarine on this date.

British Claims

15 SAAF Sqn	Bisley crew	Ca.133 destroyed on the ground at LG.121
15 SAAF Sqn	Bisley crew	Ju 52/3m destroyed on the ground at LG.121

Wednesday, 26 August 1942

At 1415, during an escort, Serg Giovanni Panizza of 83ª Squadriglia fired at a Wellington, scoring hits in the right engine. A U-Boat was seen and attacked by a 47 Squadron Wellesley flown by Flt Sgt Moore at 1218 between Port Said and Gaza. One large air bubble appeared after the explosion of the four 250lb depth charges which he dropped. This was followed by further air bubbles for 40 minutes. C-in-C Mediterranean Fleet decided that the U-Boat had probably been sunk.

Thursday, 27 August 1942

Despite being escorted by a Cant.Z.1007bis of 35° Stormo and two Ju 88s, the Italian steamer *Dielpi* of 1,527 tons heading to Benghazi was torpedoed, bombed and sunk by British aircraft, between Suda and Benghazi. Two attackers were claimed shot down, one of which was a 227 Squadron Beaufighter, reported missing on this date (see *Malta: The Spitfire Year, 1942* for more details). Back from the escort, the Cant.Z. 1007bis flown by S.Ten Giuseppe Vulcani crash-landed near Derna, the whole crew emerging unhurt.

British Claims

103 MU	Flg Off G.W.H.Reynolds	Spitfire V	e/a Damaged	Aboukir area	
227 Sqn	Sqn Ldr W.C.Wigmore	Beaufighter T4666 'Y'	Ju 88 Probable	80-90m N Derna	1845
227 Sqn	Plt Off D.W.Schmidt	Beaufighter T5150 'K'	Cant.Z.1007bis	80-90m N Derna	1845

British Casualties

227 Sqn	Beaufighter X8035 'J' MiA from shipping patrol; Flt Sgt E.O'Hara/Sgt K.Seddon KiA

Italian Claims

230ª Sq, 95°Gr, 35°St BT Cant.Z.1007bis gunners	2 Beaufighters	over convoy

Italian Casualties

230ª Sq, 95°Gr, 35°St BT	Cant.Z.1007bis MM 23406 '230-5' crash-landed near Derna, w/o, pilot S.Ten Giuseppe Vulcani, copilot Serg Magg Luigi Di Lallo and three safe

Friday, 28 August 1942

At 1600 two S.79s of 284ª Squadriglia were sent to reconnoitre over the eastern Mediterranean. One aircraft returned safely but the S.79 flown by Cap De Angelis, flying over the Fuka-El Daba area on its return course, was shot down in error by German Flak, killing the whole crew. Throughout the day 231ª Squadriglia of 95° Gruppo BT provided Cant.Z.1007bis aircraft as escorts for a tanker sailing in the central Mediterranean. In the mid-afternoon this duty was taken up by two aircraft, flown by Serg Magg Gaiardoni and S.Ten Luciani. The former returned safely at 2045, but the latter was attacked by a formation of about 15 twin-engined aircraft which shot down Luciani's bomber. No claim relating to the loss of this bomber has been found. A search for survivors next morning did not prove successful.The tanker had been spotted by Wellingtons and Liberators of 221 Squadron, following which 38 Squadron Wellingtons attacked. A flash and a column of water was seen amidship and astern, and when these cleared the tanker had reportedly disappeared, only a patch of oil remaining visible.

When searching for shipping north-east of Derna, Flt Lt Ian Slaughter, DFC of 203 Squadron, spotted three Ju 52/3ms at sea level at 1029, flying southbound. He believed these to be Red Cross aircraft, and ignored them. At 1145 two Bf 110s attacked his Maryland, the rear top gunner, Sgt Curtis, claiming hits on one from which pieces flew off the port wing. This fighter then dropped behind and broke off. The other continued to attack, using cannon from 600 yards until 1159 when it too broke off. The Maryland had been damaged by machine-gun fire, but not by the cannons, suffering hits in the wings, tailplane and fuselage. It then suffered engine trouble, but Slaughter was able to reach Gianaclis where he landed at 1410.

At 1600 three Bisleys of 15 SAAF Squadron attacked a diesel engine pulling a train of 15 trucks near Mersa Matruh, coming in from 50ft altitude and gaining a direct hit on the truck adjacent to the engine, blowing off the roof and bringing the train to a halt. The third aircraft crashed three miles away after being hit by guns mounted in the middle of the train.

Cant.Z.1007bis of 35° Stormo BT. This unit later suffered severe losses during a raid by the Long Range Desert Group at Barce during the night of 13/14 September.

British Claims					
46 Sqn	Plt Off W.H.Perinchief/ Sgt G.Naylor	Beaufighter If X7760	Ju 88	30m SW LG.224	0015-0105
203 Sqn	Sgt Curtis, gunner in Maryland AH372 'R'		Bf 110 Damaged		

British Casualties	
203 Sqn	Maryland AH372 'R' damaged by Bf 110; Flt Lt I.Slaughter, DFC, and crew safe
15 SAAF Sqn	Bisley BA149 attacking a train, 40m SW Sidi Barrani, crashed on landing; Lt N.D.Boyd and two KiA

German Casualties	
1./LG 1	Ju 88 A-4 WNr 140121 L1+EH shot down by Hurricanes, crashed S Alexandria; Lt Horst Dietze and three MiA

Italian Casualties	
284ª Sq, 131°Gr Aut AS	S.79 MM 24088 shot down in error by German Flak, pilot Cap Riccardo De Angelis, copilot S.Ten Giorgio Concato and crew KiA
231ª Sq, 95°Gr, 35°St BT	Cant.Z.1007bis MM 24532 '231-9' failed to return, pilot S.Ten Luigi Luciani, copilot Serg Magg Giuseppe Carrara and crew MiA

Saturday, 29 August 1942

A Swordfish of 815 Squadron was undertaking an anti-E-Boat patrol around RN destroyers engaged in a bombardment of the Daba area as three Albacores of 821 and 826 Squadrons illuminated the target area for the ships' gunners. The Swordfish crew then spotted an E-Boat as it torpedoed one of the destroyers, then seeking to make good its escape in the inshore waters near the port. This was at once attacked, a direct hit being obtained as a result of which the vessel later sank.

The new tactics devised at 103 MU for the interception of the high-flying Ju 86Rs were tested in action for the first time on this date. Plt Off George Genders in the striker Spitfire reached a position about 1,000 feet below the Junkers, but could only get in a brief burst before his guns jammed. After the engagement he made no claim, but according to Luftwaffe records this quick burst may have been more effective than he had thought. The Ju 86R crashed in the Port Said-Cairo area, although reportedly due to engine failure. It seems that it ditched in the sea, the two crewmen being picked up by the German rescue service. On this date also a Ju 87 of III./StG 3 was shot down over the sea by ships' AA, the pilot being rescued by an Italian torpedo-boat.

US Casualties	
83rd BS/12th BG	B-25C 41-12863 '33' damaged by Flak at night; Capt D.W.Spawn safe, one KiA

German Casualties	
2.(F)/123	Ju 86R-1 WNr 5144 crashed in Port Said-Cairo area, reportedly due to engine failure; crew picked up safely
9./StG 3	Ju 87D-1 WNr 2541 ships' AA 20km NW El Daba; Oblt Siegfried Göbel/Obfw Richard Stark WiA

Sunday, 30 August 1942

At 0137 Wellington 'E' of 38 Squadron attacked one merchant vessel with two torpedoes and claimed to have sunk it. Other Wellingtons from this unit, 221 and 458 Squadrons found it very difficult to assess the results of an attack on another convoy due to a heavy smoke screen laid by the escorting destroyers. One of the 221 Squadron aircraft dropped five 250lb bombs, claiming at least one hit and possibly two. One 459 Squadron Hudson crew reported seeing one MV on fire and believed that at least one hit had been obtained.

The Regia Aeronautica reported that at 1410 a patrol of four G.50bis of 161° Gruppc, led by Ten Ghiacci, intercepted a formation of British torpedo-bombers, escorted by heavy fighters off S.Maria di Leuca, which were attacking the shipping. After the combat they claimed three Beauforts and a fighter. The Italian tanker *Sant'Andrea* of 5,077 tons was hit and sunk on this occasion. It seems that the attacking formation comprised Beauforts of 39 Squadron, one such aircraft being reported lost during an attack on shipping off Punta Stilo on this date. There were road strafes and attacks on F-Boats almost every day by Beaufighters at this time, joined now frequently by the Bisleys of 15 SAAF Squadron.

British Casualties	
15 SAAF Sqn	Bisley BA407 'O' off 1410 for low-level attack on supply train 45m W Mersa Matruh; undercarriage shot away by return fire from flatbed truck and crash-landed on return
39 Sqn	Beaufort AW295 shot down, reportedly by Flak, during a shipping strike off Punta Stilo

Italian Claims

161° Gr CT	Ten Piero Ghiacci	G.50bis	3 Beauforts + a fighter off S.Maria di Leuca	1410
161° Gr CT	three pilots	G.50bis		

Monday, 31 August 1942

Between 0317-0617 two Ju 88s were claimed shot down by 73 Squadron and one by AA gunners. Two Luftwaffe aircraft were recorded as shot down by AA, one in the Abu Ogos area and one at Alam Shaltat airfield. Four Beaufighters of 272 Squadron strafed the Sidi Barrani-Mersa Matruh road but little was to be seen until a marching column of about 100 men was spotted. This was strafed and it was thought that about half of them were killed. Several Ju 52/3ms were then observed, flying to the right of the road. Two of these were claimed shot down and two damaged.

British Claims

272 Sqn	Plt Off C.T.H.Delcour/ Sgt E.S.Woolford	Beaufighter 'B'	Ju 52/3m	Sidi Barrani area	1619
272 Sqn	Sgt K.A.Graham/ Sgt L.J.Powdrill	Beaufighter 'E'	Ju 52/3m	Sidi Barrani area	1619
272 Sqn	unstated	Beaufighters	2 Ju 52/3ms Damaged	Sidi Barrani area	1619

German Casualties

6./LG 1	Ju 88A-4 WNr 140739 L1+FP shot down by AA, crashed Abu Ogos area; Hptm Wolfgang Voigt and one KiA, two PoW
4./KG 100	He 111H-6 WNr 7456 6N+HG shot down by AA , crashed Alam Shaltut l.g.; Fw Hans Spiering KiA, two MiA, one PoW

September 1942

September would see the departure from AHQ, Egypt, of the French GC III/2 Alsace, bound for the United Kingdom. While in its various guises in North Africa, the unit had flown some 500 sorties, claimed three victories and lost two pilots killed in action. Its duties for the defence of the Canal and its Hurricanes were now taken over by the RCAF's 417 Squadron at Shandur. Although many Canadian pilots had served, or were still serving with RAF squadrons in the Middle East, and many RCAF were now in the UK, this was the first all-Canadian unit to arrive in North Africa. With the French unit also departed the Nancy Flight which had been operating in an anti-submarine role over the further reaches of the eastern Mediterranean.

252 and 272 Squadrons were continuing to fly many sorties together, although throughout most of the coming month 252's small detachment on Malta would remain there. 15 SAAF Squadron had now joined 201 Group and moved to Maryut equipped with Bisleys (Blenheim Vs), although one flight had been left at Kufra Oasis with the unit's last few remaining Blenheim IVs.

Tuesday, 1 September 1942

Two Maryland crews of 203 Squadron found a south-bound convoy at 1257. Serg Mario Turchetti of 82ª Squadriglia, during an afternoon patrol over Tobruk harbour, sighted what he identified as a Blenheim flying at 4,500 metres (13,500 feet) off the coast. He attacked at 1630 and claimed to have shot this down into the sea, the crews of two Bf 110s observing the action. No Blenheims were lost on this date, but two Beaufighters of 252 Squadron both failed to return, though from a sortie much earlier in the day. The convoy was found by two ASV Wellingtons of 221 Squadron during the evening, and a striking force of seven torpedo Wellingtons was sent off at 2230 to relocate the ships. One supply ship and two destroyers were seen at 0130 some 30 miles north-west of Derna. One aircraft attacked and hit the merchant vessel, this being confirmed by the crew of the second aircraft to attack.

British Casualties

252 Sqn	Beaufighter T5042 left 1040: Flg Off R.G.D.Jaggard/Sgt F.G. Drewry MIA Gambut-Bardia road 1050-1425
252 Sqn	Beaufighter T4881 left 1040; Flg Off E. D.Vanier/Flt Sgt H.Asquith MIA Gambut-Bardia road 1040-1410

Italian Claims

82ª Sq, 13°Gr, 2°St CT	Serg Mario Turchetti	MC.200	Blenheim	off Ras Azzaz	1630

Wednesday, 2 September 1942

Two ASV Wellingtons again located shipping north of Derna and homed in a striking force of five bombers and seven torpedo-carriers of 38 Squadron. One attack was made by a torpedo aircraft, an explosion being seen with black smoke. A Ju 88 of 1.(F)/121 was identified approaching Suez and flying down the Gulf. Two Hurricanes of 94 Squadron were scrambled and shot it down into the sea where it blew up. Three baled out at 6,000 feet and landed in the water from where they were rescued, becoming PoWs.

British Claims					
94 Sqn	Plt Off A.E.Walker	Hurricane IIc BP346 'C'	Ju 88	10m W Suez	1250
94 Sqn	Sgt N.G.Aldardice	Hurricane IIc BP339 'F'			
German Casualties					
1.(F)/121	Ju 88D-1 WNr 430252 7A+BH MiA Suez; Obfw Adolf Hauhoff, Oblt Günther Reif and two PoW				

Thursday, 3 September 1942

Eight Beaufighters of 252 and 272 Squadrons undertook an attack on a convoy and provided cover for torpedo aircraft. Locating the convoy, the pilots claimed to have shot down an escorting He 111. On return 252 Squadron crews saw three Fi 156s, claiming one shot down and the other two as probables (according to 201 Group's records; in practice claims have been found only for one and one damaged).

A lone Cant.Z.1007bis of 191ª Squadriglia, flown by S.Ten Achille Scaduto, took off at 1515 from Mersa Matruh on a reconnaissance over enemy territory, but failed to return *(this mission is recorded as being on Sept 4th in 35° Stormo ORB)*. This aircraft was reported by 252 Wing during the evening, some ten miles south of LG.224, flying at 20,000 feet. Two Hurricanes of the Alsace unit on one of their last sorties before leaving the area, and two Spitfires of 103 MU from Heliopolis, were scrambled, the latter pair intercepting and shooting down the Italian aircraft. About three hours or so later a Ju 88 was intercepted by a 46 Squadron Beaufighter and this too was shot down, falling into the sea 15 miles NE of El Alamein.

During the night three ASV Wellingtons and two similarly-equipped Liberators, all from 221 Squadron, accompanied by six torpedo and two bomber Wellingtons of 38 Squadron were out. A convoy was seen by a 221 Squadron crew about 50 miles north-west of Tobruk and this was attacked very successfully. One large merchant ship of approximately 54,000 tons was hit and split in two by torpedoes and was known to have sunk. One other MV was sunk by HMS *Thrasher*, homed in by another of the 221 Squadron crews. A third MV was considered to have been probably sunk by torpedo Wellingtons. At dawn seven 459 Squadron Hudsons set off to strike, but found only two ships which were picking up survivors. One destroyer was found and attacked from low level, being claimed sunk. Flt Lt Slaughter of 203 Squadron searched for a convoy to be attacked by Beauforts, finding this under escort by at least six Ju 88s and comprising three MVs and four destroyers. However, no Beauforts were seen.

British Claims					
272 Sqn	Sgt G.A.Tuckwell/ Sgt K.F.Hubbard	Beaufighter Ic 'B'	He 111		1345-1900
272 Sqn	Flt Sgt S.J Kernaghan/ Sgt P.G.Andrews	Beaufighter Ic T5040 'Y'			1340-1840
252 Sqn	Flg Off I.Maclean/ Sgt T.Arnsby	Beaufighter Ic T5032 'D'	Fi 156		1340-1840
252 Sqn	Flg Off I.Maclean/ Sgt T.Arnsby	Beaufighter Ic T5032 'D'	Fi 156 Damaged		1340-1840
103 MU	Flt Lt Webb	Spitfire V BR487	Cant.Z.1007bis	50-60m S Burg el Arab	1755-1849
103 MU	Sgt Ross	Spitfire V BR586			
46 Sqn	Plt Off M.M.Davison/ Sgt A.C.Willmott	Beaufighter VIf X8165	Ju 88	10m NW Alamein	2150-2315
British Casualties					
15 SAAF Sqn	Bisley BA239 engine cut and ditched in Mediterranean				
German Casualties					
6./KG 100	He 111H-6 WNr 7635 6N+DJ shot down, crash-landed; crew returned safely on foot				
FlgLentst O.B.	Fi 156C-3 WNr 1032 D1+GK on courier flt Sicily-Derna, shot down by Beaufighters and crashed in sea; Obgfr Anton Kalezawa MiA				
4./LG 1	Ju 88A-4 WNr 140 060 L1+CM shot down by Beaufighters nr El Alamein; Lt Eugen Rolff and two KiA, one PoW				

Italian Casualties

191ª Sq, 86°Gr, 35°St BT	Cant.Z.1007bis MM 23263 failed to return, pilot S.Ten Achille Scaduto, copilot Serg Magg Vincenzo Casiello and five MiA

Friday, 4 September 1942

Seven Hudsons of 459 Squadron in a dawn strike claimed the destruction of a destroyer by Plt Off Beaton and the crew of FH242 'K', the other crews reporting that the vessel was seen to be ablaze from stem to stern.

A 203 Squadron Maryland located shipping south-west of Crete and homed in a strike force of Beauforts. A second Maryland went in to relocate the ships, followed by a third to the north of Tobruk. Two ASV Wellingtons of 221 Squadron found and illuminated a convoy, homing in 38 Squadron which reported sinking a merchant vessel with two torpedoes. To the east Sgt Smith of 203 Squadron in one of the unit's Blenheims ('Z') depth-charged a submarine while engaged in a convoy escort, seeing this crash-dive at 1100 as he approached to attack. Some time later at 1325 a Bisley from the Free French Nancy Flight attacked another submarine north-west of Jaffa, an oil patch being observed subsequently. Two days later the flight was withdrawn from operations preparatory to a move of its personnel to the United Kingdom. At the same time the 47 Squadron Air Echelon went from Kasfareet to Shandur under the operational control of 203 Squadron. Another 221 Squadron Wellington, 'X' which was flown by Flg Off White, when searching for a dinghy reported 20 miles north of Rosetta, was attacked by a Ju 88 as it left the area. The rear gunner, Sgt Atkins, opened fire and drove it off, seeing it going down with white smoke issuing from the port engine.

Saturday, 5 September 1942

Eight Cant.Z.1007bis of 30° Stormo took off from Gadurra at 0200-0215 on a night bombing mission to landing grounds in the Alexandria area. Spotted approaching between 0352-0545, some 50-80 miles north of Daba, they were intercepted by Beaufighters of 46 Squadron, Plt Off Davison and Plt Off White each claiming one shot down. During the same period a Ju 88 was also claimed by Flt Lt Coleman.

British Claims

46 Sqn	Flt Lt G.B.S.Coleman/ Plt Off W.R.Peasley	Beaufighter If V8227	Ju 88	S Amiriya	0410-0640
46 Sqn	Plt Off M.M.Davison/ Sgt A.C.Willmott	Beaufighter VI f X8165	Cant.Z.1007bis	50-60m N Aboukir	0445-0550
46 Sqn	Plt Off J.A.White/ Sgt K.F.C.Inskip	Beaufighter X7779	Cant.Z.1007bis	Alexandria area	0445-0600

Italian Casualties

193ª Sq, 87°Gr, 30°St BT	Cant.Z.1007bis failed to return from a night mission to Alexandria 0210-, pilot T.Col Mario Giuliano (87°Gr CO), copilot M.llo Emilio Cumo and crew MiA
195ª Sq, 90°Gr, 30°St BT	Cant.Z.1007bis MM 24735 failed to return from a night mission to Burg el Arab 0205-, pilot S.Ten Anacleto Del Monte, copilot Serg Magg Virgilio Genestreti and three MiA

Sunday, 6 September 1942

A Ju 86R was intercepted by a pair of 103 MU Spitfires, Plt Off Genders again in the stripped striker. He intercepted the reconnaissance aircraft about 80 miles north of Alexandria at very high altitude, and pursued it out to sea before he finally reached an attacking position. He gained some hits on the intruder which caused it to descend somewhat, and this allowed Plt Off Gold in the marker to deliver a further attack. The Ju 86R was last seen heading away over the sea and was claimed as damaged. The long chase had left the striker's limited fuel supply considerably depleted and on the way back to base this ran out. Genders continued south in a glide but when the aircraft reached 1,000 feet, still short of the coast, he baled out, 25 miles north-west of Rosetta. Here he fell into the sea where an air/sea rescue search failed to find him. He had survived, however, and after spending 21 hours in his dinghy he was washed ashore at Rosetta.

The Ju 86R had in fact failed to regain its base; having suffered serious damage, it crash-landed in an area of the desert held by German forces, and was written off. By the end of July 2(F)/123 had been down to three aircraft of this type, but only one of these had been serviceable. Despite the aircraft's impressive performance, its poor serviceability record restricted the sortie rate. By actually intercepting two aircraft

The 'team' of staff pilots at 103 Maintenance Unit who were ultimately successful in intercepting the very high-flying pressurised Ju 86Rs of 2.(F)/123, Plt Offs G.W.H.Reynolds, G.E.C.Genders and A.G.W.Gold.

in eight days, the stripped Spitfires had ended their more brazen incursions over the Nile delta area. From then on the high-flying reconnaissance aircraft flew only occasionally, and when they did appear, their crews avoided well-defended areas.

In *Malta: The Spitfire Year, 1942* detail is given of action over and around a large Italian convoy. More information regarding this action has become available, and an updated account is therefore included here. In the early hours of Sunday, 6 September, Italian Convoy N sailed from Taranto, the motor cargo vessels *Luciano Manara* and *Ravello* being escorted by six destroyers and an MTB. At much the same time, Convoy P left Brindisi, composed of the motor vessel *Sestriere* and the 4,700-ton, tank-laded German steamer *Ankara*, escorted by three destroyers and two MTBs. Mid-morning the two convoys met off Cap Santa Maria di Leuca, to become Lambda Convoy and headed for the comparative safety of the Greek coastal waters, before making the dash for Benghazi. This enlarged convoy was soon spotted by Flt Lt R.C.Mackay's 69 Squadron Baltimore crew, and to attack this formidable armada – identified as four merchant vessels and 11 destroyers in two columns – the most powerful strike force possible was put together.

At around 1230, therefore, Flt Lt Hank Sharman led off 13 torpedo-armed Beauforts, with a close escort and diversionary force of a dozen Beaufighters from 227 Squadron, six of which were armed with bombs; however, four Beauforts and three Beaufighters were forced to return early, effectively reducing the capability and potency of the strike force by 25% at a single stroke. To provide long-range fighter escort, 89 Squadron's four intruder Beaufighters were also pressed into service as top cover for the whole formation.

Thirty miles south of Cap S.Maria di Leuca the two columns of vessels were sighted, with an air umbrella of six Ju 88s, a flyingboat and Italian fighters. The fighter-bombers at once opened the attack in the face of a formidable curtain of Flak; although bombs were seen falling amongst the ships, no

Ju 86R-2 8H+LK of 2.(F)/123 at Kastelli, Crete, from where these pressurised reconnaissance aircraft had regularly been photographing Allied installations all along the Egyptian coast.

actual hits were observed. The convoy weaved and scattered, the destroyers failing to put up a smoke screen. The Beauforts followed in three flights, sweeping in from the starboard. The defending fighters swarmed all over them despite the efforts of 89 Squadron's Beaufighters; a Ju 88 was claimed shot down by Plt Off Neville Reeves, possibly M7+HL of 7./KG 54 flown by Lt Siegfried Philipp; Reeves reported:

> "Saw a Ju 88 and chased it. Squirted and missed. Saw another Ju 88 6-10 miles south of the convoy. Squirted and saw bits off the port engine and starboard wing. Broke away as another Ju 88 was shooting from the starboard behind. Turned 360° and lost attacker; looked for previous Ju 88 which was very near sea level, going slowly with smoke pouring from both engines, heading for shore. Several single-engined fighters were above so I did not dive to attack again."

Sqn Ldr P.M.J.Evans gained strikes on the fuselage of the flyingboat, which he identified as a Do 24, and this was seen to alight near one of the escorting destroyers. Flt Lt H.G.Edwards reported engaging a Macchi: "As we turned towards the convoy, I saw three single-engined fighters approaching head-on, slightly to port. I turned towards them and climbed. I attacked the nearest fighter, firing one long burst from quarter to beam. I saw bursts on the enemy fighter before I passed over the top of it. My last view of the fighter was with its wing vertical, turning away." Another fighter identified as a Macchi was claimed probably destroyed by Wg Cdr Ross Shore, who gave it a four-second burst from astern. Strikes were seen on its fuselage and pieces appeared to fall off. As it dived away, Sgt Heath (the observer) gave it a further burst with his hand-held machine gun. Sgt Phillips reported engaging a Ju 88, and seeing pieces fly off its tailplane before it dived steeply to sea level. Two of the Beaufighters were shot down, however it would appear that the opponents were not Macchis, but G.50bis from Regia Aeronautica's 161° and 24° Gruppi, the pilots of which claimed three aircraft which they identified as Beauforts, off Corfu at 1540. Bf 109s of II./JG 53 from Malta were also present, one pilot of 6.Staffel also claiming a Beaufort in the same area at 1530.

The Beaufort attack was not without effect. *Luciano Manara* sustained damage from a torpedo strike, resulting in fires breaking out, but the cost was high. Flt Lt Sharman's aircraft was hit on the run-in when still some distance from the convoy, but despite a burning engine the Canadian, who had flown the very first Beaufort strike of the war, held course until his machine eventually plunged into the sea. There were no survivors from this; nor from 'R', flown by Lt R.C.B.Evans, SAAF, which was also shot down into the sea. Seeing Sharman's aircraft crash, Flg Off Les Wordell took over the lead, despite being attacked by fighters identified as Macchis, and it was probably his torpedo which caused the damage to the cargo vessel. Meanwhile Plt Off Marshall's AW291 was also shot-up by fighters and his observer, Wt Off Hutchison, was slightly wounded; Sgt G.E.Sanderson's AW381 suffered heavier damage, being hit by fighters and Flak, one of the gunners, Sgt J.D.Cunningham, being mortally wounded. Yet another Beaufort, Flt Sgt Watlington's AW302, was hit by fighters and both air gunners, Flt Sgt McEllamy and Sgt L.H.Tester, suffered wounds; the latter, however, continued greatly to assist his pilot and the damaged machine regained base, as did the other two badly shot-up aircraft.

It was believed that the Italian fighters had not got away unscathed, however, for apart from those engaged by the Beaufighters, Plt Off Colin Milson's gunner reported one falling into the sea apparently due to his fire. Two others were claimed damaged by gunners aboard Plt Off A.F.Izzard's machine and that flown by Wt Off R.J.Dawson, the latter also reporting damage to an attacking Ju 88. The damaged *Luciano Manara* was escorted to Arilla Bay, Corfu, by the destroyer *Freccia*, where she was beached. Next morning the rest of the convoy was to be attacked by a submarine, but without loss. On the evening of the 7th, the ships again divided, Group Ankara heading for Tobruk under repeated air attack from seven North African-based Liberators of 159 Squadron, during which the destroyer *Fuciliere* was damaged by bombs (see also Chapter Eleven). The three remaining transports reached their destinations safely, delivering a combined total of 2,500 tons of fuel, 1,100 tons of ammunition and other urgently-needed supplies.

British Claims

103 MU	Plt Off G.E.C.Genders	Spitfire V BR234	Ju 86P Damaged	Aboukir area	
103 MU	Plt Off A.G.W.Gold	Spitfire V			
89 Sqn	Plt Off N.Reeves	Beaufighter If	Ju 88	30m S Cap S.Maria di Leuca	1530
89 Sqn	Sqn Ldr P.M.J.Evans	Beaufighter If	Do 24 Damaged	30m S Cap S.Maria di Leuca	1530
89 Sqn	Flt Lt H.G.Edwards	Beaufighter If	MC.200 Damaged	30m S Cap S.Maria di Leuca	1530
227 Sqn	Wg Cdr D.R.Shore/ Sgt Heath	Beaufighter Ic X8030 'Q'	MC.200 Probable	30m S Cap S.Maria di Leuca	1530
227 Sqn	Sgt A.J.Phillips	Beaufighter Ic T5050 'K'	Ju 88 Damaged	30m S Cap S.Maria di Leuca	1530
39 Sqn	Beaufort crew of Plt Off C.Milson		MC.200	30m S Cap S.Maria di Leuca	1530
39 Sqn	Beaufort crew of Plt Off A.F.Izzard		MC.200 Damaged	30m S Cap S.Maria di Leuca	1530
39 Sqn	Beaufort crew of Wt Off R.J.Dawson		MC.200 Damaged	30m S Cap S.Maria di Leuca	1530
39 Sqn	Beaufort crew of Wt Off R.J.Dawson		Ju 88 Damaged	30m S Cap S.Maria di Leuca	1530

British Casualties

103 MU	Spitfire V BR243 abandoned after interception due to fuel shortage; Plt Off G.E.C.Genders baled into sea safely
227 Sqn	Beaufighter T4666 'Y' shot down off Cap S.Maria di Leuca while escorting Beauforts; Flg Off D.de M.Partridge/Sgt A.W.Vivian KiA
227 Sqn	Beaufighter X8085 'A' shot down off Cap S.Maria di Leuca while escorting Beauforts; Lt F.C.Noone/Sgt A.J.Cusworth KiA
39 Sqn	Beaufort AW305 'Q' shot down by Flak during shipping strike off Paxos, Greece; Flt Lt D.C.Sharman and crew KiA
39 Sqn	Beaufort AW280 'R' shot down by Flak during shipping strike off Paxos, Greece; Lt R.C.B.Evans and crew KiA
39 Sqn	Beaufort AW291 damaged by fighters; Plt Off Marshall and two safe, one WiA
39 Sqn	Beaufort AW381 damaged by fighters; Sgt G.E.D. Sanderson and two safe, one WiA, died of wounds
39 Sqn	Beaufort AW302 damaged by fighters and Flak; Flt Sgt Watlington and one safe, two WiA
38 Sqn	Wellington BB477 MiA

German Claims

6./JG 53	Oblt Günther Hess	Beaufort	S Corfu	1530

German Casualties

2.(F)/123	Ju 86R-1 WNr 5101 badly damaged by Spitfire off Nile Delta; crash-landed at Bir el Abd on return and written off
7./KG 77	Ju 88A-4 WNr 5690 3Z+FR shot down by Beaufighter SE El Alamein; Uffz Hans-Oskar Battige and three MiA
6./KG 77	Ju 88A-4 WNr 140 077 3ZHP shot down by AA in Cairo area; Oblt Gustav Kasdorf and two PoWs, one KiA

Italian Claims

164ª Sq, 161°Gr Aut CT	S.Ten Iolando Suprani	G.50bis	Beaufort	off Corfu	1540
164ª Sq, 161°Gr Aut CT	Ten Giuseppe Marazio	G.50bis			
161°Gr Aut CT	Ten Giuseppe Bentivoglio	G.50bis	2 Beauforts	off Corfu	1540
355ª Sq, 24° Gr Aut CT	Ten Francesco Pantanella	G.50bis			
161°Gr Aut CT	above pilots	G.50bis	2 twin-engined a/c Damaged	off Corfu	1540

Italian Casualties

161°Gr Aut CT	2 G.50bis damaged in combat, pilots safe

Monday, 7 September 1942

Two of 203 Squadron's Marylands soon found the convoy which Malta's aircraft had been attacking during the previous day. The ships were located 120 miles west of Crete, including three merchant ships and nine destroyers. These were attacked during the night by 14 bomber and six torpedo Wellingtons of 38 Squadron when 40 miles north-east of Apollonia. Homing and illumination was successfully achieved by six torpedo-carriers of 221 Squadron, but a heavy smoke screen resulted in no sinkings being achieved, although several hits were claimed.

Meanwhile, 252 Wing reported that ten plus Bf 109s swept east from Daba, three of these engaging three Albacores four miles north of Agami. Two of the naval biplanes were damaged, but landed safely. 211 Group reported that its fighters shot down one Messerschmitt and damaged three more (see claims of 601 Squadron in Chapter Six). Two 103 MU Spitfires were directed by the wing to intercept a Ju 88 65 miles south of Burg el Arab and this was claimed shot down by Flg Off Rowland and Sgt Ross north-west of Port Said (no details). With nightfall, at least 15 enemy aircraft were reported, 46 Squadron Beaufighters and a Hurricane of 33 Squadron taking off, the night fighters claiming two bombers shot down. It appears that aircraft of 89 Squadron were also scrambled, claiming a further such success.

British Claims

46 Sqn	Sqn Ldr R.M.MacKenzie/ Plt Off A.L.Craig	Beaufighter If X8137	He 111	area LG.224	2150-2250
46 Sqn	Plt Off J.A.White/ Sgt K.F.Inskip	Beaufighter I X7708	Ju 88		2305-0035
89 Sqn	Sgt J.S.Robson/Sgt Dunn	Beaufighter If X7777	Ju 88	NW Suez	2310

British Casualties

39 Sqn	Maryland BS764 lost

German Claims

9./ZG 26	Fw Günther Wegmann	B-24	S Tympakion	1756
8./ZG 26	Uffz Heinz Susemihl	B-24		1830

German Casualties

9./KG 77	Ju 88A-4 WNr 140 112 3Z+KT shot down by night fighter Great Bitter Lake area, crashed in German lines; Uffz Walter Sohnye and two KiA, one u/i
9./KG 77	Ju 88A-4 WNr 140 035 3Z+CM shot down by night fighter Suez Canal area; Uffz Herbert Dietze and three baled out, PoW
7./KG 54	Ju 88A-4 WNr 142 219 M7+HL FTR from area W Peloponnese; Lt Siegfried Philipp and three MiA
1.(F)?121	Ju 88D-1 WNr 430 295 damaged in combat with fighter, crash-landed Fuka; crew safe

Tuesday, 8 September 1942

An even bigger operation was now undertaken, six ASV aircraft of 221 Squadron locating and illuminating the convoy north of Derna, homing in 13 bombers and three torpedo aircraft of 38 Squadron. Seven of the bombers and two torpedo-carriers attacked, but results were not observed. Six Hudsons followed at first light with a similar lack of success.

British Claims

272 Sqn	Flt Lt A.Watson/ Sgt J.E.Orchard	Beaufighter Ic T5079 'G'	S.81	coast N Barrani-Matruh road	1445-1755

German Casualties

9./KG 77	Ju 88A-4 WNr 3691 3Z+GT FTR from Great Bitter Lake area, presumed shot down; Lt Walter Forster and three MiA

Wednesday, 9 September 1942

From 0935 to 1350 nine MC.200s of 18° Gruppo, operating three at a time with each trio remaining overhead for about two hours, provided top cover to a convoy of eight F-Boats sailing to Mersa Matruh. Serg Giovanni Panizza of 83ª Squadriglia, who had taken off at 0935, failed to return. At 1120 Ten Carlo Tommasi and M.llo Paolo Franchi, who took off at 1040, sighted a formation of a dozen Beaufighters and attacked. Tommasi claimed a Beaufighter shot down near Ismailia Rocks. The formation which he had attacked appears to have been comprised of 15 SAAF Squadron Bisleys, escorted by Beaufighters from 272 Squadron, which recorded no loss. Two Cant.Z.1007bis of 195ª Squadriglia took off at 0955 on a reconnaissance mission to the eastern Mediterranean; one crashed on landing, killing the whole crew.

British Claims

272 Sqn	Flg Off R.Rankin/ Sgt R.H.Pinkerton	Beaufighter Ic 'U'	Bf 109E	escort 15 SAAF convoy strike	1045-1400

German Casualties

2.(F)/123	Ju 88D-5 WNr 430166 4U+PK presumed shot down by AA Port Said; Lt Gerhard Pichler and three KiA

Italian Claims

83ª Sq, 18°Gr, 3°St CT	Ten Carlo Tommasi	MC.200	Beaufighter	Ismailia Rocks	1120

Italian Casualties

83ª Sq, 18°Gr, 3°St CT	MC.200 MM 8797 failed to return from escort 0935-, Serg Giovanni Panizza MiA
195ª Sq, 90°Gr, 30°St BT	Cant.Z.1007bis MM 24244 crash-landed 1535 after recce mission, pilot S.Ten Isonzo Giuliarini, copilot Serg Sirio Mascanzoni and four KiA

Thursday, 10 September 1942

A detachment of three of 459 Squadron's Hudsons, fitted with ASV radar, was despatched to Aden to support Blenheims operating from that base over the approaches to the Red Sea. The latter were not so fitted, but were being maintained there in case of any incursion by Japanese submarines from the Indian Ocean. Six more such aircraft were posted to St Jean, Palestine, following an increase of U-Boat activity in the eastern Mediterranean.

British Claims

103 MU	Flg Off G.W.H.Reynolds	Spitfire V	Ju 86 Damaged	Aboukir area

Friday, 11 September 1942

Between 1035-1140 two Bf 109s attacked 108 MU at LG.222, one Boston and one Wellington being destroyed on the ground there and four other aircraft damaged. Two Hurricanes of 127 Squadron and one Spitfire from Heliopolis were scrambled. Having reached 3,000 feet, the Hurricane pilots saw the column of smoke rising from LG.172 and spotted the two Messerschmitts, shooting down one in flames; the other was also attacked, but escaped. (See also Chapter Six.)

Sunday, 13 September 1942

During the early hours, eight men of the Special Boat Section, assisted by four Greeks, divided into two groups; one led by Capt Richard Allott and the other by Lt David Sutherland, attacked the two main airfields on Rhodes. At Gadurra they destroyed five fighters of 396ª Squadriglia (three G.50bis and two CR.42s) and two Cant.Z.1007bis bombers of 194ª Squadriglia, and badly damaged two more. At Maritza a Cant.Z.1007bis of 193ª Squadriglia was destroyed. This raid was undertaken at the same time as several others were taking place in North Africa, although it did not form a part of the series of operations which will now be described.

Italian Casualties

194ª Sq, 90°Gr, 30°St BT	2 Cant.Z.1007bis (MM 24724 and 24722) destroyed and 2 damaged (MM 23762 and 24736) by commando raid at Gadurra
193ª Sq, 87°Gr, 30°St BT	Cant.Z.1007bis destroyed by commando raid at Maritza
396ª Sq, 154°Gr CT	3 G.50bis and 2 CR.42s destroyed by commando raid at Gadurra

An Ill-conceived Operation

Even before the Alam el Halfa battle (see Chapter Six), the commanders-in-chief in Cairo had devised a plan designed to keep the pressure on the Axis forces, although mainly of a psychological nature. This plan, worked up by their associated staffs, was to make the fullest possible use of all the various special forces that had come into being during the course of the North African war thus far. From the start Air Chief Marshal Tedder disliked the planned operation because it would not be possible to provide any fighter cover due to the distances involved. He did not, however, feel that he could simply dismiss it. Montgomery meanwhile had his time and attention fully taken up with plans for the defence of the Alam el Halfa area against the forthcoming Axis offensive there, which was already fully anticipated. 8th Army therefore took no part in either the planning or the implementation of a scheme which was thoroughly disliked by its commanders.

The operation was extremely bold in its concept, and would rely considerably on both surprise and a strong element of luck. Four main forces were to take part, all at much the same time. For the main initial strike the first thrust would be made by Force B which incorporated D Squadron of the 1st Special Service Regiment and supporting detachments of arms such as artillery, engineers and signals. Force B would be guided to the area immediately outside the Tobruk perimeter by elements of the Long Range Desert Group (LRDG), via the Kufra Oasis. Their task would be to get through the perimeter defences at dusk and seize an inlet known as Mersa Scuasc to the east of the harbour and just outside the boom defences. Here, if successful, they would be reinforced by Force C which comprised D Company of the 1st Argyll and Sutherland Highlanders, carried to the area from Alexandria in 16 MTBs and three MLs (motor launches). The combined force was then to work its way west, capturing coast defences and Flak batteries around the harbour. These moves were to be preceded by a heavy bombing attack by 205 Group to divert the defenders' attention.

At 0340, Force A, comprising the destroyers HMS *Sikh* and *Zulu*, with a battalion of Royal Marines on board who were to be put ashore on the coast north of Tobruk town, cross the intervening tongue of land, capture the guns on the north side of the harbour and enter the town. The beaches where they were to come ashore would be marked by 'folbotists' (one-man canoes) launched from the submarine HMS *Taku*. Meanwhile, when the bombing ceased, the MTBs were to attack shipping at the east end of the harbour. Once the guns protecting the harbour had been silenced, the destroyers would land demolition parties. By then it would be afternoon, and while some of the forces were to be re-embarked in the destroyers and returned to Alexandria by sea, the remainder were to commandeer captured Axis transport and be ready to head westwards to inflict further destruction if deemed possible.

Meanwhile, in support of these activities, Force X – L Detachment of the Special Air Service Brigade, commanded by Lt Col David Stirling, with two patrols of the LRDG and a detachment of Royal Marines – operating also from Kufra, was to raid Benghazi with the target of blocking the inner harbour and destroying an oil storage and pumping plant. The force was then to return to Jalo and continue undertaking raids from there for a period of three weeks. To secure this base for them, Jalo was to be captured during the night of the 15/16th by Force Z, a patrol of the Sudan Defence Force from Kufra, again led by an LRDG patrol. At the same time dummy parachutists were to be dropped by the RAF at Siwa where a demonstration against the defences would also be made by another element of the Sudan Defence Force from Bahariya Oasis. The dummies would be dropped by five Hudson VI transports of 216 Squadron, this unit having just been provided with these aircraft to re-quip one flight; this would be the first operation in which these new aircraft were to take part. Feint attacks were to be made on land as appeared appropriate, and finally a raid on Barce airfield was to be made by two more LRDG patrols. Well before the designated opening date for the operation, Force B, led by the LRDG, left Cairo on 22 August for the 1,700-mile journey to Tobruk. A halt was made at Kufra for a few days, and by 13 September the force was in place ready to advance.

Sunday-Monday, 13/14 September 1942

On a patrol over Tobruk harbour between 1325-1530 on Sunday, Serg Mario Turchetti of 82ª Squadriglia, sighted a British submarine off Marsa el Adua and strafed it repeatedly. The ship evaded the attack by a rapid dive. This was almost certainly HMS *Taku*, which had arrived offshore to launch the 'folbotists' who were to paddle ashore after nightfall and set up signals indicating the landing beach for Force A.

Between 2225-0330, 91 Wellingtons, Halifaxes, Liberators and Fortresses rained down 70 tons of bombs on Tobruk, starting a number of secondary fires. With Force B, 83 soldiers in three lorries were driven to an Italian checkpoint in the perimeter. A number of German-speaking men had been dressed in German uniforms and the transport had been similarly disguised, giving the impression that a group of PoWs were being brought to the 'cage' within the port. The ruse worked, and the party got through unchallenged. After the 'guards' had changed back into British uniforms, the party inside the wire and the rest of Force B attacked under cover of the air raid and rapidly took the Mersa Scuasc inlet, then awaiting the expected arrival of Force A and C. Now things started to go wrong.

The MTBs had straggled on the way up the coast and a number of their crews failed to receive the signal that success had been obtained. The guiding lights which Force B should have laid out, proved difficult to see, while the vessels also met gunfire from several of the docks. In the event only two boats managed to get in to the inlet and land a section of machine gunners.

Force A's warships had arrived two miles off the north coast shortly after 0300, but a sea swell prevented the folbotists being launched and getting to shore as planned. The destroyers were also experiencing difficulty with the improvised landing craft that were being used. By 0500 only about 70 marines had been landed near Mengar el Auda, two miles west of the designated beach. These troops fought their way towards Tobruk but were overwhelmed by the now fully-alerted defenders. In this situation no more marines were landed because the destroyers, searching for landing craft to despatch the second wave of troops in, had closed to within a mile of the shore and here they came under accurate shellfire. *Sikh*'s steering gear was hit and put out of action. *Zulu* sought to take her in tow, but a shell struck and parted the cable; in addition both ships were repeatedly hit. The naval commander then ordered *Zulu* to retire and later directed that *Sikh* should be scuttled. The result of these events was that the ship's survivors and the marines still aboard were all made prisoners.

Force B, meanwhile, unable to advance, blew up the coastal guns at Mersa Scuasc and fought against rapidly increasing odds for as long as possible. The commanding officer, Lt Col J.E.Haselden, was killed attempting to lead a breakout. By now the Axis were attacking the forces in and around Tobruk with fighter-bombers, while shipping trying to get up the coast to provide support, was heavily attacked by Luftwaffe bombers from Crete, resisted by Beaufighters operating above the warships at the extremity of their range. At 1115 on the 14th the AA cruiser HMS *Coventry*, coming up with six Hunt-class destroyers to support the retiring *Zulu*, having survived several such air attacks, was hit and sunk after a further attempt to tow her failed.

Zulu had fallen victim to MC.200 fighter-bombers of 13° Gruppo. Twenty-one of this unit's Macchis, some of which had recently been equipped with wing racks to carry 50kg bombs, had set off early in the morning in a succession of waves to attack the Allied shipping approaching Tobruk. Magg Viale led all his pilots to strafe and bomb at low level. S.Ten Gian Mario Zuccarini, at that time the unit's adjutant, recalled:

> "At 5 a.m. I was woken up by Ops Officer of 5ª Squadra and notified the order to take off as soon as possible with all available aircraft to attack a formation of Royal Navy vessels on their way to Tobruk. I immediately called Magg Viale and in a few minutes the first patrol was in the air. With Viale we planned to attack in two waves, one strafing and the second bombing the ships. I was in a bombing section with Serg Sergio Boieri and Serg Davide Zanarini as wingmen. We attacked a destroyer off the coast, releasing bombs at 1,000 metres (3,000ft), but our bombs missed the target by some hundred metres. Then we strafed some minor vessels already burning. Back at Bu Amud I asked the fitters to set the bomb fuses for a low level attack. I took off again with some wingmen and attacked the same destroyer, this time from astern, flying just 30 metres above the sea surface. Just before releasing we nosed up by a dozen metres, delivered our bombs and this time hit the ship. After a long turn I saw the destroyer, later identified as HMS *Zulu*, heeling over and starting to sink."

On conclusion of its attacks, 13° Gruppo claimed not only the destroyer, but also two motor launches (ML352 and 353), an MTB (MB308) and five landing craft. Additionally, Cap Vincenzo Sansone, 92ª Squadriglia commander, in 8° Gruppo, led five of that unit's MC.200s to strafe and bomb three motor-boats off the Egyptian coast. The attack, the first of the 8° Gruppo against shipping, was carried out at 1135 but apparently no vessels were damaged by it. In fact during the day three MTBs and the two MLs had been lost to air attack, and one of the two MTBs which had entered Mersa Scuasc was stranded and had to be abandoned.

Apart from the losses to shipping and bomber aircraft, personnel losses in killed, wounded and prisoners amounted to 280 naval officers and ratings, 300 Royal Marines and 160 members of the British Army. The main causes off this debacle included an incorrect assessment of the garrison of Tobruk which was thought to be made up mainly of second rate Italian garrison troops, coupled with a lack of experience in leading landing operations and the lack of suitable landing craft. There was much talk of the whole operation having been jeopardised by lax security. "...that there was a serious breach of security since the impending raids were the gossip of Cairo," wrote Michael Crichton-Stuart. The British official history doubted this, but noted that the sheer scale of the air attacks raised the suspicions of GenMaj Deindl, commander of the Rear Army Area, who alerted all German troops in the area, amounting to around 2,000 men. It was also noted that the Italian forces acted with speed and resolution.

What then of the other planned attacks? Although the Liberators, the only bombers with the range to reach Benghazi, attacked as planned, Force X, whose timetable had been running late, appeared to have been detected approaching, and found themselves strongly opposed. Dawn was already near and surprise had been lost, so a withdrawal was ordered. This would be followed by consistent air attacks next day (Tuesday).

Force Z reached Jalo at night, 15/16th as planned, but found the defenders alert and present in sufficient strength to resist effectively, and on the 19th Cairo ordered the force to withdraw from here also. The dummy parachutists and demonstration at Siwa brought no apparent reaction and no occupation of this oasis followed, the Sudan Defence Force returning to its base.

It was only at Barce that success was achieved. Maj J.R.Easonsmith and the two LRDG patrols comprising five Jeeps and 12 30cwt trucks, having covered the 700 miles from Faiyum, reached their objective on time and roared across the airfield, shooting-up aircraft and hurling grenades at buildings. Italian sources reported 16 aircraft destroyed and seven damaged on this date by "British armoured cars". They had actually destroyed seven Cant Z.1007bis, six Ca.311s, one S.79 and one IMAM Ro.63, and damaged two more Cant.Z.1007bis, three Ca.311s, one Ca.312 and one Ro.63. However, next day would come retribution as Italian aircraft searched for the retiring forces here too.

British Claims

272 Sqn	Flg Off R.Rankin/ Sgt R.H.Pinkerton	Beaufighter Ic 'W'	Ju 87 Probable escort HMS *Coventry* E Tobruk	1114
272 Sqn	Flg Off R.Rankin/ Sgt R.H.Pinkerton	Beaufighter Ic 'W'	2 Ju 87s Damaged escort HMS *Coventry* E Tobruk	1114
272 Sqn	Sgt W.Russell/ Sgt A.B.Wilson	Beaufighter Ic 'E'	Ju 87 Damaged escort HMS *Coventry* E Tobruk	1114
252 Sqn	Sgt S.J.Kernaghan/ Sgt P.G.Andrews	Beaufighter Ic T4987 'P'	Ju 88 Probable escort Naval force 'Agent'	1306-1705
252 Sqn	Sgt S.J.Kernaghan/ Sgt P.G.Andrews	Beaufighter Ic T4987 'P'	Ju 87 Damaged escort Naval force 'Agent'	1306-1705
252 Sqn	Flg Off D.M.Garbutt/ Sgt M.A.Lea	Beaufighter Ic T5080 'K'	Ju 88 Damaged escort Naval force 'Agent'	1740-2045

German Casualties

6./LG 1 Ju 88A-4	WNr 140 751 L1+LP shot down by Beaufighters and crashed in sea N Tobruk; Lt Alfred-Peter Auer and three MiA
4./LG 1 Ju 88A-4	WNr 140 734 L1+DM shot down by ships' AA and crashed in sea N Tobruk; Uffz Karl-Heinz Bruns and three MiA

Tuesday, 15 September 1942

Throughout the day both Forces X and Z suffered constant attack from the air by the Regia Aeronautica, the withdrawing raiders being hunted by 31 MC.200s of 13° Gruppo led by Magg Renzo Viale, 81 CR.42s, three Cant.Z.1007bis, seven S.79s and 14 Ca.311s. One CR.42 of 15° Stormo crashed, probably hit by ground fire, the pilot being killed. Five Ca.311s of 87ª Squadriglia OA strafed five LRDG vehicles in the Wadi Nagr area, but two of these were hit by intense ground fire and crash-landed in the desert; one army officer observer was hurt. Easonsmith's force was particularly hard-hit, losing 15 of its 17 vehicles destroyed, and from a strength of 47 men, 21 became casualties. However, the results caused the Axis to review the protection of their lines of communication. Following these attacks three German replenishment holding battalions were posted to Sollum and for a short time the Pavia Division was

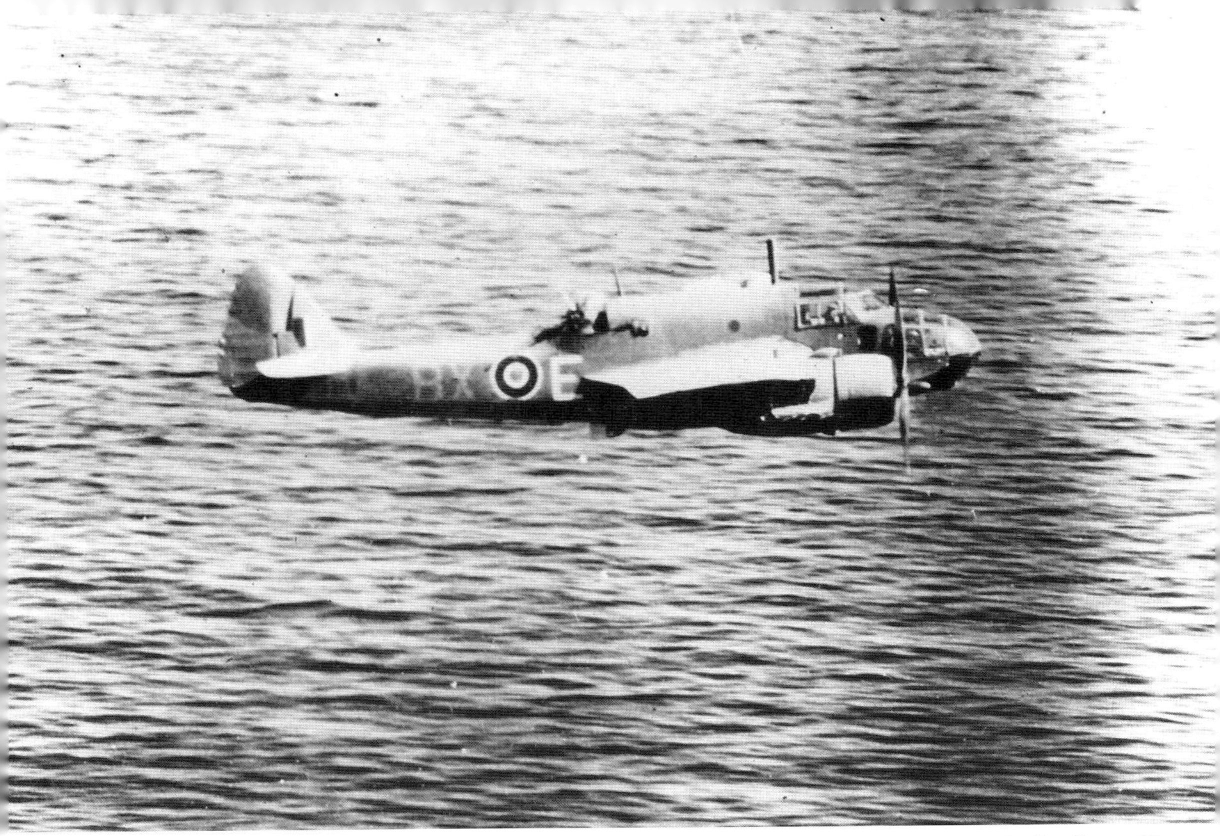

A Bristol Beaufort of 86 Squadron, operating with elements of 39 Squadron, attacks a tanker in the Ionian Sea on 15 September.

retained at Mersa Matruh instead of moving forward. There was also considerable talk of capturing Kufra, although nothing came of this. There were, however, air attacks on the oasis, of which more later.

Many miles to the east the final claim against a high-flying Ju 86R was made on this date, Plt Off Gold in the stripped aircraft and Plt Off Wilson in the marker being scrambled. Gold thought he had achieved some hits, although he noted that the aircraft seemed to be remarkably manoeuvrable in the evasive actions it took. It was last seen diving away at 34,000 feet, with black smoke trailing from its starboard engine. However, no damage was recorded by the Luftwaffe.

Yet further away, but to the west in Gibraltar some suspicious radio traffic had been picked up emanating from the area north-west of Algiers. A Sunderland of 202 Squadron was despatched to the location, Flt Lt E.P.Walshe and his crew, flying at 800 feet spotting a dark green submarine on the surface at 1430. This made no attempt to submerge, allowing Walshe to approach from astern where the vessel's main gun could not be brought to bear. The flyingboat was fired on by lighter weapons, but as it passed overhead the rear gunner put a solid burst into the conning tower which caused this to cease. Only four of the aircraft's six depth charges released, but these fell so close to the submarine that they were sufficient to ensure its destruction. At once it lost way and gushed oil; Walshe continued to circle overhead for the next 30 minutes, seeing some 40 survivors climbing into dinghies or swimming prior to the vessel sinking. He and his crew had sunk the Italian submarine *Alabastro*, a success which was instrumental in the award of a DFC to Walshe a couple of months later.

British Claims

103 MU	Plt Off A.G.W.Gold	Spitfire V	Ju 88 Damaged	Aboukir area

British Casualties

46 Sqn	Beaufighter crashed on way to LG.224; Plt Off Holme-Sumner and four KiFA

Italian Casualties

35° St BT	Cant.Z.1007bis MM 23362, 23326, 24281, 24753, 23380, 24750, 23371 destroyed; MM 23433, 23419 damaged at Barce by LRDG raid 0145

131ª Sq OA	Ca.311s MM 11688, 11720, 11764, 11687, 11610 and 11692 destroyed, MM 11488, 11601, 11642 and 11738 damaged; Ro.63 MM 11595 destroyed and MM 11596 damaged at Barce by LRDG raid
174ª Sq AS	S.79 MM 24332 destroyed at Barce by LRDG raid
87ª Sq, 66° Gr, OA	2 Ca.311s force-landed, w/o, observer Cap Natale Pesce WiA, crews rescued, returned next day

Thursday, 17 September 1942

Wellingtons of 38 Squadron attacked and claimed damage to all three ships forming a convoy north-west of Tobruk. Heavy Flak defences seriously damaged one torpedo-carrier, which managed to return safely nonetheless.

British Casualties

227 Sqn	Beaufighter T5148 shot down by ships' Flak 30m S Kalibia
38 Sqn	Welligton Ic badly damaged by Flak during shipping attack; Plt Off A.L.Wiggins and crew safe

Italian Casualties

230ª Sq, 95°Gr, 35°St BT	Cant.Z.1007bis MM 23391 '230-8' hit by AA, pilot Ten Marco Sommi-Picenardi, copilot Serg Magg Paolo D'Andrea and crew KiA

Friday, 18 September 1942

British Casualties

46 Sqn	Beaufighter X7707 crashed in force-landing at Kafr el Dairher

Monday, 21 September 1942

Serg Giacomo Magnani of 82ª Squadriglia undertaking a patrol over Tobruk at 1630, reported having intercepted an aircraft which he identified as a Blenheim, claiming to have shot it down in flames. Two Hurricanes of 274 Squadron were scrambled after a Ju 88 which was spotted and pursued. Both pilots attacked, the German aircraft last being seen in a dive with black smoke issuing from both engines.

Italian Claims

82ª Sq, 13°Gr, 2°St CT	Serg Giacomo Magnani	MC.200	Blenheim	20km NE Bu Amud	1630

Tuesday, 22 September 1942

At 1245 two Bf 109s dived on two 252 Wing Spitfires, Flt Lt Webb being wounded by a splinter in one foot when a bullet penetrated his cockpit. The Messerschmitt pilots went on to strafe Kilo 40 (LG.237), but inflicted no damage.

British Casualties

103 MU	Spitfire V slt damaged by Bf 109; Flt Lt Webb slt WiA
2 PRU	Spitfire IV BP883; Flt L.L.Ford MiA Crete; PoW
680 Sqn	Spitfire IV BR411 MiA Crete
227 Sqn	Beaufighter T5150 'K' collided with Beaufort AW350 during attack on convoy 10m W Antipaxos and crash-landed at Luqa; Sgt Phillips safe
39 Sqn	Beaufort AW350 collided with Beaufighter T5150 and crashed in sea; Flg Off A.F.Izzard and three MiA

German Claims

9./JG 27	Uffz Hans Löffler	Spitfire	S Suda Bay	0913
8./JG 27	Uffz Rudolf Moycis	Spitfire	NW Rethymnon	1520

Wednesday, 23 September 1942

Two hostile aircraft attacked a detachment of 103 MU at Edcu where three airmen were killed, three more subsequently died from wounds inflicted, and one officer was wounded.

One 38 Squadron Wellington from a force sent out to attack a convoy, failed to return. The pilot, R.V.Flanagan, was on his 40th operational sortie, but after being out for one and a half hours and before finding the target, both engines cut when the aircraft was flying at 1,200ft. Flanagan stated later that he had just handed the controls over to the second pilot, named Woods, and had just been discussing the course with him when this emergency occurred, so he ordered crash-landing stations and moved aft to the wobble pump and petrol cocks. When aft he removed the astro hatch, turned all the petrol cocks on and operated the wobble pump for a short time. He then moved forward and stood in the second pilot's position from where he advised on the best method to make a safe landing. The aircraft crashed approximately 50 miles north-north-west of Mersa Matruh, Woods being drowned at once. Flanagan meanwhile, was knocked unconscious and became entangled in the wreckage. Recovering his senses, he managed to free himself, then spotted a dinghy 50 yards away, which he reached; only he and two other members of the crew had survived. They remained floating in the dinghy for five days until seen by the crew of a Maryland. Because of their parlous situation, the latter broadcast a report of their position in clear language, and shortly afterwards they were picked by a Do 24, becoming PoWs.

British Casualties

2 PRU	Spitfire IVc BR435 MiA Crete; Flt Lt F.B.Day PoW
38 Sqn	Wellington Ic HX402 FTR from night torpedo attack on vessel off Ras el Tin; Flt Sgt R.V.Flanagan and two PoW, two KiA

Thursday, 24 September 1942

Five Wellingtons of 221 Squadron homed in nine torpedo-carriers of 38 Squadron to a convoy spotted earlier by a Maryland, 110 miles north-north-west of Tobruk. One Wellington crew attacked a large merchant vessel, claiming a possible hit, but one of the attackers failed to return. Another Maryland subsequently reported little sign of any damage to the ships which had got within 30 miles of Tobruk.

British Casualties

38 Sqn	Wellington FTR from convoy attack

Friday, 25 September 1942

The day at last brought a riposte to the use of Kufra as the base for the recent attacks on Tobruk and Benghazi by the various special forces. A force reported to have comprised eight He 111s and Ju 88s was successful in catching three Bombays of 216 Squadron on the ground there, and these were all destroyed. Several eye-witness reports of this attack exist, though they differ to varying degrees from the official sources. An instrument repairer serving on the groundcrew of 15 SAAF Squadron, Bertie Wilson, recorded in *The Aegean Pirates; The History of 15 Squadron, SAAF in WW2*:

> "It was a quiet sunny day. After lunch the groundcrews were relaxing doing odd jobs waiting for their aircraft to return. Suddenly they heard a roar and realised bullets were flying all around them. One mechanic shouted: 'Here they come, over the palm trees from the fort side of the hill!' Some members scrambled for the door while others fell flat on the floor. I got out last without my tin hat and shirt. I ran like never before with my army boots on. I saw I was not going to make the funk hole so I fell flat on the hard ground with my hands covering my head. As soon as I heard the first Heinkel pass I looked up and ran to another slit trench, which was deeper but also occasionally used as a toilet. Bombs were exploding all around us, with shrapnel flying through the air. They came over in relays, strafing, dropping bombs and anti-personnel bread baskets* in the area between the fort, the hangar and the parked Bombays. They were all destroyed. First to burn was a Sato Hut, containing all the Bombay aircraft crews' kit and other items. The drums next to the hangar were pierced with hundreds of holes. While ignoring the stench I kept my head down and prayed. Every minute seemed like an hour. The aircraft came at about 500 feet from the fort's direction, straight for us, banking towards the parked Bombay aircraft. I found I was sharing the slit trench with an RAF officer, two teenage Sudanese, and my mate Van, and that we were directly in line of everything, especially the Met Signal House.
>
> "We saw them hit the hangar and several places were burning with thick smoke adding to dust swirling all around us. Still they bombed, dropping sticks of five bombs at a time. As soon as we saw a chance, we jumped up and ran into the palm trees, to get further away from the hangar. All the time our antiaircraft guns kept firing away at the Heinkels and we noticed that one of the aircraft started to smoke.
>
> "Then there was silence. We came out of the palm trees and looked around. We stayed away from the burning hangar. Suddenly we heard them coming again. Heinkels, Ju 88s and Me 110s

216 Squadron Bristol Bombay similar to those destroyed on the ground at Kufra Oasis on 25 September. L5845 survived for many more months.

were all around us, diving towards the fort. I could not find a hole quickly enough and fell flat on the open ground. As soon as they banked I took the gap and half sailed waist deep into a water well. I could feel the sand on the shirtless body when the 500lb bombs were dropped. Then they were gone. Slowly we got out of our hide-aways to investigate. The fort got direct hits and the petrol and oil burned for days. We made sure everything was clear before investigating near the hangar area. Undetonated bombs were found in a few places. One corner of the hangar was blasted away, with our armoury, stores, instruments as well as the radio equipment room.

"Four chaps could find none of their kit. Half the asbestos hangar roof had fallen in and damaged our parked aircraft. We praised the Lord that no one was killed in the air raid that lasted about 80 minutes. Six Bombays and two Lockheed Hudsons had been burned out and our aircraft had been severely damaged. After investigating the raid the British Incendiary Squad was of the opinion that we had been saved because most of the bombs and incendiaries were dropped below 500 feet, therefore not detonating. On 26 September 1942 we received news from Al Maza that one Heinkel and a Ju 88 had been shot down by us and that the prisoners were picked up. We continued to be attacked by enemy aircraft but only as single aircraft raids. This did not deter us and allied aircraft movements took place every day. One day we had our usual air raid by a Heinkel which was shot down by a single .303 bullet which had severed an oil pipe. It crash-landed 20 miles outside the Kufra Oasis."

*The 'bread baskets' were containers packed with a large number of small anti-personnel devices, referred to at the time as 'Molotov Bread Baskets'.

Despite this detailed report there is no indication in 216 Squadron's records that more than three Bombays were destroyed on this date or that any Hudsons were lost – although one was at a later date. Further, there is no indication that any of 15 SAAF Squadron's detached aircraft were written off due to severe damage. It seems therefore, that other aircraft may have been hit, but not damaged beyond local repair.

Recorded Maj Gen David Lloyd Owen in his book *The Long Range Desert Group, 1940-1945; Providence Their Guide*:

> "The final and ironical reminder of these failures came when two days after our arrival back in Kufra, where we were sorting ourselves out, the Germans sent eight Heinkels over to bomb and strafe the place. There were more troops in Kufra on that day than there had ever been, and more machine guns too. But the enemy first destroyed the Bombays on the landing-ground and then proceeded to sweep the palm trees with cannon and machine-gun fire.
>
> "The venomous reply from the SAS and LRDG on the ground resulted in five of the eight Heinkels failing to return to base, which says quite as lot for the combined fire-power of these two units, considering we had nothing more formidable than 20mm Bredas. The only casualties on our side were four Arabs killed in the fort at Kufra, while I had a cannon shell through my back and left arm and one Guardsman was wounded rather less seriously.
>
> "I never forgave the idiot who had allowed the BBC to put out a statement about these raids. They had included the fact that they had been mounted from Kufra. Why ask for trouble ? I remember how we had specifically requested that no mention should be made of the fact that these raids had been launched from Kufra."

Five of eight Heinkels shot down? Of such reports are myths born.

British Casualties

216 Sqn	Bombay L5824 destroyed in air raid at Kufra
216 Sqn	Bombay L5843 destroyed in air raid at Kufra
216 Sqn	Bombay L5857 destroyed in air raid at Kufra

Saturday, 26 September 1942

The pilot of a 417 Squadron Hurricane IIc patrolling over Suez at 28,000 feet, spotted a Ju 88 which he shot down. Three members of the crew were seen to bale out at 6,000 feet, landing in the sea where the aircraft also crashed and blew up. The survivors were picked up safely. An He 111 was reported to have crashed between Burg el Arab and Amiriya, four prisoners being taken. This was an aircraft of 6./KG 100, one of six bombers reported over Cairo and Suez harbour. Three Beaufighters of 46 Squadron and one of 89 Squadron had been scrambled and Plt Off Perinchief shot the Heinkel down in flames 60 miles south of Cairo.

British Claims

417 Sqn	Flt Sgt J.H.G.Leguerier	Hurricane IIc HL891 'H'	Ju 88	10m SE Suez	1205
46 Sqn	Plt Off W.H.Perinchief	Beaufighter If .3352	He 111	Cairo area	2035-2335

German Casualties

1.(F)/121	Ju 88 WNr 430 049 7A+AH shot down by Hurricane 12m E Suez at 1305; Oblt Hermann Meier and three PoW
6./KG 100	He 111H-6 WNr 7222 6N+AS shot down by night fighter at El Alamein; Fw Helmut Dümmler and three PoW (listed by Luftwaffe as lost 27th)
3./LG 1	Ju 88A-4 WNr 140 301 L1+WL shot down by AA at Kufra; Fw Ernst Müller and three PoW

Monday, 28 September 1942

With evening some 35 or more bombers were reported in the Daba area, these then heading for Amiriya and LG.90. Six bombed LG.86, but caused no damage. 211 Group claimed one Bf 109 shot down and two possibles by 238 and 92 Squadrons (see Chapter Six).

German Casualties

1/126 (III./KG100)	u/k Obgfr Wolfgang Bock, Lt Hans Mass and two return from internment

Tuesday, 29 September 1942

Two Beaufighters of 272 Squadron undertook a late afternoon strafe of the Sidi Barrani-Mersa Matruh road shooting down one of two Fi 156s and strafing a convoy.

British Claims					
272 Sqn	Sgt G.A.Tuckwell/ Sgt K.F.Hubbard	Beaufighter Ic 'E'	Fi 156	Sidi Barrani road	1600-1845

British Casualties	
10 ADU	Beaufort DW823 MiA between Malta and Egypt on delivery flight
10 ADU	Beaufort DW833 MiA between Gibraltar and Malta on delivery flight

German Casualties	
7./KG 100	He 111H-6 WNr 7819 D1+FH ran out of fuel on escort sorties and force-landed in Turkey; Obgefr Wolfgang Buk and three interned. Released May 1943

Wednesday, 30 September 1942

Beaufighters of 272 Squadron took off at 0855, intercepting four bombers over the Sollum-Sidi Barrani road, three of which were claimed shot down. 203 Squadron despatched four Marylands and one new Baltimore on a reconnaissance, a convoy being spotted escorted by five Ju 88s to the south and west of Crete. The Baltimore failed to return.

British Claims				
272 Sqn	Flg Off E.E.Coate/Sgt E.W.Miles	Beaufighter Ic 'V'	He 111	0855-1140
272 Sqn	Plt Off A.I.Smith/Sgt J.P.Diaper	Beaufighter Ic 'P'	He 111	0855-1140
272 Sqn	Plt Off A.I.Smith/Sgt J.P.Diaper	Beaufighter Ic 'P'	Ju 88	0855-1140

British Casualties	
203 Sqn	Baltimore AG723 FTR from reconnaissance sortie; Flg Off T.A.A.G.Tahiwi and three MiA
2 PRU	Spitfire IV BR411 shot down; Flt Lt M.E.Leng PoW

German Claims			
8./JG 27	Uffz Rudolf Moycis	Spitfire	Tympakion, Crete 0945

At this stage 235 Wing's long-serving commanding officer, Grp Capt A.P.Revington, was replaced by Grp Capt Collins. During September the sorties undertaken under the wing's guidance included:

252 Squadron	1	47 Squadron attached flight	32
272 Squadron	1	Free French Nancy Flight	8
459 Squadron	66	203 Squadron	22
13(Hellenic) Squadron	20	701 Squadron, Fleet Air Arm	78
13(Hellenic) Squadron Gaza Det	35	815 Squadron, Fleet Air Arm	30

An unarmed Spitfire PR IV of 680 Squadron (previously2 PRU).

Other changes were also occurring at this time. In 248 Wing Wg Cdr R.A.Sprague, commanding officer of 221 Squadron, commenced torpedo training at 5 METS. On completion of this during October, he would become commanding officer of the new 47 Squadron on Beauforts. Meanwhile 221 Squadron would be taken over by Wg Cdr E.P.W.Hutton, AFC. 203 Squadron was now led by Wg Cdr E.B.Grace, formerly commanding officer of the 47 Squadron Air Echelon.

The month had been a very busy one with many reconnaissances by day and night searches by ASV radar, although these were often frustrated by cloud, bad weather and smoke screens. 815 Squadron had been particularly busy, hunting E- and F-Boats along the coast by night. 14 Squadron, having given up its Blenheims for US-built Martin Marauders, was now also commencing training for torpedo-dropping. Rather than transfer the whole squadron to Shallufa for this purpose, 5 METS moved temporarily to the unit's base at LG.224. 38 Squadron moved to Gianaclis.

October would see a number of changes. 417 Squadron, which had moved to Edcu with Hurricanes, sent four pilots to Heliopolis to fly Spitfires in defence of Cairo. 889 Squadron had now been partially re-equipped, operating seven Hurricanes and four Fulmars. The Beaufighters would once more become involved in much strafing activity during the coming month. Now, however, they would be joined by aircraft of 46 Squadron which would begin both strafing and bombing as well as continuing with their night-fighter activities.

Friday, 2 October 1942

On this date a Ju 88 was intercepted by Spitfires of 92 Squadron and shot down 40 miles north-west of Alexandria, being seen to dive into the water (see also Chapter Six).

British Casualties	
Special Ops Flt	Wellington X9734 ditched, Mediterranean

Saturday, 3 October 1942

A pair of 601 Squadron Spitfires – 211 Group aircraft under 252 Wing control – intercepted and damaged a Ju 88 in the Burg el Arab area (see also Chapter Six).

Sunday, 4 October 1942

Italian Casualties	
252ªSq, 104°Gr Aut AS	S.79 ditched 40 miles off Turkish coast, pilot Ten Piergiovanni Nannini (wounded) and crew rescued

Tuesday, 6 October 1942

Three Beaufighters of 252 Squadron attacked the Italian seaplane base at Menelao Bay where crews identified about a dozen Cant.Z.506Bs, two Do 22s and an He 115; seven of these aircraft were claimed to have been strafed. One of these was seen to catch fire and nine were claimed to have been badly damaged.

British Claims		
252 Sqn	Three Beaufighter crews	ten floatplanes strafed

Italian Casualties	
148ª Sq RM	Cant.Z.506 MM 45450 destroyed, Cant.Z 501 MM 35614, 35604, 35842 and 35566 strafed and damaged at Menelao by three Beaufighters, 1130
174ª Sq AS	2 S.79s destroyed after collision in taking-off, pilots S.Ten Ottone Sponza, Serg Magg Antonio Canis and crews unscathed

Wednesday, 7 October 1942

Four Beaufighters of 252 Squadron repeated the attack on the Menelao seaplane base, claiming to have hit four Cant.Z.506Bs moored on the water and one drawn up on the slipway. The Beaufighters then went on to attack traffic on the Gazala road. As three crews headed for home, eight fully-laden F-Boats were seen ten miles north of Sidi Barrani, covered by two fighters identified as MC.202s; these were in fact MC.200s of 8° Gruppo CT, the pilots of which attempted to provide cover as one Beaufighter hit the leading barge. S.Ten Franco Mauri and Serg Magg Giuseppe Fucci claimed to have probably shot down a Beaufighter between them. The British crews reported seeing only one Macchi attack them, but fire from this hit one Beaufighter and damaged it slightly, causing the pilot to have to belly-land on return to base.

British Claims		
252 Sqn	Beaufighter crews	5 Z.506bs hit on the water and slipway at Menelao

British Casualties	
252 Sqn	Beaufighter slightly damaged by Flak and crash-landed at base; Sgt G.M.Nettleship/Flt Sgt J.B.Blake safe

Italian Claims					
94ª Sq, 8°Gr, 2°St CT	S.Ten Franco Mauri	MC.200	Beaufighter Probable	off coast	1450
94ª Sq, 8°Gr, 2°St CT	Serg Magg Giuseppe Fucci	MC.200			

Italian Casualties	
148ªSq RM	Cant.Z.506 MM 45451 and Cant.Z.501 MM 35620 destroyed, Cant.Z.501 MM 35844 and 35632 damaged at Menelao by four Beaufighters' strafing, 1400

Thursday, 8 October 1942

During a test flight, Ten Franco Bordoni-Bisleri of 95ª Squadriglia sighted a Beaufighter flying at 19,500 feet and fired at it, until his right machine gun jammed.

Italian Claims					
95ª Sq, 18°Gr, 3°St CT	Ten Franco Bordoni-Bisleri	MC.202	Beaufighter Damaged	nr Abu Haggag	1110

Friday, 9 October 1942

Three Bisleys of 15 SAAF Squadron and four Beaufighters of 252 Squadron attacked a train comprising engine, tender and 20 trucks carrying four disassembled big guns amongst other cargo. The attack was very successful, the Bisleys gaining hits, following which the Beaufighters strafed. The train was totally destroyed and reportedly an ammunition wagon blew up so violently that the smoke and debris thrown into the air was visible from 40 miles away. It appears, however, that these aircraft were intercepted by Bf 109s which claimed one aircraft shot down, although no British or South African loss was recorded.

German Claims				
4./JG 27	Fw Heinrich Steis	Beaufighter	SE Deir el Tarfa	1220

Saturday, 10 October 1942

During a patrol over Abu Haggag, 0930-1130, two MC.200s of 85ª Squadriglia met two Beaufighters; Serg Magg Luigi Gorrini claimed two damaged. Early afternoon, Cap Solaro, during a test flight encountered three Albacores and claimed to have shot down two, which he reported were seen crashing into the sea. Solaro's Macchi was hit in the windshield by return fire but the pilot emerged unscathed.

British Casualties	
10 ADU	Beaufort DW824

Italian Claims					
85ª Sq, 18°Gr, 3°St CT	Serg Magg Luigi Gorrini	MC.200	2 Beaufighters Damaged	Abu Haggag	1000
70ª Sq, 23°Gr, 3°St CT	Cap Claudio Solaro	MC.202	2 Albacores	N Ras Kenayis	1505-1555

Italian Casualties	
70ª Sq, 23°Gr, 3°St CT	MC.202 hit by return fire from Albacores, Cap Claudio Solaro safe

Monday, 12 October 1942

Three Bisleys and four Beaufighters from the same units as on 9 October undertook a further attack on a train which had been spotted by a reconnaissance aircraft west of Capuzzo. Axis aircraft were encountered on this occasion and there was some confusion in the various reports of just what happened. 15 SAAF Squadron recorded that one Bisley was shot down by a twin-engined aircraft which was itself then shot down by the Beaufighters and left in flames near the blazing Bisley. It was also recorded that the Bisley crews forced down a Ju 52/3m, then bombing it on the ground where a direct hit was claimed; however, one Bisley was shot down by return fire.

The *Aegean Pirates* records that an attack on the target train was made first, at least four of ten trucks being destroyed before an S.81 attacked and shot down Lt Bruton-Simmonds' Bisley. Maj Pidsley then apparently attacked the S.81 which was now on the ground, his observer dropping two 250lb bombs on it and destroyed it. Amidst these reports are the claims of the Beaufighter pilots, Flt Sgt Kernaghan for a Ju52/3m, and an unidentified pilot reportedly damaging a Bf 110.

With some trepidation, it would appear that when attacking a trimotor aircraft, Bisley NA497 was shot down by return fire. This aircraft was then shot down by a Beaufighter, falling close to the Bisley, but at the same time being attacked by Maj Pidsley's Bisley. There certainly appears to have been aircraft other than the single lightly-armed trimotor present (which was definitely a Luftwaffe aircraft, there being no evidence of an Italian S.81 being anywhere in the vicinity), for apart from the apparent presence of a Bf 110, two of the Beaufighters were damaged during this engagement, one crash-landing at base.

British Claims

252 Sqn	Sgt S.J.Kernaghan/ Sgt A.Powell	Beaufighter Ic T5036	Ju 52/3m	train strafe	1340-1730
252 Sqn	Sgt S.J.Kernaghan/ Sgt A.Powell	Beaufighter Ic T5036	Bf 110 Damaged		1340-1730
252 Sqn	Flg Off C.R.McMills/ Sgt H.G.Bicknell	Beaufighter Ic			
252 Sqn	Plt Off E.S.Watson/ Sgt G.D.Hudson	Beaufighter Ic			
252 Sqn	Sgt A.B.McKeown/ Sgt G.D.Hudson	Beaufighter Ic			
15 SAAF Sqn	Maj A.W.Pidsley & crew Bisley		Ju 52/3m or S.81 forced down and destroyed by bombing		

British Casualties

15 SAAF Sqn	Bisley NA497 'H' shot down by return fire from Ju 52/3m over desert; Lt C.R.Bruton-Simmonds and two KiA
252 Sqn	Beaufighter badly damaged
252 Sqn	Beaufighter badly damaged and crash-landed on return; crew safe
203 Sqn	Maryland 'Y' FTR from search sortie; Lt Bergh and three MiA 1245

German Casualties

FlgKdo/LnRegtAfrika	Ju 52/3m lost

Wednesday, 14 October 1942

While engaged in convoy escort to the cargo steamer, *Trapani* and MTB *Medici* off Tripoli, a Beaufighter was claimed shot down by S.Ten Francesco Figini of 393ª Squadriglia. Serg Brunelli of the same unit was scrambled at 1130 and claimed a Hurricane damaged. At much the same time, but far away near Tobruk, S.Ten Cecchino Maestri of 83ª Squadriglia claimed a twin-engined aircraft damaged, and Ten Giorgio Savoia of 77ª Squadriglia claimed damage to an aircraft identified as a Stirling during a patrol over the port. Further east still, a Blenheim crew from 13 (Hellenic) Squadron reported attacking a submarine.

British Casualties

227 Sqn	Beaufighter X8030 shot down by Flak during shipping attack
248 Sqn	Beaufighter T5132 crashed in sea while attacking ships off Tripoli
267 Sqn	Lodestar EW961 damaged by bombs at Kufra

Italian Claims

393ª Sq, 160°Gr Aut CT	S.Ten Francesco Figini	G.50bis	Beaufighter	convoy escort	1150
393ª Sq, 160°Gr Aut CT	Serg Antonio Brunelli	G.50bis	Hurricane Damaged	off Tripoli	1245
77ª Sq, 13°Gr, 2°St CT	Ten Giorgio Savoia	MC.200	Stirling Damaged	nr Tobruk	1245-1345
83ª Sq, 18°Gr, 3°St CT	S.Ten Cecchino Maestri	MC.200	twin-engined Damaged	convoy escort	1445

Thursday, 15 October 1942

At 0800 eight Beaufighters of 252 Squadron carried out an offensive sweep south of Crete. One pilot returned early, reporting seeing a Beaufighter dive into the sea. He circled over the spot for 15 minutes, but saw nothing more. Meanwhile the rest of the formation flew back towards Tobruk, but in doing so spotted two Ju 52/3ms flying at 200ft some 78 miles south-east of Gavdos Island. One of these was shot down into the sea, four men clambering into their dinghy, with hits also seen on the second aircraft.

During the day a reconnaissance Baltimore of 203 Squadron failed to return from an anti-submarine patrol. Next day a search by the Sea Rescue Flight found the aircraft crashed on the coast between Haifa and Port Said, with one of the crew dead and two others badly injured.

British Claims

252 Sqn	Wg Cdr P.H.Bragg/ Flg Off E.G.Nichols	Beaufighter Ic T5137	Ju 52/3m	S Crete	0800-1200
252 Sqn	Wg Cdr P.H.Bragg/ Flg Off E.G.Nichols	Beaufighter Ic T5137	Ju 52/3m Damaged	S Crete	0800-1200

British Casualties

252 Sqn	Beaufighter X8075 crashed in sea; Plt Off K.J.A.Read/Flt Sgt C.D. Nash MiA
203 Sqn	Baltimore crashed on the coast between Haifa-Port Said; 1 killed, 2 badly injured

Saturday, 17 October 1942

British Casualties

103 MU	Hurricane HL842 missing on delivery flight between Aboukir and Wadi Natrun

Monday, 19 October 1942

Four Piaggio P.108 four-engined bombers of 274ª Squadriglia BGR (Bombardamento Grande Raggio – Long Range Bombardment) led by T.Col Gori Castellani, moved from Guidonia, near Rome, to Sardinia's Decimomannu airfield, to take part in operations. From here they were initially employed in a raid on Gibraltar.

At 1250 on this date Beaufighters of 272 Squadron swept to the south of Gavdos, attacking a two-masted schooner which was last seen blazing and sinking, some of the crew taking to a lifeboat. Fifteen minutes later four of the crews spotted 32 Ju 52/3ms with six towed gliders and a Bf 110 escort flying at 200ft west of Gavdos. Attacking head-on, at least one was shot down before three escorting Bf 110s attacked the British fighters. One of these was claimed damaged by the navigator in one Beaufighter, using his Vickers K gun from the upper fuselage blister, although one Beaufighter was also damaged; a claim for one such aircraft shot down was submitted by the pilot of one of the Messerschmitts.

During the day the Liberators of 120 Squadron on detachment with 221 Squadron, returned to the UK. That night a torpedo-carrying He 111 hit the tanker *Scalaria* at Ras Garib; the vessel sank in flames.

Four-engine Piaggio P.108 bombers of the Regia Aeronautica commenced operations in very limited numbers during late October 1942.

British Claims

272 Sqn	Sgt G.G.Patearson/ Sgt G.J.W.Simister	Beaufighter Ic 'T'	Ju 52/3m	SW Gavdos Island	1240-1730
272 Sqn	Plt Off C.F.Cutting/ Flt Lt A.Watson	Beaufighter Ic T5079 'G'	Bf 110 Damaged	SW Gavdos Island	1240-1730

British Casualties

272 Sqn	Beaufighter Ic damaged by Bf 110s
2 PRU	Spitfire IV AB312 MiA
46 Sqn	Beaufighter X7637 crashed in force-landing SW Edcu

German Claims

7./ZG 26	Fw Hubert Freiberger	Beaufighter	S of Crete	1420

Tuesday, 20 October 1942

Four P.108s took off from Decimomannu at 1635 on a long-range mission to Gibraltar. Cap Carlo Corti made an early return due to engine trouble, his aircraft then being badly damaged during the landing. The three remaining bombers, led by T.Col Castellani, carried out the planned bombing. A Maryland and a Baltimore of 203 Squadron undertook reconnaissances to the west and south of Crete. The latter aircraft returned early but the Maryland was not seen again.

British Casualties

203 Sqn	Maryland AH342 FTR from reconnaissance of Crete area, began 0632; Flg Off Young and three MiA

Italian Casualties

274ª Sq BGR	P.108 MM 22603 badly damaged on landing at Decimomannu, w/o, Cap Carlo Corti and crew safe

Wednesday, 21 October 1942

Three P.108s took off from Decimomannu at 1715 on another sortie to Gibraltar. On return two landed safely at Decimomannu, but Cap Giano Rossi force-landed near Bone due to engine failure. He and his crew then destroyed the aircraft to prevent its capture or internment.

Four 272 Squadron Beaufighters strafed vehicles on the Sidi Barrani-Mersa Matruh road, following which a Do 24 was seen north of the Ishailia Rocks heading out to sea. One pilot attacked this, but his Beaufighter was damaged by return fire. At 103 Maintenance Unit, Aboukir, Flg Off Genders, flying a Spitfire, intercepted and claimed to have shot down a reconnaissance Ju 88. Torpedo Heinkels gained another success when a dredger was hit and sunk.

British Claims

103 MU	Flg Off G.E.C.Genders	Spitfire V	Ju 88		
272 Sqn	Flg Off D.M.Garbutt/ Sgt M.A.Lea	Beaufighter Ic T6080	Do 24 Damaged	Matruh-Barrani road	1155-1455
252 Sqn	Sgt G.M.Nettleship/ Flt Sgt S.G.Deacon	Beaufighter Ic T5209			
252 Sqn	Sgt J.M.Gunn/ Plt Off L.A.Clark	Beaufighter Ic T4987 'P'			
252 Sqn	Sgt K.W.Clark/ Sgt A.Fraser	Beaufighter Ic X8068			

British Casualties

272 Sqn	Beaufighter damaged by return fire fron Do 24 N Ishailia Rocks 1145-1455
5 METS	Beaufort DD974 crashed in sea 6m S Suez

Italian Casualties

274ª Sq BGR	P.108 MM 22602 destroyed on force-landing near Bone, Cap Giano Rossi and crew safe

Thursday, 22 October 1942

Two S.79s of 252ª Squadriglia set off at 1720 over the eastern Mediterranean. Off Port Said Ten Enrico Miranda sighted a convoy and released his torpedo at a destroyer which he claimed to have sunk. Miranda's aircraft was pursued and shot-up by two fighters. With the central engine damaged, he was forced to crash-land near Koufonisi island (south of Crete). The crew was rescued by ship next day.

Italian Casualties

252ª Sq, 104°Gr, 46°St AS	S.79 ditched in sea, pilot Enrico Miranda, copilot Vincenzo Prota and three safe

Saturday, 24 October 1942

There had been a decline in Axis nocturnal bombing attacks during the month and consequently the Beaufighters of 46 Squadron began carrying out night strafing and bombing sorties against the enemy lines of communication.

British Casualties

15 SAAF Sqn	Bisley BA335 crashed in flames, Kufra Oasis

Sunday, 25 October 1942

A small convoy of merchant ships was seen making for Tobruk during the day, seven Beaufighters of 252 Squadron taking off to attack. Two Ju 88s and a Do 24 flyingboat were identified escorting the ships and these were all claimed shot down by four of the fighters, the Do 24 catching fire and blowing up; the other three Beaufighters strafed the vessels. Later in the day three more aircraft from this unit escorted Beauforts and Bisleys to make a further attack, on this occasion encountering two CR.42s, both of which were claimed shot down. The Beauforts missed with their torpedoes but a Bisley hit one merchant ship with its bombs, this vessel reportedly blowing up.

It seems that these attacks were both intercepted by Italian fighters, the pilots of three MC.200s of 8° Gruppo CT attacking four Beaufighters, two of which were claimed to have been damaged. Shortly after these claims were made, Serg Vanello of 13° Gruppo in an MC.202 reported encountering another Beaufighter 50 miles off Sidi Abeida which he claimed to have shot down. No RAF casualties were recorded during these two attacks.

However, somewhat later that morning eight Beaufighters of 272 Squadron intercepted 35 Ju 52/3ms and six escorting Bf 109s north of Tobruk. Four of the British fighters were providing top cover and the leader of this section, Flg Off Rankin, claimed hits on one Messerschmitt which dived away, smoking. A general dogfight then began as the lower four, led by Flt Lt Watson went for the transports. Watson claimed two shot down, saw another exploding and also noted two aircraft colliding. Wg Cdr White and his observer failed to return but in discussion after the rest of the crews got back to base, it was agreed that it had been White who had been in collision with a Ju 52/3m, bringing the number of transports claimed shot down to four; it also appears that Rankin's claim for a Bf 110 damaged was later upgraded to an aircraft destroyed.

British Claims

252 Sqn	Flt Lt A.D.Frecker/ Sgt T.Armstrong	Beaufighter Ic T5110	Do 24 (shared by three crews)	Tobruk area	0715-1150
252 Sqn	Sgt G.M.Nettleship/ Flt Sgt S.G.Deacon	Beaufighter Ic T4932			
252 Sqn	Plt Off F.T.Derick/ Plt Off M.J.McCann	Beaufighter Ic T4940			
252 Sqn	Wg Cdr P.H.Bragg/ Flg Off E.G.Nichols	Beaufighter Ic T5137	Ju 88	Tobruk area	0715-1150
252 Sqn	Flt Lt A.D.Frecker/ Sgt T.Armstrong	Beaufighter Ic T5110	Ju 88	Tobruk area	0715-1150
272 Sqn	Sgt G.G.Hains/ Sgt D.C.Lawton	Beaufighter Ic T4708 'P'	Ju 52/3m Damaged	Crete-N Africa	1116-1545
272 Sqn	Flg Off R.Rankin/ Sgt R.H.Pinkerton	Beaufighter Ic T4983'W'	Bf 110	Crete-N Africa	1116-1545
272 Sqn	Sgt W.Russell/ Sgt A.B.Wilson	Beaufighter Ic T5037 E'	Ju 52/3m	Crete-N Africa	1116-1545
272 Sqn	Sgt W.Russell/ Sgt A.B.Wilson	Beaufighter Ic T5037 'E'	Ju 52/3m Damaged	Crete-N Africa	1116-1545
272 Sqn	Flt Lt A.Watson/ Plt Off C.F.Cutting	Beaufighter Ic T4713 'G'	2 Ju 52/3ms	Crete- N Africa	1116-1545

British Claims

272 Sqn	Wg Cdr E.J.M.White/ Flt Sgt R.A.Francis	Beaufighter Ic T5076 'B'	Ju 52/3m	Crete-N Africa	1116-1545
252 Sqn	Flg Off D.M.Garbutt/ Sgt M.A.Lea	Beaufighter Ic T5046	CR.42	Tobruk area	1212-1745
252 Sqn	Flg Off C.R.McMills/ Sgt H.G.Bicknell	Beaufighter Ic T4990			
252 Sqn	Plt Off E.S.Watson/ Sgt G.D.Hudson	Beaufighter Ic T4872			

British Casualties

272 Sqn	Beaufighter T5078 MiA from interception of Ju 52/3ms off Crete; Wg Cdr J.M. White/Flt Sgt R.A.Francis

Italian Claims

93ª Sq, 8°Gr, 2°St CT	Ten Gioacchino Bissoli	MC.200	2 Beaufighters Damaged off coast		0740-0920
82ª Sq, 13°Gr, 2°St CT	Serg Sergio Vanello	MC.202	Beaufighter	80km N Sidi Abeida	0910-0950

Italian Casualties

148ª Sq RM	Cant.Z.501 MM 35844 shot down by fighters 20 miles N Tobruk, 1000, pilot Ten Paolo Anelli, copilot Serg Magg Francesco Tozzini and crew MiA

Monday, 26 October 1942

As recounted in *Malta: The Spitfire Year, 1942* there had been a number of quite major battles with Axis convoys during the first half of October, involving aircraft from the island almost entirely. The latest pre-offensive blitz on Malta had reduced such activity considerably, but now an extremely important convoy of critically needed fuel had been spotted on its way. This was the Axis TT convoy which comprised the 4,869-ton tanker *Proserpina*, 5,890-ton freighter *Tergestea* and the German steamer *Dora*, escorted by Regia Marina motor-torpedo boats *Partenope*, *Lira*, *Ciclope* and *Calatafimi*, with air cover provided by both the Regia Aeronautica and the Luftwaffe. With daylight Marylands soon found a convoy identified as a tanker, two merchant vessels, four barges and four destroyers 20 miles west of Tobruk. Following these sightings three strike forces were prepared.

Meanwhile, Beaufighters were out patrolling throughout the day, the first encounter occurring soon after midday when aircraft from 252 Squadron engaged Bf 109s and Ju 88s in the Tobruk area, one of each being claimed damaged for the loss of one Beaufighter which failed to return.

At 1435 four aircraft from this unit and five others of 272 Squadron escorted eight Beauforts of 47 Squadron and five Bisleys of 15 SAAF Squadron to target the convoy 18 miles north-west of Tobruk where the entire British force attacked, the Bisley crews claiming four direct hits on the stern of the tanker with 250lb bombs, while of five torpedoes launched by 47 Squadron, one hit the stern of the tanker too. An explosion was followed by flames and thick black smoke. One Bisley collided with the tanker's mast and crashed. In the face of an intense barrage of Flak, a second failed to return and a Beaufort crashed into the sea near the ships. As the attackers turned away for base, a Beaufort and a Bisley collided, both crashing into the sea; the *Proserpina* had, however, been sunk in this attack. The departing crews saw 50 Ju 52/3ms eight miles north-west of Tobruk but were not in a position to interfere.

A second strike force comprising five Beauforts of 39 Squadron escorted by eight Beaufighters drawn from the two squadrons, attacked a barge estimated to be 300ft long and carrying a cargo of barrels 15 miles north-east of Tobruk. Three torpedoes were launched but no visible damage was caused. Five He 111s of II./KG 100 were encountered en route when 50 miles north-north-east of Sidi Barrani. Assessment of claims differed, wing reporting one shot down, one badly damaged and two damaged to a lesser extent. Individual claims were made by 272 Squadron for two shot down and a third probable, additionally unstated pilots of 252 Squadron were apparently credited with one probable and three damaged; one more Beaufighter was lost during this engagement.

The third force comprised three torpedo-carrying Wellingtons of 38 Squadron which attacked at dusk, all claiming hits on the large merchant vessel one mile north of Tobruk as the remains of the convoy were about to enter harbour. There was a terrific explosion – and they had sunk *Tergestea*. One of the Wellingtons was seen to stagger as its torpedo was released and 'L' then broke away with one engine on fire, failing to return. During the night a fourth force of two bomb-laden and three torpedo-carrying Wellingtons was sent out. These found the tanker blazing from end to end and red hot, with intermittent explosions, no further attacks being deemed necessary. A 1,000lb bomb was released on the jetties by one aircraft, but a second – B of 38 Squadron – did not return.

The Axis did not receive a single litre of petrol from this effort, but although it was believed that all the vessels in the convoy had been sunk, the *Dora* did, however, manage to reach Tobruk. *Lira* and *Calatafimi* rescued 62 out of 77 sailors aboard *Proserpina*, but when *Tergestea* exploded, all her crew of 80 were killed. The day had also seen the first sortie by one of 14 Squadron's Marauders, Lt B.W.Young undertaking a reconnaissance in FK121.

British Claims

252 Sqn	Sgt K.W.Clark/Sgt A.Fraser	Beaufighter Ic T5209	Bf 109 Damaged	E Tobruk	1240-1740
252 Sqn	Sgt J.M.Stephan/ Sgt S.R.Whear	Beaufighter Ic T5036	Ju 88 Damaged	18m from Tobruk	1240-1740
272 Sqn	Plt Off G.G.Patearson/ Sgt G.J.W.Simister	Beaufighter Ic X8031 'S'	He 111 Probable	NW Sidi Barrani	1435-1915
272 Sqn	Plt Off A.I.Smith/	Beaufighter Ic T5041 'U'	He 111	NW Sidi Barrani	1435-1915
	Plt Off J.P.Diaper	Beaufighter VIf EL227	He 111	escort shipping strike	1435-1930
252 Sqn	Sgt S.J.Kernaghan/ Sgt A.Powell				
252 Sqn	Flt Lt A.D.Frecker/ Sgt T.Armstrong	Beaufighter Ic T5025	3 He 111s Damaged during shipping strike		1430-1900
252 Sqn	Sgt G.M.Nettleship/ Flt Sgt S.G.Deacon	Beaufighter Ic T5040			
252 Sqn	Flg Off C.R.McMills/ Sgt H.G.Bicknell	Beaufighter Ic T5110			
252 Sq	Plt Off E.R.Derick/ Plt Off M.J.McCann	Beaufighter Ic T4940 'B'			

British Casualties

47 Sqn	Beaufort DE110 collided with Bisley BA486 of 14 SAAF Sqn during shipping strike and crashed; Plt Off H.J.Davidson and three MiA
47 Sqn	Beaufort DW834 shot down by Flak during shipping strike near Tobruk
252 Sqn	Beaufighter T4940 'B' ditched on escort to Beauforts; Plt Off E.R.Derick/Plt Off M.J.McCann MiA
252 Sqn	Beaufighter T4987 'P' ditched on escort to Beauforts; Plt Off J.S.Adams/Sgt C.L.Barringer MiA
272 Sqn	Beaufighter 'E' damaged Cat I by MC.202 1245-1910; Sgt W.Russell/Sgt A.B.Wilson safe
15 SAAF Sqn	Bisley BA234 'P' shot down by Flak on shipping strike; Lt A.B.Groch and one PoW, one KiA
15 SAAF Sqn	Bisley BA368 'K' hit mast of tanker during attack and ditched; Lt E.C.Dustow and two KiA
15 SAAF Sqn	Bisley BA486 'Y' collided with Beaufort DE110 of 47 Sqn on shipping strike and crashed; Lt S.E.Leisegang and two KiA
38 Sqn	Wellington shot down by Flak during evening attack on convoy at Benghazi

US Claims

9th BS/1st PBG	gunners aboard B-17E '9 A', pilot 1/Lt J.J.Kramp	MC.200 Probable	off Tobruk	0800-

Italian Claims

92ª Sq, 8°Gr, 2°St CT	S.Ten C.Petrosellini	MC.200	Maryland	over sea	0900
78ª Sq, 13°Gr, 2°St CT	Serg Galileo Petti	MC.200	Liberator Damaged	over sea	1040
93ª Sq, 8°Gr, 2°St CT	S.Ten Alessandro Beretta	MC.200	Halifax	over sea	1105
93ª Sq, 8°Gr, 2°St CT	Ten Gioacchino Bissoli	MC.200	Halifax Probable	over sea	1105
93ª Sq, 8°Gr, 2°St CT	Serg Magg Ottorino Lancia	MC.200	Halifax Probable	over sea	1105
77ª Sq, 13°Gr, 2°St CT	Serg Luigi Boieri	MC.200	Stirling	70km N Ain el Gazala	1105-1200
77ª Sq, 13°Gr, 2°St CT	M.llo Fiore Mastropietro	MC.202	2 Beaufighters	150km N Ain el Gazala	1110-1205
77ª Sq, 13°Gr, 2°St CT	Serg Magg Rovero Abbarchi	MC.202	Boston	100km N Sidi Abeida	1405-1505
92ª Sq, 8°Gr, 2°St CT	Serg Silvio Moressi	MC.200	Boston	over sea	1425

Tuesday, 27 October 1942

Between 0250-0400 a raid was recorded, and was intercepted by 46 Squadron Beaufighters, Flg Off Davison shooting down a CR.42 near Burg el Arab.

British Claims

46 Sqn	Flg Off M.M.Davison / Sgt A.C.Willmott	Beaufighter If 'B'	CR.42	4-5m W Burg el Arab	0300-0415
73 Sqn	Flt Sgt R.D.Marsh	Hurricane IIc HV342	2 Ju 87s Damaged	Haneish	0430-0645
73 Sqn	Sgt D.R.Beard	Hurricane IIc HL972	Ju 88	25m W Alamein	2300-2359

Italian Casualties

208ª Sq, 101°Gr, 5°St Tuff	CR.42 failed to return from a night mission, M.llo Roberto Costantini PoW

Wednesday, 28 October 1942

Another P.108 of 274ª Squadriglia BGR flown by Ten Giuseppe Floridi on a reconnaissance mission over the western Mediterranean, force-landed in Algeria due to engine trouble. As before, the aircraft was destroyed by the crew, all six of whom were then interned by the Vichy French. During an interception patrol Sqn Ldr Read of 46 Squadron was attacked by a hostile aircraft and the Beaufighter was slightly damaged. He pursued the aircraft but it escaped. By now the fighting at El Alamein had drawn away most Axis aerial activity, and although the occasional intruder still appeared, the operations by the defensive wings were rapidly becoming quieter.

Italian Casualties

274ª Sq BGR	P.108 MM 22007 destroyed in force-landing in Algeria, pilot Ten Giuseppe Floridi, copilot Ten Gastone Sacchetto and four PoW

Oblt Iro Ilk, Kapitän of 2./LG 1, who was presented with the Ritterkreuz at Heraklion on 28 October.

Thursday, 29 October 1942

US Casualties

376th BG ?	C-47 shot down by Spitfire, Port Said, Capt Paul F.Roth and three KiA

Friday, 30 October 1942

The crew of a 203 Squadron Baltimore out on a coastal reconnaissance saw 35 Ju 52/3ms 65 miles north-east of Tobruk. The aircraft was then pursued for 30 minutes by escorting Bf 110s, two of these inflicting some damage on the fleeing machine. The gunners experienced similar problems to those of the bomber units operating the early model Baltimores when the rear defensive machine guns jammed after their first burst.

Five Beaufighters of 252 Squadron strafed El Adem airfield at 1830, crews reporting 12 Ju 52/3ms and two or three MC.202s on the ground there, six or eight of the transports with their engines running. Four were claimed destroyed, but two more were then spotted in the air after take-off and both were claimed shot down; five more were claimed damaged on the ground. Italian records noted that three Ju 52/3ms had been set on fire on the ground and that two pilots of 4° Stormo CT had been wounded during the attack; these were Ten Orlando Mandolini of 91ª Squadriglia and M.llo Salvatore Mechelli of 84ª Squadriglia. Lorries full of troops were then shot-up on the road 15 miles east of Tobruk, three of these being claimed destroyed. Two small supply ships of 500-600 tons escorted by an MTB were then seen 34 miles off Tobruk, and these were also attacked. Two of the Beaufighters from this eventful sortie landed safely, one landed on a road nearby and a fourth landed in Lake Edcu; the fifth had been badly hit and was short of fuel; it crashed north-west of Daman harbour after the crew had baled out.

Well to the east of the main action, one of 47 Squadron's elderly Wellesleys had just taken over patrol duty from a Hudson when the pilot spotted a periscope. In co-operation with nearby destroyers, he made the first drop for 235 Wing of three 274lb Torpex depth charges, just as the submarine was diving. A large oil patch was seen which it was thought might have been caused by the air attack, although it was considered very possible that this had not been the case. Later that night the U-559 – for such it was –

was forced to the surface by damage inflicted by the destroyers HMS *Pakenham*, *Petard*, *Hero*, *Dulverton* and *Hurworth*. It was then further damaged by gunfire and was subsequently inspected before being sunk. However, no conclusive proof was forthcoming that the first damage had indeed been caused by the aircraft.

Although the detached flight of 47 Squadron still operated Wellesleys with 201 Group, during September a new unit of this number had been formed at Shandur from elements of 39 and 42 Squadrons, equipped with Beauforts and commanded by Wg Cdr R.A.Sprague, DFC, previously an army co-operation pilot who had spent most of 1940 commanding 208 Squadron. Towards the end of September this new squadron despatched a detachment to Gianaclis, near Alexandria, to commence operations. Initially, attacks were made on small Axis vessels seeking to reach Tobruk.

British Claims

252 Sqn	Sgt J.M.Stephen/ Sgt S.R.Whear	Beaufighter Ic T5046	Ju 52/3m	W El Adem l.g.	1550-2036
252 Sqn	Plt Off R.S.Watson/ Sgt G.D.Hudson	Beaufighter VI T5110	Ju 52/3m	El Adem l.g.	1555-2225
252 Sqn	Sgt A.B.McKeown/ Sgt W.M.Driscoll	Beaufighter Ic X8068	Ju 52/3m Probable	El Adem l.g.	1555-2225
252 Sqn	Sgt D.R.Meldrum/ Sgt F.Hawthorne	Beaufighter Ic T5036	4 Ju 52/3ms	on the ground El Adem l.g.	1555-2225
			5 Ju 52/3ms Damaged	on ground El Adem l.g.	1555-2225

British Casualties

252 Sqn	Beaufighter T5046 damaged by Flak and abandoned N Edcu; Sgt J.M.Stephen

Italian Casualties

91ª Sq, 10° Gr, 4° St CT	Ten Orlando Mandolini wounded on ground by strafing
84ª Sq, 10° Gr, 4° St CT	M.llo Salvatore Mechelli wounded on ground by strafing

During this period 235 Wing's main duties had remained the provision of anti-submarine cover for shipping, but this had been joined by offensive anti-submarine patrolling in co-operation with destroyers. The wing was now controlling 38 and 458 Squadrons with Wellingtons, 15 SAAF Squadron with Bisleys, 162 Squadron with Wellingtons and Bisleys, 459 Squadron with Hudsons and 14 Squadrons with Marauders.

The last successes against Axis shipping by Malta's air forces prior to the victory at El Alamein occurred on the night of 28/29 October when torpedo-carrying Wellingtons attacked Italian Convoy J on its way from Taranto to Benghazi. This convoy (see also *Malta: The Spitfire Year, 1942*) comprised the 2,552-ton tanker *Luisiano*, carrying 1,460 tons of fuel, the motor vessel *Etiopia*, of 2,153 tons, carrying a cargo of aviation fuel, and an MTB. During the attack *Luisiano* was sunk and *Etiopia* was badly damaged and had to put into Navarino for immediate repairs. She later reached Tobruk where she would be bombed and set on fire on 6 November, the 341 tons of fuel still aboard being lost. Also on that latter date the 6,424-ton tanker *Portofino* was set on fire during an RAF attack on Benghazi (see also Chapter Eleven).

Sunday, 1 November 1942

Meanwhile during the night, two ASV Wellingtons of 221 Squadron with six torpedo Wellingtons of 38 Squadron and one bomb-carrier of 458 Squadron on the unit's first sortie with 247 Wing, attacked a convoy of one MV, one small MV and two destroyers north-west of Tobruk. One 38 Squadron crew got a hit on the larger vessel which was seen to blow up. Three Beauforts of 47 Squadron set off at dawn, spotting the smaller ship and a destroyer 25 miles to the north-west. One pilot got a direct hit on the MV which he believed was destroyed, the other two aircraft returning with their torpedoes still attached. These two attacks had sunk the 1,464-ton *Tripolino* which was carrying 410 tons of rations and 318 tons of ammunition, off Derna; moreover the Beaufort crew had sunk the German steamer *Ostia* (carrying 57 tons of rations and 52 tons of ammunition).

German Casualties

2.(F)/123	Ju 88D-1 WNr 430270 4U+EK MiA Alexandria; Uffz Alfred Kleinschmidt and three KiA

Monday, 2 November 1942

By night four of 221 Squadron's ASV Wellingtons located a convoy identified as two merchant vessels and one destroyer, accompanied by 13 smaller vessels. Five 38 Squadron aircraft and two of 458 Squadron were homed onto these ships, which were then illuminated by the ASV aircraft. Four bombers attacked, claiming two hits, while a torpedo-carrier targeted what was thought to be a cruiser without effect.

Two Baltimores of 203 Squadron co-operated with six 39 Squadron Beauforts and seven escorting Beaufighters on their second sortie of the day to attack the convoy of two MVs, estimated at 5,000 and 3,000 tons apiece, and two destroyers, which had earlier been attacked by the Wellingtons. The vessels were now six miles north-north-west of Tobruk, escorted by a reported two Bf 110s, two Ju 88s, two MC.202s and two MC.200s. The Beaufighters sought to chase off the air escort as the Beauforts attacked, hitting the larger vessel which poured forth a column of smoke up to 5,000ft. Crews also thought that they had possibly hit the smaller vessel as well. However, one Beaufort was seen to be shot down, apparently by Flak, the crew getting into their dinghy, and a second Beaufort and a Beaufighter failed to return. Two Baltimores then reconnoitred, confirming that the smaller vessel had been hit and was on fire.

The victims of this attack were actually an Italian naval auxiliary, the 1,976-ton *Zara*, which was sunk, and the 1,987-ton *Brioni*, which managed to enter harbour where she was then sunk by bombers; the size of both vessels had been considerably over-estimated by the torpedo-bomber crews. Both had been carrying cargoes of cased petrol and ammunition, but although *Brioni* was able to enter harbour at Tobruk, she was sunk by USAAF bombers before she could be unloaded. The defending fighters were mainly MC.200s of 77ª Squadriglia, the pilots of which reportedly prevented an attack by the Beaufighters, which, of course, had not been seeking to attack the ships, but solely to drive off these escorts. Ten Giorgio Savoia claimed one shot down, while another section of three MC.200s of 8° Gruppo, led by Cap Guglielmo Arrabito, took off at 0845 to relieve the previous patrol and they too engaged some Beaufighters. Serg Magg Filippo Baldin claimed one shot down and Arrabito one damaged. It would appear that the claims made represented the missing Beaufighter and Beauforts. Later in the morning also four CR.42s of 101° Gruppo took part in the escort: an aircraft identified as a lone Beaufighter was driven off by Serg Walter Banfi of 208ª Squadriglia. This was probably in fact one of the 203 Squadron Baltimores checking on the results of the attack.

This meant, however, that six ships had been sunk in five days, five by air-launched torpedoes and one by bombs. During this same period only two merchant vessels and five destroyers had managed to reach Tobruk unscathed, all carrying only small quantities of stores, including only about 500 tons of fuel.

British Claims					
272 Sqn	Sqn Ldr A.Watson/ Plt Off C.F.Cutting	Beaufighter Ic 'G'	Ju 88	60m N Tobruk	0630-1200

British Casualties	
272 Sqn	Beaufighter Ic T4880 'H'crash-landed; Plt Off A.J.Proctor/Plt Off E.A.C.Young ditched; picked up after eight days in dinghy
39 Sqn	Beaufort DD937 'R' shot down by fighters during strike off Tobruk; Flt Lt Grant and crew MiA
39 Sqn	Beaufort DD873 'H' shot down during shipping strike off Tobruk; Plt Off Hedley and crew MiA

German Claims		
I./LG 1	Ofw Otto Leupert	2 Beauforts

Italian Claims					
77ª Sq, 13°Gr, 2°St CT	Ten Giorgio Savoia	MC.200	Beaufighter	off Tobruk	0800-
82ª Sq, 13°Gr, 2°St CT	Serg Magg Filippo Baldin	MC.202	Beaufighter	120km N Tobruk	0845-1005
82ª Sq, 13°Gr, 2°St CT	Cap Guglielmo Arrabito	MC.202	Beaufighter Damaged	off Tobruk	0845-1005

Coupled with the losses inflicted on the Axis by the Royal Navy's submarines and surface warships, 44% of all cargoes despatched to North Africa during October had been squandered, 17 vessels with a displacement of 500 tons or more had been lost, the total amount of shipping sunk or destroyed of all classes amounting to 54,804 tons. This occasioned General Montgomery to signal 201 Group:

> "I would like to express my thanks for the way in which No 201 Group are assisting to make easier the task of the Eighth Army. Recent attacks carried out against enemy ships so vital to his effort were a wonderful achievement… I would be grateful if you would convey to those responsible our gratitude for operations carried out which must be epics against ships at sea."

As a consequence of these latest sinkings, and in response to ever more desperate pleas for fuel and supplies emanating from the Afrika Korps and its commander, Feldmarshall Kesselring now ordered the Luftwaffe to transport fuel to North Africa "day and night down to the last crew and the last aircraft". By midnight on 2 November the British were aware of this via Ultra intercepts and were able to conclude correctly that these losses – particularly of three tankers during the last few days – would seriously impair Rommel's ability to continue resisting Montgomery's offensive.

Tuesday, 3 November 1942

Five ASV Wellingtons found and directed eight torpedo-carriers of 38 Squadron, plus four bombers of 458 Squadron, to attack a south-bound convoy 110 miles north of Benghazi. A tanker, two merchant ships and several destroyers were seen and four bombing attacks made. These were concentrated on the tanker and the MV, but torpedoes hung-up on several aircraft on this occasion. One bomber pilot made seven attacks on destroyers, claiming three hits and two near misses; another released 11 bombs, but saw no results. The tanker was claimed to have been straddled by 11 bombs, but one 38 Squadron aircraft was lost. Following this attack, however, it suddenly went very quiet for the anti-shipping units. Events on the ground had overtaken matters.

British Casualties

38 Sqn	Wellington MiA

Wednesday, 4 November 1942

During a patrol over Tobruk, 1525-1620, Serg Galileo Petti of 78ª Squadriglia was attacked by Beaufighters and fired at one.

Friday, 6 November 1942

As the Axis retreat from Alamein began to gather momentum, a steady stream of movements westwards commenced for both WDAF and AHQ, RAF Egypt's units. First of the latter was 234 Wing which now arrived at Mersa Matruh, although it would be a few days until operations commenced from here. Available to the wing were 127, 335 and 889 Squadrons, all with Hurricanes, 257, 260, 274, 873 and 880 AMES, 31 and 42 WUs and 12 AAF. From here the main duty of these units would revolve around protection of coastal shipping which would soon be carrying supplies to the Cyrenaican ports as soon as these fell into Allied hands and were secured.

Following its period of considerable activity, particularly over the coastal areas, 272 Squadron now departed Edcu and its various forward bases for Malta where new duties awaited the unit. At this point 46 Squadron, so recently involved in adding ground attack to its night-fighting duties, came temporarily under the control of 201 Group to make good the departure of the coastal Beaufighter unit. 235 Wing with 47 Squadron Air Echelon, 459 Squadron and 13 (Hellenic) Squadron were all ordered to move up from St Jean to LG.39, close to LG.227; 821 Squadron moved from Dekheila to LG.21. Within a day 247 Wing also moved to LG.05 from Gianaclis, including 38 and 458 Squadrons, the Fleet Air Arm's 889 Squadron moving to Fayid from LG.20.

Amidst all these moves, the new 47 Squadron lost its new commanding officer when Wg Cdr Sprague was killed in an accident. A few days later the 47 Squadron Air Echelon was renamed 47 Squadron Wellesley Flight. Numbers of Beaufighters were despatched to Malta at this time, as were several Wellingtons. The demand for both types of aircraft by the units on the island was rising rapidly following the commencement of operations over northern Tunisia (see Volume 3).

Saturday, 7 November 1942

Italian Claims

82ª Sq, 13°Gr, 2°St CT	Serg Mario Turchetti	MC.202	Blenheim (Boston?)	Tobruk	0730

Sunday 8 November 1942

Italian Casualties

254ª Sq, 105°Gr AS	S.79 '254-6' failed to return, probably hit by AA, pilot Ten Antonio Poggi-Cavalletti, copilot M.llo Alberto Casano and three crew PoW

Monday, 9 November 1942

A Fiat G.12 of Nucleo Comunicazioni LATI, flown by Cap Felice Fenili, en route from Tobruk to Athens had the engines cut and was forced to ditch near Gaudo Island. The crew was rescued by German troops and the aircraft was tentatively towed by a landing craft to reach dry land but it sank as this was being attempted.

Italian Casualties

Nucleo Comunicazioni LATI	Fiat G.12 MM 60666 'I-FELI' ditched nr Gaudo island, pilot Cap Felice Fenili and all aboard safe

Sunday, 15 November 1942

British Casualties	
46 Sqn	4 Beaufighters detached to Malta, disappear en route. Two days later German Intelligence reported that fighters had shot down three Beaufighters near Bizerta. However, no claims by Luftwaffe units have been discovered and several of these crews appear again later. The aircraft and crews were:
46 Sqn	Beaufighter T5261 Flg Off J.A.White/Plt Off K.F.C.Inskip both KiA
46 Sqn	Beaufighter T4982 Flg Off R.Dundin/Flg Off T.R.Smith
46 Sqn	Beaufighter 4890 Plt Off G.A.Glibbvery/Sgt J.F.Roberts, both KiA
46 Sqn	Beaufighter X8007 Wg Cdr R.G.A.Reid/Plt Off W.H.Peasley
German Casualties	
III./ZG 26	Bf 110 3U+NT crashed west Crete; Uffz Erwin Seeliger, Uffz Johannes List, Gefr Kurt Enke KiA
Italian Casualties	
196ª Sq RM	Cant.Z.501 MM 35539 crashed in sea after take-off at Benghazi, pilot S.Ten Guido Gandolfini WiA and two WiA, two KiA
196ª Sq RM	Cant.Z.501 MM 35627 crashed in landing accident at Kitheyon (Greece), pilot Ten Piero Pinna and one of crew WiA, three safe

Monday, 16 November 1942

250 Wing scrambled a section of Hurricanes from 94 Squadron, vectoring the pilots onto a Ju 88 which was shot down into the sea; four survivors were rescued.

British Claims					
94 Sqn	Sgt W.G.Imrie	Hurricane IIc BP387 'J'	Ju 88	Damietta	1118-1205
94 Sqn	Sgt G.Grove	Hurricane IIc BP392			

British Casualties	
94 Sqn	Hurricane IIc BP392 shot down by Ju 88 gunner off Damietta; Sgt G.Grove MiA
German Casualties	
2.(F)/123	Ju 88D-1 WNr 430388 4U+FK MiA; Fw Friedrich Greiner WiA, two KiA, one PoW

Operation Stoneage

With the success of the Alamein battle and the Anglo-American landings in North-West Africa, the position of the Axis air forces along the Cyrenaican coast now looked far less secure and threatening than had been the case in August. Malta had received no major replenishment of stores, fuel or ammunition since that time, and the population were now close to starvation. Some small deliveries had been made, by individual fast vessels – *Parthian* and *Clyde* one each from Gibraltar, and two from Beirut by *Rorqal* during October, whilst at the start of November *Parthian* and *Clyde* made further trips with aviation fuel and torpedoes. Runs were also made by the fast minelayers *Manxman* and *Welshman* from Alexandria and Gibraltar respectively.

Much more was needed, but in the circumstances pertaining, to run a major convoy through from the west at this stage was not a possibility. It was decided therefore, that in the residual risk situation appertaining in the east, an attempt should be made from here. The main perceived threat remained the Italian Fleet, which was now even stronger than what remained of the Mediterranean Fleet. The Regia Marina could 'field' six battleships, two heavy cruisers and five light cruisers plus more than 20 destroyers.

Following the Torch landings the three Littorio-class battleships had withdrawn to Naples, but could still pose an enormous threat from there.

Available to escort a convoy, the Royal Navy could only offer two six-inch cruisers and three 5.25-inch vessels, plus seven Fleet and ten Hunt-class destroyers. This force could not begin to hold off the Italian Fleet for long by day, but the convoy could be timed to ensure that the first half of the journey (350 miles) could be undertaken by night. If the Italians sought to intercept before dark when the convoy was still off the Cyrenaican coast, heavy air attack from the Gambut airfield would have to be faced, while by next morning the ships would be within range of Malta's now-formidable air striking force. It was virtually a certainty that they would not approach at night given the Royal Navy's known superiority in night manoeuvre and radar. The possibility of success rested strongly with the air forces.

At this stage the Axis air forces, although still on the Cyrenaican airfields, were short of fuel, constantly on the move westwards, and facing serviceability problems. It was also hoped that 8th Army would have reached Tobruk by the time the ships sailed. Although in the event the airfields at Martuba were to be unusable because of heavy rain, those at Gazala proved to be adequate.

The Royal Navy and 201 Group set up a combined operations room at the latter's HQ and began planning. 201 Group had available for this operation three general reconnaissance squadrons, and three for anti-submarine patrol, the aircraft of one of which was equipped with ASV radar; there were also four torpedo-bomber squadrons – again one with ASV, and one Beaufighter squadron. AHQ, Egypt, and Desert Air Force could be relied upon to provide any short-range single-engined fighter support up to 40 miles west of Benghazi. From this point Malta would take over, additionally to support the striking force the USAAF B-24s at Gambut could be called upon.

Codenamed Stoneage, the convoy was organised in great secrecy, the four merchant ships being loaded at Port Sudan for security purposes. They were the British *Denbighshire*, US *Mormacmoon* and *Robin Locksley*, and the Dutch *Bantam*. They sailed up through the Canal, entering the Mediterranean late on 16 November. Under naval escort, with anti-submarine patrols being flown by 15 SAAF Squadron Bisleys, 459 Squadron Hudsons and Swordfish of 815 Squadron. Shore-based fighter cover was reinforced at dawn and dusk by 252 Squadron Beaufighters. Around midday, on the 18th, a small force of Ju 88s approached, but were driven off by Kittyhawks of 450 Squadron. Just as night drew near, the naval vessels were disengaging from close escort, torpedo-bombers approached and attacked both forces. The transports escaped damage, but the cruiser HMS *Arethusa* was hit forward and set on fire. She was ordered to head for Alexandria with an escort of two destroyers.

At dawn on 19 November the warships again closed on the convoy, Beaufighters and Spitfires from Malta arriving to give continuous cover. Baltimores of 203 Squadron swept ahead to spot any Italian sorties, which in the event did not appear. Within 80 miles of Malta the warships withdrew to Alexandria, and by 0300 on 20 November all vessels were safely docked in Malta's Grand Harbour. Here they were unloaded with record speed.

Tuesday, 17 November 1942

Albacores torpedoed and damaged the tanker *Giulio Giordani* (10,534 tons).

Wednesday, 18 November 1942

During the day the new commanding officer of 47 Squadron, Wg Cdr Sprague, was killed when he crashed whilst low-flying in a Beaufort.

British Casualties	
252 Sqn	Beaufighter Ic T5212 on escort to naval forces, attacked and damaged by Ju 88, crash-landed at base 1845; Plt Off F.H.Foyston/Sgt V.A.Madeley safe
47 Sqn	Beaufort DE118 'S' crashed while low-flying; Wg Cdr R.A. Sprague, DFC, KiFA

Thursday, 19 November 1942

243 Wing now moved forward to El Adem, but the unit's Hurricane squadrons were not to follow the 8th Army advance further at this time. The Wing Leader, John Darwen, was now posted to lead 244 Wing on Spitfires, his place being taken by Wg Cdr H.F. 'Billy' Burton, DFC, once a protégé of Douglas Bader in Fighter Command; he was now a highly-experienced fighter pilot on his second operational tour.

Saturday, 21 November 1942
By night the 4,537-ton *D'Annunzio* was torpedoed and damaged by Wellingtons.

Italian Casualties	
148ª Sq RM	Cant.Z.506 MM 45450 from Pisida failed to reach Stagnoni, pilot Serg Magg Antonio Raciti and crew MiA. All Squadriglia documents lost
182ª Sq RM	Cant.Z.501 MM 35295, crashed in taking off from Pisida, pilot Ten Renato Di Lorenzo, copilot Serg Magg Armando Spinetti and crew WiA
224ª Sq, 57°Gr, 18° St T	S.81 MM 20193 force-landed near Castel Benito, damaged, crew safe

Tuesday, 24 November 1942
The Algerian ports were under severe bombing attack at this time, which was proving very difficult to counter as the Beaufighters sent there from the UK had made the flight without their AI radar installed for security reasons in case any of the aircraft should be obliged to land in mainland Europe on the way. The sets were due to arrive imminently. To bridge the gap, therefore, six experienced crews of B Flight, 89 Squadron, were to fly their fully equipped aircraft to Algiers for this purpose. Meanwhile, the remains of the flight were disbanded for the time being and transferred to A Flight.

The chosen crews were:

Sqn Ldr C.W.Passy/Sgt G.H.Ward
Flg Off A.M.Spurgin/Flt Sgt D.A.Norris
Flt Lt E.J.Etherton/Sgt N.L.Gibbs
Flt Lt H.E.Mitchell/Sgt J.G.Trebell
Sgt P.T.Parks/Sgt R.N.Rumbold
Sgt P.F.Kingsnorth/Wt Off R.N.Turnbull
(details of the operations of this detachment will be included in Volume 3)

Wednesday, 25 November 1942

British Casualties	
117 Sqn	Lodestar EW945 missing on transport flight

Italian Casualties	
12ª Sq APC	Ca 309 MM 12378 ditched after combat, one crew WiA

Thursday, 26 November 1942
Many searches were still being made for Axis shipping seeking to reach Tripoli, but elsewhere in the eastern Mediterranean there was very little action. Typically on this date four 221 Squadron ASV Wellingtons and five torpedo Wellingtons of 38 Squadron searched the Gulf of Sidra, but without results. The specialist 162 Squadron also undertook some searches for raiders in this area, while 252 Squadron covered naval forces. From Castel Benito an MC.200 of 13° Gruppo was scrambled to intercept intruders, Serg Mario Turchetti claiming two Beaufighters shot down 50 miles north-east of Tripoli.

Italian Claims				
82ª Sq, 13°Gr, 2°St CT	Serg Mario Turchetti MC.202	2 Beaufighters	80km NE Tripoli	1030-1130

Saturday, 28 November 1942
459 Squadron was now reunited at Gianaclis from where only convoy escort sorties would be flown, many of them by night. The unit would be moved forward to Gambut on 18 December, but without any immediate change in duties.

Italian Casualties	
unidentified units	2 Cant.Z.506s damaged by strafing at Pisida

Sunday, 29 November 1942

Italian Casualties	
unidentified unit	Cant.Z.506 MM 45447 destroyed by strafing at Pisida, another ditched and a third damaged

Monday, 30 November 1942

By the end of the month the Beaufighters of 252 Squadron were operating from Berca Satellite strafing the retreating Axis columns. At Daba 889 Squadron was now up to a strength of 12 Hurricane IIcs, plus a pair of retained Fulmars. At this stage, however, 33, 80, 127, 208, 213, 238, 274 and 335 Squadrons (all Hurricanes) were now all on either training or patrol duties and were not to remain a part of WDAF or to follow 8th Army's further advance.

At this stage 212 Group was formed under AHQ, Egypt, with Grp Capt A.J.Rankin, OBE, AFC, taking over from Grp Capt H.A.Fenton, DFC, who had recently been promoted and posted in from 243 Wing. The new group was to control the protection of shipping along the Cyrenaican coast, air defence of the area, and administration thereof. One of the first units to move was 89 Squadron which next day sent forward a detachment to Gambut. Three days later another detachment would move further westwards to Bu Amud.

Wednesday, 2 December 1942

Flt Lt Joyce, late of 73 Squadron but now with 243 Wing Training Flight, shot down a Ju 88 in flames eight miles east of Martuba. Two such aircraft were lost by the Luftwaffe during the night. One of these was on a special mission to Tobruk with Oberstlt Franz von Benda, Kommodore of LG 1 aboard.

British Claims				
243 Wg Training Flt	Flt Lt E.L.Joyce	Hurricane I	Ju 88	Sidi Haneish area
British Casualties				
46 Sqn	Beaufighter X7638 lost			
German Casualties				
3./LG 1	Ju 88A-4 WNr 140332 L1+DL crash-landed near Derna due to fighter attack; Lt Benno Farkac and 3 PoWs			
Stab/LG 1	Ju 88-4 WNr 8610 L1+BA, shot down by AA in Tobruk area, Hptm Erwin Sy, Obstlt Franz von Benda and two MiA			

Friday, 4 December 1942

Directed by 252 Wing, a pair of Hurricanes of 417 Squadron were vectored onto a lone reconnaissance Ju 88 over Alexandria, which the two pilots claimed to have damaged. Further west a claim for damage to another Ju 88 was submitted by pilots of 274 Squadron. Two days later 252 Wing was enlarged to become a new 219 Group, taking over the fighter defence of Egypt. In this role it remained at the base so long the home of 252 Wing at Seagull Camp, Mex. The unit would be able, initially, to call on the services of 94, 127 and 889 Squadrons.

Meanwhile at dusk two S.79 torpedo-bombers of 104° Gruppo took off from Rhodes to attack a British naval convoy. The aircraft flown by Ten Guglielmo Michelotti failed to return. The day also saw 89 Squadron set up a detachment at Gambut to bring forward its night fighters.

British Claims					
417 Sqn	Wt Off H.C.Conn	Hurricane IIc HL843 'C'	Ju 88 Damaged	50m from Alexandria Bar	1043
417 Sqn	Flt Lt W.H.Pentland	Hurricane IIc BP590 'R'			
German Casualties					
9./KG 76	Ju 88A-4 WNr 144 079 F1+ET FTR from raid on Benghazi, presumed shot down; Obw Balder Kretschmann and 3 MiA				
Italian Casualties					
253ª Sq, 104°Gr Aut AS	S.79 '253-5' failed to return, pilot Ten Guglielmo Michelotti, copilot Ten Mario Faggian and crew MiA; the bodies of three crew members were recovered on 11 December on a shore at Cape Sidero (Crete)				

Saturday, 5 December 1942

Operation Portcullis

Two weeks after the Stoneage convoy to Malta, a second sailing under the name Portcullis took place. This time five cargo ships and a tanker arrived from the eastern basin without any interference from the Axis. Between them, these two convoys had brought to the island some 56,000 tons of cargo. Although there were further requirements which would be fulfilled as merchant tonnage allowed in the weeks to come, the siege really was to all intents and purposes over, leaving Malta as an increasingly strong base for Allied operations. Following Portcullis came the arrival of pairs of vessels on 11, 13 and 21 December and 2 January, including two tankers. These were achieved by arranging for the vessels to sail with one of the main supply convoys heading for Benghazi, breaking off with a local escort when approaching Malta. This methodology proved a great success and was also economical in the use of warship escorts and air cover.

Two crews of 194ª Squadriglia, 90° Gruppo, were ordered to undertake reconnaissances over the Middle East. The first Cant.Z.1007bis, flown by S.Ten Pasquale Sorrentino, carried out the sortie and landed back at Maritza at 1500. The second, flown by Ten Medardo Vincenzi, took off from Gadurra at 1035 but failed to return.

Italian Casualties

194ª Sq, 90°Gr, 30°St BT	Cant.Z.1007bis MM 23755 failed to return, 1035-, pilot Ten Medardo Vincenzi, copilot M.llo Erasmo Zamparutti, observer T.V. Arrigo Flamini and three MiA

Sunday, 6 December 1942

221 Squadron sent out three ASV Wellingtons to search for shipping off Tripoli, but nothing was seen; one Wellington failed to return. Eight Beaufighters of 252 Squadron undertook a reconnaissance and strafe in the Sollum-Sirte area, some vehicles being shot-up. Two aircraft strafed Tmimi airfield soon after midday, but both failed to return; that flown by Sqn Ldr A.D.Frecker appears to have been shot down by an Italian fighter.

At 1205 three MC.200s of 93ª Squadriglia, 8° Gruppo, operating from Tauorga, had bounced Beaufighters which were seen strafing an Italian armoured column, and Ten Bissoli (first claim on 11 June 1940) claimed one shot down in flames, which was later inspected by ground personnel. A claim for a second as a probable was made by Serg Plodari, but Bissoli's aircraft was hit by return fire, and he landed at Sirte. This second victim was probably the aircraft flown by the British unit's commanding officer, Wg Cdr Peter Bragg, who was lost with his navigator.

Flt Lt A.D.Frecker and his navigator, Plt Off T.Armstrong, were shot down on 6 December and crash-landed their 252 Squadron Beaufighter. They survived and evaded capture, being picked up safely by a British patrol.

Sqn Ldr Frecker crash-landed his Beaufighter, the three aboard then commencing the walk back to Allied lines. On the seventh day they encountered Senussi Arabs who provided them with food and shelter for eight days until they were picked up by a patrol of the 1st King's Own Dragoon Guards and transported back to base.

British Casualties

221 Sqn	Wellington VIII HK734 'J' FTR from patrol after radio message at 0427; Flt Sgt H.J.R.Walsh and crew MiA
252 Sqn	Beaufighter Ic T5045 FTR from strafing sortie; Sqn Ldr A.D.Frecker/Plt Off T.Armstrong crash-landed; walked to safety
252 Sqn	Beaufighter Ic T5137 strafing Agheila-Sirte road, seen to ditch in sea 3m off coast; Wg Cdr P.H.Bragg/Flg Off E.G.Nichols MiA

Italian Claims

93ª Sq, 8°Gr, 2°St CT	Ten Gioacchino Bissoli	MC.200	Beaufighter	over Via Balbia	1205
93ª Sq, 8°Gr, 2°St CT	Serg Mario Plodari	MC.200	Beaufighter probable	over Via Balbia	1205

Italian Casualties

93ª Sq, 8°Gr, 2°St CT	MC.200 MM 6695 belly-landed near Nofilia because of engine failure, Serg Nino Randich safe
93ª Sq, 8°Gr, 2°St CT	MC.200 hit in oil radiator, landed at Sirte, Ten Gioacchino Bissoli safe
94ª Sq, 8°Gr, 2°St CT	MC.200 MM 8806 damaged in landing at Tauorga, Ten Bruno Cartosio safe

Tuesday, 8 December 1942

RAF fighters were active over a convoy codenamed Pocket throughout the day, Beaufighters of 46 Squadron and six of 252 Squadron taking part. A Ju 88 was engaged early in the morning, Plt Off Perinchief claiming to have shot this down. Somewhat later in the morning Sgt McAll of 238 Squadron drove off another Ju 88 which he claimed to have damaged as it attempted to attack the ships, and two 252 Squadron Beaufighters also encountered Ju 88s. During this engagement one Beaufighter was shot down and a second damaged, crash-landing at base. The pilot of this latter aircraft, Sgt Kernaghan, claimed to have shot down one of the intruders. Finally, during the early afternoon, Flg Off McMills of 252 Squadron claimed damage to two more of the German bombers.

Obfw Herbert Isachsen on his return from Benghazi on 7 December in Ju 88A-4 L1+DK.

British Claims

46 Sqn	Plt Off W.H.Perinchief	Beaufighter If 'K'	Ju 88	convoy patrol	0615-1130
238 Sqn	Sgt C.T.McAll	Hurricane IIc HV549 'C'	Ju 88 Damaged	convoy patrol	0820-1130
252 Sqn	Sgt S.J.Kernaghan/ Sgt A.Powell	Beaufighter VIf EL270 'R'	Ju 88	escort convoy 'Pocket'	0825-1125
252 Sqn	Flg Off C.R.McMills	Beaufighter VIf T5209	2 Ju 88s Damaged	over convoy	1245-1550

British Casualties

252 Sqn	Beaufighter shot down; Plt Off R.S.Watson/Sgt G.D.Hudson MiA
252 Sqn	Beaufighter EL270 'R' crash-landed at base after combat over convoy with Ju 88s; Sgt S.J.Kernaghan/Sgt A.Powell safe

German Casualties

9./KG 76	Ju 88A-4 WNr 142 251 F1+CT shot down by Beaufighters, crashed in sea 70 miles NW Benghazi; Stfw Willi Fröhlich and 3 MiA
5./LG 1	Ju 88-4 WNr 141038 damaged 20% by Hurricane 10m off Benghazi; Hptm Karl-Heinz Schomann and one WiA

Wednesday, 9 December 1942

212 Group now moved from Gazala to Benghazi. Apart from providing control for the Hurricanes of 73 Squadron, the group was now operating:

15 Sector	Bu Amud	80 Squadron
16 Sector	Martuba	213, 238, 274 Squadrons
17 Sector	Benina	33 Squadron

Far away at Rhodes the Regia Aeronautica scrambled two CR.42s to intercept enemy fighters, but met nothing. On landing the CR.42 flown by S.Ten Marson crashed, killing the pilot.

British Casualties

238 Sqn	Hurricane IIs HL840 and HL885 collided on night take-off at Martuba
459 Sqn	Hudson III V8994 crashed in circuit at Gambut
15 SAAF Sqn	Bisley BA478 crashed while force-landing SW Maryut

Italian Casualties

395ª Sq, 154° Gr Aut CT CR.42 crashed to ground, S.Ten Giuseppe Marson KiA

Thursday, 10 December 1942

British Casualties

46 Sqn	Beaufighter on convoy escort FTR

Friday-Saturday, 11/12 December 1942

British Casualties

38 Sqn	Wellington HF881 'U' FTR from minelaying sortie to Tripoli; Sgt S.A.Croll and crew MiA

Saturday, 12 December 1942

During the day a section of three Spitfires from 417 Squadron moved up to Benina; Spitfires of 1 SAAF Squadron were scrambled to intercept some Ju 88s, but arrived only to see one shot down by AA fire. That night Flg Off Shipard, one of the 89 Squadron night fighters on detachment at Gambut, claimed two Ju 88s shot down over Tripoli.

British Claims

89 Sqn	Flg Off M.C.Shipard/ Flt Sgt Oxby	Beaufighter VIf X8009 'S'	Ju 88	NNW Tobruk	1815-1930
89 Sqn	Flg Off M.C.Shipard/ Flt Sgt Oxby	Beaufighter VIf X8009 'S'	Ju 88	SE Tobruk	1815-1930

German Casualties

7./KG 76	Ju 88A-4 WNr 140 363 F1+ER shot down by Beaufighter, crashed 30m SSE Agedabia; Lt Waldemar Schmitt and 3 MiA

Sunday, 13 December 1942

Whilst patrolling three miles west of Benghazi, Flt Sgt Logan of 73 Squadron spotted a Ju 88 and dived on this, closing to 1,000 feet as it entered cloud. He fired a five-second burst as it disappeared, and a report was subsequently received that an enemy aircraft had crashed at approximately the right time and place, his claim therefore being confirmed for an aircraft shot down.

British Claims

73 Sqn	Flt Sgt D.M.Logan	Hurricane IIc HV441	Ju 88	3m W Benghazi	1940

Monday, 14 December 1942

Eight Wellingtons of 38 Squadron took off in the evening to lay mines in Tripoli harbour while two of 458 Squadron searched for shipping. One of the former unit's aircraft, flown by the commanding officer, Wg Cdr Pratt, failed to return.

British Casualties

38 Sqn	Wellington VIII HF913 'R' off 1915 on shipping strike W Tripoli. Message at 0115 but FTR; Wg Cdr C.V.J.Pratt, DSO, and three MiA; one body washed ashore 26 March 1943
203 Sqn	Baltimore I AG721 FTR from anti-shipping patrol 120m NW Alexandria; Flg Off M.G.Cowan and three KiA

Tuesday, 15 December 1942

212 Group reported that although many convoys had been escorted recently, not one ship had been lost to hostile air attack during this period.

British Casualties

252 Sqn	Beaufighter X7828 lost

Wednesday-Thursday, 16/17 December 1942

Benghazi was attacked by bombers, Flt Sgt Beard of 73 Squadron claiming one Ju 88 shot down. He reported:

> "I was returning from patrol at about 1930 when I saw heavy ack-ack bursting over Benghazi. I returned to target area to investigate and called Zig Zag and told him where I was. By this time the barrage was intense. I was at 3,000 feet approx, on the edge of the barrage NE of target when Ju 88 turning out to sea some 20 yds in front of us. I fired immediately and hit the e/a in the fuselage and port engine. He dived towards the barrage and I followed him as he neared the sea. I followed him through it at 1,000 feet but was not hit. His engine began to glow and the fuselage caught fire. The aircraft hit the sea and burnt on the water for about five minutes. I claim this e/a as destroyed. Confirmed by Flg Off Davis."

While the main night defence of Egypt rested in the hands of Beaufighters, the night-flying Hurricanes of 73 Squadron also protected the area in the immediate vicinity of the 8th Army's positions and over the captured ports. During the night of 16/17 December Flt Sgt D.R.Beard (seen here as a warrant officer) claimed a Ju 88 shot down over Benghazi.

British Claims

73 Sqn	Flt Sgt Beard	Hurricane IIc	Ju 88	over Benghazi

British Casualties

14 Sqn	Marauder FK367 shot down during sea sweep 15m off Benghazi by Spitfires in error

German Casualties

4./LG 1	Ju 88A-4 WNr 140263 L1+BM shot down by Hurricane 4m W Benghazi harbour; Uffz Eckert Baumann and three MiA

German Casualties

10./KG 54	He 111H-3 WNr 3204 B3+OX crashed in sea 100m NNW Tripoli - ? combat; Lt Konrad Fritz and 3 KiA

Thursday-Friday, 17/18 December 1942

In 89 Squadron Flt Lt Edwards now led the unit's Bu Amud detachment on to Benina.

British Claims

89 Sqn	Sgt C.C.Webb/ Sgt J.V.Mather	Beaufighter If X7776 'M'	Ju 88	1910-2025

German Casualties

III./KG 26	Ju 88A-4 WNr 140 432 1T+AD shot down by night fighter, crashed in sea N Benghazi; Maj Horst Kayser, Oblt Gerhard Höland and two MiA
8./KG 76	Ju 88A-14 WNr 144 259 F1+CB missing from flight to Castel Benito, presumed shot down; Uffz Ottmar Schuler and 3 MiA

Saturday, 19 December 1942

Four Beaufighters of 46 Squadron provided escort for a convoy, as four more took off at 0720 on a reconnaissance along the Tripolitanian coast. Four F-Boats were seen and attacked, hits being claimed, but one Beaufighter was damaged by Flak from the vessels. Others were foiled in their attacks by the accurate Flak and by the arrival of three-five Bf 109s from I./JG 77 which shot down Plt Off Roe's aircraft into the sea where it sank at once. A simultaneous attack on other F-Boats was made by four more Beaufighters of 252 Squadron. Targets on the ground were strafed but the Bf 109s from I./JG 77 then attacked, shooting down Plt Off Roe's aircraft into the sea. One of the other pilots managed to get a shot at the attackers, claiming one Messerschmitt probably shot down. Two claims were submitted by the German unit. Four pilots of 97ª Squadriglia of 9° Gruppo also took part in the combat, claiming a Beaufighter shot down, shared among them.

British Claims

46 Sqn	Plt Off Banbury	Beaufighter If 'O'	Bf 109 Probable	Tripolitanian coast	0720-1150

British Casualties

46 Sqn	Beaufighter shot down in sea; Plt Off Roe KiA
46 Sqn	Beaufighter damaged by Flak

German Claims

Stab I./JG 77	Obfw Kurt Niederhagen	Beaufighter	1108
1./JG 77	Oblt Siegfried Freytag	Beaufighter	

Italian Claims

97ª Sq, 9° Gr, 4° St CT	4 pilots	MC.202s	Beaufighter	Bir Dufan area

Sunday, 20 December 1942

219 Group scrambled two Spitfires of 94 Squadron to intercept a Ju 88 which was caught 55 miles north of Port Said at 23,500 feet. Both pilots got hits on the aircraft which dived steeply into the sea; there were no survivors. At 1035 another intruder appeared, but this escaped the attentions of two Hurricanes of 417 Squadron. A Marauder of 14 Squadron undertaking an offensive reconnaissance off the Tunisian coast was attacked by two Ju 88s and a Bf 110, but the crew managed to claim one of each type shot down, although the rear gunner was wounded during the engagement. Five more of this unit's aircraft laid eight mines off La Goulette, but lost one of their number.

At 243 Wing Wg Cdr Burton was posted to lead 239 Wing of Kittyhawks with WDAF. Sqn Ldr H.A.Bartlett took temporary leadership of the wing for the time being, although it was to be quite a long time before a replacement for Burton arrived.

British Claims

94 Sqn	Flg Off M.J.Rowland	Spitfire Vc BR586	Ju 88	NW Port Said	1032-1155
94 Sqn	Flt Lt R.Webb	Spitfire V BR487			
14 Sqn	turret gunner in Marauder		Bf 110	off Tunisian coast	
14 Sqn	rear gunner in Marauder		Ju 88	off Tunisian coast	

British Casualties

14 Sqn	Marauder FK366 MiA from mine laying off La Goulette, Tunis; Flt Lt J.T.Willis PoW, five KiA
14 Sqn	Marauder damaged and rear gunner WiA in combat with German aircraft off Tunisian coast

German Casualties

2.(F)/123	Ju 88D-1 WNr 430273 4U+KK MiA Port Said; Uffz Hans Zweigert, Lt Hans Schulze and one KiA, one PoW

Monday, 21 December 1942

Flt Lt Thompson of 73 Squadron was on patrol at 5,000 feet to the south-west of Benghazi when he saw a Ju 88 beneath him, over the sea. He attacked, firing two bursts which sent it crashing into the water. This was confirmed by the crew of an 89 Squadron Beaufighter, operating close by. This latter unit was now flying from Benina.

British Claims

73 Sqn	Flt Lt A.R.F.Thompson	Hurricane IIc HL852	Ju 88 Probable		
89 Sqn	Flt Lt H.G.Edwards/ Wt Off Phillipson	Beaufighter If X8022	Ju 88		2150
89 Sqn	Flt Sgt H.F.W.Shead/ Flt Sgt Curtis	Beaufighter If X7769	Ju 88 Probable	N Benghazi	2115
89 Sqn	Flt Sgt H.F.W.Shead/ Flt Sgt Curtis	Beaufighter If X7769	Ju 88		2215
89 Sqn	Flt Sgt H.F.W.Shead/ Flt Sgt Curtis	Beaufighter If X7769	He 111		2230

German Casualties

6./LG 1	Ju 88A-4 WNr 140245 L1+XP shot down by Hurricane Benghazi harbour; Obfw Johannes Biela and three PoW
6./KG 100	He 111H-14 WNr 7948 6N+DN damaged 10% by AA N Benghazi; Lt Günther Barrett and one WiA

Wednesday, 30 December 1942

Three He 111 crews from 4./KG 100 attacked Marble Arch airfield during the night of 29/30th, taking off at 0028 on 30th. Between 0400-0410 24 SD 50, 252 SD 2 and 16 LC 50 bombs were released on aircraft parked on the ground, but heavy AA fire of all calibres was encountered and one bomber was shot down. It appears that this may also have been attacked by an 89 Squadron Beaufighter, the crew of which claimed damage to such an aircraft at this time.

British Claims

89 Sqn	Flg Off Reeves/ Wt Off O'Leary	Beaufighter X8022	He 111 Damaged	Benina	0415+

German Casualties

4./KG 100	He 111H-14 WNr 7925 6N+AN shot down (reportedly by AA) over Arco Philaenorum (Marble Arch) airfield and crashed in the desert; Uffz Siegfried Zirpel and 3 MiA

Friday, 1 January 1943

The month was to see much movement and change as 8th Army moved closer to Tripoli, bringing aerial operations nearer to those being undertaken from Malta. 219 Group noted that it now had control of 6, 46, 238, 335 and 451 Squadrons. From Berka airfield the Wellingtons of 221 and 458 Squadron (a detachment only of the latter) moved to Malta for torpedo-dropping and other anti-shipping activities, whereas at Edcu 603 Squadron, still with no aircraft or aircrews, at last began a return to full status with the arrival of some Beaufighters and their crews from the United Kingdom. At Shandur by the start of the month 7 SAAF Squadron had been brought back to a strength of eight Hurricane IIcs and eight Mark IIds. Another South African fighter unit, 3 SAAF Squadron, which had served since 1940 in East Africa (see *Dust Clouds in the Middle East*) now arrived in Egypt from Ethiopia.

When practicing anti-submarine searches with Hudsons and Bisleys, a Sunderland of 230 Squadron crashed into the sea with the loss of the complete crew; the cause was not ascertained.

British Casualties

230 Sqn	Sunderland crashed into the sea; crew KiFA

Successful Beaufighter personnel of 89 Squadron with what appears to be a captured German Kübelwagen. Flg Off E.N.Reeves (left) and Wt Off A.A.O'Leary claimed an He 111 damaged over Tripoli during the night of 29/30 December, having already claimed six confirmed victories over Axis bombers while operating from Malta during the summer. On the right is Flg Off Mervyn Shipard who had also done well over Malta but had since shot down two Ju 88s in the Tobruk area during the night of 12/13 December to raise his total to nine. Between them is Flt Sgt Douggie Oxby, Shipard's radar operator. Oxby would continue to achieve great success, ending the war as the RAF's most successful airborne radar operator.

Saturday, 2 January 1943

212 Group at Bu Amud vectored an 89 Squadron Beaufighter onto an intruder 110 miles north. Flt Sgt Peters attacked the Ju 88 at extreme range, but the cannons in his aircraft then jammed and he was able to attack only with his machine guns. He believed that his fire had killed the rear gunner, but the aircraft then got away in cloud.

British Claims

89 Sqn	Flt Sgt R.G.Peters/ Flt Sgt Halliday	Beaufighter X8101	Ju 88 Damaged	Bu Amud	0900

Sunday, 3 January 1943

At 0905 two torpedo-carrying Marauders from 14 Squadron set off on an offensive reconnaissance from Shallufa over the Aegean Sea. At 1415 five ships were seen off the Aghios Georgios Islands which appeared to be a scattered convoy with three twin-engined aircraft overhead, thought to be Ca.310s or He 111s; these were reported also to be accompanied by an autogiro. The Marauders headed in together to attack a large vessel when the leader broke away, apparently to attack two other vessels to the north. This aircraft was last seen being pursued by two twin-engined aircraft which failed to catch it. However,

An Arado Ar 196A floatplane, 7R+BK of 2./SAGr 125 of the type that shot down a 14 Squadron Marauder on 3 January 1943 is moored in a Cretan harbour. For a short period this unit became a part of III./KG 100.

the leader then sent back a message that he was force-landing south of Crete. It appears that he had actually been shot down by an Ar 196 floatplane.

British Casualties

14 Sqn	Marauder FK375 MiA from attack on convoy off Aghios Georgios Island; Capt B.W.Young and crew

German Claims

III./KG 100	B-26	off Crete	1215

Thursday, 7 January 1943

The 11,718-ton Italian vessel *Virgilio* was damaged by an air-laid magnetic mine at Tripoli which had been dropped by a 38 Squadron Wellington during December.

British Claims

89 Sqn	Flg Off M.C.Shipard/ Flt Sgt Oxby	Beaufighter VIf X8009 'S'	2 He 111s Damaged	Bu Amud	1915

Friday, 8 January 1943

Over Libya the Benina detachment of 89 Squadron saw considerable action, three He 111s and a Ju 88 being claimed shot down. The first of these, an aircraft of I./LG 1, fell to the north of Tobruk where the pilot was captured. He proved to be Obfw Isachsen, a recipient of the Ritterkreuz.

British Claims

89 Sqn	Flg Off M.C.Shipard/ Flt Sgt Oxby + Sgt Hancock	Beaufighter VI X7844 'L'	Ju 88	N Tobruk	1823
89 Sqn	Flg Off M.C.Shipard/ Flt Sgt Oxby + Sgt Hancock	Beaufighter VI X7844 'L'	He 111		1832
89 Sqn	Flt Sgt H.F.W.Shead/ Flt Sgt Curtis	Beaufighter X7769	He 111 in flames		2150
89 Sqn	Flg Off Reeves/ Wt Off O'Leary	Beaufighter X8166	He 111 in flames		2200

German Casualties

2./LG 1	Ju 88A-4 WNr 140219 L1+RK shot down by night fighter nr Tobruk; Obfw Herbert Isachsen RK and three, PoW
6./KG 100	He 111H-14 WNr 79949 6N+DP shot down in flames during Benghazi raid; Lt Gunther Barett and three MiA

Italian Casualties

60ª Sq, 33°Gr, 9°St BT	Cant.Z.1007bis shot down by Beaufighter, pilot Ten Aldemaro Valeriani and one crew KiA, copilot S.Ten Mario Fontana and two PoW

Obfw Herbert Isachsen, a Ritterkreuzträger of LG 1, was shot down and killed in Ju 88A-4 L1+RK on 8 January 1943.

Saturday, 9 January 1943

In Egypt 417 Squadron now received six Spitfire Vbs and four Mk Vcs.

Sunday, 10 January 1943

Ten Beaufighters (six of 46 Squadron and four of 252 Squadron) provided cover for convoy Survey during the day. Two of 46 Squadron arrived over their charges at 1535. A single He 111 was spotted and attacked by both pilots who claimed to have inflicted damage before their quarry escaped in cloud. One Beaufighter was hit in the starboard engine by return fire. At this stage a detachment of eight Beaufighters led by Sqn Ldr C.G.Clegg left Egypt for India where it was to form the nucleus for a new 176 Squadron for the night defence of Calcutta. A further detachment including Flt Lt Lovell and Flg Offs Kinmonth and Reeves and their radar operators moved to Bersis.

British Claims

46 Sqn	Plt Off D.Crerar	Beaufighter If 'E'	He 111 Damaged	escort convoy 'Survey'	1535-1930
46 Sqn	Flt Lt A.W.Cuddie	Beaufighter If 'P'			

British Casualties

46 Sqn	Beaufighter damaged in starboard engine by return fire from He 111

Monday, 11 January 1943

Five Wellingtons of 38 Squadron dropped 1,000lb bombs on Homs, Tanagra and Tripoli. One of the bombers failed to return. A Beaufort crew from 39 Squadron on an anti-submarine patrol ahead of a convoy 136 miles south-east of Malta, located and crippled with depth charges, a large Italian supply-carrying submarine bound for Italy from North Africa.

British Casualties

38 Sqn	Wellington crashed nr El Abiod; pilot and one KiA, rest of crew injured
	Baltimore AG742 MiA from reconnaissance over Albania ?? Plt Off J.A.Frazer of 69 Squadron, listed as Spitfire

German Casualties

2.(F)/123	Ju 88D-1 WNr 1087 crashed W Alexandria, cause unknown; Fw Rudolf Grossmayer and 3 KiA

Tuesday, 12 January 1943

73 Squadron now departed 243 Wing to be administered by the mainly-reconnaissance 285 Wing.

Friday, 15 January 1943

243 Wing finally got a new commanding officer in the person of Wg Cdr G.D.Garvin. A new squadron leader flying also arrived, Sqn Ldr R.Webb from 94 Squadron (and previously 103 MU). Four days later this unit would move from Nofilia to Tamet West. All Beaufighters of 46 Squadron flew back from

Beaufort Ia DW830 'TY' of 47 Squadron photographed either at Shandur or Misurata during the early spring of 1943.

Benghazi to rejoin the rest of the unit at Edcu.

British Casualties

47 Sqn	Beaufort Ia DD999 'K' FTR from anti-submarine patrol over convoy nr Benghazi; Plt Off F.J.Pile and crew MiA

German Casualties

9./KG 26	Ju 88A-4 1T+FT FTR from raid over Bay of Benghazi, presumed shot down; Uffz Rudolf Hanauer and three MiA

Saturday, 16 January 1943

Over Tobruk Flg Off Shipard and Flt Sgt Oxby of 89 Squadron claimed to have shot down two Ju 88s and reported seeing a third being shot down by a second Beaufighter. This latter aircraft and its crew failed to return, having collided with their victim. A large detachment of Wellingtons from 458 Squadron now moved to Malta for further operations.

British Claims

89 Sqn	Flg Off M.C.Shipard/ Flt Sgt D.Oxby	Beaufighter VIf V8447 'S'	2 Ju 88s	Gambut area	1922 & 1932 (BA)
89 Sqn	Flt Sgt R.G.Peters/ Flt Sgt F.Halliday	Beaufighter X8136	Ju 88 by collision	W Tobruk	

British Casualties

73 Sqn	Hurricane IIc HV516 shot down by Flak at Tauorga; Flg Off S.P.Davies (or Davis) KiA
89 Sqn	Beaufighter X8136 collision with Ju 88 E Tobruk; Flt Sgts R.G.Peters and F.Halliday MiA (from Bu Amud)

German Casualties

5./LG 1	Ju 88A-4 WNr 142305 L1+EN shot down by Beaufighters in Tobruk area; Ogefr Horst Scheda captured, but died 29 January; 3 crew PoW
5./LG 1	Ju 88A-4 WNr 142 319 L1+FN shot down by night fighter nr Tobruk; Lt Werner Schmitz and 3 MiA (probably the aircraft lost in collision)
II./LG 1	Ju 88A-4 WNr 140098 attacked ship nr Tobruk, damaged by night fighter and crash-landed at Heraklion airfield, 60% damaged

Sunday, 17 January 1943

Two Marauder crews from 14 Squadron on an offensive sweep over the Aegean spotted two Bf 109s, three miles north of Syros. A Ju 52/3m was then seen and attacked, damage being claimed.

British Claims			
14 Sqn	Marauder crews	Ju 52/3m Damaged	over Aegean Sea

Tuesday, 19 January 1943

Marauder crews from 14 Squadron were again out on an offensive reconnaissance over the Aegean – an increasingly frequent duty. A merchant vessel assessed as 1,500-2,000 tons was seen, escorted by a single Ar 196 floatplane. A torpedo attack was made, a hit being claimed on the ship which caused a violent explosion, the 654-ton tanker *Alfredo* then sinking almost at once.

British Claims					
73 Sqn	Sgt D.H.Thomas	Hurricane IIc HL769	Ju 87 Damaged	N Castel Benito	2325-0150
British Casualties					
238 Sqn	Hurricane II BN389				

Wednesday, 20 January 1943

13(Hellenic) Squadron moved from Gianaclis to LG.07.

Thursday, 21 January 1943

Two more 14 Squadron Marauders were out over the Aegean, the crews spotting a vessel of about 8,000 tons, escorted by two destroyers and four twin-engined aircraft 20 miles south-east of Milos. Both crews attacked but missed, following which one Marauder was engaged by the escort for 13 minutes, but escaped damage, the gunners claiming hits on a Ju 88 which broke away with smoke issuing from one engine.

British Claims					
89 Sqn	Flt Sgt H.F.W.Shead/ Flt Sgt F.W. Curtis	Beaufighter X7769	Ju 88	Libya (Benina)	2000
14 Sqn	Marauder gunners		Ju 88 possibly Damaged nr Milos		
British Casualties					
89 Sqn	Beaufighter FTR; Sgt C.C.Webb/Sgt J.A.Mathers MiA				

Friday, 22 January 1943

Five Wellingtons of 38 Squadron took off to raid Khalkis, three carrying mines and two bombs. One minelayer returned early, but two mines were laid in the south approach to Khalkis and one in the north harbour. The second bomber failed to return, the crew radioing that their aircraft had been hit by Flak.

Saturday, 23 January 1943

Next day 235 Wing, which was now operating to a considerable extent over the southern Aegean area, noted that during the month to date the units operating, and the number of sorties they had flown since the start of the year, were as follows:

459 Squadron	71	221 Squadron	2
15 SAAF Squadron	41	458 Squadron	8
Sea Rescue Flight	8	14 Squadron	3
47 Squadron	4	162 Squadron	3
38 Squadron	18		

Sunday, 24 January 1942

Four Cant.Z.1007bis of 30° Stormo from Rhodes bombed Tobruk at night (0225-0645). A vast fire was observed in the area behind the harbour.

Monday, 25 January 1943

417 Squadron went from Edcu to LG.175. A few days later 7 SAAF Squadron also moved, arriving at Benina, while 2 PRU despatched its forward flight to Castel Benito. At the start of February this latter unit was renamed 680 Squadron during a wholesale renumbering of the RAF's photographic reconnaissance units. 60 SAAF Squadron, which as a South African unit retained its existing title, received the first two Mosquitos to reach North Africa which were to be employed for similar duties.

Sunday, 31 January 1943

A detachment of Beaufighters from 46 Squadron was sent to Abu Sueir for night fighting.

British Claims

89 Sqn	Flt Sgt L.R.Blackwell/ Sgt Melrose	Beaufighter X7827?	Ju 88	Bu Amud	1510

British Casualties

213 Sqn	Hurricane IIc BM983

Tuesday, 2 February 1943

British Casualties

221 Sqn	Wellington FTR from patrol in Cap Stilo area; Plt Off Bertram and crew MiA

Wednesday, 3 February 1943

A lone Cant.Z.1007bis of 8ª Squadriglia, 25° Gruppo BT flown by Ten Abramo Pappalardo bombed the harbour of Tripoli at night. The results could not be observed due to dazzling caused by the 'Martellona' flashing devices delivered by the bomber. During the day Grp Capt (Acting Air Cdr) J.R.Scarlett-Stratfield, CBE, took over command of 201 Group from AVM L.H.Slatter, KBE, CB, DSC, DFC.

Thursday, 4 February 1943

Another Cant.Z.1007bis, this time of 9ª Squadriglia, 25° Gruppo BT flown by M.llo Giuseppe Cernuschi bombed Tripoli harbour at 0510. The results could not be observed due to haze.

Friday, 5 February 1943

As before, the dazzling effect of the Martellona flashing devices prevented the observation of the results of the bombing on the shipping in Tripoli harbour at 0340 by a Cant.Z.1007bis of 8ª Squadriglia, 25° Gruppo BT, flown by Ten Manfredo De Musis.

Saturday, 6 February 1943

British Casualties

335 Sqn	Hurricane II HL699

Sunday, 7 February 1943

Two Hurricanes of 274 Squadron on patrol in the Tripoli area, were vectored onto a Ju 88, which the pilots claimed to have damaged. At evening, Flg Off Spurgin of 89 Squadron claimed an He 111 damaged north of the port.

British Claims

89 Sqn	Flg Off A.L.M.Spurgin/ Flt Sgt Norris	Beaufighter VIf V8311	He 111 Damaged	N Tripoli	1925

British Casualties

221 Sqn	Wellington off 1830 from Luqa to illuminate convoy 60m E Sardinia, FTR; Flg Off G.F.C.Waite and five MiA

Monday, 8 February 1943

At 1907 two Beaufighters were scrambled to join a third which was already on patrol, these all being vectored towards an incoming formation reported as being composed of at least six bombers. Flt Sgt Park claimed an He 111 which crashed in flames into the sea five miles north of Tagui; two of the crew were seen to bale out. Sqn Ldr Parry claimed another in flames 150 miles east of Tripoli, again two survivors being observed to bale out. It was believed that the German aircraft had been mine-laying. The body of one member of the crew of the first aircraft shot down was later washed ashore The attack on Tripoli was actually undertaken by five II./KG 100 Heinkels, four of which returned safely after bombing, the fifth being attacked by a twin-engined fighter and failing to return. It would appear that the second bomber shot down – probably that claimed by Sqn Ldr Parry – was in fact a Ju 88 of 6./LG 1 also lost in the same area.

Four Beaufighters of 603 Squadron moved up to Berka, near Benghazi, to begin operational flying. From now on the unit would frequently despatch detachments to this base from Edcu for similar duties.

British Claims

89 Sqn	Flt Sgt P.T.Park/Sgt Rumbold	Beaufighter V8376	He 111 in flames	into sea N Tripoli	1930
89 Sqn	Sqn Ldr C.W.Passy/Flt Sgt Ward	Beaufighter V8015	He 111 in flames	ENE Tripoli 1940, crashed Mellaha	

German Casualties

4./KG 100	He 111H-14 WNr 7936 6N+GM FTR from raid on Tripoli, presumed shot down by night fighter; Lt Bruno Stange and 3 MiA
6./LG 1	Ju 88A-4 WNr 140 735 L1+AP FTR from raid on Tripoli, presumed shot down into the sea; Obfw Eduard Ott and 3 MiA

Tuesday, 9 February 1943

At Rhodes a Cant.Z.506 of 'Sezione Soccorso' (Rescue Flight) crashed in the sea just after take-off, probably due to engine trouble; all aboard were killed.

Italian Casualties

Sez Soccorso	Cant.Z.506 MM 45221 ditched into sea, pilot Cap Francesco Molteni, copilot Cap Mario Cesari and four KiA

Friday, 12 February 1943

212 Group ordered 33 and 7 SAAF Squadrons from Benina to Bersis on 10th, but two days before the move had been completed, the latter unit was to claim its first victory flying from Benina. With morning a Ju 88 of II./KG 54 attacked an Allied convoy north of El Hamma, off the Tripolitanian coast. This was being protected by a section of Hurricanes from 7 SAAF Squadron at Benina, which at once attacked the raider, shooting it down near Benghazi. However, Lt Rosholt was lost, believed shot down by ships' AA, and Lt King's aircraft received some damage to one wing. During the afternoon two Hurricanes of 33 Squadron over the same convoy, intercepted a Ju 88 15 miles west of Benghazi. This was claimed probably shot down by Sgt McKillop, although he then had to bale out into the sea from where he was safely picked up.

British Claims

7 SAAF Sqn	Lt D.J.S.W.King	Hurricane IIc HV444	} Ju 88	off Benghazi	0905
7 SAAF Sqn	Lt E.A.Rorvik	Hurricane IIc HV829			
33 Sqn	Sgt R.G.McKillop	Hurricane IIc ..144	Ju 88 Probable		1420-1555
89 Sqn	Flt Lt V.C.Lovell/ Wt Off Turnbull	Beaufighter X7849	Ju 88 Damaged	N Benghazi	1910

British Casualties

7 SAAF Sqn	Hurricane IIc HV337 shot down in error by RN corvette nr Benghazi; Lt A.C.Rosholt MiA
7 SAAF Sqn	Hurricane IIc HV444 slt damaged by return fire from Ju 88; Lt King safe
33 Sqn	Hurricane IIc shot down in sea off Bersis in combat with S.79; Sgt McKillop safe

German Casualties

6./KG 54	Ju 88A-4 WNr 140 500 B3+OP FTR from armed reconnaissance Misurata-Benghazi area, presumed shot down into the sea; Uffz Oskar Baumann and 3 MiA

Saturday, 13 February 1943

Eight Ju 88s approached Tocra from the north in formation. Two 89 Squadron Beaufighters were scrambled and one crew claimed one shot down in flames, reporting that the other German aircraft had probably collided with their victim.

British Claims

89 Sqn	Flt Sgt Dean/ Wt Off Lowther	Beaufighter X7968	Ju 88 in flames	Tobruk	1905
89 Sqn	Flt Sgt Dean/ Wt Off Lowther	Beaufighter X7968	Ju 88 Probable by collision with first claim		1905

Sunday, 14 February 1943

Four Cant.Z.1007bis of 30° Stormo took off at 1613 to bomb Tobruk. As they approached one of the Beaufighters of 46 Squadron's night-fighter detachment at Tobruk was scrambled at 1900, Flt Sgt Holmes being followed five minutes later by Flg Off Sage. Holmes climbed to 18,000 feet over the Bu Amud area where his radar operator, Flt Sgt Bell, got a contact, followed by a sighting at 19,000 feet of a Cant.Z.1007bis. He opened fire at 350 feet with five bursts, all of which hit the bomber, which exploded in flames and fell vertically into the sea. Sage also got a contact at 18,000 feet, but this was below his aircraft, and at 15,000 feet he spotted another Cant.Z.1007bis. He fired at 200 feet range, seeing strikes on the fuselage; a fire started and the starboard engine burst into flames, the aircraft then falling vertically through some clouds, well alight. Two Cant.Z.1007bis, flown by S.Ten Gino Traini and S.Ten Cesare Stagni, failed to return.

One 89 Squadron aircraft was already patrolling and another was scrambled as raiders also approached Tripoli. One was intercepted by Flt Sgt Blackwell whose fire set the starboard engine aflame, and he was awarded a probable. It seems in fact to have been shot down, II./KG 76 reporting the loss of one of its bombers in this area; Blackwell's claim was apparently later confirmed.

British Claims

46 Sqn	Flt Sgt G.J.Holmes/ Flt Sgt Bell	Beaufighter If 'W'	Cant.Z.1007	Bu Amud area	1900-2035
46 Sqn	Flg Off P.C.W.Sage/ Flt Sgt J.Cockburn	Beaufighter If 'U'	Cant.Z.1007	Bu Amud	1905-2030
89 Sqn	Flt Sgt L.R.Blackwell/ Sgt Melrose	Beaufighter V8375	Ju 88	N Tripoli	2003

German Casualties

5./KG 76	Ju 88A-4 WNr 141 105 F1+EN FTR from raid on Tripoli, presumed shot down; Fw Paul Christ and 3 MiA

Italian Casualties

193ª Sq, 87°Gr, 30°St BT	Cant.Z.1007bis MM 24256 '193-3' failed to return from a night bombing mission to Tobruk, 1613-, pilot S.Ten Gino Traini, copilot Serg Magg Gino Giacometti and crew MiA
195ª Sq, 90°Gr, 30°St BT	Cant.Z.1007bis MM 24721 failed to return from a night bombing mission to Tobruk, 1613-, pilot S.Ten Cesare Stagni, copilot M.llo Tonino Campani and crew MiA

Monday, 15 February 1943

Two S.79 torpedo-bombers of 104° Gruppo AS took off from Rhodes at 0600 on a recce mission to the African coast from Tobruk to Marsa el Mreis. At 0811 they were attacked by four fighters identified by the crews as P-39 Airacobras. One was claimed shot down by S.79's gunners. No Allied operations have been discovered which offer any clues to the possible identity of the Allied fighters involved. Certainly at this point there were no P-39s based anywhere near this part of the North African coast.

Oblt Werner Schroer, as Kapitän of 8./JG 27 was flying home over the Adriatic on 11 February 1943 on leave to get married. He intercepted and claimed to have shot down two Beauforts near Karpathos – his 62nd and 63rd victories. It is believed, however, that both the date and the identification were incorrectly recorded and that he in fact engaged a pair of 14 Squadron Marauders on 15 February.

One engagement was recorded by the RAF on this date regarding which there is some confusion. During this period III./JG 27 was based at Kastelli in western Crete, but with 8.Staffel detached to Rhodes. Apparently on 11 February the Staffelkäpitan, Oblt Werner Schroer, was granted home leave to get married, taking off in his Bf 109 to fly to Kastelli on the first leg of his journey. During his flight he encountered two torpedo-bombers, which he identified as Beauforts. He attacked, claiming to have shot down both to the north of Karpathos (also known as Scarpanto, in Italian), a small island located roughly mid-way between Rhodes and eastern Crete; he also reported that some of the crew of the second aircraft to fall were picked up by a fishing boat.

No Allied losses have been discovered on 11 February, but on the 15th at just the times and in just the area of his claims, 14 Squadron reported that two of its torpedo-carrying Marauders on a sortie to the Aegean, failed to return. One was not heard from again but the other reached Turkey on one engine and force-landed, the crew being interned. This would have been the first occasion on which Schroer, at this time the top-scoring surviving pilot of the Libyan campaign, encountered Marauders, accounting for the incorrect identification. In all other respects it seems extremely likely that these were his victims and that this combat had in fact occurred on 15 February rather than four days earlier.

British Casualties

14 Sqn	Marauder FK150 MiA from reconnaissance; Flg Off C.Truman and crew MiA
14 Sqn	Marauder FK143 damaged by Bf 109, landed in Turkey and interned; Lt L.G.Jones and crew interned

German Claims (provisional)

8./JG 27	Oblt Werner Schroer	2 Beauforts	NNE Karpathos	1330 & 1334

Italian Claims

104° Gr Aut AS	S.79 gunners	Airacobra	Tobruk-Mersa el Mreis	0811

Tuesday, 16 February 1943

243 Wing, now controlling 73, 213, 274 and 89 Squadrons, welcomed a new commanding officer, Grp Capt John Grandy (later a marshal of the RAF).

Tuesday-Wednesday, 16/17 February 1943

British Casualties

38 Sqn	Wellington HD966 'C' FTR from minelaying sortie to Candia area; Plt Off E.McDonald and crew MiA

Wednesday, 17 February 1943

Three Hudsons and two Bisleys provided anti-submarine cover to a convoy during the day. At 1045 the crew of a 13(Hellenic) Squadron Bisley saw a submarine forced to the surface by a destroyer attack west of Derna. They at once attacked with depth charges and machine-gunned the crew, forcing them back inside the conning tower. At a signal from the destroyer, the Bisley withdrew out of range as this ship pressed home the attack. The U-Boat – U-205 – was later captured and was then taken in tow by HMS *Paladin* after a boarding had taken place. Hudsons and Bisleys then escorted the destroyers towards port, but the prize was then lost when it sank in shallow water at 1640.

British Claims

89 Sqn	Flg Off J.H.Etherton/ Sgt Gibbs	Beaufighter V8315	Ju 88 Damaged	Tripoli	2000

Thursday, 18 February 1943

At Berka Satellite landing ground four Beaufighters of 603 Squadron arrived from Egypt to fly combined operations with those of 252 Squadron.

Friday, 19 February 1943

417 Squadron arrived at Castel Benito to join 244 Wing. Initially the unit remained involved in defensive patrolling.

Saturday, 20 February 1943

In 212 Group's 15 Sector four Beaufighters of 46 Squadron intercepted a raid on Tobruk, Flg Off Kemp with Sgt Cussons being scrambled at 1955 after a contact in the Bu Amud area. They caught a raider, a Ju 88 of II./LG 1, at 9,500 feet whereupon it took violent evasive action, turning south for Tobruk and going down. Kemp finally saw it at 2,500 feet, lost it again, finally catching it and opening fire from 600 feet, hitting the nose and fuselage. It turned to starboard and disappeared, but a flash and glow were then seen as it hit the ground.

Far to the east in 219 Group's area, six more bombers raided the Haifa area. Five more of 46 Squadron's Beaufighters from Abu Sueir and Edcu, were vectored to intercept, one obtaining a contact 90 miles north of Port Said at 0443, but this escaped attack. A second crew then got a contact 85 miles north of Rosetta at 0510, Flg Off Olley achieving a visual on a 30° Stormo Cant.Z.1007bis at 13,000 feet over Alexandria. Three Cant.Z.1007bis of this unit had taken off from Rhodes at 0030 to bomb oil refineries and depots at Beirut. The Italian crews were unable to see the results of their attack due to a heavy overcast. Olley opened fire at 200 yards on the Cant he had spotted, seeing strikes on the port engine which caught fire at once, gradually spreading to the fuselage as the bomber rapidly lost height. It then hit the water with a huge flash.

During the morning a Baltimore crew spotted a 10,000-ton tanker 40 miles north of Trapani. Wellingtons, Beauforts and Albacores were sent out in poor weather, although some damage was claimed to have been inflicted on the vessel. However, it was sunk that night by Beauforts of 39 Squadron.

British Claims

46 Sqn	Flg Off W.F.Kemp/ Sgt W.H.Cussons	Beaufighter If 'N'	Ju 88	Bu Amud area	1955-2055
46 Sqn	Flg Off A.G.Olley/ Sgt C.W.Baldwin	Beaufighter If 'L'	Cant.Z.1007	Alexandria area	0425-0620

German Casualties

4./LG 1	Ju 88A-4 140 057 L1+BM FTR from raid on Tobruk, presumed shot down by night fighter; Uffz Wilhelm Wilms and 3 MiA

Italian Casualties

193ª Sq, 87°Gr, 30°St BT	Cant.Z.1007bis FTR from a night bombing mission to Beirut, 0030-, pilot Cap Vincenzo Guidi, copilot S.Ten Guido Castagnoli and crew MiA

Sunday, 21 February 1943

From Egypt at 1245 14 Squadron mounted a raid on the harbour of Melos in the Aegean. The torpedo-carriers attacked ships, Plt Off Clark-Hall (FK142) claiming a direct hit on a 5,000-ton vessel which blew up and sank, while Maj Lewis (FK370) and Flg Off Lapthorne (FK151) both targeted a ship of 4,000 tons; their attack was followed by an explosion and a mass of flames and debris. Amongst the bombers, Lt Egebjerg (FK370) bombed buildings on the east side of the bay, claiming direct hits, and Flg Off C.Phillips (FK123) attacked a ship of 2,000 tons, but with unobserved results. However, he did see a Marauder in flames, gaining height and heading west. Flg Off Donovan (FK121) saw his bombs straddle another vessel, but he too then saw a Marauder in flames which crashed in the eastern part of the bay. To the west, eight bombers got through the Allied defences to drop 22 HE bombs on Tripoli harbour.

British Casualties

14 Sqn	Marauder FK399 FTR from attack on ships at Melos; Sgt B.H.Yarwood and crew KiA
14 Sqn	Marauder FK377 FTR from attack on ships at Melos; Sgt R.A.Barton and crew KiA

German Casualties

6./KG 30	Ju 88A-4 WNr 1765 4D+DP FTR from raid on Tripoli, presumed shot down; Fw Martin Scholz and three MiA

Monday, 22 February 1943

As morning arrived in the Tripoli area 15 plus Ju 88s were reported approaching, 12 bombs being dropped which failed to cause any damage. Four Hurricanes of 73 Squadron and three 89 Squadron Beaufighters had been sent up, the pilots of two of the latter claiming two Ju 88s shot down and one more damaged. The AA defences claimed three shot down and a fourth probably so. From 46 Squadron, Sqn Ldr R.M.MacKenzie, DFC, was now promoted Wg Cdr and posted to command 227 Squadron.

Two sections of Hurricanes of 451 Squadron took off at 0931, Plt Off Wallis engaging a Ju 88 20 miles north of Alexandria at 1008, pursuing this until return fire struck the windscreen of his aircraft,

14 Squadron converted to Marauders in August, frequently then operating these aircraft over the Aegean Sea initially, either in standard bomber form, or carrying a torpedo. Here FK151 'O' is seen in the latter role in the hands of Maj Eric Lewis, SAAF.

which was substantially cracked. It seems other bullets had hit home, as his cockpit filled with smoke and dripping glycol. Unable to reach Edcu, he crash-landed near Maryut, claiming to have damaged the Ju 88. An S.81 of Reparto Autonomo Volo which took off from Rhodes to carry personnel and fuel to Kos island, ditched for unknown reason. Most of the crew and passengers were killed.

British Claims

89 Sqn	Flt Lt H.G.Edwards/ Sgt D.A.Street	Beaufighter	Ju 88	Tripoli	
89 Sqn	Flg Off N.E.Reeves/ Wt Off A.A.O'Leary	Beaufighter X8166 Beaufighter X8166	Ju 88 in flames	Tripoli into sea	0538
89 Sqn	Flg Off N.E.Reeves/ Wt Off A.A.O'Leary	Beaufighter X8166	Ju 88 Damaged	Tripoli	0557
451 Sqn	Plt Off W.P.G.Longbottom	Hurricane IIc BN290	Ju 88 Damaged		1008-1025
451 Sqn	Plt Off J.D.Wallis	Hurricane IIc BP342			

German Casualties

6./KG 30	Ju 88A-4 WNr 142386 4D+FN MiA Tripoli; Oblt Erich Schulz and three MiA
4./KG 30	Ju 88A-4 WNr 141146 4D+HM MiA Tripoli; Fw Wilhelm Liebscher and three MiA
4./KG 30	Ju 88A-4 WNr 141142 4D+JM MiA Tripoli; Uffz Franz Hrncirik and three MiA
2.(F)/122	Me 210A-1 WNr 0210 F6+ZK FTR from reconnaissance to Tripoli, presumed shot down in the sea; Fw Walter Spitzner/Uffz Waldemar Küch MiA

Italian Casualties

Rep Aut Volo Egeo	S.81 ditched 36°38', 27°26', pilot M.llo Italo Miglio and two of crew safe on dinghy, copilot M.llo Vito Nizza, rest of crew and passengers killed

Wednesday, 24 February 1943

Four Cant.Z.1007bis of 107° Gruppo were despatched at 2010-2020 from Castelvetrano to bomb shipping in Tripoli bay. Two bombers, flown by Ten Giovanni Sferlazza and Ten Eugenio Giordano, failed to return.

During a two-day series of attacks on the 6,987-ton *Alcamo* (ex-French *St François*) one Beaufort was lost on each day, although the vessel was successfully sunk.

British Claims

89 Sqn	Wg Cdr J.A.Leathart/ Flt Lt C.J.Glass	Beaufighter V8579	Cant Z.1007bis in flames	N Tripoli	2215

British Casualties

39 Sqn	Beaufort a AW349 'R' shot down by Flak during shipping attack; Wt Off Dawson and crew MiA

German Casualties

5./KG 30	Ju 88A-4 WNr 140463 4D+GN FTR Tripoli; Lt Walter Inführ and three MiA

Italian Casualties

262ª Sq, 107°Gr, 47°St BT	Cant.Z.1007bis FTR, pilot Ten Giovanni Sferlazza, copilot Serg Vincenzo Sala and crew MiA
263ª Sq, 107°Gr, 47°St BT	Cant.Z.1007bis FTR, pilot Ten Eugenio Giordano, copilot M.llo Andrea Martini and crew MiA

Thursday, 25 February 1943

1 SAAF Squadron reported that 417 Squadron had now arrived at Castel Benito to join 244 Wing and that four US squadrons had also arrived. A second Greek unit, 336 Squadron, was formed at Cairo on this date, equipped with Hurricanes.

British Casualties

39 Sqn	Beaufort IIa\ DD910 'S' from shipping strike; Flg Off A.C.Hewetson and crew MiA

Friday-Saturday, 26/27 February 1943

Three Beaufighters were scrambled as several Ju 88s approached from the west of Tripoli. One was claimed shot down in flames by Flg Off Reeves.

British Claims

89 Sqn	Flg Off N.E.Reeves/ Wt Off A.A.O'Leary	Beaufighter V8309	Ju 88	N Tripoli	0430

German Casualties

5./KG 76	Ju 88A-4 WNr 140 048 F1+FN FTR from raid on Tripoli presumed shot down; Uffz Helmut Hövelmann and 3 MiA

Saturday, 27 February 1943

British Casualties

221 Sqn	Wellington HX626 off 1955 from Luqa, shipping search Marsala-Palermo, FTR; Flg Off D.H.Cochrane and five MiA

Sunday, 28 February 1943

Between 2219-2305 Flg Off Kinmonth of 89 Squadron intercepted a single He 111 which he shot down into the sea.

British Claims

451 Sqn	Plt Off A.F.Arnell	Hurricane IIc BP518	e/a Damaged	0723-0845
451 Sqn	Plt Off D.Le S.Fisher	Hurricane IIc BP172		
89 Sqn	Flg Off M.W.Kinmonth/ Flt Sgt A.J. Edgar	Beaufighter	He 111 in flames	2310

German Claims

Stab I./JG 77	Hptm Heinz Bär	Beaufighter

Tuesday-Wednesday, 2/3 March 1943

British Claims

89 Sqn	Flg Off M.C.Shipard/ Plt Off Oxby	Beaufighter VIf V8447 'S'	Ju 88 Probable	15m NE Tripoli	1800
89 Sqn	Flt Sgt Blackwell/ Sgt Melrose	Beaufighter V8375	Ju 88 Damaged		

Sunday, 7 March 1943

German Casualties

4./KG 30	Ju 88A-4 WNr 140 430 4D+KM MiA Tripoli; Obfw Heribert Bauer and two MiA, Oblt Ernst Brackelmann KiA

Monday, 8 March 1943

On this date the 47 Squadron Wellesley Flight, so long attached to 235 Wing, was finally disbanded at LG.07.

British Claims

89 Sqn	Flt Lt V.C.Lovell/ Wt Off R.H.Turnbull	Beaufighter V8330	Ju 88 into sea	off Tripoli	1850

German Casualties

6./LG 1	Ju 88A-4 WNr 142 304 hit in combat with night fighter and belly-landed at Gabes; Fw Rudolf Ascherl and 3 WiA

Thursday, 11 March 1943

Sqn Ldr J.A.A.Read, DFC, and Flt Lt W.G.Howell were posted from 46 Squadron to a new night fighter unit, 108 Squadron, which was just forming at Shandur; Read was at the same time promoted to command this unit.

British Claims

89 Sqn	Flg Off M.W.Kinmonth/ Flt Sgt A.J.Edgar	Beaufighter V88439	Ju 88	Tripoli area	1955

German Casualties

5./KG 100	He 111H-14 WNr 7923 6N+JN FTR from raid on Tripoli, presumed shot down; Fw Oskar Goldmann PoW, 3 MiA

Friday, 12 March 1942

British Casualties

39 Sqn	Beaufort IIa DD928 'E' FTR from attack on Italian tanker *Sterope* (10,496 tons); Sgt W.D.Blackmore and crew MiA
39 Sqn	Beaufort IIa DD934 'M' DBR by Flak during attack on *Sterope*; Flg Off A.M.Feast and crew safe

Monday, 15 March 1943

German Casualties

III./KG 26	Ju 888A-4 WNr 144421 1H+BD FTR from shipping strike E Tripoli, presumed shot down; Obfw Johann Lacher and one KiA, two PoW

Tuesday, 16 March 1943

Two Beaufighters of 89 Squadron were on patrol over the Tripoli area between 2030-2130. Each crew claimed to have shot down a Ju 88. III./KG 77 lost one such aircraft over the city and one over St Marie du Zit while II./KG 26 lost two He 111s over the former area.

British Claims

89 Sqn	Wt Off H.F.W.Shead/ Wt Off Curtis	Beaufighter V9330	Ju 88 in flames	N Tripoli	2105
89 Sqn	Flt Lt V.C.Lovell/ Flt Lt C.J.Glass	Beaufighter V8636	Ju 88	NW Tripoli	2112

German Casualties

7./KG 77	Ju 88A-4 WNr 142 395 3Z+KR FTR from raid on Tripoli, presumed shot down; Uffz Alfred Schmidt and 3 MiA
4./KG 26	He 111H-11 WNr 8128 1H+EM FTR from raid on Tripoli, presumed shot down; Uffz Ernst Höfer and 3 MiA
6./KG 26	He 111H-11 WNr 8099 1H+AP FTR from raid on Tripoli, presumed shot down ; Lt Karl Tschiggert KiA, 3 PoW
6./KG 26	He 111H-11 WNr 8107 1H+HP FTR from raid on Tripoli, presumed shot down; Fw Albin Bamberger and 3 MiA

Wednesday, 17 March 1942

British Casualties

39 Sqn	Beaufort IIa DD902 'D' FTR from abortive daylight shipping strike; Flt Lt D.Fraser and crew MiA

Friday, 19 March 1943

German Casualties

6./KG 30	Ju 88A-4 WNr 142 430 4D+EP MiA Tripoli; Uffz Artur Lampsatis and 3 MiA
7./KG 77	Ju 88A-4 WNr 142 352 3Z+ER FTR from raid on Tripoli, presumed shot down; Lt Fritz Schendel and 3 MiA
7./KG 77	Ju 88A-4 WNr 141 095 3Z+BR FTR from raid on Tripoli, presumed shot down; Obfw Karl Fellhöfer and 3 MiA
8./KG 77	Ju 88A-4 WNr 140 547 3Z+LSD FTR from raid on Tripoli, presumed shot down; Oblt Ulrich Prinz and 3 KiA

Monday, 22 March 1943

Four Spitfires of 417 Squadron on a convoy patrol near Tripoli intercepted a torpedo-carrying He 111 of II./KG 26. Sqn Ldr F.B.Foster attacked first, but ran out of ammunition without seeing any worthwhile damage. The other three pilots then took up the chase, the bomber bursting into flames and crash-landing on the water after the torpedo had been jettisoned. The crew climbed out and got into their dinghy; they were subsequently picked up and made prisoners.

At 0845 a Cant.Z.1007bis of 30° Stormo took off at 0845 on a recce mission along the Palestinian coast. Around 1415 the aircraft interrupted radio communications and failed to return.

British Claims

417 Sqn	Flg Off D.E.Bruce	Spitfire Vb ER634 'H'	He 111	nr Tripoli	0635
417 Sqn	Sqn Ldr F.B.Foster	Spitfire Vb EP893 'R'			
417 Sqn	Plt Off J.R.Harmer	Spitfire Vb ER364 'T'			
417 Sqn	Flt Lt W.H.Pentland	Spitfire Vb BR483 'V'			

German Casualties

5./KG 26	He 111H-11 WNr 8126 FTR from raid on Tripoli, presumed shot down; Oblt Helmut Jantzen and one PoW, two KiA

Italian Casualties

192ª Sq, 87°Gr, 30°St BT	Cant.Z.1007bis failed to return 0845-, pilot Ten Salvatore Seranella, copilot Serg Antonio Barbieri and one KiA, three others rescued by motor boat

Tuesday, 23 March 1943

In the early hours at 0330 Flg Off Kinmonth of 89 Squadron intercepted a Sicily-based Cant.Z.1007bis over the Tripoli area which he claimed to have shot down. It is possible that this was the aircraft reported lost by 30° Stormo on the previous day and that there was an error in the recording by one side or the other. Command of 212 Group was now taken over by Grp Capt D.W.Bayne.

British Claims

89 Sqn	Flg Off Kinmonth/ Flt Sgt Edgar	Beaufighter V8309	Cant.Z.1007bis in flames into sea N Tripoli		
73 Sqn	Flg Off R.J.D.Henderson	Hurricane IIc HV585	Ju 88 Damaged	10m ESE Gabes	0025-0140

British Casualties

69 Sqn	Baltimore AG815 damaged by Bf 109s and force-landed at Luqa
272 Sqn	Beaufighter VIf FTR from convoy escort; Plt Off R.R.Grimes/Sgt D.J.Dawson MiA

Wednesday, 24 March 1943

British Claims

73 Sqn	Plt Off R.Chandler	Hurricane IIc HW848	Ju 88	Sfax	2105-2315

Friday, 26 March 1943

British Claims

451 Sqn	Plt Off W.E.Goldman	Hurricane IIc HV673	Ju 88 Probable	40m N Alexandria Bar	1459-1520
451 Sqn	Plt Off T.H.S.James	Hurricane IIc HL847			
451 Sqn	Plt Off G.H.Purdy	Spitfire Vc BP982			
451 Sqn	Plt Off R.H.Sutton	Spitfire Vc BP981 'J'			

British Casualties

Baltimore AG919 lost

German Casualties

2.(F)/123	Ju 88D-1 WNr 430 531 badly shot-up by fighters and crash-landed on return, 100% damaged; crew safe

Saturday, 27 March 1943

At 1525 four Hurricanes and a single Spitfire, all from 238 Squadron, were scrambled from El Gamil to intercept a Ju 88 on reconnaissance over Port Said. The Spitfire pilot caught the intruder, making three attacks over the sea. On the third attack pieces flew off the port wing, following which a section of the wing five or six feet long broke off. Four or five bundles then fell from the aircraft following which it crashed into the water; these appear to have been crewmembers baling out and a dinghy, all of which were seen in the water but were not picked up.

British Claims

238 Sqn	Flg Off C.J.Aylott	Spitfire Vc BR586	Ju 88	El Gamil, Port Said	1525-1610

British Casualties

39 Sqn	Beaufort IIa AW348 'M' FTR from abortive shipping strike; Flg Off R.D.McAdam and crew MiA

German Casualties

2.(F)/123	Ju 88D-1 WNr 430505 4U+IK shot down by Spitfire at Alexandria; Uffz Johann Holzer, Lt Herbert Brennecke and two MiA

Sunday, 28 March 1943

British Casualties

203 Sqn	Baltimore AG724 crash-landed Luqa

CHAPTER 11

THE ALLIED HEAVY BOMBING OFFENSIVE

At the close of January 1942, 205 Group had increased in strength to six squadrons, equipped in the main with Wellington Ic bombers. The group was due to grow further in the near future, and at this point it had become appropriate to sub-divide immediate control of squadrons down to a number of new wings. Consequently, 231 (Bomber) Wing had been formed at Shallufa on 27 December 1941, initially to control 37, 70 and 108 Squadrons. This was followed on 30 January 1942 by 238 (Medium Bomber) Wing, also at Shallufa, and next day by 236 (Mobile Medium Bomber) Wing at Kabrit. The former of these two units was allocated 38 and 40 Squadrons, followed later by 104 Squadron and the detachment of Boeing Fortress Is from 220 Squadron; the latter wing incorporated 104 and 148 Squadrons. Finally, in this first phase, 242 Wing was initially formed at Fayid on 10 February with 108 Squadron from the recently formed 231 Wing, followed by the as-yet unformed 147 Squadron and with the ground party of 159 Squadron.

At this stage, 40 Squadron's air party was effectively a detachment from the United Kingdom parent unit, operating on Malta. After a period of intensive operations, it would leave the island on 14 February, flying to Shallufa to become part of 205 Group. However, after a single operation it was stood down, subsequently being reformed as a full squadron at the start of May, with the echelon in England being renumbered as 156 Squadron. The group was also about to lose 38 Squadron which, following trials in torpedo-dropping (see below) was to be transferred to 201 Naval Co-operation Group specifically for anti-shipping activities.

There was at this time one specialist unit within the group, the duties of which were of a different nature to those of the other squadrons. It will be recalled that during the recent Operation Crusader fighting a detachment of Wellingtons from 109 Squadron in the United Kingdom had taken part fitted with devices to interfere with the radios in the Axis tanks. Having proved the worth of this activity, a new unit dubbed the Special Signals Squadron had been formed at Kabrit on 6 January under the command of Wg Cdr D.H.S.Rasher. This squadron took over the remaining six Wellington Ics of the 109 Squadron detachment, led by Flt Lt C.O.V.Willis, as a nucleus. However, since these aircraft had just moved to Shallufa, formation of the new unit was immediately transferred to this airfield. At the same time came news of the award of a DFC to Willis and a Bar to this decoration for Plt Off T.J.W.Williams, in both cases for their work with 109 Squadron.

At once, on 8 January, Plt Off Fenton in aircraft 'K' undertook a special reconnaissance over Crete and the Greek islands. On 12 January Wg Cdr Simpson arrived with seven army radio operators armed with a number of captured German tank transporters and receiving sets removed from some of the tanks left on the battlefield. One of the army operators, Lt Baker, went up in a Wellington for a special signals reconnaissance over the Tripoli area. The jamming tests appeared to be very successful, and during the month operations began using LG.09 as a forward landing ground. At the same time, RDF (radar) calibration work commenced to aid in the performance of the RAF's AMES radar sets. By early February, the unit had on hand seven Wellingtons, one captured S.79 and a Hawker Hart. At this time the name Special Signals Squadron was changed to 162 Squadron and, with the beginning of a more static period on the ground, a great deal of calibration work would be undertaken during March.

It will be recalled that 108 Squadron had received some of the first Consolidated Liberator II bombers to reach the Middle East, the intention originally being that 242 Wing should become a heavy bomber wing. With this in mind 147 Squadron, which had been approved for formation in October 1941 to take over 216 Squadron's Bombays, was allocated to this role instead. In the event, due to the onset of the Far Eastern war and a general delay in obtaining more Liberators, the unit never received any aircraft and ultimately would be disbanded a little over a year later in February 1943. In the meantime, it did receive an allocation of groundcrew personnel who would be employed in supporting the aircraft of 159 and 160 Squadrons.

Endeavours to increase the number of units to be incorporated into 205 Group would be constantly thwarted during the opening months of 1943 by the demands of the new Far Eastern front. During January 1942, two new squadrons, 159 and 160, had been formed in the UK equipped with Liberator IIs, although their intended destination was India. On 12 February, the ground parties of both units departed for this destination, but the aircraft and crews remained at 1653 Heavy Conversion Unit at Polebrook to complete their training. Equipment with Liberators finally took place, 159 Squadron departing first, reaching Fayid on 7 June, followed by 160 Squadron four days later. Here the latter unit's aircraft and crews were absorbed into 159 Squadron.

Most of the groundcrews of both units had already reached India, or were on the way there, as a consequence of which the aircraft were serviced by personnel of 147, 159, 160, 454 and 458 Squadrons, those members of 147 and 454 Squadrons having no aircraft or aircrews of their own. Upon the arrival of the Liberators, those aircraft of this type already serving with 205 Group's own 108 Squadron, were passed to 159 Squadron, the former unit resuming full equipment with Wellingtons. Subsequently, in September 159 Squadron would be re-titled 160 Squadron and ultimately in mid-January 1943 the aircraft and crews of 160 Squadron, together with the remaining ground personnel of 159 and 160 Squadrons, plus those of 147 Squadron, all became a new 178 Squadron. Throughout these six months, however, despite the changes of name, etc, no more than one squadron of Liberator IIs was available to 205 Group. This composite unit had meanwhile moved from Fayid to Shandur during November 1942, where it remained for several months.

Mention was made above of the groundcrews of 454 and 458 Squadrons. These were established as units of the Royal Australian Air Force, formed in their home country at Williamstown in the summer of 1941. Almost at once 454 Squadron, at this stage a ground echelon only, was disbanded and absorbed by 458 Squadron, which during August 1941 departed for the United Kingdom. On arrival, it was at once trained and equipped as a Wellington bomber unit, undertaking three months operations as a part of Bomber Command before being posted to the Middle East. Although the groundcrews were shipped to Egypt, the unit's 17 Wellingtons made the long delivery flight to the Mediterranean via Gibraltar and Malta, departing in flights of three or four aircraft. 458 Squadron had been formed in the UK during the summer of 1941 with predominantly Australian personnel. After a short period of operations with 1 Group, Bomber Command, the unit was ordered to the Middle East at the end of January 1942. Thirty-seven Wellington Ics were flown out, all but one of these reaching Egypt safely. Before the ground party arrived at Suez in May, the aircraft and crews had been attached to the locally-based units, 37, 70, 104, 108 and 148 Squadrons all benefitting from the influx. The groundcrews, once they had arrived, were attached to 159 Squadron, and to the first USAAF unit to arrive.

Unfortunately, the one Wellington which failed to reach its destination, was that flown by the commanding officer, Wg Cdr N.G.Mulholland. When 45 miles from Malta, the aircraft was intercepted and shot down by a Ju 88, Mulholland and four of his crew being killed. The only survivor was Flg Off J.Willis-Richards, the squadron gunnery officer, who was picked up by an Italian destroyer. (See below 16 February.) Other aircraft were also lost, but those which reached Egypt were distributed on attachment amongst the resident 37, 40, 104, 108 and 148 Squadrons due to the shortage of aircraft and crews appertaining at the time. The groundcrews, on their arrival, were employed in servicing 159 Squadron's Liberators and later USAAF B-24s at Lydda. Not until September would 458 Squadron be re-established as a unit in 201 Group. 454 Squadron's adventures proved to be somewhat different, as will now be related.

During July 1942 with 205 Group almost devoid of four-engined heavy bombers, 10 and 76 Squadrons of Bomber Command, rather than being posted to the Middle East, were instructed each to despatch 16 Handley Page Halifax IIs and their crews to Palestine. On arrival, each detachment had attached to it the groundcrew parties of units in the area which had no air parties with them. 454 Squadron had meanwhile been reformed as a ground nucleus only in the United Kingdom and transported out to the area where they were 'married' to the 76 Squadron air party, forming for the time being 76/454 Squadron. Similarly, the 10 Squadron party was joined by 227 Squadron to form 10/227 Squadron. 227 Squadron had been formed in the Middle East at around this time, also with no air party. On Malta were a number of Beaufighters and their crews, the survivors of detachments sent to the island from the United Kingdom (parent units 235 and 248 Squadrons) and the Middle East (252 Squadron). All were now joined together to become a new 227 Squadron – but again, without a ground organisation being set up at the same location.

During September 1942, a further RAAF ground party formed as 462 Squadron replaced the 454 Squadron personnel. During the same month 10/227 and 76/462 (as it had become) were merged to form 462 Squadron. Thus in order to create two heavy bomber units for 205 Group at least a dozen squadron numbers had been employed!

Meanwhile, 38 Squadron, whilst continuing to operate in its bombing role, had been experimenting with carrying a pair of Mark XII torpedoes. In order to save some of the weight caused by the load thus to be carried, the nose turrets of the squadron's aircraft were being removed. During February 1942, therefore, the unit was transferred to 201 (Naval Co-operation) Group although it remained at Shallufa.

The main duty of 205 Group was to reduce the ability of the Axis forces to provide supplies and reinforcements across the Mediterranean to North Africa. In this role the group was joined by such offensive capability as could be maintained on Malta at the time, and, of course, by the units of the Royal Navy. This task required the aircrews to make frequent raids on the Axis ports both in Libya and in Sicily, southern Italy, Greece and Crete. It also required from time to time, attacks on supply convoys underway at sea. Further, on those occasions when the land battles in Cyrenaica increased substantially as one side or the other was launching major offensive action, sustained operations in support of the army were necessary. Typically, this involved attacks on airfields, supply dumps, workshops and concentrations of tanks and other vehicles.

Throughout the months to come, as had been the case during 1941, regular reinforcements of bomber aircraft were making their way by air to RAF bases. So long as Malta remained under sustained air attack, the vast majority of these were heading for North Africa, most of the Wellingtons being destined for 205 Group. However, the losses in transit remained heavy as crews became lost and ran out of fuel, aircraft were destroyed on the ground by bombing when refuelling in Malta, or suffered interception by hostile aircraft.

The conditions under which units operated above the deserts and coastal areas seemed to inflict a particularly heavy toll of Wellingtons whilst on operations or on training flights. The proportion of aircraft lost due to engine failures of various types was notable, engine fires or lost propellers seemed to be a particularly frequent hazard, while the percentage of faulty instruments – especially of altimeters – must have been a source of considerable disquiet. Certainly, the level of losses to these multifarious causes exceeded considerably those suffered to enemy action much of the time. As in Volume 1, details of all such non-operational losses have not been included here, since they are available in the excellent *Bomber Losses in the Middle East and Mediterranean* by David Gunby and Pelham Temple, at least until the end of 1942. Those losses detailed in this chapter relate essentially to those suffered during offensive operations and generally as a result of hostile action. Other losses are included where it is felt they offer a particular insight or interest to the narrative.

Despite the departure for the Indian Ocean of two of the three Fleet Air Arm fighter squadrons in Egypt, other units were to continue playing an important part, particularly associated with 205 Group's activities. 826 Squadron, equipped with Fairey Albacores and commanded at the end of January 1942 by Lt C.W.B.Smith (to be replaced early in March by Lt P.W.Compton), operated from various bases during December and January. Located mainly at Maaten Bagush at the start of February, but with detachments at Bu Amud, Berka and Martuba amongst other forward landing grounds, the unit was deeply involved in dropping flares to aid 205 Group's Wellingtons in finding their various targets.

821 Squadron which had reformed in Egypt during July 1941, would be re-equipped with six Albacores at Dekheila at the start of March, command then being taken over by Maj A.C.Newsom, RM. The unit then moved to Nicosia, Cyprus, to take part in a planned bombardment of the island of Rhodes. It would then return to Dekheila at the start of April to undertake duties similar to those being carried out by 826 Squadron.

Against the above background, operations had continued from the beginning of 1942 onwards. Despite the loss of the western portion of Cyrenaica during January, it remained possible to employ landing grounds between the main Egyptian bomber bases and the frontal area behind the Gazala Line for refuelling and despatching bombers to attack the important Axis harbour and supply base at Benghazi.

The withdrawal from that area had rendered it difficult to undertake attacks on Tripoli by anything other than the very small number of Liberators available, and once more activity here was left very much to the squadrons based on Malta (see *Malta: The Spitfire Year, 1942*).

Sunday-Monday, 1/2 February 1942

Although not an operational loss, that suffered during this night reflects how dangerous the testing of new ideas could be. The crew of Wellington 'H' of 38 Squadron undertook one of the torpedo-dropping exercises mentioned above with two Royal Navy observers aboard. However, flying low over Suez Bay their aircraft struck the water and sank almost at once.

British Casualties	
38 Sqn	Wellington Ic X9735 'H' crashed into sea while practising torpedo-dropping; two KiFA; pilot Plt Off E.W.Knowles and three rescued from dinghy by HMS *Sagitta*

Wellington Ic runs up its engines on a desert airfield.

Thursday, 5 February 1942

Two Liberators of 108 Squadron dropped 15,000lbs of bombs from 15,000ft onto Benghazi docks, the crews claiming direct hits on the Spanish Mole and adjoining quays.

It was recorded in *Malta: The Spitfire Year, 1942* that an OADU Wellington on its way from Gibraltar to the island was intercepted off Sicily at daybreak and was attacked by two Bf 109s of 6./JG 53. The bomber was claimed shot down by Obfw Otto Gröthe, but in fact survived, although damaged, the pilot managing to evade the attackers. The gunners put up a spirited defence, claiming strikes on one of the fighters. Later in the day, another pair of Messerschmitt pilots from the same unit undertook a surprise strafe of the Kalafrana seaplane base where an He 115 which was being used for espionage purposes, was destroyed at anchor by Lt Hans Möller.

British Casualties	
OADU	Wellington Ic damaged by Bf 109s when south of Sicily
	He 115 BV187 destroyed by Bf 109s when at anchor at Kalafrana seaplane base

German Claims			
6./JG 53	Obfw Otto Göthe	Wellington	S Sicily
6./JG 53	Lt Hans Möller	Fokker T.VIII	

Sunday-Monday, 8/9 February 1942

German Claims

Flak	Halifax into the sea, Crete (No further details)

Monday-Tuesday, 9/10 February 1942

British Casualties

70 Sqn	Wellington Ic Z1166 'O' from LG.104 to bomb Martuba West airfield, FTR; Sqn Ldr R.D.Davies and five MiA

Sunday, 15 February 1942

An Axis air raid on Luqa succeeded in destroying four recently arrived Wellington Ics being delivered by 1 OADU.

British Casualties

1 OADU	Wellington Ics DV413, DV414, DV454 and DV482 destroyed on the ground during a bombing raid at Luqa

Monday, 16 February 1942

British Casualties

458 Sqn	Wellington Ic DV539 shot down by Ju 88 in transit; Wg Cdr N.G.Mulholland and four KiA, one rescued and PoW

German Claims

2./NJG 2	Obfw Hermann Jung	Wellington	S Malta ??
4./NJG 2	Uffz Gerhard Wolter	Wellington	S Malta

Monday-Tuesday, 16/17 February 1942

Close behind Mulholland's Wellington came two reinforcement aircraft from 1 OADU. Leaving Malta, one flew too far north and the other similarly to the south. Plt Off King's bomber fell foul of AA fire upon reaching Sicily and force-landed near Castelvetrano, while Plt Off O'Brien's Wellington flew into mountains in North Africa with the loss of the whole crew.

British Casualties

1 OADU	Wellington Ic AD591 hit by AA, force-landed nr Castelvetrano, Sicily; Plt Off P.W.King and four PoW, one KiFA
1 OADU	Wellington Ic AD635 crashed into mountains 8m E La Calle, Algeria; Plt Off A.O'Brien and five KiFA

German Claims

4./NJG 2	Lt Robert von Keudell	Wellington	S Modica

German Casualties

I./NJG 2	Ju 88C-2 WNr –125 R4+AM lost over sea E Syracuse; Lt Robert von Keudell and two MiA

Tuesday, 17 February 1942

Three more delivery Wellingtons failed to complete their journey next day. All set off from Gibraltar, but two were intercepted by fighters. One fell victim to a Bf 109F of II./JG 53 from Sicily, coming down in the sea, whereas a second, damaged, reached the Tunisian coast and crash-landed in a lake near Bizerta; four survived to be interned by the Vichy French. The third aircraft overshot the Luqa runway on landing and was destroyed when it crashed into a quarry. Early in the night, British bombers raided Benghazi. Two Italian 5ª Squadra HQ barracks and some German HQ huts were damaged with some casualties.

British Casualties

1 OADU	Wellington Ic D458 damaged by fighters, crash-landed in lake 12km S Bizerta; Plt Off J.C.Hardy and three interned, two KiFA
1 OADU	Wellington Ic DV497 shot down into sea nr Delle Correnti Isle, Sicily; Sgt C.Dancer and five PoW

German Claims

4./JG 53	Uffz Johannes Lompa	Wellington		0825
4./NJG 2	Lt Robert von Keudell*	Wellington	S Malta	0845

*Apparently claimed by the radio operator Uffz Gerhard Wolter, with the rear guns

Saturday, 21 February 1942

A delivery Wellington flying from Gibraltar towards Malta was believed to have fallen foul of a Bf 110 when an SOS was received at 0103 hours, the crew remaining in contact for an hour and a half thereafter, but still failing to arrive. However, no claim by a Luftwaffe fighter has been found for this day.

British Casualties	
1 OADU	Wellington Ic Z8952; Sgt P.F.Monk and five KiA

Sunday-Monday, 22/23 February 1942

A special effort was called for during the night as a convoy had been reported approaching the African coast. A Liberator was ordered off first to spot the ships, but crashed on take-off when the undercarriage was retracted too soon. It was followed by 30 Wellingtons, but ten of these returned early. A single 38 Squadron aircraft found the convoy, releasing 1,500lbs of high explosive aimed at two merchant ships – but no results were observed. One 148 Squadron aircraft suffered a seizure of the port engine and crash-landed 64 miles behind Axis lines, the crew being captured after several days.

British Casualties	
148 Sqn	Wellington II Z8360 'R' crash-landed in Axis territory due to port engine failure; Sgt R.Hamilton and five PoW
108 Sqn	Wellington AD599 MiA
148 Sqn	Wellington Z8360 MiA Benghazi
German Claims	
Flak	2 Wellingtons over Western Desert

Monday-Tuesday, 23/24 February 1942

Three of 108 Squadron's Wellingtons failed to return from an attack on the Martuba airfields. Possibly these were the aircraft claimed by Flak gunners during the previous night.

British Casualties	
108 Sqn	Wellington Ic AD599 'E' MiA believed to have crashed and blown up at Martuba; Flg Off B.A.Willis and five KiA
108 Sqn	Wellington Ic AD606 'K' FTR from Martuba area; Sgt W.B.Moffat and five KiA
108 Sqn	Wellington Ic AD616 MiA took off to bomb Martuba, crashed near Derna; Flg Off B.A.Willis & crew KiA

Wellington Ic undergoing service.

Tuesday-Wednesday, 24/25 February 1942

A diversionary raid was made on Benghazi harbour to distract the defenders from mining operations by 38 Squadron. One of the latter unit's aircraft was hit and damaged by Flak which put out most of the instruments. With deteriorating weather making it impossible to control the Wellington, Plt Off E.W.Knowles gave the order to bale out. Three of the crew were later picked up by 8th Army units, but the pilot and two others were killed. One aircraft from the diversionary force also failed to return.

British Casualties	
38 Sqn	Wellington Ic Z9108 'R' hit by Flak while mining Benghazi harbour; crew baled out in worsening weather; Plt Off E.W.Knowles and two KiA, three picked up safely
104 Sqn	Wellington II W5422 'E' FTR; Sgt R.H.Richardson and five KiA

Friday-Saturday, 27/28 February 1942

Early in the morning on Friday Hptm Gerlitz of II./JG 27 intercepted a Wellington of 148 Squadron returning from a raid, which he shot down east of Gambut at 0750. Five minutes later he encountered and shot down a Hurricane in the same area. Although the details of these engagements coincide, 205 Group records indicate that this Wellington was lost on Saturday morning, though the Luftwaffe claims were recorded as occurring the day before. The combat recorded by 274 Squadron in regard to the loss of a Hurricane, also appears to fit the details of the 27th, but confusingly, there is also a loss of a 274 Squadron Hurricane flown by a different pilot next day, for which there are no German or Italian claims. It appears fairly clearly to have been one and the same set of engagements, but on which of these two dates has not been finally resolved (see Chapter One).

British Casualties	
148 Sqn	Wellington II Z8423 'V' FTR, reported shot down in flames over Benghazi; Plt Off D.Wisdom and five PoW, captured at Sidi Chalifa, 15m NE Benghazi
70 Sqn	Wellington Ic Z9025 'X' bomb exploded while bombing-up at LG.104; five groundcrew K and four injured

German Claims				
II./JG 27	Hptm Erich Gerlitz*	Wellington	E Gambut	0750
II./JG 27	Hptm Erich Gerlitz*	Hurricane	W Gambut	0755
*See these claims also listed in Chapter One				
Flak		Wellington	off Messina	0656

Wednesday, 4 March 1942

British Casualties	
37 Sqn	Wellington Ic X9886 destroyed on the ground during air raid on Luqa, Malta

Wednesday-Thursday, 4/5 March 1942

An attack was made on Giuliana and Cathedral Moles at Benghazi by 21 aircraft – six of 108 Squadron, five of 104 Squadron and ten of 148 Squadron. One crew reported an engagement with a Ju 88 over the target, but returned safely. However, from a separate raid by 70 Squadron during the night, one bomber failed to return and would appear to have fallen to a NJG 2 Ju 88 night fighter flown by Obfw Köster.

British Casualties	
70 Sqn	Wellington Ic Z1042 'S' off from LG.104 2245. Last heard from 0249; later found crashed in forward area by army personnel, 50-60m S Bomba; Flt Lt P.J.Fisher and five KiA

German Claims					
3./NJG 2	Obfw Alfons Köster	Ju 88C	Wellington	80-90km S Bomba	0119

Thursday, 5 March 1942

En route to Dekheila on a communications flight during the day in bad weather, an Albacore of 826 Squadron, carrying groundcrews, was intercepted at 300 feet over Fuka by a Ju 88 of I./LG 1 which had been bombing the airfield. Almost helpless, the Albacore was shot down, crashing at once.

British Casualties	
148 Sqn	Wellington MiA
70 Sqn	Wellington Z1042 lost

German Claims				
1./LG 1	Lt Gerhard Brenner and crew	Ju 88A	Albacore	Fuka

Wellington Ic DV554 'B' of 70 Squadron.

Friday-Saturday, 6/7 March 1942

Special radio intelligence reconnaissance by 'O' of the Special Signals Squadron over Rhodes, but the aircraft failed to return.

British Casualties	
162 Sqn	Wellington Ic Z8905 'O' FTR from Rhodes; Sgt M.H.Knowles, Lt Baker, RN, and six PoW

Italian Claims	
AA	Wellington over Rhodes; crew PoW

Saturday-Sunday, 7/8 March 1942

Aircraft 'N' of 148 Squadron returning from a sortie over Benghazi, suffered failures to both engines, obliging the pilot to ditch off Sollum. The crew took to their dinghy in which they were spotted by the crew of a Fleet Air Arm Walrus, subsequently being picked up by an ASR launch eight miles to the east. Targets during this night included Piraeus harbour, Greece.

British Casualties	
148 Sqn	Wellington II W5388 'N' ditched after failure of both engines off Sollum; Plt Off J.W.Pelletier and five rescued

Sunday-Monday, 8/9 March 1942

A pair of Wellingtons from 37 Squadron took off to lay mines off the Sicilian ports. As they did so, they collided, both catching fire at once; this caused the mines to explode after they had crash-landed.

British Casualties	
37 Sqn	Wellington Ic Z9038 'H' collided with DV483; Wt Off 1 S.J.Kozlowski and two KiFA, three injured
37 Sqn	Wellington Ic DV483 'Y' collided with Z9038; Flg Off C.J.L.Boyd and two injured, two KiFA

Italian Claims

Flak at Rhodes	Wellington, crew taken PoW

Monday, 9 March 1942

During the day Malta was heavily bombed by Luftwaffe aircraft from Sicily (see *Malta: The Spitfire Year, 1942*), five Wellingtons being destroyed or badly damaged, with a sixth less severely so.

In Egypt 205 Group units were ordered to prepare for an attack on an incoming convoy which had been reported approaching. Twenty-six Wellingtons were to operate, including five torpedo-carriers from 38 Squadron. During the afternoon this unit's commanding officer, Wg Cdr Chaplin, took off to fly to LG.05 at Bu Amud from where the bombers were to operate. South-west of Sidi Barrani, however, his aircraft was intercepted by a pair of 2/JG 27 Bf 109Fs which were undertaking a Freie Jagd (free chase) over the area, and it was shot down by Gefr Romeikat. Chaplin crash-landed the burning aircraft, which was then shot-up on the ground, two of the crew being killed. The survivors scrambled out, just in time to see the German pilots attack three Albacores of 826 Squadron which were making for the same destination. One of these was shot down and a second was extensively damaged (see also Chapter One).

British Casualties

37 Sqn	Wellington Ic Z8731 destroyed on the ground during air raids on Luqa, Malta
37 Sqn	Wellington Ic DV421 destroyed on the ground during air raids on Luqa, Malta
40 Sqn	Wellington Ic Z8417 destroyed on the ground during air raids on Luqa, Malta
38 Sqn	Wellington Ic W5646 'V' destroyed on the ground during air raids on LG.09
unspecified	Wellington destroyed or badly damaged on the ground during bombing raids on Luqa, Malta
unspecified	Wellington damaged on the ground during bombing raids on Luqa, Malta
38 Sqn	Wellington Ic Z9099 'C' shot down by Bf 109; Wg Cdr J.H.Chaplin, DFC, (slt WiA) and two walked to Allied lines; two KiA
826 Sqn	Albacore T9149 shot down by Bf 109s 20m S Sollum; crew baled out, Sub Lt R.S.Nathan and two badly WiA
826 Sqn	Albacore badly damaged by Bf 109s 20m S Sollum

German Claims

2./JG 27	Gefr Herbert Romeikat	Wellington	SW Sidi Barrani	1635
2./JG 27	Lt Friedrich Körner	Albacore	SW Sidi Barrani	1650

Fleet Air Arm Fairey Albacores played an important part in 205 Group's operations, frequently dropping flares to aid the bomber units' 'heavies'. One such aircraft has come to grief on the open desert.

Monday-Tuesday, 9/10 March 1942

With nightfall, the force of Wellingtons despatched to seek and attack the convoy, undertook their search with a high degree of failure. In the event only two of 38 Squadron's torpedo-carriers located the convoy, comprised of five ships, aircraft 'Q' and 'Z' launching attacks without observed results. Following these operations, several attacks were to be made on Heraklion and other Greek and Cretan targets. These did not prove very successful, a high proportion of returns with armaments still aboard occurring, either because the targets could not be found, or for various technical problems with the aircraft.

Thursday, 12 March 1942

British Casualties

37 Sqn	Wellington Ics Z1043 and Z8731 destroyed on the ground during an air raid on Luqa

Sunday, 15 March 1942

During a raid on Rhodes a claim was submitted by S.Ten Pappalardo, pilot of a 163ª Squadriglia CR.42 for a Wellington probably shot down. No RAF losses were actually recorded on this night.

Italian Claims

163ª Sq Aut	S.Ten Giovanni Pappalardo	Wellington Probable	Rhodes	0025

Wellington IIs proved less popular than the 'standard' Mark Ic. Powered by a pair of liquid-cooled Rolls-Royce Merlin engines instead of the Bristol Hercules, these did not provide quite the same level of performance. Aircraft of this type were ultimately all gathered into 104 Squadron with which unit W5382 'R'and Z5800 'B' were serving when photographed on 15 March.

Tuesday, 17 March 1942

British Casualties

37 Sqn	Wellington Ics W5646 and DV493 destroyed on the ground during an air raid on Luqa
40 Sqn	Wellington Ic Z9039 destroyed on the ground during an air raid on Luqa
1 OADU	Wellington Ic Z1164 destroyed on the ground during an air raid on Luqa
70 Sqn	Wellington DV485 engine cut in circuit and crash-landed LG.104

German Casualties

I./NJG 2	Ju 88C-2 WNr 0770 R4+CH engine failure, crashed nr Berka on return, destroyed; Uffz Wolfgang Teuber and 2 KiA

Thursday, 19 March 1942

British Casualties

1 OADU	Wellington 1c Z9035 destroyed on the ground during an air raid on Luqa
37 Sqn	Wellington Ic (unidentified) possibly destroyed on the ground during an air raid on Luqa

Friday-Saturday, 20/21 March 1942

Target – Eleusis, Greece.

British Casualties

104 Sqn	Wellington II Z8510 'R' took off from Kabrit 1455, FTR; Plt Off F.N.Pope and five KiA

Saturday, 21 March 1942

British Casualties

1 OADU	Wellington Ic Z9035 destroyed on the ground during an air raid on Luqa

Monday, 23 March 1942

Ten aircraft of 104 Squadron flew across to Malta on detachment, carrying with them key maintenance and armament personnel.

Friday-Saturday, 27/28 March 1942

A force of 22 bombers drawn from 37, 104 and 148 Squadrons set out to raid Benghazi. Eighteen aircraft unloaded some 51,500lbs of high explosive on the port. Meanwhile, five torpedo-carrying aircraft from 38 Squadron attacked shipping at Patras. Two crews launched their weapons at an 8,000-ton vessel, registering one hit. A third Wellington was hit during the run-in and crashed into the sea as it tried to pull away. The other two aircraft brought their torpedoes back to LG.05 with them.

British Casualties

148 Sqn	Wellington II Z8571 'V' attacked shipping at Benghazi. Technical problems on return and aircraft hit rock near Tolmeta while trying to land, and crashed; Flt Sgt E.M.Papworth (pilot) KiA, one injured, four safe
148 Sqn	Wellington II Z8337 'P' FTR from Benghazi; Sgt C.Wild and five rescued by LRDG patrol and back 13 April
38 Sqn	Wellington Ic AD596 'M' shot down by Flak attacking ships at Patras; Sgt H.Buckingham and three PoW, one KiA

Saturday-Sunday, 28/29 March 1942

During the night four CR.42s from the 154ª Squadriglia, 3° Gruppo CT undertook a sortie to Tobruk, their pilots reporting that they caused fires in the docks area. During the return flight Ten Andalò intercepted a Wellington which he claimed to have shot down.

British Casualties

148 Sqn	Wellington II Z8516 'L' departed LG.106 at 2223 hrs; crashed 59km WNW Mersa Matruh. No further details

Italian Claims

154ª Sq, 3° Gr CT	Ten Egisto Andalò	CR.42	Wellington	Tobruk area	night

Monday 30 March 1942

British Casualties

104 Sqn	Wellington Z8433 MiA Eleusis, Greece

Tuesday, 31 March 1942

British Casualties

70 Sqn	Wellington Ic Z1041 destroyed on the ground during an air raid on LG.104, Qotafiya

Wednesday, 1 April 1942

British Casualties

104 Sqn	Wellington II Z8341 lost to enemy action on the ground – details unknown

Thursday, 2 April 1942

Target – Shipping at Benghazi attacked.

British Casualties	
1 OADU	Wellington Ic DV412 damaged beyond repair on the ground during an air raid on Luqa

Saturday-Sunday, 4/5 April 1942

Benghazi was the target for 70 and 108 Squadrons. The crew of the latter unit's aircraft 'K' reported being engaged by a Ju 88 as a result of which bombs were jettisoned. One of 70 Squadron's ten Wellingtons failed to return. In the opposite direction five of 38 Squadron's torpedo-carriers undertook a sweep in the Salamis area, looking for ships. This formation also suffered one loss.

British Casualties	
70 Sqn	Wellington Ic AD632 'Z' FTR from Benghazi; Sgt G.T.L.Salmon and five PoW

Sunday-Monday, 5/6 April 1942

British Casualties

148 Sqn	Wellington II Z8359 'H' off to bomb harbour facilities at Benghazi to create a diversion for mine layers. On return one engine cut and aircraft crash-landed 150m E of Benghazi; Sgt B.Nethercote and crew walked to British lines and picked up safely by a patrol

Tuesday-Wednesday, 7/8 April 1942

Target – shipping at Benghazi.

British Casualties	
38 Sqn	Wellington Ic AD604 'U' attacked shipping in Benghazi harbour. On return descended through cloud to ascertain position. Starboard engine caught fire and aircraft crashed nr Mersa Matruh; Flt Sgt T.A.Holdsworth and two KiFA, three injured

Thursday, 9 April 1942

Italian Casualties

77ª Sq, 13°Gr, 2°St CT	4 MC.200s, MM 5235 '77-6', MM 5312 '77-2', MM 4520 '77-10', MM 7678 '77-7' damaged by bombs at Benghazi K3

Saturday-Sunday, 11/12 April 1942

British Casualties

37 Sqn	Wellington Ic DV420 raided shipping in Benghazi harbour; hydraulics damaged by Flak, resulting in undercarriage collapsing on landing at Mersa Matruh; Plt Off R.A.V.Salmon and four safe, one injured

Monday, 13 April 1942

British Casualties

148 Sqn	Wellington Ic DV502 damaged beyond repair on the ground during an air raid on Luqa
1 OADU	Wellington Ics Z1178 and DV537 damaged beyond repair on the ground during an air raid on Luqa
Unspecified	Wellington Ic BB505 damaged beyond repair on the ground during an air raid on Luqa

Tuesday, 21 April 1942

British Casualties

148 Sqn	Wellington Ic AD652 'D' destroyed on the ground during an air raid on Luqa
1 OADU	Wellingtons Z8584 and Z9032 damaged beyond repair on the ground during an air raid on Luqa

Tuesday-Wednesday, 21/22 April 1942

From Luqa Wg Cdr Rollinson led five 148 Squadron Wellingtons to attack Comiso. In very poor weather conditions, only three crews found what they believed to be the target, but in fact they bombed Gerbini airfield, killing three Italian servicemen and wounding ten Germans. The other two released their bombs on Catania.

Wednesday-Thursday, 22/23 April 1942

With darkness, two damaged 148 Squadron Wellingtons which had been rendered serviceable, joined one other again seeking to attack Comiso. On return crews reported bombs exploding close to hangars; they then handed their aircraft over to be refuelled and re-armed for a second sortie by fresh crews. These attacked in the face of intense Flak, but returned without suffering any damage. One aircraft then made a third sortie before dawn, some bombs falling near Ragusa.

British Casualties

1 OADU	Wellington Ic DV548 flying from Luqa to Egypt failed to arrive; Plt Off J.H.Reid and five KiA
1 OADU	Wellington Ic HF849 flying from Luqa to Egypt failed to arrive; Sgt A.P.Westle and five crew, plus Sqn Ldr S.O'R.Surridge, MC, and two other passengers KiA

Thursday, 23 April 1942

British Casualties

148 Sqn	Wellington Ic ES984 'C' destroyed on the ground during an air raid on Luqa
1 OADU	Wellington Ic DV412 damaged beyond repair on the ground during an air raid on Luqa

Thursday-Friday, 23/24 April 1942

Despite the constant attrition of aircraft on the ground at Luqa, two replacement Wellingtons were flown in for 148 Squadron during the day, allowing raids to be made for a third consecutive night. Joined by two serviceable survivors from the original detachment, they set off once again for Comiso at 2110. Here 'O' was shot down with the loss of the crew and a second bomber was badly damaged. On return the two surviving aircraft were readied again, setting out at 0110 with replacement crews to repeat the attack. Despite heavy fire from the ground, both returned to prepare for a third raid. On this last occasion 'Q' was shot down, three members of the crew being killed and three captured. Although a few bombs fell near Vittoria railway station, none hit Comiso airfield despite the eight sorties. Subsequently, Flt Lt Hayter, the pilot of 'Q', would take part in the Great Escape from Stalag Luft III on 6 April 1944, following which he was shot by the Gestapo on recapture.

British Casualties

148 Sqn	Wellington Ic DV573 'O' shot down; Flg Off R.McM.Harper and five KiA
148 Sqn	Wellington Ic BB483 'Q' shot down; Flt Lt A.R.H.Hayter and two PoW, three KiA

German Claims (recorded a day earlier)

Flak	Wellington	N Vittoria	2117
Flak	Wellington	Vittoria-Gela	0120

Saturday, 25 April 1942

British Casualties

104 Sqn	Wellington II Z8497 destroyed on the ground during an air raid on Kabrit

Saturday-Sunday, 25/26 April 1942

During the night a Wellington was shot down by Benghazi AA and part of the crew were captured.

British Casualties

70 Sqn	Wellington Ic Z8984 'D' attacked the harbour and shipping at Benghazi; hit and badly damaged by Flak over target and second pilot KiA. Sgt P.R.Darby and four baled out and PoW; aircraft crashed and blew up 20m S Benghazi

Italian Claims

AA at Benghazi	Wellington shot down; part of crew PoW (recorded on 24/25 night)

Sunday, 26 April 1942

British Casualties

38 Sqn	Wellington Ic DV555 destroyed on the ground during an air raid on Luqa
70 Sqn	Wellington Ic Z1045 reported lost as a result of enemy action – details unspecified; Wg Cdr J.H.T.Simpson and five safe, one injured

Tuesday-Wednesday, 28/29 April 1942

A 70 Squadron aircraft which had taken off at 2000 from LG.104, was shot down over the airfield by an intruding Ju 88C of I./NJG 2

British Casualties

70 Sqn	Wellington Ic Z8766 'Y' shot down by intruder; Plt Off A.C.White and three KiA, two WiA, one fatally
104 Sqn	Wellington II Z8500 'B' attacked airfields at Martuba. Seen caught by searchlights and Flak, going down into the sea and bursting into flames; Sgt H.J.Bennett and five KiA
37 Sqn	Wellington DV618 MiA

German Claims

2./NJG 2	Obfw Hermann Sommer	Wellington

In late April several attacks on Axis airfields had been undertaken, but during this period the group recorded a rather high proportion of 'no shows' amongst the aircraft despatched.

May brought some changes of command, starting right at the top when Air Cdr A.P.Ritchie, AFC, took over the group from Air Cdr L.L.Maclean. At the same time Wg Cdr R.H.Maw, DFC assumed command of 108 Squadron from Sqn Ldr Beare, Wg Cdr R.E.Ridgeway took over 40 Squadron, and a week later Sqn Ldr Blackburn, DFC, replaced the newly-promoted Wg Cdr Beare, DSO, DFC, in 104 Squadron.

This was but the start, for on 15 May Grp Capt G.H.Russell took over command of 242 Wing from Grp Capt May and Wg Cdr G.F.Wood was posted from Group HQ to lead 70 Squadron; Wg Cdr J.H.T.Simpson from this latter unit was promoted to command 236 Wing, Here he replaced Grp Capt J.S.T.Fall, DSC, AFC who became station commander at Kabrit. Towards the end of the month Sqn Ldr D.A.Kerr, DSO, replaced Wg Cdr J.D.Rollinson with 148 Squadron. It was at this time, as detailed in Chapter One that 2 and 4 Middle East Training Squadrons were formed within 205 Group to provide additional conversion and refresher training, mainly for crews arriving to join the unit.

Friday-Saturday, 1/2 May 1942

German Claims

Flak	Wellington	S Piraeus, Greece 0045

Sunday-Monday, 3/4 May 1942

A Liberator of 108 Squadron took off at 1830 from Fayid to attack the harbour and shipping at Tobruk. It was intercepted by one of I./NJG 2's Ju 88C night fighters and shot down, crashing near Soluch. Apart from the crew, it had been carrying Grp Capt F.M.V.May from 242 Wing for operational experience. He was one of three to survive, but had been wounded and was to die in a German hospital on 22 May.

British Casualties

108 Sqn	Liberator II AL511 'A' shot down by night fighter; Flt Lt D.H.McArthur DFC and three KiA, 3 PoWs, one of which DofW

German Claims

2./NJG 2	Hptm Heinz Harmstorf	Liberator	Derna	0209

Tuesday, 5 May 1942

British Casualties

148 Sqn	Wellington Ic DV605 'U' destroyed on the ground during an air raid on Luqa

Saturday-Sunday, 9/10 May 1942

Target – shipping at Benghazi.

British Casualties

37 Sqn	Wellington Ic Z8987 'B' MiA; Plt Off H.E.A.Scard and five MiA

Wednesday-Thursday, 13/14 May 1942

Target – Benghazi harbour.

British Casualties

104 Sqn	Wellington Z8574 'L' MiA; Plt Off A.F.O'Donnell and five KiA
104 Sqn	Wellington Z8341 MiA Benghazi

Sunday, 17 May, 1942

British Casualties

104 Sqn	Wellington Z8498 'M' raided Benghazi harbour, crashed in force-landing in desert and abandoned; Sgt R.A.Baker and crew safe
104 Sqn	Wellington Z8574 MiA Benghazi

Tuesday-Wednesday, 19/20 May 1942

British Casualties

37 Sqn	Wellington Ic AD626 MiA from raid on Heraklion, Crete; Plt Off A.D.J.Salt and five KiA

German Claims

Flak	Wellington	6km E Heraklion, Crete 0132

Wednesday, 20 May 1942

During the day 108 Squadron moved from Fayid to LG.105 while the recently-formed 2 METS went from Shallufa to Kabrit. A week later 61 RSU would leave Kabrit on posting to LG.104.

British Casualties

1 OADU	Wellington II Z8589 lost on way from Gibraltar to Malta, attacked and damaged by Ju 88. Ditched out of fuel off Filicudi Island, N Sicily and front gunner R.C.Henley KiFA, plus one badly injured. Crew in dinghy for six days. Two then swam ashore on Filicudi and rescue followed; Plt Off H.G.Bancroft and four PoW (one injured), one KiFA

Friday-Saturday, 22/23 May 1942

Five Wellingtons of 38 Squadron took off for Benghazi to lay mines. One aircraft went in below the safety height and suffered severe damage. The pilot ordered the crew to bale out, which they did to the south-east of the target, but he then managed to maintain control for three hours before baling out himself; he was picked up on the 29th near Wadi Natrun in a weak condition. The rest of the crew were helped to eventual safety by local Senussi, although one of their number died before assistance could arrive.

British Casualties

38 Sqn	Wellington Ic BB484 'X' laying mines outside Benghazi harbour; badly damaged, crash-landed at Wadi Natrun. Flt Sgt D.R.Ward and four safe; one died

German Claims

III./ZG 26	Lt Alfred Wehmeyer	Wellington	night

With the outbreak of fighting resulting from the launch of the new Axis offensive in the Gazala area, the main target in late May became the airfields at Martuba, motor transport frequently also being strafed. Before the end of the month Tmimi had also become a priority target; incendiaries and spikes were dropped in large quantities here.

Monday, 25 May 1942

German Casualties

1./NJG 2	Ju 88C-2 WNr 0833 R4+DL badly damaged by AA fire and force-landed 25km W Bardia in Allied territory; Lt Walter Riedlberger and two walked to safety in own lines

Wednesday-Thursday, 27/28 May 1942

German Casualties

1./NJG 2	Ju 88C-6 WNr 360190 R4+EL shot down by AA at 0227 near Bardia; Obfw Anton Naiss and two KiA

Thursday-Friday, 28/29 May 1942

From Malta six Wellingtons of 104 Squadron were sent off to attack Catania airfield. Five bombed from 10,000ft, two 4,000lb bombs being amongst those dropped. Returning crews reported seeing many hits on buildings and a number of fires; one He 111 bomber was destroyed during the attack. One crew reported seeing two night fighters over the target area, but these then appeared to collide, following which there was a large explosion. The bomber which had not attacked, had suffered an engine failure over Sicily, the crew jettisoning all armament and bombs in an effort to retain altitude. On approach to Malta, however, the aircraft crashed near Attard. Three members of the crew were killed and two injured, only the pilot surviving unhurt.

British Casualties

104 Sqn	Wellington II Z8366 'T' crashed on return due to engine failure; Sgt R.J.Hills safe, but three KiFA and two injured amongst crew

Friday-Saturday, 29/30 May 1942

Two Wellingtons of 148 Squadron were lost during an attack on the Tmimi landing grounds, both losses being due to technical problems, but both crews survived unharmed and reached safety.

British Casualties

148 Sqn	Wellington Ic Z8974 crash-landed in Axis territory nr Bir Hacheim due to engine failure; Flt Lt J.A.Watts and crew walked for two days, meeting a Free French patrol cut off from the main force. Broke through lines next night and returned to base
148 Sqn	Wellington Ic DV654 crash-landed 20m SSW Sidi Barrani due to engine fire; aircraft destroyed by crew who then walked to the frontier wire. Signalled a Bombay which returned and dropped message and water; later rescued by a lorry

German Claims

7./ZG 26	Oblt Alfred Wehmeyer	Wellington	Ras el Tin	2034

Saturday, 30 May 1942

British Casualties

1 OADU	Wellington Ic HX369 departed Gibraltar for Malta, but damaged by Flak over Pantelleria; force-landed Licata, Sicily and captured after several days; Flt Lt G.H.Lonnberg and five PoW
109 Sqn	Wellington Z1113 MiA

Saturday-Sunday, 30/31 May 1942

German Casualties

1./NJG 2	Ju 88C-4 WNr 0365 R4+BH damaged 30% by AA and crash-landed at Kastelli a/f, Crete; Lt Heinz Rökker and two safe

Sunday-Monday, 31 May/1 June 1942

Eleven aircraft of 148 Squadron were detailed to operate, taking off at 2125; most returned by 0315 except 'R', Flg Off Astell (AD653) and 'J', Sgt Ross. No news was received of 'R', but 'J'(DV615) landed badly shot-up at LG.05 after attacking Derna. The aircraft was unserviceable and Sgt Ross had received splinter wounds in his shoulder. News was finally received on 6 June that Flg Off W.Astell was at Gazala MDS (main dressing station), suffering from exposure, but could be expected back in two days.

It seems that both the Wellingtons had been attacked by Axis fighters – but not by radar-equipped aircraft. Between 2230-2400 Ten Renato Talamini, a pilot of the 17° Gruppo's 80ª Squadriglia, flying a CR.42 borrowed from 3° Gruppo, intercepted a Wellington over Martuba and claimed to have shot it down; the Regia Aeronautica reported that part of the crew was taken prisoner which certainly appears to indicate that he had attacked 'R'. However at 2310, in much the same time-slot, the Luftwaffe's Oblt Wehmeyer in a ZG 26 Bf 110 claimed a similar victory in the same area. Presumably he had attacked 'J', which makes for a neat conclusion – or did Talamini attack 'J' and the capture of some of the crew from 'R' come to be used as evidence of the latter's success?

A second claim was submitted by the Luftwaffe relating to these nocturnal hours when 1./NJG 2's Oblt Albert Schulz targeted a twin-engined aircraft which he identified as a Boston. No such aircraft was lost on this night, or in adjacent dates before or after. On 1 June a Maryland of 223 Squadron was reportedly struck off charge in undefined circumstances. There is a vague possibility that this aircraft, presumably on a night practice flight of some sort, may have been the victim, although this possibility must be considered unlikely.

British Casualties

148 Sqn	Wellington II AD653 'R' attacked and damaged by fighter while targeting Biret el Cheiba airfield; caught fire and crash-landed by Flg Off W.Astell and Plt Off A.W.Dodds after rest of crew baled out. Made their way to front line, but here Dodds captured; Astell safe by 5 June. One other member of crew evaded capture and returned, but three PoW
148 Sqn	Wellington Ic DV615 'J' damaged ; Sgt Ross slt WiA but he and five safe

German Claims

7./ZG 26	Oblt Alfred Wehmeyer	Wellington	Martuba	2310
I./NJG 2	Oblt Albert Schulz (unconfirmed)	Boston		

Italian Claims

80 Sq/17° Gr/1° CT	Ten Renato Talamini*	Wellington	Martuba	2230-2400

*Flying a CR.42 borrowed from 3° Gruppo CT

An extraordinary shot of bombs falling towards an Axis vessel which is taking violent evasive action far below. The bombs have just missed hitting this Liberator II which appears to carry the individual letter 'X' on the fuselage ahead of the roundel. The form of roundel (Type A) indicates that this was probably taken during the convoy battles of June and that this was an aircraft of the newly-arrived 159 Squadron.

At this time 16 Ju 88Cs of I./NJG 2 were ordered to Africa with their crews to operate from Benghazi, Derna, Qasaba, Tobruk and Heraklion. Almost at once five of the new arrivals were amongst 20 Axis aircraft destroyed at Qasaba by an LRDG patrol. Within days the Albacore crews of 826 Squadron reported an increase in night fighter activity, all of which they reported, appeared to involve Ju 88s.

Friday-Saturday, 5/6 June 1942

British Casualties

70 Sqn	Wellington Ic Z9096 'M' damaged by Flak while attacking Martuba airfields; force-landed 100m SW Tobruk; Sgt F.B.Leach and five PoW

Italian Claims

AA gunners at Derna	Wellington

Sunday-Monday, 7/8 June 1942

British Claims

148 Sqn	Wellington Ic DV618 'A' on way to attack harbour and shipping at Benghazi had engine fail due to high oil temperature and subsequently force-landed. Crew took rations from the dinghy and walked for two days before attracting the attention of a passing Baltimore. Two of the squadron's aircraft were then sent out to pick them up

Italian Claims

AA at Barce	Martin Maryland	2330

Tuesday, 9 June 1942

British Casualties

109 Sqn	Wellington Z1048 MiA
821 Sqn	Albacore N4351 damaged on landing from early flight; abandoned when enemy captured airfield

Wednesday-Thursday, 10/11 June 1942

Crete became the target during the night, Castelli Pediada being attacked by 21 aircraft of 70, 104 and 108 Squadrons. One of the 108 Squadron bombers which was carrying an artillery officer to aid in identifying Flak positions, was hit over Maleme and failed to return with the loss of all aboard.

British Casualties

108 Sqn	Wellington Ic BB482 'K' FTR from Crete; Flt Sgt R.H.McRae and crew of five plus Lt R.B.Strang of 85 Battery, RHA

German Casualties

1./NJG 2	Ju 88A-4 WNr 5678 R4+FH destroyed on ground by bombs during air raid on Kastelli

Friday-Saturday, 12/13 June 1942

Benghazi harbour was bombed as a diversion to mine-laying activities. Eighteen aircraft from 70, 104 and 108 Squadrons were involved. By dawn on the 13th 205 Group had, since 26 May, undertaken 403 sorties against Benghazi and the Axis airfields, concentrating particularly on the fighter bases at Tmimi, Martuba, Berka and Derna. From 8 June a series of attacks had also been made on Italian ports and airfields in preparation for the convoy to be run through the western Mediterranean to Malta.

British Casualties

104 Sqn	Wellington II Z8592 'Z' hit by Flak and crashed in sea SW Benghazi harbour; Plt Off F.H.Shackleton and five KiA

Sunday-Monday, 14/15 June 1942

British Casualties

108 Sqn	Wellington Ic AD624 'T' off to attack Benghazi; radioed that aircraft was force-landing 45m SE Bir Hacheim; Sgt G.Watkins and five PoW

Friday-Saturday, 19/20 June 1942

At this point 205 Group was joined by the B-24Ds of the Halverson Detachment, which was to operate initially like the RAF bombers – by night. This was not really what the American crews had been trained for, nor was it much to their taste.

British Casualties

37 Sqn	Wellington Ic DV669 'W' off to attack harbour and shipping at Benghazi; aircraft believed to be this one seen going down near the target; Flg Off W.L.Kauter and five KiA

Sunday-Monday, 21/22 June 1942

Airfields at Gazala were bombed and it was thought that some hits on aircraft had been achieved. The commanding officer's aircraft from 148 Squadron received a direct Flak hit and exploded. Flt Lt Westcott was blown out, unconscious, and awoke on the ground some five miles east of Benghazi, his parachute next to him. However, Wg Cdr Kerr and the rest of the crew had all died in the explosion. The night also saw the first raid on a North African target to be made by USAAF, when nine B-24s of the Halverson Detachment bombed Benghazi after the port had been lit up by preceding Wellingtons dropping flares and incendiaries. The crews reported seeing two large fires at the base of the Cathedral Mole and several smaller conflagrations.

British Casualties

148 Sqn	Wellington Ic ES990 'S' destroyed by Flak; Wg Cdr D.A.Kerr, DSO, and four KiA, one survived and PoW
821 Sqn	Albacore T9175 hit crashed aircraft when landing at night; burned when the airfield fell to the Axis

Tuesday-Wednesday, 23/24 June 1942

The Gazala airfields were priority again, 15 aircraft from 37 Squadron, three each from 40 and 70 Squadrons, 12 from 104 and 12 from 148 Squadrons making up the force. Eleven Halverson Detachment aircraft (now usually referred to as HalPro) attacked Benghazi again.

Wednesday-Thursday, 24/25 June 1942

The full weight of 205 Group's units was directed against Benghazi harbour in the biggest attack yet undertaken in the Middle East. Seventy-three Wellingtons drawn from all six squadrons, joined by nine Liberators of the newly-arrived 159 Squadron and ten B-24s of HalPro set off, 85 crews releasing a total of 170,900lbs of high explosive and 39,320lbs of incendiaries on the target area. Many fires and explosions were reported on return from an attack which cost only two aircraft.

British Casualties

37 Sqn	Wellington Ic DV643 MiA; Flt Lt C.P.T.Halliwell and five KiA
40 Sqn	Wellington Ic DV652 'E' ran out of fuel due to excessive consumption and crashed 15m from LG.115 when both engines cut, then catching fire; Sgt R.E.White and two injured, one KiA and one safe

Thursday, 25 June 1942

British Casualties

821 Sqn	Albacore N4244 failed to start after engine change at LG.15. Fired on by strafing Bf 109s, and enemy approaching, abandoned; Sub Lt P.F.Manders and crew departed by road

Lt Heinz Rökker of I./NJG 2 claimed a Wellington shot down near Mersa Matruh on 25 June. When the unit was ordered home to the Reich he had claimed six victories. He would end the war wearing the Ritterkreuz mit Eichenlaubs and the Deutches Kreuz im Gelt for 64 victories, all but one by night.

Thursday-Friday, 25/26 June 1942

Eighty-two Wellingtons attacked Axis MT concentrations at night, and although none of the four-engined bombers accompanied them on this occasion, a greater weight of ordnance was dropped due to the shorter distance to the target area; 288,500lbs of HE, 180 40lb fragmentation bombs, and 17 SBC 21lb incendiaries were released between 2125 and 0230; only four of the aircraft due to take part failed to operate. A second sortie was made by five aircraft from 104 Squadron and ten from 108 during which a further 67,500lbs of HE were added.

On this occasion, however, elements of I./NJG 2 had been brought up from the Gruppe's various Mediterranean bases to provide some nocturnal protection for Rommel's forces at the front. Pilots from this unit claimed three Wellingtons shot down during the course of the night. Sgt Medwin's 37 Squadron aircraft was hit by a single long burst from a fighter which started a fire. Medwin ordered the crew to prepare to bale out, but Sgt J.L.Abson misunderstood and jumped at once; he was never found. The other four stayed aboard until Medwin had crash-landed during which the Wellington was destroyed, he and his co-pilot both suffering head injuries. They all then set off for British lines and were picked up safely by a forward patrol after about three hours.

70 Squadron's 'L' undertook a successful attack on a convoy of trucks, but was then targeted by a Ju 88, fire from which fatally wounded the rear gunner. A number of small fires were extinguished by the observer, thus allowing the badly damaged aircraft to be belly-landed off the flare path on its return to base. Even as they did so, the four-engined types were out on their own account, five HalPro B-24s and four 159 Squadron Liberators dropping 31,600lbs of HE on Tobruk, which was now in Axis hands. This attack also acted as a diversion for Albacores seeking to dive-bomb two supply vessels in the harbour.

British Casualties

148 Sqn	Wellington DV646 'A' crashed in force-landing W Fuka
104 Sqn	Wellington Z8500 shot down after take-off from LG.106
M.E.	Wellington ES984 destroyed in air raid
37 Sqn	Wellington Ic DV522 attacked by fighter 30m SW Mersa Matruh and crash-landed due to damage; Sgt I.G.Medwin and four safe (two slt injured), one MiA
70 Sqn	Wellington Ic DV564 'L' attacked and damaged by Ju 88; crash-landed at base; Flt Sgt G.J.Wagner and four safe, one DofW
104 Sqn	Wellington II Z8572 'N' hit by a bomb as about to take off from LG.106; Sgt P.M.Sharplin and three WiA, two KiA

German Claims

1./NJG 2	Lt Heinz Rökker	Wellington	Mersa Matruh	2345
1./NJG 2	Lt Heinz Rökker	Wellington	50km SE Mersa Matruh	0009

Friday, 26 June 1942

Earlier in the year, following the conclusion of the Crusader operation, 231 Wing had moved its squadrons forward to be nearer to the main targets in and around Bizerta. 79 Squadron had moved up to LG.140 as early as 5 February, 37 Squadron going to LG.09 on 27 April. During May, as the prospect of major offensive action approached, 104 and 148 Squadrons moved from Kabrit to LG.106, 108 Squadron following them a few days later to LG.105.

As 8th Army fell back from the Gazala battles in ever greater confusion, a return to the bases in the Delta became ever-more imperative, and on 26 June all these units 'headed for home', 37 and 70 Squadrons (231 Wing) to LG.224, 104 and 148 Squadrons (236 Wing) to Kabrit and 108 Squadron to Fayid. At Abu Sueir 40 Squadron shifted to Shallufa, allowing 231 Wing to fly in to its unit's previous base on the 29th. The supporting units were also on the move at the same time, Advanced 37 ASP moving to LG.24, Advanced 36 ASP to Kabrit, 1 R & R party and RSU MTRS to Fayid, and 61 RSU moving to join 57 RSU at Shallufa. This quite massive administrative exercise was achieved without major loss, and all squadrons were rapidly back in action.

German Claims

I./NJG 2	Fw Heyne	Wellington	0134

British Casualties

104 Sqn	Wellingtons Z8508 and Z8580 collided at LG.106 and DBR

Friday-Saturday, 26/27 June 1942

Another big attack was made on MT concentrations, on this occasion three Wellingtons falling to German night fighters. However, only one such claim was made by Fw Heyne; another of NJG 2's night fighters failed to return, apparently claimed shot down by the crew of the 70 Squadron Wellingtons taking part in the raid. The crew of this night fighter is very likely to have been responsible for the shooting down of the other bombers. Eight Halpro B-24s raided a supply vessel in Tobruk, crews reporting a violent explosion and a large fire on one jetty.

British Claims

70 Sqn	crew of Flt Lt Stewart	Ju 88

British Casualties	
40 Sqn	Wellington Ic Z9028 'V' searching for targets in El Alamein area, shot down by night fighter and crashed near Halfaya railway station; Sgt S.H.Gunn and five KiA
70 Sqn	Wellington Ic Z9102 'A' searching for targets around El Daba, attacked by fighter. Engine caught fire and aircraft dived into ground; Sgt F.V.Charlton and one KiA, four walked NE, picked up and taken to Fuka
108 Sqn	Wellington Ic ES981 'A' seeking MT in Sidi Barrani area, shot down by Ju 88; Sgt P.K.J.Street and three KiA; two picked up by 7th Armoured Div
German Casualties	
2./NJG 2	Ju 88C-2 WNr 0752 R4+LK failed to return from mission over Egypt. Presumed crashed in Fuka area for u/k reasons; Uffz Hermann Hackhausen and two MiA

Saturday-Sunday, 27/28 June 1942

Attacks were directed against an Axis HQ, motor transport and landing grounds in the battle area generally. Eighty-one bombers were sent off, including ten of 159 Squadron's Liberators, all but ten making attacks during which 243,000lbs of HE and 39 SBC 4lb incendiaries were dropped, all without loss.

British Casualties			
108 Sqn	Wellington ES981 MiA Sidi Barrani		
40 Sqn	Wellington DV652 damaged by Flak; not repaired		
German Claims			
3./NJG 2	Obfw Alfons Köster	Blenheim	0007

Sunday-Monday, 28/29 June 1942

Axis MT concentrations were again the main targets; 242,500lbs of HE and six SBD 40lb fragmentation bombs were dropped during the night by 75 Wellingtons and seven Liberators from seven squadrons. At the same time four more 38 Squadron Wellingtons planted mines in Tobruk harbour and 19 HalPro B-24s dropped a further 39,000lbs of HE here. During the night one Wellington of 108 Squadron was intercepted by I./NJG 2's Lt Heinz Rökker, who inflicted severe damage on the British aircraft, claiming to have shot it down (it was indeed subsequently destroyed in a crash-landing). The bomber's crew fought back, the front gunner inflicting sufficient damage to bring down their attacker in a similar manner.

British Claims			
108 Sqn	front gunner of Sqn Ldr D.H.Jacklin's Wellington Ic R1029 'S'	Ju 88	
British Casualties			
104 Sqn	Wellington II Z8646 'B' took off from Kabrit but the starboard engine cut. The bombs, which were fused contrary to instructions, were jettisoned at 600-700ft and their explosions caused the aircraft to dive into the Great Bitter Lake; Flt Lt D.J.Haydon and five KiA		
108 Sqn	Wellington Ic R1029 'S' bombed Axis positions at Mersa Matruh but attacked by Ju 88 and badly damaged. Crashed while force-landing at Amiriya. Front gunner returned fire and set the night fighter on fire; Sqn Ldr D.H.Jacklin, DFC, and crew safe		
German Claims			
1./NJG 2	Lt Heinz Rökker	Wellington	60km SE Mersa Matruh 2358
German Casualties			
1./NJG 2	Ju 88C-6 WNr 360002 R4+DH crash-landed and destroyed 60km SE Mersa Matruh after combat with Wellington; Lt Heinz Rökker and one WiA, one safe		
3./NJG 2	Ju 88C-6 WNr 360231 15% damaged by AA nr Mersa Matruh; Stfw Hans Zappe and one safe; Fw Alfred Fuss panicked and baled out – KiA		
1./NJG 2	Ju 88C-6 WNr 360229 20% damaged by strafing fighter while on the ground at Derna		

Monday-Tuesday, 29/30 June 1942

Tobruk harbour was raided by three Halpro B-24s, six 159 Squadron Liberators and four of 162 Squadron's special Wellingtons. One of the American bombers was shot down over the target area, reportedly falling victim to Flak. The aircraft was actually shot down by Hptm Semrau of I./NJG 2. Semrau initially claimed a B-24 but was advised on his return that his victim must have been a Halifax.

The second four-engined type to reach the Middle East with detachments from 10 and 76 Squadrons in England, seen here preparing for a night sortie, was the Handley Page Halifax. This was probably an early Mark II version of the aircraft.

US Casualties	
HalPro	B-24D 41-1624/11 'Balls of Fire' shot down off El Fayid, reportedly by Flak; Capt Francis E.Nestor and 6 MiA

German Claims				
3./NJG 2	Hptm Paul Semrau	Halifax	Tobruk	0015
3./NJG 2	Hptm Paul Semrau	Wellington		0035

Tuesday-Wednesday, 30 June/1 July 1942

Returning from an attack on LG.17, one 37 Squadron Wellington developed an engine fire which caused the propeller to fall off. With the aircraft losing height, the crew baled out, three landing safely in the Delta area although one was injured severely due to a heavy landing. However, Plt Off G.W.Allan, the pilot, and the rear gunner fell into the Nile and both drowned.

British Casualties	
37 Sqn	Wellington Ic DV675 abandoned due to engine fire on return from a sortie to LG.17; Plt Off G.W.Allan and one drowned in Nile, three landed in Delta, one severely injured by hard landing

Wednesday-Thursday, 1/2 July 1942

During an attack on MT in the desert a very large explosion was seen, followed by a quantity of burning debris. It was believed that two Wellingtons had collided over the target area, near El Daba, and indeed two failed to return.

British Casualties	
104 Sqn	Wellington II Z8655 'B' left 0045 believed to have collided with X9986, crashed near El Alamein; Flg Off G.G.Retallack and five KiFA
162 Sqn	Wellington Ic X9986 crashed after collision over target near El Daba at 0200 with Z8655; Flg Off A.P.Ouelette RCAF and five KiFA

German Casualties	
I./NJG 2	Ju 88C-6 WNr 360246 crash-landed at Berka West, 35% damaged

Thursday-Friday, 2/3 July 1942

During this period of heavy raids by the bombers, losses were generally fairly light. The detachment of 104 Squadron on Malta also continued to operate throughout June and early July. Several special operations were undertaken against dockyards and units at Taranto. This night proved to be somewhat more costly, however, bringing at least one loss to the Luftwaffe's Nachtjagd.

The day had also seen the arrival at Lydda from India of the 7th Bombardment Squadron with its B-17s. That very night four of these had operated. A pattern quickly established itself whereby the crews of the somewhat longer-ranging B-24s concentrated most of their efforts on Benghazi, while those of the B-17s attacked the nearer of the ports, that at Tobruk.

British Casualties

37 Sqn	Wellington Ic Z1179 attacked troops in El Daba area; shot down by night fighter 14m W Daba; Plt Off F.A.Scott and four KiA, one PoW
37 Sqn	Wellington Ic Z8990 off 0025 to attack MT. Explosion nr target, starboard propeller fell off and engine caught fire . Nr LG.100 crew ordered to bale out and Flg Off S.J.Thorne left controls to open bulkhead door for front gunner, but fell through escape hatch on return; he and one KiA when parachutes failed or were not properly clipped on, just four safe 104 Sqn Wellington II Z8647 'W' off from Abu Sueir to attack MT. Lost one engine to Flak and crash-landed in desert; Flt Lt D.Ellis and five walked for three days but captured just short of Allied lines and PoWs

German Claims

1./NJG 2	Fw Werner Heyne	Wellington	N Africa	0117
3./NJG 2	Hptm Paul Semrau	Wellington	N Africa	0202

Friday-Saturday, 3/4 July 1942

British Casualties

40 Sqn	Wellington Ic HF914 'G' off to bomb tank repair shop at Mersa Matruh; hit by Flak on bombing run and down in flames; Sgt W.E.Dwyer and five KiA

Saturday-Sunday, 4/5 July 1942

Six US B-24s again raided Benghazi, claiming to have achieved two direct hits and several near misses on a convoy near the port, reporting that a tanker was left on fire.

British Casualties

821 Sqn	Albacore N4379 shot-up by Ju 88; Sub Lt W.Hardaker and one safe
70 Sqn	Wellington Ic Z1175 'L' off after targets of opportunity in El Alamein area; starboard engine cut during raid and a/c crash-landed nr Qassassin, 30m W base; Sgt J.R.Milligan and five all slt injured
70 Sqn	Wellington Ic Z8972 'B' off after targets of opportunity, but attacked by Ju 88 while bombing and had to jettison remaining bombs; overshot on landing and hit operations station; Sgt E.A.C.Barfoot and crew safe, one injured
108 Sqn	Wellington Ic DV662 'L' off to attack concentrations around El Daba. Attacked and badly damaged by Ju 88 and aircraft put into violent dive. As pilot pulled out at about 150ft, yellow flash seen behind and report possibly Ju 88 crashed. A/c swung on landing due to punctured tyre and undercarriage sheared off. One of crew fatally WiA during night-fighter attack and died soon after landing; Flt Sgt Metcalf and four safe

German Claims

I./NJG 2	Lt Georg Wiedow	Wellington	N Africa	0128
3./NJG 2	Hptm Paul Semrau	Wellington	N Africa	0210
I./NJG 2	Lt Georg Wiedow	Wellington	N Africa	0320

German Casualties

3./NJG 2	Ju 88C-6 WNr 360243 shot down in combat with Wellington nr El Daba; Lt Erwin Wolfbauer and two KiA

Sunday-Monday, 5/6 July 1942

Nine HalPro B-24s returned to Benghazi, the crews believing that they had hit an ammunition ship, a big explosion being seen.

British Casualties

37 Sqn	Wellington Ic DV508 'G' off 0100 to attack targets of opportunity in El Daba area but FTR. Other crews reported aircraft being attacked by night fighter 14m SE El Daba; Plt Off G.D.B.Raffil and five KiA

German Claims

3./NJG 2	Hptm Paul Semrau	Wellington	N Africa	0155
2./NJG 2	Hpt Heinz Harmstorf	Wellington	N Africa	0246

German Casualties

I./NJG 2	Ju 88C-6 WNr 360191 R4+DK shot down by Beaufighter night fighter; Lt Georg Wiedow and two KiA

Monday-Tuesday, 6/7 July 1942

British Casualties

14 Sqn	Blenheim IV Z7712 off to attack MT beteen Fuka-Mersa Matruh 0445-0512; shot down nr Fuka after bombing; Sqn Ldr A.N.Pirie and one safe, WOp/AG KiA
148 Sqn	Wellington Ic DV603 'H' off to attack MT but crashed on edge of Great Bitter Lake and blew up; Sgt C.Handley and four K. Turret gunner Sgt J.E.Robinson blown clear on hitting the water. Although initially trapped up to his neck in water and suffering minor burns, exposure and shock, he survived
108 Sqn	Wellington DV662 damaged by Ju 88 and crash-landed Abu Sueir; Flt Sgt J Metcalfe & four safe, one KiA

Tuesday-Wednesday, 7/8 July 1942

British Casualties

148 Sqn	Wellington Ic T2985 off to attack harbour and shipping at Tobruk, FTR; found crashed 18km SW Shallufa; Flg Off F.Tribe and five KiA

German Casualties

I./NJG 2	Ju 88C-6 WNr 360001 20% damaged crash-landing at Tobruk

Wednesday-Thursday, 8/9 July 1942

British Casualties

104 Sqn	Wellington II Z8520 'N' off to attack harbour and shipping at Tobruk. Failure of port engine, then partial failure of starboard caused belly-landing 38m S Sidi Barrani; Sgt C.S.Maxfield and five walked 200 miles through Axis lines until rescued by a Baltimore which landed in the desert to pick them up

Thursday-Friday, 9/10 July 1942

A convoy had been spotted sailing from Crete to Tobruk, eight Wellingtons of 38 Squadron being ordered out to attack, joined by five B-24Ds from the HalPro detachment, operating from Lydda. The US crews failed to see the ships but near Sidi Barrani they were attacked by an estimated 20 Bf 109s. The gunners claimed two of these downed and possibly a third, but one of the Liberators was shot down, crashing into the sea with the starboard wing ablaze and a second was missing (see also Chapter Ten).

More four-engined bombers were now on the way from the United Kingdom as described at the start of this chapter. One of the 10 Squadron Halifaxes, being delivered by 1 OADU, departed Gibraltar for the long flight direct to Aqir, but having become lost, the pilot put the aircraft down in the sea by the coast, some 25 miles east of Alexandria. Although two passengers were injured, all those aboard reached the shore safely by dinghy.

British Casualties

1 OADU/10 Sqn	Halifax II W7695 'D' ditched off Egyptian coast after becoming lost; Wt Off J.O'Driscoll, six crew and three passengers ashore safely; two injured

US Casualties

Halpro	B-24D 41-11618 or 41-11600 shot down by Bf 109s nr Sidi Barrani; 1/Lt K.W.Butler and six KiA

German Claims

1./JG 27	Fw Gunther Steinhausen	B-24	65m NW Bie el Astas

Saturday-Sunday, 11/12 July 1942

British Casualties

148 Sqn	Wellington Ic T2749 on sortie to attack Tobruk harbour and shipping; one engine hit by Flak and on fire; crash-landed on beach; pilot, Plt Off P.W.Hoad stayed with injured Sgt; rest walked for four days and captured

	nr Sidi Barrani when trying to commandeer a German truck. Hoad and five all PoWs
148 Sqn	Wellington Ic DV515 'K' off to attack Tobruk, FTR; Flt Sgt H.E.Kimball and five KiA

Sunday-Monday, 12/13 July 1942

British Casualties

40 Sqn	Wellington Ic HX373 'N' off to attack Tobruk harbour and shipping but target not found due to faulty compass. Off course on return for same reason; out of fuel, crash-landed in Qattara Depresion. Pilot and one go for help, others stay by aircraft and found by aerial recce; other two aided by Arabs, reach Arab camp at El Maghra, S of Alamein line, and picked up there by 40 Sqn crew who landed in the desert; Sqn Ldr F.J.Steel and six all returned safely
104 Sqn	Wellington II Z8588 'V' off to attack Tobruk harbour and shipping; on return crash-landed 30m SW Sidi Barrani; one died in crash; Plt Off J.E.Harlton and four PoW

Monday-Tuesday, 13/14 July 1942

A Halifax of 10/227 Squadron left Aqir to attack Tobruk but was damaged by Flak over the target and crashed on landing at Almaza where it blew up. Several Egyptian firemen were then killed when a bomb exploded in the wreckage. At dusk shipping at Benghazi was attacked by five Liberators from HalPro and two of 159 Squadron. A direct hit was claimed on the wreck known as 'George', together with two on the Central Mole. One B-24D was shot down by Flak. There had actually been a recall radioed to the attack force, but several crews failed to hear this and continued.During a patrol over Benghazi harbour, S.Ten Giovanni Dell'Innocenti chased a Liberator already hit by local AA and shot it down into the sea at 1755.

British Casualties

10/227 Sqn	Halifax II W1171 'X' damaged by Flak over Tobruk and crashed on landing, exploding; Plt Off H.C.Drake and one injured, four safe

US Casualties

HalPro	B-24D 41-11618 'Ole Rock' shot down by Flak; 1/Lt Charles O.Brown Jr and three KiA; four presumed to be PoWs

Italian Claims

364ª Sq, 150°Gr CT	S.Ten Giovanni Dell'Innocenti	MC.200	B-24	off Benghazi	1755

Tuesday-Wednesday, 14/15 July 1942

During attacks on Tobruk one Wellington was brought down by enemy action and three more were lost due to technical problems or accidents, two of them from 104 Squadron.

British Casualties

104 Sqn	Wellington II Z8649 'C' hit by Flak over Tobruk and on fire; became uncontrollable and crew baled out into sea; Plt Off G.Richards and three PoW, two K, one dying of pneumonia on 19th
104 Sqn	Wellington II Z8657 'J' attacked harbour and shipping at Tobruk; on return flew into ground in mist; Sgt D.C.Davies and two inj, three KiA
104 Sqn	Wellington II Z8658 'H' crashed-landed returning from attack on harbour and shipping at Tobruk; struck ground violently and burst into flames 45m E El Daba; rear gunner got out inj, but Plt Off R.C. Horton and four KiA
37 Sqn	Wellington Ic DV495 'U' off to attack harbour and shipping at Tobruk; engine trouble; force-landed in the desert, but on trying to take off again, crashed; Sgt R.J.Gordon and five walked to El Maghra by 22nd and rescued by army

German Casualties

1./NJG 2	Ju 88C-6 WNr 360247 R4+FH crash-landed at Tobruk, 45% damaged; Lt Heinz Rökker and crew safe

Wednesday, 15 July 1942

Six US B-24s and Liberators of 159 Squadron undertook the long flight from St Jean to attack the harbour and shipping at Benghazi. One RAF crew saw another of the unit's aircraft under attack by fighters, this spiralling down into the sea. This was also reported by the American crews (see also Chapter Ten). At 1750 two MC.200s of 150° Gruppo had intercepted Liberators over Benghazi. M.llo Augusto Manetti, of 363ª Squadriglia, claimed one shot down in flames and Serg Magg Bruno Benassi, of the same unit, chased and hit another, claimed as a probable.

British Casualties

159 Sqn	Liberator II AL566 shot down by fighters during sortie to Benghazi; Plt Off J.C.Pottie and six KiA

Italian Claims

364ª Sq, 150°Gr Aut CT	Serg Magg Augusto Manetti	MC.200	B-24	Benghazi	1750
363ª Sq, 150°Gr Aut CT	Serg Magg Bruno Benassi	MC.200	B-24 Probable	Benghazi	1750

A Ju 88C-6 of I./NJG 2 on a Cretan airfield.

Thursday-Friday, 16/17 July 1942

British Casualties

148 Sqn	Wellington Ic HX400 FTR from sortie to Tobruk; Flt Lt J.G.Brown and five KiA
821 Sqn	Albacore N4379 hit by night fighter; returned damaged

Friday, 17 July 1942

The HalPro B-24s and 9th Sqn B-17s now reverted to daylight bombing as their main modus operandi. Three days later with their combined force of 19 B-24s and nine B-17s, these units were reorganised to form the 1st Provisional Bombardment Group (Heavy) under Col Halverson's overall command. Meanwhile Serg Magg Rovero Abbarchi and Serg Davide Zanarini of 77ª Squadriglia, 13° Gruppo, on patrol over Tobruk, sighted and chased four four-engined aircraft at 1310. After a long and unsuccessful pursuit over the sea, Abbarchi force-landed near Marsa Lucch, damaging his aircraft beyond repair.

Italian Casualties

77ª Sq, 13°Gr, 2°St CT	MC.200 MM 8437 '77-8' force-landed, w/o, Serg Magg Rovero Abbarchi safe

Tuesday, 21 July 1942

Nine B-24s of the 1st Provisional Group and seven RAF Liberators raided Suda Bay, Crete, dropping 40,500lbs of bombs, claiming hits on two ships. A large fire and two smaller ones were also noted at the base end of the wharf.

Tuesday-Wednesday, 21/22 July 1942

Forty-six Wellingtons drawn from 37, 40, 70, 104 and 162 Squadrons bombed targets in the 'Battle Area'. Two crews reported being attacked by Ju 88s which damaged one of the British bombers. One gunner claimed to have gained hits on one attacker. It seems that the same night-fighter crew was involved in each action, for Obfw Alfons Köster and his crew were shot down in combat with Wellingtons, all of them surviving with wounds. However, they reported having shot down two of the bombers first, a claim not substantiated by the lack of actual British losses on this occasion.

British Claims

162 Sqn	Wellington crew claimed hit on Ju 88 night fighter

British Casualties

162 Sqn	Wellington Damaged by Ju 88
826 Sqn	Albacore T9168 crashed in bad weather nr El Alamein; Sub Lt W.L. MacKenzie and Sub Lt R.H.W.Shephard KiA c0300

German Claims

3./NJG 2	Obfw Alfons Köster	Wellington	2303
3./NJG 2	Obfw Alfons Köster	Wellington	2315

German Casualties

2./NJG 2	Ju 88C-5 WNr 360229 shot down in combat with Wellington nr El Alamein; Obfw Alfons Köster and two WiA

Wednesday-Thursday, 22/23 July 1942

Tobruk was also bombed by five Halifaxes and 25 Wellingtons. Again, night fighters were reported to have been encountered, but only one bomber suffered some damage, although it crashed on overshoot at Shallufa on return to base. It appears to have been involved in a fight with Hptm Harmstorf of I./NJG 2 who was credited with one Wellington shot down but who died during the engagement. Over Tobruk, however, four Wellingtons suffered slight damage from Flak.

British Casualties

40 Sqn	Wellington Ic HX440 'U' attacked MT nr El Alamein. Survived three attacks by night fighters, but crashed on overshoot on return to Shallufa; Sgt R.A.King and four injured, one KiFA

German Claims

2./NJG 2	Hptm Heinz Harmstorf	Wellington	N Africa	2250

German Casualties

2./NJG 2	Ju 88C-6 WNr 360250 R4+AK 40% damaged in combat with Wellington; Hptm Heinz Harmstorf KiA, engineer Uffz Schiffbänker WiA flew aircraft back to Qasaba and landed it

Thursday, 23 July 1942

By day 159 Squadron and 1st Provisional Group despatched 13 Liberators and B-24Ds to Benghazi again. Two of the American aircraft turned back early, but the rest of the formation attacked Benghazi between 1955-2040 from 32,000ft, claiming direct hits on one large supply ship and on the Central and Cathedral Moles. Defending fighters were encountered, the RAF bomber crews claiming to have shot down an MC.200 with a Bf 110 claimed as a probable. On return to Lydda, one B-24 ran out of fuel, the crew baling out, but one parachute caught the tailplane and the unfortunate crewman was killed.

A further nine B-24s went off from Fayid between 1510-1600, but only seven bombed, one having returned early after suffering engine trouble which caused the crew to jettison their bombload near the target. Benghazi was again hit with similar claims resulting. During the same period three 9th Squadron B-17s attacked Tobruk harbour. During these combats Serg Magg D'Ilio of 365ª Squadriglia, of the MC.200-equipped 150° Gruppo, claimed to have shot down a Liberator some 100km north-north-east of Benghazi.

British Claims

Bomber Gunners	MC.200	Benghazi
Bomber Gunners	Bf 110 Probable	Benghazi

British Casualties

159 Sqn	Liberator AL534, shot down by MC.200 off Benghazi at 2009; Flt Lt R.A. Malcolm & 3 PoW, 2 KiA

US Casualties

1st Prov BG	B-24D 41-11615/20 'Mona, the Lame Duck' abandoned out of fuel, crashed Lydda 0125; Cpt W.A. Fountain and five baled out safely, one KiA when parachute snagged on aircraft
1st Prov BG	B-24D 41-11814 'Pink Elephant' shot down, 2/Lt Robert G. McCormick and crew KiA

Italian Claims					
365ª Sq,150° Gr CT	Serg Magg Corrado D'Ilio	MC.200	Liberator	100km NNE Benghazi	1820

Thursday-Friday, 23/24 July 1942

Axis advanced landing grounds were the main target for 45 Wellingtons drawn from five squadrons. The attacks were believed by 205 Group staff to have been very successful.

British Casualties	
37 Sqn	Wellington Ic DV642 suffered flying battle damage; apparently lost

Friday-Saturday, 24/25 July 1942

Wellington 'R' of 104 Squadron was hit by Flak en route to attack Tobruk, coming down south of Sollum near the Halfaya Pass. The crew spent ten days in the desert, twice escaping from captivity, the second time after 36 hours. They then travelled 230 miles in a commandeered German car before being captured again. All but one member of the crew then got away again by overpowering their Italian guards and driving their truck eastwards until meeting an LRDG patrol. Two more Wellingtons were lost during the night as a consequence of engine troubles; and three more prior to take-off.

British Casualties	
108 Sqn	Wellington Ic DV655 'C' caught fire at Kabrit when 40lb incendiary bomb exploded, possibly due to incorrect handling of detonator; three ground crew K and two injured
108 Sqn	Wellington Ic Z9031 damaged beyond repair when DV655 exploded
108 Sqn	Wellington Ic DV659 'S' set on fire by debris from explosion of DV655, damaged beyond repair
104 Sqn	Wellington II Z8509 'R' shot down by Flak nr Sollum; Sgt A.J.Wills and four evaded capture and returned; one PoW
826 Sqn	Albacore X9256 FTR from night sortie; Sub Lt J.D.Nunnerley and two KiA

German Claims			
3./NJG 2	Obfw Alfons Köster	Boston	N Africa

Saturday, 25 July 1942

USMEAF was strengthened by the arrival at Ramat David of the HQ of the 98th Bombardment Group (Heavy) and the unit's 344th Squadron. The balance of the unit would arrive a few days later (see Chapter Four).

Saturday-Sunday, 25/26 July 1942

Tobruk was attacked by 11 Wellingtons from 40 and 162 Squadrons, joined by seven Halifaxes from 76/454 Squadron, six USAAF B-24s and four B-17s, 43,000lb of bombs being released on this target.

British Casualties	
108 Sqn	Wellington Ic HF944 'O' off from LG.86 to bomb Heraklion, Crete, but FTR; Plt Off O.H.Clement and five KiA

German Claims				
1./NJG 2	Oblt Heinz-Horst Hissbach	Wellington	SW Crete	2250

Sunday-Monday, 26/27 July 1942

Tobruk was the target once again, this time for three Halifaxes and 35 Wellingtons. One direct hit was achieved on a medium-sized ship, this causing a huge explosion which it was considered may have sunk the vessel.

German Claims				
2./NJG 2	Obfw Alfred Siewert	Wellington		0047

Monday-Tuesday, 27/28 July 1942

British Casualties	
40 Sqn	Wellington Ic HX370 'Y' from Shallufa to bomb LG.20; believed to have crashed in flames near the target; Sgt W.H.Mitchell and five KiA
70 Sqn	Wellington Ic HX364 'K' set off to attack Tobruk; crashed in force-landing 30m S Tobruk; Sgt H.R.Osborne and five PoW; three later drowned when *Nino Bixio* was torpedoed by an RN submarine south of Greece on 17 August

German Claims

2./NJG 2	Obfw Hermann Sommer	Wellington	50km SE Tobruk 2335

Tuesday, 28 July 1942

Twelve 1st Prov Group B-24s set off to attack a convoy at sea, but failed to find it. Instead, the American crews bombed shipping in Suda Bay, claiming hits on two merchant vessels.

Tuesday-Wednesday, 28/29 July 1942

Four Halifaxes from 10/227 Squadron joined 56 Wellingtons from six separate squadrons as Tobruk drew an ever-increasing weight of bombs. The following night brought 49 Wellingtons, six Halifaxes and three Liberators to the priority target of Tobruk.

German Claims

1./NJG 2	Lt Heinz Rökker	Wellington	10km E Tobruk	2310

Thursday, 30 July 1942

A Wellington with a crew from 458 Squadron on their second delivery trip, departed Gibraltar, heading for Luqa. It seems that they became lost as, far from reaching Malta, they found themselves off the coast of Libya, approaching El Daba early in the morning. Two Bf 109s intercepted the aircraft and it was shot down by Lt Munzert of 9./JG 53. During the engagement the tail gunner, Sgt G.W.S.Crompton, was severely wounded but fired back until a further attack killed him. The rest of the crew, all sergeants apart from Plt Off H.S.W. 'Bill'Fordyce, were captured. Fordyce, however, had been injured and was flown to Crete while the rest of the crew were transported to Europe by sea. It appears that they were among those on board the *Nino Bixio*, which was sunk by the British submarine, HMS *Turbulent*, with considerable loss of life.

Oblt Heinz-Horst Hissbach of 1./NJG 2, a future Ritterkreuzträger, claimed a Wellington shot down on 26 July for his first victory.

British Casualties

1 OADU	Wellington Ic HX580 shot down off El Daba on flight from Gibraltar, having lost way to Luqa; Sgt W.Mears, Plt Off H.S.W. Fordyce and two PoW, rear gunner Sgt G.W.S. Crompton KiA

German Claims

9./JG 53	Lt Hermann Munzert	Wellington	Mersa Matruh	0544

Thursday-Friday, 30/31 July 1942

The 'heavies' continued to concentrate on Tobruk, this time 50 Wellingtons, two Halifaxes and four B-17s keeping up the pressure. One Wellington was lost. By day five B-17s raided Tobruk with nine B-24s attacking shipping in Navarino Bay. One of 24 SAAF Squadron's day bomber Bostons operated by night on this occasion, taking off at 2343 to attack LG.13 at Sidi Haneish. Here, apparently, heavy and accurate Flak was encountered, the aircraft crashing and bursting into flames 15m SE of the unit's own base at LG.99 at about 0042. The crew was killed, and their loss was recorded as probably being due to the Flak.

British Casualties	
37 Sqn	Wellington Ic HF833's starboard engine failed over the port, so the crew bombed the airfield instead; the other engine then seized and the a/c crash-landed 30m from Tobruk. The crew walked for nine days, then split into two parties; then pilot, Flg Off C.E.L.Hoard, and one other (both RCAF) were captured on 18 August; the other four were picked up after 22 days by an 8th Army patrol. The crew were originally from 458 Squadron
24 SAAF Sqn	Boston III Z2163 'D' heavily damaged during an attack on LG.13 and crashed, reportedly probably due to Flak at 0042; Lt E.Corby and three KiA

Friday-Saturday, 31 July/1 August 1942

Tobruk was the target for 51 Wellingtons, three Halifaxes and two Liberators. Although casualties were low, the raid did cost one of the scarce four-engined bombers.A dozen B-24s were also out, and although two turned back early, the rest found and bombed a convoy at evening, claiming hits on two ships, one of which was believed to have sunk. On return to Lydda one pilot found the runway blocked, forcing him to go round again. On his second approach the aircraft was too low and struck a building, crashing and bursting into flames. The pilot, 2/Lt Sturkie, was badly burned but survived. Ground personnel pulled all the rest of the crew out of the wreckage, but all were either dead, or had died by next morning. The building which had been hit was a Palestine Police post in which five policemen and two Arab civilians also lost their lives.

British Casualties	
76/454 Sqn	Halifax II W7765 'D' bombed Tobruk harbour but port inner engine disabled by Flak over target and starboard outer failed about 200m from Alexandria on return. All removable equipment was jettisoned, but eventually, some 12m from Alexandria the two gunners were ordered to bale out; Plt Off H.Wickham then crash-landed at LG.09, he and all the crew surviving safely
148 Sqn	Wellington Ic HX527 off to bomb Tobruk harbour and shipping, FTR; Flg Off W.D.Bohl and four KiA
US Casualties	
1st Prov BG	B-24D 41-11601/23 'Hellsapoppin' crashed on landing on return from raid; 2/Lt Hood N.Sturkie badly burned but survived, seven KiA or died of injuries

German Claims			
1./NJG 2	Oblt Heinz-Horst Hissbach	Wellington	SW Crete

Sunday, 2 August 1942

A 37 Squadron Wellington was just about to take off from Abu Sueir in the hands of an attached 458 Squadron crew when Boston AL696 of 24 SAAF Squadron landed and crashed into it, causing it to catch fire and blow up, killing the crew. Three other Wellingtons were damaged beyond repair by the explosion. Losses due to such occurences were continuing to exceed those inflicted by the enemy!

British Casualties	
37 Sqn	Wellington Ic DV644 destroyed when about to take off, a SAAF Boston crashing into it when landing; Sgt J.S.Whitworth and three KiFA
37 Sqn	Wellington Ic HX480 and HF832 both damaged beyond repair by the explosion of DV644
37 Sqn	Wellington Ic DV641 damaged beyond repair by the explosion of DV644

Sunday-Monday, 2/3 August 1942

Tobruk was raided by 35 Wellingtons, six Halifaxes and nine Liberators. One Wellington failed to return.

British Casualties	
148 Sqn	Wellington Ic DV568 'L' off to attack Tobruk; engine cut over the battle area and despite jettisoning everything possible, the aircraft lost height and hit the ground within Allied territory, being wrecked; Sgt H.Tricks and three safe, two injured

Tuesday-Wednesday, 4/5 August, 1942

Ten B-24s attacked a convoy of three supply vessels with eight escorts, crews claiming hits of two of the former. Twelve more B-24s from the newly-arrived 98th Bomb Group, accompanied by RAF Liberators of 159 Squadron, set out to attack a convoy off Crete, but could not find it. The secondary target of Tobruk was bombed instead between 2137-2200.

German Claims

Flak		2 bombers

German Casualties

1./NJG 2	Ju 88C-6 WNr 360010 R4+BH crash-landed at Qasaba 50% damaged

Wednesday-Thursday, 5/6 August 1942

British Casualties

10/227 Sqn	Halifax II W7757 'W' off to bomb Tobruk harbour; one engine put out of action and another had to be feathered; remaining two overheated and a/c had to be ditched; Sgt De Clerk and crew got ashore in dinghy and safe
821 Sqn	Albacore X9154 FTR from sortie over Western Desert l.g.; forced to land nr Fuka aerodrome at night; Sub Lt W.Hardaker and two PoW; captured by Italians and flown by 9° Gruppo

Friday-Saturday, 7/8 August 1942

On Friday Col Harry A. Halverson relinquished his command of the Hal Squadron handing over to Lt Col George F.McGuire.

British Casualties

40 Sqn	Wellington Ic DV663 'U' collided with HX431 during sortie to Tobruk; Flt Sgt L.P.Kerr and five KiFA
40 Sqn	Wellington Ic HX431 'O' collided with DV663 during sortie to Tobruk; Flt Lt H.Grant and four PoW; one KiFA after baling out too low for parachute to open; two badly injured and one had leg amputated in German field hospital
104 Sqn	Wellington Z8436 off to attack Tobruk but crash-landed 25m SW of target after engine failure; attached 458 Sqn crew walked for sixteen days before being captured; Sqn Ldr J.A.H. Sargeant and five PoWs

Fiat G.50bis of 12° Gruppo CT at Castel Benito. These aircraft were employed mainly for convoy escort duties.

Sunday, 9 August 1942

Eleven B-24s from the 98th Bomb Group's 344th and 415th Squadrons were tasked with bombing Benghazi where 50,000lb of HE were released on the target. One aircraft returned early, but one failed to get back and a second crashed on return to base and was written off.

At Benghazi K3 airfield two pilots of 364ª Sq, S.Ten Fausto Filippi and Cap Mario Bellagambi, were scrambled at 1600 and 1615 to intercept a formation of Liberators. One was claimed as damaged.

Italian Claims					
364ª Sq, 150° Gr CT	Cap Mario Bellagambi	MC.200	Liberator Damaged	Benghazi area	1620
364ª Sq, 150° Gr CT	S.Ten Fausto Filippi	MC.200			
US Casualties					
415th Sq, 98th BG	B-24D 41-11808 'Root of Evil' shot down; 1/Lt Paul H.Francis and co-pilot baled out safe, crew KiA				
344th Sq, 98th BG	B-24D 41-11794 crash-landed at base on return and written off; pilot Uber and crew safe				

Tuesday-Wednesday, 11/12 August 1942

Three more Wellingtons were lost during raids on Tobruk due to engine failures, all crews becoming prisoners. However, during a raid on Abu Haggag at 2225 an MC.200 and six Italian pilots of 18° Gruppo were killed and three wounded; there were also one dead and two injured among ground personnel. Seven 98th Group B-24s had been out by day to raid Navarino Bay, attacking three warships identified as cruisers which were lying along the western shore of Spakteria Island.

British Casualties	
108 Sqn	Wellington DV667 'L' took off to bomb port and shipping at Tobruk; engine trouble over target caused aircraft to become uncontrollable; Plt Off A.Armstrong and four baled out and PoWs
108 Sqn	Wellington HX484 'P' took off to bomb port and shipping at Tobruk but turned back due to engine trouble; Sgt A.S.Graeme-Cook and four captured: Graeme-Cook and one killed on 23 August when Luftwaffe aircraft flying to Greece crashed in the sea on Hydra Island
40 Sqn	Wellington HX377 'A' took off to bomb port and shipping at Tobruk; engine failed and crew baled out; walked 86m before Sgt C.E. Hickman and five captured and PoWs
German Claims	
Flak	2 bombers
Italian Casualties	
83ª Sq, 18°Gr, 3°St CT	Serg Magg Franco Lambertini killed by bombing
83ª Sq, 18°Gr, 3°St CT	Serg Antonio Zanette wounded by bombing
83ª Sq, 18°Gr, 3°St CT	Serg Luciano Andretta wounded by bombing
85ª Sq, 18°Gr, 3°St CT	Serg Magg Nordio Scocchetti killed by bombing
85ª Sq, 18°Gr, 3°St CT	Serg Magg Mario Lingua killed by bombing
85ª Sq, 18°Gr, 3°St CT	Serg Magg Luigi Morellato killed by bombing
85ª Sq, 18°Gr, 3°St CT	Serg Savino Alghisi wounded by bombing
95ª Sq, 18°Gr, 3°St CT	Serg Magg Guerrino Boari killed by bombing
95ª Sq, 18°Gr, 3°St CT	Serg Magg Leone Casadei killed by bombing
95ª Sq, 18°Gr, 3°St CT	MC.200 MM 8832 destroyed by bombs

Wednesday, 12 August 1942

By now the Operation Pedestal convoy was on its way from Gibraltar towards Malta. With the prospect of considerable aerial action taking place throughout the western Mediterranean during the next few days, it became unsafe for OADU to direct further reinforcement Wellingtons from Gibraltar to the besieged island and they were ordered instead to fly on south towards the Gold Coast and Nigeria, from where they might follow the now well-proven cross-Africa route to Sudan and southern Egypt. Their first refuelling stop after Gibraltar would thus become Bathurst, but this would bring aircraft following this route within range of Vichy French fighters based in Senegal if their crews sought to skirt the coastline rather than stay well offshore, above the great wastes of the South Atlantic.

Thus it was that one such Wellington was intercepted by Curtiss H-75A fighters of Groupe de Chasse I/4 off Dakar, and was shot down. Two members of the crew were killed but the others, including the pilot, were picked up and were interned. A second Wellington following the same course simply disappeared. Next day a further interception took place, but on this occasion the British crew fought back, the rear gunner shooting down one of the fighters into the sea; the pilot was not found. Meanwhile, the damaged Wellington was force-landed and destroyed by the crew who were also then interned.

British Casualties

1 OADU	Wellington II W5565 shot down by French fighters; Plt Off A.B.Kidson and three interned, two KiA
1 OADU	Wellington Ic HF882 lost en route Gibraltar-Bathurst

French Claims

GC I/4	Cdt Louis Delfino	Wellington	Dakar
GC I/4	Lt Pierre Minot		
GC I/4	Lt Guy Husson		

Wednesday-Thursday, 12/13 August 1942

British Casualties

108 Sqn	Wellington Ic AD629 'J' FTR from raid on Tobruk; Flt Sgt D.M.Watts and five KiA

Thursday, 13 August 1942

British Claims

1 OADU	Wellington crew	French fighter	off Senegal

British Casualties

1 OADU	Wellington Ic HX583 damaged by French fighters, force-landed nr Tiaroye and destroyed by crew; Plt Off R.McIlraith and five interned, two injured

French Claims

GC I/4	Lt Yves Rupied	Wellington	30m S Dakar
GC I/4	Lt Alain Thomas		

French Casualties

GC I/4	Curtiss H-75A shot down by Wellington rear gunner; Lt Alain Thomas baled out but not found

Friday, 14 August 1942

Having navigated the West African coastline past Senegal safely, an OADU aircraft lost a propeller when one of its engines seized up, causing a force-landing just short of Hastings, Sierra Leone – British territory – but across the frontier in Ivory Coast where this crew too were interned.

British Casualties

1 OADU	Wellington Ic HX585 port engine seized and propeller flew off when off Hastings, Sierra Leone; force-landed on beach 50m W Bingeralle, Ivory Coast; Plt Off A.E.Beer and five interned at Jackville

Italian Claims

77ª Sq, 13°Gr, 2°St CT	Serg Magg Davide Zanarini	MC.202 MM 7893	B-24	off Tobruk	1345-1430
77ª Sq, 13°Gr, 2°St CT	Serg Magg Davide Zanarini	MC.202 MM 7893	B-24 Damaged	off Tobruk	1345-1430

Saturday, 15 August 1942

At dusk a convoy comprising two large merchant vessels and a single destroyer escort was spotted moving south across the Mediterranean. The US 98th Bomb Group and the RAF's 159 Squadron together put up 17 Liberators. Bomb aimers claimed to have achieved one hit and four near misses.

British Casualties

826 Sqn	Albacore T9172 '4L' shot down by Flak at night over Mersa Matruh harbour; force-landed in sea; Sub Lts T.J.Lister and K.Chapelow seven hours in dinghy, then PoW

Sunday-Monday, 16/17 August 1942

British Casualties

40 Sqn	Wellington Ic HX425 'H' engine failure on return from Tobruk possibly Flak. Crew baled out nr Fuka; Sgt J.Mason and five PoW
826 Sqn	Albacore X9147 flare-dropping Mersa Matruh harbour, FTR; Sub Lt J.H.Wilkinson and one PoW

German Claims

Flak	Wellington

Monday-Tuesday, 17/18 August 1942

German Claims

Flak	3 claims

Tuesday-Wednesday, 18/19 August 1942

Tobruk was the target for 36 Wellingtons, during which an aircraft of 70 Squadron was attacked by a Ju 88. After a quick exchange of fire, the night fighter broke away.

Thursday-Friday, 20/21 August 1942

British Casualties

37 Sqn	Wellington Ic Z8761 FTR from Tobruk; Sgt I.F.L.Arthur and five PoW; one KiA when a/c carrying him to Greece crashed on 23 August
70 Sqn	Wellington AD634 'N' took off to attack Tobruk, force-landed 30m S Sollum after engine trouble; Sgt P.J.King and four PoWs after ten days

Friday, 21 August 1942

Eleven B-24s from the 344th and 345th Squadrons of the 98th Bomb Group attacked a convoy south-west of Crete, claiming the probable sinking of two vessels (there had been one early return amongst the bombers). On this occasion the formation was intercepted by three fighters and one Liberator which was straggling was shot down. The rear gunner in another of this unit's aircraft claimed to have probably shot down a fighter alternately described as a Bf 109 or a Bf 110. The convoy, comprising three merchant vessels with escort, was bombed between 1920-1935, four hits, two probable hits and 11 near misses being claimed which the crews believed had probably sunk two of the transports.

US Claims

345th Sq, 98th BG	Pvt Tom F.Hamway, rear gunner in B-24D 41-11806/P	Bf 109 or Bf 110 Probable

US Casualties

345th Sq, 98th BG	B-24D 41-11763/N shot down SW Crete off Gavdos Island; 1/Lt Frank M.Newton and one PoW, seven MiA

German Claims

7./ZG 26	Uffz Fritz Lauff	B-24		1820
9./ZG 26	Obfw Walter Weiss	B-24	SW coast Gavdos	1830

Saturday, 22 August 1942

The US 12th Bomb Group despatched B-25s to bomb a tank depot by night. Returning from this raid, the IFF on one aircraft failed, resulting in it being intercepted by a Beaufighter and shot down in error; the pilot and three crew members survived, but two others lost their lives. An immediate inquiry cast no blame on the crew of the night fighter responsible.

US Casualties

82nd BS/12th BG	B-25C 41-12862 shot down in error by RAF Beaufighter after IFF failed; 1/Lt S.L.Powell Jr and three safe, two KiA

Sunday, 23 August 1942

By day nine 12th Bomb Group B-25s attacked a convoy which had arrived in Tobruk harbour. One aircraft was hit by Flak over the target and blew up.Tobruk was also the target for 11 B-24s of the 98th Bomb Group which took off 1430-1448. Three returned early with engine trouble and two crews could not find the target, but six bombed as instructed. However, since aircraft and crews were over the harbour as it was becoming dark, the results could not be observed.

At eventide, two MC.200s of 13° Gruppo were on patrol over Tobruk harbour when a formation of four-engined bombers approached, one of which was claimed shot down by the two Italian pilots, S.Ten Zuccarini and Serg Zanarini. The Gruppo also had three MC.202s available and Magg Viale scrambled in one of these, pursuing the bombers and claiming damage to one of them, landing at 1950 in almost complete darkness.

US Casualties					
81st BS/12th BG	B-25C 41-12853 hit by Flak over Tobruk harbour and blew up; Capt R.W.Carlisle and four KiA				

Italian Claims					
77ª Sq, 13°Gr, 2°St CT	S.Ten Gian Mario Zuccarini	MC.200	B-24	Tobruk	1900
77ª Sq, 13°Gr, 2°St CT	Serg Davide Zanarini	MC.200			
82ª Sq, 13°Gr, 2°St CT	Magg Lorenzo Viale	MC.202 MM 7884	B-24 Damaged	Tobruk	1900-1950

Monday-Tuesday, 24/25 August 1942

In daylight on Monday, Liberators of 159 Squadron operating from St Jean, targeted Tobruk. Aircraft 'S' was hit by Flak and was last seen shedding smoke and debris, failing to return. Eleven Hal Squadron B-24s also attacked, as did Wellingtons of 40 and 148 Squadrons, the total raiding force including 16 Wellingtons and 15 Liberators.

British Casualties	
159 Sqn	Liberator II AL537 'S' shot down by Flak over Tobruk; Flt Sgt F.D.Hamilton-Wilkes and seven KiA

Tuesday, 25 August 1942

Meanwhile, six 98th Bomb Group B-24s raided the Corinth Canal in southern Greece, seeking to attack ships and a railway bridge over the Canal, and to inflict damage on the Canal itself. In the event only hits on the southern embankment of the Canal could be claimed, with one bomber damaged by Flak.

Tuesday-Wednesday, 25/26 August 1942

Twenty-eight Wellingtons from 37 and 70 Squadrons were active over the battle area, one of these being seen to crash in flames when engaged in a special operation against concentrations of Axis vehicles here. This proved to be 'U' of 70 Squadron which had departed LG.86 to attack targets of opportunity but had been shot down by a night fighter – although all the crew baled out successfully.

At 2020 the commander of 4° Stormo, T.Col Armando François, had taken off in a CR.42 to intercept raiders at Fuka. He repeatedly attacked a twin-engined aircraft which he had identified as a Wellington, finally seeing this ditch in flames into the sea. Ten Giulio Reiner took off in another CR.42 at 2245 and was vectored by fighter control onto another Wellington flying at about 10,000ft. He fired 100 rounds at this, reporting seeing many hits, claiming this bomber shot down too. The 70 Squadron bomber was clearly that attacked by his commanding officer, but it proved to be the only loss of the night.

British Casualties	
70 Sqn	Wellington Ic DV514 'U' shot down in flames by a night fighter; Sqn Ldr E.B.Panter and five baled out, PoW

Italian Claims					
73ª Sq, 9°Gr, 4°St CT	T.Col Armando François	CR.42	Wellington	4km off Fuka	2020-2200
73ª Sq, 9°Gr, 4°St CT	Ten Giulio Reiner	CR.42	Wellington	10km off Fuka	2045-2400

Wednesday, 26 August 1942

At 2100 the commander of 9° Gruppo, Magg Roberto Fassi, took off in a CR.42 on loan from 96ª Squadriglia to intercept some raiders approaching Fuka. At about 3,000ft he sighted two intruders and fired at them repeatedly, claiming both damaged. With this increase in night flying for the Italian pilots, 238ª Squadriglia provided a temporary loan of another CR.42 (MM 8890) to 4° Stormo to be employed in this role.

Italian claims					
96ª Sq, 9°Gr, 4°St CT	Magg Roberto Fassi	CR.42	2 e/a Damaged	Fuka	2100-2220

Friday, 28 August 1942

Although the Pedestal operation had been over for several days, following the fall of the Libyan coast back into Axis hands, many delivery aircraft continued to be directed down the west coast of Africa to the Gold Coast. In following this route another Wellington fell foul of Armeé de l'Air fighters on this date.

British Casualties

1 OADU	Wellington Ic T2545 shot down by French fighters off Rabat, Morocco over international waters; Flt Lt G.H.M.Riddell injured, he and two survived; three KiA

French Claims

GC I/5	Lt Yves Le Calvez	Wellington	Port Lyautey
GC I/5	Lt Marcel Rouquette		
GC I/5	Adj Chef Jean Monchanin		
GC I/5	Adj Leon Vuillemain		

Friday-Saturday, 28/29 August 1942

Tobruk was raided by 27 Wellingtons, 11 Halifaxes and six Liberators. They were joined on this occasion by 13 B-25s of the 12th Bomb Group – unused to night bombing – which raided LG.20 during the early hours. Just before midnight two CR.42s of 13° Gruppo, flown by Magg Lorenzo Viale and S.Ten Gregorio Cinti of 77ª Squadriglia were scrambled to intercept an unidentified intruder; Cinti claimed to have scored some hits, but did not make a claim.

Saturday, 29 August 1942

Ten B-24Ds from the 343rd and 344th Squadrons of the 98th Bomb Group were despatched to attack a convoy near Crete. Nothing was found and the aircraft returned without having bombed. During the mission a Bf 110 made an attack on aircraft No 779 of the 344th near Crete at about 1915 but without causing any damage. The rear and top turret gunners returned fire, seeing no observable results.

German Claims

9./ZG 26	Obfw Helmut Haugk	B-24	1816
9./ZG 26	Obfw Helmut Haugk	B-24 Probable	

Sunday-Monday, 30/31August

British Casualties

70 Sqn	Wellington Ic ES992 'H' while seeking targets of opportunity in the battle area, twice attacked by night fighters; hydraulics damaged and port engine set on fire, belly-landed within Allied lines; Flt Lt R.E.Fawcett and five picked up safely by Household Cavalry patrol

German Claims

9./ZG 26	Uffz Heinz Tuns	Swordfish	SW El Alamein	0135

A belly-landed Fiat G.50bis of 161° Gruppo CT. Eight pilots of this unit claimed four Beauforts shot down on 20 August (see page 582).

Monday- Tuesday, 31 August/1 September

The airfields LG.104,101 and 13 were attacked during the night by Wellingtons from 37, 40, 70 and 104 Squadrons and by B-25s of the 12th Bomb Group.

Wednesday, 2 September 1942

Another delivery Wellington was lost, this one coming down in Morocco. Although the crew had reported engine trouble before, its seems that the French considered that they had forced the aircraft down, this time the claiming unit being the Groupe de Chasse I/5, again equipped with Curtiss H-75As.

British Casualties			
1 OADU	Wellington Ic HD962 en route Gibraltar-Bathurst, radioed experiencing engine trouble. Port engine failed and landed on beach at Safi, Morocco; Sgt A.L.Mayers and five destroyed aircraft and interned		
104 Sqn	Wellington Z8369 engine cut on approach to LG.237		
French Claims			
GC I/5	Cne Robert Huvet	Wellington	Safi
GC I/5	S/Lt Paul Boudier	Wellington	Safi
GC I/5	Sgt André Bouhy	Wellington	Safi

Wednesday-Thursday, 2/3 September 1942

British Casualties	
40 Sqn	Wellington Ic X9938 'T' seeking targets of opportunity in Salam el Halfa area, two 250lb bombs hung up and could not be jettisoned; on landing at LG.237 these fell off and exploded; Sgt V.Baker and one survived, injured, four KiA

Thursday, 3 September 1942

British Casualties			
826 Sqn	Albacore X9027 '4M' bombed and illuminated large MT concentration; attacked and badly damaged by three Bf 109s but landed safely; Sub Lt J.D.Murricane safe		
US Claims			
HalPro	B-24D gunners	Bf 110	1910
German Casualties			
8./ZG 26	Bf 110E-2 WNr 4504 hit by B-24 gunners 100m S Crete; belly-landed nr Kastelli on return, 50% damaged; Fw Günther Wegmann and gunner safe		
9./ZG 26	Bf 110F-2 WNr 5017 10% damaged in combat with B-24s 100m S Crete, landed safely; Fw Norbert Nedopil and gunner safe		

Friday, 4 September 1942

British Casualties	
148 Sqn	Wellington DV893 flew into high ground near LG.2

Saturday-Sunday, 5/6 September 1942

At dusk eight Halifaxes from 10/227 and 76/454 Squadrons departed to bomb Heraklion, Crete, but here two of the bombers were shot down. Little was observed of the effects of the attack due to the need to take evasive action against intercepting fighters and heavy Flak.

British Casualties		
10/227 Sqn	Halifax II W7679 'C' seen going down with an outer engine on fire and crashed at Castelli Padiada; Sqn Ldr A.H.Hacking and five KiA	
76/454 Sqn	Halifax II W1144 'Q' attacked by Bf 109s and possibly also hit by Flak nr target and caught fire; Flt Lt J.Bryan and one KiA, four PoW, two WiA	
70 Sqn	Wellington Ic BB477 'W' attacked Tobruk, brought down by Flak nr target; Flt Sgt J.D.Gordon and five KiA	
German Claims		
Flak	Halifax	Malia Bay, Heraklion, Crete
Flak	Halifax	Isle of Dia, Crete
Flak	Halifax	5km SE Archange, Crete

German Claims

Flak	Halifax	Diktis Mountains, Crete

German Casualties

III./KG 54	Ju 88A-4 WNr 140 765 destroyed on ground by bombing, Heraklion, Crete
III./KG 54	Ju 88A-4 WNr 1532 destroyed on ground by bombing, Heraklion, Crete

Monday, 7 September 1942

B-24Ds were out searching for convoys during the day, a dozen aircraft from the Hal Squadron and 22 drawn from all four squadrons of the 98th Bomb Group taking part. Crews from the former formation reported being attacked by a pair of aircraft identified as Ju 88s which made several passes without effect. These appear actually to have been a pair of III./ZG 26 Bf 110s, the pilots of which claimed two of the bombers shot down.

German Claims

9./ZG 26	Fw Günther Wegmann	B-24	S Tympakion	1756
8./ZG 26	Uffz Heinz Susemihl	B-24		1830

Monday-Tuesday, 7/8 September 1942

British Casualties

37 Sqn	Wellington Ic ES989 'A' FTR from Tobruk; Wt Off 1 S.A.G.Turner and five KiA
162 Sqn	Wellington DV489 damaged by Flak, Tobruk; not repaired

Tuesday-Wednesday, 8/9 September 1942

British Casualties

104 Sqn	Wellington II Z8374 'Z' shot down in flames over Tobruk; Wt Off C.S.Maxfield and five KiA

Wednesday, 9 September 1942

During a patrol over Tobruk, 1715-1915, two MC.200s of 82ª Squadriglia flown by Ten Camillo Luglio and Serg Giacomo Magnani intercepted a formation of Liberators flying at 23,000 feet. Magnani claimed some hits on one; however the engagement was brief due to the altitude and speed of the bombers.

Italian Claims

82ª Sq, 13°Gr, 2°St CT	Serg Giacomo Magnani	MC.200	Liberator Damaged	Tobruk	1715-1915

Sunday-Monday, 13/14 September 1942

The night saw a big combined operation against both Tobruk and Benghazi harbours, aimed to coincide with attacks on both harbours by British Special Forces (see Chaper Ten). The Tobruk raid was codenamed Agreement, while that directed at Benghazi was Bigamy. A force of 101 aircraft was sent out by 205 Group, including 66 Wellingtons, 14 Halifaxes, 16 Liberators and B-24s, and five B-17s, joined by some aircraft from 201 Group.

The raid proved to be more than usually costly, four Wellingtons being shot down, three of them from 70 Squadron. The 12th Bomb Group, which targeted LG.101 at Sidi Haneish, also suffered heavily; the unit's commanding officer, Col Goodrich, had been protesting against the use of B-25s by night since the exhausts to their engines were not adequately shrouded, the flames thereby given off proving to be aiming points for the defending Flak gunners as the aircraft made their bombing runs. This raid proved his point and thereafter a ban on night flying by these bombers was imposed. Thereafter they would operate by day and in formation with the RAF's and SAAF's Bostons and Baltimores.

British Casualties

70 Sqn	Wellington Ic Z8787 'R' shot down over Tobruk; Flt Lt E.F.W.McCartan-Mooney and five PoW; several attempts to escape but pilot and two KiA in skirmish with Axis patrol on 18th
70 Sqn	Wellington Ic Z9044 'B' damaged over Tobruk, force-landed on return; Plt Off R.B.Muirhead and five started walking; on 20th met survivor from 148 Sqn aircraft lost on 19/20th (see below); most then dropped out from exhaustion and died, only one and the 148 Sqn man reaching Allied lines
70 Sqn	Wellington Ic BB462 'G', one engine failed over Tobruk and a/c then force-landed in desert within Axis lines;

	Plt Off M.V.Hodge, Grp Capt R.Kellett, DFC, AFC, SASO 205 Group flying as 2nd pilot and four PoW; one of latter evaded until 20th, when captured
108 Sqn	Wellington Ic HF864 'S' FTR from Tobruk; message received that returning with engine trouble; Plt Off E.R.Wardley and five PoW; one died when Italian steamer *Scillin* sunk by RN submarine HMS *Sahib* on 14 November
US Casualties	
81st BS/12th BG	B-25C 41-12855 shot down by Flak over Tobruk; Capt J.G.Freeland and two KiA, two PoW
81st BS/12th BG	B-25C 41-13849 shot down by Flak over Tobruk; 1/Lt H.E.Belobraidich and three KiA, two PoW
81st BS/12th BG	B-25D 41-129681 shot down by Flak over Tobruk; Col C.G.Goodrich and three PoW, one KiA, one u/i fate; one PoW was group intelligence officer, Maj H.B.Houston
82ndBS/12th BG	B-25C 41-12858 shot down by Flak over Tobruk; 1/Lt L.P.Redburn PoW, four KiA

German Claims

Flak	9 claims

Wednesday, 16 September 1942

Another raid by the heavy bombers on Benghazi was flown by day, seven Liberators of 159 Squadron joining B-17s of the 1st Provisional Heavy Bomb Group and B-24s of the 98th Heavy Bomb Group. Benghazi was bombed where direct hits on an 8,000-ton merchant vessel were claimed. At around 1415 one bomber was attacked by a Bf 110, the right outer wing panel being hit by two 20mm shells. The attacker would appear to have been Uffz Susemihl of 8./ZG 26 who claimed a B-24 shot down at roughly the correct time.

German Claims

8./ZG 26	Uffz Heinz Susemihl	B-24	W Agedabia	1300

Wednesday-Thursday, 16/17 September 1942

British Casualties

826 Sqn	Albacore X9147 FTR from flare-dropping over Mersa Matruh harbour; Sub Lt J.H.Wilkinson and one PoW
104 Sqn	Wellington Z8582 crashed 4m Harnada (17th)

Saturday-Sunday, 19/20 September 1942

British Casualties

108 Sqn	Wellington Ic DV872 'W' FTR from Tobruk; Wg Cdr R.H.Mawe, DFC, and five PoW
148 Sqn	Wellington Ic HF840 'B' attacked Tobruk, on return crashed in desert; Sgt H.L.Curtiss and four PoW; one evaded and met crew from 70 Sqn aircraft lost on 13/14th, reaching safety

Sunday-Monday, 20/21 September 1942

British Casualties

70 Sqn	Wellington Ic DV546 'U' FTR from Tobruk; Flt Sgt W.M.Marvin and five KiA

Tuesday-Wednesday, 22/23 September 1942

German Claims

Flak	B-24

Wednesday, 23 September 1942

British Casualties

821 Sqn	Albacore X9154 captured by Italians 5 August; repaired and tested by 9° Gr/4° St CT; abandoned Tripoli u/s

Friday-Saturday, 25/26 September 1942

British Casualties

40 Sqn	Wellington Ic HF846 'P' seen to crash SW LG.146, El Gubbi, while attacking Tobruk; Flt Sgt G.F.Langham and five KiA

Sunday-Monday, 27/28 September 1942

Bostons of 24 SAAF Squadron joined the Wellingtons by night, nine being detailed to attack LGs.101 and 13 before midnight. One of the South African bombers was shot down in flames over LG.13 and a second was badly damaged bombing LG.101 (see also Chapter Six).

British Casualties

148 Sqn	Wellington Ic DV520 'O' FTR from Tobruk; Sgt N.G.Beadle and five KiA
24 SAAF Sqn	Boston III Z2288 one of nine off 2140-2215 for attacks on LG.101 anf LG.13. One of three attacking LG.101 damaged by Flak and SOC on return
24 SAAF Sqn	Boston III AL785 'S' one of nine off by night and one of four attacking LG.13; shot down by Flak over target; Lt G.Cohen and one KiA, two PoW

German Claims

Flak	1 Wellington and two other bombers shot down			
7./JG 53	Lt Jürgen Harder	Boston	NW Cairo	1945

Monday-Tuesday, 28/29 September 1942

British Casualties

70 Sqn	Wellington Ic Z1041 'W' crash-landed 35m S Tobruk after sending SOS; Sgt W.Goody and five presumed rescued
148 Sqn	Wellington Ic HD947 FTR from Tobruk; Plt Off S.C.Pearce and five KiA

German Claims

Flak		Wellington

Wednesday-Thursday, 30 September/1 October 1942

One loss to enemy fire was suffered by 148 Squadron during a raid on Tobruk, and two further Wellingtons were lost on this night to other causes.

British Casualties

148 Sqn	Wellington Ic FTR Tobruk; Sgt T.H.Billingham and five KiA
104 Sqn	Wellington Z8514 off 2115 to bomb Tobruk, on return engines failed on landing approach; Flt Sgt H.C.Hund and five KiA

Thursday, 1 October 1942

Eight Liberators of 160 Squadron undertook a daylight raid on a convoy north of Derna. They were intercepted by three Bf 110s and a Ju 88, the crews reporting that one of the former was hit and was seen to crash into the sea. A second dived away, pouring thick smoke, and was claimed as a probable, while the Ju 88 also dived away with smoke pouring from one engine. The attack was nonetheless effective, the 7,137-ton *Nino Bixio* being hit and sunk.

US Claims

415th BS/98th BG	B-24D gunner	Bf 109 Damaged	Navarino Bay	1830

Friday-Saturday, 2/3 October 1942

British Casualties

Special Duties Flt	Wellington Ic X9734 off from LG.237 to drop supplies to Cretan partisans; on return port engine failed and eventually force-landed in sea. Crew had difficulty extracting unconscious (or dead) rear gunner out of his turret and the aircraft sank; Flg Off E.R.Ridgeway and three survived in dinghy for 43 hours in bad weather and few rations until rescued by MTB 268

Saturday, 3 October 1942

US Casualties

415th BS/98th BG	B-24D 41-11842 'Ready and Willing', crashed into mountain N Beirut, Lebanon; 1/Lt R.E.Kennedy and eight KiA

Monday-Tuesday, 5/6 October 1942

British Casualties

148 Sqn	Wellington Ic DV562 'S' FTR from sortie to Tobruk; Sgt W.N.Fethers and five PoW
148 Sqn	Wellington Ic DV649 'Y' on sortie to Tobruk, crashed in Gambut area; Flt Sgt H.S.Rodgers and five KiA

Tuesday, 6 October 1942

US Casualties

HalPro	B-24D 41-11910 '4 X' 'Sag Ass Sally' out of fuel crashed Ryak, Palestine; Lt I.J.Wilhite and crew MiA
HalPro	B-24D 41-11595 '1 U' damaged by fighter over Benghazi 1815, pilot 2/Lt N.C.Appold, Sgt R.Weipert DoW, two WiA

German Casualties

I./KG 54	Ju 88A-4 WNr 2539 B3+GH shot down in combat witrh B-24s, crashed in sea; Fw Friedrich Müller and three MiA
IV./KGzbV 1	Ju 52/3m WNr 2868 destroyed on ground by bombs at Maleme
IV./KGzbV 1	Ju 52/3m WNr 7410 destroyed on ground by bombs at Maleme

Wednesday, 7 October 1942

German Casualties

KGr.zbV 400	Ju 52/3m WNr 5817 destroyed on ground by bombs at Maleme
KGr.zbV 400	Ju 52/3m WNr 6393 destroyed on ground by bombs at Maleme

Friday-Saturday, 9/10 October 1942

Forty-nine Wellingtons raided LGs.17 and 18. Twin-engined aircraft believed to have been He 111s or Ju 88s were seen on the ground, direct hits being claimed on two, a third blowing up and a fourth was set on fire at LG.17; other fires were also noted. Three night fighters were reported and one Wellington was hit in the rear turret, but escaped. Another from 104 Squadron failed to return, however.

British Casualties

104 Sqn	Wellington II Z8522 'H' FTR from attack on LG.17 and 18 at Fuka; night fighters reported to be active; Flt Sgt E.L.Anderson and five KiA

Saturday-Sunday, 10/11 October 1942

A Halifax of the new 462 Squadron set off from Fayid at 1912 to attack Maleme airfield, Crete. Over the target the nose was hit by Flak which seriously wounded the navigator and rendered all the forward electrical services out of action, the outboard engines on each side failing. When just about to ditch, the pilot managed to restart the port outer which allowed the aircraft to regain some height. The restarted engine subsequently failed again, but by this time the aircraft was close enough to base to allow a force-landing to be made 28km east of Mansoura. Subsequently the navigator, Flt Lt F.T.Collins, reportedly received an Immediate Award of the DFC for his courage in continuing with his duties despite his wounds.

British Casualties

462 Sqn	Halifax II W1183 'M' off to Maleme a/f, Crete; damaged by Flak but managed to force-land on return; Sqn Ldr P.G.B. Warner and six safe, although navigator WiA

Sunday-Monday, 11/12 October 1942

Eight Liberators of 160 Squadron were despatched to attack a convoy in Suda Bay. These were targeted by a night fighter and one was damaged. US B-24s raided Benghazi, being intercepted, but gunners claimed two of the interceptors shot down. MC.200 pilots of 150° Gruppo reported engaging eight Liberators, two of which were attacked by Serg Magg Benassi, who claimed hits on both; two B-24s were indeed damaged.

British Casualties

160 Sqn	Liberator II AL603 'T' set out at 1400 to bomb convoy in Suda Bay; attacked by night fighter and hydraulic tank holed. No.1 engine cut on approach to base and No.2 began to splutter so could not go round again; the undercarriage collapsed as the aircraft swung on landing and it was DBR; Flt Sgt R.E.Brown and seven safe

US Claims

Hal BS/1st PBG	B-24D '2 A' Maj R.C.Sanders, waist gunner	Bf 110	1828
Hal BS/1st PBG	B-24D '18 O' 1/Lt S.R.Oglesby, top turret gunner		
Hal BS/1st PBG	B-24D '5 D' Capt J.M.Toomey, top turret gunner		
Hal BS/1st PBG	B-24D '21 R' 1/Lt J.R.Wilcox, gunners	Ju 88	
Hal BS/1st PBG	B-24D '21 R' 1/Lt J.K.Brereton, gunners		

US Casualties				
344th BS/98th BG	B-24D 'C'; Sgt E.E.Del Vecchio died of wounds			
Italian Claims				
363ª Sq, 150°Gr Aut CT	Serg Magg Bruno Benassi	MC.200	2 B-24s Damaged	Benghazi
German Casualties				
7.ZG 26	Bf 110F-2 WNr 5098 3U+SR shot down in combat with B-24s, crashed into sea N Tobruk; Oblt Karl Will/Gefr Kurt Bohrer MiA			

Liberator II AL579 with the revised form of roundel (Type C1) introduced from summer 1942, came to the Middle East with 159 Squadron initially in June, but was amalgamated into 160 Squadron a couple of months later. The aircraft was similar to the US B-24D, but featured amongst its adaptations for British service, the dorsal turret mounting four .303in machine guns rather than the American aircraft's pair of .50in weapons.

Monday, 12 October 1942

Three MC.202s of 13° Gruppo, flown by Ten Savoia, S.Ten Zuccarini and S.Ten Pellegrini, were scrambled at 1140 to intercept a formation of Liberators. Zuccarini claimed one B-24 shot down while three more were believed to have been hit.

Italian Claims					
77ª Sq, 13°Gr, 2°St CT	S.Ten Gian Mario Zuccarini	MC.202 MM 7884	B-24	N Ras Azzaz	1140-1230

Monday-Tuesday, 12/13 October 1942

The Tobruk docks were again the target, on this occasion for 37 bombers. One Wellington was lost and two suffered some damage; a single CR.42 was spotted.

British Casualties	
70 Sqn	Wellington Ic DV570 'M' FTR from sortie to Tobruk; crew signalled engine trouble and might have to force-land; Sgt S.Fitton and five PoW

Tuesday-Wednesday, 13/14 October 1942

German Claims	
Flak	3 bombers shot down over Axis convoy (201 Group)

Wednesday, 14 October 1942

US Claims

Hal BS/1st PBG	3 B-17E gunners	Macchi Damaged		1400

Wednesday-Thursday, 14/15 October 1942

British Casualties

104 Sqn	Wellington II Z8594 'T' FTR from sortie to Tobruk; believed seen falling in flames near target area; Plt Off E.W.Baldwin and five KiA

German Claims

Flak	Wellington over Tobruk		

Saturday, 17 October 1942

US Claims

376th BG	B-24s formation	Bf 109 probable	S Benghazi	

Saturday-Sunday, 17/18 October 1942

German Claims

Flak	Wellington	nr Bir Mumin Busak	0210

Monday, 19 October 1942

During a patrol at 1110 over Tobruk, M.llo Guerriero Agostini of 92ª Squadriglia intercepted a formation of five Liberators coming from the north-west at 16,000ft. He immediately attacked and claimed one shot down in flames 30 miles north-east of Tobruk. He landed at 1205 on his MC.200 damaged by return fire.

Italian Claims

92ª Sq, 8°Gr, 2°St CT	M.llo Guerriero Agostini	MC.200	Liberator	off Tobruk	1125

Italian Casualties

92ª Sq, 8°Gr, 2°St CT	MC.200 damaged by B-24 return fire, M.llo Guerriero Agostini safe

Tuesday, 20 October 1942

British Casualties

108 Sqn	Wellington DV873 MiA Tobruk

Wednesday-Thursday, 21/22 October 1942

British Casualties

70 Sqn	Wellington Ic R1029 'S' FTR from sortie to Tobruk; Flt Sgt G.H.Rapson and three PoW, (one died on 29th); three KiA

Thursday, 22 October 1942

German Casualties

IV./KGzbV 1	Ju 52/3m WNr 5866 destroyed on ground by bombs at Maleme
IV./KGzbV 1	Ju 52/3m WNr 6345 damaged 25% on ground by bombs at Maleme

Thursday-Friday, 22/23 October 1942

LGs.20 and 104 were the targets for 37 Wellingtons. Aircraft 'X' of 108 Squadron was attacked by a twin-engined fighter, the tail and rear turret being riddled with fire. However, the crew reported seeing their assailant going down, pouring smoke, and a parachute was seen.

British Claims

108 Sqn	Twin-engined fighter possibly shot down

British Casualties

108 Sqn	Wellington Ic 'X' damaged by night fighter

The commencement of the El Alamein offensive saw 205 Group at peak strength:

231 Wing	
37 and 70 Squadrons	32 Wellington Ic
236 Wing	
108 and 148 Squadrons	32 Wellington Ic
238 Wing	
40 Squadron	16 Wellington Ic
104 Squadron	16 Wellington II
242 Wing	
160 Squadron	16 Liberator II
245 Wing	
14 Squadron	16 Marauder I
462 Squadron	16 Halifax II

NB: 14 Squadron would be transferred to 201 Group on 29 October for General Reconnaissance duties. 205 Group now also incorporated a Special Liberator Flight for SOE operations; this was equipped with ten Liberator IIs. 162 Squadron was still back at Shallufa but was now under the direct command of HQ, RAF Middle East.

With the battle underway, Tobruk remained the priority target although frequent calls were made for the bombers to strike at troop and vehicle concentrations behind the Axis lines, although airfields constituted frequent targets.

Monday, 26 October 1942

US Claims

9th BS/1st PBG	gunners (pil 1/Lt J.Kramp) B-17E '9-A'	MC.200	off Tobruk	around midday

Tuesday-Wednesday, 27/28 October 1942

Maleme was raided by eight Halifaxes of 462 Squadron and an equal number of 160 Squadron Liberators. One of the latter was lost.

British Casualties	
160 Sqn	Liberator II AL548 'R' shot down near Maleme, Crete; Flt Lt E.C.Cox and seven KiA
826 Sqn	Albacore BF677 'S4F' returning from illuminating and bombing panzers, force-landed due to shortage of fuel, hit an obstruction and badly damaged; Sub Lt C.R.Neville safe, TAG injured
German Casualties	
KGr zbV 600	Ju 52/3m WNr 7287 destroyed by bombs at Maleme airfield
KGr zvV 800	Ju 52/3m WNr 6430 destroyed by bombs at Maleme airfield

Thursday-Friday, 29/30 October 1942

When illuminating enemy positions for a 104 Squadron Wellington which should have been flying 500 feet higher, an 821 Squadron Albacore collided with the bomber, both aircraft being destroyed. The Albacore pilot survived to become a PoW of the Italians, but the other eight personnel were all killed. The heavy bombers of 160 and 462 Squadrons targeted Maleme by day. One of the Liberators was attacked by a Ju 88 off Gavdos Island, but suffered no damage.

British Casualties	
821 Sqn	Albacore I T9136 collided with Wellington W5478 and crashed; Sub Lt P.F.Manders PoW, but two KiA
104 Sqn	Wellington II W5478 'P' collided with Albacore T9136 over target nr El Alamein; Flg Off J.S.Martin and five KiA
US Casualties	
1st PBG	B-24D 42-22593 '18 O' 'Black Mariah II', hit by Flak, crashed at Maleme; Capt J.W.Kidd and crew safe

During October the group's Wellingtons had undertaken 700 sorties against Tobruk, the Halifaxes and Liberators adding 100 more; this combined weight of attack had dropped 850 tons of explosives on the harbour and the shipping there. During the same period 159 Squadron and the USAAF B-24s had made 50 sorties over Benghazi where 150 tons of bombs had been dropped on the target.

Sunday-Monday, 1/2 November 1942

Sixty-eight Wellingtons operated over the battle area, losing one of their number. However, November was marked by the despatch to the area from Germany of the rest of Nachtjagdgeschwader 2 which arrived at Comiso. The Stab and II.Gruppe were to employ their Ju 88Cs not only for night fighting, but for convoy escort and anti-submarine operations.

British Casualties	
40 Sqn	Wellington Ic HX385 'V' when seeking targets of opportunity, one engine failed and a/c lost height; Sgt M.McKiggin and five baled out into Allied territory nr El Alamein

Monday, 2 November 1942

Italian pilots reported that five four-engined bombers were engaged over Tobruk during a patrol between 1605 and 1730. M.llo Guerriero Agostini of 92ª Squadriglia expended his magazine of 600 rounds claiming two damaged, while S.Ten Gian Mario Zuccarini of 77ª Squadriglia fired at another, claiming some hits.

Italian Claims					
92ª Sq, 8°Gr, 2°St CT	M.llo Guerriero Agostini	MC.200	2 Liberators Damaged	off Tobruk	1655
77ª Sq, 13°Gr, 2°St CT	S.Ten Gian Mario Zuccarini	MC.200			

Tuesday-Wednesday, 3/4 November 1942

Again 68 Wellingtons prowled the battle area, seeking any likely targets. A single Ju 88 was seen which attacked one Wellington, but this made off when hit by fire from some of the gunners. Three were lost in accidents, but none to enemy action.

Wednesday, 4 November 1942

Raids on Benghazi continued by the four-engined units, five vessels being sunk during 4th and 5th, including the 6,424-ton tanker *Portofino*, the torpedo-boat *Centauro*, and the mine-layer *Selve* (ex-German M.100).

US Claims					
345th BS/98th BG	gunners aboard	B-24D 41-11886 'S'	Bf 109		1300
345th BS/98th BG	gunners aboard	B-24D 41-11886 'S'	Bf 110 Damaged		1300
German Claims					
8./JG 27	Oblt Werner Schroer	B-24		Sollum-Benghazi	1215
8./JG 27	Uffz Alfred Stückler	B-24		S Sollum	1215
German Casualties					
Stab III./JG 27	Bf 109F-4 trop WNr 13251 combat with B-24 Benghazi, 100% damaged; Lt Eberhard Schmidt KiA				

Thursday, 5 November 1942

104 Squadron now despatched six aircraft to Malta. Three days later the need for this further reinforcement of the island became clear when the Anglo-American Operation Torch landings in French North-West Africa took place. Malta's importance as a striking base athwart the Axis supply routes, not only now to Tripoli, but to Tunis and Bizerta as well, rendered the island of even greater importance.

As the Axis retreat got underway, targets became more fleeting, although still plentiful. The Halfaya Pass was taken on 11 November and two days later British forces entered Tobruk, removing the scene of so many costly attacks from the target map. Initially, of course, it was the WDAF units which moved forward behind the advancing 8th Army, but plans were in place to move 205 Group's units westward as quickly as possible to maintain the attack on the Axis supply route.

Already by this time units were on the move, 231 Wing making for LG.106 near El Daba, 236 Wing (now joined at the same time by the Halifaxes of 462 Squadron) to LG.106 and 238 Wing to LG.104, Qotaifiya. The squadrons of this latter wing were both currently maintaining detachments at Luqa, Malta. In fact the first unit to reduce its distance from the front had been 160 Squadron which had moved its Liberators forward to Shandur from Aqir on 8 November.

Tuesday-Wednesday, 10/11 November 1942

Three Wellingtons were lost during the night, but none of them fell victim to enemy fire of any sort. Aircraft from 37 and 148 Squadrons attacked MT between Tobruk and Gazala before succumbing to the so-frequent engine troubles. Similar problems beset a 40 Squadron aircraft operating to the north from Luqa. It was left to one of 462 Squadron's Halifaxes to fall foul of the Flak when attacking MT on the Tobruk-Derna road. Catching fire, the aircraft was abandoned by its crew off Tobruk from where Flt Lt J.V.Watts, the second pilot, swam ashore and hid for four days until found by an advancing British patrol. The pilot, Sqn Ldr Goldston, and two other members of the crew were killed, the remaining two becoming PoWs.

British Casualties	
462 Sqn	Halifax II DT498 'C' shot down by Flak off Tobruk; Sqn Ldr J.R.Goldston and two KiA, two PoWs, one evaded and returned

Thursday-Friday, 12/13 November 1942

Twenty-eight Wellingtons and four Halifaxes attacked retreating MT during the night. Three Wellingtons failed to return, one each from 40, 70 and 148 Squadrons – all crash-landed due to engine failures. Again not to enemy action!

Friday-Saturday, 13/14 November 1942

Nineteen Wellingtons attacked MT. 821 Squadron moved to Hal Far, Malta.

British Casualties	
108 Sqn	Wellington Ic HX380 off to attack Benghazi. Damaged by Flak near Sollum, crash-landed 35m S Fuka.
	Sgt M.J.S.Kerby and crew found an Italian lorry while walking, repaired it and drove back, arriving 14th
148 Sqn	Wellington Ic AD637 'E' despatched to bomb shipping and harbour at Benghazi but MiA; Plt Off W.G.Sharpe and five KiA

At this stage, before Benghazi could become a priority target again, it had fallen into Allied hands on 20 November. Within a week or so the Wellington squadrons had moved forward again, this time to the Gambut-Bardia area, 231 Wing to LG.140 at Bir el Gabr, the other two Wings to LG.237 at Kilo 40. Priority now became the enhancement of the striking force on Malta from where much attention was directed towards Sicily and Tripoli in support of the fighting now taking place in Tunisia.

Sunday, 15 November 1942

US Claims

345th BS/98th BG	gunners aboard	B-24D	Bf 109 + one Damaged		
415th BS/98th BG	waist gunner	B-24D '810 C'	Bf 109 Probable		1635
343th BS/98th BG	gunners aboard	B-24D '921 W'	Bf 109 Damaged	50m S Benghazi	1628

US Casualties

512th BS/376th	BG B-24D 41-11592 '37 T' 'Draggin'Lady', damaged by fighters, crashed; 1/Lt J.R.Wilcox and crew rescued by British

German Claims

2./JG 27	Fw Gustav Sturm	B-24 HSS	S El Agheila
9./JG 77	Fhj Uffz Hans-Werner Renzow	B-24	60km N Benghazi
III./JG 77	unstated	B-24	60km N Benghazi

German Casualties	
8./JG 77	Bf 109G-2 trop WNr 10651 combat with B-24, crashed in sea; Fhj Uffz Hans-Werner Renzow baled and safe

Thursday-Friday, 19/20 November 1942

British Casualties	
104 Sqn	Wellington II W5583 'E' from Luqa to attack Catania, but shot down over target; Flt Lt J.H.D.Mercer and five KiA

Monday-Tuesday, 23/24 November 1942

British Casualties	
37 Sqn	Wellington Ic X9693 'U' took off to attack Kastelli Pediada, but shot down over the target; Flg Off E.D.Fleishman and five KiA
German Casualties	
2.(F)/123	Ju 88D-1 WNr 430324 70% damaged by bombs at Kastelli airfield
2.(F)/123	Ju 88D-2 WNr 0803 95% damaged by bombs at Kastelli airfield

Thursday-Friday, 26/27 November 1942

British Casualties	
104 Sqn	Wellington II W5550 'Q' off from Luqa to attack Gerbini airfield. Ditched off Sicily on return; Plt Off F.M.Benitz, DFM, and four PoW, one KiA

Sunday, 29 November 1942

MC.202s of 13° Gruppo were scrambled to intercept a reported eight Liberators, claiming two probably shot down. During later interception one more such bomber was claimed, again as a probable, but the successful pilot was slightly wounded and force-landed.

Italian Claims					
77ª Sq, 13°Gr, 2°St CT	S.Ten Gian Mario Zuccarini	MC.202	} 2 B-24s Probable	80km N Tripoli	1215-1325
82ª Sq, 13°Gr, 2°St CT	Serg Magg Filippo Baldin	MC.202			
82ª Sq, 13°Gr, 2°St CT	Serg Mario Turchetti	MC.202			
82ª Sq, 13°Gr, 2°St CT	S.Ten Attilio Cannata	MC.202 MM 7887	B-24 Probable		1630-1715
Italian Casualties					
82ª Sq, 13°Gr, 2°St CT	MC.202 MM 7887 belly-landed, S.Ten Attilio Cannata slightly wounded				

Wednesday, 2 December 1942

British Casualties	
828 Sqn	Albacore X9094 FTR from attack on convoy 20m from Kerkenah; caught fire and blew up on water; Mdspm C.G.Taylor PoW, Sub Lt W.Guy KiA

Friday, 4 December 1942

Twenty B-24s of the 98th and 376th Bombardment Groups (Heavy), in the first attack by the USAAF against Italy, bombed the Italian fleet and docks at Naples; hits were reported on numerous harbour installations, a railroad yard, and three or four ships, including a battleship. As a matter of fact three Italian cruisers, harboured in the central dock, were hit: *Muzio Attendolo* was struck by one or two bombs and sank, *Raimondo Montecuccoli* was badly damaged, while *Eugenio di Savoia* sustained minor damage. About 350 people lost their lives, among them 200 sailors. No fighter opposition was met.

Thursday, 10 December 1942

A Halifax of 138 Squadron loaded with passengers being returned to the United Kingdom (and composed mainly of tour-expired 205 Group aircrew) was on the way from Malta to Gibraltar when engine failures occurred. Flt Lt Sutton, the pilot, ordered all aboard to bale out as the aircraft was passing over Algeria. For some reason only two passengers did so, the rest remaining in the aircraft and all surviving when Sutton undertook a crash-landing near Khebil.

Meanwhile a second Halifax had taken off from LG.224 on the first leg of the journey to Malta. This aircraft never arrived and it was presumed that it had come down in the Mediterranean, possibly falling victim to a night fighter. Flt Lt Anderle and his all-Czech crew together with eight passengers were all lost.

British Casualties	
138 Sqn	Halifax II L9618 left Luqa 0345 but crash-landed near Khebil, Algeria, after three of the four engines failed; Flt Lt J.C.K.Sutton, four crew and 11 passengers all survived safe, including two of the latter who baled out
138 Sqn	Halifax II W1002 MiA between North Africa and Malta; Flt Lt L.Anderle and six crew (like him, all Czech), with eight passengers KiA

Friday, 11 December 1942

In Italy, 18 B-24s of 98th and 376th Bomb Groups bombed the harbour and surrounding areas at Naples with good results. One aircraft was reportedly shot down by Flak. This time Regia Aeronautica fighters of 22° Gruppo, in charge of the defence of Naples, reacted. Two patrols, one of four MC.202s, led by Ten Baschiera, and one of four MC.200s, led by Ten Ferlin, took off at about 1500. Rather optimistically, the Italians claimed three Liberators shot down, for the loss of Ten Baschiera, badly hit by bombers' return fire and crash-landed.

British Casualties	
826 Sqn	Albacore X9163 '4L' force-landed in sea; dinghy found 51m SE Malta; Sub Lt J.C.Manning KiA; Sub Lt N.H.Kempson picked up by HMS *Hebe* on 20th
US Casualties	
344th BS/98th BG	B-24D 41-11797 'F', shot down by Flak; 1/Lt Lawrence C.Kennedy and seven PoW (two escaped), three KiA

Italian Claims					
371ª Sq, 22°Gr Aut CT	Ten Orazio Ferlin	MC.200	B-24	Naples	1500-
371ª Sq, 22°Gr Aut CT	Serg Magg Raffaele Nanoia	MC.200	B-24	Naples	1500-
359ª Sq, 22°Gr Aut CT	M.llo Antonino Lo Schiavo	MC.200	B-24	Naples	1500-
Italian Casualties					
371ª Sq, 22°Gr Aut CT	MC.202 MM 9579, hit by return fire, crash-landed nr Agropoli, Ten Lanfranco Baschiera DoW				

Sunday, 13 December 1942

An attack on LG.140 by a Ju 88 succeeded in destroying three Wellingtons on the ground there, one of which is believed already to have previously been serving with 108 Squadron at the time that unit was disbanded. B-24Ds of the 93rd BG flew their first mission in North Africa, to Bizerte. Over the target they were attacked by FW 190s, and 'Ambrose', piloted by 1/Lt John H.Roche, was hit in the gas line. He force-landed near Bone, Algeria, the aircraft running into a gully; the nose gear broke, and the aircraft dug its nose in, reared up and broke its back. Three crew were killed. Another aircraft, 'Flying Cock', piloted by Lt Llewellyn Brown, was damaged by Flak and the bombardier, 2/Lt John T.Sparks was badly wounded; he died of his wounds.

British Casualties	
37 Sqn	Wellington Ics DV614 and HX571 destroyed on the ground during an air raid by a Ju 88 on LG.140
108 Sqn	Wellington Ic AD633 'H' possibly destroyed at LG.140 during an attack by a Ju 88
1 OADU	Wellington Ic LA965 took off from Gibraltar to fly to Egypt, shot down over Gulf of Sirte; Sgt D.A.Roberts and four rescued unhurt
US Casualties	
93rd BG	B-24D 'Ambrose', damaged by FW 190s, crash-landed nr Bone; 1/Lt John H.Roche and six safe, three killed
409th BS/93rd BG	B-24D 41-23724 'Flying Cock', damaged by Flak, later repaired; Lt Llewellyn Brown and crew safe, but bombardier WiA, died of wounds

Thursday, 17 December 1942

A Halifax of 138 Squadron took off from Luqa, tasked with carrying a group of passengers home to England. At once, it was beset with engine troubles and turned back, but crashed east of Zetun at 0405 with the loss of everyone aboard. This included Flg Off K.Dobromirski's crew, five of the six being Poles like himself. Amongst the ten passengers were Maj Lord A.A.B.Apsley, DSO, MC, TD, Sqn Ldr J.H.Wedgwood, DFC, until recently the commanding officer of 92 Squadron and one of the most successful of the Spitfire pilots in North Africa, and Flt Lt L.A.Vaughan, DSO, DFC, a bomber pilot who had been serving with 40 Squadron and who had completed 100 operational sorties.

British Casualties

138 Sqn	Halifax II DT542 crashed trying to land back at Luqa due to engine trouble; Flg Off K.Dobromirski, six crew and ten passengers KiFA

Thursday-Friday, 17/18 December 1942

During an attack on Tunis docks and La Goulette, Wellington 'F' of 104 Squadron was intercepted and shot down by a Ju 88C of II./NJG 2, and a second damaged. This was the first engagement between aircraft of 205 Group and this Luftwaffe unit which was to take quite a toll of the group's aircraft during the coming few months.

British Casualties

104 Sqn	Wellington II Z8469 'F' shot down by Ju 88; Flg Off C.W.M.Dallas PoW, crew of five KiA
104 Sqn	Wellington II damaged by Ju 88

German Claims

II./NJG 2	Oblt Albert Schulz	2 Wellingtons

Friday, 18 December 1942

British Casualties

40 Sqn	Wellington Ic HD959 destroyed on the ground during air raid on Luqa, Malta
40 Sqn	Wellington Ic HE 108 destroyed on the ground during air raid on Luqa, Malta
40 Sqn	Wellington Ic HX382 possibly destroyed on the ground during air raid on Luqa, Malta
40 Sqn	Wellington Ic AD627* destroyed on the ground during air raid on Luqa, Malta
1 OADU	Wellington II Z8596 destroyed by 'enemy action' probably on the ground during air raid on Luqa, Malta

*Thought to be an aircraft of 108 Squadron, recently handed over to 40 Squadron

Wednesday-Thursday, 23/24 December 1942

German Casualties

II./KG 76	Ju 88 A-4 WNr 1403293 destroyed and 4 Ju 88A-4s WNr 3531, 5787, 140433 and 140351 damaged by bombs at Tympakion

Monday-Tuesday, 28/29 December 1942

Wellingtons from 104 Squadron were again despatched from Luqa to bomb Tunis docks. Again one was intercepted by a II./NJG 2 Ju 88C and was shot down, on this occasion by Hptmn Dr Horst Patuschka, the unit's Kommandeur and a very successful night fighter who had claimed circa 20 RAF aircraft shot down at this time.

British Casualties

104 Sqn	Wellington IC Z8908 'H' FTR; Sgt R.T.Cottrell and five KiA

German Claims

II./NJG 2	Hptm Dr Horst Patuschka	Wellington

Thursday-Friday, 31 December 1942/1 January 1943

104 Squadron once again flew from Luqa to attack a target in Tunisia – this time Sfax, somewhat to the south of other raids undertaken from here. Once more one of the unit's aircraft was intercepted and shot down, and as had been the case three nights earlier, the German pilot was Hptmn Patuschka.

British Casualties

104 Sqn	Wellington Ic HD955 FTR from Sfax; Wt Off D.L.Iremonger and five KiA

German Claims

I./NJG 2	Hptm Dr Horst Patuschka	Wellington	Sfax

At the year's end 205 Group – already effectively denuded by the departure of units to Malta, began to shrink further when 148 Squadron was disbanded. It would reform in March 1943 as Special Duties Flight, involved in the dropping of supplies to partisan forces – but no longer under the control of 205 Group.

Sunday, 3 January 1943
IX Bomber Command continued to direct the efforts of the Liberators which were again successful on this date, sinking the freighter *Agostino Bertani* in Tripoli harbour.

Tuesday, 5 January 1943
205 Group advised that from 7 January it would come under the operational control of Advanced HQ, Western Desert. Between 8th-23rd the units moved from Menastir to Benina. Operations under Western Desert continued until 19th, and then on 23rd reverted to HQ, RAF Middle East. At this point 37 and 70 Squadrons moved with 231 Wing to Magrun, whereas 462 Squadron, which had reformed, arrived at LG.237 as part of 236 Wing, based at Soluch.

Wednesday, 6 January 1943
All units still in North Africa were ordered to stand by for operations against targets in Sicily from 6 January, but bad weather prevented their involvement until the 19th. Meanwhile 40 Squadron returned from Malta to LG.237, but mantained a detachment at Magrun; the unit now came under the control of 236 Wing at Soluch.

Thursday, 7 January 1943
From Cyrenaica on this date the US IXth Bomber Command launched 25 B-24s to undertake the first raid on Palermo in Sicily. Bad weather affected navigation adversely, but ten bombers managed to release their bombs over the designated target, sinking the Italian destroyer *Bersagliere* at 1625.

Monday, 11 January 1943
Nine B-24Ds of 376th BG took off to attack Vittorio Emanuele Mole at Naples; one returned early. Two aircraft were lost, reportedly shot down by a Bf 109, which was then shot down by the other two B-24s. Regia Aeronautica fighters of 22° Gruppo were scrambled at 1620 from Capodichino airdrome to face the bombers. Ten Riccardo Monaco claimed two B-24s shot down, after a long chase east of Naples, up to Avellino; Ten Orfeo Mazzitelli claimed another, reportedly shot down between Procida and Ischia Islands. A fourth bomber was claimed by the Flak.

US Claims					
376th BG	B-24D, pilot Capt J.K.Brereton, bombardier 2/Lt T.V.Flynn and right waist gunner		Bf 109	E Naples	
US Casualties					
376th BG	B-24D '50/E', shot down by fighters, ditched; Lt Col John H.Payne and seven KiA, one PoW				
515th BS/376th BG	B-24D '59/J', shot down by fighters, crashed E Naples; Capt Louis A.Prchal and six KiA, two PoW				
Italian Claims					
369ª Sq, 22°Gr Aut CT	Ten Riccardo Monaco	MC.202	2 B-24s	E Naples	
371ª Sq, 22°Gr Aut CT	Ten Orfeo Mazzitelli	MC.202	B-24	NW Naples	
Flak			B-24	Naples	1652

Friday, 15 January 1943
Throughout the period under review in this volume, the activities of the heavy bombers and front-line fighters almost never coincided. This has made it easier to allow for a clearer reading of these different changes of events by keeping them separated. However, for a short time during January the front-line fighter units of the Axis, notably 3° and 4° Stormi CT and elements of JG 77, did become engaged on several occasions with formations of US heavy bombers. These involved both aircraft of IX Bomber Command from Cyrenaica and 12th Air Force aircraft based in eastern Algeria. Rather than repeat the details of these particular engagements within both WDAF chapters and this chapter devoted to the heavy bombers, we have detailed them in the former. Therefore, at this point in this particular chapter we draw your attention to relevant events on 15-19 January 1943 related in Chapter Eight which deals with several such interceptions.

Sunday, 17 January 1943

By night 50 Allied bombers raided Castel Benito where reconnaissance indicated that some 200 Axis aircraft were now concentrated. Regia Aeronautica records show that during one attack by 18 bombers, eight MC.202s and an S.82 were destroyed and a number of other aircraft damaged. Italian AA gunners claimed one four-engined bomber shot down, one member of the crew becoming a PoW. I./JG 77 lost two Bf 109s plus nine more damaged during these attacks.

Italian Claims					
AA at Tripoli			B-24	Tripoli	night

Monday, 18 January 1943

B-24s of the 98th and 376th Bomb Groups bombed Tripoli harbour.

Italian Claims					
83ª Sq, 18°Gr, 3°St CT	Ten Guglielmo Specker	MC.202	B-17	60km S Zuara	
95ª Sq, 18°Gr, 3°St CT	M.llo Felice Longhi	MC.202	}		
85ª Sq, 18°Gr, 3°St CT	Cap Giulio C.Giuntella	MC.202	} B-17	60km S Zuara	
85ª Sq, 18°Gr, 3°St CT	Serg Domenico Balduzzo	MC.202	}		
AA at Tripoli			four-engined bomber		night

Friday-Saturday, 29/30 January 1943

Six Halifaxes and 11 Wellingtons attacked targets at Catania and Messina in Sicily. One Wellington failed to return. January had generally been a period of re-organisation due to a general shortage of aircraft and crews.

British Casualties		
70 Sqn	Wellington	
Italian Claims		
AA at Catania	Wellington	0245-0451

Saturday, 30 January 1943

Five B-24 of the 98th Bomb Group bombed the railroad terminal at Messina. One Bf 109 was claimed damaged by gunners.

US Claims				
346th BS/98th BG	gunners aboard B-24D 41-11774 'O', pilot Capt L.C.Holloway	Bf 109 Damaged	Messina	1620-1622

Sunday, 31 January 1943

Nine B-24Ds took off to attack the ferry quay in Messina harbour, but on this occasion three aircraft were lost. Bombs fell in the area of the ferry gear, but appeared short. Three Bf 109s attacked just after the bomb run, four more attacked 35 minutes later. The pilot of B-24D '37' believed he hit and damaged a Bf 109 with nose guns during the second attack. The top turret and waist gunners of '32/M', pilot 1/Lt F.W.Milan, claimed hits on two Bf 109s, one of them seen smoking.

US Claims				
515th BS/376th BG	gunners aboard B-24D '4Q', pilot Capt J.K.Brereton	Bf 109	Messina	1517
US Casualties				
515th BS/376rd BG	B-24D 41-11603 '22' 'Malicious', shot down by Flak; pilot Maj John Toomey and crew MiA			
513th BS/376rd BG	B-24D 41-24000 '53' 'Poison Ivy', damaged by fighters, crashed at Luqa; pilot Lt William S.Stewart and crew safe			
514th BS/376rd BG	B-24D 41-24000 '37/J', damaged by fighters, crashed at Luqa; pilot 1/Lt George A.Ulrich and crew safe			

Monday, 1 February 1943

37 and 70 Squadrons now moved to Gardabia from Berka, 38 Squadron remaining at this latter base. 40 and 104 Squadrons now returned to Gardabia from Malta, to resume normal bombing operations.

Wednesday-Thursday, 3/4 February 1943

205 Group's new range of operations since the return of most of its units commenced with an attack on shipping at Palermo which was raided by 15 Wellingtons of 37, 40 and 70 Squadrons, and seven Halifaxes of 462 Squadron.

Friday-Saturday, 5/6 February 1943

A repeat attack on Palermo was carried out by 17 Wellingtons and nine Halifaxes.

British Casualties	
37 Sqn	Wellington FTR from Palermo

Sunday, 7 February 1943

Eight B-24Ds of 376th Bomb Group attacked Naples, hitting the docks and damaging the destroyer *Ugolino Vivaldi* and at least two freighters. One B-24 was lost to fighters and bombers' gunners claimed three Bf 109s shot down and one probable. In reality the adversaries were 19 Italian fighters of 22° Gruppo, this time mostly equipped with MC.202s, which were scrambled at 1640 to intercept the intruders. Ten Giulio Torresi, an ace already with seven claims in his bag, attacked a B-24 from below, hitting the left wing. A fire quickly started and the bomber, flown by Capt Brereton, crashed to the ground, killing the whole crew. Three Macchis were damaged by return fire in various degrees.

US Claims				
514th BS/376th BG	belly gunner aboard B-24D '34/S', pilot 1/Lt R.L.Rhoades	Bf 109 Probable	Naples	1540-1548
515th BS/376th BG	gunners aboard B-24D '39/K', pilot 1/Lt G.E.Mayfield	2 Bf 109s	Naples	1540-1548
515th BS/376th BG	belly gunner aboard B-24D '56/B', pilot Capt E.A.Crouchley	Bf 109	Naples	1540-1548
US Casualties				
515th BS/376rd BG	B-24D 41-11602 '47' 'Babe, the Big Blue Ox', shot down; pilot Capt James K.Brereton and crew MiA			

Italian Claims					
371a Sq, 22° Gr Aut CT	Ten Giulio Torresi	MC.202	B-24	Naples	1640-
Italian Casualties					
371ª Sq, 22° Gr Aut CT	MC.202 MM 7419, hit in combat, crash-landed and destroyed, Serg Bruno Biagini safe				
371ª Sq, 22° Gr Aut CT	MC.202 MM 7421, hit in combat, damaged, Ten Enrico Londei safe				
371ª Sq, 22° Gr Aut CT	MC.200 MM 8198, force-landed, M.llo Marcello Baccara safe				

Monday, 8 February 1943

The 205 Group moved to airfields in the Gardabia area:

231 Wing with 37, 40 and 70 Squadrons
236 Wing with 104 and 462 Squadrons
Group HQ, followed on 9th by 57 and 61 Rearming and Refuelling Units,
and on 13th by 437 Air Stores Park.

Monday-Tuesday, 8/9 February 1943

Palermo was raided again by 20 Wellingtons and six Halifaxes. Three Wellingtons landed at Malta on return, one Halifax crash-landed near Barce, and one Wellington was lost. However, bad weather then prevented further repeat attacks for some nights.

British Casualties	
	Wellington MiA
462 Sqn	Halifax MiA

Meanwhile, between 9-15 February 205 Group and its wings moved again, this time to Misurata in order to bring targets in Sicily and Tunisia nearer.

Monday, 15 February 1943

Nine B-24Ds of the 376th Bomb Group took off from Gambut Main to attack Naples. Five returned early and four delivered their bombload on target at 1615-1625. Results were unobserved due to a 30-minute attack by six Bf 109s and one MC.200. A fighter was claimed destroyed and another probable. All bombers suffered damage by Flak.

Twelve more B-24Ds of the 93rd Bomb Group also attacked Naples on this date, reaching their target between 1810 and 1840, but the results were again unobserved due to bad weather. One aircraft was lost. The opponents were once again the Macchis of 22° Gruppo. Eighteen fighters were scrambled and one B-24 was claimed shot down, shared among all pilots taking part in the interception. However, three MC.202s were lost, shot down by return fire.

US Claims					
515th BS/376th BG	gunners aboard B-24D '55/B', pilot 1/Lt J.R.Wilcox	fighter probable		Naples	1615-1645
515th BS/376th BG	gunners aboard B-24D '49/L', pilot Capt J.H.Wilkinson	fighter		Naples	1615-1645
US Casualties					
330th BS/93rd BG	B-24D 41-23675 'Celhalopodus', shot down; pilot Capt Charles T.Moore and crew MiA				
Italian Claims					
22° Gr Aut CT	18 pilots	MC.202	B-24	Naples	1810-
Italian Casualties					
359ª Sq, 22° Gr Aut CT	MC.202 MM 7851 shot down by B-24 gunners, S.Ten Franco Benedetti KiA				
362ª Sq, 22° Gr Aut CT	MC.202 MM 9061 shot down by B-24 gunners, Ten Frank Passerini KiA				
359ª Sq, 22° Gr Aut CT	MC.202 MM 9070 shot down by B-24 gunners, M.llo Antonino Lo Schiavo KiA				
359ª Sq, 22° Gr Aut CT	MC.202, hit in combat, Ten Eugenio Omicini WiA				
371ª Sq, 22° Gr Aut CT	MC.202 MM 9027 hit in combat, Ten Orfeo Mazzitelli safe				

Saturday, 20 February 1943

Due to bad weather efforts were made to recall the force sent out to attack Palermo again. Ten Wellington crews and one of those of 462 Squadron failed to pick up the message and continued, bombing through thick cloud. Despite the conditions, only one Wellington failed to return.

Thirty-nine B-24s of the 376th, 98th and 93rd Bomb Groups, so far the largest formation of American bombers formed in North Africa, took off to attack Naples. The primary target was closed in by cloud cover, so the B-24s bombed the secondary target of Crotone instead. Results were mostly unobserved due to haze. All (apparently) completed the mission, but one aircraft, flown by 1/Lt Story, was damaged by flak and force-landed on the beach near Pachino, Sicily, the crew being taken prisoner. The B-24 was later repaired by the Italians, and test flown by Cap Giovanni Raina as I-RAIN. It was then flown by Raina to Germany on 19 June 1943, and eventually assigned to KG 200. It was found, badly damaged, at Rechlin at the end of the war.

British Casualties	
37 Sqn	Wellington MiA
US Casualties	
330th BS/93rd BG	B-24D 41-236659 'V' 'Blonde Bomber II', damaged by Flak, force-landed at Pachino, pilot 1/Lt Daniel A.Story and crew PoW

Monday-Tuesday, 22/23 February 1943

Thirty-one Wellingtons and six Halifaxes returned to Palermo again. Once again one Wellington failed to return; on this occasion it fell victim to a CR.42 night fighter, flown by Ten Torchio. Although it has frequently been stated that Italian night fighters had achieved virtually no success apart from one or two against RAF Bomber Command raids on northern Italy, pilots in CR.42s had actually gained several successes during the past twelve months or so, as has become apparent.

British Casualties					
142 Sqn	Wellington MiA				
Italian Claims					
377ª Sq Aut CT	Ten Luigi Torchio	CR.42	Wellington	off Sicily	at night

Tuesday-Wednesday, 23/24 February 1943

Palermo was once again the target (becoming almost a 'milk run' at this stage), 25 Wellingtons and six Halifaxes making the attack this time. As before the cost was one of the former lost.

British Casualties	
	Wellington MiA (no details)

By this time 37, 40 and 70 Squadrons were operating from Gardabia East airfield, but this was found not to be suitable for heavily-loaded aircraft. Consequently 231 Wing moved with these three units to Gardabia West. At the end of the month reinforcements arrived in the shape of Wellington IIIs with Hercules XI engines. It was immediately realised that initially this would give problems with spare parts, and particularly with spare engines. This was exacerbated when Wellington Xs with Hercules VIs also began to arrive. Nonetheless, the crews were very enthusiastic about their new aircraft (of either Mark) which they felt to be very different from the old Mark Ic, the increased power greatly improving performance. As the new mounts arrived both 37 and 70 passed the Mark IIs which they had been using recently, to 40 Squadron. At this time the Group returned once more to the control of Advanced HQ, Western Desert, but received advice that this command would not call on its resources until 17 March.

Monday, 1 March 1943

Twenty B-24s of the 98th and nine of 376th Bomb Groups took off to attack Naples harbour. Seven returned early, but two from the 376th were attacked over Messina by a MC.200 of 161° Gruppo and were forced to return to base, escorted by a third. The 19 remaining delivered their bombs on target around 1630, hitting and sinking the torpedo-boat *Maestrale*. Over Naples they were intercepted by 24 fighters of 22° Gruppo which claimed three B-24s shot down.

US Casualties	
415th BS/98th BG	B-24D 41-23789 'K' shot down by fighters; pilot 1/Lt Virgil M.Anders and crew MiA

Italian Claims					
362ª Sq, 22° Gr Aut CT	Magg Vittorio Minguzzi	D 520	B-24	Naples	1735
369ª Sq, 22° Gr Aut CT	Ten Riccardo Monaco	MC.202 MM 9055	B-24	Naples	1740
362ª Sq, 22° Gr Aut CT	Ten Giulio Torresi	MC.202	} B-24	Naples	1740
22° Gruppo Aut CT	pilots	MC.202			

Monday-Tuesday, 1/2 March 1943

The attacks on Palermo continued. A raid by 22 Wellingtons during the night was followed by another by 20 Wellingtons and five Halifaxes next night – on both occasions without loss.

Monday-Tuesday, 8/9 March 1943

Palermo was the target again, but this time very heavy Flak was encountered which inflicted damage on two of the aircraft involved.

British Casualties	
	Wellington damaged
	Wellington damaged

Wednesday, 17 March 1943

It had been intimated at the end of February that AAHQ, Western Desert, would not call upon 205 Group's resources prior to 17 March. Now, that date having arrived, it ordered the Group to commence attacks against Mareth and Kettema Village which were to be the unit's first raids on Tunisian targets.

Thursday, 18 March 1943

Sixteen B-24s of the 98th Bomb Group took off between 142 0-1430 to attack Naples. Two returned early, and one aircraft was lost for unknown causes. Results were unobserved due to cloud but apparently all bombs fell far from the target.

US Casualties	
415th BS/98th BG	B-24D 41-11798 'F' lost; pilot 2/Lt Harry K.McHugh and eight MiA

Saturday, 20 March 1943

From this time there were frequent requests to 205 Group from AAHQ, Western Desert, for operations. After several cancellations, there now came a call for a maximum effort to be directed against MT concentrations in the Mareth area and to the north-west which had been spotted by Fleet Air Arm Albacores. 205 Group responded at once, sending 45 Wellingtons and 11 Halifaxes to drop 120 tons of bombs, including two of the 4,000lb 'Cookies'. The pilots of three aircraft went down low so that their gunners could strafe the beaches east of Kettema and other targets. On this occasion the cost was light; one Wellington of 104 Squadron force-landed in the sea, the crew being saved.

British Casualties	
104 Sqn	Wellington force-landed in sea; crew safe

Monday-Tuesday, 22/23 March 1943

A further request for a maximum effort to the same area, concentrating on the Mareth-Gabes road was illuminated by flare-dropping Albacores. On this occasion bad weather rendered 40 Squadron's airfield unserviceable, but 35 Wellingtons from 70 and 104 Squadrons, and ten Halifaxes from 462 Squadron managed to attack, some crews undertaking double sorties during the night.

Tuesday-Monday 23/29 March 1943

As 8th Army's assault on the Mareth Line got underway, more such requests followed. Twenty-six sorties on the 23rd were followed by 73 next night and by another 65 on the 25th, aimed mainly at concentrations south of El Hamma. Fifty-five Wellingtons and seven Halifaxes struck at the Gabes area on the 26th, but another maximum effort planned for 27 March had to be aborted due to bad weather. Following this brief nature-inspired break, 48 Wellingtons and four Halifaxes concluded a successful attack on crossroads at Oudref and Wadi Akarit on 28th. It could not be repeated next night as weather again caused a cancellation.

Thursday, 25 March 1943

In Italy, 19 B-24s of the 98th Bomb Group attacked the ferry installations at Messina. Direct hits were claimed on the target area and adjacent railroad yards, and naval oil and storage tanks were set afire. Three fighters were claimed shot down plus a probable but four bombers were damaged by Flak. Just before midnight, RAF Liberators, under operational control of the IX Bomber Command, raided the docks at Messina.

US Claims				
343rd BS/98th BG	gunners aboard B-24D '761/R', pilot G.E.Groff	2 Bf 109s	Messina	1325-1345
343rd BS/98th BG	gunners aboard B-24D '761/R', pilot Capt Kilgore	Bf 109	Messina	1330
343rd BS/98th BG	gunners aboard B-24D '913/N', pilot Capt Lawrence	two-seater Damaged	Messina	1330
344th BS/98th BG	gunners aboard B-24D '761/R', pilot Lt Gaston	Bf 109 probable	Messina	1330

Tuesday, 30 March 1943

Occupation of the Mareth defences by 8th Army troops on this date ended this series of attacks, but that same night Albacores illuminated Sfax-El Maou landing ground for 45 Wellingtons to unload 100 tons of bombs on it.

By the end of March re-equipment had been proceeding apace, aided by the low level of losses during these recent operations. By now both 37 and 70 Squadrons had full complements of Mark III or X Wellingtons, whereas 40 Squadron had 17 Mark IIIs and only three of the elderly Mark Ics.

BIBLIOGRAPHY

The Original

Fighters over the Desert Christopher Shores and Hans Ring Neville Spearman 1969

Linked Titles in the Series

Malta: The Hurricane Years, 1940-41 Christopher Shores and Brian Cull with Nicola Malizia Grub Street 1987

Air War for Yugoslavia, Greece and Crete, 1940-41 Christopher Shores and Brian Cull with Nicola Malizia Grub Street 1987

Dust Clouds in the Middle East; The Air War for East Africa, Iraq, Syria and Madagascar, 1940-42 Christopher Shores Grub Street 1996

Major Research Titles

Fighter Squadrons of the RAF and Their Aircraft John D.R.Rawlings Macdonald 1969

Bomber Squadrons of the RAF and Their Aircraft Philip Moyes Macdonald 1964

Coastal, Support and Special Squadrons of the RAF and Their Aircraft John D.R.Rawlings Jane's 1982

Royal Air Force Flying Training and Support Units Ray Sturtivant, John Hamlin and James J.Halley Air-Britain 1997

RAF Squadrons; A Comprehensive Record of the Movement and Equipment of all RAF Squadrons and their Antecedents Since 1912 Wing Commander C.G. Jefford MBE RAF Airlife 1988

The Squadrons of the Fleet Air Arm Ray Sturtivant Air-Britain 1984

RAF Bomber Losses in the Middle East & Mediterranean, Volume 1: 1939-1942 David Gunby & Pelham Temple Midland 2006

The History of the Second World War; The Mediterranean and Middle East, Volumes I, II and III Major-General I.S.O.Playfair, CB, DSO, MC and Others HM Stationery Office 1954, 1956 and 1960

Springbok Fighter Victories; SAAF Operations in 1939-1945, Volumes 1 and 2 Michael Schoeman Freeworld Publications CC 2002 and 2009

South African Forces in World War II; Volume 4 –Eagle Strike; The SAAF in Egypt, Cyrenaica, Libya, Tunisia, Tripolitania and Madagascar, 1931-1943 James Ambrose Brown Purnell 1974

Die Jagdfliegerverband 1934-1945; Volumes 5, 8/I and 8/II Jochen Prien, Gherhard Stemmer, Peter Rodeike and Winfried Bock Struve's Buchdruckerie und Verlag 2003-2004

Bomber Units of the Luftwaffe 1932-1945. Volumes 1 and 2 Henry L.de Zeng IV and Douglas G.Stankey with Eddie Creek Chevron Publishing Ltd 2007 and 2008

Dive-Bomber and Ground Attack Units of the Luftwaffe 1933-1945, Volume 1 Henry L. de Zeng IV and Douglas G.Stankey Ian Allan Publishing 2009

The Distinguished Flying Cross and How it was Won, 1918-1995, Volumes 1(A-L) and 2(M-Z) Nick and Carol Carter Savannah 1998

The Distinguished Flying Medal Register for the Second World War, Volumes 1(A-J) and 2 (K-Z) Ian Tavender Savannah 2000

Additional Research Titles

Australia in the War of 1939-1945; Air War Against Germany and Italy, 1939-1943 John Herington Australian War Memorial, Canberra 1954

Desert Warriors; Australian P-40 pilots at war in the Middle East and North Africa, 1941-1943 Russell Brown Banner Books 2000

Kittyhawks over the Sand; The Canadians & RCAF Americans; The Men & The Aircraft Michel Lavigne & W/C James F.Edwards Lavigne Aviation Publications 2002

Hurricanes over the Sands; The Canadians & The RCAF Americans; The Men and the Aircraft, Part One Michel Lavigne & W/C James F.Edwards Lavigne Aviation Publications 2003

Pictorial History of the Mediterranean Air War, Volume One Christopher F. Shores Ian Allan 1972

Hurricanes over Tobruk; The Pivotal Role of the Hurricane in the Defence of Tobruk, January-June 1941 Brian Cull with Don Minterne Grub Street 1999

The Bristol Blenheim; a Complete History Graham Warner Crécy Publishing 2002

Desert Air Force at War Chaz Bowyer and Christopher Shores Ian Allan 1981

Aces High;A Tribute to the Most Notable Fighter Pilots of the British and Commonwealth Forces in WWII Christopher Shores and Clive Williams Grub Street 1994

Those Other Eagles: A Tribute to the British.Commonwealth and Free European Fighter Pilots Who Claimed Between Two and Four Victories in Aerial Combat, 1939-1982 Christopher Shores Grub Street 2004

Fleet Air Arm Aircraft 1939 to 1945 Ray Sturtivant ISO, with Mick Burrow Air-Britain 1995

Courage Alone: The Italian Air Force 1940-1943 Chris Dunning Hikoki Publications 1998

Squadron/Unit Histories

Flat Out; The Story of 30 Squadron, Royal Air Force John F.Hamlin Air-Britain 2002

The Flying Camels; The History of No. 45 Squadron, RAF Wg Cdr C.G.Jefford, MBE, BA, RAF(Retd) C.G.Jefford 1995

The History of 73 Squadron; Part 2 November 1940 to September 1943 Don Minterne Tutor Publishing 1997

Strike True; The Story of No. 80 Squadron, Royal Air Force Christopher Shores Air-Britain 1986

Shark Squadron; The History of 112 Squadron, 1917-1975 Robin Brown Crécy Books 1994

A History of 209 Squadron Flight Lieutenant D.S.B.Marr, B.Sc(Eng), RAF Privately published 1966

The Hornet Strikes; The Story of No.213 Squadron, Royal Air Force Frank M.Leeson Air-Britain 1998

The Desert Harassers; Memoirs of 450 (RAAF) Squadron Leonard L.Barton Aston Publications 1991

Bankstown to Berlin; with 451 (RAAF) Squadron, 1941-1946 Leonard L.Barton The Committee of the 451 (RAAF) Squadron Association 1996

Theirs is the Glory; The Story of 12 Squadron, SAAF Stuart N.McCreath Widdlecombe and Ogden date unspecified

Per Noctem Per Diem; The Story of 24 Squadron, SAAF E.N.Tucker and P.M.J.McGregor 24 Squadron Album Committee 1961

Die Geschichte des Lehrgeschwaders 1; Band 1 1936-1942 Peter Taghon VDM Heinz Nickel 2004

Pilot Autobiographies or Biographies

Killer Caldwell: Australia's Greatest Fighter Pilot Jeffrey Watson Hodder 2005

Clive Caldwell, Air Ace Kristen Alexander Allen & Unwin 2006

Boy, tales of Childhood, and Going Solo Roald Dahl Penguin Books 1984

Test Pilot Neville Duke Allan Wingate 1953 republished by Grub Street in 1992

The War Diaries of Neville Duke DSO, OBE, DFC (two Bars), AFC, Czech Military Cross, 1941-1944 Edited by Norman Franks Grub Street 1995

Kittyhawk Pilot; Wing Cdr James (Stocky) Edwards J.P.A.Michel Lavign and J.F.(Stocky) Edwards Turner-Walker Publications 1983

Goon in the Block Don Edy Private publication 1961; revised edition 2010

You Live But Once; Bobby Gibbes; Autobiography Wing Commander (Retd) R.H.Gibbes, DSO, DFC & Bar Private publication 1994

Mezze (mee-zay); Little bites of flying, living and golfing Oliver Green Ryan Publishing 1999

A Lot to Fight For; The War Diaries and Letters of S/Ldr J.F.Jackson DFC Private publication by Patricia and Arthur Jackson 2001

Imshi; A Fighter Pilot's Letters to his Mother W.H.Allen & Co Ltd 1943

Messerschmitt Roulette; The Western Desert 1941-42 Wing Commander Geoffrey Morley-Mower DFC, AFC Phalanx Publishing Co Ltd 1993
Woody; A Fighter Pilot's Album Hugh A.Halliday Canav Books 1987

Air Commanders

From Sea to Sky, 1910-1945 Air Chief Marshal Sir Arthur Longmore Geoffrey Bles, 1946
With Prejudice Marshal of the Royal Air Force Lord Tedder Cassell 1966
Coningham; A Biography of Air Marshal Sir Arthur Coningham Vincent Orange Methuen 1990
Straight and Level Air Chief Marshal Sir Kenneth Cross KCB,CBE,DSO,DFC, with Professor Vincent Orange Grub Street 1993
Be Bold Air Chief Marshal Sir Frederick Rosier GCB, CBE, DSO with David Rosier Grub Street 2011
The Memoirs of Field Marshal Kesselring William Kimber and Co Ltd Reprinted by Purnell Book Services Ltd 1974

Ground Commanders

Wavell; Soldier & Statesman Victoria Schofield John Murray 2006
The Forgotten Victor; General Sir Richard O'Connor KT, GCB, DSO, MC John Baynes Brassey's (UK) 1989
Auchinleck; The Lonely Soldier Philip Warner Buchan & Enright Publishers Ltd 1981 Republished by Pen & Sword Military 2006
Armoured Crusader; The Biography of Major-General Sir Percy 'Hobo' Hobart Kenneth Macksey Hutchinson 1967 Republished by Grub Street 2004
Panzer Commander The Memoirs of Colonel Hans von Luck Cassell 2002

Related Books, Ground Operations

The Early Battles of Eighth Army; 'Crusader' to the Alamein Line 1941-1943 Adrian Stewart Leo Cooper 2002
Crusader; The Eighth Army's Forgotten Victory, November 1941-January 1942 Richard Humble Leo Cooper 1987
The Great Tank Scandal; British Armour in the Second World War Part 1 David Fletcher HM Stationery Officer 1989
The Tanks; The History of the Royal Tank Regiment; Volume Two 1939-1945 Captain B.H.Liddell Hart Cassell 1959
Leakey's Luck; A Tank Commander with Nine Lives R.E.A. Leakey with George Forty Sutton Publishing 1999
Tanks Across the Desert; The War Diary of Jake Wardrop George Forty William Kimber & Co Ltd 1981 Republished by Sutton Publishing 2003

Additional Bibliography

La guerra aerea in Africa Settentrionale, Borgiotti, A. and Gori, C., Stem Mucchi, Modena, 1973
Quelli del cavallino rampante, Duma, A., Dell'Ateneo, Roma 1970
Italian Aces of World War 2, Massimello, G. and Apostolo G., Osprey Publishing, Oxford, 2000
L'Aeronautica Italiana nella seconda guerra mondiale, Santoro, G., Ed. Esse, Roma, 1957 Tarantola, E., Il 150°, 151° e 153° Gruppo Caccia, SMA, Roma, 1987

INDEX

BRITISH AND COMMONWEALTH (including US citizens serving in Commonweath units and Free Europeans – Belgians, Free French, Greeks and Poles)

UNITED STATES SERVICE PERSONNEL

GERMAN PERSONNEL

FRENCH PERSONNEL – FREE FRENCH AND VICHY

ITALIAN PERSONNEL

SQUADRONS

FLIGHTS

MISCELLANEOUS AND SUPPORT UNITS

AIR MINISTRY EXPERIMENTAL STATIONS (RADAR)

WIRELESS UNITS

UNITED STATES ARMY AIR FORCE UNITS

INITIAL UNITS

IX FIGHTER COMMAND

XII ASC FIGHTER UNITS

ITALIAN ARMY UNITS

ITALIAN VESSELS

PLACES